COMPLETE BOOK OF
BUSINESS SCHOOLS

The Princeton Review
COMPLETE BOOK OF
BUSINESS SCHOOLS

2003 EDITION

NEDDA GILBERT

Random House, Inc.
New York
www.PrincetonReview.com

Princeton Review Publishing, L.L.C.
2315 Broadway
New York, NY 10024
E-mail: bookeditor@review.com

© 2002 by Princeton Review Publishing, L.L.C.

All rights reserved under International and Pan-American Copyright Conventions. Published in the United States by Random House, Inc., New York, and simultaneously in Canada by Random House of Canada Limited, Toronto.

ISSN: 1067-2141
ISBN: 0-375-76270-1

Editorial Director: Robert Franek
Editor: Erica Magrey
Production Coordinator: Scott Harris
Account Manager: Kevin McDonough
Production Editor: Julieanna Lambert

Manufactured in the United States of America on partially recycled paper.

9 8 7 6 5 4 3 2 1

2003 Edition

Acknowledgments

This book absolutely would not have been possible without the help of my husband, Paul. With each edition of this guide, his insights and support have been invaluable—this book continues to be as much his as it is mine. That said, I also need to thank my eight-year-old daughter, Micaela, and her four-year-old sister, Lexi, for enduring all my time immersed in this project.

The following people were also instrumental in the completion of this book: Scott Harris, Julieanna Lambert, Erica Magrey, Erik Olson, Nathan Firer, Kevin McDonough, Yojaira Cordero, Thacher Goodwin, Eric Amsler, Jose Guillermo, Jennifer Fallon, Sarah Kruchko, Jeff Adams, and Chris Wujciak for putting all the pieces together; the sales staff at The Princeton Review: Kyle Jackson, Grace Linch, Josh Escott, Thom MacLeod, Devin Sirmenis, and Vanessa Wanderlingh; Robert Franek and Pat Vance, as well as Alicia Ernst and John Katzman, for giving me the chance to write this book; and to the folks at Random House, who helped this project reach fruition.

Thanks go to all those section-A mates, HBS-92, who lent a hand and provided valuable feedback when this project first got underway. And much appreciation to Kristin Hansen (Tuck '01) and Matt Camp (Tuck '02). Thanks must also go to Claudia Tattanelli-Skeini from Universum Communications for providing access to the Universum Survey 2002 results and to Ramona Payne and all the folks at The Diversity Pipeline Alliance.

Special thanks go to the following members of the Harvard Business School, Class of '92: John Cattau, Clive Holmes, John Kim, Lionel Leventhal, Patricia Melnikoff, Jay O'Connor, Chiara Perry, and Steve Sinclair. I am also grateful for the unique insights provided by Cathy Crane-Moley, Stanford's Class of '92.

Thanks are also due to the business school folks who went far out of their way to provide essential information. They continue to make this book relevant and vital:

Linda Baldwin, director of admissions, The Anderson School, UCLA

Derek Bolton, assistant dean and director of admissions, Stanford University School of Business

Paul Danos, dean of the Tuck School of Business

Allan Friedman, University of Chicago

David Irons, University of California—Berkeley

Professor Mitch Knetter, associate dean of the Tuck School of Business

Steven Lubrano, assistant dean and director the MBA Program at the Tuck School of Business

Will Makris, Babson University

Rose Martinelli, director of admissions and financial aid of The Wharton School MBA Program

Julia Min, director of MBA admissions, Stern School of Business at New York University

Alysa Polkes, director of career management center, The Anderson School, UCLA

Carol Swanberg, director of admissions and financial aid, University of Chicago

Carol Tucker, interim director of media relations, The Anderson School, UCLA

Jeanne Wilt, assistant dean of admissions and career development at Michigan

The staff at the News and Publications Office, Stanford University

Contents

PART I: ALL ABOUT BUSINESS SCHOOL   1

Introduction   3

CHAPTER 1: THIS ISN'T YOUR FATHER'S (OR MOTHER'S) B-SCHOOL ANYMORE   5
Post-September 11: A Changed MBA Landscape   5
The Continuing Relevance of Business School   10

CHAPTER 2: PICKING THE RIGHT BUSINESS SCHOOL FOR YOU   13
Making the Decision to Go   13
Why the Rankings Aren't a Useful Guide to School Selection   14
Judging for Yourself   14
B-School Admission Goes Electronic   17
How to Use This Book   19

CHAPTER 3: WHAT B-SCHOOL IS REALLY LIKE   21
An Academic Perspective   21
The Tuck Interview (What Makes Tuck So Special)   24
Your First Year   27
Your Second Year   29
Life Outside of Class   32

CHAPTER 4: PALM PILOTS AND POWER BREAKFASTS: WHAT DOES AN MBA OFFER?   33
Nuts-and-Bolts Business Schools   33
Access to Recruiters, Entrée to New Fields   33
MBA Careers: An Interview with the Director of the MBA Career Management Center at UCLA   38
Friends Who are Going Places, Alumni Who are Already There   41

CHAPTER 5: WHERE ARE THEY NOW?   43
Harvard Business School's Class of '92: Reflections on Where They've Been and Where They're Headed, Ten Years Out   43

CHAPTER 6: MONEY MATTERS   83
How Much It Will Cost?   83
How Do I Fund My MBA?   84
Loan Specifics   86

PART II: HOW TO GET IN   89

CHAPTER 7: PREPARING TO BE A SUCCESSFUL APPLICANT   91

CHAPTER 8: ADMISSIONS   97
How the Admissions Criteria are Weighted   97
An Interview with the Director of MBA Admissions at the Anderson School   102
Making the Rounds: When to Apply   106

Quotas, Recruitment, and Diversity   107
An Interview with Cathy Crane-Moley, Stanford Graduate School of Business, Class of '92   110

CHAPTER 9: THE RIGHT STUFF   117
Common Essay Questions   117
Straight Talk from Admissions Officers:
Fifteen Sure-Fire Ways to Torpedo Your Application   124

CHAPTER 10: ESSAYS THAT WORK   127
Boston University   128
Brigham Young University   131
University of California—Berkeley   136
Case Western Reserve University   140
Dartmouth   142
University of Maryland   146
University of Michigan   149
University of Notre Dame   151
Stanford University   153
Tulane University   157
University of Virginia   161

PART III: QUICK REFERENCE LIST   165

PART IV: THE SCHOOLS   201

INDEXES   519

Alphabetical List of Schools   521
Business Program Name   525
Location   527
Cost   531
Enrollment of Business School   533
Average GMAT   535
Average Undergrad GPA   537
Average Starting Salary   539

About the Author   541

Part I

ALL ABOUT BUSINESS SCHOOL

INTRODUCTION

PROVEN STRATEGIES FOR WINNING ADMISSION

Admission to the business school of your choice, especially if your choice is among the most selective programs, will require your absolute best shot. Thousands and thousands of prospective MBA candidates spend loads of time and money making sure they select, and are in turn admitted to, the "best" school. They spend their time working in jobs they think will impress a b-school; studying and preparing for the GMAT; writing essays; interviewing; visiting prospective schools; and buying guides like—but not as good as—this one.

This book is your best bet. It takes you into the secret deliberations of the admissions committees at the top schools. You get a firsthand look at who decides your fate. More important, you learn what criteria are used to evaluate applicants. As we found out, things aren't always the way you'd expect them to be. You also get straight talk from admissions officers—what dooms an application and how to ace the interview.

In addition to getting inside information on the application process, you learn when the best time to apply is, how to answer the most commonly asked essay questions, and what key points to make in your essays. There's also loads of information on what you can do before applying to increase your odds of gaining admission.

We also give you the facts—from the most up-to-date information on major curricula changes and placement rates to demographics of the student body—for the AACSB-accredited graduate business schools in the country. And we've included enough information about them—which we gather from admissions officers and administrators—to help you make a smart decision about where to go.

For ten years, The Princeton Review has been publishing this book. We've always been able to chart the changes in the business school landscape—through the ups and downs, good times and bad. This year, things have been different and what is ahead is tough to predict. To help you navigate the waters, we've gone into greater depth and provided more analysis of recent business trends and their effect on b-school and b-school admissions. We've interviewed deans at several of the top schools to share with you their take on recent events. We also spoke with several Harvard MBAs on the eve of their tenth anniversary to find out what they had to say about their MBA experience and their lives after b-school. Reading all of this will give you added insight into the b-school world, which will, in turn, help you craft your applications, ace your interviews, and gain acceptance to the business schools you want.

CHAPTER 1

THIS ISN'T YOUR FATHER'S (OR MOTHER'S) B-SCHOOL ANYMORE

POST–SEPTEMBER 11: A CHANGED MBA LANDSCAPE

The MBA has always been seen as a golden passport, the trip-tik to romance and riches. The destination: career acceleration, power networks and recruiters, elite employers, and of course, generous paychecks.

But not everyone wants to make the trip. Several factors will always impact on the popularity of the MBA: 1) the state of the economy—interest in getting the MBA has generally waxed and waned with economic times; 2) trends and favorable or unfavorable press—in the 1980s, a rash of insider trading scandals in which MBAs were ensnared made the degree look smarmy and other graduate programs, notably law and medicine, look more appealing; 3) the immediacy of good professional opportunities—the collapse of the dot-com boom, followed by the severe retrenchment of traditional MBA destinations (such as investment banks and consulting firms) in this depressed economy, has left many current MBAs stranded; and 4) recruiter demand for newly minted MBAs—do employers see the skill sets of today's MBAs bringing measurable value to their companies?

RIDING OUT THE STORM: A WEAKENED ECONOMY SPURS NEAR-RECORD LEVELS OF APPLICANTS

"Applicants tend to seek shelter during a tumultuous time. They seek safe havens. Business schools are safe havens."

—Linda Baldwin,
director of admissions at the University of California
at Los Angeles's Anderson School of Business

So where does the MBA stand these days? Once again, it's in great demand. Recent events have made business school a great place to ride out the aftershocks of September 11 and a weakened economy.

Historically, the opportunity cost of leaving the work force for two years is minimized in a weak economy. During recessions, cutbacks in spending diminish opportunities to move up the corporate ladder, and waves of layoffs wash through corporate America. It's a no-brainer at times like these to look to b-schools to gain a key credential, develop networks of contacts, and even have some fun.

The "At-a-Glance" Version of the High-Tech Revolution

Head spinning from how fast the high-tech story unfolded? Need the abridged version? We did too, so here it is:

Early, high-visibility "liquidity events" such as initial public offerings (IPOs) showed that young people could gain extravagant wealth quickly by "scaling" their new Internet businesses and selling them to high bidders or by going public. Newly established techie business magazines competed with heavyweights like *Fortune* and *Forbes* in a race to get these stories out. The media blitz about this new unprecedented era of success stoked even greater interest in joining the dot-com race. Indifferent to gender, nationality, or race, the Nasdaq minted new millionaires daily. With all the hype, IPOs went right out of the gate to ravenous investor demand.

Continued

"Applications this year have gone up tremendously," notes Jeanne Wilt, assistant dean of admissions and career development at Michigan. "You'll see schools quote a range of percentages. Here, at Michigan we've gone up 15 percent."

This increase is in sharp contrast to the numbers in recent years, when b-school applications trailed off. Between 1999 and 2000, the perceived value of the degree to potential applicants had dropped considerably in light of the booming economic climate, and according to the Graduate Management Admissions Council (GMAC), applications at full-time b-schools had decreased by 27 percent. Just one year ago, Rose Martinelli, director of admissions for the University of Pennsylvania Wharton MBA Program, commented on this drop: "Last year [2000], our applications fell by 11 percent. While we don't have accurate reasons for why this happened, we can point to certain indicators: a soaring economy, the lure to Internet companies, and people trying to pursue get-rich-quick strategies."

Of course, back in 2000, the hi-tech economy was roaring ahead. Economic experimentation occurred across a range of industries trying to make sense of the Internet. MBA or not, these companies needed brain power and bodies. Dot-coms hired extravagantly and paid obscene levels of salaries. With the dot-com boom, the very need for the MBA was questioned. How could two years at an MBA program keep up with the impact and rapid-fire changes of the Internet?

Unsurprisingly, professionals in their mid-twenties who would have followed the traditional path to b-school took that faster route to success. Rather than work their way up through a traditional organizational ladder, they become senior managers of newly formed dot-coms. Not even the most pedigreed program could compete with the immediacy and enormity of riches that the high-tech world offered.

Fast-forward to the present and the near future. The dot-com world has long fizzled. The Nasdaq is in ruins. The economy hit the skids after the longest period of growth prosperity in history, and the September 11 attacks knocked the economy off its remaining leg. Now Wall Street (along with the rest of us) is looking with great skepticism at all of the glory technology was supposed to have wrought.

Given all this, it's no surprise that the tough job market has influenced an unprecedented increase in the volume of applications. Applicants are worried about not only the economy and the threat of layoffs, but also their ability to remain competitive in the business world. Their survival strategy? They've decided to head back to b-school to acquire a degree that turbo-charges their future.

EXTREME APPLICATIONS

This recent spike in b-school applications is far from normal, even in a time when a traditional business school education is once again perceived to be the best bet for many young professionals. The latest figures from the GMAC on the number of people taking the Graduate Management Admission Test (GMAT), the required exam for b-school applicants, confirm that the number of test-takers increased by more than 20 percent in 2001.

At the Anderson School of Business, applications came in at an astounding rate in the first round. Admissions officers saw an increase of between 50 and 60 percent more applications than they had in the same round in the previous year. "In terms of overall levels, we're about 20 percent above where we were in 2001," notes Linda Baldwin, director of admission at the University of California at Los Angeles' Anderson School of Business. "But this year is historically different than anything we've experienced in the past. We never saw individuals respond to market forces like this before. Online applications zoomed in the first three months."

"What occurred for the past year for almost all the top schools occurred unusually early in the first three months. This absolutely coincided with two forces: September 11 and the economic downturn. The online application process became a true phenomenon in that it made it very easy to apply. Given what prospective applicants were hearing in terms of the recession, by the end of January the volume of applications was still high, at a time when we typically start to see a decline. In the last rounds it finally leveled off. This showed us how sensitive applications are to market trends and world events."

Stanford's School of Business saw a similar rise in applications, with an overall increase of about 10 to 15 percent. "We saw much larger numbers in the first round—the same thing that every school saw," echoes Derrick Bolton, director of admissions at Stanford. But he suggests another factor that may have impacted this year's less-than-normal first round: the feeling that b-school was the only option. "We saw a substantial change in the number of schools applicants applied to. Instead of a candidate applying to two schools, they applied to five."

Anderson's Baldwin advises, "Looking ahead, the economy looks brighter, and there is more confidence. There are options. Now that things have come back to normalcy, people might say to themselves, 'Is this the right time to apply?'"

"As you look to what opportunities there will be in the long run, is 2004 the year in which you want to be in that job market? Some people see the ascending curve; some are a little more risk averse. Looking into a crystal ball, applicants need to think about the future and consider their risk-taking profile.

Continued

Starting with Netscape, the first high-profile Internet IPO, venture capitalists rushed their investment progeny ever faster into the hands of the investment bankers. In turn, these bankers put on "road shows" to explain the merits of their new company to analysts and investors at stops around the country. With the hype of the transformative power of the Internet, increasingly immature companies went public. Many were not even truly "revenue validated"—in other words, earning real sales dollars as opposed to just having a sizzling business concept.

As investors realized that much of the offerings coming through the pipeline were of low quality and that most of the hyped companies had little chance of earnings worthy of their valuations, the whole process came abruptly to a stop in March of 2000. The IPO window slammed shut. Companies started running out of funding from VCs and began folding in increasing numbers. And suddenly, the dot-com boom came to an ignominious end.

"I think about the people who started school in 2000. At that time everything looked bright. The peak was occurring at that point in terms of the economy, so timing is of the essence in terms of making a decision. You may not want to jump in when things are peaking. You really have to ask yourself how risk averse you are. But to reap great rewards, you have to risk."

As the economy recovers over the next year, app-happy candidates may simmer down, and b-school may lose its top spot in the hot destination rankings. For the near future however, it's likely that competition will remain stiff. Whatever tomorrow brings, one thing seems certain: in joining those who've chosen to pursue the MBA, you'll find yourself in stellar company.

YOUNGER MINDS

With this year's historically high volume of applications, 2001 may have been impossibly competitive. On the flip side, there are now some unrecognized opportunities for candidates with less than the traditional two to four years of work experience to make a strong case for admittance.

Interest in turning to b-school after September 11 reinforced a small but notable trend toward re-thinking rigid admittance standards on work experience. Many schools had already begun to assess their emphasis on work experience as the be-all and end-all.

Admissions officers at large benchmark schools such as Stanford say that at their respective institutions this trend pre-dates recent events. Stanford's Bolton notes, "The pendulum has gone too far in one direction in terms of the number of younger candidates applying to b-school. It has not kept pace with the overall pace of all applicants. We want more young applicants applying. The goal is to bring the average age down in the next couple of years."

"What's driving this is the willingness on the part of the b-schools to not be rigidly fixed on what's right for someone. We may not always be the best judge of when the best time is for a candidate to go to b-school," continues Bolton.

Wharton's Martinelli concurs: "A year ago there was a shift in that we became more tuned in to when students are ready in their leadership, professional, and personal development. We see so many nontraditional students that we don't want to have rules on when they can apply. We don't want to miss out on fabulous applicants because they don't think they can get in."

"When the applicant pool continues to get older and older, then we're closing out younger applicants who are on a fast track." Continues Martinelli, "Why should we wait? Why should they wait? We want to catch the human element in the application process."

At the Anderson School, there is a growing recognition that younger applicants can contribute as much in the classroom as their older counterparts. Baldwin notes, "We had already begun to consider, 'how much work experience do you really need?' Prior to September 11, we had done some experimenting in bringing in individuals who had less experience and we found they did very well. After September 11, we did see more students applying directly to the MBA program from undergraduate school and knew this was the result of recent events. Post–September 11 and even as the economy recovers, we'll be targeting our efforts at those undergraduates."

There may be more to the story. Because they may be less likely to be in committed relationships or have families, younger students are more active, generous alumni, and b-schools can't afford to ignore the market that these younger students represent. Despite the heightened competition, candidates with less experience are increasingly being deemed worthy of a coveted b-school seat.

FOREIGN MBA STUDENTS: WHAT HAS CHANGED

Opportunities to study abroad for part (or all) of an MBA program have become highly relevant. U.S. schools stumble over each other to provide amazing overseas options in dozens of countries. Likewise, international enrollment at U.S. business schools continues to grow. At top business schools, non-U.S. students now make up an average of 30 percent of the class.

International students represent a win-win proposition for both U.S. business schools and the foreign industries that send them here. American business schools prize the global perspective and diversity international students bring into the classroom and community; foreign businesses operating in a global economy desire expertise in U.S. business practices, which are becoming the international standard.

So how has September 11 and subsequent wartime security upset this informal but critical partnership that we've established with foreign institutions?

At Stanford, not much has changed. Stanford's Bolton observes, "We were really surprised. Among our peer schools, we talked about whether we would see fewer international students. Yet I don't think we saw a substantial change in international applications." Martinelli reports similar findings: "Our foreign applications were steady. Perhaps this year they were a little bit lower, but overall, they were very stable. International students make up 40 percent of our class."

The big change for foreign students appears to be in slogging through the new INS rules and procedures for obtaining a visa. And the snags can be considerable. Wharton's Martinelli says, "More than anything else since September 11, timing is critical. It takes so much more time to begin the process of applying for a visa, or adjusting a visa, especially if a foreign student is already in the country on a visa. The adjustment can take between three and five months. Males betweens the ages of 18 and 45 have to file additional forms and so need to build in extra time."

With so much legislation pending on guidelines for admitting foreigners and international students, non-U.S. citizens should visit the INS website (www.ins.usdoj.gov) for the latest information. Foreign applicants should anticipate delays in obtaining visas. Students from the countries on the Terrorist Countries List and nations such as Egypt and Saudi Arabia may face additional hurdles.

A Historical Perspective on B-School Curricula

Revamped curricula are nothing new. Through the 1990s, three waves of change hit curricula across the country. First, in the early part of the decade, schools reeled from criticism that their graduates lacked ethics and were only out for themselves. The result? Major overhauls included Outward-Bound-type, touchy-feely orientation programs — which continue today — and loads of programs on ethics and diversity. Then, the concept of leadership broadened to include and eventually be founded on collaboration skills. Recruiters were demanding that graduating MBAs be team players, not command-and-control business warriors. Finally, to prepare graduates for the increasingly global nature of business, programs updated their materials and course structures to emphasize global commerce and decision-making in large and small countries around the world.

The point of all this is that business schools are always going to change with the times. During times of great change, the pendulum will swing wildly. Inevitably, it will swing back to its point of equilibrium. Instead of schools focusing intensely on all the latest trends, they'll move to a more disciplined integration of what's new with what's basic.

For the foreseeable future, students wishing to obtain a visa will not be able to escape the shadow of world events but still should not be deterred. Most business schools stand firm on their commitment to foreign applicants throughout the entire process.

When applying for a visa, Wharton's Martinelli offers this advice: "Emphasize plans to return home, rather than plans to immigrate to the United States." If a visa is denied, many schools will defer admission and hold that student's spot until the visa is obtained. Sums up Martinelli, "It may take a little longer for students from some countries to get their visas. But decisions here are not made based on whether they got a visa or not. Decisions are made based on what they'll do at our school and on the contributions they'll make."

THE CONTINUING RELEVANCE OF BUSINESS SCHOOL

The MBA is such an attractive option because it *does* confer huge value on the recipient. Business schools know how to keep pace with the rapidly changing face of business. After all, that's *their* business, so you're never really out of the game. In fact, if you look at the nation's top business programs, you'll find exciting innovations in curriculum that reflect all that's new and relevant. This includes unique opportunities for teamwork, internships, and laboratory simulations that replicate real-world, real-time business scenarios.

The integration of these real-world experiences into the basics produces better-trained, more well-rounded managers, as graduates are more adept at discerning the correlation between principle and reality. Even so, this year, a turn from fad courses in search of business knowledge that is more widely applicable and more relevant long-term has caused a strong return to fundamentals.

BACKPEDALING TO THE BASICS

Many top schools are reviving the old classics: it's back to basics. Both schools and students now have enough of a perspective to look back at the frenzy of the last business cycle and understand that enduring values are rooted in a solid foundation. Gone is the frothy demand for trendy courses on e-commerce and other hype-driven topics. Just two years ago, a class at Stanford on the principles of Internet marketing was oversubscribed. This year, only two people signed up for it.

So here's a sampler of the back-to-basics you'll get at b-school: an in-depth immersion in all of the key functional areas of an organization: marketing, management, sales, finance, operations, logistics, etc. And you'll look at these areas across dozens of industries and organizational types, from start-ups to Fortune 500 companies.

But the renewed focus on basics doesn't mean that you'll find yourself shorted on current events. Expect plenty of case study debate on corporate governance and the Enron debacle, and expect the themes of global perspective and technological competence to permeate many programs. You'll also find classes and seminars on leadership gaining popularity. "We're seeing a resurgence of leadership courses as students seek out professions and business models that are other-oriented," notes Stanford's Bolton. "This may be a new generation. But these are students who look at business as a positive force in the world, a more noble calling."

SURVIVOR POWER

Once you have your MBA, you can expect to hit the ground running. You'll start off your post b-school career with a load of contacts that you will periodically leverage over your career. Many graduates use the degree to embark on entirely new career paths than those that brought them to the school; consultants become bankers, entrepreneurs become consultants, marketers become financiers, and so on. The MBA has and will continue to be a terrific opportunity to reinvent oneself.

"An MBA is unlike any other professional degree because the breadth of knowledge poises you for a multitude of career choices," says Julia Min, director of MBA admissions for NYU Stern School of Business. "You can be an investment banker, yet two years from that point, segue into nonprofit work. You can move from banking to corporate finance to a venture-capital proposition to ultimately having an entrepreneurial experience. So it's a credential that allows you the flexibility to explore different industries; it's a long-term investment that will give you the tools to transition if you want to."

"What's wonderful about the MBA is that it provides fundamental skills that you can use whenever and wherever you need them," champions Martinelli. "I'm a cheerleader for the nontraditional because I feel the MBA is such a fundamental tool. It offers an ability to enter the business world and link passion with functionality."

"For example, for folks who want to go into public service or nonprofit, even the arts industry, they're very narrow fields. You need the passion and vision to be successful in them. But often credibility is undermined when you don't understand the business world's perspective," states Martinelli.

"You've got to know that industry if you're going to make it viable for the future. But you have to be able to know how to talk to the business world in order to get those investments to make it happen. And that's one of the reasons why an MBA is so valuable. It bestows credibility in the marketplace and helps us maintain these organizations in a world that doesn't often respect passion over the bottom line," she continues.

As the economy reaches bottom after a record-setting ten years of growth, companies are taking a more cautious approach to hiring. That means even at the top schools recruiting has been deeply affected. Jeanne Wilt, assistant dean of admissions and career development at Michigan, says, "A weak economy, lay-offs, a year's worth of turmoil, the whole combination has made the job market for MBAs tougher, there's no question about that. That means that at the top schools, students maybe not getting the two or three offers they might have, but just one or two. Students are really having to use their networks to go after what they want."

Even so, hundreds of companies continue to visit and recruit from business school campuses. Many can ill afford the cost of bypassing campus recruiting for fear that when their hiring needs increase, MBA students will be less receptive to their offers. Thus, MBA programs remain one of the most effective means to get oneself in front of recruiters and senior managers from the most desirable companies. And while that may not grant you "immunity" from an economy of ups and downs, it will guarantee you survivor power.

GETTING INTO THE BEST SCHOOLS IS STILL TOUGH

With economic recovery at hand (and maybe well underway at the time of this book's publication) the opportunity to dive right into the corporate milieu may once again lure a percentage of young professionals away from the MBA, and application numbers may return to normal. Despite this possibility, if you want to be competitive, you'll need to develop a solid application strategy and apply to a diverse portfolio of schools.

LET US HELP YOU DECIDE

There are many factors to consider when deciding whether or not to pursue an MBA, and we'll help you make that decision in the following chapters. We'll also tell you a bit about each school in our profiles and prepare you for further research into the schools on your list. We've worked hard to provide you with thorough information on every angle of the MBA, but you don't have to take our word for it—see for yourself. Stanford's Bolton advises future applicants, "Start early. Visit as many schools as you can, because it's very hard to differentiate among programs from websites, books, and marketing materials. You need to get a feeling from walking down the halls."

After you decide to go, finding the right program can be extremely difficult. Bolton explains, "Applicants really have to dig beneath the programs they're looking at to determine what's going to make them happy. A lot of people wind up going to the wrong school. A lot of external factors contribute to that. People shouldn't worry about justifying the decision to others, but to themselves."

Chapter 2

Picking the Right Business School for You

MAKING THE DECISION TO GO

The next step for you may be b-school. Indeed, armed with an MBA you may journey far. But the success of your trip and the direction you take will depend on knowing exactly why you're going to b-school and just what you'll be getting out of it.

The most critical questions you need to ask yourself are the following: Do you really want a career in business? What do you want the MBA to do for you? Are you looking to gain crediblity, accelerate your development, or move into a new job or industry? Perhaps you're looking to start your own business, and entrepreneurial study will be important.

Knowing what you want doesn't just affect your decision to go, it also affects your candidacy; admissions committees favor applicants who have clear goals and objectives. Moreover, once at school, students who know what they want make the most of their two years. If you're uncertain about your goals, opportunities for career development—such as networking, mentoring, student clubs, and recruiter events—are squandered.

You also need to find a school that fits your individual needs. Consider the personal and financial costs. This may be the single biggest investment of your life. How much salary will you forego by leaving the workforce? What will the tuition be? How will you pay for it? If you have a family, spouse, or significant other, how will getting your MBA affect them?

If you do have a spouse, you may choose a program that involves partners in campus life. If status is your top priority, you should simply choose the most prestigious school you can get into.

The MBA presents many opportunities but no guarantees. As with any opportunity, you must make the most of it. Whether you go to a first-tier school or to a part-time program close to home, you'll acquire the skills that can jump-start your career. But your success will have more to do with you than with the piece of paper your MBA is printed on.

WHY THE RANKINGS AREN'T A USEFUL GUIDE TO SCHOOL SELECTION

All too many applicants rely on the magazine rankings to decide where to apply. Caught up with winners, losers, and whoever falls in between, their thinking is simply: Can I get into the top five? Top ten? Top fifteen?

But it's a mistake to rely on the rankings. Benjamin Disraeli once said, "There are lies, damn lies, and statistics." Today, he'd probably add b-school rankings. Why? Because statistics rarely show the whole picture. When deciding on the validity of a study, it's wise to consider how the study was conducted and what exactly it was trying to measure.

First, the rankings have made must-read news for several years. Not surprisingly, some of the survey respondents—current b-school students and recent grads—now know there's a game to play. The game is this: Give your own school the highest marks possible. The goal: that coveted number-one spot. Rumor has it that some schools even remind their students of how their responses will affect the stature of their program. This kind of self-interest is known as respondent bias, and b-school rankings suffer from it in a big way.

The rankings feature easy-to-measure differences such as selectivity, placement success, and proficiency in the basic disciplines. But these rankings don't allow for any intangibles—such as the progressiveness of a program, the school's learning environment, and the happiness of the students.

To create standards by which comparisons can be made, the rankings force an evaluative framework on the programs. But this is like trying to evaluate a collection of paintings—impressionist, modern, classical, and cubist—with the same criteria. Relying on narrow criteria to evaluate subjective components fails to capture the true strengths and weaknesses of each school.

The statistically measurable differences that the magazines base their ratings on are often so marginal as to be insignificant. In other words, it's too close to call the race. Perhaps in some years two schools should be tied for the number-one spot. What would the tie-breaker look lie? A rally cry of "We're number one" with the loudest school winning?

A designation as the number-one, number-five, or number-ten school is almost meaningless when you consider that it changes from year to year—and from magazine to magazine. (At least Olympic medalists enjoy a four-year victory lap.)

JUDGING FOR YOURSELF

Depending on what you're looking for, the rankings may tell you something about the b-schools. But it's wise to use them as approximations rather than the declarations of fact they're made out to be.

The rankings don't factor in your values or all of the criteria you need to consider. Is it selectivity? The highest rate of placement? The best starting salary? Surprise: The number-one school is not number one in all these areas. No school is.

The best way to pick a program is to do your homework and find a match. For example, if you have limited experience with numbers, then a program with a heavy quantitative focus may round out your resume. If you want to stay in your home area, then a local school that's highly regarded by the top regional companies may be best for you. If you know that you want to go into a field typified by cutthroat competition, or a field in which status is all-important . . . well, obviously, keep your eyes on those rankings.

You also need to consider your personal style and comfort zone. Suppose you get into a "top-ranked" school, but the workload is destroying your life, or the mentality is predatory. It won't matter how prestigious the program is if you don't make it through. Do you want an intimate and supportive environment, or are you happy to blend in with the masses? Different schools will meet these needs. Lecture versus case study, specialization versus broad-based general management curriculum, and heavy finance versus heavy marketing are other kinds of trade-offs.

One last thing to consider is social atmosphere. What is the spirit of the student body? Do students like each other? Are they indifferent? Perhaps a bit hostile? If you go through graduate school in an atmosphere of camaraderie, you'll never forget those two years. But if you go through school in an atmosphere of enmity . . . okay, you'll still remember those two years. It's up to you to decide how you want to remember them.

Remember when you applied to college? You talked to friends, alumni, and teachers. You visited the campus and sat in on classes (or should have). It's not all that different with b-school. Here are some of the things you should check out:

ACADEMICS

- Academic reputation
- International reputation
- Primary teaching methodology
- Renown and availability of professors
- General or specialized curriculum
- Range of school specialties
- Opportunities for global/foreign study
- Emphasis on teamwork
- Fieldwork/student consulting available
- Student support—extra study sessions, accessible faculty, tutoring
- Academic support—libraries, computer facilities, and expertise
- Grading/probation policy
- Workload/hours per week in class
- Class and section size
- Pressure and competition

CAREER

- Summer and full-time job placement (number of companies recruiting on and off campus)
- Placement rate
- Average starting salaries
- Salaries at five-year mark
- Career support—assistance with career planning, resume preparation, interview skills
- Networking with visiting executives

QUALITY OF LIFE

- Location
- Campus
- Orientation
- Range of student clubs/activities
- Diversity of student body
- Housing
- Social life
- Spouse/partner group
- Recreational facilities

EXPENSE

- Tuition
- Books, computer
- Cost of living
- Financial aid

B-SCHOOL ADMISSION GOES ELECTRONIC

Universities were among the first organizations on the Internet, and most MBA programs have a lot of useful information online. B-school websites typically include detailed information about the program, course offerings, housing options, and campus life. If you are at all interested in a school, checking out its website is an essential way to gather more facts.

PRINCETON REVIEW ON THE WEB

One of the best places to start your search for b-school information on the Internet is at The Princeton Review's website—www.PrincetonReview.com. The site has everything you need to manage your admissions process from researching schools to filling out applications to finding ways to pay for it all.

RESEARCH SCHOOLS

Using The Princeton Review's powerful search tools you can narrow your search to those schools that best meet your interests. With the simple search, you can look up specific schools by name. In return, you'll get a list of the school's basic stats. Advanced School Search will allow you to target your search by selecting from an array of criteria. The search results will show you how closely each school fits your requirements by displaying a percentage of how many of your criteria were matched.

MY REVIEW

My Review lets you manage the entire application process online. As you research business schools, save those schools you wish to target in your own personal list. Gain access to a free GMAT practice resources, and if you are a student in a Princeton Review GMAT course, get access to all your online course tools. When it's time to apply, check for online applications to the schools you have selected. My Review will keep track of your applications and their deadlines. My Review will also store your results from our financial aid tools and more.

LET B-SCHOOLS FIND YOU

Your search for a school doesn't have to be one-sided anymore. With The Princeton Review you can enter information about yourself—academic record, work history, etc.— along with information about what you want in a school, and let the schools find you. Using the School Match service, you can allow schools to search your criteria just like you search through theirs. It takes just a few minutes to fill out the information, and then you sit back while schools send you e-mail extolling the virtues of their institution.

DISCUSSION

Visitors to our discussion group post messages describing their experiences as they go through the admissions process. It's the most popular MBA admissions discussion area anywhere on the Internet.

THE GMAT

The Princeton Review combines cutting-edge technology with its standardized-testing expertise to accommodate the needs of GMAT-takers everywhere. Access fantastic resources, free practice material, and information on Princeton Review's classroom and online courses. Start off by taking a free full-length, timed GMAT to see just how you'd do.

THE FINANCIAL CENTER

The Princeton Review's financial center is a unique resource for students. You'll find everything from helpful tips on saving money, tax forms, aid, loans, scholarships, and personal finance to a host of helpful financial tools. You should get started with the Tuition Cost Calculator, which will help you figure out how much your b-school tuition will cost, including the yearly tuition increases, for the duration of your enrollment. The Expected Family Contribution Calculator (a revamped calculator comes online in October) allows you to calculate your approximate Expected Family Contribution (EFC), which both schools and the federal government use to determine what they think you should be able to pay for a year's worth of business school. The FAFSA Worksheet (the 2003 version will be online in December) is a virtual dress rehearsal for the official FAFSA form, which you'll need to complete to receive any financial aid. We even have an excellent Scholarship Search that gives you access to millions of dollars of scholarship money.

APPLYING TO B-SCHOOL VIA ELECTRONIC APPLICATION

Once you've gathered all the school information you need and decided where to apply, you may not need to leave The Princeton Review's website. Business schools are scrambling to make electronic versions of their applications available, and many schools have those apps available on www.PrincetonReview.com. The best thing about applying from The Princeton Review website is the efficiency. Simply fill out the application profile once and any application you start will be prepopulated with that information. Many schools will also allow you to submit your application and pay the fees electronically. For those that don't, you can print out the application and drop it in the mail.

A final note of advice: No matter which form of electronic application you choose, you should still contact the admissions office for an application packet. This guarantees that you will have all the information and materials that you need to put together the strongest candidacy possible. Some, but not all, schools will let you download this information at their websites; usually, such information is packaged as a .pdf file, which can only be read by a free, downloadable program called Adobe Reader (www.adobe.com/acrobat). Still, despite the increasing online presence of business schools and the convenience of the electronic medium, "snail mail" remains an integral part of the process.

If you have any questions, comments, or suggestions, please e-mail your insights to us at businesseditor@review.com. We appreciate your input and want to make our books as useful to you as they can be.

HOW TO USE THIS BOOK

Each of the business schools listed in this book has its own page. Each page comprises ten sections, though if a school did not supply us with the particular information for certain sections, we simply omitted it from the page. Here's what's on each page:

CONTACT INFORMATION
Included in this shaded section at the top of each page is the admissions contact—that person to whom a possible applicant should address all correspondence—and his or her title. The school's physical address comes next, followed by the admission office's phone and fax numbers. Finally, this section includes the admission office's e-mail and Web addresses.

INSTITUTIONAL INFORMATION
This portion gives the nitty-gritty of the school's character. Is it a public or private school? Are evening classes available? How many total faculty does the school boast? What percent are female? Minority? Part time? What's the student/faculty ratio—important to know if you're one of those students who desire personal interaction with your professors—and how many other students (undergrads, other grad students) at the parent institution are you going to have to wade through to get to class? Finally, is the school on a semester, trimester, or quarter calendar?

PROGRAMS
In this section we tell you what single and joint degrees the school offers (MBA, EMBA, JD/MBA, etc.). Each school has academic specialties—like finance, marketing, or accounting—and we include these so you can judge whether the school's programs fit your needs. Any special academic or extracurricular opportunities are also listed in this section. Finally, for those interested in studying abroad, we provide a list of countries in which the school sponsors a program.

STUDENT INFORMATION
The essentials of the student body are listed here. How many total business students are enrolled in this school? What percentage are full time? Female? Minority? Out of state? International? Finally, what's the average age of the b-school students?

A Glossary of Insider Lingo

B-school students, graduates, and professors—like most close-knit, somewhat solipsistic groups—seem to speak their own weird language. Here's a sampler of MBA jargon (with English translations):

B2B: "Business to Business"—a company that sells not to retail consumers, but to other enterprises. With the renewed focus on more traditional industries, this now stands for "Back to Basics."

B2C: "Business to Consumer"—a company that sells primarily to individual retail consumers. As with the above joke about B2B, business students occasionally say this really means "Back to Consulting."

Four Ps: Elements of a marketing strategy: Price, Promotion, Place, Product.

Rule of Three: You should not talk more than three times in any given class, but you should participate at least once over the course of three classes.

The Five Forces: Michael Porter's model for analyzing the strategic attractiveness of an industry.

Three Cs: The primary forces considered in marketing: Customer, Competition, Company.

COMPUTER AND RESEARCH FACILITIES

Because research and computer facilities are an absolute necessity for the modern b-school student, we present data on the facilities of each school. What libraries and special research centers or institutes are supported by the school? What percentage of b-school dedicated classrooms are wired for laptops and provide Internet access? Does the school have a campuswide network? What type of computer (laptop, desktop, notebook) does the school recommend to or require of its students? Does the school have a purchasing agreement with any hardware companies? If so, with whom? Finally, will you have to pay a fee to be connected to the Internet?

EXPENSES/FINANCIAL AID

Don't worry, we didn't forget about money. We've tried to provide as much cost information as possible, including tuition (in and out of state, when applicable), room and board (on and off campus), and books and supplies. On the flip side, you'll find the amount of the average scholarship/grant (free money) and loan (not free money) awarded, as well as the percentages of first-year and total students who receive financial aid.

ADMISSIONS INFORMATION (OR, WHAT ARE YOUR CHANCES OF GETTING IN?)

This section lists all the various and sundry details you may want to know when applying to a particular b-school. What's the application fee? Does the school have an electronic application? Do they have an early decision program? When is the regular application deadline? How does the b-school notify its students, i.e., do they admit on a rolling basis or not? Can accepted students defer? If so, for how long? Can students apply for entry in the spring semester rather than the fall? Are transfer students accepted? If so, how many credits can he or she have transferred? Are admissions need-blind? How many applications did the school receive the previous year? Of that number, what percent were accepted? What percentage of accepted applicants actually enrolled? What was the average GPA of incoming students? GMAT scores? Average years of business experience? We also provide a section for the schools to highlight other factors they consider during the admissions process (e.g., communication and leadership skills). Finally, a list of other schools to which accepted and enrolled students applied is included.

INTERNATIONAL STUDENTS

This one's quick and easy. For those international students interested in applying, the b-school reports whether the Test of English as a Foreign Language (TOEFL) is required, and if it is, the minimum score the school will accept.

EMPLOYMENT INFORMATION

We've included some valuable information on post-grad employment expectations students might have. Here's where you will find whether each school has a placement office, the percentage of graduates who have jobs after three months and after one year, and the companies who frequently employ graduates. We also graph the most popular fields students enter upon graduation. Finally, in case you have seriously high aspirations, we list any prominent alumni.

SCHOOL BLURB

Finally, we've offered a few words about what to expect at each school. We tell you if there is one particular attribute for which a program is renowned and we disclose details about the curriculum, student body, campus, or location to add a little flavor to your search. We've concocted these informative blurbs from both the schools' websites and our student surveys.

CHAPTER 3

WHAT B-SCHOOL IS REALLY LIKE

AN ACADEMIC PERSPECTIVE

The objective of all MBA programs is to prepare students for a professional career in business. One business school puts it this way:

Graduates should be all of the following:

1. Able to think and reason independently, creatively, and analytically
2. Skilled in the use of quantitative techniques
3. Literate in the use of software applications as management tools
4. Knowledgeable about the world's management issues and problems
5. Willing to work in and successfully cope with conditions of uncertainty, risk, and change
6. Astute decision makers
7. Ethically and socially responsible
8. Able to manage in an increasingly global environment
9. Proficient in utilizing technology as a mode of doing business

Sound like a tall order? Possibly. But this level of expectation is what business school is all about.

Nearly all MBA programs feature a core curriculum that focuses students on the major disciplines of business: finance, management, accounting, marketing, manufacturing, decision sciences, economics, and organizational behavior. Unless your school allows you to place out of them, these courses are mandatory. Core courses provide broad functional knowledge in one discipline. To illustrate, a core marketing course covers pricing, segmentation, communications, product-line planning, and implementation. Electives provide a narrow focus that deepens the area of study. For example, a marketing elective might be entirely devoted to pricing.

Students sometimes question the need for such a comprehensive core program. But the functional areas of a real business are not parallel lines. All departments of a business affect each other every day. For example, an MBA in a manufacturing job might be asked by a financial controller why the company's product has become unprofitable to produce. Without an understanding of how product costs are accounted for, this MBA wouldn't know how to respond to a critical and legitimate request.

At most schools, the first term or year is devoted to a rigid core curriculum. Some schools allow first-years to take core courses side by side with electives. Still others have come up with an entirely new way of covering the basics, integrating the core courses into one cross-functional learning experience, which may also include sessions on topics such as globalization, ethics, and managing diversity. Half-year to year-long courses are team-taught by professors who see you through all disciplines.

TEACHING METHODOLOGY

Business schools employ two basic teaching methods: case study and lecture. Usually, they employ some combination of the two. The most popular is the case study approach. Students are presented with either real or hypothetical business scenarios and are asked to analyze them. This method provides concrete situations (rather than abstractions) that require mastery of a wide range of skills. Students often find case studies exciting because they can engage in spirited discussions about possible solutions to given business problems and because they get an opportunity to apply newly acquired business knowledge.

On the other hand, lecturing is a teaching method in which—you guessed it—the professor speaks to the class and the class listens. The efficacy of the lecture method depends entirely on the professor. If the professor is compelling, you'll probably get a lot out of the class. If the professor is boring, you probably won't listen, which isn't necessarily a big deal since many professors make their class notes available on computer disc or in the library.

THE CLASSROOM EXPERIENCE

Professors teaching case methodology often begin class with a "cold call." A randomly selected student opens the class with an analysis of the case and makes recommendations for solutions. The cold call forces you to be prepared and to think on your feet.

No doubt, a cold call can be intimidating. But unlike law school, b-school professors don't use the Socratic method to torture you, testing your thinking with a pounding cross-examination. They're training managers, not trial lawyers. At worst, particularly if you're unprepared, a professor will abruptly dismiss your contribution.

More Insider Lingo

Back of the Envelope: A quick analysis of numbers, as if scribbled on the back of an envelope.

Benchmarking: Comparing a company to others in the industry.

Burn Rate: Amount of cash a money-losing company consumes during a period of time.

Cycle Time: How fast you can turn something around.

Deliverable: Your end product.

Fume Date: Date the company will run out of cash reserves.

Low Hanging Fruit: Tasks or goals that are most easy to achieve (consultant jargon).

Net Net: End result.

Pro Forma: Financial presentation of hypothetical events, such as projected earnings.

Slice and Dice: Running all kinds of quantitative analysis on a set of numbers.

Value-Based Decision Making: Values and ethics as part of the practice of business.

Alternatively, professors ask for a volunteer to open a case, particularly someone who has had real industry experience with the issues. After the opening, the discussion is broadened to include the whole class. Everyone tries to get in a good comment, particularly if class participation counts heavily toward the grade. "Chip shots"—unenlightened, just-say-anything-to-get-credit comments—are common. So are "air hogs," students who go on and on because they like nothing more than to hear themselves pontificate.

Depending on the school, class discussions can degenerate into wars of ego rather than ideas. But for the most part, debates are kept constructive and civilized. Students are competitive, but not offensively so, and learn to make their points succinctly and persuasively.

THE TUCK INTERVIEW (WHAT MAKES TUCK SO SPECIAL)

In 2001, the Tuck School of Business at Dartmouth received the top ranking in a survey of 1,600 recruiters from around the globe conducted by *The Wall Street Journal*, in collaboration with Harris Interactive. We interviewed Paul Danos, dean of Tuck, to find out why recruiters value Tuck MBAs so much.

"What employers want from their top-performing people are leadership characteristics that relate to how you treat other people."

Q: **Dean Danos, in a study commissioned by *The Wall Street Journal*, Tuck was lauded by corporate recruiters as the country's number-one business school. Congratulations. Recruiters said you are the school that most successfully graduates students with attributes such as: teamwork, communication, problem-solving skills, and the ability to drive results. Can you comment?**

A: Thank you. You know, a lot of people are on the side of the small school. For many, Tuck is an idealized image of what education should be. I don't think too many people would say, "Oh my idealized image of an education is to be with 2,000 other people in a class." We have worked hard to have this setting and this history. And we will stick to our philosophy, our program, and we are fortunate to have the resources that make our school exceptional.

There are many great schools in this world. But I think our model of a small-scale program, with very high-quality education, and still being competitive at the recruiter level, which is obvious from this *Wall Street Journal* study, is a viable alternative.

One of the categories in which we are very strong, and one which I thought was a clever question, asked the recruiters, "Where would you have liked to have gotten your MBA?" We beat the next school by something like thirty points. That says quite a lot about our program because the people surveyed were all highly experienced, selective recruiters.

Clearly, there is an experience at Tuck that you just can't make up and that is very hard to duplicate—the combination of our history, the personal scale of our program, the teamwork of our students. This place resonates with that idealized image of what an MBA education should be.

Q: **So is it the overall experience at Tuck that imbues students with characteristics that make them so highly valued?**

A: Absolutely. What I believe is this: You have to have a prestigious faculty, very good teaching, and a relevant and strong curriculum—we have all of that. So you have to be in a high-end, worldclass game in terms of all of that, and most of the top schools are. But then I think you have to distinguish yourself.

The way Tuck distinguishes itself is a combination of the way the students live here, the way they interact with each other, and their success with the major blue-ribbon employers of the world that hire MBAs.

If you listen to what those employers say, they say Tuck students meet the test for technical and analytical skills. But Tuck students have something special when it comes to working with other diverse people. And that something is very important.

Most companies want to hire people who can work well with other people. I think the biggest differential treatment people get when they come to Tuck is this ability to be sensitive to others. A very interesting comment we hear from recruiters is when we ask about what they thought about the class they just interviewed. They will say, "You know this is what's unusual about this school: You never hear a Tuck student putting down another just for personal advantage."

The other component to this is, I'll bet every MBA at a top school in the country would say, "I learned as much from my colleagues here as I learned from the faculty." Because the colleagues at a top school are an average of twenty-eight years old, they have had lots of business experience. I think Tuck is one of the best at bringing those people together, in creating teams that truly work together. The teamwork aspect is enhanced because of our location, because students learn to live together and work together a lot more closely.

Q: **But many schools, including those that are small and intimate like Tuck, have attempted to instill a genuine one-for-all feeling among their students. Why have you succeeded?**

A: Well, I believe that there is no school in the world that's better at it. I'm not saying there might not be a few that are close, but if you think about what you want from a business school, which is for all these diverse students to come together and work harmoniously in various teams and also as a whole class, I think we do it as well as, if not better than, anyone.

So to answer your question, Tuck students have an edge because they've been living in this community that fosters sensitivity, respect, communication, and working well with others. Even if you came to this community without such instincts, you have to develop some or else you're going to find you're not going to operate too well. Of course, there's self-selection too. The students who choose to come to Tuck are the ones who want this kind of experience.

But we operate and live as a family here. They all know each other and you will not find that closeness at every school.

Q: **All of this is somewhat surprising. I mean it runs counter-intuitive to what you think of business school. When you think about a business school student, you don't think of sensitivity training.**

A: There's no doubt in my mind that the number-one attribute the best employers want from MBAs beyond a high level of technical skill and knowledge is the ability to lead groups. MBAs must know how to be humane in their management styles; they must know how to be sensitive.

Even in the hardest–nosed industry, that's what people want, that's what the bankers want, that's what the consultants want.

This is something every company wants: What employers want from their top-performing people are leadership characteristics that relate to how you treat other people. This has a huge impact on how employers view and evaluate the people who will come into their organizations.

YOUR FIRST YEAR

The first six months of b-school can be daunting. You're unfamiliar with the subjects. There's a tremendous amount of work to do. And when you least have the skills to do so, there's pressure to stay with the pack. All of this produces anxiety and a tendency to over-prepare. Eventually, students learn shortcuts and settle into a routine, but until then much of the first year is just plain tough. The programs usually pack more learning into the first term than they do into each of the remaining terms. For the schools to teach the core curriculum (which accounts for as much as 70 percent of learning) in a limited time, an intensive pace is considered necessary. Much of the second year will be spent on gaining proficiency in your area of expertise and on searching for a job.

The good news is that the schools recognize how tough the first year can be. During the early part of the program, they anchor students socially by placing them in small sections, sometimes called "cohorts." You take many or all of your classes with your sectionmates. Sectioning encourages the formation of personal and working relationships and can help make a large program feel like a school within a school.

Because so much has to be accomplished in so little time, getting an MBA is like living in fast-forward. This is especially true of the job search. No sooner are you in the program than recruiters for summer jobs show up, which tends to divert students from their studies. First-years aggressively pursue summer positions, which are linked with the promise of a permanent job offer if the summer goes well. At some schools, the recruiting period begins as early as October, at others in January or February.

Even More Insider Lingo

Air Hogs: Students who monopolize classroom discussion and love to hear themselves speak.

Case Study Method: Popular teaching method that uses real-life business cases for analysis.

Cold Call: Unexpected, often dreaded request by the professor to open a case discussion.

Functional Areas: The basic disciplines of business (e.g., finance, marketing, R&D).

HP12-C: A calculator that works nothing like a regular one, used by finance types when they don't have Excel handy.

Power Nap: Quick, intense, in-class recharge for the continually sleep deprived.

Power Tool: Someone who does all the work and sits in the front row of the class with his or her hand up.

Pre-enrollment Courses: Commonly known as MBA summer camp—quantitative courses to get the numerically challenged up to speed.

Quant Jock: A numerical athlete who is happiest crunching numbers.

Run the Numbers: Analyze quantitatively.

Soft Skills: Conflict resolution, teamwork, negotiation, oral and written communication.

Take-aways: The key points of a lecture or meeting that participants should remember.

A DAY IN THE LIFE

Matt Camp, First Year

Tuck School of Business, Dartmouth College

7:00 A.M.: Get dressed. Out of the door by 7:45 to head to the campus dining hall for breakfast. If I have time, I'll grab the *Financial Times* and *Wall Street Journal* and gloss over the front page. Today, I have an informal get-to-know-you-better meeting with marketing professor over breakfast.

8:30 A.M.: Core class in Corporate Finance. Grab any seat in a tiered classroom set-up. I'm usually in the middle toward the side. If possible, the front row stays empty.

10:00 A.M.: Go to e-mail kiosk on campus and check messages. Hang out or do a quick run to the library to read more of the *Times*.

10:30 A.M.: Macroeconomics lecture/case study class. Again, no assigned seating. Expect cold calls on case. Cold calls are not terrifiying. Professors are supportive, not out to embarass you. Class discussion is lively, with a mix of people offering their view.

Noon: Back to the cafeteria. Tuck may be one of the few schools where everyone eats together at the same place. There isn't much in town, and you're tight on time, so it doesn't make sense to go back home or elsewhere. It's crowded, so I look for friends, but basically grab a seat anywhere at one of the large tables that seat six to seven. Professors, administrators, and students all eat at the same place. Food is above average.

1:15 P.M.: Classes are over for the day. From this point here, I begin to start homework; there's a lot of work to do. I can go to a study room on campus, but they get booked up pretty quickly for groups, so I head to the library. The majority of the people are doing work for tomorrow. It's rare to have someone working on a project that's due the following week. It's pretty much day-to-day.

4:00 P.M.: I head off to one of the scheduled sports I've signed up for. Today it's soccer, played about one mile from campus. I drive; friends hitch a ride with me. This is a big international scene, mostly men, but there's a small group of women too. It's definitely a game we play hard, but in a very congenial way.

6:00 P.M.: Head back to campus. I'm hungry. It's off to the dining hall again. Most first-years live in dorms, so home cooking is not an option. Almost all second-years live off-campus, so they head back for a home-cooked meal. Cafeteria is not crowded; I may eat alone.

7:00 P.M.: Head home for a quick shower and change. The night is just beginning.

7:30 P.M.: Meet with study group at school to flesh out rest of work that needs to be done in preparation for tomorrow's classes.

11:00 P.M.: Students and their wives/husbands or partners head out to play ice hockey at one of the two rinks here. Wives/husbands and partners play. Because there are different levels, there are different games going on for different skill levels. It's a lot of fun.

Midnight: Time to go and celebrate either a hard game or a sore butt, but everyone goes to get some wings and a beer. There are only two bars on campus, and they close at 1:00 A.M. so we head to one of them.

1:00 A.M.: After the bar closes, people head home.

1:15 A.M.: Exhausted, I go to bed. No TV. I've forgotten what that is.

YOUR SECOND YEAR

Relax, the second year is easier. By now, students know what's important and what's not. Second-years work more efficiently than first-years. Academic anxiety is no longer a factor. Having mastered the broad-based core curriculum, students now enjoy taking electives and developing an area of specialization.

Anxiety in the second year has more to do with the arduous task of finding a job. For some lucky students, a summer position has yielded a full-time offer. But even those students often go through the whole recruiting grind anyway because they don't want to cut off any opportunities prematurely.

Most MBAs leave school with a full-time offer. Sometimes it's their only offer. Sometimes it's not their dream job, which may be why most grads change jobs after just two years. One student summed up the whole two-year academic/recruiting process like this: "The first-year students collapse in the winter quarter because of on-campus recruiting. The second-years collapse academically in the first quarter of their second year because it's so competitive to get a good job. And when a second-year does get a job, he or she forgets about class entirely. That's why pass/fail was invented."

Just a Bit More Insider Lingo

Admissions Mistake: How each student perceives him or herself until getting first-year grades back from midterms.

Chip Shot: Vacant and often cheesy comments used not to truly benefit class discussion, but rather to get credit for participation.

Lingo Bingo: A furtive game of Bingo whereby he who "wins" must work a decided upon, often trite phrase (see "chip shot") into the class discussion. For example: "I didn't actually read the case last night, but the protagonist is two beers short of a six-pack." The winner also earns a prize and the admiration of classmates.

Skydeck: Refers to the back row of the classroom, usually when it's amphitheater style.

Monitize: To turn an idea into a moneymaking scheme.

Shrimp Boy: A student who comes to a corporate event just to scarf down the food.

A DAY IN THE LIFE

Kristin Hansen, Second-Year

Tuck School of Business, Dartmouth College

9:00 A.M.: Wake-up (my first class is at 10:30 A.M.) and finish work for Monday classes.

10:15 A.M.: Ride my bike to campus for 10:30 class.

10:30 A.M.: Head to International Economics class, an elective. I have only three classes this semester, my last. Prior to this I had four and a half classes each term. I front-loaded so I would have a light last semester. Grab a yogurt and juice on way in. Eat in class. We discuss a currency crisis case.

Noon: Head to study room to plug my personal computer into one of the many networked connections on campus to check e-mail. Finish work for next class.

1:00 P.M.: Grab a quick lunch in the dining hall. Will bring it to eat during class.

1:15 P.M.: Managerial Decision Making class, another elective. Today is the very last class that second-years will have at Tuck; we're off to graduation! Our professor brings in strawberries and champagne to celebrate. We all hang out and toast each other. This obviously doesn't happen everyday, but this is just the kind of thing a Tuck professor would do.

2:45 P.M.: I'm one of four Tuck social chairpersons, so I use this time to send e-mails to my co-chairs about the upcoming chili cook-off and farm party. Then I send a message to the school regarding other social events for the weekend. I get an e-mail from the New York office of CS First Boston, with whom I've accepted a job offer, with a calendar of the dates for my private client-services training.

3:00 P.M.: Go for a run, swim, or bike.

5:00 P.M.: Head home to shower and change. Usually I'd make dinner at home and eat, but tonight, I'm heading out to a social event. So I relax a bit and do an hour of preparation for the next day. On Monday, Tuesday, and Wednesday nights, the workload is heavier.

7:00 P.M.: Off to a Turkey Fry Dinner. This is a meal that will be prepared by my two Economics professors. They donated this "dinner" for the charity student auction. Friends of mine bid on it and won. Each of eight bidders gets to bring a guest, and I'm one of the guests. The professors are hosting this at one of their homes. Basically, they're taking three large turkeys and fry-o-lating them.

8:30 P.M.: We all head out to an "open-mic" night, led by the same two Economics professors that hosted the Turkey Fry. It's held at a local bar. Anyone in the audience can get onstage and perform. I'm a member of the Tuck band, so I get up on stage with my acoustic guitar and play various folk and bluegrass songs. This is a great warm-up for the Open Mic night at Tuck.

10:45 P.M.: We head out for Pub Night in downtown Hanover.

1:00 A.M.: The bar closes, so we head to "The End Zone," one of the second-year houses close to campus. All the second-year houses are named; these are names that have been passed down from generation to generation. On a typical Thursday night at Tuck, a small number of students will stay out until 3:00 A.M. I'm usually one of them.

3:00 A.M.: I walk home. My house, called "Girls in the Hood," is just a ten-minute stroll away. I may grab a 3:00 A.M. snack. Then, I quickly fall asleep, exhausted.

RECIPE FOR FRIED TURKEY AT TUCK

Prepared by Professor Andrew Bernard and Professor Michael Knetter, who was recently promoted to associate dean of the MBA Program.

From the chefs: "Students would say it's the best turkey they've ever had."

Equipment:

10-gallon aluminum pot with lid

Iron stand to sit pan in, Bunsen burner underneath

Large poultry syringe

Ingredients:

Coca-Cola

Bottle of onion juice

Couple of cans of beer

Garlic powder

Cajun spices

6 gallons peanut oil for frying

12-pound turkey

Directions:

The night before, combine the first four ingredients and bring to a boil. Let cool. Using a big poultry injector/syringe, inject bird with 16 to 20 ounces of marinade. Rub down the outside of the bird with the Cajun spices. Let sit overnight.

Heat the 6 gallons of oil in 10-gallon pot until bubbly. Carefully submerge turkey into 350-degree oil. Leave pot uncovered while turkey is cooking. Cook for about 4 minutes per pound. Repeat process as needed (once the oil is hot, it's easy to cook additional birds). *For a special treat:* try placing a chicken or duck in the cavity of your turkey.

Top Ten Most Desirable Employers

According to a recent survey of students at 40 top U.S. business schools by the academic consulting firm Universum, the top ten most desirable employers for 2002 are (2001 rankings are in parentheses):

1. McKinsey and Company (1)
2. The Boston Consulting Group (2)
3. Goldman Sachs (4)
4. General Electric (25)
5. Bain and Company (5)
6. Citigroup (37)
7. Morgan Stanley (10)
8. Walt Disney (13)
9. IBM (11)
10. Coca-Cola (38)

The following employers dropped out of the top ten:

12. Booz-Allen Hamilton (7)
17. Accenture (6)
29. Intel (8)
33. Cisco Systems (3)
48. Hewlett-Packard (9)

The top three most desirable industries are:

1. Management Consulting (preferred by 30%)
2. Consumer Goods (preferred by 20%)
3. Investment Banking (preferred by 19%)

LIFE OUTSIDE OF CLASS

Business school is more than academics and a big-bucks job. A spirited community provides ample opportunity for social interaction, extracurricular activity, and career development.

Much of campus life revolves around student-run clubs. There are groups for just about every career interest and social need—from "MBAs for a Greener America" to the "Small Business Club." There's even a group for Significant Others on most campuses. The clubs are a great way to meet classmates with similar interests and to get in on the social scene. They might have a reputation for throwing the best black-tie balls, pizza-and-keg events, and professional mixers. During orientation week, these clubs aggressively market themselves to first-years.

Various socially responsible projects are also popular on campus. An emphasis on volunteer work is part of the overall trend toward good citizenship. Perhaps to counter the greed of the 1980s, "giving back" is the b-school style of the moment. There is usually a wide range of options—from tutoring in an inner-city school to working in a soup kitchen to renovating public buildings.

Still another way to get involved is to work on a school committee. Here you might serve on a task force designed to improve student quality of life. Or you might work in the admissions office and interview prospective students.

For those with more creative urges there are always the old standbys: extracurriculars such as the school paper, yearbook, or school play. At some schools, the latter takes the form of the b-school follies and is a highlight of the year. Like the student clubs, these are a great way to get to know your fellow students.

Finally, you can play on intramural sports teams or attend the numerous informal get-togethers, dinner parties, and group trips. There are also plenty of regularly scheduled pub nights, just in case you thought your beer-guzzling days were over.

Most former MBA students say that going to b-school was the best decision they ever made. That's primarily because of nonacademic experiences. Make the most of your classes, but take the time to get involved and enjoy yourself.

Chapter 4

Palm Pilots and Power Breakfasts: What Does an MBA Offer?

NUTS-AND-BOLTS BUSINESS SKILLS

Graduate business schools teach the applied science of business. The best business schools combine the latest academic theories with pragmatic concepts, hands-on experience, and real-world solutions.

B-schools also teach the analytical skills used to make complicated business decisions. You learn how to define the critical issues, apply analytical techniques, develop the criteria for decisions, and make decisions after evaluating their impact on other variables.

After two years, you're ready to market a box of cereal. Or prepare a valuation of the cereal company's worth. You'll speak the language of business. You'll know the tools of the trade. Your expertise will extend to many areas and industries. In short, you will have acquired the skills that open doors.

ACCESS TO RECRUITERS, ENTRÉE TO NEW FIELDS

Applicants tend to place great emphasis on "incoming" and "outgoing" statistics. First they ask, "Will I get in?" Then they ask, "Will I get a job?"

Obviously, the first is largely dependent on how selective the school is and the quality of your credentials. The latter question can almost assuredly be answered in the positive, "Yes, you will."

But the real question is how many offers will you receive? Again, that is dependent on the appeal of the school to recruiters (which is a readily available statistic you can get from each school) and the particular industry you elect to pursue. For example, investment banks and consulting firms are always going to come to the schools for formal recruiting periods, whereas more off-the-beaten-path choices will possibly require you to go off campus in search of opportunity.

Location, Location, Location

Universum's 2002 respondents named the U.S. and international cities in which they'd prefer to work. Note that New York holds this top ranking despite the fact that most survey responses were received after September 11.

In the U.S.:

1. New York (20%)
2. Boston (11%)
3. San Francisco (11%)
4. Chicago (10%)
5. Los Angeles (7%)
6. Washington, D.C. (6%)
7. Atlanta (5%)
8. Seattle (3%)
9. Austin (2%)
10. Minneapolis (2%)

Overseas:

1. London (23%)
2. Paris (7%)
3. Hong Kong (6%)
4. Sydney (5%)
5. Madrid (5%)

I don't want to work abroad (10%)

GOODBYE GET-RICH-QUICK SCHEMES, HELLO REALITY

Unhappily, the immediate, economic value of the MBA remains in flux. Although MBAs continue to be in demand, a weak economy and flat national job market have depressed recruiter appetite for new grads. The latest figures suggest a tough job market for newly minted MBAs. And first- and second-year business students are feeling the pinch of a tight job market as both full-time and summer positions become more difficult to obtain.

For the last several years, cash-heavy dot-coms and investment banks flush with business deals made a heavy play for MBAs. The loss of one of these recruitment sources and the downsizing of the other has further shrunk the recruiter pool and made for a more anxious recruiting period. Where once students were awash in three or more job offers apiece, the latest figures are more sobering: students are working hard to receive one or two offers. Of course with fewer offers, the jobs students get, and have to accept, may not be their first choice.

"The statistics that we've seen indicate that placement is pretty much on track. But it's really persistence, it's students who are really committed in their job search who are successful," says Rose Martinelli, director of admissions at the Wharton School. "Students who have a strong focus are still finding a lot of opportunity. But it's sort of a tale of two cities. Some students will wind up with five or so offers each. Others who are still unsure are getting beaten out in the job process. And that's the difference—one student knows what they want to do and takes advantage of all the networking opportunities and getting paired up with an alumni mentor. Another just scrambles and has unrealistic expectations."

Linda Baldwin, director of admission at the University of California at Los Angeles' Anderson School of Business echoes a similar note: "This year recruiting has been difficult. Many of the standard industries are hiring less. There are still positions in high tech and biotech, but in many areas things have not been rosy and students have had to use different strategies and engage their networks."

Although the stress of job hunting may be greater, that doesn't mean that hiring has come to a complete standstill. Steven Lubrano, assistant dean and director of the MBA Program at the Tuck School of Business, best summed up the career placement picture: "There are two issues at stake here: what the market has to offer students and what students come to expect when they enroll."

If you really want the current numbers, they're daunting. At many of the nation's top schools, spring placement rates are at about 50 percent to 60 percent, when only a year ago, more than three-quarters of the graduating class had a job. That means that roughly 40 percent of the graduating class is still jobless. "The stalwart recruiters may not hire ten students, but they may hire eight," says Lubrano. "The question is, are you one of the eight?"

As we write this book, many schools still have a month or so to go until graduation. If past downturns offer us any insight, it is that students will continue to receive job offers up until and right past graduation into the summer months. Roughly 90 percent of the graduating class will be employed by the fall, and it's likely that that first job out will earn them a solid return on their b-school investment. Adds Lubrano, "Some of the best jobs come very late in the academic year. Our goal at Tuck is we don't rest until everybody has a job and is happy at that job."

At less prominent schools, the picture may not be as optimistic. Heavy hirers of MBAs who have few spots available during this recruiting go-around may bypass these schools.

The good news is that even in an uncertain economy, top schools will continue to produce in-demand MBAs for the marketplace. These schools tend to have an extensive history with big recruiting companies because the schools are a steady source of exceptional talent. Even during an economic downturn, big recruiters can't afford to lose face on these campuses. They need a constant presence at these schools to ensure that they'll have top picks when good times return. In fact, to cement that relationship, recruiters often have a partnership with the schools that includes sponsoring academic projects and hosting school club functions and informational cocktail hour events.

GOOD TIMES, BAD TIMES: GETTING THE MBA FOR THE LONG RUN

You'd be hard-pressed to find a year as turbulent as this one. The events of September 11 flattened an economy already on its knees from the washout of the high-tech world. This past year was so tumultuous that it should be seen as something of an aberration. But that's just it—labor markets will warm and cool periodically. The tables can turn at any time. Although this year's events were unusual, as you make plans to go to b-school, you need to accept that there is some risk that the labor market won't greet you with open arms at graduation.

Consider the plight of this year's MBA graduates. When they entered b-school two years ago, the economy was roaring ahead. The immediate future looked exceptionally bright. Most MBAs probably thought that once they got in, they had it made, and they looked forward to generous starting salaries and bonuses. Few probably anticipated that tough times could hit so dramatically.

The best way to consider the value of the degree is by focusing on its long-lasting benefits. "When people come here for their MBA, they talk about re-tooling for their life. They think about the long term and recognize that there are some short term hurdles," says Rose Martinelli, director of admissions at the Wharton School. "Just out of business school, this is the very first job in a long career. This is really about building blocks and going for the long run. You may have to work harder to find a job now, but building your career is a lifelong process." The MBA gives you the tools, networking, and polish to meaningfully enhance your long-term prospects and earning potential.

"There is real opportunity here. The opportunity right now is to pursue your passion and perhaps not your wallet," continues Martinelli. "We're seeing more of an equalization in salary. Those high-paying jobs in finance, investment banking, and consulting are fewer and harder to find. So here you have an opportunity for a job with a true learning experience rather than one that just pays a lot. More people are going into nonprofit and government and making contributions back to the community."

Salary Expectations

Universum's 2002 Survey also asked business students about their salary expectations. When students were asked, "What annual base salary do you expect at your first job after graduation?" the results were as follows (last year's responses in parentheses):

Less than $60,000	9%	(8%)
$60,000–$69,999	6%	(7%)
$70,000–$79,999	14%	(14%)
$80,000–$89,999	29%	(24%)
$90,000–$99,999	16%	(14%)
$100,000–$109,999	16%	(16%)
$110,000–$119,999	3%	(6%)
$120,000 and more	7%	(10%)

According to Universum's findings, the recent economic downturn hasn't dampened the average salary expectations of MBA grads, up $10,000 from 2000, while hopes of earning top salaries right out of school have dropped from 32 percent in 2001 to only 26 percent this year. Universum also found that only 74 percent of students expect to receive a signing bonus, down from 87 percent in 2001, and that men are more confident that they will receive a signing bonus than are women.

Universum is a Stockholm-based firm that specializes in graduate recruitment and student relations. The 2002 Universum survey reflects the responses of 2,807 MBA students at 40 top b-schools in the U.S. For more information, visit Universum's website at www.universum.se.

SHOW ME THE MONEY

After several years of hefty salary increases, 2001 and 2002 starting salaries have clearly leveled. Pundits argue that this is a natural progression of events. During the dot-com craze, e-commerce start-ups, as well as the more traditional industries, had to compete for students. To get their attention, hefty salaries and option packages were thrown at them. The hiring binge, career placement officers observe, and the over-inflated salaries that went with them, was an anomaly. This year, they argue, will be more typical, and students will have to re-adjust their expectations.

Ironically, salaries for new MBAs in the next few years will seem higher. But again, this is another remnant of the dot-com world that requires a closer look. Because dot-coms offered lower base pay and big options, dollar to dollar, the base salaries in other industries seem higher.

But not all the news is bad. A survey of placement offices reveals that salaries are holding steady, ranging from $60,000 to $130,000 for average first-year packages offered to MBA grads from top-flight schools.

The majority also receive a generous relocation package. Indeed, if you were fortunate enough to have spent the summer in between your first and second year at a consulting company, then you will, in all likelihood, also receive a "rebate" on your tuition. These companies pick up student's second-year tuition bill. The big enchilada, however, goes to those MBA students who worked at the firm before b-school. These lucky capitalists get their whole tuition paid for.

GETTING A JOB

For most would-be MBAs, b-school represents a fresh beginning—either in their current profession or in an entirely different industry. Whatever promise the degree holds for you, it's wise to question what the return on your investment will be.

As with starting salary, several factors affect job placement. School reputation and ties to industries and employers are important. At the top programs, the lists of recruiters read like a "Who's Who" of American companies. These schools not only attract the greatest volume of recruiters, but consistently get the attention of those considered "blue chip."

Not to be overlooked are lesser-known, regional schools that often have the strongest relationships with local employers and industries. Some b-schools (many of them state universities) are regarded by both academicians and employers as number one in their respective regions. In other words, as far as the local business community is concerned, these programs offer as much prestige and pull as a nationally ranked program.

Student clubs also play a big part in getting a job because they extend the recruiting efforts at many schools. They host a variety of events that allow you to meet leading business people, so that you can learn about their industries and their specific companies. Most important, these clubs are very effective at bringing in recruiters and other interested parties that do not recruit through traditional mainstream channels. For example, the high-tech, international, and entertainment student clubs provide career opportunities not available through the front door.

Your background and experiences also affect your success in securing a position. Important factors are academic specialization, academic standing, prior work experience, and intangibles such as your personal fit with the company. These days, what you did before b-school is particularly important; it helps establish credibility and gives you an edge in competing for a position in a specific field. For those using b-school to switch careers to a new industry, it's helpful if something on your resume ties your interest to the new profession. It's smart to secure a summer job in the new area.

Finally, persistence and initiative are critical factors in the job search. Since the beginning of this decade, many fast tracks have been narrowed. Increasingly, even at the best schools, finding a job requires off-campus recruiting efforts and ferreting out the hidden jobs.

MBA CAREERS: AN INTERVIEW WITH THE DIRECTOR OF THE MBA CAREER MANAGEMENT CENTER AT UCLA

The recruitment of MBAs has always been tied to the state of the economy. To better gauge the current tenor of MBA hiring, we spoke to Alysa Polkes, the director of the MBA Career Management Center at the Anderson School at UCLA. She shares with us her thoughts on the MBA job search process and provides insight into how things have evolved over the last few years.

Q: Alysa, I would think the Career Management Center is the epicenter of the MBA program. What's the mood on campus as students search for jobs? How have things changed from last year—for example, the number of offers students are getting?

A: The number of offers is always a tough one for me because I feel that we sometimes focus on it as the measuring stick of success. I think a student with just one offer that's exactly what he/she wanted to do is better off than the student with ten offers if none of those offers are what the student really wants to do.

So let me focus on the mood and how things are different from last year. When you look at the landscape of MBA career management over the last decade, I would say that overall, except for a little dip in 1991, we have a very stable thing going.

Then last year, we got a whack on the side of the head with the whole dot-com revolution. It created numerous challenges for those of us in the career management field. The primary one was that students were not taking the time for what we consider the necessary first step in this process: self-assessment. The market was so strong and the economy was so hot there really was no need to sit back and reflect on interests, skills, values, and strengths, all that stuff we believe is the foundation to a long-term successful career.

Of course it's true that we still had the bankers, consultants, and brand managers who followed their paths. But for the folks who were in the other categories of undecided or high-tech, they fell into the whole dot-com world.

It was interesting to watch this happen. Our traditional recruiters came in and asked us to help them attract top talent given what was happening. And we had dot-coms calling us who hadn't a clue about the MBA recruiting process, much less scheduling interviews six months in advance and reserving rooms.

Q: Did the more traditional companies up salaries to compete with the lure of the dot-coms?

A: That was one of the consequences. It was not completely out of control. We heard of one instance where a bank had offered a million dollars if you sign a contract that you'll stay for two or three years. But other than that, I didn't hear of anything that ludicrous.

Q: **That's pretty ludicrous. But obviously I'm in the wrong field.**

A: Exactly. You can suffer anything for two years if you're going to get a million dollars. But beyond that, we saw that what the traditional companies were offering was very competitive.

The problem was that you would think that students would be making a trade-off to go to a dot-com. You would think that, okay, there's a promise of all these options, but the base is not very high.

Q: **What do you mean by a trade-off?**

A: That the students who opted to go to a dot-com would trade off a strong base salary for the promise of rewards down the road. And they didn't, which made the whole thing more complicated.

They didn't have the trade-off. The dot-com base salaries were $75,000 to $80,000. No one was going to suffer at a salary like that, and then there was still the promise of the options.

The year before was a little different. The class of 1999 had to make some trade-offs for those packages. The dot-com salaries weren't yet what they were in 2000. In 1999, the salaries were fifties, sixties, and the promise of options. In 2000, the dot-com salaries were competitive. And then the lure was the millions.

Q: **So . . . fast-forwarding to now . . .**

A: Well, having done this for eleven years, you really get a big-picture perspective. Over the course of the summer, the dot-coms started to wind down, and then we heard about banks buying each other out and consolidating, so that raised some flags.

Students began to become cautious about banking opportunities and realized there were would be fewer spots. Then we started to see the demise of the e-commerce consulting firms, like March First. When they were on campus recruiting, the company filed bankruptcy, and they got a call to go home. Then the other dot-coms started going under, and that included the incubators. Then we started to see the venture capital money dry up. Then, we started hearing that the good old Fortune 500 companies had depressed earnings and were not making their targets.

At the same time, all these high-tech wannabe students realized they weren't going to be going to work for dot-coms or cool, new high-tech companies. So it seems that almost all at once they were going to hit companies like Intel, Dell, Hewlett Packard, Microsoft, and those kinds of companies. Sure enough, those companies turned around and said, "We're suffering too, and we're not going to be able to hire in the numbers that we thought." I've since that heard that some of these firms are pulling back offers.

Q: They rescinded them? I've never heard of that. How often have you?

A: Maybe three times in eleven years. It's not common, but they do get paid off.

Q: Oh, that's not bad.

A: It is if you turned down other offers. In any case, the Dells and Ciscos cut out recruiting. What this meant in the end is that we did have huge turnout for consulting and banking this year. And we do have more students at this time of year (April, May) without positions than last year. But again, last year was not normal.

I would say that we are down off an average year. But I wouldn't say it's dramatically so. People are just having to work harder to find their job

Q: Isn't entertainment a big draw at your school?

A: Yes. We are in a unique situation where we have a higher than average percentage of students who are interested in entertainment, real estate, entrepreneurial ventures, digital media, and optical networking. Where we stand now, three-quarters of each class has an offer.

Q: With the economic slump, the dot-com meltdown, and MBAs out there pounding the pavement hard, what would you say to someone trying to decide whether to go to business school?

A: I think if you look at how quickly things have changed in the past twenty-four to thirty-six months you can't possibly predict what the economy will be in twelve to twenty-four months. So making a decision based on the current state of the economy when you're looking at a two-year program is probably not a reasonable way to make a decision.

The better way to make a decision is to sit down and think about where you, as an individual, want to be in your career down the road. Draw a picture of what you already have in your portfolio to help you get there, and of what is missing. If you can say conclusively that you're missing a set of skills such as quantitative skills or leadership development skills that you would get from an MBA program, then waiting won't help propel your career.

There are always going to be jobs for the people who can't be turned down.

FRIENDS WHO ARE GOING PLACES, ALUMNI WHO ARE ALREADY THERE

Most students say that the best part about b-school is meeting classmates with whom they share common goals and interests. Many students claim that the "single greatest resource is each other." Not surprisingly, with so many bright and ambitious people cocooned in one place, b-school can be the time of your life. It presents numerous professional and social opportunities. It can be where you find future customers, business partners, and mentors. It can also be where you establish lifelong friendships. And after graduation, these classmates form an enduring network of contacts and professional assistance.

Alumni are also an important part of the b-school experience. While professors teach business theory and practice, alumni provide insight into the real business world. When you're ready to interview, they can provide advice on how to get hired by the companies recruiting at your school. In some cases, they help secure the interview and shepherd you through the hiring process.

B-schools love to boast about the influence of their alumni network. To be sure, some are very powerful. But this varies from institution to institution. At the very least, alumni will help you get your foot in the door. A resume sent to an alum at a given company, instead of to "Sir or Madam" in the personnel department, has a much better chance of being noticed and acted on.

After you graduate, the network continues to grow. Regional alumni clubs and alumni publications keep you plugged in to the network with class notes detailing who's doing what, where, and with whom.

Throughout your career, an active alumni relations department can give you continued support. Post-MBA executive education series, fund-raising events, and continued job-placement efforts are all resources you can draw on for years to come.

Chapter 5

Where Are They Now?

HARVARD BUSINESS SCHOOL'S CLASS OF '92: REFLECTIONS ON WHERE THEY'VE BEEN AND WHERE THEY'RE HEADED, TEN YEARS OUT

It takes a monumental leap of faith to go to business school, to take two years out of your professional life, go to zero income, and drop $60,000 or more on tuition. By contrast, making the decision to go to medical or law school is more straightforward. Of the three so-called primary professions—business, medicine, and law—business is the only one you can pursue without a degree. In fact, you can become highly successful (and may already be) without an MBA. So how do you decide?

Perhaps the best way to assess the value of the MBA is to talk to the people who have already gone through the program and can reflect on the experience and the credential.

This next section features tape-edited interviews with eight executives who are ten years out of the MBA program. These interviews resonate with real-life lessons and insights. As these men and women reflect on their prospects out of business school and then bring us up to speed ten years later, you get a personal and candid look at how the MBA has served them. *These* are the human stories behind all those big-number statistics.

What is most interesting about these MBAs is how what matters to them has broadened and deepened beyond money, immediate gratification, and career acceleration. Their experiences reflect the conflicts and yearnings that are natural to all striving professionals.

The one common element these interviewees share is an MBA from Harvard Business School, perhaps one of the most sought after business degrees in the world. These individuals are exceptionally intelligent, savvy, successful professionals. It is no accident they went to Harvard. As you will see, their life choices, experiences, and reflections on the value of the MBA are widely divergent, though all believe the MBA continues to serve them well in a variety of areas. Without a doubt, the MBA was a transforming experience in their lives.

As divergent as some of their paths have been, there are common themes to their stories:

- Where you go to school matters. A lot.
- Technical or knowledge-content learning at business school may be limited; the real learning is in how to approach a situation and think it through.

- Business school provides unimaginably rich social opportunities. Friendships made there offer a lifetime of personal and professional support.
- Like the network of friendships, the network of alumni offers continued social and professional opportunities.
- The desire for high level of achievement and success is great.
- They are highly competitive.
- There is some pressure to follow the money-making herd.
- Money is important, but its importance diminishes over time.
- Women often choose to disengage fromt he fast track and modify their career aspirations when they want to have a family.
- Family starts to matter, usually above all else.
- Time matters, and working 24/7 is a lifestyle all labor to leave behind.
- Over the years, the value of the MBA changes from the knowledge gained to the networks that can be leveraged.
- All agree, though not for all the same reasons, that the MBA was worth it.

Clive Holmes

Managing Director, Investment Banking Division, Deutsche Bank

"All this hype about everyone rushing off at twenty years old to become a billionaire and all that kind of stuff, that is a classic example of a very short-lived fad. You don't plan your career based on fads."

Q: Clive, fresh out of business school, what were your expectations about what your MBA could do for your business career?

A: I think I saw the degree as a way to open doors that weren't open before. I believe in optionality. You should have as many options in your career and in your life as possible open to you at all times. What I saw the MBA as doing is increasing that optionality because things I wouldn't have been able to do career-wise without the MBA would now be added to the list of things I could do. It was a great way to meet people, make contacts, network, and all that sort of stuff. The reach of the alumni network is amazing. But it's all part of the same increased optionality equation.

Q: How did you see the value of the degree at the five-year mark?

A: I think the degree itself was of declining value at that point because people were putting more emphasis on what your job experience is rather than your life experience. But without a doubt because of the field I went into, it was valuable. And the degree gives you credibility, meaning it allows you to skip questions that no longer need to be asked because you have that name on your resume.

Q: Did you use Harvard's alumni network in the first five years out to advance your career?

A: I really did not in any formal way. But without a shadow of a doubt, other Harvard people, when they know you're from Harvard, stick together. You just get treated differently. Things might be offered to you, or made available to you, that are not made available to people who did not go to that school by other people who did.

Q: Can you give an example?

A: There was a client company we were pursuing, and I was the junior guy on the deal. The client was choosing between our firm and a couple of other firms. At our first meeting, we went around the room for introductions, and the client wanted to know not only about our backgrounds, but where we went to school, that sort of stuff. I was the only one who had gone to Harvard. Well, so had he.

He was a big fan of Harvard, and he and I hit it off very well. He went on to award us the piece of business. I think quite a bit of that was a result of the personal relationship that he and I quickly developed. That goes to the spine of the Harvard alumni connection.

Q: Not a bad benefit of being a HBS alum.

A: Absolutely. And this stuff plays out subtly all the time in the financial world, and still plays out today, ten years later. People from HBS, even though you may not know each other personally, have an immediate kind of camaraderie. Now, you've got a slight leg up on someone you've never met before and know nothing about. That is an incredibly powerful business tool.

It really does work that way. Other grads from other schools have said, "Well on occasions this happens," or "There is some advantage that I feel I'm being afforded by being from Wharton or Duke or somewhere else." But this is not on occasion for Harvard. This happens all the time.

Q: Switching subjects, how many jobs did you hold in your first five years out of school?

A: Two.

Q: Both of them were in finance?

A: Yes.

Q: What was the reason for getting the second job?

A: Simply going to a better firm at the time. I went from Merrill Lynch to Morgan Stanley because I was doing mergers and acquisitions, and Merrill Lynch was number six or seven on the table while Morgan Stanley was number number one. Morgan Stanley approached me.

As someone relatively new to the business, exposure to deal flow and transactions and experience is what you want, and Morgan Stanley had more of that than anybody else.

Q: You went into finance, a discipline that can be studied in a school setting fairly well. Did you learn a lot about finance at Harvard? Did that impact on how well you did in business in the financial arena?

A: No. And no. Harvard is not a great finance school. I was an accountant before I went to Harvard, and there wasn't really a great deal about finance or the mechanical tools of finance that Harvard taught me.

What Harvard really taught me was a way to think. It taught me how to deal with vast amounts of information and to be able to discern what is important and what to focus on. Rather than giving me the tools to directly discern the answer, it gave me the tools to identify what 80 percent or 90 percent is just noise, and this is the piece you need to focus on. Focus your analysis in this area, and you'll get your answer. That sort of macro tool set was frankly more useful than something that you can pull out of a finance textbook and that you don't need to go to Harvard to get in the first place.

Q: On a scale of 1 to 10, how important would you say that learning "how to think" was in your first five years out?

A: A 9. That's the point I'm making. It really wasn't finance tools that they taught me. I knew a lot of that stuff. But the methodology of going about the problem solving, that was the key take-away from Harvard for me. And that I use every single day.

Q: How has family or personal life impacted on your career choices?

A: I think it's actually been the other way around for me in that my career choices have impacted family and personal life. To be honest, this wasn't a whole lot because at the time I was making those kinds of career choices, earlier on in my career, family and friends were sort of on the periphery for me. They followed what else was going on in my life.

That's why we came to New York, so I could work on Wall Street. My partner at the time, now my wife, followed me.

Q: And now, ten years out, have your priorities changed?

A: Absolutely. I think there comes a point for a lot of people where you reassess what your absolute priorities are in life.

I mean, I'm a banker by trade, so understand that, however you cut the pie, more money is better than less money. My instincts tell me more is better than less. That's the first thing I would tell you about priorities. But then after a while it becomes, well, just how much money is enough money, and what sacrifices are you willing to make to get more money.

The answer for me after a while was, I don't need to be a member of the BBC, the Billionaire Boys Club. But I need to be financially secure and comfortable, and I'm probably at that point in my career at this moment. And so that causes a reassessment, having reached that sort of critical level of what is acceptable in terms of sacrifice.

What has happened now is that the end does not in all instances justify the means, and by that I mean, when I didn't have that financial security, I would sacrifice everything to succeed in my job to make sure I got it. Having reached a level of financial security, I'm still very competitive, I want to do very well in my job, but I'm not prepared to work a hundred hours a week anymore.

So I guess my priorities have changed because that was not on the top of my mind right out of business school. You would simply do what it took to get the job done. Nowadays, you start to question what it takes to get the job done, and whether you're the best person to be doing it.

Q: Speaking of nowadays, how many jobs have you held in the last five to ten years?

A: Just one more.

Q: You've stayed on a very straight course of banking?

A: Correct. Now I've done things outside of banking as well; I'm not sure you're aware of that. I've started two or three companies, and I did private investing for my own accounts.

So I've done a little bit of this and that. We took a company public on the Nasdaq a couple of years back. We've had some fun. So if you look at my career, I've only had three jobs, yes.

Q: I'm curious, when you say "we" took a company public, who's the "we"? Are you talking about peers outside of work?

A: Yes. Six of us started a company in 1996, and in the following two years—now you know what I do with my weekends—we grew it from a start-up to four-and-a-half thousand employees and $100 million of revenue and $150 million of market capital as we sold it on the Nasdaq in '98.

Q: Are these business partners from Harvard?

A: No. None of these were. These were just good old-fashioned friends of mine that I went drinking with.

Q: Did any of these friends have MBAs?

A: Not all of them; half of them did. Three MBAs and three not MBAs.

Q: Would you say a side business is a common experience for a b-school grad like yourself?

A: Not really for investment banking. Other people were much more focused, which is not really the right word, but narrow maybe in their views.

My view was that investment banking would create another tool set that would be applicable across a wide range of opportunities of which this was one. And so I was the acting chief financial officer until we took it public, whereupon someone else stepped into that role, and I stepped back to just pure investment banking again until the next opportunity came up.

Q: There's that optionality again. Okay, so you're not part of the BBC. But you're part of the MMC, the Millionaire Men's Club.

A: Ah, thank you for that.

Q: There's a tremendous amount of uncertainty in the business world now about the state of the economy, the future of technology. What advice would you have for today's business school applicant?

A: I think I would say definitely go to business school. You still want to do that. And the answer is because all this hype about everyone rushing off at twenty years old to become a billionaire and all that kind of stuff, that is a classic example of a very short-lived fad.

You don't plan your career based on fads. You plan your career, as I've said, on optionality. You want to have as many options open to you and available to you throughout your professional career. You want to try and avoid the temptation to chase what's hot, what's there today, and really look to the future and say to yourself, "How will this opportunity, if it doesn't work out, prepare me for the rest of me career? "

To that I would say, first up, do go to business school. The reason is, you will meet people and learn processes that will benefit you throughout your career, no matter what you do, because of the network, the way of thinking, and the added maturity that you'll get during those couple of years interacting with some very, very, smart people. It's just good.

Coming out of business school think hard about what you want. Don't get revved up with what everyone else is doing. I went into investment banking because I liked finance. And I went into investment banking back in '92. Nineteen ninety-two was a terrible year on the street. They just weren't hiring, and everybody was going into consulting. I mean McKinsey was there interviewing 500 Harvard people. But the answer was, I didn't want to do that because it wasn't me, it wasn't what I was about. I'm not a consultant; that's not my nature. I like numbers. I'm facile with them. They're easy for me. So for me, going off and being an investment banker was what I really wanted to do, and I stuck to my goals, and I've stuck with it since. I've been very happy with my decision.

So I would tell MBAs coming out of school: Think hard about that you want to do. Don't do what everyone else is doing just cause it seems like a good idea. And if you go do what everyone else is doing, rather than what you really want to do, think hard about what happens next. Always be thinking one, two, three steps up the road. Because if you go off to start-up an Internet company at nineteen years old and it goes bust, and now you're a nineteen-year-old with no real business experience, no MBA, and no money in the bank, just exactly what are you going to do for the next twenty-five years? And how are you going to reach that level of financial security that everyone aspires to? Not the BBC, just that level of security that lets you know your kids will be able to go to good colleges and you'll be able to retire one day.

As for the young people that ran off and blew off getting their MBAs and everything else, for every one wonderful story you hear of going off and striking it rich in the millions, there are thousands that you don't hear about that crashed and burned. So unless you think you're that one special person, go out and do it properly. Go to business school and get it in the bag.

Jay O'Connor

Vice President, Marketing and Product Management for an Internet start-up

"The network value of my friends and classmates from business school increases with time."

Q: Jay, are you happy you got an MBA?

A: I'm very glad I went to business school. I felt that way when I graduated, and I continue to feel that way now. But I certainly don't think that everyone needs to get an MBA. There are some industries where an MBA is not that highly valued, and you might be better off getting two extra years of work experience rather than the MBA.

Q: Can you give us some examples?

A: Real estate, the entertainment industry, and perhaps the advertising business are examples of industries that may not place a high "credential" value on an MBA degree.

Q: What kinds of people get the most benefit from an MBA program?

A: Almost everyone learns something valuable. In terms of pure learning, I would say that the people who seem to learn relatively less from an MBA program are people who have been consultants or investment bankers, or who received an undergraduate business degree from a great undergrad business school like Wharton or Berkeley—anyone who already has had broad exposure to a range of different industries and who understands accounting and finance. People like this can still get lots of value from going to business school, but for them, the value is probably less about the "hard science" portion of the curriculum and more about the "soft sciences"—e.g., organizational behavior—the credential itself, and the network.

But if you think you might ever want the flexibility to shift industries or job functions, or if you feel you would learn a tremendous amount from the b-school curriculum, an MBA is very helpful.

Q: What about choosing a school?

A: I think it matters where you go. Not all MBAs are equal. This may sound elitist to some people, but over the years I've talked to lots of people who've attended different MBA programs. I consistently heard about much better experiences from people who went to, say, a top-five school, versus a lower-level school.

One of the biggest differences I hear people talk about is the quality of your fellow students. At a top-five school, you can be pretty sure that 90 percent of the people there are pretty darn sharp! Having case discussions can be much less interesting and educational if your fellow students aren't as sharp. And since some of the value of the MBA program is the network of friends and classmates you'll have access to over the years, going to school with a strong network will provide more long-term value.

I would say that if you're planning on going to a lower-ranked program, talk to some of their grads to find out what they got out of it.

Q: How did you feel about the value of your degree and career prospects upon graduation from Harvard?

A: Getting out of business school, I definitely felt that I had more career options than before. In fact, for me the MBA program at Harvard Business School (HBS) allowed me to make a seamless transition from one industry to another. My goal at Harvard was to develop a deep functional expertise in marketing and product management in the software industry.

Before business school, I had worked as an investment banker, a real estate developer, and a marketer. Afterwards, I went into the software industry as a marketing and product manager. I've stayed in that industry ever since and am now the vice president of marketing and product management for an Internet-based company in Silicon Valley.

Q: So you used the degree to make a significant career change?

A: A reasonably large percentage of people who went to HBS changed industries or functions after business school. Business school was a seamless way for them to do so without losing lots of valuable time in their career.

When they came to business school, many of my classmates didn't really know what they wanted to do *after* business school. They felt the MBA program would be a great way to help figure that out, by getting broad exposure to what industries are out there, interacting with lots of smart young people who've worked in different industries, and having tons of ready-made interview opportunities with the large number of companies that come to campus to interview.

Q: How helpful was getting the MBA in terms of finding a job in your specific area of interest—the software field?

A: For me, since I was interested in the software/technology industry, the career center wasn't very useful in my job search. Remember, this is ten years ago. But HBS did help my career search indirectly.

In business school, I was 100 percent focused on the software industry. At the same time, software and technology was not yet a big deal on campus, and only one or two software firms came to campus to interview people, either for summer jobs or full-time jobs. So I had to do a totally self-directed job search—had to figure out who the good companies were, find a contact at my target companies, and get someone to say yes to giving me an interview.

Since I didn't have any real background in software, I knew I would need to get some relevant experience during business school. So I worked hard to get a summer job with a software company, and during my second year, I did a four-month consulting project (field study) for a hot, local software company. Between these two experiences, I gained about seven months worth of experience in the field, had learned enough about business to be somewhat knowledgeable about it, and had demonstrated a commitment to the industry.

Getting out of business school, I felt confident that I would end up with an interesting job in my target industry. And I did. I went to work for Intuit, a leading financial software firm and the maker of Quicken, QuickBooks, and Turbo Tax. I loved my experience there.

Q: What else did you get out of the MBA?

A: The learning itself, especially the confidence that comes from exposure to so many different business situations through the case method at HBS. The case method builds your intuitive feel for business and your confidence. After two years, you've looked at literally thousands of different companies and business cases and scenarios.

It is a very useful synthesis of business knowledge, jam-packed into two years. The pace of the learning is so great, you learn about things you otherwise would not have been exposed to for a long time in the business world, for example production issues at a company. And you learn lots about what you don't know that you don't know, so you have fewer "blind spots" in future business situations.

I will say that the MBA program certainly doesn't teach you all the details about everything in business that there is to know. But you do get exposed to some very important ways of thinking about business and looking at business. You develop a set of helpful "tools," and you learn enough business basics across the spectrum of many subjects to develop an intuitive sense of what you need to know.

As a credential, an MBA can tell people you're pretty sharp and capable. Assuming there is some relevant experience on your resume, an MBA from a good school helps signal to people that you may be worth talking to.

Q: How did you feel about the value of your MBA degree at the five-year mark out of business school? Did anything change?

A: I would say the big difference was that at five years out, my career goals had changed. Upon leaving business school, my near-term career goal was to become a functional expert in marketing and product management in the software industry. By the five-year mark, I felt I had accomplished that goal.

At that point, I wanted to leverage the skills I had mastered and apply them to new businesses, and at a higher level of responsibility. I ended up staying at Intuit another year and a half, and had the chance to help create and to lead an interesting new Internet business at the company.

After six and a half years at Intuit, I developed a new career goal. I felt it was time for me to join a promising start-up where I would be the senior marketing person, would be on the senior management team, and would have a significant equity opportunity. So I left the company for the chance to apply what I'd learned at a higher level, and to have a real stake in the outcome.

Q: **You stayed at your first job after business school for six and a half years. Was that unusually long compared to your peers?**

A: Yes. I would guess that less than 20 percent of my graduating class stayed at one company six years or more out of business school. A lot of people changed jobs within two or three years of graduation. For me, I really enjoyed the company and the industry, and felt I was continually learning and developing important new skills, so I was happy to stay at one company for many years.

Q: **And after ten years, how many jobs in total have you held?**

A: I've worked for a total of three companies: Intuit and two different start-ups.

Q: **As you approach the ten-year mark, how do you feel about the value of your business school training?**

A: Ten years out, I'm still very glad I went to HBS. Over time, the relative importance of different aspects of the MBA change. In my experience, the value of the business network goes up over time, and the value of the learning goes down relative to when you first go out of school. The credential value is most useful early on. But the more senior you are, the more people are primarily concerned about your work experience and track record rather than your educational degrees.

Q: **So the business network of friends and classmates matters more now?**

A: Yes. I would say that the network value of my friends and classmates from HBS increases with time. There are a couple of examples that illustrate the point: A number of my HBS peers are now at prominent venture capital firms, and through them, I've heard about interesting start-up job opportunities. At my newest company, I'm now approaching those same contacts about investing in our company.

My HBS network provides many ongoing, useful contacts. All it takes is a quick call, or e-mail, to get a friendly introduction to the right person at a given company, as well as some inside perspective on how to best position a particular proposal to that company.

Q: Looking back, if you could do anything over again differently, what would it be?

A: I would have gotten my MBA a bit sooner. I went to business school about six years after college. I had been reluctant to get an MBA because I was skeptical about how much learning I would get out of the program. I thought most of the value would be from the getting the credential and the network aspects rather than the learning itself. I was pleasantly surprised by how much I learned at HBS.

Also, I would have spent more time getting to know more people outside of my section. HBS has a big class, so you need to make an effort to get to know most of your classmates. Unless you try hard, you may not get to know more than 30 percent of your classmates very well, 250 or 300 people. The way it works, you probably end up getting to know the same total number of people as at a smaller MBA program, but as a percentage of the class, it's a smaller number.

Q: Any regrets or complaints?

A: The two-year program was a bit long in my opinion. I think it could have been just as effective in about fifteen to eighteen months. By the end of the second year, it started feeling repetitive.

At the time, HBS didn't seem very attentive to student concerns, seemed to stick with tradition in response to a rapidly changing business environment, and was slow to innovate. The school seems to have responded and improved significantly in these areas in recent years, benefiting from more creative leadership.

Q: What advice do you have for today's MBA?

A: Focus on building your skills and developing a true, relevant expertise in a field that interests you.

If you want a senior-level role at a new company, know that hiring companies—especially early-stage companies—are looking for true experts in a given functional role. If they are looking to hire a vice president of a specific area—e.g., VP of marketing or business development—the vast majority of times they are NOT looking for well-rounded generalists. They want the expert. Being a generalist is a nice plus. But nine times out of ten, it won't get you the job you're looking for. If you are talking about a CEO or GM—general manager—role, it might be a different story.

Q: How has family or personal life affected your career development and the choices you've made?

A: You know, I'm still single. So compared to a lot of my peers who are married, it's been less of an issue so far. I worked really hard, really long hours. But family and personal issues have become more important to me over time, and I've definitely cut way back on the brutal hours.

John Kim

Co-Founder and CFO of an Internet start-up

"I think, without a question, my family is the priority in my life."

Q: **What were your goals and ambitions as a newly minted MBA?**

A: I have always had an entrepreneurial bent to my personality, and I didn't want to go the traditional investment banking or consulting route. I wanted to be involved in starting up a company or having some business of my own. So my primary goal in coming out of business school was to understand where there might be an opportunity in the future in terms of what industries would show significant areas of growth. I wanted to position myself within an operating unit to learn more about opportunities that might then actually arise from having been involved in that industry.

Coming out of business school, one of the areas I wanted to get involved in was called, at that point, "multi-media." This eventually evolved into the Internet space. I was fortunate enough to get a job working at Sony for one of the presidents of one of the operating units (within Sony).

Q: **Did Harvard help you get your job with Sony?**

A: I had worked the prior summer for Sony, (the summer between the first and second year of business school). That actually came through an alum of Harvard who worked at Sony. He saw my resume, and then he took me into Sony as a summer intern. That's how I networked within Sony to get a better position coming out of business school.

Q: **What was the biggest surprise in your first couple of years about the value of your MBA?**

A: My view on an MBA and a Harvard education was always that this was going to be about more than just the curriculum or education itself. What is really important about Harvard Business School is the network of people you meet while at school, as well as the network of alums outside of school. These are some of the advantages of going to HBS.

Business school gives you a pedigree and gives you access to a network. But to be honest, I assumed that was going to be the case, so I guess I had no real surprises.

Q: **So the degree did for you what you thought it should?**

A: Yeah, I think so. Again, I always thought that it's the network of people and friends that you meet that are the great lure, and permanent aspects that you take away from business school. My closest friends are the ones whom I met at HBS.

Q: **How did your goals and ambitions change at the five-year mark out of business school?**

A: I don't know if my goals changed all that dramatically. Basically, at the five-year mark, it's just a time to position yourself to see if you can really try to accomplish what you wanted to.

In my case, at the five-year mark I had the opportunity to go off and start a firm. I had the opportunity to go off with a handful of partners and start a merchant bank based in Asia. So I don't think the goals really necessarily changed; it was really just the opportunities were different at the five-year mark.

Q: How different? They sound very different. You came out wanting to be in multi-media and wound up starting an investment fund.

A: Well, I think some people are very good at taking a very long, slow, methodical approach and going step by step within an organization, or going step by step and trying to plan their life exactly. I think in my case, it was much more than trying to go from one step to another. It was trying to take advantage of opportunities that presented themselves to me.

So I started out in an operating unit in a media group, and then I had the opportunity to work more in an investment banking, advisory role for media companies pursuing cross-border transactions. From that I was able to raise a fund to invest in companies. It was not a direct progression of events, but kind of just taking advantage of opportunities.

In my case, I was much more opportunistic than methodical in my planning.

Q: That leads to my next question. How many jobs did you have in your first five years out of school and what caused you to change jobs?

A: I had three jobs in my first five years. Changing jobs was really a combination of trying to progress up, as well as address some personal issues in my life.

For example, my first job was at Sony, but it was on the West Coast. My wife was on the East Coast in a medical residency. So I decided that I had to move to the East Coast. That led me to my next job, which was in the investment space.

My next job change was a result of that investment job, which did not pan out to be what I expected it to be, so I didn't want to linger there too long. Within the first twelve months, I left for my third job.

Q: How else has family and personal life continued to affect your career and the choices you make?

A: Once you have a family your goals change. You not only have additional factors you want to take into consideration in your career plans, but there are other things which become a lot more important to you in life. I think, without a question, my family is the priority in my life.

In terms of career choices, I wouldn't say it's necessarily swayed me one way or the other. The only major move that we made as a family was to move back from Singapore to San Francisco. I wouldn't say that was the primary reason for that move. But in the back of my mind, I wanted my kids to grow up in a friendlier environment where they can play outside without suffering from the oppressive heat.

Q: In terms of what you learned at business school, do you find that your learning was relevant to the work you do now?

A: In the finance world, what I learned from HBS had minimal applicability since Harvard takes the case-study approach. I don't know whether that has changed dramatically, but my view on that has always been that certain tools have to be taught, and learning through the case-study method is not the best way to learn corporate finance. The case-study approach doesn't go deep enough. So at least in corporate finance, you learn much more on the job than you do at HBS.

Q: What was the case study good for then?

A: Arguably, it's very good for being able to assess a situation and problem and then to try to address it. More than anything else, it's great for learning how to try and communicate your viewpoint effectively to others.

Q: What about analytical skills?

A: I'm just not convinced. I don't know whether the people who were good at case studies were good before they were introduced to case studies, or whether they actually were able to progress and learn from the case studies.

Q: Approaching the ten-year mark, where do you find yourself?

A: I'm now involved in a start-up software company. I had a little bit of experience working in technology working in places like Sony and IBM. So when I moved back from San Francisco, I sought out an opportunity in technology. I met a good partner, who was a very strong engineer, and we started a software company. So the immediate goals are to position the company to be successful. I don't have any goals other than to try and make the company viable and succeed.

Q: Sounds like you reached your goal of ten years ago, which was to start up a business?

A: Yes.

Q: What advice do you have for today's MBA?

A: You have to be passionate about what you are doing. Since you'll be spending a significant portion of your time at work, try to be involved with something that you are truly excited about. Try to learn as much as you can from as many experiences as possible.

Chiara Perry

Senior Pricing Analyst, a division of United Technologies

"I think ten years later, it's very helpful to have Harvard up there on your resume. It will probably get you a least a second look if an employer is flipping through resumes. . . . [P]eople look at the school you've gone to and are impressed with you. And I have to be honest, that will make you feel good."

Q: **In 1992, the nation was in a recession. Jobs, even for Harvard B-School grads, were scarce. What was your mindset coming out of the program?**

A: Well, I was fortunate in that I had a job in place before graduating. And I was thinking about the opportunities and challenges I'd face in that position. The company that made me the offer was part of United Technologies, and they had come on campus looking for MBAs. I was really happy to already have the offer by graduation so I didn't have to worry about looking for some great job over the summer.

It's true that in 1992 the economy wasn't in great shape, so many people were heading into graduation without an offer yet. I had a lot of things going on in my life at that time: I got married and moved a thousand miles away from the east coast to the middle of the Midwest [Indiana].

In terms of my expectations about the degree, I think they were that it put me into an elevated position and salary compared to the people I would be working with at my new job.

Q: **Given your job offer, were you happy with what the MBA did for you?**

A: Oh, absolutely. The company was excited to have hired me, and I was excited to work for them. I still work for the same company in the same location.

Q: **For ten years straight?**

A: Yes. I'm probably not your typical Harvard MBA in that regard.

Q: **To what do you attribute having stayed with the same company for ten years?**

A: I think it's several things. It's a great place to work. They treat their employees really well. And I don't like to play the sexist card, but it's a wonderful company to work for if you're a woman. My husband and I also really love Bloomington, Indiana. We have two children, and this is a great place to raise a family. So it's been several factors, including having children come into the equation. I only work three days a week now, but I have a professional position.

Q: **Switching subjects, what kind of person is ideally suited for an MBA?**

A: I think the type of person that benefits from the MBA is someone who wants to learn a lot, but also realizes that this isn't rocket science. Yes, there are challenging courses, and I learned a tremendous amount when I was at school. But I thought it was hard because of the overwhelming amount of work, the perceived competitiveness within the class, at least the first year. It wasn't necessarily hard academically. There was only one class I felt a bit overwhelmed by. Mostly, I pretty much felt, "Oh, I can do this."

So, back to your question. Someone who can go into a business school program with the attitude that this is a good thing to have, that you're going to challenge yourself and expand your expertise is going to benefit the most. It's great if you can do it full-time because you can really devote yourself to the program and figure out what you want to do with your life. But don't think that afterwards you're going to be like this NASA engineer.

Q: **Are you saying there are not huge intellectual gains, and that you shouldn't expect to be made into a great mind by the MBA?**

A: Yes. From the intellectual point, I was challenged. It definitely broadened my thinking, and it was very interesting. I had some classes I didn't have as an undergrad, and so that was valuable. There were new concepts in my learning, but overall, I don't think it's the most cerebral experience in terms of content.

Q: **But don't you think that's because for most people who go to a school like Harvard, there's a pre-selection factor, so they're already coming in so high above the bar . . .**

A: Well, that's probably right to a certain degree. Someone who's going to get the MBA at a school like Harvard is probably going to be of higher caliber. They expect more. They not only want to further their development and education, but they also want to get the financial benefit.

Q: **So how important is it to go to a really good school?**

A: I think it is important because people look at the school you've gone to and are impressed with you. And I have to be honest, that will make you feel good. People will say, "Oh my gosh, you went to Harvard!" In a social setting, when people ask me where I went to school, I almost hesitate, because I know there will be this big reaction, especially out here in the Midwest. Not very many people out here went to Harvard.

But after that big reaction, I say, wait; I'm just a person here. But from a career perspective, it definitely helps for the recognition. There is somewhat of an expectation that you may be super intelligent or talented, so you have to tame them. But I have to say, one of the reasons I went to Harvard was that I got in. I said, 'Wow, I got into Harvard; I'm going to go.'

This may relate back to your other question, but right out of business school, I felt, you know, if this job doesn't work, I can go almost anywhere I want with this degree. I know that sounds kind of arrogant but I knew that with my business experience before I went to Harvard, and now with my MBA, I could take a risk. I could come out to this small town in the Midwest and if I needed to, I could leave and be okay.

Even ten years later, I think that's still true. A Harvard MBA certainly is helpful when you're trying to move to the next place or job. I don't think I can go anywhere I want now, because I've taken a little curve in my career track to be with my children. I've been working part time for three years now, three days a week. But the MBA from Harvard is going to be very helpful if we decide to leave.

Q: **That's a Mommy "curve"?**

A: Yes absolutely. And it's been great. The job, the flexibility, my schedule . . . I love every minute of it. It would be very hard for me to give it up.

Q: **What, specifically?**

A: The part-time schedule. Going back to full time.

Q: **Do you ever anticipate re-entering the workforce as a full-time person or leaving your job? And if so, how do you think the opportunities will be enhanced with the MBA?**

A: It's actually good you ask that question, because right now I'm grappling with that. Our factory is moving all of its manufacturing to Mexico. And so the question is, what will happen to the office staff? Will we go, have some role, or be laid off? That's an unanswered question right now.

Because we'd like to stay in the area, my husband and I have been thinking about different things I can do. So the MBA will be very beneficial as I face these issues.

Q: **What else did you get out of the two years you were at school?**

A: I met a lot of wonderfully diverse and interesting people. Many people were like Wall Street–Harvard–back to Wall Street, or consulting–Harvard–back to consulting. Or people were switching careers. There were people who had been in the Peace Corps, done public not-for-profit work, or come from the military. So from that perspective, it was just wonderful to meet all those incredible people.

And how many smart people can you put in a room? I mean students were just incredibly bright. It was impressive and added tremendously to the classes.

Q: **As you approach the ten-year mark, how do you feel about the value of your business school training?**

A: I absolutely still utilize it. I still think back on cases and situations and examples that I use to resolve issues going on in work. For example, we are moving some aspect of the business to Mexico, and I can remember that I did a case on that. Plus, with this colleague of mine who is currently getting his MBA, we'll chat even more about some of those issues from class.

But looking back, I can still remember comments I made in class, and my teachers and the classes themselves. It was a very valuable, memorable time in my life. But it wasn't always pleasant . . .

Q: Why wasn't it pleasant?

A: The first year class set-up and the overwhelming desire to make value-added comments was an immense amount of pressure on me. I mean I'm probably obsessive, but I even think of comments now!

Q: Someone reading this book might not understand what this comment thing is all about.

A: Comments you made to contribute to classroom discussion which, depending on the class, counted toward your grade. Comments could almost define the class—coming up with comments to be brilliant, or prove yourself to the others. I remember I was always second-guessing what I said in class. I could have said it better, or I could have said it a different way, that kind of thing.

Q: So you felt some pressure to prove yourself. Was it difficult to be a woman at Harvard?

A: No. I think it was hard to be a woman or man at Harvard. I didn't find that being a woman made it easier or harder. It had more to do with me, because I can be concerned about those kinds of things.

Q: How many women were in your section of ninety classmates?

A: You know, I want to say, twenty-three comes to mind, but I might be a little off on that. It was less than 50 percent for sure.

Q: Were your closest friends women?

A: No, I had women and men friends.

Q: We may have covered some of this, but how has family affected the career choices you've made?

A: Greatly. I'm totally off the fast track. I'm just on kind of a maintain track. I'm not a manger anymore; I'm a worker bee. I work about thirty hours a week, but I'm paid for twenty-four, which is fine because I love the work. I have a great boss, a flexible schedule. It all fits.

I don't feel like I'm wasting the MBA at all. I have a wonderful, challenging job that's very cerebral. I've managed exciting projects. I've trained people. I do a lot of great things at my job, that would typically be the province of a full-time person, but I get to do them as this part-timer. And that's very rewarding.

I feel extremely lucky. I don't make a pile of money, but I have a good balance. I have time with my kids, and then I get some time to go and work and be challenged at a very high level.

Q: Looking back, if you could do anything differently, what would it be?

A: Well, probably I would do a little better at networking and then keeping in touch with section mates, because I may need to call them at some point. I think if you have those networks in place, it's not really calling to ask for a job, it's talking about your situation, and then those people know what's going on and may be able to let you know about an opportunity.

Having been at the same job for ten years, and being out in the Midwest, I'm a little less connected to the pipeline of, "Hey, do you need someone like me at your company?" And that goes both ways. You know, time is a problem, and when kids come along, things change greatly. It's just hard to fit everything in.

Q: Summing up, what advice do you have for someone reading this book?

A: The MBA gives you an extra couple of years to go and figure out what you want to do. I liken it to what college does for you, but this is your second breath. And it's a very valuable one. I recommend you go full time, so you can really focus.

John Cattau

Vice-President, Inventory Management Services, PartMiner

"The herd mentality at a business school is very difficult to distance yourself from.... Think hard about what you really want. Don't get distracted by what's going on around you. Remember, you're the person that has to show up for work at the job that you accept."

Q: **John, what were your goals and ambitions right out of business school?**

A: I came out of business school looking at a general management position but with a focus on marketing. I specifically did not want to interview at any consulting firms and really avoided anything other than brand management and marketing positions.

The surprise that I had was that I thought coming out of Harvard Business School, I'd have a decent shot at switching from, say, a finance field to a marketing field. But in fact, when it came time to recruit, I had to force my way into the American Express recruiters lunch hour and make a hard sell on why I thought I would be the right person for the job.

Q: **What do you mean you had to force your way into a recruiter meeting?**

A: I wasn't allowed to get on the list because I was blocked out by all the people who had pre-business school work experience from P&G and McNeil Pharmaceuticals, and by all the students from the brand companies who wanted to switch from marketing soap to marketing credit cards. So they got on the recruiter sign-up list and I did not. I had to beg, borrow, and steal my way onto it.

I guess the guy running the session felt sorry for me, and so he said he had a few minutes to chat with me while he was eating his sandwich.

Q: **And you won him over.**

A: I guess. I basically told him, "Whatever you have, I'll take the job." And I got one; they were probably looking to pick up a couple of people. This was for a summer internship. So I was focused on making that career switch early on while I was at business school. And I stuck to it.

I ended up having a great experience at American Express. I stumbled into a great opportunity to the extent that I was able to move quickly though several different functional areas within American Express and in a number different settings.

Q: **Can I interupt for a moment and take you back to the comment you made about your focusing on marketing while at school? How does that work?**

A: Well, I guess if you're thinking about what you want to do, then you're focusing on particular opportunities. You're specifically not spending time interviewing or contemplating different directions from where you want to go. For me that meant not even considering the consulting firms.

Q: Did you focus your elective study on marketing?

A: Yes, I did, and I also pursued a group-study project that was in marketing. I went with three other students and did an extensive service-oriented marketing study for Steamboat Springs. It was also a great opportunity to travel all around the West and ski at all these mountains and ski resorts.

Q: Did that study help you when you went to get a job?

A: No, it didn't really have much of an impact. It was just a good learning opportunity.

Q: What made you so interested in American Express?

A: In my second year, I had some job opportunities in marketing in New Jersey and Philadelphia, but I was engaged and my fiancée was based in the New York area. So I focused my search on marketing positions in New York, where American Express is.

I wasn't about to jeopardize that kind of serious relationship by moving to Hong Kong or something.

Q: What happened at the five-year mark?

A: At the five-year mark I was openly questioning whether I should be staying at American Express.

It was '95 and a lot was just starting to happen with the Internet. But a lot was also happening inside of American Express. One opportunity in particular was focusing on a direct financial services unit that was a start-up within a large company. There was an opportunity for me to move into that unit, and it was a great fit for me. So faced with this new opportunity within American Express, versus going outside and starting over with a smaller company, I chose to stay.

So at the five-year mark I was contemplating leaving because obviously I had been there three years or so. Meanwhile, my business school colleagues had held at least two jobs by then, and some had held three after just three years out. I thought, "Am I really slow here or should I be moving on?"

But the opportunities just kept coming. After awhile, I was given some options on shares, so I started to get attached to the idea that if I stayed a little bit longer I might be able to reap some of those gains.

I stayed there long enough to get just a taste of that. Then they came more quickly after 1997, which made it even harder to leave.

Q: So how long were you there?

A: Eight years. The advantage to me was that I was able to cycle through a number of different areas. I was promoted and advanced rapidly through the organization and was made vice-president just after the five-year mark. Typically, the vice-president promotion takes six or seven years.

Q: Having stayed at one job right out of business school for eight years, is that something you've felt you've had to defend to peers or recruiters?

A: Well there were people with whom I was interviewing when I was considering leaving American Express who said, "What's taken you so long? What's wrong with you?" But I think that perspective was in the minority relative to others who said, "I'm looking for someone that really has demonstrated significant depth in one particular area."

What I found was that people were looking not so much for people who had done a year or two at this company, or a year or two at that company, and who had accumulated experiences at different places, as they were looking for someone who had sort of a spike if you will within a particular function.

Many of the opportunities both at small and larger companies were for someone who had eight to ten years of solid brand, service-marketing experience. So I really had very little difficulty interviewing with the American Express experience on my resume.

Q: What was the biggest surprise in your first couple of years out of school about the value of your MBA?

A: On selected occasions there were things that I was able to draw from early on right out of school. But everything that I started at American Express was so new there wasn't a whole lot that I was bringing from my business school training, especially from a marketing and branding perspective. I had to spend a lot of time learning the business.

And you ask yourself, "Gee, you know, I'm not really drawing on some of the things I learned at school." But what is true is you're not really aware of the learning you picked up at school and how it's impacting your thinking.

Even in my third or fourth year out and later on, there were many times I would go back to checklists and case notes and say, "Yeah, I've dealt with this issue before." I found that to be even more so after I moved into my different positions after American Express. It's particularly been the case in my current position here at PartMiner.

Q: What do they do?

A: We're an an electronic components distributor that has a market in semiconductors.

Q: So you left American Express. When?

A: In May of 2000, I became quite ill. At the time I was working as the vice president of American Express in the brokerage unit, and I had to go on disability. It took two or three months to recover. While I was home recuperating, I thought through what I really wanted to do.

There were different opportunities to look at. One of them was PartMiner, which I officially joined in October of 2000. QTopics, a polling service that was Internet-dependent, was an opportunity that came up right when I was ready to return to work at American Express, though it turned out to be a short-lived opportunity.

In retrospect, with QTopics, I probably overlooked some things in my due diligence of the company. If I had looked at it with a case-study approach, I would have said something doesn't feel right. In fact, I did several role-plays with a Harvard business school friend, and he pointed out several flaws with the business plan.

Getting caught up in the hype of moving to a new job, I ignored my friend's advice and said thanks, but I took the job anyway.

Well, probably sixty days after I started, his insights and predictions came to be.

Q: So you went from a very stable, long-term employment situation to one which went south quickly?

A: Yes. Where I had decided to go after American Express was an important issue to share with my wife because of it's potential to impact on our finances and our lifestyle.

One of the things I remember in having that conversation with her—and I look to my wife as an equal and powerful voice—is: What is the downside if this blows up right away? You know what, not a lot of damage. Sometimes you need to take a risk, and you're not going to have complete information.

Well, basically, ninety days after I started at QTopics, the company imploded.

Q: Sounds like the fate of many Internet companies.

A: Yeah. The burn rate, things I should have picked up on but didn't, was crazy. We were not managing our cash appropriately, though there were many issues.

Q: Switching subjects, what would do differently with your two years at business school if you could do it again?

A: If I had an extra hour of time, which I didn't, I would have further deepened relationships with colleagues at school. Also, probably equally, I would have looked at what opportunities I could have pursued on my own, what areas might have made sense, and how I could have worked through a network to build that up.

Also, on that marketing study, it was a great experience, I learned a lot. But I might have looked at other opportunities in more entrepreneurial areas. I could have used all that research and legwork to give me a leg up on something more viable than the ski industry, something I really wanted to pursue.

But the reality is, from a financial standpoint, starting a company was a pipe dream. I was already significantly in debt from school. Just the thought of having to further borrow to fund a small start-up that really was not something I could have done.

But overall I would not have changed much.

Q: What advice do you have for someone reading this book?

A: The advice I typically give is to think very carefully about the balance they want between work and what they want to do personally, either relationships or the direction they want to go in. It won't happen by accident.

The herd mentality at a business school is very difficult to distance yourself from. And frankly, I felt pretty uncomfortable focusing on a marketing position when almost half the class was going into consulting.

Think hard about what you really want. Don't get distracted by what's going on around you. Remember, you're the person that has to show up for work at the job that you accept.

The best advice I ever heard was from two professors at Harvard. The first was from Robin Cooper, who said, "Every three months or so look in the mirror and ask yourself are you happy? And if you're not, go do something about it." It's pretty simple, but [it's] about the best advice I've ever gotten.

The other advice that sticks in my head is from Professor Michael Jansen. He basically said, "Look at yourself and accept the fact that you will fail." It may not be in five years. It may not be in ten years. But you will fail. You will be put in circumstances that you cannot overcome. So get over the fact that you may have a failure in your experiences.

My QTopics experience did not work out as well as I hoped. But that's an ongoing tension that I think people in MBA programs have, balancing risk and trying to understand what is the probability that I'm going to fail, relative to the potential reward that I might gain.

That is an ongoing tension you have to get comfortable with. Some MBAs have a risk tolerance that really is low, like mine was right out of school. It seems these days, people have higher tolerances. Either way, getting in touch with that is going to help you choose the right path.

Steve Sinclair

Operations Director for the Channel Sales Force, Cisco Systems

"I'm sure that competitiveness exists on an unpleasant level sometimes, but it is only competitive if you let it be. At the end of the day you need to compete more with yourself and think about what you're trying to achieve. If you do that, you're fine and on the right track."

Q: Coming out of business school, Steve, what were your expectations?

A: I guess when I was in business school and thinking about what would happen afterwards, I was hoping that it would do two key things: 1) It would help me in terms of knowledge, so I would have certain skill sets, and 2) it would open some doors for networking.

Q: How relevant has your learning been?

A: It's hard to take specific classes and attach them to specific things I do everyday. So I don't typically go, "Oh, I remember this from a marketing class," or "I should do this a certain way," especially because I'm in sales, and we really didn't have any classes in sales *per se*.

That said, I find myself often thinking back to specific discussions we might have had in classes, or to the way that people interacted together, and other learning experiences we had. It gives me a pretty good comfort level that there's a general base of knowledge that I don't doubt is helping me at some level, every day.

Q: How many jobs have you held since business school?

A: Well, I've been at two companies since business school. The first was for about nine months, which didn't work out. Then I've been at Cisco for a little over seven years, and at Cisco I've held a couple of different jobs.

Q: Is it unusual to stay at one company as long as you have compared to your peers?

A: Yeah, I think so. It's probably also unusual to still be at a fairly large company. I guess it's a combination of the fact that I ended up at a company that was at the sweet spot at the right place at the right time. I've been lucky enough to work for some good people here, so things have stayed interesting to me, and I've had room to grow and do different things.

It's kind of interesting. As I look at people who have changed jobs a lot, some of them have been very, very, happy, as they've done a bunch of different things. But I would say it's more the case that people are now at the point where they're a little frustrated that they've held four or five jobs and haven't found something yet that they really liked.

Q: You mean it's ten years out and they're still wondering when they're going to hit it?

A: Yes, and I don't know if "hit it" from a making-money perspective is the real issue, as much as it is finding something that they really enjoy. It's hard with jobs because often the first year or two, you're just getting your hands around it, figuring out the company, the industry, and the job, and so it really is years three through five when you feel like your hitting your stride, adding a lot of value, and having an impact, at least at a somewhat larger company.

Q: How have your priorities changed in the last five years, if at all?

A: I'm not sure that my priorities have changed that much. When I came out of business school, I didn't really understand what financial freedom would mean. I was living in a $1,000-a-month apartment in New York City, and I didn't even own a car, so except for a little debt from business school, there wasn't a lot to worry about.

Now that I'm a little further along, that would be a higher priority, though where I'm at is fine. The point is, had things not worked out at Cisco, which has enjoyed a great ride, I think that having financial freedom would be a lot higher on my mind than it is.

In terms of the salary you want to make coming out of business school, making a ton of money wasn't the highest priority for me. I wanted a job that I liked. Obviously, I wanted to be comfortable. But I didn't say, "Okay, I'm going to take this particular job because in five years I'm going to make a bazillion dollars."

If anything, I took my first job because I thought it would make sense for the family business and that was my immediate priority.

Q: What happened with that job?

A: Well, I went into an investment management job straight out of business school because I thought that I would take over my family's business eventually. But it turned out that I really didn't like it, although there were some other considerations as well. And I chose not to pursue that fairly quickly.

So again, I didn't really go into that first job with the idea of making a ton of money. I went into it to see if it was something I really wanted to do longer term.

So neither was it a higher priority to begin with, nor is it today, but for different reasons at both points.

The other comment I would make is that I went to business school pretty young, and that probably had an impact on my priorities. I was the first or second youngest person in our section I believe.

Q: How old were you?

A: I graduated when I was just a little over twenty-four.

Q: That's unusual. The average age is twenty-eight.

A: Yeah. So I think other people who were three and four years older had their priorities a little more worked out.

I think that was the difference. I think other people may have come out of business school with a little more specificity about where they were headed. And I was still in the mode of "Hey, I'm twenty-four years old. Let's party."

Being younger has its pluses and minuses. You can make an argument that it's a good thing to go to business school when you have an idea of exactly what you want to get out of it and where you're going. Because if you do, then you can be focused about the two years. And afterwards, I think folks that went in like myself, that were on the younger side, maybe weren't quite as determined or knew exactly what they wanted to do.

Q: Let's switch gears, Steve. If you could go back to business school and do your two years all over again, what would you do differently?

A: While I was at Harvard a lot of people said, "Gee, you really need to take the organizational behavior classes and the negotiation classes." I didn't do that that much. I took classes more like finance and marketing and very specific skill-set classes.

In retrospect, now that I'm managing a lot of people and having to work within a bigger organization, I wish I had done more of that kind of what we used to call "soft" or "fuzzy" classes. Because some of that stuff would have been pretty helpful the last few years here at Cisco. So, that's one thing.

Another is that I was kind of backwards at Harvard. By that I mean, during my first year at school, I didn't work very hard. I had been working my butt off in consulting prior to school, and so in the first year it was just like a big playground to me. In my second year, I worked a lot harder and didn't go out as much. In retrospect, I would probably have cranked up the focus a little bit more in year one because time is fleeting, and it's such a huge investment.

I would say that the biggest challenge to the whole place is clearly that there is so much that you can take advantage of, whether it's figuring out your career, making friends, getting in shape, taking classes, interacting with professors, or getting involved extracurricularly. And then there's Boston. The reality is, you just can't do everything well. You're probably better off picking three or four things and doing them well. Say to yourself, "Well, at least I did those well," rather than just taking a complete sampling, without achieving any depth.

Q: Do you have any regrets?

A: In my mind the experience I got out of Harvard was just great. It was well worth the investment, just for the two years alone, not even for what it would do for me afterwards.

If you can't justify the investment, and you don't think you're going to get enough out of it in those two years, then don't approach it just to justify the investment. I'm not sure the ROI will ever really be there. I think you can figure out a way to make more money, skip the two years of business school, and go right to what you want.

I justify the dollars I spent based on the fun I had, the friends I made, the experience I had. So I have no real regret about school—it was great.

Q: Is the business school environment intimidating?

A: One of the things about business school is that you have a lot of people with a lot of very diverse experience. They tend to be pretty self-confident, or at least they appear to be on the surface, and certainly people have one or two areas where they really excel. You can get into a situation where you kind of go, "Boy, how do I hang with everyone here?" But then, when you get to know people and understand where they're at, you realize that everyone has their challenges and their issues, and things they're good at and not so good at. And we're all kind of human as we go through this. Trying to work through that with people, and get through that façade, and not act like you know everything yourself, and being open about it, that's hard to do, but it's where you really break through barriers and learn.

Q: Well what about the competitiveness you hear about business schools? Was that a problem for you?

A: You know that's a funny one for me. People talk about how competitive Harvard is all the time. I didn't feel it, maybe because I had a study group of maybe seven or eight guys that I really got along with well who had a pretty balanced outlook on what was going on.

I remember the very first night of cases we had to do, four of us went to a Red Sox game because we wanted to see them play in Fenway Park, and so we sort of walked into class not very prepared on that first day of classes. And you know, we got away with it. And it was fine. And maybe that set a little bit of the tone in terms of not getting too stressed about the whole thing.

I'm sure that competitiveness exists on an unpleasant level sometimes, but it is only competitive if you let it be. At the end of the day you need to compete more with yourself and think about what you're trying to achieve. If you do that, you're fine and on the right track.

Patricia Melnikoff

Vice President, Marketing and Business Development,

Ariat International, a Manufacturer of Equestrian Footwear and Apparel

"Over a decade ago, I sat in a classroom and discussed for 90 minutes how to approach a crisis. Somehow that exercise of analyzing and debating potential scenarios left an impression on me that helped me years later. . . . I was told by several people that I would understand the true value of my MBA after 10 years. I would say that is mostly true."

Q: Patty, what kind of opportunities were you looking for post-MBA?

A: I was looking for an opportunity with a consumer-oriented company that sold goods and services. I was seeking product management, marketing, or strategic planning opportunities.

I was interested in working for a large multinational company, so I interviewed with companies like Disney and Sara Lee Corporation.

Q: Did they come on campus?

A: Yes they did.

Q: So you relied heavily on on-campus recruiters?

A: Very heavily. My second year I attended quite a few corporate presentations from different sectors: technology, packaged goods, and so forth.

At that time, we had the opportunity to attend recruiting presentations and the weekly Q&A sessions with well-known business leaders that are part of the second-year general management course. So by going to the more general presentations and learning about the companies or going to specific recruiting presentations, I actually came across quite a varied group of organizations.

Q: What was your summer position between your first and second year?

A: I participated in a fellowship in Eastern Europe. I worked with a group that was consulting with factories in Poland that were at risk of going out of business. It was 1991, so it was right after the fall of the communist system in Poland and there were a number of state-run factories and businesses that were in a state of collapse.

Q: How did you find your way to Poland?

A: I had worked previously with two of the founders of a consulting practice in Poland.

Q: You learned of this opportunity for a fellowship in Poland at Harvard? How did you unearth that?

A: Actually, it was a formalized program of doing nonprofit work. There were a number of HBS students who participated in the program.

I had to complete an application that explained the nature of the nonprofit work, and upon my return, I was required to write a summary report.

Q: Why did you seek out this particular opportunity in Europe for your summer job? A lot of MBAs expect that summer job to be the one that leads to a final job offer.

A: I'm always looking for interesting experiences in my life. I wanted to work overseas. I figured I probably wouldn't end up living my life in Eastern Europe, and so it was a unique opportunity at the time.

Q: How was Poland?

A: It was great fun. I ended up in a footwear factory, of all places, which is funny because now I work for a footwear company. It must have been fate.

Q: Okay, enough about Poland and you and shoes. What was your first position right out of school?

A: I took a position with the Sara Lee Corporation in Chicago. What drew me to them was that they were growing significantly in their international markets. Their largest revenue stream at the time was in apparel and accessories like Hanes, L'eggs, and Coach. While I was in business school, they were on an acquisition hunt in Europe and had acquired quite a few different brands. I thought that would be an interesting opportunity.

Coming out of Bain & Co. I had worked on quite a few acquisitions and big-picture European strategy projects. I had been in London with Bain before business school, so for me, there was a particular interest in working for a U.S.-based company with international interests.

Q: What was your title in that first job?

A: Senior Financial Analyst, Corporate Development.

Q: In plain English what does that mean?

A: That meant that I worked for a corporate staff group that reported to the CEO. We looked at acquisitions and divestitures and we also did long range and strategic planning. For example, I worked with the CEO of Coach on potential acquisitions and new business opportunities.

Q: How relevant were the things you learned at business school for your first job out?

A: I probably learned more basic analytical, communication, and process management skills from my experience at Bain & Co. My HBS education helped me to understand many of the big-picture issues facing the corporation.

Q: What did you learn at business school?

A: (Long pause) I can tell you more about how business school helps me today than how it helped me then. I was told by several people that I would understand the true value of my MBA after 10 years. I would say that is mostly true.

In the short term however, I did find that the finance courses I took helped me in my first job. I chose to take several finance courses at HBS because I wanted to develop a more in-depth understanding of that area. I did not plan on working in finance post-HBS, and I didn't think I would ever have another opportunity to learn about it.

Ten years out, it's all about the leadership and people issues. For example, my company was facing a potential product recall recently. I found myself drawing upon the case we studied on the Tylenol recall at J&J. I asked myself, what were the big picture decisions they had to make? How fast? How serious? What is the potential damage? What is the action plan and how will we communicate it? Being able to draw from that exposure to a crisis management situation was very helpful. Over a decade ago, I sat in a classroom and discussed for 90 minutes how to approach a crisis. Somehow that exercise of analyzing and debating potential scenarios left an impression on me that helped me years later.

Q: How long were you at Sara Lee?

A: Two years.

Q: Why did you change jobs?

A: I got married and moved out west.

Q: What did you do then?

A: I worked as a consultant while I looked for a position with a small company. I wanted an opportunity to work with a start-up company.

Q: Was that when you took the position at Ariat?

A: Yes. Three years out from HBS, I joined Ariat as a product manager and director of marketing.

Q: So you've been there now . . .

A: Seven years.

Q: So you've held only two jobs since school.

A: Yes, although I think I've held four different positions since I've been here.

Q: Do you think women switch jobs less so they can have more stability?

A: I can't speak to the experience of all women, but it has been true in my case. The organization has been very flexible in allowing me to make my family a priority, and at the same time, it has given me opportunities that keep me interested.

What has been critical for me as a mother of two young children is that I have a predictable work schedule while being professionally challenged. I am lucky to have found a company that offers that combination.

What I have found is that a lot of the women who aren't working feel like it's an either/or situation for them: "Either I work in a high-pressure, unpredictable job and never see my children, or I just quit altogether." I don't think it has to be that way, but you do have to be willing to make tradeoffs in compensation and promotions to strike the balance.

Q: **If there were anything you could go back and do differently at business school what would it be?**

A: I would take more of those organizational behavior classes that I laughed at.

Q: **Because?**

A: Oh you know, power, "group norms," and other people issues. None of those issues seemed that important to me at the time. I was still focused on mastering my knowledge in academic disciplines.

Q: **Did you all laugh at them?**

A: I don't think we valued those courses as much as other courses in the curriculum. But now I see the value, having managed so many people. In the second year, I might have taken more leadership courses and those organizational behavior courses.

Q: **Do you have any regrets?**

A: No, not at all.

Q: **Do you think it was more intimidating for you to go to business school as a woman?**

A: No. But I think I had to work harder in certain ways earlier on to establish myself as a credible voice in the class. Somehow I felt that if a woman was perceived to be too harsh or too focused, there was a natural tendency not to like her. And so I do think that women have to work harder at finding their place and fitting in.

Q: **Overall would you say business school is an intimidating place?**

A: No. I enjoyed it. I made great friends at HBS. I think the first week is terrifying for everyone, but overall, no.

Q: **What would you say to someone who said, should I get my MBA today?**

A: I think it depends on their circumstances. If they're very successful in business already and they are financially secure, I'm not sure business school is necessary. I meet incredible business people all the time who don't have MBAs.

But I think if you're younger in your career, or you're trying to make a career change, or you've found yourself limited, then I think it's a wonderful opportunity to go for two years and get the MBA.

Q: Do you think you went at the right time for the right reasons?

A: Absolutely. I was 25. It was perfect for a young woman with three years of business experience post-college, with my objectives, to go and get the MBA from the very best school I could.

Lionel Leventhal

Principal, $300 million private equity fund

"Spend every minute trying to think about how you get the most out of this experience, both in terms of content and people, but on content in particular. Try to understand how everything fits together because business school is not about taking however many courses you can in different subject areas. You go to business school to learn how businesses are built and run."

Q: Lionel, after graduating from Harvard Business School, what were your expectations about the value of your MBA at that time?

A: Having come from investment banking, like a lot of people in our class, what was interesting was that virtually none of them went back into that industry after graduating.

My objective for business school, from a curriculum perspective, had been to get exposure to the various elements of general management with a long-term goal of either starting a business or, in the private equity area, to be able to buy businesses and fix them up. So those were my expectations as to how to apply what I learned in school.

I didn't have any expectation about the period of time it would take to utilize everything I learned at business school or to network because I really was focused on that long-term goal.

But my first job out of school was amazing. With no experience in managing operations or people, I was given the opportunity to fix a $25 million business in New Jersey, at a can factory employing about 150 people that was losing money.

Q: Was that a manufacturing company?

A: Yes. I'm sure I was one of the few people in our year to do something as mundane as that. My summer in between my first and second year of business school was equally mundane because I worked in a plastics/chemical factory in Baton Rouge, Louisiana, to test whether being in that environment—maybe not in the long term—was something I would enjoy.

Q: Plastics and can companies, that doesn't sound like a typical MBA career path. How did you find those positions? Did Harvard help?

A: The summer job came from contacts at my investment banking job prior to business school. While at business school I wrote to some of the LBO groups that I had helped to buy businesses about working in the operations of some of the companies they had bought.

At the plastics company, I worked for two gentlemen who had previously been executives for a German chemical company. We had helped them buy a couple of plastics companies while I was at First Boston. They gave me a job in the summer of helping them to integrate two of these plastics businesses.

Q: Would you have been able to take on those positions without that business school experience?

A: No way, because I would say in particular the Operations Management class I had was critical to my understanding of these businesses.

I would think one of the major take-aways from business school is that management is not a science, but more a practical application of common sense and working with people to solve problems and set and reach goals. People always underestimate how important the working-with-people part is.

But again, my work that summer demonstrated to myself that someone without an engineering background could feel comfortable assessing how to change things in that environment.

Q: What about the can manufacturing business—how did you get that job?

A: Well, I had a very unique approach to looking for jobs at business school. Basically, the consulting firms came to me to interview. But I didn't really focus on that. I interviewed with Bain and got an open offer to join them whenever I wanted to.

My approach to interviewing was primarily focused on finding interesting smaller businesses where I could work for the owner with an objective of one time running the business.

I think it was the SBNE, the Small Business New Enterprise Club, at Harvard that sponsored a cocktail party with some of the people with YPO, The Young Presidents Organization.

I met this guy, started talking to him, and had dinner. After we spent some time talking, he offered me an opportunity. He was a steel trader who bought shiploads of steel. One of his customers was going bankrupt and offered him this can factory in lieu of the debt he owed him. So he ended up taking on this can factory even though it was in New Jersey and he lived in Boston. He had gone through three managers in five years. And the business wasn't doing any better.

We talked about common sense being more important than anything else in managing people and managing businesses. And he gave me the opportunity to fix the business.

It was overwhelming for the first few months because it involved renegotiating labor contracts, firing very senior people, and having people much older than I work for me, which was a new experience as well. At the factory, of the 150 people, I think two had gone to college. So, on a day-to-day basis I didn't really have a lot of people to bounce ideas off of. I did end up talking to a bunch of HBS professors, three in particular, during the first six months bouncing ideas off of them.

Q: Then the actual content learning at business school was very valuable to you?

A: Oh, yeah. It was essential. But I would say equally important to the content was the self-confidence that you could apply common sense to solve problems. And working with people is not something you can study.

Q: Are you saying you already had a style and a way of working with people that was effective?

A: I wouldn't say that because I had never managed anyone other than an analyst when I was at First Boston.

But one of the things business school did, outside of teaching actual course content, was expose us to many cases in which people with totally different backgrounds founded and managed businesses. Rather than having a technical background, such as engineering for example, they applied a common sense approach to solving problems.

Q: What caused you to leave that position and where did you go next?

A: We turned the can company around and went from losing money to breaking even to making money. And we sold the business to the largest company in the industry—US Can. That is what I was hired to do. It was a natural end to the job because I accomplished what I set out to accomplish.

I had an open-ended offer to join Bain, so I was keeping in touch with them as the process of selling the company started. Bain said, "Great! Sounds like you had a great experience, and come here when you are done."

The fellow I worked for who owned the can factory became a great mentor of mine. He'll be a second father to me for life. He's an investor in the fund I manage now.

Q: Bring me up to speed from Bain to this fund you manage now.

A: It was all part of the same long-term plan. At Bain I spent thee years helping to manage case teams in various industries. Three quarters of the three years there was spent working on ten different projects for a $2.5 billion company that made various building products. But I would say I wasn't focused on a lifetime of consulting. I was focused on learning a lot and contributing a lot.

At the end of the three years the CEO of my primary client offered me the number-two marketing position at a $1.5 billion division, which made me feel pretty good. I had never held a marketing management job before, but they felt comfortable offering me the job.

Since that time, I have spent the last six years in the private equity area. Private equity is by definition providing equity privately to companies, both private and public. It's putting capital at risk that you've raised from investors. I spent a little over three years working at a small buyout fund in New York. It was a very small group, basically five of us. One of the guys, who I thought was a genius, taught me a ton about how to be very creative in terms of structuring transactions to protect the return to investors and provide money to companies.

A little more than two years ago, somebody I worked with fifteen years ago at First Boston invited me to join a very novel private equity fund that is focused on the pharmaceutical industry, on providing capital to companies that develop drugs. I came in to be the person who negotiated and structured the deals.

Q: Jumping around a bit, how valuable have your business school friendships been in your career?

A: I'd say extremely. I would never have had this first opportunity at the can factory without having been at business school and meeting the YPO people.

I would say the real value of your business school network starts to become apparent seven years out because that's when all your classmates are in positions where they have a lot of influence. I've worked on transactions with many classmates at various points and times. I've also served as an aide to a ton of my classmates from my year in an informal capacity.

Q: What do you mean by aide?

A: Just helping people to raise money for ventures they're starting, helping with their careers, helping people find jobs, and thinking through issues they face managing their businesses.

Q: How have your priorities changed since you got your MBA?

A: I'd say that every year I constantly have more control over my life. Even though I work hard, I try to have control over when I'm working and when I'm not working. I still spend an enormous amount of time with my parents and my brothers. I probably have dinner with them once a week. That's always been a priority. And when I get married it will be the same, that family will be a priority.

So the goal is more and more each year to get more control over my schedule. That's very important. My priorities haven't really changed, just the amount of control I have over my time and life have changed.

Q: Do you have any regrets?

A: Job-wise in terms of what I've done, I have zero regrets. I've been very lucky. You can never plan life. You can sort of say, "I'd like to do this, I'd like to do that," but you don't know when you turn around to the left who you're going to happen to meet.

I think life is setting goals, preparing to meet those goals, and reacting to chaos. Generally you have an objective of what you want to achieve, but you don't really control what opportunities are going to be created. What I'm trying to say is that if I got up one hour later, everything might be different, so there really isn't much I would change.

As for school, I had an outstanding group of people in my section and in my study group who I keep in contact with quite a bit. So I think the only thing I would have done a little differently would have been spending more time with people outside my section.

Q: What advice do you have for someone considering going to business school?

A: Well, a lot of people go to business school for the wrong reason. They go to a particular business school because someone else wants them to go or because they haven't thought it through. And it needs to be thought through. Where you go really impacts your career.

I've also seen people who've had completely different experiences at Harvard. Some people come away and haven't invested much of themselves in it and say, you know, it wasn't such an amazing experience. Well that's not a surprise. You get out what you put in.

Some people just go because they just got in, and that's not a reason to go. I saw a lot of mismatches that got through, and they just hated it.

My advice is this: I would spend every minute trying to think about how you get the most out of this experience, both in terms of content and people, but on content in particular. Try to understand how everything fits together because business school is not about taking however many courses you can in different subject areas. You go to business school to learn how businesses are built and run, which is understanding how everything has to fit together and be integrated. So, I would spend a lot of energy in all the classes trying to figure out, for example, if it's a marketing class, how things fit in with operations and finance and everything else.

CHAPTER 6

MONEY MATTERS

HOW MUCH WILL IT COST?

THE TRUTH
To say that business school is an expensive endeavor is an understatement. In fact, to really gauge how expensive business school is, you need to look not only at your tuition costs and living expenses, but also at the opportunity cost of foregoing a salary for the length of your program. Think about it: You'll have a net outflow of money.

But keep in mind that, unlike law school or medical school, business school is just a two-year program. And once those two years are over, you can expect to reap the rewards of your increased market value. Unfortunately, business school differs from law school and medical school in a much less desirable way as well—there are serious limitations on the amount of money available through scholarships and grants. Most of you will be limited to loans, and lots of them.

Try not to get too upset about borrowing the money for business school; think of it as an investment in yourself. But, like all investments, it should be carefully thought out and discussed with everyone (spouse, partner, etc.) concerned. This is especially important for those of you considering business school. You need a law degree to practice law, and a medical degree to practice medicine, but a business degree is not required to work in business. That said, certain professional opportunities may be tougher to pursue without an MBA on your resume.

THE COST OF B-SCHOOL
So get out some paper, a pencil, and a calculator, and figure out how much it will cost you to attend school. What should you include? Your opportunity cost (lost income) and your cost of attending b-school (tuition and fees). One more thing: For a more accurate assessment of your investment, you should figure taxes into the equation by dividing tuition cost by .65 (this assumes taxes of about 35 percent). Why? Because in order to pay tuition of $25,000, you would have to make a pre-tax income of about $38,500. If you are lucky enough to have a source of aid that does not require repayment, such as a grant, scholarship, or wealthy benefactor, subtract that amount from the cost of attending b-school.

For example, if you currently make $50,000 and plan to attend a business school that costs $25,000 per year, your investment would be approximately $177,000.

$$(50,000 \times 2) + [(25,000 \times 2)/.65] = 177,000$$

Now say you receive an annual grant of $5,000. Your investment would now be approximately $161,500.

$$(50,000 \times 2) + [(20,000 \times 2)/.65] = 161,500$$

HOW LONG WILL IT TAKE YOU TO RECOUP YOUR INVESTMENT?

To estimate this figure, you first need to estimate your expected salary increase post-MBA. Check out the average starting salaries for graduates of the programs you are looking at and adjust upward/downward based on the industry you plan to enter. Subtract your current salary from your expected salary and you'll get your expected salary increase.

Once you complete the step above, divide your investment (tuition and fees plus lost income) by your expected salary increase, and then add 2 (the length of a full-time MBA program). If you are contemplating a one-year MBA program, just add 1.

Going back to the example above, if your pre-MBA salary is $50,000 and you expect to make $75,000 when you graduate, your expected salary increase is $25,000 (a 50 percent increase). Let's assume you did not receive a grant and that your investment will be about $177,000.

$$(177,000/25,000) + 2 = 9.08$$

It will take you approximately nine years to earn back your investment.

Keep in mind, these are approximations and don't take into account annual raises, inflation, etc. But it is interesting, isn't it?

While business school is an expensive proposition, the financial rewards of having your MBA can be immensely lucrative as we discussed before. You won't be forced into bankruptcy if you finance it correctly. There are tried-and-true ways to reduce your initial costs, finance the costs on the horizon, and manage the debt you'll leave school with—all without selling your soul to the highest bidder.

COMPARISON SHOPPING

While cost shouldn't be the first thing on your mind when you are choosing a school, depending on your goals in getting an MBA, it might be fairly high on your list. Private schools aren't the only business schools. Many state schools have fantastic reputations. Regional schools may be more generous with financial aid. Tuition costs will vary widely between public and private schools, especially if you qualify as an in-state student. Keep in mind, however, that salary gains tend to be less dramatic at more regional schools.

HOW DO I FUND MY MBA?

The short answer: loans. Unless your company is underwriting your MBA, or you're able to pay your way in cash, you'll be financing your two years of business school through a portfolio of loans. Loans typically come in one of two forms: federal and private. Only a few of you will be lucky enough to qualify for, and get, grants and scholarships.

Anyone with reasonably good credit, regardless of financial need, can borrow money for business school. If you have financial need, you will probably be eligible for some type of financial aid if you meet the following basic qualifications:

- You are a United States citizen or a permanent U.S. resident.
- You are registered for Selective Service if you are a male, or you have documentation to prove that you are exempt.

- You are not in default on student loans already.
- You don't have a horrendous credit history.

International applicants to business school should take note: Most U.S. business schools will require all international students to pay in full or show proof that they will be able to pay the entire cost of the MBA prior to beginning the MBA program.

FEDERAL LOANS
The federal government funds federal loan programs. Federal loans are usually the "first resort" for borrowers since many are subsidized by the federal government and offer generous interest rates. Some do not begin charging you interest until after you complete your degree. Most federal loans are need-based, but some higher interest federal loans are available regardless of financial circumstances. Your business school's financial aid office will determine what, if any, your need is.

PRIVATE LOANS
Don't think private loans are available only from banks. There are programs that exist for the express purpose of lending money to business students. These loans are expensive and interest accumulates during your studies. You will also be responsible for many extra charges (guarantees and insurance fees).

ALTERNATIVE SOURCES OF FUNDING
We've already mentioned these in one form or other, but they are worthy of a bit more attention.

The first alternative is sponsorship of your employer or educational reimbursement. Not all companies treat this the same way, but if you are able to get your employer to kick in a portion of the cost, you are better off than before. But beware, this benefit also comes with strings attached. Most companies that pay for your MBA will require a commitment of several years upon graduation. If you renege, you could be liable for the full cost of your education. Others will require that you attend business school part time, which you may or may not want to do. Often, part-time students are ineligible to participate in on-campus recruiting efforts to the same extent as full-time students.

Educational reimbursement can come in another form as well. Some companies will provide sign-on bonuses to new MBAs that will cover the cost of a year's tuition. This is a fantastic development from the years of a robust economy, but it is by no means a guarantee during tougher times. Don't assume that you will have this option open to you just because it has been a common occurrence in past years.

The other "alternative" source of funding is a financial gift from family or another source. Either you have a resource that is willing and able to fund all or part of your MBA, or you don't. If you do, be thankful.

APPLYING FOR FINANCIAL AID
In order to become eligible for financial aid of any kind, you will need to complete the Free Application for Federal Student Aid, also known as the FAFSA. You complete and submit this form after January 1 of the year in which you plan to enter business school. You should aim to complete and submit this form as soon as possible after the first of the year to avoid any potential delays. The FAFSA is available from a school's financial aid office. You can also download the form directly from the website of the U.S. Department of Education at www.fafsa.ed.gov. A third option is to use

the FAFSA Express software (also downloadable from the website) and transmit the application electronically.

It is important to note that the form requires information from your federal income tax returns. Plan to file your taxes early that year.

In addition to the FAFSA form, most schools will have their own financial aid form that you will be required to complete and submit. These often have their own deadlines, so it is wise to keep careful track of all the forms you must complete and all their respective deadlines. Yes, it's a lot of paperwork, but get over it. You'll be much happier when the tuition bill arrives.

LOAN SPECIFICS

GUIDE TO FEDERAL LOANS

Stafford Loans
Stafford loans require you to complete the FAFSA form in order to qualify. These are very desirable loans because they offer low-interest rates capped at 8.25 percent and are federally guaranteed. There is a limit to how much you can borrow in this program. The maximum amount per year you may borrow as a graduate student is $18,500 ($10,000 of this must be unsubsidized loans). The maximum amount you may borrow in total is $138,500 (only $65,500 of this may be in subsidized loans). The aggregate amount includes any Stafford loans you may have from your undergraduate or other graduate studies.

The loans come in two types: subsidized and unsubsidized. Subsidized loans are need-based as determined by your business school. They do not charge interest while you are in school or in authorized deferment period (such as the first six months after graduation). This cost is picked up by the government (hence the name "subsidized"). Repayment begins at that time. Unsubsidized loans are not need-based and do charge interest from the time of disbursement to the time of full repayment. You can pay the interest while you are in school or opt for capitalization, in which case the interest is added to the principal. You will pay more in the long run if you choose capitalization. Interest payments may be tax deductible, so be sure to check. The standard repayment period for both is ten years.

You will pay a small origination and guarantee fee for each loan, but this is not an out-of-pocket expense. It is simply deducted from the loan amount. Some schools will allow you to borrow the money under the Stafford program directly from them, while others will require you to borrow from a bank. For more information on federal loans, call the Federal Student Aid Information Center at 1-800-433-3243.

Perkins Loans
Perkins loans are available to graduate students who demonstrate exceptional financial need. The financial aid office will determine your eligibility for a Perkins Loan. If you qualify for a Perkins Loan as part of your financial aid package, take it. The loans are made by the schools and are repaid to the schools, though the federal government provides a large portion of the funds. You can borrow up to $6,000 for each year of graduate study up to a total of $40,000 (this includes any money borrowed under this program during undergraduate study). The interest rates on this loan are low, usually 5 percent. There are no fees attached. The grace period is nine months upon graduation.

GUIDE TO PRIVATE/COMMERICAL LOANS

This is expensive territory. Not only are interest rates high, but terms are also quite different from those found with federal loans. You may not be able to defer payment of interest or principal until after graduation. Origination and guarantee fees are also much higher since these loans are unsecured. After all, banks and other specialized lenders exist to loan money to folks like you and, unlike the federal government, want to make money doing it. If you go this route, shop around diligently. Think of it as good practice for your post-MBA executive career.

Some of the more popular programs are listed below. *Please note, rates can vary and most programs require the borrower to be attending an approved graduate program at least halftime.* If you choose to investigate loans outside of the educational market, such as a personal line of credit, credit card, or a loan against an insurance plan, be aware that these can be quite costly.

The Access Group, Business Access Loan
Can borrow up to the amount certified by your school. Interest rate is the three-month London Interbank Offered Rates (LIBOR) + 2.7 percent. There is no guarantee or origination fee upon disbursement, but a guarantee fee between 7.5 and 12.9 percent is added to the principal at the time of repayment. Defer interest until repayment begins up to nine months after graduation. Repayment period can be as long as twenty years. For more information, call 1-800-282-1550 or go to www.accessgroup.org.

The Education Resources Institute (TERI) PEP Program
$15,000 annual limit. Prime rate for interest. Guarantee fee is 11 percent or 6.5 percent with a creditworthy cosigner. Repayment begins six months after graduation and can be up to twenty-five years. For more information go to www.teri.org.

Citibank CitiAssist® Loan
No minimum loan amount and no annual limit. Aggregate limit of $110,000. Prime rate + 0.5 percent. No guarantee or origination fees. Can defer interest while in school or make interest payments as you go. Repayment period up to fifteen years. Six-month grace period. For more information call 1-800-692-8200 or visit www.studentloan.citibank.com/slcsite/.

Nellie Mae EXCEL Grad Loan
Students can borrow up to $15,000 on their own or more with a qualified co-signer. Aggregate limit of $100,000 (without co-signer). No aggregate limit with co-signer. Guarantee fee is 6 percent (without co-signer) and 2 percent (with co-signer). Prime rate + 0 percent (monthly variable) or prime rate + 2 percent (annual variable). All loan payments may be deferred until six months following graduation. Interest payments may be made during school or capitalized. Repayment period up to twenty years. Call 1-800-9-TUITION or visit www.nelliemae.com.

Sallie Mae MBA Loans
Interest rates start at prime and depend on borrower's credit history. Disbursement fee from 0 to 4 percent based on credit rating. Repayment period up to twenty-five years. International students are eligible. For more information call 1-888-440-4622 or go to www.salliemae.com.

GUIDE TO SCHOLARSHIPS AND GRANTS
The usual sources for this type of funding are alumni groups and civic organizations. This funding is limited, and actual awards tend to be small. Even if you benefited from generous scholarship funding as an undergraduate, it would be unwise to assume you'll have the same experience as a graduate student. But do investigate. You never know what's out there. Schools will frequently list any scholarships and grants that are available at the back of their financial aid catalog.

Part II

HOW TO GET IN

CHAPTER 7

PREPARING TO BE A SUCCESSFUL APPLICANT

GET GOOD GRADES
If you're still in school, concentrate on getting good grades. A high GPA says you've got not only brains, but also discipline. It shows the admissions committee you have what you need to make it through the program. If you're applying directly from college or have limited job experience, your grades will matter even more. The admissions committee will have little else on which to evaluate you.

It's especially important that you do well in courses such as economics, statistics, and calculus. Success in these courses is more meaningful than success in classes like "Monday Night at the Movies" film appreciation. Of course, English is also important; b-schools want students who communicate well.

STRENGTHEN MATH SKILLS
Number-crunching is an inescapable part of b-school. If your work experience has failed to develop your quantitative skills, take an accounting or statistics course for credit at a local college or b-school. If you have a liberal arts background and did poorly in math, or got a low GMAT math score, this is especially important. Getting a decent grade will go a long way toward convincing the admissions committee you can manage the quantitative challenges of the program.

WORK FOR A FEW YEARS—BUT NOT TOO MANY
Business schools have traditionally favored applicants who have worked full-time for several years. There are three primary reasons for this: 1) with experience comes maturity; 2) you're more likely to know what you want out of the program; 3) your experience enables you to bring real-work perspectives to the classroom. Since business school is designed for you to learn from your classmates, each student's contribution is important.

Until recently, b-schools preferred to admit only those students with two to five years of work experience. The rationale was that at two years you have worked enough to be able to make a solid contribution, while beyond four or five, you might be too advanced in your career to appreciate the program fully. However, as we noted earlier in this book, there is a new trend among top schools toward admitting "younger" applicants—that is, candidates with limited work experience as well as those straight from college.

Depending on the schools you're applying to and the strength of your resume of accomplishments, you may not need full-time, professional work experience. Of course, there's a catch: the younger you are, the harder you'll have to work to supply supporting evidence for your case as a qualified applicant. Be prepared to convince admissions committees that you've already done some incredible things, especially if you're hailing straight from college.

If you've targeted top-flight schools like Wharton, Columbia, or Stanford, applying fresh out of college is still a long shot. While your chances of gaining admission with little work experience have improved, your best shot is still to err on the conservative side and get a year or two of some professional experience under your belt.

If you're not interested in the big league or you plan on attending a local program, the number of years you should work before applying may vary. Research the admissions requirements at your target school. There's no doubt the MBA will jumpstart your career and have long-lasting effects on your business (and perhaps personal) outlook. If you're not ready to face the real world after college, plenty of solid b-schools will welcome you to another two years of academia.

There is one caveat to this advice, however. If your grades are weak, consider working at least three years before applying. The more professional success you have, the greater the likelihood that admissions committees will overlook your GPA.

LET YOUR JOB WORK FOR YOU

Many companies encourage employees to go to b-school. Some of these companies have close ties to a favored b-school and produce well-qualified applicants. If their employees are going to the kinds of schools you want to get into, these may be smart places to work.

Other companies, such as investment banks, feature training programs, at the end of which trainees go to b-school or leave the company. These programs hire undergraduates right out of school. They're known for producing solid, highly skilled applicants. Moreover, they're full of well-connected alumni who may write influential letters of recommendation.

Happily, the opposite tactic—working in an industry that generates few applicants—can be equally effective. Admissions officers look for students from underrepresented professions. Applicants from biotechnology, health care, not-for-profit, and even the Peace Corps are viewed favorably.

One way to set yourself apart is to have had two entirely different professional experiences before business school. For example, if you worked in finance, your next job might be in a different field, like marketing. Supplementing quantitative work with qualitative experiences demonstrates versatility.

Finally, what you do in your job is important. Seek out opportunities to distinguish yourself. Even if your responsibilities are limited, exceed the expectations of the position. B-schools are looking for leaders.

MARCH FROM THE MILITARY

A surprising number of b-school students hail from the military (although the armed forces probably had commanders in mind, not CEOs, when they designed their regimen). Military officers know how to be managers because they've held command positions. And they know how to lead a team under the most difficult of circumstances.

Because most have traveled all over the world, they also know how to work with people from different cultures. As a result, they're ideally suited to learn alongside students with diverse backgrounds and perspectives. B-schools with a global focus are particularly attracted to such experience.

The decision to enlist in the military is a very personal one. However, if you've thought of joining those few good men and women, this may be as effective a means of preparing for b-school as more traditional avenues.

CHECK OUT THOSE ESSAY QUESTIONS NOW

You're worried you don't have interesting stories to tell. Or you just don't know what to write. What do you do?

Ideally, several months before your application is due, you should read the essay questions and begin to think about your answers. Could you describe an ethical dilemma at work? Are you involved in anything outside the office (or classroom)? If not, now is the time to do something about it. While this may seem contrived, it's preferable to sitting down to write the application and finding you have to scrape for or, even worse, manufacture situations.

Use the essay questions as a framework for your personal and professional activities. Look back over your business calendar, and see if you can find some meaty experiences for the essays in your work life. Keep your eyes open for a situation that involves questionable ethics. And if all you do is work, work, work, get involved in activities that round out your background. In other words, get a life.

Get involved in community-based activities. Some possibilities are being a big brother/big sister, tutoring in a literacy program, or initiating a recycling project. Demonstrating a concern for others looks good to admissions committees, and hey, it's good for your soul, too.

It's also important to seek out leadership experiences. B-schools are looking for individuals who can manage groups. Volunteer to chair a professional committee or run for an office in a club. It's a wide-open world; you can pick from any number of activities. The bottom line is this: The extracurriculars you select can show that you are mature, multifaceted, and appealing.

We don't mean to sound cynical. Obviously, the best applications do nothing more than describe your true, heartfelt interests and show off your sparkling personality. We're not suggesting you try to guess which activity will win the hearts of admissions directors and then mold yourself accordingly. Instead, think of projects and activities you care about, that maybe you haven't gotten around to acting on, and act on them now!

PICK YOUR RECOMMENDERS CAREFULLY

By the time you apply to business school, you shouldn't have to scramble for recommendations. Like the material for your essays, sources for recommendations should be considered long before the application is due.

How do you get great recommendations? Obviously, good work is a prerequisite. Whom you ask is equally important. Bosses who know you well will recommend you on both a personal and professional level. They can provide specific examples of your accomplishments, skills, and character. Additionally, they can convey a high level of interest in your candidacy.

There's also the issue of trust. B-school recommendations are made in confidence; you probably won't see exactly what's been written about you. Choose someone you can trust to deliver the kind of recommendation that will push you over the top. A casual acquaintance may fail you by writing an adequate, yet mostly humdrum letter.

Cultivate relationships that yield glowing recommendations. Former and current professors, employers, clients, and managers are all good choices. An equally impressive recommendation can come from someone who has observed you in a worthwhile extracurricular activity.

We said before you won't see *exactly* what's being written about you, but that doesn't mean you should just hand a blank piece of paper to your recommender. Left to their own devices, recommenders may create a portrait that leaves out your best features. You need to prep them on what to write. Remind them of those projects or activities in which you achieved some success. You might also discuss the total picture of yourself that you are trying to create. The recommendation should reinforce what you're saying about yourself in your essays.

About "Big Shot" recommendations: Don't bother. Getting some professional golfer who's a friend of your dad's to write you a recommendation will do you no good if he doesn't know you very well, even if he is President of the Universe. Don't try to fudge your application—let people who really know you and your work tell the honest, believable, and impressive truth.

PREPARE FOR THE GRADUATE MANAGEMENT ADMISSION TEST (GMAT)

Most b-schools require you to take the GMAT. The GMAT is now a three-and-a-half-hour computer adaptive test (CAT) with multiple-choice math and verbal sections as well as an essay section. It's the kind of test you hate to take and schools love to require.

Why is the GMAT required? B-schools believe it measures your verbal and quantitative skills and predicts success in the MBA program. Some think this is a bunch of hooey, but most schools weigh your GMAT scores heavily in the admissions decision. If nothing else, it gives the school a quantitative tool to compare you with other applicants.

The test begins with the Analytical Writing Assessment (AWA) containing two essays questions. In the past, all questions that have appeared on the official GMAT have been drawn from a list of about 150 topics that appear in *The Official Guide to the GMAT* (published by the Educational Testing Service). Review that list and you'll have a pretty good idea of what to expect from the AWA. You will have thirty minutes to write each essay. By the way, you will be required to type your essay at the computer. Depending on how rusty your typing skills are, you may want to consider a bit of practice.

Next comes the multiple-choice section which has two parts: a seventy-five-minute math section and a seventy-five-minute verbal section. The math section includes problem-solving questions (e.g. "Train A leaves Baltimore at 6:32 A.M. . . .") and data-sufficiency questions. Data-sufficiency questions require you to determine whether you have been given enough information to solve a particular math problem. The good news about these types of questions is that you don't actually have to solve the problem; the bad news is that these questions can be very tricky. The verbal section tests reading skills (reading comprehension), grammar (sentence correction), and logic (critical reasoning).

For those unfamiliar with CAT exams, here's a brief overview of how they work: On multiple-choice sections, the computer starts by asking a question of medium difficulty. If you answer it correctly, the computer asks you a question that is slightly more difficult than the previous question. If you answer incorrectly, the computer asks a slightly easier question next. The test continues this way until you have answered enough questions that it can make an accurate (or so they say) assessment of your performance and assign you a score.

Most people feel they have no control over the GMAT. They dread it as the potential bomb in their application. But relax; you have more control than you think. You can take a test-preparation course to review the math and verbal material, learn test-taking strategies, and build your confidence. Test-prep courses can be highly effective. The Princeton Review offers what we think is the best GMAT course available. Even better, it offers two options for online preparation in addition to the traditional classroom course and one-on-one tutoring. Another option is to take a look at our book *Cracking the GMAT CAT*, which reviews all the subjects and covers all the tips you would learn in one of our courses.

How many times should you take the GMAT? More than once if you didn't ace it on the first try. But watch out: Multiple scores that fall in the same range make you look unprepared. Don't take the test more than once if you don't expect a decent increase, and don't even think of taking it the first time without serious preparation. Limiting your GMAT attempts to two is best. Three tries are okay if there were unusual circumstances or if you really need another shot at it. If you take it more than three times, the admissions committee will think you have an unhealthy obsession. A final note: If you submit more than one score, most schools will take the highest.

If you don't have math courses on your college transcript or numbers-oriented work experience, it's especially important to get a solid score on the quantitative section. There's a lot of math between you and the MBA.

CHAPTER 8

ADMISSIONS

HOW THE ADMISSIONS CRITERIA ARE WEIGHTED

Admissions requirements vary from institution to institution. Most rely on the following criteria (not necessarily in this order): GMAT score, college GPA, work experience, essays, letters of recommendation, interviews, and extracurriculars, of which the first four are the most heavily weighted. The more competitive the school, the less room there is for weakness in any one of these areas.

Most applicants suspect that the GMAT score or GPA pushes their application into one of three piles: "yes," "no," or "maybe." But that's not the way it is. Unless one or more of your numbers is so low it forces a rejection, the piles are "looks good," "looks bad," "hmmm, interesting," and all variations of "maybe." In b-school admissions, the whole is greater than the sum of the parts. Each of the numbers has an effect but doesn't provide the total picture.

What's fair about the system is that you can compensate for problem areas. Even if you have a low GMAT score, a high GPA, evidence of quantitative work experience, or the completion of an accounting or statistics course will provide a strong counterbalance.

As we've said, no one single thing counts more than everything else. Your scores, work experience, and essays should give the admissions committee a clear idea of your capabilities, interests, and accomplishments. Any particular weakness can be overcome by a particular strength in another area—so make sure you emphasize whatever strengths you have, and don't take them for granted.

THE GMAT AND GPA

The GMAT score and GPA are used in two ways. First, they're used as "success indicators" for the academic work. In other words, if admitted, will you have the brain power and discipline to make it through the program? Second, they're used to compare applicants with the larger pool. In particular, the top schools like applicant pools with high scores. They think that having an incoming class with high scores and grade profiles is an indicator of their program's prestige and selectivity.

> **Reminder:**
>
> We've done our best to give you solid advice on winning admission to *any* school in this book. But that doesn't mean these schools share the same standards for admission.
>
> As you read through the next few sections, think about your personal list of schools. Contact each program directly to determine just how selective it is. This information will help you make the best use of our admissions advice.
>
> Again, the less competitive the school is, the more easily you may be able to breeze through (or completely omit) the rigorous requirements we identify as crucial in the application process for top programs.

Some schools look more closely at junior and senior year grades than the overall GPA. Most consider the academic reputation of your college and the difficulty of your curriculum. A transcript loaded with courses like "Environmental Appreciation" and "The Child in You" isn't valued as highly as one with a more substantive agenda.

WORK EXPERIENCE

B-schools pay particularly close attention to your work history. It provides tangible evidence of your performance in the business world thus far and hints at your potential. This helps b-schools determine whether you're going to turn out to be the kind of graduate they'll be proud to have as an alum. Your work experience reveals whether you've progressed enough (or too far) to benefit from a b-school education. It is also telling of the industry perspective you'll bring to the program.

Five elements are considered. First, the stature of your company: Does it have a good reputation? Does it produce well-qualified applicants?

Second, diversity of work experience. Have you done something extraordinary like starting your own business or inventing a new software program? Or maybe you've lucked out to work in an industry that is underrepresented at the prospective school?

Third, your advancement: Did you progress steadily to ever more responsible positions, or did you just tread water? Do your salary increases prove that you are a strong performer? Did you put in your time at each job, or just jump from company to company?

Fourth, your professional and interpersonal skills: Did you get along well with others? Work as part of a team? Do your recommenders see you as future manager material?

Fifth (and this is critical), your leadership potential: Did you excel in your positions, go beyond the job descriptions, save the day, lead a team?

THE ESSAYS

Admissions committees consider the essays the clincher, the swing vote on the "admit/deny" issue. Essays offer the most substance about who you really are. The GMAT and GPA reveal little about you, only that you won't crash and burn. Your work history provides a record of performance and justifies your stated desire to study business. But the essays tie all the pieces of the application together and create a summary of your experiences, skills, background, and beliefs.

The essays do more than give answers to questions. They create thumbnail psychological profiles. Depending on how you answer a question or what you present, you reveal yourself in any number of ways—creative, witty, open-minded, articulate, mature—to name a few. Likewise, your essay can reveal a negative side, such as arrogance, sloppiness, or an inability to think and write clearly.

THE RECOMMENDATIONS

Admissions committees expect recommendations to support and reinforce the rest of the application. They act as a sort of reality check. When the information from your recommender doesn't match up with the information you've provided, it looks bad.

Great recommendations are rarely enough to save a weak application from doom. But they might push a borderline case over to the "admit" pile.

Mediocre recommendations are potentially harmful: an application that is strong in all other areas now has an inconsistency that's hard to ignore.

Bad recommendations—meaning that negative information is provided—cast doubt on the picture you've created. In some cases they invalidate your claims. This can mean the end for your application. Again, be careful whom you ask for recommendations.

THE INTERVIEW

Like the recommendations, the interview is used to reinforce the total picture. But it is also used to fill in the blanks, particularly in borderline cases.

Not all b-schools attach equal value to the interview. For some, it's an essential screening tool. For others, it's used to evaluate those hovering in the purgatory between accept and reject. Still others strongly encourage, but do not require, the interview. Some schools make it simply informative. If you can't schedule an on-campus interview, the admissions office may find an alum to meet with you in your hometown.

If an interview is offered, take it. In person, you may be an entirely more compelling candidate. You can further address weaknesses or bring dull essays to life. Most important, you can display the kinds of qualities—enthusiasm, sense of humor, maturity—that often fill in the blanks and sway a decision.

Our strongest advice: act quickly to schedule your interviews. Admissions officers lack the staffing to interview every candidate who walks through their doors. So interview slots go faster than tickets to the Final Four. Grab a slot early by phoning the schools in September. You don't want your application decision delayed by several months (and placed in a more competitive round) because your interview was scheduled late in the filing period. Worse, you don't want to hear that your opportunity for face-to-face selling and convincing is gone, because all time slots are booked.

A great interview can tip the scale in the "admit" direction. How do you know if it was great? You were calm and focused. You expressed yourself and your ideas clearly. Your interviewer invited you to go rock climbing with him next weekend. (Okay, let's just say you developed a solid personal rapport with the interviewer.)

A mediocre interview may not have much impact, unless your application is hanging on by a thread. In such a case, the person you're talking to (harsh as it may seem) is probably looking for a reason not to admit you, rather than a reason to let you in. If you feel your application may be in that hazy, marginal area, try to be extra-inspired in your interview.

Did you greet your interviewer by saying, "Gee, are all admissions officers as pretty as you?" Did you show up wearing a Karl Marx T-shirt? Did you bring your mother with you? If so, it's probably safe to say you had a poor interview. A poor interview can doom even a straight-A, high-GMAT, strong-work-history candidate. Use good taste, refrain from belching, avoid insulting the interviewer's tie, and you'll probably be okay.

B-school interviews with alumni and admissions officers rarely follow a set formula. The focus can range from specific questions about your job responsibilities to broad discussions of life. Approach the interview as an enjoyable conversation, not as a question-and-answer ordeal that you're just trying to get through. You can talk about your hobbies or recent cross-country trip. This doesn't mean that it won't feel like a job interview. It just means you're being sized up as a person and future professional in all your dimensions. Try to be your witty, charming, natural self.

THE TYPICAL COURSE A BUSINESS SCHOOL APPLICATION RUNS

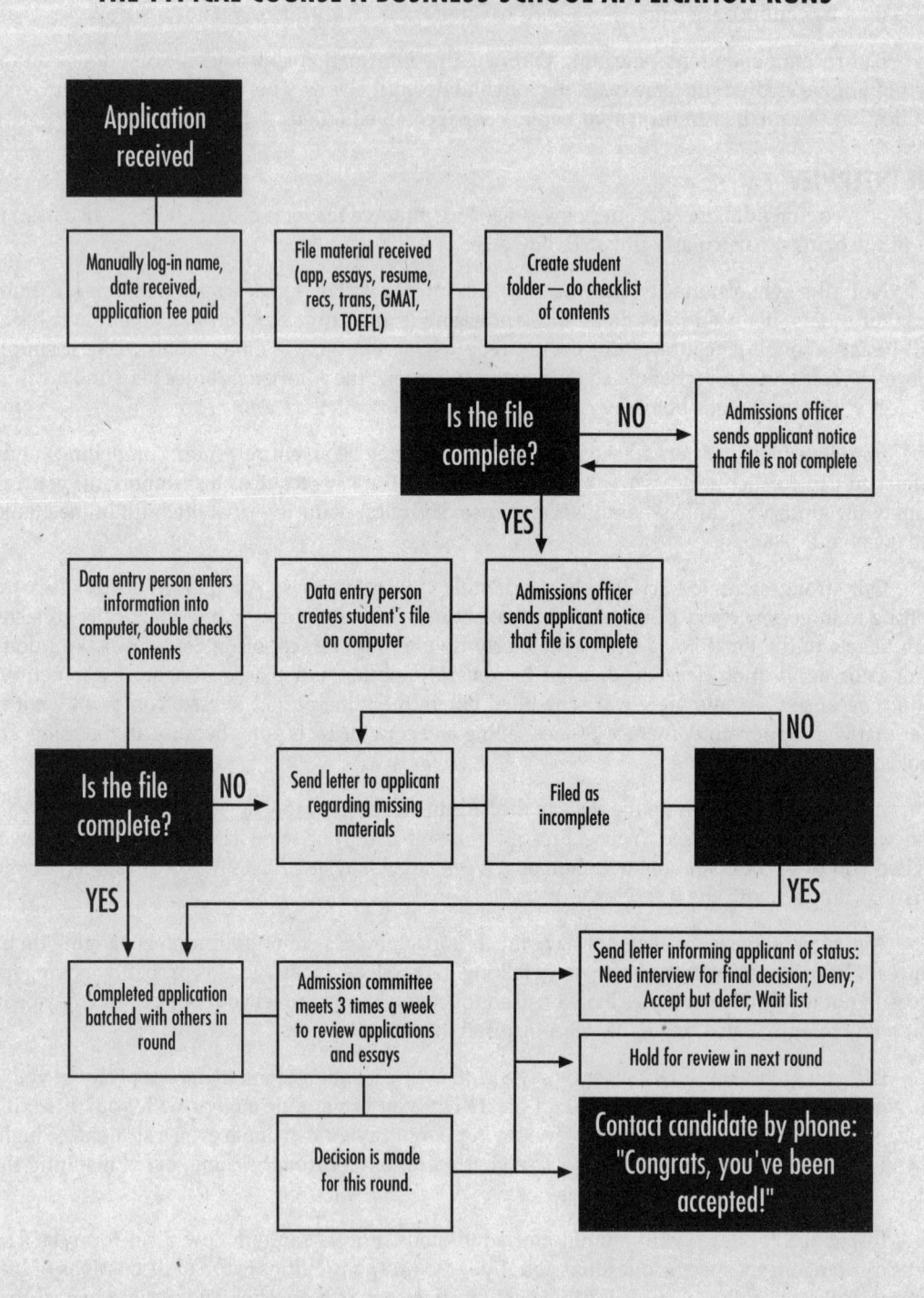

Application received

- Manually log-in name, date received, application fee paid
- File material received (app, essays, resume, recs, trans, GMAT, TOEFL)
- Create student folder — do checklist of contents

Is the file complete?
- NO → Admissions officer sends applicant notice that file is not complete
- YES ↓

- Data entry person enters information into computer, double checks contents
- Data entry person creates student's file on computer
- Admissions officer sends applicant notice that file is complete

Is the file complete?
- NO → Send letter to applicant regarding missing materials → Filed as incomplete → NO (loop) / YES ↓
- YES ↓

- Completed application batched with others in round
- Admission committee meets 3 times a week to review applications and essays
- Decision is made for this round.

→ Send letter informing applicant of status: Need interview for final decision; Deny; Accept but defer; Wait list

→ Hold for review in next round

→ **Contact candidate by phone: "Congrats, you've been accepted!"**

100 • COMPLETE BOOK OF BUSINESS SCHOOLS

Students, faculty, admissions personnel, and alumni conduct interviews. Don't dismiss students as the lightweights; they follow a tight script and report back to the committee. However, because they're inexperienced beyond the script, their interviews are most likely to be duds. You may have to work harder to get your points across.

Prepare for the interview in several ways: Expect to discuss many things about yourself. Be ready to go into greater depth than you did in your essays (but don't assume the interviewer has read them). Put together two or three points about yourself that you want the interviewer to remember you by. Go in with examples, or even a portfolio of your work, to showcase your achievements. Practice speaking about your accomplishments without a lot of "I did this; I did that." Finally, be prepared to give a strong and convincing answer to the interviewer's inevitable question, "Why here?"

HOW TO BLOW THE INTERVIEW

1. Wear casual clothes.
This is an automatic ding. Wearing anything but professional attire suggests you don't know or don't want to play by the rules of the game.

2. Bring your mom or dad. Or talk about them.
Business schools value maturity. If Mom or Dad takes you to the interview, or your answer to the question "Why an MBA," begins with "Dad always told me . . . ," the interviewer is going to wonder how ready you are for the adult world of b-school.

3. Talk about high school.
Again, they'll question your maturity. Stories about high school, and even college, suggest you haven't moved on to more mature, new experiences. Exceptions: Explaining a unique situation or a low GPA.

4. Show up late.
This is another automatic ding at some schools. Short of a real catastrophe, you won't be excused.

5. Say something off the wall or inappropriate.
No doubt, the conversation can get casual, and you may start to let your guard down. But certain things are still off-limits: profanity, ethnic jokes, allusions to sex, your romantic life, and anything else that might signal to the interviewer that the cheese fell off your cracker.

6. Chew gum or munch on one of those new designer mints.
Your teacher always said, "Don't chew gum in class." The same rule applies here.

7. Forget to write a thank-you note to your interviewer.
Sending a thank-you note means you know how to operate in the business world, and it goes a long way toward convincing the interviewer you belong there.

AN INTERVIEW WITH THE DIRECTOR OF MBA ADMISSIONS AT THE ANDERSON SCHOOL

To get some perspective on the most recent group of applicants, we sat down with Linda Baldwin, the director of MBA admissions at the Anderson School. We asked her to comment on the dot-com era, dispense some advice for prospective MBAs, and give out special words of wisdom for international applicants.

Q: What are some of your thoughts on the dot-com era?

A: The dot-com phenomenon allowed a number of individuals to dream in new ways. For some individuals, they pulled up their stake in very traditional jobs to work with entrepreneurial start-ups populated with other talented, educated, and skilled dreamers. For others, they began their career in the start-up environment never knowing traditional workplaces. For the most part, those who have worked for dot-coms enjoyed the high energy associated with these start-up organizations, the flow of ideas, the collaboration, the involvement in everything, and even the excitement of the uncertain payoff. They were young enough and strong enough to step out there and take on the risk associated with great reward or failure. They wanted a creative environment and in many cases they got that manifolds over.

I can't say they're any worse off, if they learned about themselves and have a better sense of what they need to know in the future. In fact we're now seeing a lot of those individuals saying, "Based on what I learned out there, I now know that I need to learn more, and an MBA will help me understand business fundamentals, and perhaps come up with better business models." Interestingly enough, these young people have plans of working in entrepreneurial environments whether it's with a start-up or within a larger organization.

Q: In a smaller entrepreneurial environment you have a huge impact; that's pretty heady stuff.

A: It's about having an impact, being able to see things take shape and knowing that you have contributed. Often in these environments there is a tremendous amount of collaboration and creativity; you're not alone in doing your work. That can be very exciting for individuals who may have worked in an organization where the daily work entailed mostly interacting with a monitor within a cubicle.

What's interesting in looking at the career aspirations of individuals who've left dot-coms is what they want to do with their lives after the MBA. They continue to have a strong preference for technology-related industries and they want to work within entrepreneurial environments.

Q: **How does someone coming from a dot-com or entrepreneurial environment convince you that their prior experience was meaningful and that they're ready for the MBA?**

A: Through essays and/or the interview process an applicant from a dot-com or entrepreneurial environment can persuasively position their work accomplishments by addressing the scope of their responsibilities; their assessment of their impact on their work environment/their company; they can address the business model driving their start-up, perhaps analyzing what went right and what went wrong.

We're looking for their understanding of the bigger picture, and not just a description of their day-to-day activities. We ask open-ended questions to give them every opportunity to elaborate on their leadership experiences/challenges in these environments. If they are able to answer with a level of self-awareness about what occurred to them within that industry—that's great! Their understanding of the skills they developed, including soft skills; their role and how it evolved over time; as well as their rationale for MBA study—all can reveal a lot about the individual's readiness for MBA study.

Q: **Are you wary of having an applicant pool for which the MBA is their only resort now?**

A: I'm not wary at all. I've talked to many of these ex-dot-com prospectives and I think they've given the MBA a lot of thought. Their recent experiences have made them reflect on their situation. They have had numerous conversations with other ex-dot-com types about career directions. In most instances they have thought very carefully about their next step, having taken a risky one with questionable results.

Q: **I guess these dot-com-ers are coming into your program more like mini-CEOs.**

A: I believe they will come in with a greater desire to understand the business fundamentals because they were so personally impacted.

Q: **In the next chapter we have a section called "Fifteen Sure-Fire Ways to Torpedo Your Application." What mistakes do you commonly see in applicants' essays or presentation?**

A: Most candidates are quite savvy. However, I've seen a few individuals err in the interview or essays by denigrating others. When an applicant speaks poorly of a boss, a company, or colleagues in order to enhance him/herself it usually backfires.

Q: **I bet it's hard not to, though. It's one of those things you slip into.**

A: It's one of those things where you might start by describing a situation revealing the problems or errors, and suddenly the story is more about "what they did wrong," and "what they did not do," or "how they messed up" rather than your story. Venting is not a good way to impress anyone. Instead, my advice is to explain a failure objectively. Ask yourself what lessons you learned from the situation and how has that positioned you to take on future challenges.

Negative comments about employers—anyone—will get you nowhere. You can be critical, but also remember to be constructive. The moment you start to blame others, you're telling the admissions staff in a very obvious way that you may not be capable of working with people, and moreover you're not emotionally ready for the MBA. At Anderson you have to take responsibility for your behavior and the situation. We're always looking for the person who is the problem-solver as opposed to the person who is the naysayer/critic.

Q: We are frequently asked by readers, "How many times can someone take the GMAT before it's becomes a turn-off?"

A: Typically two times is acceptable. A third time might be acceptable if there's a good reason for it.

Q: Speaking of another admissions turn-off, when applicants describe their accomplishments, how easy is it to cross over into bragging?

A: In the application process you do have some leeway to toot your own horn. You should remember your recommenders are also on your side, so you need not go overboard.

Q: Well, that's assuming the recommenders did a decent job of recommending. It's a blind process.

A: Well you know, it isn't as blind as you might think. The applicant selects the recommenders and we would assume she or he would select someone who would have a balanced perspective of the applicant. You would not necessarily just leave your recommendation form without some discussion.

I would think that you would select a recommender with whom you have cultivated a relationship. You would spend some time with that person, perhaps discussing why you want to pursue an MBA degree, and maybe highlighting some of your accomplishments/achievements that relate to why you are now interested in pursuing an MBA. You manage that process of recommendations just like you manage the entire application process.

Q: What is a common mistake international applicants make?

A: Most international candidates don't make a lot of mistakes. However, among international candidates, two minor mistakes/misunderstandings occur from time to time.

First, they can be extremely persistent about wanting to communicate via e-mail or fax or phone about their accomplishments or unique situations. Our decision is based on the contents of the "completed application" and not these additional "lobbying" communications. All of these efforts to be familiar or to make a positive impression might be better spent doing an excellent job on the application.

Along this same line of thought, e-mailing information about one's background, test scores, accomplishments, and work experiences in order to get some feedback on one's viability in the applicant pool is a big no-no.

Q: **So how do you answer that person? Do you re-direct them?**

A: We tell the prospective applicant that it can't be done via a letter/e-mail. We do a comprehensive review of their application that requires submission of a completed application.

Q: **This year the GMAC reported a big spike in the number of people taking the GMAT. Is the bulk of that increase international students?**

A: Based on data provided by GMAC, I would say it certainly is. During the last five years, international test-takers have increased by 11 percent for men and 8 percent for women. U.S. men test-takers have declined by 21 percent, and U.S. women test-takers have declined by 16 percent.

Q: **You said above that two or three is an acceptable number of times for domestic students to take the GMAT. What do you consider the acceptable number for international students?**

A: Two times or three given special circumstances. Because the GMAT is offered monthly, we have noted that some international applicants are taking the GMAT every month, basically utilizing it as a practice test. This is not a good idea because the scores will be averaged, and all scores are reported to the school.

Q: **Linda, what other advice would you give to someone considering business school today?**

A: One piece of advice . . . in thinking about when to begin MBA study, each individual has a different timeframe. Each of us is ready at different points in time to pursue the MBA. One needs to think about how and why the MBA will serve them at this particular juncture. They should not be afraid of the fact that they have less than two years of work experience and they should not assume that just because the average is four years of work experience, that they're ready.

What is important to us is what you've accomplished in life thus far and how you see the MBA contributing to your further development . . . that is critical in deciding when to apply to The Anderson School at UCLA.

MAKING THE ROUNDS: WHEN TO APPLY

You worked like a dog on your application—is there anything else you can do to increase your odds of getting accepted? Perhaps. The filing period ranges anywhere from six to eight months. Therefore, the timing of your application can make a difference. Although there are no guarantees, the earlier you apply, the better your chances. Here's why:

First, there's plenty of space available early on. As the application deadline nears, spaces fill up. The majority of applicants don't apply until the later months because of procrastination or unavoidable delays. As the deadline draws close, the greatest number of applicants compete for the fewest number of spaces.

Second, in the beginning, admissions officers have little clue about how selective they can be. They haven't reviewed enough applications to determine the competitiveness of the pool. An early application may be judged more on its own merit than how it stacks up against others. This is in your favor if the pool turns out to be unusually competitive. Above all, admissions officers like to lock their classes in early; they can't be certain they'll get their normal supply of applicants. Admissions decisions may be more generous at this time.

Third, by getting your application in early you're showing a strong interest. The admissions committee is likely to view you as someone keen on going to their school.

To be sure, some admissions officers report that the first batch of applications tend to be from candidates with strong qualifications, confident of acceptance. In this case, you might not be the very first one on line; but closer to the front is still better than lost in the heap of last-minute hopefuls.

Of course, if applications are down that year at all b-schools or—thanks to the latest drop in its ranking—at the one to which you are applying, then filing later means you can benefit from admissions officers desperately filling spaces. But this is risky business, especially since the rankings don't come out until the spring.

Conversely, if the school to which you are applying was recently ranked number one or two, applying early may make only a marginal difference. Swings in the rankings from year to year send school applications soaring and sagging. From beginning to end, a newly crowned number-one or two school will be flooded with applications. Regardless, do not put in your application until you are satisfied that it is the best you can make it. Once a school has passed on your application, it will not reconsider you until the following year.

ROUNDS AND ROLLING ADMISSIONS

Applications are processed in one of two ways: rounds admissions or rolling admissions. With rounds, the filing period is divided into three to four timed cycles. Applications are batched into the round in which they are received and reviewed competitively with others in that grouping. A typical round might go from February 15th to March 15th.

With rolling admissions, applications are reviewed on an ongoing basis as they are received. The response time for a rolling admissions decision is usually quicker than a decision with rounds. And with rolling admissions, when all the spaces are full, admissions stop.

QUOTAS, RECRUITMENT, AND DIVERSITY

B-schools don't have to operate under quotas—governmental or otherwise. However, they probably try harder than most corporations to recruit diverse groups of people. Just as the modern business world has become global and multicultural, so too have b-schools. They must not only teach diversity in the classroom but also make it a reality in their campus population and, if possible, faculty.

Schools that have a diverse student body tend to be proud of it. They tout their success in profiles that demographically slice and dice the previous year's class by sex, race, and geographic and international residency. Prospective students can review this data and compare the diversity of the schools they've applied to.

But such diversity doesn't come naturally from the demographics of the applicant pool. Admissions committees have to work hard at it. In some cases, enrollment is encouraged with generous financial aid packages and scholarships.

While they don't have quotas per se, they do target groups for admission, seeking a demographic balance in many areas. Have they admitted enough women, minorities, foreign students, marketing strategists, and liberal arts majors? Are different parts of the country represented?

As we've said before, the best b-schools tend to attract top talent, students, and recruiters to their campus. Women and minorities are the most sought-after groups targeted for admission. So it's no surprise that programs that report higher-than-average female and minority enrollments tend to be among the very best.

FEMALES WANTED

The ratio of women to men enrolled in business school hasn't changed much in recent years, despite the attempts of b-schools to draw women to their campuses. A recent study by Michigan's Business School, Michigan's Center for the Education of Women, and Catalyst, Inc., found that women experience key barriers to b-school. Some of the reasons women shy away are the myth that the MBA is still really a male domain, lack of support from employers, lack of career opportunity and flexibility, lack of access to powerful business networks and role models, and concerns that b-school is overloaded with number-crunching. Armed with these findings, a new consortium has emerged whose sole focus is to attract more women to b-school.

"The mission of this new organization is to substantially increase the number of women business owners and leaders by increasing the flow of women into key education gateway and business networks," says Jeanne M. Wilt, executive director of the consortium and assistant dean of admissions and career development at the University of Michigan. A major area of activity for the consortium will be communication and education.

"One of the key barriers to business education is the lack of knowledge women have about the value and flexibility of business careers and education. There will be tremendous outreach about that. We also need to make more positive role models available to women and girls so that they can make good decisions about their career paths. So leadership development is a priority. This will involve mentorship and program internships for girls as sophomores and juniors in college," notes Wilt.

Also on the consortium's to-do list is to provide significant financial assistance to MBAs. To make all this happen, they've formed partnerships with market leaders Dell, Goldman Sachs, and Procter and Gamble. In the near future, they hope to expand these alliances to dozens of other b-schools and companies.

Women MBA Enrollments at Leading MBA Programs (1988–2000)
Top 20 Schools (as ranked by Business Week)

1988		1990		1992		1994		1996		1998		2000	
Kellogg	30%	Kellogg	30%	Kellogg	29%	Wharton	27%	Wharton	28%	Wharton	29%	Wharton	29%
Harvard	27%	Wharton	30%	Chicago	23%	Kellogg	30%	Michigan	25%	Kellogg	32%	Kellogg	31%
Dartmouth	26%	Harvard	28%	Harvard	29%	Chicago	20%	Kellogg	31%	Chicago	22%	Harvard	31%
Wharton	27%	Chicago	28%	Wharton	30%	Stanford	27%	Harvard	26%	Michigan	28%	MIT	27%
Cornell	23%	Stanford	31%	Michigan	23%	Harvard	29%	Virginia	34%	Harvard	30%	Duke	38%
Michigan	25%	Dartmouth	30%	Dartmouth	33%	Michigan	27%	Columbia	35%	Columbia	36%	Michigan	28%
Virginia	26%	Michigan	28%	Stanford	29%	Indiana	26%	Stanford	29.5%	Duke	33%	Columbia	37%
UNC	35%	Columbia	34%	Indiana	22%	Columbia	32%	Chicago	23%	Cornell	26%	Cornell	27%
Stanford	27%	Carnegie Mellon	19%	Columbia	32%	UCLA	29%	MIT	28%	Stanford	29%	Virginia	28%
Duke	25%	UCLA	33%	UNC	25%	MIT	25%	Dartmouth	29.7%	Dartmouth	29%	Chicago	23%
Chicago	23%	MIT	24%	Virginia	34%	Duke	30%	Duke	30%	Virginia	30%	Stanford	35%
Indiana	27.5%	UNC	30%	Duke	28%	Virginia	31%	UCLA	27%	UCLA	28%	UCLA	28%
Carnegie Mellon	21%	Duke	25%	MIT	25%	Dartmouth	31%	Berkeley	34%	NYU	38%	NYU	39%
Columbia	31%	Virginia	29%	Cornell	25%	Carnegie Mellon	20%	NYU	26%	Carnegie Mellon	24%	Carnegie Mellon	26%
MIT	20%	Indiana	30%	NYU	29%	Cornell	24%	Indiana	23%	MIT	27%	UNC	31%
UCLA	35%	Cornell	25%	UCLA	31%	NYU	28%	Washington	30%	Berkeley	38%	Dartmouth	32%
Berkeley	38%	NYU	31%	Carnegie Mellon	19%	Texas	31%	Carnegie Mellon	19.1%	Washington	26%	Texas	24%
NYU	39%	Texas	30%	Berkeley	30%	UNC	31%	Cornell	32%	Texas	25%	Berkeley	34%
Yale	37%	Berkeley	32%	Vanderbilt	23%	Berkeley	34%	UNC	36%	UNC	27%	Yale	30%
Rochester	30%	Rochester	30%	Washington	25%	Purdue	31%	Texas	25%	Yale	32%	Indiana	24%
Average	28.6%	Average	28.9%	Average	27.2%	Average	28.2%	Average	28.6%	Average	29.5%	Average	30.1%

If you're a woman, consider aiming high. You'll find yourself in solid company—almost 4 out of 10 classmates at top schools are female. At other programs, you may stick out. How much? That depends. The percentage of female MBAs at b-school can be as high as 38 percent, and in fact, at NYU's Stern School of Business, that's been the average for the last several years. Stern's director of admissions, Julia Min, notes, "We've been very proactive in our female representation. In the 1900s we were one of the very first schools to admit women."

Our advice: Look at the number of female MBA students attending your targeted school and evaluate whether you would feel comfortable there. Research the number and range of student organizations for women only and speak with female MBAs about school life.

AN INTERVIEW WITH CATHY CRANE-MOLEY, STANFORD GRADUATE SCHOOL OF BUSINESS, CLASS OF '92

While there remains a shortage of women in b-school, those who go the distance are not shorted on opportunity. We spoke with Cathy Crane-Moley, an outstanding MBA with the talent, passion, and drive that have made her one of America's most successful businesswomen. In fact, Entelos, Inc., which Cathy co-founded in 1996, has recently been named one of the 13 coolest companies in the nation by *Fortune* magazine.

Ten years out, Cathy is the co-founder and senior VP strategy, Entelos, Inc. and former CFO and head of corporate development.

Q: Cathy, as a newly minted MBA, what were your thoughts on what the degree could do for you?

A: At that point in time, I didn't have a 10-plus-year horizon in my view. My thoughts were more about the immediate future of my career. I was a molecular biology major as an undergrad. I had worked in sales and in the field and had a big passion for health care. So that's really why I went to get an MBA, to follow through on my passion and vision for a business career in the health care sector.

Q: How did you target Stanford as the school that would deliver on that vision?

A: That's an interesting question. I lived in Virginia at the time and I did a lot of research on schools. I had a number of goals, some of which changed once I got to business school, but one of the goals was to go to a top school—which Stanford is. And I was really interested in somehow combining international business and entrepreneurship, so another goal was to find an environment that would support my exposure to that. So I applied to Stanford and Harvard and Wharton and all the types of schools that would have recruiters coming on campus from an international background. And I chose Stanford as the best environment for my combined vision.

Q: But what was it about Stanford that fit with your career aspirations in particular?

A: What I really wanted from the MBA was to have the credibility to go build a company in health care. I had an expectation that business school would help me be a better businessperson in science. My goal was to be able to tie together the business and science and pursue a business career in biotechnology health care.

When I went to Stanford I was pretty nervous because all these investment bankers and consultants were using intimidating terms like "run the numbers." When I got to business school I learned that it just meant 2 + 2. So for me it was really about learning a whole new language.

Every domain has it's own jargon and half the battle is learning the language. Business isn't rocket science. It has some very pragmatic, practical, and even intuitive components to it. So putting a language to it was a critical step for me.

Q: Did you utilize Stanford's formal on-campus recruiting to get your first job or did you have to do a one-of-a-kind type of job search?

A: I did a little bit of both. The on-campus recruiting I did that was formalized was more for the sake of exposure. Mostly, I created my own job search, which touches on the MBA and how important the school's networks are. The Stanford community was pivotal to my getting the job. There is no question that if I hadn't come out of Stanford, I would not have had the job I had.

Q: Why?

A: A couple of things. Right out of school I went to become an entrepreneur-in-residence at the Mayfield Fund, a venture firm on Sand Hill Road [one of the most nationally prominent addresses for ventures funding]. The combination of my background and MBA was a big plus, but mostly getting my foot in the door was the result of befriending a wonderful woman who was from Stanford's Class of '87. She became a really strong mentor and made endless introductions in the venture community for me. She is now a dear friend of mine and was instrumental in my soul-searching.

Q: You met her while you were a student?

A: I did. She was panelist at a Stanford corporate event on biotech that was sponsored by a student-run club. She was extremely helpful.

Q: Who else influenced your path?

A: At Stanford, and I'm sure other schools are the same way, there were a number of visiting lecturers who came into class. During my second year, I took a venture capital class taught by Peter Wendell who was a partner at Sierra Ventures [a venture fund]. During that class, two of my classmates and I wrote a business plan for a scientist at [University of California at San Francisco]. This plan eventually became the biotech company Khepri Pharmaceuticals.

So interestingly enough, after I graduated I first became an entrepreneur-in-residence, working for a man at Mayfield Fund named Mark Levin who is now the CEO of Millennium Pharmaceuticals, but at that point was a very well-known health-care venture capitalist. I worked with him on a number of deals and then Mayfield, along with Sierra Ventures, ended up funding Khepri Pharmaceuticals, the company that I had written the plan for while at Stanford.

Q: What did you do at that point?

A: I went from doing the entrepreneur-in-residence to becoming the first business/operational person at Khepri.

Q: And how long did you do that for?

A: Until 1995, when we merged with a public company. Then I started my current company with my four co-founders in 1996, which is also in the biotechnology sector.

Q: It sounds as though the Stanford networks were invaluable to this first experience out. What about this next stage?

A: Absolutely invaluable. Not just because of the connections—that's one component—but in your own brainstorming about what you want to be in your life.

At business school, you are surrounded by people who have done everything. There were people in my environment that had been entrepreneurs, venture capitalists, investment bankers, and international marketers at pharmaceutical companies. There were incredibly helpful connected professors and alumni. It was all at your fingertips as you were solidifying your own vision.

Q: I'm guessing that you would advise students beginning their MBA studies to think hard about why they're there and to take advantage of all the opportunities?

A: Absolutely. What can happen is that it's easy to do it [pursue the opportunities], but it's also easy not to do it.

Stanford is a classic example. It's in such a beautiful location and people want to experience California; you can easily be distracted. But this is two years when anyone will return your call. You have heads of state, heads of corporations visiting, people in the nonprofit area showing up. And all you have to do is get on your bike and ride over there.

The other thing is, there are people who have come from a particular background, like investment banking and consulting, who know they intend to return to those careers after business school. But even if that is your goal, you still should use the two years to check everything out. You should use the two years to get more exposure and think about long term.

Q: Would you have traveled this same road had you not gone to business school?

A: Not a chance.

Q: You knew that going in?

A: I don't know if I knew that going in. My path as a molecular biology undergrad was more limited and linear; I couldn't have been exposed to all the things I could become. So I doubt I could have done all that I have post-MBA. I think that's what business school does for you. It gives you exposure to multiple pathways, all of which are attainable.

Q: **You founded a second company, Entelos?**

A: That's correct. Entelos is a leader in biosimulation and predictive biology. We work with major pharmaceutical companies to test out whether their drugs will work or not on virtual people in a computer before they are tested on real people in clinical trials.

Q: **What is your role as a founder? How has it changed over the last several years?**

A: For most of our company's growth, I was the CFO and head of corporate development. As you can imagine, in a start-up this role includes raising money, doing deals, hiring, and everything that's internal too.

About a year and a half ago I decided that I did not want to travel as much as I had when we started the company, so I migrated towards the role of strategy. At that point, we also brought in a CEO to help lead the company to its next level of operations and I ended up hiring two guys, one to take the CFO role and one to take the business development role.

Q: **You scaled back on your responsibilities. I know you have children, so did that drive this change?**

A: It did. My job now is really great, it's all the things I love: to help with strategy direction on where we take this revolutionary technology, to evaluate technology, to help our fundraising strategy, to do deal structure.

But what did I think I'd be when I left b-school? I thought I'd run a biotech company, or would be a CEO of a company; there was no question in my mind. I had the abilities.

But when kids came along, I thought, to be the CEO I want to be, I can't be that right now. I have a vision for what the CEO should be, and it's someone for whom the company is an all-encompassing focus. I have small children and for me, they are my top priority at this point in my life. Hence, at this point, I wouldn't be able to be the kind of CEO/leader that I believe a young company deserves.

Q: **What was it like to go from leading a high growth start-up in your professional career to scaling back for personal reasons?**

A: When you are passionate about what you do, it is hard to scale back. My transition has not been overnight. I have really migrated to a new role. I love leading-edge technologies and of course, Entelos, and I think I have created a role in which I can still make a significant contribution to our growth.

Q: **So your priorities have changed?**

A: There's no question in life, it may be kids, it may be your health, but there comes a time when you need to strike a balance. Ten years out I feel I have a really great base and a solid set of skills, so much so that I can now turn around and help other people out. This is one of the things I've started doing out over the last years, helping people who are at the same place I was ten years ago. And that's been very important to me.

Q: Switching gears a bit, it's clear the networking opportunities were critical to your future career developments, but how important would you say actual content learning at school was?

A: It actually was. But you'll see differences depending on people's backgrounds. For my husband, who was an undergrad at Wharton (I met him at Stanford), he could do corporate finance with his eyes closed. But for me, a molecular biology major as an undergrad, I had never taken business classes, so the academic training was critical. Take corporate finance, for example. I cannot imagine anyone being in the business world without formal corporate finance. Our strategy classes, entrepreneurial classes, small business classes were all great for me. Anything like cost accounting, I could have done without. Some of the options theory too. But the pragmatic fundamentals gave me the tools to build two businesses from nothing.

Q: How was being a woman at Stanford?

A: It was wonderful. The quality of people, male and female, was superb. I believe we have a ratio of 33 percent female. We had strong women and we did great. I never noticed any sort of difference in abilities based on gender.

Q: Was the business school environment intimidating?

A: I didn't think so. I felt very inspired by the people around me.

Q: What advice do you have for someone thinking about going to business school now?

A: I think it comes back to the theme we've already touched on: make the most of the community that you can, way over and above what the classes offer. Business school is a very unique opportunity—live it while you are there.

AN INITIATIVE FOR MINORITIES

Some schools report higher minority enrollments than others, so our advice is consistent: you need to thoroughly research the program you've set your sights on. Consider your goals. Do you simply want to attend the most prestigious program? How will social factors impact your goals and experiences on campus?

As you explore the schools in this book, you'll find that one program is especially noteworthy for it's unfaltering commitment to diversity. Unsurprisingly, it is the University of Michigan, which recently won the Outstanding Educational Institution of the Year Award from the National Black MBA Association (NBMBA). This award is presented to an institution that has made the greatest contribution toward encouraging African Americans to enter the field of business.

We don't want to single out just one school, as most business schools aspire to diversify their programs. It's the number of minorities applying to business school that has remained consistently low. The number of minorities taking the GMAT, a key indicator of how many will go on to b-school, was just roughly 14 percent of test administrations from 1999–2000.

An initiative of the Graduate Management Admissions Council called The Diversity Pipeline Alliance (www.diversitypipeline.org) was formed to reverse this trend and increase the number of African Americans, Hispanic Americans, and Native Americans pursuing a business career. Much like the initiative for women, this organization plans a powerful marketing campaign with a pro-business career message for students from middle school to graduate school. It offers information on current opportunities for mentorships, internships, and financial assistance and provides an impressive roster of member organizations, services, and educational opportunities.

Minority enrollment at business schools is still quite low, so in all likelihood, you will not experience the dramatic upward shift in b-school demographics in the near future that initiatives like the Diversity Pipeline Alliance hope to influence. However, by recognizing the disparity between the minority presence in the U.S. and minority involvement in business education and practice, we are working toward a solution.

As you make up your mind about where you want to go, know that the scenario is positive and that new infrastructures exist to support your business career.

CHAPTER 9

THE RIGHT STUFF

CREATING PERFECTION TAKES TIME

"Essays are the love letter of why a student wants to attend business school"

—Julia Min,
Director of MBA Admissions at Stern School of Business,
New York University

No one ever said it was going to be easy. Depending on where you're applying and how prolific a writer you are, a b-school application will take anywhere from 50 to 100 hours to complete. Sound excessive? Go ahead and try it. You'll probably scrap and rewrite an essay many times over. It takes time for thoughts to gestate. Indeed, it might feel like a fine wine ages faster than it takes you to write an essay.

This chapter should speed the process along. It deciphers some of the most commonly asked essay questions. It also provides you with a list of the mistakes applicants make most often.

COMMON ESSAY QUESTIONS

WHAT THEY'RE REALLY ASKING

Each school has its own set of essay questions. Although posed differently, all search for the same insights. Here's a list of commonly asked questions and what's behind them.

1. **Theme: Career Goals and the MBA**

    Describe your specific career aspirations. How will your goals be furthered by an MBA degree and by our MBA program in particular?

    How do you feel the X school MBA degree can help you attain your specific career and personal goals for the five years after you graduate?

    Discuss your career progression to date. What factors have influenced your decision to seek a general management education? Based on what you know about yourself at this time, how do you envision your career progressing after receiving the MBA degree? Please state your professional goals, and describe your plan to achieve them.

> **Reminder:**
>
> It's unlikely that all the schools in this book will require you to write such exhaustive essays. The more selective a school is, the more rigid and demanding their standard for admission will be.
>
> The information in this next section is geared toward helping you master the application process at a top-notch school. If you're applying to a less selective program, you'll find this section helpful, but not entirely applicable. One bit of advice: Almost all schools require you to compose an essay on why you want an MBA. So pay particular attention to our tips on this issue.

Translation:

What do I want to be when I grow up, and how will the MBA get me there?

This may be the most important essay question. It lays out the reasons why you should be given one of the cherished spots in the program. Even if your post-MBA future is tough to envision, this question must be answered.

A good way to frame this essay is to discuss how the MBA makes sense in light of your background, skills, and achievements to date. Why do you need this degree? Why now? One common reason is being stymied in your work by a lack of skills that can be gained in their program. Or you may want to use the MBA as a bridge to the next step. For example, an actress wants an MBA to prepare for a career in theater management. The more specific, the better.

It may be easier to provide specifics by breaking your plans into short-term and long-term objectives.

Don't be afraid to present modest goals. If you're in accounting and want to stay there, say so. Deepening your expertise and broadening your perspective are solid reasons for pursuing the degree. On the other hand, feel free to indicate you'll use the MBA to change careers; 70 percent of all students at b-school are there to do just that.

If you aspire to lofty goals, like becoming a CEO or starting your own company, be especially careful that you detail a sensible, pragmatic plan. You need to show you're realistic. No one zooms to the top. Break your progress into steps.

Finally, this essay question asks how a particular program supports your goals. Admissions committees want to know why you've selected their school. That means you not only have to know, but also show, what's special about their program and how that relates specifically to your career aspirations.

(Hint: Many admissions officers say they can tell how much someone wants to go to their school by how well their essays are tailored to the offerings in their program.)

2. **Theme: Extracurriculars and Social Interaction: Our Nonwork Side**

What do you do for fun?

What are your principal interests outside of your job or school?

What leisure and/or community activities do you particularly enjoy?
Please describe their importance in your life.

Translation:
Would we like to have you over for dinner? Do you know how to make friends? What are your special talents—the b-school Follies needs help. Are you well balanced, or are you going to freak out when you get here?

B-school is not just about business, case studies, and careers. The best programs buzz with the energy of a student body that is talented and creative and that has personality. You won't be spending all your time in the library.

Are you interesting? Would you contribute to the school's vitality? Are you the kind of person other MBAs would be happy to meet? Describe activities you're involved in that might add something to the b-school community.

Are you sociable? B-school is a very social experience. Much of the work is done in groups. Weekends are full of social gatherings. Will you participate? Initiate? Get along with others? Communicate that people, not just your job, are an important part of your life.

Can you perform at a high level without being a nerd?

B-school can be tough. It's important to know when to walk away and find some fun. Do you know how to play as hard as you work?

How well rounded are you? Business leaders have wide-angle perspectives; they take in the whole picture. How deep or broad are your interests?

(A warning: Don't just list what you've done. Explain how what you've done has made you unique.)

3. Theme: The Personal Statement

Does this application provide the opportunity to present the real you?

The admissions committee would welcome any additional comments you may wish to provide in support of your application.

What question should we have asked you?

Translation:
What did we miss? Appeal to us in any way you want; this is your last chance. Be real.

If you have an experience or personal cause that says something interesting about you, and it hasn't found a place in any other essay, this is the time to stick it in. Keep in mind that you are hoping to present yourself as unique—so show some passion!

4. Theme: Whom You Most Admire

If you were able to choose one person from the business world, past or present, to be your personal professor throughout the MBA program, who would this person be and why?

Describe the characteristics of an exceptional manager, using an example of someone whom you have observed or with whom you have worked. Illustrate how his or her management style has influenced you.

Translation:
What are your values? What character traits do you admire?

This is the curve-ball question. The committee isn't looking to evaluate your judgment in selecting some famous, powerful person in your firm or in the world. What they're really after, which you reveal in your selection of the person, are the qualities, attributes, and strengths you value in others, as well as in yourself. Some important qualities to address: Drive, discipline, vision, ethics, and leadership. As always, provide specific examples, and avoid choosing anyone too obvious.

Since the person you select is not as important as what you say about him or her, your choices can be more humble. You might write about a current boss, business associate, or friend. Bad choices are your mother or father.

If you like, it's perfectly fine to go for a famous figure. Indeed, there may be someone whose career and style you're passionate about. Make sure your essay explains why you find this person so compelling.

5. Theme: Teamwork—How Do You Work with Others in a Group Setting?

At X School, a team, which consists of approximately five first-year students, is often assigned group projects and class presentations. Imagine that, one year from now, your team has a marketing class assignment due at 9:00 am on Monday morning. It is now 10:00 pm on Sunday night; time is short, tension builds, and your team has reached an impasse. What role would you take in such a situation? How would you enable the team to meet your deadline? [Note: The specific nature of the assignment is not as important here as the team dynamic.] Feel free to draw on previous experiences, if applicable, in order to illustrate your approach.

Translation:
We need cooperative, one-for-all and all-for-one students here. Are you cut out to be one, or are you a take-over type who has all the answers? Are you likely to help everyone get along and arrive at solutions? (We like those kinds of students). Can you lead others to order and synergy? (We especially like leaders). Or do you retreat or become a follower?

This too is a curveball question. But you can't afford to get it wrong. After the career goals question, it probably ranks as the most critical essay you write. Here the committee isn't looking to see how you save the team (so put yourself on ego-alert as you sit down to write this one). They want to see how you can create an environment in which everyone contributes so the sum is greater than its parts. Bottom line—the admissions committee is looking to see whether you have "emotional intelligence." Understand that schools today believe that emotional intelligence, the ability to navigate emotion-laden situations, is as important as strategic and analytical skills. This question is intended to illustrate this particular type of intelligence.

Expect to shift gears with this essay. Almost the entire application process thus far has asked you to showcase *me-me-me*. Now the focus of your story needs to be on the *we* and how you made the *we* happen.

As you write your essay, consider that when you get to school, some team members will be from different countries where cultural attitudes play into team dynamics. Your sensitivity to these cultural differences, as well as to personality types, will go a long way toward demonstrating your emotional intelligence. For example, a team member hailing from a certain culture may withhold an opinion in an attempt to foster consensus. How can you help this person make a contribution? Likewise, consider differences among team members in terms of their academic and professional strengths. If the assignment is heavy on numbers, finance students may dominate teammates from softer sciences. How can you ensure that everyone feels valued? Teams are inspired to success when everyone is motivated and taking ownership within a context of respect.

Remember: the team in this particular essay is at an impasse, as most teams are at some point and time. Write about how you unjammed the jam. Ideas: a change of scene, food, twenty push-ups, a quick round-the-room confessional about why you came to b-school. Introducing some *process* is also useful: ground rules such as voting, speaking times, a division of labor and a timeline, all create a method out of the madness. Perhaps you encourage members to adopt roles—business or otherwise. Hint: the leader or CEO in this case might be your most soft-spoken team member. Whatever you do in this essay, be careful not to present yourself as the one who single handedly gets the team dynamic going.

6. Theme: Diversity and What Makes You Unique

Our Business School is a diverse environment. How will your experiences contribute to this?

During your years of study in the X program, you will be part of a diverse multicultural, multiethnic community within both the Business School and the larger university. What rewards and challenges do you anticipate in this environment, and how do you expect this experience to prepare you for a culturally diverse business world?

Translation:
What about you is different in terms of your background, your experience, or your cultural or geographic heritage? Can we count on your unique voice and perspective in our wide-ranging classroom discussions? How will you support the diverse, cultural climate we are fostering here?

This essay gets at two concerns for the admissions committee: 1) how will you enrich the student body at this school and 2) what is your attitude toward others' diverse backgrounds? Today's business leaders must be able to make decisions in situations that cut across geographic and cultural boundaries. If your essay reveals that you have dinosaur-era, only-white-males-rule thinking, you're going to close the door on your candidacy.

So what if you are a white male? Or you have no immediate point of distinction? Maybe a grandparent or relative is an immigrant to this country and you can discuss the impact of his or her values on your life. Perhaps you are the first individual in your family to attend college or to attend graduate school. What does that mean to you? Perhaps you are involved in a meaningful or unusual extracurricular activity. How has this changed your perspective? Perhaps you did a business deal with a foreign country—what did you observe about that culture, and how did it affect your decisions?

Whatever you write about need not be dramatic—maybe you take art classes, coach a little league team, or race a motorcycle. Sound goofy? It's all in the framing. Racing a motorcycle might be about the physical and mental stamina, the ability to take risk, the commitment to learning something new.

This question can be relatively easy to answer if, of course, you have diversity or some unique element in your background. If you don't have something obvious, then you're going to have to dig a bit and find something you can amplify to suggest you bring a unique voice to the school.

7. Theme: Your Greatest Personal Achievement/Accomplishment

Describe a personal achievement that has had a significant impact on your life. In addition to recounting this achievement, please analyze how the event has changed your understanding of yourself and how you perceive the world around you.

In reviewing the last five years, describe one or two accomplishments in which you demonstrated leadership.

Translation:

Do you know what an achievement is? Have you done anything remarkable? What made it remarkable to you? Bonus points if you showed leadership or inspired others in some way.

This is one of those maddening essay questions. On the one hand, b-schools seek out applicants whose average age is 27 (a relatively young age to have achieved much of anything). On the other hand, the schools want to know what miracles you've performed. Don't pull your hair out yet. There is a way out. Like all the others, this essay is just one more prove-to-us-you-have-some-character hoop you'll have to jump through. It's less about the achievement and more about who you are and how you see yourself.

Again, this question can be easy to answer if you have some clear accomplishment or event in your background. But if you're like the rest of us—you guessed it—you'll have to rely on framing.

Let's cover bad essay topics for achievements. Getting straight A's in college is not an achievement because every one else at b-school has probably done the same. Surviving a divorce or breakup is a bad accomplishment topic. Personal stories are acceptable—but one taboo area is romance and marriage. If this is all you can come up with, you're going to look like you're as deep as a donut.

The accomplishment you choose might show some of the following qualities: character, sacrifice, humility, dedication, high-personal stakes, perseverance over obstacles, insight, and learning. You need not have published a business article or won an award to answer this question. *This essay is not about excellence of outcome, but what it took for you to reach some personal worthy objective.* Maybe you didn't lead a sports team to a victory. The victory may be just that you made it onto the team.

8. Theme: Failure/ What Mistakes Have You Made?

Discuss a nonacademic personal failure. In what way were you disappointed in yourself? What did you learn from the experience?

Translation:
Can you admit to a genuine failure? Do you have enough self-awareness to know what one is real? Can you learn from your mistakes? Do they lead to greater maturity and self-awareness? Do you take accountability when the fault is yours?

Many applicants make the mistake of answering this question with a failure that is really a positive, "I'm a perfectionist and so therefore I was too demanding on a friend when she was in a crisis." Or, they never really answer the question, fearful that any admission of failure will throw their whole candidacy into jeopardy. The truth is, if you don't answer this question with a genuine failure or mistake, one that the committee will recognize as authentic, you may have jinxed your application.

In this essay you want to write about a failure that had some high stakes for you. Demonstrate what you learned from your mistake and how it matured you. What's the relevance to b-school here? Your ability to be honest, take accountability, and face your failures head on reflects what kinds of decisions and judgments you will make as a business professional.

Can't think of a time you failed? Discuss the essay question with a friend or family member. An outsider's perspective may jar your memory. Remember, if your whole application has been about work, work, work, this is a great place to convince the committee you're a real person.

MUST-FOLLOW CHECKLIST FOR THE ESSAYS

- Communicate that you're a proactive, can-do sort of person. Leaders take initiative and aren't thwarted by roadblocks.

- Put yourself on ego alert; stress what makes you unique, not what makes you great. You want admissions officers to respect and like you.

- Position yourself as a stand-out from the crowd; emphasize your distinctiveness.

- Make sure your leadership qualities really come through. Admissions officers want to hear about skills that enabled you to rally folks around your solution.

- Communicate specific reasons why you're a "fit" for a school (but avoid pompous, fluff statements such as "I am the ideal or perfect candidate for your program").

- Use your gender, ethnicity, minority, or foreign background—but only if it has affected your outlook or experiences.

- Bring passion to your writing—admissions officers want to know what you're really excited about.

- Avoid too many sentences that begin with "I." Use examples and anecdotes instead.

- Play up an unorthodox path to b-school. Admissions officers appreciate risk-takers. But be convincing about your ability to handle the program, especially quantitative skills that schools can take for granted in applicants in finance.

STRAIGHT TALK FROM ADMISSIONS OFFICERS: FIFTEEN SURE-FIRE WAYS TO TORPEDO YOUR APPLICATION

1. Write about the high school glory days.

Unless you're right out of college, or you've got a great story to tell, resist using your high-school experiences for the essays. What does it say about your maturity if all you can talk about is being editor of the yearbook or captain of the varsity team?

2. Submit essays that don't answer the questions.

An essay that does no more than restate your resume frustrates the admissions committees. After reading 5,000 applications, they get irritated to see another long-winded evasive one.

Don't lose focus. Make sure your stories answer the question.

3. Fill essays with industry jargon and detail.

Many essays are burdened by business-speak and unnecessary detail. This clutters your story. Construct your essays with only enough detail about your job to frame your story and make your point. After that, put the emphasis on yourself—what you've accomplished and why you were successful.

4. Write about a failure that's too personal or inconsequential.

Refrain from using breakups, divorces, and other romantic calamities as examples of failures. What may work on a confessional talk show is too personal for a b-school essay.

Also, don't relate a "failure" like getting one C in college (out of an otherwise straight-A average). It calls your perspective into question. Talk about a failure that matured your judgment or changed your outlook.

5. Reveal half-baked reasons for wanting the MBA.

Admissions officers favor applicants who have well-defined goals. Because the school's reputation is tied to the performance of its graduates, those who know what they want are a safer investment.

If b-school is just a pit stop on the great journey of life, admissions committees would prefer you make it elsewhere. However unsure you are about your future, it's critical that you demonstrate that you have a plan.

6. Exceed the recommended word limits.

Poundage is not the measure of value here. Exceeding the recommended word limit suggests you don't know how to follow directions, operate within constraints, organize your thoughts, or all of the above.

Get to the crux of your story and make your points. You'll find the word limits adequate.

7. Submit an application full of typos and grammatical errors.

How you present yourself on the application is as important as what you present. Although typos don't necessarily knock you out of the running, they suggest a sloppy attitude. Poor grammar is also a problem. It distracts from the clean lines of your story and advertises poor writing skills.

Present your application professionally—neatly typed and proofed for typos and grammar. And forget gimmicks like a videotape. This isn't *America's Funniest Home Videos*.

8. *Send one school an essay intended for another—or forget to change the school name when using the same essay for several applications.*

Double check before you send anything out. Admissions committees are (understandably) insulted when they see another school's name or forms.

9. *Make whiny excuses for everything.*

Admissions committees have heard it all—illness, marital difficulties, learning disabilities, test anxiety, bad grades, pink slips, putting oneself through school—anything and everything that has ever happened to anybody. Admissions officers have lived through these things, too. No one expects you to sail through life unscathed. What they do expect is that you own up to your shortcomings.

Avoid trite, predictable explanations. If your undergraduate experience was one long party, be honest. Discuss who you were then, and who you've become today. Write confidently about your weaknesses and mistakes. Whatever the problem, it's important you show you can recover and move on.

10. *Make the wrong choice of recommenders.*

A top-notch application can be doomed by second-rate recommendations. This can happen because you misjudged the recommendors' estimation of you or you failed to give them direction and focus.

As we've said, recommendations from political figures, your uncle's CEO golfing buddy, and others with lifestyles of the rich and famous don't impress (and sometimes annoy) admissions folk—unless such recommenders really know you or built the school's library.

11. *Let the recommender miss the deadline.*

Make sure you give the person writing your recommendation plenty of lead time to write and send in their recommendation. Even with advance notice, a well-meaning but forgetful person can drop the ball.

It's your job to remind them of the deadlines. Do what you have to do to make sure they get there on time.

12. *Be impersonal in the personal statement.*

Each school has its own version of the "Use this space to tell us anything else about yourself" personal statement question. Yet many applicants avoid the word "personal" like the plague. Instead of talking about how putting themselves through school lowered their GPA, they talk about the rising cost of tuition in America.

The personal statement is your chance to make yourself different from the other applicants, further show a personal side, or explain a problem. Take a chance and be genuine; admissions officers prefer sincerity to a song and dance.

13. Make too many generalizations.

Many applicants approach the essays as though they were writing a newspaper editorial. They make policy statements and deliver platitudes about life without giving any supporting examples from their own experiences.

Granted, these may be the kind of hot-air essays that the application appears to ask for, and probably deserves. But admissions officers dislike essays that don't say anything. An essay full of generalizations is a giveaway that you don't have anything to say, don't know what to say, or just don't know how to say whatever it is you want to say.

14. Neglect to communicate that you've researched the program and that you belong there.

B-schools take enormous pride in their programs. The rankings make them even more conscious of their academic turf and differences. While all promise an MBA, they don't all deliver it the same way. The schools have unique offerings and specialties.

Applicants need to convince the committee that the school's programs meet their needs. It's not good enough to declare prestige as the primary reason for selecting a school (even though this is the basis for many applicants' choice).

15. Fail to be courteous to employees in the admissions office.

No doubt, many admissions offices operate with the efficiency of sludge. But no matter what the problem, you need to keep your frustration in check.

If you become a pest or complainer, this may become part of your applicant profile. An offended office worker may share his or her ill feelings about you with the boss—that admissions officer you've been trying so hard to impress.

CHAPTER 10

ESSAYS THAT WORK

WRITING YOUR WAY INTO BUSINESS SCHOOL

CASE EXAMPLES:
ADMISSIONS OFFICERS CRITIQUE WINNING ESSAYS

To show you how some applicants have answered the essay questions, we asked the b-schools for samples of "winning" essays. To show you what worked, we also asked the admissions officers to provide a critique.

As you read through the essays, keep in mind that each was but one of several submitted by an applicant for admission. Moreover, they were part of a package that included other important components. One essay alone did not "win" admission.

One other reminder. The purpose of including essays in this book is to give you a nudge in the right direction, not to provide you with a script or template for your own work. It would be a mistake to use them this way.

Obviously, this collection is by no means all-encompassing. There are thousands of winning essays out there; we just couldn't include them all.

BOSTON UNIVERSITY

ESSAY #1:
Imagine a straight line of infinite length, stretching out of sight in two directions. Assuming the line represents time, one can stand at any present moment and simultaneously look back at past experience and project one's sight into the future.

The time line is an assumption that makes planning possible. Though it may someday be proven a false, or at least incomplete, model, it can be useful for both personal and professional planning. For this essay, I'll limit myself to the latter.

Where I Stand

Looking back at what I've done and ahead to what I'd like to do, I can find great sense in beginning a graduate management program.

I have: a foundation of experience in the administration of educational and cultural institutes. Past jobs have ranged from directing a college admissions office to promoting an opera company, to managing a modern dance company, to running a day care center, to editing a weekly newspaper.

I have: an understanding of how groups function, what makes an organization healthy, and various ways people can organize to accomplish a goal. This has come from work experience as well as graduate study in organization theory and design at Harvard and at M.I.T.

I have: dreams and plans for a range of jobs and enterprises that extend ahead through my life.

From Here to There

Among many goals, I would like to direct a major cultural institution. I would also like to head a major educational institution, run a major foundation, and start and run my own cultural or educational organization—not necessarily all at the same time.

To achieve the above, there are skills and arenas of knowledge and experience that I'd like to have in my grasp. Some of these are presently out of reach, others are at my fingertips, but none are firmly in hand.

Financial management is, for me, perhaps the largest arena of knowledge in which I want, but do not have, agility. A course of study that refreshes my quantitative skills and teaches me principles of economics, fiscal planning, and other financial management skills would be very useful.

Another such arena includes management information systems and computer programming. I presently work on word processing equipment with comfort and joy. I hope, with time and guidance, to do the same with other systems at an even deeper level.

I would also like more personal contact with professional peers, particularly in the Boston and New England region. The public management program appears to offer that.

Some of my more obvious strengths and weaknesses should be evident from the above. I have confidence in myself. I have a great deal of curiosity. I generate ideas and develop interests, and can usually turn these into realistic, well-organized, and flexible plans. These I consider my strengths.

I can also stretch myself too thin, which can be a problem. Though I realize taking on the new demands some letting go of the old, I also believe experience increases capacity. There seems to me a need for more trained generalists to protect against overspecialization and fragmentation.

One great tool for that kind of protection is humor. My own sense of the comic can be quite dry and subtle, or broad and bizarre. Regardless of the form in which it spills out, it provides me perspective, balance, and spontaneity.

Cooperation, too, is a central motivation for me, and I am glad to see it stressed in the public management literature.

Arrivals

To accept two accomplishments and to label these significant runs counter to my way of assessing substance. I try to resist measuring my achievement by individual moments of arrival. Still, when pressed, I can come up with a few.

Performing professional theater at the age of 17 is an accomplishment that seems more significant now than it did at the time. Being appointed a college admissions director at 23 seems similarly significant. Both provided a sense of competence at a young age, and both provided peer experience with people older and more experienced than myself.

Doing well in a graduate program at Harvard feels notable in that the school was an environment very different from any in which I had worked before. The program became a test of adaptability as well as intellect. Other accomplishments might include a few backpacking ventures taken in severe conditions, some of which became life threatening. These provided dramatic tests of my reserves, and gave me confidence in my capacity for survival.

Less dramatic, and not quite finished, is a quilting project that I have worked on for more than six years. I have just completed the top sheet, a multipieced pattern in fabric. Still ahead is the quilting process itself, stitching the top sheet to a sturdy backing, with a layer of batting between the two. When done, the quilt takes on an identity far greater than the sum of its many parts.

The work on this piece has been a teacher of patience and harmony. The quilt, with its assortment of shapes and fabric, can serve as a model for the organization for one's life and the people and activities in it.

Now, imagine a fine thread of infinite length weaving in and out of all those pieces.

CRITIQUE

Admissions officers review several hundreds or thousands of applications each year. Due to this high volume, any given applicant should formulate a creative approach in composing the essay to attract attention to its quality and content. Unfortunately, many applicants write essays that are similar to a detailed resume or a cover letter. This not only discourages a thorough review but also eliminates the opportunity for the individual to express his or her own uniqueness. The admissions officers are also usually interested in how an applicant responds to a specific question, rather than to a general statement.

This essay creatively suggests the applicant's general outlook on his life, what he hopes to achieve, and how he will do it. He does not go into great detail about any of these issues but allows what he does say to have a powerful impact. Reading this essay gives the evaluator the opportunity to get to know the values as well as interests and accomplishments the candidate has. This is particularly helpful when applying to a school that does not have evaluative interviews as part of the application process.

The essay is also brief and concise and makes an effort to link all the topics mentioned in the essay to create a well-defined image. The use of subtitles introduces the outline and scope of the essay.

BRIGHAM YOUNG UNIVERSITY

Essay #1

Donald J. Buehner

MBA Admissions Committee
640 TNRB
Brigham Young University
Provo, UT 84602

Dear Members of the BYU MBA Admissions Committee:

In response to your request, I am writing to inform you of my intentions for this coming year as well as to describe my employment experience acquired during the past year.

I plan to attend the MBA program commencing in September 1991. You should have already received my Bishops Form.

During the past year I have had extensive international and national work experience. In February of 1990 I was promoted by Franklin International Institute Inc. to assist in opening a European Distribution Center in England. My specific assignment was to establish and manage the order entry and customer service departments as well as to hire and train British employees in the various operational functions. Inclusive with this training assignment was to implement the corporate values, philosophies, and quality, and to instill in our employees the high standards of excellence and consumer satisfaction for which the Franklin International Institute strives. During my six-month assignment, I worked under pressured time constraints.

The international exposure in Europe during historic times as Britain and the other eleven continental countries prepare for the economic union in 1992 was extremely beneficial for me. Combined with my work experience in Japan and my mission to South Africa, as well as my ability to speak Japanese, Dutch, and Afrikaans, working in the British Isles increased my confidence and desire to pursue a career in international business.

My next promotion came in September last year, which was to help open and manage the first Franklin Day Planner Retail center to be situated in a mall. This opportunity is providing me with more valuable experience in hiring, training, and management skills, as well as useful retail understanding including sales, stock control, and profit and loss flows. Working with the extremely qualified and professional upper management of Franklin International has been valuable in shaping my career goals.

Regarding my decision to defer attendance at Brigham Young for one year, I believe Dr. Peter Clarke's counsel that additional exposure in the workforce would only enhance my graduate experience was wise advice. I feel better prepared to both learn from and be a progressive participant in the Master of Business Administration program at Brigham Young University. I request admittance for the fall of 1991.

Essay #2

Dean of Business School
Brigham Young University
Provo, UT 84601

Dear Sir:

In preparation for a career as an International Businessman, I am seeking entrance into the graduate program at Brigham Young University. This letter will provide the requested information regarding my wish to study at BYU.

My family experience has significantly influenced my preparation for a career in business administration. As the youngest of six children I have shared family responsibilities of managing our 48-acre farm. Because my father worked full-time, my brothers and I learned at a young age to operate a farm. At fourteen, being the only son left at home, I learned to creatively utilize my resources and to seek expert advice from local farmers in managing the farm. I learned other important business principles, such as hard work, commitment, and honesty. I also learned frugality by saving a portion of my earnings in order to attend University and in addition, support myself for two years as a voluntary missionary in South Africa.

I have actively sought for balance by being involved in school plays, learning to play the trumpet and guitar, and to sing. I have sought excellence in athletics: baseball, football, track and field, and swimming. I was actively involved in scouting and obtained the Eagle Scout award and the Order of the Arrow, an award earned through leadership, service, and courage. Such activities taught me self-discipline and team unity.

At sixteen, I was selected to go for one year as a High School Rotary International Exchange student to South Africa. My responsibility was to represent America while there, and then upon returning home, to be an ambassador for South Africa to enhance world peace and understanding. In this effort, I made presentations about America to business clubs, high schools, and social groups. I also became immersed in South African culture by learning to speak Afrikaans, play their sports, enjoy their food, and listen carefully to their interesting and unique perspectives. From this experience in such a diverse land, I learned to respect foreign cultures, and I feel I developed a special talent to communicate with and relate to a wide variety of people.

As a missionary to South Africa, I served as a district and Zone leader, and Assistant to the President. As an Assistant, I became responsible for the mission's 52-car fleet, the supply and distribution of mission products, and the transportation arrangements for more than 130 missionaries. Working both in an intimate and business level in a foreign country was exciting and challenging. On my mission I decided I could best serve my fellow men as an international businessman. This decision was based on my passion for South Africa and my ability to relate with and influence a variety of people for good.

During the summer of my sophomore year at Brigham University, I decided to enhance my international marketability by going to Japan and learning Japanese. After arriving in Japan, I negotiated to establish and to teach an English program to an expanding Japanese company. Through this experience, I became excited and confident in my ability to learn languages, and to conduct business in foreign cultures by being understanding and alert to their traditions and values.

One of my major accomplishments has been financing and completing a college education. In this pursuit, I demonstrated creativity in my capacity to see business opportunities and make them profitable. For example, I installed security door-viewers in apartment complexes in exchange for rent by discovering existing trends of vacancy of various apartments, as well as installing door-viewers in a cost-effective manner. While working ten to thirty hours a week, I maintained an average of fifteen credit hours, I achieved an overall 3.61 GPA with a 3.74 GPA in my major. I feel this reflects my commitment to achieving excellence under challenging situations.

In addition to the university curriculum I have had a valuable experience in the work field. As a salesman for an insulation company in San Francisco, I succeeded at and learned to love honest sales by being competent in my service and by discovering the true needs of the people. My marketing experience as a sales rotator for Karl Lagerfeld products in Utah included direct selling as well as overseeing advertising displays in department stores such as Nordstrom's.

As a full-time employee of Franklin International, I have demonstrated total commitment. I have also sought creative ways to better the company through my organizational behavior training at BYU. Recently, I helped restructure the leadership responsibilities in my department in order for more on-going training and less busywork. As a result of the confidence of my superiors, I have been offered positions of trust and leadership. In March until August, I will be establishing the customer service/order entry department for our company in England. My responsibilities will include hiring, training, and managing a British team of fifteen employees.

I am extremely enthusiastic about the future of international business administration. I believe there are major breakthroughs yet to be made in the field. After completing an MBA, I hope to gain practical experience and exposure with a major international business firm. Eventually, I intend to establish resorts, clinics, and camps in which to motivate and train people of all cultures. To incorporate values and thought patterns conducive to healthier, happier, and more productive lifestyles. Such training would include a physical appreciation of body and environment, as well as a spiritual appreciation of fundamental values such as honesty and integrity. I envision training focused at salvaging youth from drug abuse and inspiring them to become producers. I believe this personal passion can best be accomplished as a professional and competent businessman.

I want to attend the graduate program at BYU for many reasons. I understand the working relationship between local corporations and the business school is conducive to consistent business exposure and experience combined with serious academic study. I desire a top-quality accredited program that incorporates high moral values as part of the curriculum. I am also impressed with the close working association with professors and students at the Business School. I look forward to a challenging and stimulating relationship with professors and peers and feel my unique exposure to business in South Africa, Japan, England, and America will allow me to contribute interesting insight and comparisons.

Thank you for your consideration.

CRITIQUE

Don's letter of intent gives us a picture of a well-rounded human being. He talks about his preparation in terms of his work experience as a youth as well as an adult, his high school activities in music, sports, and travel, his community experience in scouting and service to his church, as well as his academic preparation.

International Experience: Since 85 percent of our students speak second languages and 35 percent speak a third, we are interested in international experiences that enrich the class. Don mentions four experiences of significance.

The first was his high school exchange student experience in South Africa. He not only explains how he presented information about America to business clubs and social groups, he also talks about what he has learned individually in playing South African sports, learning Afrikaans, and relating to people of different cultures.

The second experience was Don's voluntary mission for the Church of the Jesus Christ of Latter-day Saints to South Africa. The admissions committee is well aware of the growth and maturity that occurs on a mission, but Don chose to elaborate by explaining his specific responsibilities as a leader and manager for the mission's fleet of cars.

The third was a choice Don made as a college student to learn Japanese and Japanese ways. He explains his work with a Japanese company in helping to expand their English program.

The fourth experience was Don's assignment in England to open a new branch of the Franklin International (now Franklin Quest) office.

Work Experience: Don shows valuable work experience from his youth. He supports his assertion that he learned how to work early with specifics about being in charge of a farm at fourteen because his brothers had grown up, looking to neighboring farmers for advice, and saving his earnings for his own future plans.

Don financed his own college education. He mentions creative part-time work—installing door-viewers.

After college Don gained marketing and sales experience with some well-known companies before he joined Franklin International and was promoted to management positions.

Leadership: Evidence of Don's leadership skills is shown in his experience as district and Zone leader and eventually Assistant to the President on his church mission in South Africa.

Future Plans: Don has some definite ideas about what he would like to do in international business administration. He presents his plan to establish resorts and camps to train people. This information gives the admissions committee some idea about whether our program can contribute to what he has in mind.

Good Writing Skills: Don's writing indicates an ability to express himself well and reflect on his undergraduate preparation. He frames his letter in the first paragraph by telling us what the letter is about and he concludes in the final paragraph by pulling together the reasons the Marriot School of Management is attractive to him. This indicates he has done his homework to find out what our program is about. Within the framing are clear paragraphs explaining Don's experiences that make him a viable candidate.

What the Student Brings to the Class: Don shows he has something to contribute to his peers. He shows diversity in his experiences, a teachableness, some definite goals, and an ability to work hard. His international experiences show an ability to cooperate and get along with people and demonstrate good problem-solving skills.

This area is very important. The Admissions Committee works at building a class with diversity in backgrounds and educational experiences that will enrich and contribute to the whole class.

UNIVERSITY OF CALIFORNIA—BERKELEY

Question #1: *What seminal influences, broadly defined, have especially contributed to your personal development? What correlation, if any, has your personal development to your professional goals? In your response to this question, please do not discuss the influence of members of your immediate family, athletic endeavors, or professional experiences.*

Essay #1:

Bangkok, Vientiane, Malaysia, Singapore, Tokyo, Washington D.C., Manhattan, Boston, Camden, and San Francisco are the places where I have grown up. My father was a diplomat, my mother a teacher, and I am the youngest of four children. Together, my family moved every two or three years to a new city. Growing up was an adventure: as children, my brothers, sister, and I did not choose to move so frequently, but we became accustomed to it. We learned to assimilate quickly, make new friends, adjust to unfamiliar customs, even speak foreign languages.

The diverse cultural experiences that are part of my childhood have shaped the way I think about the world and my purpose in it. Living abroad cultivated my curiosity in politics and international relations, and moving frequently developed my interpersonal skills and created a strong personal motivation to make the best of a new situation.

Living abroad and moving frequently influenced who I am today, yet they are facts about my life that I have had little control over. When I think about who I am today, I focus on the choices I have made, the actions I have taken, and the guidance I have received from relatives and friends through various struggles. One choice I made stands out as an important influence because it resulted in challenges that stretched me in new directions and dramatically changed my perspective.

* * * *

Following High School graduation, I worked as a roustabout out on an offshore oil rig in the Gulf of Mexico, 125 miles off the coast of Louisiana. For graduation, my family had pitched in for a round-trip plane ticket to Europe. I had been preparing for a trip across the continent when my oldest brother called about a job opportunity on an oil rig. I opted for the job because it was both an adventure and an opportunity to earn a lot of money for college (my savings amounted to one year at Harvard).

Within a week I was on a helicopter heading for Block 352, an oil field leased from the government by Chevron. I had several lasting impressions of the experience. The first is primarily sensory as I recall the physical conditions under which we lived and worked. The incessant noise of power generators and welding machines hummed in our ears day and night. Every species of dirt and grime thrived on the rig. The platform was characterized by its oppressive heat, magnified by the flames from the acetylene torches and welding rods and by the exhaust from the welding machines. The only activity we looked forward to was mealtime in an air-conditioned bunkhouse.

The work was dangerous, and if it were not for luck and the other hands who kept a close eye on me, I certainly would have been injured. That summer seven people died on Block 352, four in a helicopter accident, two in a crane accident; the seventh was a close friend of mine. At twenty-one, Eric was the closest person to my age. When I first started, he and I worked closely together and he explained everything he knew about work on the rig. Eric was related in one way or another to many of the people in our crew, and as Eric's friend, I became one of the clan. Most of the elder clans looked out for me as they did for Eric.

One day Eric was hurrying around a corner when he tripped on the extra slack of his torch line and he fell through a hole he had just cut in the deck. He fell 200 plus feet, hit the structure before landing, and drowned, taken swiftly under either by the current or the barracuda that circle below waiting for kitchen trash.

The lawyers and the search party came and went, and work began as usual the next morning. I was struck by two reactions to Eric's death. The first was the other hands barely spoke of it. It was as though the danger of the job was something they had all accepted and put behind them so they could carry on. I will never know if I could have helped Eric if I were there, but I still wonder why it wasn't me. The other response was an unusual step taken by the foreman that morning: someone still needed to descend through the hole that Eric had fallen through and climb out to the very end of the structure to attach a cable. Without a word, our foreman joined us, climbed through the hole, attached the cable, and was back before we realized the spell was broken. His action made me realize that to earn respect as a leader, never ask another person to attempt what you might not try yourself.

Another lasting impression I have of work on the rig, in direct contrast to the harsh conditions, is the strong personal relationships that made the experience memorable. The men I worked with from 5:00 a.m. to 10:00 p.m. were an extraordinary crew, all Cajuns from southern Louisiana, all hard working, all part of a team. On my first day, one of the hands later told me, they thought I was an engineer because I came dressed with new Chevron hard-hat, clean Levi's, and a clean T-shirt. Far from an engineer, I was worse than a 'worm' (someone new on the rig) because I had no training. As a young kid from Maine who did not know how to cut, weld, fit, grind, or stack steel pipe, I had a lot of ground to cover. The interests that had been a strong part of my identity in high school: student athlete, leader, etc. were suddenly irrelevant. Where I had come from and where I was going at the end of the summer had no bearing in the context of working offshore. All that mattered was what I could accomplish that summer. The way to join this crew was straightforward: work hard, learn quickly, and interact during mealtime.

Initially I was a "rigger," someone who supports welders by hauling steel and creating safe, makeshift platforms for welders to stand on as they weld. Early in the summer I asked our foreman, Henry Calais, if I could learn to weld. I did not know about the months of training it takes to become a certified pipe welder, but Henry was kind and offered instead to have me work with Charlie Reitenger as his assistant. Charlie was the crew's "fitter" and, after Henry, was the most experienced person on the platform. A fitter measures and cuts pipe to length so that when the ends of two sections meet, they are adjacent, plumb, and square.

Charlie never wore a shirt, just a jeans jacket with cut-off sleeves. Charlie was an intense man with a subtle sense of humor; on the morning of our first day working together, immediately after a healthy breakfast (at an unhealthy 5:00 a.m.) Charlie opened his first can of Skoal Long cut, pinched a lip full of tobacco, and then offered me a can. We were hanging mid-air, about 200 feet above the water, and descending rapidly toward the workboat below as the crane operator lowered us. I smiled declining: "Thanks, no, maybe after a second cup of coffee." This exchange became a morning routine with us.

Charlie and I did not start off with a lot in common. I was not sure how to create a common ground between us, but I began by showing interest in what he had to teach me. For the first week I hauled steel all over the platform for Charlie to measure and cut. Over time Charlie taught me everything there is to know about cutting and fitting pipe, and I, in turn, taught him some of the basic concepts of trigonometry. I was less successful with physics. One day I was trying to calculate how high we were above the water by dropping a welding rod and counting how many seconds it took to hit the water. For a moment Charlie thought I was an idiot. He argued that my methodology was flawed because a heavier object would fall faster.

I tried to explain that gravity exerts the same force on all objects, but as our discussion progressed other hands took an interest, and Charlie prevailed by the sheer weight of popular opinion. Galileo would have been empathetic; we eventually conducted an experiment from the heliport, which is the highest level on the rig. We dropped several objects of varying mass before the debate was finally resolved and a basic law of physics restored. It was quite a revelation, and I was surprised by how it consumed the conversation that evening, interrupting the usual ribald dinner talk.

The summer spent offshore was unique preparation for college and for life. I still have not taken a summer off to travel in Europe, but I have never regretted passing up that opportunity to work on the oil rig. The experience exposed me to the human drama of a working class that I had not had contact with. The extreme working conditions and contact with a much older group of peers accelerated a period of growth and maturity for me. Working on the rig gave me an opportunity to reexamine what I wanted to accomplish in college and who I wanted to become. When the summer was over I felt like a completely changed person. In the helicopter heading back to Morgan City, Louisiana, I realized how fortunate I was to have the opportunity to go to college.

CRITIQUE

In reviewing Haas's MBA application essays, the admissions committee places considerable weight on intellectual performance and potential; a sense of purposiveness; evidence of ethical character; and skill in the development, organization, and presentation of thoughts and ideas. We seek candidates who demonstrated initiative, creativity, thoughtfulness, receptiveness, and resourcefulness in the conduct of their personal and professional lives. We look for individuals who can provide a satisfactory account of who they are, what they have accomplished in the context of their own experiences and opportunities, and what they intend to accomplish during graduate school and beyond. Most compelling are those candidates whose reflections on their experiences and on their record of accomplishments, however defined, suggest an adaptability to make significant contributions to their class and to the Haas School.

The previous essay ostensibly describes a summer job following graduation from high school. Although the nature of the job may be unusual by MBA-application standards, it is not merely the novelty or drama of the situation that makes this essay successful. Its principal strengths are the degree of thought and writing skill the author exhibits in this composition. The essay is compelling because the author imparts a deep insight, wry humor, and a seemly modest ability to work successfully with people of widely different backgrounds, education, and cultures to the mutual benefit of all concerned. It is exceptional because while the author suggests that he was the principal beneficiary of that summer job on the oil rig in the Gulf, it is clear that his account is as instructive to the reader as his participation was to his colleagues.

CASE WESTERN RESERVE UNIVERSITY

Question #1: *Describe the most difficult personal or professional challenge that you have faced in the past five years. What did you learn from that experience?*

Essay #1:

In 1990, I formed my own company, Asian Profiles, Inc., to conduct research on the automotive industry, focusing primarily on East Asian markets. The compiled research is stored in a computer database system which allows me to analyze the data and forecast future automotive trends. Through the evaluation of automotive markets, I am able to construct "profiles" of East Asian nations and determine their relative potential as manufacturing sites and/or consumer markets for American automobile manufacturers and suppliers. My position as a research consultant and president of the company has given me the opportunity to test my professional and personal strengths as well as verify my leadership abilities.

Asian Profiles, Inc., has created a multitude of professional challenges for me. Running a small business of any kind requires a great deal of resourcefulness and ingenuity. When I started my business, my company had a database system with zero information. Four of the major management decisions I was confronted with at the time were: assessing the type of information my clients required, determining the availability of such information, selecting appropriate sources for the information, and choosing the methods for retrieving such information. I take pleasure in the fact that my company now has an extensive operating database. However, I am still faced with the above management decisions in addition to the daily challenge of determining the speed at which I need to retrieve information, and the price I am willing to pay for it. I have to constantly ask myself, "Is there a better, quicker, more cost-effective way to find this information?" Often the answer is yes, and I have found that local resources can offer more practical means of information retrieval than other sophisticated sources such as computer network systems and expensive publications. Ultimately, though, I have come to realize that people are the most valuable resource in the business. Since incorporating my company, I have carefully developed useful contacts whom I can call upon for professional advice. (To date) my company has enjoyed great success primarily because I have learned when to seek advice, when to give it, and when to solve a problem on my own. During this period I have learned that networking is an important part of any successful business career.

Being self-employed is a true test of one's personal character. When I first made the decision to go into business for myself, many questions ran through my mind. I wondered where I was going to find reliable data, how I was going to compile it, and when I would find time to learn new computer programs. One thing I never questioned, though, was whether I was capable of attaining my goals. From the outset I understood that being self-employed would require incredible self-discipline and emotional maturity. Because I did not have the years of work experience behind me, I have had to learn to rely on my own judgment. For example, soon after incorporating Asian Profiles, Inc., I was faced with the challenge of negotiating business contracts, setting up the company's finances, and deciding which computer system to purchase. With advice from experts and personal research, I found that lack of experience did not have to be a stumbling block to success but, rather, was a challenge to overcome. As company president, I have had to become my own supervisor and supporter, which has been the most challenging aspect of the position. Employing a healthy level of self-judgment has allowed me to improve my job performance by acknowledging and working with my strengths and weaknesses.

In addition to the professional challenges Asian Profiles, Inc., has created for me, it has also given me the opportunity to test my leadership abilities. Although I perform all the research and manage the company myself, I am fortunate to have the support of two secretaries. Being a manager has been a novel and rewarding experience for me. I have learned that in any working relationship, being a good manager is more about leading people and less about being a boss. I have worked hard to establish a consistent and professional management style for dealing with my clients and employees. With the personal and professional responsibilities required of a small business manager, I have had the opportunity to realistically assess my leadership capabilities. I am confident that I do possess leadership potential, but I recognize the need for expanded experience and new challenges. Asian Profiles, Inc., has fostered in me a tremendous amount of self-reliance and business know-how which I will continue to draw upon in my future endeavors.

CRITIQUE

We gave this essay high marks on the following dimensions:

Style: Well-constructed essay; gave succinct but sufficient background information about the experience, then described the challenge, how she met the challenge, and what she learned. Tone of the essay was honest and eminently readable.

Content: Situation was unique and interesting to the reader. Descriptions provided specifics, which made the challenge more believable. Cause and effect between the situation and the learning process were made clear.

Reader would have liked to have seen reference to any measurable success resulting from meeting the challenge and learning from the experience.

DARTMOUTH

Question #1: *Discuss your career progression to date. What factors have influenced your decision to seek a general management education? Based on what you know about yourself at this time, how do you envision your career progressing after receiving the MBA degree? Please state your professional goals, and describe your plans to achieve them.*

Essay #1:

As a senior, my initial goal was to gain a thorough education in finance, which I could then apply in a field related to my personal interest in the outdoors. The most efficient way to achieve this education was as an analyst at a major investment bank. Most of the available positions were in New York. Although I was offered an analyst position there, I realized that I was unwilling to sacrifice my personal interest in order to move into the city. Instead I headed West and dedicated a year of fulfillment of these interests before beginning my professional career.

I spent the summer and fall as a professional river guide on the Snake River in Wyoming. Guiding more than 2,000 people in class IV white water rafting and fly-fishing trips taught me to interact comfortably with clients and to effectively promote myself and my abilities. I often draw upon these marketing skills in my current career when soliciting new clients. I then spent the following winter and spring in California managing a cross-country ski touring center. In this position, I gained valuable experience managing people and an appreciation for the numerous responsibilities of running a business, regardless of its size and purpose. More importantly, both experiences instilled within me an appreciation for our natural environment and an obligation to help preserve it.

Shortly thereafter, I began my professional career at Drexel Burnham Lambert in San Francisco. I was one of the first junior members to join its innovative debt restructuring group. The culture was highly entrepreneurial. Since we were the first group on Wall Street to enter the debt restructuring field, we had no standard operating procedures to rely on and therefore created our own. Our success has been a function of our creativity in developing innovative restructuring techniques as well as our cooperative group dynamics. All members of the team are encouraged to contribute to the creative process, regardless of their position. I performed well in this environment and was rewarded with a promotion from analyst to associate, a position usually reserved for MBA graduates. As the business flourished and the group expanded, I had the opportunity to train and manage several second- and third-year associates who were new to the group and therefore junior to me in experience. When Drexel entered bankruptcy, I was the only one out of ten junior members invited to join the senior group in their move to another investment bank, Smith Barney. Our group's continued success at Smith Barney has allowed me to further expand my responsibilities. We recently closed the largest public debt restructuring ever completed, which resulted in the sale of one of America's oldest and largest publishing companies. In this transaction I led our team of associates and analysts from Smith Barney and two other investment banks representing the buyer in a comprehensive financial review and valuation of our client. In collaborating with senior team members, I presented these analyses to our client's Board of Directors, who relied upon them in determining the viability of the offer.

In the last four and a half years, I have gained a solid background in finance, experience in line management, and strong negotiating skills by executing numerous transactions in a wide variety of industries. Clearly, I have surpassed the original goal I set out as a senior in college. I now plan to pursue other professional goals that I have developed during my tenure at Drexel and Smith Barney.

My next professional goal is to combine my desire to run my own business with my passion for mountaineering, as a manufacturer of outdoor recreational equipment. Mountaineering has advanced at such a rapid pace that athletes in several technique disciplines have exceeded the limits of the equipment available to them. Modern technologies have only been applied to improve the equipment in such recently popular areas as technical rock climbing where sufficient demand has justified the cost of implementation. My focus would be on product development through technology-based innovation in other areas of mountaineering that are gaining popularity, such as back-country skiing. I believe that the increased costs of such technology can be offset by more efficient production management. For example, back-country ski boots are still made of leather, which freezes when wet and must be hand-stitched. A lightweight plastic boot with a removable synthetic liner, however, would not only improve performance but reduce production costs as well through automation of the manufacturing process. I plan to enter the outdoor recreational equipment market with lines through a) additional technological innovations, b) joint ventures with or acquisitions of other specialty manufacturers, and c) leveraging my brand recognition to promote related clothing and accessories which typically yield a higher profit margin.

Clearly, my goal is not to run a Fortune 500 company. I believe the future of American manufacturing lies in small, highly specialized companies that can not only quickly respond to technological change but also help direct the public's shifting values regarding our natural environment. To create this type of enterprise, I plan to assemble a small team of individuals with diverse skills but common interests. The structure of this enterprise will combine the many positive organizational aspects of my current organization. I will create a "meritocracy" in which personal and professional growth will be rewarded with increased responsibility. All members of the team will be encouraged to contribute to the creative process regardless of their position. Compensation will be based strictly on performance rather than tenure, so that all members who share the responsibilities may also share the profits. Personal profit, however, will not be the sole motivation. The team will also be motivated by a common interest in environmental protection.

My mentor in the outdoor is Yvon Chouinard, founder of Patagonia, a leading manufacturer of outdoor equipment and clothing. Through product innovation he has advanced the sport of mountaineering and achieved a position at the forefront of the outdoor industry. As an industry leader, he has become a vocal proponent of "sustainable development," which encourages managers to balance economic growth with environmental concerns. I agree with his thesis that our country's current business practices are generally not sustainable. In the past several years, I have witnessed the effects of irresponsible growth at Drexel and many of its clients that I helped restructure. Currently we are all witnessing the effects of irresponsible growth on our natural environment. Through the success of my own company, I could fulfill the obligation to the environment I developed years ago as a river guide. As an industry leader, I would be in a position to promote responsible and sustainable growth at all levels—by example within my own organization and industry, by communication with other industry leaders, and by volunteering my time and skills to increase public awareness of the need to protect the wilderness areas on which my industry and interests depend.

I understand that, in order to pursue my entrepreneurial interest in manufacturing, I will need the skills to manage across an entire organization, from finance and production to sales and marketing. I have developed strong financial skills and gained experience in line management in my current career. An MBA education is clearly not a perfect substitute for experience, but I believe it will provide me with the framework necessary for effective decision-making in these areas. An MBA program would also allow me to further research my business ideas through the experience of my peers, independent study, and related summer employment. Education and experience may not change my goals, but they may well change the means by which I achieve them. Finally, since I will not be able to create this organization alone, I look forward to the opportunity to meet other individuals who share my interests in entrepreneurship, manufacturing, and sustainable development.

CRITIQUE

The admissions essay is a critical component in an application to the Amos Tuck School's MBA program. Throughout the process of reviewing an application, which includes careful reading of essays, the admissions committee will seek compelling reasons to admit the applicant. Although writing an excellent essay will not guarantee an applicant admission into Tuck, submitting a poorly organized or badly written essay as part of an otherwise good application will significantly reduce his or her chances for acceptance.

In addition to meeting our more immediate and obvious expectations of a well-organized, articulate presentation of his candidacy, the applicant who wrote our example essay offers (1) compelling reasons for the admissions committee to accept him and (2) convincing evidence that he would both thrive in, and contribute to, the academic and social environment at Tuck. In evaluating any essay, however, keep in mind that we judge neither the experiences nor the goals an applicant presents. Instead, we judge (1) how well the applicant presents these experiences and goals, (2) how well the applicant's accomplishments support his long-term goals, and (3) how the applicant's rationale for wanting an MBA fits into his or her overall career plan.

There are a number of indicators throughout the example essay that the writer possesses attributes that Tuck seeks: (1) the types of experiences and interests that demonstrate sufficient intellectual preparation for a rigorous curriculum of professional study, (2) a high motivational level for achievement, (3) a creative approach to problem solving, (4) a blend of leadership skills to successfully manage multiple aspects of an organization, (5) the interpersonal skills needed to work successfully with diverse groups of people, and (6) an appreciation of a need to balance one's professional and personal lives.

The applicant demonstrates these attributes in describing his career progress, relating each stage to long-term goals. He explains why general management training, central to Tuck's educational mission, is essential for implementing the next stage of his plan toward reaching those goals. The applicant knows what he wants—skills to manage an R&D-based manufacturing operation in close proximity to the great outdoors—and has a clear-cut idea of how to get it. In his essay, he indicates that he made a steady progression of conscious choices that supported his long-term goals by strategically identifying: (1) Where to live and work (on a river in Wyoming, near a ski area in California, then in a major financial center in California), (2) What types of industries were most valuable to gain experience in for his personal and professional interests (an outdoor excursion outfit, a customer-service oriented sports operation, an investment banking firm), (3) What roles would prove useful for the future (leader of white-water rafting trips, general management of a cross-country ski touring center, a member of a team in an investment bank's new debt-restructuring group), and (4) What issues to monitor (the environmental consequences of commercial land development, growth pattern of technological innovations in the sports-equipment industry, how manufacturing factors into the overall national economy).

The applicant asserts that he is management material and backs up this assertion in describing how his superiors at Drexel Burnham Lambert promoted him to a level of responsibility normally reserved for MBAs. He also demonstrates familiarity with current consequences of a slow economy by showing successful adjustment to a new position in another company after his own employer went bankrupt. This flexibility, along with his varied experiences, will enable him to offer an interesting perspective in class discussions.

In conclusion, this particular applicant's attitude, experience, goals, and interests all provided a close match with what Tuck seeks in prospective MBAs. The admissions committee was confident that his interests and abilities provided a close fit with our requirements and that he would be happy in the type of environment that Tuck offers: a rural, residential lifestyle; small classes emphasizing cooperative, highly interactive group learning; a close-knit and cohesive community that welcomes people from diverse backgrounds; and the ability to take full advantage of the career placement services and connections one would expect from an Ivy League business school.

UNIVERSITY OF MARYLAND

Essay #1:

My multi-page application answered the question, "Who am I?" Now it is the time to answer another one—"Why am I here, in the pool of applicants to the Maryland MBA program?" That's a question many people have asked me.

My friends' confusion is understandable. Why would a graduate student who enjoys doing research and teaching, with an expertise in a politically important part of the world and who allegedly would be able to get full funding in any school if he chose to go all the way to the Ph.D. in political science, want to change his career to take an unknown road in business? Quite a legitimate question. Let me explain why I chose to apply to the Maryland MBA Program and not to do something else; first revisit my life history.

In 1990 I joined the analytical division of a trading firm in Moscow—International Secondary Resources Exchange. I discovered consulting as a career and developed an interest in assessment of market potential, including a degree of political risk. At the time, Russia and other former communist countries were opening their markets and it was fascinating, but also very important to try to predict how promising the Russian market was. So I decided to get my masters in political science in order to be able to competently assess such important categories for estimating market potential as government capacity, public administration competence, political risk (legal and other obstacles to foreign investment), entrepreneurial culture, and economic training of the population.

Still working on projects with the exchange, I started a graduate program with concentration in international relations, comparative politics (Europe), and economics. It has been an important part of my education, given the importance of the political situation and, therefore, political forecasting for the business future of the former communist world.

My education now has to enter its most critical stage—actual study of business. This would let me have a deep understanding, as I hope, of financial and other market structures, competitiveness, and other factors that a consultant needs to take into account when recommending whether to conduct business in a foreign country.

Taking advantage of my bi-cultural background, long study of international relations and foreign languages, and business experience, I plan to pursue a career as an international business consultant. The UMCP certainly has a focus on global business. I am attracted by the Center for International Business Education and Research—I work for CIBER at the University of Utah and my colleagues spoke highly of the Maryland Program. At the same time the School offers a strong general management program—something I need, coming from a country with no free market traditions.

These are the "career" reasons to apply to Maryland. But there is also a "character" reason. It is critically important for me to be challenged. Only when sufficiently challenged, can I work at full capacity and deliver results. Without doubt, Maryland provides enough challenge, without mentioning that an application process itself is very stimulating.

Business schools' quality criteria are no secret. From these I pay special attention to location. The Washington-Baltimore metropolitan area is a perfect location for somebody interested in an international business career. It is also the place to be for a person, who, coming from Utah, is just hungry for student body diversity and culture attractions. I visited the area on two occasions during my first year in this country and just fell in love with the place.

Add to these advantages a critical one for me—generous financial aid options. Unfortunately, without financial aid, I will not be able to attend school.

The Program's diverse environment is of special importance for me. I appreciate diversity and I think I could add something myself to the already culturally rich Maryland MBA Program—after two years in the United States I am a walking example of cultural interaction. I picked up a lot of American practices, keeping at the same time some of my old ones. I do not protest anymore when my friends take me out to dinner around my birthday, but on my birthday itself, I, as the Russian tradition goes, have them over for dinner. I try not to go with the flow and never say "how are you?" when I do not care and "nice to meet you" when I do not mean it, but sometimes I am supposed to say these meaningless phrases. I still pass with my face, rather than my back, to people sitting in a theater. I use Kleenex tissues, but still have a handkerchief in my pocket just in case. I kept my main dining habit—never putting down a knife when having salad and a main course. I changed, on the other hand the way I approach desert [sic], when I dine by myself; I still eat it with a spoon, as the Russians do. And I drink both hot tea and coke.

From my Russian background I keep moral integrity, industriousness, strong attachment to my family, self-reliance, cooperative spirit, sense of humor, strong interest in spending time with children, and my three other hobbies—movies, soccer, and travel. My American present made me friendly, punctual, conscientious, self-disciplined, law-abiding, determined to help people who are less lucky than I am (first of all, my fellow Russians), and two more past-times—basketball and hiking. I hope that a person combined with two cultures will be a good edition to the School's environment.

I believe that the Maryland MBA Program will provide me with a training I need and enough challenges to launch me into a new intellectual orbit. And, also, it would just be nice to be back East.

CRITIQUE

One important way MBA programs strengthen their international focus is by attracting talented students from different parts of the world. Indeed, a priority of the Maryland Business School is actively to recruit such students, because they increase both the breadth and depth of the school's international perspective.

In addition to fulfilling the basic requirement of every application's essay section—i.e., answer the questions asked (a surprising number of people fail to do this)—"Andrei's" statement also provided the admissions director with a vivid glimpse into his personality. And though English is obviously not his first language, his command of "Americanisms" is impressive and his sense of humor engaging. He comes across as a bright, self-motivated, high-energy individual. Just the type for Maryland.

He also did his homework. For instance, he mentions Maryland's Center for International Business Education and Research and the fact that the university is located in the culturally rich Washington D.C. area. To the admissions director, this means he is serious about his application to the program; that he is not using the shotgun approach in applying to graduate school.

Had he wanted to make an even stronger impression, however, "Andrei" should have asked a native English speaker to read over his essay. One or two native speakers, for that matter. They would have helped him smooth over some of his sentences with proper punctuation and usage. For though his message is clear to the reader, his occasional lapses into fractured English somewhat detract from his many fine qualities.

UNIVERSITY OF MICHIGAN

Question #1: *During your years of study in the Michigan MBA program, you will be part of a diverse multicultural, multi-ethnic community within both the Business School and the larger University. What rewards and challenges do you anticipate in this campus environment, and how do you expect this experience to prepare you for a culturally diverse business world?*

Essay #1:

High return on investment...

One quality I have always admired is independent thinking. I always strive to be different and befriend those who share the same goal. I see conformity as a moral deficiency. "Group think" is the enemy of creativity and innovation. In contrast, diversity in thought is the key to any successful endeavor. I want to be a part of creative concepts proposed from a wide array of sources. These creative concepts can only be reached by assembling individuals with discordant views and from varying backgrounds. For this reason, I find the growing diversity of Michigan's student body to be one of its greatest selling points. I feel that understanding a wide range of views, opinions, and judgments on a variety of subject matter broadens the base of experience from which effective solutions may be derived. Therefore, learning, sharing, and growing within the context of diverse individuals is an avenue for developing a successful manager.

While there will be rewards from this melting pot, there is always the potential for difficulty when assembling people with divergent views and from different cultures. As a member of an international exchange program, in both training and travel, I was able to witness the glaring problems of cultural bias, prejudice, and close-mindedness. One thing I learned through this experience is that nobody is above prejudice of some kind, myself included. Everyone has some innate sense that they are superior to other individuals in some manner. When people feel superior because of their intellect, we call them arrogant. When people feel superior because of their nationality or culture, we call them elitists. And when people feel superior because of their race, we call them racists. The first step in understanding each other is to better understand ourselves and develop an understanding of our own prejudices. This will be the challenge facing every student in the melting pot. For some this challenge will be great and for some it may be overcome easily, but in either case I feel that the rewards from integration of people and ideas provide a great return on the time and energy invested to make it so.

Beyond the hallowed halls...

I expect my time at Michigan to enhance my understanding and appreciation of the benefits of mixing ideas and opinions among people from different backgrounds. The business community I will enter is a global-, multinational-, multicultural-based body. Any business manager willing to shun certain peoples or ideas because they are foreign will be injuring his company. And yet, I have every reason to believe that I will inevitably encounter these types of individuals.

While universities are taking the lead in cultural and ethnic diversification, the business world is somewhat behind. The reasons for this are twofold: those people who are fearful of new ideas tend to fight diversity, while those individuals in favor of diversity often find developing it a daunting task. For this reason, many companies concede to the status quo, to the old way of doing business. Yet there are firms willing to shift paradigms of current thinking. These are the companies that will prosper in the future. The company that takes the initiative to broaden its personnel base will find that any short-term expenses it may incur in this diversification process are easily offset by the long-term benefits of having a dynamic, progressive, and enterprising staff. This is the type of firm I would like to associate with. Just as I expect to do at Michigan, I hope in the business company to be an active part of the melting pot of ideas, developing creative concepts, and forging new paths by engaging divergent viewpoints.

CRITIQUE

Originality, insight, and graceful writing immediately capture the reader of this essay. Tackling the topic directly and substantively, the author effectively relates the subject to past personal experiences and future career aspirations. The writer avoids the platitudes that slide all too easily into application essays. With admirable honesty, he acknowledges the challenges posed by a multicultural environment, admits the prejudices he has felt, and identifies the personal rewards of being part of the Michigan community.

The essay goes beyond any superficial treatment of the issue and reveals how the author thinks. Indeed, the independent thinking admired by the writer emerges from the piece. The reader finds clear evidence of the analytical reasoning skills so critical to success and leadership in management. Finally, the writing style, characterized by flowing, balanced prose and apt word choice, is eloquent. The essay convinces the reader that this is someone whose thinking and ability to convey thoughts will enrich the learning process in and out of the classroom.

UNIVERSITY OF NOTRE DAME

Question #1: *As a Notre Dame student, what contributions would you make to the life of the program, both inside and outside the classroom? How will an MBA from Notre Dame help you achieve your short-term career goals and long-term professional aspirations?*

Essay #1

As a Notre Dame M.B.A. student there are many contributions I will make to enhance the excellence of the program. These contributions include attributes such as professional insight, an inquisitive mind, and innovative ideas along with high moral and ethical standards.

My two years' experience with Sikorsky Aircraft has given me a good understanding of multifunctional disciplines within American aerospace firms. I have grown from these experiences, and I will bring them to the classroom in the form of anecdotes. My job has helped me to gain a good perception of some of the best and worst ways to run a business. These experiences are ones you could never pick up from a textbook, but they will enhance the lessons found in one.

To the classroom I also bring an inquisitive mind. I am never satisfied with the statements of "that's the way it is" or "if it's not broke don't fix it." I feel that if you do not ask why or try to completely appreciate a theory or technique, you may never truly understand it. There is always an alternative to any method or theory, and questioning is a way of developing new understandings.

Outside the classroom I bring innovation. I enjoy adding to the competitiveness of the organization of which I am a part, and I am always willing to try new things. For example, while at Michigan State, I assisted in developing the first annual Materials and Logistics student/faculty retreat. This retreat is now an event supported by both the University and the professional world. In the same respect, as an intern at Sikorsky Aircraft, I worked in our Overhaul and Repair facility (O&R). One of my first observations was that O&R had no definitive way of tracking our suppliers' performance. Every individual department had a different tracking system. I combined the best attributes of each system to form a consolidated tracking run which is now used throughout the entire 600-person facility.

Two other contributions I will bring to Notre Dame cannot be labeled either inside or outside of the classroom because they pertain to both. Number one, I am a good team player. I have a good disposition, which helps me not only get along with many different types of people but to enjoy working with them. Number two, through my business trips and experience of serving on MSU's Anti-Discrimination Judicial Board I have developed a unique appreciation of others' cultures and beliefs. I enjoy learning about other people and what makes them tick.

A Notre Dame M.B.A. will help me obtain my short-term and long-term goals by providing a solid foundation and setting a direction from which I can build. Before choosing the M.B.A. programs to which I would apply, I sat down with a former professor to obtain his insight into this decision. He told me that when choosing an M.B.A. program, I am choosing a label to carry with me throughout my career. This label aligns me with the beliefs and practices of my M.B.A. institution. I chose to apply to Notre Dame because of the school's strong stand on ethics and the international market. At Notre Dame I will be exposed to people not only from the Midwest but from around the world. This will further help me to broaden my horizons and understanding of people.

My long-term professional aspiration is to enter into a field of management consulting. An M.B.A. from Notre Dame in Interdisciplinary Studies will enhance my understanding of all aspects of business. This will contribute significantly to becoming effective in the consulting profession.

In conclusion, as a Notre Dame M.B.A. candidate I will bring a sincere attitude to succeed in the classroom, high ethical standards, and the willingness to go the extra mile. Upon graduation from Notre Dame, I will represent the university as a sign of excellence a Notre Dame M.B.A. portrays in the professional world.

CRITIQUE

We chose Ed's essay because it was clearly and concisely written, using examples from college and career to make his points. For example, he used his experience in O&R at his current employment to highlight his technical and analytical abilities with the establishment of a tracking system now used throughout the facility. He backed up his claim for being innovative by citing his assistance in developing the first faculty and student retreat in his college department.

He dealt with both the short-term and long-term orientation of the program. In seeking advice from his professor, he showed seriousness about making his choice of schools. He wanted an international thrust to his studies and chose Notre Dame because of its reputation in that area as well as its commitment to ethics in business. That fit in nicely with what he learned from his experience on the Anti-Discrimination Judicial Board of his university. And his choice of Interdisciplinary Studies reinforces Notre Dame's focus on preparing students for General Management. Finally, his choice of consulting for a career flows naturally from his prior experiences and his curricular choices.

We like Ed's essay because it was to the point, responded to the essay question, and in a subtle but concrete way "sold" the candidate to the admissions committee. Ed managed to weave in accomplishments on the job with commitments he planned to make to the Notre Dame program. He demonstrated college leadership in a large, public, "anonymous" kind of school in which students often get lost. Based on his experience, his career goals and aspirations appear to be realistic. While he has high ideals, they do not seem to be "pie in the sky" notions, and he displayed a certain kind of maturity and sensitivity that we liked.

STANFORD UNIVERSITY

Question #1: *Tell us about those influences that have significantly shaped who you are today.*

Essay #1:

I am a descendant of a long line of Quaker business people. My family, the Xs, have been Quaker since 1630. The common punch line about this group, at gathering of Friends, is that Quaker business people set out to do good and ended up doing very well. I am just beginning to emerge as a Quaker in business.

Relating to background about my Quaker heritage should help to illustrate how values of the Religious Society of Friends (the official name of "Quakers") have shaped my sense of who I am. Quakers have particular ethics that I try to develop in myself and live out. Quakers believe that there is a God in every person—they often call it the "Inner Light"—and that all people, regardless of rank and position, should be treated with dignity and integrity. This vision has helped me to see the potential in other people, even those who may be difficult to work with. It has also helped me to relate comfortably to people of every rank; in my current job, I enjoy friendships with everyone from secretaries to the president. In addition, a belief in my own Inner Light helped my self-confidence, especially in those situations where intuition must complement facts and objective measures in making decisions.

This faith in the Inner Light has many other implications, of course, but two of the most important ones involve how group decisions should be made, and the equality of women.

As a way of doing business, Quakers believe in consensus decision-making; in fact, they don't believe in hiring or paying ministers. All administration for Quaker Meeting is done by voluntary committees. From participating in consensus decision-making, I have learned to work with diverse groups of people, to negotiate between individual agendas, and to build effective teamwork between people. Consensus decision-making gives everyone a chance to contribute, and helps all members of the group to understand and articulate both the problem and the solution.

Because of the Quaker belief that all people possess an Inner Light, they have traditionally believed in the full equality of men and women. In fact, Quakers held separate business meetings for men and women until about 50 years ago, because it was felt that otherwise women would be overshadowed by the men. This separation allowed Quaker women to develop leadership skills in speaking and administration. Strong Quaker women like Lucretia Mott, a leader in the movement to abolish slavery, and Elizabeth Cady Stanton, a leader among the suffragettes, were products of this culture.

Several other characteristic Quaker beliefs are placing a high value on simplicity, and on speaking and living the truth. For example, Quakers refuse to swear to anything, even at a trial or for a marriage license, because it implies that at other times one might not tell the truth. Being practical and "grounded" are Quaker values that discourage otherwordly or naive thinking. As a general rule,

Quakers don't proselytize or even talk very much about their religion. They believe that their lives should speak of their convictions.

Quaker values can interact with business priorities in many ways, mostly positive, but some potentially negative as well. For example, because Quakers didn't limit their business contacts to the highest social echelon, they found opportunities for more customers and a wider circle of business associates. As Quaker women developed leadership skills, their ingenuity contributed to the success of Quaker businesses. Quaker businesses put a high value on providing products that truly add value for consumers, rather than devising ways to trick them into buying something. In the days before *Consumer Reports*, people saw many advantages to doing business with Quakers, because it was widely known that they wouldn't cheat you. Since Quakers were known to try to seek the truth regardless of the cost to themselves or whether the news was welcome, their word was trusted. Of course, being honest didn't prevent Quakers from being shrewd business people.

But although Quakers tend to be highly ethical, they can also be somewhat naive. Consensus decision-making can be far too slow and unwieldy for some decisions, and it runs a risk that people will feel coerced by the group into settling for less than they want. Rather than making everyone responsible, it can end up making no one responsible. Even people with an Inner Light can behave badly. "Speaking truth to power," to use the common catch-phrase for Quakers, can either increase long-run credibility or can be a cover for venting harsh feelings at inappropriate times.

My mother has told me that she married my father partially because he had been raised Quaker and was comfortable with strong, independent women. During my senior year at college, I was disheartened to find that many men of my own age found me intimidating. It was also a time when my mother was diagnosed with serious and potentially life-threatening breast cancer. Now I'm happily married, and my mother has at least survived the chemotherapy, but I still keep and reread a letter I received from my father that year about the strong women in my family. Here's an excerpt.

"Let's start with this generalization: Highly articulate, handsome, intelligent women are not terribly rare. No doubt you yourself have many friends that would easily fit such categorization. But if you add two further adjectival phrases, then such women are rare indeed. Namely, passionate commitment and courageous. (I'm willing to concede that these may even be redundant... they, in your case, certainly go together.) Obviously these same characteristics are very rare in men too.

"The problem arises primarily for women. These characteristics scare the bejabbers out of others . . . they may be admired by some, vilified by others, and wholly misunderstood by the majority. But even those that admire them generally want to do it at a safe distance. Let's face it—sparks are given off by such people. The prudent man usually decides that the warmth and excitement isn't worth the high risk of being consumed in a conflagration set off by so many sparks.

"You are the fourth in line of such women."

I am enclosing a photocopy of this letter with application (Attachment I) because it illuminates the way Quakers like my father can support and encourage women in leadership. Also, it provides some insight into my family.

Another important influence is my new husband, Timothy. We were married July 6 of this year. Tim is the managing editor of the *Journal of Economic Perspectives*, which is based at Stanford. My husband's background in economics informs and counterbalances my perspectives.

My career has forced me to balance the idealistic qualities of Quakerism with real-life experience, where the rubber meets the road. My first job out of college was as editor and then executive director for a nonprofit foundation called Fellowship in Prayer (FIP), whose purpose was to "encourage the practice of prayer or meditation among people of all faiths." This nonprofit was a rare one; it actually had an endowment that grew from $2.7 to $3.5 million during my three-year tenure. My job was to organize the programs and facilities from complete chaos to something more effective and methodical. I managed the budgets so that operating expenditures came only from the interest on the endowment, not from the capital. I also learned some lessons that went well beyond business. I was sexually harassed by two members of the Board of Trustees, and had to face the problem of other Board members stealing from the endowment.

Perhaps my biggest lesson from Fellowship in Prayer was that systems—the way information is transferred, decisions are made and reporting relationships defined—largely determine the effectiveness of the organization. When I started working there, the organization had no functioning systems in place, and no objectives or strategies beyond the general mission statement quoted a moment ago. I had previously looked on things like standard operating procedures and methods of reporting and accountability as necessary evils. But I found that it's not nearly enough to have an operating budget and some staff. An organization also needs some definite goals, strategies for achieving them, and ways of measuring success. While working at FIP, I came to understand that structure is enabling: without it, people spend too much time wondering what they are supposed to be doing or reinventing the wheel. Now I appreciate the need to organize structures, and the significance when such systems work well.

My position as executive director at FIP forced me to learn a wide range of business skills and responsibilities. I wrote the annual budget and the annual report and oversaw expenditures. I bought a $300,000 property for headquarters of the foundation (previously, it had rented space), arranged for $20,000 of structural repairs and another $20,000 for redecorating and furnishing, and moved the office. I edited the bimonthly magazine for nine months, until I became executive director. I supervised other staff. I tried to create a counterbalance to the power of the Board of Trustees, some of whom had been stealing from the foundation, by recruiting a lawyer with financial expertise to the Board. I also formed an advisory board composed of Christians, Jews, Baha'is, Buddhists, a Mohawk Chief, and others to improve the programs and create a balance of power with the Board of Trustees. Also, this group helped in generating ideas for programs, like lectures and retreats.

I also worked on developing my own speaking and writing skills; I gave lectures, workshops, and retreats myself. I have continued to pursue my interest in designing programs and giving talks that help people deepen their spirituality and fulfill their potential. During the past few years, for example, I have led retreats at the Quaker Center in Ben Lomond, California, and for Faith at Work, a national ecumenical group with which I continue to do volunteer work. With my application, I have enclosed some flyers publicizing these retreats (attachment II). I wrote the ones for Quaker Center.

CRITIQUE

General Guidelines—The strongest essays give us a real sense of who the applicant is. Because we do not offer interviews, this is the applicant's only opportunity to provide insight into who they are; in a way, it is like an interview on paper. But it should be more personal and less resume-like. Ideally, after reading the essay, we should have a good idea of what this person would like to discuss if we (hypothetically) met over coffee. We're looking for who someone is rather than what he or she has done. This is the fundamental distinction we make: We want to get to know the person behind the grades, scores, and job accomplishments—what are his or her passions, values, interests, and goals? We expect applicants to get beyond the standard "I did this; I did that" model to share with us what they care about and what has shaped them. We look for an honest and natural tone, hoping to find essays that are engaging and immediate rather than dry and distant—ideally, a conversation on paper.

For this student, being Quaker has been the most significant influence in her life. She does a good job of focusing deeply on that single influence, extracting specific insight from its effects on her. She ties it in to her values (simplicity, truthful living, living one's convictions), her social/emotional experiences (dating, equality of women), and even her philosophy of business (consensus decision-making, honesty). For her, being Quaker is more than a religious faith; it is a life choice, and by explaining its influences on her she provides insight into who she is and why she developed that way.

This essay is honest and immediate; she opens up about personal matters in a way that allows us to get to know the real her; for example, she shares a personal and emotional letter her father sent her during a difficult time for her family. She has analyzed the positives and negatives that her Quaker upbringing has fostered, further showing intelligent self-analysis and thoughtfulness. Overall, she presents a picture of a smart, committed woman who has thought hard about who she is and is able (and willing) to communicate what she cares about and why.

Toward the end of the essay she shifts from the personal to the professional (from the "who" to the "what"), but does so relatively effectively. We learn how she puts her passions into action, as well as some key lessons she has learned from her initial work experiences. There is a bit too much "I did this; I did that" at the end of the essay; it would have been stronger had she let her resume tell us her accomplishments, focusing here only on personal introspection. However, as a whole the essay is strong because some of that introspection is present, and even the "what" section tells us something about her.

TULANE UNIVERSITY

Question 1: *Why are you seeking a Tulane MBA at this time? In your answer, please include critical academic and professional experiences that led to your decision, a self-assessment of your suitability for graduate management school, your career goals, and your specific interest in the Freeman School.*

Essay #1:

I am seeking a Tulane MBA because the curriculum and international programs offered by the A.B. Freeman School of Business at Tulane University will expand my knowledge of core business concepts while allowing me to focus on the area in which I plan to make my career: international business. As the national accounts officer at ABC Bank, I serve as the account handling officer for the bank's national and multinational corporate customers, such as General Motors Acceptance Corporation, Anheuser-Busch, and Westinghouse Electric. In working with these firms, both now as an officer and previously as a credit card analyst, I have observed that many of them plan to increase their international presence, especially in Mexico and Europe. My career objective is to work for a multinational firm for several years to gain the experience needed to ultimately establish my own international service-related firm. The knowledge needed and experience offered by the programs at the Freeman School will help me achieve this goal.

After working at ABC Bank for three years, I have decided that I need more academic training in order to pursue a more challenging career. The will and drive to succeed has characterized my tenure at ABC Bank. I attribute my success to two of my personal strengths that will be equally important in future careers: persistence and interpersonal skills.

After graduating from the University of XYZ in August of 1986, my goal was to secure a credit analyst position with ABC Bank. I believed the analyst position would help me build a foundation for making credit decisions as a lender, as well as allow me to study the operations of many industries. Upon applying for the position, however, I was told that no analyst positions were available and that the bank preferred to hire internally for such jobs. With this guideline in mind, I asked for any available job at the bank. I was offered a commercial-vault teller position and accepted it. Although the work of processing commercial deposits for eight hours a day was monotonous, I kept my strategy in mind: perform my teller duties well, be persistent with credit management, and thereby earn the credit analyst job. After nine months in the vault, my determination was rewarded; the credit manager offered me the position that I sought. As an analyst, I was responsible for writing detailed analyses of a firm's operations to assist the commercial lenders with credit decisions. After working only eleven months in the credit area (the normal tenure is eighteen to twenty-four months), I was elected national accounts officer, thus becoming the bank's youngest officer. Although I wrote very good credit reviews, I was not promoted for this reason; there were several other analysts who also wrote good reviews. I was promoted largely because of my strong interpersonal and communications skills, since the National Accounts position requires an officer who can work well with both current and prospective customers. The National Accounts position entails handling the lending and cash management needs of the bank's national customers.

At ABC Bank, I have moved from a teller to an officer position in a short time. I have used my intelligence, persistence, and interpersonal skills to move up rapidly, and now I wish to pursue a more challenging career. I am ready to use my past experience, combined with my strengths that I have discussed above, to obtain a graduate management degree and then excel in the area of international business.

Goal: Career in International Business

I want to build on my three years of banking experience and my travels, literally around the world, in preparation for an international management position either within the United States or abroad. My travels to Australia, Latin America, and South Africa on behalf of my family's cattle ranch first stimulated my interest in international business and trade. This interest has subsequently evolved during my three years in the banking business.

While I was a credit analyst, I learned much more about the international direction in which many firms are increasingly moving. Some of the firms that I reviewed are aggressively pursuing opportunities in Mexico because of their proximity to the border, the probable free trade agreement between the United States and Mexico, and the burgeoning maquiladora industry along the international border. The common denominator among these firms is a desire to take advantage of Mexico's abundance of labor and natural resources. I believe these two resources, coupled with Mexico's progressive government and an increasing interest in Mexico by U.S. business, will provide great opportunity in this emerging area of trade.

In addition, the National Accounts position has afforded me the opportunity to travel nationwide to call on my customers' home offices, and, in the course of conducting the bank's affairs, inquire about each firm's international operations. Although noting the obstacles, political and economic, many customers have eagerly outlined their plans to expand into Latin America, Eastern Europe, and China. They made it clear to me that trends such as the movement toward common markets and the increasing capability of long-distance communication via satellite will further encourage foreign trade. Furthermore, most noted their company's need to employ more personnel in the international area; the general consensus among my contacts is that there will be an increasing demand for international managers in the next decade.

At present, I am undecided as to which path I will choose in international business. Some possibilities that I have considered are finance-related and should capitalize on my lending and cash management experience with a multinational bank. Another option I am considering is to establish a firm that provides translation services to companies wishing to conduct business abroad. As more firms enter the international market, the language barrier could be an obstacle to many U.S. businesses. A translation service would overcome this problem and innovations such as video teleconferencing make this idea quite feasible.

Why a Tulane MBA?

Clearly, there are a number of options available to someone pursuing a career in international business in order to be an effective manager. The Freeman School's curriculum provides the opportunity for me to obtain this knowledge.

The program's first year of required core courses, such as Financial Accounting and Marketing Management, followed by a flexible course scheduled in the second year appeals to my desire to expand my knowledge in the areas of finance and accounting, and then focus on international topics. I also hope to take advantage of the school's international internship program or the study abroad program. It is important that I take advantage of one of these programs, since I believe one should have a sense of culture and economic climate of a region if she or he hopes to conduct business in that area.

Since I will spend almost two years in a master's program and the school I choose could well determine my career options, I have treated the selection of schools to which I will apply with great care. I am quite aware of the Freeman School's outstanding reputation for international studies. Furthermore, since New Orleans is one of the nation's largest ports, I will have the opportunity to obtain first-hand knowledge about international commerce. Finally, several of the school's alumni have highly recommended the Freeman School to me due to its significant global focus.

In summary, the combination of my three years of banking experience, international travels, and completion of the MBA program at Tulane should prepare me quite well to succeed as an international manager. As you can see, I have demonstrated both motivation and initiative during my tenure at ABC Bank. I realize that my grade point average is below the published median 3.1 for a recently entering class. I attribute my relatively low GPA to lack of career focus and immaturity during my undergraduate years. I want to assert my belief, however, that I have as much character, determination, and will to succeed as any student in the MBA program. I might note that there are several credit analysts who obtained their jobs before I did mainly due to higher GPAs; most of these analysts are still in the credit department writing reviews while I travel nationwide representing the bank. I can successfully complete the MBA program at Tulane and would certainly like the opportunity to do so.

CRITIQUE

Our admissions committee felt that this was an extremely strong essay. Many applications have the tendency to treat this as an open-ended "tell us about yourself" kind of question and write very general essays that elaborate on their backgrounds without providing adequate rationale regarding their suitability for MBA studies, an outline of their of their goals, or how a Freeman MBA can help them attain these goals. Although often cleverly written, such essays do not help the committee in making an admissions decision.

This essay is well structured, well written, and gives us a clear picture of the applicant as an individual who is both motivated and focused. The description of his rapid progression at ABC Bank from commercial vault teller to credit analyst (his initial goal) to national accounts officer clearly shows that the applicant is able to assess his options, set goals and successfully develop and execute a strategy to reach them. These are characteristics we seek in our MBA students. The essay also shows that the applicant has gained important knowledge and insights along the way which have helped him formulate his goals for the future. These goals include a Freeman MBA and a career in international business.

Although this applicant confesses that he is still weighing two options in the area of international business (rather refreshing, since many of the very specific career goals we read about are obviously contrived or not well supported in the essay), he makes a convincing case for his interest in the field. He also explains his interest in the Freeman School well, citing our global focus, locations in one of the nation's largest port cities, and some of our specific international programs. The applicant shows a strong interest in the Freeman MBA program. He has researched the program and has clearly taken the time to speak with alumni.

Finally, the applicant acknowledges a weakness (his GPA), and, without making excuses, emphasizes the characteristics he has which he believes will make him a strong candidate for our program. These characteristics were amply demonstrated throughout the essay, but he does a nice job of summarizing them and "closing the sale" at the end.

UNIVERSITY OF VIRGINIA

Question #1: *What is the most difficult ethical dilemma you have faced in your professional life? Articulate the nature of the difficulty. Upon present reflection, would you have resolved this dilemma in a different manner?*

Essay #1:

Upon graduation from college, my sense of adventure and quest for learning continued when I accepted a nontraditional position with the Bank of Credit and Commerce International (BCCI). I accepted a position with BCCI with the understanding that overseas placements were the requirement, given the bank's limited U.S. presence. BCCI was founded in 1972 by Pakistani financier Agha Hasan Abedi, whose goal was to create the first multinational bank for the Third World. Its shareholders were rich Middle Eastern oil sheiks. Healthy growth fueled by increasing international trade helped BCCI expand to $20 billion in assets that circled the globe in a 70-country branch network.

After completing BCCI's international trade finance training program with distinction at Pace University in New York, I received my first placement in London, England, working as a trainee in bank branch operations and special country-analysis projects. After quickly completing my London assignment in three months, BCCI management promoted me to a marketing role at their main offices in the United Arab Emirates (UAE). The ruling sheiks of each of the emirates were BCCI's major stockholders and had enormous international political and economic clout.

By quickly absorbing the local culture and the basics of the Arabic language, I earned the respect of my peers at the bank and in the local business community. Through my efforts, I marketed and received commitments for trade financing and investing from many multinational businesses operating in the UAE.

It was right after my third month working in the UAE that I was faced with a major ethical dilemma. During my search for new business, I learned from a contact at the government ministry of trade that a European sportswear manufacturer had applied for permission to start up a business in the UAE. (An application to do business is required of all foreigners along with the requirement to find a local partner.) I immediately informed bank management of the prospect and began my research into the company. After an initial meeting with the company in the UAE a few weeks later, I learned that the firm required a $30 million line facility. I requested the necessary financial information from the company and began my analysis of the company to assess its creditworthiness. My recommendation to bank management was not to proceed any further with the company, given its losses over the past three years and very high leverage. The risks posed by the company's profiles were too great.

My manager, who had always valued my credit skills, mysteriously ignored my recommendation and ordered me to negotiate a loan facility with the company. I was puzzled by my manager's actions, especially since he offered no explanation. I structured a smaller facility at a premium interest rate with adequate primary and secondary fallback collateral to protect the bank from any credit risks. After presenting the new proposal to my bank manager, he dismissed it without comment and made the necessary arrangements to grant the company a $30 million unsecured line of credit at an interest rate reserved for the bank's highest creditworthy clients. A new provision was added, though. A finder's fee of one percent of the loan ($300,000) was due. Even though the fee was paid, there existed no mention of it in the loan documents. Through a search of the bank's accounting records, I learned that the fee was transferred out of the UAE to my manager's personal account abroad. I was naive to think that the manager did not have his contacts in the bank who would report my inquiring.

My manager explained that the fee was not to be considered extorted funds, rather it was his finder's fee. Further, he explained that this was a customary practice. In fact, to show good will, he offered to share his fee with me and suggested $50,000. The only stipulation was that I had to keep the matter quiet from "jealous" employees.

My dilemma was whether to accept part of my manager's illegally obtained funds and keep quiet or to report the matter to a higher level of bank management. Being only 23 years of age and in a foreign country 8,000 miles away from home, I was scared. If this was a customary practice and the branch was covering up for him, then my reporting this incident would put my job in jeopardy as well as my life. I was always taught by my family to practice high ethical and moral standards and to obey the law. This was my guiding principle in refusing the illegal funds and notifying the bank's London headquarters of this serious matter. Immediately, I was transferred back to London within 48 hours, and no mention of the incident was ever made to me either in the UAE or in London. My newly assigned job in London was nonmarketing related and consisted of counting checks in a windowless basement room. Even though it felt like BCCI management was punishing me for good ethical conduct, I still believed that my decision was right. I resigned from the bank one month later and returned to the United States, where I obtained a banking job with an organization that, I feel proud to say, has never presented me with a choice of compromising my ethics and moral standards.

If, in the future, I am unfortunately presented with an ethical dilemma of any degree, I feel confident in holding my ethical and moral standards as priority.

CRITIQUE

What makes an application to the Darden School stand out from among the thousands received each year? One important key is well-written essays. As with many business school applications, the essay portion is the applicant's chance to showcase his or her writing talents while at the same time communicating a lot of explicit (and sometimes implicit) information to the admissions committee.

Many b-schools offer the first-year student traditional courses in such functional areas as accounting, marketing, and operations, but Darden was one of the first to include required, graded courses in both communications and ethics. Nowhere at Darden do these two disciplines dovetail more perfectly than in Essay #4 of Darden's application, which asks: "What is the most difficult ethical dilemma you have faced in your professional life? Articulate the nature of the difficulty. Upon present reflection, would you have resolved this dilemma in a different manner?"

While this essay question often prompts the most reflection and introspection on the part of the applicant, it is also often the least understood. The admissions committee is looking not necessarily to judge the nature of the dilemma but rather the candidate's ability to articulate an often personal and complex decision-making process. The key to an effective Essay #4 is in dissecting the terms *ethical* and *dilemma*. Too often, themes reflected in this essay are of a legal nature: Should I disagree with my boss? Should I turn a co-worker in who's stealing office supplies? Should I break the law? And many situations do not accurately present a true dilemma in which there is no clear right or wrong answer but two or more possible solutions, none of which are necessarily better than another.

The essay above serves as an outstanding example by setting the scene, explaining clearly the nature of the dilemma and summing up the candidate's experience in a concise and well-written essay. The admissions committee was particularly impressed by the author's honest approach and engaging writing style. The firm does not have to be well-known, in this case BCCI, nor must the dilemma involve large sums of money or shady characters. Rather, the essay should reflect the candidate's personal and professional commitment to ethics, a commitment that also underlies the foundation of the Darden School.

Part III

QUICK REFERENCE LIST

AMERICAN GRADUATE SCHOOL OF BUSINESS (SWITZERLAND)
Master of International Business Administration Program

Web Address: www.agsb.ch/
Total Business Students: 33
Annual Tuition: $26,000

AMERICAN UNIVERSITY
Kogod School of Business

Address: 4400 Massachusetts Avenue NW, Washington, DC 20016
Admissions Phone: 202-885-1913 • Web Address: www.kogod.american.edu
Public/Private: Private
Average GMAT: 560
Annual Tuition: $19,080

APPALACHIAN STATE UNIVERSITY
Walker College of Business

Address: ASU Box 32004, Boone, NC 28608
Admissions Phone: 828-262-2120 • Web Address: www.business.appstate.edu
Public/Private: Public
Total Business Students: 39
Average GMAT: 502
% Full Time: 90
Annual Tuition (Resident/Nonresident): $1,285/$8,400

ARIZONA STATE UNIVERSITY
College of Business—ASU MBA Program

Address: PO Box 874906, Tempe, AZ 85287-4906
Admissions Phone: 480-965-3332 • Web Address: www.cob.asu.edu/mba
Public/Private: Public
Total Business Students: 477
Average GMAT: 644
% Full Time: 43
Annual Tuition (Resident/Nonresident): $9,344/$17,800

ARIZONA STATE UNIVERSITY WEST
School of Management

Address: PO Box 37100, Phoenix, AZ 85069-7100
Admissions Phone: 602-543-6201 • Web Address: www.west.asu.edu/som/mba
Public/Private: Public
Total Business Students: 445
Average GMAT: 580
% Full Time: 0

ARKANSAS STATE UNIVERSITY
College of Business

Address: PO Box 60, State University, AR 72467
Admissions Phone: 870-972-3029 • Web Address: business.astate.edu
Public/Private: Public
Total Business Students: 104
Annual Tuition (Resident/Nonresident): $1,488/$3,744

AUBURN UNIVERSITY
College of Business

Address: 503 Lowder Business Building, Auburn University, AL 36849
Admissions Phone: 334-844-4060
Web Address: www.mba.business.auburn.edu
Public/Private: Public
Total Business Students: 500
Average GMAT: 578
% Full Time: 25
Annual Tuition (Resident/Nonresident): $1,630/$4,890

AUBURN UNIVERSITY AT MONTGOMERY
AUM School of Business

Web Address: www-biz.aum.edu
Public/Private: Public
Total Business Students: 227
Annual Tuition (Resident/Nonresident): $3,400/$10,056

AUDREY COHEN COLLEGE
Graduate School of Business

Address: 1 Hudson Square (75 Varick Street), New York, NY 10013
Admissions Phone: 212-343-1234 • Web Address: www.audreycohen.edu/html/businessmbas.shtml
Public/Private: Private

AUGUSTA STATE UNIVERSITY
College of Business Administration

Address: MBA Office, 2500 Walton Way, Augusta, GA 30904-2200
Admissions Phone: 706-737-1565 • Web Address: www.aug.edu/coba/
Public/Private: Public
Total Business Students: 133
Average GMAT: 520
% Full Time: 29
Annual Tuition (Resident/Nonresident): $2,096/$7,316

BABSON COLLEGE
F. W. Olin Graduate School of Business

Address: Olin Hall, Babson Park (Wellesley), MA 02457-0310
Admissions Phone: 781-239-4317 • Web Address: www.babson.edu/mba
Public/Private: Private
Total Business Students: 1,696
Average GMAT: 638
% Full Time: 27
Annual Tuition: $25,710

BALL STATE UNIVERSITY
College of Business

Address: WB 146, Muncie, IN 47306
Admissions Phone: 765-285-1931 • Web Address: www.bsu.edu/mba
Public/Private: Public
Total Business Students: 175
Average GMAT: 520
% Full Time: 23
Annual Tuition (Resident/Nonresident): $4,100/$10,000

BARUCH COLLEGE (CITY UNIVERSITY OF NEW YORK)
Zicklin School of Business

Address: One Bernard Baruch Way, Box H-0820, New York, NY 10010
Admissions Phone: 646-312-1300
Web Address: www.zicklin.baruch.cuny.edu
Public/Private: Public
Total Business Students: 1,445
Average GMAT: 650
% Full Time: 43
Annual Tuition (Resident/Nonresident): $6,000/$13,300

BAYLOR UNIVERSITY
Hankamer School of Business

Address: PO Box 98013, Waco, TX 76798-8013
Admissions Phone: 254-710-3718
Web Address: www.gradbusiness.baylor.edu
Public/Private: Private
Total Business Students: 112
Average GMAT: 590
% Full Time: 100
Annual Tuition: $14,000

BENTLEY COLLEGE
The Elkin B. McCallum Graduate School of Business

Address: 175 Forest Street, Waltham, MA 02452
Admissions Phone: 781-891-2108 • Web Address: www.bentley.edu
Public/Private: Private
Total Business Students: 722
Average GMAT: 545
% Full Time: 22
Annual Tuition: $23,300

BINGHAMTON UNIVERSITY (STATE UNIVERSITY OF NEW YORK)
School of Management

Address: School of Management, Binghamton, NY 13902
Admissions Phone: 607-777-2317 • Web Address: som.binghamton.edu
Public/Private: Public
Total Business Students: 133
Average GMAT: 585
% Full Time: 86
Annual Tuition (Resident/Nonresident): $5,100/$8,416

BOCCONI UNIVERSITY
SDA Bocconi

Web Address: www.sda.uni-bocconi.it
Total Business Students: 291
% Full Time: 76

BOISE STATE UNIVERSITY
College of Business and Economics

Address: 1910 University Drive B117, Boise, ID 83725-1600
Admissions Phone: 208-426-1126 • Web Address: http://cobe.boisestate.edu/graduate
Public/Private: Public
Total Business Students: 257
% Full Time: 20

BOSTON COLLEGE
The Carroll School of Management

Address: Fulton Hall 315, Chestnut Hill, MA 02467
Admissions Phone: 617-552-3920 • Web Address: www.bc.edu\mba
Public/Private: Private
Total Business Students: 766
Average GMAT: 640
% Full Time: 30
Annual Tuition: $25,792

BOSTON UNIVERSITY
School of Management

Address: 595 Commonwealth Avenue, Boston, MA 02215
Admissions Phone: 617-353-2670 • Web Address: management.bu.edu
Public/Private: Private
Total Business Students: 1,158
Average GMAT: 635
% Full Time: 53
Annual Tuition: $25,700

BOWLING GREEN STATE UNIVERSITY
College of Business Administration

Address: 369 Business Administration Building, Bowling Green, OH 43403
Admissions Phone: 419-372-2488
Web Address: www.cba.bgsu.edu/gsb/gradprg/
Public/Private: Public
Total Business Students: 150
Average GMAT: 526
% Full Time: 29
Annual Tuition: $9,552

BRADLEY UNIVERSITY
Foster College of Business Administration

Address: Baker Hall, Peoria, IL 61625
Admissions Phone: 309-677-2253 • Web Address: www.bradley.edu
Public/Private: Private
Annual Tuition: $13,880

BRIGHAM YOUNG UNIVERSITY
Marriott School of Management

Address: 640 TNRB, Provo, UT 84602
Admissions Phone: 801-422-3509 • Web Address: marriottschool.byu.edu/mba
Public/Private: Private
Total Business Students: 251
Average GMAT: 660
% Full Time: 100
Annual Tuition: $6,140

BRYANT COLLEGE
School of Business Administration

Address: 1150 Douglas Pike, Smithfield, RI 02917-1284
Admissions Phone: 401-232-6230 • Web Address: www.bryant.edu
Public/Private: Private
Total Business Students: 318
Average GMAT: 521
% Full Time: 23

BUTLER UNIVERSITY
College of Business Administration

Address: 4600 Sunset Avenue, Indianapolis, IA 46208-3485
Admissions Phone: 317-940-9221 • Web Address: www.butler.edu/www/cba
Public/Private: Private
Total Business Students: 405
% Full Time: 5

CALIFORNIA POLYTECHNIC STATE UNIVERSITY—SAN LUIS OBISPO
College of Business

Web Address: www.cob.calpoly.edu
Public/Private: Public
Total Business Students: 106
Average GMAT: 558

CALIFORNIA STATE POLYTECHNIC UNIVERSITY—POMONA
College of Business Administration

Address: 3801 West Temple Avenue, Pomona, CA 91768
Admissions Phone: 909-869-3210 • Web Address: www.csupomona.edu/~mba/
Public/Private: Public
Total Business Students: 600
Average GMAT: 520
Annual Tuition (Resident/Nonresident): $2,100/$4,100

CALIFORNIA STATE UNIVERSITY—BAKERSFIELD
School of Business and Public Administration

Address: 9001 Stockdale Highway, Bakersfield, CA 93311-1099
Admissions Phone: 661-664-2326 • Web Address: www.csubak.edu/bpa/
Public/Private: Public
Total Business Students: 718
Annual Tuition (Resident/Nonresident): $1,887/$9,233

CALIFORNIA STATE UNIVERSITY—CHICO
College of Business

Address: BGAD@CSU, Chico 041, Chico, CA 95929
Admissions Phone: 530-898-4425 • Web Address: www-cob.csuchico.edu
Public/Private: Public
Total Business Students: 80
Average GMAT: 560
% Full Time: 70
Annual Tuition (Resident/Nonresident): $2,120/$7,500

CALIFORNIA STATE UNIVERSITY—FRESNO
Sid Craig School of Business

Address: 5245 North Backer Avenue, Fresno, CA 93740
Admissions Phone: 559-278-2107 • Web Address: www.craig.csufresno.edu/
Public/Private: Public
Total Business Students: 318
Average GMAT: 500
% Full Time: 13

CALIFORNIA STATE UNIVERSITY—FULLERTON
College of Business and Economics

Address: PO Box 6848, Fullerton, CA 92834
Admissions Phone: 714-278-2211 • Web Address: business.fullerton.edu
Public/Private: Public
Total Business Students: 511
Average GMAT: 550
% Full Time: 10
Annual Tuition (Resident/Nonresident): $0/$246

CALIFORNIA STATE UNIVERSITY—HAYWARD
School of Business and Economics

Address: 25800 Carles Bee Boulevard, Hayward, CA 94542
Admissions Phone: 510-885-2624 • Web Address: sbegrad.csuhayward.edu
Public/Private: Public
Total Business Students: 579
Average GMAT: 530
% Full Time: 20
Annual Tuition (Resident/Nonresident): $2,460/$10,332

CALIFORNIA STATE UNIVERSITY—LONG BEACH
College of Business Administration

Address: 1250 Bellflower Boulevard, Long Beach, CA 90840-0119
Admissions Phone: 562-985-7988 • Web Address: www.csulb.edu/~cba/
Public/Private: Public
Total Business Students: 430
% Full Time: 20

CALIFORNIA STATE UNIVERSITY—LOS ANGELES
College of Business and Economics

Address: 5151 State University Drive, Los Angeles, CA 90032
Admissions Phone: 323-343-3901 • Web Address: http://sbela.calstatela.edu
Public/Private: Public
Total Business Students: 330
% Full Time: 0

CALIFORNIA STATE UNIVERSITY—NORTHRIDGE
College of Business and Economics

Address: 18111 Nordhoff Street, Northridge, CA 91330-8380
Admissions Phone: 818-677-2467 • Web Address: mba.csun.edu
Public/Private: Public

CALIFORNIA STATE UNIVERSITY— SACRAMENTO
College of Business Administration

Address: College of Business Administration, Sacramento, CA 95819-6088
Admissions Phone: 916-278-6772
Web Address: www.csus.edu/cbagrad/index.html
Public/Private: Public
Total Business Students: 385
Average GMAT: 576
% Full Time: 35
Annual Tuition (Resident/Nonresident): $1,949/$6,377

CALIFORNIA STATE UNIVERSITY— SAN BERNARDINO
College of Business & Public Administration

Address: 5500 University Parkway, San Bernardino, CA 92407
Admissions Phone: 909-880-5703 • Web Address: www.csusb.edu
Public/Private: Public
Total Business Students: 334
Average GMAT: 511
% Full Time: 69
Annual Tuition (Resident/Nonresident): $2,000/$10,000

CANISIUS COLLEGE
Richard Wehle School of Business

Address: 2001 Main Street, 220 Lyons Hall, Buffalo, NY 14208-9989
Admissions Phone: 716-888-2140 • Web Address: www.canisius.edu
Public/Private: Private
Total Business Students: 353
Average GMAT: 510
% Full Time: 18
Annual Tuition: $27,756

CAPELLA UNIVERSITY
School of Business

Address: 222 South 9th Street, Minneapolis, MN 55402
Admissions Phone: 888-227-3552 • Web Address: www.capellauniversity.edu
Total Business Students: 300
% Full Time: 25
Annual Tuition: $12,000

CARNEGIE MELLON UNIVERSITY
Graduate School of Industrial Administration

Address: 5000 Forbes Avenue, Pittsburgh, PA 15213
Admissions Phone: 412-268-2272 • Web Address: www.gsia.cmu.edu
Public/Private: Private
Total Business Students: 607
Average GMAT: 660
% Full Time: 73
Annual Tuition: $28,250

CASE WESTERN RESERVE UNIVERSITY
Weatherhead School of Management

Address: 310 Enterprise Hall, 10900 Euclid Av., Cleveland, OH 44106
Admissions Phone: 216-368-2030 • Web Address: www.weatherhead.cwru.edu
Public/Private: Private
Total Business Students: 1,039
Average GMAT: 608
% Full Time: 35
Annual Tuition: $24,500

CENTRAL MICHIGAN UNIVERSITY
College of Business Administration

Address: 105 Warriner Hall, Mount Pleasant, MI 48859
Admissions Phone: 517-774-3150 • Web Address: www.cba.cmich.edu
Public/Private: Public
Total Business Students: 471
% Full Time: 50

CENTRAL MISSOURI STATE UNIVERSITY
Harmon College of Business Administration

Web Address: www.cmsu.edu/academic/hcba.htm
Public/Private: Public
Total Business Students: 88
% Full Time: 58
Annual Tuition (Resident/Nonresident): $3,840/$7,632

CHAPMAN UNIVERSITY
The George L. Argyros School of Business and Economics

Address: Beckman Hall, One University Dr., Orange, CA 92866
Admissions Phone: 714-997-6745 • Web Address: chapman.edu/argyros
Public/Private: Private
Total Business Students: 148
Average GMAT: 535
% Full Time: 29
Annual Tuition: $15,240

CHINESE UNIVERSITY OF HONG KONG
Faculty of Business Administration

Web Address: www.cuhk.edu.hk/baf/graduate.html
Total Business Students: 514
Annual Tuition: $42,100

THE CITADEL
College of Graduate and Professional Studies

Web Address: www.citadel.edu
Public/Private: Public
Total Business Students: 143

CLAREMONT GRADUATE UNIVERSITY
The Peter F. Drucker Graduate School of Management

Address: 1021 North Dartmouth Avenue, Claremont, CA 91711
Admissions Phone: 800-944-4312 • Web Address: www.drucker.cgu.edu
Public/Private: Private
Total Business Students: 200
Average GMAT: 582
% Full Time: 65
Annual Tuition: $30,984

CLARION UNIVERSITY
College of Business Administration

Address: 302 Still Hall, Clarion University, Clarion, PA 16214
Admissions Phone: 814-393-2605 • Web Address: www.clarion.edu/mba
Public/Private: Public
Total Business Students: 57
Average GMAT: 494
% Full Time: 88
Annual Tuition (Resident/Nonresident): $4,600/$7,554

CLARK ATLANTA UNIVERSITY
School of Business

Address: James P. Brawley Drive at Fair Street, Atlanta, GA 30314
Admissions Phone: 404-880-8447 • Web Address: www.cau.edu\cau\ctsps.html
Public/Private: Private
Total Business Students: 155
% Full Time: 90
Annual Tuition: $13,237

CLARK UNIVERSITY
Graduate School of Management

Address: 950 Main Street, Worcester, MA 01610
Admissions Phone: 508-793-7406 • Web Address: www.clarku.edu/mba
Public/Private: Private
Total Business Students: 329
Average GMAT: 540
% Full Time: 42
Annual Tuition: $19,900

CLARKSON UNIVERSITY
School of Business

Address: CU Box 5770, Potsdam, NY 13699
Admissions Phone: 315-268-6613 • Web Address: phoenix.som.clarkson.edu
Public/Private: Private
Total Business Students: 75
Average GMAT: 550
% Full Time: 91
Annual Tuition: $21,984

CLEMSON UNIVERSITY
Graduate School of Business and Behavioral Science

Address: 124 Sirrine Hall, Box 341315,
Clemson University, Clemson, SC 29634-1315
Admissions Phone: 864-656-3975
Web Address: www.clemson.edu/business/mba/
Public/Private: Public
Total Business Students: 255
Average GMAT: 594
% Full Time: 32
Annual Tuition (Resident/Nonresident): $5,310/$11,284

CLEVELAND STATE UNIVERSITY
James J. Nance College of Business Administration

Address: 1860 East 18th Street, BU 219, Cleveland, OH 44114
Admissions Phone: 216-687-3730 • Web Address: csuohio.edu/cba/
Public/Private: Public
Total Business Students: 527
Average GMAT: 505
% Full Time: 22
Annual Tuition (Resident/Nonresident): $6,312/$12,624

COLLEGE OF CHARLESTON
School of Business and Economics

Web Address: www.cofc.edu
Public/Private: Public

COLLEGE OF WILLIAM AND MARY
Graduate School of Business

Address: Blow Hall, Room 254, Williamsburg, VA 23187
Admissions Phone: 757-221-2900 • Web Address: www.business.wm.edu
Public/Private: Public
Total Business Students: 306
Average GMAT: 616
% Full Time: 52
Annual Tuition (Resident/Nonresident): $9,322/$19,670

COLORADO STATE UNIVERSITY
College of Business

Web Address: www.biz.colostate.edu
Public/Private: Public
Total Business Students: 543
% Full Time: 8
Annual Tuition (Resident/Nonresident): $3,937/$12,967

COLUMBIA UNIVERSITY
Columbia Business School

Address: 216 Uris Hall, 3022 Broadway, New York, NY 10027
Admissions Phone: 212-854-1961 • Web Address: www.gsb.columbia.edu
Public/Private: Private
Total Business Students: 1,225
Average GMAT: 705
Annual Tuition: $30,334

CONCORDIA UNIVERSITY
John Molson School of Business

Address: 1455 de Maisonneuve Blvd. West, GM 710, Montreal, QC H3G 1M8 Canada
Admissions Phone: 514-848-2708 • Web Address: www.johnmolson.concordia.ca
Total Business Students: 323
Average GMAT: 634
% Full Time: 44
Annual Tuition (Resident/Nonresident): $1,330/$12,500

CORNELL UNIVERSITY
Johnson Graduate School of Management

Address: 111 Sage Hall, Ithaca, New York 14853, NY 14853
Admissions Phone: 607-255-4526 • Web Address: www.johnson.cornell.edu
Public/Private: Private
Total Business Students: 554
Average GMAT: 669
% Full Time: 100
Annual Tuition: $29,500

CREIGHTON UNIVERSITY
College of Business Administration

Address: 2500 California Plaza, Omaha, NE 68178
Admissions Phone: 402-280-2829 • Web Address: cobweb.creighton.edu
Public/Private: Private
Total Business Students: 111
Average GMAT: 550
% Full Time: 33
Annual Tuition: $8,532

DARTMOUTH COLLEGE
Tuck School of Business at Dartmouth

Address: 100 Tuck Hall, Hanover, NH 03755
Admissions Phone: 603-646-3162 • Web Address: www.tuck.dartmouth.edu
Public/Private: Private
Total Business Students: 435
Average GMAT: 693
% Full Time: 100
Annual Tuition: $30,250

DEPAUL UNIVERSITY
Kellstadt Graduate School of Business

Address: 1 East Jackson Boulevard, Chicago, IL 60604
Admissions Phone: 312-362-8810 • Web Address: www.depaul.edu
Public/Private: Private
Total Business Students: 2,537
Average GMAT: 561
% Full Time: 53
Annual Tuition: $14,400

DRAKE UNIVERSITY
College of Business and Public Administration

Address: 2507 University Avenue, Des Moines, IA 50311
Admissions Phone: 515-271-2188 • Web Address: www.drake.edu/cbpa/grad
Public/Private: Private
Total Business Students: 336
% Full Time: 20
Annual Tuition: $6,120

DREXEL UNIVERSITY
The Bennett S. LeBow College of Business

Address: 3141 Chestnut Street, Philadelphia, PA 19104-2875
Admissions Phone: 215-895-6704 • Web Address: www.coba.drexel.edu
Public/Private: Private
Total Business Students: 850
% Full Time: 37

DUKE UNIVERSITY
The Fuqua School of Business

Address: Towerview Road, A-08 Academic Center, Durham, NC 27708
Admissions Phone: 919-660-7705 • Web Address: www.fuqua.duke.edu
Public/Private: Private
Total Business Students: 679
Average GMAT: 690
% Full Time: 100
Annual Tuition: $29,600

DUQUESNE UNIVERSITY
John F. Donahue Graduate School of Business

Address: 600 Forbes Avenue, Pittsburgh, PA 15282
Admissions Phone: 412-396-6276 • Web Address: www.bus.duq.edu/grad/
Public/Private: Private
Total Business Students: 688
% Full Time: 20
Annual Tuition: $14,112

EAST CAROLINA UNIVERSITY
School of Business

Web Address: www.business.ecu.edu/grad
Public/Private: Public
Total Business Students: 200
% Full Time: 64
Annual Tuition (Resident/Nonresident): $918/$8,188

EAST TENNESSEE STATE UNIVERSITY
College of Business

Address: PO Box 70699, Johnson City, TN 37614
Admissions Phone: 423-439-5314
Web Address: www.etsu.edu/gradstud/index.htm
Public/Private: Public
Total Business Students: 211
% Full Time: 26
Annual Tuition (Resident/Nonresident): $1,280/$3,693

EASTERN ILLINOIS UNIVERSITY
Lumpkin College of Business and Applied Science

Address: 600 Lincoln Avenue, 337 Lumpkin Hall, Charleston, IL 61920-3099
Admissions Phone: 217-581-3028 • Web Address: www.eiu.edu/~mba/
Public/Private: Public
Total Business Students: 133
% Full Time: 25
Annual Tuition (Resident/Nonresident): $3,360/$7,970

EASTERN MICHIGAN UNIVERSITY
College of Business

Address: PO Box 970, Ypsilanti, MI 48197
Admissions Phone: 734-487-3060 • Web Address: www.emich.edu/public/gradcatolog
Public/Private: Public
Total Business Students: 760
Average GMAT: 495
% Full Time: 36
Annual Tuition (Resident/Nonresident): $5,160/$10,560

EASTERN WASHINGTON UNIVERSITY
College of Business & Public Administration

Address: EWU 206 Showalter Hall, Cheney, WA 99004
Admissions Phone: 509-359-6297 • Web Address: www.ewu.edu
Public/Private: Public
Total Business Students: 82
Average GMAT: 479
% Full Time: 35
Annual Tuition (Resident/Nonresident): $4,470/$13,161

EMORY UNIVERSITY
Goizueta Business School

Address: 1300 Clifton Road, Atlanta, GA 30322
Admissions Phone: 404-727-6311 • Web Address: www.goizueta.emory.edu
Public/Private: Private
Total Business Students: 584
Average GMAT: 651
% Full Time: 78
Annual Tuition: $27,760

ERASMUS GRADUATE SCHOOL OF BUSINESS
Rotterdam School of Management

Address: Burgemeester Oudlaan 50, 3062 PA Rotterdam, The Netherlands
Admissions Phone: 011-31-10-408-2222 • Web Address: www.rsm.nl
Total Business Students: 550
Average GMAT: 622
% Full Time: 60
Annual Tuition: $30,000

ESADE

Address: Av. d'Esplugues, 92-96, Barcelona, 08034 Spain
Admissions Phone: 011-34-934-952-088 • Web Address: www.esade.edu
Total Business Students: 270
Average GMAT: 640
% Full Time: 65
Annual Tuition: $19,000

FAIRFIELD UNIVERSITY
Charles F. Dolan School of Business

Address: 1073 North Benson Road, Fairfield, CT 06430
Admissions Phone: 203-254-4070 • Web Address: www.fairfield.edu
Public/Private: Private
Total Business Students: 191
Average GMAT: 548
% Full Time: 12
Annual Tuition: $19,100

FIU COLLEGE OF BUSINESS ADMINISTRATION
Alvah H. Chapman, Jr., Graduate School of Business

Address: 11200 S. W. 8th Street, RB 310, Miami, FL 33199
Admissions Phone: 305-348-6631 • Web Address: www.fiu.edu\~cba\
Public/Private: Public
Total Business Students: 489
Average GMAT: 546
% Full Time: 33
Annual Tuition: $24,000

FLORIDA ATLANTIC UNIVERSITY
College of Business

Address: 777 Glades Road, Boca Raton, FL 33431
Admissions Phone: 561-297-3624
Web Address: www.collegeofbusiness.fau.edu
Public/Private: Public
Total Business Students: 510
Average GMAT: 525
% Full Time: 32
Annual Tuition (Resident/Nonresident): $4,152/$13,920

FLORIDA STATE UNIVERSITY
Florida State University College Of Business

Address: FSU College of Business, Tallahassee, FL 32306-1110
Admissions Phone: 850-644-6458 • Web Address: www.cob.fsu.edu
Public/Private: Public
Total Business Students: 178
Average GMAT: 569
% Full Time: 23

FORDHAM UNIVERSITY
Graduate School of Business Administration

Web Address: www.bnet.fordham.edu
Public/Private: Private
Total Business Students: 1,534
% Full Time: 23
Annual Tuition: $21,060

FRANCIS MARION UNIVERSITY
School of Business

Address: Box 100547, Florence, SC 29501-0547
Admissions Phone: 843-661-1436 • Web Address: alpha1.fmarion.edu/~mba/
Public/Private: Public
Total Business Students: 61
% Full Time: 5
Annual Tuition (Resident/Nonresident): $3,460/$6,920

GEORGE MASON UNIVERSITY
School of Management

Address: 4400 University Drive, MSN 5A2, Enterprise Hall, Room 156, Fairfax, VA 22030
Admissions Phone: 703-993-2140 • Web Address: www.som.gmu.edu
Public/Private: Public
Total Business Students: 65
Average GMAT: 605
% Full Time: 30
Annual Tuition (Resident/Nonresident): $7,788/$12,696

THE GEORGE WASHINGTON UNIVERSITY
School of Business and Public Management

Address: 710 21st Street, NW Suite 209, Washington, DC 20052
Admissions Phone: 202-994-5536 • Web Address: www.sbpm.gwu.edu
Public/Private: Private
Total Business Students: 784
Average GMAT: 606
% Full Time: 52
Annual Tuition: $17,820

GEORGETOWN UNIVERSITY
Georgetown MBA

Address: Box 571148, Washington, DC 20057-1221
Admissions Phone: 202-687-4200 • Web Address: www.mba.georgetown.edu
Public/Private: Private
Total Business Students: 502
Average GMAT: 662
% Full Time: 100
Annual Tuition: $24,440

GEORGIA COLLEGE & STATE UNIVERSITY
The J. Whitney Bunting School of Business

Address: GC&SU Campus Box 23, Milledgeville, GA 31061
Admissions Phone: 478-445-6289 • Web Address: www.gcsu.edu
Public/Private: Public
Total Business Students: 138
Average GMAT: 490
% Full Time: 25
Annual Tuition (Resident/Nonresident): $4,557/$18,228

GEORGIA INSTITUTE OF TECHNOLOGY
DuPree School of Management

Address: 755 Ferst Drive, Atlanta, GA 30332
Admissions Phone: 404-894-8713 • Web Address: www.dupree.gatech.edu
Public/Private: Public
Total Business Students: 203
Average GMAT: 645
Annual Tuition (Resident/Nonresident): $5,128/$18,046

GEORGIA SOUTHERN UNIVERSITY
College of Business Administration

Address: PO Box 8113, Statesboro, GA 30460-8113
Admissions Phone: 912-681-5483 • Web Address: www2.gasou.edu/mba
Public/Private: Public
Total Business Students: 313
Average GMAT: 488
% Full Time: 27
Annual Tuition (Resident/Nonresident): $1,702/$6,768

GEORGIA STATE UNIVERSITY
J. Mack Robinson College of Business

Address: Office of Academic Assistance, University Plaza, Atlanta, GA 30303
Admissions Phone: 404-651-1913 • Web Address: robinson.gsu.edu
Public/Private: Public
Total Business Students: 2,625
Average GMAT: 590
% Full Time: 58

GOLDEN GATE UNIVERSITY
Edward S. Ageno School of Business

Address: 536 Mission Street, San Francisco, CA 94105-2968
Admissions Phone: 415-442-7800 • Web Address: www.ggu.edu
Public/Private: Private

GONZAGA UNIVERSITY
School of Business Administration

Address: 502 East Boone Avenue, AD Box 9, Spokane, WA 99528
Admissions Phone: 509-323-3403
Web Address: www.gonzaga.edu/mba-macc
Public/Private: Private
Total Business Students: 158
% Full Time: 67

GRAND VALLEY STATE UNIVERSITY
Seidman School of Business

Address: 401 W. Fulton, Grand Rapids, MI 49504
Admissions Phone: 616-336-7400 • Web Address: www.gvsu.edu/ssb
Public/Private: Public
Total Business Students: 311
Average GMAT: 575
% Full Time: 11
Annual Tuition (Resident/Nonresident): $3,700/$7,900

GROUPE ESC TOULOUSE
Graduate School of Management

Web Address: www.esc-toulouse.fr
Total Business Students: 850
% Full Time: 100

HARVARD UNIVERSITY
Harvard Business School

Address: Soldiers Field, Boston, MA 02163
Admissions Phone: 617-495-6127 • Web Address: www.hbs.edu
Public/Private: Private
Total Business Students: 1,770
Annual Tuition: $28,500

HEC SCHOOL OF MANAGEMENT
HEC MBA Program

Web Address: www.mba.hec.edu
Total Business Students: 162
% Full Time: 100
Annual Tuition: $21,867

HENDERSON STATE UNIVERSITY
School of Business Administration

Web Address: www.hsu.edu/dept/bus/index.html
Public/Private: Public

HOFSTRA UNIVERSITY
Frank G. Zarb School of Business

Address: 134 Hofstra University, Hempstead, NY 11549
Admissions Phone: 516-463-6700 • Web Address: www.hofstra.edu/business
Public/Private: Private
Total Business Students: 600
Average GMAT: 570
% Full Time: 30
Annual Tuition: $16,000

HONG KONG UNIVERSITY OF SCIENCE & TECHNOLOGY
School of Business & Management

Admissions Phone: 011-852-2358-7539 • Web Address: www.bm.ust.hk/mba
Total Business Students: 196
% Full Time: 19

HOWARD UNIVERSITY
School of Business

Address: 2600 Sixth Street, NW, Washington, DC 20059
Admissions Phone: 202-806-1725
Web Address: www.bschool.howard.edu/mba
Public/Private: Private
Total Business Students: 93
Average GMAT: 539
% Full Time: 100
Annual Tuition: $11,900

IDAHO STATE UNIVERSITY
College of Business

Address: Box 8020, Pocatello, ID 83209
Admissions Phone: 208-282-2966 • Web Address: cob.isu.edu
Public/Private: Public
Total Business Students: 127
% Full Time: 23
Annual Tuition (Resident/Nonresident): $2,940/$8,920

ILLINOIS STATE UNIVERSITY
College of Business

Web Address: http://gilbreth/cob.ilstu.edu
Public/Private: Public
Total Business Students: 214
% Full Time: 25
Annual Tuition (Resident/Nonresident): $2,600/$7,801

ILLLINOIS INSTITUTE OF TECHNOLOGY
Stuart Graduate School of Business

Address: 565 W. Adams Street, Chicago, IL 60616
Admissions Phone: 312-906-6544 • Web Address: www.stuart.iit.edu
Public/Private: Private
Total Business Students: 284
Average GMAT: 568
% Full Time: 38
Annual Tuition: $19,000

IMD (INTERNATIONAL INSTITUTE FOR MANAGEMENT DEVELOPMENT)

Address: Chemin de Bellerive 23, PO Box 915, 1001 Lausanne, Switzerland
Admissions Phone: 011-41-21-6180298 • Web Address: www.imd.ch/mba
Total Business Students: 90
Average GMAT: 670
% Full Time: 100
Annual Tuition: $28,000

INCAE
Graduate Program

Web Address: www.incae.ac.cr
Total Business Students: 441
% Full Time: 80
Annual Tuition: $11,500

INDEPENDENT INSTITUTION
The American Graduate School of Business

Web Address: www.agsb.ch
Total Business Students: 14
Annual Tuition: $16,000

INDIANA STATE UNIVERSITY
School of Business

Address: Indiana State University, Terre Haute, IN 47802
Admissions Phone: 812-237-2002
Web Address: web.indstate.edu/schbus/mba.html
Public/Private: Public
Total Business Students: 105
Average GMAT: 530
% Full Time: 60
Annual Tuition (Resident/Nonresident): $2,720/$5,920

INDIANA UNIVERSITY—BLOOMINGTON
Kelley School of Business

Address: 1309 East Tenth Street, Bloomington, IN 47405
Admissions Phone: 812-855-8006
Web Address: www.kelley.indiana.edu/mba
Public/Private: Public
Total Business Students: 596
Average GMAT: 651
% Full Time: 100
Annual Tuition (Resident/Nonresident): $10,004/$20,007

INDIANA UNIVERSITY—KOKOMO
School of Business

Address: PO Box 9003, Kokomo, IN 46904-9003
Admissions Phone: 765-455-9465 • Web Address: www.iuk.edu/academic_program/business/index.html
Public/Private: Public
Total Business Students: 235
Average GMAT: 575
% Full Time: 2
Annual Tuition (Resident/Nonresident): $4,206/$9,619

INDIANA UNIVERSITY—NORTHWEST
Division of Business and Economics

Address: 3400 Broadway, Gary, IN 46408-1197
Admissions Phone: 219-980-6635 • Web Address: www.iun.edu/~busnw
Public/Private: Public
Total Business Students: 196
% Full Time: 2

INDIANA UNIVERSITY—PURDUE UNIVERSITY FORT WAYNE
School of Business and Management

Address: Neff 366, 2101 Coliseum Boulevard East, Fort Wayne, IN 46805
Admissions Phone: 219-481-6498 • Web Address: www.ipfw.indiana.edu/bms/
Public/Private: Public
Total Business Students: 191
% Full Time: 9

INDIANA UNIVERSITY—PURDUE UNIVERSITY INDIANAPOLIS
Kelley School of Business

Web Address: www.iupui.edu/~business/
Public/Private: Public
Total Business Students: 304
% Full Time: 0

INDIANA UNIVERSITY—SOUTH BEND
Division of Business and Economics

Address: IUSB PO Box 7111, South Bend, IN 46634-7111
Admissions Phone: 219-237-4138 • Web Address: www.iusb.edu/~gradbus
Public/Private: Public
Total Business Students: 267
% Full Time: 17

INSEAD
The European Institute of Business Administration

Web Address: www.insead.fr/mba
Total Business Students: 601
Annual Tuition: $25,500

INSTITUTO TECNOLOGICO Y DE ESTUDIOS SUPERIORES DE MONTERREY (ITESM)
EGADE School of Business

Web Address: www.itesm.mx
Total Business Students: 140
% Full Time: 0

IONA COLLEGE
Hagan School of Business

Address: 715 North Avenue, New Rochelle, NY 10801
Admissions Phone: 914-633-2288 • Web Address: www.iona.edu/hagan
Public/Private: Private
Total Business Students: 295
% Full Time: 12
Annual Tuition: $0

IOWA STATE UNIVERSITY
College of Business

Address: 218 Carver Hall, Ames, IA 50011
Admissions Phone: 515-294-8118 • Web Address: www.bus.iastate.edu/grad/
Public/Private: Public
Total Business Students: 254
Average GMAT: 591
% Full Time: 29
Annual Tuition (Resident/Nonresident): $3,702/$10,898

JACKSON STATE UNIVERSITY
School of Business

Address: PO Box 18660, Jackson, MI 39217
Admissions Phone: 601-432-6315 • Web Address: www.jsums.edu
Public/Private: Public
Total Business Students: 1,104
Annual Tuition (Resident/Nonresident): $2,688/$2,858

JACKSONVILLE STATE UNIVERSITY
College of Commerce and Business Administration

Web Address: www.jsu.edu
Public/Private: Public
Total Business Students: 100
Average GMAT: 470
% Full Time: 30
Annual Tuition (Resident/Nonresident): $2,940/$5,880

JAMES MADISON UNIVERSITY
College of Business

Address: Zane Showker Hall, MSC 0206, Room 620, Harrisonburg, VA 22807
Admissions Phone: 540-568-3253 • Web Address: cob.jmu.edu/mba
Public/Private: Public
Total Business Students: 180
Average GMAT: 565
% Full Time: 22

JOHN CARROLL UNIVERSITY
John M. and Mary Jo Boler School of Business

Address: 20700 North Park Boulevard, University Heights, OH 44118-4581
Admissions Phone: 216-397-4391 • Web Address: bsob.jcu.edu
Public/Private: Private
Total Business Students: 256
Average GMAT: 504
% Full Time: 7
Annual Tuition: $11,304

KANSAS STATE UNIVERSITY
College of Business Administration

Address: 110 Calvin Hall, Manhattan, KS 66506-0501
Admissions Phone: 785-532-7190 • Web Address: www.cba.ksu.edu
Public/Private: Public
Total Business Students: 91
Average GMAT: 548
% Full Time: 82
Annual Tuition (Resident/Nonresident): $3,305/$10,508

KENNESAW STATE UNIVERSITY
Michael J. Coles College of Business

Address: 1000 Chastain Road, Kennesaw, GA 30144
Admissions Phone: 770-420-4377 • Web Address: coles.kennesaw.edu/
Public/Private: Public
Total Business Students: 557
Average GMAT: 510
% Full Time: 0
Annual Tuition (Resident/Nonresident): $1,160/$4,640

KENT STATE UNIVERSITY
Graduate School of Management

Address: PO Box 5190, Kent, OH 44242-0001
Admissions Phone: 330-672-2282 • Web Address: business.kent.edu/grad
Public/Private: Public
Total Business Students: 328
Average GMAT: 547
% Full Time: 35
Annual Tuition (Resident/Nonresident): $6,848/$11,736

LA SALLE UNIVERSITY
School of Business Administration

Address: 1900 West Olney Avenue, Philadelphia, PA 19141
Admissions Phone: 215-951-1057
Web Address: www.lasalle.edu/academ/sba/sba.htm
Public/Private: Private
Total Business Students: 687
% Full Time: 10

LAMAR UNIVERSITY
College of Business

Address: PO Box 10009, Beaumont, TX 77710
Admissions Phone: 409-880-8350
Web Address: www.lamar.edu
Public/Private: Public
Total Business Students: 77
% Full Time: 35
Annual Tuition (Resident/Nonresident): $1,200/$5,200

LEHIGH UNIVERSITY
College of Business and Economics

Address: 621 Taylor Street, Bethlehem, PA 18015
Admissions Phone: 610-758-5280 • Web Address: www.lehigh.edu/mba
Public/Private: Private
Total Business Students: 292
Average GMAT: 614
% Full Time: 13
Annual Tuition: $14,640

LOUISIANA STATE UNIVERSITY— BATON ROUGE
E.J. Ourso College of Business Administration

Address: 3170 CEBA Building, Baton Rouge, LA 70803
Admissions Phone: 225-578-8867 • Web Address: www.bus.lsu.edu/mba
Public/Private: Public
Total Business Students: 121
Average GMAT: 570
Annual Tuition (Resident/Nonresident): $2,551/$7,851

LOUISIANA STATE UNIVERSITY— SHREVEPORT
College of Business Administration

Address: One University Place, Shreveport, LA 71115
Admissions Phone: 318-797-5213 • Web Address: www.lsus.edu/ba/
Public/Private: Public
Total Business Students: 150
% Full Time: 7

LOUISIANA TECH UNIVERSITY
College of Administration and Business

Address: PO Box 10318, Ruston, LA 71272
Admissions Phone: 318-257-4526 • Web Address: www.cab.latech.edu
Public/Private: Public
Total Business Students: 84
Annual Tuition (Resident/Nonresident): $3,356/$7,256

LOYOLA COLLEGE IN MARYLAND
Sellinger School of Business and Management

Address: 4501 North Charles Street, Baltimore, MD 21210
Admissions Phone: 410-617-2000 • Web Address: sellinger.loyola.edu
Public/Private: Private
Total Business Students: 948
Average GMAT: 528
Annual Tuition: $6,570

LOYOLA MARYMOUNT UNIVERSITY
MBA Program

Address: 7900 Loyola Boulevard, Los Angeles, CA 90045-8387
Admissions Phone: 310-338-2848 • Web Address: www.mba.lmu.edu
Public/Private: Private
Total Business Students: 420
Average GMAT: 570
% Full Time: 80
Annual Tuition: $12,780

LOYOLA UNIVERSITY NEW ORLEANS
The Joseph A. Butt, S.J. College of Business Administration

Address: 6363 St. Charles Avenue, Campus Box 15, New Orleans, LA 70118
Admissions Phone: 504-864-7965 • Web Address: cba.loyno.edu
Public/Private: Private
Total Business Students: 144
Annual Tuition: $12,984

MARQUETTE UNIVERSITY
College of Business Administration

Address: PO Box 1881, Milwaukee, WI 53201-1881
Admissions Phone: 414-288-7145 • Web Address: www.busamm.mu.edu/mba
Public/Private: Private
Total Business Students: 804
% Full Time: 10

MARSHALL UNIVERSITY
College of Business

Address: Corby Hall 217, 400 Hal Greer Boulevard, Huntington, WV 25755
Admissions Phone: 304-696-2613 • Web Address: lcob.marshall.edu/
Public/Private: Public
Total Business Students: 80
Average GMAT: 530
Annual Tuition (Resident/Nonresident): $2,884/$8,158

MASSACHUSETTS INSTITUTE OF TECHNOLOGY
Sloan School of Management

Address: E52-126, Cambridge, MA 02139
Admissions Phone: 617-253-3730 • Web Address: web.mit.edu/sloan/www
Public/Private: Private
Total Business Students: 711
Average GMAT: 663
% Full Time: 100
Annual Tuition: $25,800

MCMASTER UNIVERSITY
Michael G. DeGroote School of Business

Address: MGD 104, 1280 Main St. West, Hamilton, Ontario, ON L8S 4M4 Canada
Admissions Phone: 905-525-9140 • Web Address: www.degroote.mcmaster.ca
Total Business Students: 279
Average GMAT: 630
Annual Tuition (Resident/Nonresident): $7,040/$15,340

MCNEESE STATE UNIVERSITY
MBA Program

Address: PO Box 92495, Lake Charles, CA 70609-2495
Admissions Phone: 337-475-5153
Web Address: www.mcneese.edu/colleges/business/mba
Public/Private: Public
Total Business Students: 82
Average GMAT: 459
Annual Tuition (Resident/Nonresident): $1,987/$3,530

MIAMI UNIVERSITY
Richard T. Farmer School of Business

Address: Richard T. Farmer School of Business, Oxford, OH 45056
Admissions Phone: 513-529-6643
Web Address: www.sba.muohio.edu/mbaprogram
Public/Private: Public
Total Business Students: 135
% Full Time: 61
Annual Tuition (Resident/Nonresident): $4,896/$11,356

MICHIGAN STATE UNIVERSITY
The Eli Broad Graduate School of Management

Address: 215 Eppley Center, East Lansing, MI 48824-1221
Admissions Phone: 517-355-7604 • Web Address: mba.bus.msu.edu
Public/Private: Public
Total Business Students: 206
Average GMAT: 641
% Full Time: 100
Annual Tuition (Resident/Nonresident): $12,800/$16,900

MILLSAPS COLLEGE
Else School of Management

Address: 17 North State Street, Jackson, MS 39110
Admissions Phone: 601-974-1253 • Web Address: www.millsaps.edu/som
Public/Private: Private
Total Business Students: 151
Annual Tuition: $16,200

MISSISSIPPI STATE UNIVERSITY
College of Business and Industry

Address: PO Drawer 5288, Mississippi State, MS 39762
Admissions Phone: 662-325-1891
Web Address: www.cbi.msstate.edu/cobi/gsb/index2.html
Public/Private: Public
Total Business Students: 85
Average GMAT: 501
% Full Time: 64
Annual Tuition (Resident/Nonresident): $3,586/$8,128

MONMOUTH UNIVERSITY
School of Business Administration

Address: 400 Cedar Ave, West Long Branch, NJ 07764-1898
Admissions Phone: 732-571-3452
Web Address: www.monmouth.edu/academics/business.asp
Public/Private: Private
Total Business Students: 269
Average GMAT: 491
% Full Time: 61
Annual Tuition: $9,414

MONTANA STATE UNIVERSITY
College of Business

Address: 338 Reid Hall, PO Box 173040, Bozeman, MT 59717-3040
Admissions Phone: 406-994-4681 • Web Address: www.montana.edu/cob/
Public/Private: Public
Total Business Students: 40
Average GMAT: 530
% Full Time: 92
Annual Tuition (Resident/Nonresident): $3,080/$8,352

MORGAN STATE UNIVERSITY
Earl Graves School of Business and Management

Web Address: www.morgan.edu
Public/Private: Public
Total Business Students: 103
% Full Time: 0

MURRAY STATE UNIVERSITY
College of Business and Public Affairs

Address: PO Box 9, Murray, KY 42071
Admissions Phone: 270-762-6970 • Web Address: www.murraystate.edu
Public/Private: Public
Total Business Students: 160
% Full Time: 47
Annual Tuition (Resident/Nonresident): $2,300/$6,260

NATIONAL UNIVERSITY OF SINGAPORE
Graduate School of Business

Web Address: www.fba.nus.edu.sg/
Total Business Students: 942
% Full Time: 30
Annual Tuition (Resident/Nonresident): $7,170/$14,340

NEW JERSEY INSTITUTE OF TECHNOLOGY
School of Management

Web Address: www.njit.edu
Public/Private: Public
Total Business Students: 442
% Full Time: 15
Annual Tuition (Resident/Nonresident): $3,476/$4,885

NEW MEXICO STATE UNIVERSITY
College of Business Administration and Economics

Address: PO Box 173040, Dept 3GSP, La Cruces, NM 88003-8001
Admissions Phone: 505-646-8003 • Web Address: cbae.nmsu.edu/~mba/
Public/Private: Public
Total Business Students: 125
% Full Time: 56
Annual Tuition (Resident/Nonresident): $2,502/$8,166

NEW YORK UNIVERSITY
Leonard N. Stern School of Business

Address: 44 West 4th Street, Suite 10-160, New York, NY 10012
Admissions Phone: 212-998-0600 • Web Address: www.stern.nyu.edu
Public/Private: Private
Total Business Students: 2,724
Average GMAT: 686
% Full Time: 31
Annual Tuition: $29,800

NICHOLLS STATE UNIVERSITY
College of Business Administration

Address: PO Box 2004, Thibodaux, LA 70310
Admissions Phone: 877-642-4655 • Web Address: www.nicholls.edu
Public/Private: Public
Total Business Students: 105
Average GMAT: 469
% Full Time: 33
Annual Tuition (Resident/Nonresident): $2,400/$7,800

NORTH DAKOTA STATE UNIVERSITY

Web Address: www.ndsu.nodak.edu/graduate/
Public/Private: Public
Total Business Students: 537
% Full Time: 11
Annual Tuition: $7,632

NORTHEASTERN UNIVERSITY
Graduate School of Business Administration

Address: 360 Huntington Avenue, Boston, MA 02115
Admissions Phone: 617-373-5992 • Web Address: www.cba.neu.edu/gsba
Public/Private: Private
Total Business Students: 616
Average GMAT: 557
% Full Time: 36
Annual Tuition: $25,850

NORTHERN ARIZONA UNIVERSITY
College of Business Administration

Address: 70 McConnell Circle, PO Box 15066, Flagstaff, AZ 86011-5066
Admissions Phone: 928-523-7342
Web Address: www.cba.nau.edu/mbaprogram
Public/Private: Public
Total Business Students: 74
Average GMAT: 548
% Full Time: 57
Annual Tuition (Resident/Nonresident): $3,906/$13,268

NORTHERN ILLINOIS UNIVERSITY
College of Business, Office of MBA Programs

Address: Wirtz 140, Dekalb, IL 60115
Admissions Phone: 800-323-8714
Web Address: www.cob.niu.edu/grad/grad.html
Public/Private: Public
Total Business Students: 528
Average GMAT: 535
% Full Time: 1

NORTHERN KENTUCKY UNIVERSITY
College of Business

Address: PO Box 9, Highland Heights, KY 41099
Admissions Phone: 859-572-5165 • Web Address: www.nku.edu/~mbusiness
Public/Private: Public
Total Business Students: 192
% Full Time: 7

NORTHWESTERN UNIVERSITY
J. L. Kellogg Graduate School of Management

Address: 2001 Sheridan Road, 2nd Floor, Evanston, IL 60208
Admissions Phone: 847-491-3308 • Web Address: www.kellogg.nwu.edu
Public/Private: Private
Average GMAT: 660
% Full Time: 49
Annual Tuition: $25,872

OAKLAND UNIVERSITY
School of Business Administration

Address: 432 Elliott Hall, Rochester, MI 48309-4493
Admissions Phone: 248-370-3287 • Web Address: www.sba.oakland.edu
Public/Private: Public
Total Business Students: 536
Average GMAT: 537
% Full Time: 24
Annual Tuition (Resident/Nonresident): $4,428/$9,144

OHIO STATE UNIVERSITY
Fisher College of Business

Address: 100 Gerlach Hall 2108 Neil Avenue, Columbus, OH 43210
Admissions Phone: 614-292-8511 • Web Address: fisher.osu.edu
Public/Private: Public
Total Business Students: 477
Average GMAT: 638
% Full Time: 59

OHIO UNIVERSITY
College of Business

Address: 514 Copeland Hall, Athens, OH 45701
Admissions Phone: 740-593-4320 • Web Address: www.cob.ohiou.edu/grad/
Public/Private: Public
Total Business Students: 83
Average GMAT: 560
% Full Time: 100
Annual Tuition (Resident/Nonresident): $8,780/$16,872

OKLAHOMA STATE UNIVERSITY
College of Business Administration

Address: 102 Gundersen Hall, Stillwater, OK 74078-4011
Admissions Phone: 405-744-2951 • Web Address: mba.okstate.edu
Public/Private: Public
Total Business Students: 338
Average GMAT: 601
% Full Time: 33
Annual Tuition (Resident/Nonresident): $2,576/$5,752

OLD DOMINION UNIVERSITY
College of Business and Public Administration

Address: 203A Technology Building, Norfolk, VA 23529
Admissions Phone: 757-683-3585 • Web Address: www.odu-cbpa.org
Public/Private: Public
Total Business Students: 450
Average GMAT: 520
% Full Time: 34
Annual Tuition (Resident/Nonresident): $3,528/$9,468

OREGON STATE UNIVERSITY
School of Business Administration

Address: 200 Bexell Hall, Corvallis, OR 97330
Admissions Phone: 541-737-6031 • Web Address: www.bus.orst.edu
Public/Private: Public
Total Business Students: 81
Average GMAT: 552
% Full Time: 78
Annual Tuition (Resident/Nonresident): $7,413/$12,465

PACE UNIVERSITY
Lubin School of Business

Address: 1 Martine Avenue, White Plains, NY 10606-1909
Admissions Phone: 914-422-4283 • Web Address: www.pace.edu
Public/Private: Private
Total Business Students: 1,473
% Full Time: 32
Annual Tuition: $0

PACIFIC LUTHERAN UNIVERSITY
School of Business

Address: Office of Admissions, Tacoma, WA 98447
Admissions Phone: 253-535-7151 • Web Address: www.plu.edu
Public/Private: Private
Total Business Students: 108
Average GMAT: 542
% Full Time: 65
Annual Tuition: $13,296

PENNSYLVANIA STATE UNIVERSITY—ERIE, THE BEHREND COLLEGE
School of Business

Address: 5091 Station Road, Erie, PA 16563
Admissions Phone: 814-898-6100 • Web Address: www.pserie.psu.edu
Public/Private: Public
Total Business Students: 159
Average GMAT: 508
% Full Time: 5

PENNSYLVANIA STATE UNIVERSITY—GREAT VALLEY CAMPUS
School of Graduate Professional Studies

Address: 30 East Swedesford Road, Malvern, PA 19355
Admissions Phone: 610-648-3248 • Web Address: www.gv.psu.edu

PENNSYLVANIA STATE UNIVERSITY—HARRISBURG
School of Business Administration

Address: 777 West Harrisburg Pike, Middletown, PA 17057
Admissions Phone: 717-948-6250 • Web Address: www.hbg.psu.edu/sbus
Public/Private: Public
Total Business Students: 207
Average GMAT: 520
% Full Time: 12
Annual Tuition (Resident/Nonresident): $9,264/$17,592

PENNSYLVANIA STATE UNIVERSITY—UNIVERSITY PARK
The Smeal College of Business Administration

Address: 106 Business Administration Building, University Park, PA 16802
Admissions Phone: 814-863-0474 • Web Address: www.smeal.psu.edu/mba
Public/Private: Public
Total Business Students: 108
Average GMAT: 624
% Full Time: 100
Annual Tuition (Resident/Nonresident): $9,076/$17,334

PEPPERDINE UNIVERSITY
The Graziadio School of Business and Management

Address: 24255 Pacific Coast Highway, Malibu, CA 90263
Admissions Phone: 310-568-5535
Web Address: www.bschool.pepperdine.edu
Public/Private: Private
Total Business Students: 1,796
Average GMAT: 630
% Full Time: 8
Annual Tuition: $25,315

PITTSBURG STATE UNIVERSITY
Gladys A. Kelce College of Business

Address: 1701 South Broadway, Pittsburg, KS 66762-7540
Admissions Phone: 620-235-4222 • Web Address: www.pittstate.edu
Public/Private: Public
Total Business Students: 86
Average GMAT: 515
% Full Time: 78
Annual Tuition (Resident/Nonresident): $2,466/$6,268

PORTLAND STATE UNIVERSITY
School of Business Administration

Address: 631 SW Harrison St., Portland, OR 97201
Admissions Phone: 503-725-3712 • Web Address: www.sba.pdx.edu
Public/Private: Public
Total Business Students: 363
Average GMAT: 598
% Full Time: 23
Annual Tuition (Resident/Nonresident): $6,834/$11,613

PURDUE UNIVERSITY
Krannert Graduate School of Management

Address: 1310 Krannert Building, West Lafayette, IN 47907
Admissions Phone: 765-494-4365 • Web Address: www.mgmt.purdue.edu
Public/Private: Public
Total Business Students: 211
Average GMAT: 642
% Full Time: 100
Annual Tuition (Resident/Nonresident): $10,064/$19,868

PURDUE UNIVERSITY CALUMET
School of Management

Address: School of Management, Hammond, IN 46323-2094
Admissions Phone: 219-989-2425 • Web Address: www.calumet.purdue.edu
Public/Private: Public
Total Business Students: 539
% Full Time: 24

QUEEN'S UNIVERSITY
Queen's School of Business

Address: Mackintosh-Corry Hall, Queen's University,
Kingston, ON K7L 3N6 Canada
Admissions Phone: 613-533-2302 • Web Address: www.business.queensu.ca
Public/Private: Public
Total Business Students: 60
Average GMAT: 665
% Full Time: 100
Annual Tuition: $24,200

RADFORD UNIVERSITY
College of Business and Economics

Address: PO Box 6956, Radford, VA 24142
Admissions Phone: 540-831-5258
Web Address: www.runet.edu/~gradcoll/index
Public/Private: Public
Total Business Students: 114
% Full Time: 34
Annual Tuition (Resident/Nonresident): $2,369/$5,863

RENSSELAER POLYTECHNIC INSTITUTE
Lally School of Management and Technology

Address: 110 Eighth St., PI 3218, Troy, NY 12180
Admissions Phone: 518-276-6586 • Web Address: www.lallyschool.rpi.edu
Public/Private: Private
Total Business Students: 255
Average GMAT: 635
% Full Time: 63
Annual Tuition: $21,000

RICE UNIVERSITY
Jesse H. Jones Graduate School of Management

Address: 6100 Main Street, MS 531 (Herring Hall, Suite 245),
Houston, TX 77005-1892
Admissions Phone: 713-348-4918 • Web Address: www.jonesgsm.rice.edu
Public/Private: Private
Total Business Students: 323
Average GMAT: 640
% Full Time: 100
Annual Tuition: $23,250

RIDER UNIVERSITY
College of Business Administration

Address: LIB 137, 2083 Lawrenceville Road, Lawrenceville, NJ 08648-3099
Admissions Phone: 609-896-5033
Web Address: www.rider.edu/academic/ccs/gradbus/index.htm
Public/Private: Private
Total Business Students: 321
Average GMAT: 517
% Full Time: 16
Annual Tuition: $5,820

ROCHESTER INSTITUTE OF TECHNOLOGY
College of Business

Address: 105 Lomb Memorial Drive, Rochester, NY 14623
Admissions Phone: 585-475-2229 • Web Address: www.ritmba.com
Public/Private: Private
Total Business Students: 360
Average GMAT: 567
% Full Time: 50
Annual Tuition: $20,928

ROLLINS COLLEGE
Crummer Graduate School of Business

Address: 1000 Holt Ave. 2722, Winter Park, FL 32789-4499
Admissions Phone: 407-646-2405 • Web Address: www.crummer.rollins.edu
Public/Private: Private
Total Business Students: 365
Average GMAT: 569
% Full Time: 43
Annual Tuition: $22,400

RUTGERS, THE STATE UNIVERSITY OF NEW JERSEY — CAMDEN
School of Business

Address: MBA Program, Camden, NJ 08102-1401
Admissions Phone: 856-225-6452 • Web Address: camden-www.rutgers.edu
Public/Private: Public
Total Business Students: 264
% Full Time: 15

RUTGERS, THE STATE UNIVERSITY OF NEW JERSEY — NEWARK
Rutgers Business School

Address: 190 University Avenue, Newark, NJ 07102-1813
Admissions Phone: 973-353-1234 • Web Address: business.rutgers.edu
Public/Private: Public
Total Business Students: 1,520
Average GMAT: 609
% Full Time: 24
Annual Tuition (Resident/Nonresident): $9,864/$14,708

ST. CLOUD STATE UNIVERSITY
Herberger College of Business

Address: 720 4th Ave. South, St. Cloud, MN 56301-4498
Admissions Phone: 320-255-2113 • Web Address: www.stcloudstate.edu
Total Business Students: 98
Average GMAT: 546
% Full Time: 88
Annual Tuition (Resident/Nonresident): $2,862/$4,356

ST. JOHN'S UNIVERSITY
The Peter J. Tobin College of Business

Address: 8000 Utopia Parkway, Jamaica, NY 11439
Admissions Phone: 718-990-1345
Web Address: www.tobincollege.stjohns.edu
Public/Private: Private
Total Business Students: 672
Average GMAT: 515
% Full Time: 25
Annual Tuition: $15,120

SAINT JOSEPH'S UNIVERSITY
The Erivan K. Haub School of Business

Address: 5600 City Avenue, Philadelphia, PA 19131
Admissions Phone: 610-660-1101 • Web Address: www.sju.edu
Public/Private: Private
Total Business Students: 552
Average GMAT: 520
% Full Time: 10
Annual Tuition: $10,260

SAINT LOUIS UNIVERSITY
John Cook School of Business

Address: 3674 Lindell Blvd., St. Louis, MO 63108
Admissions Phone: 314-977-2013
Web Address: http://mba.slu.edu
Public/Private: Private
Total Business Students: 295
Average GMAT: 580
% Full Time: 19
Annual Tuition: $25,500

SAINT MARY'S COLLEGE OF CALIFORNIA
School of Economics and Business Administration

Address: 1928 Saint Mary's Road, PO Box 4240, Moraga, CA 94575-4240
Admissions Phone: 925-631-4500
Web Address: www.stmarys-ca.edu/mba/index.html
Public/Private: Private
Total Business Students: 351
% Full Time: 56

SAINT MARY'S COLLEGE OF KANSAS
Department of Business, Economics, and Information Technology

Address: 11413 Pflumm Road, Overland Park, KS 66125
Admissions Phone: 913-345-8288 • Web Address: www.smcks.edu
Public/Private: Private
Total Business Students: 36
% Full Time: 69

SAINT MARY'S UNIVERSITY OF CANADA
Frank H. Sobey Faculty of Commerce

Address: Loyola Building, Robie Street, Halifax, NS B3H 3C3 Canada
Admissions Phone: 902-420-5729
Web Address: www.stmarys.ca/academic/commerce
Total Business Students: 268
% Full Time: 55

ST. MARY'S UNIVERSITY OF MINNESOTA
School of Business and Social Sciences

Address: 2500 Park Avenue, Minneapolis, MN 55404-4403
Admissions Phone: 612-728-5135 • Web Address: www.smumn.edu
Public/Private: Private
Total Business Students: 300

SAINT MARY'S UNIVERSITY OF SAN ANTONIO
School of Business and Administration

Address: 1 Camino Santa Maria, San Antonio, TX 78228-8507
Admissions Phone: 210-431-2027 • Web Address: www.stmarytx.edu
Public/Private: Private
Total Business Students: 210
% Full Time: 7

SALISBURY STATE UNIVERSITY
Franklin P. Perdue School of Business

Address: 1101 Camden Avenue, Salisbury, MD 21801-6837
Admissions Phone: 410-548-3983
Web Address: www.ssu.edu/schools/perdue.html
Public/Private: Public
Total Business Students: 116
% Full Time: 21

SAM HOUSTON STATE UNIVERSITY
College of Business Administration

Address: PO Box 2056, Huntsville, TX 77341-2056
Admissions Phone: 936-294-1246
Web Address: coba.shsu.edu/mba-home.htm
Public/Private: Public
Total Business Students: 164
% Full Time: 29
Annual Tuition (Resident/Nonresident): $648/$4,464

SAMFORD UNIVERSITY
School of Business

Address: DBH 322, School of Business, 800 Lakeshore Drive, Birmingham, AL 35209
Admissions Phone: 205-726-2931
Web Address: www.samford.edu/schools/business.html
Public/Private: Private
Total Business Students: 128
Average GMAT: 500
% Full Time: 0
Annual Tuition: $8,000

SAN DIEGO STATE UNIVERSITY
Graduate School of Business

Address: 5500 Campanile Drive, San Diego, CA 92182
Admissions Phone: 619-594-8073 • Web Address: www.sdsu.edu
Public/Private: Public
Total Business Students: 718
Average GMAT: 603
% Full Time: 55
Annual Tuition (Resident/Nonresident): $2,000/$8,000

SAN FRANCISCO STATE UNIVERSITY
Graduate School of Business

Address: 1600 Holloway Avenue, San Francisco, CA 94132
Admissions Phone: 415-338-1279 • Web Address: www.sfsu.edu/~mba
Public/Private: Public
Total Business Students: 900
Average GMAT: 536
% Full Time: 35
Annual Tuition (Resident/Nonresident): $1,904/$7,808

SAN JOSE STATE UNIVERSITY
Collge of Business

Address: One Washington Square, San Jose, CA 95192-0162
Admissions Phone: 408-924-3420 • Web Address: www.cob.sjsu.edu/graduate
Public/Private: Public
Total Business Students: 765
Average GMAT: 560
Annual Tuition (Resident/Nonresident): $1,990/$6,418

SANTA CLARA UNIVERSITY
Leavey School of Business

Address: MBA Office, Kenna Hall #223, Santa Clara, CA 95053-0001
Admissions Phone: 408-554-4539 • Web Address: business.scu.edu
Public/Private: Private
Total Business Students: 853
Average GMAT: 614
% Full Time: 18
Annual Tuition: $14,533

SEATTLE PACIFIC UNIVERSITY
School of Business & Economics

Address: 3307 Third Ave. W., Seattle, WA 98119
Admissions Phone: 206-281-2753 • Web Address: www.spu.edu/sbe
Public/Private: Private
Total Business Students: 150
Average GMAT: 491
% Full Time: 30
Annual Tuition: $12,255

SEATTLE UNIVERSITY
Albers School of Business and Economics

Address: 900 Broadway, Seattle, WA 98122
Admissions Phone: 206-296-2000 • Web Address: www.seattleu.edu/asbe
Public/Private: Private
Total Business Students: 511
Average GMAT: 557
% Full Time: 17
Annual Tuition: $13,932

SETON HALL UNIVERSITY
Stillman School of Business

Address: 400 South Orange Avenue, South Orange, NJ 07079-2692
Admissions Phone: 973-761-9262 • Web Address: www.business.shu.edu
Public/Private: Private
Total Business Students: 522
Average GMAT: 527
% Full Time: 15
Annual Tuition: $19,380

SIMMONS COLLEGE
Simmons Graduate School of Management

Address: 409 Commonwealth Avenue, Boston, MA 02215
Admissions Phone: 617-521-3840 • Web Address: www.simmons.edu/gsm
Public/Private: Private
Total Business Students: 250
Average GMAT: 550
% Full Time: 25
Annual Tuition: $31,000

SOUTHEAST MISSOURI STATE UNIVERSITY
Donald L. Harrison College of Business

Address: MBA Office, Cape Girardeau, MO 63701
Admissions Phone: 573-651-5116
Web Address: www.semo.edu
Public/Private: Public
Total Business Students: 100
Average GMAT: 510
% Full Time: 68
Annual Tuition (Resident/Nonresident): $2,000/$4,000

SOUTHEASTERN LOUISIANA UNIVERSITY
College of Business & Technology

Address: SLU 10752, Hammond, LA 70402
Admissions Phone: 800-222-7358 • Web Address: www.selu.edu/academics/business
Public/Private: Public
Total Business Students: 234
% Full Time: 63
Annual Tuition (Resident/Nonresident): $2,374/$6,370

SOUTHERN ILLINOIS UNIVERSITY— CARBONDALE
College of Business Administration

Address: Rehn Hall 133, Carbondale, IL 62901-4625
Admissions Phone: 618-453-3030 • Web Address: www.cba.siu.edu
Public/Private: Public
Total Business Students: 128
Average GMAT: 533
Annual Tuition (Resident/Nonresident): $4,000/$8,200

SOUTHERN ILLINOIS UNIVERSITY—EDWARDSVILLE
School of Business

Address: Campus Box 1051, Edwardsville, IL 62026
Admissions Phone: 618-650-3840 • Web Address: www.siue.edu/business
Public/Private: Public
Total Business Students: 255
Average GMAT: 520
% Full Time: 32
Annual Tuition (Resident/Nonresident): $2,034/$4,068

SOUTHERN METHODIST UNIVERSITY
Cox School of Business

Address: PO Box 750333, Dallas, TX 75275
Admissions Phone: 214-768-1214 • Web Address: mba.cox.smu.edu
Public/Private: Private
Total Business Students: 843
Average GMAT: 651
% Full Time: 27
Annual Tuition: $26,090

SOUTHWEST MISSOURI STATE UNIVERSITY
College of Business Administration

Address: 901 S. National, Springfield, MO 65804
Admissions Phone: 417-836-5335 • Web Address: www.coba.smsu.edu
Public/Private: Public
Total Business Students: 299
Average GMAT: 520
% Full Time: 50
Annual Tuition (Resident/Nonresident): $2,835/$5,670

SOUTHWEST TEXAS STATE UNIVERSITY
Graduate School of Business

Address: 105 Derrick Hall, San Marcos, TX 78666
Admissions Phone: 512-245-3591 • Web Address: www.business.swt.edu
Public/Private: Public
Total Business Students: 343
Average GMAT: 550
% Full Time: 10
Annual Tuition (Resident/Nonresident): $5,552/$15,872

STANFORD UNIVERSITY
Stanford Graduate School of Business

Address: 518 Memorial Way, Stanford, CA 94305-5015
Admissions Phone: 650-723-2766 • Web Address: www.gsb.stanford.edu
Public/Private: Private
Total Business Students: 755
Average GMAT: 718
% Full Time: 100
Annual Tuition: $31,002

STATE UNIVERSITY OF WEST GEORGIA
Richards College of Business

Address: 1600 Maple Street, Carrollton, GA 30118-3000
Admissions Phone: 770-836-6467 • Web Address: www.westga.edu
Public/Private: Public
Total Business Students: 64
% Full Time: 52
Annual Tuition (Resident/Nonresident): $2,770/$9,526

STEPHEN F. AUSTIN STATE UNIVERSITY
College of Business

Address: PO Box 13004, Nacogdoches, TX 75962
Admissions Phone: 936-468-3101 • Web Address: www.cob.sfasu.edu
Public/Private: Public
Total Business Students: 65
Average GMAT: 482
% Full Time: 10
Annual Tuition (Resident/Nonresident): $432/$2,976

STETSON UNIVERSITY
School of Business Administration

Address: 421 North Woodland Boulevard, Unit 8398, DeLand, FL 32720-7413
Admissions Phone: 904-822-7410 • Web Address: www.stetson.edu
Public/Private: Private
Total Business Students: 160
% Full Time: 50
Annual Tuition: $1

SUFFOLK UNIVERSITY
Frank Sawyer School of Management

Address: 8 Ashburton Place, Boston, MA 02108
Admissions Phone: 617-573-8302 • Web Address: www.sawyer.suffolk.edu
Public/Private: Private
Total Business Students: 774
Average GMAT: 505
% Full Time: 21
Annual Tuition: $20,440

SYRACUSE UNIVERSITY
School of Management

Address: 900 South Crouse Avenue, Suite 100, Syracuse, NY 13244-2130
Admissions Phone: 315-443-9214 • Web Address: www.som.syr.edu
Public/Private: Private
Total Business Students: 521
Average GMAT: 636
% Full Time: 36
Annual Tuition: $19,410

TCU
M. J. Neeley School of Business

Address: PO Box 298540, Fort Worth, TX 76129
Admissions Phone: 817-257-7531 • Web Address: www.mba.tcu.edu
Total Business Students: 243
Average GMAT: 601
% Full Time: 49
Annual Tuition: $11,340

TEL AVIV UNIVERSITY
Leon Recanati Graduate School of Business Administration

Web Address: www.tau.ac.il/gsba
Total Business Students: 2,196

TEMPLE UNIVERSITY
Fox School of Business and Management

Address: 1810 North 13th Street, Speakman Hall, Room 5, Philadelphia, PA 19122
Admissions Phone: 215-204-7678 • Web Address: www.sbm.temple.edu
Public/Private: Public
Total Business Students: 1,198
% Full Time: 19
Annual Tuition (Resident/Nonresident): $8,760/$12,288

TENNESSEE STATE UNIVERSITY
School of Management

Address: School of Management, Nashville, TN 37209-1561
Admissions Phone: 615-963-7146 • Web Address: www.cob.tnstate.edu
Public/Private: Public
Total Business Students: 250
Average GMAT: 510

TENNESSEE TECHNOLOGICAL UNIVERSITY
College of Business Administration

Address: Box 5023, Cookeville, TN 38505
Admissions Phone: 931-372-3600 • Web Address: www2.tntech.edu/mba/
Public/Private: Public
Total Business Students: 122
Average GMAT: 515
% Full Time: 57
Annual Tuition (Resident/Nonresident): $0/$6,472

TEXAS A&M UNIVERSITY—COLLEGE STATION
Mays College and Graduate School of Business

Address: TAMU 4117, College Station, TX 77845
Admissions Phone: 979-845-4714 • Web Address: http://mba.tamu.edu
Public/Private: Public
Total Business Students: 208
Average GMAT: 628
% Full Time: 100
Annual Tuition (Resident/Nonresident): $2,120/$7,818

TEXAS A&M UNIVERSITY—COMMERCE
Graduate Programs in Business

Address: PO Box 3011, Commerce, TX 75429
Admissions Phone: 903-886-5167
Web Address: www.tamu-commerce.edu/mba
Total Business Students: 253
Average GMAT: 460
% Full Time: 35
Annual Tuition (Resident/Nonresident): $2,828/$7,942

TEXAS A&M UNIVERSITY—CORPUS CHRISTI
College of Business Administration

Web Address: www.enterprise.tamucc.edu
Public/Private: Public
Total Business Students: 144
% Full Time: 30

TEXAS TECH UNIVERSITY
Jerry S. Rawls College of Business Administration

Address: Box 42101, Lubbock, TX 79409-2101
Admissions Phone: 806-742-3184 • Web Address: grad.ba.ttu.edu
Public/Private: Public
Total Business Students: 213
Average GMAT: 580
% Full Time: 86
Annual Tuition (Resident/Nonresident): $1,920/$6,984

THESEUS INTERNATIONAL MANAGEMENT INSTITUTE

Address: BP 169 Rue Albert Einstein, Sophia Antipolis, 06903, France
Admissions Phone: 011-334-9294-5107 • Web Address: www.theseus.edu

THUNDERBIRD
American Graduate School of International Management

Address: 15249 North 59th Avenue, Glendale, AZ 85306-6000
Admissions Phone: 602-978-7100 • Web Address: www.thunderbird.edu
Total Business Students: 1,100
Average GMAT: 600
% Full Time: 100
Annual Tuition: $25,500

TRUMAN STATE UNIVERSITY
Division of Business and Accountancy

Address: VH 2400, 100 East Normal, Kirksville, MO 63501-4221
Admissions Phone: 660-785-4378 • Web Address: www.truman.edu
Public/Private: Public
Total Business Students: 16
Average GMAT: 600
Annual Tuition (Resident/Nonresident): $4,072/$7,400

TULANE UNIVERSITY
A. B. Freeman School of Business

Address: 7 McAlister Drive, Suite 401, New Orleans, LA 70118
Admissions Phone: 504-865-5410 • Web Address: freeman.tulane.edu
Public/Private: Private
Total Business Students: 150
Average GMAT: 653
% Full Time: 93
Annual Tuition: $24,675

UNION COLLEGE
MBA @ Union

Address: Lamont House, Schenectady, NY 12308
Admissions Phone: 518-388-6238 • Web Address: www.mba.union.edu
Public/Private: Private
Total Business Students: 118
Average GMAT: 570
% Full Time: 67
Annual Tuition: $14,640

UNIVERSITAT POMPEU FABRA
Department of Economics & Business MBA Programme

Address: Ramon Trias Fargas, 25-27, Barcelona, 08005, Spain
Admissions Phone: 011 34 93 542 2912 • Web Address: mba.upf.es
Annual Tuition: $12,500

UNIVERSITAT RAMON LLULL
ESADE

Address: Av. Pedralbes, 60-62, Barcelona, 08034, Spain
Admissions Phone: 011-349-328-02995 • Web Address: www.esade.edu

UNIVERSITE LAVAL
Faculte des sciences de l'Administration

Address: Universite Laval, Quebec, QC G1K 7P4, Canada
Admissions Phone: 418-656-3080
Web Address: www.fsa.ulaval.ca/formation/2ecycle.html
Total Business Students: 963
% Full Time: 49
Annual Tuition: $2,250

UNIVERSITY AT ALBANY (STATE UNIVERSITY OF NEW YORK)
School of Business

Address: UAB 121 1400 Washington Ave., Albany, NY 12222
Admissions Phone: 518-442-4961 • Web Address: www.albany.edu/business
Public/Private: Public
Total Business Students: 148
Average GMAT: 528
% Full Time: 35
Annual Tuition (Resident/Nonresident): $2,550/$4,208

UNIVERSITY AT BUFFALO (STATE UNIVERSITY OF NEW YORK)
School of Management

Address: 206 Jacobs Management Center, Buffalo, NY 14260
Admissions Phone: 716-645-3204 • Web Address: www.mgt.buffalo.edu
Public/Private: Public
Total Business Students: 791
Average GMAT: 609
% Full Time: 75
Annual Tuition (Resident/Nonresident): $5,100/$8,416

UNIVERSITY OF AKRON
Graduate Programs in Business

Address: The University of Akron, CBA 412, Akron, OH 44325-4805
Admissions Phone: 330-972-7043 • Web Address: www.uakron.edu/cba/grad
Public/Private: Public
Total Business Students: 306
Average GMAT: 561
% Full Time: 36
Annual Tuition (Resident/Nonresident): $7,786/$13,396

UNIVERSITY OF ALABAMA AT BIRMINGHAM
Graduate School of Management

Address: 1530 3rd Avenue South HUC 511, Birmingham, AL 35294-1150
Admissions Phone: 205-934-8817 • Web Address: www.business.uab.edu
Public/Private: Public
Total Business Students: 334
Average GMAT: 525
% Full Time: 0

UNIVERSITY OF ALABAMA AT HUNTSVILLE
College of Administrative Science

Address: ASB 102, Huntsville, AL 35899
Admissions Phone: 256-824-6024
Web Address: www.uah.edu/colleges/adminsci
Public/Private: Public
Total Business Students: 1

UNIVERSITY OF ALABAMA AT TUSCALOOSA
Manderson Graduate School of Business

Address: Box 870223, Tuscaloosa, AL 35487-0223
Admissions Phone: 205-348-6517 • Web Address: www.cba.ua.edu/~mba
Public/Private: Public
Total Business Students: 114
Average GMAT: 607
% Full Time: 100
Annual Tuition (Resident/Nonresident): $3,292/$8,912

UNIVERSITY OF ALASKA—ANCHORAGE
College of Business and Public Policy

Address: 3211 Providence Drive, Anchorage, AK 99508-8060
Admissions Phone: 907-786-4129 • Web Address: www.cbpp.uaa.alaska.edu
Public/Private: Public
Total Business Students: 27
% Full Time: 71
Annual Tuition (Resident/Nonresident): $3,096/$2,688

UNIVERSITY OF ALBERTA
School of Business

Address: 2-30 Business Building, Edmonton, AB T6G 2R6, Canada
Admissions Phone: 780-492-3946 • Web Address: www.bus.ualberta.ca/mba
Public/Private: Public
Total Business Students: 295
Average GMAT: 627
% Full Time: 48
Annual Tuition: $2,870

UNIVERSITY OF ARIZONA
Eller Graduate School of Management

Address: McClelland Hall 210, 1130 E Helen, Tucson, AZ 85721-0108
Admissions Phone: 520-621-4008 • Web Address: www.eller.arizona.edu/mba
Public/Private: Public
Total Business Students: 316
Average GMAT: 656
% Full Time: 100
Annual Tuition (Nonresident): $15,804

UNIVERSITY OF ARKANSAS AT FAYETTEVILLE
Sam M. Walton College of Business

Address: BA Suite 475, Fayetteville, AR 72701
Admissions Phone: 501-575-2851
Web Address: waltoncollege.uark.edu/gsb/mba/
Public/Private: Public
Total Business Students: 74
Average GMAT: 575
% Full Time: 51
Annual Tuition (Resident/Nonresident): $9,272/$19,038

UNIVERSITY OF ARKANSAS AT LITTLE ROCK
College of Business Administration

Address: 2801 South University Avenue, Little Rock, AR 72204
Admissions Phone: 501-569-3048 • Web Address: www.ualr.edu/~cbadept/
Public/Private: Public
Total Business Students: 225
% Full Time: 13

UNIVERSITY OF BALTIMORE
Merrick School of Business

Address: 1420 North Charles Street, Baltimore, MD 21201
Admissions Phone: 877-277-5982 • Web Address: www.ubalt.edu
Public/Private: Public
Total Business Students: 506
Average GMAT: 500
% Full Time: 46
Annual Tuition (Resident/Nonresident): $5,941/$8,533

UNIVERSITY OF BATH
University of Bath School of Management

Address: MBA Office, School of Management, Claverton Dewr., Bath, BA2 7AY, United Kingdom
Admissions Phone: 011 44 (0) 225 383432 • Web Address: www.bath.ac.uk/management
Total Business Students: 293
Average GMAT: 580
% Full Time: 27

UNIVERSITY OF CALGARY
Faculty of Management

Address: 2500 University Drive, NW, Calgary, AB T2N 1N4, Canada
Admissions Phone: 403-220-3808 • Web Address: www.ucalgary.ca/mg/mba
Total Business Students: 398
Average GMAT: 598
% Full Time: 33
Annual Tuition (Resident/Nonresident): $6,000/$12,000

UNIVERSITY OF CALIFORNIA—BERKELEY
Haas School of Business

Address: 440 Student Services Building #1902, Berkeley, CA 94720-1902
Admissions Phone: 510-642-1405 • Web Address: haas.berkeley.edu
Public/Private: Public
Total Business Students: 477
Average GMAT: 675
% Full Time: 100

UNIVERSITY OF CALIFORNIA—DAVIS
Graduate School of Management

Address: One Shields Ave., Davis, CA 95616
Admissions Phone: 530-752-7658 • Web Address: www.gsm.ucdavis.edu
Public/Private: Public
Total Business Students: 131
Average GMAT: 662
% Full Time: 98
Annual Tuition (Resident/Nonresident): $10,782/$21,027

UNIVERSITY OF CALIFORNIA—IRVINE
Graduate School of Management

Address: 202 GSM, Irvine, CA 92697-3125
Admissions Phone: 949-824-4622 • Web Address: www.gsm.uci.edu
Public/Private: Public
Total Business Students: 638
Average GMAT: 654
% Full Time: 38
Annual Tuition (Resident/Nonresident): $0/$10,244

UNIVERSITY OF CALIFORNIA—LOS ANGELES
The Anderson School at UCLA

Address: 110 Westwood Plaza, Los Angeles, CA 90095-1481
Admissions Phone: 310-825-6944 • Web Address: www.anderson.ucla.edu
Public/Private: Public
Total Business Students: 1,388
Average GMAT: 700
% Full Time: 47
Annual Tuition (Resident/Nonresident): $11,744/$22,448

UNIVERSITY OF CALIFORNIA—RIVERSIDE
A. Gary Anderson Graduate School of Management

Address: Anderson Hall, Riverside, CA 92521-0203
Admissions Phone: 909-787-4551 • Web Address: www.agsm.ucr.edu
Public/Private: Public
Total Business Students: 130
Average GMAT: 594
% Full Time: 82

UNIVERSITY OF CAPETOWN
Graduate School of Business

Web Address: www.gsb.uct.ac.za
Total Business Students: 157
% Full Time: 70
Annual Tuition: $34,400

UNIVERSITY OF CENTRAL ARKANSAS
College of Business Administration

Address: Burdick Business Building, Room 224, Conway, AR 72035
Admissions Phone: 501-450-5316 • Web Address: www.business.uca.edu
Public/Private: Public
Total Business Students: 60
% Full Time: 40

UNIVERSITY OF CENTRAL FLORIDA
College of Business Administration

Address: PO Box 161400, Orlando, FL 32816
Admissions Phone: 407-823-2184 • Web Address: www.bus.ucf.edu
Public/Private: Public
Total Business Students: 725
Average GMAT: 556
% Full Time: 13
Annual Tuition (Resident/Nonresident): $4,000/$14,000

UNIVERSITY OF CHICAGO
Graduate School of Business

Address: 1101 East 58th Street, Chicago, IL 60637
Admissions Phone: 773-702-7369 • Web Address: gsb.uchicago.edu
Public/Private: Private
Total Business Students: 3,060
Average GMAT: 695
% Full Time: 34
Annual Tuition: $30,500

UNIVERSITY OF CHICAGO
The University of Chicago GSB—Europe Campus

Address: Arago 271, Barcelona, 08007, Spain
Admissions Phone: 011-34 93 505 21 54
Web Address: gsb.uchicago.edu/execmbaeurope
Total Business Students: 3,000
Average GMAT: 684

UNIVERSITY OF CINCINNATI
College of Business Administration

Address: Carl H. Linder Hall, Suite 103, Cincinnati, OH 45221
Admissions Phone: 513-556-7020 • Web Address: www.cba.uc.edu/mba
Public/Private: Public
Total Business Students: 307
Average GMAT: 579
% Full Time: 27
Annual Tuition (Resident/Nonresident): $12,916/$16,348

UNIVERSITY OF COLORADO AT BOULDER
Leeds School of Business

Address: Business 204, UCB 419, Boulder, CO 80309
Admissions Phone: 303-492-8397 • Web Address: leeds.colorado.edu
Public/Private: Public
Total Business Students: 181
Average GMAT: 648
% Full Time: 61
Annual Tuition (Resident/Nonresident): $4,418/$17,750

UNIVERSITY OF COLORADO AT COLORADO SPRINGS
Graduate School of Business Administration

Address: 1420 Austin Bluffs Parkway, Colorado Springs, CO 83918
Admissions Phone: 719-262-3408 • Web Address: web.uccs.edu/business
Public/Private: Public
Total Business Students: 290
Average GMAT: 550
% Full Time: 0

UNIVERSITY OF COLORADO AT DENVER
Graduate School of Business Administration

Address: Campus Box 165, PO Box 173364, Denver, CO 80217-3364
Admissions Phone: 303-556-5900 • Web Address: www.business.cudenver.edu
Public/Private: Public
Total Business Students: 1,249
% Full Time: 29
Annual Tuition (Resident/Nonresident): $3,956/$13,818

UNIVERSITY OF CONNECTICUT
School of Business

Address: 2100 Hillside Road Unit 1041, Storrs, CT 06269-1041
Admissions Phone: 860-486-2872 • Web Address: www.business.uconn.edu
Public/Private: Public
Total Business Students: 783
Average GMAT: 640
% Full Time: 11
Annual Tuition (Resident/Nonresident): $5,478/$14,230

UNIVERSITY OF DALLAS
Graduate School of Management

Address: 1845 E. Northgate Dr., Irving, TX 75062
Admissions Phone: 972-721-5174 • Web Address: gsm.udallas.edu
Public/Private: Private
Total Business Students: 2,000
Average GMAT: 550
Annual Tuition: $15,984

UNIVERSITY OF DAYTON
School of Business Administration

Address: 300 College Park Avenue, Dayton, OH 45469
Admissions Phone: 937-229-3733 • Web Address: www.sba.udayton.edu/mba
Public/Private: Private
Total Business Students: 431
Average GMAT: 543
% Full Time: 21
Annual Tuition: $8,658

UNIVERSITY OF DELAWARE
MBA Programs—College of Business and Economics

Address: 103 MBNA America Hall, Newark, DE 19716
Admissions Phone: 302-831-2221 • Web Address: www.mba.udel.edu
Public/Private: Public
Total Business Students: 302
Average GMAT: 555
% Full Time: 24
Annual Tuition (Resident/Nonresident): $6,020/$13,860

UNIVERSITY OF DENVER
Daniels College of Business

Address: 2101 South University Blvd. #255, Denver, CO 80208
Admissions Phone: 303-871-3416 • Web Address: www.daniels.du.edu
Public/Private: Private
Total Business Students: 180
Average GMAT: 560
% Full Time: 66
Annual Tuition: $21,456

UNIVERSITY OF DETROIT MERCY
College of Business Administration

Address: College of Business Administration, Detroit, MI 48219-0900
Admissions Phone: 313-993-1202 • Web Address: www.business.udmercy.edu
Public/Private: Private
Total Business Students: 235
Average GMAT: 513
% Full Time: 9

UNIVERSITY OF FINDLAY
College of Business

Address: 1000 N. Main Street, Findlay, OH 45840
Admissions Phone: 419-434-4676 • Web Address: www.findlay.edu/academic_programs/business/index.html
Public/Private: Private
Total Business Students: 450
Average GMAT: 550
% Full Time: 12
Annual Tuition: $13,572

UNIVERSITY OF FLORIDA
Warrington College of Business

Address: 134 Bryan Hall, PO Box 117152, Gainesville, FL 32611-7152
Admissions Phone: 352-392-7992 • Web Address: www.floridamba.ufl.edu
Public/Private: Public
Total Business Students: 457
Average GMAT: 655
% Full Time: 76
Annual Tuition (Resident/Nonresident): $4,620/$16,018

UNIVERSITY OF GEORGIA
Terry College of Business, Graduate School of Business Administration

Address: 346 Brooks Hall, Athens, GA 30602-6264
Admissions Phone: 706-542-5671 • Web Address: www.terry.uga.edu/mba
Public/Private: Public
Total Business Students: 368
Average GMAT: 659
% Full Time: 68
Annual Tuition (Resident/Nonresident): $3,549/$13,017

UNIVERSITY OF HARTFORD
The Barney School of Business

Address: Office of Academic Service, 200 Bloomfield Avenue, West Hartford, CT 06117
Admissions Phone: 860-768-4390 • Web Address: www.hartford.edu
Public/Private: Private

UNIVERSITY OF HAWAII—MANOA
College of Business Administration

Address: 2404 Maile Way A303, Honolulu, HI 96822
Admissions Phone: 808-956-8266 • Web Address: www.cba.hawaii.edu
Public/Private: Public
Total Business Students: 329
% Full Time: 50

UNIVERSITY OF HOUSTON
College of Business Administration

Address: 4001 West McNichols Road, Houston, TX 77204-6282
Admissions Phone: 713-743-4876 • Web Address: www.cba.uh.edu
Public/Private: Public
Total Business Students: 1,088
% Full Time: 40

UNIVERSITY OF HOUSTON—CLEAR LAKE
School of Business and Public Administration

Address: BA 122, Houston, TX 77058-1098
Admissions Phone: 281-283-3110
Web Address: www.cl.uh.edu/bpa/index.html
Public/Private: Public
Total Business Students: 1,083
% Full Time: 42

UNIVERSITY OF ILLINOIS AT CHICAGO
UIC MBA Program

Address: 815 West Van Buren, Suite 220, Chicago, IL 60607
Admissions Phone: 312-996-4573 • Web Address: www.uic.edu/cba/mba
Public/Private: Public
Total Business Students: 499
Average GMAT: 580
% Full Time: 40
Annual Tuition (Resident/Nonresident): $11,078/$18,334

UNIVERSITY OF ILLINOIS AT URBANA-CHAMPAIGN
College of Commerce & Business Administration

Address: 410 David Kinley Hall, Champaign, IL 61820
Admissions Phone: 217-244-8019 • Web Address: www.mba.uiuc.edu
Public/Private: Public
Total Business Students: 201
Average GMAT: 621
% Full Time: 100
Annual Tuition (Resident/Nonresident): $11,050/$18,776

UNIVERSITY OF IOWA
Henry B. Tippie School of Management

Address: 108 Pappajohn Business Administration Building, Iowa City, IA 52242-1000
Admissions Phone: 319-335-1039 • Web Address: www.biz.uiowa.edu/mba
Public/Private: Public
Total Business Students: 910
Average GMAT: 631
% Full Time: 25
Annual Tuition (Resident/Nonresident): $7,440/$15,752

UNIVERSITY OF KANSAS
School of Business

Address: 206 Summerfield Hall, Lawrence, KS 66045
Admissions Phone: 785-864-3844 • Web Address: www.business.ku.edu
Public/Private: Public
Total Business Students: 477
Average GMAT: 606
% Full Time: 21
Annual Tuition (Resident/Nonresident): $3,434/$11,212

UNIVERSITY OF KENTUCKY
Gatton College of Business and Economics

Address: 145 Carol Martin Gatton College of Business and Economics, Lexington, KY 40506-0034
Admissions Phone: 859-257-5889 • Web Address: gatton.uky.edu
Public/Private: Public
Total Business Students: 233
Average GMAT: 613
% Full Time: 64
Annual Tuition (Resident/Nonresident): $3,610/$10,830

UNIVERSITY OF LOUSIANA AT LAFAYETTE
Graduate School

Address: Martin Hall, Room 260 PO Box 44610, Lafayette, LA 70504
Admissions Phone: 337-482-6965 • Web Address: www.louisiana.edu
Public/Private: Public

UNIVERSITY OF LOUISIANA AT MONROE
College of Business Administration

Address: 700 University Avenue, Monroe, LA 71209-0100
Admissions Phone: 318-342-1100 • Web Address: ele.ulm.edu/mba/
Total Business Students: 78
Average GMAT: 500
% Full Time: 81
Annual Tuition (Resident/Nonresident): $1,900/$7,858

UNIVERSITY OF LOUISVILLE
College of Business and Public Administration

Address: CBPA Student Academic Support Services, Louisville, KY 40292
Admissions Phone: 502-852-7765 • Web Address: www.louisville.edu
Public/Private: Public
Total Business Students: 652
% Full Time: 34

UNIVERSITY OF MAINE
Maine Business School

Address: 5723 DP Corbett Business Building, Orono, ME 04469-5723
Admissions Phone: 207-581-1973 • Web Address: www.umaine.edu/business
Public/Private: Public
Total Business Students: 95
Average GMAT: 530
% Full Time: 42
Annual Tuition (Resident/Nonresident): $3,780/$10,728

UNIVERSITY OF MANITOBA
Faculty of Management

Address: 268 Drake Center, Winnipeg, MB R3T 5V4 Canada
Admissions Phone: 204-474-8448
Web Address: www.umanitoba.ca/management/mbapage.html
Public/Private: Public
Total Business Students: 102
% Full Time: 16

UNIVERSITY OF MARYLAND—COLLEGE PARK
Robert H. Smith School of Business

Address: 2308 Van Munching Hall, College Park, MD 20742-1871
Admissions Phone: 301-405-2278 • Web Address: www.rhsmith.umd.edu
Public/Private: Public
Total Business Students: 1,111
Average GMAT: 658
% Full Time: 38
Annual Tuition (Resident/Nonresident): $11,466/$16,992

UNIVERSITY OF MASSACHUSETTS AT AMHERST
Isenberg School of Management

Address: 209 Isenberg School of Management, UMass, Amherst, MA 01003
Admissions Phone: 413-545-5608 • Web Address: www.umass.edu/mba
Public/Private: Public
Total Business Students: 260
Average GMAT: 640
% Full Time: 26
Annual Tuition (Resident/Nonresident): $2,640/$9,937

UNIVERSITY OF MASSACHUSETTS AT BOSTON
Graduate College of Management

Address: 100 Morrissey Boulevard, Boston, MA 02125-3393
Admissions Phone: 617-287-7720 • Web Address: www.mgmt.umb.edu
Public/Private: Public
Annual Tuition (Resident/Nonresident): $6,624/$14,488

UNIVERSITY OF MASSACHUSETTS AT LOWELL
College of Management

Address: 1 University Avenue, Lowell, MA 01854-2881
Admissions Phone: 978-934-2848
Web Address: www.uml.edu/college/management/
Public/Private: Public
Total Business Students: 322
Average GMAT: 525
% Full Time: 9
Annual Tuition (Resident/Nonresident): $1,600/$6,400

UNIVERSITY OF MEMPHIS
Fogelman College of Business and Economics

Address: Graduate School Administration Building, Rm. 216, Memphis, TN 38152-3370
Admissions Phone: 901-678-2911 • Web Address: www.fcbe.memphis.edu
Public/Private: Public
Total Business Students: 645
Average GMAT: 530
% Full Time: 53
Annual Tuition (Resident/Nonresident): $3,964/$8,968

UNIVERSITY OF MIAMI
School of Business Administration

Address: PO Box 248505, Coral Gables, FL 33124-6524
Admissions Phone: 305-284-2510 • Web Address: bus.miami.edu/grad
Public/Private: Private
Total Business Students: 529
% Full Time: 75
Annual Tuition: $21,576

UNIVERSITY OF MICHIGAN
Business School

Address: 701 Tappan Street, Ann Arbor, MI 48109
Admissions Phone: 734-763-5796 • Web Address: www.bus.umich.edu
Public/Private: Public
Total Business Students: 1,813
Average GMAT: 676
% Full Time: 48
Annual Tuition (Resident/Nonresident): $25,500/$30,500

UNIVERSITY OF MICHIGAN—DEARBORN
School of Management

Address: School of Management, 4901 Evergreen Road, Dearborn, MI 48128-1491
Admissions Phone: 313-593-5460 • Web Address: www.som.umd.umich.edu
Public/Private: Public
Total Business Students: 396
Average GMAT: 565
% Full Time: 5
Annual Tuition (Resident/Nonresident): $10,700/$19,955

UNIVERSITY OF MICHIGAN—FLINT
School of Management

Address: UM-F, MBA Office, 364 French Hall, 303 E Kearsley, Flint, MI 48502-1950
Admissions Phone: 810-761-3163
Web Address: www.flint.umich.edu/departments/som/mba
Public/Private: Public
Total Business Students: 225
Average GMAT: 530
Annual Tuition: $8,420

UNIVERSITY OF MINNESOTA—MINNEAPOLIS
Curtis L. Carlson School of Management

Address: 321 19th Avenue South, Minneapolis, MN 55455
Admissions Phone: 612-625-5555 • Web Address: www.carlsonschool.umn.edu
Public/Private: Public
Total Business Students: 1,243
Average GMAT: 645
% Full Time: 19
Annual Tuition (Resident/Nonresident): $14,683/$19,200

UNIVERSITY OF MINNESOTA—DULUTH
School of Business and Economics

Address: 431 Darland Administration Building, Duluth, MN 55812-2496
Admissions Phone: 218-726-7523
Web Address: sbe.d.umn.edu/sem_description
Public/Private: Public

UNIVERSITY OF MISSISSIPPI
School of Business Administration

Address: 319 Conner Hall, University, MS 38677
Admissions Phone: 662-915-5483 • Web Address: www.bus.olemiss.edu/mba
Public/Private: Public
Total Business Students: 90
Average GMAT: 560
% Full Time: 100

UNIVERSITY OF MISSOURI—COLUMBIA
College of Business

Address: 303 Middlebush Hall, 4901 Evergreen Road, Columbia, MO 65211
Admissions Phone: 573-882-2750 • Web Address: mba.missouri.edu
Public/Private: Public
Total Business Students: 121

UNIVERSITY OF MISSOURI—KANSAS CITY
Henry W. Bloch School of Business & Public Administration

Address: 5100 Rockhill Road, Kansas City, MO 64110
Admissions Phone: 816-235-1111 • Web Address: www.umkc.edu/bloch
Public/Private: Public
Total Business Students: 403
Average GMAT: 559
% Full Time: 31
Annual Tuition (Resident/Nonresident): $3,582/$9,842

UNIVERSITY OF MISSOURI—ST. LOUIS
School of Business Administration

Address: 8001 Natural Bridge Road, 461 Social Science and Business, St. Louis, MO 63121-4499
Admissions Phone: 314-516-5885
Web Address: www.umsl.edu/business/busgrad/sabagrad.htm
Public/Private: Public
Total Business Students: 388
Average GMAT: 565
% Full Time: 10
Annual Tuition (Resident/Nonresident): $4,890/$14,700

UNIVERSITY OF MONTANA—MISSOULA
School of Business Administration

Address: School of Business Administration, Missoula, MT 59812
Admissions Phone: 406-243-4983 • Web Address: www.mba-macct.umt.edu
Public/Private: Public
Total Business Students: 132
Average GMAT: 550
% Full Time: 60
Annual Tuition (Resident/Nonresident): $3,500/$9,400

UNIVERSITY OF NEBRASKA—OMAHA
College of Business Administration

Address: 6001 Dodge Street, Omaha, NE 68182-0048
Admissions Phone: 402-554-2303 • Web Address: cba.unomaha.edu/mba
Public/Private: Public
Total Business Students: 362
Average GMAT: 533
% Full Time: 0

UNIVERSITY OF NEBRASKA—LINCOLN
College of Business Administration

Address: CBA 126, Lincoln, NE 68588-0405
Admissions Phone: 402-472-2338 • Web Address: www.cba.unl.edu
Public/Private: Public
Total Business Students: 159
Average GMAT: 596
% Full Time: 51
Annual Tuition (Resident/Nonresident): $3,216/$8,298

UNIVERSITY OF NEVADA—LAS VEGAS
College of Business

Address: 4505 Maryland Parkway, Box 456031, Las Vegas, NV 89154-6031
Admissions Phone: 702-895-3655 • Web Address: www.unlv.edu
Public/Private: Public
Total Business Students: 191
Average GMAT: 588
% Full Time: 46
Annual Tuition (Resident/Nonresident): $0/$7,215

UNIVERSITY OF NEVADA—RENO
College of Business Administration

Web Address: www.coba.unr.edu/mba/
Public/Private: Public
Total Business Students: 167
% Full Time: 26
Annual Tuition (Nonresident): $3,750

UNIVERSITY OF NEW HAMPSHIRE
Whittemore School of Business and Economics

Address: 116 McConnell Hall, 15 College Road, Durham, NH 03824
Admissions Phone: 603-862-1367 • Web Address: www.mba.unh.edu
Public/Private: Public
Total Business Students: 210
Average GMAT: 560
% Full Time: 32
Annual Tuition (Resident/Nonresident): $6,300/$15,720

UNIVERSITY OF NEW MEXICO
Robert O. Anderson Graduate School of Management

Address: The University of New Mexico, Albuquerque, NM 87131
Admissions Phone: 505-277-3147 • Web Address: asm.unm.edu
Public/Private: Public
Total Business Students: 431
Average GMAT: 562
% Full Time: 57
Annual Tuition (Resident/Nonresident): $3,301/$11,737

UNIVERSITY OF NEW ORLEANS
College of Business Administration

Address: Administration Building, Room 103, New Orleans, LA 70148
Admissions Phone: 504-280-6595 • Web Address: www.uno.edu
Public/Private: Public
Total Business Students: 792
Average GMAT: 461
% Full Time: 44
Annual Tuition (Resident/Nonresident): $2,748/$9,792

UNIVERSITY OF NORTH CAROLINA AT CHAPEL HILL
Kenan-Flagler Business School

Address: CB #3490, McColl Building, Chapel Hill, NC 27599-3490
Admissions Phone: 919-962-3236 • Web Address: www.kenan-flagler.unc.edu
Public/Private: Public
Total Business Students: 554
Average GMAT: 674
% Full Time: 100
Annual Tuition (Resident/Nonresident): $12,082/$25,524

UNIVERSITY OF NORTH CAROLINA AT CHARLOTTE
Belk College of Business Administration

Address: 9201 University City Boulevard, Charlotte, NC 28223-0001
Admissions Phone: 704-687-3366 • Web Address: www.belkcollege.uncc.edu/
Public/Private: Public
Total Business Students: 372
Average GMAT: 552
% Full Time: 23
Annual Tuition (Resident/Nonresident): $2,526/$10,456

UNIVERSITY OF NORTH CAROLINA AT GREENSBORO
Joseph M. Bryan School of Business & Economics

Address: PO Box 26165, Greensboro, NC 27402-6165
Admissions Phone: 336-334-5390 • Web Address: www.uncg.edu/bae/mba
Public/Private: Public
Total Business Students: 214
Average GMAT: 573
% Full Time: 32
Annual Tuition (Resident/Nonresident): $2,675/$12,057

UNIVERSITY OF NORTH CAROLINA AT WILMINGTON
Cameron School of Business

Web Address: www.csb.uncwil.edu
Public/Private: Public
Total Business Students: 120
% Full Time: 0
Annual Tuition (Resident/Nonresident): $1,122/$6,488

UNIVERSITY OF NORTH DAKOTA
College of Business Administration

Address: PO Box 7659, Winston-Salem, NC 27109
Admissions Phone: 336-758-5422 • Web Address: www.mba.wfu.edu
Public/Private: Public
Total Business Students: 90
% Full Time: 17

UNIVERSITY OF NORTH FLORIDA
College of Business Administration

Web Address: www.unf.edu
Public/Private: Public
Total Business Students: 388
% Full Time: 25

UNIVERSITY OF NORTH TEXAS
College of Business Administration

Address: PO Box 311160, Denton, TX 76203
Admissions Phone: 940-369-8977 • Web Address: www.coba.unt.edu
Public/Private: Public
Total Business Students: 412
Average GMAT: 560
% Full Time: 45

UNIVERSITY OF NORTHERN IOWA
College of Business Administration

Web Address: www.cba.uni.edu
Public/Private: Public
Total Business Students: 118
% Full Time: 37
Annual Tuition (Resident/Nonresident): $3,166/$7,805

UNIVERSITY OF NOTRE DAME
Mendoza College of Business

Address: 276 Mendoza College of Business, Notre Dame, IN 46556-4656
Admissions Phone: 219-631-8488 • Web Address: www.nd.edu/~mba
Public/Private: Private
Total Business Students: 332
Average GMAT: 659
% Full Time: 100
Annual Tuition: $24,969

UNIVERSITY OF OKLAHOMA
Michael F. Price College of Business

Web Address: www.ou.edu/mba/
Public/Private: Public
Total Business Students: 261
% Full Time: 50

UNIVERSITY OF OREGON
Charles H. Lundquist College of Business

Address: 300 Gilbert Hall, 1208, Eugene, OR 97403-1208
Admissions Phone: 541-346-1462 • Web Address: http://biz.uoregon.edu
Public/Private: Public
Total Business Students: 139
Average GMAT: 601
% Full Time: 100
Annual Tuition (Resident/Nonresident): $7,056/$11,958

UNIVERSITY OF OXFORD
Saïd Business School

Address: Park End Street, Oxford, OX1 1HP, United Kingdom
Admissions Phone: 0044-1865-288830 • Web Address: www.sbs.ox.ac.uk
Total Business Students: 120
Average GMAT: 671
Annual Tuition: $27,440

UNIVERSITY OF PENNSYLVANIA
The Wharton School Graduate Division

Address: 102 Vance Hall, 3733 Spruce Street, Philadelphia, PA 19104-6361
Admissions Phone: 215-898-6183
Web Address: www.wharton.upenn.edu/mba
Public/Private: Private
Total Business Students: 1,573
Average GMAT: 703
Annual Tuition: $28,970

UNIVERSITY OF PITTSBURGH
Katz Graduate School of Business

Address: 272 Mervis Hall, Roberto Clemente Drive, Pittsburgh, PA 15260
Admissions Phone: 412-648-1700 • Web Address: www.katz.pitt.edu
Public/Private: Public
Total Business Students: 633
Average GMAT: 621
% Full Time: 22
Annual Tuition (Resident/Nonresident): $19,707/$33,570

UNIVERSITY OF PORTLAND
Pamplin School of Business Administration

Address: 5000 N Willamette Blvd., Portland, OR 97203
Admissions Phone: 503-943-7147 • Web Address: www.up.edu
Public/Private: Private
Total Business Students: 94
% Full Time: 15

UNIVERSITY OF RHODE ISLAND
College of Business Administration

Address: 210 Flagg Road, Kinsgton, RI 02881
Admissions Phone: 401-874-5000
Web Address: www.cba.uri.edu/graduate/mba.htm
Public/Private: Public
Total Business Students: 220
Average GMAT: 620
% Full Time: 10
Annual Tuition (Resident/Nonresident): $7,800/$22,155

UNIVERSITY OF RICHMOND
The Robins School of Business

Address: Richard S. Reynolds Graduate School, Richmond, VA 23173
Admissions Phone: 804-289-8553 • Web Address: www.richmond.edu
Public/Private: Private
Total Business Students: 205
Average GMAT: 595
% Full Time: 0
Annual Tuition: $20,360

UNIVERSITY OF ROCHESTER
William E. Simon Graduate School of Business Administration

Address: 305 Schlegel Hall, Rochester, NY 14627
Admissions Phone: 585-275-3533 • Web Address: www.simon.rochester.edu
Public/Private: Private
Total Business Students: 703
Average GMAT: 640
% Full Time: 68
Annual Tuition: $28,320

UNIVERSITY OF SAN DIEGO
School of Business Administration

Address: 5998 Alcala Park, San Diego, CA 92110
Admissions Phone: 619-260-4524 • Web Address: business.sandiego.edu
Public/Private: Private
Total Business Students: 266
Average GMAT: 550
% Full Time: 47
Annual Tuition: $11,340

UNIVERSITY OF SAN FRANCISCO
School of Business and Management

Address: 2130 Fulton Street, San Francisco, CA 94117-1045
Admissions Phone: 415-422-4723 • Web Address: www.usfca.edu/sobam
Public/Private: Private
Total Business Students: 460
Average GMAT: 541
% Full Time: 63
Annual Tuition: $19,200

UNIVERSITY OF SCRANTON
Kania School of Management

Address: The Graduate School, University of Scranton, Scranton, PA 18510
Admissions Phone: 570-941-7600 • Web Address: www.scranton.edu
Public/Private: Private
Total Business Students: 114
Average GMAT: 517
% Full Time: 30
Annual Tuition: $12,936

UNIVERSITY OF SOUTH ALABAMA
College of Business and Management Studies

Web Address: bus.usouthal.edu
Public/Private: Public
Total Business Students: 147
% Full Time: 23

UNIVERSITY OF SOUTH CAROLINA
Darla Moore School of Business

Address: Darla Moore School of Business, Columbia, SC 29208
Admissions Phone: 803-777-4346 • Web Address: darlamoore.badm.sc.edu
Public/Private: Public
Total Business Students: 653
Average GMAT: 610
% Full Time: 62

UNIVERSITY OF SOUTH DAKOTA
School of Business

Address: 414 E. Clark, School of Business, Vermillion, SD 57069
Admissions Phone: 605-677-5232 • Web Address: www.usd.edu
Public/Private: Public
Total Business Students: 257
Average GMAT: 490
% Full Time: 47
Annual Tuition (Resident/Nonresident): $5,200/$11,000

UNIVERSITY OF SOUTH FLORIDA
College of Business Administration

Address: 4202 E. Fowler Ave. BSN 3403, Tampa, FL 33620
Admissions Phone: 813-974-8800 • Web Address: www.coba.usf.edu
Public/Private: Public
Total Business Students: 503
Average GMAT: 560
% Full Time: 34
Annual Tuition (Resident/Nonresident): $2,789/$9,606

UNIVERSITY OF SOUTHERN CALIFORNIA
Marshall School of Business

Address: Popovich Hall Room 308, Los Angeles, CA 90089-2633
Admissions Phone: 213-740-7846 • Web Address: www.marshall.usc.edu
Public/Private: Private
Total Business Students: 1,477
Average GMAT: 670
Annual Tuition: $28,677

UNIVERSITY OF SOUTHERN INDIANA
School of Business

Address: 8600 University Boulevard, Evansville, IN 47712
Admissions Phone: 812-465-7015 • Web Address: business.usi.edu
Public/Private: Public
Total Business Students: 113
Average GMAT: 545
% Full Time: 4

UNIVERSITY OF SOUTHERN MAINE
School of Business

Address: PO Box 9300, Portland, ME 04104
Admissions Phone: 207-780-4184 • Web Address: www.usm.maine.edu/sb
Public/Private: Public
Total Business Students: 121
Average GMAT: 566
% Full Time: 17
Annual Tuition (Resident/Nonresident): $4,620/$12,912

UNIVERSITY OF SOUTHERN MISSISSIPPI
College of Business Administration

Address: Box 5096, Hattiesburg, MS 39406-5096
Admissions Phone: 601-266-4677 • Web Address: www.usm.edu
Public/Private: Public
Total Business Students: 77
% Full Time: 87
Annual Tuition (Resident/Nonresident): $3,439/$6,500

UNIVERSITY OF SOUTHWESTERN LOUISIANA
College of Business Administration

Web Address: www.usl.edu
Total Business Students: 151
Annual Tuition (Resident/Nonresident): $1,100/$3,700

UNIVERSITY OF TAMPA
John H. Sykes College of Business

Address: 401 W. Kennedy Blvd., Tampa, FL 33606-1490
Admissions Phone: 813-258-7409 • Web Address: mba.ut.edu
Public/Private: Private
Total Business Students: 387
Average GMAT: 529
% Full Time: 37
Annual Tuition: $8,400

UNIVERSITY OF TENNESSEE AT CHATTANOOGA
College of Business

Address: Dept 5305, 114 Race Hall, 615 McCallie Avenue, Chattanooga, TN 37403
Admissions Phone: 423-755-4667 • Web Address: www.utc.edu
Public/Private: Public
Total Business Students: 316
Average GMAT: 495
% Full Time: 21
Annual Tuition (Resident/Nonresident): $1,876/$4,909

UNIVERSITY OF TENNESSEE AT KNOXVILLE
College of Business Administration

Address: 527 Stokely Management Center, Knoxville, TN 37996-0552
Admissions Phone: 423-974-5033 • Web Address: mba.bus.utk.edu
Public/Private: Public
Total Business Students: 195
Average GMAT: 625
% Full Time: 100

UNIVERSITY OF TENNESSEE AT MARTIN
School of Business Administration

Web Address: www.utm.edu/departments/soba/home.html
Public/Private: Public
Total Business Students: 200
Annual Tuition (Resident/Nonresident): $2,962/$4,826

UNIVERSITY OF TEXAS—ARLINGTON
College of Business Administration

Address: Box 19167, Arlington, TX 76019
Admissions Phone: 817-272-2688 • *Web Address:* www2.uta.edu/gradbiz
Public/Private: Public
Total Business Students: 536
Average GMAT: 542
% Full Time: 30
Annual Tuition (Resident/Nonresident): $2,400/$9,180

UNIVERSITY OF TEXAS—AUSTIN
McCombs School of Business

Address: MBA Program Office, CBA 2.316, Austin, TX 78712
Admissions Phone: 512-471-7612 • *Web Address:* texasmba.bus.utexas.edu
Public/Private: Public
Total Business Students: 783
Average GMAT: 680
% Full Time: 100
Annual Tuition (Resident/Nonresident): $3,600/$14,850

UNIVERSITY OF TEXAS—EL PASO
College of Business Administration

Address: Room 102, El Paso, TX 79968
Admissions Phone: 915-747-5174 • *Web Address:* www.utep.edu
Public/Private: Public
Total Business Students: 245
% Full Time: 24
Annual Tuition (Resident/Nonresident): $2,350/$7,294

UNIVERSITY OF TEXAS—PAN AMERICAN
College of Business Administration

Address: 1201 West University, Edinburg, TX 78539-2999
Admissions Phone: 956-381-3313
Web Address: www.coba.panam.edu/mba/index.htm
Public/Private: Public
Total Business Students: 127
Average GMAT: 420
% Full Time: 51
Annual Tuition (Resident/Nonresident): $1,570/$6,658

UNIVERSITY OF TEXAS—SAN ANTONIO
College of Business

Address: 6900 N. Loop 1604 West, San Antonio, TX 78249-0603
Admissions Phone: 210-458-4330 • *Web Address:* business.utsa.edu
Public/Private: Public
Total Business Students: 311
Average GMAT: 564
% Full Time: 36
Annual Tuition (Resident/Nonresident): $2,268/$6,066

UNIVERSITY OF TEXAS—TYLER
School of Business Administration

Address: 3900 University Boulevard, Tyler, TX 75799
Admissions Phone: 903-566-7433 • *Web Address:* www.uttyl.edu
Public/Private: Public
Total Business Students: 101
% Full Time: 2

UNIVERSITY OF THE PACIFIC
Eberhardt School of Business

Address: MBA Program, 3601 Pacific Avenue, Stockton, CA 95211
Admissions Phone: 800-952-3179 • *Web Address:* www.uop.edu/esb
Public/Private: Private
Total Business Students: 61
Average GMAT: 553
% Full Time: 52
Annual Tuition: $19,830

UNIVERSITY OF TOLEDO
College of Business Administration

Address: College of Business Administration, University of Toledo, Toledo, OH 43606
Admissions Phone: 419-530-2775
Web Address: www.business.utoledo.edu/degrees/mba
Public/Private: Public
Total Business Students: 313
Average GMAT: 517
% Full Time: 30
Annual Tuition (Resident/Nonresident): $6,335/$13,694

UNIVERSITY OF TORONTO
Joseph L. Rotman School of Management

Address: 105 St. George Street, Toronto, ON M5S 3E6, Canada
Admissions Phone: 416-978-3499 • *Web Address:* www.rotman.utoronto.ca
Public/Private: Public
Total Business Students: 264
Average GMAT: 674
% Full Time: 100
Annual Tuition (Resident/Nonresident): $41,000/$47,150

UNIVERSITY OF TULSA
College of Business Administration

Address: BAH 215, 600 S. College Avenue, Tulsa, OK 74104-3189
Admissions Phone: 918-631-2242 • *Web Address:* www.utulsa.edu
Public/Private: Private
Total Business Students: 203
Average GMAT: 520
% Full Time: 22
Annual Tuition: $0

UNIVERSITY OF UTAH
David Eccles School of Business

Address: 1645 East Campus Center Drive, Room 101,
Salt Lake City, UT 84112-9301
Admissions Phone: 801-581-7785
Web Address: www.business.utah.edu/masters
Public/Private: Public
Total Business Students: 370
Average GMAT: 600
% Full Time: 49
Annual Tuition (Resident/Nonresident): $4,300/$11,900

UNIVERSITY OF VERMONT
School of Business Administration

Address: 333 Waterman Building, Burlington, VT 05405
Admissions Phone: 802-656-2699
Web Address: www.bsad.emba.uvm.edu/mba
Public/Private: Public
Total Business Students: 76
% Full Time: 34

UNIVERSITY OF VIRGINIA
Darden Graduate School of Business Administration

Address: PO Box 6550, Charlottesville, VA 22906
Admissions Phone: 804-924-3220 • Web Address: www.darden.virginia.edu
Public/Private: Public
Total Business Students: 491
Average GMAT: 660
% Full Time: 100

UNIVERSITY OF WARWICK
Warwick Business School

Address: Warwick Business School, Coventry, CV4 7AL, United Kingdom
Admissions Phone: 011-44 (0)24 7652 4306
Web Address: www.wbs.warwick.ac.uk
Total Business Students: 2,500
Average GMAT: 600
% Full Time: 4
Annual Tuition: $34,650

UNIVERSITY OF WASHINGTON
Business School

Address: 110 Mackenzie Hall, Box 353200, Seattle, WA 98195-3200
Admissions Phone: 206-543-4661 • Web Address: www.mba.washington.edu
Public/Private: Public
Total Business Students: 417
Average GMAT: 657
% Full Time: 64
Annual Tuition (Resident/Nonresident): $5,859/$15,988

UNIVERSITY OF WEST FLORIDA
College of Business

Web Address: www.uwf.edu/~enserv\b.htm
Public/Private: Public
Total Business Students: 260
% Full Time: 22
Annual Tuition (Resident/Nonresident): $3,379/$11,491

UNIVERSITY OF WESTERN ONTARIO
Richard Ivey School of Business

Address: 1151 Richmond Street North, London, ON N6A 3K7, Canada
Admissions Phone: 519-661-3212 • Web Address: www.ivey.uwo.ca/mba
Total Business Students: 600
Average GMAT: 660
% Full Time: 100
Annual Tuition: $22,000

UNIVERSITY OF WISCONSIN—EAU CLAIRE
School of Business

Web Address: www.uwec.edu
Public/Private: Public
Total Business Students: 61
% Full Time: 3

UNIVERSITY OF WISCONSIN—LA CROSSE
College of Business Administration

Address: 1725 State Street, La Crosse, WI 54601
Admissions Phone: 608-785-8067 • Web Address: www.uwlax.edu
Public/Private: Public
Total Business Students: 81
Average GMAT: 520
% Full Time: 20
Annual Tuition (Resident/Nonresident): $5,000/$14,000

UNIVERSITY OF WISCONSIN—MADISON
Business School

Address: 2266 Grainger Hall, 975 University Avenue, Madison, WI 53706
Admissions Phone: 608-262-4000 • Web Address: www.wisc.edu/bschool
Public/Private: Public
Total Business Students: 489
Average GMAT: 612
% Full Time: 93
Annual Tuition (Resident/Nonresident): $5,950/$16,230

UNIVERSITY OF WISCONSIN—MILWAUKEE
School of Business Administration

Address: PO Box 742, Milwaukee, WI 53201-0742
Admissions Phone: 414-229-5403
Web Address: www.uwm.edu/dept/business/sba
Public/Private: Public
Total Business Students: 274
Average GMAT: 535
% Full Time: 16
Annual Tuition (Resident/Nonresident): $7,471/$20,839

UNIVERSITY OF WISCONSIN—OSHKOSH
College of Business Administration

Web Address: www.uwosh.edu/grad_school/mba
Public/Private: Public
Total Business Students: 525
% Full Time: 5
Annual Tuition (Resident/Nonresident): $3,800/$11,200

UNIVERSITY OF WISCONSIN—PARKSIDE
School of Business and Technology

Address: 900 Wood Road, Box 2000, Kenosha, WI 53141-2000
Admissions Phone: 262-595-2046
Web Address: www.uwp.edu/academic/business.technology
Public/Private: Public
Total Business Students: 93
Average GMAT: 500
% Full Time: 10
Annual Tuition (Resident/Nonresident): $4,540/$14,364

UNIVERSITY OF WISCONSIN—WHITEWATER
College of Business and Economics

Address: 800 West Main Street, Whitewater, WI 53190
Admissions Phone: 262-472-1945 • Web Address: www.uww.edu
Public/Private: Public
Total Business Students: 405
Average GMAT: 523
% Full Time: 21
Annual Tuition (Resident/Nonresident): $5,023/$14,871

UNIVERSITY OF WYOMING
College of Business

Address: PO Box 3275, Laramie, WY 82071
Admissions Phone: 307-766-2449
Web Address: www.business.uwyo.edu/grad/mba
Public/Private: Public
Total Business Students: 90
Average GMAT: 555
% Full Time: 49

UTAH STATE UNIVERSITY
College of Business

Address: 0900 Old Main Hill, Logan, UT 84322-0900
Admissions Phone: 435-797-1189
Web Address: www.usu.edu/mba/pages/main.html
Public/Private: Public
Total Business Students: 370
Average GMAT: 590
% Full Time: 39
Annual Tuition (Resident/Nonresident): $2,426/$7,438

VALDOSTA STATE UNIVERSITY
College of Business Administration

Address: 903 N. Patterson Street, Valdosta, GA 31698-0005
Admissions Phone: 229-333-5694
Web Address: www.valdosta.edu/coba/grad
Public/Private: Public
Total Business Students: 50
Average GMAT: 512
% Full Time: 0
Annual Tuition (Resident/Nonresident): $4,395/$13,095

VANDERBILT UNIVERSITY
Owen Graduate School of Management

Address: 401 21st Avenue South, Nashville, TN 37203
Admissions Phone: 615-322-6469 • Web Address: mba.vanderbilt.edu
Public/Private: Private
Total Business Students: 438
Average GMAT: 638
% Full Time: 100
Annual Tuition: $27,560

VILLANOVA UNIVERSITY
College of Commerce and Finance

Address: 800 Lancaster Avenue, Bartley Hall, Villanova, PA 19085
Admissions Phone: 610-519-4336 • Web Address: www.mba.villanova.edu
Public/Private: Private
Total Business Students: 585
Average GMAT: 582
% Full Time: 7
Annual Tuition: $15,000

VIRGINIA COMMONWEALTH UNIVERSITY
School of Business

Address: Box 844000 University Hill, Richmond, VA 23284-4000
Admissions Phone: 804-828-1741 • Web Address: www.vcu.edu/busweb/gsib
Public/Private: Public
Total Business Students: 289
% Full Time: 20

VIRGINIA POLYTECHNIC INSTITUTE AND STATE UNIVERSITY
Pamplin College of Business

Address: 1044 Pamplin Hall, Virginia Tech, Blacksburg, VA 24061
Admissions Phone: 540-231-6152 • Web Address: www.mba.vt.edu
Public/Private: Public
Total Business Students: 393
Average GMAT: 630
% Full Time: 37
Annual Tuition: $2,174

WAKE FOREST UNIVERSITY
Babcock Graduate School of Management

Address: PO Box 7659, Winston-Salem, NC 27109
Admissions Phone: 336-758-5422 • Web Address: www.mba.wfu.edu
Public/Private: Private
Total Business Students: 660
Average GMAT: 643
% Full Time: 35
Annual Tuition: $23,000

WASHINGTON STATE UNIVERSITY
College of Business and Economics

Address: PO Box 644744, Pullman, WA 99164-4744
Admissions Phone: 509-335-7617 • Web Address: www.cbe.wsu.edu/graduate
Public/Private: Public
Total Business Students: 119
% Full Time: 93

WASHINGTON UNIVERSITY
John M. Olin School of Business

Address: Campus Box 1133, One Brookings Drive, St. Louis, MO 63130
Admissions Phone: 314-935-7301 • Web Address: www.olin.wustl.edu
Public/Private: Private
Total Business Students: 664
Average GMAT: 660
% Full Time: 45
Annual Tuition: $28,300

WAYNE STATE UNIVERSITY
School of Business Administration

Address: Office of Student Services, 5201 Cass, Room 200, Detroit, MI 48202
Admissions Phone: 313-577-4505 • Web Address: www.busadm.wayne.edu
Public/Private: Public
Total Business Students: 1,677
Average GMAT: 515
% Full Time: 10
Annual Tuition (Resident/Nonresident): $4,410/$8,520

WEBER STATE UNIVERSITY
John B. Goddard School of Business and Economics

Address: 3806 University Circle, Ogden, UT 84408-3806
Admissions Phone: 801-626-7545 • Web Address: goddard.weber.edu/dp/mba
Public/Private: Public
Total Business Students: 75
Average GMAT: 571
Annual Tuition (Resident/Nonresident): $6,000/$13,000

WEST VIRGINIA UNIVERSITY
College of Business and Economics

Address: PO Box 6025, Morgantown, WV 26506-6025
Admissions Phone: 304-293-5408 • Web Address: www.be.wvu.edu
Public/Private: Public
Total Business Students: 187
Average GMAT: 560
% Full Time: 28
Annual Tuition (Resident/Nonresident): $11,300/$30,800

WESTERN CAROLINA UNIVERSITY
College of Business

Address: 112 Forsyth Building, Cullowhee, NC 28723
Admissions Phone: 828-227-7402
Web Address: www.wcu.edu/cob/gradprograms.html
Public/Private: Public
Total Business Students: 126
Average GMAT: 509
% Full Time: 38
Annual Tuition (Resident/Nonresident): $1,072/$8,704

WESTERN ILLINOIS UNIVERSITY
College of Business and Technology

Web Address: www.wiu.edu
Public/Private: Public
Total Business Students: 132
% Full Time: 63
Annual Tuition (Resident): $1,152

WESTERN MICHIGAN UNIVERSITY
Haworth College of Business

Web Address: www.hcob.wmich.edu
Public/Private: Public
% Full Time: 100

WESTERN WASHINGTON UNIVERSITY
College of Business and Economics

Address: 516 High St., Parks Hall 419, Bellingham, WA 98225-9072
Admissions Phone: 360-650-3898 • Web Address: www.cbe.wwu.edu/mba
Public/Private: Public
Total Business Students: 53
Average GMAT: 533
% Full Time: 79
Annual Tuition (Resident/Nonresident): $5,114/$15,035

WICHITA STATE UNIVERSITY
Barton School of Business

Address: 1845 N. Fairmount, Wichita, KS 67260-0048
Admissions Phone: 316-978-3230 • Web Address: business.twsu.edu
Public/Private: Public
Total Business Students: 222
Average GMAT: 520
Annual Tuition (Resident/Nonresident): $3,095/$8,856

WIDENER UNIVERSITY
School of Business Administration

Address: 1 University Place, Chester, PA 19013
Admissions Phone: 610-499-4305 • Web Address: www.sba.widener.edu
Public/Private: Private
Total Business Students: 318
Average GMAT: 500
Annual Tuition: $12,800

WILLAMETTE UNIVERSITY
Atkinson Graduate School of Management

Address: 900 State Street, Salem, OR 97301
Admissions Phone: 503-370-6167 • Web Address: www.willamette.edu/agsm
Public/Private: Private
Total Business Students: 168
Average GMAT: 564
% Full Time: 90
Annual Tuition: $17,150

WINTHROP UNIVERSITY
College of Business Administration

Web Address: http://cba.winthrop.edu
Public/Private: Public
Total Business Students: 250
% Full Time: 40
Annual Tuition (Resident/Nonresident): $1,964/$3,530

XAVIER UNIVERSITY
Williams College of Business

Address: 3800 Victory Parkway, Cincinnati, OH 45207
Admissions Phone: 513-745-3525 • Web Address: www.xavier.edu/mba
Public/Private: Private
Total Business Students: 997
Average GMAT: 550
% Full Time: 19
Annual Tuition: $7,830

YALE UNIVERSITY
Yale School of Management

Address: 135 Prospect Street, PO Box 208200, New Haven, CT 06520-8200
Admissions Phone: 203-432-5932 • Web Address: www.mba.yale.edu
Public/Private: Private
Total Business Students: 440
Average GMAT: 686
Annual Tuition: $31,500

Part IV

THE SCHOOLS

AMERICAN UNIVERSITY
Kogod School of Business

Admissions Contact: Sondra Smith, Director of Graduate Admissions and Financial Aid
Address: 4400 Massachusetts Avenue NW, Washington, DC 20016
Admissions Phone: 202-885-1913 • Admissions Fax: 202-885-1078
Admissions E-mail: mbakogod@american.edu • Web Address: www.kogod.american.edu

Like many MBA programs, American University boasts an emphasis on the hot topics in today's MBA market: global business and information technology. But with its prime Washington, D.C., location and proximity to tech powerhouses in Virginia and Maryland such as AOL, American is well positioned to deliver that promise. Come ready for cultural interaction and leadership opportunities galore; in an unusual democratic twist, American expects its students to contribute to the running of the program. More than 40 percent of the student body is international.

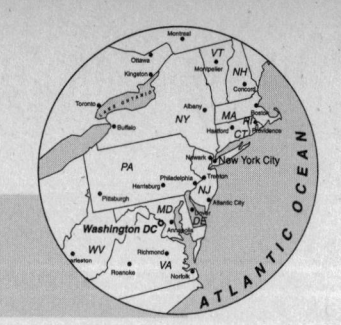

INSTITUTIONAL INFORMATION
Public/Private: Private
Evening Classes Available? Yes
Total Faculty: 78
% Faculty Part Time: 27
Student/Faculty Ratio: 6:1
Academic Calendar: Semester

PROGRAMS
Degrees Offered: MBA with concentrations in Accounting, Developmental Economics, Entrepreneurship, Finance, Human Resources, International Business, Management, Management Information Systems, Marketing, Real Estate, International Finance, and International Marketing (full time or part time, 41 to 54 credits, minimum of 18 months); Master of Science in Accounting (MS) (full time or part time, 60 credits, 12 months to 2 years); Master of Science in Taxation (MS) (full time or part time, 30 credits, 12 months to 2 years); Master of Science in Finance (MS) (full time or part time, 30 credits, 12 months to 2 years)

STUDENT INFORMATION
Total Business Students: 506
% Female: 46
% Minority: 17

COMPUTER AND RESEARCH FACILITIES
Campuswide Network? Yes
Internet Fee? No

EXPENSES/FINANCIAL AID
Annual Tuition: $19,080
Room & Board (On/Off Campus): $9,000/$12,000

ADMISSIONS INFORMATION
Application Fee: $50
Electronic Application? Yes
Regular Application Deadline: Rolling
Regular Notification: Rolling
Deferment Available? Yes
Length of Deferment: 1 year
Non-fall Admissions? Yes
Non-fall Application Deadline(s): Rolling; for international students, 6/1 fall and 10/1 spring

Transfer Students Accepted? Yes
Transfer Policy: They must meet the same requirements as a nontransfer student; 9 credits may be transferred into the program.
Need-Blind Admissions? No
Number of Applications Received: 581
% of Applicants Accepted: 76
% Accepted Who Enrolled: 32
Average GPA: 3.2
Average GMAT: 560
Other Admissions Factors Considered: A résumé, work experience, and computer experience are all recommended for application.

INTERNATIONAL STUDENTS
TOEFL Required of International Students? Yes
Minimum TOEFL: 550 (213 computer)

EMPLOYMENT INFORMATION
Placement Office Available? Yes
% Employed Within 3 Months: 82

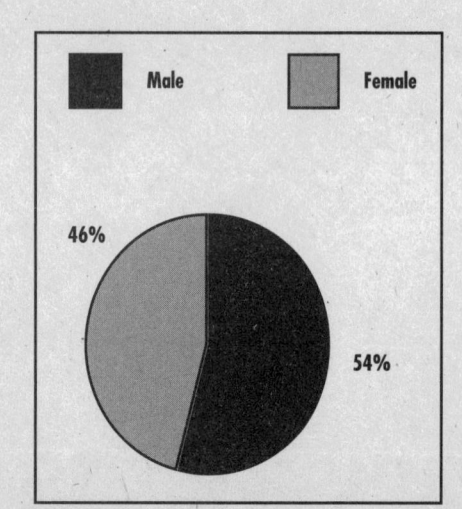

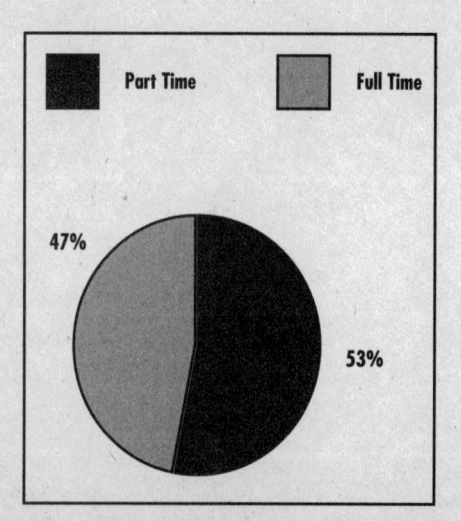

APPALACHIAN STATE UNIVERSITY
Walker College of Business

Admissions Contact: T. Joseph Watts, Director
Address: ASU Box 32004, Boone, NC 28608
Admissions Phone: 828-262-2120 • Admissions Fax: 828-262-3296
Admissions E-mail: admissions@appstate.edu • Web Address: www.business.appstate.edu

With an enrollment of less than 50 students, the MBA program at Walker College of Business offers a more intimate education, especially for the prospective female students, who account for approximately half of the student body. Students are required to attend an "enrichment experience," an orientation that includes workshops, a "team-building outdoor experience," and plenty of downtime for social acclimation. Walker expects that its high-quality instruction will yield graduates that are competent in areas across the board, emphasizing information technology, global economy, communication, professional development, and ethical responsibility. The Distinguished CEO Lecture Series gives students a chance to learn from and engage with future employers, as a majority of Walker's graduates gain employment with North Carolina corporations.

INSTITUTIONAL INFORMATION
Public/Private: Public
Evening Classes Available? No
Total Faculty: 48
% Faculty Female: 16
Student/Faculty Ratio: 35:1
Students in Parent Institution: 12,500
Academic Calendar: Semester

PROGRAMS
Degrees Offered: Master of Business Administration (MBA) (full time or part time, 39 credits, 12 to 18 months); Master of Science in Accounting (MS) (full time or part time, 30 credits, 12 months to 2 years); concentrations in accounting and taxation; Master of Arts in Industrial Organizational Psychology and Human Resources (MA) (full time or part time, 30 credits, 12 months to 2 years)
Academic Specialties: Case study, computer-aided instruction, computer analysis, computer simulations, field projects, group discussion, lecture, role playing, seminars by members of the business community, student presentations, team projects

STUDENT INFORMATION
Total Business Students: 39
% Full Time: 90
% Female: 46
% Minority: 1

COMPUTER AND RESEARCH FACILITIES
Computer Facilities: Carol Gotnes Belk Library plus 2 on-campus libraries, access to online bibliographic retrieval services
Campuswide Network? Yes
% of MBA Classrooms Wired: 100
Computer Model Recommended: Laptop
Internet Fee? No

EXPENSES/FINANCIAL AID
Annual Tuition (Resident/Nonresident): $1,285/$8,400
Books and Supplies: $1,000

ADMISSIONS INFORMATION
Application Fee: $35
Electronic Application? No
Regular Application Deadline: 4/15
Regular Notification: Rolling
Deferment Available? Yes
Length of Deferment: 1 year
Non-fall Admissions? No
Transfer Students Accepted? Yes
Transfer Policy: Six credit hours can be transferred.

Need-Blind Admissions? No
Number of Applications Received: 54
% of Applicants Accepted: 78
% Accepted Who Enrolled: 81
Average GPA: 3.0
GPA Range: 2.7-3.8
Average GMAT: 502
GMAT Range: 310-756
Average Years Experience: 3
Other Admissions Factors Considered: Minimum GMAT 450; interview, résumé, work experience, and computer experience recommended
Other Schools to Which Students Applied: University of North Carolina-Greensboro

INTERNATIONAL STUDENTS
TOEFL Required of International Students? Yes
Minimum TOEFL: 550

EMPLOYMENT INFORMATION
Placement Office Available? Yes
% Employed Within 3 Months: 99

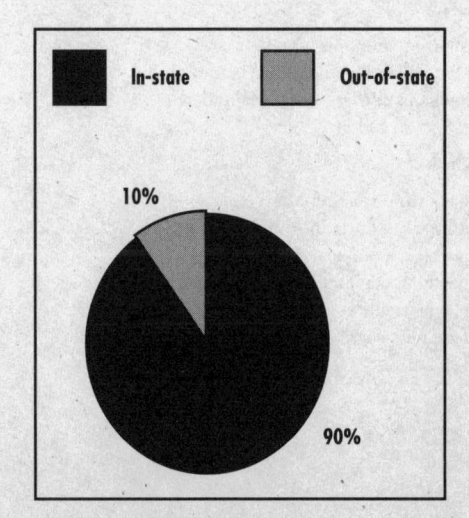

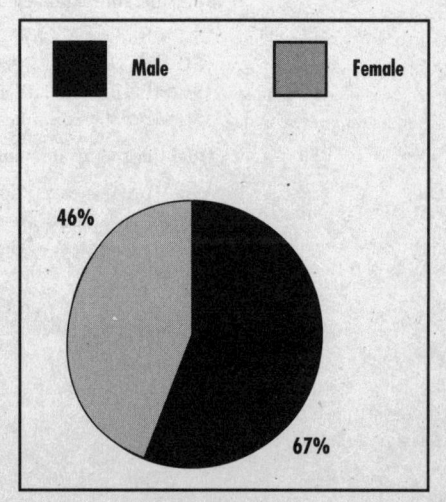

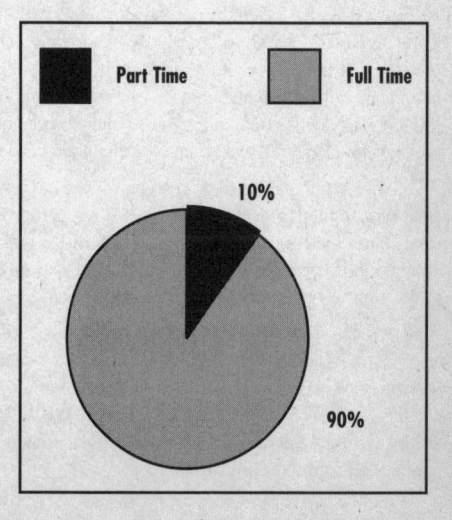

In-state 90% / Out-of-state 10%

Male 67% / Female 46%

Part Time 10% / Full Time 90%

ARIZONA STATE UNIVERSITY

THE UNIVERSITY AT A GLANCE

Today's managers face an increasingly global landscape that is continuously transformed by technology. This dynamic environment presents opportunity, but also challenge, as managers grapple with the demands of efficiency, quality, and profit. The ASU MBA prepares you for this exciting world by grounding you with business essentials and developing immediately useable specialized knowledge based on your career goals.

The intensive first year of the ASU MBA is an integrated academic experience that builds advanced managerial knowledge and skills, essential for your career. The second year specializations, with their elective options, fill the immediate need for value-added knowledge and skills that you can offer an employer in a new position immediately upon graduation. The ASU MBA emphasizes experiential, applied knowledge and best practices from a faculty with a wealth of cumulative experience, scholarship, and expertise. In the technology-rich ASU MBA environment you will learn to make decisions and evaluate tools and systems. This is a global business environment, and the ASU MBA faculty is comprised of internationally respected teachers and scholars who stand ready to share their expertise and experience.

Alumni tell us year after year that the ASU MBA prepared them well; upon graduation they were able to add value to their employers immediately; yet the ASU MBA has continued to support them in their career advancement years later. I am proud to introduce you to this vibrant academic institution closely linked to a fast-growing population center in the high-tech U.S. West. I invite you to visit us at our beautiful, semi-tropical campus in the Sonoran Desert and learn how you can become an ASU MBA.

STUDENTS

In the first-year ASU MBA prepares students with advanced managerial and leadership skills as well as knowledge of the functional areas of business. The core curriculum delves into management of technology, operational and logistical supply chain management, marketing, e-business issues, global economics, financial decision-making, product and project management, organizational strategy, and legal, ethical and political components of business decisions.

ASU MBA students put their new knowledge into practice through case competitions, applied projects, and business presentations. ASU MBA full-time students participate in two major case competitions each year. One is held in November and is open to both first- and second-year ASU MBAs; the other is held in May and is open only to first-year ASU MBAs.

Students are automatically members of the ASU MBA Association. They may participate in community service through the Collegiate Volunteer Council or join the Graduate Women in Business organization, Graduate Latin Business Exchange, Black Student MBA Association, ASU MBAsia, or the Master's Consulting Group. Other important aspects of the program include working on field projects and summer internships.

Ninety-six percent of the ASU MBA graduating class is employed within three months after graduation. The ASU MBA and Graduate Business Career Management Center partner with the ASU MBA students and alumni in personal career development at the executive level. The Career Management Center and ASU Career Services partner with well over 100 companies that schedule on-campus interviews annually. Resources offered by the Career Management Center to help students compete successfully in the employment marketplace include individual career consulting, seminars, and opportunities to network with local business professionals. In 2000, ASU MBA graduates' average salary was $73,000.

Distinguished alumni include:

Craig Weatherup, CEO, PepsiCo
Tom Evans, chairman and CEO, Official Payments Corp.
Steve Marriott, vice president of corporate marketing, Marriott Hotels
Scott Wald, president, Romar Services, LLC
Wayne Doran, chairman of the board, Ford Motor Company
Linda Brock-Nelson, president-manager, LBN & Associates, LLC
Jack Furst, managing director/partner, Hicks, Muse, Tate & Furst, Inc.

ACADEMICS

ASU MBA is an enriching educational experience, providing lifelong value. The program builds and strengthens a student's knowledge, skills, and managerial abilities by means of technical, analytical, and case materials that inform about the functional areas of business.

During the first year, students acquire fundamental business management knowledge and skills through a core curriculum that stresses collaboration and teamwork, analysis, ethical decision-making, and written and oral communication. In the second year, students prepare for careers in service marketing and management, supply chain management, financial management and markets, and sports business or dual degrees in Master of Accountancy, Taxation, Information Management, Health Services Administration, and Economics. An MIM with Thunderbird (AGSIM) may also be completed in the second year. Other master's programs may be considered for concurrent degrees (e.g., MS in Engineering).

Dual degrees that take more than two years are the Arizona State University MBA/Juris Doctorate and MBA/MS in Architecture. Application must be made separately to each program for acceptance. The ASU MBA Evening, High Technology, and Executives programs and the PhD degree in Business Administration and in Economics are also available.

ASU MBA full-time students focus on one area of specialization or dual degree that they may tailor with electives to fit individual career aspirations.

Specialization choices include:

ASU MBA/Supply Chain Management Specialization
ASU MBA/Services Marketing & Management Specialization
ASU MBA/Financial Management & Markets Specialization
ASU MBA/Sports Business Specialization

Dual degree options include:

ASU MBA/Master of Science in Information Management
ASU MBA/Master of Health Services Administration
ASU MBA/Master of Science in Economics
ASU MBA/Master of Science in Accountancy
ASU MBA/Master of Science in Taxation
ASU offers additional dual degree programs.

College of Business—MBA Program

The internationally renowned ASU MBA faculty come from four continents and remain continuously in touch with other scholars around the world. ASU MBA faculty are in the top ranks for research productivity as measured by the premier academic journals. For example, an international listing of 50,000 publishing economists places two ASU MBA professors among the top 100. The School of Accountancy and Information Management has one of the largest faculties in the United States. Full-time faculty members teach all courses.

Faculty travel the globe to present research in leading conferences. These scholars also develop new knowledge through research, consulting, and other interactions with major corporations. They bring these experiences into the classroom, creating timely cases and generating lively discussions. Their efforts have helped earn ASU the highest research designation awarded by the Carnegie Foundation's Classification of Institutions of Higher Education.

Students may combine their ASU MBA with specialized training in international management during their second year of study. ASU has developed several partnerships with outstanding institutions abroad:

- ESC Toulouse—Toulouse, France
- Universidad Carlos III de Madrid—Madrid, Spain
- Instituto Technologico Y De Estudios Superiores De Monterrey-Campus Estado de Mexico (ITESM-CEM)—Mexico City, Mexico
- Escuela de Administracion de Negocios Para Graduados—Lima, Peru

CAMPUS LIFE

Arizona State University is a leading metropolitan research institution, creating cutting-edge knowledge in areas such as cancer research, astrobiology, bioengineering, urban ecology, nanoelectronics, and business, and translating this knowledge in meaningful ways for the community. With nearly 50,000 students from all states and more than 120 countries, ASU is a diverse scholarly and cultural environment, and a center for cultural and social activities.

The College of Business has been accredited for more than 30 years by AACSB International—The Association to Advance Collegiate Schools of Business. It offers highly ranked undergraduate degrees, doctoral degrees, and professional masters's degrees, including the internationally respected ASU MBA.

The College of Business is a longstanding leader in developing technological facilities at an institution known for its technology. The ASU business campus is equipped with Cisco wireless access points (WAP) throughout its two buildings including the external patio and fountain areas. Citrix Thin Client servers allow students to utilize complex software programs wirelessly as well as remotely from home or office. Additionally, a $6.9 million renovation project completed in 2001 included a new computer lab outfitted with 113 IBM 1.7/2.2 GHz personal computers and six fully mediated presentation rooms for the master's program in the Ford Graduate Suite.

ASU has one of the largest and most comprehensive computing facilities of all U.S. universities. The Computing Commons provides access to MacIntosh and IMB PCs. A variety of Internet software packages provide students with access to e-mail and Internet newsgroups and resources.

The University's Charles Trumbull Hayden Library is one of the largest research libraries in North America. It contains more than 2.9 million volumes, including many in business and economics, and the specialized Arthur C. Young Tax Collection.

The College of Business is housed in two adjacent buildings that contain an auditorium; lecture halls; seminar rooms; faculty, administrative, and graduate offices; and several computer resource centers. The ASU MBA Program Suite includes the ASU MBA Student Center, the Project Room, conference rooms, student organization offices, and classrooms. A media services center is also located in the College. The College is home to the L. William Seidman Research Institute, whose affiliated centers and programs conduct specialized research on business topics such as entrepreneurship, economics, finance, ethics, and quality.

ASU has one of the largest and most comprehensive computing facilities of all U.S. universities. The Computing Commons provides access to Macintosh and IBM PCs. All printers are laser printers. A variety of Internet software packages provide students with access to e-mail and Internet news groups and opportunities to browse the Internet. There are numerous other computer sites on campus, including a fully equipped project room in the Ford Graduate Suite of the College of Business. Wireless capability is now operational at the College.

COSTS

Estimated tuition and fees for 2002–2003 are $11,585 for Arizona residents and $20,105 for nonresidents. Books and supplies average $1,500 per year. Most ASU MBA students live off campus in nearby apartment complexes and married couples find suitable housing in the local community. Average rents for apartments range from $550 to $800 (one to two bedrooms) per month. On-campus residential facilities are available on a limited basis for graduate students.

The ASU MBA is fortunate to have a well-endowed array of financial resources such as grants, fellowships, scholarships, assistantships, and out-of-state tuitions waivers available to students based on various criteria including need and merit. Approximately 95 percent of last year's entering class received at least one scholarship award. The PepsiCo Scholarship is a "full-ride" award.

ADMISSIONS

ASU MBA has implemented a fully online application. For information or to begin your application, go to www.cob.asu.edu/mba. Application submission target dates are January 1, February 1 (for non-U.S. citizens), and April 30. However applications will be accepted until all seats are filled. Admission is for the fall term only.

Application to the ASU MBA Program is open to individuals with at least two years of work experience who hold a bachelor's degree or its equivalent in any discipline from an accredited college or university. During evaluation of candidates, the Admissions Committee looks for well-rounded individuals with leadership skills, strong academic credentials, managerial experience or potential, and the ability to contribute to the diversity of the class. Transcripts, GMAT scores, TOEFL scores (for international students), work history, a personal statement, and letters of recommendation all influence the decision. The entering class of fall 2001 had an average GPA of 3.3 on a 4.0 scale, an average GMAT score of 645, an average TOEFL score of 630 (paper-based)/270 (computer-based), and average post-baccalaureate work experience of five years. Due to the high volume of applications and the limited size of the entering class, students are strongly encouraged to apply as early as possible.

Admissions Contact: Judith K. Heilala, Director of Recruiting and Admissions
Address: MBA Program Office, Main Campus, PO Box 874906, Tempe, AZ 85287-4906
Admissions Phone: 480-965-3332 • Admissions Fax: 480-965-8569
Admissions E-mail: asu.mba@asu.edu • Web Address: www.cob.asu.edu/mba

Arizona State University
College of Business—MBA Program

Admissions Contact: Judith Heilala, Director of Recruiting and Admissions
Address: PO Box 874906, Tempe, AZ 85287-4906
Admissions Phone: 480-965-3332 • *Admissions Fax:* 480-965-8569
Admissions E-mail: asu.mba@asu.edu • *Web Address:* www.cob.asu.edu/mba

The "very quick" trimester academic calendar at affordable Arizona State University makes the MBA program a bit hectic, but "an enormous number of companies recruit here"—especially from the Southwest—and students leave "well equipped to work with top-level executives as well as loading dock or field representatives." Also, "living in Phoenix is great," and Computerworld recently ranked ASU's joint degree program in information management 15th in the nation.

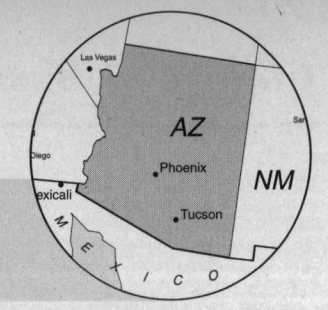

INSTITUTIONAL INFORMATION
Public/Private: Public
Evening Classes Available? Yes
Total Faculty: 84
% Faculty Female: 15
% Faculty Minority: 11
Student/Faculty Ratio: 25:1
Students in Parent Institution: 47,325
Academic Calendar: Trimester

PROGRAMS
Degrees Offered: MBA, MS in Accounting, MS in Taxation, MS in International Management, MS in Economics, PhD in Economics, PhD in Business
Joint Degrees: MB/Master of Economics, MBA/Master of International Management, MBA/Master of Accountancy, MBA/MS in International Management, MBA/Master of Taxation, MBA/Master of Health Services Administration, MBA/Juris Doctor, MBA/Master of Architecture
Academic Specialties: Services Marketing and Management, Supply Chain Management, Information Management, Financial Management and Markets, Health Administration, and Sports Business
Study Abroad Options: Groups Esc Toulouse-Toulouse, France; Instituto Technologico y De Estudios Superiores De Monterrey (ITESM), Mexico City, Mexico; Escuela de Administracion de Negocios (ESAN), Lima, Peru; Universidad Carlos III-Madrid, Spain

STUDENT INFORMATION
Total Business Students: 477
% Full Time: 43
% Female: 29
% Minority: 12
% Out of State: 56
% International: 33
Average Age: 29

COMPUTER AND RESEARCH FACILITIES
Research Facilities: ASU Research Park, Center for Business Research, Center for Services Marketing and Management, Bank One Economic Outlook Center, Arizona Real Estate Center, L. William Seidman Research Institute, Center for Advanced Purchasing Studies, ASU Manufacturing Institute
Computer Facilities: Effective fall 2001, wireless capability will be fully operational at the College of Business. The MBA Program Suite has 2 MBA Labs, an MBA Project Room, and a lounge available only to MBA students. The College of Business and the Computing Commons have additional computer labs, bringing the total number of available computers to 733, which is approximately 1 computer per MBA student.
Campuswide Network? Yes
% of MBA Classrooms Wired: 100
Computer Model Recommended: Laptop
Internet Fee? No

EXPENSES/FINANCIAL AID
Annual Tuition (Resident/Nonresident): $9,344/$17,800
Room & Board (Off Campus): $6,950
Books and Supplies: $2,500
Average Grant: $6,750
Average Loan: $15,000

ADMISSIONS INFORMATION
Application Fee: $45
Electronic Application? Yes
Early Decision Application Deadline: 12/15
Regular Application Deadline: 5/1
Regular Notification: Rolling
Length of Deferment: 1 year
Non-fall Admissions? No
Transfer Students Accepted? No
Need-Blind Admissions? Yes
Number of Applications Received: 1,059
% of Applicants Accepted: 41
% Accepted Who Enrolled: 49
Average GPA: 3.4
GPA Range: 3.2-3.7
Average GMAT: 644
Average Years Experience: 4
Other Admissions Factors Considered: Applicant's ability for placement, desire for offered specializations, ability to fit with the program
Minority/Disadvantaged Student Recruitment Programs: PepsiCo scholarships, graduate tuition scholarships, graduate academic scholarships, graduate assistantships, graduate fellowships

INTERNATIONAL STUDENTS
TOEFL Required of International Students? Yes
Minimum TOEFL: 580 (237 computer)

EMPLOYMENT INFORMATION

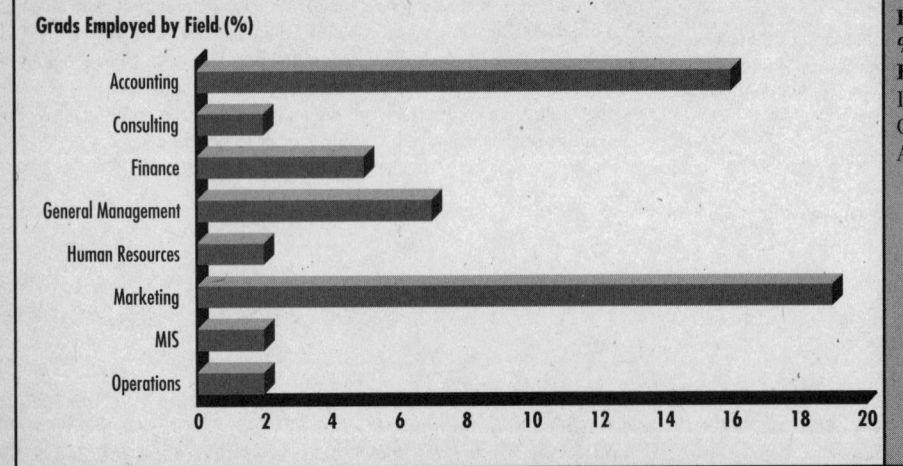

Grads Employed by Field (%)
- Accounting: ~16
- Consulting: ~2
- Finance: ~3
- General Management: ~7
- Human Resources: ~1
- Marketing: ~19
- MIS: ~2
- Operations: ~2

Placement Office Available? Yes
% Employed Within 3 Months: 96
Frequent Employers: IBM, Hewlett-Packard, Intel, Honeywell, Motorola, Apple Computers, Cisco Systems, Ford Motor Co., America West Airlines, Integrated Information Systems

Arizona State University West
School of Management

Admissions Contact: MBA Admissions
Address: PO Box 37100, Phoenix, AZ 85069-7100
Admissions Phone: 602-543-6201 • Admissions Fax: 602-543-6249
Admissions E-mail: mba@asu.edu • Web Address: www.west.asu.edu/som/mba

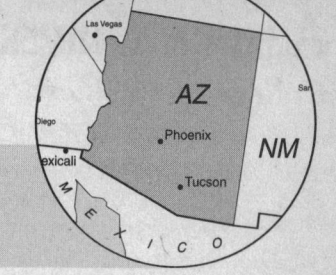

ASU West is a part-time, flexible MBA program designed specifically for working professionals. As expected, the average age of the student body, at 33, is considerably higher than that of the traditional, full-time MBA student, and admission emphasis is on the applicant's work experience. Through its new connectMBA program, ASU West offers an innovative, technology-based, weekend-only MBA program. Joint degrees with nearby Thunderbird lend an international flavor to the classroom.

INSTITUTIONAL INFORMATION
Public/Private: Public
Evening Classes Available? Yes
Total Faculty: 25
% Faculty Female: 28
% Faculty Minority: 12
% Faculty Part Time: 2
Student/Faculty Ratio: 20:1
Academic Calendar: Semester

PROGRAMS
Degrees Offered: MBA with 3 delivery options: scottsdaleMBA (27 months), connectMBA (24 months), pmMBA (2.5 to 6 years)
Joint Degrees: MBA/MIM (jointly offered with Thunderbird, 3 years)
Academic Specialties: We are fully AACSB-accredited and so our faculty are research-qualified in their fields. Our curriculum provides a general business education rather than a specialty-focused one.

STUDENT INFORMATION
Total Business Students: 445
Average Age: 34

COMPUTER AND RESEARCH FACILITIES
Research Facilities: The ASU West library has nearly 300,000 books, 3,400 journal subscriptions, and about 1.5 million microforms available locally. In addition, we are linked to the library on the main campus so that students have the full range of library support as do full-time students on the main campus.
Computer Facilities: ASU West has a state-of-the-art computing center with networked computers, laser printers, scanners, and other high-quality peripherals available free of charge to students. We are linked to the main campus so that students have the full range of computer/technology support as do full-time students on the main campus.
Campuswide Network? Yes
% of MBA Classrooms Wired: 100
Computer Model Recommended: No
Internet Fee? No

EXPENSES/FINANCIAL AID
Tuition Per Credit (Resident/Nonresident): $126/$428
% Receiving Financial Aid: 20
% Receiving Aid Their First Year: 5

ADMISSIONS INFORMATION
Application Fee: $45
Electronic Application? No
Early Decision Application Deadline: 1/1
Early Decision Notification: 1/1
Regular Application Deadline: 6/1
Regular Notification: 7/1
Deferment Available? Yes
Length of Deferment: 1 year
Non-fall Admissions? Yes
Non-fall Application Deadline(s): 11/1, 4/1
Transfer Students Accepted? Yes
Transfer Policy: 9 credit hours of transfer credit from AACSB-accredited programs
Need-Blind Admissions? Yes
Number of Applications Received: 169
% of Applicants Accepted: 77
% Accepted Who Enrolled: 75
Average GPA: 3.5
GPA Range: 2.6-3.7
Average GMAT: 580
GMAT Range: 500-700
Average Years Experience: 8
Other Schools to Which Students Applied: Arizona State University

INTERNATIONAL STUDENTS
TOEFL Required of International Students? Yes
Minimum TOEFL: 600 (250 computer)

EMPLOYMENT INFORMATION
Placement Office Available? No
% Employed Within 3 Months: 100

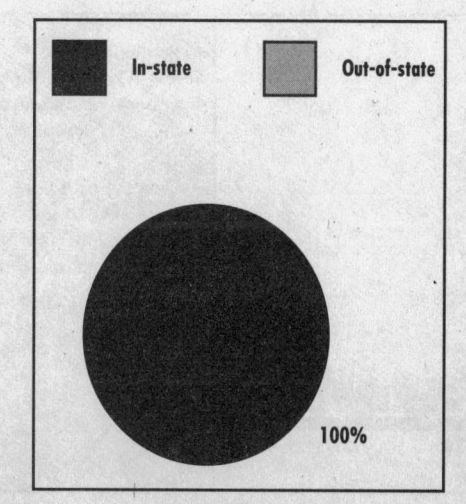

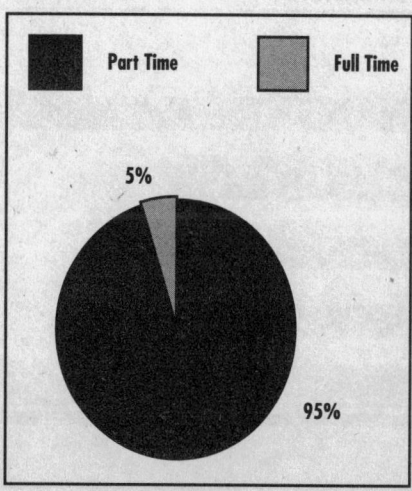

AUBURN UNIVERSITY
College of Business

Admissions Contact: MBA Director of Admissions
Address: 503 Lowder Business Building, Auburn University, AL 36849
Admissions Phone: 334-844-4060 • Admissions Fax: 334-844-2964
Admissions E-mail: mbainfo@auburn.edu • Web Address: www.mba.business.auburn.edu

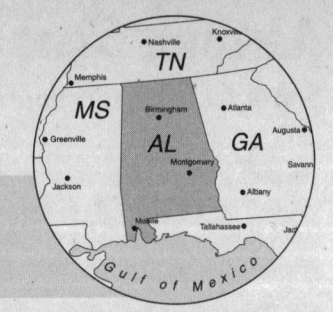

Auburn is one of the better MBA values around. At less than one-tenth the price of other MBA programs, Auburn offers a flexible calendar (students can enter at four times during the year), a distance learning option (MBA via the Internet), and a curriculum that emphasizes teamwork and the fundamentals. A challenging team capstone project is required to get the degree.

INSTITUTIONAL INFORMATION
Public/Private: Public
Evening Classes Available? No
Total Faculty: 8
% Faculty Female: 11
% Faculty Minority: 2
% Faculty Part Time: 2
Student/Faculty Ratio: 35:1
Students in Parent Institution: 21,860
Academic Calendar: Semester

PROGRAMS
Degrees Offered: MBA (36 to 42 semester hours, 16 months to 2 years) with available concentrations in Agribusiness, Aviation Management, Economic Development, Finance, Health Care Administration, Human Resource Development, Management Information Systems, Management of Technology, Marketing, Production/Operations Management, and Sports Management; Executive MBA Program (22 months); Physicians Executive MBA Program (22 months); Techno Executive MBA Program (22 months)
Joint Degrees: Dual-degree program with Industrial and Systems Engineering
Academic Specialties: Business Strategy, Information Systems, Operations Management
Special Opportunities: Internship program for domestic as well as international placements
Study Abroad Options: No formal study-abroad exchange programs are available. However, study-abroad programs are generally accommodated and approved on an individual student basis in Czech Republic, Germany, Hungary, Japan, UK, and France.

STUDENT INFORMATION
Total Business Students: 500
% Female: 22
% Minority: 6
% International: 7
Average Age: 24

COMPUTER AND RESEARCH FACILITIES
Research Facilities: Dedicated MBA computer lab and study room accessible 24 hours a day, 7 days a week
Computer Facilities: Access to online bibliographic retrieval services and online databases
Campuswide Network? Yes
% of MBA Classrooms Wired: 50
Computer Model Recommended: No
Internet Fee? No

EXPENSES/FINANCIAL AID
Annual Tuition (Resident/Nonresident): $1,630/$4,890
Room & Board (Off Campus): $2,650
Books and Supplies: $1,500
Average Grant: $1,000
Average Loan: $10,000
% Receiving Financial Aid: 30

ADMISSIONS INFORMATION
Application Fee: $25
Electronic Application? No
Regular Application Deadline: 3/1
Regular Notification: Rolling
Deferment Available? Yes
Length of Deferment: 1 year
Non-fall Admissions? Yes
Non-fall Application Deadline(s): 9/1 spring (Distance Learning MBA only)
Transfer Students Accepted? Yes
Transfer Policy: AACSB schools only; case-by-case basis; elective courses only
Need-Blind Admissions? Yes
Number of Applications Received: 159
% of Applicants Accepted: 60
% Accepted Who Enrolled: 48
Average GPA: 3.2
GPA Range: 3.0-3.4
Average GMAT: 578
GMAT Range: 530-610
Average Years Experience: 2
Other Admissions Factors Considered: 2 years of full-time work experience encouraged but not required.
Minority/Disadvantaged Student Recruitment Programs: Recruiting visits to minority campuses; particularly in-state

INTERNATIONAL STUDENTS
TOEFL Required of International Students? Yes
Minimum TOEFL: 550 (213 computer)

EMPLOYMENT INFORMATION

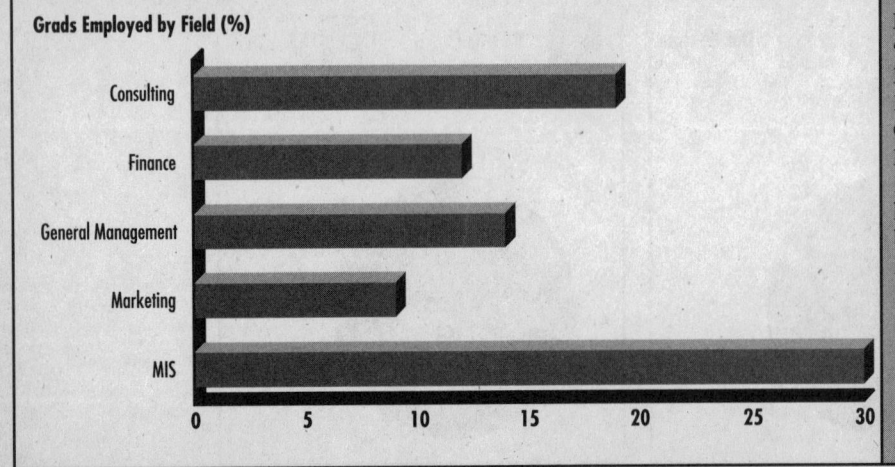

Grads Employed by Field (%):
- Consulting: ~19
- Finance: ~12
- General Management: ~19
- Marketing: ~9
- MIS: ~30

Placement Office Available? Yes
% Employed Within 3 Months: 86
Frequent Employers: IBM, Sapient, BellSouth, PricewaterhouseCoopers, Accenture, Chick-fil-A, Daleen Technologies, Home Depot
Prominent Alumni: Mohamed Mansour, CEO, Mansour Group in Egypt; Joanne P. McCallie, head coach, Michigan State U. Women's Basketball; Wendell Starke, vice chairman of the board, EntreMed, Inc.

AUGUSTA STATE UNIVERSITY
College of Business Administration

Admissions Contact: Miyoko Jackson, Degree Program Specialist
Address: MBA Office, 2500 Walton Way, Augusta, GA 30904-2200
Admissions Phone: 706-737-1565 • Admissions Fax: 706-667-4064
Admissions E-mail: mbainfo@aug.edu • Web Address: www.aug.edu/coba

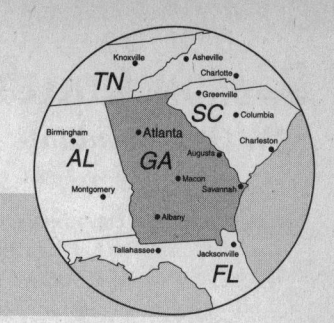

Come to Augusta State's College of Business Administration ready to be called on—the outstanding student/faculty ratio of 9:1 makes class sizes uncommonly small. The MBA program is basically designed for working professionals—it offers only night classes for its students, and the average age of matriculation is 30. COBA's competitive curriculum provides core business knowledge and problem-solving solutions and addresses important global and ethical business perspectives.

INSTITUTIONAL INFORMATION
Public/Private: Public
Evening Classes Available? Yes
Total Faculty: 12
% Faculty Female: 42
Student/Faculty Ratio: 9:1
Students in Parent Institution: 5,317
Academic Calendar: Trimester

PROGRAMS
Degrees Offered: Master of Business Administration (MBA) (36 credits, 16 months to 6 years)

STUDENT INFORMATION
Total Business Students: 133
% Full Time: 29
% Female: 11
% Minority: 2
% International: 7
Average Age: 30

COMPUTER AND RESEARCH FACILITIES
Computer Facilities: Online bibliographic retrieval services
Campuswide Network? Yes
Internet Fee? No

EXPENSES/FINANCIAL AID
Annual Tuition (Resident/Nonresident): $2,096/$7,316
Tuition Per Credit (Resident/Nonresident): $97/$387
Room & Board (Off Campus): $9,500
Books and Supplies: $500

ADMISSIONS INFORMATION
Application Fee: $20
Electronic Application? No
Regular Application Deadline: Rolling
Regular Notification: Rolling
Deferment Available? Yes
Length of Deferment: 1 year
Non-fall Admissions? Yes
Non-fall Application Deadline(s): 11/15 spring, 4/15 summer, 7/15 fall
Transfer Students Accepted? Yes
Transfer Policy: Must meet our regular MBA admission standards; up to 9 semester credit hours may be accepted for transfer.
Need-Blind Admissions? No
Number of Applications Received: 44
% of Applicants Accepted: 80
% Accepted Who Enrolled: 89
Average GPA: 3.1
GPA Range: 2.8-3.4
Average GMAT: 520
GMAT Range: 450-590
Average Years Experience: 6
Other Admissions Factors Considered: Computer experience required in word processing, spreadsheet, and database; work experience recommended; minimum 400 GMAT

INTERNATIONAL STUDENTS
TOEFL Required of International Students? Yes
Minimum TOEFL: 500 (173 computer)

EMPLOYMENT INFORMATION
Placement Office Available? Yes
% Employed Within 3 Months: 90

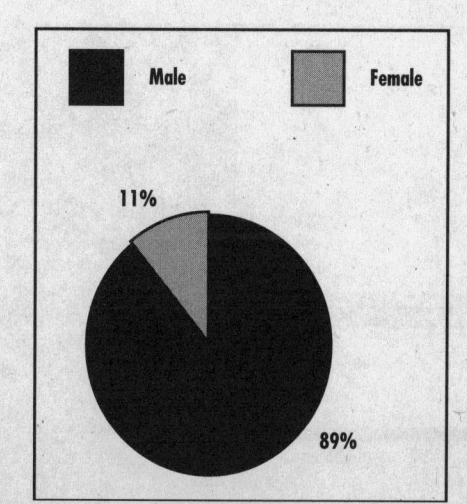

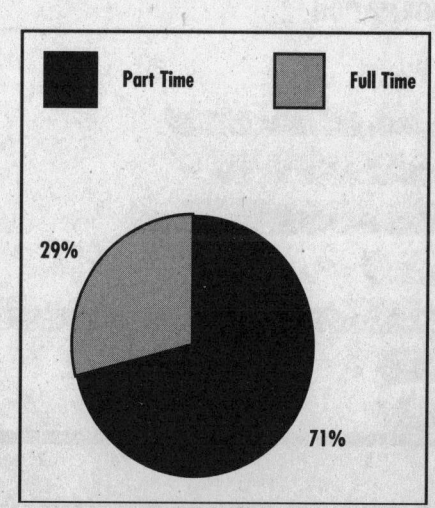

BABSON COLLEGE
F.W. Olin Graduate School of Business

Admissions Contact: Kate Klepper, Director of Admissions
Address: Olin Hall, Babson Park (Wellesley), MA 02457-0310
Admissions Phone: 781-239-4317 • *Admissions Fax:* 781-239-4194
Admissions E-mail: mbaadmission@babson.edu • *Web Address:* www.babson.edu/mba

Not for nothing is Babson College synonymous with entrepreneurial studies. Budding capitalists here enjoy "outstanding" course offerings, abundant opportunities for "in-the-field" learning, and access to the many perks of the "entrepreneurial incubator space" in newly built Olin Hall. Other highlights include a "tough, fun," and "committed" faculty and a Business Mentor program, which allows students to work as consultants for companies in the Boston area.

INSTITUTIONAL INFORMATION
Evening Classes Available? Yes
Total Faculty: 155
% Faculty Female: 25
% Faculty Minority: 10
% Faculty Part Time: 17
Student/Faculty Ratio: 12:1
Academic Calendar: Semester

PROGRAMS
Degrees Offered: 2-year MBA (21 months); 1-year MBA (12 months); evening MBA (4 years); Intel MBA (2 years); Lucent MS in Finance (3 years)
Academic Specialties: Entrepreneurship, Marketing, Finance, and Consulting. 2-year MBA stresses opportunity recognition, innovation, and creative problem solving. Field-based programs, mentor program, international internships, and management consulting programs provide opportunities for hands-on application of classroom learning.
Special Opportunities: Global Management Program, Management Consulting Field Experience, Consulting Alliance Program, International Independent Study
Study Abroad Options: Argentina, Chile, China, France, Germany, Japan, Russia, Switzerland, UK

STUDENT INFORMATION
Total Business Students: 1,502
% Full Time: 33
% Female: 33
% Minority: 5
% International: 34
Average Age: 29

COMPUTER AND RESEARCH FACILITIES
Research Facilities: Centers for Entrepreneurial Studies, Global Entrepreneurial Leadership, Real Estate, Information Management Studies, Language and Culture, Technology and Enterprise, and Women's Leadership; Asian Institute of Business, Institute for Latin American Business
Computer Facilities: 7 computer lab/classrooms (with 180 computers), 24-hour-access lab, wireless access, electronic online and CD-ROM subscriptions, electronic services including Bloomberg, etc.
Campuswide Network? Yes
% of MBA Classrooms Wired: 100
Computer Model Recommended: Laptop

EXPENSES/FINANCIAL AID
Annual Tuition: $27,124
Tuition Per Credit: $819
Room & Board: $11,796
Books and Supplies: $1,850
Average Grant: $15,570
Average Loan: $30,362
% Receiving Financial Aid: 55
% Receiving Aid Their First Year: 53

ADMISSIONS INFORMATION
Application Fee: $75
Electronic Application? Yes
Regular Application Deadline: 4/15
Regular Notification: 5/31
Length of Deferment: 1 year
Non-fall Application Deadline(s): 10/15, 1/31 for 1-year MBA, beginning in May
Transfer Policy: Credit from AACSB-accredited program into Evening MBA program.
Need-Blind Admissions? Yes
Number of Applications Received: 707
% of Applicants Accepted: 41
% Accepted Who Enrolled: 47
Average GPA: 3.1
Average GMAT: 637
Average Years Experience: 5
Other Admissions Factors Considered: Fit with Babson's team orientation, modular curriculum, entrepreneurial focus, and global mind-set
Minority/Disadvantaged Student Recruitment Programs: GMASS, scholarship program
Other Schools to Which Students Applied: Boston College, Boston U., Dartmouth, Harvard, MIT, Northwestern, U. of Pennsylvania

INTERNATIONAL STUDENTS
TOEFL Required of International Students? Yes
Minimum TOEFL: 600 (250 computer)

EMPLOYMENT INFORMATION

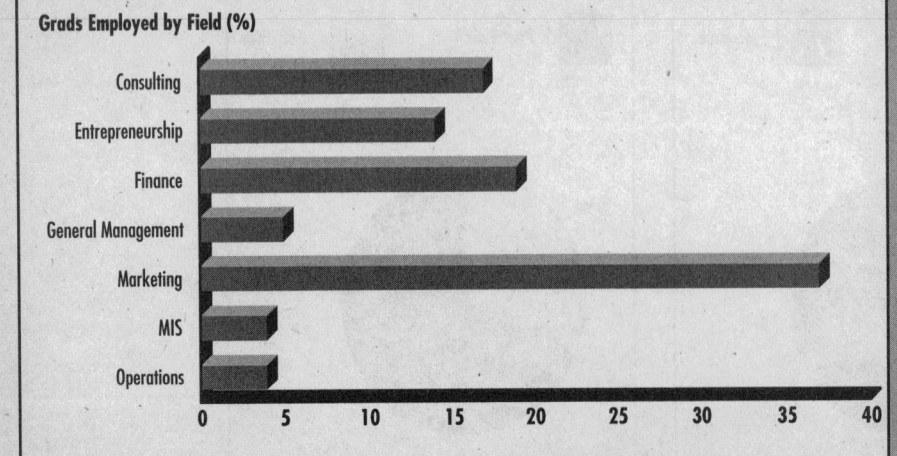

Grads Employed by Field (%)

Field	%
Consulting	~17
Entrepreneurship	~14
Finance	~18
General Management	~4
Marketing	~37
MIS	~2
Operations	~4

Placement Office Available? Yes
% Employed Within 3 Months: 81
Frequent Employers: Fidelity Investments, Fidelity Capital, FleetBoston, AT Kearney, Digitas, EMC Corporation, Adventis, Bose Corporation, Boston Scientific Corporation, Charles River Associates, Genuity, The Hartford, IBM, International Data Corporation (IDC), Liberty Mutual Group, Merrill Lynch, Our Group, Philips Medical Systems, PricewaterhouseCoopers, Staples, Inc., Strategic Pricing Group, Inc.
Prominent Alumni: Robert Davis, founder, Lycos; Mark Holowesko, president, Templeton Holdings Ltd; Deborah A. McLaughlin, executive VP, NSTAR; Junichi Murata, president, Murata Machinery, Ltd; Michael Smith, chairman and CEO, Hughes Electronics

BALL STATE UNIVERSITY
College of Business

Admissions Contact: Staci L. Davis, Associate Director of Graduate Business Programs
Address: WB 146, Muncie, IN 47306
Admissions Phone: 765-285-1931 • Admissions Fax: 765-285-8818
Admissions E-mail: mba@bsu.edu • Web Address: www.bsu.edu/mba

Best known as a leader in the jump to distance learning MBA programs, Ball State offers a fully accredited off-site MBA in four states. Ball State's other claim to fame is its nationally ranked Entrepreneurship Program.

INSTITUTIONAL INFORMATION
Public/Private: Public
Evening Classes Available? No
Total Faculty: 63
Student/Faculty Ratio: 25:1
Students in Parent Institution: 19,070
Academic Calendar: Semester

PROGRAMS
Degrees Offered: MBA in Entrepreneurship (36 credits); MBA in Operations and Technology Management (36 credits); MBA in Finance (36 credits); MBA in Information Systems (36 credits)

STUDENT INFORMATION
Total Business Students: 175
% Full Time: 23
% Female: 8
% Minority: 1
% Out of State: 1
% International: 2
Average Age: 29

COMPUTER AND RESEARCH FACILITIES
Campuswide Network? Yes
Computer Model Recommended: No
Internet Fee? No

EXPENSES/FINANCIAL AID
Annual Tuition (Resident/Nonresident): $4,100/$10,000
Room & Board (On/Off Campus): $7,100/$5,200
Books and Supplies: $1,300

ADMISSIONS INFORMATION
Application Fee: $35
Electronic Application? No
Regular Application Deadline: Rolling
Regular Notification: Rolling
Deferment Available? Yes
Length of Deferment: 2 years
Non-fall Admissions? Yes
Non-fall Application Deadline(s): 12/1 spring, 4/1 summer
Transfer Students Accepted? Yes
Transfer Policy: Up to 9 credit hours may be considered for transfer.
Need-Blind Admissions? No
Number of Applications Received: 81
% of Applicants Accepted: 73
% Accepted Who Enrolled: 58
Average GPA: 3.2
GPA Range: 2.9-3.4
Average GMAT: 520
GMAT Range: 480-570
Average Years Experience: 7
Other Schools to Which Students Applied: Indiana University-Purdue University at Indianapolis, Butler University, Indiana University-Purdue University at Fort Wayne, Indiana University-Kokomo

INTERNATIONAL STUDENTS
TOEFL Required of International Students? Yes
Minimum TOEFL: 550 (213 computer)

EMPLOYMENT INFORMATION
Placement Office Available? No

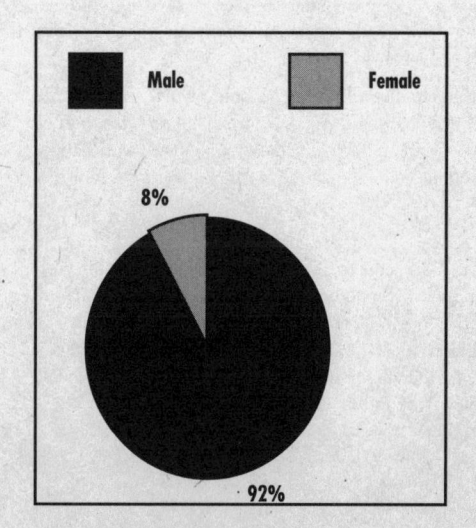

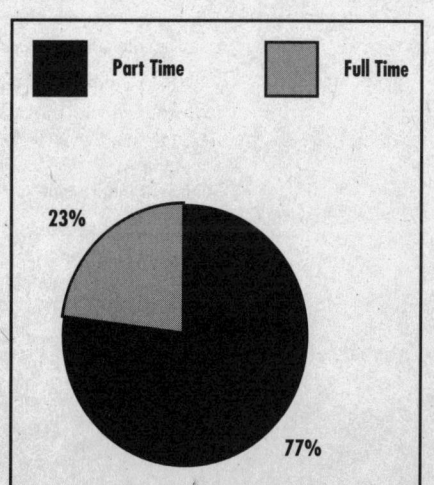

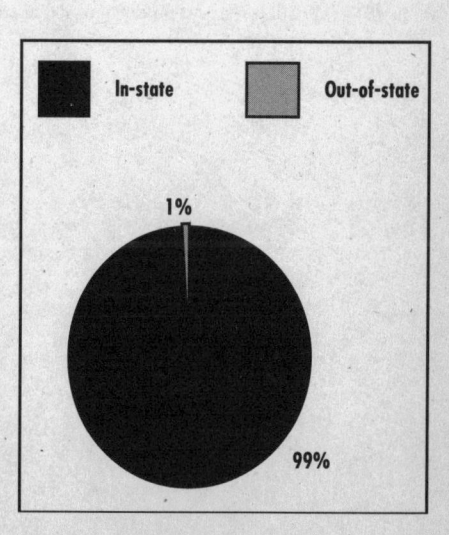

BARUCH COLLEGE (CITY UNIVERSITY OF NEW YORK)

THE SCHOOL AT A GLANCE

"Baruch College is proud of its place in New York City, the world's most dynamic financial and cultural center. We are uniquely positioned to provide students with an excellent education at a very reasonable cost in a global environment. Our outstanding faculty, flexible full- and part-time programs, and convenient location offer students unequaled access to opportunities for both learning and professional advancement."

—Sidney Lirtzman, Vice President and Dean, Zicklin School of Business

STUDENTS

Baruch's reputation for excellence extends to all parts of the world, attracting students from New York, neighboring states, and abroad. The cohort-style MBA program offers students the option of full-time or part-time study. Full-time students complete the degree program in two years, part-time students average four. The diverse group of men and women doing graduate work at Baruch hold undergraduate degrees from more than 200 colleges and universities. There are more than 400 international graduate students, who represent approximately 50 countries.

The average graduate student is 28 years old. At least two years of full-time work experience before applying is strongly encouraged. Many MBA students at Baruch have undergraduate degrees in business, but the majority have majored in the liberal arts, the sciences, or engineering. Professional experience varies widely. Forty percent of the students are women, while members of minority groups represent almost 30 percent of the student body. International students make up 50 percent of the full-time MBA student population.

The Baruch degree is highly valued. Graduates may be found at all levels in business, industry, and public life. Notable graduates include Laura Altschuler, president, New York City League of Women Voters; the Honorable Abraham D. Beame, former mayor of the City of New York; Lawrence Zicklin, chairman of the board, Neuberger Berman Inc.; Matthew Blank, chairman of the board and CEO, Showtime Networks; Irving Schneider, vice chairman, Helmsley Spear; and Sally Guido, CEO, Lee Myles.

ACADEMICS

Zicklin's premier program is the Full-Time MBA, a very selective honors format that evolved from the successful Jack Nash Honors MBA program. The MBA is also offered in the FlexTime format for full- or part-time students who need a wider range of options in scheduling their graduate study. Eighteen courses (54 credits) are required. The nine-course core curriculum is designed to provide students with an understanding of the basic principles of both management and the environment in which managerial decisions are made. Courses include accountancy, economics, finance, behavioral sciences, quantitative methods, information systems, production, and marketing.

Supplementing the core are nine credits of elective courses, including one international elective, one quantitative elective, and one general elective. Beyond the core, students can specialize in accountancy, computer information systems, economics, entrepreneurship, finance and investments, health care administration, industrial/organizational psychology, international business, management, marketing, operations research, statistics, or taxation.

Those who wish to design their own MBA programs can select unique, cross-disciplinary combinations of courses to fulfill the 18-credit specialization requirement. These combinations are useful for students interested in careers in such fields as marketing in financial institutions or banking operations. A few examples of the many specialization courses available to students are Futures and Forwards Markets, Options Markets, Mergers and Acquisitions, International Trade and Investment Law, International Commodity Trading, International Corporate Finance, Computer Simulation for Solving Business Problems, Product Planning and Development, and Entrepreneurial Ventures. The Zicklin School also offers a strategic management Executive MBA as well as Executive MS programs in finance and industrial and labor relations.

The faculty at Baruch is top-notch, with strong academic credentials and ties to New York's business and financial communities. All share a commitment to teaching. Baruch's retired Harry Markowitz held the Marvin M. Speiser Professorship when he earned the Nobel Prize in Economics in 1990. Other faculty members recognized for outstanding honors include Robert Schwartz, University Distinguished Professor of Finance, an expert on market microstructures; Prakash Sethi, University Distinguished Professor of Management, an expert on business ethics and corporate policy; E. S. Savas, an expert on privatization of public enterprises; and Yoshihiro Tsurumi, an authority on cultural and economic relations between the United States and Japan.

CAMPUS LIFE

With a prime location in Manhattan's historic Gramercy Park neighborhood and the leading-edge Flatiron District, Baruch is at the heart of one of the world's most dynamic business and cultural centers—within easy reach of Wall Street, "Silicon Alley," and the headquarters of major business and financial firms and nonprofit organizations. This real-world environment adds immeasurably to the value of a Baruch education and offers unparalleled internship and career opportunities. The campus extends from East 22nd Street to East 26th Street (Madison and Third Avenues) and is surrounded by a variety of ethnic restaurants and stores of all kinds. All of New York City's museums, theaters, concert halls, clubs, sports arenas, and beaches are easily accessible by public transportation.

The College has just moved into a 17-floor academic complex that is now the home of the Zicklin School. The award-winning design encloses modern, multimedia-equipped classrooms; all faculty members' offices; two large production-level theaters; a fitness center with a gym and a swimming pool; a television studio; and an enhanced Center for Student Life.

Baruch's Information and Technology Building, which opened on East 25th Street in 1994, houses The William and Anita Newman Library, the Baruch Computing and Technology Center (which includes 400 computer workstations in an open-access lab), student and administrative offices, and a state-of-the-art multimedia center.

More than three times the size of its predecessor, the 1,450-seat library has local area networks that provide access to a wide variety of electronic information resources. Students and faculty members can access the Internet and hundreds of online databases through the Dow Jones News/Retrieval, Lexis-Nexis, and Dialog services, in addition to its traditional holdings. The Baruch community also has access to the 4.5 million volumes in the CUNY library system and to the collections of the New York Public Library.

Zicklin School of Business

In March 2000, Baruch opened the Subotnick Financial Services Center/Bert W. and Sandra Wasserman Trading Floor, a unique educational facility for students and the financial community that features a fully equipped simulated trading environment with continuous live data feeds by Reuters, integrating financial services practice into the MBA curriculum.

The placement office offers students a range of job search services. A core curriculum of workshops is offered to all students and covers topics such as job search strategies, resume writing, interviewing techniques, networking strategies, and job search correspondence. Individual career counseling and consultation are also available. On-campus recruiting is held in the fall and spring semesters, and career fairs are held throughout the year. Students have unlimited access to the various full-time and internship position openings that are posted in the office on a daily basis. Special events, such as career seminars, company information sessions, and other networking opportunities, are also held throughout the year.

COSTS

Tuition for New York State residents in 2000–2001 was $2,175 per semester for full-time and $185 per credit for part-time study. For out-of-state residents and international students, tuition was $3,800 for full-time and $320 per credit for part-time study. Tuition and fees are subject to change without notice. Average estimated annual cost for books, supplies, transportation, and personal expenses is $12,000 per year.

Financial aid is available and is merit based. Nash Tuition Scholarships of $2,000 to $5,000 per year are awarded to 20 to 25 of the most qualified students in the Full-Time MBA (honors) program. Graduate assistantships require 15 hours of work for a faculty member or administrative area each week for a $5,000 annual stipend. They are awarded primarily to honors students and do not include a tuition waiver. International students are eligible for both Nash Scholarships and graduate assistantships.

In the fall, the Mitsui USA Foundation awards two annual scholarships of $5,000 each to newly admitted full-time students pursuing an MBA degree in international business. Applicants for the Mitsui Scholarships must be United States citizens or permanent residents. The Carl Spielvogel Scholarship offers an annual award of $5,000 in the fall to newly admitted full-time students pursuing an MBA degree in international marketing.

Financial aid is also available to graduate students through other sources, including various state, federal, and College programs, although international students are not eligible for most of these programs.

ADMISSIONS

Applicants for any program must take the GMAT. The average student entering the program in 1999–2000 had a GMAT score of 585 and an undergraduate grade point average of 3.2. For the honors Full-Time MBA program, the average GMAT is 647 and the GPA is 3.4. International students whose native language is not English must take the Test of English as a Foreign Language (TOEFL) and the Test of Written English (TWE). In addition to test scores, applicants must submit application forms, an essay, a resume, official transcripts from every college or university attended, two letters of recommendation, and a nonrefundable application fee of $40.

Application deadlines for fall admission are February 28 for Full-Time MBA students (honors program, fall entry only), domestic students, and international students; April 30 for full- or part-time international FlexTime students; and May 31 for domestic students. For spring, the deadlines are October 31 for international students and November 30 for domestic students. Applicants are encouraged to submit their applications as early as possible, particularly if they wish to be considered for a graduate assistantship or scholarship.

To request application materials, applicants should contact:

Office of Graduate Admissions
Baruch College of the City
University of New York
17 Lexington Avenue, Box H-0880
New York, NY 10010-5518
Telephone: 212-802-2330
Fax: 212-802-2335
E-mail: zicklingradadmissions@baruch.cuny.edu
World Wide Web: www.zicklin.baruch.cuny.edu

For Executive Programs information, applicants should contact:

Zicklin School Executive Programs
Baruch College of the City
University of New York
17 Lexington Avenue, Box F-1215
New York, NY 10010-5518
Telephone: 212-802-6700
Fax: 212-802-6705
E-mail: exprog_bus@baruch.cuny.edu
World Wide Web: www.zicklin.baruch.cuny.edu

Admissions Contact: Frances Murphy, Director of Admissions
Address: One Bernard Baruch Way, Box H-0820, New York, NY 10010
Admissions Phone: 646-312-1300 • Admissions Fax: 646-312-1301
Admissions E-mail: ZicklinGradAdmissions@baruch.cuny.edu • Web Address: www.zicklin.baruch.cuny.edu

BARUCH COLLEGE (CITY UNIVERSITY OF NEW YORK)
Zicklin School of Business

Admissions Contact: Frances Murphy, Director of Admissions
Address: One Bernard Baruch Way, Box H-0820, New York, NY 10010
Admissions Phone: 646-312-1300 • Admissions Fax: 646-312-1301
Admissions E-mail: ZicklinGradAdmissions@baruch.cuny.edu • Web Address: www.zicklin.baruch.cuny.edu

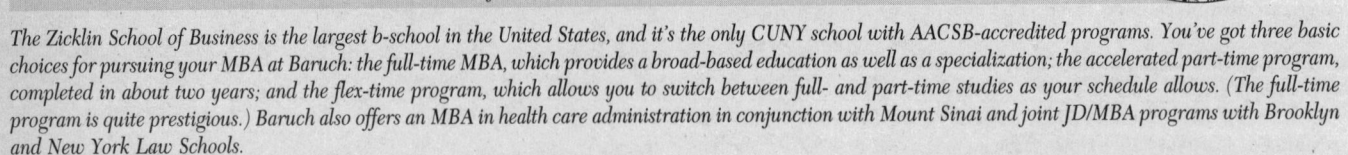

The Zicklin School of Business is the largest b-school in the United States, and it's the only CUNY school with AACSB-accredited programs. You've got three basic choices for pursuing your MBA at Baruch: the full-time MBA, which provides a broad-based education as well as a specialization; the accelerated part-time program, completed in about two years; and the flex-time program, which allows you to switch between full- and part-time studies as your schedule allows. (The full-time program is quite prestigious.) Baruch also offers an MBA in health care administration in conjunction with Mount Sinai and joint JD/MBA programs with Brooklyn and New York Law Schools.

INSTITUTIONAL INFORMATION
Public/Private: Public
Evening Classes Available? Yes
Total Faculty: 200
% Faculty Female: 24
% Faculty Minority: 22
% Faculty Part Time: 30
Student/Faculty Ratio: 40:1
Students in Parent Institution: 16,600
Academic Calendar: Semester

PROGRAMS
Degrees Offered: MBA (2 years full time, 4 years part time; 28 months accelerated part-time program), MS (1.5 years full time, 3 years part time), Executive MBA (2 years), Executive MS in Finance (1 year)
Joint Degrees: JD/MBA (full time, 4.5 years)
Academic Specialties: Large, diverse faculty holds degrees from NYU, Columbia, Penn, MIT, Harvard, Cornell, UC Berkeley, Yale, Stanford, and others. Curriculum features deep 6-course specializations.
Study Abroad Options: Sweden, Korea, Germany, England, France, Mexico

STUDENT INFORMATION
Total Business Students: 1,445
% Full Time: 12
% Female: 40
% Minority: 3
% Out of State: 80
% International: 55
Average Age: 28

COMPUTER AND RESEARCH FACILITIES
Research Facilities: Financial Services Center, Center for International Business, Center for Logistics and Transportation, Center for Entrepreneurship and Small Business, Communication Institute
Computer Facilities: Laptop loan program, wireless networking, Lexis-Nexis, CRSP, Compustat, S&P NetAdvantage, Business & Company Resource Center, Global Access, and Simmons Choices II. Training on the use of Reuters databases.
Campuswide Network? Yes
Computer Model Recommended: No
Internet Fee? No

EXPENSES/FINANCIAL AID
Annual Tuition (Resident/Nonresident): $6,000/$13,300
Tuition Per Credit (Resident/Nonresident): $265/$475
Room & Board (Off Campus): $16,500
Books and Supplies: $1,000
Average Grant: $3,152
Average Loan: $10,000
% Receiving Financial Aid: 50
% Receiving Aid Their First Year: 50

ADMISSIONS INFORMATION
Application Fee: $40
Electronic Application? Yes
Regular Application Deadline: 4/30
Regular Notification: 6/15
Length of Deferment: 1 year
Non-fall Application Deadline(s): 10/31 spring
Transfer Policy: Up to 4 courses from an AACSB-accredited institution
Need-Blind Admissions? Yes
Number of Applications Received: 654
% of Applicants Accepted: 22
% Accepted Who Enrolled: 58
Average GPA: 3.3
GPA Range: 2.8-4.0
Average GMAT: 650
GMAT Range: 590-700
Average Years Experience: 5
Other Admissions Factors Considered: TWE scores for international applicants
Minority/Disadvantaged Student Recruitment Programs: No specific programs; City University of New York affiliation and unusually low tuition rates makes us well known to these groups.
Other Schools to Which Students Applied: Columbia, Fordham, Hofstra, NYU, Pace, Rutgers, St. John's

INTERNATIONAL STUDENTS
TOEFL Required of International Students? Yes
Minimum TOEFL: 580 (237 computer)

EMPLOYMENT INFORMATION

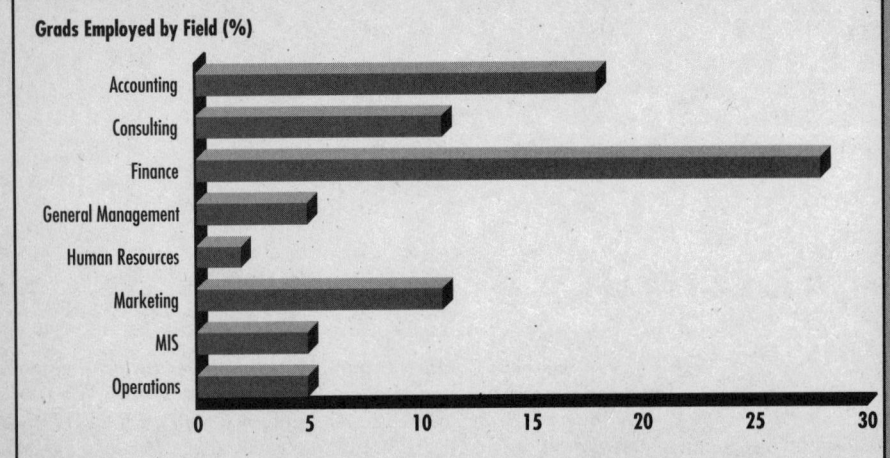

Grads Employed by Field (%)

Field	%
Accounting	~18
Consulting	~11
Finance	~28
General Management	~3
Human Resources	~1
Marketing	~11
MIS	~3
Operations	~5

Placement Office Available? Yes
% Employed Within 3 Months: 86
Frequent Employers: Andersen, Citigroup, Deloitte & Touche, Ernst & Young, PricewaterhouseCoopers, Salomon Smith Barney
Prominent Alumni: Larry Zicklin, chairman, Neuberger Berman; Mark Kurland, chairman and CEO, Bear Stearns; Donald Marron, chairman and CEO, PaineWebber; Bernard Schwartz, chairman and CEO, Loral Space Corporation; Matthew Blank, chairman and CEO, Showtime Networks

BAYLOR UNIVERSITY
Hankamer School of Business

Admissions Contact: Laurie Wilson, Director, Graduate Business Admissions
Address: PO Box 98013, Waco, TX 76798-8013
Admissions Phone: 254-710-3718 • Admissions Fax: 254-710-1066
Admissions E-mail: mba@hsb.baylor.edu • Web Address: www.gradbusiness.baylor.edu

Dedicated professors, a strong Baptist influence, and a standout accounting program are the hallmarks of the Hankamer School of Business at Baylor University in Waco. Each semester, MBA students analyze a "focus firm" inside and out, giving students "the chance to solve real-world business problems from several aspects at once." In fall 1998, Baylor's focus firm was Dell Computers, headquartered in (relatively) nearby Austin.

INSTITUTIONAL INFORMATION
Public/Private: Private
Evening Classes Available? No
Total Faculty: 30
% Faculty Female: 20
% Faculty Minority: 2
Student/Faculty Ratio: 14:1
Students in Parent Institution: 14,221
Academic Calendar: Semester

PROGRAMS
Degrees Offered: MBA (16 to 21 months), MBA in Information Systems Management (16 to 21 months), MBA in International Management (16 to 21 months), MS-ECO (12 months), MAcc (12 months), MTax (12 months), MS in Information Systems (12 to 16 months)
Joint Degrees: JD/MBA (4 years), MBA/MS in Information Systems (2 years), JD/MTax (4 years)
Academic Specialties: Customer Relationship Management specialization features elective courses, internship, and scholarships; E-Commerce specialization features entrepreneurship focus, elective courses and a business plan competition.
Special Opportunities: The Integrated Management Seminar (1-semester seminar satisfies all business prerequisites), "Focus Firm" approach (provides real-time delivery of theoretical applications, technological advances, global awareness, functional integration, and team-centered learning)
Study Abroad Options: Mexico, France, Australia, China, Japan, Korea, Thailand, UK, Netherlands

STUDENT INFORMATION
Total Business Students: 112
% Full Time: 100
% Female: 36
% Minority: 4
% Out of State: 26
% International: 33
Average Age: 25

COMPUTER AND RESEARCH FACILITIES
Research Facilities: Videoconferencing sessions with corporate executives are held regularly. Distance learning is also integral to classroom activity.
Computer Facilities: Graduate Computer Lounge with wireless network access, wireless networking in all MBA classrooms, approximately 100 desktop PCs, scanning equipment, color printers, approximately 4,200 computers.
Campuswide Network? Yes
% of MBA Classrooms Wired: 100
Computer Model Recommended: Laptop
Internet Fee? No

EXPENSES/FINANCIAL AID
Annual Tuition: $15,700
Room & Board: $10,000
Books and Supplies: $8,000
Average Grant: $16,128
Average Loan: $18,551
% Receiving Financial Aid: 80
% Receiving Aid Their First Year: 80

ADMISSIONS INFORMATION
Application Fee: $50
Electronic Application? Yes
Regular Application Deadline: 7/1
Regular Notification: Rolling
Length of Deferment: 1 year
Non-fall Application Deadline(s): 11/1 spring, 4/1 summer
Transfer Policy: A student who has been admitted to a graduate program at another university, and who desires admission to Baylor, must present a transcript that presents the student's active, satisfactory work toward the same degree. Only 6 credits may be transferred into the program.
Need-Blind Admissions? Yes
Number of Applications Received: 173
% of Applicants Accepted: 62
% Accepted Who Enrolled: 62
Average GPA: 3.1
GPA Range: 2.5-4.0
Average GMAT: 590
GMAT Range: 510-700
Average Years Experience: 3
Other Admissions Factors Considered: Work experience, leadership skills, community service
Other Schools to Which Students Applied: Rice, Southern Methodist, Texas A&M, TCU, Thunderbird, University of North Texas, University of Texas—Arlington

INTERNATIONAL STUDENTS
TOEFL Required of International Students? Yes
Minimum TOEFL: 600 (250 computer).

EMPLOYMENT INFORMATION

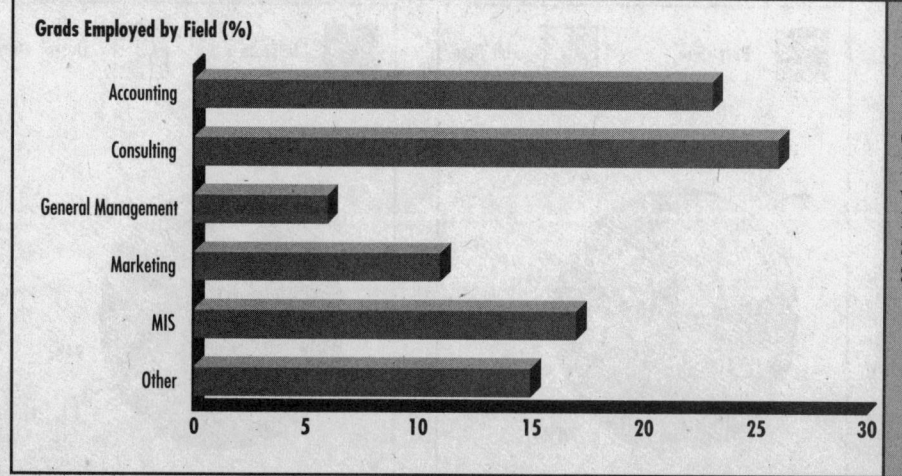

Grads Employed by Field (%)
- Accounting: ~23
- Consulting: ~26
- General Management: ~6
- Marketing: ~11
- MIS: ~17
- Other: ~15

Placement Office Available? Yes
% Employed Within 3 Months: 91
Frequent Employers: Accenture, Alltel, AT&T, Bank One, Cap Gemini, JP Morgan Chase, Conoco, Continental Airlines, Deloitte & Touche, Dynegy, El Paso Energy, ExxonMobil, HBK Investments, H.E.B. Grocery, IBM, Intecap, Lockheed Martin, Microsoft, Raytheon, Shell, Southwest Airlines, SBC Communications, Sprint, Tivoli, Tucker Alan, TXU, VHA Inc.

BENTLEY COLLEGE
The Elkin B. McCallum Graduate School of Business

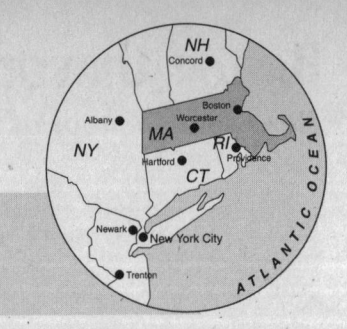

Admissions Contact: Paul J. Vaccaro, Director
Address: 175 Forest Street, Waltham, MA 02452
Admissions Phone: 781-891-2108 • *Admissions Fax:* 781-891-2464
Admissions E-mail: gradadm@bentley.edu • *Web Address:* www.bentley.edu

Bentley College offers three MBA tracks. The Information Age MBA is Bentley's answer to the traditional two-year multidisciplinary MBA. As expected, a heavy emphasis on information technology (IT) is included in the curriculum. IT is part of every course, and students utilize the hot technology of enterprise resource planning software to integrate the various disciplines of each lesson. Students can also choose from the popular part-time Self-Paced MBA or the One-Year MBA, designed to give those with an undergraduate business degree an intensive MBA education in one calendar year. Bentley is a hit with foreign students, giving the program a true international flavor.

INSTITUTIONAL INFORMATION
Public/Private: Private
Evening Classes Available? Yes
Total Faculty: 243
% Faculty Female: 35
% Faculty Minority: 14
% Faculty Part Time: 42
Student/Faculty Ratio: 14:1
Students in Parent Institution: 5,587
Academic Calendar: Semester

PROGRAMS
Degrees Offered: Self-paced MBA (MBA) (30 to 57 credits, 12 months to 7 years); MS in Accountancy (MS) (30 to 60 credits, 12 months to 7 years); Master of Science in Information Technology (MSIT) (30 to 36 credits, 12 months to 7 years); MS in Finance (MS) (30 to 57 credits, 12 months to 7 years); MS in Taxation (MS) (30 to 36 credits, 12 months to 7 years); MS in Personal Financial Planning (MS) (30 to 36 credits, 12 months to 7 years); Information Age Master of Business Administration (IAMBA) (58 credits, 2 years); MS in Global Financial Analysis (MSGFA) (30 to 36 credits, 2 to 7 years); MS in Information Age Marketing (MSIAM) (30 credits, 12 months to 5 years); MS in Accounting Information Systems (MSAIS) (30 to 39 credits, 12 months to 7 years); MS in Human Factors in Information Design (MSHFID) (30 credits, 2 to 5 years)
Special Opportunities: Internship program, study electives in the summer

Study Abroad Options: Australia, Austria, Belgium, England, Estonia, France, Italy, Mexico, Spain

STUDENT INFORMATION
Total Business Students: 722
% Full Time: 22
% Female: 40
% Minority: 4
% Out of State: 6
% International: 9
Average Age: 27

COMPUTER AND RESEARCH FACILITIES
Computer Facilities: Access to online bibliographic retrieval services and online databases
Campuswide Network? Yes
Computer Model Recommended: Laptop
Internet Fee? No

EXPENSES/FINANCIAL AID
Annual Tuition: $23,300
Tuition Per Credit: $777
Room & Board (On/Off Campus): $3,880/$3,580
Books and Supplies: $980

ADMISSIONS INFORMATION
Application Fee: $50
Electronic Application? No
Regular Application Deadline: 6/1
Regular Notification: Rolling
Deferment Available? Yes
Length of Deferment: 1 year
Non-fall Admissions? Yes
Non-fall Application Deadline(s): 11/1 spring, 3/1 summer
Transfer Students Accepted? No
Need-Blind Admissions? No
Number of Applications Received: 516
% of Applicants Accepted: 57
% Accepted Who Enrolled: 62
Average GMAT: 545
GMAT Range: 480-600
Average Years Experience: 4
Other Admissions Factors Considered: Interview, résumé

INTERNATIONAL STUDENTS
TOEFL Required of International Students? Yes
Minimum TOEFL: 600

EMPLOYMENT INFORMATION
Placement Office Available? Yes
% Employed Within 3 Months: 98
Frequent Employers: Aetna Inc., Accenture (formerly Andersen) Consulting, Goldman Sachs, Johnson & Johnson, Merrill Lynch, Polaroid Corporation, PricewaterhouseCoopers
Prominent Alumni: Charles E. Peters, Jr. (MSF '85), senior VP and CFO, Burlington Industries; Ullas Naik (MBA '93), managing director, JAFCO Ventures

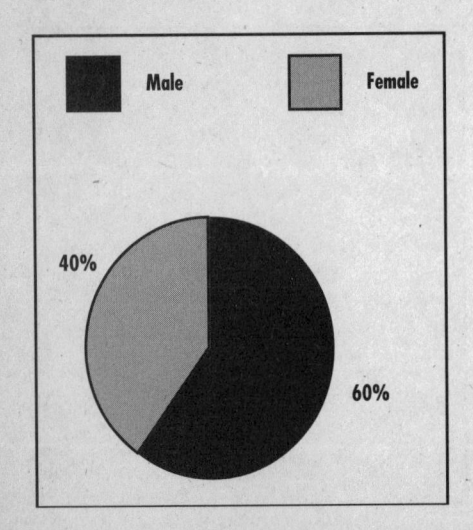

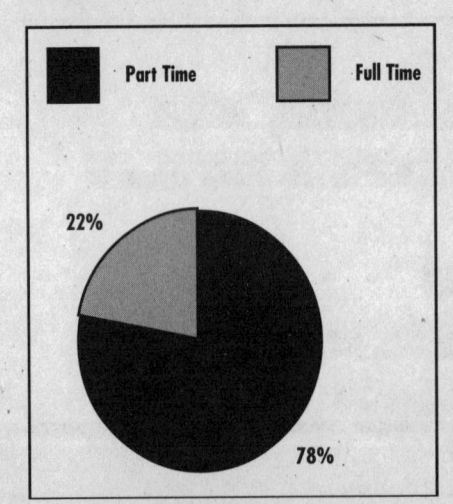

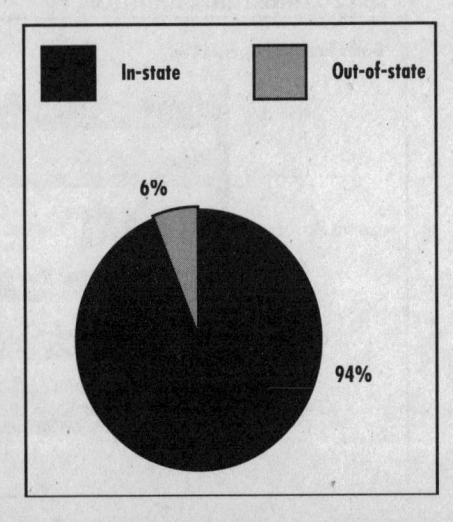

BINGHAMTON UNIVERSITY (SUNY)
School of Management

Admissions Contact: Alesia Wheeler, Assistant Director, MBA/MS Program
Address: School of Management, Binghamton, NY 13902
Admissions Phone: 607-777-2317 • Admissions Fax: 607-777-4872
Admissions E-mail: somadvis@binghamton.edu • Web Address: som.binghamton.edu

Binghamton's MBA program builds on its excellent undergraduate reputation as one of the top 25 public universities in the United States. The four-semester program emphasizes general management skills with a special focus on teamwork. Binghamton stresses communication skills, understanding of group dynamics, and conflict resolution. Close ties with the local business community provide readily available internships and real-world expertise. A Fast-Track Program is available for those overachieving business undergraduates who want to be in and out in two semesters.

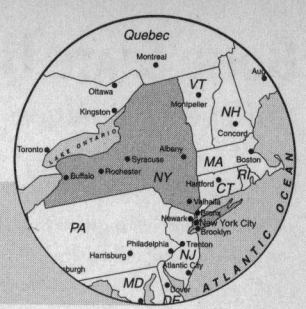

INSTITUTIONAL INFORMATION
Public/Private: Public
Evening Classes Available? No
Total Faculty: 57
% Faculty Female: 10
% Faculty Part Time: 30
Student/Faculty Ratio: 20:1
Students in Parent Institution: 12,820
Academic Calendar: 2-semester

PROGRAMS
Degrees Offered: Master of Business Administration (2 years or 9 months), Master of Science in Accounting (1 year), Executive MBA for Corporate Professionals (21 months), Executive MBA in Health Care (21 months)
Academic Specialties: World-renowned leadership research center; one of the top 15 percent research institutions with regard to finance publications
Special Opportunities: Leadership Certificate Program, Management Development Program

STUDENT INFORMATION
Total Business Students: 133
% Full Time: 86
% Female: 40
% Minority: 5
% Out of State: 5
% International: 60
Average Age: 25

COMPUTER AND RESEARCH FACILITIES
Computer Facilities: Access to online bibliographic retrieval services, ACCESS, SQL server, Oracle
Campuswide Network? Yes
% of MBA Classrooms Wired: 100
Computer Model Recommended: No
Internet Fee? No

EXPENSES/FINANCIAL AID
Annual Tuition (Resident/Nonresident): $5,100/$8,416
Tuition Per Credit (Resident/Nonresident): $213/$351
Room & Board (Off Campus): $10,077
Books and Supplies: $1,000
Average Grant: $13,556
Average Loan: $12,000
% Receiving Financial Aid: 20
% Receiving Aid Their First Year: 15

ADMISSIONS INFORMATION
Application Fee: $60
Electronic Application? Yes
Regular Application Deadline: 4/15
Regular Notification: Rolling
Deferment Available? Yes
Length of Deferment: 1 year
Non-fall Admissions? No
Transfer Students Accepted? No
Need-Blind Admissions? Yes

Number of Applications Received: 375
% of Applicants Accepted: 61
% Accepted Who Enrolled: 39
Average GPA: 3.3
GPA Range: 3.0-3.6
Average GMAT: 585
GMAT Range: 510-671
Average Years Experience: 3
Minority/Disadvantaged Student Recruitment Programs: Through the Clifford D. Clark Graduate Fellowship Program for Underrepresented Minority Students, the State University of New York has provided graduate fellowships for outstanding minority students from groups historically underrepresented in the university's graduate and professional programs (African American, Hispanic, Native American). These fellowships are granted to students entering both master's and doctoral degree programs and carry stipends between $6,800 and $12,750 (depending on discipline) for the academic year plus a full tuition scholarship. Renewals or graduate assistantships may be awarded in subsequent years, depending upon availability of funds.
Other Schools to Which Students Applied: Baruch College (City University of New York), Syracuse University, State University of New York-Albany, State University of New York-Buffalo

INTERNATIONAL STUDENTS
TOEFL Required of International Students? Yes
Minimum TOEFL: 570 (233 computer)

EMPLOYMENT INFORMATION

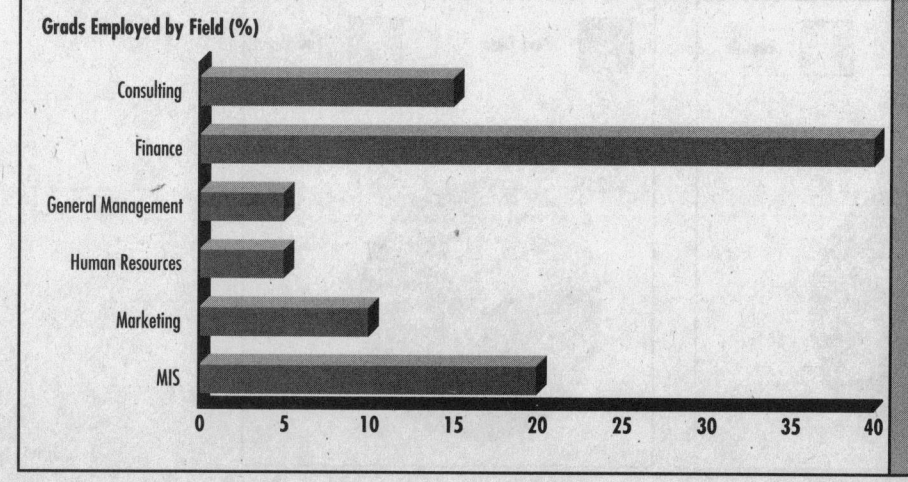

Grads Employed by Field (%)

Field	%
Consulting	15
Finance	40
General Management	5
Human Resources	10
Marketing	10
MIS	20

Placement Office Available? No
% Employed Within 3 Months: 75
Frequent Employers: IBM, PricewaterhouseCoopers, Deloitte & Touche, Merrill Lynch, Arthur Andersen, Ernst & Young, KPMG Peat Marwick, Lockheed Martin

BOISE STATE UNIVERSITY
College of Business and Economics

Admissions Contact: Mrs. J. Renee Anchustegui, Program Coordinator
Address: Graduate Business Studies, 1910 University Drive, B117, Boise, ID 83725-1600
Admissions Phone: 208-426-1126 • Admissions Fax: 208-426-4989
Admissions E-mail: ranchust@boisestate.edu • Web Address: http://cobe.boisestate.edu/

Accountancy is at the forefront of Boise State's graduate business school, with two of its four programs focused on bottom lines. And new number-crunchers will be thrilled to calculate their own bottom-line tuition and fees at this bargain school. Boise State is unusually student-focused, as demonstrated by the Student of the Month awards it regularly gives to outstanding undergraduate and graduate students who the school believes "will represent the college well in their chosen profession." Each student chosen has his or her "photograph displayed in the foyer of the Business Building and are taken to lunch by the Dean to celebrate their award."

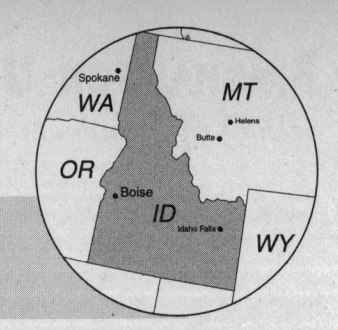

INSTITUTIONAL INFORMATION
Public/Private: Public
Evening Classes Available? No
Total Faculty: 55
% Faculty Part Time: 2
Students in Parent Institution: 14,883
Academic Calendar: Semester

PROGRAMS
Degrees Offered: MBA (33 to 54 credits, 12 months to 7 years), Master of Science in Taxation (MS) (30 credits, 12 months to 7 years), Master of Science in Accountancy (MS) (30 credits, 12 months to 7 years), Master of Science in Management Information Systems (MS) (30 credits)
Academic Specialties: Computer-aided instruction, computer analysis, computer simulations
Special Opportunities: Internship program
Study Abroad Options: France, Germany, and Spain

STUDENT INFORMATION
Total Business Students: 257
% Full Time: 20
% Female: 44
% Minority: 15
% International: 16
Average Age: 32

COMPUTER AND RESEARCH FACILITIES
Research Facilities: CD players
Computer Facilities: Access to online bibliographic retrieval services and online databases
Number of Student Computers: 300
Campuswide Network? Yes
Computer Proficiency Required? Yes
Special Purchasing Agreements? No

EXPENSES/FINANCIAL AID
Annual Tuition (Resident/Nonresident): $3,500/ $11,000
Room & Board (On/Off Campus): $5,600/ $11,800
% Receiving Financial Aid: 6

ADMISSIONS INFORMATION
Application Fee: $20
Electronic Application? No
Regular Application Deadline: 3/1
Regular Notification: Rolling
Deferment Available? No
Non-fall Admissions? Yes
Non-fall Application Deadline(s): 1/1 spring
Transfer Students Accepted? No
Need-Blind Admissions? No
Number of Applications Received: 122
% of Applicants Accepted: 65
% Accepted Who Enrolled: 90
Average GPA: 3.1
Average GMAT: 535
Other Admissions Factors Considered: Computer experience required in word processing, spreadsheet, and database; minimum GPA 2.9 recommended; minimum 2 years of work experience recommended

INTERNATIONAL STUDENTS
TOEFL Required of International Students? Yes
Minimum TOEFL: 587

EMPLOYMENT INFORMATION
Placement Office Available? Yes
% Employed Within 6 Months: 95

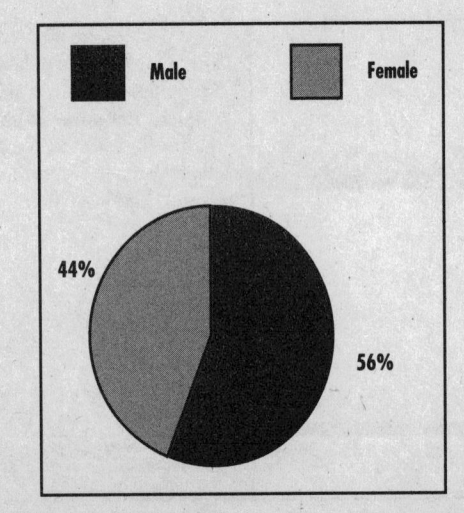

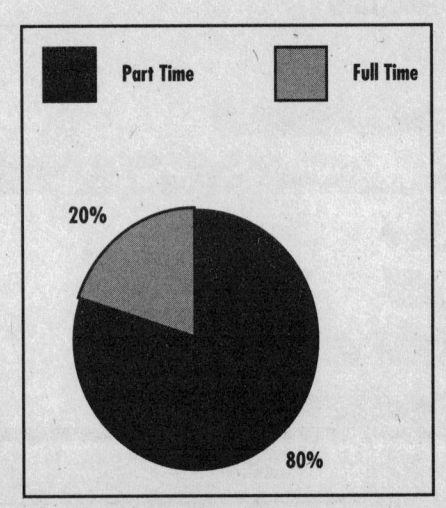

Boston College
The Carroll School of Management

Admissions Contact: Shelley Conley, Director of Graduate Enrollment and MBA Admissions
Address: Fulton Hall 315, Chestnut Hill, MA 02467
Admissions Phone: 617-552-3920 • Admissions Fax: 617-552-8078
Admissions E-mail: bcmba@bc.edu • Web Address: www.bc.edu\mba

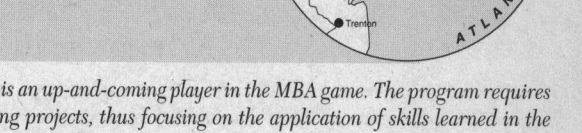

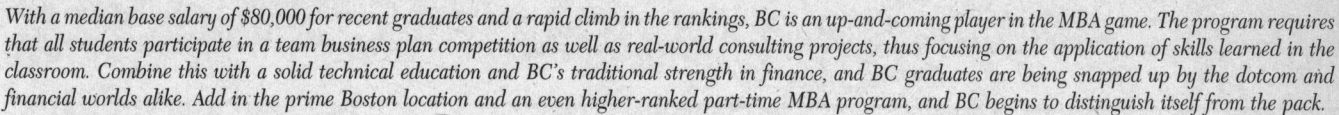

With a median base salary of $80,000 for recent graduates and a rapid climb in the rankings, BC is an up-and-coming player in the MBA game. The program requires that all students participate in a team business plan competition as well as real-world consulting projects, thus focusing on the application of skills learned in the classroom. Combine this with a solid technical education and BC's traditional strength in finance, and BC graduates are being snapped up by the dotcom and financial worlds alike. Add in the prime Boston location and an even higher-ranked part-time MBA program, and BC begins to distinguish itself from the pack.

INSTITUTIONAL INFORMATION
Public/Private: Private
Evening Classes Available? Yes
Total Faculty: 90
Students in Parent Institution: 14,419
Academic Calendar: Semester

PROGRAMS
Degrees Offered: Full-Time MBA (2 years), Part-Time MBA (3 years), Full-Time MS in Finance (1 year), Part-Time MS in Finance (2 years), MBA/MS in Finance (24 months), PhD in Finance (4 years), PhD in Organizational Studies (4 years)
Joint Degrees: MBA/MS in Finance (24 months); MBA/Juris Doctor (48 months); MBA/Master of Social Work (3 years); MBA/MS in Nursing (36 to 48 months); MBA/MS in Biology, Geology, Geophysics (36 months); MBA/MA in Math, Slavic Studies, Russian, Linguistics (36 months)
Academic Specialties: Finance, Information Technology, Global Management, Consulting
Special Opportunities: MBA Program offers dual-degree with Robert E. Schuman University in Stratsbourg, France (MBA and the Diplome degree).
Study Abroad Options: China, France, Ireland, Spain, Mexico, The Netherlands

STUDENT INFORMATION
Total Business Students: 766
% Full Time: 30
% Female: 37
% Minority: 19
% International: 27
Average Age: 27

COMPUTER AND RESEARCH FACILITIES
Research Facilities: Retirement Research Center, Center for Corporate Community Relations, Small Business Development Center, Center for Work and Family
Computer Facilities: Latest financial and trade data in electronic form and more than 500 databases.
Campuswide Network? Yes
% of MBA Classrooms Wired: 100
Computer Model Recommended: No
Internet Fee? Yes

EXPENSES/FINANCIAL AID
Annual Tuition: $25,792
Books and Supplies: $1,500
Average Grant: $13,330

ADMISSIONS INFORMATION
Application Fee: $50
Electronic Application? Yes
Early Decision Application Deadline: 12/1
Early Decision Notification: 1/31
Regular Application Deadline: 4/1
Regular Notification: Rolling
Length of Deferment: 1 year
Non-fall Application Deadline(s): July to Sept.
Transfer Policy: 4 courses (with a grade of B or higher) accepted from AACSB MBA programs.
Need-Blind Admissions? Yes
Number of Applications Received: 793
% of Applicants Accepted: 40
% Accepted Who Enrolled: 34
Average GPA: 3.2
Average GMAT: 640
Average Years Experience: 4
Other Admissions Factors Considered: Applicant's interests match school's core competencies
Minority/Disadvantaged Student Recruitment Programs: Graduate Management Admission Search Service search mailings nationally to identify underrepresented candidates; active participation in National Black MBA Association case competitions, regional conferences, and national meetings

INTERNATIONAL STUDENTS
TOEFL Required of International Students? Yes
Minimum TOEFL: 600 (250 computer)

EMPLOYMENT INFORMATION
Placement Office Available? Yes
% Employed Within 3 Months: 97

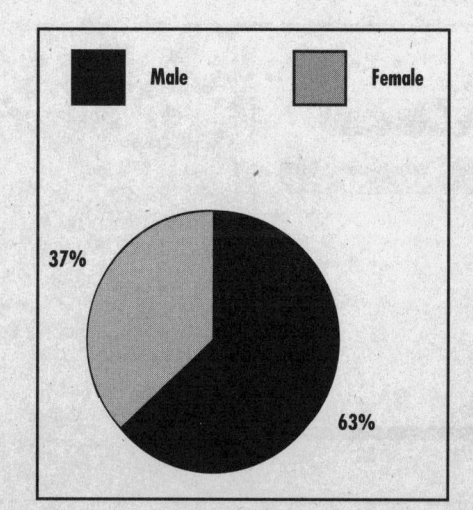

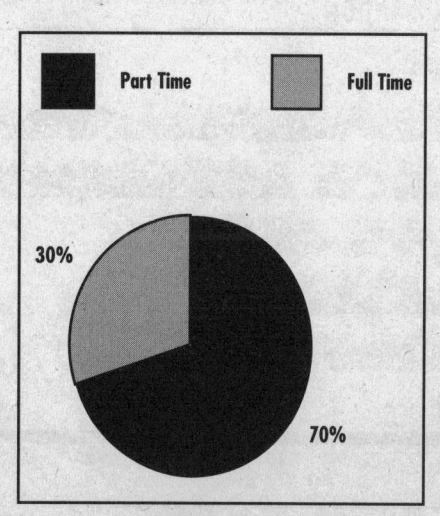

BOSTON UNIVERSITY
School of Management

Admissions Contact: Evelyn Tate, Director of Graduate Admissions and Financial Aid
Address: 595 Commonwealth Avenue, Boston, MA 02215
Admissions Phone: 617-353-2670 • Admissions Fax: 617-353-7368
Admissions E-mail: mba@bu.edu • Web Address: management.bu.edu

The School of Management at Boston University is one of the largest in the country, and students here say it offers a "beautifully organized," "almost flawless" MBA program that stresses teamwork and practical, hands-on education. Professors are "extremely helpful, open for discussion," and "enthusiastic," and BU boasts a spiffy new building as well as a wide array of resources and dual degree programs.

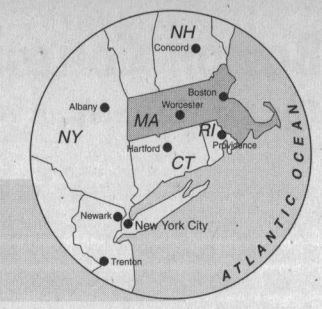

INSTITUTIONAL INFORMATION
Public/Private: Private
Evening Classes Available? Yes
Total Faculty: 116
% Faculty Female: 19
Student/Faculty Ratio: 14:1
Students in Parent Institution: 27,767
Academic Calendar: Semester

PROGRAMS
Degrees Offered: MBA (2 years full time, 3 to 6 years part time), Executive MBA (17 months), MS in Information Systems (12 months), MS in Investment Management (17 months)
Joint Degrees: MBA/MS, MBA/MPH in Television Management, MBA/MA International Relations, MBA/MS Manufacturing Engineering, MBA/MA Economics, MBA/MA Medical Sciences (80 credits), MBA/MIS (84 credits), MBA/JD (124 credits), MBA/MPH, MS/MBA (MS in Information Systems and traditional MBA) (84 credits, 21 months)
Academic Specialties: Health Care Management, Finance, MIS, Entrepreneurship, Public and Nonprofit Management
Special Opportunities: MS/MIS programs
Study Abroad Options: International Management Programs in Kobe, Japan, and Shanghai, China; study abroad in France and UK

STUDENT INFORMATION
Total Business Students: 1,158
% Full Time: 53
% Female: 34
% Minority: 11
% International: 42
Average Age: 27

COMPUTER AND RESEARCH FACILITIES
Research Facilities: Systems Research Center, Entrepreneurial Management Institute, Executive Development Roundtable, Center for Enterprise Leadership, Human Resources Policy Institute, Institute for Leading in a Dynamic Economy, Health Care Management Research Center, Leadership Institute, Bronner e-Business Center and Hatchery, Center for Team Learning
Computer Facilities: 3,800 Data Parts, 5 computer labs, multimedia lab, and 28 classrooms with complete computing and A/V systems.
Campuswide Network? Yes
% of MBA Classrooms Wired: 100
Computer Model Recommended: No
Internet Fee? No

EXPENSES/FINANCIAL AID
Annual Tuition: $25,700
Tuition Per Credit: $809
Books and Supplies: $900
Average Grant: $12,900
Average Loan: $40,728
% Receiving Financial Aid: 60
% Receiving Aid Their First Year: 60

ADMISSIONS INFORMATION
Application Fee: $90
Electronic Application? Yes
Regular Application Deadline: 4/1
Regular Notification: 5/15
Length of Deferment: 1 year
Non-fall Application Deadline(s): 11/15 spring (part time only)
Transfer Policy: Part time only
Need-Blind Admissions? Yes
Number of Applications Received: 1,115
% of Applicants Accepted: 36
% Accepted Who Enrolled: 41
Average GPA: 3.1
Average GMAT: 635
Average Years Experience: 5
Other Admissions Factors Considered: Leadership skills, movement in career, team skills
Minority/Disadvantaged Student Recruitment Programs: Advertisements placed in periodicals that target specific communities, scholarships offered to minority students, partnership with the National Black MBA Association, student outreach to the ALANA community concerning NBMBAA and the National Hispanic MBA Association, attendance at minority recruiting events
Other Schools to Which Students Applied: Babson College, Boston College, Case Western Reserve University, Duke University, Georgetown University, New York University

INTERNATIONAL STUDENTS
TOEFL Required of International Students? Yes
Minimum TOEFL: 600 (250 computer)

EMPLOYMENT INFORMATION

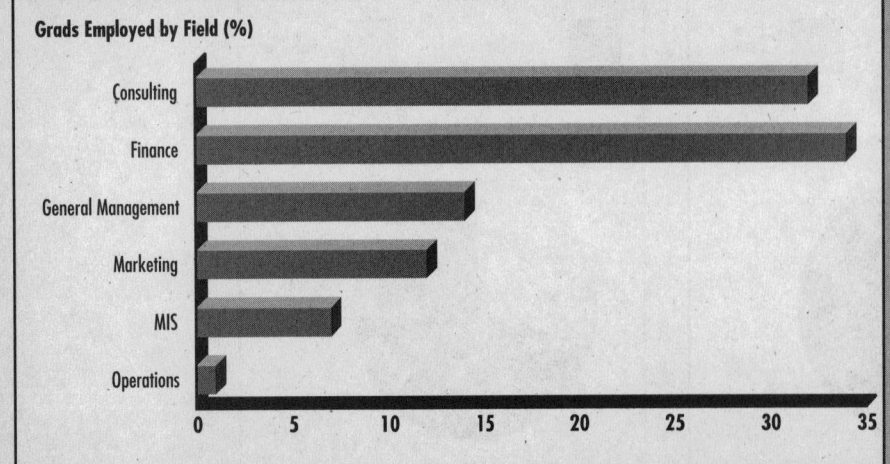

Grads Employed by Field (%)

Field	%
Consulting	~33
Finance	~34
General Management	~8
Marketing	~14
MIS	~6
Operations	~1

Placement Office Available? Yes
% Employed Within 3 Months: 98
Frequent Employers: Acorn Systems, Andersen Consulting, Boston Consulting Group, Citibank, Citizens Bank, Deloitte Consulting, Digitas, EMC Corp., Fidelity Investments, JPMorgan Chase, Lehman Bros. Holdings, Liberty Mutual, PricewaterhouseCoopers, State Street Corp., Teradyne Inc.
Prominent Alumni: Jack F. Smith, Jr. (GSM '65), chairman and CEO, General Motors; Millard Mickey Drexler, president and CEO, The Gap; Ed Zander (GSM '75), president and COO, Sun Microsystems; Allen Questrom (SMG '64), chairman and CEO, JC Penney

BOWLING GREEN STATE UNIVERSITY
College of Business Administration

Admissions Contact: Carmen Castro-Rivera, Director, Graduate Studies in Business
Address: 369 Business Administration Building, Bowling Green, OH 43403
Admissions Phone: 419-372-2488 • Admissions Fax: 419-372-2875
Admissions E-mail: mba-info@cba.bgsu.edu • Web Address: www.cba.bgsu.edu/gsb/gradprg

It at first seems incongruous that you'd find a business school with a diverse range of graduate programs and student body in a small town in northern Ohio. But if you take time to look closely at Bowling Green State University's b-school, you'll find a student body that's 50 percent international and five very distinct graduate business programs. Practically any student with an interest in studying business will find a track of study appropriate to his or her skills and interests.

INSTITUTIONAL INFORMATION
Public/Private: Public
Evening Classes Available? Yes
Total Faculty: 66
% Faculty Female: 27
% Faculty Minority: 15
Student/Faculty Ratio: 30:1
Students in Parent Institution: 19,900
Academic Calendar: Semester

PROGRAMS
Degrees Offered: MBA (14 months full time, 2.5 years part time), EMBA (18 months), Master of Accountancy (12 months), Master of Organization Development (18 months), MS in Applied Statistics, MS in Computer Science (Operations Research), MA in Economics
Special Opportunities: Specializations in MIS, Finance, and Accounting
Study Abroad Options: France—ESC Nantes

STUDENT INFORMATION
Total Business Students: 150
% Full Time: 29
% Female: 36
% Minority: 14
% Out of State: 11
% International: 50
Average Age: 29

COMPUTER AND RESEARCH FACILITIES
Research Facilities: Institute for Organizational Effectiveness, Statistical Consulting Center, Supply Chain Management Institute
Computer Facilities: The campus supports a comprehensive network of academic computing resources, including DEC/VAX and IBM major systems, along with IBM and Apple microcomputers. This business computing network includes 4 state-of-the-art computer classroom laboratories featuring advanced computer systems and Internet connections for students.
Campuswide Network? Yes
Internet Fee? No

EXPENSES/FINANCIAL AID
Annual Tuition: $9,552
Tuition Per Credit: $295
Room & Board (Off Campus): $5,800
Books and Supplies: $800
% Receiving Aid Their First Year: 33

ADMISSIONS INFORMATION
Application Fee: $30
Electronic Application? Yes
Regular Application Deadline: Rolling
Regular Notification: Rolling
Length of Deferment: 1 year
Non-fall Application Deadline(s): 11/1 spring, 11/1 summer, 3/1 fall
Transfer Students Accepted? Yes

Transfer Policy: Maximum of 6 graduate hours of transfer credit from AACSB-accredited institutions. Some restrictions apply.
Need-Blind Admissions? Yes
Number of Applications Received: 184
% of Applicants Accepted: 67
% Accepted Who Enrolled: 65
Average GPA: 3.1
GPA Range: 2.9-3.3
Average GMAT: 526
GMAT Range: 483-590
Average Years Experience: 6
Other Admissions Factors Considered: Interview, work experience, undergraduate major
Minority/Disadvantaged Student Recruitment Programs: Project Search is a program in the Graduate College at BGSU that recruits students for university graduate programs (primarily full time) and then coordinates an array of services designed to lead these students from enrollment through graduation.

INTERNATIONAL STUDENTS
TOEFL Required of International Students? Yes
Minimum TOEFL: 550 (213 computer)

EMPLOYMENT INFORMATION
Placement Office Available? Yes
Frequent Employers: American Express, American Greetings, Ernst & Young, Marathon Ashland, National City Corporation, Nationwide Insurance, Owens Corning, Plante & Moran, Progressive Insurance, State Farm Insurance

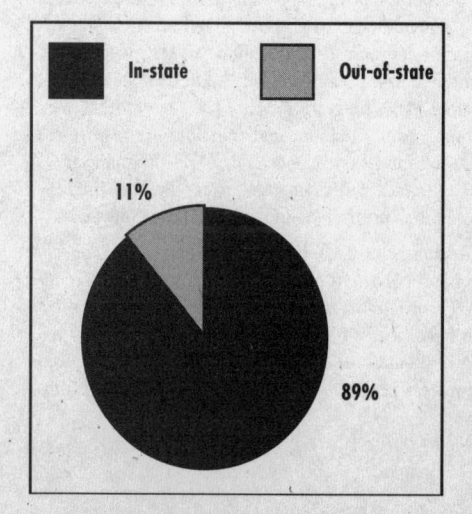

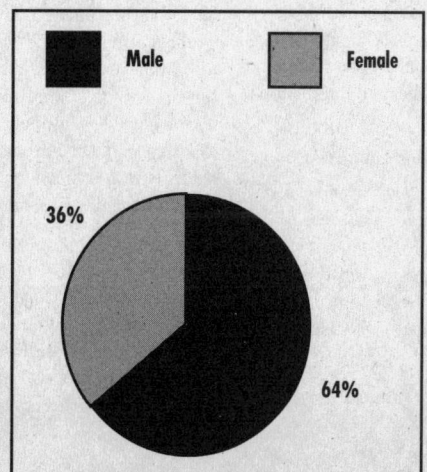

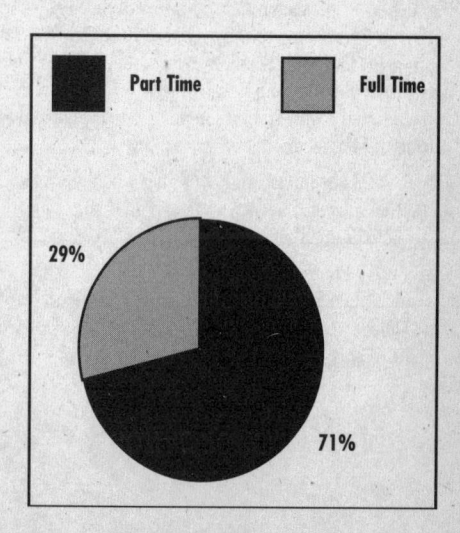

In-state 89% / Out-of-state 11%

Male 64% / Female 36%

Part Time 29% / Full Time 71%

BOWLING GREEN STATE UNIVERSITY

STUDENTS

The BGSU MBA program, accredited by the AACSB, is recognized nationally and internationally for the quality of its students and faculty. The incoming class of full-time MBA students is limited to a maximum of 40 students to maintain the small class sizes and faculty accessibility for which the MBA program is known. The program works to foster an "espirit de corps" among the students. Within each semester, full-time students will be a part of a cohort that shares a common schedule. This cohort experience is vital to the development of communication and teamwork skills and promotes valuable networking abilities that will be critical in any business professional career.

The student body in the MBA program is very diverse, and this diversity enhances the learning environment. The current MBA student population includes people from 16 countries and 6 states. In addition, approximately 34 percent of our students are international. Across all programs, students range in age from 22 to 52, with an average of 29. The average work experience of full-time, part-time and executive students is 3, 6, and 10 years, respectively, but work experience is not required of full-time or part-time students. BGSU's MBA programs do not require undergraduate degrees in business for admission, so participants' academic backgrounds vary.

ACADEMICS

MBA Program Philosophy

MBA programs are as varied as the business schools that offer them. Some are big. Bowling Green State University's MBA is not. The incoming class of full-time students consists of only 40 people. This means small class sizes and easy access to faculty. Some programs appear to prefer an undergraduate business degree. BGSU does not. The full-time MBA can be completed in 14 months with or without an undergraduate business degree. A specialization requires only an additional semester. Some schools require business experience for admission. BGSU does not. The full-time program is designed for students who will be new to their chosen fields. Most business schools (75 percent) are not AACSB accredited. BGSU is AACSB accredited. Accreditation is one way to demonstrate how serious BGSU is about their business programs.

The College of Business Administration has created a small-school atmosphere within a major research university. The outstanding students who comprise the MBA cohort reap the benefits of these resources without facing the cutthroat competition common in larger programs.

The College of Business Administration

The College of Business Administration serves approximately 2,300 undergraduate students and 300 graduate students. The College offers two undergraduate degrees (BS Business Administration and BS Economics) and six master's programs (Master of Business Administration, Master of Organization Development, Master of Accountancy, Master of Science in Applied Statistics, Master of Arts in Economics, and Operations Research Specialization in the Master of Science in Computer Science). The College consists of seven academic departments: Accounting and Management Information Systems, Applied Statistics and Operations Research, Economics, Finance, Legal Studies and International Business, Management, and Marketing.

The Business Administration building is a modern facility providing classrooms and office space for faculty, staff, and graduate assistants. MBA classes are generally held in small seminar-style classrooms or computer laboratory classrooms.

University Overview

Bowling Green State University is a diverse, mid-size institution located in northwest Ohio, approximately 23 miles south of Toledo. BGSU was founded in 1910. The 1,338-acre campus houses more than 100 buildings in a small-town setting.

The University serves approximately 17,000 undergraduate and 2,900 graduate students. BGSU combines the resources of a first-rate research institution with the friendliness and ambience of a small college. The work of MBA students is supported by excellent facilities, including a modern Business Administration Building, an outstanding library collection, excellent computing facilities, and a network of campus research centers.

The University's degree offerings include more than 165 undergraduate degrees, 15 master's in more than 60 fields, 2 specialist degrees, the EdD, and 16 PhD programs. The heart of the University is its 550 full-time faculty members, who are engaged in teaching, research, and public service activities.

In order to function effectively in a professional world that is more diverse, more team-oriented, more global, and more dynamic than ever before, the BGSU MBA program is designed to prepare graduates who:

- Know the fundamentals of business well.
- Recognize the ethical obligations of leadership.
- Engage problems creatively.
- Learn on their own, continuously.
- Work well in teams with diverse memberships.
- Understand change and know how to adapt and succeed in the midst of change.
- Communicate effectively, both orally and in writing.

The MBA program provides a broad curriculum organized around three principle components: foundation, core, and capstone courses. The foundation courses cover Financial and Managerial Accounting, Economic Analysis, Statistics, Quantitative Analysis, and Information Technology. The core courses include Financial Management, Operations Management, Marketing Management, and Ethics and Law in Business. The capstone courses cover Economic Policy, Leadership and Change, Strategy Design and Implementation, and International Business and Management. For full-time students, the program includes modules on Computer Skills, International Business Principles, and the Foundations of Ethical Leadership. In addition, students take part in a series of co-curricular professional development seminars dealing with topics such as presentations and report writing, team facilitation, effective negotiations, career planning, and organizational politics.

Although students may choose to do a general MBA, they also may pursue a formal specialization in Accounting, Finance, or Management Information Systems. Or, a student may pursue the dual degree option and earn a second master's degree in any of a variety of fields, such as Organization Development, Public Health, Industrial Technology, or Public Administration.

The MBA degree requires a minimum of 42 semester hours (47 semester hours for full-time students). The general MBA may be completed in 14 months regardless of the student's prior undergraduate preparation. An MBA with a specialization requires 12 additional semester hours (one additional semester of full-time study). The full-time MBA program primarily serves students who will be entry-level professionals upon graduation and does not require business experience as a requirement for admission. The evening MBA program serves students with professional experience and an ongoing career. Neither the full-time nor evening program requires prior academic preparation in business.

Bowling Green State University has been offering an Executive MBA program since 1977. The EMBA program is a rigorous, accelerated program that requires 12 graduate courses. The program serves students with extensive professional experience and is designed to accomodate the demmands of professional travel and relocation. Prior academic preparation in business is not required for the EMBA program. However, candidates must be nominated by their employers, unless self-employed.

College of Business Administration

A comprehensive and carefully designed career planning and placement program is an integral part of the BGSU MBA experience. Career planning activities begin during orientation week and continue throughout the year.

The Career Services office, which has been recognized nationally and regionally for the quality of its programming, assists with career development and job placement from the student's first semester through actual job placement.

Career Services provides students with personal help with interviewing skills, resume preparation, alumni and professional networking skills and opportunities, and access to on-campus recruiters. These services are provided using state-of-the-art Web-based computer systems that have received national recognition.

COSTS

Tuition and fees for 2001–2002 for 12 semester hours per semester (full-time) for Ohio residents total $3,728. Nonresidents pay $6,854. Tuition per credit hour is $350 for residents. Nonresidents pay $648 per credit hour. Room and board for off-campus accommodations is approximately $5,800 per year. Additional costs for books and other academic expenses vary from $500 to $800 for the academic year.

Financial aid is available to full-time students in a variety of forms, including graduate assistantships, loans, student employment, and scholarships. The College of Business Administration, in cooperation with the Graduate College, offers a significant number of assistantships to outstanding full-time MBA candidates. These positions provide a cash stipend and scholarship covering all tuition and fees for the semesters of appointment. A student serving in the fall and spring semesters also receives a scholarship covering instructional fees for the program's summer sessions. The cash stipends for 2001–2002 range from $3,550 to $7,100.

ADMISSIONS

Graduate Studies in Business at BGSU welcomes applications from individuals regardless of their undergraduate major. Applicants must submit an application, transcripts of all previous college work, GMAT scores (and TOEFL when applicable), two letters of recommendation, a personal statement, a current resume, and a $30 application fee. Prior work experience is also reviewed when making assistantship decisions, although it is not required.

Application Facts and Dates

For full-time domestic students, the program begins in July with two courses. For international students, the session begins in late June with a one-week intensive orientation program followed by the same two courses. As a result of the limited admissions and mid-summer starting date, completed application materials including test scores (GMAT, TOEFL) must be received by the following deadlines:

January 15 for **international** applicants applying for a graduate assistantship award.

February 15 for **international** applicants who are NOT applying for a graduate assistantship award.

February 15 for **domestic** applicants applying for a graduate assistantship award.

March 15 for **domestic** applicants who are NOT applying for a graduate assistantship award.

International applications received or completed after the February 15 deadline are unlikely to be processed in time for admitted students to apply for and receive their student visas and begin the program in late June/early July. Domestic applications received or completed after the March 15 deadline will be accepted for consideration on a space-available basis.

Admissions Contact: Carmen Castro-Rivera, Director, Graduate Studies in Business
Address: Room 369 Business Administration Building, Bowling Green, OH 43403
Admissions Phone: 419-372-2488 • Admissions Fax: 419-372-2875
Admissions E-mail: mba-info@cba.bgsu.edu • Web Address: www.cba.bgsu.edu/gsb/gradprg

BRIGHAM YOUNG UNIVERSITY
Marriott School of Management

Admissions Contact: Debra Ruse, Program Administrator
Address: 640 TNRB, Provo, UT 84602
Admissions Phone: 801-422-3509 • Admissions Fax: 801-422-0513
Admissions E-mail: mba@byu.edu • Web Address: marriottschool.byu.edu/mba

Students at Brigham Young University's "remarkably" ethics-oriented Marriott School say their professors constantly emphasize the importance of character and the moral responsibilities of leadership. Marriott is also a tremendous place to study international business because many students have acquired foreign work experience, cross-cultural knowledge, and proficiency in a second (or third) language as missionaries for the Church of Jesus Christ of Latter-day Saints.

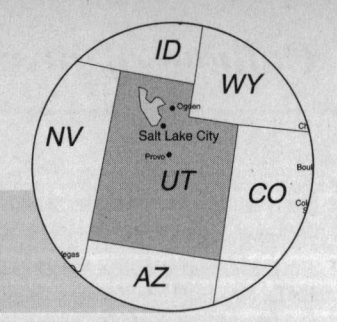

INSTITUTIONAL INFORMATION
Public/Private: Private
Evening Classes Available? No
Total Faculty: 63
% Faculty Female: 6
% Faculty Minority: 1
% Faculty Part Time: 9
Student/Faculty Ratio: 4:1
Students in Parent Institution: 33,645
Academic Calendar: 2-semester

PROGRAMS
Degrees Offered: EMBA (2 years), MBA (2 years), MOB (2 years), EMPA (3 years), MISM and MAcc (5 years including undergraduate years), MPA (2 years)
Joint Degrees: MBA/JD (4 years); MBA/MS, IPD Program with Engineering Department (4 years); MBA/International (4 years); MAcc/JD (4 years); MOB/JD (4 years); MPA/JD (4 years)
Academic Specialties: Entrepreneurship, Corporate Finance, Investment Management, Management of Financial Institutions, Marketing Management, Information Systems, Organizational Behavior, Strategic Management, Production and Operations Management, Quantitative Methods, International Business, Accounting, White Collar Fraud, E-Business
Special Opportunities: Executive Lecture Series, Computer Summer Prep, 9 Business Language Programs, Computer Business Simulation, Field Study Program, Faculty-Hosted International Business Study in Asia and Latin America
Study Abroad Options: China, Vietnam, Russia, Sweden, Germany, UK, Czech Republic

STUDENT INFORMATION
Total Business Students: 251
% Female: 15
% Minority: 4
% International: 14
Average Age: 28

COMPUTER AND RESEARCH FACILITIES
Research Facilities: Center for Entrepreneurship; Center for E-Business; Center for International Business Education and Research; Institute of Retail, Sales and Marketing; Financial Services Inst.
Computer Facilities: Computer labs, Lexis-Nexis, Bloomberg, EDGAR
Campuswide Network? Yes
% of MBA Classrooms Wired: 100
Computer Model Recommended: Laptop

EXPENSES/FINANCIAL AID
Annual Tuition: $6,140
Tuition Per Credit: $341
Room & Board (On/Off Campus): $5,340/$5,640
Books and Supplies: $1,260
Average Grant: $4,053
Average Loan: $9,139
% Receiving Financial Aid: 72
% Receiving Aid Their First Year: 80

ADMISSIONS INFORMATION
Application Fee: $50
Electronic Application? Yes
Early Decision Application Deadline: 1/15
Early Decision Notification: 2/28
Regular Application Deadline: 3/1
Regular Notification: Rolling
Length of Deferment: 2 years
Non-fall Admissions? No
Transfer Policy: 15 credit hours of grad-level courses (minimum grade of B, no pass/fail)
Need-Blind Admissions? Yes
Number of Applications Received: 468
% of Applicants Accepted: 37
% Accepted Who Enrolled: 72
Average GPA: 3.5
Average GMAT: 660
Average Years Experience: 3
Other Admissions Factors Considered: International experience, evidence of leadership skills
Minority/Disadvantaged Student Recruitment Programs: Ford Motor Co. Extended Reach Scholarship; the diversity recruitment office is partnering with more than 10 companies through a diversity initiative to provide financial assistance to minority students; focus on recruitment for minority students in large urban areas
Other Schools to Which Students Applied: Utah State, University of Utah, Idaho State

INTERNATIONAL STUDENTS
TOEFL Required of International Students? Yes
Minimum TOEFL: 580 (230 computer)

EMPLOYMENT INFORMATION

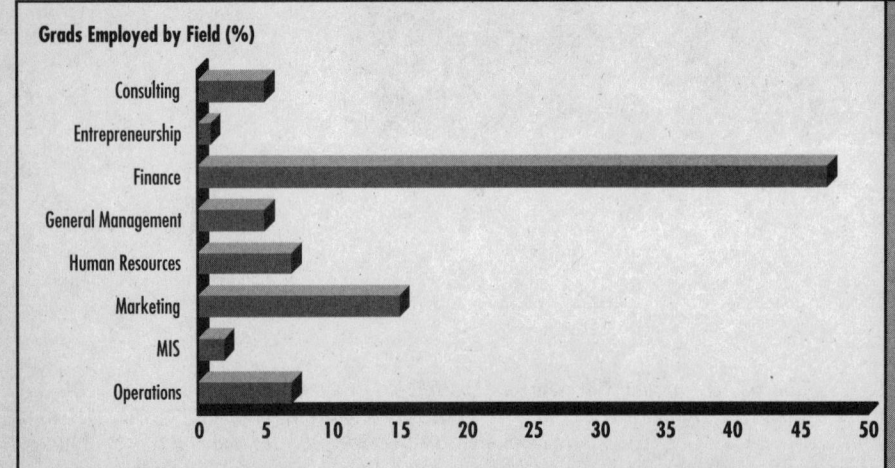

Grads Employed by Field (%)

Field	%
Consulting	~2
Entrepreneurship	~1
Finance	~47
General Management	~3
Human Resources	~2
Marketing	~15
MIS	~2
Operations	~7

Placement Office Available? Yes
% Employed Within 3 Months: 98
Frequent Employers: AMD, Bear Stearns, Cintas, Citigroup, Dell Computers, Deloitte & Touche, Dow Chemical, Ford Motor Co., Gateway, GE, Goldman Sachs, Hewlett-Packard, IBM, Intel, Iomega, Marriott International, Motorola, Payless Shoes, DaimlerChrysler, Partners Group, Eli Lilly, SBC, Honeywell, Ernst & Young, Target
Prominent Alumni: Kevin Rollins, vice chairman, Dell Computer Corporation; Matt Mosman, senior VP of corporate development, Oracle Corp.; Warren Jenson, CFO, Amazon.com

CALIFORNIA POLYTECHNIC STATE UNIVERSITY—SAN LUIS OBISPO

College of Business

Admissions Contact: David Peach, Director, Graduate Programs
Address: Graduate Management Programs, San Luis Obispo, CA 93407
Admissions Phone: 805-756-2637 • Admissions Fax: 805-756-0110
Admissions E-mail: dpeach@calpoly.edu • Web Address: www.cob.calpoly.edu

This small MBA program (106 students) offers the requisite courses in all the usual suspects: finance, accounting, marketing, and so on. However, the program's competitive advantage lies in the opportunity it offers MBA students to focus on agribusiness. Cal Poly is an aggie school and it plays to this strength. Several other dual degrees are offered with other departments/schools ranging from architecture to engineering. The MBA/MS in Engineering program offers the option to concentrate on manufacturing management.

INSTITUTIONAL INFORMATION
Public/Private: Public
Evening Classes Available? No
Total Faculty: 58
% Faculty Female: 22
% Faculty Minority: 38
Academic Calendar: Quarter

PROGRAMS
Degrees Offered: MBA with concentrations in Agribusiness and Management (full time, 96 credits, 2 years)
Joint Degrees: MBA/MS in Engineering Management (full time, 96 to 98 credits, 2 years); MBA/MS in Computer Science (full time, 105 credits, 2 to 3 years); MBA/MS in Electrical Engineering (full time, 101 credits, 2 to 3 years); MBA/MS in Mechanical Engineering (full time, 101 credits, 2 to 3 years)
Study Abroad Options: Hungary, Israel, Mexico, Taiwan, France

STUDENT INFORMATION
Total Business Students: 106
% Female: 28
% Minority: 8
% Out of State: 12
% International: 9
Average Age: 27

COMPUTER AND RESEARCH FACILITIES
Computer Facilities: Full range of facilities and resources
Campuswide Network? Yes
% of MBA Classrooms Wired: 100
Computer Model Recommended: Laptop
Internet Fee? No

EXPENSES/FINANCIAL AID
Books and Supplies: $2,000

ADMISSIONS INFORMATION
Application Fee: $55
Electronic Application? Yes
Regular Application Deadline: 7/1, 4/1 for international applicants
Regular Notification: Rolling
Deferment Available? Yes
Length of Deferment: 2 years
Non-fall Admissions? No
Transfer Students Accepted? Yes
Transfer Policy: 8-unit transfer
Need-Blind Admissions? No
Number of Applications Received: 144
% of Applicants Accepted: 44
% Accepted Who Enrolled: 78
Average GPA: 3.3
GPA Range: 2.6-3.9
Average GMAT: 558
GMAT Range: 480-700
Average Years Experience: 5
Other Admissions Factors Considered: Minimum GPA of 3.0; minimum of 3 years of work experience and computer experience are recommended

INTERNATIONAL STUDENTS
TOEFL Required of International Students? Yes
Minimum TOEFL: 550 (213 computer)

EMPLOYMENT INFORMATION
Placement Office Available? Yes
% Employed Within 3 Months: 100

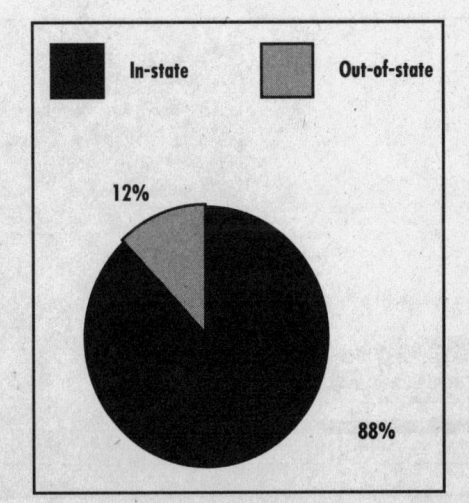

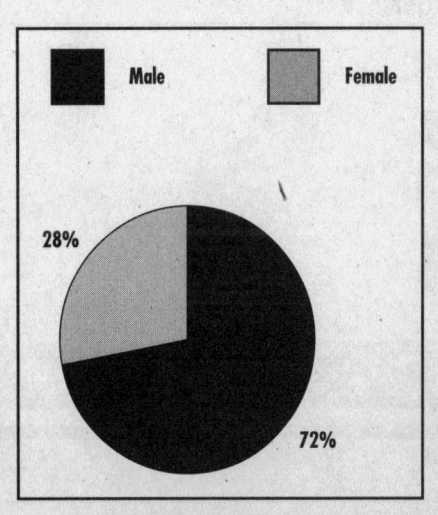

In-state: 88% / Out-of-state: 12%

Male: 72% / Female: 28%

CALIFORNIA STATE UNIVERSITY — CHICO
College of Business

Admissions Contact: Sandy Jensen, Advisor, Business Graduate Programs
Address: CSU, Chico 041, Chico, CA 95929
Admissions Phone: 530-898-4425 • Admissions Fax: 530-898-5889
Admissions E-mail: sjensen@csuchico.edu • Web Address: www.cob.csuchico.edu

The MBA program at CSU—Chico is designed for students with undergraduate study in any major or concentration. The program is traditional and comprehensive, and it fosters a strong intellectual focus on managerial preparation and real-world business skills. CSU—Chico's College of Business declares that its graduates have the "distinctive quality of 'extraordinary effectiveness'" that makes them appealing to recruiters.

INSTITUTIONAL INFORMATION
Public/Private: Public
Evening Classes Available? No
Total Faculty: 10
% Faculty Female: 20
% Faculty Minority: 5
% Faculty Part Time: 20
Student/Faculty Ratio: 35:1
Students in Parent Institution: 16,000
Academic Calendar: Semester

PROGRAMS
Degrees Offered: Master of Business Administration (MBA) (full time or part time, 30 credits, 18 months to 5 years), with concentrations in Finance, Human Resources, Management, Management Information Systems, Production Management, and Marketing; Master of Science in Accountancy (MS) (full time or part time, 30 credits, 18 months to 5 years), with concentrations in Accounting and Management Information Systems
Joint Degrees: MBA with MIS emphasis (2 years)
Academic Specialties: SAP, real-world consulting experience, team projects, project management, cutting-edge MIS applications

STUDENT INFORMATION
Total Business Students: 80
% Full Time: 70
% Female: 35
% Minority: 4
% Out of State: 1
% International: 45
Average Age: 27

COMPUTER AND RESEARCH FACILITIES
Computer Facilities: More-than-adequate computer facilities are available on campus.
Campuswide Network? Yes
% of MBA Classrooms Wired: 100
Computer Model Recommended: No
Internet Fee? No

EXPENSES/FINANCIAL AID
Annual Tuition (Resident/Nonresident): $2,120/$7,500
Room & Board (On/Off Campus): $7,500/$8,500
Books and Supplies: $1,000
Average Grant: $1,000
Average Loan: $5,000
% Receiving Financial Aid: 65
% Receiving Aid Their First Year: 50

ADMISSIONS INFORMATION
Application Fee: $55
Electronic Application? Yes
Regular Application Deadline: Rolling
Regular Notification: Rolling
Deferment Available? Yes
Length of Deferment: 1 year
Non-fall Admissions? Yes
Non-fall Application Deadline(s): Rolling
Transfer Students Accepted? Yes
Transfer Policy: Must meet our admissions criteria
Need-Blind Admissions? Yes
Number of Applications Received: 100
% of Applicants Accepted: 70
% Accepted Who Enrolled: 50
Average GPA: 3.3
GPA Range: 2.7-3.7
Average GMAT: 560
GMAT Range: 540-650
Average Years Experience: 3
Other Admissions Factors Considered: Computer experience required (word processing, spreadsheet, database); minimum score in the 50th percentile on the GMAT and minimum GPA of 2.75 for the last 60 units required; 3 letters of recommendation required; minimum of 2 years of work experience recommended
Other Schools to Which Students Applied: San Francisco State University, California State University—Sacramento

INTERNATIONAL STUDENTS
TOEFL Required of International Students? Yes
Minimum TOEFL: 550 (213 computer)

EMPLOYMENT INFORMATION

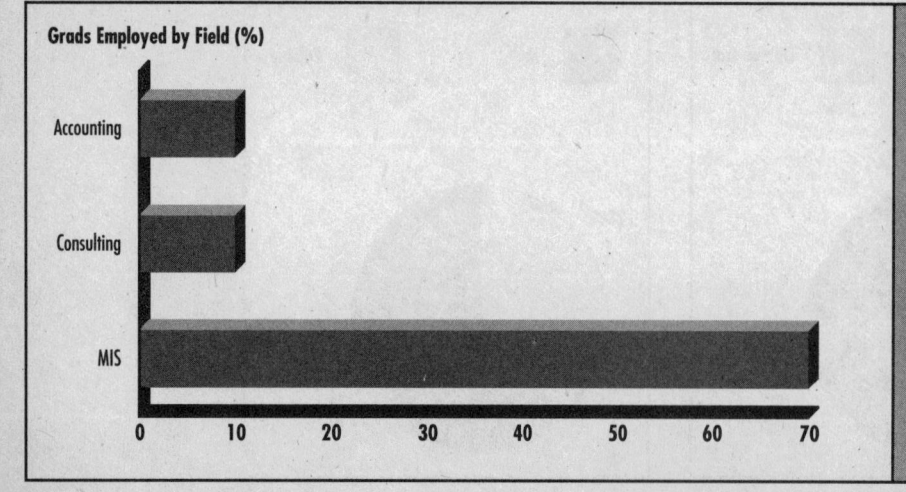

Grads Employed by Field (%):
- Accounting: ~10
- Consulting: ~10
- MIS: ~70

Placement Office Available? Yes
% Employed Within 3 Months: 95
Frequent Employers: Chevron, Intel, Ernst & Young, Deloitte & Touche, Accenture, Micron, Apple, Hewlett-Packard

CALIFORNIA STATE UNIVERSITY — FULLERTON
College of Business and Economics

Admissions Contact: Pre-Admission Advisor
Address: PO Box 6848, Fullerton, CA 92834
Admissions Phone: 714-278-2211 • Admissions Fax: 714-278-7101
Admissions E-mail: mba@fullerton.edu • Web Address: business.fullerton.edu

The Fullerton MBA offers three plans for the attainment of a Master in Business Administration. The MBA Generalist plan is constructed for those applicants who have little or no business course work or work experience; the MBA Specialist plan is designed for applicants who have recent business course work or experience and allows them to select an area of concentration; and the MBA International Business plan is designed for students with prior business education who wish to specialize in international business. Most Fullerton MBA students are working professionals, commuting to campus from work and attending afternoon or evening classes.

INSTITUTIONAL INFORMATION
Public/Private: Public
Evening Classes Available? Yes
Total Faculty: 44
% Faculty Female: 18
% Faculty Minority: 7
% Faculty Part Time: 7
Student/Faculty Ratio: 20:1
Students in Parent Institution: 25,550
Academic Calendar: Semester

PROGRAMS
Degrees Offered: Master of Business Administration, Specialist (MBA) (part time, 33 credits, 12 months to 5 years), with concentrations in Accounting, Finance, Management, Management Science, Management Information Systems, and Marketing; Master of Business Administration (MBA) (part time, distance learning option, 57 credits, 2 to 5 years); Master of Science in Taxation (MS) (full time or part time, 30 credits, 12 months to 5 years); Master of Science in Management Science (MS) (full time or part time, 33 credits, 12 months to 5 years), with concentration in Management Information Systems; Master of Science in Accountancy (MS) (full time or part time, 30 credits, 12 months to 5 years)
Academic Specialties: Financial Accounting, Auditing, Managerial Accounting, Cost Accounting, Accounting Systems, Tax, Advanced Accounting, Governmental Accounting, International Economics, Macroeconomics, Money and Banking, International Trade, Economic Development, Economic Theory, Social Security, Financial Institutions, Corporate Finance, Real Estate, Business Law, Small Business Management, Strategic Management, Operations Management, Organizational Behavior, Human Resource Management, Strategic Management, Marketing Management, Marketing Analysis and Planning, Marketing Research, Marketing Technology, Computer Science, Microcomputers, Multivariate Analysis, Operations Research, Statistics, Information Systems, Supply Chain Management

STUDENT INFORMATION
Total Business Students: 511
% Female: 44
% Minority: 30
% International: 28

COMPUTER AND RESEARCH FACILITIES
Research Facilities: SAP, XBRL, Center for Entrepreneurship, Center for the Study of Emerging Financial Markets, Center for Insurance Studies, Center for International Business Program, Family Business Council, Institute for Economic & Environmental Studies, Real Estate and Land Use Institute, Small Business Council
Computer Facilities: Computer labs, areas on campus of wireless Internet access, individual student portals for Internet access, numerous databases available through the library on the Internet
Campuswide Network? Yes
% of MBA Classrooms Wired: 100
Internet Fee? No

EXPENSES/FINANCIAL AID
Tuition Per Credit (Nonresident): $246
Room & Board (On/Off Campus): $9,056/$10,810
Books and Supplies: $810
Average Grant: $1,772
Average Loan: $8,750
% Receiving Financial Aid: 52
% Receiving Aid Their First Year: 18

ADMISSIONS INFORMATION
Application Fee: $55
Electronic Application? Yes
Regular Application Deadline: Rolling
Regular Notification: Rolling
Deferment Available? No
Non-fall Admissions? Yes
Non-fall Application Deadline(s): 11/1 spring
Transfer Students Accepted? Yes
Transfer Policy: Students must apply as new students; courses will be evaluated.
Need-Blind Admissions? No
Number of Applications Received: 498
% of Applicants Accepted: 63
% Accepted Who Enrolled: 52
Average GPA: 3.2
Average GMAT: 550
Other Admissions Factors Considered: Admission is competitive and depends on personal information, letters of recommendation, GPA, and GMAT score. Admission is based on the caliber of applicants applying each semester, and the most qualified students are offered admission.

INTERNATIONAL STUDENTS
TOEFL Required of International Students? Yes
Minimum TOEFL: 570 (230 computer)

EMPLOYMENT INFORMATION
Placement Office Available? Yes
Frequent Employers: Ernst & Young, Home Depot, Mercury, Target
Prominent Alumni: Steve Charton, president and CEO; Kevin Costner, businessman and actor; Robert Grant, managing partner; Maurice Myers, president and CEO; Shirley Reel Caldwell, president

CALIFORNIA STATE UNIVERSITY—HAYWARD
School of Business and Economics

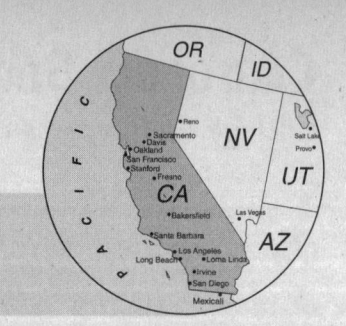

Admissions Contact: Maria De Anda-Ramos, Director of Enrollment Services, Admissions, and Recruitment
Address: 25800 Carles Bee Boulevard, Hayward, CA 94542
Admissions Phone: 510-885-2624 • Admissions Fax: 510-885-4059
Admissions E-mail: adminfo@csuhayward.edu • Web Address: sbegrad.csuhayward.edu

Hayward's MBA program proudly houses a student body with female and minority populations of more than 50 percent. The MBA has a multitude of concentrations, from new venture management and telecommunications to materials management and taxation. Hayward MBA students can participate in a great selection of study abroad options, should they wish to leave Hayward, known locally as the "Heart of the Bay." Graduates of CSU—Hayward have been hired by Bay Area companies such as Chevron and Pacific Gas & Electric.

INSTITUTIONAL INFORMATION
Public/Private: Public
Evening Classes Available? No
Total Faculty: 75
% Faculty Part Time: 45
Students in Parent Institution: 12,705
Academic Calendar: Quarter

PROGRAMS
Degrees Offered: Master of Business Administration (MBA) (part time, 45 credits, 12 months to 5 years), with concentrations in Accounting, Economics, Entrepreneurship, Finance, Human Resources, International Business, Management Information Systems, Management Science, Marketing, Operations Management, Taxation, Management, Materials Management, New Venture Management, Strategic Management, and Telecommunications Management; Executive MBA in Vienna (EMBA) (part time, 47 credits, 12 months); Master of Science in Taxation (MS) (part time, 45 credits, 12 months to 5 years), with concentration in Taxation; Master of Science in Business Administration: Computer Information Systems/Quantitative (MS) (part time, 45 credits, 12 months to 5 years), with concentrations in Decision Sciences and Management Information Systems; Master of Arts in Economics (MA) (part time, 45 credits, 12 months to 5 years), with concentration in Economics; Master of Science in Telecommunication Systems (MS) (part time, 45 credits, 12 months to 5 years)

Study Abroad Options: Australia, Canada, Denmark, France, Germany, Japan, Philippines, Thailand, Zimbabwe, Israel, Italy, Korea, New Zealand, Spain, Sweden

STUDENT INFORMATION
Total Business Students: 579
% Female: 55
% Minority: 55
% International: 20
Average Age: 32

COMPUTER AND RESEARCH FACILITIES
Research Facilities: Alameda Center for Environmental Technologies, China America Business and Education Center, Center for Business and Environmental Studies, Center for Economics Education, Center for Sustaining Development and Environmental Technologies, California Urban Environmental Research Center, Center for Entrepreneurship, Environmental Finance Center Region IX, Human Investment Research and Education Center, Institute for Research and Business Development, Small Business Institute, Smith Center for Private Enterprise Studies, Institute for Telecommunications Technologies
Campuswide Network? Yes
Internet Fee? No

EXPENSES/FINANCIAL AID
Annual Tuition (Resident/Nonresident): $2,460/$10,332
Books and Supplies: $10,000

ADMISSIONS INFORMATION
Application Fee: $55
Electronic Application? Yes
Regular Application Deadline: 6/1
Deferment Available? Yes
Non-fall Application Deadline(s): 9/1 winter, 1/1 spring, 4/1 summer; international: 4/1 fall, 10/1 spring
Transfer Students Accepted? No
Need-Blind Admissions? No
Number of Applications Received: 307
% of Applicants Accepted: 76
% Accepted Who Enrolled: 68
Average GPA: 3.1
Average GMAT: 530
Average Years Experience: 8
Other Admissions Factors Considered: Computer experience required; GMAT and letters of recommendation recommended
Minority/Disadvantaged Student Recruitment Programs: Educational Opportunity Program

INTERNATIONAL STUDENTS
TOEFL Required of International Students? Yes
Minimum TOEFL: 550 (213 computer)

EMPLOYMENT INFORMATION
Placement Office Available? Yes
% Employed Within 3 Months: 99
Frequent Employers: Arthur D. Little, Hewlett-Packard, IBM, Mitsubishi, Pricewaterhouse-Coopers, Sony, Sun Microsystems

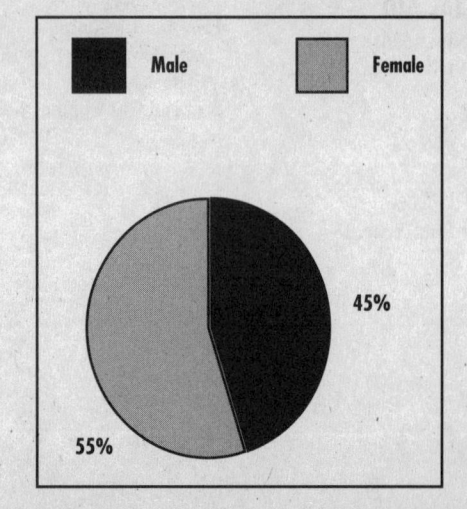

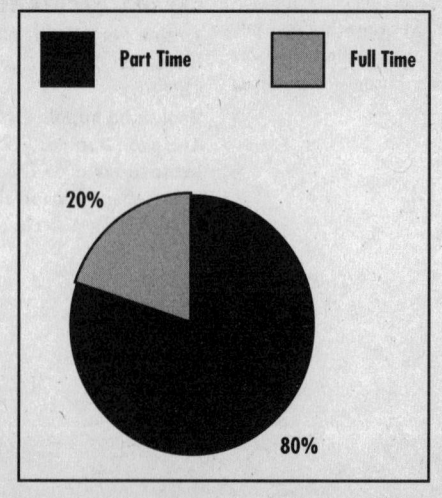

CALIFORNIA STATE UNIVERSITY — SACRAMENTO
College of Business Administration

Admissions Contact: Jeanie Allam, Graduate Program Advisor
Address: College of Business Administration, Sacramento, CA 95819-6088
Admissions Phone: 916-278-6772 • Admissions Fax: 916-278-4979
Admissions E-mail: cbagrad@csus.edu • Web Address: www.csus.edu/cbagrad/index.html

Educated on the banks of the American River, Sacramento MBA students will thrive in this leadership-oriented program, not only from the high-quality education designed to meet the needs of working professionals, but also from the multiple degree options offered within the business school. CSU Sacramento is affiliated with many international business schools, affording the student several study abroad options, along with several additional educational opportunities at any of the Cal State universities in the region. New students will reap the benefits of an ambitious construction project involving a new alumni center and the expansion of the student union.

INSTITUTIONAL INFORMATION
Public/Private: Public
Evening Classes Available? Yes
Total Faculty: 26
% Faculty Female: 27
% Faculty Part Time: 7
Student/Faculty Ratio: 14:1
Students in Parent Institution: 26,923
Academic Calendar: Semester

PROGRAMS
Degrees Offered: Master of Business Administration (MBA) (33 to 55 credits, 1 year full time or 2 years part time), with concentrations in Accounting, Finance, Human Resources, Management Information Systems, Marketing, and Urban Land Development; Master of Science in Accountancy (MS) (30 to 49 credits, 1 year full time or 2 years part time), with concentrations in Accounting and Taxation; Master of Science in Business Administration (MS) (30 to 55 credits, 1.5 years full time or 2.5 years part time), with concentrations in Management Information Systems and Taxation
Joint Degrees: MBA/JD, McGeorge School of Law, (approximately 4 years full time)
Academic Specialties: The faculty at CSUS are focused on teaching.
Special Opportunities: Certificate of Advanced Business Studies (19 to 21 units of general business studies, 1 year)

STUDENT INFORMATION
Total Business Students: 385
% Female: 46
% Minority: 22
% International: 20
Average Age: 28

COMPUTER AND RESEARCH FACILITIES
Campuswide Network? Yes
Computer Model Recommended: No
Internet Fee? No

EXPENSES/FINANCIAL AID
Annual Tuition (Resident/Nonresident): $1,949/$6,377
Books and Supplies: $9,000
Average Grant: $800

ADMISSIONS INFORMATION
Application Fee: $55
Electronic Application? Yes
Regular Application Deadline: 4/1
Regular Notification: 5/15
Deferment Available? Yes
Length of Deferment: 1 semester
Non-fall Admissions? Yes
Non-fall Application Deadline(s): 10/1 spring
Transfer Students Accepted? No
Need-Blind Admissions? No
Number of Applications Received: 275
% of Applicants Accepted: 34
% Accepted Who Enrolled: 55
Average GPA: 3.2
Average GMAT: 576

INTERNATIONAL STUDENTS
TOEFL Required of International Students? Yes
Minimum TOEFL: 550 (213 computer)

EMPLOYMENT INFORMATION
Placement Office Available? Yes
Frequent Employers: Hewlett-Packard, EDS Corporation, Franklin Templeton, Investors Bank & Trust, Franchise Tax, State Board of Equalization, State Controllers Office, Chevron
Prominent Alumni: Dennis Gardemeyer, executive VP, Zuckerman-Hertog; Tom Weborg, CEO, Cucina Holdings; William Keever, president, Vodafone Airtouch; Margo Murray, president and CEO, MMHA, The Mangers' Mentors Inc.; Scott Syphax, president, CEO/Nehemiah Corporation

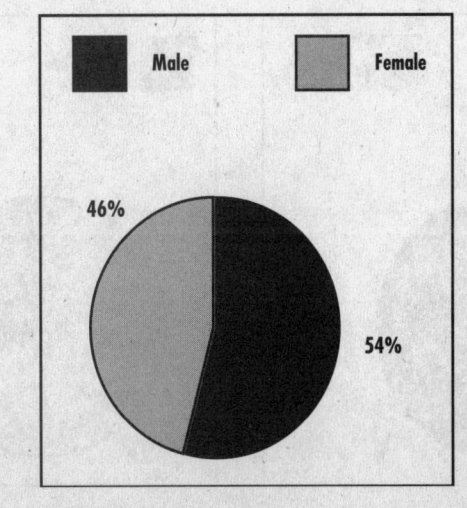

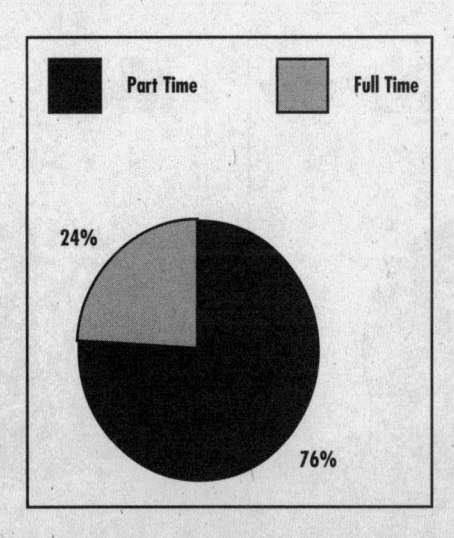

Male 54% / Female 46%

Part Time 76% / Full Time 24%

CALIFORNIA STATE UNIVERSITY—SAN BERNARDINO
College of Business & Public Administration

Admissions Contact: Director of Admissions and Recruitment
Address: 5500 University Parkway, San Bernardino, CA 92407
Admissions Phone: 909-880-5703 • Admissions Fax: 909-880-7582
Admissions E-mail: sgreenfe@csusb.edu • Web Address: www.csusb.edu

Another of the many California State system MBA programs, the San Bernardino MBA stands its ground with a student body that's a whopping 80 percent international students from 24 foreign countries and a sweeping view of the San Bernardino Mountains from any point on campus. The MBA program is known for its small class sizes, student/faculty relationships, and affordable in-state business education.

INSTITUTIONAL INFORMATION
Public/Private: Public
Evening Classes Available? Yes
Total Faculty: 65
% Faculty Female: 15
% Faculty Minority: 10
Student/Faculty Ratio: 17:1
Students in Parent Institution: 15,985

PROGRAMS
Degrees Offered: Master of Business Administration (approximately 1.5 years full time; evening, 3 to 4 years part time)
Academic Specialties: 9 concentrations in specific areas of Information Systems, Finance, Accounting, Entrepreneurship, Corporate Management, Management and Human Resources, Management of Conflict, Operations, and Marketing

STUDENT INFORMATION
Total Business Students: 334
% Full Time: 69
% Female: 45
% Minority: 5
% Out of State: 80
% International: 80
Average Age: 27

COMPUTER AND RESEARCH FACILITIES
Campuswide Network? Yes
% of MBA Classrooms Wired: 50
Computer Model Recommended: No
Internet Fee? No

EXPENSES/FINANCIAL AID
Annual Tuition (Resident/Nonresident): $2,000/$10,000
Tuition Per Credit (Nonresident): $164
Room & Board (On Campus): $6,700
Books and Supplies: $2,000
Average Grant: $1,000
Average Loan: $6,000

ADMISSIONS INFORMATION
Application Fee: $55
Electronic Application? Yes
Early Decision Application Deadline: 2/1
Early Decision Notification: 6/1
Regular Application Deadline: 7/1
Regular Notification: 9/1
Deferment Available? Yes
Length of Deferment: 1 year
Non-fall Admissions? Yes
Non-fall Application Deadline(s): 10/1, 1/1
Transfer Students Accepted? Yes
Transfer Policy: Only 3 graduate courses may be transferred into the MBA program.
Need-Blind Admissions? Yes
Number of Applications Received: 290
% of Applicants Accepted: 69
% Accepted Who Enrolled: 53
Average GPA: 3.2
Average GMAT: 511
Average Years Experience: 4
Other Schools to Which Students Applied: California State Polytechnic University-Pomona, California State University-Fullerton, California State University-Los Angeles

INTERNATIONAL STUDENTS
TOEFL Required of International Students? Yes
Minimum TOEFL: 550 (213 computer)

EMPLOYMENT INFORMATION
Placement Office Available? Yes
Frequent Employers: Arrowhead Credit Union; Citizens Bank; Community Bank; GTE; Southern California Edison; Kaiser Permanente; ESRI; Arthur Andersen; almost all regional accounting firms, banks, credit unions, etc.

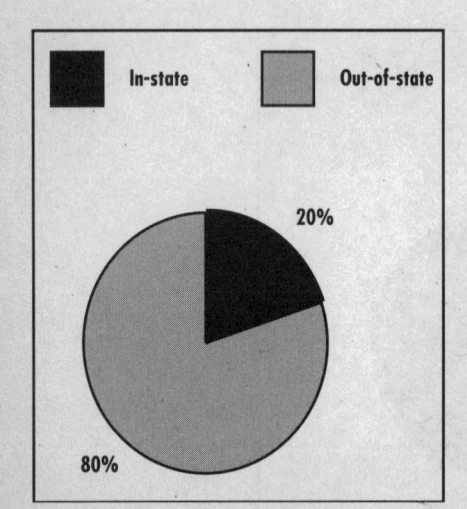

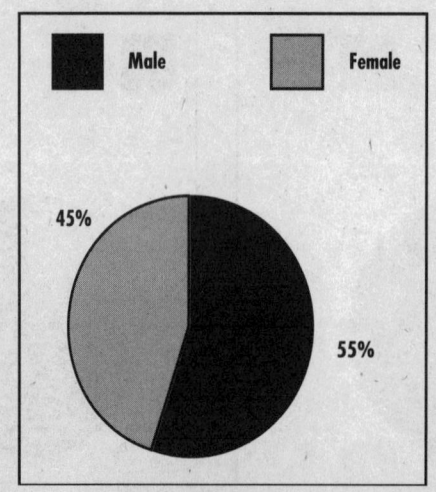

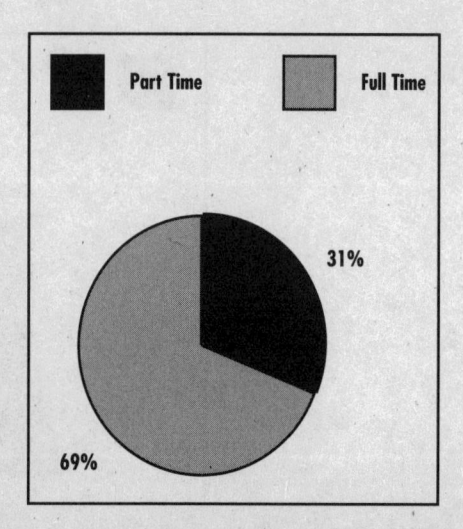

In-state 20% / Out-of-state 80%

Male 55% / Female 45%

Part Time 31% / Full Time 69%

CANISIUS COLLEGE
Richard Wehle School of Business

Admissions Contact: Laura McEwen, Director, Graduate Business Program
Address: 2001 Main Street, 220 Lyons Hall, Buffalo, NY 14208-9989
Admissions Phone: 716-888-2140 • Admissions Fax: 716-888-2145
Admissions E-mail: gradbus@canisius.edu • Web Address: www.canisius.edu

The Richard Wehle School of Business is a private institution, renowned for its strong Jesuit tradition of ethical responsibility and hard work; in fact, Canisius College is named for St. Peter Canisius, who established multiple colleges and seminaries in the United States and in Europe, fueled by "his zeal for education as an agent for change." The Canisius MBA offers both a full-time one-year MBA and a part-time evening MBA. Students can look forward to frequent intimate interactions with their professors, some of whom are consultants with prestigious corporations such as Fisher Price, Mattel, and Federal Express.

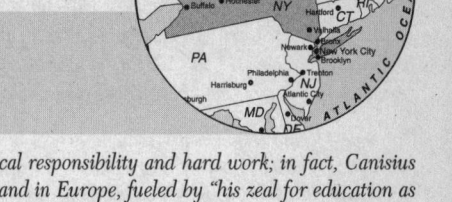

INSTITUTIONAL INFORMATION
Public/Private: Private
Evening Classes Available? Yes
Total Faculty: 48
% Faculty Female: 17
% Faculty Minority: 4
% Faculty Part Time: 25
Student/Faculty Ratio: 15:1
Students in Parent Institution: 4,589
Academic Calendar: Semester

PROGRAMS
Degrees Offered: MBA, MBA in Professional Accounting, Master of Science in Telecommunications Management, Master of Science in Taxation
Joint Degrees: Bachelor degree/MBA (5 years)
Academic Specialties: AACSB-certified (only 30% of U.S. business schools have this certification); students can finish in as little as 12 months or as long as 5 years; Jesuit tradition of engaging students as individuals

STUDENT INFORMATION
Total Business Students: 353
% Full Time: 18
% Female: 40
% Minority: 10
% Out of State: 1
% International: 5
Average Age: 28

COMPUTER AND RESEARCH FACILITIES
Computer Facilities: Library lab, Wehle Lab, Amherst Lab, many databases available in 400,000-volume library
Campuswide Network? Yes
% of MBA Classrooms Wired: 100
Computer Model Recommended: No
Internet Fee? No

EXPENSES/FINANCIAL AID
Annual Tuition: $27,756
Room & Board: $5,000
Books and Supplies: $500

ADMISSIONS INFORMATION
Application Fee: $25
Electronic Application? Yes
Regular Application Deadline: Rolling
Regular Notification: Rolling
Deferment Available? Yes
Length of Deferment: 1 year
Non-fall Admissions? Yes
Non-fall Application Deadline(s): Spring, summer
Transfer Students Accepted? Yes
Transfer Policy: Case by case
Need-Blind Admissions? No
Number of Applications Received: 206
% of Applicants Accepted: 72
% Accepted Who Enrolled: 68
Average GPA: 3.1
GPA Range: 2.8-3.4
Average GMAT: 510
GMAT Range: 460-557
Other Schools to Which Students Applied: Northeast Louisiana University, University at Buffalo (State University of New York)

INTERNATIONAL STUDENTS
TOEFL Required of International Students? Yes
Minimum TOEFL: 500 (200 computer)

EMPLOYMENT INFORMATION
Placement Office Available? Yes

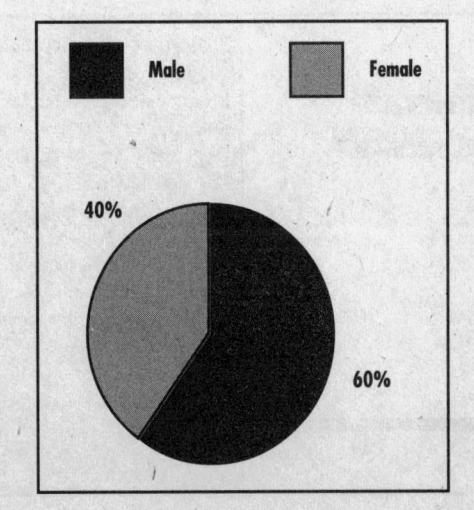

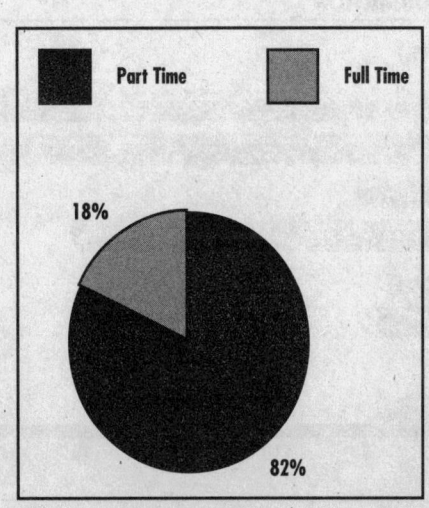

Male / Female: 60% / 40%

Part Time / Full Time: 82% / 18%

CARNEGIE MELLON UNIVERSITY
Graduate School of Industrial Administration

Admissions Contact: Laurie Stewart, Director of MBA Admissions
Address: 5000 Forbes Avenue, Pittsburgh, PA 15213
Admissions Phone: 412-268-2272 • Admissions Fax: 412-268-4209
Admissions E-mail: gsia-admissions@andrew.cmu.edu • Web Address: www.gsia.cmu.edu

Carnegie Mellon's renowned Graduate School of Industrial Administration is "boot camp for the brain," and its innovative, Nobel Prize–winning faculty are excellent. Particularly noteworthy is the "real world–oriented" Management Game, in which students negotiate mock contracts with actual union reps and secure "financing" through Pittsburgh banks. Students say "no task is too complicated, intense, or daunting" if you have "already survived Management Game."

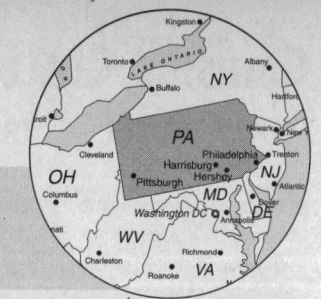

INSTITUTIONAL INFORMATION
Public/Private: Private
Evening Classes Available? Yes
Total Faculty: 120
% Faculty Female: 11
% Faculty Minority: 22
% Faculty Part Time: 25
Student/Faculty Ratio: 5:1
Students in Parent Institution: 8,500
Academic Calendar: Mini-Semester

PROGRAMS
Degrees Offered: MBA (2 years); PhD (4-5 years); MS in Computational Finance (1 year); Master of Business/Master of Software Engineering (3 years); MS in Electronic Commerce (1 year).
Joint Degrees: MS in Information Networking; JD/MSIA; joint master's program with the Engineering College; collaborative program with the School of Urban and Public Affairs
Academic Specialties: Production/Operations Management, Management Information Systems, Entrepreneurship, Finance, Electronic Commerce, Economics, Quantitative Analysis, Corporate Strategy
Study Abroad Options: Germany, Slovakia

STUDENT INFORMATION
Total Business Students: 709
% Full Time: 62
% Female: 27
% Minority: 5
% International: 38
Average Age: 28

COMPUTER AND RESEARCH FACILITIES
Research Facilities: Carnegie Bosch Institute, Center for E-Business Innovation, Center for Financial Markets, Center for Interactive Simulations, Center for the Management of Technology, Center for the Study of Public Policy, Donald H. Jones Center for Entrepreneurship, Green Design Initiative, Institute for Electronic Commerce, Institute for Strategic Management, Technology Transfer Office, Center for Interactive Simulations, Center for Business Communication.
Computer Facilities: Business Dateline, Commerce Biz Daily, Dunn & Bradstreet's, EconLit, FISonline, Hoover's Online, Lexis/Nexis, INFORMS PubOnline, InfoTrac, Investext, Knowledge Max, Net Advantage, ProQuest Direct, Statistical Universe, STAT/USA, Wilson Business Abstracts, Worldscope Global, Ethnic Newswatch, NetFirst, NetLibrary, OCLC.
Campuswide Network? Yes
% of MBA Classrooms Wired: 100
Computer Model Recommended: Laptop
Internet Fee? No

EXPENSES/FINANCIAL AID
Annual Tuition: $28,250
Tuition Per Credit: $312
Room & Board (Off Campus): $10,090
Books and Supplies: $3,950
Average Grant: $7,500
Average Loan: $21,500
% Receiving Financial Aid: 44
% Receiving Aid Their First Year: 42

ADMISSIONS INFORMATION
Application Fee: $100
Electronic Application? Yes
Regular Application Deadline: 3/31
Regular Notification: 5/15
Deferment Available? Yes
Length of Deferment: 2 years
Non-fall Admissions? No
Transfer Students Accepted? No
Need-Blind Admissions? Yes
Number of Applications Received: 1,300
% of Applicants Accepted: 28
% Accepted Who Enrolled: 60
Average GPA: 3.0
GPA Range: 3.0-3.6
Average GMAT: 652
GMAT Range: 620-690
Average Years Experience: 5
Minority/Disadvantaged Student Recruitment Programs: Challenge Weekend, Member of the Consortium for Graduate Study in Management
Other Schools to Which Students Applied: Cornell University, Massachusetts Institute of Technology, New York University, University of Michigan, University of Pennsylvania, University of Texas at Austin

INTERNATIONAL STUDENTS
TOEFL Required of International Students? Yes
Minimum TOEFL: 600 (250 computer)

EMPLOYMENT INFORMATION

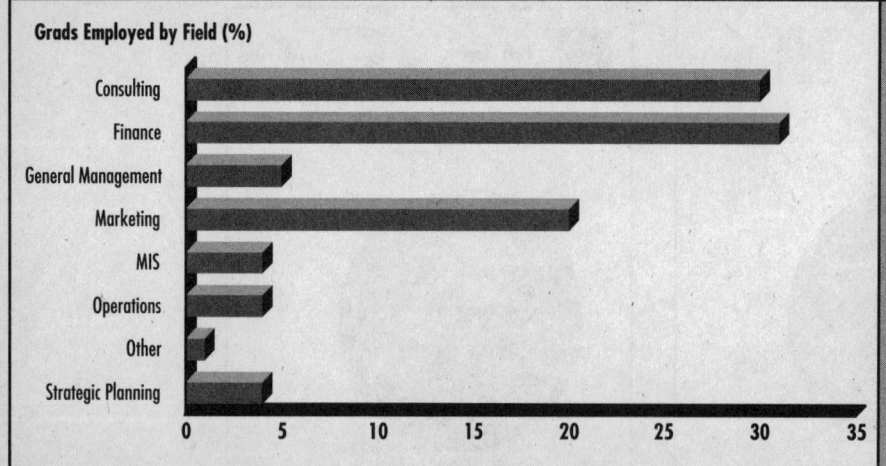

Grads Employed by Field (%)

Field	%
Consulting	~31
Finance	~32
General Management	~5
Marketing	~20
MIS	~3
Operations	~3
Other	~2
Strategic Planning	~4

Placement Office Available? Yes
% Employed Within 3 Months: 92
Frequent Employers: Deloitte Consulting, A.T. Kearney, Deutsche Bank, Alex Brown, DiamondCluster International, Booz Allen & Hamilton, McKinsey & Company, PricewaterhouseCoopers, Exxon Mobil, Federated Investors, IBM Consulting, KPMG Consulting, Goldman Sachs, Intel Corporation, Johnson & Johnson
Prominent Alumni: Francois De Carbonnel, president, private client services in Europe, CSO Global Corporation; Frank Risch, VP and treasurer, Exxon Corporation Headquarters; Dina Dublon, CFO, Chase Bank Headquarters

CASE WESTERN RESERVE UNIVERSITY
Weatherhead School of Management

Admissions Contact: Christine L. Gill, Director of Marketing and Admissions
Address: 310 Enterprise Hall, 10900 Euclid Avenue, Cleveland, OH 44106-7235
Admissions Phone: 216-368-2030 • Admissions Fax: 216-368-5548
Admissions E-mail: questions@exchange.cwru.edu • Web Address: www.weatherhead.cwru.edu

Outstanding aspects of Case Western Reserve's Weatherhead School of Management include its administrative "flexibility," a faculty "open to new course ideas and curriculum enhancements," and a cutting-edge, wavy-looking new building designed by Frank O. Gehry. The "team-oriented" classes here are "very challenging, but rewarding" as well, and "you'll be up to your ears in group projects with students from many other countries" from day one.

INSTITUTIONAL INFORMATION
Evening Classes Available? Yes
Total Faculty: 99
% Faculty Female: 18
% Faculty Minority: 2
% Faculty Part Time: 2
Student/Faculty Ratio: 10:1
Academic Calendar: Semester

PROGRAMS
Degrees Offered: MSM-IS (1 year), EDM (3 years), Executive MBA (2 years), MBA (2 years), Accelerated MBA (11 months), MNO (2 years), MAcc (1 year), MSM-Operations Research (1 year), MSM-Supply Chain (1 year)
Joint Degrees: MBA/JD (4 years), MD/MBA (5 years), MSN/MBA (2.5 years), MSM/MBA (2.5 years), MNO/JD (4 years), MNO/MA (2.5 years), MNO/MSSA (2.5 years), MBA/MIM (2.5 years), MAcc/MBA (2 years), MBS/MA Bio-Ethic (2.5 years)
Academic Specialties: Leadership Assessment and Development, Emotional Intelligence, Competency-Based Learning, Appreciative Inquiry
Special Opportunities: Weatherhead Mentor Program; certificates in Community Service, Public Policy, Health Systems Management, Nonprofit Management, and E-Business; Professional Fellows Program
Study Abroad Options: Israel, Mexico, Costa Rica, South Africa, and many in Europe and Asia

STUDENT INFORMATION
Total Business Students: 1,039
% Full Time: 35
% Female: 28
% Minority: 10
% Out of State: 60
% International: 43
Average Age: 28

COMPUTER AND RESEARCH FACILITIES
Research Facilities: Centers for regional economic issues, enterprise development, health systems management, nonprofit organizations, and entrepreneurial studies
Computer Facilities: Multimedia access in all classrooms; wireless Internet access
Campuswide Network? Yes
% of MBA Classrooms Wired: 100
Computer Model Recommended: Laptop

EXPENSES/FINANCIAL AID
Annual Tuition: $24,500
Tuition Per Credit: $955
Room & Board (On/Off Campus): $9,200/$10,900
Books and Supplies: $1,200
Average Grant: $13,800
Average Loan: $18,500
% Receiving Financial Aid: 79
% Receiving Aid Their First Year: 77

ADMISSIONS INFORMATION
Application Fee: $50
Electronic Application? Yes
Early Decision Application Deadline: 1/31
Early Decision Notification: 3/1
Regular Application Deadline: 3/22
Regular Notification: 4/15
Deferment Available? No
Non-fall Application Deadline(s): Full time accelerated: 4/19 summer; part time: 7/1 fall, 12/7 spring, 5/3 summer
Transfer Policy: 6 hours from an AACSB program
Need-Blind Admissions? Yes
Number of Applications Received: 707
% of Applicants Accepted: 45
% Accepted Who Enrolled: 49
Average GPA: 3.2
Average GMAT: 608
Average Years Experience: 6
Minority/Disadvantaged Student Recruitment Programs: On-campus scholars weekends; networking with professional associations and alumni
Other Schools to Which Students Applied: Ohio State, U. of Michigan, Notre Dame, U. of Pittsburgh, U. of Virginia, Vanderbilt, Washington U.

INTERNATIONAL STUDENTS
TOEFL Required of International Students? Yes
Minimum TOEFL: 600 (250 computer)

EMPLOYMENT INFORMATION

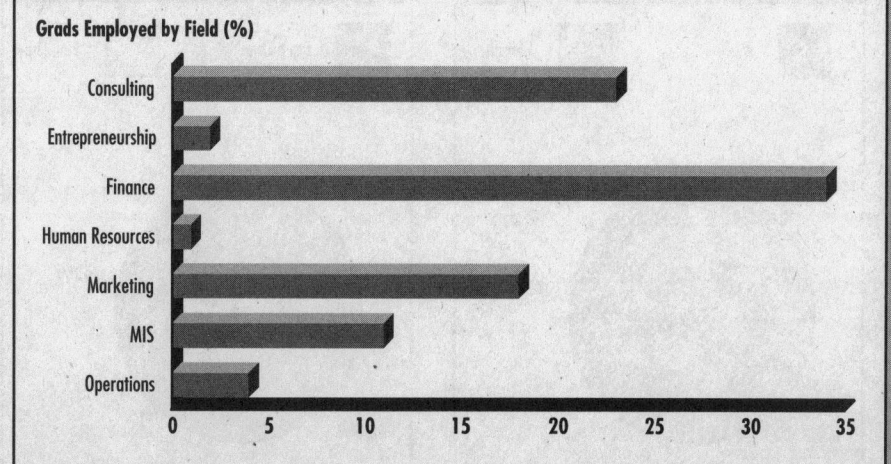

Grads Employed by Field (%)

Field	%
Consulting	~23
Entrepreneurship	~2
Finance	~34
Human Resources	~2
Marketing	~18
MIS	~11
Operations	~4

Placement Office Available? Yes
% Employed Within 3 Months: 92
Frequent Employers: IBM, Accenture, American Express, AT Kearney, Deloitte & Touche, Ethicon (Johnson & Johnson), JP Morgan, TRW, Key Bank
Prominent Alumni: John Breen, CEO (retired), Sherwin Williams; Clayton Deutsch, managing partner, McKinsey & Co., Chicago; David Daberko, chairman and CEO, National City Bank; John Neff, CEO (retired), Vanguard Fund; Joseph Sabatini, managing director, JP Morgan

CENTRAL MISSOURI STATE UNIVERSITY
Harmon College of Business Administration

Admissions Contact: Terry Hazen (Graduate School), Admissions Evaluator
Address: Humphreys 410, Warrensburg, MO 64093
Admissions Phone: 660-543-4621 • Admissions Fax: 660-543-8333
Admissions E-mail: gradinfo@cmsu1.cmsu.edu • Web Address: www.cmsu.edu/academic/hcba.htm

The average age of graduate students at the Harmon College of Business Administration is 35, as the MBA program is designed for the working professional. The students can expect a tightly knit educational community thanks to the MBA Association, a student-run organization that coordinates a renowned mentorship program, bridging MBA students with business managers in Kansas City and west central Missouri. The traditional MBA curriculum is complemented by a prestigious and competitive internship program.

INSTITUTIONAL INFORMATION
Public/Private: Public
Evening Classes Available? Yes
Total Faculty: 43
% Faculty Female: 23
% Faculty Minority: 5
Students in Parent Institution: 1,820
Academic Calendar: Semester

PROGRAMS
Degrees Offered: MBA with concentrations in Accounting, Information Systems, Finance, Marketing, and Management
Academic Specialties: Integration of core MBA courses
Special Opportunities: Internships
Study Abroad Options: Study abroad available based on student interest

STUDENT INFORMATION
Total Business Students: 88
% Full Time: 58
% Female: 55
% Minority: 47
% Out of State: 33
% International: 47
Average Age: 35

COMPUTER AND RESEARCH FACILITIES
Research Facilities: Center for Business and Economic Research, Research Institute, Small Business Development Center
Computer Facilities: On-campus computer facilities: Business Computing Center, College of Education & Human Services Lab, College of Arts and Sciences Lab, Comp. U Center, Harmon Computer Commons, Learning Center, Safety Science and Technology lab, Writing Center Lab, Psychology Lab. Databases Available: Lexis-Nexis, Eric, Infotrac, MLA Bibliography, First Search, Ebsco Host, Criminal Justice Periodical Index, RSC (Chemistry Journals), Math Sci Net (Mathematics Journals), Shepard's Citations, CC Infoweb (Chemical Data), Gale Literary Index, College Source (College Catalogs)
Number of Computer Labs: 29
Number of Student Computers: 385
Campuswide Network? Yes
Computer Proficiency Required? Yes
Special Purchasing Agreements? Yes
Companies with Agreements: All software is specially priced for educational use. Primary computer vendors are Compaq and Apple.
Internet Fee? No

EXPENSES/FINANCIAL AID
Annual Tuition (Resident/Nonresident): $3,840/$7,632

ADMISSIONS INFORMATION
Application Fee: $25
Electronic Application? No
Regular Application Deadline: Rolling
Regular Notification: Rolling
Deferment Available? No
Non-fall Admissions? Yes
Non-fall Application Deadline(s): Rolling
Transfer Students Accepted? Yes
Transfer Policy: A maximum of 8 hours may be transferred and a "B" average or higher is required.
Need-Blind Admissions? Yes
Average GPA: 3.0
GPA Range: 2.6-3.5
Average GMAT: 491
GMAT Range: 440-540
Minority/Disadvantaged Student Recruitment Programs: None
Other Schools to Which Students Applied: University of Kansas, University of Missouri—Columbia, University of Missouri—Kansas City, University of New Orleans

INTERNATIONAL STUDENTS
TOEFL Required of International Students? Yes
Minimum TOEFL: 550

EMPLOYMENT INFORMATION
Placement Office Available? Yes
Frequent Employers: Sprint, Enterprise Rent-a-Car, Sherwin Williams
Prominent Alumni: John Clark, CEO, United Foods; John Lenox, president, Shelter Insurance; Keith Province, president, Sales & Marketing Group

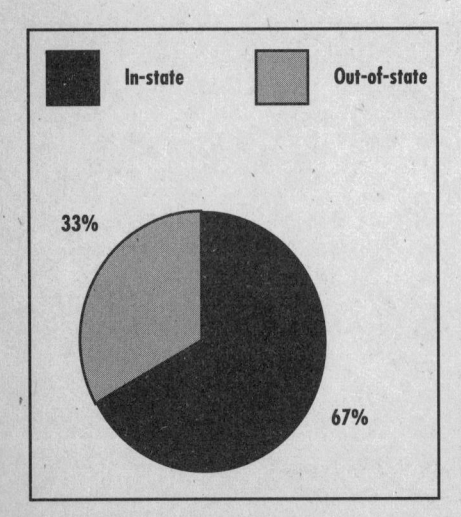

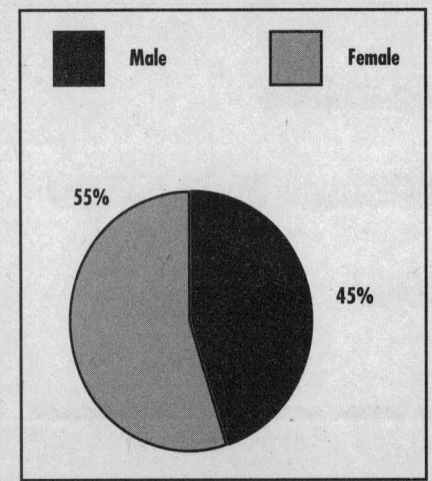

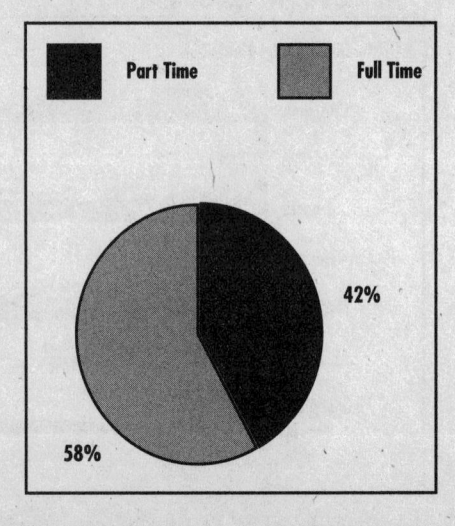

In-state 67% / Out-of-state 33%

Male 45% / Female 55%

Part Time 58% / Full Time 42%

CHAPMAN UNIVERSITY
The George L. Argyros School of Business and Economics

Admissions Contact: Debra Gonda, Associate Director
Address: Beckman Hall, One University Dr., Orange, CA 92866
Admissions Phone: 714-997-6745 • Admissions Fax: 714-532-6081
Admissions E-mail: gonda@chapman.edu • Web Address: chapman.edu/argyros

If you're a mid-career manager or a senior level exec, you may want to get on board the Executive MBA program at the George L. Argyros School of Business and Economics. The EMBA offers a competitive, private education with a class size of about 50, and it takes only 22 months to complete. The program includes a trip to China to attend residential seminars and gain on-site education of the global economic community. The slightly younger applicants to the MBA program have the advantage of being under the tutelage of faculty with doctorates from prestigious institutions such as MIT and Cornell.

INSTITUTIONAL INFORMATION
Public/Private: Private
Evening Classes Available? Yes
Total Faculty: 21
% Faculty Female: 14
% Faculty Minority: 5
Student/Faculty Ratio: 20:1
Students in Parent Institution: 4,012
Academic Calendar: Semester

PROGRAMS
Degrees Offered: MBA (2 years full time, 3 years part time), Executive MBA (22 months)
Joint Degrees: JD/MBA (4 years)
Academic Specialties: The school has three centers that represent the strength of the school: Anderson Center for Economic Research, Ralph Leatherby Center for Entrepreneurship and Ethics, and Walter Schmid Center for International Business.

STUDENT INFORMATION
Total Business Students: 148
% Full Time: 29
% Female: 36
Average Age: 27

COMPUTER AND RESEARCH FACILITIES
Computer Facilities: Computer labs with state-of-the-art IBM and Macintosh computers
Campuswide Network? Yes
% of MBA Classrooms Wired: 100
Computer Model Recommended: No
Internet Fee? No

EXPENSES/FINANCIAL AID
Annual Tuition: $15,240
Tuition Per Credit: $635
Books and Supplies: $1,600
Average Grant: $3,000
Average Loan: $13,570
% Receiving Financial Aid: 35

ADMISSIONS INFORMATION
Application Fee: $40
Electronic Application? Yes
Regular Application Deadline: Rolling
Regular Notification: Rolling
Deferment Available? Yes
Length of Deferment: 1 year
Non-fall Admissions? Yes
Non-fall Application Deadline(s): Spring, rolling
Transfer Students Accepted? Yes
Transfer Policy: Transfer up to 9 units of course work
Need-Blind Admissions? Yes
Number of Applications Received: 114
% of Applicants Accepted: 63
% Accepted Who Enrolled: 56
Average GPA: 3.1
Average GMAT: 535
Other Schools to Which Students Applied: California State University-Fullerton, Pepperdine University, University of California-Irvine, University of Southern California

INTERNATIONAL STUDENTS
TOEFL Required of International Students? Yes
Minimum TOEFL: 550

EMPLOYMENT INFORMATION
Placement Office Available? Yes

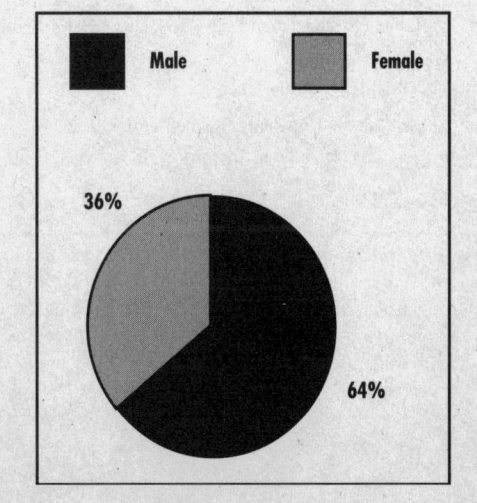

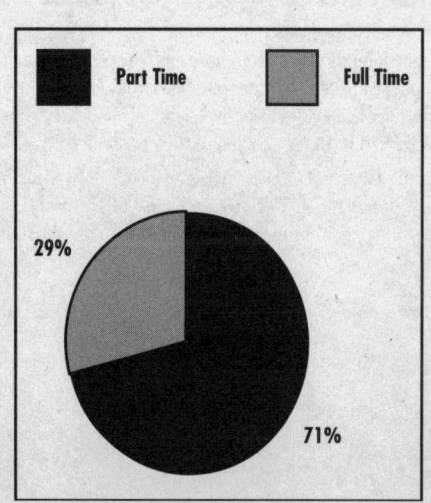

Male 64% / Female 36%

Part Time 71% / Full Time 29%

CLAREMONT GRADUATE UNIVERSITY

THE SCHOOL AT A GLANCE
The Peter F. Drucker Graduate School of Management at Claremont Graduate University, located in beautiful Claremont, California, is a unique management school dedicated to training people to become effective and ethical leaders, strategists, and visionaries in whatever organization they serve. Our focus stems from the belief that management is a liberal art, a human enterprise encompassing perspectives from the social and behavioral sciences. This positions Drucker as a "Different School of Thought" and not just another business school.

In his book, *The New Realities,* Peter Drucker explains why management is a liberal art:

"Management is thus what tradition used to call a liberal art—'liberal' because it deals with the fundamentals of knowledge, self-knowledge, wisdom, and leadership; 'art' because it is practice and application. Managers draw on all the knowledge and insights of the humanities and the social sciences—on psychology and philosophy, on economics and history, on the physical sciences and ethics. But they have to focus this knowledge on effectiveness and results—on healing a sick patient, teaching a student, building a bridge, designing and selling a user-friendly software program."

Named after the most prominent management thinker of the twentieth century, Peter F. Drucker, the Drucker MBA program offers a high quality interactive educational experience: small classes averaging 25 students per class and instruction from world-renowned professors. Approximately 70 percent of our classroom instruction is either in discussion or case analysis format, and we incorporate team building in classroom projects and presentations. In a nutshell, our classes are highly interactive. Additionally, we are ranked 20th nationally by the 2003 *U.S. News & World Report* in General Management.

STUDENTS
Student life at the Drucker School is busy and diverse. In addition to challenging academic programs, students can also participate in a number of special interest clubs designed to further both academic and career interest. Clubs include the Consulting Club, the Finance Club, the Marketing Club, Professional Women's Networking Club, Net Impact, and Business Entertainment Association among others.

The Drucker School Student Association is the student-run governance body that works with the Dean and his staff to ensure that student interests and needs are being addressed. Student study rooms, computer labs, and common areas give our students places to gather to exchange ideas and develop friendships.

Most of our students live near the campus, many within walking distance. The variety of events taking place both at the Claremont Colleges and around the Los Angeles basin give students a tremendous range of social, cultural, and sports activities from which to choose.

The Drucker School prides itself on its diverse, talented, and proactive student population. Drawn from a pool of exceptional people, the Drucker MBA students have a wide range of interests, besides the usual rigors of academia; they are involved in many activities within the program and the university.

There are numerous opportunities for Drucker MBAs to be associated with leadership roles through the various student organizations and clubs. Most clubs and student organizations are elected and run by students based on the mission of that particular organization.

ACADEMICS
Degrees Offered
- MBA
- Master of Science in Financial Engineering
- Dual Degrees
- Executive MBA
- Certificate Series
- PhD in Management

MBA Program
Consistent with our vision, we attract students who already exhibit strong leadership and achievement skills or who clearly show the potential to develop such skills. These students typically wish to develop themselves both as individuals and as professional executives fully competent in the complex, globally connected economy, and recognize our focus on strategy, leadership, and risk management and our philosophy of management as a liberal art. The effectiveness of this positioning strategy is confirmed by the fact the Drucker School's MBA program was ranked 20th nationally in the General Management category in the *U.S. News & World Report*'s 2003 rankings.

Curriculum
The Drucker MBA curriculum is designed in a layered yet integrated fashion, allowing the student to sequentially build knowledge and develop professional skills. Core courses or foundation level courses provide candidates with an understanding of the fundamental disciplines of management. Advanced core courses are geared to help students integrate key concepts and skills necessary for Strategic or General Management. And elective courses enable students to specialize in a particular field of interest.

Our flexible MBA curriculum allows both full-time and part-time students to select an area of emphasis in strategic management, risk management/finance, leadership, marketing, information sciences, and human resources. Students are also able to take courses outside of the management program in the areas of psychology, politics and policy, economics, and biosciences, and other disciplines through the various schools in the Claremont Graduate University and the Claremont College Consortium that consists of Claremont McKenna College, Pomona College, Harvey Mudd College, Scripps College, Pitzer College, and the Keck Graduate Institute of Applied Life Sciences.

We offer courses overseas and have several semester exchange programs.

Overseas Courses:
1) Global Operations Management (1 week in Monterrey, Mexico)
2) Strategic Risk Management in an Emerging Economy (1 week in Mexico City)
3) Global Strategy and Trade (4 weeks at Oxford University)

Semester Exchanges:
1) Theseus Institute (Nice, France)
2) St. Gallens University (Switzerland)
3) Hitotsubashi University (Tokyo, Japan)

Peter F. Drucker sets the standard for a faculty whose teaching and research is consistently influencing management practice. Our globally renowned faculty write groundbreaking books and serve as consultants to organizations worldwide. A professor may counsel a Fortune 100 CEO in the morning and share the insights with you in class that evening. Being a teaching university—as opposed to a research university—our faculty have time outside of class to meet with students, and have time outside of school to maintain their own consulting practice.

The Peter F. Drucker Graduate School of Management

Professors such as Mihaly Csikszentmihalyi, Vijay Sathe, Richard Smith, Jean Lipman-Blumen, and Richard Ellsworth comprise the core faculty who are globally renowned in their respective areas of research and interest.

Special Programs
- *Dual Degree:* Dual degrees allow students to obtain two degrees in an accelerated period of time. The dual degrees Drucker School offers are MBA/MSMIS, MBA/MSFE, MBA/MSHRD, MBA/MS, and MBA/MA.
- *Course Auditing:* Students who take 12 credits or more are allowed to audit a course of their choice at no cost at any of our seven colleges within the Claremont College Consortium. The audited course will not count for credit, however, it will appear in the transcripts as an audit course.
- *IF Program:* The International Fellows Program helps students adapt quickly to learning in a different culture, build the level of confidence needed for success in the classroom and beyond, and develop sophisticated spoken and written English skills for academic and professional purposes.
- *Alumni Mentoring Program:* Each admitted student is assigned an alumnus to share his experience at the Drucker School, as well as his life and opportunities as part of the Drucker School Alumni.
- *Student Mentoring Program:* Each admitted student is assigned a current student to mentor him from the moment he/she is admitted to the moment he/she is enrolled. Current students share their experience at the Drucker School with new coming students.
- *Drucker Board-Student Mentoring Program:* The Drucker Board of Visitors Mentoring Program rewards the top 10 percent of our students. This mentoring program connects top students one on one with board members, who are high-ranking executives from companies such as JP Morgan Chase, McKinsey & Co., Bain & Co., Wells Fargo Bank, Edward D. Jones, Deloitte and Touche, Dimensional Fund Advisors, and Forbes. These mentoring programs assist students with anything ranging from course selection and student associations to internship opportunities, and with the possibility for full-time job offers.

Career Services and Placement

The ultimate objective of any successful career services function within a business school is the successful transition of students out of the classroom and into the working world with job and career opportunities closely aligned with the graduates' interests and capabilities. The career services provided to students at the Peter F. Drucker Graduate School of Management are designed to provide the tools needed to successfully navigate a course into the working world and beyond. While the department has brought some of the major US corporations on campus to interview—companies such as Andersen Consulting, GE Capital, Deloitte & Touche, Johnson & Johnson, Wedbush Morgan Securities—our strength has been in training students to successfully conduct a significant portion of their own job and career search. Students have available to them a ready arsenal of programs, workshops, and company information sessions to help them define their short and long-term objectives and provide significant information about companies, industries, and career paths. We invite you to learn more about our capabilities and programs by visiting our website http://careers.cgu.edu.

CAMPUS LIFE

Location: approximately 25 miles east of the City of Los Angeles and 6 miles west of Ontario International Airport in a small suburban college-town community.

Population: 34,000

Area and elevation: 14 square miles at an elevation of between 1,100 and 1,800 feet above sea level.

Climate: average yearly temperature of 63 degrees with average annual rainfall of 17 inches.

Nestled in the foothills of the San Gabriel Mountains, this charming community is famous for its tree-lined streets, world-renowned colleges, and charming "old town" restaurants and shops. Claremont provides the atmosphere of a New England college town within comfortable driving distance of major Southern California attractions and sports stadiums.

COSTS

Tuition: $16,174 full time (16 credits); $1,044/credit part time

Fees: $80

Books & Supplies: $400

Health Insurance: $225

Average Rent: $600–$700/month (not including meals). We have on-campus graduate apartments (first come first serve) and numerous off-campus housing resources/assistance.

Expenses: expected expenses are approximately $12,000 per year, including housing, meals and entertainment.

Financial Aid: merit- and need-based scholarships are available for U.S. and international students alike. Institutional financial aid is based on the applicant's professional work experience, academic qualifications, and GMAT score. To be considered, applicants must complete the Application for Institutional Financial Aid and have their entire application materials submitted by the financial aid deadline. Government loans (FAFSA—for U.S. citizens and permanent residents) and International Student loans are also available. Please contact Rosie Ruiz at: rosie.ruiz@cgu.edu.

ADMISSIONS

The Peter F. Drucker Graduate School of Management at Claremont Graduate University prides itself in being "A Different School of Thought." Our student body is academically, professional, racially, and geographically diverse, and we do not require an undergraduate background in business or economics. Our aim is to create an environment that more realistically reflects the world around us.

We do not have minimum cut-offs for the GMAT and GPA as we attempt to individualize each student's application by evaluating the "whole person."

In order for an application to be complete, applicants must submit:

1) Application
2) Student profile sheet and application for institutional financial aid (if applicable)
3) 3 letters of reference (recommendation letters)
4) Official transcripts from every college/university attended
5) Personal statement (3–5 pages double-spaced)
6) Current resume
7) GMAT score
8) TOEFL score (for international students)
9) $50 application fee

Application Deadlines

Fall semester (financial aid applicants): February 15
Fall semester (regular applicants): May 1
Spring semester (international and financial aid applicants): October 1
Spring semester (regular applicants): November 15

If you are applying for financial aid, all documents must be in by the above dates. We also have rolling admissions based on space availability.

CLAREMONT GRADUATE UNIVERSITY
The Peter F. Drucker Graduate School of Management

Admissions Contact: Go Yoshida, Assistant Director, MBA Admissions
Address: 1021 North Dartmouth Avenue, Claremont, CA 91711
Admissions Phone: 800-944-4312 • *Admissions Fax:* 909-607-9104
Admissions E-mail: drucker@cgu.edu • *Web Address:* www.drucker.cgu.edu

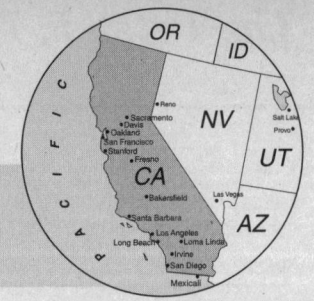

The chief draw of the Peter F. Drucker Graduate School of Management is the school's namesake. Mr. Drucker wrote The Practice of Management, the sacred writ of MBAs the world over and the first book to recognize management as a distinct and important business skill. Students tell us there is a real "family atmosphere" here and a "super-high emphasis on hands-on learning," and "if you plan carefully, you can assemble a schedule of world-class professors."

INSTITUTIONAL INFORMATION
Public/Private: Private
Evening Classes Available? Yes
Total Faculty: 12
% Faculty Female: 29
% Faculty Minority: 5
Student/Faculty Ratio: 12:1
Students in Parent Institution: 2,200
Academic Calendar: Semester

PROGRAMS
Degrees Offered: MBA (60 units); 4+1 accelerated program for undergraduates (48-60 units); MS in Financial Engineering (48 units); Executive MBA (60 units); Doctorate in Executive Management (60 units).
Joint Degrees: Dual-degree programs in Human Resources, Information Sciences, Economics, Education, Psychology, and Public Policy, and by special arrangement in other disciplines
Academic Specialties: Strategic Management, Leadership/Ethics, Cost Management, Marketing, Finance, Risk Management
Special Opportunities: International Fellows Program in Advanced English and Cultural Proficiency for Management
Study Abroad Options: England, France, Mexico, Japan, Switzerland

STUDENT INFORMATION
Total Business Students: 220
% Full Time: 84
% Female: 34
% Minority: 24
% Out of State: 10
% International: 57
Average Age: 28

COMPUTER AND RESEARCH FACILITIES
Research Facilities: Center for Advanced Studies in Leadership, New Venture Finance Institute, Quality of Life Research Center
Computer Facilities: Computer lab in the Burkle Building dedicated to management students' use with full range of software. Academic computing lab accesible 24 hours per day. Off-campus dial-in accounts available.
Campuswide Network? Yes
% of MBA Classrooms Wired: 35
Computer Model Recommended: Laptop
Internet Fee? No

EXPENSES/FINANCIAL AID
Annual Tuition: $32,348
Tuition Per Credit: $1,044
Room & Board: $12,000
Books and Supplies: $810
Average Grant: $8,000
Average Loan: $18,500
% Receiving Financial Aid: 80
% Receiving Aid Their First Year: 55

ADMISSIONS INFORMATION
Application Fee: $50
Electronic Application? Yes
Regular Application Deadline: Rolling
Regular Notification: Rolling
Deferment Available? No
Non-fall Application Deadline(s): October 1 (spring) and April 15 (summer)
Transfer Students Accepted? Yes
Transfer Policy: Maximum of 10 credits
Need-Blind Admissions? Yes
Number of Applications Received: 350
% of Applicants Accepted: 71
% Accepted Who Enrolled: 48
Average GPA: 3.1
GPA Range: 2.8-3.4
Average GMAT: 579
GMAT Range: 500-660
Average Years Experience: 4
Other Admissions Factors Considered: Leadership potential as indicated by experience and/or references
Minority/Disadvantaged Student Recruitment Programs: The Albrecht Endowed Fellowship awarded to students who demonstrate academic and professional potential and financial need; other minority funding sources are available.
Other Schools to Which Students Applied: USC, UCLA

INTERNATIONAL STUDENTS
TOEFL Required of International Students? Yes
Minimum TOEFL: 600 (250 computer)

EMPLOYMENT INFORMATION

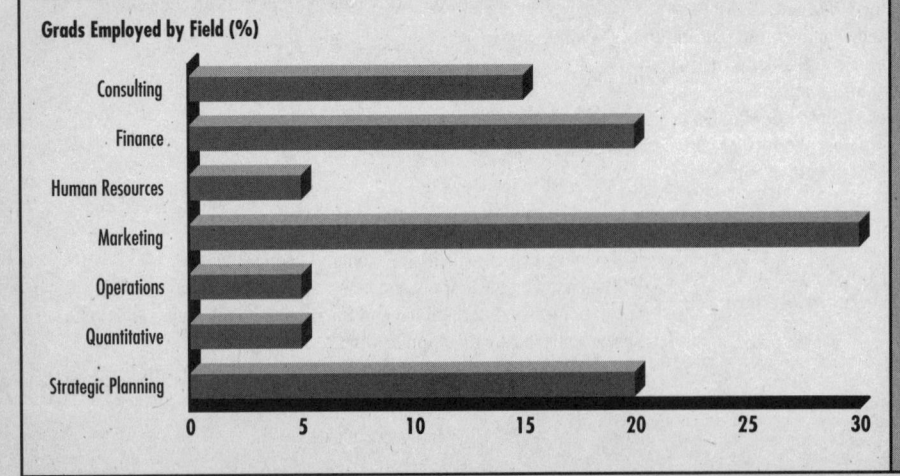

Grads Employed by Field (%):
- Consulting: 15
- Finance: 20
- Human Resources: 5
- Marketing: 30
- Operations: 5
- Quantitative: 5
- Strategic Planning: 20

Placement Office Available? Yes
% Employed Within 3 Months: 62
Frequent Employers: Avery Dension, Deloitte and Touche, Rainbird, Accenture, Aerojet, Boeing
Prominent Alumni: Charles Emery, senior VP & CEO, Horizon Blue CrossBlue Shield NJ; Stephen Rountree, executive VP & COO, J. Paul Getty Trust; Rajiv Dutta, chief financial officer, eBay, Inc.; Colin Forkner, president and CEO, California First National Bank; Brian Mulvaney, executive vice president, Aramark Corporation

CLARKSON UNIVERSITY
School of Business

Admissions Contact: Brenda Kozsan, Associate Director of Graduate Programs
Address: CU Box 5770, Potsdam, NY 13699
Admissions Phone: 315-268-6613 • Admissions Fax: 315-268-3810
Admissions E-mail: gradprog@clarkson.edu • Web Address: phoenix.som.clarkson.edu

This private school located in New York is renowned for its remarkable ratio of 32 faculty members to nearly 100 business students. Clarkson is proud of its "team-intensive learning communities," and it aims to "educate leaders who are energized by the entrepreneurial spirit and encouraged to serve the community." MBA students can participate in any of several experiential learning programs, including the Internet Consulting Group and the Corporate Partnership Program.

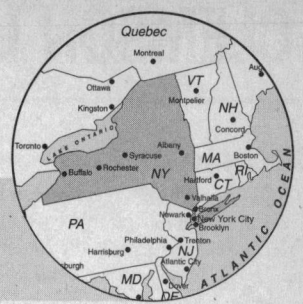

INSTITUTIONAL INFORMATION
Public/Private: Private
Evening Classes Available? No
Total Faculty: 32
% Faculty Female: 16
% Faculty Minority: 28
% Faculty Part Time: 9
Student/Faculty Ratio: 3:1
Students in Parent Institution: 2,539

PROGRAMS
Degrees Offered: Master of Business Administration (MBA) (1 year); Master of Business Administration (MBA) (2 years); Master of Science (1 year) in Manufacturing Management (MSMM), Information Systems (MSIS), or Human Resources (MSHR); MS in Engineering and Manufacturing Management (EMM) (32 credits over 5 summers)
Joint Degrees: MBA/MS in Environmental Manufacturing (EvMM) (2 years)
Academic Specialties: Accounting and Law, Economics and Finance, Marketing, Management Information Systems, Operations and Production Management, Organizational Studies, Strategy, Leadership Assessment and Development
Study Abroad Options: L'Ecole Superieure de Commerce de Grenbole, France; Reims Business School in Reims, France

STUDENT INFORMATION
Total Business Students: 75
% Full Time: 90
% Female: 40
% Minority: 4
% Out of State: 35
% International: 10
Average Age: 24

COMPUTER AND RESEARCH FACILITIES
Campuswide Network? Yes
% of MBA Classrooms Wired: 100
Internet Fee? No

EXPENSES/FINANCIAL AID
Annual Tuition: $21,984
Tuition Per Credit: $687
Books and Supplies: $1,100
Average Grant: $10,180
Average Loan: $15,000
% Receiving Financial Aid: 90
% Receiving Aid Their First Year: 90

ADMISSIONS INFORMATION
Application Fee: $25
Electronic Application? Yes
Regular Application Deadline: Rolling
Regular Notification: Rolling
Deferment Available? Yes
Length of Deferment: 1 year
Non-fall Admissions? Yes
Non-fall Application Deadline(s): Only if students are applying for our MS in Management Systems program; MBA students, fall term only
Transfer Students Accepted? Yes
Transfer Policy: Graduate students who need to complete foundation course work may enroll in the courses at Clarkson before entering the advanced MBA program. Students doing graduate work at another university are allowed to transfer 9 credit hours of graduate work.
Need-Blind Admissions? Yes
Number of Applications Received: 126
% of Applicants Accepted: 57
% Accepted Who Enrolled: 92
Average GPA: 3.3
Average GMAT: 550
Average Years Experience: 2
Other Admissions Factors Considered: Test of Spoken English is required or can be waived by the Graduate Office conducting a telephone interview.

INTERNATIONAL STUDENTS
TOEFL Required of International Students? Yes
Minimum TOEFL: 600 (250 computer)

EMPLOYMENT INFORMATION

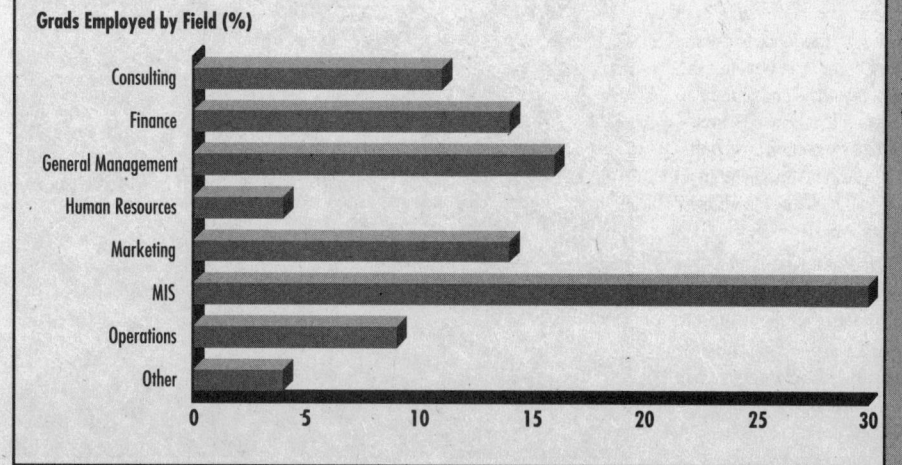

Grads Employed by Field (%):
- Consulting: ~11
- Finance: ~14
- General Management: ~16
- Human Resources: ~3
- Marketing: ~14
- MIS: ~30
- Operations: ~9
- Other: ~4

Placement Office Available? Yes
% Employed Within 3 Months: 73
Frequent Employers: Accenture, General Electric, IBM

CLEMSON UNIVERSITY

THE SCHOOL AT A GLANCE
The Clemson MBA Program offers both a full-time, two-year (21-month) degree and an off-campus, part-time, evening program for working professionals. Chosen by *Time* magazine as the 2001 Public College of the Year, Clemson University is consistently named as the best college value in South Carolina by *Money* magazine, is listed in America's 100 Best Buys, and is named a top national public university by *U.S. News & World Report*'s Best Colleges edition.

STUDENTS
Clemson's MBA students hail from all over the world. The average evening student is 29 years old with seven years of work experience. Full-time students average 25 years of age with two years of work experience. Overall, about 39 percent have degrees in business, 27 percent in engineering and pure sciences, and 24 percent in social sciences and humanities. Almost 40 percent are women. Approximately 30 percent of the students are international, representing more than 15 countries. The domestic students come from the South (60 percent), Northeast (20 percent), Midwest (15 percent), and West (5 percent).

On average, between 55 and 70 percent of the full-time MBAs have jobs at graduation. Hiring companies typically include PricewaterhouseCoopers, Michelin, Bank of America, American Management Systems, GE, and many other well-known companies. Clemson's MBA Career Services Center assists students in identifying and obtaining professional positions through a variety of placement services, including job fairs, résumé books, Web-based résumés, résumé and cover letter assistance, placement counseling, and workshops.

ACADEMICS
The Clemson MBA Program, accredited by AACSB International, enables individuals to study advanced, integrated concepts of business, industry, and government. Students include active managers as well as recent graduates interested in expanding their analytical, business, and interpersonal skills.

Participants in the full-time program on the Clemson campus take a highly intensive and rigorous 62-semester-hour program over two years. The first year (32 semester hours) provides foundation knowledge in core business areas: accounting, business communications, marketing, finance, economics, operations management, statistics, information systems, and law. Courses are taught in a condensed seven-week format during the first year. The second year (30 semester hours) is flexible, with tracks such areas as entrepreneurship, technology management, or a student-designed area of specialization. Areas of specialization can follow traditional disciplinary lines such as finance, marketing, or human resources; or they can target areas of current global and business interest such as sports marketing, e-commerce, supply chain management, or information technology. These courses are supplemented by a choice of tools courses and free electives. Diverse learning environments offer approaches that include role playing, simulations, internships, consulting, teamwork, and case studies.

The Clemson Evening MBA Program is a part-time, evening program that allows working business professionals with at least two years of work experience to pursue a degree in Greenville, South Carolina, at the University Center or in Greenwood, South Carolina, on the campus of Lander University. Students with no undergraduate business courses can expect to complete the 4 core courses and 11 advanced courses, which include 3 electives, in approximately three years. Course content and delivery are similar to the full-time program, but provide more flexibility for the nontraditional student. Students, who are all working professionals, actively enrich class learning by contributing and integrating personal business experience.

Clemson's distinguished faculty are highly qualified to bring outstanding learning opportunities to students by offering superb teaching skills, applied business research and professional experience, and high-quality student interaction. Clemson faculty are dedicated to sharing the practical aspects of academic theories as they relate to real-world situations. They are actively engaged in scholarly research and publication for leading academic journals, and many regularly serve as consultants to businesses around the globe.

CAMPUS LIFE
Clemson is a public university located in South Carolina's lake and mountain region. The campus consists of more than 1,400 wooded acres on the former plantation of John C. Calhoun. Founded in 1889, the University has a student population of approximately 17,000 and offers more than 100 graduate degrees in almost 70 areas. The town of Clemson is a small college community of 25,000 located on the shores of Lake Hartwell. Large population centers are conveniently located within 20 to 40 minutes of the area.

Clemson has one of the largest (based on number of individual user accounts) Novell networks in the world, linking all student labs and University departments to each other and the Internet with both wired and wireless networking access. Student labs, which are strategically located throughout the campus, contain state-of-the-art, networked, Windows-based personal computers. All lab computers have access to laser-quality printers, mainframe applications, e-mail, and a large selection of current software, including Microsoft Office. The University supports in excess of 100 "smart classrooms," which offer students and faculty the latest in learning technologies. The university's Collaborative Learning Environment (myCLE) is an integrated comprehensive university portal that has received national acclaim and is widely used by students and faculty in the teaching and research environment.

Graduate School of Business and Behavioral Science

COSTS

The 2001–2002 tuition and fees for the full-time program were $2,655 per semester for South Carolina residents and $5,642 per semester for nonresidents. Graduate assistants pay $696 per semester. Books and supplies cost approximately $1,200 per year extra, and all MBA students in the full-time program are required to purchase a notebook computer meeting minimum specifications at an average cost of $1,800. On-campus housing ranges from $920 per semester for a residence hall to $1,895 for an on-campus apartment. Off-campus apartments typically cost around $550 per month. A limited number of competitive graduate assistantships are available. Awards are based on personal interviews and candidate qualifications. Tuition for the evening program in 2001–2002 was $312 per credit hour for South Carolina residents and $562 per hour for nonresidents.

ADMISSIONS

Acceptance is based on academic background, the GMAT, letters of recommendation, a statement of purpose, and work experience. The admission process is highly personalized, with emphasis on each applicant's accomplishments. A score of at least 550 on the TOEFL is required for all students whose native language is not English. Calculus is a prerequisite for the MBA programs.

Application deadlines for the full-time program are February 15 for international students and May 15 for domestic students. For the part-time program, deadlines are April 15, July 15, and November 15. Visit our admissions and application website at www.clemson.edu/business/mba/apply.htm for last-minute details.

Admissions Contact: MBA Office—Admissions, Associate Director of MBA Programs
Address: 124 Sirrine Hall, Clemson, SC 29634-1315
Admissions Phone: 864-656-3975 • Admissions Fax: 864-656-0947
Admissions E-mail: mba@clemson.edu • Web Address: www.clemson.edu/business/mba

CLEMSON UNIVERSITY
Graduate School of Business and Behavioral Science

Admissions Contact: MBA Office—Admissions, Associate Director of MBA Programs
Address: 124 Sirrine Hall, Box 341315, Clemson University, Clemson, SC 29634-1315
Admissions Phone: 864-656-3975 • Admissions Fax: 864-656-0947
Admissions E-mail: mba@clemson.edu • Web Address: www.clemson.edu/business/mba

The Clemson MBA provides a standard business education with a specific focus on the practical application of learned business knowledge, and students participate in computer-based simulations, role-playing scenarios, casework, and field study. The student body is 35 percent international, giving students a prime opportunity to learn about global business cultures and the true international marketplace of ideas. The part-time evening MBA program offers flexibility for working professionals and a choice between two locations where Clemson faculty provide quality instruction: Greenwood and Greenville.

INSTITUTIONAL INFORMATION
Public/Private: Public
Evening Classes Available? Yes
Total Faculty: 123
Student/Faculty Ratio: 3:1
Students in Parent Institution: 16,900

PROGRAMS
Degrees Offered: PhD in Industrial Management (4 years); PhD in Management Science (4 years); PhD in Applied Economics (4 years); MBA (2 years full time, 3 years evening part time); Master of Professional Accounting (MPAcc) (2 years); Master of Electronic Commerce (MECOM) (1.5 years); Master of Science in Industrial Management (MSIM) (1 year); MA in Economics (2 years)
Joint Degrees: Dual degrees are allowed. Up to one-sixth of the total hours in both programs combined may be double-counted. Dual degrees must be declared by the middle of the first semester of graduate school.
Study Abroad Options: A second master's can be earned in Australia.

STUDENT INFORMATION
Total Business Students: 255
% Full Time: 32
% Female: 32
% Minority: 3
% Out of State: 55
% International: 35
Average Age: 25

COMPUTER AND RESEARCH FACILITIES
Research Facilities: Center for International Trade, Technology Transfer Institute, Spiro Center for Entrepreneurial Leadership
Campuswide Network? Yes
% of MBA Classrooms Wired: 100
Computer Model Recommended: Laptop
Internet Fee? No

EXPENSES/FINANCIAL AID
Annual Tuition (Resident/Nonresident): $5,310/$11,284
Tuition Per Credit (Resident/Nonresident): $312/$562
Room & Board (On/Off Campus): $8,000/$9,200
Books and Supplies: $1,600
Average Grant: $5,000
Average Loan: $11,000
% Receiving Financial Aid: 85
% Receiving Aid Their First Year: 81

ADMISSIONS INFORMATION
Application Fee: $40
Electronic Application? Yes
Regular Application Deadline: 4/15
Regular Notification: 5/15
Deferment Available? Yes
Length of Deferment: 1 year
Non-fall Admissions? No
Transfer Students Accepted? Yes
Transfer Policy: Must meet all admission requirements; can transfer a maximum of 6 semester hours of acceptable course work
Need-Blind Admissions? Yes
Number of Applications Received: 338
% of Applicants Accepted: 44
% Accepted Who Enrolled: 61
Average GPA: 3.4
GPA Range: 3.1-3.5
Average GMAT: 594
GMAT Range: 560-640
Average Years Experience: 2

INTERNATIONAL STUDENTS
TOEFL Required of International Students? Yes
Minimum TOEFL: 580 (237 computer)

EMPLOYMENT INFORMATION

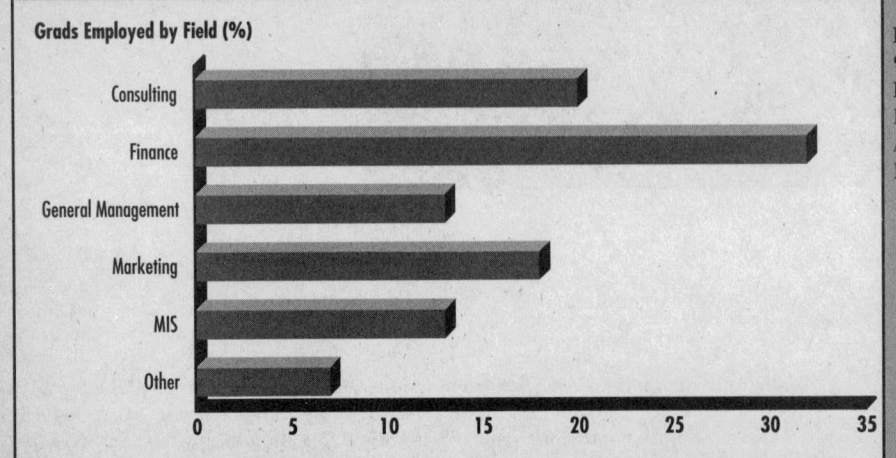

Grads Employed by Field (%)
- Consulting: ~20
- Finance: ~32
- General Management: ~13
- Marketing: ~18
- MIS: ~13
- Other: ~7

Placement Office Available? Yes
% Employed Within 3 Months: 62
Frequent Employers: General Electric, Michelin, First Union, Ingersol Rand, Bank of America, Fluor Daniel, Avis, Accenture, Milliken, AC Neilsen

CLEVELAND STATE UNIVERSITY
James J. Nance College of Business Administration

Admissions Contact: Bruce M. Gottschalk, MBA Programs Administrator
Address: 1860 East 18th Street, BU 219, Cleveland, OH 44114
Admissions Phone: 216-687-3730 • Admissions Fax: 216-687-5311
Admissions E-mail: cbacsu@csuohio.edu • Web Address: csuohio.edu/cba

The James J. Nance College of Business Administration offers several MBA programs. The Accelerated Program is a "fast-paced weekend program, ideal for management-track professionals." The Executive MBA offers working professionals the opportunity to continue their careers while enhancing their knowledge and acquiring a degree. The Off-Campus Program allows students extreme schedule/location flexibility, enabling them to take courses at any of the four off-campus centers.

INSTITUTIONAL INFORMATION
Public/Private: Public
Evening Classes Available? Yes
Total Faculty: 76
% Faculty Female: 22
% Faculty Minority: 15
% Faculty Part Time: 17
Student/Faculty Ratio: 26:1
Students in Parent Institution: 15,620
Academic Calendar: Semester

PROGRAMS
Degrees Offered: Master of Accountancy (2 years), Master of Business Administration (1 to 2 years), Master of Computer and Information Science (2 years), Master of Labor Relations and Human Resources (2 years), Master of Public Health (2 years)
Joint Degrees: JD/MBA (4 years)
Academic Specialties: Comprehensive multidisciplinary method of instruction
Study Abroad Options: England, Germany

STUDENT INFORMATION
Total Business Students: 527
% Full Time: 22
% Female: 40
% Minority: 8
% Out of State: 58
% International: 56
Average Age: 27

COMPUTER AND RESEARCH FACILITIES
Research Facilities: Executive Development Center, Labor Relations Center, Real Estate Institute, Small Business Institute
Computer Facilities: The university has a networked laboratory of basic and advanced personal computers, plus a networked laboratory of workstations including Sun Sparc, SGI Indy, and a DEC 3100/5100. There are SAS and SPSS databases available for statistical research applications.
Campuswide Network? Yes
% of MBA Classrooms Wired: 12
Computer Model Recommended: No
Internet Fee? No

EXPENSES/FINANCIAL AID
Annual Tuition (Resident/Nonresident): $6,312/$12,624
Tuition Per Credit (Resident/Nonresident): $263/$526
Room & Board (On/Off Campus): $8,100/$9,500
Books and Supplies: $1,000
% Receiving Financial Aid: 3
% Receiving Aid Their First Year: 7

ADMISSIONS INFORMATION
Application Fee: $30
Electronic Application? Yes
Regular Application Deadline: 7/1
Regular Notification: Rolling
Deferment Available? Yes
Length of Deferment: 1 year
Non-fall Admissions? Yes
Non-fall Application Deadline(s): 11/2 spring, 4/2 summer
Transfer Students Accepted? Yes
Transfer Policy: Must be in good academic standing
Need-Blind Admissions? Yes
Number of Applications Received: 333
% of Applicants Accepted: 79
% Accepted Who Enrolled: 80
Average GPA: 3.1
GPA Range: 2.8-3.3
Average GMAT: 505
GMAT Range: 460-590
Average Years Experience: 4
Other Schools to Which Students Applied: Case Western Reserve University, John Carroll University, Kent State University, University of Akron

INTERNATIONAL STUDENTS
TOEFL Required of International Students? Yes
Minimum TOEFL: 525 (197 computer)

EMPLOYMENT INFORMATION

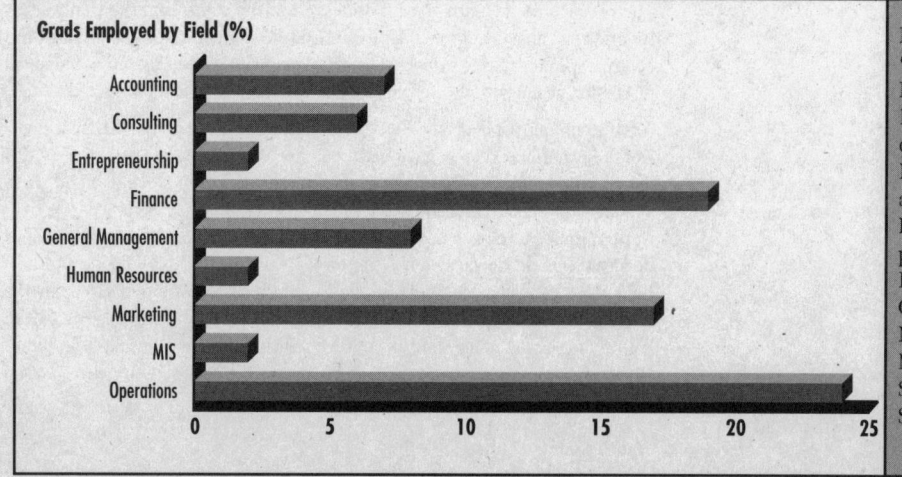

Grads Employed by Field (%)

Field	%
Accounting	6
Consulting	6
Entrepreneurship	2
Finance	19
General Management	8
Human Resources	2
Marketing	17
MIS	2
Operations	23

Placement Office Available? No
% Employed Within 3 Months: 93
Frequent Employers: American Greetings, Banc One, Cleveland Clinic, IMG, KeyCorp, Lincoln Electric, MBNA, Moen Inc., NASA Glenn, National City Bank, Nestle, Progressive Insurance, Sherwin Williams, Steris, Swagelok
Prominent Alumni: Monte Ahuja, chairman, president, and CEO, Transtar Industries; Michael Berthelot, chairman and CEO, Transtechnolgy Corporation; Ted Hlavaty, chairman and CEO, Neway Stamping & Manufacturing; Thomas Moore, president, Wolf Group; Kenneth Semelsberger, president, COO, and director, Scott Fetzer, Inc.

COLLEGE OF WILLIAM AND MARY

THE SCHOOL AT A GLANCE

"The blend of opportunities afforded by the William and Mary School of Business is unmatched; the College is within easy reach of some of the world's most vibrant business centers, the MBA program's small size fosters interaction, and the school's passionate faculty is dedicated to facilitating an MBA experience based on partnerships. Ours is a cutting-edge approach to global business education; we provide a real-world perspective, impressive corporate connections, and unfettered access to some of the sharpest minds teaching business today. We invite you to preview our MBA program; one of the most challenging and intimate graduate business educations offered."

—Lawrence B. Pulley
Dean and T.C. and Elizabeth Clarke
Professor of Business Administration

Founded in 1693, The College of William and Mary is the second oldest educational institution in the U.S. and has educated four U.S. Presidents: George Washington, Thomas Jefferson, James Monroe, and John Tyler. Other alumni range from American luminaries like John Marshall to modern business trailblazers such as Mark McCormack, Founder, Chairman, and CEO of IMG. The striking architecture of the William and Mary campus provides a tour through three hundred years of history and tradition located in the heart of colonial Williamsburg, Virginia. Although it retains its traditional title of "College," William and Mary is in reality a small public university with approximately 5,500 undergraduate and 2,000 graduate students. The College is just a 45-minute drive from Virginia Beach, Norfolk, or Richmond, which are home to a broad array of industries, just over two hours from Washington, D.C., and half a day from New York City.

STUDENTS

The William and Mary student body exhibits diverse academic and professional achievements, which adds great richness to the environment. The small class size, usually two sections of 50 students each, facilitates a fellowship among students, faculty, alumni, and corporate leaders. The average entering full-time student is 28 years old with approximately five years of post-undergraduate work experience. Thirty-seven percent of the class is women, 33 percent is international, and U.S. minority students comprise 10 percent of the class.

The program emphasizes teamwork; student teams designed to link MBA candidates with varying strengths provide a preview of the cross-functional work groups they will encounter in professional settings. Through live case studies, students analyze trends as they develop in the business world. Students and faculty manage information as it unfolds and participate together in examining the complexities of alternative scenarios. This immersion in teamwork and collaboration prepares William and Mary MBAs to develop comprehensive business solutions in the classroom and the real world.

ACADEMICS

The College of William and Mary offers the MBA degree in three formats: full-time, evening, and executive. William and Mary provides a broad management education that offers immediate access to faculty and one-on-one interaction with some of today's most intriguing corporate leaders and risk-taking entrepreneurs. The MBA curriculum reflects the complexities of the business world, where everyday problems are not separated into academic disciplines.

In the full-time MBA program, the first year provides a thorough grounding in management theory and practice. Proceeding through a uniquely integrated curriculum, MBA candidates examine business problems from every possible angle until a comprehensive understanding is achieved. This method requires intense collaboration among faculty, as well as a flexible schedule that changes to accommodate topic modules and to allow for interaction with visiting business executives. Second-year MBA candidates return from internships having mastered the fundamentals and pursue specialized study in accounting, finance, economics, marketing, information technology, operations, organizational behavior and human resource management, or general management.

Joint degree programs that combine the MBA with law (MBA/JD) or public policy (MBA/MPP) are offered cooperatively with William and Mary's Marshall-Wythe School of Law and the Thomas Jefferson Program in Public Policy.

To meet the needs of working professionals, the evening and executive MBA programs offer the same high-quality education available to full-time students. Through the evening program, students pursue the MBA during the evening hours over three to four years in the centrally located Peninsula Center in Newport News, Virginia. The Executive MBA is an intensive program, meeting on alternate Fridays and Saturdays with four residency periods over 20 months.

Accessibility to faculty makes the William and Mary MBA experience truly exceptional. William and Mary MBA students benefit from engaged faculty who are extraordinary educators. They are practitioners who are recognized for outstanding achievements within their chosen fields and award winners who are committed to delivering graduate management programs that are superior on every level. Due to the carefully crafted size of the MBA programs, faculty members are attentive to the aspirations of each student and are easily accessible for consultation. They challenge students to reframe business concepts and processes in the context of currently developing corporate strategy. This approach is the backbone of a quality MBA education and one of the many reasons why William and Mary graduates excel.

The MBA Association is the representative organization for graduate business students; it maintains a committee structure, representing all facets of business, which allows students with common academic and professional goals to come together with faculty and experienced business executives in a focused, team-based environment.

The opportunity to learn about business trends straight from the trendsetters themselves enhances the MBA programs at William and Mary. The MBA Executive Speaker Series brings corporate leaders into the classroom and small discussion group settings for one-on-one interaction with students.

Another unique aspect is the Senior Executive Resource Corps (SERC), a network of experienced executives with senior-level expertise representing 22 different industries. The members of this volunteer group serve as mentors to William and Mary MBAs and share their considerable business acumen as real-world resources. SERC members collaborate with faculty to advise student teams during the Field Studies consulting projects, conducted by second-year, full-time MBA students. The Field Studies program requires students to apply the knowledge and skills gained from the first year and internship experiences in identifying, researching, and proposing solutions for real business problems faced by national and regional clients. Additional information can be found online at http://business.wm.edu/corporate.

Graduate School of Business

CAMPUS LIFE

While many MBA courses encompass a global perspective, the student body (approximately 38 percent international) provides additional insight into global business issues. Several options for further internationalizing the William and Mary MBA are available, including course work that features hands-on study tours to international locations and exchange partnerships—with ESCP-EAP, the European School of Management in France; INCAE in Costa Rica; the Norwegian School of Economics and Business Administration; and the Otto Beisheim Graduate School in Germany—that offer international immersion experiences.

The College of William and Mary works to help students clarify their goals and recognizes that they expect to achieve a challenging professional position with excellent compensation following the academic rigor of the MBA program. The MBA Career Services Office, in partnership with alumni and corporate leaders, provides exposure and access to Fortune 500 recruiters through a comprehensive Career Management Program including participation in MBA Consortium events in Atlanta, New York City, Washington, D.C., and the Silicon Valley, as well as a full range of on- and off-campus recruiting activities. Career forums bring corporate representatives to campus for panel discussions; alumni encourage networking and provide mock interviews, resume reviews, and mentoring relationships. SERC members work closely with the MBA Career Services team to provide corporate contacts and expert guidance on professional opportunities. Current placement profiles and recruiter lists can be found online at http://business.wm.edu.

A modern graduate housing complex designed specifically for graduate students offers two-, three-, or four-bedroom apartments within walking distance to the School of Business Administration. Early applications for on-campus housing are encouraged. Students living off-campus can choose from a variety of privately managed living options in Williamsburg, or commute from neighboring cities.

Entering full-time MBA students are required to bring a laptop computer; minimum specification requirements can be found online at http://business.wm.edu. Each classroom seat is equipped with power and network hookups, with wireless technology available in some areas. The School of Business facilities includes modern, executive-style classrooms, a computer lab, and team-study and conference rooms housed within the historic section of the William and Mary campus.

COSTS

William and Mary provides exceptional academic programs with comparatively low tuition and fees. Considering the success of our graduates, our programs offer a compelling return on investment. Full-time MBA students will find some resources made available through scholarships, loans, and graduate assistantships. Scholarship and graduate assistantship awards are based solely on merit. Loan eligibility is based on need as determined by filing the U.S. Department of Education's Free Application for Federal Student Aid (FAFSA). Although participation in some loan programs is limited to U.S. Citizens and Permanent Residents, international students may be eligible for private or alternative loans.

The total annual, full-time, in-state student budget for 2002–2003 is $25,808, which includes tuition and fees of $9,978, room and board of $8,330, computer and software totalling $3,500, miscellaneous expenses of $3,000, and books and supplies totalling $1,000. The total annual, full-time, out-of-state and international student budget for 2002–2003 is $37,088. This includes tuition and fees, $21,258; room and board, $8,330; computer and software $3,500; miscellaneous, $3,000; and books and supplies, $1,000.

Evening MBA tuition and fees for 2002–2003 are $306 per credit hour (in state) and $620 per credit hour (out of state), up to 8 credit hours per semester.

ADMISSIONS

The full-time and evening MBA programs are small by design; the effectiveness of these programs depends on the relationships developed within student teams and those forged between students and faculty. While some MBA candidates enter the program with business-related degrees or experience, many students enter from an array of different academic and professional disciplines. Admission decisions are based on the applicant's academic record, professional experience, GMAT scores, recommendations, interview, essays, and other indicators of aptitude for graduate study in business. Applicants are encouraged to apply online at http://business.wm.edu/mba.

Admission to the full-time MBA program is granted for the fall term only. There are three formal application review periods, followed by a rolling admission process. Applicants for fall 2003 who apply by November 15 are notified by February 1; January 15 applicants are notified by March 15; March 15 applicants are notified by May 1; April 15 applicants are notified by June 1; May 15 applicants are notified by July 1. Those who apply after May 15 are notified on a rolling basis. Applicants are encouraged to apply early for full scholarship consideration.

Admission to the evening MBA program is offered for both the fall and spring semesters on a rolling basis. Applicants who apply for spring 2003 admission by November 15 are notified by December 15. Those who apply for fall 2003 admission by July 1 are notified by August 1. Interested students should contact:

Admissions Contact: Kathy Williams Pattison, Director, MBA Admissions
Address: Blow Hall, Room 254, Williamsburg, VA 23187
Admissions Phone: 757-221-2900 • Admissions Fax: 757-221-2958
Admissions E-mail: admissions@business.wm.edu • Web Address: www.business.wm.edu

COLLEGE OF WILLIAM AND MARY
Graduate School of Business

Admissions Contact: Kathy Williams Pattison, Director, MBA Admissions
Address: Blow Hall, Room 254, Williamsburg, VA 23187
Admissions Phone: 757-221-2900 • Admissions Fax: 757-221-2958
Admissions E-mail: admissions@business.wm.edu • Web Address: www.business.wm.edu

A "smaller program," "non-competitive attitude," and state-school prices attract MBAs to the College of William and Mary Graduate School of Business, where "very enthusiastic, very capable," and "very tough" professors offer "a great deal of personal attention." Incoming students here participate in an Outward Bound–style Orientation Week, during which they divide into teams and compete in, among other things, a high-ropes course and a raft-building exercise.

INSTITUTIONAL INFORMATION
Public/Private: Public
Evening Classes Available? Yes
Total Faculty: 45
% Faculty Female: 20
% Faculty Minority: 5
Student/Faculty Ratio: 4:1
Students in Parent Institution: 7,560
Academic Calendar: Semester

PROGRAMS
Degrees Offered: MBA (2 years full time, 3.5 years evening), Executive MBA (20 months), Master of Accounting (1 year)
Joint Degrees: MBA/JD (4 years), MBA/MPP (3 years)
Academic Specialties: Finance, Operations Management, Information Technology, Marketing, leadership, and team-building
Special Opportunities: Field Study (team consulting project), international trips to Southeast Asia or Paris
Study Abroad Options: Norway, France, Germany, Costa Rica

STUDENT INFORMATION
Total Business Students: 306
% Full Time: 53
% Female: 40
% Minority: 9
% Out of State: 53
% International: 34
Average Age: 29

COMPUTER AND RESEARCH FACILITIES
Research Facilities: State-of-the-art electronic reference resource area, investment management center with Bloomberg and Baseline
Computer Facilities: Wireless Internet receivers and networked laser printers. Databases include Lexis-Nexis, Compustat, CRSP, ProQuest ABI/Inform, STAT-USA, Hoover's Online, Piranhaweb, Global Access, and others. Every course has its own Web page and news server.
Campuswide Network? Yes
% of MBA Classrooms Wired: 100
Computer Model Recommended: Laptop

EXPENSES/FINANCIAL AID
Annual Tuition (Resident/Nonresident): $9,322/$19,670
Tuition Per Credit (Resident/Nonresident): $280/$571
Room & Board: $8,330
Books and Supplies: $4,000
Average Grant: $5,775
Average Loan: $17,597
% Receiving Financial Aid: 79
% Receiving Aid Their First Year: 75

ADMISSIONS INFORMATION
Application Fee: $50
Electronic Application? Yes
Early Decision Application Deadline: 12/1
Early Decision Notification: 12/31
Regular Application Deadline: 5/1
Regular Notification: Rolling
Length of Deferment: 1 year
Non-fall Admissions? No
Transfer Students Accepted? No
Need-Blind Admissions? Yes
Number of Applications Received: 224
% of Applicants Accepted: 79
% Accepted Who Enrolled: 44
Average GPA: 3.2
GPA Range: 2.7-3.9
Average GMAT: 616
GMAT Range: 580-690
Average Years Experience: 5
Other Admissions Factors Considered: Managerial and leadership potential, personal and professional achievements, communications skills, academic promise, academic record, recommendations, work experience, interview
Minority/Disadvantaged Student Recruitment Programs: Attend minority recruitment fairs locally and nationally; attend international MBA forums; presentations to HBCs (undergraduate business students)
Other Schools to Which Students Applied: North Carolina—Chapel Hill, Wake Forest, U. of Maryland—College Park, U. of Virginia, Georgetown, Babson

INTERNATIONAL STUDENTS
TOEFL Required of International Students? Yes
Minimum TOEFL: 600 (250 computer)

EMPLOYMENT INFORMATION

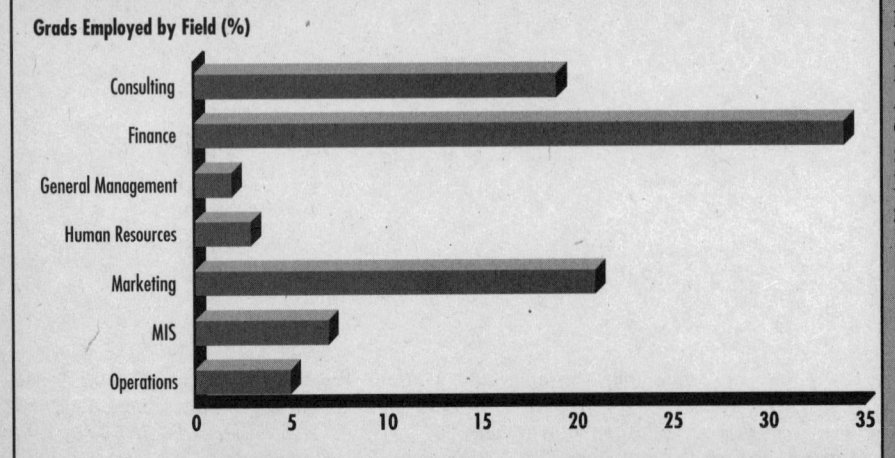

Grads Employed by Field (%)

Field	%
Consulting	~19
Finance	~34
General Management	~3
Human Resources	~3
Marketing	~21
MIS	~7
Operations	~5

Placement Office Available? Yes
% Employed Within 3 Months: 92
Frequent Employers: Dominion Energy, Booz Allen Hamilton, National City, Align 360, Capital One, IBM, William M. Mercer, Bristol-Myers Squibb, PricewaterhouseCoopers, BB&T
Prominent Alumni: Charles Horner, lieutenant general; Steve Umberger, president, ValueClick International; Bill Fricks, chairman and CEO, Newport News Shipbuilding

COLUMBIA UNIVERSITY
Columbia Business School

Admissions Contact: Linda Meehan, Assistant Dean for Admissions
Address: 216 Uris Hall, 3022 Broadway, New York, NY 10027
Admissions Phone: 212-854-1961 • *Admissions Fax:* 212-662-5754
Admissions E-mail: apply@claven.gsb.columbia.edu • *Web Address:* www.gsb.columbia.edu

Columbia Business School's candle continues to burn brighter and brighter, thanks to its "truly outstanding professors" and a wealth of "very strong" resources and programs, especially in international business. Best of all, though, is Columbia's unbeatable New York City location. Internship opportunities are staggering and "several of the 'big guns' from Wall Street serve as adjunct faculty for many second-year courses."

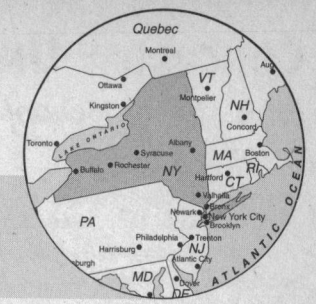

INSTITUTIONAL INFORMATION
Public/Private: Private
Evening Classes Available? No
Total Faculty: 207
% Faculty Female: 16
% Faculty Part Time: 39
Student/Faculty Ratio: 6:1
Students in Parent Institution: 22,892
Academic Calendar: Trimester

PROGRAMS
Degrees Offered: PhD (4 to 5 years), Executive Master of Business Administration (EMBA) (20 months), MBA (16 to 20 months)
Joint Degrees: MBA/MS Urban Planning, MBA/DDS, MBA/MS Engineering, MBA/Master of International Affairs, MBA/MS Journalism, MBA/Juris Doctor, MBA/MS Nursing, MBA/MD, MBA/Master of Public Health, MBA/MS Social Work, MBA/EdD Educational Administration and Higher Education
Academic Specialties: 4 overarching themes: total quality management, ethics, human resource management, and globalization.
Special Opportunities: EMBA with London Business or UC Berkeley, Executive Education Program
Study Abroad Options: Australia, Austria, Brazil, China, Finland, France, Germany, Israel, Italy, Japan, Mexico, Netherlands, Philippines, Singapore, South Africa, Spain, Sweden, Switzerland, UK

STUDENT INFORMATION
Total Business Students: 1,225
% Female: 36
% Minority: 19
% International: 27
Average Age: 27

COMPUTER AND RESEARCH FACILITIES
Research Facilities: Centers and institutes for for Accounting Research, International Business Education, Futures Markets, Global Brand Leadership, Japanese Economy and Business, Entrepreneurship, Tele-Information, International Business, Banking and Financial Institutions, Real Estate, and Quality, Productivity, and Competitiveness
Computer Facilities: The Student Notebook Computer Initiative requires every student to own a notebook computer. Students have access to more than 20 economic databases, Web-based instructional and administrative applications, and Web-based e-mail listservers for all courses, clusters, clubs, and administrative committees. A Trading Room utilizes real-time financial data trading simulation software.

EXPENSES/FINANCIAL AID
Annual Tuition: $30,334
Room & Board: $13,546
Books and Supplies: $1,116
% Receiving Financial Aid: 70

ADMISSIONS INFORMATION
Application Fee: $175
Electronic Application? Yes
Early Decision Application Deadline: 10/15
Early Decision Notification: 11/30
Regular Application Deadline: 4/20
Regular Notification: Rolling
Length of Deferment: 1 year
Non-fall Application Deadline(s): 10/1 for January entry
Transfer Students Accepted? No
Need-Blind Admissions? Yes
Number of Applications Received: 5,277
% of Applicants Accepted: 13
% Accepted Who Enrolled: 69
Average GPA: 3.4
Average GMAT: 705
Average Years Experience: 4
Other Admissions Factors Considered: Varied business and other backgrounds, potential to become successful global leader, record of achievement, demonstrated leadership, ability to work as member of a team
Minority/Disadvantaged Student Recruitment Programs: Fellowships for minority students, information sessions and receptions for prospective students
Other Schools to Which Students Applied: Harvard, Penn, Stanford

INTERNATIONAL STUDENTS
TOEFL Required of International Students? Yes

EMPLOYMENT INFORMATION

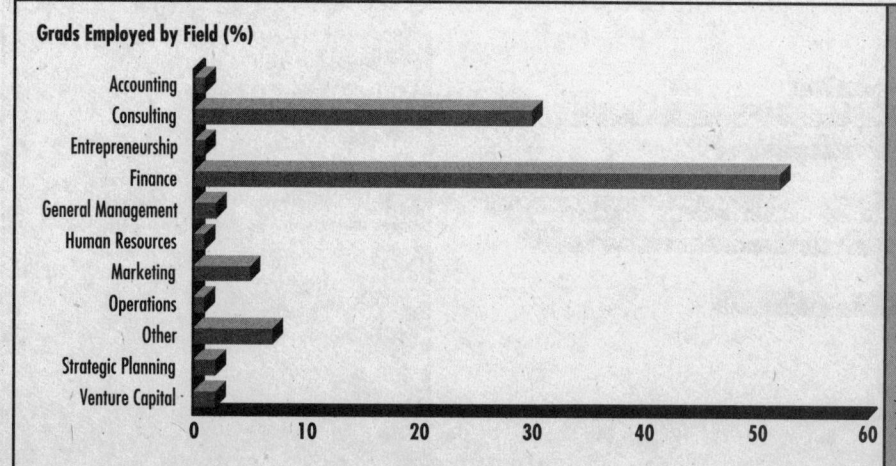

Grads Employed by Field (%)
- Accounting
- Consulting
- Entrepreneurship
- Finance
- General Management
- Human Resources
- Marketing
- Operations
- Other
- Strategic Planning
- Venture Capital

Placement Office Available? Yes
% Employed Within 3 Months: 94
Frequent Employers: McKinsey & Co.; Goldman Sachs; Citicorp/Citibank; Booz Allen Hamilton; Morgan Stanley Dean Witter; Deutsche Bank; Bear Stearns; Lehman Brothers, Inc.; Merrill Lynch & Co., Inc.; American Express; Credit Suisse
Prominent Alumni: Warren Buffett, chairman, Berkshire Hathaway Inc.; Henry Kravis, founding partner, Kohlberg, Kravis; Rochelle Lazarus, chairman and CEO, Ogilvy & Mather; Michael Gould, chairman and CEO, Bloomingdales; Benjamin Rosen, chairman emeritus, Compaq Computer

CONCORDIA UNIVERSITY
John Molson School of Business

Admissions Contact: Cynthia Law, MBA Program Admissions Officer
Address: 1455 de Maisonneuve Boulevard West, GM 710, Montreal, PQ H3G 1M8
Admissions Phone: 514-848-2708 • *Admissions Fax:* 514-848-2816
Admissions E-mail: mba@mercato.concordia.ca • *Web Address:* www.johnmolson.concordia.ca

Welcome to the John Molson School of Business, where you can attain an MBA and do just about anything else: The Concordia MBA opportunity comes packaged with an extravagant host of study abroad options, numerous academic specialties, and a growing number of degrees offered within the business school. Concordia is a private institution located in Quebec, so come prepared with your English-French dictionary.

INSTITUTIONAL INFORMATION
Public/Private: Private
Evening Classes Available? Yes
Total Faculty: 266
% Faculty Female: 26
% Faculty Part Time: 53
Student/Faculty Ratio: 12:1
Students in Parent Institution: 26,000
Academic Calendar: Trimester

PROGRAMS
Degrees Offered: MBA (16 months to 5 years), Executive MBA (20 months), International Aviation MBA (12 months), Global E-based Aviation MBA (2 years), Master of Science in Administration (16 months to 5 years), PhD (4 to 5 years), Diploma in Accountancy (1 year), Diploma in Administration (1 year), Diploma in Sport Administration (1 year), MBA Investment Management Option (3 to 5 years), Master in Investment Management (3 to 5 years), Graduate Diploma in Investment Management (3 to 4 years), Graduate Certificate in E-Business (1 year)
Academic Specialties: Accounting, Finance, International Business, Aviation Management, Investment Management, E-Business, Portfolio Management, Not-for-Profit, Sport Administration
Special Opportunities: CREPUQ University Agreements, Faculty of Commerce and Administration Bilateral Exchange Programs

Study Abroad Options: Australia, China, Denmark, France, Germany, Hungary, Italy, Mexico, New Zealand, Spain, Sweden, Switzerland, United Kingdom, United States

STUDENT INFORMATION
Total Business Students: 323
% Full Time: 44
% Female: 39
% Out of State: 68
% International: 41
Average Age: 28

COMPUTER AND RESEARCH FACILITIES
Research Facilities: Webster Library, Vanier Library with 1,700,000 holdings; 992,581 microforms; and 6070 current serials
Computer Facilities: Computer lab with Pentium computers
Campuswide Network? Yes
% of MBA Classrooms Wired: 25
Computer Model Recommended: Laptop
Internet Fee? No

EXPENSES/FINANCIAL AID
Annual Tuition: $12,500
Room & Board (On/Off Campus): $10,000/$11,000
Books and Supplies: $1,000
Average Grant: $9,000
Average Loan: $8,000
% Receiving Financial Aid: 15
% Receiving Aid Their First Year: 15

ADMISSIONS INFORMATION
Application Fee: $50
Electronic Application? Yes
Early Decision Application Deadline: 3 deadlines throughout year
Regular Application Deadline: Rolling
Regular Notification: Rolling
Deferment Available? Yes
Length of Deferment: 1 year
Non-fall Admissions? Yes
Non-fall Application Deadline(s): 6/1 for September, 10/1 for January, 2/28 for May
Transfer Students Accepted? No
Need-Blind Admissions? Yes
Number of Applications Received: 660
% of Applicants Accepted: 17
% Accepted Who Enrolled: 81
Average GPA: 3.3
GPA Range: 3.0-4.0
Average GMAT: 634
GMAT Range: 600-740
Other Admissions Factors Considered: Awards, career potential, personality and fit, level of maturity, communication skills
Minority/Disadvantaged Student Recruitment Programs: Noncredit courses and certificate programs for members of minority communities
Other Schools to Which Students Applied: University of Toronto, University of Western Ontario

INTERNATIONAL STUDENTS
TOEFL Required of International Students? Yes
Minimum TOEFL: 600 (250 computer)

EMPLOYMENT INFORMATION

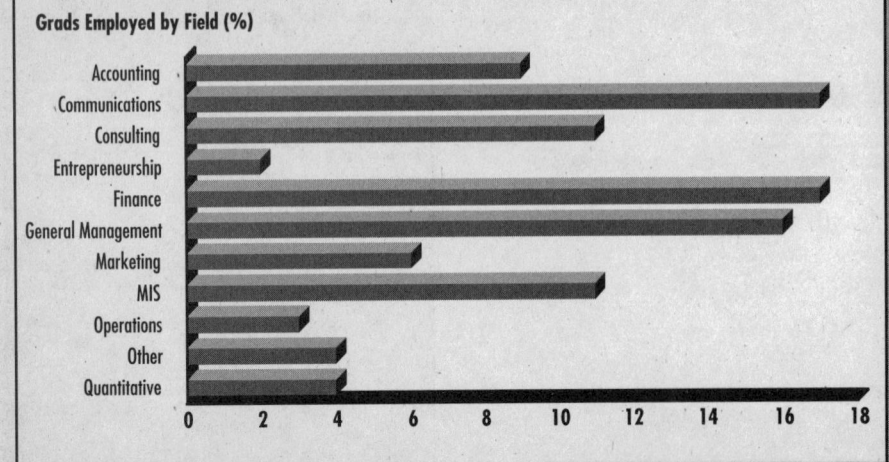

Grads Employed by Field (%): Accounting, Communications, Consulting, Entrepreneurship, Finance, General Management, Marketing, MIS, Operations, Other, Quantitative

Placement Office Available? Yes
% Employed Within 3 Months: 95
Frequent Employers: Royal Bank, Bombardier, Air Canada, Merck Frosst, Novartis, TD Bank, Andersen Consulting, CAP Gemini Ernst & Young, Nortel Networks
Prominent Alumni: Brian Steck, former vice chairman, Bank of Montreal; David Goldman, COO, Noranda Inc.; Jonathan Weiner, CEO, Canderel Inc.; Lawrence Bloomberg, former COO, National Bank; Christine Sirsley, executive vice president, Via Rail

Cornell University
Johnson Graduate School of Management

Admissions Contact: Natalie Grinblatt, Director, Office of Admissions and Financial Aid
Address: 111 Sage Hall, Ithaca, NY 14853
Admissions Phone: 607-255-4526 • Admissions Fax: 607-255-0065
Admissions E-mail: mba@johnson.cornell.edu • Web Address: www.johnson.cornell.edu

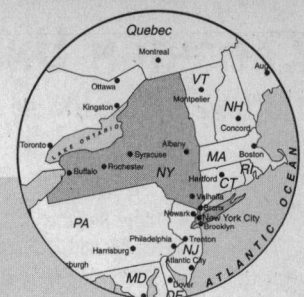

Selecting classes every semester is like attending a mile-long buffet table at Cornell University's Johnson School, where joint degree programs and specialized concentrations are legion. The "thrilling" pace of instruction here is "phenomenal," and students tell us "there hasn't been teaching this good since Socrates." Also noteworthy are the Johnson School's Immersion Learning courses, which come complete with "real-world" problems and time pressure.

INSTITUTIONAL INFORMATION
Public/Private: Private
Evening Classes Available? No
Total Faculty: 77
% Faculty Female: 23
% Faculty Minority: 16
% Faculty Part Time: 31
Student/Faculty Ratio: 7:1
Students in Parent Institution: 19,924
Academic Calendar: Semester

PROGRAMS
Degrees Offered: MBA (2 years; 12-month option with advanced degree in science or technical field), EMBA (2 years), PhD (5 years)
Joint Degrees: MBA/MILR (5 semesters), MBA/MEng (5 semesters), MBA/MA in Asian Studies (6 to 7 semesters), JD/MBA (4 years)
Academic Specialties: Finance, Accounting, and Entrepreneurship. Strengths include flexibility of core program, "reality-based" education such as immersion programs, and Cayuga MBA Fund.
Special Opportunities: Park Leadership Fellows Program; Leadership Skills Program; Executive Education; Immersion programs in Brand Management, Manufacturing, Investment Banking, Managerial Finance, eBusiness, Entrepreneurship, and Private Equity
Study Abroad Options: Australia, Belgium, England, France, Hong Kong, Italy, Spain, Netherlands, Norway, South Africa, Sweden, Switzerland, Thailand, Venezuela

STUDENT INFORMATION
Total Business Students: 554
% Full Time: 100
% Female: 28
% Minority: 21
% International: 33
Average Age: 29

COMPUTER AND RESEARCH FACILITIES
Research Facilities: Parker Center for Investment Research, Center for Leadership Development
Computer Facilities: Quick Stations, MS Office Suite, Business Simulation Lab, Business and Industry, Datastream, Dow Jones Interactive, EIU Country Data, Global Access, Global Market Information Database, Lexis-Nexis, Market Insight, Marketresearch.com, Academic Sourcebook America
Campuswide Network? Yes
% of MBA Classrooms Wired: 100
Computer Model Recommended: Laptop
Internet Fee? No

EXPENSES/FINANCIAL AID
Annual Tuition: $29,500
Room & Board (On Campus): $7,850
Books and Supplies: $1,100
Average Grant: $18,500
Average Loan: $29,800
% Receiving Financial Aid: 73
% Receiving Aid Their First Year: 74

ADMISSIONS INFORMATION
Application Fee: $200
Electronic Application? Yes
Regular Application Deadline: 3/15
Regular Notification: 5/31
Deferment Available? No
Non-fall Application Deadline(s): 11/15, 12/15, 1/15 for TMO only
Transfer Students Accepted? No
Need-Blind Admissions? Yes
Number of Applications Received: 2,271
% of Applicants Accepted: 26
% Accepted Who Enrolled: 51
Average GPA: 3.3
GPA Range: 2.8-3.8
Average GMAT: 669
GMAT Range: 599-730
Average Years Experience: 5
Other Admissions Factors Considered: Leadership, demonstrated record of achievement, creative problem solving, team skills, interpersonal skills, analytical thinking
Minority/Disadvantaged Student Recruitment Programs: Tiogo Fellowship; NSH MBA Membership; Johnson Means Business for Minority Students; MBA Alliance with Duke, Yale, NYU, and Berkeley
Other Schools to Which Students Applied: Michigan, Penn, Columbia, Dartmouth, Harvard

INTERNATIONAL STUDENTS
TOEFL Required of International Students? Yes
Minimum TOEFL: 600 (250 computer)

EMPLOYMENT INFORMATION

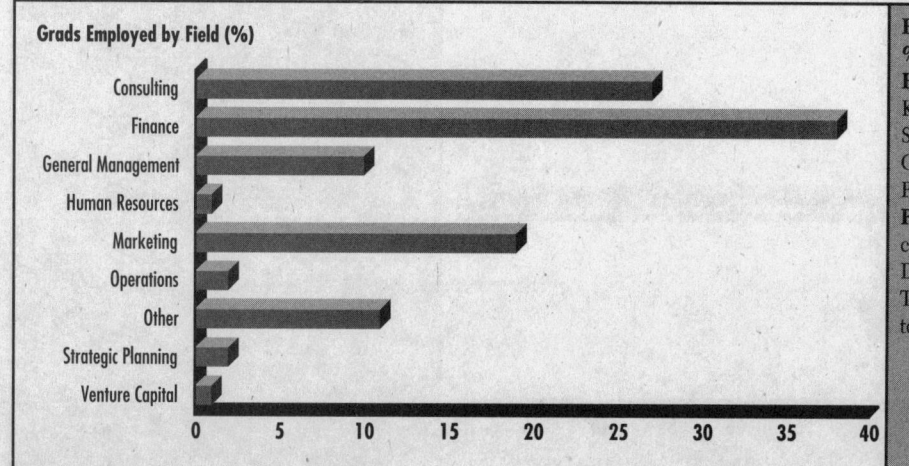

Grads Employed by Field (%)
- Consulting: ~27
- Finance: ~38
- General Management: ~10
- Human Resources: ~1
- Marketing: ~19
- Operations: ~2
- Other: ~11
- Strategic Planning: ~2
- Venture Capital: ~1

Placement Office Available? Yes
% Employed Within 3 Months: 91
Frequent Employers: American Express, AT Kearney, PricewaterhouseCoopers, Salomon Smith Barney, McKinsey & Co., PRTM, Bain & Co., Accenture, Goldman Sachs, Hewlett-Packard
Prominent Alumni: David Duffield (MBA '64), cofounder and chairman, PeopleSoft, Inc.; Daniel Hesse (MBA '77), president and CEO, Terabeam Corp.; Rick Sherlund, managing director, Goldman Sachs.

CREIGHTON UNIVERSITY
College of Business Administration

Admissions Contact: Gail Hafer, Coordinator of Graduate Business Programs
Address: 2500 California Plaza, Omaha, NE 68178
Admissions Phone: 402-280-2829 • Admissions Fax: 402-280-2172
Admissions E-mail: cobagrad@creighton.edu • Web Address: cobweb.creighton.edu

Creighton University is a private Catholic school run by the Jesuits, so it's no surprise that the school prides itself on its awareness of ethics and its value-centered learning environment. With just over 100 MBA students per class, COBA's MBA program provides quality instruction and easy access to professors and community business leaders.

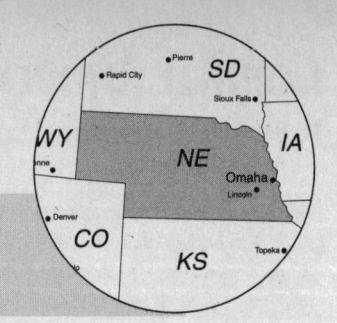

INSTITUTIONAL INFORMATION
Public/Private: Private
Evening Classes Available? Yes
Total Faculty: 35
% Faculty Female: 14
% Faculty Part Time: 11
Student/Faculty Ratio: 2:1
Students in Parent Institution: 6,297

PROGRAMS
Degrees Offered: Master of Business Administration (2 years); Master of Science in Information Technology Management; Master of Science in Electronic Commerce (2 years).
Joint Degrees: JD/MBA (3 years); MBA/Master of International Relations (3 years); JD/MS in Electronic Commerce (3 years); MBA/MS in Information Technology Management (3 years); MS in Information Technology Management/Master of Computer Science (3 years); MBA/PharmD (4 years)
Academic Specialties: Investments, leadership, electronic commerce
Special Opportunities: Mentor Program, Anna Tyler Waiter Graduate Leadership Fellow
Study Abroad Options: China; Beijing International MBA Program

STUDENT INFORMATION
Total Business Students: 111
% Full Time: 33
% Female: 30
% Minority: 10
% Out of State: 21
% International: 35
Average Age: 26

COMPUTER AND RESEARCH FACILITIES
Research Facilities: Carl Reinert Alumni Memorial Library
Computer Facilities: Seagate/Wad Labs, Computer Center Lab
Campuswide Network? Yes
% of MBA Classrooms Wired: 100
Internet Fee? No

EXPENSES/FINANCIAL AID
Tuition Per Credit: $474
Books and Supplies: $1,000
Average Grant: $1,422

ADMISSIONS INFORMATION
Application Fee: $40
Electronic Application? Yes
Regular Application Deadline: Rolling
Regular Notification: Rolling
Deferment Available? Yes
Length of Deferment: 1 year
Non-fall Admissions? Yes
Non-fall Application Deadline(s): 10/1
Transfer Students Accepted? Yes
Transfer Policy: Maximum of 6 hours of electives accepted from AACSB-accredited schools
Need-Blind Admissions? No
Number of Applications Received: 44
% of Applicants Accepted: 100
% Accepted Who Enrolled: 64
Average GPA: 3.2
Average GMAT: 550
Average Years Experience: 5
Other Admissions Factors Considered: 2 to 3 years work experience strongly preferred
Other Schools to Which Students Applied: University of Nebraska-Omaha

INTERNATIONAL STUDENTS
TOEFL Required of International Students? Yes
Minimum TOEFL: 550

EMPLOYMENT INFORMATION

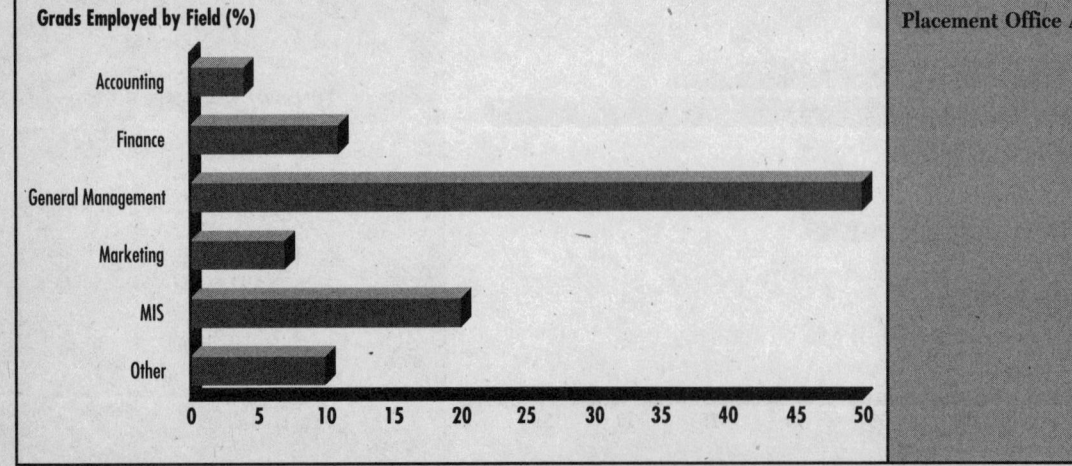

Grads Employed by Field (%)

Field	%
Accounting	3
Finance	10
General Management	50
Marketing	7
MIS	20
Other	10

Placement Office Available? Yes

DARTMOUTH COLLEGE
Tuck School of Business

Admissions Contact: Sally O. Jaeger, Director of Admissions
Address: 100 Tuck Hall, Hanover, NH 03755
Admissions Phone: 603-646-3162 • Admissions Fax: 603-646-1441
Admissions E-mail: Tuck.Admissions@dartmouth.edu • Web Address: www.tuck.dartmouth.edu

The workload is "humbling" and teamwork is essential at Tuck School of Business Administration, the world's first graduate school of management and the only top U.S. business school that offers an MBA and nothing else. The ridiculously happy students here report off-the-Richter-scale terrific teachers, an amazing array of resources, and "no such thing as not getting into a class." Also notable is Tuck's annual alumni giving rate of 63 percent (the highest in the country).

INSTITUTIONAL INFORMATION
Public/Private: Private
Evening Classes Available? No
Total Faculty: 67
% Faculty Female: 20
% Faculty Minority: 16
Student/Faculty Ratio: 6:1
Students in Parent Institution: 5,388
Academic Calendar: Quarter

PROGRAMS
Degrees Offered: MBA (21 months)
Joint Degrees: Tuck offers dual- and joint-degree programs and other creative curricular options.
Academic Specialties: Tuck Leadership Forum is a unique blend of traditional general management class sessions, experiential exercises (including a major field project focused on business development), and career-oriented instruction.
Special Opportunities: Alumnae Mentoring Program, International Field Study Program, Visiting Executive Program
Study Abroad Options: London, Japan, Paris, Barcelona, and Germany

STUDENT INFORMATION
Total Business Students: 435
% Full Time: 100
% Female: 24
% Minority: 18
% Out of State: 98

% International: 30
Average Age: 28

COMPUTER AND RESEARCH FACILITIES
Research Facilities: Feldberg Library and Bloomberg Professional Service, Center for Asia and Emerging Economics, Foster Center for Private Equity, Center for Corporate Governance, Achtmeyer Center for Global Leadership, Glassmeyer/McNamee Center for Digital Strategies, Initiative for Corporative Citizenship
Computer Facilities: More than 450 power ports, plus library databases, online information services, bulletin boards, file services, high-speed laser printers, and 75 public-access computers
Campuswide Network? Yes
% of MBA Classrooms Wired: 100
Computer Model Recommended: Laptop
Internet Fee? No

EXPENSES/FINANCIAL AID
Annual Tuition: $30,250
Room & Board: $11,600
Books and Supplies: $2,250
Average Grant: $9,500
Average Loan: $30,000
% Receiving Financial Aid: 73
% Receiving Aid Their First Year: 73

ADMISSIONS INFORMATION
Application Fee: $175
Electronic Application? Yes
Regular Application Deadline: 4/17
Regular Notification: 5/15
Length of Deferment: Case-by-case basis
Non-fall Admissions? No
Transfer Students Accepted? No
Need-Blind Admissions? Yes
Number of Applications Received: 2,819
% of Applicants Accepted: 16
% Accepted Who Enrolled: 51
Average GPA: 3.4
GPA Range: 2.4-4.0
Average GMAT: 693
GMAT Range: 530-800
Average Years Experience: 5
Minority/Disadvantaged Student Recruitment Programs: Member of the Consortium for Graduate Study in Management, member school of the Robert F. Toigo Fellowship Foundation, and a number of scholarships are marked for minority students
Other Schools to Which Students Applied: Columbia, Harvard, Northwestern, Stanford, Penn

INTERNATIONAL STUDENTS
TOEFL Required of International Students? Yes
Minimum TOEFL: 580 (237 computer)

EMPLOYMENT INFORMATION

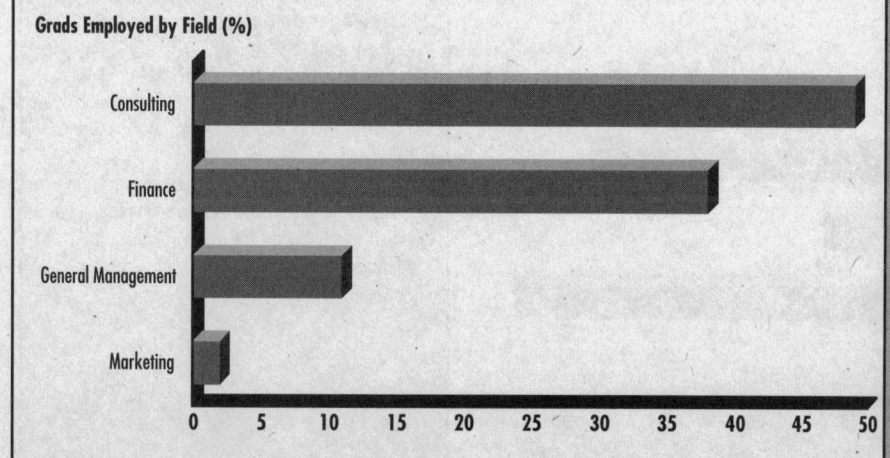

Grads Employed by Field (%)

Field	%
Consulting	~50
Finance	~38
General Management	~11
Marketing	~2

Placement Office Available? Yes
% Employed Within 3 Months: 96
Frequent Employers: Goldman Sachs, Bain & Co., McKinsey and Co., Booz Allen Hamilton, Accenture, BCG, Parthenon Group, Morgan Stanley, Credit Suisse First Boston Corporation, JPMorgan Chase
Prominent Alumni: Alexander M. Cutler, chairman and CEO, Eaton Corporation; Peter R. Dolan, president and CEO, Bristol-Myers Squibb; Noreen Doyle, deputy VP, European Bank; Roger B. McNamee, partner, Integral Capital Partners; Charles O. Schetter, managing director, McKinsey & Co.

DePaul University
Kellstadt Graduate School of Business

Admissions Contact: C.A. Munoz, Director of Admission
Address: 1 East Jackson Blvd., Chicago, IL 60604
Admissions Phone: 312-362-8810 • Admissions Fax: 312-362-6677
Admissions E-mail: mbainfo@depaul.edu • Web Address: www.depaul.edu

You'll enjoy a solid education at the Kellstadt Graduate School of Business, one of the oldest b-schools in the United States. Kellstadt has earned national recognition for its MBA programs, which offer day, evening, and weekend classes. In addition, the MBA program in International Marketing and Finance (MBA/IMF) is the only existing program of its kind. If the campus location near bustling Chicago doesn't satisfy, Kellstadt also offers MBAs in Hong Kong, Bahrain, and Prague.

INSTITUTIONAL INFORMATION
Public/Private: Private
Evening Classes Available? Yes
Total Faculty: 195
% Faculty Part Time: 38
Student/Faculty Ratio: 28:1
Students in Parent Institution: 21,363
Academic Calendar: Quarter

PROGRAMS
Degrees Offered: Day MBA (full time, 88 credits, 18 months), with concentrations in International Finance and International Marketing; evening MBA (full time or part time, 60 to 80 credits, 18 months to 6 years), with concentrations in Accounting, Economics, Entrepreneurship, Finance, Human Resources, International Business, Management Information Systems, Marketing, and Operations Management; weekend MBA (full time or part time, 60 to 80 credits), with concentration in Strategic Management; Master of Accountancy (MAcc) (full time or part time, 45 credits, 18 months to 6 years), with concentration in Accounting; MS in Accountancy (full time or part time, 60 to 64 credits, 15 months to 6 years); MS in Finance (full time or part time, 48 credits, 18 months to 6 years); MS in Taxation (full time or part time, 45 to 60 credits, 18 months to 6 years); MS in Management Information Systems (full time or part time, 116 credits, 2 to 6 years); Master of E-Business (full time or part time, 48 credits, 2 to 6 years); MS in Human Resources (full time or part time, 48 credits, 2 to 6 years)

Joint Degrees: MBA/JD (full time or part time, 140 credits, 2.8 to 3.8 years), with concentrations in Accounting, Economics, Entrepreneurship, Finance, Human Resources, International Business, Management Information Systems, Marketing, Operations Management, and E-Business

STUDENT INFORMATION
Total Business Students: 2,537
% Female: 36
% Minority: 16
% International: 3
Average Age: 27

COMPUTER AND RESEARCH FACILITIES
Research Facilities: Main library plus 3 additional on-campus libraries; access to online bibliographic retrieval services
Campuswide Network? Yes
% of MBA Classrooms Wired: 100
Computer Model Recommended: No
Internet Fee? Yes

EXPENSES/FINANCIAL AID
Annual Tuition: $14,400
Books and Supplies: $7,200
Average Grant: $8,000
Average Loan: $18,500
% Receiving Financial Aid: 40
% Receiving Aid Their First Year: 40

ADMISSIONS INFORMATION
Application Fee: $40
Electronic Application? Yes
Regular Application Deadline: 7/1
Regular Notification: Rolling
Length of Deferment: 1 year
Non-fall Admissions? Yes
Non-fall Application Deadline(s): 10/1 winter, 2/1 spring, 4/1 summer; international applicants: 6/1 fall, 9/1 winter, 1/1 spring, 3/1 summer
Transfer Students Accepted? Yes
Transfer Policy: Must apply like any other applicant
Need-Blind Admissions? Yes
Number of Applications Received: 721
% of Applicants Accepted: 78
% Accepted Who Enrolled: 70
Average GPA: 3.1
Average GMAT: 561
Average Years Experience: 5
Other Admissions Factors Considered: Interview, 2 letters of recommendation, résumé, work experience recommended
Other Schools to Which Students Applied: University of Chicago, Northwestern University

INTERNATIONAL STUDENTS
TOEFL Required of International Students? Yes
Minimum TOEFL: 550 (213 computer)

EMPLOYMENT INFORMATION

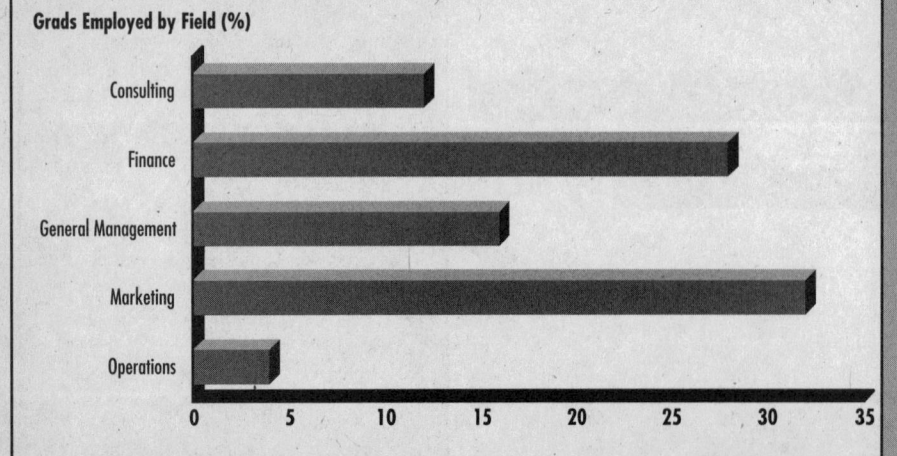

Grads Employed by Field (%)
- Consulting: ~12
- Finance: ~28
- General Management: ~16
- Marketing: ~32
- Operations: ~3

Placement Office Available? Yes
% Employed Within 3 Months: 90
Frequent Employers: CNA, Baxter, BP, ABN Amro, KPMG, International Truck & Engine, Accenture, McDonald's Corporation, Bank One, Cigna, Abbott Laboratories
Prominent Alumni: Jaclyn Winship, director of strategy; Rosario Perrelli, executive VP and CFO; Christopher Piesko, Sr., VP; Frank Ptak, vice chairman; Jeffrey Rohr, managing partner

DUKE UNIVERSITY
The Fuqua School of Business

Admissions Contact: Liz Riley, Director of Admissions
Address: Towerview Road, A-08 Academic Center, Durham, NC 27708
Admissions Phone: 919-660-7705 • Admissions Fax: 919-681-8026
Admissions E-mail: admissions-info@mail.duke.edu • Web Address: www.fuqua.duke.edu

Liberal arts majors with no experience in business courses should be prepared to hit the ground running at Duke University's Fuqua School of Business. Here, "the pace is very fast"—what with "six-week terms"—and students need a working knowledge of calculus just to survive the first year. Also, you heard it here first: The correct pronunciation of Fuqua is "few-kwa" and definitely not "foo-kwa." They really hate that.

INSTITUTIONAL INFORMATION
Public/Private: Private
Evening Classes Available? No
Total Faculty: 78
% Faculty Female: 23
% Faculty Minority: 2
% Faculty Part Time: 9
Student/Faculty Ratio: 18:1
Students in Parent Institution: 11,200
Academic Calendar: Terms

PROGRAMS
Degrees Offered: MBA (day, 2 years); PhD (4 to 5 years); MBA—Global Executive (19 months); MBA—Weekend Executive (20 months); MBA—Cross Continent (20 months)
Joint Degrees: MBA/JD (4 years); MBA/Master of Public Policy (2 to 3 years); MBA/Master of Forestry (2 to 3 years); MBA/Master of Environmental Management (3 years); MBA/MS Engineering (2 to 3 years); MBA/MD (5 years); MBA/MSN in Nursing (3 years)
Academic Specialties: Integrative, general management curriculum emphasizing cross-functional, strategic, and global perspectives—particular strength in Corporate Finance, Marketing Investments, General Management Decision Science, and Operations
Special Opportunities: MBA Enterprise Corps, GATE (Global Academic Travel Experiences) programs

Study Abroad Options: Australia, Belgium, Costa Rica, Denmark, France, Hong Kong, Italy, Mexico, Netherlands, Norway, South Africa, Spain, Sweden, Thailand, UK, Switzerland, India

STUDENT INFORMATION
Total Business Students: 679
% Full Time: 100
% Female: 30
% Minority: 21
% International: 34
Average Age: 28

COMPUTER AND RESEARCH FACILITIES
Research Facilities: Center for International Business Education & Research, North Carolina Family Business Forum, Hartman Center midsize company, Accounting Research Center, Futures and Options Research Center, Computer-Mediated Learning Center
Computer Facilities: 147 Pentium-class systems and 262 plug-in access points to FuquaNet for laptop systems.
Campuswide Network? Yes
% of MBA Classrooms Wired: 38
Computer Model Recommended: No
Internet Fee? No

EXPENSES/FINANCIAL AID
Annual Tuition: $29,600
Books and Supplies: $13,124
Average Grant: $11,700
Average Loan: $28,875
% Receiving Financial Aid: 90
% Receiving Aid Their First Year: 91

ADMISSIONS INFORMATION
Application Fee: $150
Electronic Application? Yes
Regular Application Deadline: 12/1
Regular Notification: 2/1
Length of Deferment: 1 year
Non-fall Admissions? No
Transfer Students Accepted? No
Need-Blind Admissions? Yes
Number of Applications Received: 3,207
% of Applicants Accepted: 20
% Accepted Who Enrolled: 53
Average GPA: 3.5
GPA Range: 2.8-3.8
Average GMAT: 690
GMAT Range: 630-750
Average Years Experience: 5
Minority/Disadvantaged Student Recruitment Programs: Ford MBA Workshop for Minority Applicants; aggressive minority scholarship program

INTERNATIONAL STUDENTS
TOEFL Required of International Students? Yes
Minimum TOEFL: 600

EMPLOYMENT INFORMATION

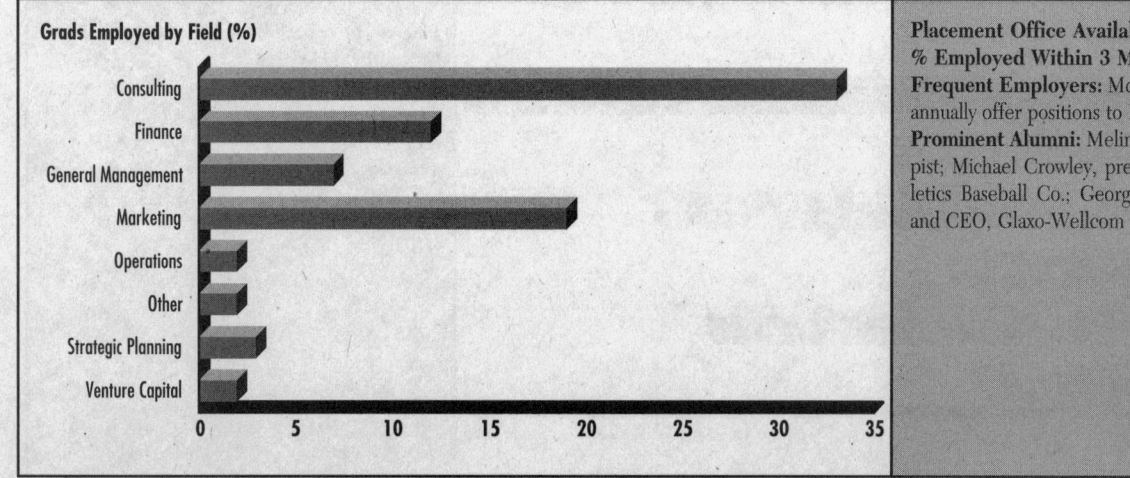

Grads Employed by Field (%)
- Consulting: ~33
- Finance: ~12
- General Management: ~7
- Marketing: ~19
- Operations: ~2
- Other: ~3
- Strategic Planning: ~3
- Venture Capital: ~2

Placement Office Available? Yes
% Employed Within 3 Months: 99
Frequent Employers: More than 400 law firms annually offer positions to Duke Law students.
Prominent Alumni: Melinda Gates, philanthropist; Michael Crowley, president, Oakland Athletics Baseball Co.; George Morrow, president and CEO, Glaxo-Wellcom

EASTERN MICHIGAN UNIVERSITY
College of Business

Admissions Contact: Christie Montgomery, Assistant Dean
Address: PO Box 970, Ypsilanti, MI 48197
Admissions Phone: 734-487-3060 • Admissions Fax: 734-487-1484
Admissions E-mail: graduate.admissions@emich.edu • Web Address: www.emich.edu/public/catalogs

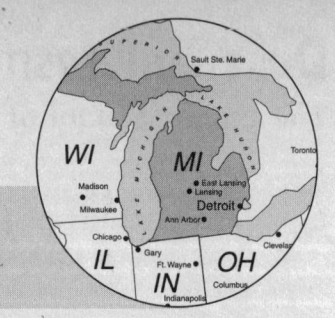

The Eastern Michigan University MBA program has a trimester academic calendar, an intimate educational setting, and affordable tuition rates. The faculty members are nearly all full time, allowing the student body great accessibility to their professors, who are more than willing to lend a helping mind. EMU's Entrepreneurship Center is a fantastic resource for information, support for innovative ideas, and opportunities to interact with the entrepreneurial community.

INSTITUTIONAL INFORMATION
Public/Private: Public
Evening Classes Available? Yes
Total Faculty: 66
% Faculty Female: 24
% Faculty Minority: 8
% Faculty Part Time: 32
Student/Faculty Ratio: 25:1
Students in Parent Institution: 23,000
Academic Calendar: Trimester

PROGRAMS
Degrees Offered: Master of Business Administration (12 months to 6 years), Master of Science in Information Systems (12 months to 6 years), Master of Science in Accounting (12 months to 6 years), Master of Science in Human Resources/Organizational Development (12 months to 6 years)
Academic Specialties: Case study, computer-aided instruction, computer analysis, computer simulations, faculty seminars, field projects, group discussion, lecture, research, seminars by members of the business community, simulations, student presentations, team projects
Study Abroad Options: Canada, France, Germany, Mexico, Spain

STUDENT INFORMATION
Total Business Students: 760
% Female: 45
% Minority: 7
% International: 24
Average Age: 28

COMPUTER AND RESEARCH FACILITIES
Research Facilities: Alumni network, career counseling/planning, career fairs, career library, career placement, electronic job bank, job interviews arranged, job search course, résumé referral to employers, résumé preparation
Computer Facilities: Lexus/Nexus (EMU), WSJ Online (Web), Reference USA (EMU), Wilson Business Abstracts (Web)
Campuswide Network? Yes
Internet Fee? No

EXPENSES/FINANCIAL AID
Annual Tuition (Resident/Nonresident): $5,160/$10,560
Tuition Per Credit (Resident/Nonresident): $215/$440
Books and Supplies: $600

ADMISSIONS INFORMATION
Application Fee: $30
Electronic Application? Yes
Regular Application Deadline: 5/1
Regular Notification: 8/1
Deferment Available? No
Non-fall Admissions? Yes
Non-fall Application Deadline(s): 10/1, 3/1
Transfer Students Accepted? Yes
Transfer Policy: 6 credits may be accepted upon approval.
Need-Blind Admissions? Yes
Number of Applications Received: 286
% of Applicants Accepted: 85
% Accepted Who Enrolled: 100
Average GPA: 3.0
Average GMAT: 495
GMAT Range: 410-590
Average Years Experience: 3
Other Admissions Factors Considered: work experience, computer experience
Other Schools to Which Students Applied: Central Michigan University, Michigan State University, Oakland University, University of Michigan, University of Michigan-Dearborn, Wayne State University, Western Michigan University

INTERNATIONAL STUDENTS
TOEFL Required of International Students? Yes
Minimum TOEFL: 550 (213 computer)

EMPLOYMENT INFORMATION

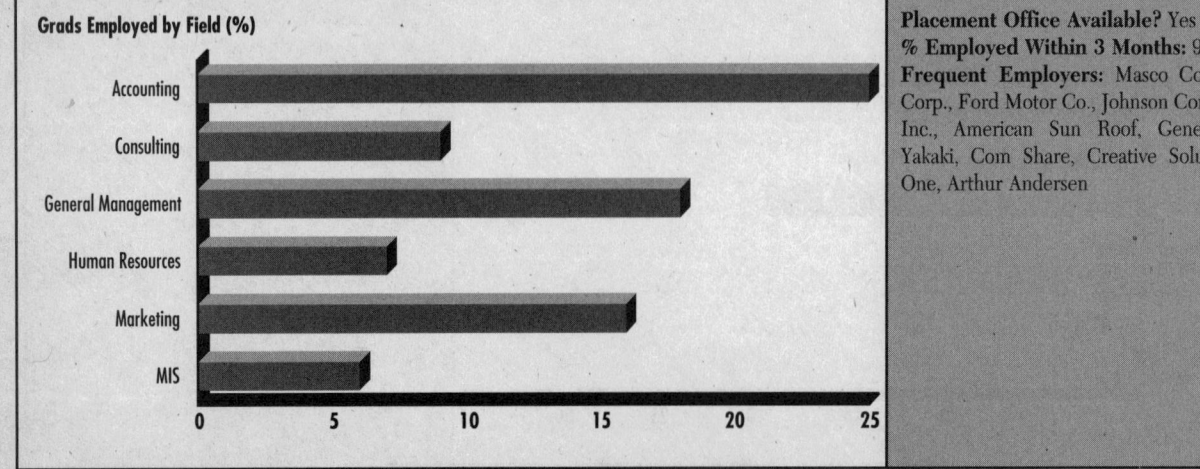

Placement Office Available? Yes
% Employed Within 3 Months: 98
Frequent Employers: Masco Corp., Visteon Corp., Ford Motor Co., Johnson Controls, Pfizer Inc., American Sun Roof, General Motors, Yakaki, Com Share, Creative Solutions, Bank One, Arthur Andersen

EASTERN WASHINGTON UNIVERSITY
College of Business and Public Administration

Admissions Contact: Diana Teague, Program Assistant
Address: EWU 206 Showalter Hall, Cheney, WA 99004
Admissions Phone: 509-359-6297 • Admissions Fax: 509-359-6044
Admissions E-mail: gradprograms@ewu.edu • Web Address: www.ewu.edu

The EWU College of Business and Public Administration is a small school with less than 100 students that provides an intimate classroom experience and an accessible faculty of "nationally renowned scholars with strong ties to the local business community." Much of the student body comes from out of state, allowing for a diversified learning experience. Unlike other graduate programs at EWU, the MBA program's courses are taught from within each of their respective departments at the business school. This approach benefits its students, enabling them to acquire "unique and interdisciplinary business expertise." Classes are available in the evenings and on weekends.

INSTITUTIONAL INFORMATION
Public/Private: Public
Evening Classes Available? Yes
Total Faculty: 13
% Faculty Female: 46
Student/Faculty Ratio: 15:1
Students in Parent Institution: 8,597
Academic Calendar: Quarter

PROGRAMS
Degrees Offered: MBA (49 credits, 1 year), Master of Public Administration (60 credits, 1.5 years)
Joint Degrees: MBA/ Master of Public Administration (69 credits, 2 years)
Academic Specialties: Entrepreneurship, Nonprofit Marketing, Health Services, Accounting Information Systems

STUDENT INFORMATION
Total Business Students: 82
% Full Time: 35
% Female: 45
% Minority: 8
% Out of State: 80
% International: 55
Average Age: 28

COMPUTER AND RESEARCH FACILITIES
Campuswide Network? Yes
Internet Fee? No

EXPENSES/FINANCIAL AID
Annual Tuition (Resident/Nonresident): $4,470/$13,161
Room & Board (On/Off Campus): $5,567/$7,000
Books and Supplies: $1,200

ADMISSIONS INFORMATION
Application Fee: $35
Electronic Application? No
Regular Application Deadline: 1/1
Regular Notification: Rolling
Deferment Available? Yes
Length of Deferment: 1 year
Non-fall Admissions? Yes
Non-fall Application Deadline(s): 1/1
Transfer Students Accepted? Yes
Transfer Policy: Up to 12 transfer credits
Need-Blind Admissions? Yes
Number of Applications Received: 44

% of Applicants Accepted: 50
% Accepted Who Enrolled: 91
Average GPA: 3.2
GPA Range: 2.9-3.7
Average GMAT: 479
GMAT Range: 420-600
Average Years Experience: 5
Other Admissions Factors Considered: Formula: GMAT (minimum of 450) + GPA (minimum of 3.0)

INTERNATIONAL STUDENTS
TOEFL Required of International Students? Yes
Minimum TOEFL: 580 (237 computer)

EMPLOYMENT INFORMATION
Placement Office Available? Yes

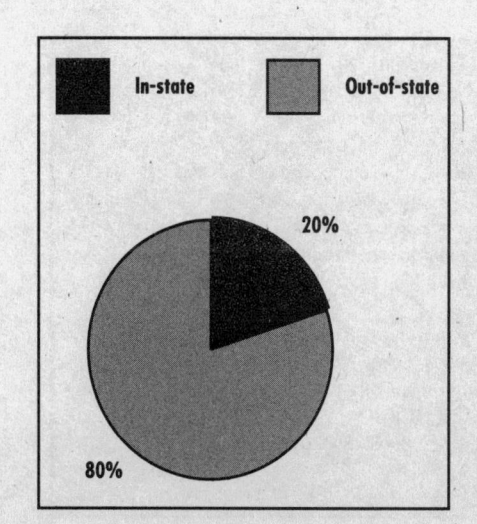

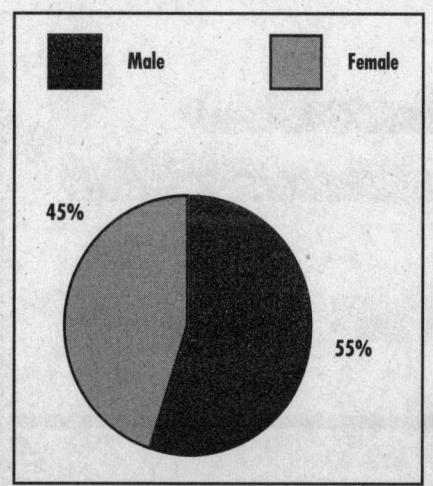

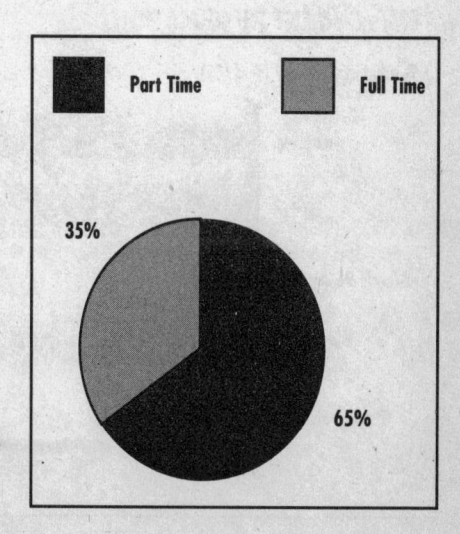

EMORY UNIVERSITY
Goizueta Business School

Admissions Contact: Julie R. Barefoot, Assistant Dean and Director of Admissions
Address: 1300 Clifton Road, Atlanta, GA 30322
Admissions Phone: 404-727-6311 • Admissions Fax: 404-727-4612
Admissions E-mail: Admissions@bus.emory.edu • Web Address: www.goizueta.emory.edu

Students at Emory University's Goizueta Business School "love" its "up-and-coming" reputation, and they are thrilled about the "exceptional" as well as "brand-new and state-of-the-art business center" that houses the school. Goizueta includes a unique international business component in its core, and it offers several flexible programs of study. Students with an undergraduate business degree might consider Goizueta's intensive one-year accelerated MBA.

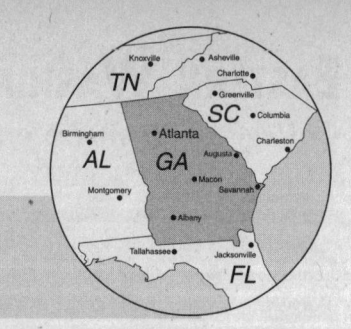

INSTITUTIONAL INFORMATION
Public/Private: Private
Evening Classes Available? Yes
Total Faculty: 83
% Faculty Female: 28
% Faculty Minority: 7
% Faculty Part Time: 7
Student/Faculty Ratio: 5:1
Students in Parent Institution: 11,443
Academic Calendar: Semester

PROGRAMS
Degrees Offered: MBA Program (1 to 2 years, evening 3 years), Weekend Executive MBA Program (16 months), Modular Executive MBA Program (20 months)
Joint Degrees: Master of Business Administration/Doctor of Jurisprudence (MBA/JD) (4 years), Master of Business Administration/Master of Public Health (MBA/MPH) (5 semesters), Master of Business Administration/Master of Divinity (MBA/MDiv) (4 years)
Academic Specialties: Marketing, Strategy/Entrepreneurship, Finance, Consulting
Special Opportunities: We offer our students Regional Studies Concentrations as a way to gain an in-depth understanding of tomorrow's emerging economies. Students can earn a certificate of specialization along with an MBA in Latin American and Caribbean Studies and Russian/East European Studies.

Study Abroad Options: Austria, Australia, Chile, China, Costa Rica, Finland, France, Germany, Hungary, India (pending), Korea, Mexico, Netherlands, Singapore, South Africa, Spain, Venezuela, United Kingdom

STUDENT INFORMATION
Total Business Students: 584
% Female: 26
% Minority: 13
% International: 24
Average Age: 27

COMPUTER AND RESEARCH FACILITIES
Research Facilities: Goizueta Business Library
Computer Facilities: Computer lab
Campuswide Network? Yes
% of MBA Classrooms Wired: 100
Computer Model Recommended: Laptop
Internet Fee? No

EXPENSES/FINANCIAL AID
Annual Tuition: $27,760
Tuition Per Credit: $1,157
Room & Board (Off Campus): $11,340
Books and Supplies: $1,900
Average Grant: $14,567
Average Loan: $26,531
% Receiving Financial Aid: 66
% Receiving Aid Their First Year: 41

ADMISSIONS INFORMATION
Application Fee: $100
Electronic Application? Yes
Regular Application Deadline: 3/31
Regular Notification: Rolling
Deferment Available? Yes
Length of Deferment: 1 year
Non-fall Admissions? No
Transfer Students Accepted? No
Need-Blind Admissions? Yes
Number of Applications Received: 1,161
% of Applicants Accepted: 32
% Accepted Who Enrolled: 47
Average GPA: 3.3
GPA Range: 3.0-3.7
Average GMAT: 651
GMAT Range: 590-700
Average Years Experience: 5
Minority/Disadvantaged Student Recruitment Programs: The school is a member of Consortium of Graduate Study in Management. Additionally, the school hosts Inside Goizueta: A Conference for Prospective Minority Students.
Other Schools to Which Students Applied: Duke University, Georgetown University, Michigan State University, New York University, University of North Carolina-Chapel Hill, University of Virginia, Vanderbilt University

INTERNATIONAL STUDENTS
TOEFL Required of International Students? Yes
Minimum TOEFL: 633 (250 computer)

EMPLOYMENT INFORMATION

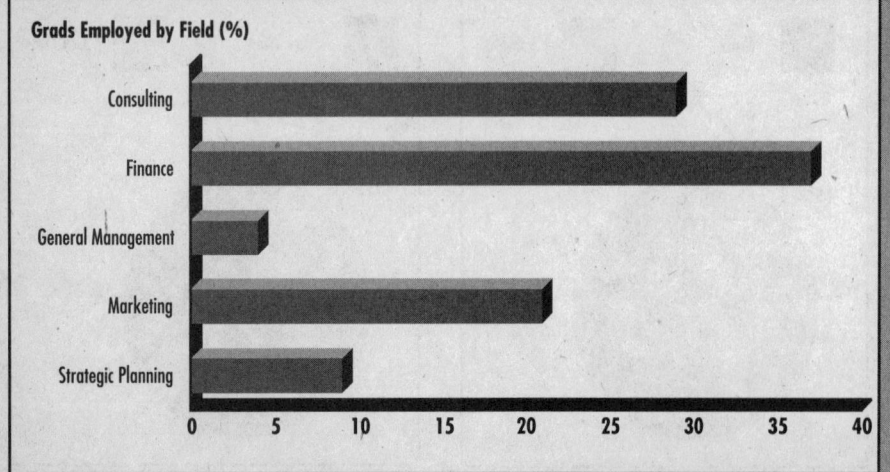

Grads Employed by Field (%)
- Consulting: ~29
- Finance: ~37
- General Management: ~4
- Marketing: ~21
- Strategic Planning: ~9

Placement Office Available? Yes
% Employed Within 3 Months: 94
Frequent Employers: Accenture, AT Kearney, Bank of America, Bear Stearns, Cap Gemini Ernst & Young, Credit Suisse First Boston, Deloitte Consulting, Eastman Kodak Company, Equant, GE Capital, Honeywell, IBM, ING, Johnson & Johnson, JPMorgan Chase, Kurt Salmon Associates, Lehman Brothers, McKinsey & Co.
Prominent Alumni: Alan Lacy (MBA '77), CEO, Sears; Michael Golden (EMBA '84), vice chairman and senior VP, New York Times Company; Charles Jenkins, Jr. (BBA '64, MBA '65), CEO, Publik Super Markets, Inc.

ERASMUS GRADUATE SCHOOL OF BUSINESS
Rotterdam School of Management

Admissions Contact: Connie Tai, Director, Marketing and MBA Admissions
Address: Burgemeester Oudlaan 50, 3062 PA Rotterdam, Netherlands
Admissions Phone: 011-31-10-408-2222 • Admissions Fax: 011-31-10-452-9509
Admissions E-mail: info@rsm.nl • Web Address: www.rsm.nl

The Erasmus Graduate School of Business is located in Rotterdam, home of the world's largest port, with access to a myriad of multinational businesses. The MBA program houses a mostly international student body, with more than 90 percent of the students coming from more than 50 countries around the globe. The classes are group-oriented, and there are study abroad opportunities in more than 30 countries. Erasmus offers multiple MBA options, including the Full-Time MBA, the Executive MBA, and the OneMBA program, "designed for achievement-oriented executives with increasing international responsibilities," with demanding admissions requirements.

INSTITUTIONAL INFORMATION
Evening Classes Available? No
Total Faculty: 240
% Faculty Female: 20
% Faculty Part Time: 25
Students in Parent Institution: 16,000
Academic Calendar: Semester

PROGRAMS
Degrees Offered: International MBA and MBA/MBI (full time, 15 months); Weekend Executive MBA (part time, 24 months); Modular Executive MBA (part time, 21 months); Master in Financial Management (full time, 12 months); Master of HR Leadership (part time, 18 months)
Academic Specialties: RSM offers broadly based MBA programs with functional strengths in Finance, Information Technology, and Strategy. The innovative MBA/MBI program offers the possibility to specialize in the managerial aspects of information technology.
Study Abroad Options: Australia, Canada, China, France, Germany, Italy, Japan, Mexico, Philippines, Republic of South Africa, Spain, United Kingdom, United States, Thailand (31 schools total)

STUDENT INFORMATION
Total Business Students: 550
% Female: 25
% International: 95
Average Age: 29

COMPUTER AND RESEARCH FACILITIES
Research Facilities: Area 31, a business "incubator" for start-ups; Centre of Business History; Center for Technology and Innovation Management; Econometric Institute; Erasmus Business Support Centre; Erasmus Centre for Financial Research; Erasmus Institute for Philosophy and Economics; Erasmus Research Institute of Management; Erasmus University Research Institute for Decision and Information Systems; European Institute for Comparative Urban Research; Institute for Sociologic Economic Research; Institute of Globalization, International Economic Law and Dispute Settlement; Research Centre for Economic Policy; Netherlands Research School for Transport Infrastructure and Logistics Research; School Safety & Security in Society; Rotterdam Institute for Business Economic Studies; Rotterdam Institute of Modern Asian Studies; Thomas Stieltjes Institute for Mathematics; Tinbergen Institute
Computer Facilities: In-building computer labs have 75 computers and 55 connections for laptop computers. Databases include online access to Erasmus University's library databases and catalogs, plus online content providers such as Lexis-Nexis Academic Universe and Hoovers.com. The Trading Room has simulation facilities, group systems, and videoconferencing.

Campuswide Network? Yes
% of MBA Classrooms Wired: 100
Computer Model Recommended: Laptop
Internet Fee? No

EXPENSES/FINANCIAL AID
Annual Tuition: $30,000
Books and Supplies: $1,500

ADMISSIONS INFORMATION
Application Fee: $75
Electronic Application? Yes
Regular Application Deadline: 6/15
Regular Notification: Rolling
Deferment Available? No
Non-fall Admissions? No
Transfer Students Accepted? No
Need-Blind Admissions? Yes
Number of Applications Received: 650
% of Applicants Accepted: 35
% Accepted Who Enrolled: 67
Average GMAT: 622
GMAT Range: 550-700
Average Years Experience: 6
Other Admissions Factors Considered: International outlook, leadership potential, motivation, contribution to the program

INTERNATIONAL STUDENTS
TOEFL Required of International Students? Yes
Minimum TOEFL: 600 (250 computer)

EMPLOYMENT INFORMATION

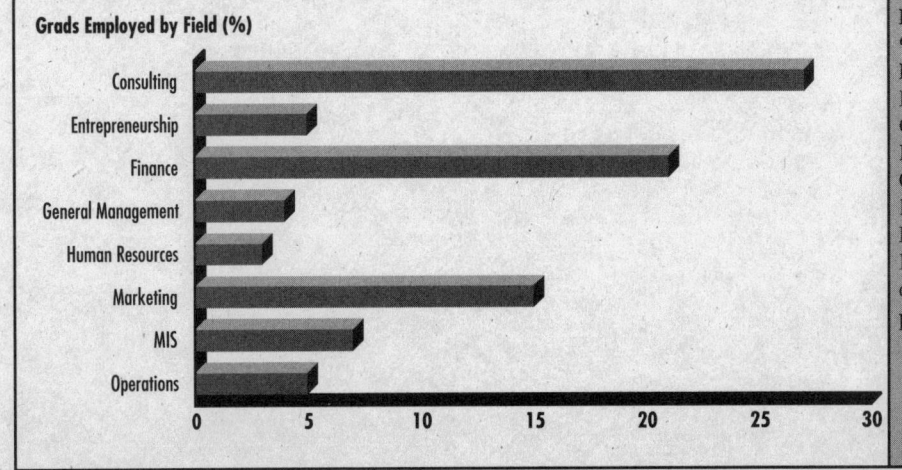

Grads Employed by Field (%):
- Consulting: ~27
- Entrepreneurship: ~3
- Finance: ~21
- General Management: ~7
- Human Resources: ~3
- Marketing: ~15
- MIS: ~7
- Operations: ~4

Placement Office Available? Yes
% Employed Within 3 Months: 97
Frequent Employers: ABN Amro, Accenture, Bain & Co., Barclays Capital, Boston Consulting Group, Citibank, McKinsey & Co., KPN Qwest, Ford Motor Company, Roland Berger Strategy Consultants, AT Kearney, Dresdner Kleinwort Benson, Bertelsmann, Eli Lilly
Prominent Alumni: Durk Jager, ex-CEO, Procter & Gamble; Bert van den Bergh, president of European operations, Eli Lilly; Hans Smit, president, Rabobank

ERASMUS GRADUATE SCHOOL OF BUSINESS

THE SCHOOL AT A GLANCE

"The ability to innovate and to remain at the leading edge of developments in management theory and practice are critical for the success of MBA participants and of MBA programs. The Rotterdam School of Management continuously strives to build upon the success we have achieved through a continuous focus on issues of international business, information technology, and soft management skills. These features complement an in-depth, integrated MBA curriculum aimed at creating managers capable of leading global companies."

—Kai Peters, Dean

STUDENTS

The Rotterdam School of Management is a business school that attracts students from all over the world. About 50 different nationalities are represented in the current student population of 280 (140 students per year). Only 8 percent of the students are Dutch; the remaining 92 percent are international. Students come from a wide variety of academic backgrounds. An average breakdown is 30 percent engineering, 25 percent business, 20 percent science and medicine, 20 percent humanities and social sciences, and 5 percent law. The average age of students is 29, and the average number of years of work experience is five.

Working in groups is an essential element of the MBA programs. The emphasis on teamwork provides a realistic model for the way in which management issues are handled in the business world. Students learn the vital significance of teamwork and the value of cooperation when they are confronted with a wide range of approaches to a single problem. By forming teams of students with different cultural and educational backgrounds, various problem-solving techniques are recognized and appreciated. This enriches the learning experience of all students.

All RSM activities are international by definition, as the student body represents so many nationalities. Students can receive assistance with applications for visa and housing matters.

The Rotterdam School of Management was founded with the support of major Dutch multinationals and has since developed close ties with the international business community. Companies such as Citibank, Arthur D. Little, and ABN AMRO Bank actively take part in the curriculum of the MBA program.

The RSM Alumni Network is a very international network of all RSM graduates. Alumni are closely involved in the School's activities and are always pleased to meet potential students and discuss their experiences at the RSM with them.

ACADEMICS

The Rotterdam School of Management (RSM) offers two full-time MBA programs: the International MBA Program in General Management and the International MBA/MBI (Master of Business Administration/Master of Business Informatics) Program. These 18-month programs start each September and are taught entirely in English.

The curriculum of the International MBA Program in General Management covers all major aspects of general management. The first year consists of mandatory courses in management basics and functional areas and includes communication workshops.

The International MBA/MBI Program is designed for students who, in addition to a general management education, wish to receive theoretical and practical training in the managerial aspects of information technology (IT). MBA/MBI graduates help bridge the gap between specialist in information technology and managers who are the main users of information systems. It is clearly a management program, not a technical program. The MBA/MBI program is largely identical to the MBA program but includes MBI-exclusive class blocks later in the program. During the summer, students are required to undertake an in-company project. MBA/MBI students take a required MBI block of courses before performing an IT in-company project.

The second year allows students to tailor their studies to areas of their interest. Through electives and mini-courses, they can focus on areas such as corporate finance, marketing, entrepreneurship, or IT. Students also have the opportunity to participate in an exchange program with top business schools worldwide.

The Rotterdam School of Management is consistently ranked as one of Europe's top business schools. The Economist's "Which MBA?" describes the School as innovative, interesting, friendly, and representing excellent value.

In addition to the functionally based courses, the MBA programs include extensive workshops, seminars, and mini-courses aimed at building practical skills. Furthermore, students undertake consultancy projects for companies and non-profit organizations.

In the third semester of the MBA programs, students can choose to participate in a business school exchange program. Currently, more than 30 business schools around the globe are partnered with RSM.

The academic faculty represents a mix of professors from the Rotterdam School of Management and Erasmus University, visiting faculty members of prestigious international universities, and consultants and managers active in various industries. Faculty members are international professionals who bring up-to-date management techniques and practices into the classroom. They are committed to a wide range of teaching methods, such as lectures, case studies, field trips, group work, management games, and real-life projects.

Rotterdam School of Management

CAMPUS LIFE

The Rotterdam School of Management is a foundation of Erasmus University Rotterdam, which is renowned for its business orientation. The University was founded in 1913 by Rotterdam entrepreneurs and named after Erasmus Desiderius Roterodamus. Erasmus was born in Rotterdam in the late fifteenth century. He was a leader of the liberal reform movement in Europe and dreamed of democracy of the intellect and correct use of free will. It is this humanist tradition that still lives on in the university, which today has more than 16,000 students, of whom some 1,600 are enrolled in postgraduate studies.

The Rotterdam School of Management is located on the Woudestein Campus of the Erasmus University. The University campus is situated close to the center of Rotterdam. The RSM offers housing services for all international students near the University campus. The language laboratory, sports center, libraries, restaurant, shops, and information services at Erasmus University are available to RSM students.

The new, dedicated RSM building on the Erasmus Woudestein campus officially opened in March 2000. Dedicated facilities include eight large theater-style classrooms, break-out rooms, student lounges, a cafeteria, and staff offices.

Facilities in the RSM building also include three computer labs with 70 desktop personal computers as well as connections for an additional 55 laptop computers. The main theater-style classrooms are equipped with professional and state-of-the-art audiovisual and multimedia facilities, including high-speed video conferencing, cable television, and laptop plug-ins. Every student receives an account to access the Internet from home. The network supports numerous Windows NT applications including Microsoft Office 2000, online databases, Internet access, and specialized business programs.

RSM provides an online library for students. Erasmus University library databases and catalogues, along with online content providers such as Hoovers.com and Lexis/Nexis Academic Universe form RSM's online library facilities. RSM is continually updating the online library content with information relevant to business students and in fact is the first European business school to offer the Lexis/Nexis Academic Universe to students.

The Career Management Center (CMC) is dedicated to the career development needs of all MBA students while serving the recruitment requirements of international companies. The yearly organization of on-campus company presentations and selection interviews provides an important recruitment tool for students.

Career planning is an integral part of the curriculum. At the start of the program, students receive the Career Management Guide. This guide contains information about services offered, guidelines for the job search process, and information about interviewing and job offers, which helps students to find a challenging career.

COSTS

Tuition fees for students starting in September 2001 are CE27,500 for the entire MBA program and CE30,000 for the entire MBA/MBI program. Other expenses, such as room rent, books, and living expenses, are estimated to be CE17,675 for the entire program duration of 18 months.

ADMISSIONS

The RSM welcomes applications from outstanding men and women whose intellectual ability, management potential, and personal qualities indicate that they will benefit from and contribute to the learning environment. Eligibility requirements include a recognized university degree, GMAT scores, two letters of recommendation (academic and/or professional), work experience, proficiency in English, and a personal interview with one of RSM's alumni in the applicant's country of residence.

The application deadline is June 15. Applications are processed on a continuous basis in order of receipt. Late applicants are placed on a waiting list. Applicants should contact:

Ms. Connie Tai, MBA
Director, Admissions
Rotterdam School of Management
Erasmus Graduate School of Business
PO Box 1738
3000 DR Rotterdam
The Netherlands
Telephone: +31-(0)10-408-2222
Fax: +31-(0)-452-9509
E-mail: Petersons@rsm.nl
World Wide Web: www.rsm.nl

Admissions Contact: Connie Tai, Director, Marketing and MBA Admissions
Address: Burgemeester Oudlaan 50, 3062 PA Rotterdam, Netherlands
Admissions Phone: 011-31-10-408-2222 • Admissions Fax: 011-31-10-452-9509
Admissions E-mail: info@rsm.nl • Web Address: www.rsm.nl

ESADE

Admissions Contact: Nuria Guilera, MBA Admissions Director
Address: Av. d'Esplugues, 92-96, Barcelona, Spain 08034
Admissions Phone: 011-34-934-952-088 • Admissions Fax: 011-34-934-953-828
Admissions E-mail: mba@esade.edu • Web Address: www.esade.edu

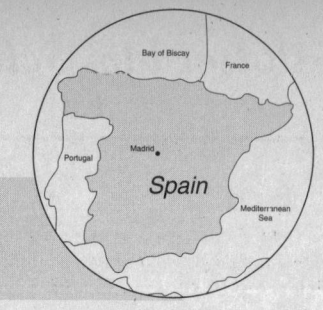

The ESADE MBA program is a "truly international education" with an incredible student/faculty ratio and study abroad opportunities at more than 30 schools. ESADE has a bilingual Spanish/English full-time MBA program and a part-time MBA available only in Spanish. Students can look forward to the professional demands of the curriculum, which requires each student to perform a filed consulting project and participate in an international corporate internship. ESADE is located in Barcelona, where the average temperature is 61 degrees Fahrenheit and the metropolitan population is 4,654,000.

INSTITUTIONAL INFORMATION

Evening Classes Available? Yes
Total Faculty: 552
% Faculty Part Time: 70
Student/Faculty Ratio: 3:1
Students in Parent Institution: 720
Academic Calendar: Annual

PROGRAMS

Degrees Offered: MBA (language is mainly Spanish) (part time, 2 years); Executive MBA (language is mainly Spanish) (18 months) PhD in Management Science (4 years)
Academic Specialties: Finance, Business Politics and Strategy, Marketing
Study Abroad Options: France, United Kingdom, Germany, Belgium, Norway, Netherlands, Italy, United States, Canada, Brazil, Venezuela, Mexico, Chile, Australia, China, Philippines, Singapore, Korea, Japan, India, Malaysia, Israel, Cape Town/South Africa

STUDENT INFORMATION

Total Business Students: 270
% Female: 25
% International: 60
Average Age: 28

COMPUTER AND RESEARCH FACILITIES

Computer Facilities: Digital Library; European Documentation Centre; Corporate Information Centre; databases including ABI/Inform, Datastream, ProQuest, STAT-USA
Campuswide Network? Yes
% of MBA Classrooms Wired: 100
Computer Model Recommended: Laptop
Internet Fee? No

EXPENSES/FINANCIAL AID

Annual Tuition: $19,000
Books and Supplies: $150

ADMISSIONS INFORMATION

Application Fee: $65
Electronic Application? Yes
Regular Application Deadline: 6/30
Regular Notification: Rolling
Deferment Available? Yes
Length of Deferment: 1 year
Non-fall Admissions? No
Transfer Students Accepted? No
Need-Blind Admissions? Yes
Number of Applications Received: 825
% of Applicants Accepted: 20
% Accepted Who Enrolled: 65
Average GMAT: 640
GMAT Range: 600-680
Average Years Experience: 4
Other Admissions Factors Considered: Motivation of the candidate, potential for development and leadership

INTERNATIONAL STUDENTS

TOEFL Required of International Students? Yes
Minimum TOEFL: 600 (250 computer)

EMPLOYMENT INFORMATION

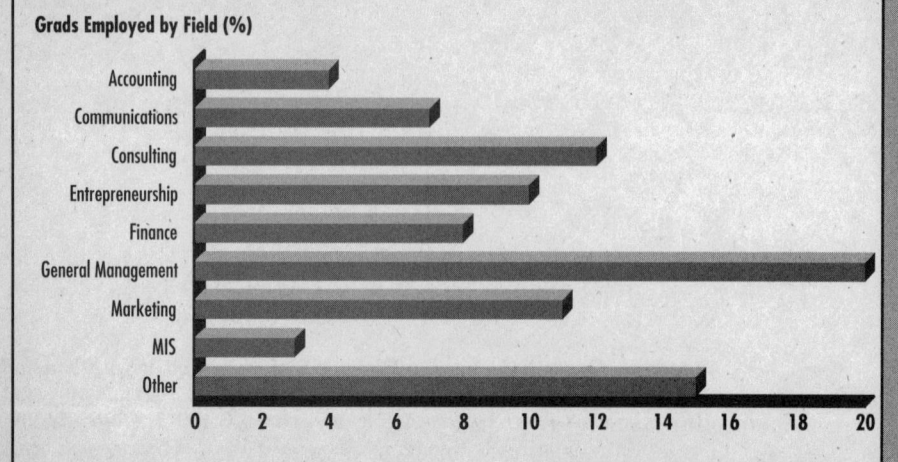

Grads Employed by Field (%)

Field	%
Accounting	3
Communications	7
Consulting	12
Entrepreneurship	8
Finance	3
General Management	20
Marketing	11
MIS	3
Other	15

Placement Office Available? Yes
% Employed Within 3 Months: 100
Frequent Employers: McKinsey & Co., Boston Consulting Group, KPMG Peat Marwick, General Electric, Hewlett-Packard, Henkel, Arthur Andersen

FAIRFIELD UNIVERSITY
Charles F. Dolan School of Business

Admissions Contact: Colleen Kupchick, MBA Program Assistant
Address: 1073 North Benson Road, Fairfield, CT 06430
Admissions Phone: 203-254-4070 • Admissions Fax: 203-254-4029
Admissions E-mail: mba@mail.fairfield.edu • Web Address: www.fairfield.edu

It's private, it's Jesuit, it's got an exceedingly high acceptance rate, and it's located on a beautiful 200-acre campus in Fairfield, Connecticut. The MBA program at the Charles F. Dolan School of Business requires that all students begin the full MBA at the same level. "Leveling" demands that students who do not have adequate grades or business course work take fundamental competency classes before commencing study at Fairfield. This process allows all students the chance to learn in an equal and ethical learning environment.

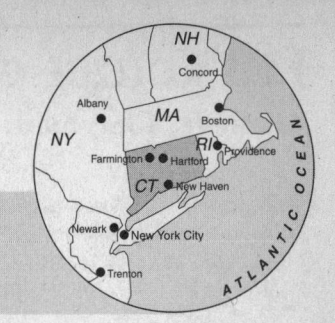

INSTITUTIONAL INFORMATION
Public/Private: Private
Evening Classes Available? Yes
Total Faculty: 44
% Faculty Female: 36
% Faculty Minority: 2
% Faculty Part Time: 9
Student/Faculty Ratio: 23:1
Students in Parent Institution: 5,154
Academic Calendar: Semester

PROGRAMS
Degrees Offered: Master of Business Administration (MBA) (12 months to 5 years), Master of Science in Finance (MS) (1 to 3 years)
Academic Specialties: Business ethics, gender differences in role modeling, e-marketing, information visualization, supply chain management
Study Abroad Options: China, France, Germany, Japan, Netherlands, United Kingdom

STUDENT INFORMATION
Total Business Students: 191
% Female: 9
% Minority: 5
% International: 17
Average Age: 29

COMPUTER AND RESEARCH FACILITIES
Computer Facilities: Nyselius Library, Lexis-Nexis Academic Universe, Business and Company Resource Center (Gale), Disclosure Global Access (Primark), STAT-USA, ABI/Inform
Campuswide Network? Yes
% of MBA Classrooms Wired: 100
Internet Fee? No

EXPENSES/FINANCIAL AID
Annual Tuition: $19,100
Tuition Per Credit: $510
Room & Board (On/Off Campus): $18,000/$20,000
Books and Supplies: $1,000

ADMISSIONS INFORMATION
Application Fee: $55
Electronic Application? Yes
Regular Application Deadline: 8/15
Regular Notification: Rolling
Deferment Available? Yes
Length of Deferment: 1 year
Non-fall Admissions? Yes
Non-fall Application Deadline(s): Rolling
Transfer Students Accepted? Yes
Transfer Policy: 6 credits or Jesuit University
Need-Blind Admissions? No
Number of Applications Received: 94
% of Applicants Accepted: 79
% Accepted Who Enrolled: 72
Average GPA: 3.2
GPA Range: 2.9-3.8
Average GMAT: 548
GMAT Range: 490-650
Average Years Experience: 6
Other Admissions Factors Considered: Students are required to have taken a introductory course in Computer Information Systems.
Other Schools to Which Students Applied: University of Connecticut

INTERNATIONAL STUDENTS
TOEFL Required of International Students? Yes
Minimum TOEFL: 550 (213 computer)

EMPLOYMENT INFORMATION
Placement Office Available? Yes
Frequent Employers: GE, People's Bank, American Skandia, United Technologies, Pitney Bowes, The Common Fund, Bayer Corporation, UBS Warburg, Gartner, Unilever, Cendant Corporation, Pfizer
Prominent Alumni: Dr. E. Gerald Corrigan, managing director, Goldman Sachs; Joseph Berardino, former CEO, Arthur Andersen; Robert Murphy, Jr., senior VP, Walt Disney Company Foundation; Christopher McCormick, president and CEO, LL Bean, Inc.; Dr. Francis Tedesco, president, Medical College of Georgia

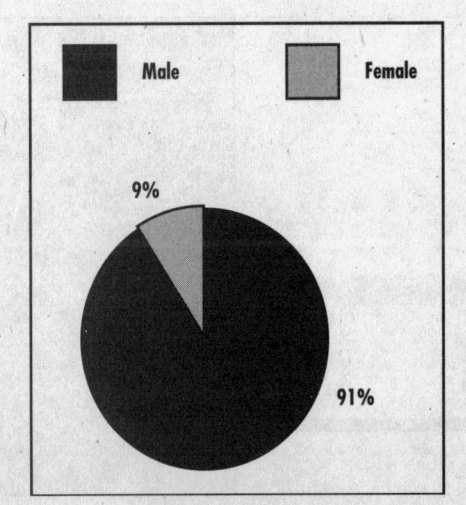

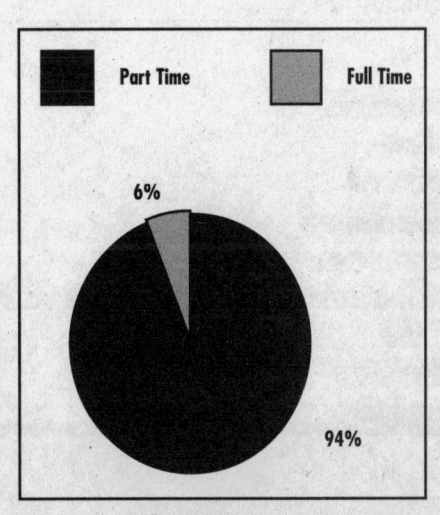

FIU College of Business Administration
Alvah H. Chapman, Jr., Graduate School of Business

Admissions Contact: Sally Gallion, Assistant Dean
Address: 11200 S.W. 8th Street, RB 310, Miami, FL 33199
Admissions Phone: 305-348-6631 • Admissions Fax: 305-348-3278
Admissions E-mail: cba@fiu.edu • Web Address: www.fiu.edu/~cba

It's no surprise that FIU's Global Executive MBA for managers in the Americas is so popular—not only is the College of Business Administration known for its expertise in Latin American commerce, it's been ranked the best business school for Hispanics in the United States by Hispanic Business magazine, with a student body that's 58 percent Hispanic American. Miami is a major center of international commerce, technology, travel and tourism, and real estate, but if you'd rather study abroad, you can get your Executive MBA in Kingston, Jamaica, your MIB in Cochabamba, Bolivia, or your International MBA in Saint-Etienne, France.

INSTITUTIONAL INFORMATION
Public/Private: Public
Evening Classes Available? Yes
Total Faculty: 125
% Faculty Female: 31
% Faculty Minority: 30
% Faculty Part Time: 11
Student/Faculty Ratio: 40:1
Students in Parent Institution: 32,500

PROGRAMS
Degrees Offered: Executive MBA (12 months); Global (Web-based) Executive MBA (13 months); Evening MBA (full time and part time, 2 to 3 years); International MBA (full time, 12 months); Master of Accounting (1 to 2 years); Executive MS in Taxation (70 weeks); MS in Finance Fast Track (12 months); MS in Management Information Systems (12 months); MS in Human Resource Management (16 months); Master of International Business (8 to 15 months)
Academic Specialties: Strongest in global/international business and strategic uses/management of IT. Also enterprise resource planning, e-business, operations research, knowledge management, financial derivatives, international trade and banking, consumer behavior, global management and marketing, and corporate responsibilities.
Study Abroad Options: France, Spain, Bulgaria, Croatia, Greece, Japan, Italy, Latin America, Caribbean countries

STUDENT INFORMATION
Total Business Students: 489
% Full Time: 33
% Female: 60
% Minority: 58
% Out of State: 85
% International: 69
Average Age: 28

COMPUTER AND RESEARCH FACILITIES
Research Facilities: Center for International Business Education and Research, Center for Excellence in Management, Center for Supply Chain Systems, Real Estate Institute, Latin American and Caribbean Center, Entrepreneurship Center, a number of additional specialized research centers
Computer Facilities: A number of business-related databases, wireless networking, computer labs are equipped with multimedia projectors for instructors, videoconferencing over IP.
Campuswide Network? Yes
% of MBA Classrooms Wired: 100
Computer Model Recommended: Laptop

EXPENSES/FINANCIAL AID
Annual Tuition: $24,000
Tuition Per Credit (Resident/Nonresident): $162/$570
Room & Board (On/Off Campus): $12,000/$18,000
Books and Supplies: $1,800
Average Grant: $5,000
Average Loan: $8,000

ADMISSIONS INFORMATION
Application Fee: $20
Electronic Application? No
Regular Application Deadline: Rolling
Regular Notification: Rolling
Deferment Available? No
Non-fall Application Deadline(s): Spring, summer
Transfer Students Accepted? No
Need-Blind Admissions? Yes
Number of Applications Received: 688
% of Applicants Accepted: 45
% Accepted Who Enrolled: 98
Average GPA: 3.3
GPA Range: 2.4-3.8
Average GMAT: 546
GMAT Range: 490-700
Average Years Experience: 5
Other Schools to Which Students Applied: U. of Miami, U. of South Carolina, U. of Florida, Arizona State, Thunderbird, ESADE, INCAE

INTERNATIONAL STUDENTS
TOEFL Required of International Students? Yes
Minimum TOEFL: 580 (237 computer)

EMPLOYMENT INFORMATION

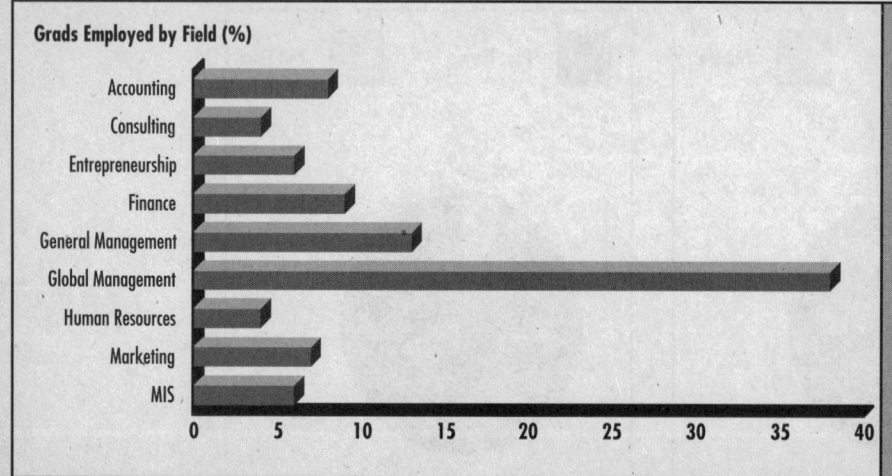

Grads Employed by Field (%):
- Accounting: 3
- Consulting: 3
- Entrepreneurship: 2
- Finance: 7
- General Management: 8
- Global Management: 38
- Human Resources: 2
- Marketing: 7
- MIS: 6

Placement Office Available? No
% Employed Within 3 Months: 99
Frequent Employers: Ryder, Exxon-Mobil, Amadeus North America, Andrx Pharmaceuticals, Blue Cross/Blue Shield of Florida, AT&T, Bank of America, Burdines, Citibank, The Corranino Group, DaimlerChrysler Financial Services, Gomez-Acebo & Pombo, Harcos International, IBM-Lotus Latin America, Kroll Associates, Latin Venture Partners, Mercedes-Benz, Motorola, Merrill Lynch, Morgan Stanley Dean Witter, U.S. Coast Guard, U.S. Department of Commerce,
Prominent Alumni: Augusto Vidaurreta, founder, Systems Consulting Group & Adjoined Technology; Carlos Migoya, president, First Union Bank, Miami

FLORIDA ATLANTIC UNIVERSITY
College of Business

Admissions Contact: Fredrick Taylor, Graduate Advisor
Address: 777 Glades Road, Boca Raton, FL 33431
Admissions Phone: 561-297-3624 • Admissions Fax: 561-297-3686
Admissions E-mail: mba@fau.edu • Web Address: www.collegeofbusiness.fau.edu

Boca Raton's Florida Atlantic University provides a suite of options for the MBA-hungry working professional. The most unique option is the Environmental MBA, which focuses on corporate responsibility with the belief that it's "possible for companies to create value for both society and shareholders." Other options include the Health Administration MBA; the MBASport, which aims to train sports executives and administrators; and the Executive MBA. Online programs are also available, including FAUMBA.net, the standard MBA course delivered both on campus and online.

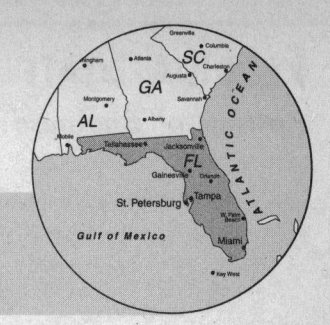

INSTITUTIONAL INFORMATION
Public/Private: Public
Evening Classes Available? Yes
Total Faculty: 111
% Faculty Part Time: 6
Student/Faculty Ratio: 12:1
Students in Parent Institution: 23,716

PROGRAMS
Degrees Offered: Master of Business Administration (MBA) (40 to 52 credits, 12 months to 7 years); Executive MBA (48 credits, 20 months); Weekend MBA (39 credits, 2 years); Environmental MBA (40 credits, 15 months); Master of Science in International Business (MSIB) (33 credits, 2 years); Master of Accounting (MAcc) (33 credits, 12 months to 5 years); Master of Taxation (MTax) (33 credits, 12 months to 5 years)
Study Abroad Options: Australia, Chile, Ecuador, China, Denmark, Finland, France, Germany, Greece, Israel, Japan, Lithuania, Mexico, Russia, Spain, Sweden, United Kingdom, Italy, Brazil

STUDENT INFORMATION
Total Business Students: 510
% Full Time: 31
% Female: 48
Average Age: 29

COMPUTER AND RESEARCH FACILITIES
Computer Facilities: FAU libraries offer more than 100 electronic databases and other computer resources to all FAU students.
Campuswide Network? Yes
% of MBA Classrooms Wired: 5
Computer Model Recommended: No
Internet Fee? No

EXPENSES/FINANCIAL AID
Annual Tuition (Resident/Nonresident): $4,152/$13,920
Tuition Per Credit (Resident/Nonresident): $173/$580
Books and Supplies: $1,500
Average Loan: $5,000

ADMISSIONS INFORMATION
Application Fee: $20
Electronic Application? No
Regular Application Deadline: 6/15
Regular Notification: Rolling
Deferment Available? Yes
Length of Deferment: 1 year
Non-fall Admissions? Yes
Non-fall Application Deadline(s): 6/15 fall, 10/15 spring, 3/15 summer
Transfer Students Accepted? No
Need-Blind Admissions? Yes
Number of Applications Received: 330
% of Applicants Accepted: 57
% Accepted Who Enrolled: 68
Average GPA: 3.3
GPA Range: 3.0-3.6
Average GMAT: 525
GMAT Range: 474-568
Average Years Experience: 4
Other Admissions Factors Considered: GMAT score, GPA, PC literacy, work experience
Other Schools to Which Students Applied: Florida International University, Florida State University, Miami University, University of Central Florida, University of Florida, University of South Florida

INTERNATIONAL STUDENTS
TOEFL Required of International Students? Yes
Minimum TOEFL: 600 (250 computer)

EMPLOYMENT INFORMATION
Placement Office Available? Yes

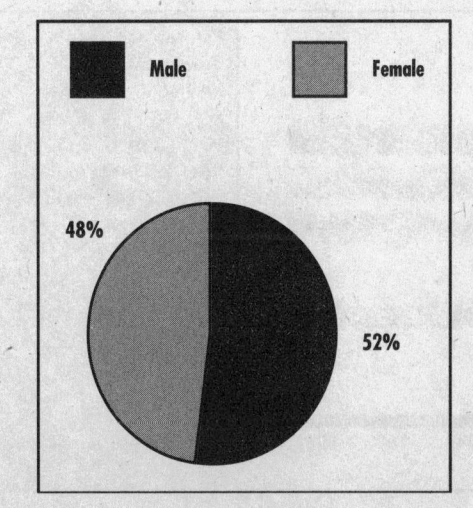

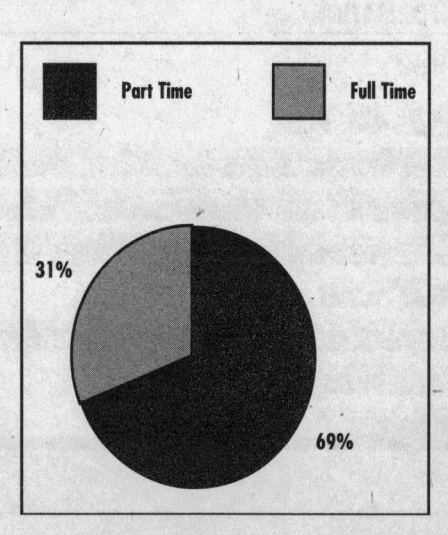

Male / Female: 52% / 48%

Part Time / Full Time: 69% / 31%

FLORIDA STATE UNIVERSITY
College of Business

Admissions Contact: Scheri L. Martin, Coordinator of Graduate Programs
Address: FSU College of Business, Tallahassee, FL 32306-1110
Admissions Phone: 850-644-6458 • Admissions Fax: 850-644-0915
Admissions E-mail: gradprog@cob.fsu.edu • Web Address: www.cob.fsu.edu

The MBA program at FSU's College of Business offers a full-time curriculum (1 year) and a part-time curriculum (2.5 years) at the Tallahassee campus and, if enrollment is high, a part-time evening curriculum (2.5 years) at the Panama City campus as well. FSU is home to the Jim Moran Institute of Global Entrepreneurship and the DeSantis Center of Executive Management Education, and is proud to announce its new Technology Center, equipped with three new computer labs and two computer classrooms.

INSTITUTIONAL INFORMATION
Public/Private: Public
Evening Classes Available? Yes
Total Faculty: 85
% Faculty Female: 13
Student/Faculty Ratio: 40:1
Students in Parent Institution: 35,000
Academic Calendar: Semester

PROGRAMS
Degrees Offered: MBA with concentrations in Finance, Global Entrepreneurship, Marketing and Supply Chain Management; JD/MBA; Master of Accounting with majors in Accounting Information Systems, Assurance Services, Corporate Accounting, Taxation; Master of Science in Management with a major in Management Information Systems; Master of Science in Management with a major in Risk and Insurance; Master of Science in Management with a major in Hospitality and Tourism; Corporate MBA; PhD in Business Administration with majors in Accounting, Finance, Information and Management Sciences, Marketing, Organizational Behavior, Risk Management and Insurance, Strategic Management
Joint Degrees: JD/MBA

STUDENT INFORMATION
Total Business Students: 178
% Full Time: 23
% Female: 30
% Minority: 18
% Out of State: 30
% International: 15
Average Age: 27

COMPUTER AND RESEARCH FACILITIES
Research Facilities: Jim Moran Institute for Entrepreneurship
Computer Facilities: Strozier Library
Campuswide Network? Yes
% of MBA Classrooms Wired: 100
Computer Model Recommended: Laptop
Internet Fee? No

EXPENSES/FINANCIAL AID
Room & Board (On/Off Campus): $10,000/$13,000
Books and Supplies: $4,750
Average Grant: $10,000
% Receiving Financial Aid: 37
% Receiving Aid Their First Year: 37

ADMISSIONS INFORMATION
Application Fee: $20
Electronic Application? Yes
Regular Application Deadline: 2/1
Regular Notification: 4/15
Deferment Available? Yes
Length of Deferment: 12 months
Non-fall Admissions? Yes
Non-fall Application Deadline(s): Spring 10/1, summer 2/1
Transfer Students Accepted? Yes
Transfer Policy: Transfer applicants must complete the same application process as other applicants.
Need-Blind Admissions? No
Number of Applications Received: 153
% of Applicants Accepted: 42
% Accepted Who Enrolled: 63
Average GPA: 3.2
Average GMAT: 569
Average Years Experience: 5
Other Admissions Factors Considered: Bachelor's degree with minimum 3.0 GPA, applicant's statement, work experience and resume, college transcripts, letters of recommendation, GMAT score, and interview
Minority/Disadvantaged Student Recruitment Programs: FAMU Feeder Program, FAMU Graduate and Professional Days, PT-Program Seminars through the FSU Center for Professional Development, Minority Student Orientation Program, Leslie Wilson Assistantships, Delores Auzenne Minority Fellowship, University Fellowship

INTERNATIONAL STUDENTS
TOEFL Required of International Students? Yes
Minimum TOEFL: 600 (250 computer)

EMPLOYMENT INFORMATION

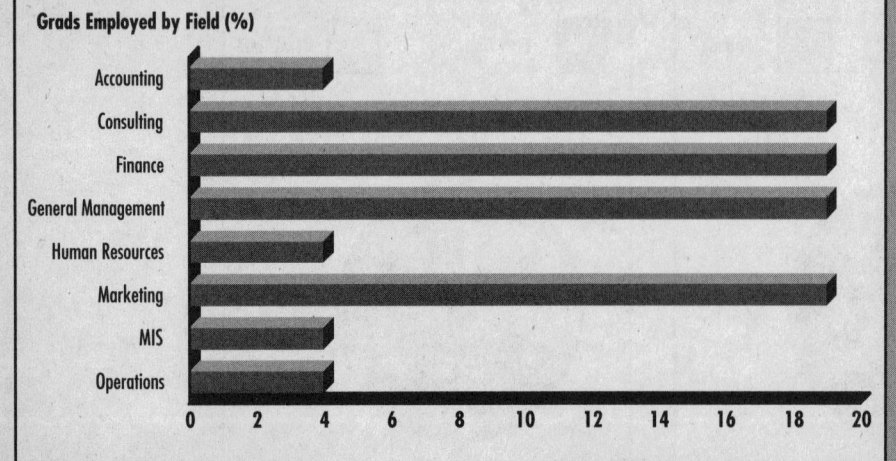

Grads Employed by Field (%)
- Accounting: 4
- Consulting: 19
- Finance: 19
- General Management: 19
- Human Resources: 4
- Marketing: 19
- MIS: 4
- Operations: 4

Placement Office Available? Yes
% Employed Within 3 Months: 77
Frequent Employers: Accenture, Am South Banks, Bank of America
Prominent Alumni: Gary Rogers, president and CEO, GE Plastics; Craig Wardlaw, executive vice president and CIO, Bank of America; Craig Ramsey, partner, Accenture

FORDHAM UNIVERSITY
Graduate School of Business Administration

Admissions Contact: Christine Elliott, Administrative Assistant
Address: 33 West 60th Street, 4th floor, New York, NY 10023
Admissions Phone: 212-636-6200 • Admissions Fax: 212-636-7076
Admissions E-mail: admissionsgb@fordham.edu • Web Address: www.bnet.fordham.edu

The Fordham MBA student needs only to step outside to begin his or her financial education in New York City, the corporate mecca of the twenty-first century. Offering a multitude of degree concentrations, an MBA student can specialize in areas ranging from accounting to media management to information and communications systems. Fordham also has a suburban campus located just a short train ride from the city campus, in Westchester County. A few big-time employers of Fordham MBA graduates are Ernst & Young, Chase Manhattan Bank, and G.E. Capital Citibank.

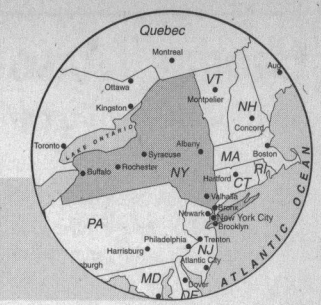

INSTITUTIONAL INFORMATION
Public/Private: Private
Evening Classes Available? Yes
Total Faculty: 180
% Faculty Part Time: 49
Student/Faculty Ratio: 4:1
Academic Calendar: Trimester

PROGRAMS
Degrees Offered: MBA-Deming Scholars (60 credits), MBA-Global Professional (69 credits), MBA-Transnational (Executive) (69 credits), MBA-Accounting (60 credits), MBA-Professional Accounting (60 credits), MBA-Taxation and Accounting (90 credits), MS-Taxation (54 credits), MBA-Communications and Media Management (60 credits), MBA-Finance and Business Economics (60 credits), MBA-Information and Communications Systems (60 credits), MBA-Management Systems (60 credits), MBA-Marketing (60 credits), MBA-Beijing International (60 credits)
Joint Degrees: Joint Juris Doctor/MBA
Special Opportunities: Dual-concentration programs, Global Professional MBA Program, Masters in Taxation and Accounting
Study Abroad Options: Russia, England, France, Finland, Chile, Switzerland, Poland, China, Spain, Brazil, Holland, Ireland, India

STUDENT INFORMATION
Total Business Students: 1,534
% Full Time: 23
% Female: 38
% Minority: 16
% International: 26
Average Age: 28

COMPUTER AND RESEARCH FACILITIES
Number of Computer Labs: 3
Number of Student Computers: 40
Campuswide Network? Yes
% Who Own Computers: 95
Computer Proficiency Required? Yes
Special Purchasing Agreements? Yes
Companies with Agreements: University Computer Store
Internet Fee? No

EXPENSES/FINANCIAL AID
Annual Tuition: $21,060
Room & Board (Off Campus): $14,000
Books and Supplies: $1,495
Average Grant: $3,000
Average Loan: $20,000

ADMISSIONS INFORMATION
Application Fee: $65
Electronic Application? Yes
Regular Application Deadline: 6/1
Regular Notification: 7/31
Deferment Available? Yes
Length of Deferment: 1 year
Non-fall Admissions? Yes
Non-fall Application Deadline(s): 11/1, 3/1
Transfer Students Accepted? Yes
Transfer Policy: ACCSB-accredited school; prerequisite and core courses only can be waived
Need-Blind Admissions? Yes
Number of Applications Received: 822
% of Applicants Accepted: 62
% Accepted Who Enrolled: 63
Average GPA: 3.3
GPA Range: 2.7-3.7
Average GMAT: 600
GMAT Range: 540-680
Average Years Experience: 6
Other Schools to Which Students Applied: Baruch College (CUNY), Boston College, Columbia University, Georgetown University, New York University

INTERNATIONAL STUDENTS
TOEFL Required of International Students? Yes
Minimum TOEFL: 600

EMPLOYMENT INFORMATION

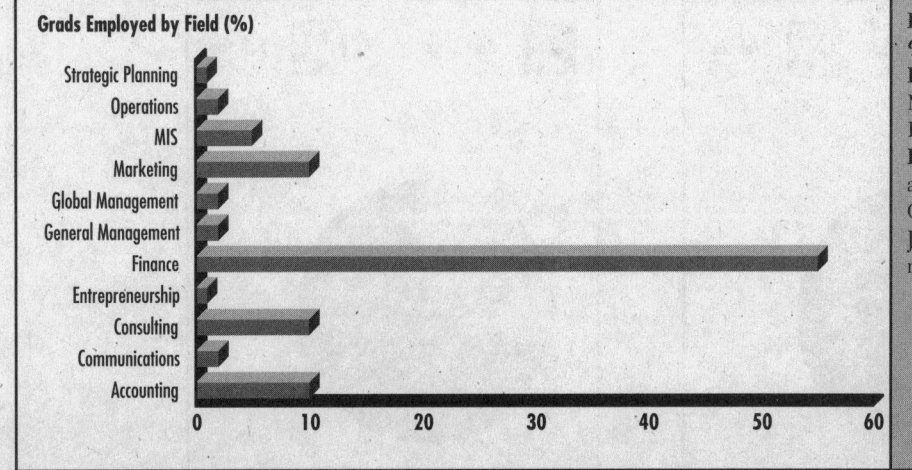

Grads Employed by Field (%)

Field	%
Strategic Planning	1
Operations	2
MIS	3
Marketing	5
Global Management	2
General Management	3
Finance	55
Entrepreneurship	1
Consulting	5
Communications	2
Accounting	10

Placement Office Available? Yes
% Employed Within 6 Months: 97
Frequent Employers: Ernst & Young, Chase Manhattan Bank, G.E. Capital Citibank, Rechetl Block Drugs
Prominent Alumni: Nemir Kirdar, president and CEO, Investcorp Bank E.C.; Mary Louise Quinlan, vice chairman, MacManus Group; James Fernandez, executive vice president of Finance and CEO, Tiffany & Co.

GEORGE MASON UNIVERSITY
School of Management

Admissions Contact: Carol Hoskins, MBA Program Coordinator
Address: 4400 University Drive, MSN 5A2, Enterprise Hall, Room 156, Fairfax, VA 22030
Admissions Phone: 703-993-2140 • Admissions Fax: 703-993-1778
Admissions E-mail: masonmba@som.gmu.edu • Web Address: www.som.gmu.edu

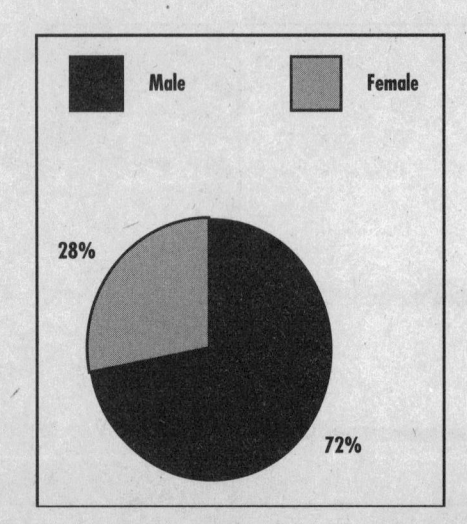

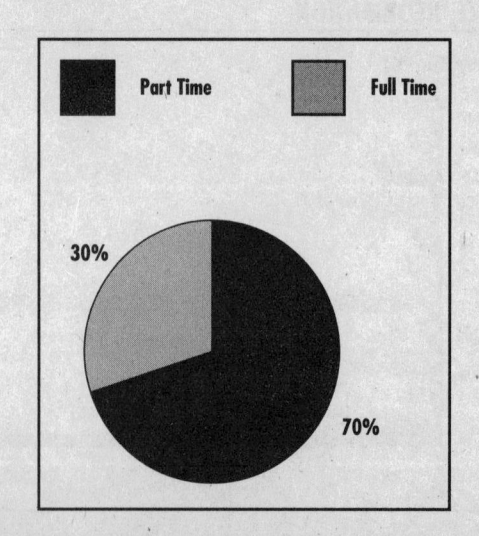

The George Mason University School of Management provides superb educational training in finance and leadership skills and acts as a supportive resource center for career information and placement. The George Mason MBA is generally completed over the course of two years and nine months, taking two classes per week, but students can opt for the accelerated course, completed in 24 months, taking three courses per semester. All MBA courses take place in the evening and utilize cohort groups of about 35 students. One unique feature of the program is that, prior to taking any MBA electives, students are required to pass an exam that tests their proficiency in the use of Web resources and knowledge of basic information technology.

INSTITUTIONAL INFORMATION
Public/Private: Public
Evening Classes Available? Yes
Total Faculty: 96
% Faculty Part Time: 24
Academic Calendar: Semester

PROGRAMS
Degrees Offered: Executive MBA (EMBA) (full time, 48 credits, up to 22 months); MBA (full time, 48 credits, 24 months to 6 years), with concentrations in Accounting, Decision Sciences, Entrepreneurship, Finance, International Business, Management, Management Information Systems, Marketing, and Organizational Behavior/Development; Fast Track MBA (part time, 48 credits, 2.8 years), with concentrations in Entrepreneurship, International Business, International Finance, Accounting, Management, Decision Sciences, Finance, International Business, Management Information Systems, Marketing, and Organizational Behavior/Development

STUDENT INFORMATION
Total Business Students: 65
% Female: 28
% Minority: 12
% International: 10
Average Age: 28

COMPUTER AND RESEARCH FACILITIES
Research Facilities: Fenwick library plus 1 additional on-campus library; total holdings of 635,284 volumes, 1,683,847 microforms, 9,191 current periodical subscriptions; CD player(s) available for graduate student use; access to online bibliographic retrieval services
Campuswide Network? Yes
Internet Fee? No

EXPENSES/FINANCIAL AID
Annual Tuition (Resident/Nonresident): $7,788/$12,696
Tuition Per Credit (Resident/Nonresident): $325/$529
% Receiving Financial Aid: 19

ADMISSIONS INFORMATION
Application Fee: $50
Electronic Application? Yes
Regular Application Deadline: 4/1
Regular Notification: 1/1
Deferment Available? Yes
Length of Deferment: 2 years
Non-fall Admissions? Yes
Non-fall Application Deadline(s): 11/1 spring; international applicants: 3/1 fall, 9/1 spring
Transfer Students Accepted? Yes
Transfer Policy: Applicants must submit all required application documents.
Need-Blind Admissions? No
Number of Applications Received: 210
% of Applicants Accepted: 54
% Accepted Who Enrolled: 58
Average GPA: 3.1
Average GMAT: 605
Average Years Experience: 6
Other Admissions Factors Considered: A minimum GPA of 3.1 and 2 years of work experience are required. Experience with PC software is recommended.

INTERNATIONAL STUDENTS
TOEFL Required of International Students? Yes
Minimum TOEFL: 600 (230 computer)

EMPLOYMENT INFORMATION
Placement Office Available? Yes
% Employed Within 3 Months: 90
Frequent Employers: Hunton & Williams; McGuire, Woods, Battle & Boothe; Finnegan, Henderson, Farabow, Garret & Dunner, LLP; U.S. government; Shaw Pittman; Wiley, Rein, and Fielding; Sterne, Kessler, Goldstein, and Fox; Sutherland, Asbill, and Brennan

THE GEORGE WASHINGTON UNIVERSITY
School of Business and Public Management

Admissions Contact: Mr. David Toomer, Director, Graduate Enrollment Management
Address: 710 21st Street NW, Suite 301, Washington, DC 20052
Admissions Phone: 202-994-5536 • Admissions Fax: 202-994-3571
Admissions E-mail: mbaft@gwu.edu • Web Address: www.mba.gwu.edu

The location of GW's School of Business and Public Management in Washington, D.C., grants the MBA student the benefits of an international atmosphere and a continuous opportunity to interact with a truly global city. GW is a renowned academic institution that offers an outstanding financial education to working professionals and full-time students. Frequent employers of GW MBA graduates are Deloitte & Touche, Accenture, PricewaterhouseCoopers, and the U.S. government—Colin Powell is an alumnus of the program.

INSTITUTIONAL INFORMATION
Public/Private: Private
Evening Classes Available? Yes
Total Faculty: 120
% Faculty Female: 17
% Faculty Minority: 5
% Faculty Part Time: 9
Student/Faculty Ratio: 20:1
Students in Parent Institution: 20,346
Academic Calendar: Semester

PROGRAMS
Degrees Offered: MBA (full time 21 months, part time 2 to 5 years, accelerated 24 months, executive 21 months), MAcc (21 months), MPA (21 months), Master of Public Policy (21 months), MS in Finance (full time 1 year, part time 2 years), MS in Information Systems Technology (21 months), MS in Project Management (21 months), Master of Tourism Administration (21 months)
Joint Degrees: MBA/JD (4 years), MBA/MA in International Affairs (30 months)
Academic Specialties: International Business, Finance and Investments, Entrepreneurship and Small Business, Public Administration, Organizational Behavior, Development Accountancy

STUDENT INFORMATION
Total Business Students: 784
% Full Time: 52
% Female: 45
% Minority: 17
% Out of State: 80
% International: 41
Average Age: 27

COMPUTER AND RESEARCH FACILITIES
Research Facilities: Centers and institutes for Global Management and Research, European Union Research, Financial Markets, Latin American Issues, Real Estate and Urban Analysis, Advancement of Small Business, Family Enterprise, NAFTA/EU Project, Social and Organizational Learning, Tourism Studies, Municipal Management, Law Practice Strategy, and Management
Computer Facilities: MBA Computer Labs, various research databases, alumni databases
Campuswide Network? Yes
% of MBA Classrooms Wired: 75
Computer Model Recommended: Laptop
Internet Fee? No

EXPENSES/FINANCIAL AID
Annual Tuition: $19,464
Tuition Per Credit: $810
Room & Board (Off Campus): $14,400
Books and Supplies: $2,280
Average Grant: $10,000
Average Loan: $18,000
% Receiving Financial Aid: 90
% Receiving Aid Their First Year: 44

ADMISSIONS INFORMATION
Application Fee: $55
Electronic Application? Yes
Regular Application Deadline: 4/1
Regular Notification: Rolling
Deferment Available? No
Non-fall Application Deadline(s): 10/2
Transfer Students Accepted? Yes
Need-Blind Admissions? Yes
Number of Applications Received: 981
% of Applicants Accepted: 28
% Accepted Who Enrolled: 49
Average GPA: 3.1
GPA Range: 2.7-3.7
Average GMAT: 610
GMAT Range: 550-680
Average Years Experience: 5
Other Admissions Factors Considered: Country diversity
Other Schools to Which Students Applied: Boston U., Case Western, Georgetown, NYU, Thunderbird, U. of Maryland College Park, University of Rochester

INTERNATIONAL STUDENTS
TOEFL Required of International Students? Yes
Minimum TOEFL: 600 (250 computer)

EMPLOYMENT INFORMATION

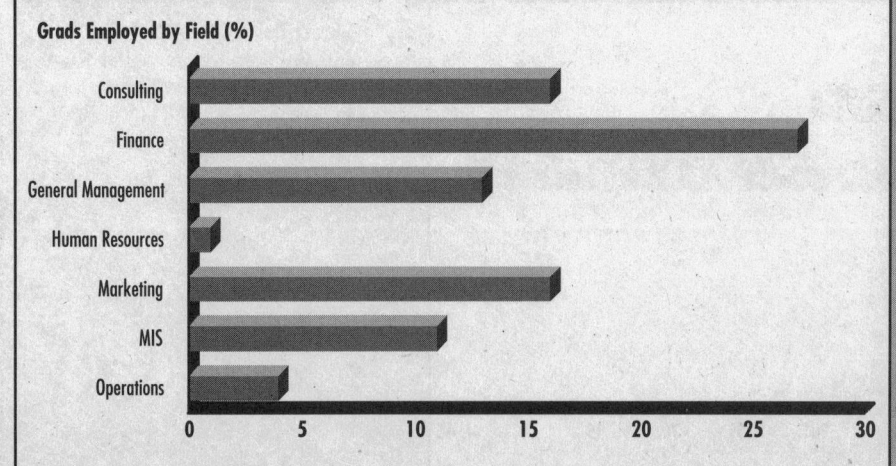

Grads Employed by Field (%)
- Consulting: ~16
- Finance: ~27
- General Management: ~14
- Human Resources: ~2
- Marketing: ~16
- MIS: ~11
- Operations: ~4

Placement Office Available? Yes
% Employed Within 3 Months: 65
Frequent Employers: Accenture, Andersen, Pcubed, KPMG, Deloitte & Touche, Lehman Brothers, Citigroup, FedEx, Pricewaterhouse Coopers, Taylor Dejongh, Ernest & Young, IBM, World Bank Group, Johnson and Johnson
Prominent Alumni: Colin Powell, U.S. secretary of state; Henry Duques, president & CEO, First Data Corp.; Edward M. Liddy, chairman & CEO, Allstate Insurance; Darla A. Moore, president, Rainwater, Inc.; Clarence B. Rogers, Jr., chairman, president, and CEO, Equifax, Inc.

GEORGETOWN UNIVERSITY
School of Business

Admissions Contact: Robert Wheeler, Assistant Dean
Address: Box 571148, Washington, DC 20057-1221
Admissions Phone: 202-687-4200 • Admissions Fax: 202-687-7809
Admissions E-mail: mba@georgetown.edu • Web Address: www.mba.georgetown.edu

Georgetown's School of Business has an "unbelievably dedicated" faculty and a tremendous Washington, D.C., location, but without a doubt, international business is its strong suit. Students here can take electives at the School of Foreign Service, and there is a strong "international flavor" among the students, as "nearly a quarter are foreign and almost everyone else has lived or worked abroad and speaks a second language."

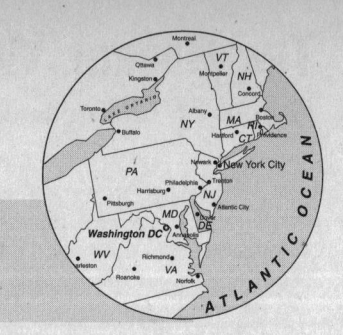

INSTITUTIONAL INFORMATION
Public/Private: Private
Evening Classes Available? No
Total Faculty: 76
% Faculty Female: 23
% Faculty Minority: 9
% Faculty Part Time: 12
Student/Faculty Ratio: 8:1
Students in Parent Institution: 12,000
Academic Calendar: Module

PROGRAMS
Degrees Offered: MBA (21 months)
Joint Degrees: MBA/MSFS (3 years); MBA/JD (4 years); MBA/MPP (3 years); MBA/MD (5 years); BS, BA/MBA (5 years); MBA/MA Physics (3 years); MBA/PhD Physics (5 years)
Academic Specialties: Curriculum is new (as of fall 1998) with integrated modules of varying lengths. An international experience is required of all second-years.
Special Opportunities: International Business Diplomacy Certificate, Area Studies Certificate, Summer Study Abroad Opportunities, International Exchange Opportunities, Summer Pre-Enrollment "Prep" Workshops
Study Abroad Options: Spain, France, Australia, Germany, Mexico, Belgium, England, Denmark, Netherlands, Italy

STUDENT INFORMATION
Total Business Students: 502
% Female: 33
% Minority: 66
% International: 35
Average Age: 28

COMPUTER AND RESEARCH FACILITIES
Research Facilities: Capital Markets Research Center
Computer Facilities: The school maintains its own local area network, decision support center, Boland Information Systems Laboratory, MBA Lounge computer centers, numerous databases (Georgetown University), and full Internet services. The school uses a Windows 2000 applications environment.
Campuswide Network? Yes
% of MBA Classrooms Wired: 100
Computer Model Recommended: Laptop
Internet Fee? No

EXPENSES/FINANCIAL AID
Annual Tuition: $24,440
Room & Board (Off Campus): $14,000
Books and Supplies: $1,250
Average Grant: $12,500
Average Loan: $26,000
% Receiving Financial Aid: 90
% Receiving Aid Their First Year: 90

ADMISSIONS INFORMATION
Application Fee: $75
Electronic Application? Yes
Regular Application Deadline: 4/16
Regular Notification: 5/29
Deferment Available? No
Non-fall Admissions? No
Transfer Students Accepted? No
Need-Blind Admissions? Yes
Number of Applications Received: 2,816
% of Applicants Accepted: 21
% Accepted Who Enrolled: 45
Average GPA: 3.4
Average GMAT: 662
Average Years Experience: 5
Minority/Disadvantaged Student Recruitment Programs: Specific, targeted marketing efforts made in this area

INTERNATIONAL STUDENTS
TOEFL Required of International Students? Yes
Minimum TOEFL: 600 (250 computer)

EMPLOYMENT INFORMATION

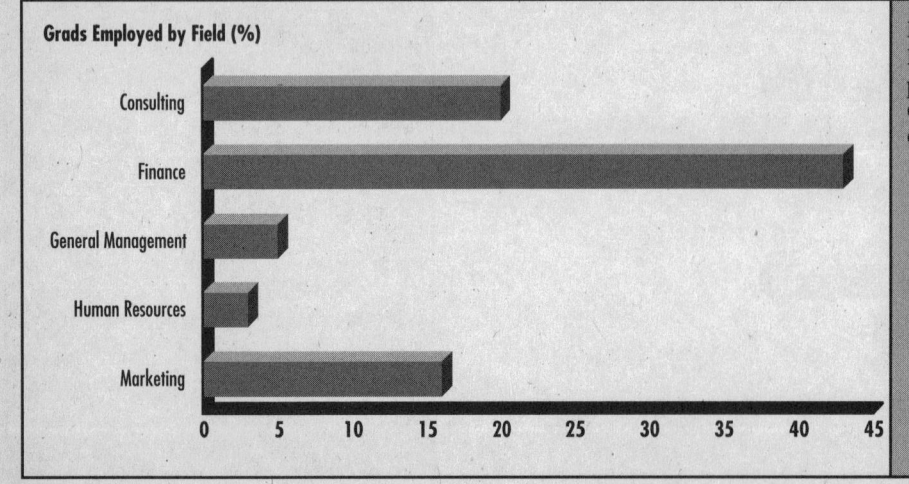

Grads Employed by Field (%)
- Consulting: 20
- Finance: 43
- General Management: 5
- Human Resources: 3
- Marketing: 15

Placement Office Available? Yes
Frequent Employers: Pricewaterhouse-Coopers, Chase Manhattan, Citicorp, Cosmiar, Goldman Sachs, Johnson & Johnson, Procter & Gamble, Toyota

GEORGIA COLLEGE & STATE UNIVERSITY
The J. Whitney Bunting School of Business

Admissions Contact: Maryllis Wolfgang, Director of Admissions
Address: GC&SU Campus Box 23, Milledgeville, GA 31061
Admissions Phone: 478-445-6289 • Admissions Fax: 478-445-1914
Admissions E-mail: mcmillan@gcsu.edu • Web Address: www.gcsu.edu

The J. Whitney Bunting School of Business allows in-state residents of Georgia to enjoy quality education with low tuition rates. Originally founded as a women's college, the Bunting School now has a student body that's 41 percent female. The part-time and full-time MBA programs emphasize practical financial knowledge and provide decision-making simulations to prepare MBA students for the real world.

INSTITUTIONAL INFORMATION
Public/Private: Public
Evening Classes Available? Yes
Total Faculty: 36
% Faculty Part Time: 2
Student/Faculty Ratio: 15:1
Students in Parent Institution: 5,079
Academic Calendar: Semester

PROGRAMS
Degrees Offered: Master of Business Administration (MBA) (full time or part time, 30 to 57 credits, 12 months to 7 years); Master of Management Information Systems (MMIS) (full time or part time, 36 to 60 credits, 12 months to 7 years); Master of Accountancy (MAcc) (full time or part time, 30 to 57 credits, 12 months to 7 years)
Academic Specialties: AACSB-accredited
Study Abroad Options: Brazil, Hungary, Mexico, People's Republic of China, Spain, United Kingdom

STUDENT INFORMATION
Total Business Students: 138
% Full Time: 25
% Female: 41
% Minority: 32
% Out of State: 5
% International: 38
Average Age: 32

COMPUTER AND RESEARCH FACILITIES
Research Facilities: Ina Dillard Russell Library; total holdings of 170,834 volumes, 515,123 microforms, 1,137 current periodical subscriptions; CD player(s) available for graduate student use; access to online bibliographic retrieval services and online databases
Computer Facilities: Georgia Libraries Learning On-Line (GALILEO), JSTOR
Campuswide Network? Yes
% of MBA Classrooms Wired: 100
Internet Fee? No

EXPENSES/FINANCIAL AID
Annual Tuition (Resident/Nonresident): $4,557/$18,228
Tuition Per Credit (Resident/Nonresident): $127/$506
Room & Board (On/Off Campus): $9,000/$15,000
Books and Supplies: $900

ADMISSIONS INFORMATION
Application Fee: $25
Electronic Application? Yes
Regular Application Deadline: Rolling
Regular Notification: Rolling
Deferment Available? Yes
Length of Deferment: 1 year
Non-fall Admissions? Yes
Non-fall Application Deadline(s): 12/1 spring, 7/15 fall, 5/1 summer
Transfer Students Accepted? Yes
Transfer Policy: Minimum of 9 semester hours if equivalent to GC&SU curriculum
Need-Blind Admissions? No
Number of Applications Received: 63
% of Applicants Accepted: 63
% Accepted Who Enrolled: 65
Average GPA: 3.3
Average GMAT: 490
GMAT Range: 460-535
Other Admissions Factors Considered: Computer experience recommended
Minority/Disadvantaged Student Recruitment Programs: We recruit at seminars developed for minority students.

INTERNATIONAL STUDENTS
TOEFL Required of International Students? Yes
Minimum TOEFL: 500

EMPLOYMENT INFORMATION
Placement Office Available? No

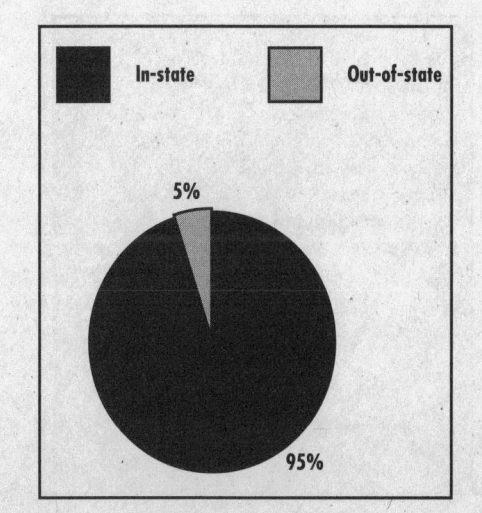

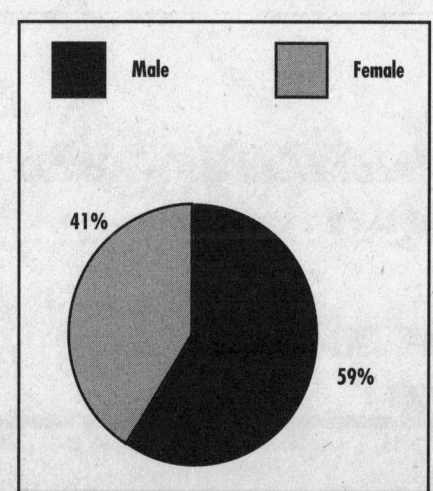

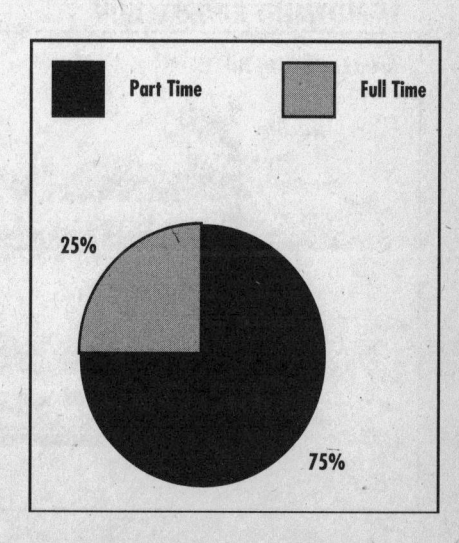

GEORGIA INSTITUTE OF TECHNOLOGY
DuPree School of Management

Admissions Contact: Paula Wilson, Assistant Director, MSM Program
Address: 755 Ferst Drive, Atlanta, GA 30332
Admissions Phone: 404-894-8713 • Admissions Fax: 404-894-4199
Admissions E-mail: msm@mgt.gatech.edu • Web Address: www.dupree.gatech.edu

Georgia Tech's DuPree School of Management offers an MSM, which is pretty much identical to an MBA. There is an "emphasis on analytic skills and technology" here—not surprising given Georgia Tech's prominence in engineering and the sciences—and "the operations faculty is one of the school's great strengths." Professors at DuPree all do extensive work in their industries" yet are "always available to students for support and advice."

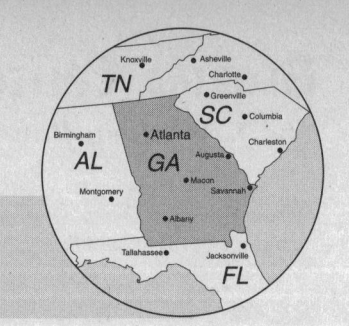

INSTITUTIONAL INFORMATION
Public/Private: Public
Evening Classes Available? No
Total Faculty: 53
% Faculty Female: 20
Student/Faculty Ratio: 4:1
Students in Parent Institution: 14,000
Academic Calendar: Semester

PROGRAMS
Degrees Offered: Master of Science in Management (MSM) (60 credits, 2 years); Executive Master of Science in Management of Technology (EMSMOT) (54 credits, 18 months); PhD in Management (4 to 5 years),, with concentration in Technology and Management
Joint Degrees: Dual-degree programs with any master's degree or PhD at Georgia Tech
Academic Specialties: Finance, Accounting, Operations Management, Information Technology
Special Opportunities: Management of Technology, Entrepreneurship and New Venture Development, International Business
Study Abroad Options: France, Germany, Netherlands, People's Republic of China, Japan, Denmark, Colombia, Poland

STUDENT INFORMATION
Total Business Students: 203
% Female: 28
% Minority: 13
% International: 32
Average Age: 27

COMPUTER AND RESEARCH FACILITIES
Research Facilities: MOT Program, Entrepreneurship Center, CIBER, Center for Quality
Computer Facilities: Numerous on-campus computer labs, comprehensive online databases maintained by the University System of Georgia, SAP R/3 Lab
Campuswide Network? No
Internet Fee? No

EXPENSES/FINANCIAL AID
Annual Tuition (Resident/Nonresident): $5,128/$18,046
Room & Board: $10,000
Books and Supplies: $1,400

ADMISSIONS INFORMATION
Application Fee: $50
Electronic Application? Yes
Regular Application Deadline: 3/5
Regular Notification: Rolling
Deferment Available? Yes
Length of Deferment: 1 year
Non-fall Admissions? No
Transfer Students Accepted? No
Need-Blind Admissions? Yes
Number of Applications Received: 530
% of Applicants Accepted: 38
% Accepted Who Enrolled: 51
Average GPA: 3.3
GPA Range: 2.7-3.7
Average GMAT: 645
GMAT Range: 570-730
Average Years Experience: 4
Other Admissions Factors Considered: We look at all factors in evaluating applicants.
Minority/Disadvantaged Student Recruitment Programs: FOCUS programs on campus; information sessions; Regents Opportunity Scholarships; minority student outreach
Other Schools to Which Students Applied: Emory University, University of Georgia, University of Texas-Austin, Purdue University, Indiana University, Carnegie Mellon University, Massachusetts Institute of Technology

INTERNATIONAL STUDENTS
TOEFL Required of International Students? Yes
Minimum TOEFL: 600 (250 computer)

EMPLOYMENT INFORMATION

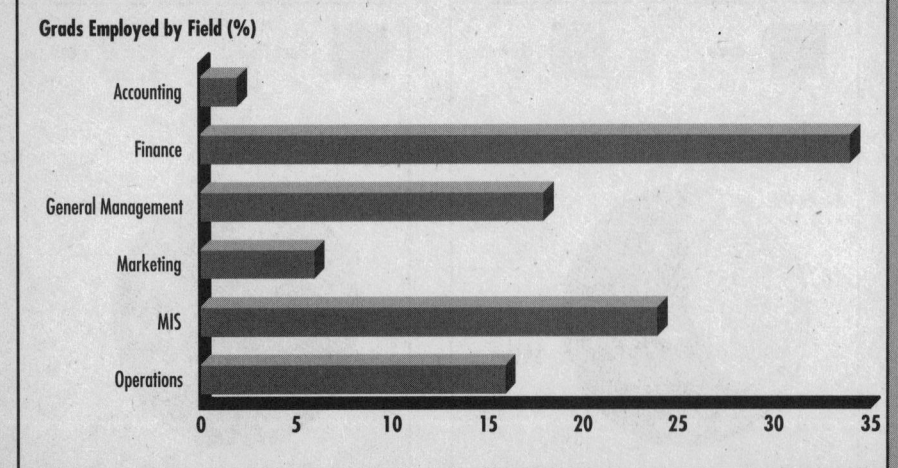

Grads Employed by Field (%)

Field	%
Accounting	~2
Finance	~34
General Management	~18
Marketing	~6
MIS	~24
Operations	~16

Placement Office Available? Yes
% Employed Within 3 Months: 98
Frequent Employers: AT Kearney, Accenture, Lam Research, PricewaterhouseCoopers, Radient Systems, Barclays Capital, AMVESCAP, Delta Airlines, Cintas Corp., United Parcel Service
Prominent Alumni: Jimmy Carter, former U.S. President; Sam Nunn, former U.S. Senator; Ivan Allen, Jr., former mayor of Atlanta and CEO of Ivan Allen Jr. Co.; David Dornan, president and CEO of AT&T; John Young, astronaut

GEORGIA SOUTHERN UNIVERSITY
College of Business Administration

Admissions Contact: Dr. John R. Diebolt, Associate Vice President, Graduate Studies
Address: PO Box 8113, Statesboro, GA 30460-8113
Admissions Phone: 912-681-5483 • Admissions Fax: 912-681-0740
Admissions E-mail: diebolt@gsvms2.cc.gasou.edu • Web Address: www2.gasou.edu/mba

Located in historic Statesboro, Georgia, GSU's College of Business has a high acceptance rate and a campus teeming with educational entertainment, ranging from a planetarium to a university museum and on to a botanic garden and wildlife education center. The GSU MBA provides working professionals with several part-time evening MBA program options, including the option to take classes at the Statesboro, Hinesville, Savannah, and Dublin campuses, depending on the program. GSU also offers a Web Exclusive Collaborative MBA, which began in the spring of 2002.

INSTITUTIONAL INFORMATION
Public/Private: Public
Evening Classes Available? Yes
Total Faculty: 50
% Faculty Female: 20
% Faculty Minority: 1
Student/Faculty Ratio: 7:1
Students in Parent Institution: 14,700

PROGRAMS
Degrees Offered: Master of Business (evening/part time, 2 years); Web-based Lockstep MBA (2 years); Weekend Lockstep MBA (2 years); Master of Accounting (2 years), rolling admission

STUDENT INFORMATION
Total Business Students: 313
% Full Time: 60
% Female: 47
% Minority: 10
% Out of State: 12
% International: 12
Average Age: 31

COMPUTER AND RESEARCH FACILITIES
Computer Facilities: Coastal Georgia Center computer labs (offsite teaching location)
Campuswide Network? Yes
% of MBA Classrooms Wired: 100
Internet Fee? No

EXPENSES/FINANCIAL AID
Annual Tuition (Resident/Nonresident): $1,702/$6,768
Tuition Per Credit (Resident/Nonresident): $94/$376
Room & Board (On/Off Campus): $4,154/$2,301
Books and Supplies: $950

ADMISSIONS INFORMATION
Electronic Application? Yes
Regular Application Deadline: 7/1
Regular Notification: 7/2
Deferment Available? Yes
Length of Deferment: 1 year
Non-fall Admissions? Yes
Non-fall Application Deadline(s): 11/15, 4/1
Transfer Students Accepted? Yes

Transfer Policy: No more than 6 semester hours of graduate credit may be transferred to a graduate program at GSU. Only grades of B or higher will be accepted for transfer.
Need-Blind Admissions? Yes
Number of Applications Received: 62
% of Applicants Accepted: 100
% Accepted Who Enrolled: 100
Average GPA: 3.0
GPA Range: 2.0-3.0
Average GMAT: 488
GMAT Range: 310-740
Average Years Experience: 3
Other Schools to Which Students Applied: Auburn University

INTERNATIONAL STUDENTS
TOEFL Required of International Students? Yes
Minimum TOEFL: 530

EMPLOYMENT INFORMATION
Placement Office Available? Yes
Frequent Employers: Gulfstream Aerospace Inc., Memorial Medical Hospital, Great Dane Trucking Inc., SunTrust Bank

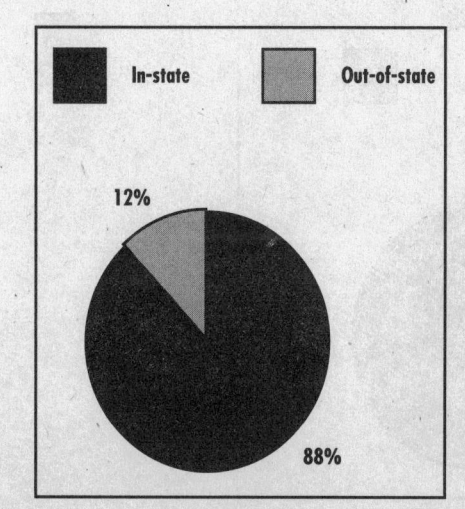

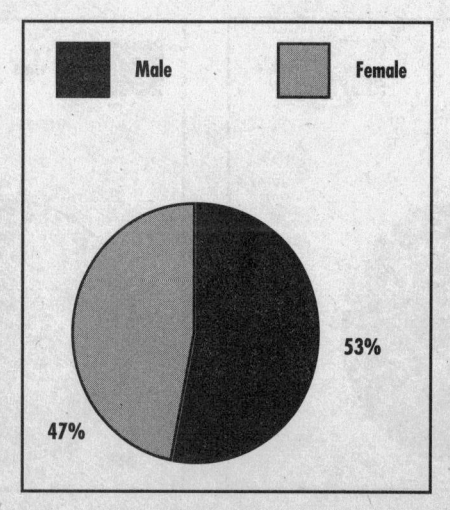

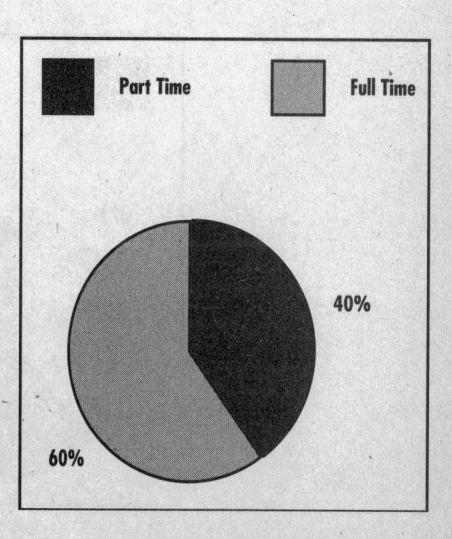

In-state / Out-of-state: 88% / 12%

Male / Female: 53% / 47%

Part Time / Full Time: 60% / 40%

GEORGIA STATE UNIVERSITY
J. Mack Robinson College of Business

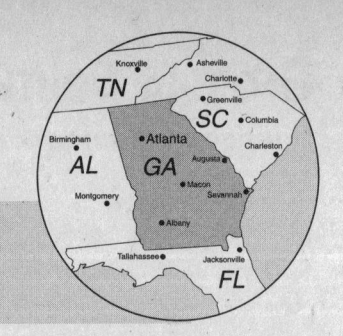

Admissions Contact: Master's Admissions Counselors, Master's Counseling Staff
Address: RCB Office of Academic Assistance, University Plaza, Atlanta, GA 30303-3083
Admissions Phone: 404-651-1913 • Admissions Fax: 404-651-0219
Admissions E-mail: rcb-oaa@gsu.edu • Web Address: robinson.gsu.edu

The J. Mack Robinson College of Business is located in downtown Atlanta, a metropolis surrounded by financial corporations and elite businesses such as Coca-Cola, Home Depot, UPS, and BellSouth. Several options are available for the prospective MBA applicant: the Flexible MBA for working professionals, the Executive MBA for professionals with 7 to 10 years of business experience, and the Global e-Management Executive MBA, designed for working professionals with a concentration in e-commerce and technology. The GSU MBA program is well known for the excellence of its curriculum, faculty, and diverse student body.

INSTITUTIONAL INFORMATION
Public/Private: Public
Evening Classes Available? Yes
Total Faculty: 206
% Faculty Part Time: 14
Students in Parent Institution: 24,300
Academic Calendar: Quarter

PROGRAMS
Degrees Offered: Master of Business Administration (MBA) (full time or part time, 85 credits, 12 months to 5 years); Master of Science (MS) (full time or part time, 75 credits, 12 months to 4 years); Master of Actuarial Science (MAS) (full time, 50 credits, 15 months to 2.5 years); Master of Professional Accountancy (MPA) (full time or part time, 45 credits, 12 months to 2.3 years); Master of Science in Real Estate (MS) (full time or part time, 60 credits, 12 months to 3 years); Master of Taxation (MTax) (full time or part time, 50 credits, 12 months to 2.5 years); Executive MBA (full time, 66 credits, 18 months); Concentrated MBA (full time, 80 credits, 12 months); Master of Science in Health Administration (MS) (full time or part time, 55 credits, 12 months to 2.8 years); Master of International Business (MIB) (full time or part time, 60 credits, 12 months to 3 years)

Joint Degrees: Master of Business Administration/Doctor of Jurisprudence (MBA/JD) (full time or part time, 95 credits, 12 months to 5 years); Master of Business Administration/Master of Health Administration (MBA/MHA) (full time, 110 credits, 2.8 to 6 years)
Study Abroad Options: France, Germany

STUDENT INFORMATION
Total Business Students: 2,625
% Female: 37
% Minority: 22
% International: 15
Average Age: 28

COMPUTER AND RESEARCH FACILITIES
Research Facilities: William R. Pullen Library plus 1 additional on-campus library; total holdings of 1,215,397 volumes, 1,973,138 microforms, 11,283 current periodical subscriptions; CD player(s) available for graduate student use; access to online bibliographic retrieval services
Campuswide Network? Yes
Internet Fee? No

ADMISSIONS INFORMATION
Application Fee: $25
Electronic Application? Yes
Regular Application Deadline: 5/1
Regular Notification: 6/15
Deferment Available? No
Non-fall Admissions? Yes
Non-fall Application Deadline(s): 10/1 spring, 2/1 summer
Transfer Students Accepted? No
Need-Blind Admissions? Yes
Number of Applications Received: 1,077
% of Applicants Accepted: 61
% Accepted Who Enrolled: 76
Average GPA: 3.1
Average GMAT: 590
Other Admissions Factors Considered: Letters of recommendation are permitted; work experience is recommended.

INTERNATIONAL STUDENTS
TOEFL Required of International Students? Yes
Minimum TOEFL: 580 (240 computer)

EMPLOYMENT INFORMATION
Placement Office Available? Yes
% Employed Within 3 Months: 85

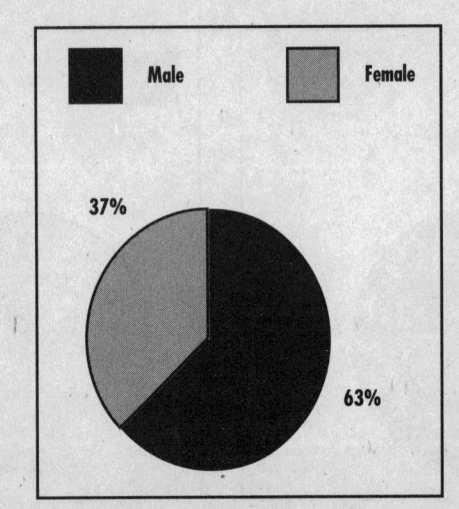

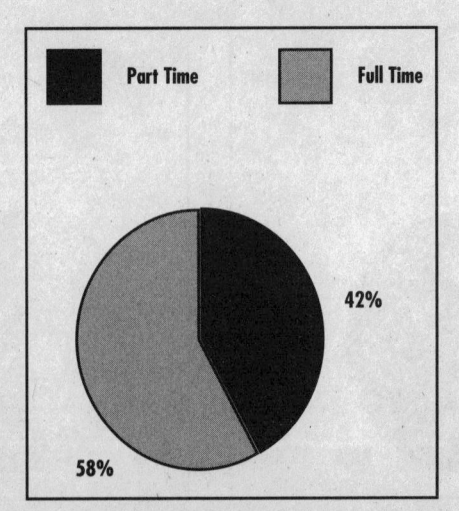

272 • COMPLETE BOOK OF BUSINESS SCHOOLS

GOLDEN GATE UNIVERSITY
Edward S. Ageno School of Business

Admissions Contact: Cherron Hoppes, Director of Admissions
Address: 536 Mission Street, San Francisco, CA 94105-2968
Admissions Phone: 415-442-7800 • Admissions Fax: 415-442-7807
Admissions E-mail: admissions@ggu.edu • Web Address: www.ggu.edu

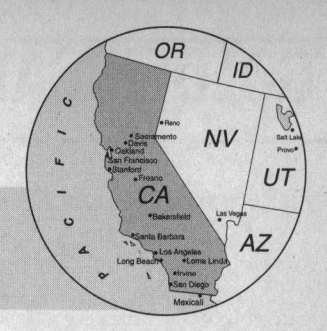

INSTITUTIONAL INFORMATION
Public/Private: Private
Evening Classes Available? Yes
Total Faculty: 400
% Faculty Female: 20
% Faculty Part Time: 80
Student/Faculty Ratio: 16:1

PROGRAMS
Degrees Offered: Executive Master of Business Administration (16 months); Executive Master of Public Administration (9 4-unit courses); Master of Accountancy (MAcc) (48 units); MA in Applied Psychology (36 units), with a concentration in Counseling; MA in Applied Psychology (36 units) with a concentration in Industrial/Organizational Management; MA in Psychology (48 units); Master of Business Administration (MBA) (30 units); MBA (48 units) with concentrations in Accounting, Electronic Business, Finance, Human Resource Management, Information Systems, International Business, Management, Marketing, Operations and Supply Chain Management, and Telecommunications; MS in Computer Information Systems (33 units); MS in Database Development and Administration (42 units); MS in Digital Security (30 units); MS in Electronic Business Systems and Technologies (33 units); MS in Enterprise Information Technology (48 units); MS in Finance (45 units); MS in Financial Planning (42 units); MS in Human Resource Management (33 units); MS in Integrated Marketing Communications (42 units) with a concentration in Public Relations; MS in Management of Technology (33 units); MS in Marketing (45 units); MS in Software Engineering (45 units); MS in Taxation (30 units); MS in Telecommunications Management (30 units); MS in Web Design and Development (36 units)
Joint Degrees: MBA/JD

COMPUTER AND RESEARCH FACILITIES
Campuswide Network? Yes
Internet Fee? No

ADMISSIONS INFORMATION
Application Fee: $55
Electronic Application? Yes
Regular Application Deadline: Rolling
Regular Notification: Rolling
Deferment Available? Yes
Length of Deferment: 1 year
Non-fall Admissions? Yes
Non-fall Application Deadline(s): Rolling
Transfer Students Accepted? Yes
Transfer Policy: May be able to transfer 6 units
Need-Blind Admissions? Yes
Number of Applications Received: 360
% of Applicants Accepted: 49
Other Schools to Which Students Applied: San Francisco State University, University of San Francisco, San Jose State University, California State University—Hayward, Santa Clara University, University of California—Berkeley

INTERNATIONAL STUDENTS
TOEFL Required of International Students? Yes
Minimum TOEFL: 550 (213 computer)

EMPLOYMENT INFORMATION
Placement Office Available? No
Frequent Employers: Arthur Andersen, Ernst & Young, Burr Pilger and Mayer, Franchise Tax Board
Prominent Alumni: Richard Belluzzo, president, Microsoft; George Christopher, former mayor, city and county of San Francisco; Richard Rosenberg, former CEO and chairman, Bank of America; Terence Henricks and Charles Precourt, NASA astronauts, Space Shuttle Columbia; Phillip Burton, former U.S. Representative, 8th District

GOLDEN GATE UNIVERSITY

THE UNIVERSITY AT A GLANCE
At Golden Gate University (GGU), students explore the global business environment and launch their futures in the graduate business program. Students are surrounded by motivated and experienced classmates who bring as much richness to the learning environment as the professors. Students apply what they learn before they graduate, and the skills they learn work for them as they pursue their studies.

STUDENTS
Students are one of GGU's finest resources. The students accepted into the program are mature and self-directed. They take their education seriously. Working students in the School of Business represent a wide variety of occupations and companies. They are often the nexus of an invaluable network of professional contacts for their classmates.

The School's student population is known for its diversity in culture, ethnicity, age, and work experience. Through working and studying with a variety of different people, students gain an edge in the international business world of today. This makes for an enriching classroom environment, where discussions are challenging and informative on many levels.

Approximately 16 percent of Golden Gate University students are from outside the United States. They come from countries in Asia, the Pacific Rim, and elsewhere throughout the world. Many international students bring with them working experience from their countries, creating a dynamic global learning environment.

ACADEMICS
The MBA program has three parts: the foundation; the advanced program, or core courses; and the area of concentration. The foundation and advanced programs focus on the fundamentals of business operation and management techniques, providing a general, but critical, knowledge of business functions. The concentration component of the MBA allows students to select an area of interest from eight different concentrations or select a general course of study.

The general MBA is also offered as a 16-month Executive MBA, designed for working managers with at least five years of management experience. This program is a cohort program, which means that a carefully selected group of students begins the program together, takes the same courses, and shares the same experiences.

The MBA degree is broad and inclusive. More specialized options are the Master of Science (MS) degrees. The goal of these degrees is to provide the students with a depth of expertise within their particular fields of specialization. These professional degree programs focus on the systems, processes, and administrative concerns relevant to the student's area of specialization. The MS degree is often referred to as a depth degree because all of the courses are in the student's field of study.

One of the features of the GGU graduate business program is the opportunity to choose from several areas of specialization either in the MBA program or in an MS degree program. Students can choose to specialize in accounting, e-commerce, finance, human resource management, information systems, international business, management, marketing, operations management, or telecommunications management. A general course of study is also available.

Another important feature is CyberCampus, the University's online program. Students at GGU can choose to complete an entire degree online from anywhere in the world or complement online classes with in-person classes. CyberCampus combines convenience with academic rigor in a highly interactive learning process.

Integral to the program is the hands-on, practical application of theoretical knowledge. The faculty is composed of teacher-practitioners and full-time professors. All members of the faculty have practiced in their fields and a significant number of adjunct faculty members bring current business trends and information directly from their work environments into the classroom. This creates a dynamic and uncommon teaching partnership.

In the rapidly changing business environment of today and tomorrow, some things will remain constant. Success continues to depend upon students' ability to quickly and accurately analyze the market and respond to fluctuations. Success depends upon their ability to recognize and seize opportunities. Everything GGU teaches is designed to impart to students these critical tools.

At GGU, global perspectives are always emphasized. The curriculum, frequently updated to reflect changing situations in the global marketplace, includes an increasing focus on international business and multinational companies. The University's international reputation brings many faculty members and students from other countries to its campuses.

At the Ageno School, students learn to work effectively in the global environment. The laboratory is the student's classroom, where working professionals bring the global strategies they encounter directly into class discussions. Students learn how to work in culturally diverse groups through team-based class projects. The skills and sensitivity learned in an internationally focused university environment enhance not only the business worldview and acumen, but also everyday life.

The Ageno School of Business curriculum is continuously updated by using feedback from students, alumni, and the business community. Advisory boards composed of corporate and industry executives provide valuable input in each management discipline that helps keep the curriculum current.

Since GGU primarily serves working adult students, classrooms become a network of professionals where learning is applied to day-to-day problems encountered in the workplace, and classmates become lifelong career contacts. Faculty members, most of whom come from the business community, also become excellent sources of career advice.

Edward S. Ageno School of Business

CAMPUS LIFE

Golden Gate University traces its origins to the founding of the San Francisco YMCA in 1853. It is a fully accredited, nonprofit, independent university. A pioneer in the case-study method of instruction, GGU is recognized for applied education for the professions. The University provides instruction for more than 6,000 students in California, at sites in San Francisco, Silicon Valley, Sacramento, Monterey, and Los Angeles. Programs are also offered in Seattle and online via CyberCampus.

The skilled staff in the Career Services Center works closely with students and employers. Students benefit from professional career counseling, job-search workshops and programs, computerized skills assessment, placement services, networking opportunities, and annual career fairs that feature on-campus recruiting by major corporations. In addition, students are encouraged to participate in internships as an integral part of their program, which allows for exploration of new career areas and opportunities to see the inside workings of a target company.

COSTS

Golden Gate University is one of the most affordable private universities in Northern California. Tuition includes all standard fees and is the same for California residents and nonresidents. Tuition is charged by the course (most courses are three units), and costs vary by program. Graduate tuition for 2001–2002 was $1,590 per course. Books, supplies, and living expenses are additional.

ADMISSIONS

Applicants to the master's program must have a bachelor's degree from a regionally accredited college or university in the United States or the equivalent from a recognized international institution. Students must also satisfy basic mathematics, writing, and computer proficiency requirements.

Applicants to the MBA program must submit an official score report from the GMAT, official transcripts from all schools previously attended, a statement of purpose, and a completed graduate application form along with the appropriate application fee (some applicants are not required to provide a GMAT score). Applicants whose native language is not English are required to meet the English language proficiency requirement by submitting TOEFL scores. University admissions information and online applications can be found on the Web at www.ggu.edu.

GGU accepts applications on a rolling admissions basis beginning up to one year prior to enrollment, and applications are reviewed as they become complete. International students should apply by the following dates: June 1 for fall trimester, October 1 for spring trimester, and February 1 for summer trimester. For more information, students should contact:

Office of Admissions
Golden Gate University
536 Mission Street
San Francisco, CA 94105-2968
Telephone: 415-442-7800 (San Francisco campus)
800-GGU-4YOU (toll-free for any campus within the U.S.)
Fax: 415-442-7807 (San Francisco campus)
E-mail: info@ggu.edu
World Wide Web: www.ggu.edu

Admissions Contact: Cherron Hoppes, Director of Admissions
Address: 536 Mission Street, San Francisco, CA 94105-2968
Admissions Phone: 415-442-7800 • Admissions Fax: 415-442-7807
Admissions E-mail: admissions@ggu.edu • Web Address: www.ggu.edu

GRAND VALLEY STATE UNIVERSITY
Seidman School of Business

Admissions Contact: Claudia Bajema, MBA Program Director
Address: 401 W. Fulton, Grand Rapids, MI 49504
Admissions Phone: 616-336-7400 • Admissions Fax: 616-336-7389
Admissions E-mail: go2gvmba@gvsu.edu • Web Address: www.gvsu.edu/ssb

The Seidman School of Business has a student body with an international population of 90 percent, giving the MBA program a global flavor. Classes are offered in four of the Greater Grand Rapids areas: Allendale, Muskegon, Downtown Grand Rapids, and Holland. Dual degrees are available with the MBA, including a Master of Science in Nursing (MSN). The unique MBA/MSN allows the student to fit the increasing need for managers who understand nursing and health care. Students may also obtain a JD/MBA via Grand Valley's partnership with nearby Michigan State University's Detroit College of Law.

INSTITUTIONAL INFORMATION
Public/Private: Public
Evening Classes Available? Yes
Total Faculty: 33
% Faculty Female: 3
% Faculty Minority: 3
% Faculty Part Time: 10
Student/Faculty Ratio: 22:1
Students in Parent Institution: 18,579
Academic Calendar: Semester

PROGRAMS
Degrees Offered: Master of Business Administration (MBA) (1.5 years), Master of Science in Taxation (MST) (1.5 years)
Joint Degrees: Master of Science in Nursing/Master of Business Administration (MSN/MBA) (4 years)
Academic Specialties: Operations, Accounting, Finance, Economics, Marketing, Organizational Behavior

STUDENT INFORMATION
Total Business Students: 311
% Female: 33
% Minority: 5
Average Age: 32

COMPUTER AND RESEARCH FACILITIES
Campuswide Network? Yes
% of MBA Classrooms Wired: 100
Internet Fee? No

EXPENSES/FINANCIAL AID
Annual Tuition (Resident/Nonresident): $3,700/$7,900
Tuition Per Credit (Resident/Nonresident): $202/$437
Room & Board (On/Off Campus): $5,000/$4,000
Books and Supplies: $1,500

ADMISSIONS INFORMATION
Application Fee: $20
Electronic Application? Yes
Early Decision Application Deadline: 1/1
Early Decision Notification: 1/1
Regular Application Deadline: 8/1
Regular Notification: Rolling
Deferment Available? Yes
Length of Deferment: 1 year
Non-fall Admissions? Yes
Non-fall Application Deadline(s): 8/1, 12/1, 4/1
Transfer Students Accepted? Yes
Transfer Policy: Students may transfer up to 9 credits with grades of B or better.
Need-Blind Admissions? Yes
Number of Applications Received: 179
% of Applicants Accepted: 82
% Accepted Who Enrolled: 88
Average GPA: 3.3
Average GMAT: 575
GMAT Range: 500-680
Average Years Experience: 10
Minority/Disadvantaged Student Recruitment Programs: Scholarship for African American and Hispanic students
Other Schools to Which Students Applied: Western Michigan University

INTERNATIONAL STUDENTS
TOEFL Required of International Students? Yes
Minimum TOEFL: 550

EMPLOYMENT INFORMATION

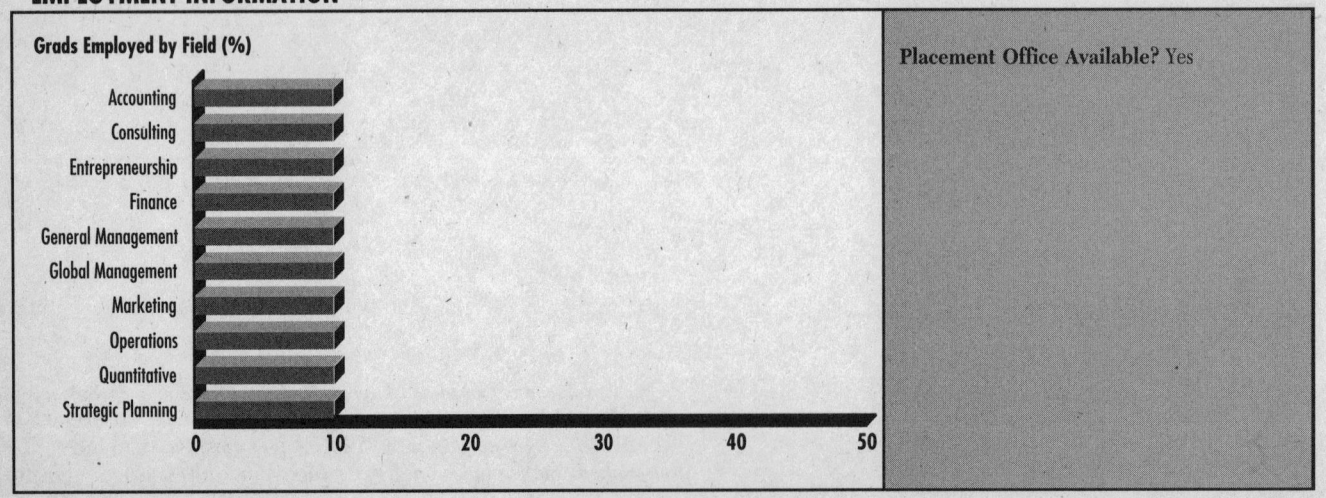

Grads Employed by Field (%)

Field	%
Accounting	10
Consulting	10
Entrepreneurship	10
Finance	10
General Management	10
Global Management	10
Marketing	10
Operations	10
Quantitative	10
Strategic Planning	10

Placement Office Available? Yes

HARVARD UNIVERSITY
Harvard Business School

Admissions Contact: Admissions Office
Address: Soldiers Field, Boston, MA 02163
Admissions Phone: 617-495-6127 • Admissions Fax: 617-496-9272
Admissions E-mail: admissions@hbs.edu • Web Address: www.hbs.edu

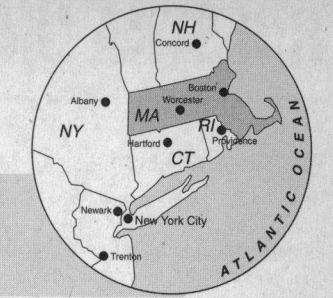

Harvard Business School is indisputably the nation's most famous business school and arguably its best as well. HBS boasts more CEO alums than any other program, a nationally renowned faculty that have penned more than 90 percent of the case materials used worldwide, uncommonly loyal and generous alumni, and a ridiculously enormous endowment to boot. HBS students also get an average 3.8 job offers each—the highest average of any b-school.

INSTITUTIONAL INFORMATION
Public/Private: Private
Evening Classes Available? No
Total Faculty: 224
% Faculty Female: 20
Academic Calendar: September-May

PROGRAMS
Degrees Offered: MBA (four 15-week terms), Doctor of BA (4 years)
Joint Degrees: Juris Doctor/MBA (4 years)
Academic Specialties: Entrepreneurship, General Management, Finance, Technology and Operations Management, Service Management

STUDENT INFORMATION
Total Business Students: 1,770
% Female: 32
% Minority: 19
% Out of State: 53
% International: 34

COMPUTER AND RESEARCH FACILITIES
Research Facilities: Research centers in Silicon Valley, Hong Kong, and Buenos Aires
Computer Facilities: 2 on-campus computer labs containing 150 machines; Harvard Business School's library has more than 600,000 volumes and 7,001 periodicals as well as numerous databases and other electronic resources
Campuswide Network? Yes
Computer Model Recommended: No
Internet Fee? No

EXPENSES/FINANCIAL AID
Annual Tuition: $28,500
% Receiving Financial Aid: 66

ADMISSIONS INFORMATION
Application Fee: $175
Electronic Application? Yes
Regular Application Deadline: 3/2
Regular Notification: Rolling
Deferment Available? No
Non-fall Admissions? No
Transfer Students Accepted? No
Need-Blind Admissions? Yes
Number of Applications Received: 8,124
Average GPA: 3.5
Average Years Experience: 4.5
Minority/Disadvantaged Student Recruitment Programs: Summer Venture in Management Program for minority college juniors, minority open-house events

INTERNATIONAL STUDENTS
TOEFL Required of International Students? Yes

EMPLOYMENT INFORMATION

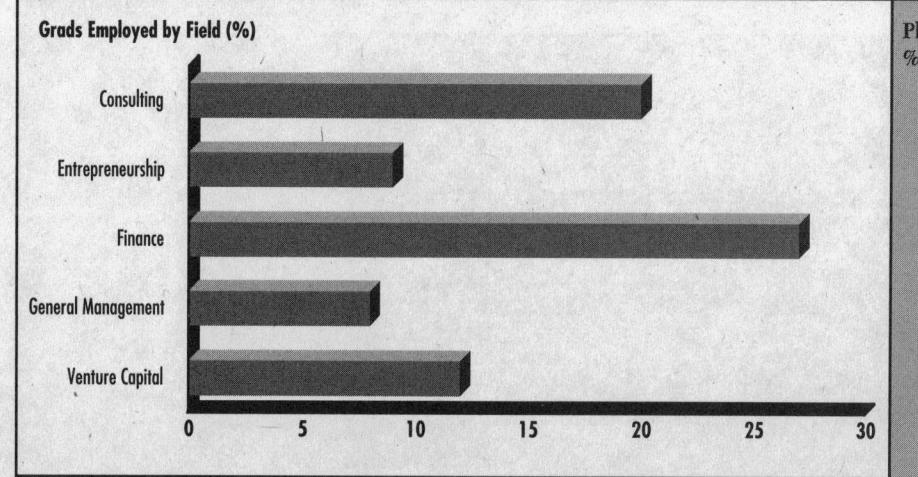

Grads Employed by Field (%)

Field	%
Consulting	20
Entrepreneurship	8
Finance	27
General Management	8
Venture Capital	12

Placement Office Available? Yes
% Employed Within 3 Months: 99

HOFSTRA UNIVERSITY

THE SCHOOL AT A GLANCE
Hofstra University is an independent, nonprofit, coed university. It was founded in 1935 and has an enrollment of 12,591 graduate, professional, and undergraduate students; 1,259 full-time matriculated graduate/professional students; and 2,403 part-time matriculated graduate/professional students. The graduate business unit is set in a suburban environment and is on a 4-1-4 calendar. Students are taught by 48 full-time faculty and 2 part-time faculty.

STUDENTS
Many students entering the Zarb MBA program have at least two years of full-time work experience. Eight states and 25 countries are represented among the student body. About 10 percent of the full-time students are members of minority groups, 31 percent are international, and 37 percent are women. Numerous organizations are open to MBA students, including the MBA Association, the Graduate Women in Business Organization, the Minority Student Organization, AIESEC, and the Organization of International Students. One of the most popular student organizations is the Hofstra Business Consulting Group. Membership in this group is by application and "hire" only, and the organization is run in a manner similar to external consulting practices. The Group provides students with hands-on consulting experience and remuneration for their services.

Team projects and the application of technology to business in a dynamically changing world are all critical to the Zarb MBA program, as is the program of internships and study abroad opportunities. The location of the University on Long Island and within a 40-minute commute from Manhattan provides extraordinary opportunities for employment, internships, and social and cultural activities.

ACADEMICS
The MBA program at the Zarb School reflects the actual environment in which contemporary managers must make decisions, often under conditions of uncertainty. Course work exposes students to innovative strategies, group interaction, and simulated business situations. The curriculum emphasizes a cross-functional approach to teaching. It also provides an experiential learning component within which students engage in business consulting and corporate internships as a means of refining their managerial skills. Students gain hands-on experience with technology, acquire a perspective on international business practices, and study environmental and ethical factors as they pertain to business, government, and not-for-profit organizations.

The MBA program is comprised of six tiers. The first is residency requirements, which establish facility with computer technology, information resources, and calculus. The second is the core competencies, which establish a basic functional understanding of business. The third is an advanced core, which provides students with a more sophisticated understanding of the functional areas of business and how they are applied across the organization. The fourth component is a cluster of courses called The Contemporary Business Environment, which is a fully interdisciplinary component of the program and includes coverage of communications skills and leadership, and an appreciation for and understanding of a truly diverse and global marketplace. The fifth component of the program enables students to focus on one of seven areas of specialization: accounting, business computer information systems, banking and finance, marketing, management, international business, or taxation. The sixth and final component is a project-based course, which may take the form of a consulting engagement, internship, research project, or management game.

A one-year, 42-credit program is available for students who hold a baccalaureate degree in business. The regular program is two years and 66 credits. Both part-time and full-time programs are available, as is a JD/MBA, which is offered in conjunction with the Hofstra School of Law. An Executive MBA program is also offered, through which full-time administrators who have a minimum of seven years' managerial experience can complete their degree on alternating Fridays and Saturdays over a period of 20 months.

Networking with the local, regional, and international business communities has traditionally been an important part of the Zarb School MBA experience, and that tradition continues. Linkages with these communities are manifested through a variety of means, including the Dean's Executive Council, which is composed of business leaders; an active alumni network, which includes senior officers at a number of multinational corporations; and the Dean's Lecture Series on topics of timely importance to the business community and to students.

In addition, Hofstra's Business Development Center, which houses the Merrill Lynch Center for the Study of International Financial Services and Markets, the Family Business Forum, the Long Island Venture Group, the Small Business Institute, and other entities, provides an additional platform for enhanced networking opportunities.

A series of conferences that address United States trade issues in the context of other countries throughout the world offers MBA students and alumni access to senior managers and faculty members from a host of organizations. Recent conferences organized to examine American trade relationships were co-sponsored by Erasmus/The Rotterdam School of Management (the Netherlands) and SDA Bocconi (Italy). Distinguished alumni of the School include its namesake, Frank G. Zarb, chairman, chief executive officer, and president of the National Association of Securities Dealers.

Frank G. Zarb School of Business

CAMPUS LIFE

Hofstra is located on a park-like, 240-acre campus in a suburban, residential area of Long Island, New York. The campus has been designated as an arboretum by the American Association of Botanical Gardens and Arboreta. It is within a 40-minute train ride of Manhattan. In addition to the enormous opportunities for cultural, professional, and social activities offered by virtue of Hofstra's location near New York City, the University hosts more than 500 cultural events each year. Athletic facilities include the only indoor Olympic-size pool on Long Island, the fully equipped Physical Fitness and Recreation Center, a 5,000-seat indoor arena, and a stadium that seats 15,000.

The Axinn Library serves the Zarb School of Business through a fully computerized system featuring LEXICAT, an online listing that includes more than 500,000 records of books, periodicals, microfilms, and media. Other services offered are Business Periodical on Disk, ABI/Inform, Newspaper Abstracts on Disk, and the Dow Jones News Retrieval Service. Extensive computer lab facilities that support a variety of software applications are available.

Microsoft Windows is the operating platform utilized most extensively by the Zarb School. Upon enrollment, every MBA student is immediately assigned an e-mail account, which may be utilized for Internet access. No additional charge is assessed for this service. The McGraw-Hill Technology Laboratory in the Axinn Library consolidates all of McGraw-Hill's proprietary software and databases into one facility available to students and faculty members for research and educational purposes.

The School subscribes to Standard & Poor's Compustat database, which contains company reports and market information for more than 8,000 companies as well as PDE Bank, Full Coverage, and Global Vantage Files. The Center for Research in Security Prices (CRSP) database, which includes daily and monthly price and volume information for more than 8,000 firms, is also available to MBA students. The main classroom building for the Zarb School is Breslin Hall, which contains rooms equipped for full computer demonstration and instruction. On-campus housing is readily available to MBA students in the form of apartments and dormitories.

A full complement of career development services is available to MBA students. These services include on- and off-campus recruiting, general job-search information (e.g., interviewing, resume preparation), a comprehensive interview and placement library, videotaping of interview simulations, computerized job banks, career planning seminars, and assistance with internships and part-time employment.

COSTS

Tuition is assessed on a per-credit basis, and is $495 for each credit for 2000–2001, with courses carrying three credits each. Hofstra is a private institution, so tuition is the same for residents and nonresidents of New York State. Room, board, books, and supplies bring the annual cost of an MBA education to approximately $24,000. Financial aid is available in the form of fellowships, which provide partial tuition credit, and graduate assistantship positions. There is no aid available for international students.

ADMISSIONS

Admission is selective. Candidates are required to complete the graduate application and all supporting forms and to submit two letters of recommendation, a resume, a statement of professional objectives, official transcripts from every college or university attended, and scores obtained on the Graduate Management Admission Test (GMAT). International students are also required to submit scores obtained on the TOEFL.

For the most recently admitted class, the middle 80 percent range of GMAT scores was from 430 to 610; the average undergraduate grade point average was 3.2 on a 4.0 scale. All credentials submitted in support of the application for admission are carefully considered in making the admission decision.

Hofstra subscribes to a rolling admissions policy, with suggested filing deadlines of May 1 for fall admission and November 1 for spring admission. Students planning to apply for financial aid should file both admission and financial aid forms no later than March 1 for fall and October 1 for spring. Candidates are generally advised of admission decisions no later than six weeks after the application is completed.

Admissions Contact: Associate Dean for Graduate Programs
Address: 134 Hofstra University, Hempstead, NY 11550
Admissions Phone: 516-463-5678 • Admissions Fax: 516-463-5268
Admissions E-mail: humba@hofstra.edu • Web Address: www.hofstra.edu/business

HOFSTRA UNIVERSITY
Frank G. Zarb School of Business

Admissions Contact: Associate Dean for Graduate Programs
Address: 134 Hofstra University, Hempstead, NY 11550
Admissions Phone: 516-463-5678 • Admissions Fax: 516-463-5268
Admissions E-mail: humba@hofstra.edu • Web Address: www.hofstra.edu/business

Students at Hofstra's "dynamic and intense" Zarb School of Business in parking-impaired Hempstead, New York (about 25 miles from New York City), are able to participate in consulting projects and engagements for companies ranging from small start-up shops to large, multinational firms. In addition, the faculty here receive great reviews for both brilliance and accessibility.

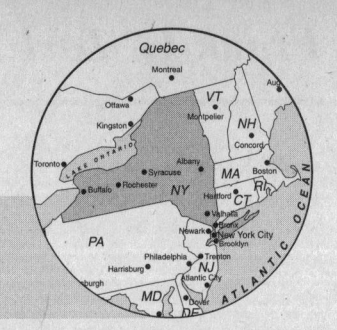

INSTITUTIONAL INFORMATION
Public/Private: Private
Evening Classes Available? Yes
Total Faculty: 80
% Faculty Female: 30
% Faculty Minority: 3
% Faculty Part Time: 2
Student/Faculty Ratio: 18:1
Students in Parent Institution: 13,000
Academic Calendar: Semester

PROGRAMS
Degrees Offered: MBA (1 to 2 years), MS (1 year), Executive MBA (21 months)
Joint Degrees: Juris Doctor/MBA (4 years)
Academic Specialties: Strengths of faculty and curriculum in Accounting, Finance, Marketing, International Business
Special Opportunities: Hofstra University Consulting Group, Association of Students of Economics and International Commerce, Merrill Lynch Center for the Study of International Financial Markets
Study Abroad Options: Finland, Korea, Netherlands, Sweden

STUDENT INFORMATION
Total Business Students: 600
% Full Time: 30
% Female: 39
% Minority: 7
% International: 24
Average Age: 26

COMPUTER AND RESEARCH FACILITIES
Research Facilities: Merrill Lynch Center for the Study of Financial Markets, Small Business Institute, Business Development Center
Computer Facilities: All of the databases and software proprietary to the McGraw-Hill companies (gift of Hofstra Alumus Joseph Dionne, former CEO of McGraw-Hill); GIS (Geographic Information System); C.V. Starr Hall, a newly opened state-of-the-art instructional facility that provides Internet access at every seat in each team room, community area, and classroom through ports installed at all seats
Campuswide Network? Yes
% of MBA Classrooms Wired: 35
Computer Model Recommended: Laptop
Internet Fee? No

EXPENSES/FINANCIAL AID
Annual Tuition: $16,000
Books and Supplies: $1,500
Average Grant: $6,000
Average Loan: $8,000
% Receiving Financial Aid: 55
% Receiving Aid Their First Year: 60

ADMISSIONS INFORMATION
Application Fee: $40
Electronic Application? Yes
Regular Application Deadline: 6/1
Regular Notification: Rolling
Deferment Available? Yes
Length of Deferment: 1 year
Non-fall Admissions? Yes
Non-fall Application Deadline(s): 11/1
Transfer Students Accepted? Yes
Transfer Policy: Maximum of 9 credits may be transferred
Need-Blind Admissions? Yes
Number of Applications Received: 400
% of Applicants Accepted: 59
% Accepted Who Enrolled: 37
Average GPA: 3.2
GPA Range: 2.8-3.4
Average GMAT: 570
GMAT Range: 480-630
Average Years Experience: 5
Other Admissions Factors Considered: Evidence of leadership, communications skills, analytical writing assessment of GMAT
Minority/Disadvantaged Student Recruitment Programs: Special consideration in the application process is given to minority students from disadvantaged backgrounds.
Other Schools to Which Students Applied: Baruch College (City University of New York), Columbia University, Fordham University, Rensselaer Polytechnic Institute

INTERNATIONAL STUDENTS
TOEFL Required of International Students? Yes
Minimum TOEFL: 600

EMPLOYMENT INFORMATION

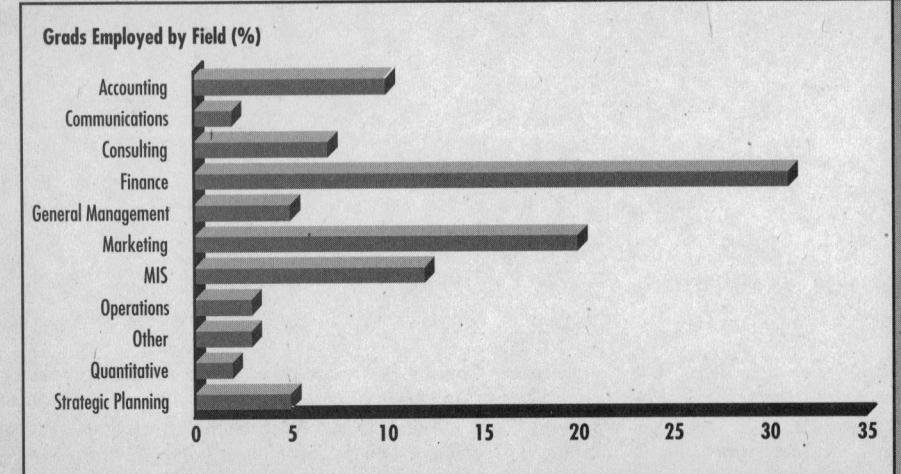

Grads Employed by Field (%):
- Accounting: ~10
- Communications: ~2
- Consulting: ~3
- Finance: ~31
- General Management: ~2
- Marketing: ~20
- MIS: ~12
- Operations: ~2
- Other: ~3
- Quantitative: ~2
- Strategic Planning: ~5

Placement Office Available? Yes
% Employed Within 3 Months: 95
Frequent Employers: Andersen Consulting, Fleet Bank, KPMG Peat Marwick, Goldman Sachs, CPC Bestfoods Baking, Deloitte & Touche, Johnson and Johnson
Prominent Alumni: Frank G. Zarb, chair & CEO, National Association of Securities Dealers; Salvatore Sodano, CEO, the American Stock Exchange

HONG KONG UNIVERSITY OF SCIENCE & TECHNOLOGY
School of Business & Management

Admissions Contact: Executive Officer
Address: Clearwater Bay, Kowloon, Hong Kong
Admissions Phone: 011-852-2358-7539 • Admissions Fax: 011-852-2705-9596
Admissions E-mail: mba@ust.hk • Web Address: www.bm.ust.hk/mba

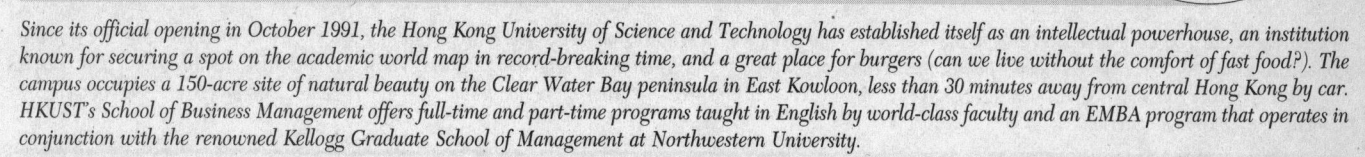

Since its official opening in October 1991, the Hong Kong University of Science and Technology has established itself as an intellectual powerhouse, an institution known for securing a spot on the academic world map in record-breaking time, and a great place for burgers (can we live without the comfort of fast food?). The campus occupies a 150-acre site of natural beauty on the Clear Water Bay peninsula in East Kowloon, less than 30 minutes away from central Hong Kong by car. HKUST's School of Business Management offers full-time and part-time programs taught in English by world-class faculty and an EMBA program that operates in conjunction with the renowned Kellogg Graduate School of Management at Northwestern University.

INSTITUTIONAL INFORMATION
Evening Classes Available? No
Total Faculty: 127
% Faculty Female: 7
% Faculty Part Time: 1
Student/Faculty Ratio: 19:1

PROGRAMS
Degrees Offered: MPhil (full time, 2 years); PhD (full time, 4 years); MS Investment Management (part time, 2 years); MS Information Systems Management (part time, 2 years); MS Electronic Commerce Management (part time, 16 months); Executive MBA (part time, 16 months)
Joint Degrees: MBA/MS Investment Management (part time, 3 years); MBA/MS Information Systems Management (part time, 3 years); MBA/MS Electronic Commerce Management (part time, 3 years)
Academic Specialties: The quality of research produced by scholars of the Business School is judged according to international standards. Our MBA program's model is based on top business schools in North America; adopting a pedagogical approach combines scientific and analytical methods with case studies. Students have the opportunity to concentrate in China Business. China-focused electives have been developed for this purpose. But more than course development, China Business and Management has been designated as a critical area for research and teaching at the HKUST Business School. Toward this end, the school has received strong support from the university as well as corporations in setting up supporting research centers such as the Hang Lung Center for Organization Research and the Shui-On Center for China Business and Management. In addition, Asia elements are built into individual courses and Asian cases and frequently used.
Study Abroad Options: Currently we have 37 MBA exchange partners from top business schools from China, Japan, India, Singapore, Israel, Australia, Denmark, Spain, France, United Kingdom, Germany, United States, and Canada.

STUDENT INFORMATION
Total Business Students: 196
% Female: 50
% International: 42
Average Age: 29

COMPUTER AND RESEARCH FACILITIES
Research Facilities: The Business School runs five research centers to promote research in specific areas as well as multi-disciplinary studies. These centers also serve as outreach centers for the co-ordination of faculty's involvement in consultancy or services to government, commercial or professional organizations.
Computer Facilities: The campus is operated with powerful servers to provide campus wide network services such as emails, network printing, World-Wide Web and an electronic notice board. There are three computer barns all equipped with advanced computer and printing facilities. In addition to the central computing facilities, the Business School runs specialized laboratories with advanced computing facilities to serve different course purposes. Moreover, a number of online business databases are available through the University Library.
Campuswide Network? Yes
Computer Model Recommended: No
Internet Fee? No

ADMISSIONS INFORMATION
Application Fee: $45
Electronic Application? No
Regular Application Deadline: 3/15
Regular Notification: 5/15
Length of Deferment: 1 year
Non-fall Admissions? No
Transfer Students Accepted? No
Need-Blind Admissions? No
Number of Applications Received: 718
% of Applicants Accepted: 36
% Accepted Who Enrolled: 76
Average Years Experience: 7

EMPLOYMENT INFORMATION

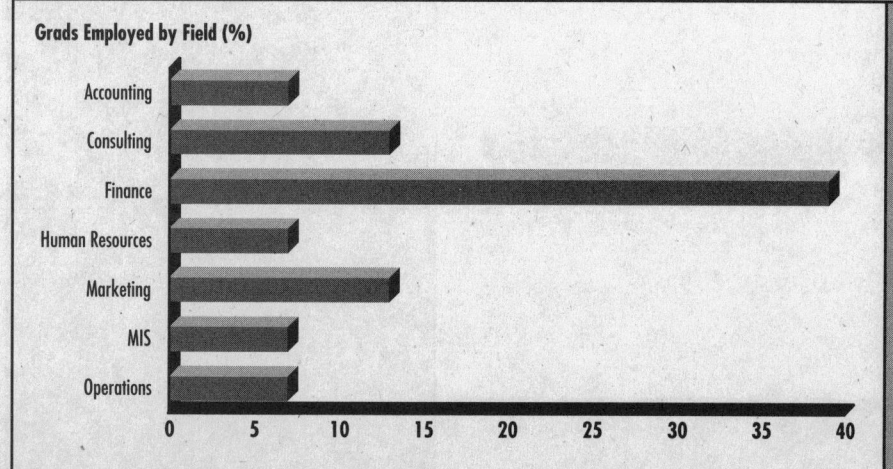

Grads Employed by Field (%)

Field	%
Accounting	~7
Consulting	~13
Finance	~40
Human Resources	~7
Marketing	~13
MIS	~7
Operations	~7

Placement Office Available? Yes
% Employed Within 3 Months: 92
Frequent Employers: UBS Warburg, Salomon Smith Barney, Morgan Stanley, Watson Wyatt, Federal Express, Citibank N.A., ExxonMobil, Coca-Cola, ABN Amro
Prominent Alumni: Estella Ng, senior VP of listing, HK Exchanges & Clearing Ltd.; Arthur Yuen, head of banking supervision, HK Monetary Authority; Terence Ma, director of business development and strategy, Motorola; Andy Yuen, VP and head of warrants, HK, Citibank N.A.; Pascale Brunet, VP, Morgan Stanley

HOWARD UNIVERSITY
School of Business

Admissions Contact: Donna Mason, Administrative Assistant
Address: 2600 Sixth Street NW, Washington, DC 20059
Admissions Phone: 202-806-1725 • Admissions Fax: 202-986-4435
Admissions E-mail: dmason@howard.edu • Web Address: www.bschool.howard.edu/mba

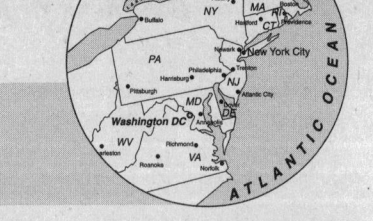

Where else would a highly accredited African American university reside but in Washington, D.C.? Here, Martin Luther King Jr. asked for something that Howard University is helping to deliver: freedom—that is, the freedom of education. The vision of the School of Business, Vision 21, is to "develop an agenda that reflects the needs of its core constituency (African Americans and people of color)." The MBA program offers a multitude of rigorous classes with professors who truly engage students with business material.

INSTITUTIONAL INFORMATION
Public/Private: Private
Evening Classes Available? Yes
Total Faculty: 37
% Faculty Female: 19
% Faculty Minority: 19
% Faculty Part Time: 13
Student/Faculty Ratio: 7:1
Academic Calendar: Semester

PROGRAMS
Degrees Offered: MBA (2 years full time, 4 years part time)
Joint Degrees: JD/MBA (4 years)
Academic Specialties: Accounting, Entrepreneurship, Finance, Finance/International Business/Insurance, Health Services Administration, Information Systems, International Business, Management (Human Resource Management), Marketing, Supply Chain Management

STUDENT INFORMATION
Total Business Students: 93
% Female: 47
% Minority: 50
% International: 50
Average Age: 26

COMPUTER AND RESEARCH FACILITIES
Research Facilities: Small Business Development Center, Center for Banking, Center for Entrepreneurship, Center for Supply Chain Management, Center for Technology, Center for Professional Development, 21st Advantage Program
Computer Facilities: Howard University I-Lab, School of Business Computer Lab, wireless access in all dorms, SPSS, SAS, Access 97/2000, Summer Enrichment Program, Federal Student Internship Program
Campuswide Network? Yes
% of MBA Classrooms Wired: 53
Computer Model Recommended: No
Internet Fee? No

EXPENSES/FINANCIAL AID
Annual Tuition: $11,900
Tuition Per Credit: $622
Room & Board (On/Off Campus): $9,000/$11,000
Books and Supplies: $1,000
Average Grant: $12,000
Average Loan: $15,216
% Receiving Financial Aid: 95
% Receiving Aid Their First Year: 95

ADMISSIONS INFORMATION
Application Fee: $45
Electronic Application? No
Regular Application Deadline: 4/30
Regular Notification: 5/31
Deferment Available? Yes
Length of Deferment: 2 semesters
Non-fall Admissions? Yes
Non-fall Application Deadline(s): 10/31 spring (part time)
Transfer Students Accepted? No
Need-Blind Admissions? No
Number of Applications Received: 207
% of Applicants Accepted: 29
% Accepted Who Enrolled: 61
Average GPA: 3.0
GPA Range: 2.8-3.3
Average GMAT: 539
GMAT Range: 470-610
Average Years Experience: 3
Other Admissions Factors Considered: GMAT scores, undergraduate GPA, work experience
Minority/Disadvantaged Student Recruitment Programs: Purchasing of mailing lists from GMAC, being a predominantly African American institution, recruiting at HBCU and the National Association for Hispanic MBA Association
Other Schools to Which Students Applied: George Mason University, Georgetown University, University of Maryland-College Park

INTERNATIONAL STUDENTS
TOEFL Required of International Students? Yes
Minimum TOEFL: 550 (213 computer)

EMPLOYMENT INFORMATION

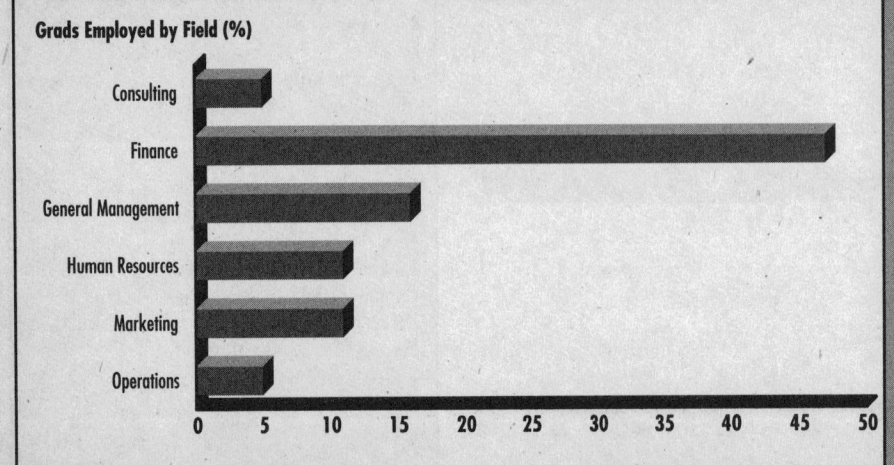

Grads Employed by Field (%)

Field	%
Consulting	~10
Finance	~47
General Management	~16
Human Resources	~10
Marketing	~10
Operations	~5

Placement Office Available? Yes
Frequent Employers: Bayer, JPMorgan Chase, IBM, PricewaterhouseCoopers, Lucent, United Technology Corp., Bank of America, General Motors, SC Johnson, Dow Chemical, Travelers Insurance, Philip Morris, Pfizer, KPMG, Texaco, Securities and Exchange Commission

Illinois Institute of Technology
Stuart Graduate School of Business

Admissions Contact: Lynn Miller, Associate Dean
Address: 565 W. Adams Street, Chicago, IL 60616
Admissions Phone: 312-906-6544 • Admissions Fax: 312-906-6549
Admissions E-mail: lmiller@stuart.iit.edu • Web Address: www.stuart.iit.edu

The Stuart MBA provides a "thorough grounding" in the major functional business areas, an understanding of technological and analytical approaches to business problem-solving, and a whole bunch of concentrations to choose from, all "within a holistic, global management perspective." Small classes allow for personal student-faculty and student-student interaction, increasing the ability to network and inherit valuable personal lessons from experienced faculty who "bring a practical point of view to management issues."

INSTITUTIONAL INFORMATION
Public/Private: Private
Evening Classes Available? Yes
Total Faculty: 37
% Faculty Female: 8
% Faculty Part Time: 51
Student/Faculty Ratio: 15:1
Students in Parent Institution: 6,100
Academic Calendar: Quarter

PROGRAMS
Degrees Offered: MBA (72 credits, 12 to 20 months); Fast Track MBA (58 credits, 12 to 15 months); MS Environmental Management (50 credits, 12 to 15 months); MS Finance (50 credits, 12 to 15 months); MS Marketing Communication (50 credits, 12 to 15 months); PhD in Management (94 credits, 3 to 6 years)
Joint Degrees: JD/MBA (4 to 6 years); MBA/MS (2 to 3 years); JD/MS Environmental Management (3 to 5 years)
Academic Specialties: Technology management, integrated marketing communication, financial markets, e-business, environmental management, quality management, entrepreneurial management, cross-functional teamwork, mathematical and computer modeling, strategic marketing planning, project financing, the impacts of technology on business strategy, finance, information management, international business, management science, marketing

STUDENT INFORMATION
Total Business Students: 284
% Female: 24
% Minority: 5
% International: 73
Average Age: 30

COMPUTER AND RESEARCH FACILITIES
Research Facilities: Center for Research on the Impacts of Information Systems, Center for Research on Industrial Strategy and Policy, Center for Sustainable Enterprise, Center for the Management of Medical Technology
Computer Facilities: IIT was ranked number 27 in *Yahoo! Internet Life* magazine's 100 most wired colleges. Labs include the Quantitative Research Lab (QRL), a state-of-the-art interactive teaching lab with real-time market feeds, financial industry databases, a simulated trading environment, software in areas such as enterprise resource planning, marketing simulation, and simulated manufacturing environments. E-commerce lab is equipped with leading-edge software for developing e-commerce transactions and marketspaces.
Campuswide Network? Yes
Computer Model Recommended: No
Internet Fee? No

EXPENSES/FINANCIAL AID
Annual Tuition: $19,000
Tuition Per Credit: $585
Room & Board (On/Off Campus): $6,631/$13,866
Books and Supplies: $890
Average Grant: $10,000
Average Loan: $17,843
% Receiving Financial Aid: 32
% Receiving Aid Their First Year: 39

ADMISSIONS INFORMATION
Application Fee: $50
Electronic Application? Yes
Regular Application Deadline: 6/15
Regular Notification: Rolling
Length of Deferment: 1 year
Non-fall Admissions? Yes
Non-fall Application Deadline(s): 10/1 winter, 1/5 spring, 4/15 summer
Transfer Policy: May transfer up to 4 core courses and 2 elective courses with advisor approval
Need-Blind Admissions? Yes
Number of Applications Received: 316
% of Applicants Accepted: 59
% Accepted Who Enrolled: 47
Average GPA: 3.0
Average GMAT: 568
GMAT Range: 490-650
Average Years Experience: 5

INTERNATIONAL STUDENTS
TOEFL Required of International Students? Yes
Minimum TOEFL: 550 (213 computer)

EMPLOYMENT INFORMATION

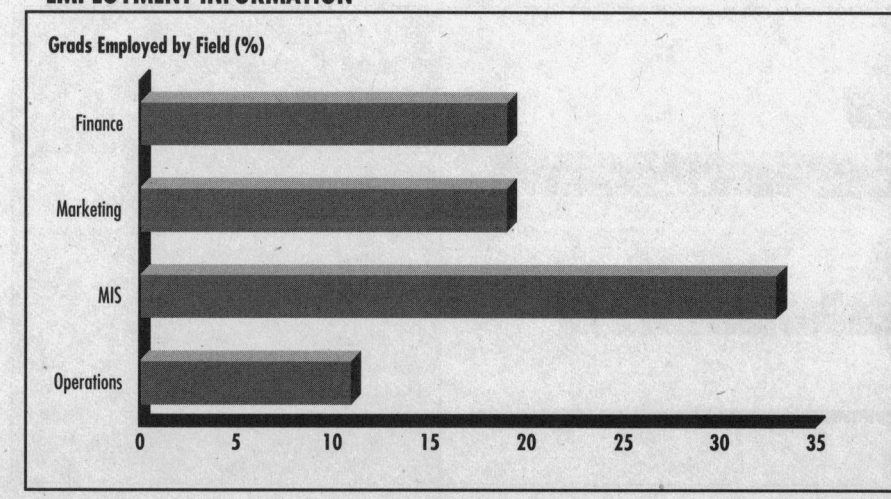

Grads Employed by Field (%)

Field	%
Finance	~19
Marketing	~19
MIS	~34
Operations	~11

Placement Office Available? Yes
% Employed Within 3 Months: 45
Frequent Employers: Bank One, Northern Trust, Bank of America, ABN Amro, Lucent Technologies, JP Morgan, Navistar, Zenith, Vankampen, Environmental Protection Agency, Reuters, Cantor Fitzgerald, McLagan Partners, Motorola, Akamal Trading
Prominent Alumni: Robert Growney, president and COO, Motorola; John Calamos, president, CIO, and founder, Calamos Asset Management; Ajva Taulananda, president, TelecomASIA Corp.; Carl Spetzler, chairman and founder, Strategic Decisions Group; Les Jezuit, president, Quixote Corp.

INDIANA UNIVERSITY
Kelley School of Business

Admissions Contact: James Holmen, Director of Admissions and Financial Aid
Address: 1309 East Tenth Street, Bloomington, IN 47405
Admissions Phone: 812-855-8006 • Admissions Fax: 812-855-9039
Admissions E-mail: mbaoffice@indiana.edu • Web Address: www.kelley.indiana.edu/mba

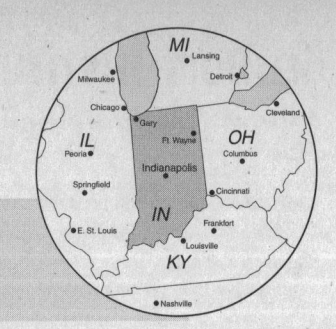

Students at Indiana University's Kelley School of Business are well prepared "to analyze business issues from a broad perspective," and there is a strong emphasis on teamwork and collaborative learning. Professors at IU are "really absorbed," and the deans "make every effort to ensure that the business school is run like a small business" ("not a large bureaucracy").

INSTITUTIONAL INFORMATION
Public/Private: Public
Evening Classes Available? No
Total Faculty: 210
% Faculty Female: 25
% Faculty Minority: 10
% Faculty Part Time: 17
Student/Faculty Ratio: 24:1
Students in Parent Institution: 37,000
Academic Calendar: Semester

PROGRAMS
Degrees Offered: MBA (21 months)
Joint Degrees: MBA/JD (4 years) MBA/MS (3 years) (area studies)
Academic Specialties: Finance and marketing are the most popular majors. Integrated approach gives the curriculum an applied force. Faculty emphasize teamwork and skill development.
Study Abroad Options: Australia, Denmark, France, Spain, Germany, Switzerland, Hong Kong, Mexico, England, Singapore, Norway, Chile, Italy, Belgium, Nurnberg, South Africa, South Korea, Austria

STUDENT INFORMATION
Total Business Students: 596
% Full Time: 100
% Female: 21
% Minority: 9
% Out of State: 84
% International: 35
Average Age: 28

COMPUTER AND RESEARCH FACILITIES
Research Facilities: Facilities in Leadership Development, Entrepreneurship and Innovation, Retailing, International Business Education and Research, Real Estate Studies, Global Business Information, Urban Transportation, Econometric Model Research
Computer Facilities: Private lab has notebook computer network connections and workstations. More than 500 network connections are available in classrooms and common areas.
Campuswide Network? Yes
% of MBA Classrooms Wired: 100
Computer Model Recommended: Laptop
Internet Fee? No

EXPENSES/FINANCIAL AID
Annual Tuition (Resident/Nonresident): $10,004/$20,007
Room & Board: $6,690
Books and Supplies: $4,854
Average Grant: $9,305
Average Loan: $12,885
% Receiving Financial Aid: 69
% Receiving Aid Their First Year: 73

ADMISSIONS INFORMATION
Application Fee: $75
Electronic Application? Yes
Regular Application Deadline: 3/1
Regular Notification: 4/30
Length of Deferment: 1 year
Non-fall Admissions? No
Transfer Students Accepted? No
Need-Blind Admissions? Yes
Number of Applications Received: 2,364
% of Applicants Accepted: 25
% Accepted Who Enrolled: 50
Average GPA: 3.3
GPA Range: 3.0-3.5
Average GMAT: 651
GMAT Range: 610-690
Average Years Experience: 5
Minority/Disadvantaged Student Recruitment Programs: Member of the Consortium for Graduate Study in Management
Other Schools to Which Students Applied: University of Michigan, University of North Carolina—Chapel Hill, University of Texas—Austin, Vanderbilt, Washington University in St. Louis

INTERNATIONAL STUDENTS
TOEFL Required of International Students? Yes
Minimum TOEFL: 580 (237 computer)

EMPLOYMENT INFORMATION

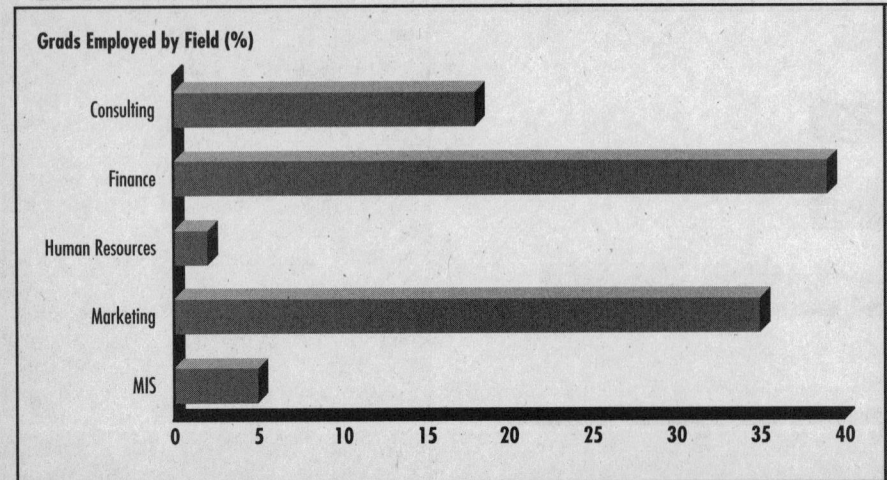

Grads Employed by Field (%)

Field	%
Consulting	18
Finance	40
Human Resources	2
Marketing	35
MIS	5

Placement Office Available? Yes
% Employed Within 3 Months: 86
Frequent Employers: Deloitte Consulting, Eli Lilly, Procter & Gamble, American Airlines, PricewaterhouseCoopers, Accenture, Samsung, Bank of America Securities, Cisco Systems, Citibank, Samsung, Sears, Ford Motor Co., Brown & Williamson, IBM, Bristol-Myers Squibb
Prominent Alumni: John T. Chambers (MBA '76), president and CEO, Cisco Systems; Ronald W. Dollens (MBA '72), president and CEO, Guidant Corporation; Jeff M. Fettig (MBA '81), president and COO, Whirlpool Corporation; Harold A. Poling (MBA '51), retired chairman and CEO, Ford Motor Co.; Frank P. Popoff (MBA '59), retired chairman and CEO, Dow Chemical

INSEAD
The European Institute of Business Administration

Admissions Contact: MBA Information Office
Address: Boulevard de Contstance, Fontainbleau, France 77305
Admissions E-mail: mbainfo@insead.fr
Web Address: www.insead.fr/mba

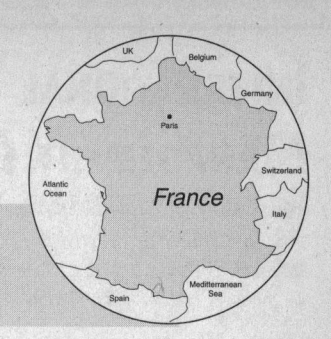

INSTITUTIONAL INFORMATION
Public/Private: Private
Evening Classes Available? No
Total Faculty: 166
% Faculty Female: 13
% Faculty Part Time: 35
Students in Parent Institution: 601

PROGRAMS
Degrees Offered: MBA (average 10 months), PhD (average 4 years)
Academic Specialties: General Management; intensive, 10-month MBA programs; truly international, and no dominant culture; teaching and reasearch are given equal weight, so pedagogical material is always realevant and up to date
Study Abroad Options: For 89 percent of our students, France is a foreign country and INSEAD is "study abroad." In addition, INSEAD will open a campus in Singapore in January 2000, and there will be exchange possibilities with the campus in Fontainbleau.

STUDENT INFORMATION
Total Business Students: 601
% Full Time: 100
% Female: 15
% International: 89
Average Age: 29

COMPUTER AND RESEARCH FACILITIES
Research Facilities: INSEAD Euro Asia Centre is a knowledge, information, and communication resource, created to enhance understanding among all communities doing business in Asia. The INSEAD EAC houses a dedicated library and documentation center. CEDEP is an independent center in partnership with INSEAD. The European Centre for Continuing Education is a consortium formed in 1971 by 6 European companies. Today, CEDEP has 23 member companies in the industry and service sector.
Computer Facilities: INSEAD (Fontainbleau): 150 PCs available for student use. INSEAD (Singapore) starting January 2000: 10 PCs will initially be available for 45 participants. Users on both campuses are connected to a messaging system for use on and off campus, and access to the Internet and Intranet is available through Netscape. Access to the main online information providers (Reviers, MAID, Datastream, and Dialog)
Campuswide Network? No
Computer Proficiency Required? No
Special Purchasing Agreements? No

EXPENSES/FINANCIAL AID
Annual Tuition: $25,500
Room & Board (On Campus): $16,600
Average Grant: $10,000
% Receiving Aid Their First Year: 50

ADMISSIONS INFORMATION
Application Fee: $110
Electronic Application? Yes
Regular Application Deadline: Rolling
Regular Notification: Rolling
Deferment Available? Yes
Length of Deferment: 1 year
Non-fall Admissions? Yes
Non-fall Application Deadline(s): Rolling
Transfer Students Accepted? No
Need-Blind Admissions? Yes
Average GMAT: 677
GMAT Range: 550-800
Other Admissions Factors Considered: Computer experience
Minority/Disadvantaged Student Recruitment Programs: Everyone is a "minority," because there are 56 nationalities in attendance. The largest representation makes up only 12% of the student body.

INTERNATIONAL STUDENTS
TOEFL Required of International Students? Yes
Minimum TOEFL: 620

EMPLOYMENT INFORMATION

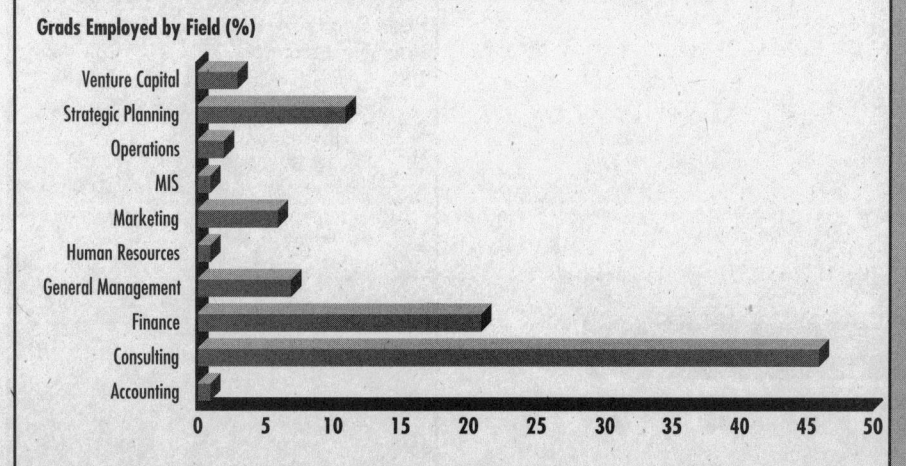

Grads Employed by Field (%)

Field	%
Venture Capital	~2
Strategic Planning	~11
Operations	~6
MIS	~1
Marketing	~5
Human Resources	~1
General Management	~7
Finance	~21
Consulting	~46
Accounting	~1

Placement Office Available? Yes
% Employed Within 6 Months: 93
Frequent Employers: McKinsey, Andersen, Booz-Allen & Hamilton, Credit Suisse, First Boston, Goldman Sachs, Morgan Stanley, Bertelsman, Pearson, F. Hoffman, La Roche
Prominent Alumni: Lord David Simon of Highbury, minister for trade and competitiveness, Department of Trade and Industry, London; Ms. Helen A. Alexander, chief executive, The Economist Group, London; Mr. Lindsay Owen-Jones, CEO L'Oreal, Paris

International Institute for Management Development

Admissions Contact: MBA Marketing Officer
Address: Chemin de Bellerive 23, PO Box 915, 1001 Lausanne, Switzerland CH-1001
Admissions Phone: 011-41-21-6180298 • Admissions Fax: 011-41-21-6180615
Admissions E-mail: mbainfo@imd.ch • Web Address: www.imd.ch/mba

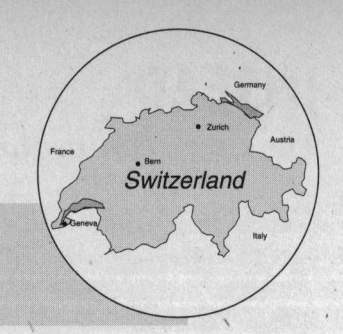

INSTITUTIONAL INFORMATION
Evening Classes Available? No
Total Faculty: 50
Student/Faculty Ratio: 2:1
Academic Calendar: January-December

PROGRAMS
Degrees Offered: MBA in General Management (11 months), Executive MBA (16 months to 3 years)
Academic Specialties: Faculty is experienced and international with a strong sense of practical reality. Members remain close to management practice through their field-based research and consulting work. The curriculum is integrative, intensive, and international.
Special Opportunities: Executive Development Program

STUDENT INFORMATION
Total Business Students: 85
% Full Time: 100
% Female: 20
% International: 97
Average Age: 31

COMPUTER AND RESEARCH FACILITIES
Computer Facilities: Information center on campus provides access to online services including databases, CD-ROMs, and catologs.
Campuswide Network? Yes
Internet Fee? No

EXPENSES/FINANCIAL AID
Annual Tuition: $45,000
Average Grant: $28,000
Average Loan: $31,000

ADMISSIONS INFORMATION
Application Fee: $150
Electronic Application? Yes
Regular Application Deadline: Rolling
Deferment Available? No
Non-fall Admissions? Yes
Non-fall Application Deadline(s): 2/1, 4/1, 6/1, 8/1, 9/1
Transfer Students Accepted? No
Need-Blind Admissions? Yes
Number of Applications Received: 800
% of Applicants Accepted: 11
% Accepted Who Enrolled: 100
Average GMAT: 660
Average Years Experience: 5
Other Admissions Factors Considered: Professional achievement, intellectual ability, leadership potential, international outlook

EMPLOYMENT INFORMATION

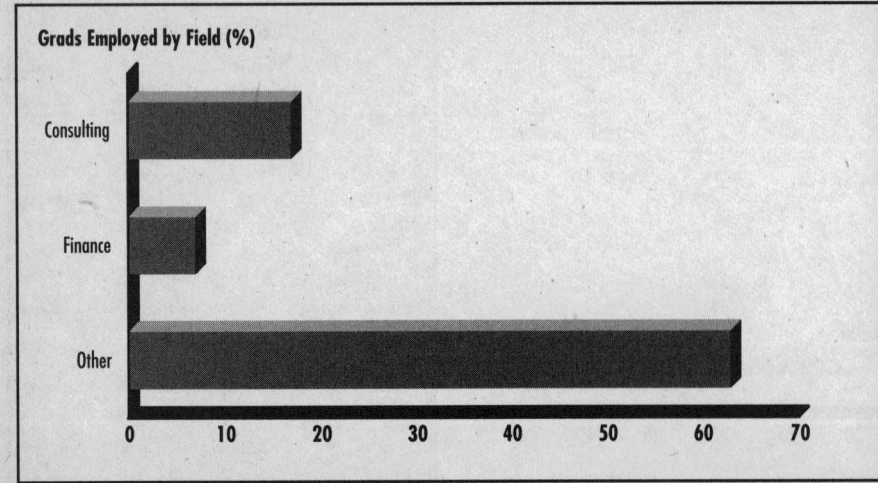

Grads Employed by Field (%)
- Consulting: ~17
- Finance: ~7
- Other: ~63

Placement Office Available? Yes
Frequent Employers: Mckinsey & Co, Nestle, UBS, Fidelity Investrient, Hilt AG

IOWA STATE UNIVERSITY
College of Business

Admissions Contact: Ronald J. Ackerman, Director of Graduate Admissions
Address: 218 Carver Hall, Ames, IA 50011
Admissions Phone: 515-294-8118 • Admissions Fax: 515-294-2446
Admissions E-mail: busgrad@iastate.edu • Web Address: www.bus.iastate.edu/grad

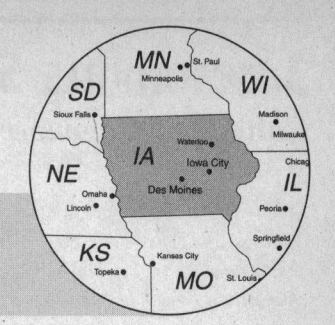

*Iowa State's Saturday MBA program, offering MBA classes on the weekends in Ames, Iowa, is an excellent option for busy working professionals who wish to maintain their full-time careers. ISU also offers employed professionals in the greater Des Moines area the option of earning their MBA in the **evenings**, right after work. These evening classes are held in downtown Des Moines, the financial aorta of Iowa. While researching schools, don't forget to check out the cartoon history of Iowa on the ISU website.*

INSTITUTIONAL INFORMATION
Public/Private: Public
Evening Classes Available? Yes
Total Faculty: 65
% Faculty Female: 9
% Faculty Minority: 12
% Faculty Part Time: 9
Student/Faculty Ratio: 4:1
Students in Parent Institution: 27,823
Academic Calendar: Semester

PROGRAMS
Degrees Offered: MBA (48 credits, 2 years); Saturday MBA (part time, 48 credits, 31 months); Evening MBA in Des Moines (part time, 48 credits, 31 months); Master of Accounting (32 credits, 1 to 3 years); MS in Information Assurance (30 credits, 1 to 2 years); MS in Information Systems (32 credits, 1 to 2 years); MS in Industrial Relations (30 to 36 credits, 1 to 3 years)
Joint Degrees: MBA/MS in Statistics (72 credits, 3 years); MBA/MS in Community and Regional Planning (73 credits, 3 years)
Academic Specialties: Accounting, Agribusiness, Finance, Human Resources, Information Systems, Marketing, Production and Operations, Transportation and Logistics
Special Opportunities: International MBA Consortium, Asolo, Italy; Summer Internship Programs in the United Kingdom and Australia; European Summer School for Advanced Management; Asian Intensive School for Advanced Management
Study Abroad Options: Italy, Mexico, Scotland, Denmark, Malaysia

STUDENT INFORMATION
Total Business Students: 254
% Full Time: 29
% Female: 30
% Minority: 8
% Out of State: 18
% International: 48
Average Age: 27

COMPUTER AND RESEARCH FACILITIES
Research Facilities: Pappajohn Center for Entrepreneurship, Murray G. Bacon Center for Ethics in Business, Center for Transportation Research and Education
Computer Facilities: Durham Computation Center, College of Business, 2 computer labs
Campuswide Network? Yes
Internet Fee? No

EXPENSES/FINANCIAL AID
Annual Tuition (Resident/Nonresident): $3,702/$10,898
Tuition Per Credit (Resident/Nonresident): $268/$668
Room & Board (On/Off Campus): $4,400/$5,000
Books and Supplies: $1,800
% Receiving Financial Aid: 50
% Receiving Aid Their First Year: 50

ADMISSIONS INFORMATION
Application Fee: $20
Electronic Application? Yes
Regular Application Deadline: Rolling
Regular Notification: Rolling
Deferment Available? Yes
Length of Deferment: 1 year
Non-fall Admissions? No
Transfer Students Accepted? No
Need-Blind Admissions? Yes
Number of Applications Received: 132
% of Applicants Accepted: 42
% Accepted Who Enrolled: 50
Average GPA: 3.3
Average GMAT: 591
Average Years Experience: 3
Minority/Disadvantaged Student Recruitment Programs: Graduate Minority Assistantship Program

INTERNATIONAL STUDENTS
TOEFL Required of International Students? Yes
Minimum TOEFL: 570 (230 computer)

EMPLOYMENT INFORMATION

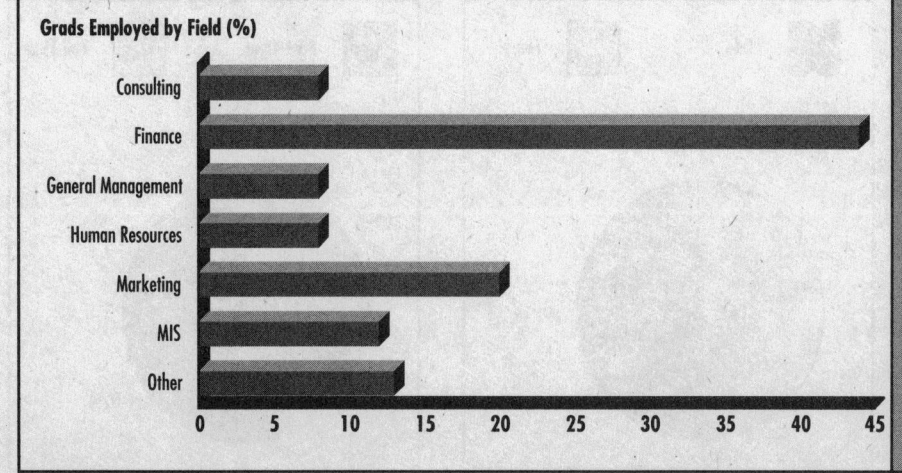

Grads Employed by Field (%)

Field	%
Consulting	7
Finance	44
General Management	7
Human Resources	5
Marketing	20
MIS	13
Other	13

Placement Office Available? Yes
% Employed Within 3 Months: 81
Frequent Employers: AmerUs Group, Andersen Consulting, Cap Gemini America Inc., Deere & Co., Dynegy Inc., Ecolab Inc., Enron, Equitable Life of Iowa, Ernst & Young, Hewitt Associates, Norwest Bank/Wells Fargo, Principal Financial Group, Sprint, Union Pacific Corporation, U.S. Gypsum Company, Utilicorp United/Aquila Energy

JACKSONVILLE STATE UNIVERSITY
College of Commerce and Business Administration

Admissions Contact: Kathy Cambron, Acting Registrar
Address: 700 Pelham Road N, Jacksonville, AL 36265
Admissions Phone: 256-782-5400 • Admissions Fax: 256-782-5121
Admissions E-mail: kcambron@jsucc.jsu.edu • Web Address: www.jsu.edu

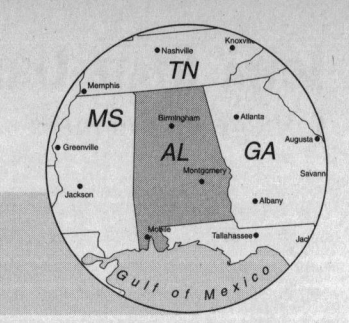

Located at the foothills of the Appalachians, about an hour and a half northeast of Birmingham and two hours west of Atlanta, JSU offers a general MBA program with good accessibility to the faculty and absolutely no teaching assistants. The school is very open about its admissions policies, offering prospective students two different formulas that they can meet to receive automatic, unconditional admission.

INSTITUTIONAL INFORMATION
Public/Private: Public
Evening Classes Available? Yes
Total Faculty: 19
% Faculty Female: 33
Student/Faculty Ratio: 15:1
Students in Parent Institution: 8,400

PROGRAMS
Degrees Offered: MBA (1.5 years), MBA with concentration in Accounting (2 years)

STUDENT INFORMATION
Total Business Students: 100
% Full Time: 30
% Female: 50
% Minority: 10
% Out of State: 10
% International: 75
Average Age: 37

COMPUTER AND RESEARCH FACILITIES
Campuswide Network? Yes
% of MBA Classrooms Wired: 20
Internet Fee? No

EXPENSES/FINANCIAL AID
Annual Tuition (Resident/Nonresident): $2,940/$5,880
Tuition Per Credit (Resident/Nonresident): $147/$294
Books and Supplies: $1,500
Average Grant: $1,000
Average Loan: $10,000

ADMISSIONS INFORMATION
Application Fee: $20
Electronic Application? Yes
Early Decision Application Deadline: 3 months prior to term
Early Decision Notification: 5/30
Regular Application Deadline: 6/30
Regular Notification: 7/31
Deferment Available? No
Non-fall Admissions? Yes
Non-fall Application Deadline(s): 3 months prior to term

Transfer Students Accepted? Yes
Transfer Policy: 6 hours of approved courses with grade of A or B
Need-Blind Admissions? Yes
Number of Applications Received: 40
% of Applicants Accepted: 80
% Accepted Who Enrolled: 78
Average GPA: 2.7
GPA Range: 2.2-4.0
Average GMAT: 470
GMAT Range: 250-650
Average Years Experience: 5
Other Admissions Factors Considered: A formula score of 200 x undergraduate GPA + GMAT must be at least 950 for unconditional admission to the MBA program.

INTERNATIONAL STUDENTS
TOEFL Required of International Students? Yes
Minimum TOEFL: 500

EMPLOYMENT INFORMATION
Placement Office Available? Yes

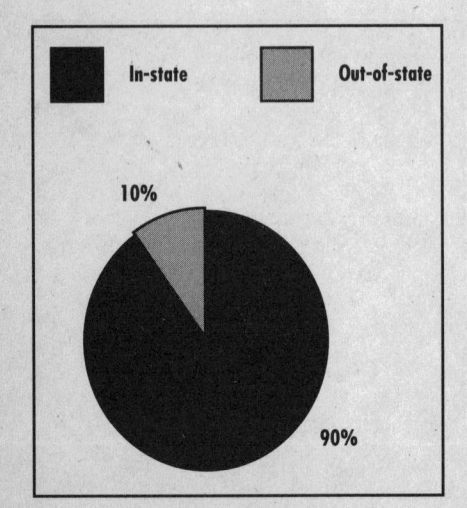

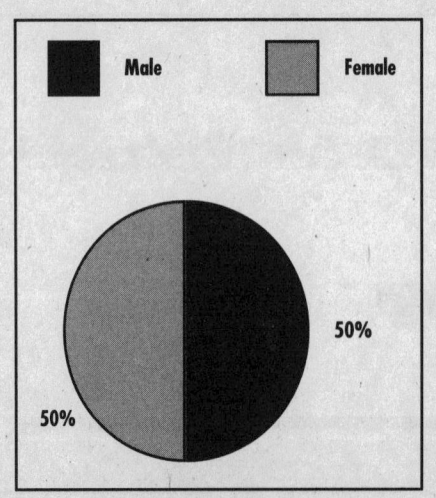

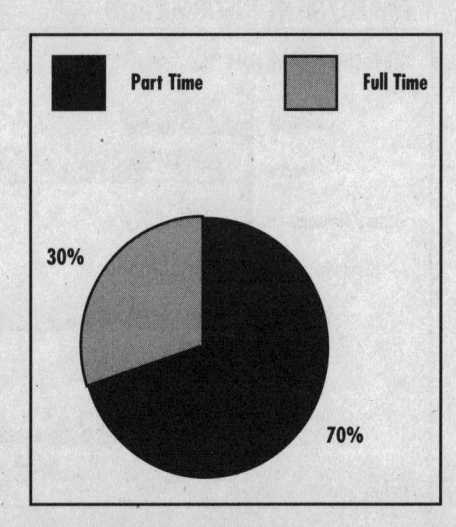

JOHN CARROLL UNIVERSITY
John M. and Mary Jo Boler School of Business

Admissions Contact: Dr. James M. Daley, Associate Dean and Director, MBA Program
Address: 20700 North Park Boulevard, University Heights, OH 44118-4581
Admissions Phone: 216-397-4391 • Admissions Fax: 216-397-1728
Admissions E-mail: mmauk@jcu.edu • Web Address: bsob.jcu.edu

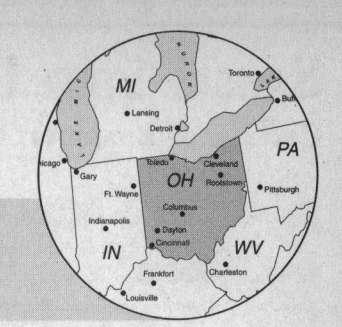

JCU offers the Mellen Series, where "chief executive officers of Ohio-headquartered, publicly traded firms meet with students and make a public presentation on the financial and strategic plans for their companies." John Carroll has agreements with 21 other American Jesuit business schools that allow for the transfer of graduate school credits. So if you started your MBA at the University of San Diego and your job transferred you from California to Ohio, you could complete your degree without having to start from scratch or agonize over lost credits.

INSTITUTIONAL INFORMATION
Public/Private: Private
Evening Classes Available? Yes
Total Faculty: 37
% Faculty Female: 19
% Faculty Minority: 2
% Faculty Part Time: 21
Student/Faculty Ratio: 16:1
Students in Parent Institution: 4,301
Academic Calendar: Semester

PROGRAMS
Degrees Offered: MBA (60 credits, 2 to 6 years)
Joint Degrees: Communications Management (33 credits, 2 to 3 years)
Special Opportunities: Beijing International MBA Program
Study Abroad Options: China—University of Peking

STUDENT INFORMATION
Total Business Students: 256
% Full Time: 19
% Female: 26
% Minority: 11
Average Age: 26

COMPUTER AND RESEARCH FACILITIES
Computer Facilities: 5 computer labs on campus; online databases: ABI/Inform, BNA HR Library, Business & Industry, CCH International Tax Research Network, Compustat PC Plus, EconLit, EconLit Database, FIS Online, Global Access, International Financial Statistics, Moody's Company Data Direct, Moody's International, NBER Working Papers
Campuswide Network? Yes
% of MBA Classrooms Wired: 100
Internet Fee? No

EXPENSES/FINANCIAL AID
Annual Tuition: $11,304
Tuition Per Credit: $628
Books and Supplies: $600

ADMISSIONS INFORMATION
Application Fee: $25
Electronic Application? No
Regular Application Deadline: Rolling
Regular Notification: Rolling
Deferment Available? Yes
Length of Deferment: 1 year
Non-fall Admissions? Yes
Non-fall Application Deadline(s): spring, summer A, summer B
Transfer Students Accepted? Yes
Transfer Policy: Applicants from members of the Network of MBA Programs at Jesuit Universities and Colleges will have all credits transferred. Otherwise, applications are reviewed on a case-by-case basis.
Need-Blind Admissions? Yes
Number of Applications Received: 84
% of Applicants Accepted: 74
% Accepted Who Enrolled: 82
Average GPA: 3.2
GPA Range: 2.2-3.9
Average GMAT: 504
GMAT Range: 390-640
Other Schools to Which Students Applied: Case Western Reserve University, Cleveland State University

INTERNATIONAL STUDENTS
TOEFL Required of International Students? Yes
Minimum TOEFL: 550 (215 computer)

EMPLOYMENT INFORMATION
Placement Office Available? Yes

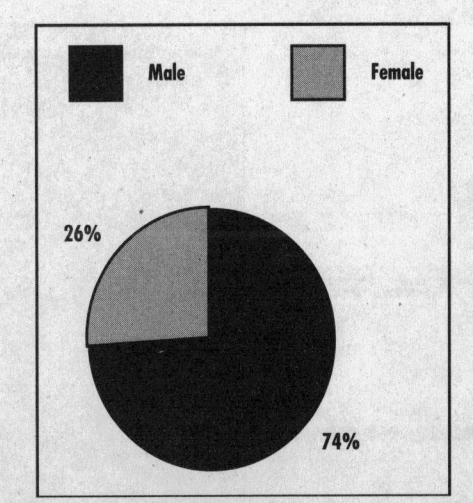

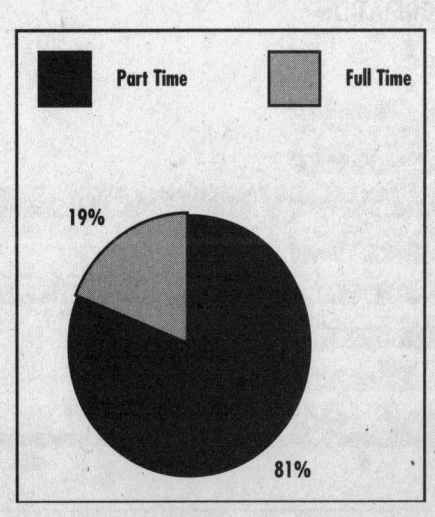

KANSAS STATE UNIVERSITY
College of Business Administration

Admissions Contact: Lynn Waugh, Graduate Studies Assistant
Address: 110 Calvin Hall, Manhattan, KS 66506-0501
Admissions Phone: 785-532-7190 • Admissions Fax: 785-532-7216
Admissions E-mail: flynn@ksu.edu • Web Address: www.cba.ksu.edu

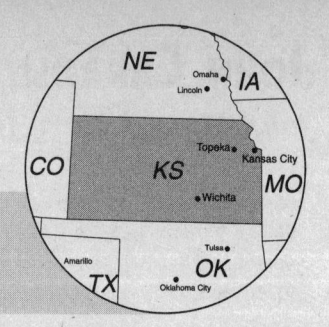

The Kansas State University MBA curriculum is designed to accommodate students who did not obtain an undergraduate degree in business; while a large percentage of students at KSU do possess a business degree, other MBAs have backgrounds as varied as food technology and modern language. The class size is capped to 70 full-time equivalent students and up to 35 new students each year to ensure a close-knit environment for students and faculty. The focus of the MBA program is simply "what you need to know to run a business."

INSTITUTIONAL INFORMATION
Public/Private: Public
Evening Classes Available? No
Total Faculty: 27
% Faculty Female: 22
% Faculty Minority: 4
% Faculty Part Time: 100
Student/Faculty Ratio: 5:1
Academic Calendar: Semester

PROGRAMS
Degrees Offered: MBA (52 credit hours, 2 years), Certificate of Business Administration offered to KSU graduate students in other fields (15 credit hours from Business core courses)
Academic Specialties: MBA Business Practicum, capstone to curriculum
Study Abroad Options: Leipzig & Giessen, Germany; CIMBA, Italy (administered by University of Kansas)

STUDENT INFORMATION
Total Business Students: 91
% Full Time: 82
% Female: 30
% Minority: 9
% Out of State: 4
% International: 22
Average Age: 24

COMPUTER AND RESEARCH FACILITIES
Computer Facilities: KSU library provides access to most major academic databases via any campus computer or via a home computer using KSU as the ISP.
Campuswide Network? No
% of MBA Classrooms Wired: 100
Internet Fee? No

EXPENSES/FINANCIAL AID
Annual Tuition (Resident/Nonresident): $3,305/$10,508
Room & Board (On/Off Campus): $5,000/$6,000
Books and Supplies: $1,000
Average Grant: $2,500
Average Loan: $3,000
% Receiving Financial Aid: 18
% Receiving Aid Their First Year: 12

ADMISSIONS INFORMATION
Application Fee: $45
Electronic Application? Yes
Regular Application Deadline: 3/1
Regular Notification: 6/1
Deferment Available? Yes
Length of Deferment: 1 year
Non-fall Admissions? No
Transfer Students Accepted? Yes
Transfer Policy: Up to 9 graduate credit hours from an AACSB-accredited institution accepted
Need-Blind Admissions? Yes
Number of Applications Received: 86
% of Applicants Accepted: 40
% Accepted Who Enrolled: 100
Average GPA: 3.4
Average GMAT: 548
Average Years Experience: 2
Other Admissions Factors Considered: Index created based on Adv. GPA x 200 + minimum GMAT of 1150
Minority/Disadvantaged Student Recruitment Programs: Exchange program with Grambling State University
Other Schools to Which Students Applied: Oklahoma State University, University of Kansas, University of Nebraska—Lincoln, University of Oklahoma, Wichita State University

INTERNATIONAL STUDENTS
TOEFL Required of International Students? Yes
Minimum TOEFL: 550 (213 computer)

EMPLOYMENT INFORMATION

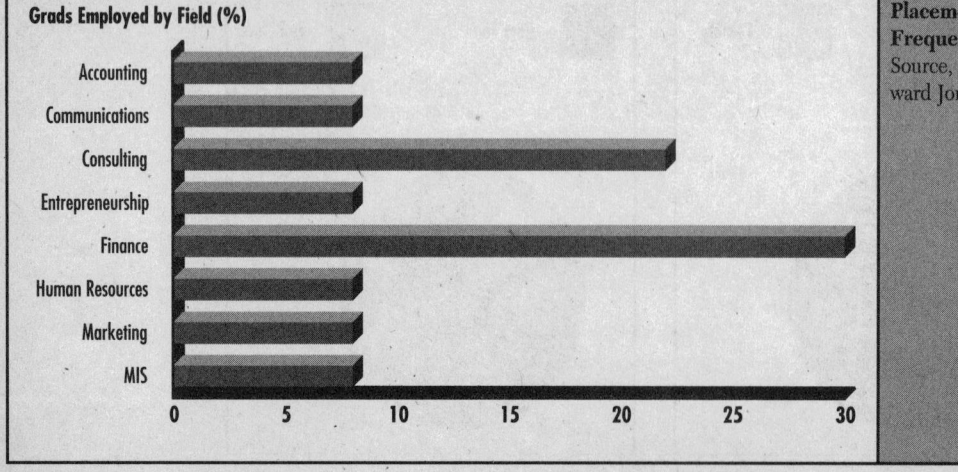

Grads Employed by Field (%)

Placement Office Available? Yes
Frequent Employers: Sprint, Payless Shoe Source, Hallmark, U.S. Military, Phillips, Edward Jones

KENT STATE UNIVERSITY
Graduate School of Management

Admissions Contact: Louise Ditchey, Director, Master's Programs
Address: PO Box 5190, Kent, OH 44242-0001
Admissions Phone: 330-672-2282 • Admissions Fax: 330-672-7303
Admissions E-mail: gradbus@bsa3.kent.edu • Web Address: business.kent.edu/grad

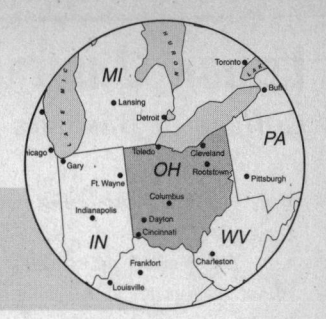

The KSU Professional MBA program is designed for students who wish to obtain an advanced financial education on a part-time basis while holding on to their day jobs. The Kent State Traditional MBA program offers a comparable curriculum for full-time students but places greater emphasis on the internships. An Executive MBA is also offered, consisting of courses that alternate between Friday and Saturday for middle managers. Kent focuses on preparing students for management positions and recognizes that adjusting teaching methods to best serve the needs of each program group is key to providing relevant business experience.

INSTITUTIONAL INFORMATION
Public/Private: Public
Evening Classes Available? Yes
Total Faculty: 54
% Faculty Female: 26
% Faculty Minority: 6
% Faculty Part Time: 7
Student/Faculty Ratio: 15:1
Students in Parent Institution: 22,828
Academic Calendar: Semester

PROGRAMS
Degrees Offered: Master of Business Administration (60 credits, 2 years); Master of Arts in Economics (30 credits, 1 year); Master of Science in Accounting (30 to 55 credits, 1 to 2 years); Doctor of Philosophy (4 to 5 years)
Joint Degrees: MBA/Master of Science in Nursing (70 credits, 3 years), MBA/Master of Library Science (70 credits, 3 years)
Academic Specialties: Concentrations in MBA program: Finance, Marketing, Information Systems, Human Resource Management, International Business
Study Abroad Options: France—Groupe Ecole Superieure de Commerce de Rennes

STUDENT INFORMATION
Total Business Students: 328
% Full Time: 35
% Female: 29
% Minority: 5
% Out of State: 15
% International: 39
Average Age: 26

COMPUTER AND RESEARCH FACILITIES
Computer Facilities: The College of Business local area network supports e-mail, spreadsheets, graphics, word processing, various specialized packages, and Internet access. University buildings are networked via a high-speed ATM backbone. The department of Academic Computing Technology supports computing on the IBM UNIX environment. It offers statistical packages such as SAS and SPSS and datasets such as CRSP, Compustat, and ICPSR.
Campuswide Network? Yes
% of MBA Classrooms Wired: 90
Internet Fee? No

EXPENSES/FINANCIAL AID
Annual Tuition (Resident/Nonresident): $6,848/$11,736
Tuition Per Credit (Resident/Nonresident): $280/$530
Room & Board (On/Off Campus): $5,580/$5,500
Books and Supplies: $900
% Receiving Financial Aid: 40
% Receiving Aid Their First Year: 30

ADMISSIONS INFORMATION
Application Fee: $30
Electronic Application? Yes
Regular Application Deadline: 4/1
Regular Notification: 4/15
Length of Deferment: 1 year
Non-fall Application Deadline(s): 12/15, 5/15
Transfer Policy: Transfer credits must be from an AACSB-accredited program, less than 6 years old by the time the Kent degree is conferred, and approved by the graduate committee and dean.
Need-Blind Admissions? Yes
Number of Applications Received: 141
% of Applicants Accepted: 79
% Accepted Who Enrolled: 37
Average GPA: 3.0
GPA Range: 2.0-3.0
Average GMAT: 547
GMAT Range: 470-620
Average Years Experience: 3
Other Schools to Which Students Applied: Bowling Green, Case Western, Cleveland State, John Carroll, Ohio State, University of Akron

INTERNATIONAL STUDENTS
TOEFL Required of International Students? Yes
Minimum TOEFL: 550 (213 computer)

EMPLOYMENT INFORMATION

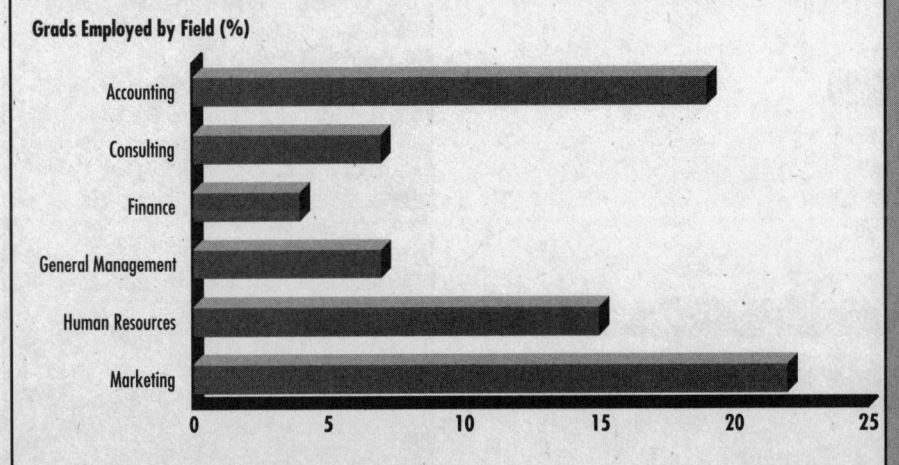

Grads Employed by Field (%)
- Accounting
- Consulting
- Finance
- General Management
- Human Resources
- Marketing

Placement Office Available? No
% Employed Within 3 Months: 85
Frequent Employers: Ernst & Young, Progressive Insurance, Key Bank, Little Tikes, Jo-Ann Stores Inc., Summa Health System, FedEx Systems, The Timken Company, Diebold Inc.
Prominent Alumni: Yank Heisler, CEO, Key Bank Corporation, Cleveland; Leigh Herington, U.S. Senator, Columbus, Ohio; M.R. Rangaswami, cofounder, Sand-Hill Venture Capital LLC; Richard Ferry, chairman, Korn-Ferry International, Los Angeles; George Stevens, dean, College of Business, Kent State University

LEHIGH UNIVERSITY
College of Business and Economics

Admissions Contact: Mary Theresa Taglang, Director of Recruitment and Admissions
Address: 621 Taylor Street, Bethlehem, PA 18015
Admissions Phone: 610-758-5280 • Admissions Fax: 610-758-5283
Admissions E-mail: mba.admissions@lehigh.edu • Web Address: www.lehigh.edu/mba

Lehigh's College of Business and Economics is a private institution with decent tuition rates and an average student age of around 30. The Lehigh MBA program offers two unique joint programs: MBA/Master of Education (MBA & Ed), and MBA/Engineering (MBA & E). Frequent employers of Lehigh graduates are Lucent Technologies, Merrill Lynch, PricewaterhouseCoopers, and Andersen Consulting.

INSTITUTIONAL INFORMATION
Public/Private: Private
Evening Classes Available? Yes
Total Faculty: 60
% Faculty Part Time: 12
Student/Faculty Ratio: 5:1
Students in Parent Institution: 6,437
Academic Calendar: Credit hours

PROGRAMS
Degrees Offered: MBA (36 credits); MS in Accounting and Information Analysis (30 credits); MS in Economics (30 credits); PhD in Business and Economics (72 credits)
Joint Degrees: MBA and Engineering (MBA and E) (45 credits); MBA and Educational Leadership (MBA/MEd) (45 credits)

STUDENT INFORMATION
Total Business Students: 292
% Female: 32
% International: 32
Average Age: 30

COMPUTER AND RESEARCH FACILITIES
Computer Facilities: ABI/Inform, Compustat/Research Insight, CRSP, Dow Jones Interactive
Campuswide Network? Yes
% of MBA Classrooms Wired: 100
Internet Fee? No

EXPENSES/FINANCIAL AID
Annual Tuition: $14,640
Tuition Per Credit: $610
Books and Supplies: $1,300
Average Grant: $11,000

ADMISSIONS INFORMATION
Application Fee: $50
Electronic Application? Yes
Regular Application Deadline: 5/1
Regular Notification: Rolling
Deferment Available? Yes
Length of Deferment: 1 year
Non-fall Admissions? Yes
Non-fall Application Deadline(s): 12/1 spring, 4/30 summer 1, 5/30 summer 2
Transfer Students Accepted? Yes
Transfer Policy: 6 credits from an AACSB-accredited school
Need-Blind Admissions? Yes
Number of Applications Received: 253
% of Applicants Accepted: 69
% Accepted Who Enrolled: 77
Average GPA: 3.2
Average GMAT: 614
Average Years Experience: 7

INTERNATIONAL STUDENTS
TOEFL Required of International Students? Yes
Minimum TOEFL: 580 (237 computer)

EMPLOYMENT INFORMATION

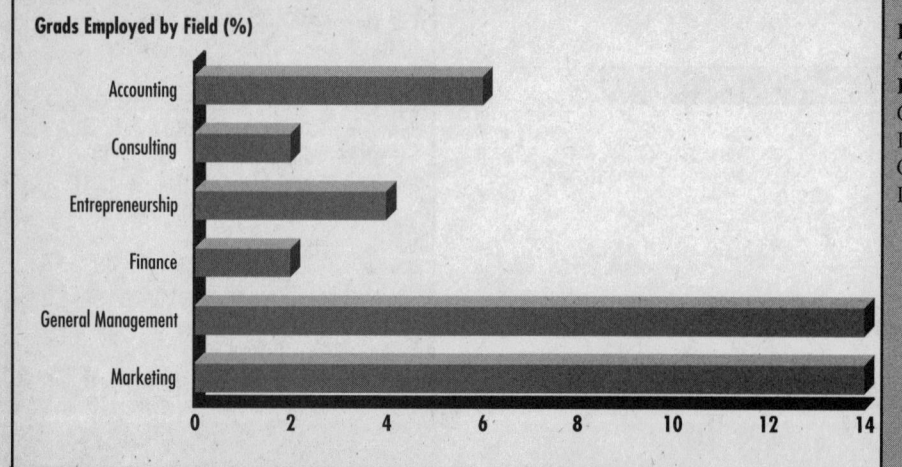

Grads Employed by Field (%)
- Accounting: 6
- Consulting: 2
- Entrepreneurship: 4
- Finance: 2
- General Management: 14
- Marketing: 14

Placement Office Available? Yes
% Employed Within 3 Months: 94
Frequent Employers: Accenture; Andersen Consulting; Air Products & Chemicals, Inc.; Bethlehem Steel; Lucent Technologies; Merck & Co., Inc.; PricewaterhouseCoopers; Merrill Lynch; Lehman Brothers

LOUISIANA STATE UNIVERSITY
E.J. Ourso College of Business Administration

Admissions Contact: Dr. P. David Shields, Director, Flores MBA Programs
Address: 3170 CEBA Building, Baton Rouge, LA 70803
Admissions Phone: 225-578-8867 • Admissions Fax: 225-578-2421
Admissions E-mail: busmba@lsu.edu • Web Address: www.bus.lsu.edu/mba

Small classes, incredible job placement, competitive internships—this is only the beginning of the list of great benefits of a Louisiana State University graduate business education. The E.J. Ourso College of Business Administration, located in the red-hot city of Baton Rouge, offers three different tracks (full-time, professional, and executive) leading to a distinctly LSU Flores MBA. Because many credits overlap curricula, students seeking a joint JD/MBA full time can expect to graduate in four years instead of the usual five.

INSTITUTIONAL INFORMATION
Public/Private: Public
Evening Classes Available? Yes
Total Faculty: 106
% Faculty Female: 25
% Faculty Minority: 10
% Faculty Part Time: 3
Student/Faculty Ratio: 19:1
Students in Parent Institution: 31,000

STUDENT INFORMATION
Total Business Students: 121
% Female: 36
% Minority: 9
% International: 14
Average Age: 24

COMPUTER AND RESEARCH FACILITIES
Research Facilities: Internal Audit Center, Louisiana Institute for Entrepreneurial Education and Family Business Studies, Louisiana Business & Technology Center
Computer Facilities: All MBA students have access to 2 computer labs and the general-access area housed in the Microcomputer Lab. MBA students also have access to all public-access areas on campus. The College of Business supports Compustat/Research Insight and the CRISP databases, as well as some accounting simulations.
Campuswide Network? Yes
Computer Model Recommended: No
Internet Fee? No

EXPENSES/FINANCIAL AID
Annual Tuition (Resident/Nonresident): $2,551/$7,851
Books and Supplies: $1,000

ADMISSIONS INFORMATION
Application Fee: $25
Electronic Application? Yes
Regular Application Deadline: 5/15
Regular Notification: Rolling
Deferment Available? No
Non-fall Admissions? No
Transfer Students Accepted? No
Need-Blind Admissions? No
Number of Applications Received: 315
% of Applicants Accepted: 40
% Accepted Who Enrolled: 66
Average GPA: 3.3
GPA Range: 3.1-3.6
Average GMAT: 570
GMAT Range: 533-598

INTERNATIONAL STUDENTS
TOEFL Required of International Students? Yes
Minimum TOEFL: 550 (213 computer)

EMPLOYMENT INFORMATION

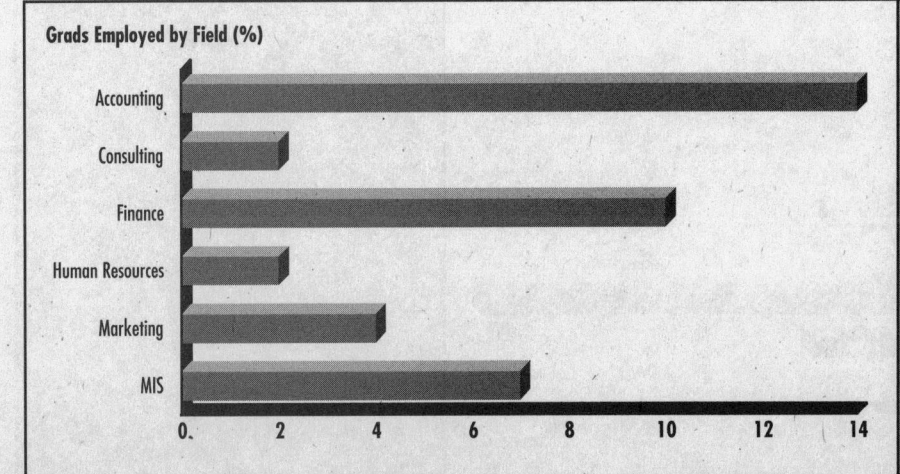

Grads Employed by Field (%):
- Accounting: 14
- Consulting: 2
- Finance: 10
- Human Resources: 2
- Marketing: 4
- MIS: 7

Placement Office Available? Yes
% Employed Within 3 Months: 84
Frequent Employers: Arthur Andersen, Accenture, Entergy Corporation, Exxon, Mobil, KPMG

LOYOLA COLLEGE IN MARYLAND
Sellinger School of Business and Management

Admissions Contact: Scott Greatorex, Graduate Admissions Director
Address: 4501 North Charles Street, Baltimore, MD 21210
Admissions Phone: 410-617-2000 • Admissions Fax: 410-617-2002
Admissions E-mail: mba@loyola.edu • Web Address: sellinger.loyola.edu

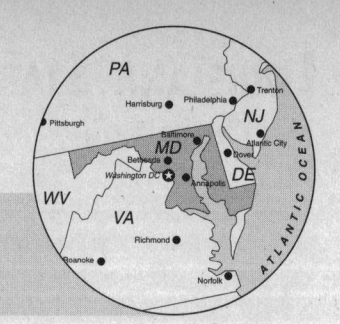

The Sellinger School of Business and Management is inspired by Jesuit values and guided by the principles of cura personalis (care for the whole person). The general MBA program is broad-based, and the graduate programs (Evening MBA, Executive MBA, and MBA Fellows Program) usually serve working professionals in the Baltimore/Washington region. Expect to pay very little for a quality, private-school business education.

INSTITUTIONAL INFORMATION
Public/Private: Private
Evening Classes Available? No
Total Faculty: 59
% Faculty Part Time: 17
Student/Faculty Ratio: 10:1
Students in Parent Institution: 6,181
Academic Calendar: Semester

PROGRAMS
Degrees Offered: MBA (51 credits, 12 months to 7 years); Executive MBA (51 credits, 21 months); MBA Fellows Program (51 credits, 28 months); Master of Science in Finance (42 credits, 12 months to 7 years)

STUDENT INFORMATION
Total Business Students: 948
% Minority: 14
% Out of State: 4
% International: 3
Average Age: 31

COMPUTER AND RESEARCH FACILITIES
Campuswide Network? Yes
Internet Fee? No

EXPENSES/FINANCIAL AID
Tuition Per Credit: $365
% Receiving Financial Aid: 10

ADMISSIONS INFORMATION
Application Fee: $50
Electronic Application? No
Regular Application Deadline: 8/20
Regular Notification: Rolling
Deferment Available? Yes
Length of Deferment: 1 year
Non-fall Admissions? Yes
Non-fall Application Deadline(s): 11/20, 4/20
Transfer Students Accepted? No
Need-Blind Admissions? No
Number of Applications Received: 688
% of Applicants Accepted: 83
% Accepted Who Enrolled: 86
Average GMAT: 528
Other Admissions Factors Considered: Letters of recommendation, work experience

INTERNATIONAL STUDENTS
TOEFL Required of International Students? Yes
Minimum TOEFL: 550 (213 computer)

EMPLOYMENT INFORMATION

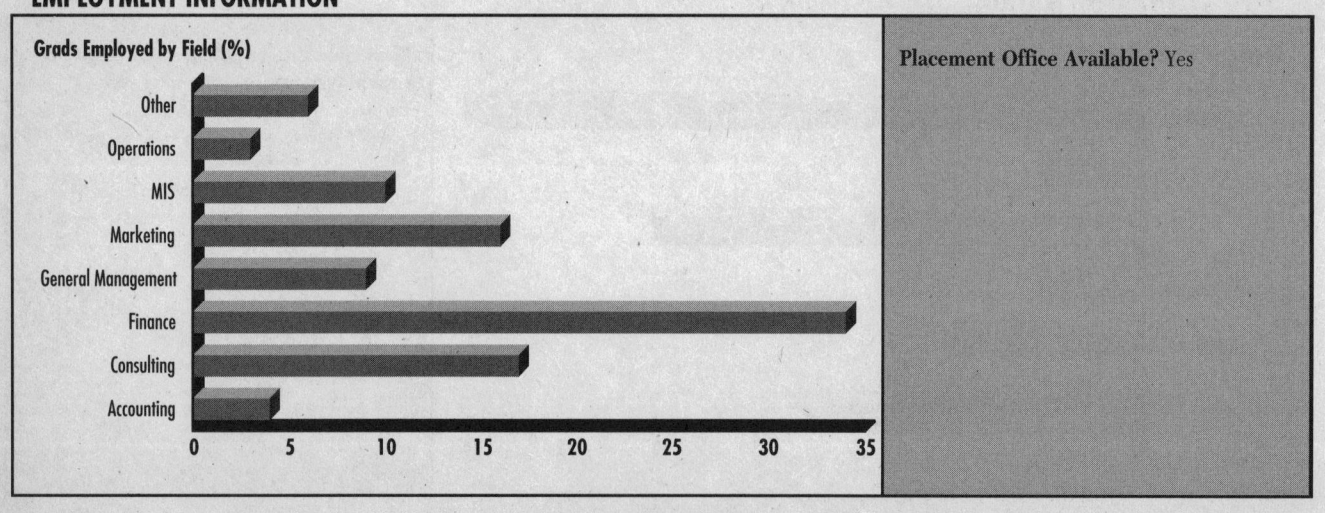

Grads Employed by Field (%)

Field	%
Other	6
Operations	3
MIS	10
Marketing	17
General Management	9
Finance	34
Consulting	17
Accounting	4

Placement Office Available? Yes

LOYOLA MARYMOUNT UNIVERSITY
MBA Program

Admissions Contact: Charisse Woods, MBA Program Coordinator
Address: 7900 Loyola Boulevard, Los Angeles, CA 90045-8387
Admissions Phone: 310-338-2848 • *Admissions Fax:* 310-338-2899
Admissions E-mail: mbapc@lmu.edu • *Web Address:* www.mba.lmu.edu

Most of Loyola Marymount's MBA students live in Los Angeles while attending school full time. The MBA education includes small classes with accessible professors and cutting-edge technology. Enabling the student to take courses catered to his or her current standing in the business world, LMU offers a general MBA, an Executive MBA, and an MBA for International Managers.

INSTITUTIONAL INFORMATION
Public/Private: Private
Evening Classes Available? Yes
Total Faculty: 50
% Faculty Female: 16
% Faculty Minority: 8
% Faculty Part Time: 20
Student/Faculty Ratio: 25:1
Students in Parent Institution: 7,151
Academic Calendar: Semester

PROGRAMS
Degrees Offered: MBA, MBA for International Managers (1 to 3 years); Executive MBA (21 months)
Joint Degrees: MBA/Doctor of Jurisprudence (4 years)
Academic Specialties: Flexible, evening classes; noncompetitive environment
Special Opportunities: Comparative Management Systems, Master of Science in European Business
Study Abroad Options: Beijing, China; EDHEC Graduate School of Management in Lille or Nice, France

STUDENT INFORMATION
Total Business Students: 420
% Full Time: 80
% Female: 40
% Minority: 30
% International: 9
Average Age: 27

COMPUTER AND RESEARCH FACILITIES
Computer Facilities: Computer labs on campus, "nooks" to check e-mail
Campuswide Network? Yes
Internet Fee? No

EXPENSES/FINANCIAL AID
Annual Tuition: $12,780
Room & Board (Off Campus): $14,000
Books and Supplies: $500
Average Grant: $2,500
Average Loan: $12,000
% Receiving Financial Aid: 39
% Receiving Aid Their First Year: 50

ADMISSIONS INFORMATION
Application Fee: $35
Electronic Application? Yes
Regular Application Deadline: Rolling
Regular Notification: Rolling
Deferment Available? Yes
Length of Deferment: 1 year
Non-fall Admissions? Yes
Non-fall Application Deadline(s): Fall, spring, summer I or II
Transfer Students Accepted? Yes
Transfer Policy: Students from other Jesuit MBA programs through the Jesuit Multilateral Agreement or students who attend an AACSB-accredited MBA program with equivalent course work of B or better may transfer in only 6 units of upper-division course credit.
Need-Blind Admissions? Yes
Number of Applications Received: 331
% of Applicants Accepted: 67
% Accepted Who Enrolled: 58
Average GPA: 3.2
Average GMAT: 570
GMAT Range: 450-680
Average Years Experience: 4
Other Admissions Factors Considered: Work experience not required but could help an application

INTERNATIONAL STUDENTS
TOEFL Required of International Students? Yes
Minimum TOEFL: 600 (250 computer)

EMPLOYMENT INFORMATION
Placement Office Available? Yes

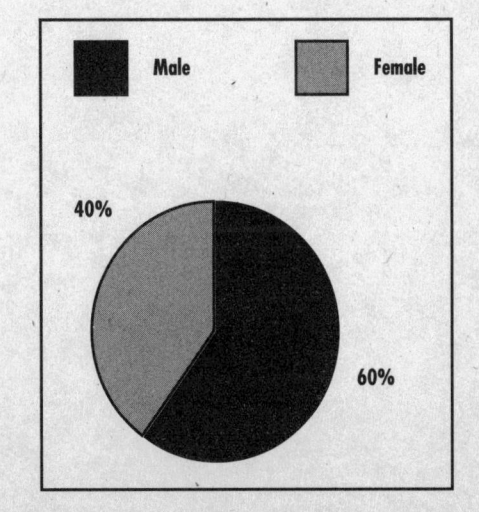

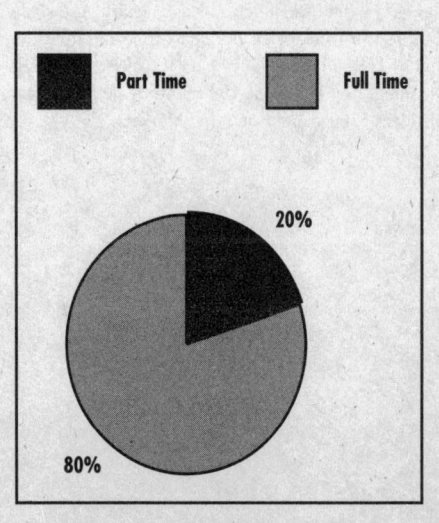

LOYOLA UNIVERSITY CHICAGO

THE SCHOOL AT A GLANCE
At Loyola, we provide an excellent faculty, a diversity of students, the resources of a great university, and individualized attention to create a superb learning environment. By studying with us, you will enhance your ability to think critically, solve problems, work in a team environment, think strategically about technology, and effectively communicate your ideas. Consistent with 450 years of Jesuit education, we emphasize the foundation necessary to make ethical decisions in today's complex business environment.

Student Organizations and Activities
Alpha Kappa Psi (AKP) is a national co-ed business fraternity with the purpose of uniting business students into a group representing high professional standards. Students will be exposed to various projects and activities to prepare them for the business environment. Our organization is a complete, well-integrated, and capably administered national business fraternity, standing for the highest ideals of conduct and achievement in university and professional life.

American Marketing Association is an organization created to help students understand the opportunities in marketing and promote the ethical and professional practice of marketing through adherence to the standards espoused by American Marketing Association.

Delta Sigma Pi Fraternity is a professional business fraternity organized to foster the study of business in universities and augment the educational experiences with "real-world" applications. It aims to encourage scholarship, social activity, and the association of students; to promote mutual advancement through research practice and close affiliation between the commercial world and students of commerce; and to further high standards of commercial ethics, culture, and the civic and commercial welfare of the community.

Financial Management Association (FMA) is an organization whose intent is to assist in the professional, educational, and social development of college students interested in finance, banking, and investments. FMA also provides an association for college students actively interested in these fields, and encourages interaction between business executives, faculty, and students of business and finance.

ACADEMICS
At Loyola, we help prepare you for the global demands of business by routinely including international considerations in all our courses and by offering courses that singularly focus on the international dimensions of a topic. Students whose career goals demand an intensive grounding in international business can take advantage of our innovative study abroad programs. Under these programs we offer intensive, two-week summer courses at the Loyola campus in Rome, Italy; the East Asian Studies Institute of Thammasat University in Bangkok, Thailand; and at the University of Piraeus in Greece. Each course focuses on topical international issues and is taught by the best of our Chicago faculty. And since each session is compressed into a two-week block, both part-time and full-time students have the opportunity to attend. Past courses have focused on issues such as International Management, the European Union, Strategic Marketing in Europe, International Business Ethics, and Emerging Markets.

In addition to Loyola's unique two-week summer programs in Italy, Thailand, and Greece, MBA students can attend overseas programs through the AJCU (the Association of Jesuit Colleges and Universities). Sites for these fully accredited courses include Florence, Hong Kong, Paris, Tokyo, and Antwerp.

Loyola's Graduate School of Business offers:

- The MBA degree with a choice of 15 specializations: Accounting, Business Ethics, Derivative Markets, Economics, Electronic Commerce, Environmental Management, Finance, Health Care Administration, Information Systems and Management Science, International Business, Legal Environment, Management, Marketing, Production and Operations, and Strategic Management and Decision Making
- MS degree in Integrated Marketing Communications
- MS degree in Information Systems Management
- MS degree in Accountancy
- 3 Graduate Certificates, in E-commerce, Data Warehousing and Business Intelligence, and Ethics
- Dual Degrees: MBA/MSIM, MBA/MSIMC, MBA/MSA, MBA/MS Pharmacology, MBA/MSN, and MBA/JD

The Loyola University Chicago faculty is strongly committed to teaching as well as research. Because 70 percent of the faculty members are full time and 95 percent of those have a PhD or equivalent degree, classes are taught by experienced, highly trained leaders in their fields. Loyola also augments the regular faculty with practicing managers and consultants who teach classes in special topics such as emerging technologies and negotiations. Class size is purposely kept small in order to ensure that the faculty is accessible to students both inside and outside the classroom.

As leaders in their fields, many faculty members have important industry and community ties in such areas as financial and policy studies, consulting, and marketing and communications. In the classroom, they offer a scholarly approach gained through research as well as practical business experience.

The faculty's dedication to research invigorates the MBA experience by developing new ideas that can be applied in the classroom. The faculty is involved in an impressive range of research projects in all major areas of business and is also widely published. Our faculty are internationally known for their research, have written many books and contributed to many journals, and have won awards for their publications. To see sampling of their expertise, visit the faculty website at www.gsb.luc.edu/research.

Graduate School of Business

CAMPUS LIFE

The Graduate School of Business campus is located adjacent to Chicago's Magnificent Mile. Chicago is home to the Chicago Board of Trade, Chicago Board Options Exchange, and Chicago Mercantile Exchange, making the city one of the largest financial trading centers in the world. Many national and multinational companies in a broad range of industries are headquartered in Chicago. As a result, job opportunities at major firms abound throughout the Chicago area, in fields as diverse as manufacturing, retailing, health care, and consulting.

The Graduate School of Business is located at the Water Tower Campus, and all classes are taught in a state-of-the-art, 15-story building. The building houses classrooms, computer labs, a library, conference rooms, an auditorium, and faculty and administrative offices. The Loyola Library system offers numerous computerized resources including the Internet, Lexis-Nexis, Legal Index, FirstSearch, and LUIS (the Loyola Library computerized catalog). Databases on CD-ROM include Business Periodicals on Disc, General Business File, and others.

The Graduate School of Business Placement Services provides current students and alumni with a career development framework to assist with assessment, collecting career information, decision making, and developing effective job search strategies. In addition, GSB Placement Services develops and maintains employer relationships in an effort to develop job leads, employment opportunities, and networking/mentor relationships for students and alumni.

Services offered are the following: one-on-one career counseling, group job-search skills workshops, employer presentations and panel discussions, job fairs, Career Consultants Network, job and internship opportunities on the Web, and resume referrals and database. Some of the Chicago-area recruiting companies that visit our campus are IBM, MarchFirst, PricewaterhouseCoopers, Andersen Consulting, and McDonald's Corp.

COSTS

Tuition for 2000–2001 is $2,186 per course for both full- and part-time students. A wide variety of housing is available both on and off campus. Many full-time students live in the Gold Coast area of Chicago, which is within walking distance of the Graduate School of Business. Other graduate students choose to live in graduate housing facilities that are located 10 miles north of the Water Tower Campus at Loyola's Lake Shore Campus. The estimated cost of room and board for 12 months is between $8,000 and $12,000.

Financial Aid

Tuition scholarships and monetary stipends are available through the Graduate Business Scholars Program. All full-time students are automatically considered for the program, which awards merit-based research assistantships and graduate assistantships.

Other financial assistance is available from a variety of sources. Some students can rely on employer support through reimbursement programs, but others must seek different options. At Loyola, we can help you explore scholarship and financing opportunities, including a variety of subsidized and unsubsidized federal loan programs. The Office of Student Financial Assistance administers these programs.

ADMISSIONS

A student may enter the program at the beginning of any of the four quarters. Prospective students should apply well in advance of the quarter in which they plan to enter. Loyola functions on a rolling admission basis; however, applications are accepted until July 1 for the fall quarter, September 1 for the winter quarter, December 1 for the spring quarter, and March 1 for the Summer quarter.

Students are admitted into the GSB programs on the basis of interest, aptitude, and capacity for business study as indicated by their previous academic record, achievement scores on the GMAT, three recommendations, and pertinent information from their applications. Our average student's undergraduate GPA is 3.0, with a range from 2.5 to 4.0. The average GMAT score is 540, and average work experience of the entering students is three to five years.

Loyola welcomes applications from international students who have completed a four-year bachelor's degree or its equivalent. A minimum TOEFL score of 550 is required.

Admissions Contact: Alan Young, Director of Recruiting and Admissions, Graduate School of Business
Address: 820 North Michigan Avenue, Chicago, IL 60611
Admissions Phone: 312-915-6120 • Admissions Fax: 312-915-7207
Admissions E-mail: mba-loyola@luc.edu • Web Address: www.gsb.luc.edu

LOYOLA UNIVERSITY CHICAGO
Graduate School of Business

Admissions Contact: Alan Young, Director of Recruiting and Admissions, Graduate School of Business
Address: 820 North Michigan Avenue, Chicago, IL 60611
Admissions Phone: 312-915-6120 • Admissions Fax: 312-915-7207
Admissions E-mail: mba-loyola@luc.edu • Web Address: www.gsb.luc.edu

Great facilities abound for MBA students at Loyola University Chicago, a school with a strong "Jesuit tradition" and an emphasis on "ethics in business." The student body includes "part-time students with significant work experience," "international students," and people who generally "differ greatly in age, work experience, and cultural backgrounds." Beyond the campus is Chicago, one of the world's most active financial trading centers and a great American city.

INSTITUTIONAL INFORMATION
Public/Private: Private
Evening Classes Available? Yes
Total Faculty: 59
% Faculty Female: 17
% Faculty Minority: 8
% Faculty Part Time: 11
Student/Faculty Ratio: 11:1
Students in Parent Institution: 11,788
Academic Calendar: Quarter

PROGRAMS
Degrees Offered: MBA (14 to 18 courses, 2 years full time, 3.5 years part time); MS in Accountancy (12 courses, 1 year full time, 2 years part time); MS in Information Systems (14 courses, 1 year full time, 2 years part time); MS in Integrated Marketing Communications (14 courses, 1 year full time, 2 years part time)
Joint Degrees: MBA/JD (4 years full time, 6 years part time); MBA/MSISM (2 years full time, 4 years part time); MBA/MSIMC (2 years full time, 4 years part time); MBA/MS in Nursing (2 years full time, 4 years part time); MBA/MS in Pharmacology (2 years full time, 4 years part time)
Academic Specialties: Finance, Derivatives, Business Ethics, Information Systems Management, Integrated Marketing Communications, Health Care Administration, E-Commerce, International Business, Strategic Management, Accountancy

Special Opportunities: Multicultural advisors for minority students
Study Abroad Options: Loyola Programs in Rome, Italy; Athens, Greece; Bangkok, Thailand

STUDENT INFORMATION
Total Business Students: 626
% Full Time: 19
% Female: 44
% Minority: 9
% Out of State: 53
% International: 46
Average Age: 27

COMPUTER AND RESEARCH FACILITIES
Research Facilities: Family Business Center, Center for Information Management & Technology, Center for Business Ethics, Center for Financial & Policy Study
Computer Facilities: 3 computer classrooms, wide range of applications software available to students
Campuswide Network? Yes
% of MBA Classrooms Wired: 50
Computer Model Recommended: No
Internet Fee? No

EXPENSES/FINANCIAL AID
Annual Tuition: $20,250
Tuition Per Credit: $750
Room & Board (On/Off Campus): $7,550/$9,500

Books and Supplies: $900
Average Grant: $9,900
Average Loan: $10,100

ADMISSIONS INFORMATION
Application Fee: $50
Electronic Application? Yes
Regular Application Deadline: 7/1
Regular Notification: Rolling
Length of Deferment: 1 year
Non-fall Application Deadline(s): 9/1, 12/1, 3/1
Transfer Policy: AACSB schools only; Jesuit MBA consortium agreement
Need-Blind Admissions? Yes
Number of Applications Received: 379
% of Applicants Accepted: 86
% Accepted Who Enrolled: 56
Average GPA: 3.1
GPA Range: 2.7-3.8
Average GMAT: 542
GMAT Range: 490-670
Average Years Experience: 5
Other Admissions Factors Considered: Work experience
Other Schools to Which Students Applied: DePaul, Northwestern, U. of Chicago, University of Illinois at Urbana-Champaign, University of Illinois at Chicago

INTERNATIONAL STUDENTS
TOEFL Required of International Students? Yes
Minimum TOEFL: 550 (213 computer)

EMPLOYMENT INFORMATION

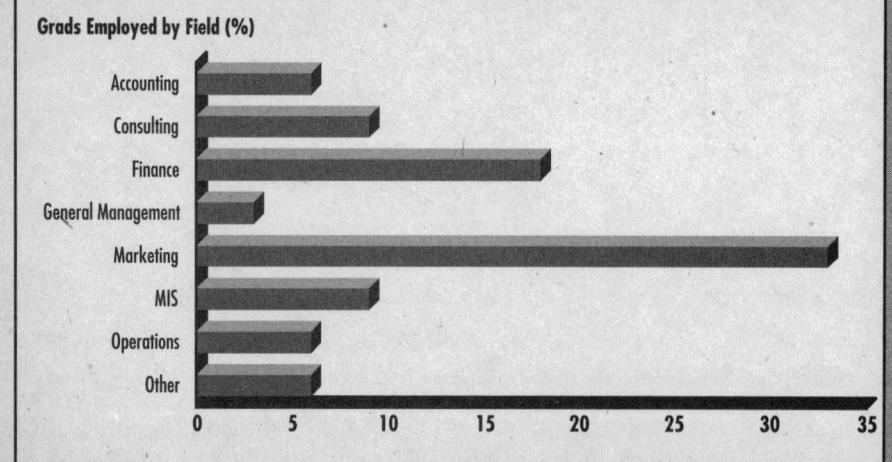

Grads Employed by Field (%)
- Accounting
- Consulting
- Finance
- General Management
- Marketing
- MIS
- Operations
- Other

Placement Office Available? Yes
% Employed Within 3 Months: 48
Frequent Employers: Accenture, Allstate, American Medical Association, Bank One, Boeing, Citicorp, Deloitte & Touche, FBOP, Kraft Foods, McDonald's, Merrill Lynch, National City, Ortho-McNeil Pharmaceuticals, PricewaterhouseCoopers, RR Donnelley, Sara Lee
Prominent Alumni: Michael Quinlan, chairman of the board, McDonald's Corp.; Robert Parkinson, former president and CEO, Abbott Laboratories; John Menzer, president and CEO, Wal-Mart International; Carl Koenemann, executive VP and CFO, Motorola; John Rooney, president and CEO, US Cellular

LOYOLA UNIVERSITY NEW ORLEANS
The Joseph A. Butt, S.J. College of Business Administration

Admissions Contact: Jan Moppert, Coordinator of Graduate and External Programs
Address: 6363 St. Charles Avenue, Campus Box 15, New Orleans, LA 70118
Admissions Phone: 504-864-7965 • Admissions Fax: 504-864-7970
Admissions E-mail: jamopper@loyno.edu • Web Address: cba.loyno.edu

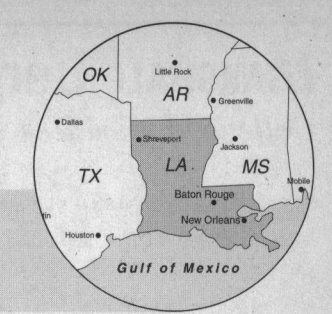

The Jesuit-centered tradition of Loyola University New Orleans offers the MBA student a solid business education in a great southern city. The curriculum is strengthened by the school's dedication to ethical responsibility and critical thinking. The school's mission statement indicates that Loyola aims to produce graduates who "possess a love for, the critical intelligence to pursue, and the eloquence to articulate truth."

INSTITUTIONAL INFORMATION
Public/Private: Private
Evening Classes Available? Yes
Total Faculty: 20
Student/Faculty Ratio: 14:1
Students in Parent Institution: 5,396
Academic Calendar: Semester

PROGRAMS
Degrees Offered: Master of Business Administration (12 months to 7 years), with concentrations in Management, Accounting, Finance, International Business, and Quality Management; Master of Quality Management (3 years);
Joint Degrees: Master of Business Administration/Doctor of Jurisprudence (5 years)
Academic Specialties: Case study, computer simulations, faculty seminars, group discussion, lecture, research, seminars by member of the business community, simulations, student presentation, team projects
Study Abroad Options: Belgium, Spain

STUDENT INFORMATION
Total Business Students: 144

COMPUTER AND RESEARCH FACILITIES
Campuswide Network? No
Internet Fee? No

EXPENSES/FINANCIAL AID
Annual Tuition: $12,984
Tuition Per Credit: $541
Books and Supplies: $2,800
% Receiving Financial Aid: 16

ADMISSIONS INFORMATION
Application Fee: $50
Electronic Application? Yes
Regular Application Deadline: 6/30
Regular Notification: Rolling
Deferment Available? Yes
Length of Deferment: 1 year
Non-fall Admissions? Yes
Non-fall Application Deadline(s): 11/30
Transfer Students Accepted? Yes
Transfer Policy: In applicant comes from an AACSB-accredited program, the foundation work may apply to our program. Also, a maximum of 6 credit hours may be applied to the advanced level. Only B's or better are accepted.
Need-Blind Admissions? Yes
Number of Applications Received: 56
% of Applicants Accepted: 63
% Accepted Who Enrolled: 37
Other Admissions Factors Considered: Work experience, though not required, is strongly recommended. The interview is optional.

INTERNATIONAL STUDENTS
TOEFL Required of International Students? Yes
Minimum TOEFL: 237

EMPLOYMENT INFORMATION
Placement Office Available? Yes
% Employed Within 3 Months: 97

MARSHALL UNIVERSITY
College of Business

Admissions Contact: Dr. Michael A. Newsome, MBA Director
Address: Corby Hall 217, 400 Hal Greer Boulevard, Huntington, WV 25755-2305
Admissions Phone: 304-696-2613 • *Admissions Fax:* 304-696-3661
Web Address: lcob.marshall.edu

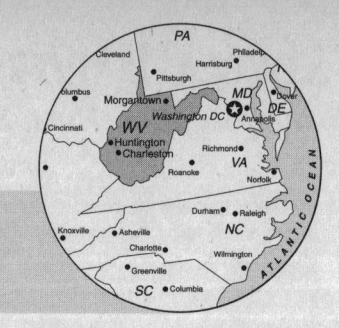

The Marshall University Elizabeth McDowell Lewis College of Business has a long name, a great school song titled "Sons of Marshall," and a long list of educational amenities like technological sophistication and a delightful campus. Named for U.S. Supreme Court Chief Justice John Marshall, MU allows its students to obtain a solid education without having to sacrifice their souls to pay the bill.

INSTITUTIONAL INFORMATION
Public/Private: Public
Evening Classes Available? Yes
Total Faculty: 20
% Faculty Female: 10
% Faculty Minority: 10
% Faculty Part Time: 25
Student/Faculty Ratio: 5:1
Academic Calendar: Semester

PROGRAMS
Degrees Offered: MBA (36 credits, 12 months to 5 years); Executive MBA (18 months to 2 years)
Special Opportunities: Internships are available.

STUDENT INFORMATION
Total Business Students: 80
% Female: 60
% Minority: 15
% International: 30

COMPUTER AND RESEARCH FACILITIES
Research Facilities: Center for Business and Economic Research, Marshall University Research Corporation
Computer Facilities: College of Business Computer Libaratories, library computer labs, Student Center computer labs

Campuswide Network? Yes
% of MBA Classrooms Wired: 25
Computer Model Recommended: No
Internet Fee? No

EXPENSES/FINANCIAL AID
Annual Tuition (Resident/Nonresident): $2,884/$8,158
Tuition Per Credit: $150
Room & Board (Off Campus): $4,000
Books and Supplies: $1,000
% Receiving Financial Aid: 50
% Receiving Aid Their First Year: 50

ADMISSIONS INFORMATION
Application Fee: $20
Electronic Application? No
Regular Application Deadline: Rolling
Regular Notification: Rolling
Deferment Available? No
Non-fall Admissions? Yes
Non-fall Application Deadline(s): Rolling
Transfer Students Accepted? Yes
Transfer Policy: When a student's Plan of Study is approved, credit may be transferred with the approval of the Graduate Dean. The work must have been completed at another regionally accredited graduate institution and must be appropriate to the student's program. Grades earned must be at the grade level of B or better, and acceptable to the advisor and the Graduate Dean. A maximum of 12 hours will be accepted, provided that they meet time limitation requirements. Graduate credit transferred from other institutions will not become part of the Marshall University grade point average and will simply meet credit hour requirements toward graduation.
Need-Blind Admissions? No
Number of Applications Received: 100
% of Applicants Accepted: 84
% Accepted Who Enrolled: 95
Average GPA: 3.5
Average GMAT: 530
Average Years Experience: 2
Other Admissions Factors Considered: Interview, letters of recommendation, and résumé are recommended.

INTERNATIONAL STUDENTS
TOEFL Required of International Students? Yes
Minimum TOEFL: 525 (195 computer)

EMPLOYMENT INFORMATION
Placement Office Available? No
% Employed Within 3 Months: 90
Frequent Employers: Steel of West Virginia, CSX Transportation, Ernst & Young, BB&T

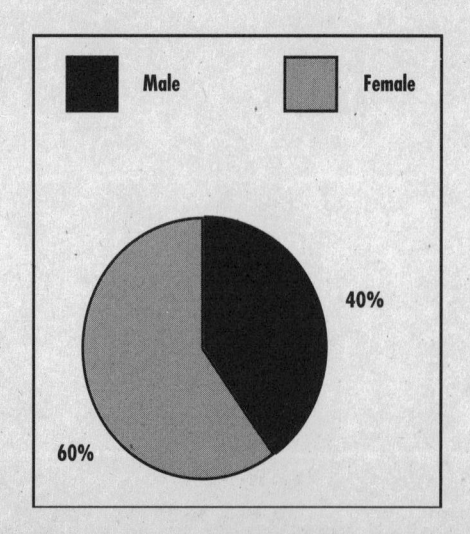

Male — 40%
Female — 60%

300 • COMPLETE BOOK OF BUSINESS SCHOOLS

MASSACHUSETTS INSTITUTE OF TECHNOLOGY
Sloan School of Management

Admissions Contact: Rod Garcia, Admissions Director
Address: E52-118, Cambridge, MA 02139
Admissions Phone: 617-258-5434 • Admissions Fax: 617-253-6405
Admissions E-mail: mbaadmissions@sloan.mit.edu • Web Address: mitsloan.mit.edu

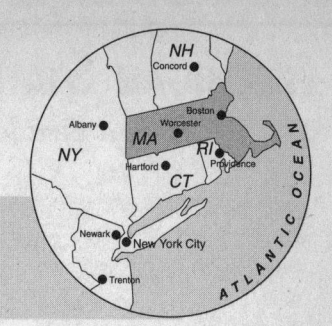

You know that the vaunted Sloan School of Management is home to arguably "the best" economics department "in the world" and "high-tech business" galore (including a nifty $3.5 million virtual trading floor). We bet you didn't know that "entrepreneurial spirit and activities pervade" Sloan. For example, the annual $50K Entrepreneurship Competition here "has spawned such successful companies as Direct Hit Technologies," the power behind the Lycos search engine.

INSTITUTIONAL INFORMATION
Public/Private: Private
Evening Classes Available? No
Total Faculty: 96
% Faculty Female: 9
% Faculty Minority: 7
Student/Faculty Ratio: 10:1
Students in Parent Institution: 9,947
Academic Calendar: Semester

PROGRAMS
Degrees Offered: MBA (2 years), Master of Science (2 years), PhD (5 years)
Combined Degrees: SM in Management/SM in Engineering (one of six departments) (2 years)
Academic Specialties: Strengths of faculty and curriculum in Financial Engineering, Financial Management, Strategic Management/Consulting, Product and Venture Development, Strategic Information Technology, Operations Management/Manufacturing.
Special Opportunities: The MIT-Japan Program in Science, Technology, and Management
Study Abroad Options: London Business School and IESE

STUDENT INFORMATION
Total Business Students: 733
% Full Time: 100
% Female: 26
% Minority: 3
% Out of State: 81
% International: 38
Average Age: 28

COMPUTER AND RESEARCH FACILITIES
Research Facilities: Dewey Library plus 14 additional on-campus libraries; 2,532,175 volumes, 2,225,281 microforms, 18,359 current periodicals. Access provided to online bibliographic retrieval services and online databases.
Internet Fee? No

EXPENSES/FINANCIAL AID
Annual Tuition: $31,200

ADMISSIONS INFORMATION
Application Fee: $175
Electronic Application? Yes
Regular Application Deadline: 1/31
Regular Notification: 3/30
Deferment Available? No
Non-fall Admissions? No
Transfer Students Accepted? No
Need-Blind Admissions? Yes
Number of Applications Received: 2,940
% of Applicants Accepted: 18
% Accepted Who Enrolled: 70
Average GPA: 3.5
GPA Range: 3.2-3.9
Average GMAT: 663
GMAT Range: 610-740
Other Admissions Factors Considered: Previous course work in calculus and economics

EMPLOYMENT INFORMATION

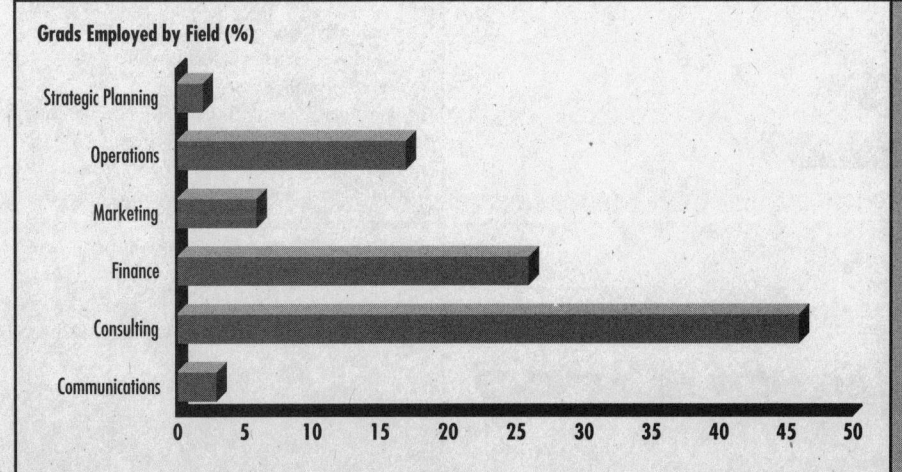

Grads Employed by Field (%):
- Strategic Planning: ~2
- Operations: ~17
- Marketing: ~5
- Finance: ~26
- Consulting: ~47
- Communications: ~3

Placement Office Available? Yes
% Employed Within 3 Months: 90
Frequent Employers: McKinsey and Co., Booz-Allen and Hamilton, AT Kearney, Merrill Lynch, Intel Corp, Boston Consulting Group, Accenture, Citigroup, Microsoft Corp., Siebel Systems, Bain and Company.

MICHIGAN STATE UNIVERSITY
The Eli Broad Graduate School of Management

Admissions Contact: Randall Dean, Director, MBA Admissions
Address: 215 Eppley Center, East Lansing, MI 48824-1221
Admissions Phone: 517-355-7604 • Admissions Fax: 517-353-1649
Admissions E-mail: mba@msu.edu • Web Address: mba.bus.msu.edu

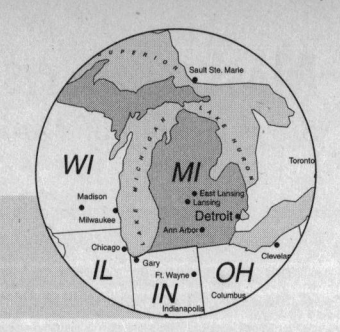

A strong national reputation, low tuition, "approachable" professors, and "a solid alumni base around the world" are a few reasons to consider the Eli Broad Graduate School of Management. Also notable is the Leadership Alliance Program, which provides students with "firsthand knowledge about a specific industry." Students say East Lansing "is a great place to live," too, thanks to its "very social atmosphere" and "shockingly beautiful" campus.

INSTITUTIONAL INFORMATION
Public/Private: Public
Evening Classes Available? No
Total Faculty: 95
% Faculty Female: 12
% Faculty Minority: 5
Student/Faculty Ratio: 2:1
Academic Calendar: Semester

PROGRAMS
Degrees Offered: MBA Program (day, full time, 21 months); MS Accounting (1 year); MBA Program in Integrative Management (weekend, 17 months); MS Manufacturing Engineering/Management (1 year); 8 doctoral programs; Executive MBA Program (21 months); MS in Foodservice Management
Joint Degrees: JD/MBA with MSU—Detroit College of Law (4 years), MBA/Master in International Management with Thunderbird (25 months)
Academic Specialties: Supply Chain Management, Finance, Marketing in Technology, Human Resource Management, Information Systems, Corporate Accounting, Hospitality Business
Special Opportunities: Leadership Alliance Program, numerous case competitions
Study Abroad Options: Japan, Mexico, Norway, Germany

STUDENT INFORMATION
Total Business Students: 206
% Full Time: 100
% Female: 25
% Minority: 14
% Out of State: 23
% International: 37
Average Age: 28

COMPUTER AND RESEARCH FACILITIES
Research Facilities: Centers for International Business and Education Research, Business and Technology, Executive Education, Management Education
Computer Facilities: Business volumes and subscriptions, high-technology classrooms with laptop and Ethernet connections, dedicated Information Systems Microlab, Financial Analysis Laboratory
% of MBA Classrooms Wired: 100
Computer Model Recommended: Laptop

EXPENSES/FINANCIAL AID
Annual Tuition (Resident/Nonresident): $12,800/$16,900
Books and Supplies: $1,500
Average Grant: $10,193
Average Loan: $12,658
% Receiving Financial Aid: 91
% Receiving Aid Their First Year: 88

ADMISSIONS INFORMATION
Application Fee: $30
Electronic Application? Yes
Early Decision Application Deadline: 12/15, 1/31, 2/28, 3/30
Early Decision Notification: 5/1
Regular Application Deadline: 6/15
Regular Notification: 7/15
Length of Deferment: 1 year
Non-fall Admissions? No
Transfer Students Accepted? No
Need-Blind Admissions? Yes
Number of Applications Received: 906
% of Applicants Accepted: 23
% Accepted Who Enrolled: 54
Average GPA: 3.4
Average GMAT: 641
Average Years Experience: 5
Other Admissions Factors Considered: Team skills and good understanding and fit with school.
Minority/Disadvantaged Student Recruitment Programs: Academic Achievement Graduate Assistantship Program, Educational Opportunity Fellowship Program, Multicultural Business Programs Scholarships. Also, Broad School and MSU Graduate School sponsor qualified minority candidates to visit the Broad School during admissions process.
Other Schools to Which Students Applied: Arizona State, Indiana University, Ohio State, Penn State—Great Valley, Purdue, U. of Michigan, U. of Wisconsin—Madison.

INTERNATIONAL STUDENTS
TOEFL Required of International Students? Yes
Minimum TOEFL: 600 (250 computer)

EMPLOYMENT INFORMATION

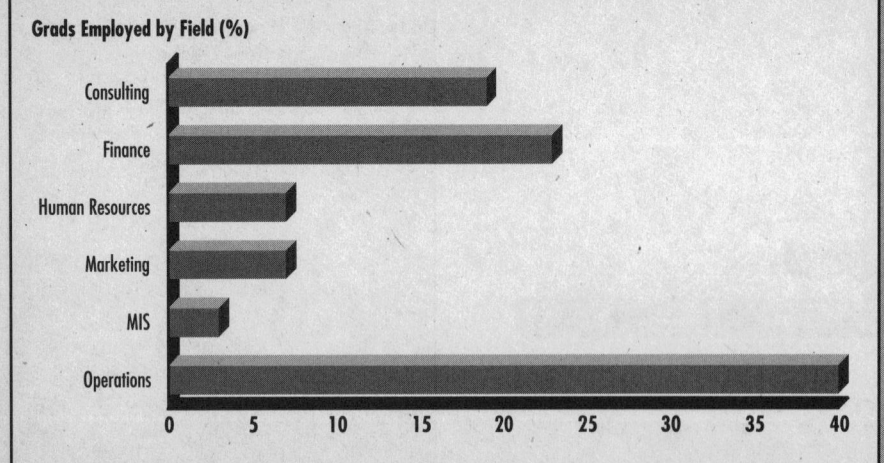

Grads Employed by Field (%)
- Consulting: ~19
- Finance: ~23
- Human Resources: ~6
- Marketing: ~7
- MIS: ~2
- Operations: ~40

Placement Office Available? Yes
% Employed Within 3 Months: 97
Frequent Employers: Intel, Ford Motor Co., IBM, Honeywell International, General Motors, Cap Gemini Ernst & Young, Northwest Airlines, Kmart Corporation, AT Kearney, Accenture, Visteon Corporation, Dow Chemical, Steelcase, Corning Incorporated, Guidant
Prominent Alumni: Eli Broad, chairman and CEO, SunAmerica, Inc.; Drayton McClane, CEO, McClane Group, and owner, Houston Astros; James Miller, president, Mazda Motor Corporation

MISSISSIPPI STATE UNIVERSITY
College of Business and Industry

Admissions Contact: Dr. Barbara Spencer, Director of Graduate Studies in Business
Address: PO Drawer 5288, Mississippi State, MS 39762
Admissions Phone: 662-325-1891 • *Admissions Fax:* 662-325-8161
Admissions E-mail: gsb@cobilan.msstate.edu • *Web Address:* www.cbi.msstate.edu/cobi/gsb/index2.html

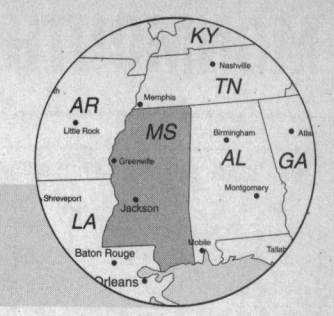

Due to its strong leadership-oriented approach, the new MBA in project management at Mississippi State attracts many applicants. Mississippi State University's emphasis on technology management is fitting, as the school offers interactive video courses to students in Columbus, Meridian, Vicksburg, and Gautier. Most students attend full time and are Mississippi natives.

INSTITUTIONAL INFORMATION
Public/Private: Public
Evening Classes Available? Yes
Total Faculty: 72
% Faculty Female: 22
% Faculty Minority: 7
% Faculty Part Time: 11
Student/Faculty Ratio: 3:1
Academic Calendar: Semester

PROGRAMS
Degrees Offered: MBA (30 credits, 12 months to 6 years); MS in Business Administration (30 credits, 12 months to 6 years); Master of Professional Accountancy (30 credits, 12 months to 6 years); Master of Taxation (30 credits, 12 months to 6 years); MS in Information Systems (30 credits, 12 months to 6 years); MBA in Project Management (32 credits, 12 months to 6 years); PhD in Business Administration (3 to 10 years); PhD in Applied Economics (3 to 10 years); MA in Applied Economics (12 months to 6 years)
Academic Specialties: Strategic Management, Human Resource Management, Leadership, Taxation, Real Estate, Insurance, E-Commerce, Marketing Management, Consumer Behavior

STUDENT INFORMATION
Total Business Students: 85
% Full Time: 64
% Female: 39
% Out of State: 39
% International: 13
Average Age: 27

COMPUTER AND RESEARCH FACILITIES
Research Facilities: A state-of-the-art instructional media center, multimedia software and computer terminals, free workshops, government depository material including statistical CD-ROMs
Computer Facilities: A large number of electronic databases, including ABI/Inform, BNA Environmental Library, Business Source Elite, CCH Internet Tax Research, Choices II (Simmons Market Research), Compustat, Disclosure Corporate Snapshots, Dissertation Abstracts, EconLit, General Business File ASAP, and Journal Citation Reports
Campuswide Network? Yes
% of MBA Classrooms Wired: 100
Internet Fee? No

EXPENSES/FINANCIAL AID
Annual Tuition (Resident/Nonresident): $3,586/$8,128
Tuition Per Credit (Resident/Nonresident): $199/$452
Room & Board (On/Off Campus): $3,000/$6,000
Books and Supplies: $600
Average Grant: $920
Average Loan: $9,461
% Receiving Financial Aid: 66
% Receiving Aid Their First Year: 68

ADMISSIONS INFORMATION
Electronic Application? Yes
Regular Application Deadline: 7/1
Regular Notification: Rolling
Length of Deferment: 1 year
Non-fall Application Deadline(s): 11/1 spring, 4/1 summer
Transfer Policy: 6 hours of transfer credit from accredited institutions.
Need-Blind Admissions? Yes
Number of Applications Received: 176
% of Applicants Accepted: 60
% Accepted Who Enrolled: 80
Average GPA: 3.4
GPA Range: 3.1-3.7
Average GMAT: 501
GMAT Range: 430-560
Average Years Experience: 1
Minority/Disadvantaged Student Recruitment Programs: We visit several minority schools.

INTERNATIONAL STUDENTS
TOEFL Required of International Students? Yes
Minimum TOEFL: 575

EMPLOYMENT INFORMATION
Placement Office Available? Yes
Frequent Employers: BellSouth, Accenture, International Paper, WorldCom, JC Penney
Prominent Alumni: Jerry Thames, former CEO, GTS, currently at Lehman Brothers; Cynthia A. Tucker, manager, Strategy and Portfolio Management

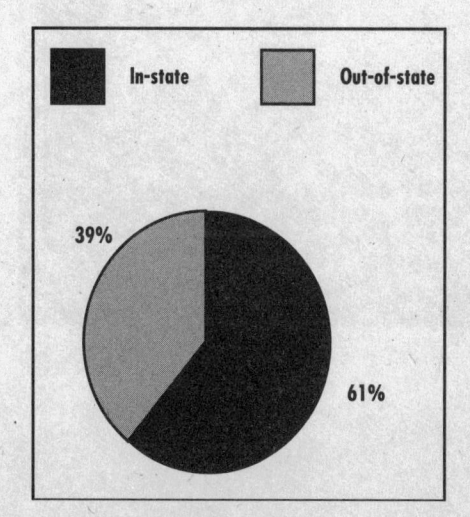

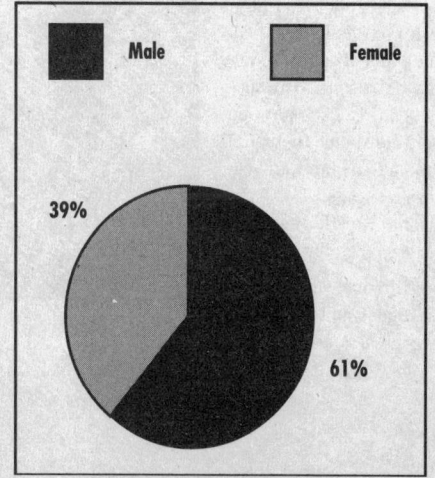

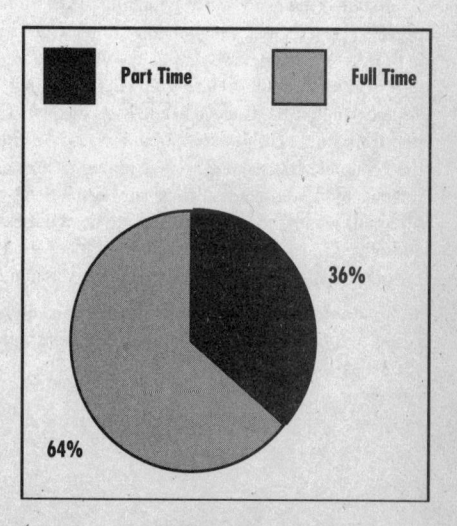

MONMOUTH UNIVERSITY

GRADUATE BUSINESS EDUCATION AT MONMOUTH UNIVERSITY
Now, more than ever, an advanced degree is key to success in the business world. At Monmouth, we educate business students by integrating scholarship and real-world experience in academic programs that are continuously reviewed and improved. If you seek to acquire the knowledge, skills, and practical judgment necessary for a rewarding career in business, consider our graduate programs.

Master of Business Administration: Theory and practice of management in national and international economies

Master of Business Administration-Healthcare Management Concentration: Healthcare systems, economics, financial management, and application of theory to practice

Whether you are breaking into a new career or moving up the administrative ladder, an advanced degree in business from Monmouth University is what you'll need.

- Learn directly from highly qualified faculty members, gaining insight from their years of business experience.
- Make contacts that will last a lifetime as you attend classes with other business professionals seeking advancement.
- Gain expertise in business administration in a wide array of topics including management, accounting, finance, and marketing. Explore international and technological dimensions.
- With an MBA, stand out from your peers as a sought-after professional in the business world.

THE UNIVERSITY
Monmouth University, as described in its mission statement, is an independent, comprehensive institution of higher learning emphasizing teaching and scholarship at the undergraduate and graduate levels. The University is dedicated to service in the public interest and, in particular, to the enhancement of the quality of life. Monmouth University is committed to providing a learning environment that enables men and women to pursue their educational goals, to reach their full potential, to determine the direction of their lives, and to contribute actively to their community and society.

Seven schools within the University—the School of Business Administration; the Edward G. Schlaefer School; the School of Education; the Graduate School; the Marjorie K. Unterberg School of Nursing and Health Studies; the School of Science, Technology and Engineering; and the Wayne D. McMurray School of Humanities and Social Sciences—provide a wide variety of academic programs at both the undergraduate and graduate levels.

Monmouth University was founded in 1933 with federal assistance, largely to provide opportunity for higher education for area high school graduates who—in those Depression days—could not afford to go away to college. It was a two-year institution holding classes only in the evening. For a time it appeared uncertain whether the College would have adequate funds to continue. With support from students and the community, however, the fledgling College survived the economic crisis and quickly assumed its present private status. In 1956 it was renamed Monmouth College and accredited by the state to offer four-year programs leading to the baccalaureate degree. Less than a decade later, it was authorized to offer master's degree programs. In 1995, the New Jersey Commission on Higher Education designated Monmouth a teaching university.

Today Monmouth offers 26 undergraduate and numerous graduate degree programs and concentrations. Within its student body, 22 states and 31 foreign countries are represented. More than 1,700 undergraduates are resident students.

ACCREDITATION
The University is licensed by the New Jersey Commission on Higher Education, and accredited by the Middle States Association of Colleges and Schools. In addition, the Chemistry Program is on the Approved List of the American Chemical Society (ACS); the Nursing Program is accredited by the New Jersey State Board of Nursing, Commission on Collegiate Nursing Education, and the National League for Nursing (NLN); the Social Work Undergraduate Program is accredited by the Council on Social Work Education (CSWE); and the School of Business Administration and its MBA program are accredited by AACSB—the Association to Advance Collegiate Schools of Business.

THE GRADUATE FACULTY
The graduate faculty provide the core of instruction in the graduate program at Monmouth University. Recognized for their scholarly achievements by peers in their fields, the members of the faculty provide a challenging classroom environment. The faculty's mission is to ensure that Monmouth graduates leave the University ready to exercise socially responsible leadership in their professions and the community. The faculty bring the insight from research and professional experience into the classroom. Graduate students are drawn into the ongoing, creative work of the faculty through classroom demonstration, as research assistants, and through attendance at professional meetings. The graduate faculty also serve as advisors and mentors to students, in many cases not only during the course of their studies but also after they graduate from the University.

Working directly with senior faculty who are engaged in research is a key element in graduate-level study. In recent interviews, a group of student leaders on campus unanimously agreed that the opportunity to work closely with faculty is the greatest single benefit of Monmouth's small class size and engaged faculty. Students are able to achieve a comfortable rapport with the professors.

LOCATION
The University is located in a quiet, residential area of an attractive community near the Atlantic Ocean, about an hour and a half from the metropolitan attractions of New York City and Philadelphia. Monmouth enjoys the advantage of proximity, within its home county, to many high-technology firms and financial institutions, and a thriving business-industrial sector. These provide employment possibilities for Monmouth University graduates.

The University's 147-acre campus, considered one of the most beautiful in New Jersey, includes among approximately 50 buildings a harmonious blend of historic and contemporary architectural styles. Bey Hall, the School of Business Administration building, which contains case study classrooms, seminar rooms, and computer laboratories, houses the MBA program.

School of Business Administration

SCHOOL OF BUSINESS ADMINISTRATION

The mission of the School of Business Administration is to excel in educating business students by integrating scholarship and business experience in academic programs that are subject to continuous review and improvement. The School of Business Administration is accredited by the AACSB—The International Association for Management Education. The primary purpose of our programs is to enable graduates to acquire the knowledge, skills, and practical judgment necessary for responsible and rewarding careers in business. The School of Business Administration prepares its graduates for positions of leadership in both the private and public sectors. Faculty with strong academic and business experience have developed curricula that stress critical thinking, sophisticated communications skills, and a flexible managerial perspective.

Within the School of Business Administration is the Kvernland Chair in Philosophy and Corporate Social Policy, which has been endowed through generous gifts in the name of Jack T. Kvernland, a late trustee of the College. Professor Guy Oakes of the management department currently occupies this chair. Professor Oakes is studying problems concerning the relationship between corporate, public, and private values in American life. The School also administers the Real Estate Institute, which is directed by Professor Donald Moliver of the economics and finance department.

MASTER OF BUSINESS ADMINISTRATION (MBA)

The purpose of the MBA program is to serve well-qualified graduate students who are committed to the pursuit of more demanding and extensive responsibilities, the enhancement of their competencies, and an improvement in their value to the organizations they serve. The graduate program combines theory and practice of management and concentrates on contemporary managerial responsibilities. The curriculum underscores the complexity and diversity of managerial decisions in both the national and international economy. The MBA student learns in small classes that promote close interaction with our business faculty, and benefits from special contributions by visiting lecturers. In addition, Monmouth's $6.5 million business administration building, Bey Hall (which opened in 1991), provides business students with a contemporary learning environment.

The MBA program includes two options: the MBA and the MBA with a concentration in Healthcare Management. A student must complete a minimum of 30 to 36 credits, which include core courses, beyond the core courses, the integrative capstone course, and elective courses where applicable. After admission, permission is required to take courses at another institution. Nonmatriculated students are prohibited from enrolling in graduate business courses.

MBA Requirements: 30 to 48 credits, depending on previous course work. The specific requirements are as follows:

a) Core courses (0 to 18 credits): BE501, BM502, BA503, BM506, BM507, and BK509. Core course(s) may be waived if equivalent undergraduate or graduate course(s) were completed within seven years with a grade of B or better.

b) Beyond the core courses (30 credits°): BF511, BM515, BA541, BM563 or BK535, BM590, a technology course (BM520 or 565), a business environment course (BE561 or 571 or 572 or 575 or BF517 or an elective°°), a behavioral course (BM525 or an elective°°), a marketing course (BK533 or 535 or 539 or 540 or 541 or an elective°°), and a quantitative course (BM549 or 556 or an elective°°).

Notes:

° *In courses beyond the core, excluding BM515, 520, 563, 565, and 590, there cannot be more than two (2) BA or BE or BF or BM or BK courses.*

°° *Indicates that an elective may be taken instead of one of the specified courses if the student has completed a related core course at Monmouth University as follows: BE501 is related to the business environment course requirement, BM502 is related to the behavioral course requirement, BK509 is related to the marketing course requirement, and BM506 is related to the quantitative course requirement.*

MBA Healthcare Management Requirements: 33 to 54 credits, depending on previous course work. The specific requirements are as follows:

a) Core courses (0 to 18 credits): BE501, BM502, BA503, BM506, BM507, and BK509. Core course(s) may be waived if equivalent undergraduate or graduate course(s) were completed within seven years with a grade of B or better.

b) Beyond the core courses (21 credits): BM515, BA541, BF511, BM590, an international course (BM563 or 535), a technology course (BM520 or 565), a marketing course (BK533 or 535 or 539 or 540 or 541 or a related elective). Elective may be taken in place of the required course if the related course was completed at Monmouth University.

c) Concentration in Healthcare Management (12 to 15 credits): BH571, BH572, BH573, BH574, and BH575 (course may be waived with sufficient relevant healthcare experience).

ADMISSION REQUIREMENTS

The School of Business Administration requires candidates for admission to the MBA and MBA-Healthcare Management programs to take the Graduate Management Admission Test (GMAT) prior to admission, achieving a score of at least 450. A total minimum score of 1000—comprising the sum of the baccalaureate GPA multiplied by 200 plus the GMAT total score—and a four-year baccalaureate degree are required for admission. The exceptions to the general rule above are as follows:

(a) A four-year baccalaureate degree and a minimum GMAT total score of 500.

(b) A recipient of a baccalaureate degree more than eight years ago; adequate business experience at the managerial level; completion of the GMAT with a minimum score of 450; and two letters of recommendation. The student must submit an autobiographical résumé detailing his or her work experience to date.

(c) A master's degree or a doctorate degree (PhD, EdD, MD, or JD).

(d) A four-year baccalaureate degree and CPA or CFA licensure.

(e) Conditional admission will be granted to a small number of qualified applicants. The MBA program director should be consulted for specific criteria.

TUITION AND FEES

For 2002–2003, cost is $549 per credit, and the comprehensive fee is $284 per semester.

MONMOUTH UNIVERSITY

Admissions Contact: Kevin Roane, Director, Graduate Admission
Address: 400 Cedar Ave., West Long Branch, NJ 07764-1898
Admissions Phone: 732-571-3452 • Admissions Fax: 732-263-5123
Admissions E-mail: gradadm@monmouth.edu • Web Address: www.monmouth.edu/academics/business.asp

MONMOUTH UNIVERSITY
School of Business Administration

Admissions Contact: Kevin Roane, Director, Graduate Admission
Address: 400 Cedar Ave., West Long Branch, NJ 07764-1898
Admissions Phone: 732-571-3452 • Admissions Fax: 732-263-5123
Admissions E-mail: gradadm@monmouth.edu • Web Address: www.monmouth.edu/academics/business.asp

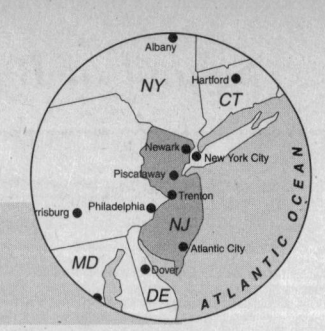

The School of Business Administration is one of the seven colleges of Monmouth University, located on a 147-acre campus only five minutes by car from the Atlantic Ocean. Monmouth's MBA comes in the broad-based, general format or with a concentration in accounting or health care management, and all classes are offered in the evening for part-time students. Emphasis is placed on ethical, global, and technological perspectives in an MBA program that "combines management practice and theory in a contemporary managerial context." One of the highlights of the School of Business Administration is the Business Council, which acts as a student resource for training and consulting, while also working to ensure that business students at the university can reciprocate these services and act as a resource for the community.

INSTITUTIONAL INFORMATION
Public/Private: Private
Evening Classes Available? Yes
Total Faculty: 26
% Faculty Female: 16
% Faculty Part Time: 15
Student/Faculty Ratio: 10:1
Students in Parent Institution: 5,753
Academic Calendar: Semester

PROGRAMS
Degrees Offered: MBA (30 to 48 credits, 12 months to 5 years); Master of Business Administration (33 to 54 credits, 12 months to 5 years), with a concentration in Health Care Management; Master of Business Administration (30 to 48 credits, 12 months to 5 years), with a track in Accounting

STUDENT INFORMATION
Total Business Students: 269
% Full Time: 10
% Female: 46
% Minority: 14
% International: 18
Average Age: 30

COMPUTER AND RESEARCH FACILITIES
Campuswide Network? Yes
% of MBA Classrooms Wired: 18
Internet Fee? No

EXPENSES/FINANCIAL AID
Annual Tuition: $9,414
Tuition Per Credit: $523
Books and Supplies: $250
Average Grant: $1,416
Average Loan: $11,095
% Receiving Financial Aid: 36
% Receiving Aid Their First Year: 54

ADMISSIONS INFORMATION
Application Fee: $35
Electronic Application? Yes
Regular Application Deadline: 8/15
Regular Notification: Rolling
Deferment Available? Yes
Length of Deferment: 1 year
Non-fall Admissions? Yes
Non-fall Application Deadline(s): 12/15 spring, 5/15 summer
Transfer Students Accepted? Yes
Transfer Policy: Must complete at least 30 credits at Monmouth; transfer credits must be within 7 years and with acceptable grade
Need-Blind Admissions? Yes
Number of Applications Received: 245
% of Applicants Accepted: 60
% Accepted Who Enrolled: 57
Average GPA: 3.1
GPA Range: 2.8-3.4
Average GMAT: 491
GMAT Range: 450-540
Other Admissions Factors Considered: Résumé; letters of recommendation required of students who graduated more than 8 years ago

INTERNATIONAL STUDENTS
TOEFL Required of International Students? Yes
Minimum TOEFL: 550 (213 computer)

EMPLOYMENT INFORMATION
Placement Office Available? Yes

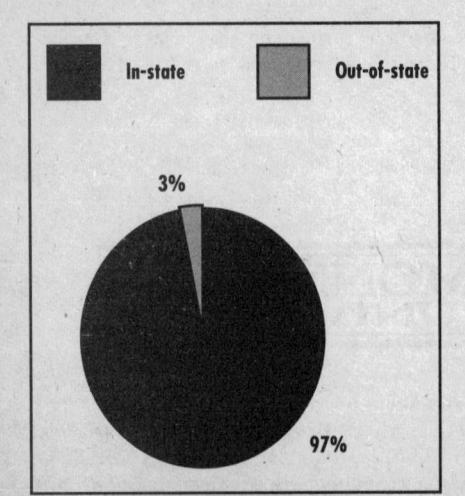

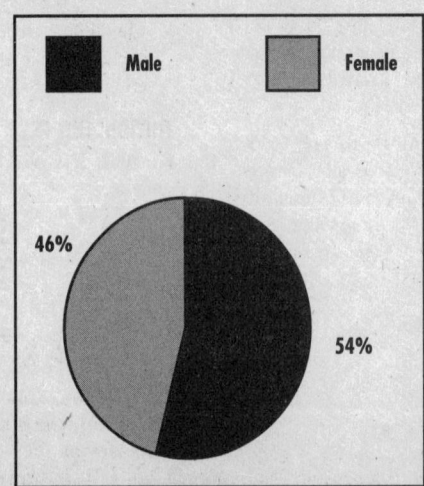

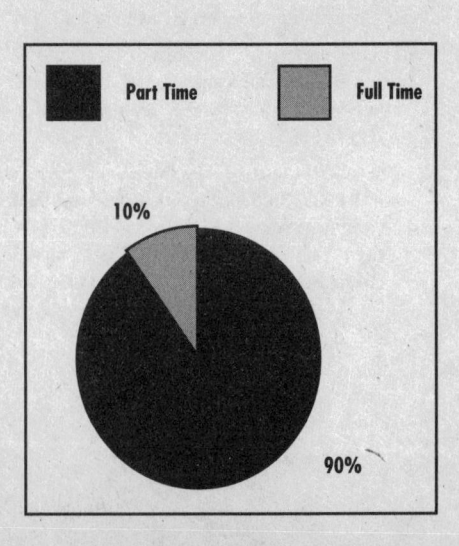

In-state: 97% / Out-of-state: 3%

Male: 54% / Female: 46%

Part Time: 90% / Full Time: 10%

NEW JERSEY INSTITUTE OF TECHNOLOGY
School of Management

Admissions Contact: Dr. Macolm Worrell, Assistant Dean for Graduate Programs
Address: University Heights, Newark, NJ 07102-1982
Admissions Phone: 973-596-3262 • Admissions Fax: 973-596-3074
Web Address: www.njit.edu

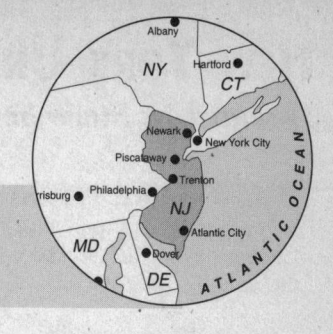

All graduate business energy at NJIT is tunneled into its single MBA program: the MBA in Management of Technology. MBA students are trained to increase the productivity and competitiveness of technology-based organizations, while recognizing the importance of ethical business standards and a global perspective. The future technology managers of the MBA program can specialize in e-commerce, infrastructure management, financial management, or management information systems, and can attend courses at the main Newark campus or at three other convenient locations. The quality of all educational programs at NJIT, undergrad or graduate, is enhanced by its 17 state-of-the-art research centers.

INSTITUTIONAL INFORMATION
Public/Private: Public
Evening Classes Available? No
Total Faculty: 38
% Faculty Part Time: 54
Students in Parent Institution: 7,504
Academic Calendar: Semester

PROGRAMS
Degrees Offered: Executive Master of Science in Management (39 credits, 14 months), Master of Science in Management (30 to 48 credits, 12 months to 7 years), MBA in Management of Technology (48 to 60 credits, 18 months to 7 years)

STUDENT INFORMATION
Total Business Students: 442
% Full Time: 15
Average Age: 32

COMPUTER AND RESEARCH FACILITIES
Number of Student Computers: 150
Campuswide Network? Yes
Computer Proficiency Required? No
Special Purchasing Agreements? No

EXPENSES/FINANCIAL AID
Annual Tuition (Resident/Nonresident): $3,476/$4,885
Room & Board (On/Off Campus): $6,873/$6,873

ADMISSIONS INFORMATION
Application Fee: $50
Electronic Application? No
Regular Application Deadline: Rolling
Regular Notification: Rolling
Deferment Available? No
Non-fall Admissions? Yes
Non-fall Application Deadline(s): Rolling
Transfer Students Accepted? No
Need-Blind Admissions? No
Number of Applications Received: 150
% of Applicants Accepted: 86
% Accepted Who Enrolled: 74
Average GPA: 3.2
Average GMAT: 500
Average Years Experience: 5
Other Admissions Factors Considered: For international students, proof of adequate funds, proof of health/immunizations required

INTERNATIONAL STUDENTS
TOEFL Required of International Students? Yes
Minimum TOEFL: 525

EMPLOYMENT INFORMATION
Placement Office Available? Yes
% Employed Within 6 Months: 100

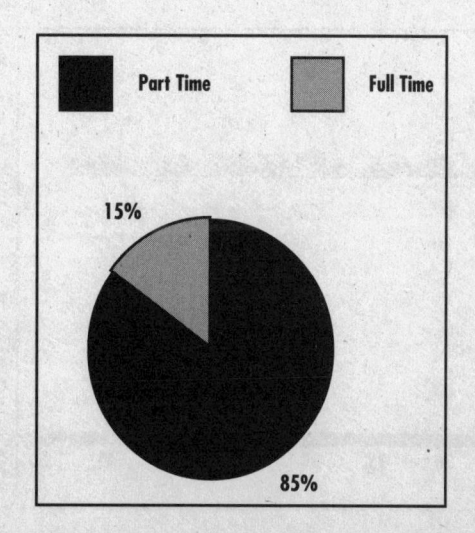

Part Time 85% | Full Time 15%

NEW YORK UNIVERSITY
Leonard N. Stern School of Business

Admissions Contact: Julia Min, Director, MBA Admissions
Address: 44 West 4th Street, Suite 10-160, New York, NY 10012
Admissions Phone: 212-998-0600 • Admissions Fax: 212-995-4231
Admissions E-mail: sternmba@stern.nyu.edu • Web Address: www.stern.nyu.edu

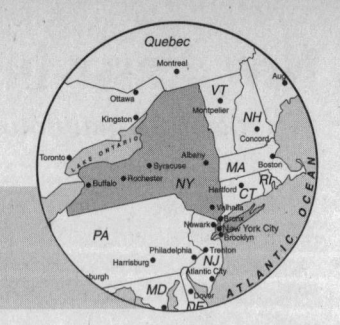

The "street-smart, focused" students at NYU's Stern School of Business love its location near "the heart of" diverse and glittering New York City's "bustling financial, consumer-products, and media industries." With nearly 30 exchange programs and international research centers, international business is especially noteworthy at Stern, as is the Management Consulting Program, in which corporations like Reebok and IBM hire teams of students to do consulting work.

INSTITUTIONAL INFORMATION
Public/Private: Private
Evening Classes Available? Yes
Total Faculty: 209
% Faculty Female: 18
% Faculty Minority: 19
Student/Faculty Ratio: 11:1
Students in Parent Institution: 51,901
Academic Calendar: Semester

PROGRAMS
Degrees Offered: PhD (average 4 to 5 years, must be completed in 6 years)
Combined Degrees: JD/MBA (4 years), MBA/MA French (3 years), MBA/MA Politics (3 years), MBA/Master of Public Administration (3 years), MBA/MS Biology (3 years)
Academic Specialties: Finance, Entrepreneurship and Innovation, Information Systems, Marketing, International Business, Accounting, Economics, Management and Organizational Behavior, Operations Management, Statistics and Operations Research
Special Opportunities: Program Initiatives in Digital Economy, Entertainment, Media and Technology, Law and Business, Quantitative Finance, Real Estate Finance
Study Abroad Options: Australia, Austria, Belgium, Brazil, Chile, Costa Rica, Denmark, England, France, Germany, Hong Kong, Israel, Italy, Japan, Mexico, The Netherlands, Norway, Singapore, South Africa, South Korea, Spain, Sweden, Switzerland, Venezuela

STUDENT INFORMATION
Total Business Students: 2,779
% Full Time: 35
% Female: 34
% Minority: 7
Average Age: 27

COMPUTER AND RESEARCH FACILITIES
Research Facilities: Centers and Institutes for Financial Institutions, Research in Securities Markets, Japan-U.S. Business and Economic Studies, Accounting Research, Entrepreneurial Studies, Digital Economy Research, Law and Business
Computer Facilities: Computer labs and electronic classrooms offer approximately 200 Pentium PCs; all are networked and provide access to time sharing and the Internet. All classroom spaces and some public study/lounge areas offer wireless internet access.
Campuswide Network? Yes
Computer Model Recommended: Laptop
Internet Fee? No

EXPENSES/FINANCIAL AID
Annual Tuition: $30,600
Tuition Per Credit: $1,130
Books and Supplies: $2,163
Average Grant: $7,600
Average Loan: $25,000
% Receiving Financial Aid: 95
% Receiving Aid Their First Year: 85

ADMISSIONS INFORMATION
Application Fee: $150
Electronic Application? Yes
Early Decision Application Deadline: 12/1
Regular Application Deadline: 3/15
Regular Notification: Rolling
Deferment Available? No
Non-fall Application Deadline(s): September 15 (spring), part-time program only
Transfer Students Accepted? No
Need-Blind Admissions? Yes
Number of Applications Received: 4,039
% of Applicants Accepted: 22
% Accepted Who Enrolled: 48
Average GPA: 3.4
Average GMAT: 689
Other Admissions Factors Considered: At least two years of work experience, undergraduate course work, involvement in community, professional progression, goals in pursuing an MBA, and letters of recommendation
Minority/Disadvantaged Student Recruitment Programs: Member of consortium for graduate study in management, which sponsors underrepresented minorities in business schools; member of The Robert A. Toigo Foundation; minority scholarship programs available

INTERNATIONAL STUDENTS
TOEFL Required of International Students? Yes
Minimum TOEFL: 600 (250 computer)

EMPLOYMENT INFORMATION

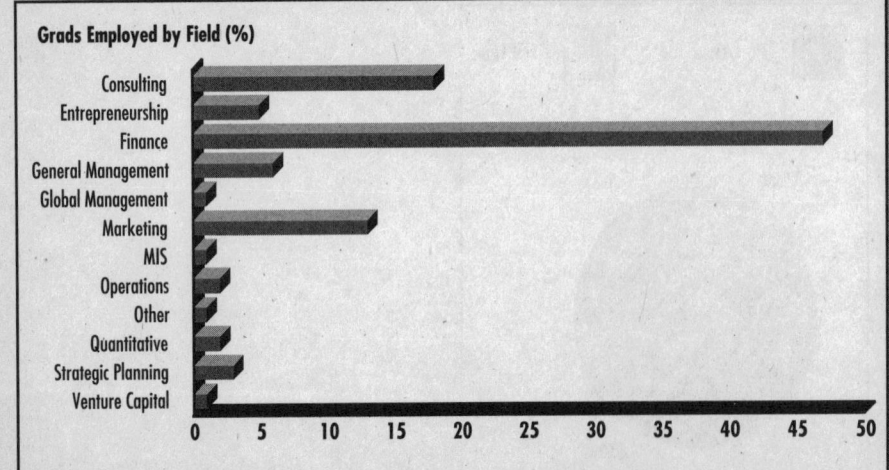

Grads Employed by Field (%)

Field	%
Consulting	~18
Entrepreneurship	~2
Finance	~47
General Management	~3
Global Management	~2
Marketing	~14
MIS	~1
Operations	~2
Other	~2
Quantitative	~1
Strategic Planning	~3
Venture Capital	~1

Placement Office Available? Yes
% Employed Within 3 Months: 93
Frequent Employers: Lehman Brothers; JP Morgan; Chase; Deutsche Bank; McKinsey & Company; Salomon Smith Barney; American Express; Bear Stearns; Goldman Sachs; Merrill Lynch; Booz Allen & Hamilton; Credit Suisse First Boston; Pfizer; Deloitte & Touche; IBM; Morgan Stanley; Citigroup; Johnson & Johnson; PriceWaterhouseCoopers; UBS Warburg; Nabisco; Unilever; Standard's & Poor
Prominent Alumni: Allen Wheat, chairman and CEO, Credit Suisse First Boston; Joseph Nacchio, chairman and CEO of Qwest Communications; Abby F. Kohnstamm, senior vice president of Marketing, IBM.

NICHOLLS STATE UNIVERSITY
College of Business Administration

Admissions Contact: Becky LeBlanc-Durocher, Director of Admissions
Address: PO Box 2004, Thibodaux, LA 70310
Admissions Phone: 877-642-4655 • *Admissions Fax:* 985-448-4929
Admissions E-mail: esai-bl@nicholls.edu • *Web Address:* www.nicholls.edu

Nicholls State University takes its name from Francis T. Nicholls, governor of Louisiana in the late nineteenth century and later chief justice to the Louisiana Supreme Court, who is known for reestablishing Louisiana's "Home Rule" political status and campaigning against the corrupt Louisiana State lottery. Nicholls is primarily an undergraduate institution, but it offers select graduate programs and insists that all students across the board be encouraged to lead responsible lives and be given the opportunity to develop character through advanced education. The MBA program, available full time or part time, emphasizes an ethical and technological approach to problem solving, critical thinking, effective communication, and maintaining a global perspective.

INSTITUTIONAL INFORMATION
Public/Private: Public
Evening Classes Available? Yes
Total Faculty: 26
% Faculty Female: 27
Student/Faculty Ratio: 15:1
Students in Parent Institution: 7,206

PROGRAMS
Degrees Offered: Master of Business Administration (33 to 69 credits)
Study Abroad Options: France—Ecole Superieure du Commerce Exterier, Paris; Ecole Superieure de Commerce, Saint Etienne; University of Paris IX, Dauphine

STUDENT INFORMATION
Total Business Students: 105
% Full Time: 26
% Female: 41
% Minority: 3
% Out of State: 6
% International: 14

COMPUTER AND RESEARCH FACILITIES
Campuswide Network? Yes
Internet Fee? No

EXPENSES/FINANCIAL AID
Annual Tuition (Resident/Nonresident): $2,400/$7,800
Room & Board (On Campus): $3,902
Books and Supplies: $2,000
% Receiving Financial Aid: 20

ADMISSIONS INFORMATION
Application Fee: $20
Electronic Application? Yes
Regular Application Deadline: 6/30
Regular Notification: Rolling
Deferment Available? Yes
Length of Deferment: 1 semester
Non-fall Admissions? Yes
Non-fall Application Deadline(s): Spring, summer
Transfer Students Accepted? Yes
Transfer Policy: Maximum of 9 hours may be transferred from an accredited institution.
Need-Blind Admissions? Yes
Number of Applications Received: 55
% of Applicants Accepted: 100
% Accepted Who Enrolled: 58
Average GPA: 3.1
Average GMAT: 469

INTERNATIONAL STUDENTS
TOEFL Required of International Students? Yes
Minimum TOEFL: 550 (213 computer)

EMPLOYMENT INFORMATION
Placement Office Available? Yes
Prominent Alumni: Barry Melancon, president, AICPA

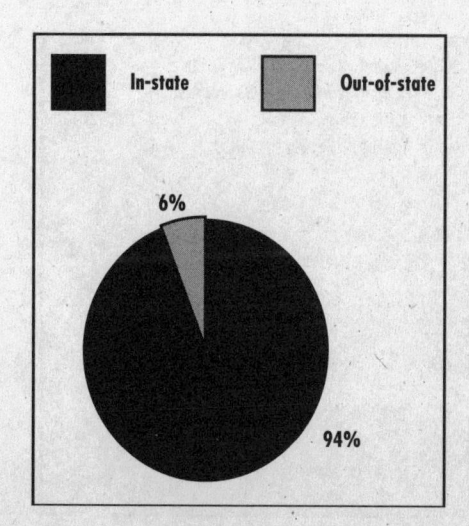

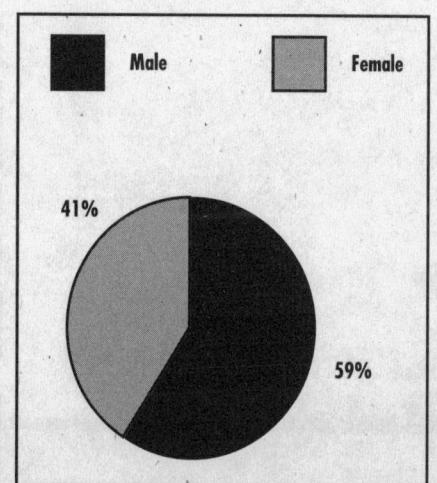

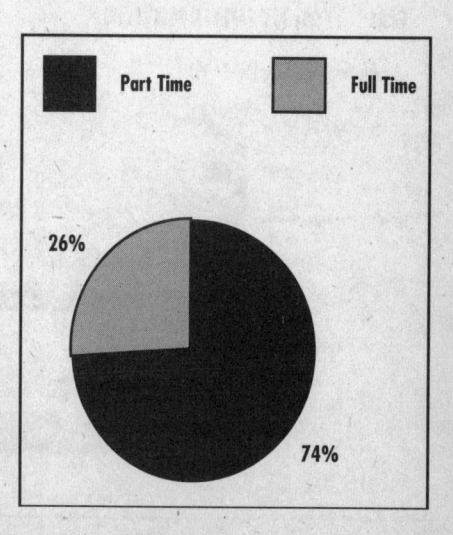

NORTHEASTERN UNIVERSITY
Graduate School of Business Administration

Admissions Contact: Jennifer Kott, Manager, Full-time MBA Programs
Address: 360 Huntington Avenue, Boston, MA 02115
Admissions Phone: 617-373-5992 • Admissions Fax: 617-373-8564
Admissions E-mail: gsba@neu.edu • Web Address: www.cba.neu.edu/gsba

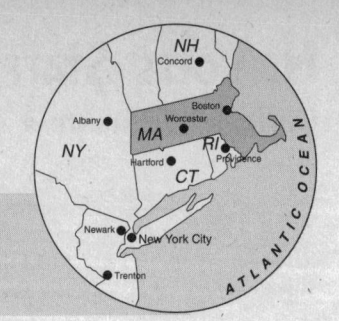

The competitive MBA students at Northeastern in "intellectually exciting" Boston have many options. There is a part-time program, an Executive MBA, a two-year full-time MBA, an "excellent" High Technology MBA for technical professionals, and the fast-paced, popular, unique, and "challenging and rewarding" Cooperative Education MBA, which provides "invaluable," paid, MBA-level employment during part of the program. After graduation, most students go into finance or consulting.

INSTITUTIONAL INFORMATION
Public/Private: Private
Evening Classes Available? Yes
Total Faculty: 148
% Faculty Part Time: 25
Student/Faculty Ratio: 12:1
Students in Parent Institution: 26,105
Academic Calendar: Quarter

PROGRAMS
Degrees Offered: Cooperative MBA (21 months), High Technology MBA (21 months), Executive MBA (18 months), Master of Science in Finance (12 to 21 months), Part-time MBA (30 to 84 months)
Joint Degrees: Juris Doctor/MBA, MS/MBA in Nursing Administration, MS/MBA in Accounting
Academic Specialties: Finance, Accounting, Marketing, Logistical and Transportation Management, Information Resources Management, International Business, Entrepreneurship
Special Opportunities: Executive MBA Program, Cooperative MBA Program, MS in Finance, High Technology MBA
Study Abroad Options: Eastern Europe, France, Southeast Asia

STUDENT INFORMATION
Total Business Students: 616
% Full Time: 36
% Female: 46
% Minority: 9
% Out of State: 1
Average Age: 28

COMPUTER AND RESEARCH FACILITIES
Computer Facilities: Snell Library plus 4 additional libraries with 870,475 volumes; 2,057,538 microforms; 8,417 current periodicals; CD players available; access provided to online bibliographic retrieval services
Campuswide Network? Yes
% of MBA Classrooms Wired: 100
Internet Fee? No

EXPENSES/FINANCIAL AID
Annual Tuition: $25,850
Books and Supplies: $850
Average Grant: $20,000
Average Loan: $13,000

ADMISSIONS INFORMATION
Application Fee: $50
Electronic Application? Yes
Regular Application Deadline: Rolling
Regular Notification: Rolling
Deferment Available? Yes
Length of Deferment: 1 year
Non-fall Admissions? Yes
Non-fall Application Deadline(s): Rolling
Transfer Students Accepted? Yes
Transfer Policy: Please visit website for transfer policy.
Need-Blind Admissions? Yes
Number of Applications Received: 190
% of Applicants Accepted: 64
% Accepted Who Enrolled: 47
Average GPA: 3.2
Average GMAT: 557
Average Years Experience: 3
Minority/Disadvantaged Student Recruitment Programs: Provost Minority Scholarship Program

INTERNATIONAL STUDENTS
TOEFL Required of International Students? Yes
Minimum TOEFL: 600 (250 computer)

EMPLOYMENT INFORMATION

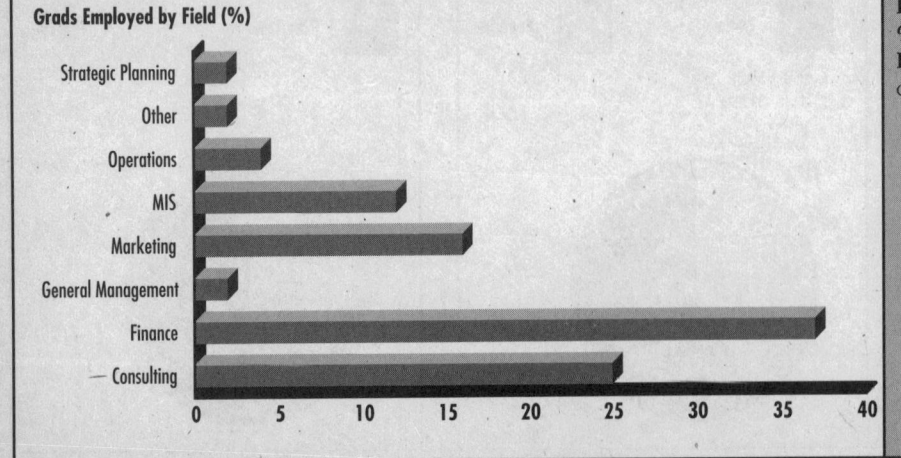

Grads Employed by Field (%):
- Strategic Planning
- Other
- Operations
- MIS
- Marketing
- General Management
- Finance
- Consulting

Placement Office Available? Yes
% Employed Within 3 Months: 95
Frequent Employers: State Street Bank, Lucent Technology, EMC Corp., Fidelity

NORTHERN ARIZONA UNIVERSITY
College of Business Administration

Admissions Contact: Joe Anderson, Director, MBA Program
Address: 70 McConnell Circle, PO Box 15066, Flagstaff, AZ 86011-5066
Admissions Phone: 928-523-7342 • Admissions Fax: 928-523-7331
Admissions E-mail: MBA@nau.edu • Web Address: www.cba.nau.edu/mbaprogram

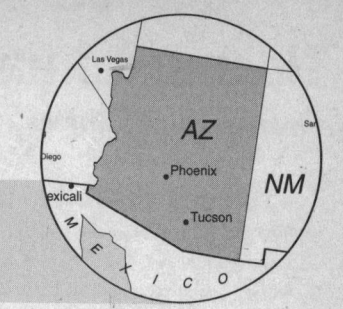

Flagstaff, home of Northern Arizona University, has a comfortable climate and an average of 288 sunny days each year, creating "excellent conditions for study and recreation." The MBA program has several different options: full time (10 months), half time (2 years), or quarter time (4 years). Frequent employers of NAU graduates are IBM, Motorola, Andersen, and Ernst & Young.

INSTITUTIONAL INFORMATION
Public/Private: Public
Evening Classes Available? No
Total Faculty: 54
% Faculty Part Time: 2
Student/Faculty Ratio: 22:1
Students in Parent Institution: 19,728

PROGRAMS
Degrees Offered: Master of Business Administration (MBA) (full time or part time, 31 credits, 10 months to 6 years), with concentrations in Management Information Systems, International Business, Finance, and International Finance

STUDENT INFORMATION
Total Business Students: 74
% Female: 28
% Minority: 16
% International: 16
Average Age: 27

COMPUTER AND RESEARCH FACILITIES
Research Facilities: Counseling and Testing Center
Computer Facilities: MBA Lab, Online Library, NAU Learning Assistance Centers
Campuswide Network? Yes
% of MBA Classrooms Wired: 100
Computer Model Recommended: No
Internet Fee? No

EXPENSES/FINANCIAL AID
Annual Tuition (Resident/Nonresident): $3,906/$13,268
Tuition Per Credit (Resident/Nonresident): $126/$428
Room & Board (On Campus): $7,216
Books and Supplies: $1,115

ADMISSIONS INFORMATION
Application Fee: $45
Electronic Application? Yes
Regular Application Deadline: 3/1
Regular Notification: 4/1
Deferment Available? Yes
Length of Deferment: 1 year
Non-fall Admissions? Yes
Non-fall Application Deadline(s): 10/15 spring, 1/15 summer
Transfer Students Accepted? Yes
Transfer Policy: 9 hours towards electives only
Need-Blind Admissions? No
Number of Applications Received: 90
% of Applicants Accepted: 51
% Accepted Who Enrolled: 91
Average GPA: 3.4
Average GMAT: 548
Average Years Experience: 5
Other Admissions Factors Considered: computer experience

INTERNATIONAL STUDENTS
TOEFL Required of International Students? Yes
Minimum TOEFL: 600 (250 computer)

EMPLOYMENT INFORMATION
Placement Office Available? Yes
% Employed Within 3 Months: 95
Frequent Employers: IBM, Motorola, Arthur Andersen, Axlam, Ernst & Young

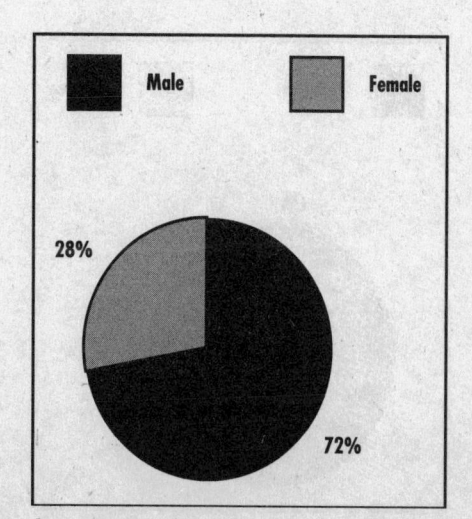

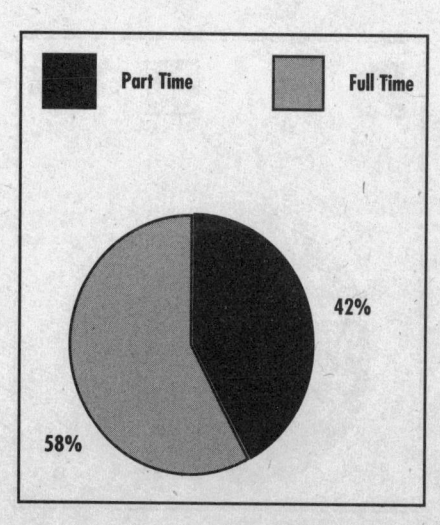

NORTHERN ILLINOIS UNIVERSITY
College of Business, Office of MBA Programs

Admissions Contact: Mona Salmon, Assistant Director
Address: Wirtz 140, Dekalb, IL 60115
Admissions Phone: 800-323-8714 • Admissions Fax: 815-753-3300
Admissions E-mail: cobgrads@niu.edu • Web Address: www.cob.niu.edu/grad/grad.html

Northern Illinois University offers two MBA programs: an Evening MBA curriculum, designed for part-time students, and an Executive MBA curriculum, offered on Saturdays and designed for mid-career working professionals. NSU has a professional, cooperative learning environment and a student body comprised of motivated part-time students—full-time professionals who wish to advance their education and gain more experience. The evening program offers study abroad options in Italy, China, and Korea as well as international business seminars that tour Europe.

INSTITUTIONAL INFORMATION
Public/Private: Public
Evening Classes Available? Yes
Total Faculty: 57
% Faculty Female: 19
% Faculty Minority: 4
Student/Faculty Ratio: 24:1
Students in Parent Institution: 23,248

PROGRAMS
Degrees Offered: AACSB-accredited: MBA (30 to 40 semester hours, 10 to 18 courses), Master of Accounting Science (30 to 67 semester hours, 10 to 25 courses), MS in Management Information Systems (30 to 51 semester hours, 10 to 20 courses). Not AACSB-accredited: MS in Taxation (30 semester hours, 10 courses)
Academic Specialties: Accounting, Finance, Management Information Systems, International Business, short-term international experience available for part-time students
Special Opportunities: International Business Seminars in Europe; Business and Culture Seminars in China and Korea
Study Abroad Options: Shanghai University of Finance and Economics, China,
Kyung Hee University, Seoul, Korea

STUDENT INFORMATION
Total Business Students: 528
% Full Time: 1
% Out of State: 20
Average Age: 32

COMPUTER AND RESEARCH FACILITIES
Computer Facilities: Computer labs at each campus: Hoffman Estates, Naperville, Rockford
Campuswide Network? Yes
Computer Model Recommended: Desktop
Internet Fee? No

ADMISSIONS INFORMATION
Application Fee: $30
Electronic Application? No
Regular Application Deadline: 6/1
Regular Notification: Rolling
Deferment Available? Yes
Length of Deferment: 24 months
Non-fall Admissions? Yes
Non-fall Application Deadline(s): 11/1 spring, 4/1 summer. International: 5/1 fall, 10/1 spring
Transfer Students Accepted? Yes
Transfer Policy: A limit of 9 semester hours accepted for phase-2 credit from AACSB-accredited schools only

Need-Blind Admissions? Yes
Number of Applications Received: 262
% of Applicants Accepted: 97
% Accepted Who Enrolled: 70
Average GPA: 3.2
Average GMAT: 535
Average Years Experience: 4.5

INTERNATIONAL STUDENTS
TOEFL Required of International Students? Yes
Minimum TOEFL: 550 (213 computer)

EMPLOYMENT INFORMATION
Placement Office Available? No

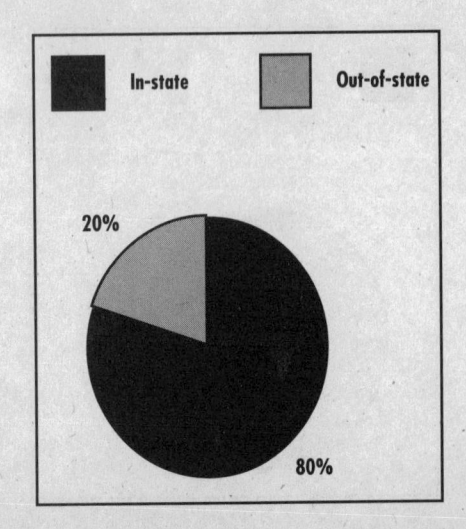

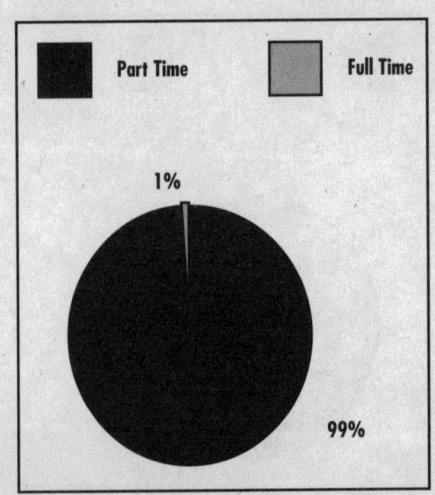

NORTHWESTERN UNIVERSITY
J. L. Kellogg Graduate School of Management

Admissions Contact: Michele Rogers, Assistant Dean, Director of Admissions and Financial Aid
Address: 2001 Sheridan Road, Evanston, IL 60208-2001
Admissions Phone: 847-491-3308 • Admissions Fax: 847-491-4960
Admissions E-mail: kellogg.admissions@nwu.edu • Web Address: www.kellogg.nwu.edu

Northwestern University's Kellogg Graduate School of Management has a strong reputation in marketing and finance, and it offers many areas of professional specialization including health services, transportation, and real estate. The "very friendly and helpful" students here are "generally laid-back about life, but somewhat serious about school," and they rate Kellogg "great in every respect." Employment prospects for Kellogg grads are tremendous. More than 300 firms conduct more than 13,000 on-campus interviews annually.

INSTITUTIONAL INFORMATION
Public/Private: Private
Evening Classes Available? Yes
Total Faculty: 261
% Faculty Female: 19
% Faculty Minority: 15
% Faculty Part Time: 17
Student/Faculty Ratio: 12:1
Students in Parent Institution: 16,018
Academic Calendar: Quarter

PROGRAMS
Degrees Offered: PhD (4 years+)
Joint Degrees: Master of Management/RN (nursing school) (4 years), MM/Doctor of Medicine (medical school) (4 years), Doctor of Medicine/Juris Doctor (law school) (4 years), and Master of Management/Manufacturing (engineering school) (4 years)
Academic Specialties: All areas of business and entrepreneurship; special strengths in General Management, Finance, and Marketing
Special Opportunities: Pre-enrollment math "prep"
Study Abroad Options: Austrailia, Austria, Belgium, Chile, Denmark, France, Germany, Hong Kong, Israel, Italy, Japan, Mexico, Norway, Spain, Thailand, United Kingdom

STUDENT INFORMATION
% Full Time: 49
% Female: 32
% Minority: 21
% Out of State: 61
% International: 24
Average Age: 27

COMPUTER AND RESEARCH FACILITIES
Research Facilities: Evanston Research Park
Computer Facilities: Visit NU homepage on the World Wide Web at www.nwu.edu
Campuswide Network? No
Computer Proficiency Required? No
Special Purchasing Agreements? No

EXPENSES/FINANCIAL AID
Annual Tuition: $25,872
Room & Board (On/Off Campus): $18,984/$18,984
% Receiving Financial Aid: 60

ADMISSIONS INFORMATION
Application Fee: $160
Electronic Application? Yes
Early Decision Application Deadline: 12/1
Early Decision Notification: 2/21
Regular Application Deadline: 3/16
Regular Notification: Rolling
Deferment Available? Yes
Length of Deferment: Case by case
Non-fall Admissions? Yes
Non-fall Application Deadline(s): 3/15
Transfer Students Accepted? No
Need-Blind Admissions? Yes
Average GPA: 3.4
GPA Range: 2.5-4.0
Average GMAT: 660
GMAT Range: 490-790
Minority/Disadvantaged Student Recruitment Programs: Annual conference sponsored by the Black Management Association includes activities intended to recruit minorities. Admission minority recruitment counselor on staff.
Other Schools to Which Students Applied: Henderson State University, Stanford University, University of Pennsylvania

INTERNATIONAL STUDENTS
TOEFL Required of International Students? Yes

EMPLOYMENT INFORMATION

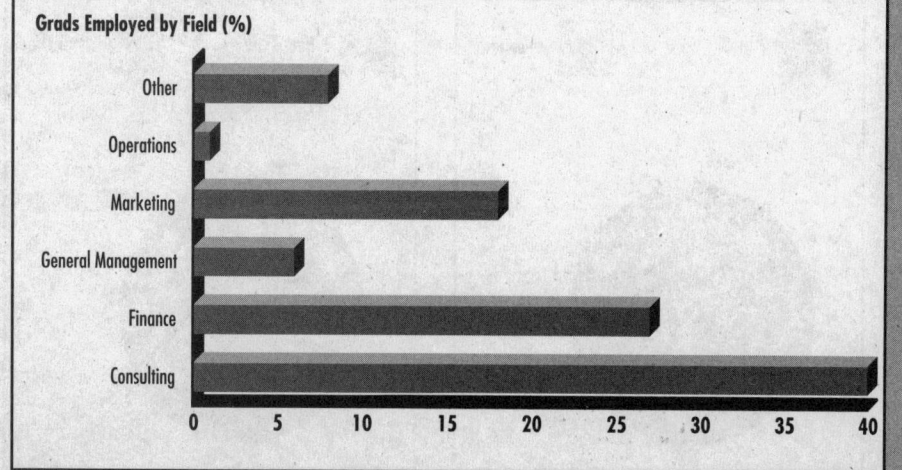

Grads Employed by Field (%)
- Other: ~8
- Operations: ~2
- Marketing: ~18
- General Management: ~5
- Finance: ~27
- Consulting: ~40

Placement Office Available? Yes
% Employed Within 6 Months: 99
Frequent Employers: McKinsey & Co., Inc. Booz-Allen & Hamilton
Prominent Alumni: Chris Galvin, CEO, Motorola; Scott Smith, CEO, publisher, *Chicago Tribune*

OAKLAND UNIVERSITY
School of Business Administration

Admissions Contact: Darla M. Null, Coordinator of Graduate Business Programs
Address: 432 Elliott Hall, Rochester, MI 48309-4493
Admissions Phone: 248-370-3287 • Admissions Fax: 248-370-4964
Admissions E-mail: gbp@oakland.edu • Web Address: www.sba.oakland.edu

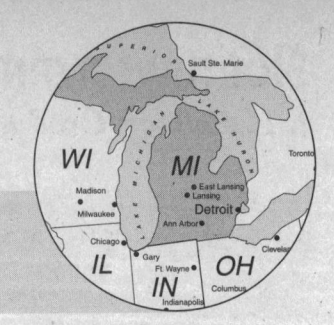

The MBA program at Oakland University's School of Business and Administration emphasizes information technology and international business and has an almost all-male student body. The OU MBA curriculum is designed for undergraduate majors from any discipline. Internships with many major corporations are available, including DaimlerChrysler Corporation, which has a brand-new Tech Center close by.

INSTITUTIONAL INFORMATION
Public/Private: Public
Evening Classes Available? Yes
Total Faculty: 57
% Faculty Female: 19
% Faculty Minority: 3
Student/Faculty Ratio: 19:1
Students in Parent Institution: 15,875
Academic Calendar: Semester

PROGRAMS
Degrees Offered: Master of Accounting (2 to 6 years), Master of Business Administration (2 to 6 years), Master of Science in Information Technology Management (1 to 6 years), Executive MBA in Health Care (21 months to 6 years)
Academic Specialties: Case study, computer-aided instruction, computer analysis, group discussion, lecture, research, role playing, seminars by members of the business community, student presentations, study groups, team projects

STUDENT INFORMATION
Total Business Students: 536
% Full Time: 5
% Female: 2
% Out of State: 5
% International: 5
Average Age: 30

COMPUTER AND RESEARCH FACILITIES
Research Facilities: Alumni network, career counseling/planning, career fairs, career library, career placement, electronic job bank, job interviews arranged, résumé referral to employers, résumé preparation
Campuswide Network? Yes
Internet Fee? No

EXPENSES/FINANCIAL AID
Annual Tuition (Resident/Nonresident): $4,428/$9,144
Tuition Per Credit (Resident/Nonresident): $246/$508
Room & Board (On Campus): $7,500
Books and Supplies: $800
Average Grant: $3,600

ADMISSIONS INFORMATION
Application Fee: $30
Electronic Application? Yes
Regular Application Deadline: 8/1
Regular Notification: Rolling
Deferment Available? Yes
Length of Deferment: 1 year
Non-fall Admissions? Yes
Non-fall Application Deadline(s): 4/2, 6/2, 12/2
Transfer Students Accepted? Yes
Transfer Policy: Up to nine credits of relevant course work may be transferred (3.0 or better)
Need-Blind Admissions? Yes
Number of Applications Received: 182
% of Applicants Accepted: 82
% Accepted Who Enrolled: 80
Average GPA: 3.1
Average GMAT: 537
Other Admissions Factors Considered: résumé, minimum of 2 years of work experience
Other Schools to Which Students Applied: Wayne State University.

INTERNATIONAL STUDENTS
TOEFL Required of International Students? Yes
Minimum TOEFL: 550 (213 computer)

EMPLOYMENT INFORMATION
Placement Office Available? Yes
% Employed Within 3 Months: 98

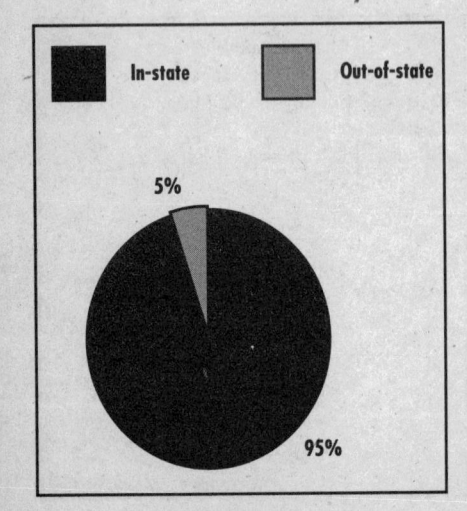

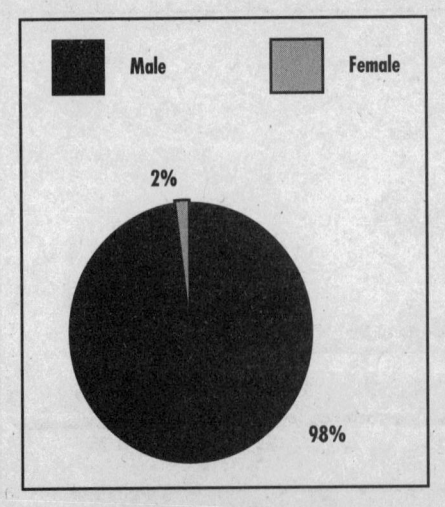

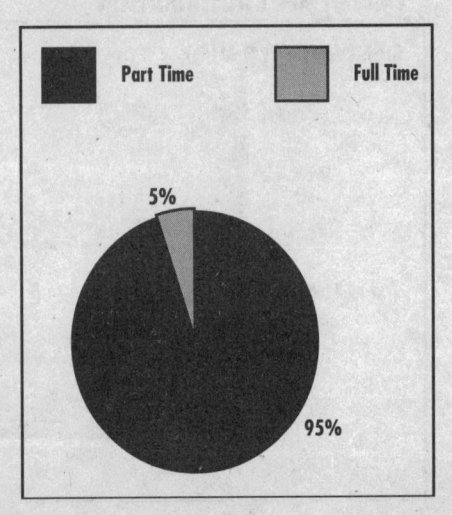

OHIO STATE UNIVERSITY
Fisher College of Business

Admissions Contact: Associate Director, Graduate Programs Office
Address: 100 Gerlach Hall, 2108 Neil Avenue, Columbus, OH 43210
Admissions Phone: 614-292-8511 • Admissions Fax: 614-292-9006
Admissions E-mail: cobgrd@osu.edu • Web Address: fisher.osu.edu

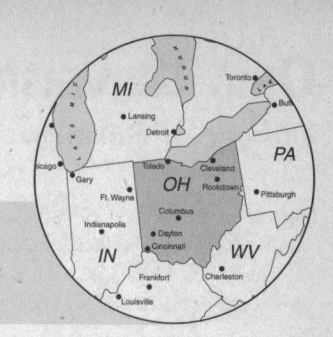

Students entering the MBA program at Ohio State's Fisher College of Business must complete a pre-enrollment review of accounting, economics, statistics, and computer literacy. It's a rigorous start to a tightly integrated and fairly exhaustive program that remains extremely challenging throughout the first-year core curriculum. Campus life is "fun," though, especially during football season, and "the campus is beautiful during spring and summer." Golf facilities are "fantastic" as well, and unmarried students report an active and satisfying social life.

INSTITUTIONAL INFORMATION
Public/Private: Public
Evening Classes Available? Yes
Total Faculty: 100
% Faculty Female: 16
% Faculty Minority: 16
Student/Faculty Ratio: 5:1
Students in Parent Institution: 54,989
Academic Calendar: Quarter

PROGRAMS
Degrees Offered: PhD in Business (4 years), PhD in Accounting (4 years), MIS in Labor and Human Resources (4 years), Master of Accounting (1 year), Master of Labor and Human Resources (5 quarters)
Joint Degrees: MBA/JD (4 years), MBA/MHA (3 years)
Academic Specialties: Accounting, Finance, Consulting, Human Resources, International Business, Logistics, MIS, Marketing, Operations, Real Estate
Special Opportunities: Business Solution Team, Student Investment Management, Executive Luncheon Series, Mentoring Program
Study Abroad Options: Italy, Germany, Chile, South Korea, China, Mexico

STUDENT INFORMATION
Total Business Students: 477
% Full Time: 59
% Female: 33
% Minority: 13

% Out of State: 39
% International: 27
Average Age: 28

COMPUTER AND RESEARCH FACILITIES
Research Facilities: Center for International Business & Research, Center for Real Estate Education & Research, Supply Chain Management Research Group
Computer Facilities: MBA classrooms allow access to college and university networks through laptops. Computer labs include state-of-the-art hardware, software, and databases. The college has more than 3,000 computer ports.
Campuswide Network? Yes
% of MBA Classrooms Wired: 100
Internet Fee? No

EXPENSES/FINANCIAL AID
Room & Board (On Campus): $7,000
Books and Supplies: $1,200
Average Grant: $4,000
Average Loan: $9,000
% Receiving Financial Aid: 70
% Receiving Aid Their First Year: 35

ADMISSIONS INFORMATION
Application Fee: $30
Electronic Application? Yes
Early Decision Application Deadline: 1/15
Early Decision Notification: 2/28
Regular Application Deadline: 4/30

Regular Notification: 5/30
Deferment Available? Yes
Length of Deferment: 1 year
Non-fall Admissions? No
Transfer Students Accepted? No
Need-Blind Admissions? Yes
Number of Applications Received: 990
% of Applicants Accepted: 29
% Accepted Who Enrolled: 72
Average GPA: 3.3
GPA Range: 3.0-3.6
Average GMAT: 638
GMAT Range: 600-690
Average Years Experience: 4
Other Admissions Factors Considered: Caliber of undergraduate institution/major, quality of work experience, evidence of leadership and teamwork, recommendations, GPA, GMAT score, essay questions, communication skills
Minority/Disadvantaged Student Recruitment Programs: Graduate and Professional Schools Visitation Day, Graduate Enrichment Fellowship Program, Targeted Minority Recruitment Initiative, Minority Student Visitation Weekend
Other Schools to Which Students Applied: Case Western Reserve University, Indiana State University, Michigan State University, Northwestern University, Purdue University, University of Michigan

INTERNATIONAL STUDENTS
TOEFL Required of International Students? Yes
Minimum TOEFL: 600 (250 computer)

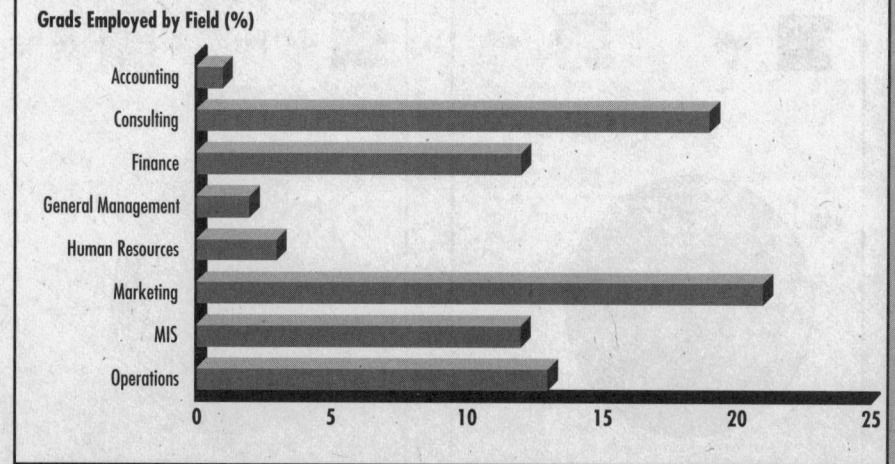

EMPLOYMENT INFORMATION

Grads Employed by Field (%)
- Accounting
- Consulting
- Finance
- General Management
- Human Resources
- Marketing
- MIS
- Operations

Placement Office Available? Yes
% Employed Within 3 Months: 98
Frequent Employers: Ford Motor Co., Andersen Consulting, Bank One, Procter & Gamble, IBM, Kimberly Clark, Hewlett-Packard, Wells Fargo, The Scotts Company, Cinergy, Lexmark, Owens Corning, John Deere, National City Bank, 3M
Prominent Alumni: Leslie Wexner, chairman and CEO, The Limited, Inc.; Alan J. Patricof, chairman, Patricof & Company Ventures, Inc.; Lionel Nowell, executive VP and CFO, Pepsi Bottling; Ray Groves, chairman, Legg Mason Merchant Banking; Max Fisher, industrialist and philanthropist

OHIO UNIVERSITY
College of Business

Admissions Contact: Jan Ross, Assistant Director, Graduate Program
Address: 514 Copeland Hall, Athens, OH 45701
Admissions Phone: 740-593-4320 • Admissions Fax: 740-597-2995
Admissions E-mail: rossj@Ohio.edu • Web Address: www.cob.ohiou.edu/grad

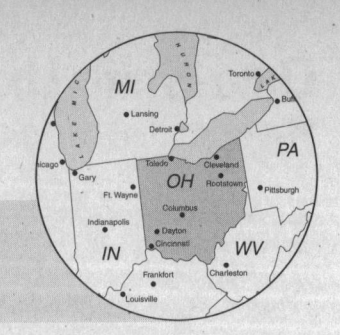

Ohio University offers a Full-Time MBA, an Executive MBA for busy working professionals, foreign MBAs, and the MBA Without Boundaries program (MBAWB), created for working professionals who wish to earn their master's degree through a combination of residential experiences and Internet-based learning. The traditional MBA requires an intensive 10-week prerequisite educational training for those without an undergrad degree in business.

INSTITUTIONAL INFORMATION
Public/Private: Public
Evening Classes Available? No
Total Faculty: 10
% Faculty Female: 10
% Faculty Minority: 10
Student/Faculty Ratio: 7:1
Students in Parent Institution: 19,000
Academic Calendar: Quarter

PROGRAMS
Degrees Offered: MBA (12 months)
Joint Degrees: MBA/MSp Ad (24 months); MBA/MA International Affairs (24 months)
Academic Specialties: Interactive, problem-based curriculum with 6 to 8 client-based experiences
Study Abroad Options: Hungary, South Africa, India, Brazil, China

STUDENT INFORMATION
Total Business Students: 83
% Full Time: 100
% Female: 43
% Minority: 5
% Out of State: 52
% International: 24
Average Age: 25

COMPUTER AND RESEARCH FACILITIES
Campuswide Network? Yes
% of MBA Classrooms Wired: 100
Computer Model Recommended: Laptop
Internet Fee? Yes

EXPENSES/FINANCIAL AID
Annual Tuition (Resident/Nonresident): $8,780/$16,872
Room & Board: $10,000
Books and Supplies: $4,700
Average Grant: $8,000
Average Loan: $15,000
% Receiving Financial Aid: 70
% Receiving Aid Their First Year: 70

ADMISSIONS INFORMATION
Application Fee: $30
Electronic Application? No
Regular Application Deadline: 3/1
Regular Notification: 4/1
Deferment Available? Yes
Length of Deferment: 1 year
Non-fall Admissions? No
Transfer Students Accepted? No
Need-Blind Admissions? Yes
Number of Applications Received: 223
% of Applicants Accepted: 50
% Accepted Who Enrolled: 74
Average GPA: 3.4
GPA Range: 3.0-3.8
Average GMAT: 560
GMAT Range: 470-670
Average Years Experience: 2

INTERNATIONAL STUDENTS
TOEFL Required of International Students? Yes
Minimum TOEFL: 600 (250 computer)

EMPLOYMENT INFORMATION
Placement Office Available? No

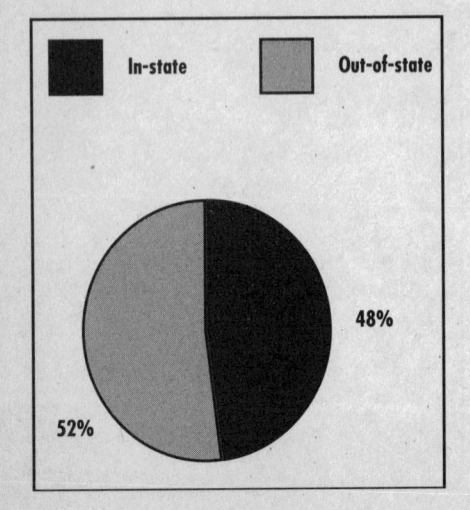

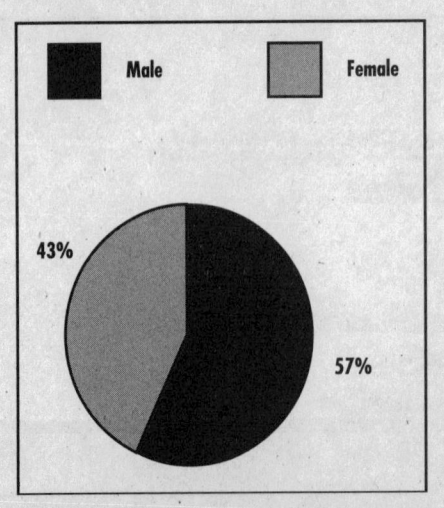

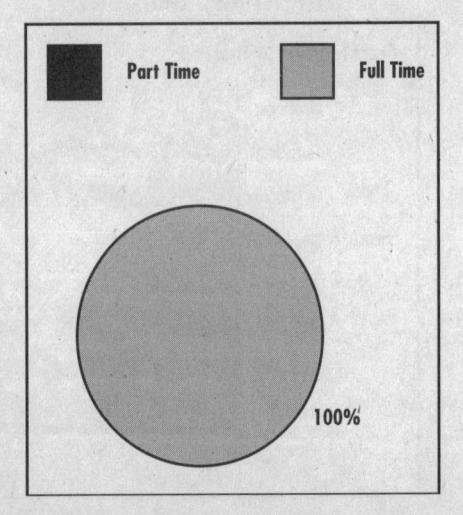

OKLAHOMA STATE UNIVERSITY
College of Business Administration

Admissions Contact: Brooks Thomas, Assistant Director, MBA Program
Address: 102 Gundersen Hall, Stillwater, OK 74078-4011
Admissions Phone: 405-744-2951 • Admissions Fax: 405-744-7474
Admissions E-mail: mba-osu@okstate.edu • Web Address: mba.okstate.edu

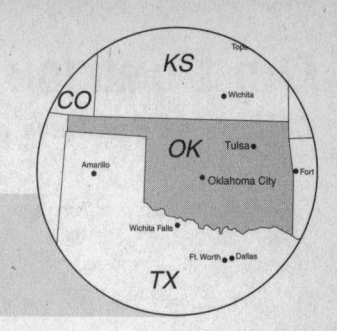

The Oklahoma State University MBA program makes no assumptions about the previous business experience of its applicants, so students from any undergraduate discipline are encouraged to apply. Thanks to a generous donation from Dynegy and its CEO, Chuck Watson, MBA students can learn on a professional-quality trading floor with 36 workstations; this is the only one of its kind in Oklahoma and one of only a few nationally. OSU also offers a Certificate in International Studies as an addition to an MBA degree, as well as a part-time study option at the Tulsa campus.

INSTITUTIONAL INFORMATION
Public/Private: Public
Evening Classes Available? Yes
Total Faculty: 20
% Faculty Female: 15
% Faculty Minority: 5
Student/Faculty Ratio: 7:1
Students in Parent Institution: 21,750
Academic Calendar: Semester

PROGRAMS
Degrees Offered: MBA (full time, 49 to 55 credits, 2 years); MBA (part time, 39 to 45 credits, 3 to 5 years); MS in Telecommunications Management (33 to 35 credits, 12 to 18 months); MS in Accounting (24 to 32 credits, 12 months to 5 years); MS in Economics (30 to 33 credits, 12 months to 5 years); MS MIS/AIS (33 to 35 credits, 12 to 18 months)
Joint Degrees: MBA/MSTM (60 credits, 2 years)
Academic Specialties: Finance, MIS, Accounting, Marketing, E-Business, Telecommunications, Venture Management, International Business
Study Abroad Options: England, Canada, Mexico, Italy, France

STUDENT INFORMATION
Total Business Students: 338
% Full Time: 34
% Female: 34
% Minority: 6
% Out of State: 8
% International: 33
Average Age: 27

COMPUTER AND RESEARCH FACILITIES
Research Facilities: Dynegy Trading Floor, Center for Research on Information Technology Transfer
Computer Facilities: Computer labs, Dow Jones
Campuswide Network? Yes
% of MBA Classrooms Wired: 80
Computer Model Recommended: Laptop
Internet Fee? Yes

EXPENSES/FINANCIAL AID
Annual Tuition (Resident/Nonresident): $2,576/$5,752
Tuition Per Credit (Resident/Nonresident): $92/$205
Room & Board (On/Off Campus): $11,000/$12,500
Books and Supplies: $1,000
Average Grant: $1,000
Average Loan: $4,000
% Receiving Financial Aid: 40
% Receiving Aid Their First Year: 45

ADMISSIONS INFORMATION
Application Fee: $25
Electronic Application? No
Regular Application Deadline: 7/1
Regular Notification: Rolling
Deferment Available? Yes
Length of Deferment: 1 year
Non-fall Admissions? Yes
Non-fall Application Deadline(s): 11/1
Transfer Students Accepted? Yes
Transfer Policy: They must be a student in good standing at an AACSB-accredited university.
Need-Blind Admissions? Yes
Number of Applications Received: 125
% of Applicants Accepted: 66
% Accepted Who Enrolled: 59
Average GPA: 3.5
GPA Range: 2.6-4.0
Average GMAT: 601
GMAT Range: 500-720
Average Years Experience: 6
Other Admissions Factors Considered: Work experience, undergraduate institution, letters of recommendation
Minority/Disadvantaged Student Recruitment Programs: minority scholarships
Other Schools to Which Students Applied: University of Arkansas at Fayetteville, University of Kansas, University of Oklahoma.

INTERNATIONAL STUDENTS
TOEFL Required of International Students? Yes
Minimum TOEFL: 575

EMPLOYMENT INFORMATION

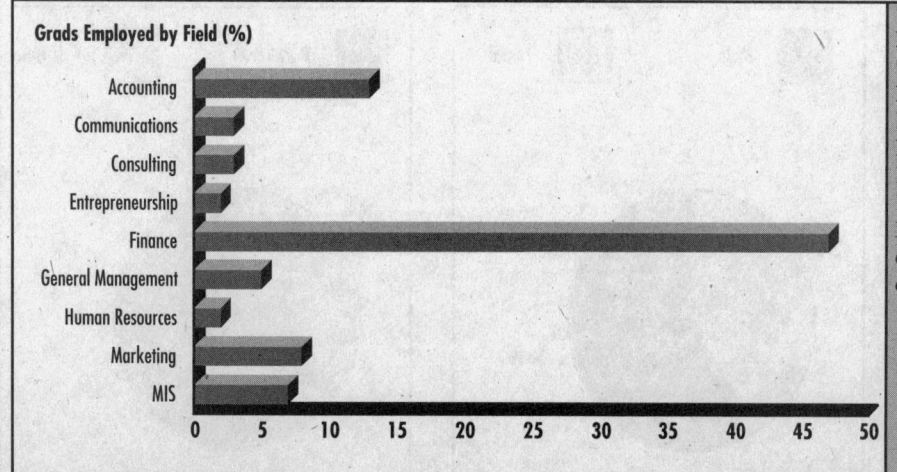

Grads Employed by Field (%)
- Accounting
- Communications
- Consulting
- Entrepreneurship
- Finance
- General Management
- Human Resources
- Marketing
- MIS

Placement Office Available? Yes
% Employed Within 3 Months: 85
Frequent Employers: ExxonMobil, Accenture, KPMG, Dynegy, Halliburton, American Airlines, Payless Shoes, Hilti, IBM, Phillips Petroleum, Bank of Oklahoma, Williams Inc., WorldCom, Koch Industries, Midfirst Bank
Prominent Alumni: Mike Holder, head golf coach, Oklahoma State University; Jim Alcock, controller, ExxonMobil

OLD DOMINION UNIVERSITY
College of Business and Public Administration

Admissions Contact: Jean Turpin, MBA Program Manager
Address: 203A Technology Building, Norfolk, VA 23529
Admissions Phone: 757-683-3585 • Admissions Fax: 757-683-5750
Admissions E-mail: mbainfo@odu.edu • Web Address: www.odu-cbpa.org

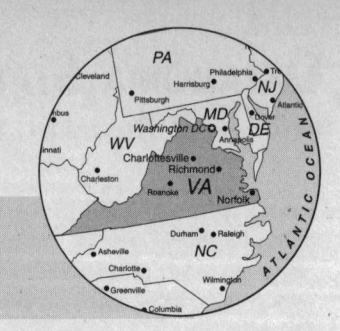

Old Dominion University offers its MBA students the chance to study year-round at any of four different locations in the greater Norfolk area, taking classes full time or part time. Currently, there are about 10 specializations within the MBA program, ranging from accounting to decision science to maritime and port management, and Old Dominion plans to add an e-commerce specialization in the near future.

INSTITUTIONAL INFORMATION
Public/Private: Public
Evening Classes Available? Yes
Total Faculty: 85
% Faculty Part Time: 6
Student/Faculty Ratio: 14:1
Students in Parent Institution: 19,500

PROGRAMS
Degrees Offered: Master of Business Administration (48 credits), Master of Taxation (30 credits), Master of Science in Accounting (30 credits), Master of Arts in Economics (30 credits), Master of Public Administration (39 credits), Master of Urban Studies (36 credits), Doctorate of Philosophy in Business (48 credits), Doctorate of Philosophy in Urban Studies
Academic Specialties: E-Commerce, Finance, Marketing
Study Abroad Options: Denmark, Korea, China, Philippines, England, Belgium

STUDENT INFORMATION
Total Business Students: 450
% Full Time: 34
% Female: 42
% Minority: 13
% Out of State: 70
% International: 65
Average Age: 29

COMPUTER AND RESEARCH FACILITIES
Campuswide Network? Yes
% of MBA Classrooms Wired: 100
Computer Model Recommended: No
Internet Fee? Yes

EXPENSES/FINANCIAL AID
Annual Tuition (Resident/Nonresident): $3,528/$9,468
Tuition Per Credit (Resident/Nonresident): $202/$534
Room & Board (On Campus): $5,232
Books and Supplies: $1,000
Average Grant: $5,000

ADMISSIONS INFORMATION
Application Fee: $30
Electronic Application? No
Regular Application Deadline: 7/1
Regular Notification: Rolling
Deferment Available? Yes
Length of Deferment: 1 year
Non-fall Admissions? Yes
Non-fall Application Deadline(s): 4/1, 11/1, 7/1
Transfer Students Accepted? Yes
Transfer Policy: Credits accepted from AACSB-accredited schools only.
Need-Blind Admissions? Yes
Number of Applications Received: 333
% of Applicants Accepted: 87
% Accepted Who Enrolled: 52
Average GPA: 3.1
Average GMAT: 520
Average Years Experience: 6

INTERNATIONAL STUDENTS
TOEFL Required of International Students? Yes
Minimum TOEFL: 550

EMPLOYMENT INFORMATION
Placement Office Available? Yes
% Employed Within 3 Months: 33

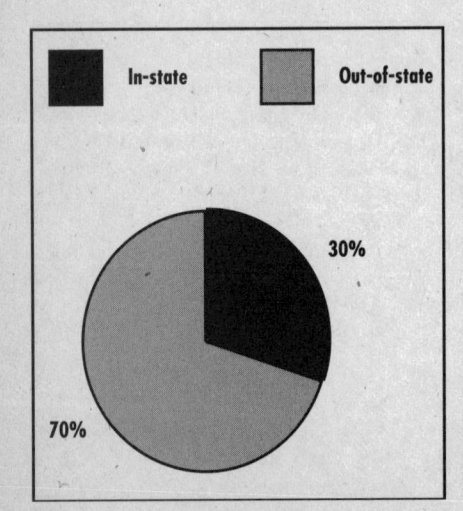

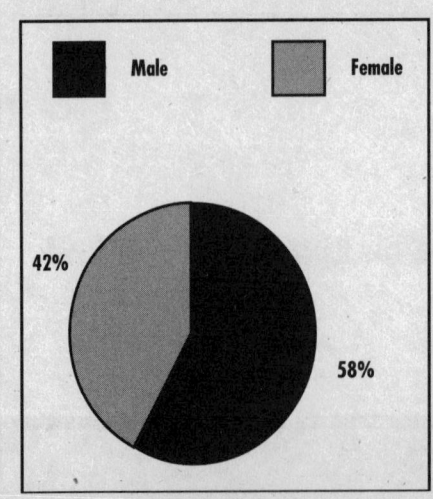

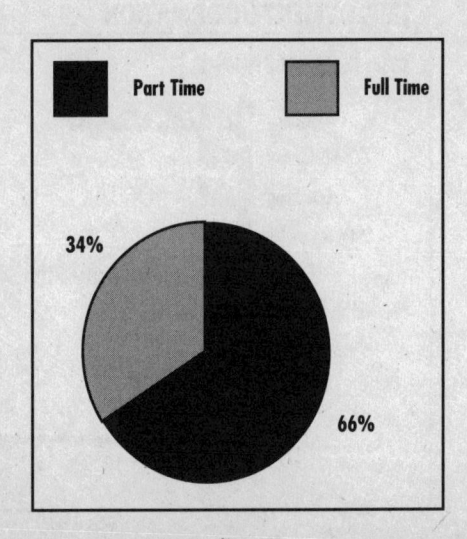

OREGON STATE UNIVERSITY
School of Business Administration

Admissions Contact: Fran Saveriano, MBA Program Coordinator
Address: 200 Bexell Hall, Corvallis, OR 97330
Admissions Phone: 541-737-6031 • Admissions Fax: 541-737-4890
Admissions E-mail: osumba@bus.orst.edu • Web Address: www.bus.orst.edu

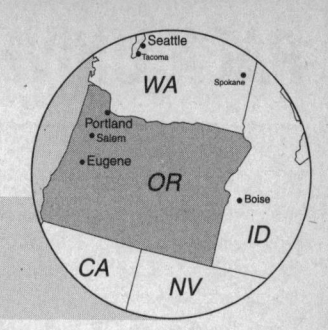

OSU's MBA is an accelerated management program heavy on technology. It aims to enable students not only to recognize situations where advanced technology is appropriate but also to know "which technologies are viable in various business contexts." Although the program is ideal for those students with technical backgrounds wishing to boost their biz savoir faire, other students looking for an education in technology management will find that the "practical value-added content" of the program suits their needs as well. Hewlett-Packard, Nike, and Procter & Gamble are just a few of the major corporations that provide great internship opportunities for Oregon State MBA students.

INSTITUTIONAL INFORMATION
Public/Private: Public
Evening Classes Available? Yes
Total Faculty: 33
% Faculty Female: 15
% Faculty Minority: 24
Student/Faculty Ratio: 3:1
Students in Parent Institution: 18,396
Academic Calendar: Quarter

PROGRAMS
Degrees Offered: MBA (45 credits, 3 terms)
Academic Specialties: Technology focus

STUDENT INFORMATION
Total Business Students: 81
% Full Time: 94
% Female: 3
% Minority: 1
% Out of State: 1
% International: 25
Average Age: 28

COMPUTER AND RESEARCH FACILITIES
Computer Facilities: College of Business and other colleges on campus
Campuswide Network? Yes
% of MBA Classrooms Wired: 100
Internet Fee? No

EXPENSES/FINANCIAL AID
Annual Tuition (Resident/Nonresident): $7,413/$12,465
Tuition Per Credit (Resident/Nonresident): $445/$633
Room & Board (On Campus): $5,000
Books and Supplies: $3,763

ADMISSIONS INFORMATION
Application Fee: $50
Electronic Application? No
Regular Application Deadline: 3/1
Regular Notification: Rolling
Deferment Available? Yes
Non-fall Admissions? Yes
Non-fall Application Deadline(s): 50 days before terms starts
Transfer Students Accepted? Yes
Transfer Policy: up to 15 credits of approved course work (AACSB-accredited)
Need-Blind Admissions? Yes
Number of Applications Received: 212
% of Applicants Accepted: 38
% Accepted Who Enrolled: 58
Average GPA: 3.3
GPA Range: 3.0-3.6
Average GMAT: 552
GMAT Range: 510-590
Average Years Experience: 3
Other Admissions Factors Considered: Résumé, work experience, computer experience
Other Schools to Which Students Applied: Portland State University, University of Oregon.

INTERNATIONAL STUDENTS
TOEFL Required of International Students? Yes
Minimum TOEFL: 575 (233 computer)

EMPLOYMENT INFORMATION
Placement Office Available? Yes
% Employed Within 3 Months: 95

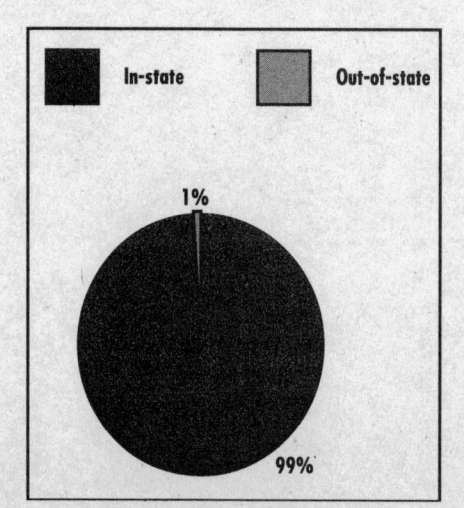

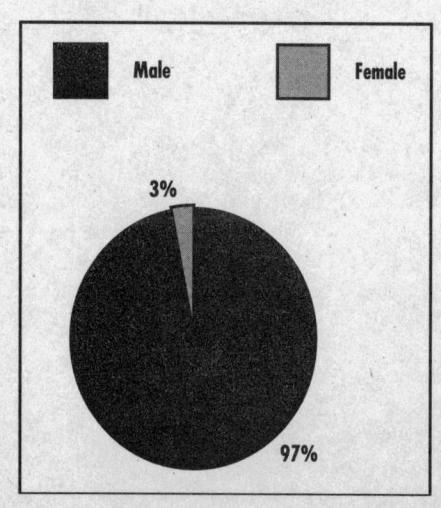

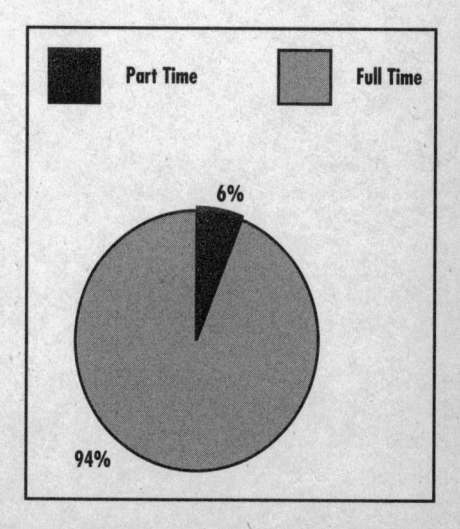

In-state 99% / Out-of-state 1%

Male 97% / Female 3%

Part Time 6% / Full Time 94%

PACE UNIVERSITY

THE SCHOOL AT A GLANCE
Founded in 1906 by brothers Homer and Charles Pace, Pace University is a private, nonsectarian, coeducational institution that embraces its motto Opportunitas. Originally founded as a school of accounting, Pace Institute was designated Pace College in 1973. Through growth and various successes, Pace College was renamed Pace University as approved by the New York State Board of Regents. Today, Pace offers comprehensive undergraduate, graduate, doctoral, and professional-level programs, at several campus locations, through six schools and colleges.

STUDENTS
Highly motivated, Pace students represent diversified personal, cultural, and educational backgrounds. Many students are employed and pursue graduate study for personal growth and career advancement opportunities, and nearly 75 percent are enrolled part-time in evening classes. Current enrollment in the business program is approximately 1,700 students.

ACADEMICS
The Lubin School of Business, one of six schools within Pace University, offers distinguished graduate full-time and part-time programs leading to the Master of Science (MS), Master of Business Administration (MBA), and Doctor of Professional Studies (DPS), in addition to the Advanced Graduate Certificate program. Lubin continues to receive national recognition, with U.S. News & World Report ranking Lubin's part-time MBA program among the top 11 nationwide and second in New York City in its "Best Graduate Schools 2002" survey.

The MS program, which provides fundamental principles and advanced technical knowledge, is designed for students who seek intensive study in a specialized area of business. Concentrations are offered in accounting, accounting information systems, business economics, investment management, management science, operations planning and analysis, personal financial planning, and taxation.

The MBA program prepares students for broad management responsibilities, with an introduction to a career concentration. Uniquely innovative and flexible, the practitioner-oriented curriculum evolves in response to the constantly changing demands of the international world and provides students with the analytical skills and conceptual understanding needed for continued professional development and career success. Concentrations include accounting, business economics, e-business, financial management, information systems, international business, management, marketing, operations planning and analysis, and taxation. MBA and MS programs may be completed in as few as 30–36 credit hours.

The e.MBA@PACE is a fully accredited, two-year, Web-based online executive MBA program that combines online learning with brief residencies to achieve an effective balance of virtual and human interaction. In a recent survey of the best online graduate programs, U.S. News & World Report lists Lubin's e.MBA@PACE among the top 25 online graduate business programs nationwide.

The Doctoral Program in Business (DPS) is a 57-credit program that encompasses a balance of theory and practice and offers full-time business executives the opportunity to advance their education to the highest level. The complexity and context of business decisions receive significant emphasis. A comprehensive examination and dissertation culminate the doctoral experience.

Certificate programs are also offered to professionals with advanced degrees who want to stay current with development in the industry, acquire new responsibilities, or qualify for licensing or certification. Concentrations are offered in accounting, business economics, financial management, information systems, international business, management, marketing, and taxation.

The Lubin School of Business is accredited by the AACSB International—The Association to Advance Collegiate Schools of Business, the premier accrediting organization for business schools in the world.

Lubin School of Business

CAMPUS LIFE

Pace University is a multi-campus institution with campuses in both New York City and Westchester County. All locations are within reach of cultural, business, and social resources and opportunities. The downtown Manhattan campus is adjacent to the financial district and City Hall. Pace's Midtown Center, located on Fifth Avenue, is within a short distance of Times Square, the theatre district, art museums, and Grand Central Station. The Pleasantville/Briarcliff campus in Westchester County is a suburban setting, surrounded by towns and villages offering various forms of recreation. The Graduate Center and the School of Law are located in White Plains, New York, among major retail districts and many corporate headquarters. Pace also offers courses at a satellite campus in Hudson Valley, New York. All locations are accessible by public transportation. Programs are available on both the New York City and Westchester campuses.

The Pace University Library is a comprehensive teaching library and student-learning center. The Pace library embodies the attributes of the "virtual library," combining the development of strong core collections with ubiquitous access and seamless connectivity to global Internet resources in support of the University's broad and diversified curricula. Reciprocal borrowing and access accords, traditional interlibrary loan services, and commercial document delivery options supplement the aggregate holdings of the libraries. Pace offers Instructional Services Librarians, sophisticated computing technologies, a state-of-the-art electronic classroom, major information literacy initiatives, digital reference services, and multimedia applications.

Pace University's computer laboratories are linked to our high-speed data network and feature sophisticated hardware utilizing the network and the Internet to facilitate learning. Pace University has been recognized by Yahoo/Internet Life Survey for the past two years as one of America's "Most Wired" Universities. Pace supports high-speed Internet and Internet-2 access on every campus; every dorm room is wired for high-speed data networking, as well as classrooms and offices. Most public areas are "wireless" accessible. There are almost 600 student-accessible PCs equipped with the latest hardware and software enhancements available. Pace University provides e-mail, Web space, and file storage space to its student body, as well as support for their PCs. Numerous rooms are connected with real-time video for interactive distance classes. Pace features an online, Web-based registration system, as well as many Web-enhanced (and some totally Web-supported) courses using Blackboard.

COSTS

Tuition for graduate courses is $625 per credit in 2001–2002.

Pace University strives to provide opportunities to students of diverse backgrounds and varied circumstances. To that end, the University is committed to offering financial aid to students to the fullest extent of its resources. Pace's comprehensive student financial aid assistance program includes scholarship, graduate assistantships, student loans (federal and alternative plans), and tuition payment plans. Scholarships are awarded to students in recognition of superior academic achievement and are available for full- and part-time study. Highly qualified students may be eligible for assistantships awarded by departments, which paid stipends up to $5,100 and tuition remission up to 24 credits during the 2001–2002 academic year.

Pace participates in all major federal and state financial aid programs, such as Direct Loans, New York State Tuition Assistance Program (TAP), Perkins Loans, and Federal Work Study. All students are encouraged to apply for these programs by filing the Free Application for Federal Student Aid (FAFSA), which can be obtained from any of the University's financial aid offices or on the Web at www.fafsa.ed.gov. For further information, prospective students should contact the Financial Aid Office and visit the Pace University website at www.pace.edu.

ADMISSIONS

Admission to Pace University graduate programs requires successful completion of a U.S. baccalaureate degree or its equivalent from an accredited institution. Students must submit a completed application, application fee ($65), official transcripts from all institutions attended since high school graduation, a personal statement, a résumé, and two letters of recommendation. International students are encouraged to apply. International students must submit official TOEFL score reports and transcripts in the native language with a professional English translation. Students applying to MS, MBA, or doctoral programs must demonstrate satisfactory performance on the GMAT.

Applications may be submitted throughout the year, and should be submitted by August 1 for the fall semester, December 1 for the spring semester, and May 1 for summer sessions. Applications for the DPS program should be submitted by July 1 for the fall semester and November 1 for the spring semester. Applications for the e.MBA@PACE program should be submitted by July 15 for the fall semester. International applications should be submitted one month prior to these dates for the respective semesters.

Admissions Contact: Ms. Joanna Broda, Director of Graduate Admission
Address: Office of Graduate Admission, 1 Martine Ave., White Plains, NY 10606-1909
Admissions Phone: 914-422-4283 • Admissions Fax: 914-422-4287
Admissions E-mail: gradwp@pace.edu • Web Address: www.pace.edu

PACE UNIVERSITY
Lubin School of Business

Admissions Contact: Ms. Joanna Broda, Director of Graduate Admission
Address: Office of Graduate Admission, 1 Martine Ave., White Plains, NY 10606-1909
Admissions Phone: 914-422-4283 • Admissions Fax: 914-422-4287
Admissions E-mail: gradwp@pace.edu • Web Address: www.pace.edu

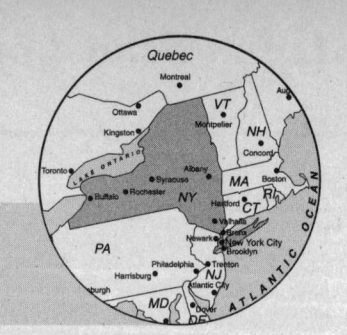

The Lubin School of Business, one of Pace's six schools, is located within a half hour of New York City, providing the "opportunity for all" that Pace's motto, "Opportunitas," promises. Alumni employed by leading corporations nearby know that graduates of the "practitioner-oriented" Lubin MBA program will be prepared for responsible management positions from the get-go. Established as an accounting school in 1906, the Lubin School of Business prepares its students for positions in a global economy at multiple NYC and Westchester County campus locations.

INSTITUTIONAL INFORMATION
Public/Private: Private
Evening Classes Available? No
Total Faculty: 126
% Faculty Female: 13
% Faculty Minority: 19
% Faculty Part Time: 25
Student/Faculty Ratio: 22:1
Students in Parent Institution: 13,461
Academic Calendar: Semester

PROGRAMS
Degrees Offered: MBA, One-Year MBA in Finance, Master of Science (MS), Advanced Professional Certificate (APC), Doctor of Professional Studies (DPS), Executive MBA
Joint Degrees: Doctor of Jurisprudence/MBA (JD/MBA)
Academic Specialties: Finance majors have proximity to Wall Street, faculty with specialties in Finance, Management, Management Science, Marketing and Tax
Study Abroad Options: China; ESC Grenoble, France; Karl Rubrechts University, Heidelberg, Germany

STUDENT INFORMATION
Total Business Students: 1,473
% Full Time: 32
% Female: 48
% Minority: 18
% International: 47
Average Age: 29

COMPUTER AND RESEARCH FACILITIES
Research Facilities: Center for Global Finance
Off-Campus Resources: Lexis-Nexis, CRSP Tapes
Number of Computer Labs: 10
Number of Student Computers: 700
Campuswide Network? Yes
Computer Proficiency Required? Yes
Computer Model Recommended: Laptop
Special Purchasing Agreements? Yes
Internet Fee? No

EXPENSES/FINANCIAL AID
Room & Board (On/Off Campus): $7,100/$11,300
Books and Supplies: $540
Average Grant: $5,038
Average Loan: $12,663
% Receiving Financial Aid: 28
% Receiving Aid Their First Year: 35

ADMISSIONS INFORMATION
Application Fee: $60
Electronic Application? No
Regular Application Deadline: 8/1
Regular Notification: Rolling
Deferment Available? No
Non-fall Admissions? No
Transfer Students Accepted? No
Need-Blind Admissions? No
Number of Applications Received: 1,307
% of Applicants Accepted: 61
% Accepted Who Enrolled: 46
Average GPA: 3.2
Average GMAT: 518
Other Schools to Which Students Applied: City University of New York—Baruch College; Fordham University; New York University; St. John's University

INTERNATIONAL STUDENTS
TOEFL Required of International Students? Yes
Minimum TOEFL: 550

EMPLOYMENT INFORMATION
Placement Office Available? Yes
% Employed Within 6 Months: 95

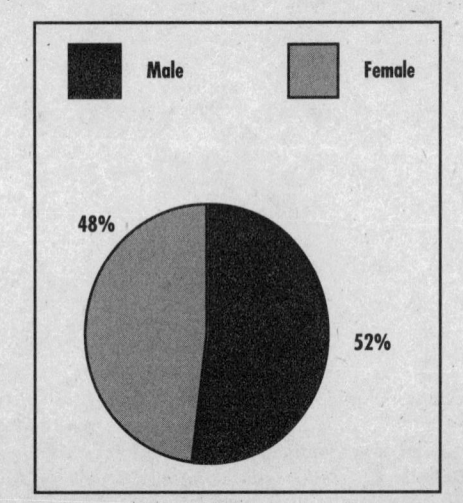

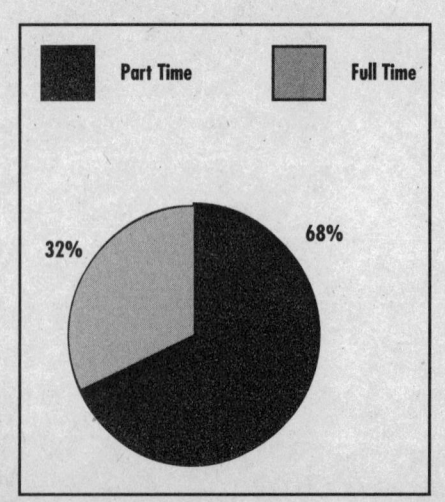

PENNSYLVANIA STATE UNIVERSITY— ERIE, BEHREND COLLEGE
School of Business

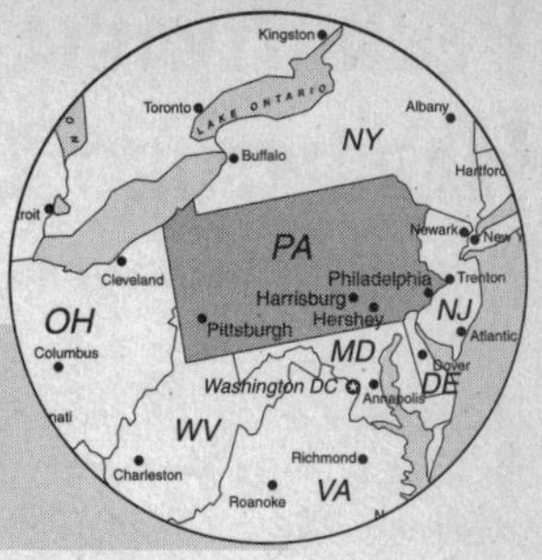

Admissions Contact: Ann M. Burbules, Graduate Admissions Counselor
Address: 5091 Station Road, Erie, PA 16563
Admissions Phone: 814-898-6100 • Admissions Fax: 814-898-6044
Admissions E-mail: behrendadmissions@psu.edu • Web Address: www.pserie.psu.edu

The Penn State Erie campus is home to the unique, newly developed Knowledge Park, a 200-acre research and development area reserved for organizations that wish to create knowledge-based partnerships and collaborate on projects with university students and faculty. Students can earn their degree in two to five years, but most are working professionals pursuing their MBA on a part-time basis. The education at the College of Business is comprehensive, and teachers are willing to dedicate one-on-one attention via independent study courses.

INSTITUTIONAL INFORMATION
Public/Private: Public
Evening Classes Available? No
Total Faculty: 22
% Faculty Female: 18
% Faculty Minority: 23
% Faculty Part Time: 9
Student/Faculty Ratio: 25:1
Students in Parent Institution: 3,500
Academic Calendar: Semester

PROGRAMS
Degrees Offered: MBA (48 credits, 18 months to 8 years)
Academic Specialties: To help students succeed in an increasingly global marketplace, Penn State—Erie has assembled an exceptional MBA faculty who have business experience in nearly every part of the industrialized world, which gives them an international perspective. Penn State—Erie faculty members have been educated at leading universities and value high-quality teaching and research. To further ensure excellent instruction, almost all MBA classes are taught by full-time faculty.

STUDENT INFORMATION
Total Business Students: 159
% Full Time: 5
% Female: 37
% Minority: 1
% International: 1
Average Age: 33

COMPUTER AND RESEARCH FACILITIES
Research Facilities: Knowledge Park, Economic Research Institute of Erie
Campuswide Network? Yes
Internet Fee? No

ADMISSIONS INFORMATION
Application Fee: $45
Electronic Application? Yes
Regular Application Deadline: 8/1
Regular Notification: Rolling
Deferment Available? Yes
Non-fall Admissions? Yes
Non-fall Application Deadline(s): 12/15, 4/15
Transfer Students Accepted? Yes
Transfer Policy: Up to 10 credits of relevant graduate work completed at any accredited institution may be applied toward the Penn State—Erie MBA. Credits earned to complete a previous graduate degree may not be used to fulfill MBA degree requirements. Transferred graduate work must have been completed no more than 5 years before the student is fully admitted as a degree candidate at Penn State—Erie. Course work must be of at least a B quality and appear on the graduate transcript of a regionally accredited institution. Pass/fail grades are not transferable.
Need-Blind Admissions? No
Number of Applications Received: 46
% of Applicants Accepted: 89
% Accepted Who Enrolled: 88
Average GPA: 3.3
Average GMAT: 508

INTERNATIONAL STUDENTS
TOEFL Required of International Students? Yes
Minimum TOEFL: 550

EMPLOYMENT INFORMATION
Placement Office Available? Yes

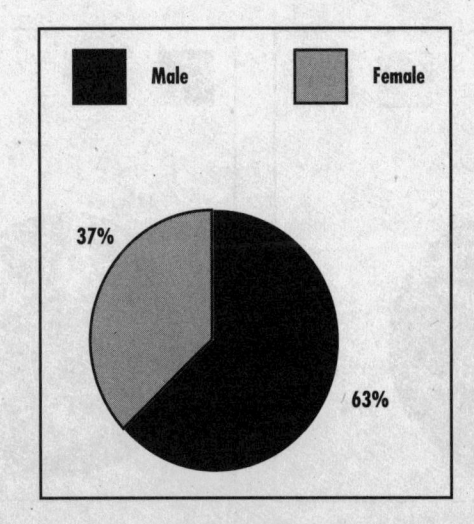

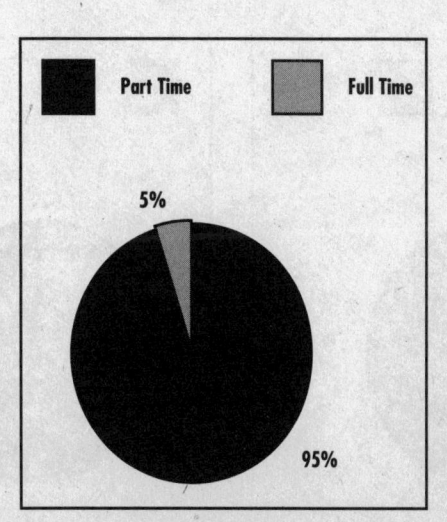

PENNSYLVANIA STATE UNIVERSITY— HARRISBURG CAMPUS

School of Business Administration

Admissions Contact: Dr. Thomas Streveler, Director of Enrollment Services
Address: 777 West Harrisburg Pike, Middletown, PA 17057
Admissions Phone: 717-948-6250 • Admissions Fax: 717-948-6325
Admissions E-mail: hbgadmit@psu.edu • Web Address: www.hbg.psu.edu/sbus

Most of Penn State Harrisburg's MBA students reside in south central Pennsylvania and are part-time students. Courses are offered primarily in the evening to allow working professionals to maintain their careers. MBA applicants will need to prove their proficiency in mathematics, composition, and computer skills before they can write out the check for their education. Penn State Harrisburg has designed its MBA curriculum not only to satisfy the immediate educational needs of its students but also to promote lifelong learning.

INSTITUTIONAL INFORMATION
Public/Private: Public
Evening Classes Available? Yes
Total Faculty: 28
Student/Faculty Ratio: 12:1
Students in Parent Institution: 3,239
Academic Calendar: Semester

PROGRAMS
Degrees Offered: MBA (30 credits, 18 months to 6 years); MS in Information Systems (30 credits, 18 months to 6 years)

STUDENT INFORMATION
Total Business Students: 207
% Full Time: 12
% Female: 36
% Minority: 7
% Out of State: 5
% International: 5
Average Age: 27

COMPUTER AND RESEARCH FACILITIES
Campuswide Network? Yes
% of MBA Classrooms Wired: 100
Computer Model Recommended: Laptop
Internet Fee? No

EXPENSES/FINANCIAL AID
Annual Tuition (Resident/Nonresident): $9,264/$17,592
Books and Supplies: $4,170
Average Grant: $4,200
Average Loan: $6,873

ADMISSIONS INFORMATION
Application Fee: $50
Electronic Application? Yes
Regular Application Deadline: 7/18
Regular Notification: Rolling
Deferment Available? Yes
Length of Deferment: 3 years
Non-fall Admissions? Yes
Non-fall Application Deadline(s): 11/18, 4/18
Transfer Students Accepted? Yes
Transfer Policy: 10 credits max will transfer
Need-Blind Admissions? Yes
Number of Applications Received: 76
% of Applicants Accepted: 91
% Accepted Who Enrolled: 90
Average GPA: 3.0
Average GMAT: 520
Average Years Experience: 3
Other Admissions Factors Considered: Prior business experience

INTERNATIONAL STUDENTS
TOEFL Required of International Students? Yes
Minimum TOEFL: 550 (213 computer)

EMPLOYMENT INFORMATION
Placement Office Available? Yes
% Employed Within 3 Months: 100

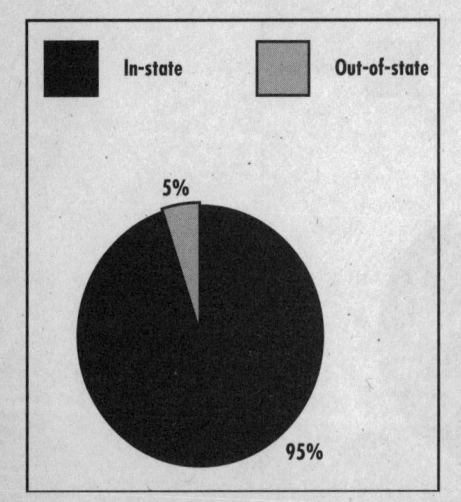

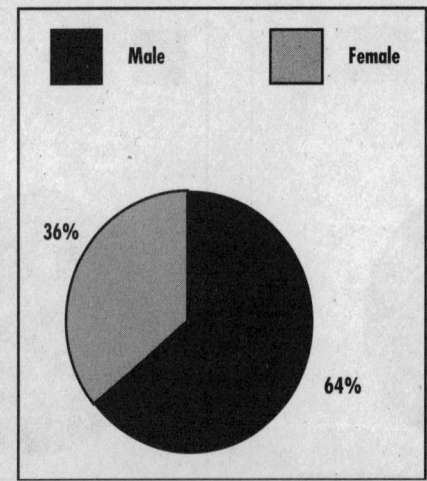

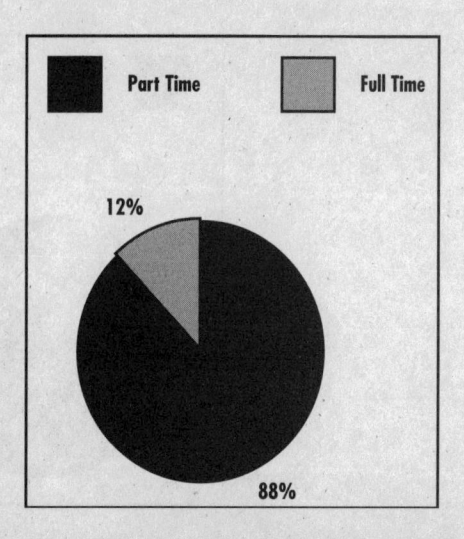

In-state 95% / Out-of-state 5%

Male 64% / Female 36%

Part Time 88% / Full Time 12%

PENNSYLVANIA STATE UNIVERSITY — UNIVERSITY PARK
The Smeal College of Business Administration

Admissions Contact: Kathleen M. Welch, Director of Marketing, MBA Program
Address: 106 Business Administration Building, University Park, PA 16802-3000
Admissions Phone: 814-863-0474 • Admissions Fax: 814-863-8072
Admissions E-mail: kmw204@psu.edu • Web Address: www.smeal.psu.edu/mba

Professors are "very accessible and willing to offer help"; team teaching and seven-week "blocks" keep things fast-paced and dynamic; and "everybody knows everybody" within the tiny, affordable confines of the MBA program at Penn State. Meanwhile, Smeal also provides "the resources of one of the largest universities in the nation." Students also laud the finance department and its "strong Wall Street alumni network," which is especially worth investigating "if you are interested in investment banking but don't want to pay $35,000 a year to get there."

INSTITUTIONAL INFORMATION
Public/Private: Public
Evening Classes Available? No
Total Faculty: 97
% Faculty Female: 18
% Faculty Minority: 19
Student/Faculty Ratio: 40:1
Students in Parent Institution: 40,828
Academic Calendar: Semester

PROGRAMS
Degrees Offered: MBA (21 months); MS in most disciplines (1 to 2 years); PhD (4 years)
Joint Degrees: BS/MBA Science (5 years), Quality and Manufacturing Management (3 years); MHA/MBA (3 years); JD/MBA (5 years); MBA/HRIM (2years)
Academic Specialties: Corporate Financial Analysis and Planning, eBusiness, Information Technologies for Management, Investment Management and Portfolio Analysis, Product and Market Development, Supply Chain Management, Strategic Consulting, Entrepreneurship
Study Abroad Options: Australia, Austria, Belgium, Denmark, England, Finland, France, Germany, Mexico, New Zealand, Norway, Singapore, Spain

STUDENT INFORMATION
Total Business Students: 108
% Full Time: 100
% Female: 24
% Minority: 15
% Out of State: 62
% International: 32
Average Age: 28

COMPUTER AND RESEARCH FACILITIES
Research Facilities: Smeal College Trading Room; centers and institutes for Global Business Studies, Logistics Research, Management of Technological and Organizational Change, Research in Conflict and Negotiation, Study of Business and Public Issues, Real Estate Studies, Study of Business Markets, Study of Organizational Effectiveness, Risk Management Research, and Venture Capital among other specialties
Computer Facilities: Wide range of databases, including ABI/Inform, CRSP, Dow Jones, EconLit, Multex, and Zacks University Analyst Watch
Campuswide Network? Yes
% of MBA Classrooms Wired: 100
Computer Model Recommended: Laptop
Internet Fee? No

EXPENSES/FINANCIAL AID
Annual Tuition (Resident/Nonresident): $9,076/$17,334
Room & Board (On/Off Campus): $5,875/$12,396
Books and Supplies: $1,500
Average Grant: $10,000

ADMISSIONS INFORMATION
Application Fee: $60
Electronic Application? Yes
Early Decision Application Deadline: 12/1
Early Decision Notification: 1/2
Regular Application Deadline: 6/2
Regular Notification: 6/2
Length of Deferment: 1 year
Non-fall Admissions? No
Transfer Policy: Maximum number of transferable credits is 6, with a minimum GPA of 3.0.
Need-Blind Admissions? Yes
Number of Applications Received: 953
% of Applicants Accepted: 25
% Accepted Who Enrolled: 46
Average GPA: 3.2
GPA Range: 2.7-3.7
Average GMAT: 624
GMAT Range: 550-693
Average Years Experience: 5
Other Admissions Factors Considered: Demonstrated leadership
Minority/Disadvantaged Student Recruitment Programs: Program awarding 10 graduate assistantships (tuition waiver plus stipend) each year to incoming minority students

INTERNATIONAL STUDENTS
TOEFL Required of International Students? Yes
Minimum TOEFL: 600 (250 computer)

EMPLOYMENT INFORMATION

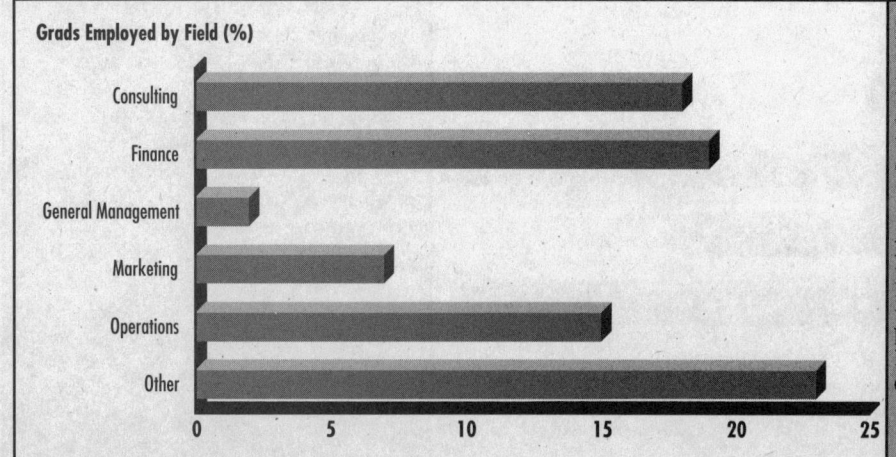

Grads Employed by Field (%)
- Consulting: ~19
- Finance: ~20
- General Management: ~2
- Marketing: ~7
- Operations: ~15
- Other: ~23

Placement Office Available? Yes
% Employed Within 3 Months: 93
Frequent Employers: IBM, Ford Motor Co., Accenture, Intel, Citibank, Flextronics International, Chatham Financial Corporation, Cap Gemini Ernst & Young, Lucent Technologies, Northwest Airlines, Owens Corning, Andersen, Hewlett-Packard, Lexmark International
Prominent Alumni: (Ret.) Lt. Gen. William G. Pagonis (MBA '70), chief logistician, Operation Desert Storm; Alexander Goldberg (MBA '64), president (retired), Ford Motor Land Services; J. David Rogers (MBA '80), founder and CEO, J.D. Capital Management LLC

PEPPERDINE UNIVERSITY
The Graziadio School of Business and Management

Admissions Contact: Darrell Eriksen, Director of Admissions
Address: 24255 Pacific Coast Highway, Malibu, CA 90263
Admissions Phone: 310-568-5535 • Admissions Fax: 310-568-5779
Admissions E-mail: gsbm@pepperdine.edu • Web Address: www.bschool.pepperdine.edu

The "brilliant, eccentric," and eclectic students at Pepperdine's Graziadio School of Business love its "conservative curriculum" that stresses "practical knowledge." Students in the "very effective" Master in International Business program are especially happy (perhaps because they get to spend a year overseas). Stateside, Pepperdine offers a "wonderful alumni network" and a "very fast-paced" one-year program to students who qualify. To top everything off, Pepperdine's paradise location in Malibu provides "one of the most beautiful settings in the world."

INSTITUTIONAL INFORMATION
Public/Private: Private
Evening Classes Available? Yes
Total Faculty: 147
% Faculty Female: 15
% Faculty Minority: 5
% Faculty Part Time: 49
Student/Faculty Ratio: 20:1
Students in Parent Institution: 7,637
Academic Calendar: Trimester

PROGRAMS
Degrees Offered: Full-time MBA (12-month, 15-month, and 2-year programs available); Evening MBA (6 trimesters); Executive MBA (5 trimesters); Presidential/Key Executive MBA (5 trimesters); Master of Science in Organization Development (6 trimesters); Executive MBA in Technology Management (5 trimesters); Master of International Business (5 trimesters)
Joint Degrees: JD/MBA (4 years); MBA/Master of Public Policy (3 years)
Academic Specialties: Strategic Management, Organization Development, Marketing, Finance, Global/International Business, Technology
Special Opportunities: MBA concentrations; mentorship program; internships; nonprofit consulting projects; business fluency in French, German, or Spanish; communication workshop; strategy simulation; Integration and Application seminars

Study Abroad Options: Belgium, France, Germany, Netherlands, Spain, UK, Brazil, Chile, Mexico, China, Hong Kong, Philippines, Thailand

STUDENT INFORMATION
Total Business Students: 1,796
% Full Time: 8
% Female: 39
% Minority: 39
% Out of State: 60
% International: 39
Average Age: 26

COMPUTER AND RESEARCH FACILITIES
Research Facilities: Teleconferencing unit
Computer Facilities: 6 computer facilities, research through more than 700 online journals and electronic databases, Intranet portal
Campuswide Network? Yes
% of MBA Classrooms Wired: 100
Computer Model Recommended: Laptop

EXPENSES/FINANCIAL AID
Annual Tuition: $25,315
Tuition Per Credit: $890
Room & Board (Off Campus): $12,709
Books and Supplies: $1,000
Average Grant: $16,700
Average Loan: $19,800
% Receiving Financial Aid: 43
% Receiving Aid Their First Year: 50

ADMISSIONS INFORMATION
Application Fee: $45
Electronic Application? Yes
Early Decision Application Deadline: 12/15
Early Decision Notification: 1/15
Regular Application Deadline: 5/1
Regular Notification: Rolling
Length of Deferment: 1 year
Non-fall Admissions? No
Transfer Policy: No more than 2 courses may be transferred, upon approval of policy committee.
Need-Blind Admissions? Yes
Number of Applications Received: 418
% of Applicants Accepted: 44
% Accepted Who Enrolled: 52
Average GPA: 3.1
GPA Range: 2.7-3.4
Average GMAT: 630
GMAT Range: 580-665
Average Years Experience: 4
Other Admissions Factors Considered: Leadership qualities, professional portfolio, managerial experience, promotions, full-time work experience is required for the 12- and 15-month MBA programs.

INTERNATIONAL STUDENTS
TOEFL Required of International Students? Yes
Minimum TOEFL: 550 (213 computer)

EMPLOYMENT INFORMATION

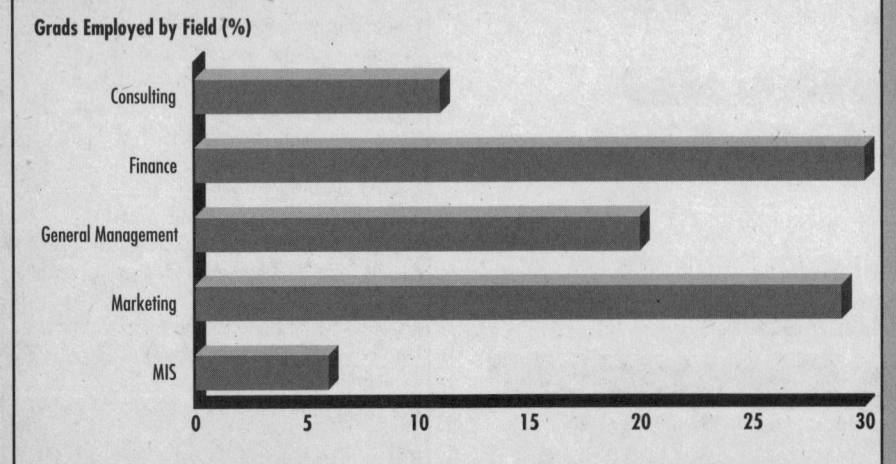

Grads Employed by Field (%)
- Consulting: ~11
- Finance: ~30
- General Management: ~20
- Marketing: ~29
- MIS: ~6

Placement Office Available? Yes
% Employed Within 3 Months: 90
Frequent Employers: Oracle, Infonet, Allergan, Bank of America, Warner Bros., Boeing, E*Trade, Pacific Bell, Merrill Lynch, EMI Music Distribution, Pricewaterhouse-Coopers, Ernst & Young
Prominent Alumni: Christos M. Cotsakos, chairman and CEO, E*Trade Group; David Mount, chairman and CEO, WEA Inc.; Dirk Gates, chairman, president, and CEO, Xircom Inc.; James Q. Crowe, president and CEO, Level 3 Communications; Shirley Choi, CEO, Seapower Group

PITTSBURG STATE UNIVERSITY
Gladys A. Kelce College of Business

Admissions Contact: Marvene Darraugh, Administrative Officer-Graduate Studies
Address: 1701 South Broadway, Pittsburg, KS 66762-7540
Admissions Phone: 620-235-4222 • Admissions Fax: 620-235-4219
Admissions E-mail: grad@pittstate.edu • Web Address: www.pittstate.edu

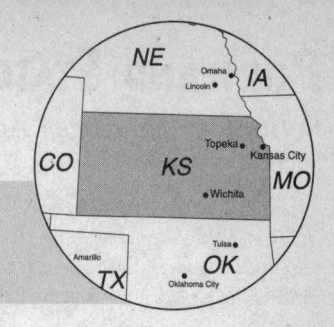

The Kelce College of Business in Pittsburg, Kansas, offers an affordable education and boasts sizable populations of women, minorities, and international students. An interesting aside: Pittsburg State University is the only college in the country with a gorilla as its mascot; in 1920, at the time of the mascot's inception, "gorilla" was a slang term for roughnecks.

INSTITUTIONAL INFORMATION
Public/Private: Public
Evening Classes Available? Yes
Total Faculty: 27
% Faculty Female: 15
% Faculty Minority: 10
Student/Faculty Ratio: 4:1
Students in Parent Institution: 6,300
Academic Calendar: Semester

PROGRAMS
Degrees Offered: MBA with concentrations in General Administration (34 semester hours, 1 year full-time), Accounting (34 semester hours, 1 year full-time)
Academic Specialties: Faculty have specialties in Finance, Marketing, Management, Accounting, MIS, and Economics.
Study Abroad Options: Australia, China, Finland, Korea, Paraguay

STUDENT INFORMATION
Total Business Students: 86
% Full Time: 78
% Female: 33
% Out of State: 55
% International: 53
Average Age: 24

COMPUTER AND RESEARCH FACILITIES
Research Facilities: Axes Library: total holdings of 350,000 volumes; 624,000 microforms; 1,600 current periodical subscriptions; CD players available
Computer Facilities: ABI/Inform, Dialogue, Compact Disclosure, Accounting and Tax Index, Infotrac, Lexis-Nexis
Campuswide Network? Yes
% of MBA Classrooms Wired: 5
Internet Fee? No

EXPENSES/FINANCIAL AID
Annual Tuition (Resident/Nonresident): $2,466/$6,268
Room & Board (On/Off Campus): $4,570/$6,000
Books and Supplies: $1,200
Average Grant: $3,500
Average Loan: $5,000
% Receiving Financial Aid: 50
% Receiving Aid Their First Year: 25

ADMISSIONS INFORMATION
Electronic Application? No
Regular Application Deadline: 7/15
Regular Notification: 8/1
Deferment Available? Yes
Length of Deferment: 1 year
Non-fall Admissions? Yes
Non-fall Application Deadline(s): 12/15, 5/1
Transfer Students Accepted? Yes
Transfer Policy: Up to 9 semester hours may be transferred from another program.
Need-Blind Admissions? Yes
Number of Applications Received: 250
% of Applicants Accepted: 76
% Accepted Who Enrolled: 45
Average GPA: 3.5
GPA Range: 2.7-4.0
Average GMAT: 515
GMAT Range: 400-690
Average Years Experience: 1

INTERNATIONAL STUDENTS
TOEFL Required of International Students? Yes
Minimum TOEFL: 550

EMPLOYMENT INFORMATION

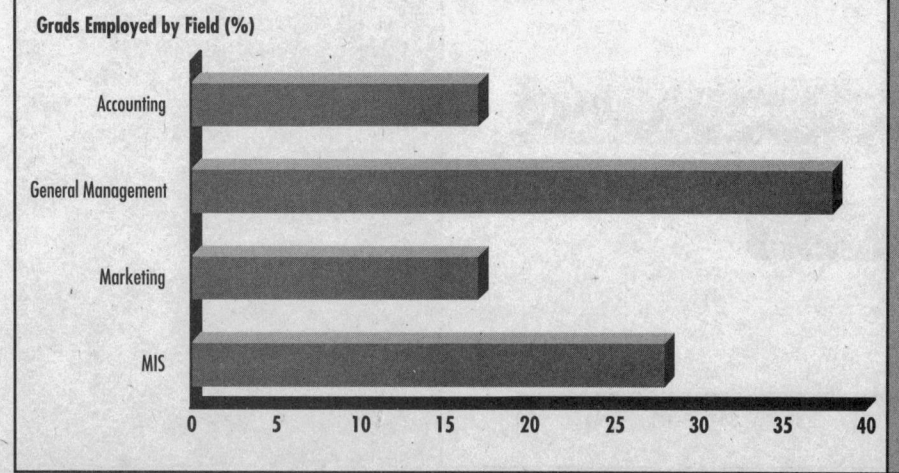

Grads Employed by Field (%)
- Accounting: ~17
- General Management: ~38
- Marketing: ~17
- MIS: ~28

Placement Office Available? Yes
Frequent Employers: Deloitte & Touche, PricewaterhouseCoopers, Payless Shoe Source, Core-Mark, Sprint, Hallmark, Cessna

PORTLAND STATE UNIVERSITY
School of Business Administration

Admissions Contact: Pam Mitchell, Graduate Programs Administrator
Address: 631 SW Harrison St., Portland, OR 97201
Admissions Phone: 503-725-3712 • Admissions Fax: 503-725-5740
Admissions E-mail: info@sba.pdx.edu • Web Address: www.sba.pdx.edu

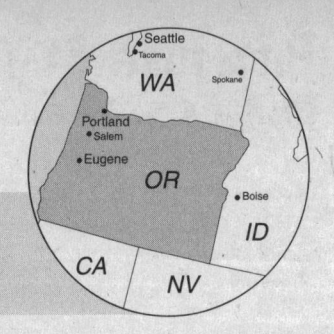

MBA students at Portland State can choose from programs in innovation and technology, finance, and international business, as well as an online program, the eMBA, that parallels Portland's on-site education. The Master of International Management, focusing on the Pacific Rim markets, is also available. The support of the business community allows the School of Business Administration to combine "academic integrity with practical, hands-on experience," and the school strives to serve the community in return.

INSTITUTIONAL INFORMATION
Public/Private: Public
Evening Classes Available? Yes
Total Faculty: 35
% Faculty Female: 23
% Faculty Minority: 9
Student/Faculty Ratio: 35:1

PROGRAMS
Degrees Offered: Master of Business Administration (MBA (2 years full time, 3 years part time/online), Master of Science in Financial Analysis (MSFA) (5 to 6 quarters), Master of International Management (MIM) (1 year full time, 2 years part time)
Academic Specialties: PSU Online MBA Program on US News Top 25 list; PSU accounting students ranked fifth in the nation on the CPA exam in 1999
Special Opportunities: 3 options offered in conjunction with the MBA program: Management of Innovation and Technology, Finance, International Business; specialized studies in Food Industry
Study Abroad Options: France, Italy, Denmark

STUDENT INFORMATION
Total Business Students: 363
% Full Time: 23
% Female: 44
% Minority: 13
% Out of State: 12
% International: 41
Average Age: 30

COMPUTER AND RESEARCH FACILITIES
Computer Facilities: MBA computer lab with 30 computers on campus for MBA students, Compustat, Standard & Poor's Research Insight, all PSU library databases (including Infotrac, EDGAR, Global Access)
Campuswide Network? Yes
Internet Fee? No

EXPENSES/FINANCIAL AID
Annual Tuition (Resident/Nonresident): $6,834/$11,613
Tuition Per Credit: $259
Room & Board (On/Off Campus): $14,268/$14,286
Books and Supplies: $1,200

ADMISSIONS INFORMATION
Application Fee: $50
Electronic Application? Yes
Regular Application Deadline: 3/1
Regular Notification: 6/30
Deferment Available? No
Non-fall Admissions? No
Transfer Students Accepted? Yes
Transfer Policy: Maximum of 1/3 of the total number of PSU credits may transfer from a US accredited university.
Need-Blind Admissions? No
Number of Applications Received: 340
% of Applicants Accepted: 39
% Accepted Who Enrolled: 88
Average GPA: 3.2
Average GMAT: 598
Average Years Experience: 6
Other Admissions Factors Considered: 2 years of business work experience preferred.
Other Schools to Which Students Applied: Oregon State University, University of Oregon, University of Portland.

INTERNATIONAL STUDENTS
TOEFL Required of International Students? Yes
Minimum TOEFL: 550 (213 computer)

EMPLOYMENT INFORMATION

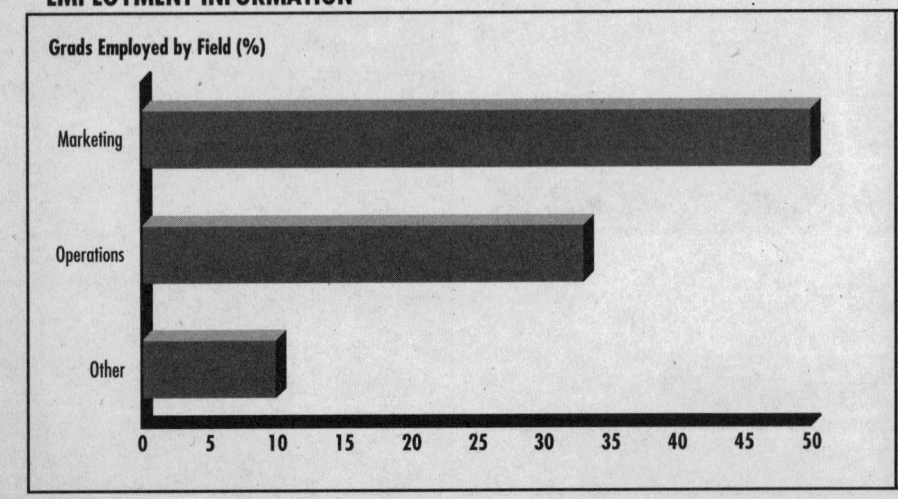

Grads Employed by Field (%)
- Marketing: ~50
- Operations: ~33
- Other: ~10

Placement Office Available? No
% Employed Within 3 Months: 67
Frequent Employers: Arthur Andersen, IBM (Sequent), Intel, Mentor Graphics, Nike-Tektronix, US Bancorp, Wells Fargo, Xerox

PURDUE UNIVERSITY — CALUMET
School of Management

Admissions Contact: Paul McGrath, Coordinator, Graduate Management Programs
Address: School of Management, Hammond, IN 46323-2094
Admissions Phone: 219-989-2425 • Admissions Fax: 219-989-3158
Admissions E-mail: pmcgrat@calumet.purdue.edu • Web Address: www.calumet.purdue.edu

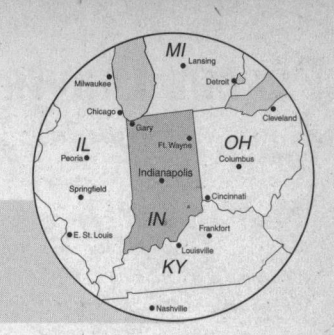

Located just 25 miles southeast of downtown Chicago, Purdue University Calumet's School of Management accommodates students with a variety of undergraduate backgrounds. The MBA program consists of three stages: foundation course work, the core program, and electives, and together they form a strong foundation of financial knowledge. Purdue's MBA program has a curriculum that fosters managerial growth in each of the functional areas and accommodates students from a multitude of undergraduate and professional backgrounds.

INSTITUTIONAL INFORMATION
Public/Private: Public
Evening Classes Available? No
Total Faculty: 52
% Faculty Part Time: 6
Students in Parent Institution: 23,676
Academic Calendar: Semester

PROGRAMS
Degrees Offered: Master of Business Administration (MBA) (full time or part time, 31 to 52 credits, up to 7 years), with concentrations in Accounting, Finance, Human Resources, Management Information Systems, Marketing, and Real Estate; Master of Science in Accountancy (MS) (full time or part time, 30 to 49 credits, up to 7 years), with concentrations in Accounting and Taxation; Master of Science in Business Administration (MS) (full time or part time, 30 to 49 credits, up to 7 years), with concentrations in Management Information Systems and Taxation

STUDENT INFORMATION
Total Business Students: 539
% Full Time: 24
% Female: 45
% Minority: 23
% International: 14
Average Age: 32

COMPUTER AND RESEARCH FACILITIES
Research Facilities: Total library holdings of 205,000 volumes, 1,361 current periodicals subscriptions; access to online bibliographic retrieval services
Campuswide Network? Yes
Internet Fee? No

EXPENSES/FINANCIAL AID
Tuition Per Credit (Resident/Nonresident): $128/$280

ADMISSIONS INFORMATION
Application Fee: $30
Electronic Application? No
Regular Application Deadline: 5/1
Regular Notification: 1/1
Deferment Available? Yes
Non-fall Admissions? Yes
Non-fall Application Deadline(s): 11/1 spring
Transfer Students Accepted? No
Need-Blind Admissions? No
Number of Applications Received: 296
% of Applicants Accepted: 60
% Accepted Who Enrolled: 61
Other Admissions Factors Considered: Computer experience required: word processing, spreadsheet, database. A minimum GMAT score of 420 and GPA of 2.5 are required. A GRE score, personal statement, résumé, and work experience are all recommended.

INTERNATIONAL STUDENTS
TOEFL Required of International Students? Yes
Minimum TOEFL: 550

EMPLOYMENT INFORMATION

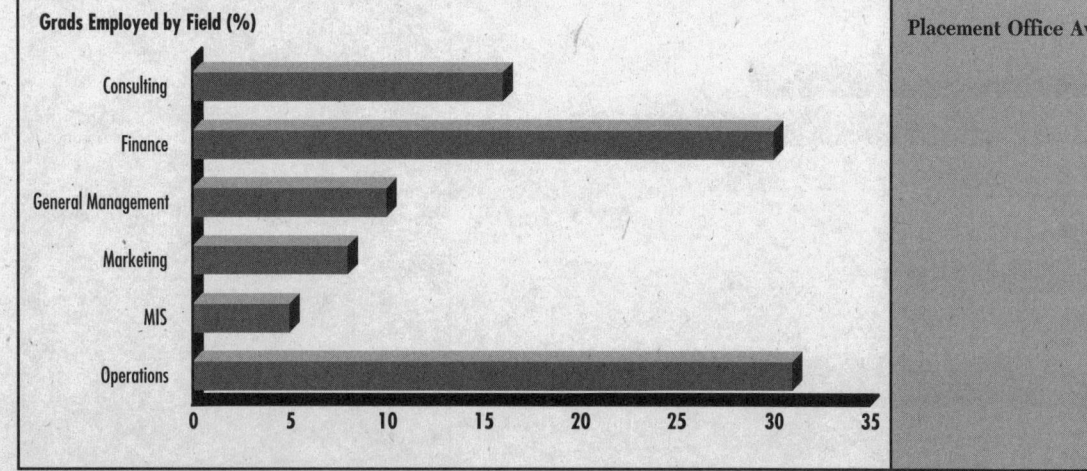

Grads Employed by Field (%)

Field	%
Consulting	~16
Finance	~30
General Management	~10
Marketing	~7
MIS	~5
Operations	~31

Placement Office Available? No

PURDUE UNIVERSITY — WEST LAFAYETTE
Krannert Graduate School of Management

Admissions Contact: Ward Snearly, Director of Admissions
Address: 1310 Krannert Building, West Lafayette, IN 47907
Admissions Phone: 765-494-4365 • Admissions Fax: 765-494-9841
Admissions E-mail: krannert_ms@mgmt.purdue.edu • Web Address: www.mgmt.purdue.edu

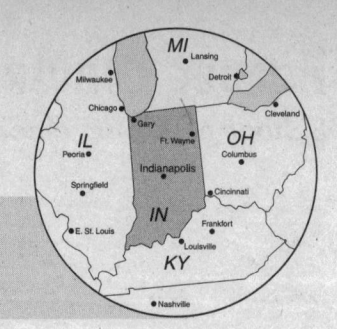

The "state-of-the-art" Krannert Graduate School of Management offers its small "technically oriented, hardworking, focused" student body "an intense program leading to a great technology MBA" and arguably "the strongest" program "in the country when it comes to using computers for quantitative analysis." There is an intimate atmosphere here, which means you'll "know everyone," and few students anywhere graduate with more job offers on average than Krannert MBAs.

INSTITUTIONAL INFORMATION
Public/Private: Public
Evening Classes Available? No
Total Faculty: 90
% Faculty Female: 16
% Faculty Minority: 10
% Faculty Part Time: 6
Student/Faculty Ratio: 4:1
Students in Parent Institution: 37,000
Academic Calendar: Semester

PROGRAMS
Degrees Offered: MS in Industrial Administration (11 months), MS in Human Resource Management (2 years), MS in Management, Executive MS in Management (2 years), PhD in Economics and Management
Joint Degrees: Agribusiness Executive MBA (in approval process now)
Academic Specialties: All major functional areas represented; especially strong in Operations/Manufacturing Management, Corporate Finance, and Applications of IT, including E-Commerce
Special Opportunities: International Multidisciplinary Management Program, Washington Campus Program, Plus Leadership Program, Management Volunteer Program, Burton Morgan Entrepreneurship Competition, Technology Transfer Initiative, SAP Alliance Program, Business Opportunity Program, Student Managed Investment Fund, MBA Enterprise Corps
Study Abroad Options: Germany

STUDENT INFORMATION
Total Business Students: 211
% Female: 28
% Minority: 17
% International: 44
Average Age: 27

COMPUTER AND RESEARCH FACILITIES
Research Facilities: Dauch Center for the Management of Manufacturing Enterprises, Center for International Business Economics Research and Education, Center for Research on Contracts and the Structure of Enterprises, Institute of Industrial Compulsiveness, SEAS
Computer Facilities: Agricola, Beilstein, Compendex, Current Contents, Humanities Index, MathSci Index, WorldCat, CRSP, Datastream, and hundreds more; all PDAs supported
Campuswide Network? Yes
% of MBA Classrooms Wired: 100
Computer Model Recommended: Laptop
Internet Fee? No

EXPENSES/FINANCIAL AID
Annual Tuition (Resident/Nonresident): $10,064/$19,868
Books and Supplies: $1,200
Average Grant: $11,012
Average Loan: $11,000
% Receiving Financial Aid: 50
% Receiving Aid Their First Year: 51

ADMISSIONS INFORMATION
Application Fee: $30
Electronic Application? Yes
Early Decision Application Deadline: 11/1
Early Decision Notification: 12/15
Regular Application Deadline: 5/1
Regular Notification: Rolling
Length of Deferment: 2 years
Non-fall Admissions? No
Transfer Students Accepted? No
Need-Blind Admissions? Yes
Number of Applications Received: 1,686
% of Applicants Accepted: 100
% Accepted Who Enrolled: 13
Average GPA: 3.2
GPA Range: 2.3-4.0
Average GMAT: 642
GMAT Range: 430-770
Average Years Experience: 4
Minority/Disadvantaged Student Recruitment Programs: Business Opportunity Program
Other Schools to Which Students Applied: Ohio State, U. of Chicago, U. of Michigan, UNC Chapel Hill, U. of Southern California, UT Austin.

INTERNATIONAL STUDENTS
TOEFL Required of International Students? Yes
Minimum TOEFL: 575 (230 computer)

EMPLOYMENT INFORMATION

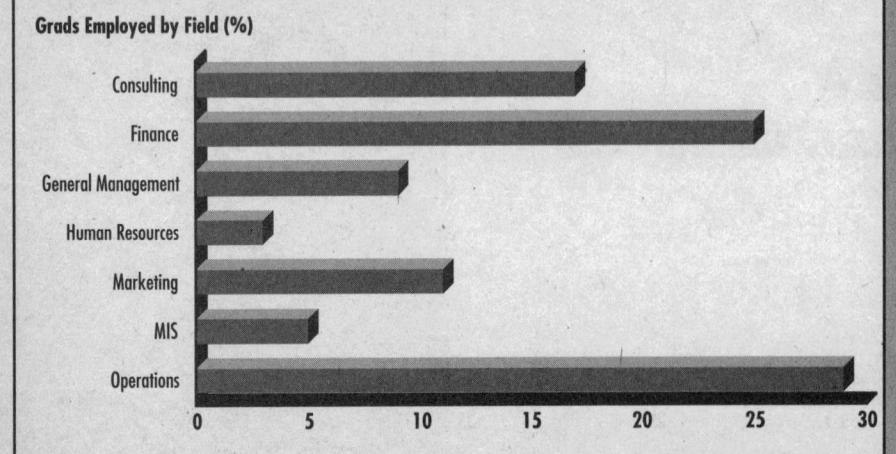

Grads Employed by Field (%)

Field	%
Consulting	17
Finance	25
General Management	8
Human Resources	3
Marketing	11
MIS	5
Operations	29

Placement Office Available? Yes
% Employed Within 3 Months: 95
Frequent Employers: IBM, Intel, Hewlett-Packard, Ford Motor Co., Pricewaterhouse-Coopers, Merrill Lynch, United Technologies, Owens Corning, Accenture, Ernst & Young, Ingersoll-Rand, TRW, HB Fuller, Deloitte & Touche, Sun Microsystems, Eli Lilly, Thomson Consumer Electronics, TRW, Cummins Engine, American Axle, Reflect.com, i2 Technologies
Prominent Alumni: Karl Krapek, president and COO, United Technologies; Joseph Forehand, managing partner and CEO, Accenture; James Perrella, CEO, Ingersoll-Rand; Jerry Rawls, founder and CEO, Finisar; Norm Blake, CEO, ComDisco

Queen's University
Queen's School of Business

Admissions Contact: Program Coordinator
Address: Mackintosh-Corry Hall, Queen's University, Kingston, ON K7L 3N6 Canada
Admissions Phone: 613-533-2302 • Admissions Fax: 613-533-6281
Admissions E-mail: admin@mbast.queensu.ca • Web Address: www.business.queensu.ca

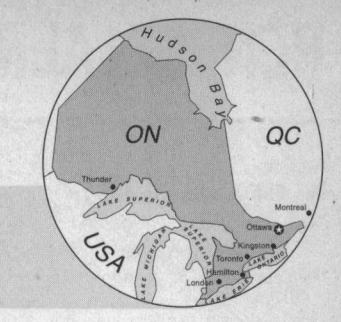

An interesting program option at Queen's University is the MBA for Science and Technology, which prepares students for management positions in areas as wide-ranging as pharmaceutical industries and aerospace. Another option is the Queen's Executive MBA, which is earned in two years and can be taken in person in downtown Ottawa or via real-time interactive videoconference by executives in other major metropolitan areas throughout Canada.

INSTITUTIONAL INFORMATION
Public/Private: Public
Evening Classes Available? No
Total Faculty: 24
Student/Faculty Ratio: 3:1
Students in Parent Institution: 17,510
Academic Calendar: Annual

PROGRAMS
Degrees Offered: MBA for Science and Technology (MBA) (minimum 12 months); Executive MBA (EMBA) (minimum 2 years); National Executive Master of Business Administration (NEMBA) (minimum 2 years)
Special Opportunities: Bachelor of Commerce undergraduate degree (4 years)
Study Abroad Options: Australia, Belgium, Canada, Chile, Denmark, Finland, France, Germany, Japan, Mexico, Norway, China, Scotland, Singapore, Sweden, Switzerland, Taiwan

STUDENT INFORMATION
Total Business Students: 60
% Full Time: 100
% Female: 25
% Minority: 5
% International: 20
Average Age: 30

COMPUTER AND RESEARCH FACILITIES
Research Facilities: Queen's Centre for Enterprise Development, Queen's Centre for Knowledge-Based Enterprise, Queen's Executive Decision Centre, CGA Ontario International Business Research Centre
Campuswide Network? Yes
% of MBA Classrooms Wired: 100
Computer Model Recommended: Laptop
Internet Fee? No

EXPENSES/FINANCIAL AID
Annual Tuition: $24,200
Room & Board (On/Off Campus): $5,500/$6,500
Books and Supplies: $1,700
Average Loan: $24,200

ADMISSIONS INFORMATION
Application Fee: $100
Electronic Application? Yes
Regular Application Deadline: 1/31
Regular Notification: 12/22
Length of Deferment: 1 year
Non-fall Application Deadline(s): May
Transfer Students Accepted? No
Need-Blind Admissions? Yes
Number of Applications Received: 297
% of Applicants Accepted: 27
% Accepted Who Enrolled: 75
Average GPA: 3.2
Average GMAT: 665
GMAT Range: 630-700
Average Years Experience: 6
Other Admissions Factors Considered: Demonstrated desire for challenging, team-based environment.
Other Schools to Which Students Applied: University of Toronto, University of Western Ontario

INTERNATIONAL STUDENTS
TOEFL Required of International Students? Yes
Minimum TOEFL: 600 (250 computer)

EMPLOYMENT INFORMATION
Placement Office Available? Yes
% Employed Within 3 Months: 95
Frequent Employers: Bell Canada Enterprises, Nortel Networks, PRTM (Boston), Deloitte Consulting, Accenture, AT Kearney, JDS Uniphase
Prominent Alumni: Mel Goodes, retired chairman and CEO, Warner-Lambert Co.; Don Carty, chairman, president, and CEO, AMR Corp. and American Airlines; Michael Ball, president, Allergan Inc.

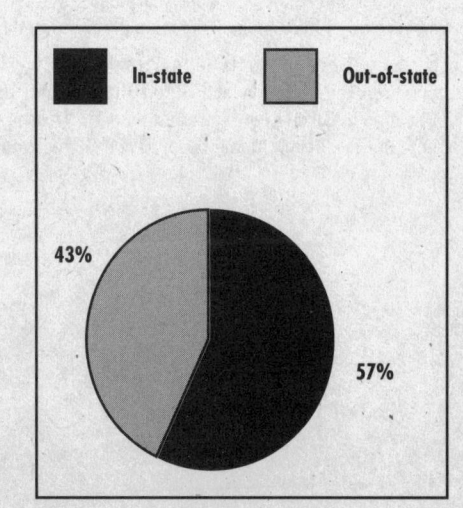

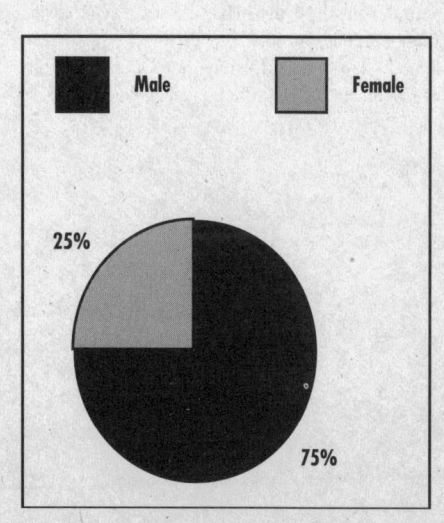

In-state: 57% / Out-of-state: 43%

Male: 75% / Female: 25%

RENSSELAER POLYTECHNIC INSTITUTE

THE SCHOOL AT A GLANCE

"The Lally School's mission is to develop technically sophisticated business leaders who are prepared to guide their organizations in the integration of technology for new products, new businesses, and new systems."

—Robert A. Baron, Interim Dean

Aspiring business leaders must be both managerially and technologically astute. Select admissions criteria result in a relatively small MBA class, and provide added value for students who choose to study at Rensselaer to develop these management tools.

Seminars offer a rigorous academic environment and personal interaction between students, faculty members, and guest speakers. Students may participate in cutting-edge research, such as our Radical Innovation Project (featured in *Business Week*), studying the commercialization of next-generation products and services by established firms.

STUDENTS

Lally's diverse student population offers a variety of cultural, educational, and business perspectives. An active Graduate Management Student Association sponsors social, career, and recreational activities, including Network International, intramural sports, and community service.

Students may work on projects or cooperative work experiences with companies at the Rensselaer Incubator Center, the Rensselaer Technology Park, or area firms that include GE, Lockheed Martin, Allied Signal, Albany International, First Albany, and a host of smaller companies. Companies at the Rensselaer Technology Park represent technologies ranging from electronic to physics research, from biotechnology to software. Our nationally acclaimed Incubator Center provides even more opportunity. Founded in 1980 as the first university-based incubator in the nation, the Incubator provides a unique entrepreneurial environment—harnessing academic, research, and community resources to assist technology start-up enterprises.

ACADEMICS

Innovation and technology create a path to corporate competitive advantage. The Lally MBA at Rensselaer provides professional management training infused with Rensselaer's 178-year history of discovery, invention, and innovation. The Lally MBA is ideal for those who want a comprehensive business education emphasizing the strategic role of technology.

A comprehensive set of core courses introduces the non-business major to the language and tools of business. MBA course work may include studies throughout the Rensselaer campus in our schools of Humanities, Architecture, Science, and Engineering—including studies in information technology and biotechnology. Areas of concentration in the Lally MBA include Technological Entrepreneurship, Management of Innovation and New Product Development, MIS, E-Business, Environmental Management, Finance, and Operations Management (the integration of management with information technology and quantitative techniques).

The MBA combines studies in traditional business tools, global corporate strategy, and technological capability (20 courses/60 credits). Our emphasis on innovation and entrepreneurship is apparent in "Design, Manufacturing, and Marketing" (DMM), a two-semester, team-based product development course. Under the leadership of a cross-disciplinary team of faculty members, students become familiar with all aspects of product development in a competitive global environment. It is not unusual for these team projects to become the seed of a new incubator business, or to re-emerge as presentations in venture capital competitions.

An MBA is a professional degree program, enabling our graduates to provide leadership in the corporate sector. The MBA curriculum combines research and development, practica-oriented experience, and corporate case study. The second year of the MBA includes a strategy sequence, business/legal ethics, an international business class, and six elective courses.

Entrepreneurship is a mainstream activity of the Lally School. For example, as the science of biotechnology grows on a global scale, we offer management seminars on the challenges of founding new ventures in the life sciences area. Faculty research suggests that competitive advantage is intimately connected to a culture of innovation. *Success* magazine ranked the Lally School sixth nationally in entrepreneurship. We foment that culture here.

The Severino Center for Technological Entrepreneurship leads this mission, with an emphasis on commercializing technology for the global marketplace. Activities include the Entrepreneur Intern program, Women in Entrepreneurship, Innovation and Technology Forums, and the $25,000 Lucent Business Plan competition, which may lead to new business creation in our world-class Incubator Center and Rensselaer Technology Park.

Student teams enter the annual Business Plan Competition seeking an award of seed-stage capital plus the opportunity to present their proposals to venture capitalists in Boston, New York, and/or California.

Management Information Systems is one of the Lally School's strong points. *U.S. News & World Report* ranked Lally in the top 30 MIS programs. This focus integrates Lally's historical strengths in operations research and statistics with Rensselaer's technological pre-eminence in IT and computer science.

The concentration in E-business evaluates the impact of new technologies on business models, supply chain management, customer relationship, and marketing. Environmental Management and Policy, recognized internationally by the World Resources Institute, provides a concentration of courses that integrate environmental issues within a framework of business strategy.

A dual degree, combining an MBA with an MS in science or engineering (72 credits total), allows students to add business acumen to emerging technologies, such as biotechnology, while sharpening their technological expertise. The Lally School of Management is nationally accredited by AACSB International.

The Rensselaer Plan, initiated by President Shirley Ann Jackson, is a cornerstone to linking the Lally School to RPI's strengths in technology, innovation, and commercializing new ventures. Says Dr. Jackson, "It is a watershed time, where our leadership in innovation is converging with unprecedented technological impact."

Lally School of Management and Technology

Lally's corporate partners help align our curriculum to the needs of hiring managers and provide high-level networking opportunities. Students regularly meet with alumni for mentoring and career advice. Classes feature guest speakers, senior managers and policy makers, and an Executive-in-Resident Program.

Our faculty are recruited for world-class capabilities to strengthen both our instructional programs (MBA, PhD) and our research foci, including entrepreneurship and information technology, E-business with decision and engineering sciences, and IT radical innovation and marketing with product innovation and design. Most full-time faculty members have substantial managerial experience in business or government.

Biotechnology entrepreneurship, an emerging focus, is closely tied to Rensselaer's future.

CAMPUS LIFE

Rensselaer is located on a 260-acre campus overlooking the Hudson River and the historic Hudson River Valley. Only 10 minutes from Albany, the New York State capital, the campus is a 2.5-hour commute to New York City; accessible to Boston, Montreal, and Washington D.C. Skiing and hiking are close by in the Adirondack, Catskill, Berkshire, and Green mountains. Amtrak and the Albany International Airport offer newly renovated facilities. The Capital District Region is a major center for government, industry, research, and academic life.

The Lally School is housed in the Pittsburgh Building, a 35,000-square-foot, state-of-art teaching and research facility. Online services include Bloomberg Data, Wharton Research Data Services, and Zacks Investment Research. Recently reconstructed, it is technology-intensive with multimedia classrooms, computer and distance learning facilities, and student lounges and food service. *Yahoo Internet Life* has consistently ranked Rensselaer as one of the top most wired campuses; we continue add on-campus infrastructure and student support services.

MBA project teams use state-of-the-art Information Technology Tools that include development tools, enterprise databases (Microsoft SQL server), IIS web servers, and Visual Interdev and Access 2000 to build hands-on technical solutions to real world business problems.

At Rensselaer, computing is an integral part of the everyday educational experience and students have broad access to computing tools for use in a variety of courses. Many of the core courses use computing intensively. The Rensselaer Computing System (RCS) has over 500 public IBM, SUN, and Silico Graphic workstations and personal computers, which form the backbone of Rensselaer's computing labs.

The Lally Career Resources Office works with each student on their job-placement strategy. These include corporate interviews, career fairs, and alumni mentoring and networking. Ongoing support includes professional resume development and situation-specific interviewing skills. A resume book is distributed to corporate recruiters. All MBA students enroll in the Craig '68 Professional and Leadership Development seminar, which includes training with a corporate recruiter using videotaped mock interviews, understanding business etiquette and protocol, and interactions with senior corporate executives.

Students have access to two job-search databanks. Rensselaer's campuswide Career Development Office and the Archer Center for Leadership Development complement our office with corporate career days, executive roundtable discussions, a Cooperative Job-Educational Program (COOP), and professional development seminars.

COSTS

Rensselaer is committed to supporting full-time graduate students with tuition support combined with a stipend awarded on a competitive basis, based on merit. Additional fellowships and other financial support may also be available. Tuition for 2002–2003 is based on a flat academic year tuition of $26,400 for full-time students. Living expenses are estimated at $9,500 per year. International students should contact Graduate Admissions, admissions@rpi.edu, or 518-276-6216 for I-20 and financial aid information.

ADMISSIONS

The Lally School values a culturally diverse student body. We are committed to the professional development of women and minorities, and seek a strong international representation. Applicants are not limited to a degree in science or engineering, but should possess quantitative skills, a strong interest in technology, and significant work experience. Each year a select number of recent college graduates are also considered for admission.

The GMAT is mandatory. All international students are required to take the TOEFL and obtain a minimum score of 600.

Applications are accepted year-round, and admission decisions are made on a rolling basis. Early submission is strongly encouraged, preferably by January 15, for consideration to receive tuition support and a stipend. Full-time MBA students must begin their program in the fall semester. MS students ideally should begin in a fall semester due to course sequencing.

The academic year runs from late August through mid-May. The full-time program may be completed in two years. A summer session allows for additional flexibility, including internships.

Visit our web site http://lallymba.mgmt.rpi.edu for an online application and program information.

Admissions Contact: Zamiul Haque, Director of MBA/MS Admissions
Address: 110 Eighth St., PI 3218, Troy, NY 12180
Admissions Phone: 518-276-6586 • Admissions Fax: 518-276-2665
Admissions E-mail: management@rpi.edu • Web Address: www.lallyschool.rpi.edu

RENSSELAER POLYTECHNIC INSTITUTE
Lally School of Management and Technology

Admissions Contact: Zamiul Haque, Director of MBA/MS Admissions
Address: 110 Eighth St., PI 3218, Troy, NY 12180
Admissions Phone: 518-276-6586 • Admissions Fax: 518-276-2665
Admissions E-mail: management@rpi.edu • Web Address: www.lallyschool.rpi.edu

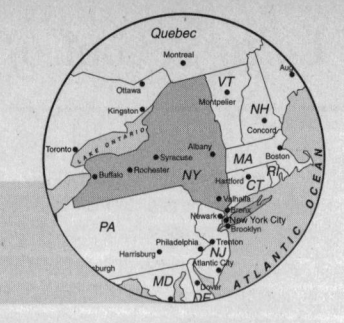

Rensselaer's intimate Lally School of Management and Technology is not for technophobes or the fainthearted. Nearly everyone here has an extensive background in computers and engineering, and the "friendly but busy" students study like crazy. RPI boasts small classes, great computing facilities, and a lot of student/faculty interaction, and its "top-notch" professors "have a wealth of both academic and professional experience."

INSTITUTIONAL INFORMATION
Public/Private: Private
Evening Classes Available? Yes
Total Faculty: 38
% Faculty Female: 15
% Faculty Minority: 7
% Faculty Part Time: 5
Student/Faculty Ratio: 15:1
Students in Parent Institution: 6,200
Academic Calendar: Semester

PROGRAMS
Degrees Offered: MBA (2 years), MS (1 year), PhD (3 to 5 years)
Joint Degrees: BS/MBA (5 years); MBA/MS (2.5 to 3 years); MBA/Master in Engineering (2.5 to 3 years); MBA/JD (3 to 4 years)
Academic Specialties: Management and Technology Emphasis, with strengths in Value Creation Systems and Financial Technology
Special Opportunities: International exchange in 7 countries; Executive MBA
Study Abroad Options: Denmark, Finland, Hong Kong, Australia, France, Italy, Spain

STUDENT INFORMATION
Total Business Students: 255
% Full Time: 63
% Female: 30
% Minority: 2
% Out of State: 75
% International: 51
Average Age: 29

COMPUTER AND RESEARCH FACILITIES
Research Facilities: Linked with the Design and Manufacturing Institute, the Severino Center for Technological Entrepreneurship, the Radical Innovation Project, and the Center for Services Research and Education Study of Financial Technology
Computer Facilities: Rensselaer library systems allow access to collections, databases, and Internet resources from campus terminals. Rensselaer Computing System permeates the campus with a coherent array of advanced workstations, a shared tool kit of applications for interactive learning and research, and high-speed Internet connectivity.
Campuswide Network? Yes
% of MBA Classrooms Wired: 100
Computer Model Recommended: Laptop
Internet Fee? No

EXPENSES/FINANCIAL AID
Annual Tuition: $21,000
Tuition Per Credit: $700
Room & Board: $7,859
Books and Supplies: $1,750
Average Grant: $22,467
% Receiving Financial Aid: 70
% Receiving Aid Their First Year: 50

ADMISSIONS INFORMATION
Application Fee: $45
Electronic Application? Yes
Early Decision Application Deadline: 2/1
Early Decision Notification: 3/1
Regular Application Deadline: Rolling
Regular Notification: Rolling
Length of Deferment: 1 year
Non-fall Application Deadline(s): 4/1 fall, 11/1 spring, 5/1 summer; full-time MBA: fall start only
Transfer Policy: Maximum number of transferable credits is 6; up to 12 credits may be waived.
Need-Blind Admissions? Yes
Number of Applications Received: 255
% of Applicants Accepted: 51
% Accepted Who Enrolled: 45
Average GPA: 3.2
Average GMAT: 635
Average Years Experience: 5
Other Admissions Factors Considered: Desire for Management and Technology focus
Minority/Disadvantaged Student Recruitment Programs: Rensselaer Minority Scholarship Program, Herman Family Fellowship for Women in Entrepreneurship
Other Schools to Which Students Applied: Babson, Boston U., Carnegie Mellon, Cornell, MIT, NYU, University of Illinois—Chicago

INTERNATIONAL STUDENTS
TOEFL Required of International Students? Yes
Minimum TOEFL: 600

EMPLOYMENT INFORMATION

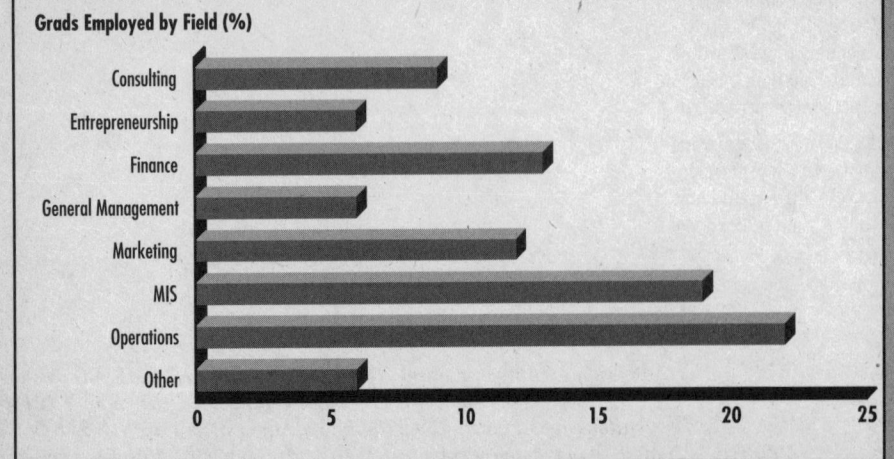

Placement Office Available? Yes
% Employed Within 3 Months: 89
Frequent Employers: Allied Signal, GE, American Management Systems, Numetrix, Citibank, Johnson & Johnson, Ernst & Young, American Express, Lucent Technologies, Samsung Inc., KPMG Peat Marwick, Pratt & Whitney, Procter & Gamble, IBM, Evonyx, American Express, Lord Corporation,

Rice University
Jesse H. Jones Graduate School of Management

Admissions Contact: Peter Veruki, Executive Director of Career Planning and Admissions
Address: 6100 Main Street, MS 531 (Herring Hall, Suite 245), Houston, TX 77005-1892
Admissions Phone: 713-348-4918 • *Admissions Fax:* 713-348-6147
Admissions E-mail: ricemba@rice.edu • *Web Address:* www.jonesgsm.rice.edu

Thanks to an "excellent faculty" and a "challenging curriculum," Rice University's Jones School enjoys a well-deserved reputation as an excellent place to get an MBA, albeit one that draws students primarily from its immediate region. Rice's surprisingly tranquil and beautiful 300-acre campus is located in a residential section of Houston, and the "highly intelligent," "competitive" students call themselves "mostly very friendly, sociable, and fun."

INSTITUTIONAL INFORMATION
Public/Private: Private
Evening Classes Available? No
Total Faculty: 90
% Faculty Female: 19
% Faculty Minority: 11
Student/Faculty Ratio: 8:1
Students in Parent Institution: 4,367
Academic Calendar: Semester

PROGRAMS
Degrees Offered: MBA (21 months)
Joint Degrees: MBA/Master of Electrical Engineering (24 months); MBA/Master of Computer Science; MBA/Master of Chemical Engineering; MBA/Master of Civil Engineering; MBA/Master of Environmental Engineering; MBA/Master of Science in Mechanical Engineering; MBA/Master of Engineering; MBA/MD (with Baylor College of Medicine) (60 months)
Academic Specialties: Finance, Entrepreneurship (part of the core curriculum), Marketing. Action Learning Project—as part of the core curriculum, first-years are placed in companies to perform specific projects. Classes are broken into 5- and 10-week modules throughout the MBA program. Emphasis on an integrated curriculum with both leadership and communication-skills development coordinated throughout.
Study Abroad Options: Costa Rica—INCAE

STUDENT INFORMATION
Total Business Students: 323
% Full Time: 100
% Female: 38
% Minority: 12
% Out of State: 23
% International: 29
Average Age: 28

COMPUTER AND RESEARCH FACILITIES
Research Facilities: Rice Alliance for Technology and Entrepreneurship, Center on Management Information Technology
Computer Facilities: Global Researcher, SEC/Worldscope, Business Dateline, Bloomberg, ABI/Inform, Wall Street Journal, Infotrac EF, PAIS, Business ASAP, Lexis-Nexis, Dow Jones News Retrieval Service, RDS, S&P DIALOG, Compustat PC Plus, Market Guide, Morningstar (Mutual Funds and VS Stock Tools), Investext, Datastream, Bridge, Insite 2, Reference USA, Disclosure Company Select, Global Access, FIS Company Data Direct
Campuswide Network? Yes
% of MBA Classrooms Wired: 100
Computer Model Recommended: Laptop
Internet Fee? No

EXPENSES/FINANCIAL AID
Annual Tuition: $23,250
Room & Board (On/Off Campus): $7,000/$9,000
Books and Supplies: $1,225

Average Grant: $5,000
Average Loan: $18,500
% Receiving Financial Aid: 65
% Receiving Aid Their First Year: 65

ADMISSIONS INFORMATION
Application Fee: $100
Electronic Application? Yes
Early Decision Application Deadline: 10/26
Early Decision Notification: 11/20
Regular Application Deadline: 3/15
Regular Notification: 4/24
Deferment Available? No
Non-fall Admissions? No
Transfer Students Accepted? No
Need-Blind Admissions? Yes
Number of Applications Received: 790
% of Applicants Accepted: 37
% Accepted Who Enrolled: 61
Average GPA: 3.3
GPA Range: 3.0-3.6
Average GMAT: 640
GMAT Range: 580-660
Average Years Experience: 5
Other Admissions Factors Considered: Leadership experience and team-based experiences. Unique qualities that the candidate will contribute to the program.

INTERNATIONAL STUDENTS
TOEFL Required of International Students? Yes
Minimum TOEFL: 600 (250 computer)

EMPLOYMENT INFORMATION

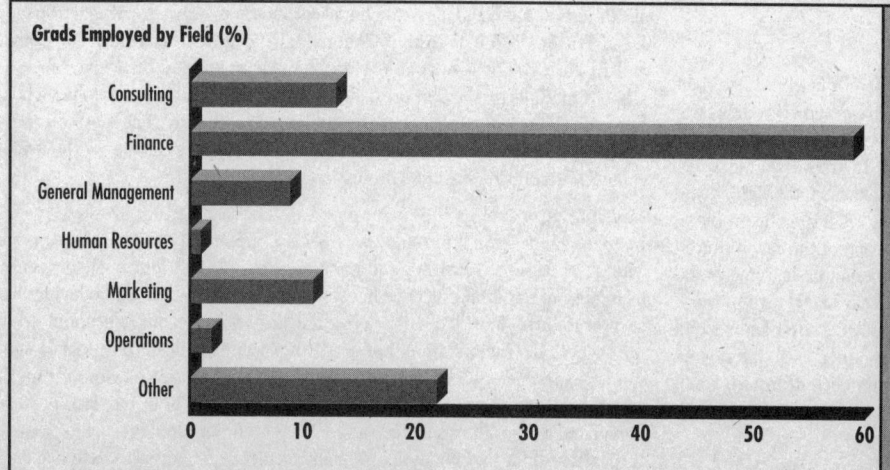

Grads Employed by Field (%)

Field	%
Consulting	~13
Finance	~58
General Management	~5
Human Resources	~8
Marketing	~12
Operations	~3
Other	~22

Placement Office Available? Yes
% Employed Within 3 Months: 100
Frequent Employers: JPMorgan Chase, Reliant Energy, Compaq Computer, Credit Suisse First Boston, BP, BMC Software, Deutsche Bank Alex. Brown, Duke Energy, Entergy Corporation, Mirant Corporation, AT Kearney, Goldman Sachs, Lehman Brothers Holdings., ExxonMobil
Prominent Alumni: James S. Turley, chairman, Ernst & Young Worldwide; Abby Rodgers, VP of innovation, Coca-Cola; Flint Brenton, VP of e-commerce, Compaq Computer Corp.; Doug Foshee, chairman, president, and CEO, Nuevo Energy Company; Caroline Caskey, founder and CEO, Identigene

RICE UNIVERSITY

THE SCHOOL AT A GLANCE
Rice MBA: Turning knowledge into action to create leaders

"Classroom learning is only one aspect of a complete business education. In this era of rapid globalization, change is the only constant, and companies want more than good managers; they want great leaders who can resolve issues with a multidisciplinary approach.

"While many business schools continue to emphasize theory, the Jones School curriculum builds on theory with an experiential learning process we call Action Learning. We're one of two business schools that require all our students to take their classroom knowledge into real business settings.

"We've applied this philosophy of change as the only constant to ourselves as well. After seeking input from our faculty, students, and industry leaders—including top management at major corporations to determine which skills they consider most valuable—we've designed an innovative course of study that provides all you'll need to excel in the global business environment. Our focus on leadership has been widely recognized, including by the Wall Street Journal."

—Gilbert R. Whitaker, Jr., Dean

Class of 2003 Profile
Number of Nationalities: 35

Ratio of men to women: 2:1

Average age: 27 years

Average work experience: 4.5 years

Degree Background:
- Business and economics: 40%
- Engineering, science, and math: 40%
- Liberal arts: 20%

ACADEMICS
Why Rice?
Choosing the right graduate business program is a decision with lasting implications. People who choose the Jones School can do well anywhere. Here are the top reasons alumni and students are glad they chose the Rice MBA program:

Personal attention
One of the hallmarks of Rice University's Jones School is its moderate class size, which creates a highly unusual learning environment that differentiates it from other top-tier business schools. Each year the entering class consists of approximately 180 exemplary students; this allows close working relationships between you and our outstanding faculty. Even outside the classroom, *Business Week* says, "Rice scores among the leaders for having faculty who are accessible to students."

Leading-edge curriculum
The Jones School action learning curriculum is at the forefront of management education. The methodology and modular structure are designed to help you develop crucial leadership and managerial skills, such as negotiating effectively and learning when to partner and when to compete. In your action learning project toward the end of the first year, you'll integrate these tools with a team of classmates, consulting full-time with a company to solve a specific problem. The required second-year entrepreneurship course—one of the few required courses of its kind in the nation—and numerous experiential-learning-based electives will provide additional opportunities to put your knowledge to work. When it comes to getting your summer internship between first and second years, you'll find that your action learning project is regarded as an internship, giving you an advantage in securing an interesting summer internship. You'll have twice as much internship experience as most MBA graduates when you're exploring your job options in your second year.

Reputation
Rice University is consistently ranked as one of America's best teaching and research universities. It has the fifth largest endowment per student among American universities. The Jones School is among the world's best business schools. In 2002 the *Financial Times* ranks the Jones School among the top 25 business schools in the U.S. and top 40 in the world. In 2002 *The Economist* ranked our faculty third best in the U.S. and fourth best in the world. Our finance program was ranked the best in the U.S. and tied for the second best in the world by *The Economist*, and ranked in the top ten by the *Financial Times* in 2002. Our marketing program was ranked second in the U.S. and tied for eighth in the world by *The Economist*. Employers also recognize the quality of our graduates—the Jones School is ranked among the top ten by *U.S. News* for employment at three months in 2002. Professor Ed Williams was named one of the two best entrepreneurial instructors in the U.S. by *Business Week*. Faculty in other areas have also been honored as leaders in their fields. The Jones School has been singled out for its support of women and minority students by *The Economist*, the *Financial Times*, and *Time* magazine.

First-class facilities
The Jones School occupies its new home as of summer 2002. The 167,000-square-foot building offers state-of-the-art facilities, including the best, broadest, and most in-depth trading room of any business school. Most school trading rooms are basically equity desks. Rice's El Paso Trading Room is designed to bring the markets to students and the students to the markets and will have four desks: energy, equity, fixed income, and currency. Other facilities include a 14,000-square-foot Business Information Center providing students with everything from periodicals and annual reports to online access retrieval of the latest financial information; tiered classrooms to enhance case-study-method instruction; behavioral research and observation rooms for focus-group research and interviews; comfortable breakout rooms for group study and discussion; a 425-seat auditorium where students and faculty can gather together as a group; a "cyber-commons" where students and faculty can meet with both coffee and ports for computer and network connectivity; and a career-planning suite, where advisors can help students develop their interviewing and job search skills and where corporations can interview students for internships or permanent positions. Student are given fully loaded laptops as part of their tuition, and the new building is equipped to make the most sophisticated use of electronic access.

Business connections
Houston is second only to New York in Fortune 500 corporate headquarters and is also an operating center for more than half of the world's largest, non-U.S.-based corporations. Among the growth industries in the city's well-diversified economy are finance, high technology, biotechnology, engineering/design services, energy, and health care services. And with the Jones school right at their doorstep, these companies recognize the value of a Rice MBA. Annually the city's largest and most influential corporations—Dynegy, Morgan-Stanley Dean Witter, CS First Boston, Continental, Booz-Allen & Hamilton, Chase, and El Paso Energy—host an evening for the area's most attractive business school applicants for the purpose of encouraging them to choose the Jones School for their studies. *Business Week*'s most recent edition of The Best Business Schools rated the Jones School 11 of 61 for providing graduates with "useful contact with outside business professionals."

Multiple approaches to learning
In every course, you'll have an unparalleled opportunity to work one-on-one with an accessible, involved, and energetic faculty. The Jones School faculty maintains an important balance between teaching and research, believing that current industry knowledge is as critical as textbooks to your education. All of the school's instructors are either academics with significant business or consulting experience, or business executives with significant classroom experience who teach specialized elective courses. In 2002, 24 of our faculty were nominated by the Classes of 2000 and 1997 for our outstanding teaching award. It speaks well for the school that so many faculty were judged to have had last-

Jesse H. Jones Graduate School of Management

ing impact on students they taught two and five years ago. Depending on what's most appropriate for each course, Jones School instructors use multiple instructional methods to enhance your learning: process-case-method study, analytical and quantitative approaches, lectures and discussions, oral and written reports, theoretical studies, management simulation games, individual study, and teamwork.

Curriculum profile
A comprehensive core curriculum focuses on managerial and leadership skills, ethics, information technology, and communication skills in addition to the functional areas. An Action Learning Project in first year gives students the opportunity to learn how to integrate disciplines and turn knowledge into action. A modular format promotes flexibility in course structure. A core entrepreneurship course in second year further refines integration of business disciplines. Students take 25 credit hours of electives in their second year, which allows them to custom design their curriculum to suit career goals.

Personalized career planning
The Jones School's Career Planning Center (CPC) is an extremely valuable advocate for your future. The CPC offers more campus interviews per student and more personalized service than any "top 10" MBA program in the U.S. *U.S. News & World Report*, April 2002, ranks the Jones School one of the top 10 business schools for grads employed at three months, along with Stanford, Harvard, and Yale. Rice MBA grads are consistently among the top 20 business schools for total compensation offers.

Close-knit community
At Rice you'll have a wealth of cultural, social, and athletic activities in the stimulating intellectual atmosphere of one of the nation's premier academic institutions. On campus, you can choose among concerts at the renowned Shepherd School of Music, dramatic productions, diverse art exhibitions, and lectures by world-class leaders in business, politics, and the arts. In the academic year 1999–2000, for example, Nelson Mandela was among the world leaders speaking here and Doug Daft, CEO of Coca-Cola, gave his first public talk at the Jones School. In 2001 Vladimir Putin and Alan Greenspan were among the speakers; in 2002 Bill Cosby, King Abdullah II of Jordan, and Robert Caro. Intercollegiate athletics, exercise, and intramural sports are available at the University's spacious fitness facilities. Get-togethers at the campus pubs as well as weekly, corporate-sponsored "partios"—parties on the Jones School patio—provide relaxation and opportunities to network. New graduate student housing was opened in 1999. Ranging from efficiencies to four-bedrooms, the graduate apartments are within an easy walking distance and are also served by a University shuttle. Rice's beautiful 300-acre campus is just a few miles from the downtown business district, across the street from the world-renowned Texas Medical Center, and within one of Houston's most attractive neighborhoods. Within walking distance are several superlative museums, the Houston Zoo, Hermann Park, a golf course and outdoor theater, and Rice Village, an eclectic shopping community with excellent restaurants.

And dynamic city
Houston, the nation's fourth largest city, is a young, dynamic place with first-class theater, opera, ballet, and symphony companies—one of the few American cities to have residential companies in all the arts. It's green; the climate is very pleasant during the school year. Gulf beaches are less than an hour's drive away. Professional sports action includes the NBA Rockets, National League Astros (a new ballpark opened in 2000), NHL Aeros, and WNBA Comets, and a new NFL football team, the Houston Texans. Houston will host the Superbowl in 2004. Houston is exceptionally affordable, with a cost of living 17 percent below the national average for cities of comparable size and average annual pay of nearly 8 percent above the national average. Housing costs fall almost 30 percent below the average for large urban areas. Texas has no state income tax.

COSTS
Application fee: $100

Tuition: $28,000 (for the class entering in fall 2002; $28,000 a year for both years, for a total of $56,000)

Total estimated expenses: $39,855 a year

Financial aid: About 65 percent of each class receives financial aid from the school. We offer a limited amount of aid to international students. An independent association, RICE-TMS, funds two minority scholarships for Jones School students.

ADMISSIONS
Admission requirements are a bachelors degree; GMAT (no minimum, average scores are 630–660); TOEFL for international applicants (minimum score of 600); no work experience required of exceptionally qualified students (up to 5 percent of the class) and the average work experience is four to five years. Deferred admission is possible for one year.

The admission selection criteria:

Academic background: You must have a four-year undergraduate degree from an accredited college or university if you received your education in the United States. If you are an international applicant, your undergraduate degree must be the equivalent of a U.S. four-year degree. If you have completed a three-year Bachelor of Commerce (BCom) degree, we also require a two-year Master of Commerce (MCom) degree. Your undergraduate and graduate GPAs, GMAT scores (or GRE scores if you are applying to the joint MBA/ME degree program or MCAT scores if you are applying to the MBA/MD program), choice of major, electives, course load, and grade patterns are all considered.

Leadership potential: Your demonstrated leadership and management experiences, both on the job and through extracurricular activities, will help us assess your leadership potential.

Confidential evaluations: Evaluations from employers and/or professors shed perspective on your capabilities, enabling us to assess your qualifications more accurately.

A personal statement: Three essays that articulate your career goals, work experience, and reasons for choosing Rice University's Jones School are a crucial component of your application. Use them to convey intangibles: Why are you pursuing an MBA? How have you benefited from your academic, professional, and personal opportunities? What qualities will you bring to the Jones School, and what will you seek from us?

For more information, contact:

Admissions Director, Rice University
Jones Graduate School of Management
MS-531
6100 Main
Houston, TX 77005-1892 USA
Telephone (toll free): 888-844-4773
Fax: 713-737-6147
E-mail: ricemba@rice.edu
Web: www.jonesgsm.rice.edu
Electronic applications are available—please visit our website.
Rice offers MBA, MBA for Executives, and two joint degrees, an MBA/MD with Baylor College of Medicine and an MBA/ME with Rice's School of Engineering.

RIDER UNIVERSITY
College of Business Administration

Admissions Contact: Dr. John Carpenter, Dean, College of Continuing Studies
Address: LIB 137, 2083 Lawrenceville Road, Lawrenceville, NJ 08648-3099
Admissions Phone: 609-896-5033 • Admissions Fax: 609-896-5261
Admissions E-mail: grdsrv@rider.edu • Web Address: www.rider.edu/academic/ccs/gradbus/index.htm

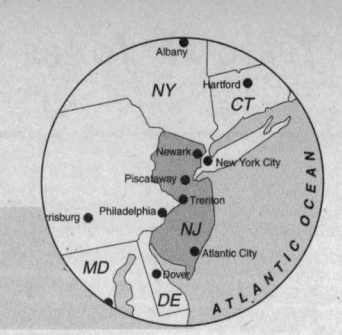

The Rider University MBA program has a flexible curriculum, whereby students may choose to pursue a general program, a concentration in the basic functional business disciplines, or an interdisciplinary concentration; if none of these options seems suitable, students may mix courses to accommodate their specific needs and interests. Rider also boasts great computer facilities and small classes in the evenings and on weekends, taught by a faculty composed almost entirely of PhD-holding scholars and researchers. Rider's main campus in Lawrenceville, New Jersey, is conveniently located between New York and Philadelphia.

INSTITUTIONAL INFORMATION
Public/Private: Private
Evening Classes Available? Yes
Total Faculty: 28
% Faculty Female: 32
% Faculty Minority: 14
% Faculty Part Time: 14
Student/Faculty Ratio: 12:1
Students in Parent Institution: 5,456
Academic Calendar: Semester

PROGRAMS
Degrees Offered: Master of Business Administration (30 to 51 credits); Master of Accounting (30 to 57 credits)
Joint Degrees: BS/BA/MBA (5 years); BS/BA/MAcc (5 years)
Academic Specialties: Faculty specialties: Accounting, Finance, Management; special strengths of curriculum: Leadership, Interpersonal Skills

STUDENT INFORMATION
Total Business Students: 321
% Full Time: 16
% Female: 55
% Out of State: 7
% International: 14
Average Age: 28

COMPUTER AND RESEARCH FACILITIES
Computer Facilities: Labs; Bloomberg and full complement of major databases via library
Campuswide Network? Yes
% of MBA Classrooms Wired: 100
Internet Fee? No

EXPENSES/FINANCIAL AID
Annual Tuition: $5,820
Tuition Per Credit: $485
Room & Board (On Campus): $8,930
Books and Supplies: $700
Average Grant: $6,067
Average Loan: $13,301
% Receiving Financial Aid: 54

ADMISSIONS INFORMATION
Application Fee: $40
Electronic Application? No
Regular Application Deadline: 8/1
Regular Notification: 1/1
Deferment Available? Yes
Length of Deferment: 1 year
Non-fall Admissions? Yes
Non-fall Application Deadline(s): 12/1 spring, 5/1 summer
Transfer Students Accepted? Yes
Transfer Policy: Each case is evaluated individually. No more than 24 transferred credits against 51 required maximum. Maximum of 6 credits against 30 in the advance portion.

Need-Blind Admissions? Yes
Number of Applications Received: 154
% of Applicants Accepted: 57
% Accepted Who Enrolled: 66
Average GPA: 3.4
GPA Range: 3.1-3.7
Average GMAT: 517
GMAT Range: 450-580
Average Years Experience: 5
Other Admissions Factors Considered: Experience, as demonstrated via résumé and interview may positively affect admin/deny decision and potential waiver of requirements.

INTERNATIONAL STUDENTS
TOEFL Required of International Students? Yes
Minimum TOEFL: 585 (240 computer)

EMPLOYMENT INFORMATION
Placement Office Available? No
Prominent Alumni: Dennis Longstreet, company group chairman, Johnson & Johnson; Robert Christie, president and CEO, Thomson Corp.; Bernard V. Vonderschmitt, chairman of the board, Xilinx, Inc.; Anne Sweigart, chairwoman, president, and CEO, D&E Communications; Kenneth Burenga, former president and CEO, Dow Jones & Co.

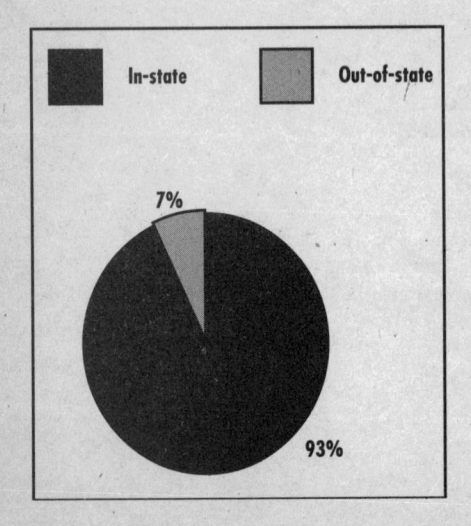

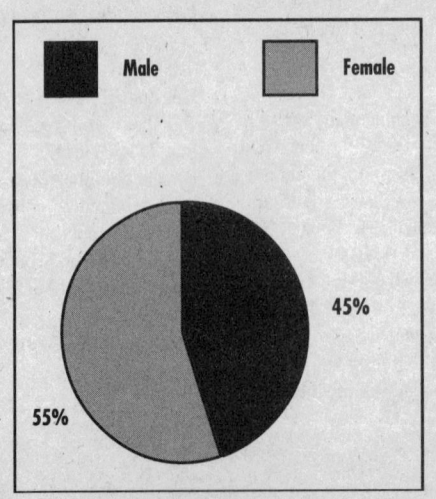

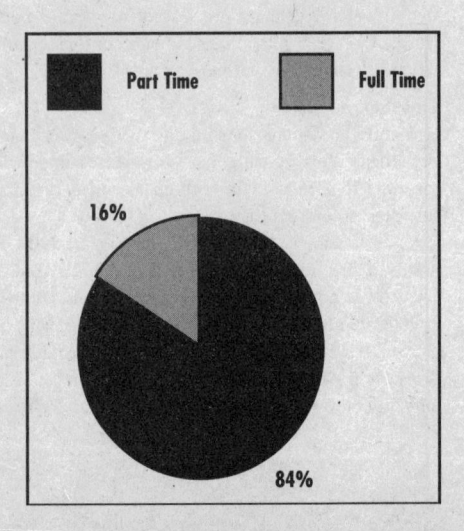

In-state 93% / Out-of-state 7%

Male 55% / Female 45%

Part Time 84% / Full Time 16%

ROCHESTER INSTITUTE OF TECHNOLOGY
College of Business

Admissions Contact: Nancy Woebkenberg, Marketing Manager
Address: 105 Lomb Memorial Drive, Rochester, NY 14623
Admissions Phone: 585-475-2229 • Admissions Fax: 585-475-5476
Admissions E-mail: gradinfo@rit.edu • Web Address: www.ritmba.com

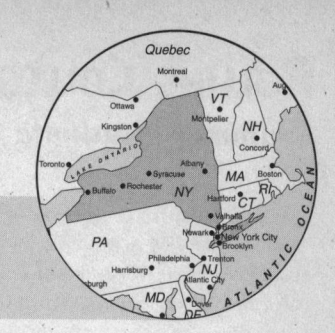

RIT is a national leader in classroom technology, it has an MBA program in Prague to bolster students' global exposure, and RIT's philosophy of quality translates into treating its students "as partners and customers." Flexible part-time and full-time curricula are taught in classrooms of only about 25 heads and feature almost as many concentration options.

INSTITUTIONAL INFORMATION
Public/Private: Private
Evening Classes Available? Yes
Total Faculty: 39
% Faculty Female: 13
% Faculty Minority: 5
Student/Faculty Ratio: 9:1
Students in Parent Institution: 13,517
Academic Calendar: Quarter

PROGRAMS
Degrees Offered: Master of Business Administration (MBA) (6 quarters); Master of Science (MS) (4 quarters); Executive MBA (2 years)
Study Abroad Options: U.S. Business School, Prague, Czech Republic; E.M. Lyon Graduate School of Management, Lyon, France

STUDENT INFORMATION
Total Business Students: 360
% Full Time: 50
% Female: 34
% Minority: 1
% Out of State: 12
% International: 25
Average Age: 28

COMPUTER AND RESEARCH FACILITIES
Research Facilities: Center for International Business and Economic Growth, Technology Management Center
Computer Facilities: Wallace Library has an extensive database.
Campuswide Network? Yes
% of MBA Classrooms Wired: 100
Internet Fee? No

EXPENSES/FINANCIAL AID
Annual Tuition: $20,928
Tuition Per Credit: $587
Room & Board (On Campus): $7,100
Books and Supplies: $1,500
Average Grant: $10,000
% Receiving Financial Aid: 26

ADMISSIONS INFORMATION
Application Fee: $50
Electronic Application? Yes
Regular Application Deadline: 8/1
Regular Notification: Rolling
Deferment Available? Yes
Length of Deferment: 1 year
Non-fall Admissions? Yes
Non-fall Application Deadline(s): 10/31, 1/31, 5/1
Transfer Students Accepted? Yes
Transfer Policy: Transfer up to 3 courses if relevant to program. Grade of B or better
Need-Blind Admissions? Yes
Number of Applications Received: 292
% of Applicants Accepted: 31
% Accepted Who Enrolled: 97
Average GPA: 3.2
GPA Range: 3.0-3.7
Average GMAT: 567
GMAT Range: 530-630
Average Years Experience: 4

INTERNATIONAL STUDENTS
TOEFL Required of International Students? Yes
Minimum TOEFL: 575 (230 computer)

EMPLOYMENT INFORMATION

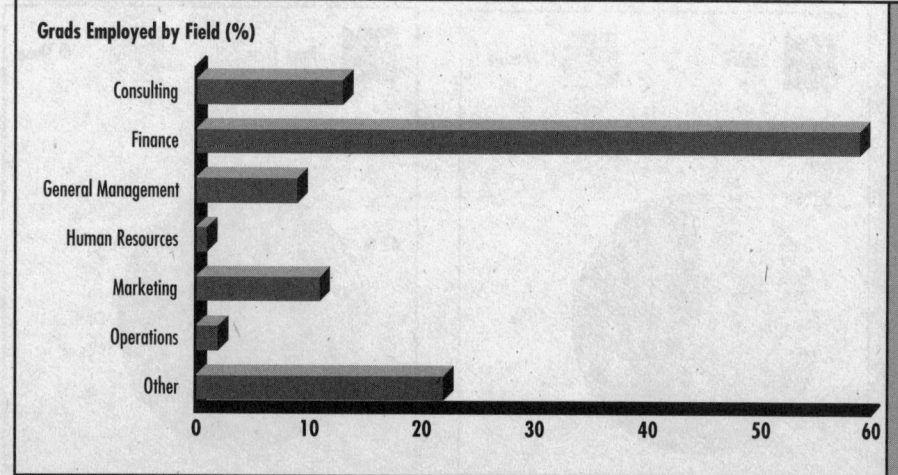

Grads Employed by Field (%)
- Consulting: ~13
- Finance: ~60
- General Management: ~5
- Human Resources: ~2
- Marketing: ~3
- Operations: ~3
- Other: ~22

Placement Office Available? Yes
Frequent Employers: Eastman Kodak Company, IBM, Johnson & Johnson, Deloitte & Touche, Xerox Inc., PricewaterhouseCoopers
Prominent Alumni: Daniel Carp, chairman and CEO, Eastman Kodak Company; Thomas Curley, president and publisher, USA Today

ROLLINS COLLEGE
Crummer Graduate School of Business

Admissions Contact: Craig Domeck, Director of Full-Time MBA Programs
Address: 1000 Holt Ave., - 2722, Winter Park, FL 32789-4499
Admissions Phone: 407-646-2405 • Admissions Fax: 407-646-2522
Admissions E-mail: crummer@rollins.edu • Web Address: www.crummer.rollins.edu

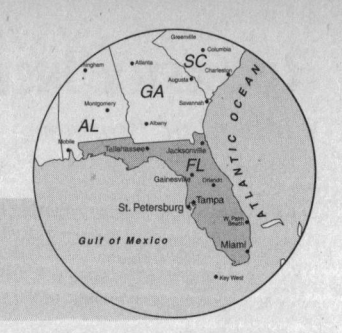

Arguably Florida's most prestigious MBA program, the Crummer Graduate School of Business offers four MBA options: a one-year program, a two-year program, a part-time take-your-time program, and an Executive MBA program designed for business professionals with 10 or more years of experience. Rollins College is located on the shores of Lake Virginia in Winter Park, a lovely upscale suburb of Orlando, Florida.

INSTITUTIONAL INFORMATION
Public/Private: Private
Evening Classes Available? Yes
Total Faculty: 20
% Faculty Female: 10
% Faculty Minority: 5
Student/Faculty Ratio: 17:1
Students in Parent Institution: 2,500
Academic Calendar: Semester

PROGRAMS
Degrees Offered: Executive MBA Program (20 months), Professional MBA Program (2.5 years), Accelerated MBA Program (11 months), Early Advantage MBA Program (20 months)
Academic Specialties: Electronic Commerce, Finance, and International Business
Special Opportunities: Global Business Consulting Projects, National Business Consulting Projects, Crummer SunTrust Portfolio
Study Abroad Options: Sweden—Vaxjo University; England—Nottingham University

STUDENT INFORMATION
Total Business Students: 365
% Full Time: 42
% Female: 51
% Minority: 10
% Out of State: 35
% International: 25
Average Age: 26

COMPUTER AND RESEARCH FACILITIES
Computer Facilities: Olin Online Catalog; electronic databases: ProQuest Direct, Wilson Databases, Academic Universe, Britannica, DIALOG, FirstSearch, Westlaw
Campuswide Network? Yes
% of MBA Classrooms Wired: 86
Computer Model Recommended: Laptop
Internet Fee? No

EXPENSES/FINANCIAL AID
Annual Tuition: $22,400
Tuition Per Credit: $750
Room & Board (Off Campus): $14,520
Books and Supplies: $1,500
Average Grant: $12,000
Average Loan: $10,000
% Receiving Financial Aid: 50
% Receiving Aid Their First Year: 50

ADMISSIONS INFORMATION
Electronic Application? Yes
Regular Application Deadline: Rolling
Regular Notification: Rolling
Length of Deferment: 1 year
Non-fall Application Deadline(s): Spring, PMBA; June, AMBA
Transfer Students Accepted? Yes
Transfer Policy: Up to 6 credits transferred from an MBA program accredited by the AACSB.
Need-Blind Admissions? Yes

Number of Applications Received: 205
% of Applicants Accepted: 85
% Accepted Who Enrolled: 57
Average GPA: 3.0
Average GMAT: 569
Average Years Experience: 3
Other Admissions Factors Considered: Previous academic records, test scores, recommendations, and evidence of maturity and motivation.
Minority/Disadvantaged Student Recruitment Programs: Scholarships and grad. assistantships
Other Schools to Which Students Applied: Florida State, Stetson, U. of Central Florida, U. of Florida, U. of Miami, Purdue, U. of South Florida

INTERNATIONAL STUDENTS
TOEFL Required of International Students? Yes

EMPLOYMENT INFORMATION
Placement Office Available? Yes
% Employed Within 3 Months: 80
Frequent Employers: Walt Disney, Radiant, CNL Group, Federal Express, Harris Corporation, Johnson & Johnson, Marriott International, Darden Restaurant Group, AT&T, Andersen Consulting, Seimens Westinghouse, SunTrust Bank
Prominent Alumni: Al Weiss, president; Thomas Jones, senior VP of operations; Ronald Gelbman, worldwide committee member and chairman; Charles Rice, president

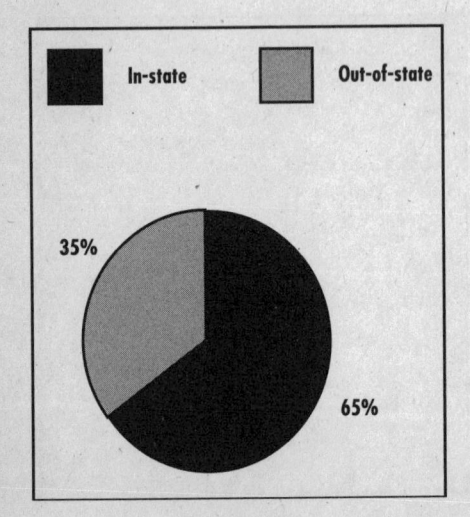

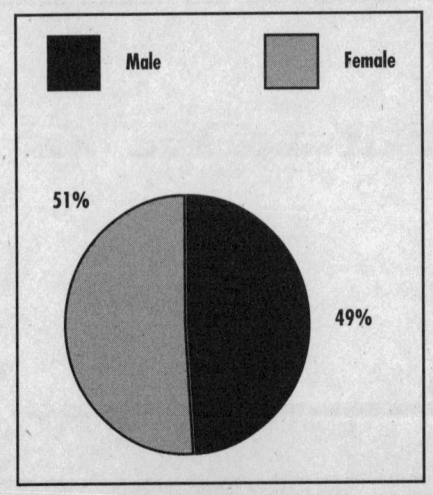

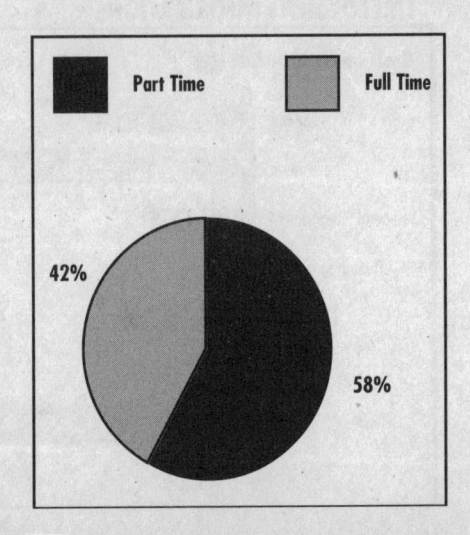

Rutgers University — Camden
School of Business

Admissions Contact: Dr. Izzet Kenis, MBA Program Director
Address: Rutgers University, School of Business, MBA Program, Camden, NJ 08102-1401
Admissions Phone: 609-225-6216 • Admissions Fax: 609-225-6231
Admissions E-mail: kenis@crab.rutgers.edu • Web Address: camden-www.rutgers.edu

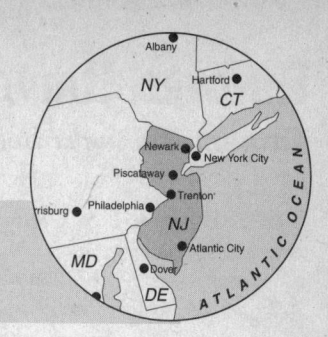

The MBA curriculum asserts that its broad educational strategy provides students with comprehensive business knowledge as well as the critical thinking skills necessary to make it in today's evolving economy. Strategically located within minutes of Center City in the heart of Philadelphia, Rutgers offers the benefits of a small campus environment with big-city options. Concentrations are available in health care management and international business, and courses are also offered in Atlantic City.

INSTITUTIONAL INFORMATION
Public/Private: Public
Evening Classes Available? No
Total Faculty: 38
% Faculty Part Time: 16
Students in Parent Institution: 5,052
Academic Calendar: Semester

PROGRAMS
Degrees Offered: MBA (60 credits, 18 months to 2 years),
Joint Degrees: MBA/Juris Doctor (108 to 120 credits, 3 to 5 years)

STUDENT INFORMATION
Total Business Students: 264
% Full Time: 15
% Female: 28
% Minority: 9
% International: 15
Average Age: 28

COMPUTER AND RESEARCH FACILITIES
Number of Student Computers: 158
Campuswide Network? Yes
Computer Proficiency Required? No
Special Purchasing Agreements? No

EXPENSES/FINANCIAL AID
Annual Tuition (Resident/Nonresident): $9,000/$13,420
Room & Board (On/Off Campus): $6,471/$8,140

ADMISSIONS INFORMATION
Application Fee: $40
Electronic Application? No
Regular Application Deadline: Rolling
Regular Notification: Rolling
Deferment Available? No
Non-fall Admissions? No
Transfer Students Accepted? No
Need-Blind Admissions? No
Number of Applications Received: 158
% of Applicants Accepted: 84
% Accepted Who Enrolled: 61
Average GPA: 3.2
Average GMAT: 563
Other Admissions Factors Considered: Work experience, computer experience

INTERNATIONAL STUDENTS
TOEFL Required of International Students? Yes
Minimum TOEFL: 550

EMPLOYMENT INFORMATION

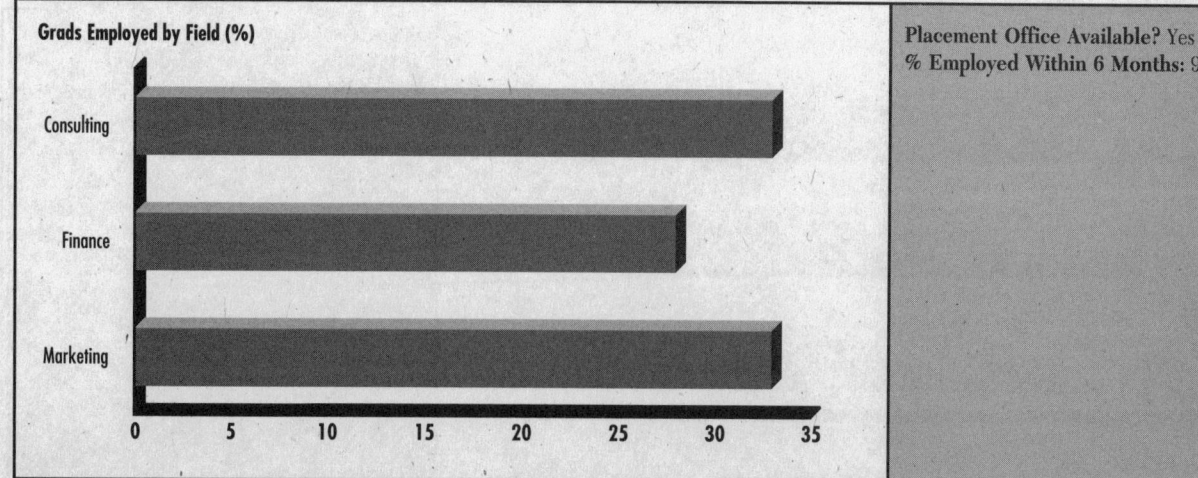

Grads Employed by Field (%):
- Consulting: ~33
- Finance: ~28
- Marketing: ~33

Placement Office Available? Yes
% Employed Within 6 Months: 98

RUTGERS UNIVERSITY — NEWARK
Rutgers Business School

Admissions Contact: Glenn S. Berman, Director of Admissions
Address: 190 University Avenue, Newark, NJ 07102-1813
Admissions Phone: 973-353-1234 • Admissions Fax: 973-353-1592
Admissions E-mail: admit@business.rutgers.edu • Web Address: business.rutgers.edu

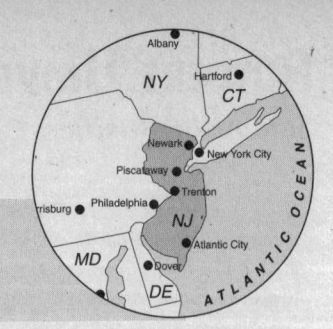

Rutgers Graduate School of Management has a large student body, a host of research centers catered to various business disciplines, and many options for MBA study, including a number of joint degrees. The MBA program is rigorous, especially for those students who need to compensate for deficiencies in calculus and/or statistics. MBA applicants are greatly discouraged from working during their first year of studies, but can expect a solid education in return for their diligence and academic labor.

INSTITUTIONAL INFORMATION
Public/Private: Public
Evening Classes Available? Yes
Total Faculty: 200
% Faculty Female: 23
% Faculty Part Time: 31
Student/Faculty Ratio: 15:1
Students in Parent Institution: 48,399
Academic Calendar: Trimester

PROGRAMS
Degrees Offered: MBA in Management (60 credits, 15 months to 2 years); Master of Accountancy (in Governmental Accounting, Financial Accounting, and Taxation) (30 credits, 10 months to 2.5 years); PhD in Management (72 credits,ota 2 to 6 years); MBA in Professional Accounting (62 credits, 14 months); Executive MBA (54 credits, 20 months); Master of Quantitative Finance (30 credits, 1 year)
Joint Degrees: MPH/MBA, MD/MBA, JD/MBA, MS/MBA in Biomedical Sciences

STUDENT INFORMATION
Total Business Students: 1,163
% Full Time: 17
% Female: 38
% Minority: 11
% International: 13
Average Age: 26

COMPUTER AND RESEARCH FACILITIES
Research Facilities: Center for Entrepreneurial Management; Center for Governmental Accounting Education and Research; Center for Information Management, Integration, and Connectivity; Center for Middle East/North Africa Business Studies; Center for Research in Regulated Industries; New Jersey Center for Research in Financial Services; Rutgers Accounting Research Center; Technology Management Research Center; Center for Management Development; University Ventures
Computer Facilities: 85 networked computers with Internet and WAN access and 3 high-quality networked printers. The ADP electronic classroom also permits the distribution of the image on the instructor's computer screen to the students' computer screens. Rutgers University Computer Services (RUCS) offers systems based on the Windows Intel platform and also Apple and UNIX systems.
Campuswide Network? Yes
Computer Model Recommended: Laptop
Internet Fee? No

EXPENSES/FINANCIAL AID
Annual Tuition (Resident/Nonresident): $10,358/$15,444
Tuition Per Credit (Resident/Nonresident): $428/$640
Room & Board (On Campus): $8,000
Books and Supplies: $3,000
Average Grant: $3,000

ADMISSIONS INFORMATION
Application Fee: $50
Electronic Application? Yes
Regular Application Deadline: 6/1
Regular Notification: Rolling
Length of Deferment: 1 year
Non-fall Application Deadline(s): 11/15 spring (part-time only), 5/1 summer (MBA in Prof. Acct.)
Transfer Policy: Credits earned at an AACSB-accredited school with a "B" or better.
Need-Blind Admissions? Yes
Number of Applications Received: 834
% of Applicants Accepted: 61
% Accepted Who Enrolled: 64
Average GPA: 3.2
Average GMAT: 613
Average Years Experience: 3
Other Admissions Factors Considered: Work experience is a major factor in admissions decisions. Also considered are community activities and awards or honors.
Other Schools to Which Students Applied: Baruch College/City University of New York, Columbia, Fordham, NYU, Seton Hall

INTERNATIONAL STUDENTS
TOEFL Required of International Students? Yes
Minimum TOEFL: 600 (250 computer)

EMPLOYMENT INFORMATION

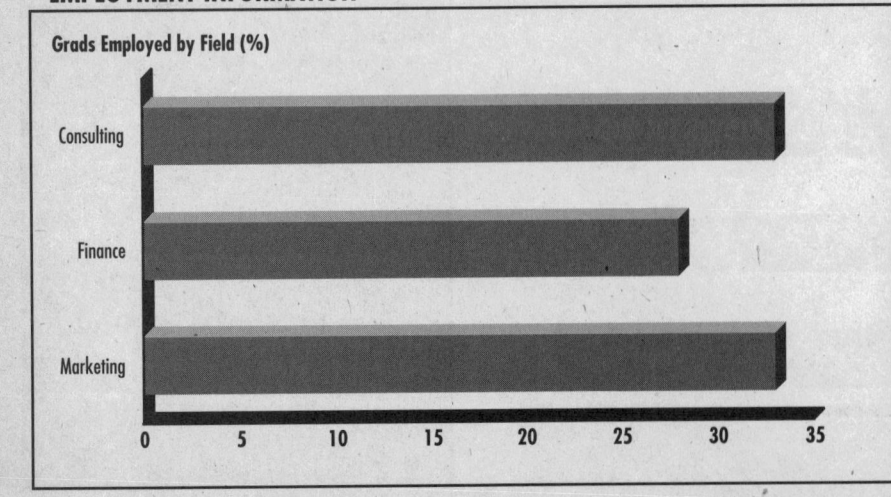

Grads Employed by Field (%)

Field	%
Consulting	~33
Finance	~28
Marketing	~33

Placement Office Available? Yes
% Employed Within 3 Months: 80
Prominent Alumni: Tom Renyi, chairman and CEO; Coary Cohen, division president; Irwin Learner, CEO

ST. CLOUD STATE UNIVERSITY
Herberger College of Business

Admissions Contact: Graduate Admissions Manager, Graduate Studies Office
Address: 720 4th Avenue South, St. Cloud, MN 56301-4498
Admissions Phone: 320-255-2113 • Admissions Fax: 320-654-5371
Admissions E-mail: grads@condor.stcloudstate.edu • Web Address: www.stcloudstate.edu

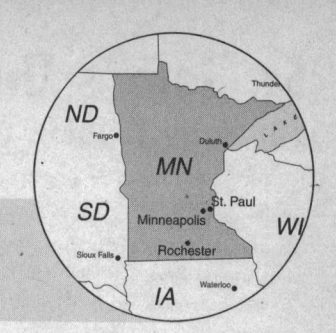

Located on the banks of the Mississippi River, St. Cloud State University is 131 years old and is Minnesota's second largest university. The MBA program at St. Cloud involves two phases: In the first, a set of foundation-type business courses must be completed, and in the second, students move on to advanced graduate course work. The MBA program has a broad-based curriculum that aims to educate students on all of the functional areas of business and teaches students how to quantify, analyze, interpret, and communicate effectively. If on-campus facilities are a major concern on your list of prospective b-school features, have a peek at the new $32.5 million high-tech James W. Miller Learning Resources Center.

INSTITUTIONAL INFORMATION
Evening Classes Available? Yes
Total Faculty: 63
% Faculty Female: 14
Student/Faculty Ratio: 20:1
Students in Parent Institution: 15,000
Academic Calendar: Semester

PROGRAMS
Degrees Offered: MBA with concentrations in Accounting, Business Information Science, Economics, Finance, Insurance, International Business, Management, Marketing, Real Estate, Taxation (18 months to 5.3 years)
Academic Specialties: Case study, computer-aided instruction, group discussion, lecture, research, student presentations, team project

STUDENT INFORMATION
Total Business Students: 98
% Full Time: 88
% Female: 26
% Minority: 35
% Out of State: 37
% International: 35

COMPUTER AND RESEARCH FACILITIES
Campuswide Network? Yes
% of MBA Classrooms Wired: 5
Computer Model Recommended: No
Internet Fee? No

EXPENSES/FINANCIAL AID
Annual Tuition (Resident/Nonresident): $2,862/$4,356
Books and Supplies: $300

ADMISSIONS INFORMATION
Application Fee: $20
Electronic Application? No
Early Decision Application Deadline: 4/15, 6/15
Regular Application Deadline: Rolling
Deferment Available? No
Non-fall Admissions? Yes
Non-fall Application Deadline(s): 4/15, 6/15
Transfer Students Accepted? No

Need-Blind Admissions? No
Number of Applications Received: 49
% of Applicants Accepted: 73
% Accepted Who Enrolled: 53
Average GPA: 3.2
GPA Range: 2.7-4.0
Average GMAT: 546
GMAT Range: 470-700
Average Years Experience: 7
Other Admissions Factors Considered: Personal statement, recommendation letters
Minority/Disadvantaged Student Recruitment Programs: Recruiting events

INTERNATIONAL STUDENTS
TOEFL Required of International Students? Yes
Minimum TOEFL: 550 (213 computer)

EMPLOYMENT INFORMATION
Placement Office Available? No
% Employed Within 3 Months: 80
Frequent Employers: IBM, Target, Andersen Consulting, General Mills, Bankers Systems, Cargill, Federated Insurance

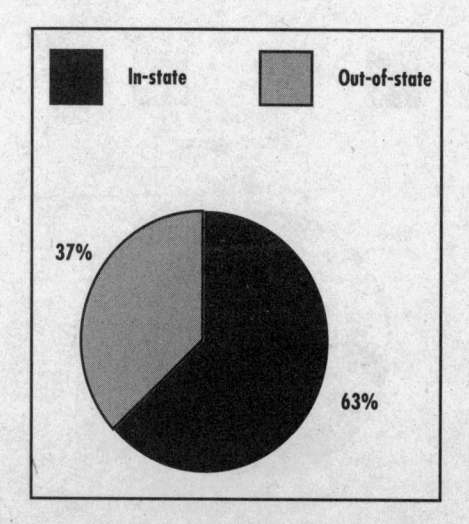

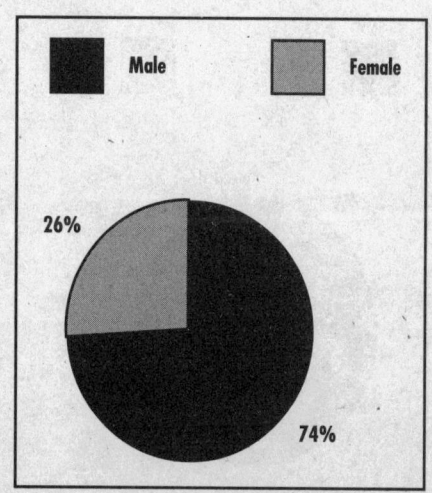

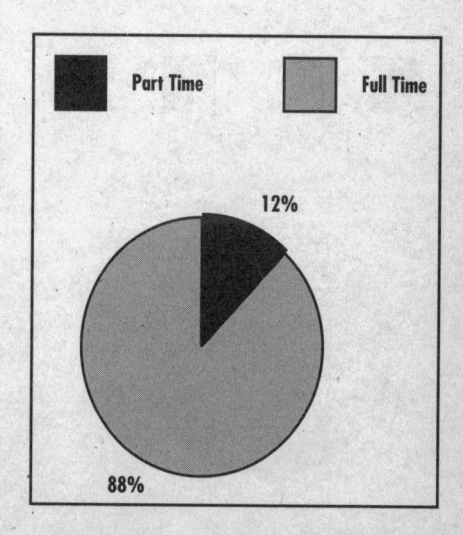

St. John's University
The Peter J. Tobin College of Business

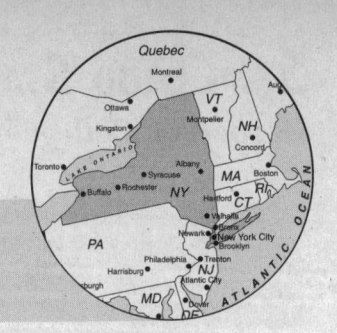

Admissions Contact: Sheila Russell, Assistant Director of MBA Admissions
Address: 8000 Utopia Parkway, Jamaica, NY 11439
Admissions Phone: 718-990-1345 • Admissions Fax: 718-990-5242
Admissions E-mail: mbaadmissions@stjohns.edu • Web Address: www.tobincollege.stjohns.edu

A private Catholic university, St. John's provides several New York campuses—historic Queens, the financial district of Manhattan, eastern Long Island, and Staten Island. In addition to these campuses, students wishing to pursue an MBA in international finance and marketing have the option of doing so in Rome. The Peter J. Tobin College of Business Administration is proud of the progressive technology found in its classrooms and research centers. The Financial Services Institute, with its courses, seminars, conferences, and publications, aims to prepare students for careers in the global financial industry after graduation.

INSTITUTIONAL INFORMATION
Public/Private: Private
Evening Classes Available? Yes
Total Faculty: 101
% Faculty Female: 18
% Faculty Minority: 10
% Faculty Part Time: 15
Student/Faculty Ratio: 9:1
Students in Parent Institution: 18,621
Academic Calendar: Semester

PROGRAMS
Degrees Offered: MBA (full time, 1 to 2 years), with concentrations in Accounting, Computer Information Sciences for Managers, Decision Sciences, Executive Management, Finance, Financial Services, International Business, International Finance, Marketing Management, Taxation, Risk Management, Risk Financing, and Insurance Management; MS (33 to 60 credits), with concentrations in Forecasting and Planning, Taxation, Accountancy
Joint Degrees: JD/MBA (full time, 4 years)
Study Abroad Options: Rome, Italy; London, United Kingdom; Rio de Janeiro, Brazil

STUDENT INFORMATION
Total Business Students: 672
% Full Time: 25
% Female: 17
% Minority: 15
% Out of State: 40
% International: 45
Average Age: 26

COMPUTER AND RESEARCH FACILITIES
Research Facilities: Total university library collections number 1.7 million volumes and include more than 6,000 periodic subscriptions. Other resources include government documents, audiovisual materials, indexes, abstracts, and full-text databases.
Computer Facilities: 4 newly upgraded microcomputer laboratories, multimedia classrooms, microcomputer classrooms, cyberlounge for resident students, 825+ Intel-based workstations, 125+ high-end Macintosh computers, and a variety of educational, business, statistical, and other electronic information resources
Campuswide Network? Yes
% of MBA Classrooms Wired: 85
Computer Model Recommended: Laptop
Internet Fee? No

EXPENSES/FINANCIAL AID
Annual Tuition: $15,120
Tuition Per Credit: $630
Room & Board (On/Off Campus): $12,000/ $15,000
Books and Supplies: $3,000
Average Grant: $1,812
Average Loan: $6,937
% Receiving Financial Aid: 55
% Receiving Aid Their First Year: 47

ADMISSIONS INFORMATION
Application Fee: $40
Electronic Application? Yes
Regular Application Deadline: 5/1
Regular Notification: Rolling
Length of Deferment: 1 year
Non-fall Admissions? Yes
Non-fall Application Deadline(s): 3/1 spring, 5/1 summer
Transfer Policy: Must use regular application; individual review of transfer credits
Need-Blind Admissions? Yes
Number of Applications Received: 565
% of Applicants Accepted: 62
% Accepted Who Enrolled: 43
Average GPA: 3.1
Average GMAT: 515
Average Years Experience: 4
Other Schools to Which Students Applied: Fordham, Hofstra, NYU

INTERNATIONAL STUDENTS
TOEFL Required of International Students? Yes
Minimum TOEFL: 500

EMPLOYMENT INFORMATION
Placement Office Available? Yes
% Employed Within 3 Months: 89
Frequent Employers: JPMorgan Chase, American Express, Citigroup, Accenture, Revlon, City of

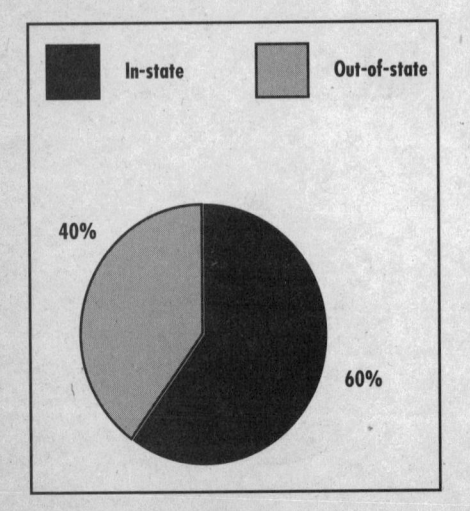

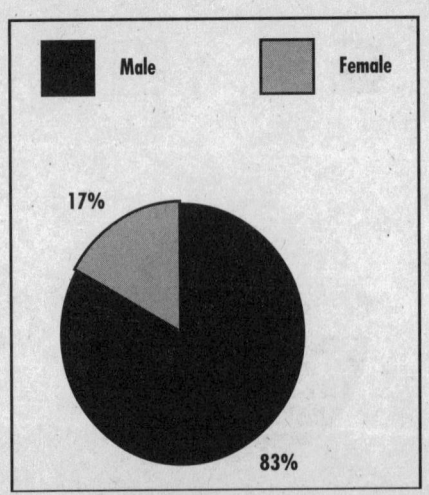

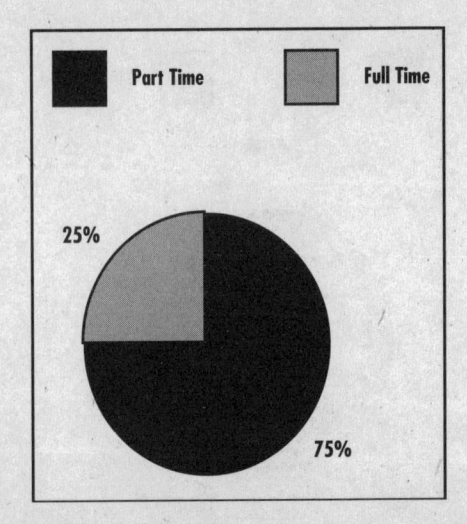

SAINT JOSEPH'S UNIVERSITY
The Erivan K. Haub School of Business

Admissions Contact: Susan Kassab, Director
Address: 5600 City Avenue, Philadelphia, PA 19131
Admissions Phone: 610-660-1101 • Admissions Fax: 610-660-1224
Admissions E-mail: graduate@sju.edu • Web Address: www.sju.edu

The Erivan K. Haub School of Business is a nationally recognized private Jesuit university in Philadelphia that promises to teach the ideals and philosophies of Jesuit education. The MBA program is a part-time program designed for working professionals and guarantees faculty concerned with each individual student. Other MBAs offered are two different Executive MBAs (one is a two-year program, and the other is completed in only one year) and the industry-specific Pharmaceutical Marketing MBA. More than 40 percent of graduates have a starting salary higher than $65,000 per year.

INSTITUTIONAL INFORMATION
Public/Private: Private
Evening Classes Available? Yes
Total Faculty: 80
% Faculty Female: 20
% Faculty Minority: 10
% Faculty Part Time: 20
Student/Faculty Ratio: 20:1
Students in Parent Institution: 3,550

PROGRAMS
Degrees Offered: Professional MBA, Master of Science in Financial Services, Master of Science in Human Resource Management, Executive MBA (21 months), Executive MBA (1 year), Master of Science in International Marketing, Executive Pharmaceutical Marketing MBA, Executive Online Pharmaceutical Marketing MBA
Joint Degrees: DO/MBA Program with Philadelphia College of Osteopathic Medicine

STUDENT INFORMATION
Total Business Students: 552
% Full Time: 10
% Female: 40
% Minority: 9
% Out of State: 9
% International: 9
Average Age: 28

COMPUTER AND RESEARCH FACILITIES
Research Facilities: Francis A. Drexel Library, Campbell Collection in Food Marketing
Computer Facilities: ABI/Inform Global, Business Source Elite, EconLit, FirstSearch, FIS Online, Hoover's Online, Lexis-Nexis Academic Universe, NetLibrary (e-books collection), New York Times, Political Risk Yearbook, Polling the Nations (survey database), The Red Books Online, STAT-USA, TableBase, Wall Street Journal
Campuswide Network? Yes
% of MBA Classrooms Wired: 67
Internet Fee? No

EXPENSES/FINANCIAL AID
Annual Tuition: $10,260
Tuition Per Credit: $570
Books and Supplies: $800
Average Loan: $7,200
% Receiving Financial Aid: 12

ADMISSIONS INFORMATION
Application Fee: $35
Electronic Application? No
Regular Application Deadline: Rolling
Regular Notification: Rolling
Deferment Available? No
Non-fall Admissions? Yes
Non-fall Application Deadline(s): 4/1 summer 1; 5/1 summer 2; 11/15 spring
Transfer Students Accepted? Yes
Transfer Policy: They must provide a completed application including original test scores.
Need-Blind Admissions? Yes
Number of Applications Received: 267
% of Applicants Accepted: 70
% Accepted Who Enrolled: 51
Average GPA: 3.2
Average GMAT: 520
Average Years Experience: 4
Other Schools to Which Students Applied: La Salle University, Penn State University-Great Valley Campus, Temple University, Villanova University.

INTERNATIONAL STUDENTS
TOEFL Required of International Students? Yes
Minimum TOEFL: 550 (213 computer)

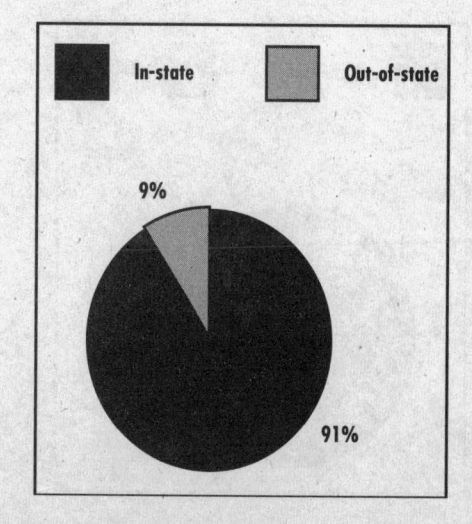

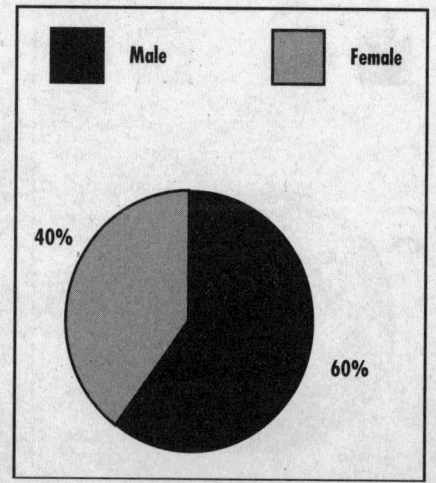

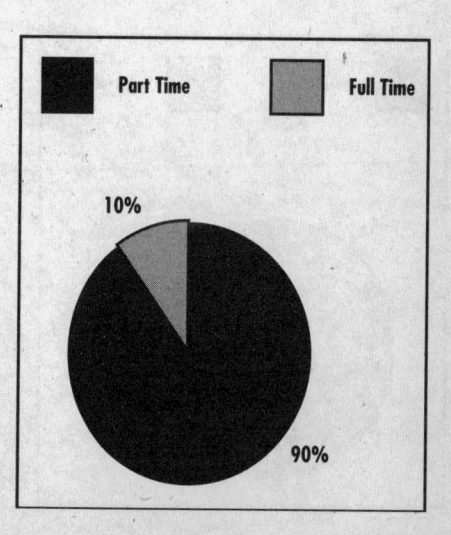

SAINT LOUIS UNIVERSITY
John Cook School of Business

Admissions Contact: Janell Kiel Nelson, Manager of Admissions and Recruitment
Address: 3674 Lindell Blvd., St. Louis, MO 63108
Admissions Phone: 314-977-2013 • Admissions Fax: 314-977-1416
Admissions E-mail: mba@slu.edu • Web Address: mba.slu.edu

Located just west of downtown St. Louis, the John Cook School of Business offers a private, Jesuit-centered business education that is well worth the investment. To top that off, SLU provides nearly half of its students with financial assistance. The MBA curriculum allows the student to choose from many concentrations, including less common areas such as decision sciences and industrial/labor relations and the more standard management information systems.

INSTITUTIONAL INFORMATION
Public/Private: Private
Evening Classes Available? Yes
Total Faculty: 60
% Faculty Female: 20
% Faculty Minority: 2
Student/Faculty Ratio: 22:1
Students in Parent Institution: 11,112
Academic Calendar: Semester

PROGRAMS
Degrees Offered: Master of Business Administration, with areas of emphasis available in Accounting, E-Commerce, Operations and Supply Chain Management, Entrepreneurial Studies, Economics, Finance, International Business, Management, Management Information Systems, and Marketing; Day MBA Program (full time, 2 years); Professional Evening MBA Program (part time, 3 to 5 years); Master of Finance (12 months to 5 years); Master of Accounting (12 months to 5 years); Executive Master of International Business (2 years)
Joint Degrees: JD/MBA (3.5 to 4 years), MHA/MBA (3 years), MD/MBA (5 years)
Academic Specialties: Case study, computer-aided instruction, experimental learning, field projects, group discussion, lecture, research, simulations, student presentations, study groups, team projects, capstone consulting projects
Study Abroad Options: Hong Kong, China; Madrid, Spain

STUDENT INFORMATION
Total Business Students: 295
% Female: 42
% Minority: 7
% International: 30
Average Age: 26

COMPUTER AND RESEARCH FACILITIES
Research Facilities: Boeing Institute of International Business, Firstar Women's Leadership Suite, Emerson Electric Center for Business Ethics, Center for Entrepreneurial Studies
Computer Facilities: Business school computer lab open 7 days a week (for business students only); additional labs available throughout campus
Campuswide Network? Yes
% of MBA Classrooms Wired: 100
Internet Fee? No

EXPENSES/FINANCIAL AID
Annual Tuition: $25,500
Tuition Per Credit: $725
Room & Board (Off Campus): $11,000
Books and Supplies: $750
Average Grant: $8,400
% Receiving Financial Aid: 84
% Receiving Aid Their First Year: 85

ADMISSIONS INFORMATION
Application Fee: $55
Electronic Application? Yes
Regular Application Deadline: 3/1
Regular Notification: 3/21
Deferment Available? Yes
Length of Deferment: 1 year
Non-fall Admissions? No
Transfer Students Accepted? Yes
Transfer Policy: 6 credits only from another AACSB-accredited school
Need-Blind Admissions? Yes
Number of Applications Received: 134
% of Applicants Accepted: 38
% Accepted Who Enrolled: 59
Average GPA: 3.2
Average GMAT: 580
Average Years Experience: 4
Other Admissions Factors Considered: Work experience plays a large role. For applicants with limited or no work experience, the GMAT and GPA become very important. Interviews are recommended for all applicants but are required for applicants with no work experience.
Other Schools to Which Students Applied: Washington University in St. Louis

INTERNATIONAL STUDENTS
TOEFL Required of International Students? Yes
Minimum TOEFL: 550 (213 computer)

EMPLOYMENT INFORMATION
Placement Office Available? Yes
% Employed Within 3 Months: 89

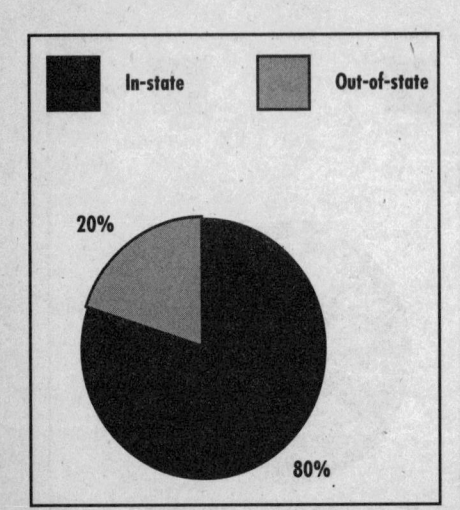

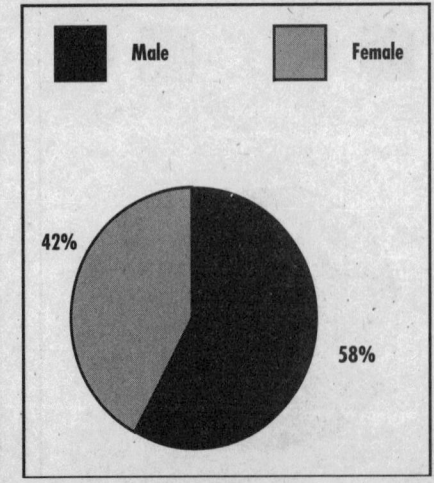

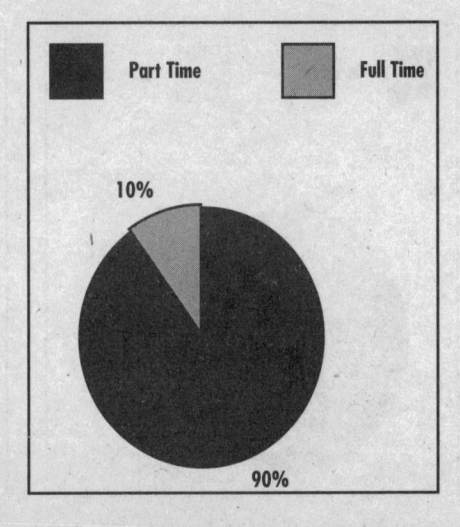

In-state 80% / Out-of-state 20%

Male 58% / Female 42%

Part Time 90% / Full Time 10%

SAN DIEGO STATE UNIVERSITY
Graduate School of Business

Admissions Contact: S. Scott or S. Temores-Valdez, MBA Program Coordinator/MSBA Program Coordinator
Address: 5500 Campanile Drive, San Diego, CA 92182
Admissions Phone: 619-594-8073 • Admissions Fax: 619-594-1863
Admissions E-mail: SDSUMBA@mail.sdsu.edu • Web Address: www.sdsu.edu

SDSU is located in the heart of San Diego, "a hotbed of entrepreneurship in biotech, telecommunications, software, and several other high-growth industries." The SDSU MBA is designed for students who do not have an undergraduate business degree. In addition to a broad range of courses in the curriculum, students are required to take one class in each of four themes: interpersonal skills, the environment, information and technology, and globalization. For the older, more experienced crowd, an EMBA is also offered.

INSTITUTIONAL INFORMATION
Public/Private: Public
Evening Classes Available? Yes
Total Faculty: 97
% Faculty Female: 14
% Faculty Minority: 3
% Faculty Part Time: 25
Student/Faculty Ratio: 35:1

PROGRAMS
Degrees Offered: Master of Business Administration (MBA) (2 to 4 years); Master of Science in Business Administration (MS) (1 to 2 years); Master of Science in Accountancy (MS) (1 to 2 years)
Joint Degrees: Master of Business Administration/Master of Arts in Latin American Studies (MBA/MA) (2 to 4 years)

STUDENT INFORMATION
Total Business Students: 718
% Full Time: 55
% Female: 41
% Minority: 15
% Out of State: 14
% International: 40
Average Age: 28

COMPUTER AND RESEARCH FACILITIES
Campuswide Network? No
Computer Model Recommended: No
Internet Fee? No

EXPENSES/FINANCIAL AID
Annual Tuition (Resident/Nonresident): $2,000/$8,000
Room & Board (On Campus): $6,318
Books and Supplies: $800

ADMISSIONS INFORMATION
Application Fee: $55
Electronic Application? Yes
Regular Application Deadline: 4/15
Regular Notification: 6/15
Deferment Available? No
Non-fall Admissions? Yes
Non-fall Application Deadline(s): 11/1 spring
Transfer Students Accepted? Yes
Transfer Policy: Transfer students apply through the normal admissions process and then will transfer courses according to our discretion.

Need-Blind Admissions? Yes
Number of Applications Received: 720
% of Applicants Accepted: 49
% Accepted Who Enrolled: 56
Average GPA: 3.2
GPA Range: 2.7-3.6
Average GMAT: 603
GMAT Range: 560-620
Average Years Experience: 5
Other Admissions Factors Considered: Undergraduate institution's reputation, major
Other Schools to Which Students Applied: University of San Diego

INTERNATIONAL STUDENTS
TOEFL Required of International Students? Yes
Minimum TOEFL: 570 (230 computer)

EMPLOYMENT INFORMATION
Placement Office Available? Yes

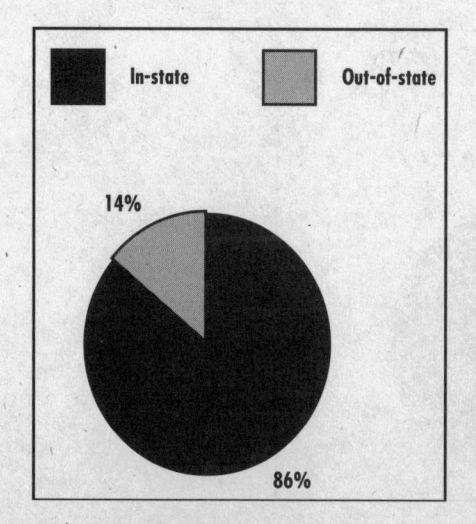

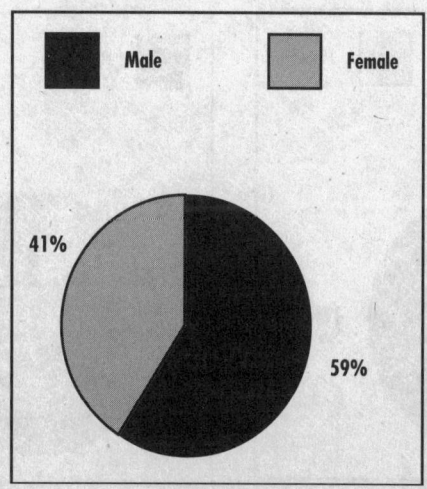

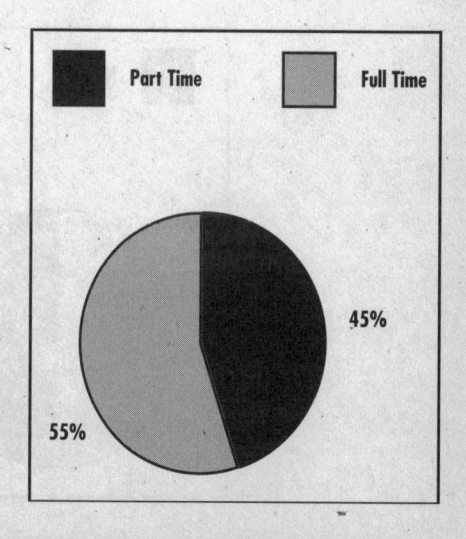

SAN FRANCISCO STATE UNIVERSITY
Graduate School of Business

Admissions Contact: Albert Koo, Admissions Coordinator
Address: 1600 Holloway Avenue, San Francisco, CA 94132
Admissions Phone: 415-338-1279 • Admissions Fax: 415-405-0495
Admissions E-mail: mba@sfsu.edu • Web Address: www.sfsu.edu/~mba

Rolling hills, trolleys, Fisherman's Wharf, perpetual spring/autumn—all of this could be yours for a great low price while obtaining an MBA from San Francisco State. The most popular program is the straight-up MBA, geared toward students working full time, but SF State also offers the Alliance MBA, delivered partially online, and the Accelerated MBA. The San Francisco State MBA aims to equip students with a broad understanding of management and a balanced knowledge base and encourages creativity, imagination, and lifelong learning.

INSTITUTIONAL INFORMATION
Public/Private: Public
Evening Classes Available? Yes
Total Faculty: 150
% Faculty Female: 36
% Faculty Minority: 40
% Faculty Part Time: 35
Student/Faculty Ratio: 25:1
Students in Parent Institution: 26,500

PROGRAMS
Degrees Offered: Master of Business Administration (2 years); Master of Science in Business Administration (2 years)
Academic Specialties: Accounting, Business Analysis, Computer Information System, Electronic Commence, Finance, Hospitality Management, Human Resources Management, International Business, Management, Marketing, Transportation/Logistics
Special Opportunities: Accelerated MBA Program
Study Abroad Options: Japan, Korea, France, Germany

STUDENT INFORMATION
Total Business Students: 900
% Female: 51
% Minority: 25
Average Age: 30

COMPUTER AND RESEARCH FACILITIES
Campuswide Network? No
Internet Fee? No

EXPENSES/FINANCIAL AID
Annual Tuition (Resident/Nonresident): $1,904/$7,808
Room & Board (On Campus): $7,000
Books and Supplies: $1,500

ADMISSIONS INFORMATION
Electronic Application? Yes
Regular Application Deadline: 5/15
Regular Notification: 6/15
Deferment Available? No
Non-fall Admissions? Yes
Non-fall Application Deadline(s): 11/15
Transfer Students Accepted? Yes
Need-Blind Admissions? No
Number of Applications Received: 1,017
% of Applicants Accepted: 53
% Accepted Who Enrolled: 46
Average GPA: 3.2
GPA Range: 2.7-4.0
Average GMAT: 536
GMAT Range: 470-700
Average Years Experience: 4

INTERNATIONAL STUDENTS
TOEFL Required of International Students? Yes
Minimum TOEFL: 550 (213 computer)

EMPLOYMENT INFORMATION
Placement Office Available? Yes

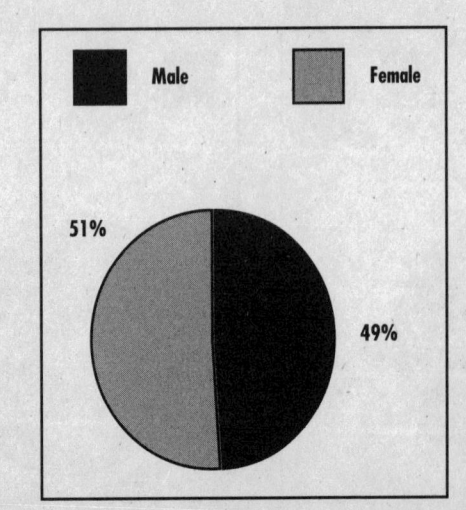

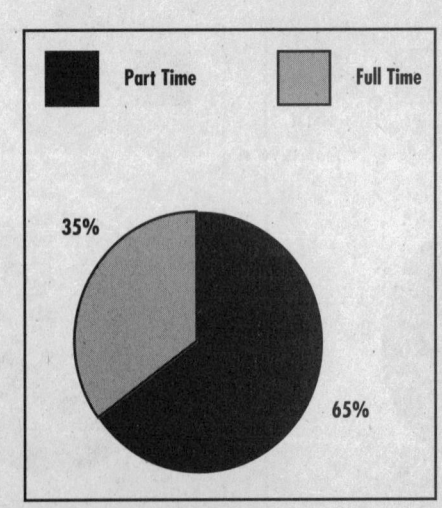

Male / Female: 49% / 51%

Part Time / Full Time: 65% / 35%

SAN JOSE STATE UNIVERSITY
College of Business

Admissions Contact: Amy Kassing, Admissions Coordinator
Address: One Washington Square, San Jose, CA 95192-0162
Admissions Phone: 408-924-3420 • Admissions Fax: 408-924-3426
Admissions E-mail: mba@cob.sjsu.edu • Web Address: www.cob.sjsu.edu/graduate

San Jose State University is situated in illustrious Silicon Valley. SJSU offers a few MBA program options, including an accelerated off-campus Evening MBA with classes in Rose Orchard Tech Center; an on-campus, traditional MBA program; and MBA One, a full-time day program. SJSU is a branch of the California State university system.

INSTITUTIONAL INFORMATION
Public/Private: Public
Evening Classes Available? Yes
Student/Faculty Ratio: 40:1

PROGRAMS
Degrees Offered: MBA-One (12 months); MBA On-Campus (18 to 48 months); MBA Off-Campus (30 months, variable); MS Transportation Management (24 to 36 months); MS Taxation (9 to 48 months); MS Accountancy (12 months)
Joint Degrees: MBA/MSE (32 months, lockstep)

STUDENT INFORMATION
Total Business Students: 765

EXPENSES/FINANCIAL AID
Annual Tuition (Resident/Nonresident): $1,990/$6,418
Books and Supplies: $1,000

ADMISSIONS INFORMATION
Application Fee: $55
Electronic Application? Yes
Regular Application Deadline: 5/1
Regular Notification: 6/14
Deferment Available? No
Non-fall Admissions? Yes
Non-fall Application Deadline(s): 10/15 spring
Transfer Students Accepted? Yes
Transfer Policy: Applicant must meet admission requirements. Up to 6 units can be transferred from previous institution.
Need-Blind Admissions? No
Number of Applications Received: 461
% of Applicants Accepted: 44
Average GPA: 3.5
Average GMAT: 560

INTERNATIONAL STUDENTS
TOEFL Required of International Students? Yes
Minimum TOEFL: 550 (213 computer)

SAN JOSE STATE UNIVERSITY

THE UNIVERSITY AT A GLANCE

San Jose State University is California's oldest institution of public higher education. Founded in 1857 in San Francisco as a teacher training school, it was named the California State Normal School in 1862 and moved to San Jose in 1871. Today, SJSU is a large university serving more than 27,000 students.

SJSU's scope has changed to meet the needs of today's society, but its long tradition of excellence in teaching remains. The early-day teacher's training school became San Jose State College in 1935 and a member of the California State system in 1961. It began awarding master's degrees in 1949 and achieved university status in 1972.

As the Santa Clara Valley evolved from a rich agricultural region into Silicon Valley, an internationally known high-technology research and development center, the University's mission expanded to fill the ever-widening educational needs.

Today, the multicultural student body prepares for careers in business, social work, engineering, science, technology, education, social sciences, arts, and humanities. The University offers degrees and professional credentials in more than 150 disciplines.

The mission of the College of Business Graduate Programs is to provide advanced business and professional education to high-potential individuals with diverse backgrounds and work experiences. Graduates are prepared to make decisions that are socially and fiscally responsible, personally enriching, and professionally advantageous. We offer a choice of academically challenging, multidisciplinary programs, each of which continuously improves to keep pace with a dynamic environment.

STUDENTS

SJSU has an active MBA Association. The MBA Association is a student organization that exists for three reasons: to increase and enhance networking among students; to aid in the dissemination of information among the students and the MBA program; and to strengthen the links between the students and the business community. The group hosts many social and academic events each year, including new-student orientation, Silicon Valley speakers, and career events.

ACADEMICS

The evening **On-Campus MBA** program consists of 13 to 16 three-unit courses, each 15 weeks long. This program is designed for students who prefer the University educational atmosphere or who are attending graduate school full-time.

The evening **Off-Campus MBA** program delivers the same courses in eight-week modules throughout the calendar year. This format allows students to complete six courses per year. Courses are held at the College of Business off-campus site located in the heart of Silicon Valley's high-tech corridor.

The **MBA-One** is a one-year, full-time, daytime MBA program designed for nonworking individuals who prefer an executive cohort style of learning. The lock-step program design allows the completion of the MBA degree in one year.

The MBA programs are open to individuals are from all undergraduate disciplines.

The daytime **Master of Science in Accountancy** (MSA) degree program is for full-time students with nonbusiness baccalaureate degrees. This is an 11-month lock-step program that begins in June of each year. The program includes a professional, paid internship component.

The evening **Master of Science in Taxation** (MST) degree program is designed to provide tax professionals with conceptual understanding and technical knowledge to compete in the dynamic tax world. This program is offered in modules to accommodate full-time professionals. A full-time student who has earned an undergraduate degree in business or passed the CPA exam can complete the MST in 11 months.

The accelerated evening **Master of Science in Transportation Management** (MSTM) degree program is designed to meet the career education needs of working transportation professionals by using "distance learning" technology.

The **MBA/MSE Off-Campus** accelerated evening dual degree program is a combined program for engineering professionals who wish to pursue technical and executive management positions.

All Business Graduate Programs are accredited by the AACSB International—The Association to Advance Collegiate Schools of Business, and the Western Association of Schools and Colleges.

The College of Business has over 100 full-time equivalent faculty positions and takes advantage of its Silicon Valley location by hiring local-area professionals to teach part time. Full-time faculty are encouraged to establish industry connections to inform their teaching and research, most of which is applied. Faculty are evaluated on their teaching performance and take pride in teaching well. They assign classroom projects that enable students to make Silicon Valley connections and work one-to-one with interested students on research and teaching projects. No courses are taught by teaching assistants.

College of Business

CAMPUS LIFE

The main campus is comprised of 10 closed city blocks adjacent to downtown San Jose. The buildings are a mix of "Old Spanish" and "Modern Government" architecture separated by many fountains, trees, and spacious lawns.

Business classes are held in the newly renovated Boccardo Business Education Center. All rooms in the 82,000-square-foot building are now wired for computer access. In addition, 18 of the 46 classrooms are equipped with "smart podia" containing Internet and television access, document cameras, and VCRs. Each room is also fully American Disabilities Act compliant with wheelchair stations and a public address system that accommodates hearing-impaired students.

The Clark Library and special collection libraries on campus house almost a million volumes and approximately 3,500 periodical titles. Clark Library serves as a federal and state repository. Special interest libraries include the Steinbeck Center, Beethoven Center, and the Chicano Library Resource Center. A collaborative effort between the City of San Jose and San Jose State University has resulted in the construction of a new joint library, the Dr. Martin Luther King Jr. library, scheduled to open in fall 2003.

The off-campus location at Rose Orchard Technology Center is approximately 12 miles from the main campus. The Rose Orchard site is located in a technology park setting in the heart of the Silicon Valley high-tech corridor, making it convenient to many working adults.

Staffed by 15 full-time professionals, SJSU's Career Center offers a range of resources to help students and recent graduates meet with success in the search for employment. Services include career advising and assistance with resume preparation and interview skills. The center maintains a resource library, a career lab with workstations and career guidance software, and a job bank with more than 100,000 listings. Graduate employment reports, containing information on the job placement rate of SJSU graduates and average starting salaries are also available. On-campus recruiting and job fairs are organized by the center, putting students and recent graduates in touch with potential employers.

COSTS

Fees for in-state residents enrolled in the On-Campus program are $680 for one to six units per semester. Resident students enrolled for more than six units pay $995 per semester. Nonresidents pay an additional $246 per unit. Students in the Off-Campus program pay fees of $1,260 per course. The program fee for the MBA-One is $20,160.

Financial aid eligibility for U.S. residents is determined after completing the Free Application for Federal Student Aid (FAFSA), available from the University Financial Aid Office.

ADMISSIONS

Prospective business graduate students must complete and submit an application, the application fee, and one official transcript from every post secondary school attended. Application due dates for U.S. residents are May 1 for the fall semester and September 15 for the spring semester. International students must apply by March 1 for the fall semester and by August 31 for the spring semester. San José State requires international applicants for whom English was not the medium of instruction to take the TOEFL exam. Scores required are 213 computer-based or 550 paper-based. The Business Graduate Programs office requires applicants to have a GMAT score of 500 with balanced verbal and quantitative scores in the 50th percentile. A GPA of 3.0 is also required.

For more information, contact:

San José State University
Business Graduate Programs
One Washington Square
San José, CA 95192-0162
Telephone: 408-924-3420
Fax: 408-924-3426
E-mail: mba@cob.sjsu.edu
World Wide Web: www.cob.sjsu.edu/graduate

Admissions Contact: Amy Kassing, Admissions Coordinator
Address: One Washington Square, San Jose, CA 95192-0162
Admissions Phone: 408-924-3420 • Admissions Fax: 408-924-3426
Admissions E-mail: mba@cob.sjsu.edu • Web Address: www.cob.sjsu.edu/graduate

Santa Clara University
Leavey School of Business

Admissions Contact: Jana Hee, Director, Graduate Business Admissions
Address: MBA Office, Kenna Hall #223, Santa Clara, CA 95053-0001
Admissions Phone: 408-554-4539 • Admissions Fax: 408-544-2332
Admissions E-mail: mbaadmissions@scu.edu • Web Address: business.scu.edu

Calling itself "the premier business program for Silicon Valley," SCU, a Jesuit business school, emphasizes the education of the whole person, along with establishing managerial leadership skills and critical thinking capabilities. One unique degree offered is an MBA in agribusiness, available through Santa Clara U's Food and Agribusiness Institute. Silicon Valley business leaders are frequent contributors to classroom discussions and are frequent employers of Santa Clara MBA graduates.

INSTITUTIONAL INFORMATION
Public/Private: Private
Evening Classes Available? Yes
Total Faculty: 70
% Faculty Female: 20
% Faculty Minority: 15
% Faculty Part Time: 15
Student/Faculty Ratio: 28:1
Students in Parent Institution: 7,350
Academic Calendar: Quarter

PROGRAMS
Degrees Offered: MBA (2 to 6 years), EMBA (16 months)
Joint Degrees: JD/MBA (4 years)
Academic Specialties: Entrepreneurship, Consulting, High-Tech

STUDENT INFORMATION
Total Business Students: 853
% Full Time: 18
% Female: 40
% Minority: 10
% Out of State: 1
% International: 20
Average Age: 29

COMPUTER AND RESEARCH FACILITIES
Campuswide Network? Yes
Internet Fee? No

EXPENSES/FINANCIAL AID
Annual Tuition: $15,500
Tuition Per Credit: $571
Books and Supplies: $500
% Receiving Financial Aid: 50

ADMISSIONS INFORMATION
Application Fee: $75
Electronic Application? Yes
Early Decision Application Deadline: 3/1 (fall only)
Early Decision Notification: 5/1
Regular Application Deadline: Rolling
Regular Notification: Rolling
Deferment Available? Yes
Length of Deferment: 2 quarters
Non-fall Admissions? Yes
Non-fall Application Deadline(s): 9/1 winter, 12/1 spring
Transfer Students Accepted? Yes
Transfer Policy: Apply as all others

Need-Blind Admissions? Yes
Number of Applications Received: 378
% of Applicants Accepted: 71
% Accepted Who Enrolled: 80
Average GPA: 3.2
GPA Range: 2.7-3.7
Average GMAT: 614
GMAT Range: 530-690
Average Years Experience: 7
Other Admissions Factors Considered: level of work experience; undergraduate institution and major; level of commitment determined by essay responses
Other Schools to Which Students Applied: University of California-Berkeley, San Jose State University, University of San Francisco, University of California-Davis, University of Pittsburgh

INTERNATIONAL STUDENTS
TOEFL Required of International Students? Yes
Minimum TOEFL: 250 computer

EMPLOYMENT INFORMATION
Placement Office Available? No

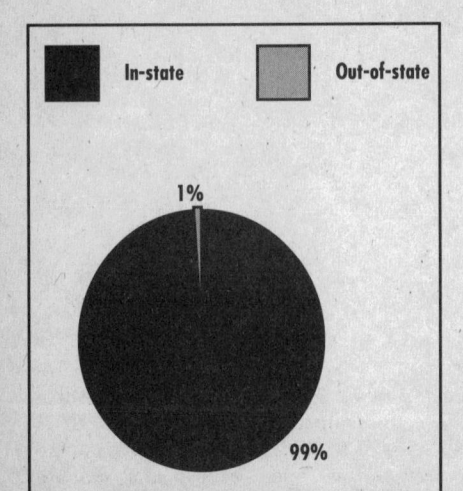

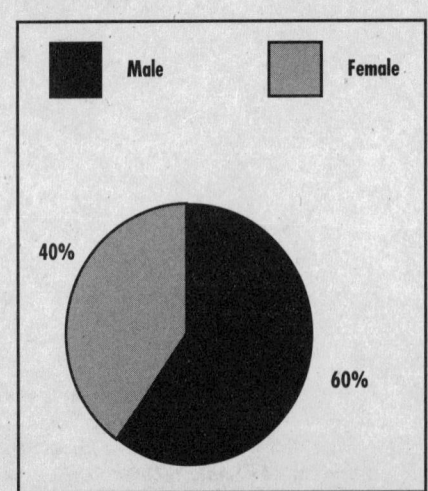

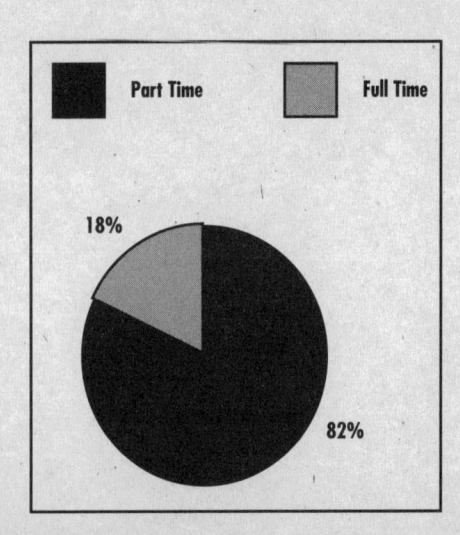

SEATTLE UNIVERSITY
Albers School of Business and Economics

Admissions Contact: Michael McKeon, Dean of Admissions
Address: 900 Broadway, Seattle, WA 98122
Admissions Phone: 206-296-2000 • Admissions Fax: 206-296-5656
Admissions E-mail: admissions@seattleu.edu • Web Address: www.seattleu.edu/asbe

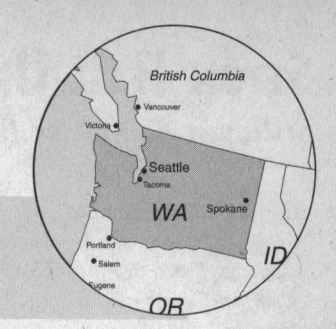

Facing ethical issues in business and completing service projects are priorities in the MBA curriculum at Seattle University, one of 28 Jesuit colleges in the United States. The learning environment at Seattle U is "diverse and culturally rich" with "a wide range of religious and ideological viewpoints" and nurturing faculty who dedicate personal attention to students. A noteworthy on-campus landmark is the Chapel of St. Ignatius, a scale model of which has been selected for inclusion in the permanent collection of the Museum of Modern Art in New York City. Architect Steven Hull's concept for the chapel was "A Gathering of Different Lights," as it refers to the "consolations and desolations" St. Ignatius believed comprised spiritual life and describes the mission of Seattle University.

INSTITUTIONAL INFORMATION
Public/Private: Private
Evening Classes Available? Yes
Total Faculty: 43
Student/Faculty Ratio: 12:1
Students in Parent Institution: 5,851
Academic Calendar: Quarter

PROGRAMS
Degrees Offered: Master of Business Administration (MBA); Master of International Business (MIB); Master of Professional Accounting (MPAcc); Master of Finance (MSF)
Joint Degrees: JD/MBA (4 years)
Study Abroad Options: France, Netherlands

STUDENT INFORMATION
Total Business Students: 511
% Female: 40
% Minority: 5
% International: 9
Average Age: 30

COMPUTER AND RESEARCH FACILITIES
Research Facilities: ECIS computer lab
Computer Facilities: There are several computer labs situated around the campus that MBA students can utilize. The following databases are available: ABI/Inform, Compustat, CRSP, DIALOG, Disclosure, Dissertation Abstracts, Ebsco, FirstSearch, Lexis-Nexis Academic Universe, ProQuest, Public Affairs Information Service, and STAT-USA.
Campuswide Network? Yes
Computer Model Recommended: No
Internet Fee? No

EXPENSES/FINANCIAL AID
Annual Tuition: $13,932
Tuition Per Credit: $516
Room & Board (On Campus): $6,318
Books and Supplies: $1,500
Average Grant: $5,265
Average Loan: $14,558
% Receiving Financial Aid: 20
% Receiving Aid Their First Year: 24

ADMISSIONS INFORMATION
Application Fee: $55
Electronic Application? Yes
Regular Application Deadline: 8/20
Regular Notification: 9/1
Deferment Available? Yes
Length of Deferment: 1 year
Non-fall Admissions? Yes
Non-fall Application Deadline(s): 11/20 winter, 2/20 spring, 5/20 summer
Transfer Students Accepted? Yes
Transfer Policy: Applicants must meet standard admission requirements (GMAT 500 or greater, 1 year work experience, undergraduate GPA of 3.0 or greater). University will accept 9 quarter credits.
Need-Blind Admissions? Yes
Number of Applications Received: 192
% of Applicants Accepted: 71
% Accepted Who Enrolled: 65
Average GPA: 3.2
GPA Range: 2.2-3.8
Average GMAT: 557
GMAT Range: 490-670
Average Years Experience: 9
Other Schools to Which Students Applied: Eastern Washington University, Pacific Lutheran University, Seattle Pacific University, University of Washington, Washington State University, Western Washington University

INTERNATIONAL STUDENTS
TOEFL Required of International Students? Yes
Minimum TOEFL: 580 (237 computer)

EMPLOYMENT INFORMATION
Placement Office Available? Yes
Prominent Alumni: Leo Hindery, CEO, Yankee Entertainment & Sports Network; Frank Murkowski, U.S. Senator, Alaska; Jim Whittaker, first American to reach the summit of Mt. Everest; Carolyn Kelly, general manager, Seattle Times; William Foley, Jr., chairman and CEO, Fidelity National Financial

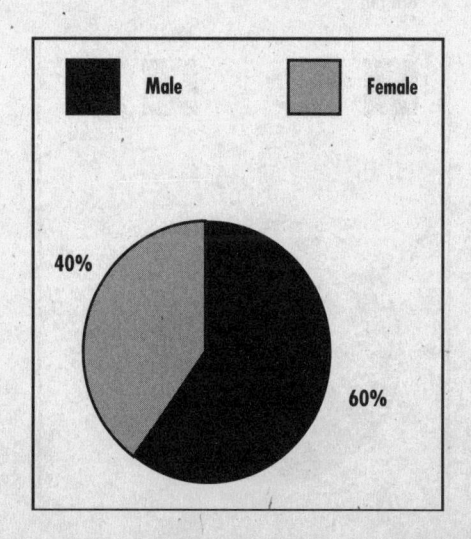

Seton Hall University
Stillman School of Business

Admissions Contact: Lorrie Dougherty, Director of Graduate Admissions
Address: 400 South Orange Avenue, South Orange, NJ 07079-2692
Admissions Phone: 973-761-9262 • Admissions Fax: 973-761-9208
Admissions E-mail: stillman@shu.edu • Web Address: www.business.shu.edu

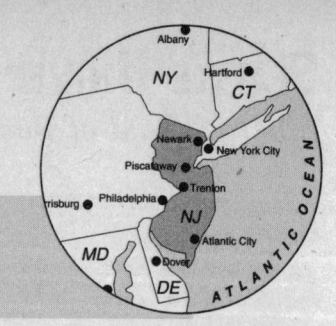

Seton Hall is a Catholic university, located in South Orange, New Jersey, just a train ride away from New York City. The Stillman School of Business at Seton Hall offers four joint degrees, including the MBA/MADIR, a Master in Business Administration coupled with a Master of Arts in Diplomacy and International Relations. Frequent employers of Seton Hall grads are AT&T, Pfizer, and Deloitte & Touche. Applicants to the Stillman School of Business also apply to Fordham University, New York University, and Pace University.

INSTITUTIONAL INFORMATION
Public/Private: Private
Evening Classes Available? Yes
Total Faculty: 94
% Faculty Female: 23
% Faculty Minority: 24
% Faculty Part Time: 38
Student/Faculty Ratio: 6:1
Students in Parent Institution: 8,324
Academic Calendar: Semester

PROGRAMS
Degrees Offered: MBA (2 to 5 years); MS International Business (18 months to 5 years); MS Taxation (12 months to 5 years); MS Accounting (12 months to 5 years); MS Professional Accounting (12 months to 5 years)
Joint Degrees: MBA/MS International Business (3 to 5 years); MBA/JD (4 years); MBA/MSN (2.5 to 5 years); MS International Business/MA Diplomacy and International Relations (2.5 to 5 years); MBS/MA Diplomacy and International Relations (2.5 to 5 years)
Academic Specialties: Sport Management (contact Dr. Ann Mayo, mayoann@shu.edu)
Study Abroad Options: Italy, China, Poland, Ireland

STUDENT INFORMATION
Total Business Students: 522
% Full Time: 15
% Female: 34
% Minority: 12
% Out of State: 14
% International: 10
Average Age: 29

COMPUTER AND RESEARCH FACILITIES
Computer Facilities: ABI/Inform, Lexis-Nexis, ProQuest, Ebsco Online, ERIC Education, FIS Online, and many others
Campuswide Network? Yes
% of MBA Classrooms Wired: 100
Computer Model Recommended: Laptop
Internet Fee? Yes

EXPENSES/FINANCIAL AID
Annual Tuition: $19,380
Tuition Per Credit: $646
Room & Board (Off Campus): $10,200
Books and Supplies: $1,100
Average Grant: $20,904
Average Loan: $12,500
% Receiving Financial Aid: 22
% Receiving Aid Their First Year: 17

ADMISSIONS INFORMATION
Application Fee: $75
Electronic Application? Yes
Regular Application Deadline: 6/1
Regular Notification: Rolling
Length of Deferment: 1 year
Non-fall Admissions? Yes
Non-fall Application Deadline(s): 11/1 spring, 3/15 summer
Transfer Policy: Must submit formal application, which is reviewed by the dean to determine how many credits would transfer (maximum of 12).
Need-Blind Admissions? Yes
Number of Applications Received: 255
% of Applicants Accepted: 58
% Accepted Who Enrolled: 78
Average GPA: 3.3
Average GMAT: 527
Average Years Experience: 5
Other Admissions Factors Considered: Interview, computer experience
Minority/Disadvantaged Student Recruitment Programs: Graduate Access Program for Business (contact Ms. Carol McMillan at mcmillca@shu.edu or 973-761-9162)
Other Schools to Which Students Applied: Fordham, NYU, Pace, Rutgers, Boston College, Villanova, Columbia

INTERNATIONAL STUDENTS
TOEFL Required of International Students? Yes
Minimum TOEFL: 550 (213 computer)

EMPLOYMENT INFORMATION
Placement Office Available? Yes
Frequent Employers: Prudential, AT&T, Pfizer, Arthur Andersen, KPMG, Lucent Technologies
Prominent Alumni: L. Dennis Kozlowski, CEO, Tyco International; Gerald P. Buccino, chairman and CEO, Buccino & Associates

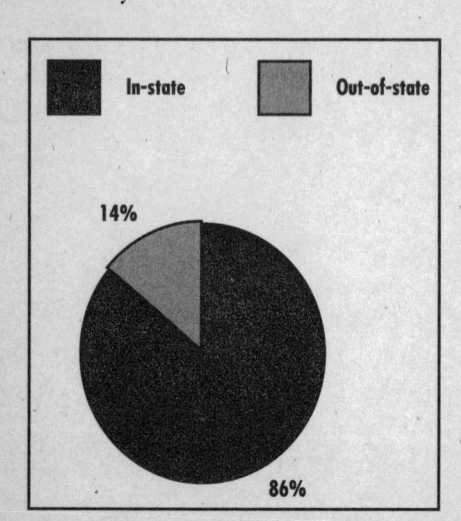

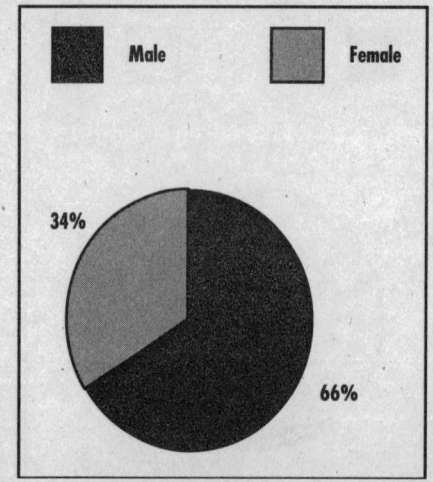

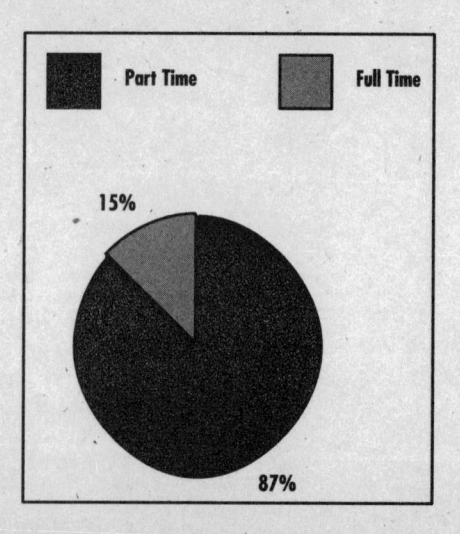

SIMMONS COLLEGE
Simmons Graduate School of Management

Admissions Contact: Andrea Bruce, Director of Admissions
Address: 409 Commonwealth Avenue, Boston, MA 02215
Admissions Phone: 617-521-3840 • Admissions Fax: 617-521-3880
Admissions E-mail: gsmadm@simmons.edu • Web Address: www.simmons.edu/gsm

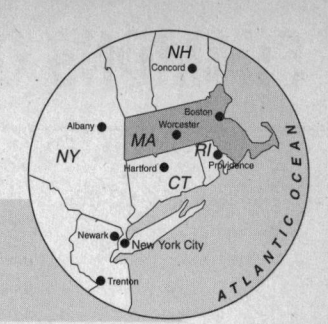

INSTITUTIONAL INFORMATION
Public/Private: Private
Evening Classes Available? Yes
Total Faculty: 16
% Faculty Part Time: 25
Student/Faculty Ratio: 16:1
Students in Parent Institution: 3,000

PROGRAMS
Degrees Offered: MBA (1, 1.5, 2 years, 2.5 years, 3, or 3.5 years)
Academic Specialties: Gender Dynamics, Leadership, Negotiations

STUDENT INFORMATION
Total Business Students: 250
% Female: 100
% Minority: 15
% International: 30
Average Age: 32

COMPUTER AND RESEARCH FACILITIES
Research Facilities: Simmons Graduate School of Management houses the Center for Gender in Organizations (CGO), an innovative research center that analyzes gender dynamics in organizations and focuses on the conditions required for women's success. Through research, educational programs, convening conferences, seminars, and workshops, CGO is committed to improving organizational effectiveness by strengthening gender equity for people of diverse racial and ethnic backgrounds in both the profit and not-for-profit sectors worldwide.

Computer Facilities: The school is equipped with its own microcomputer lab. The computer lab also offers terminals exclusively for work on the Internet and e-mail. Additional microcomputing terminals are available in the undergraduate computing facility. Through the library's online computer terminals, students can access more than 50 Boston-area university and public library catalogs and 40 subject-divided databases, including the Business Periodical Index, Business News Abstracts, Wilson Business Abstracts, and Paperchase (medical information). ABI/Inform, Business Dateline, Morningstar Mutual Funds, SEC/Disclosure, and the National Trade Data Bank are all available on CD-ROM computer workstations. Simmons is a member of the Fenway Library Consortium.
Campuswide Network? Yes
Computer Model Recommended: No
Internet Fee? No

EXPENSES/FINANCIAL AID
Annual Tuition: $31,000
Tuition Per Credit: $686
Room & Board (On Campus): $10,980
Books and Supplies: $3,000
Average Grant: $8,600
Average Loan: $10,000
% Receiving Aid Their First Year: 25

ADMISSIONS INFORMATION
Application Fee: $75
Electronic Application? Yes
Regular Application Deadline: 6/30
Regular Notification: Rolling
Deferment Available? Yes
Length of Deferment: 1 year
Non-fall Admissions? Yes
Non-fall Application Deadline(s): 11/15 (January entry)
Transfer Students Accepted? Yes
Transfer Policy: Reviewed on case-by-case basis
Need-Blind Admissions? Yes
Number of Applications Received: 120
% of Applicants Accepted: 88
% Accepted Who Enrolled: 91
Average GPA: 3.0
Average GMAT: 550
Average Years Experience: 8
Other Schools to Which Students Applied: Babson College, Bentley College, Boston College, Boston University

INTERNATIONAL STUDENTS
TOEFL Required of International Students? Yes
Minimum TOEFL: 550 (213 computer)

EMPLOYMENT INFORMATION

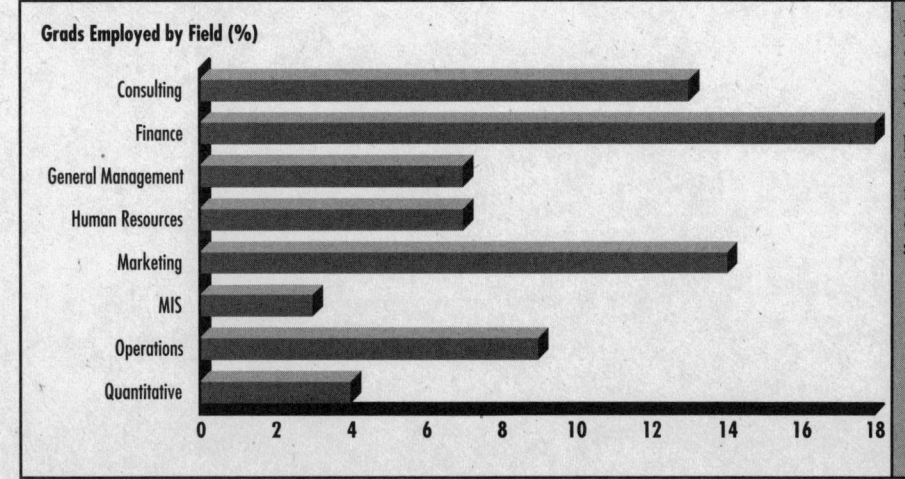

Grads Employed by Field (%)

Field	%
Consulting	13
Finance	18
General Management	7
Human Resources	7
Marketing	14
MIS	3
Operations	9
Quantitative	4

Placement Office Available? Yes
% Employed Within 3 Months: 80
Prominent Alumni: Gail Snowden, executive VP, Fleet Boston Financial; Maryann Tocio, president and COO, Bright Horizon; Donna Fernandes, director, Buffalo Zoo; Gail Deegan, former CFO and executive VP, Houghton Mifflin; Sue Paresky, senior VP, Dana Farber Cancer Institute

SIMMONS COLLEGE

THE SCHOOL AT A GLANCE

"A quarter of a century ago, the Simmons Graduate School of Management (GSM) was among the first to educate women for positions of power and leadership. Today, we remain the only business school in the world designed exclusively for women. Our challenge is the same: to help women succeed in business and to move from middle management into the most senior positions in organizations of every kind. Wherever senior managers meet, Simmons is determined to position skilled and confident women among them, competing equally, with insight and a real understanding of the business environment."

—Dr. Patricia O'Brien, Dean

STUDENTS

Thirty percent of Simmons' full-time MBA students come from outside the United States, with representation this year from Europe, Asia, Africa, and the Caribbean.

Alumnae and current students assist international students on their arrival in the United States, and alumnae have often hosted students until they secure permanent housing. On a limited basis, the School offers temporary suite housing for new students until they secure housing.

ACADEMICS

In its emphasis on functional knowledge and quantitative skills, the Simmons MBA program is identical to those offered at other business schools. What sets Simmons apart is its distinctive behavioral focus. This is available nowhere else, and it is available to full-time and part-time students alike.

Simmons offers several options for earning the MBA. An accelerated one-year program allows a woman to take a sabbatical from her career to earn the degree, while the two- and three-year tracks make it possible to parallel work and earnings with learning. Students may also complete the program in 18 months by starting in January. Students may begin in September or January.

The MBA curriculum is a structured sequence of courses, carefully integrated to build upon and reinforce one another. Students take courses in economics, quantitative analysis, accounting, finance, marketing, operations, and strategic planning with a special focus on national and international markets and competition; in the management of organizations—with courses in team strategies, organizational structure, human resources management, communication, and negotiations; and in individual career development. There are electives in advanced accounting, entrepreneurship, corporate and international finance, health-care management, and leadership. Students may also elect to pursue an internship or a market research project.

Fifteen faculty members teach in the MBA program; 12 are women. They are graduates of leading doctoral and MBA programs. The same faculty members teach classes for full-time and part-time students.

CAMPUS LIFE

The School is centrally located in Boston's vibrant academic and cultural Back Bay community just across the Charles River from Cambridge and is within walking distance of the world-renowned Boston Symphony Orchestra and the Museum of Fine Arts.

Relatively compact among major cities, Boston is a walkable city with an old seaport that is now a completely revitalized waterfront with marinas, shops, theaters, island ferries, seafood restaurants, miniparks, and walkways.

The School is housed in a historic complex of turn-of-the-century townhouses. Classrooms, administrative and faculty offices, the computer laboratory, and the library are situated within one city block. The GSM library contains the latest volumes and periodicals in business and business-related fields as well as a media center with videotaping facilities. Students also have access to the Simmons College main campus library as well as several major libraries in the immediate area, including the famous Kirstein Business Library in Boston's financial district.

The College's new Sports Center offers a running track, swimming pool, squash and racquetball court, and exercise equipment. All the facilities of Simmons College, including the new sports center, are available to GSM students at the main campus, a short distance away.

Simmons Graduate School of Management

Technology Environment

The School is equipped with its own microcomputer lab. The computer lab also offers terminals exclusively for work on the Internet and e-mail. Additional microcomputing terminals are available in the undergraduate computing facility.

Through the library's online computer terminals, students can access more than 50 Boston-area university and public library catalogs and 40 subject-divided databases, including the Business Periodical Index, Business News Abstracts, Wilson Business Abstracts, Paperchase (medical information). In addition, ABI/Inform, Business Dateline, Morningstar Mutual Funds, SEC/Disclosure, and the National Trade Data Bank are all available on CD-ROM computer workstations. Simmons is a member of the Fenway Library Consortium.

Career Services

The Office of Career Services, dedicated to the MBA program, provides personalized and comprehensive career planning and placement services. Advice on appropriate career direction, resume writing, interview preparation, and salary negotiation is integrated with a required Career Strategies course. The office provides students with access to job opportunities through its on-campus recruiting program, functions, and industry panels; correspondence recruiting services; job bank; and job fairs that are attended by a wide range of companies.

COSTS

The cost of tuition for the 2001–2002 academic year is $686 per credit hour. Forty-five credits are required for the degree. The estimated cost for fees, books, and supplies is $3,000.

Financial assistance consists of scholarships, graduate assistantships, grants, and federal loans, which may be offered separately or in combination. Deans' Scholarships are available and candidates applying to the program are automatically considered. These awards are based on merit.

ADMISSIONS

Admission is competitive. The Admissions Committee measures potential for both academic success in the program and professional success thereafter. The committee looks closely at the candidate's preparation for a highly quantitative course of study. It does not follow a formula in making its decisions; rather it evaluates the candidate's ability, aptitude, and promise by examining the whole as revealed in the application materials. An applicant must have at least two years of full-time work experience.

The following materials are needed to fulfill application requirements: a completed application form, an application fee, three letters of recommendation, official transcripts of all academic study beyond high school, and an official score report from the GMAT. International students whose native language is not English must submit a TOEFL score. Interviews are strongly encouraged.

The School has a rolling admission policy designed to let students choose their admission decision date. Students may enroll in September or January. For more information on applying and deadline dates, students should contact:

Admission Office
Simmons Graduate School of Management
409 Commonwealth Avenue
Boston, MA 02215
Telephone: 617-521-3840
800-597-1622 (toll-free)
Fax: 617-521-3880
E-mail: gsmadm@simmons.edu
World Wide Web: www.simmons.edu/gsm/index.html

Admissions Contact: Andrea Bruce, Director of Admissions
Address: 409 Commonwealth Avenue, Boston, MA 02215
Admissions Phone: 617-521-3840 • Admissions Fax: 617-521-3880
Admissions E-mail: gsmadm@simmons.edu • Web Address: www.simmons.edu/gsm

SOUTHEAST MISSOURI STATE UNIVERSITY
Donald L. Harrison College of Business

Admissions Contact: Dr. Kenneth Heischmidt, Director, MBA Program
Address: MBA Office, Cape Girardeau, MO 63701
Admissions Phone: 573-651-5116 • Admissions Fax: 573-651-5032
Admissions E-mail: mba@semo.edu • Web Address: www.semo.edu

Southeast Missouri State University is the proud home of the internationally recognized Golden Eagles Marching Band. More important, it's the home of Harrison College of Business, where tuition rates are low and 99 percent of graduates are placed within a year of graduation. SMSU emphasizes the strength of its assistantship opportunities, which enable a graduate student to teach, research, or assist with administrative duties in the business school; for the student's services, the school will provide a stipend and a waiver of all fees. Most applicants to the MBA program possess an undergrad degree in business, although without one, admission is possible under certain circumstances.

INSTITUTIONAL INFORMATION
Public/Private: Public
Evening Classes Available? Yes
Total Faculty: 45
Student/Faculty Ratio: 20:1
Students in Parent Institution: 9,000
Academic Calendar: Semester

PROGRAMS
Degrees Offered: Master of Business Administration (part time, 33 to 63 credits, 12 months to 6 years), with concentrations in Accounting and Management
Academic Specialties: Case study, computer analysis, computer simulations, experimental learning, field projects, group discussion, lecture, research, seminars by members of the business community, student presentations, study groups, team projects
Study Abroad Options: International exchange program in various countries in western Europe

STUDENT INFORMATION
Total Business Students: 100
% Female: 45
% Minority: 21
% International: 44

COMPUTER AND RESEARCH FACILITIES
Computer Facilities: Several campuswide computer labs
Campuswide Network? Yes
Internet Fee? No

EXPENSES/FINANCIAL AID
Annual Tuition (Resident/Nonresident): $2,000/$4,000
Tuition Per Credit (Resident/Nonresident): $138/$252
Room & Board: $4,500
% Receiving Financial Aid: 38

ADMISSIONS INFORMATION
Application Fee: $20
Electronic Application? Yes
Regular Application Deadline: Rolling
Regular Notification: Rolling
Deferment Available? Yes
Length of Deferment: 1 year
Non-fall Admissions? Yes
Non-fall Application Deadline(s): Spring, summer
Transfer Students Accepted? Yes
Transfer Policy: May transfer 9 hours as authorized by director of MBA program
Need-Blind Admissions? No
Number of Applications Received: 53
% of Applicants Accepted: 79
% Accepted Who Enrolled: 93
Average GPA: 3.2
Average GMAT: 510
Other Schools to Which Students Applied: Saint Louis University, Southern Illinois University, University of Missouri-Columbia, Southwest Missouri State University

INTERNATIONAL STUDENTS
TOEFL Required of International Students? Yes
Minimum TOEFL: 550 (213 computer)

EMPLOYMENT INFORMATION

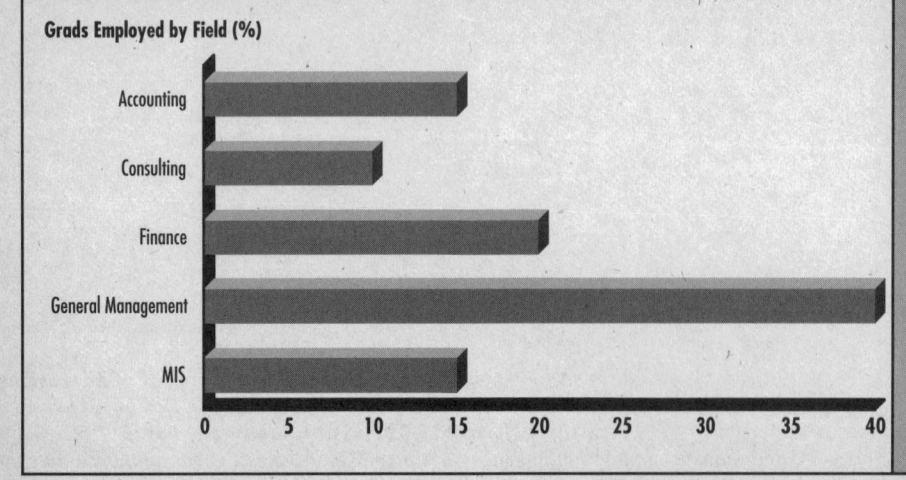

Grads Employed by Field (%)
- Accounting: 15
- Consulting: 10
- Finance: 20
- General Management: 40
- MIS: 15

Placement Office Available? Yes
% Employed Within 3 Months: 100
Frequent Employers: Accenture, Dow Jones, PricewaterhouseCoopers, TG Missouri, Bausch & Lomb, Texas Instruments

SOUTHEASTERN LOUISIANA UNIVERSITY
College of Business & Technology

Admissions Contact: Sandra Meyers, Graduate Admissions Specialist
Address: SLU 10752, Hammond, LA 70402
Admissions Phone: 800-222-7358 • Admissions Fax: 985-549-5632
Admissions E-mail: smeyers@selu.edu • Web Address: www.selu.edu/Academics/Business

The MBA program at Southeastern Louisiana University's College of Business stresses the practical aspects of business leadership and prepares students for leadership positions in both business and government. Every classroom is wired for laptop use, and the MBA curriculum has recently expanded to include new courses on international business and e-commerce. Graduation from the MBA program is contingent upon the completion of 30 hours of undergraduate business prerequisites in addition to 33 hours of MBA course work. Apart from a general MBA, SLU also offers an Executive MBA, which meets on Saturdays and includes frequent interaction with Hammond County business managers.

INSTITUTIONAL INFORMATION
Public/Private: Public
Evening Classes Available? Yes
Total Faculty: 34
% Faculty Female: 18
Student/Faculty Ratio: 7:1
Students in Parent Institution: 14,522
Academic Calendar: Semester

PROGRAMS
Degrees Offered: MBA with concerations in Accounting, Marketing, Finance (12 months to 6 years); Executive MBA lock-step program meeting mainly on weekends (17 months)
Academic Specialties: Case study, computer aided instruction, computer analysis, experimental learning, faculty seminars, field projects, group discussion, lecture, research, role playing, seminars by members of the business community, simulations, study groups, team projects
Study Abroad Options: Germany and Costa Rica

STUDENT INFORMATION
Total Business Students: 248
% Full Time: 63
% Female: 48
% Minority: 48
% Out of State: 1
% International: 37
Average Age: 28

COMPUTER AND RESEARCH FACILITIES
Research Facilities: Business Research Center
Computer Facilities: On-campus computer labs, St. Tammany Center (EMBA program)
Campuswide Network? Yes
% of MBA Classrooms Wired: 100
Internet Fee? No

EXPENSES/FINANCIAL AID
Annual Tuition (Resident/Nonresident): $2,457/$6,453
Room & Board (On Campus): $3,440
% Receiving Aid: 24
% Receiving Aid Their First Year: 8

ADMISSIONS INFORMATION
Application Fee: $20
Electronic Application? Yes
Regular Application Deadline: 7/15
Regular Notification: Rolling
Deferment Available? Yes
Length of Deferment: 1 year
Non-fall Admissions? Yes
Non-fall Application Deadline(s): 12/1, 5/1
Transfer Students Accepted? Yes

Transfer Policy: Must earn 12 hours of graduate credit at Southeastern before applying for any transfer credit from another university. That university must be an accredited institution that regularly grants the master's degree, or an equivalent foreign institution. The student must be eligible for readmission to the institution from which the credits are to be transferred and must have earned a minimum grade of B in each course to be transferred. No more than one-third of the hours required for graduation may be transferred.
Need-Blind Admissions? No
Number of Applications Received: 124
% of Applicants Accepted: 69
% Accepted Who Enrolled: 73
Average GPA: 2.9
Average GMAT: 470

INTERNATIONAL STUDENTS
TOEFL Required of International Students? Yes
Minimum TOEFL: 525 (195 computer)

EMPLOYMENT INFORMATION
Placement Office Available? Yes
Prominent Alumni: Robin Roberts, ESPN Sportscaster; Russell Carollo, Pulitzer Prize winner; Harold Jackson, president (retired), Sunsweet Products; James J. Brady, former president, National Democratic Party; Carl Barbier, federal judge

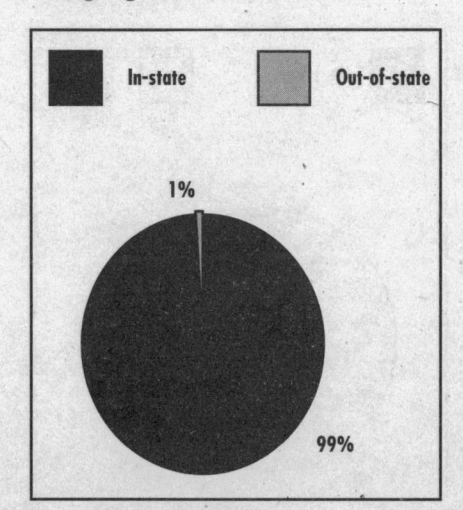

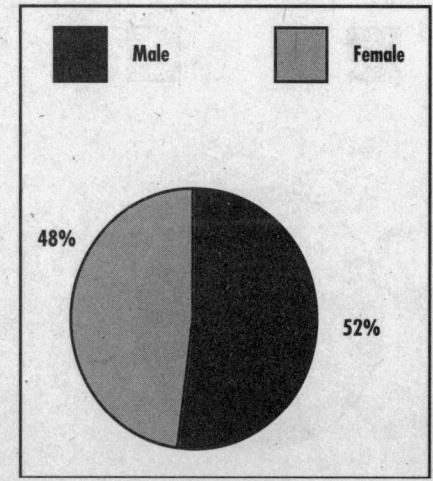

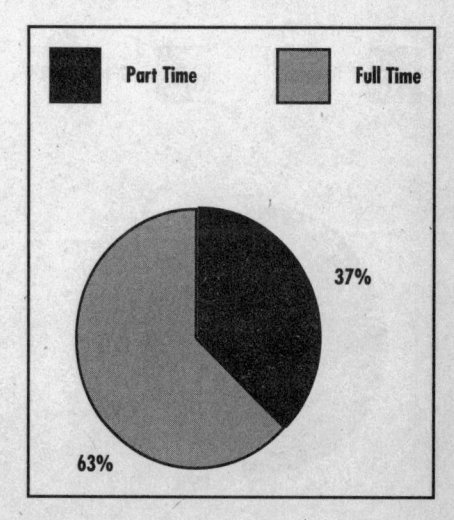

SOUTHERN ILLINOIS UNIVERSITY — CARBONDALE
College of Business Administration

Admissions Contact: Joe Pineau, Coordinator, MBA Program
Address: Rehn Hall 133, Carbondale, IL 62901-4625
Admissions Phone: 618-453-3030 • Admissions Fax: 618-453-7961
Admissions E-mail: mbagp@cba.siu.edu • Web Address: www.cba.siu.edu

The focus of Southern Illinois University—Carbondale's MBA program is to prepare students for managerial positions in profit and nonprofit organizations and in business, government, education, and health sectors. Whether or not a student possesses an undergrad business degree, SIU is willing to impart upon him or her problem-solving and decision-making skills that lead to success in management. SIU is proud to provide a comprehensive business education focusing on the political, social, legal, and economic forces at work in business environments.

INSTITUTIONAL INFORMATION
Public/Private: Public
Evening Classes Available? No
Total Faculty: 40
Student/Faculty Ratio: 6:1
Students in Parent Institution: 22,250
Academic Calendar: Semester

PROGRAMS
Degrees Offered: Master of Business Administration (MBA) (33 credits, 12 months to 2 years); Executive Master of Business Administration (EMBA) (33 credits, 18 months)
Joint Degrees: MBA/JD (105 credits, 3 to 4 years); MBA/Master of Science in Agribusiness Economics (MBA/MS) (51 credits, 12 months to 2.5 years); MBA/Master of Arts in Communication (MBA/MA) (51 credits, 12 months to 2.5 years)
Study Abroad Options: France—ESC Grenoble and Sup de Co Montpellier

STUDENT INFORMATION
Total Business Students: 128
% Full Time: 88
% Female: 43
% Minority: 8
% Out of State: 11
% International: 50
Average Age: 26

COMPUTER AND RESEARCH FACILITIES
Research Facilities: Pontikes Center
Computer Facilities: 3 university computer labs, including 1 in the College of Business
Campuswide Network? No
% of MBA Classrooms Wired: 100
Computer Model Recommended: Laptop
Internet Fee? No

EXPENSES/FINANCIAL AID
Annual Tuition (Resident/Nonresident): $4,000/$8,200

ADMISSIONS INFORMATION
Application Fee: $35
Electronic Application? No
Regular Application Deadline: 6/15
Regular Notification: 1/1
Deferment Available? Yes
Length of Deferment: 1 year
Non-fall Admissions? Yes
Non-fall Application Deadline(s): 11/15, 4/15, 9/15, 2/15

Transfer Students Accepted? Yes
Transfer Policy: Maximum number of transfer credits accepted for core curriculum is 6.
Need-Blind Admissions? No
Number of Applications Received: 278
% of Applicants Accepted: 52
% Accepted Who Enrolled: 46
Average GPA: 3.3
GPA Range: 2.4-3.7
Average GMAT: 533
GMAT Range: 470-590
Average Years Experience: 4
Other Schools to Which Students Applied: Eastern Illinois University, University of Illinois at Urbana-Champaign, University of Missouri-Columbia, Western Illinois University

INTERNATIONAL STUDENTS
TOEFL Required of International Students? Yes
Minimum TOEFL: 550 (220 computer)

EMPLOYMENT INFORMATION
Placement Office Available? Yes

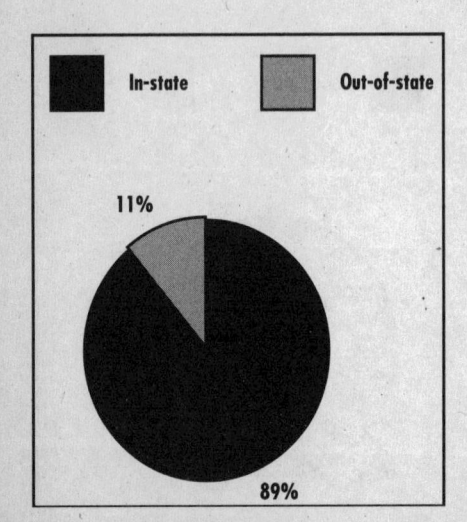

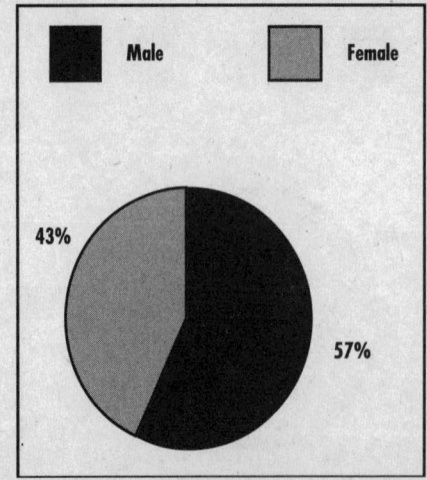

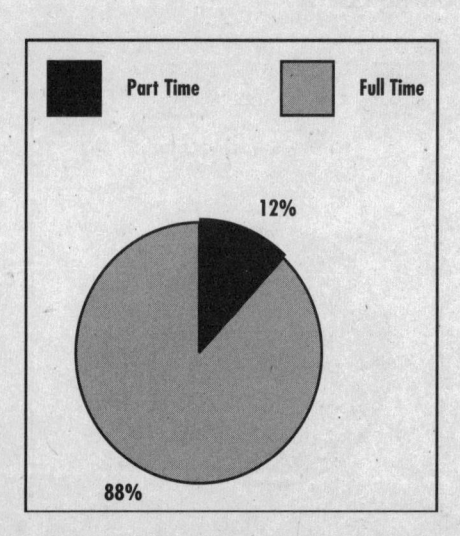

---

360 • COMPLETE BOOK OF BUSINESS SCHOOLS

SOUTHERN ILLINOIS UNIVERSITY — EDWARDSVILLE
School of Business

Admissions Contact: Dr. Kathryn Martell, Associate Dean for Academic Affairs
Address: Campus Box 1051, Edwardsville, IL 62026
Admissions Phone: 618-650-3840 • Admissions Fax: 618-650-3979
Admissions E-mail: mba@siue.edu • Web Address: www.siue.edu/BUSINESS

The SIU—Edwardsville MBA education encompasses "the social, economic, political, regulatory, and cultural forces that shape the external environment in which an organization operates." MBA students at Southern Illinois—Edwardsville can choose between a general MBA and an MBA specializing in either e-commerce or management information systems. SIU also hosts a notable lecture series called Executive Business Hour, which grants students the opportunity to meet and learn from successful business leaders and then bring their enriching lessons back to class, where they may be applied to the curriculum.

INSTITUTIONAL INFORMATION
Public/Private: Public
Evening Classes Available? Yes
Total Faculty: 56
% Faculty Female: 19
% Faculty Minority: 12
Student/Faculty Ratio: 19:1
Students in Parent Institution: 12,442

PROGRAMS
Degrees Offered: Master of Business Administration (12 months to 6 years); Master of Science in Accounting (12 months to 6 years); Master of Science in Economics and Finance (12 months to 6 years); Master of Arts in Economics and Finance (12 months to 6 years); Master of Science in Computing and Information Systems (12 months to 6 years); Master of Science in Marketing Research (12 months to 6 years); MBA with Management Information System Specialization (12 months to 6 years); MBA with E-Business Specialization (12 months to 6 years)
Special Opportunities: The calendar is divided into 10-week semesters beginning in August, November, February, and May.
Study Abroad Options: Europe, Mexico

STUDENT INFORMATION
Total Business Students: 255
% Female: 45
% Minority: 5
% International: 16
Average Age: 32

COMPUTER AND RESEARCH FACILITIES
Research Facilities: Lovejoy library; 20 million items at 45 member libraries as well as 800 other Illinois libraries can be identified and borrowed.
Computer Facilities: 400 on-campus computer terminals/PCs are available for student use, and all or some are linked by a campuswide network. The network has full access to the Internet.
Campuswide Network? Yes
Internet Fee? No

EXPENSES/FINANCIAL AID
Annual Tuition (Resident/Nonresident): $2,034/$4,068
Tuition Per Credit (Resident): $339
Room & Board (On Campus): $4,552
Books and Supplies: $1,000

ADMISSIONS INFORMATION
Application Fee: $30
Electronic Application? Yes
Regular Application Deadline: 7/15
Regular Notification: 1/1
Deferment Available? Yes
Non-fall Admissions? Yes
Non-fall Application Deadline(s): 30 days prior to first day of class
Transfer Students Accepted? Yes
Transfer Policy: Up to 9 credits from an accredited school
Need-Blind Admissions? No
Average GPA: 3.2
Average GMAT: 520
Average Years Experience: 9
Other Admissions Factors Considered: Bachelor's degree, minimum GPA of 2.5, college transcripts
Other Schools to Which Students Applied: Saint Louis University, Washington University in St. Louis, University of Missouri-St. Louis

INTERNATIONAL STUDENTS
TOEFL Required of International Students? Yes
Minimum TOEFL: 550 (213 computer)

EMPLOYMENT INFORMATION
Placement Office Available? Yes
Prominent Alumni: Robert Baer, president and CEO, United Van Lines; Wilton Heylinger, dean, School of Business, Morris Brown College; Ralph Korte, president, Korte Construction Company; Mitch Meyers, president, Zipatoni Company; James Milligan, president (retired), Spalding Sports Center

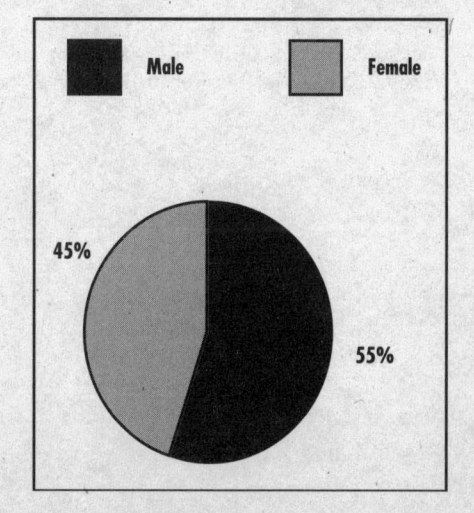

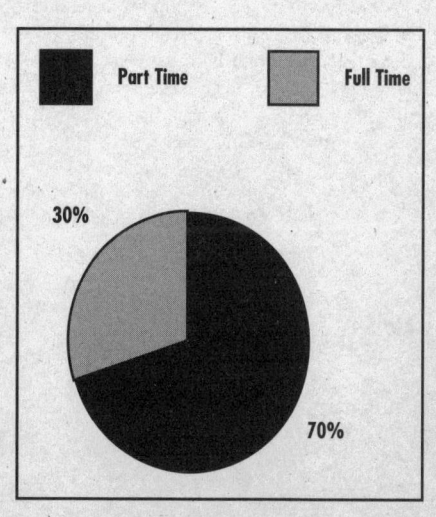

Male / Female: 55% / 45%
Part Time / Full Time: 70% / 30%

SOUTHERN METHODIST UNIVERSITY

THE SCHOOL AT A GLANCE

"In the new economy of the twenty-first century, the MBA Program at the Cox School of Business in Dallas, Texas, is positioned to provide you with all of the benefits of an exciting and rewarding business career. Through our unique combination of programs and extensive connections to the business community, the Cox School will prepare you to be a leader in this rapidly changing and globally oriented economy. The American Airlines Global Leadership Program will provide you with a hands-on experience in one of the three major business regions of the world—Asia, Latin America, and Europe. Our e-Business Initiative at Cox (ebi@cox) supplements traditional business training with a curriculum focused on the role of emerging technologies. Cox's unique Business Leadership Center hones your leadership and management skills, and our Executive Mentor Program matches you with a senior-level business executive who can act as a career coach and role model. Only the MBA Program at the Cox School offers these programs to enhance your career, provide hands-on business learning, and enrich your personal experience."

—Albert W. Niemi Jr., Dean

STUDENTS

Cox students come from all regions of the United States and the world. The MBA program consists of more than 230 full-time students, with 27 percent hailing from countries other than the U.S. Students have a wide variety of academic disciplines and professional experiences. The average amount of work experience prior to entering the MBA program is slightly more than four years, and the average age is approximately 27. Women comprise more than 30 percent of the population, and minorities account for 14 percent of the student body.

Cox's small size not only promotes collaboration among students, it also creates a close and supportive environment for students, the faculty, and the staff. The small size also gives students significant opportunities to assume leadership roles in MBA student organizations, such as the Finance Club, the Investment Club, the Marketing Club, the Consulting Club, Women in Business, and the Hi Tech Club.

At Cox, interaction with the business community is encouraged and formalized for students. The School established the Associate Board Executive Mentor Program with nearly 200 top business executives who actively serve as mentors to Cox MBA students.

In addition to being a valuable source of business contacts, a mentor relationship provides students with insightful career advice, an inside track on current business trends, and a valuable perspective from an experienced business person.

Prominent Cox alumni include Howard M. Dean, CEO and director, Dean Foods; Martin Flanagan, senior vice president and CFO, Franklin Resources; Charles Hansen Jr., chairman and CEO, Pillowtex Corporation; James MacNaughton, managing director, Salomon Smith Barney; Megan Pryor, vice president of sales, Pepsi Cola; John J. Murphy, former chairman, president, and CEO, Dresser Industries; William O'Neill, chairman, Investor's Business Daily; and John Tolleson, former chairman and CEO, First USA.

ACADEMICS

The Cox MBA Program provides an integrated curriculum that helps students establish a solid foundation for success in business. The small class size encourages students to work closely with the faculty and individualize their MBA experience. Located in Dallas, a national and international business center, the Cox School MBA Program offers nationally recognized faculty members, a global focus, and close ties with the business community. At Cox, MBAs gain much more than a business education—they gain a personalized business experience.

The new, two-year MBA curriculum began in the fall of 2000. Composed of 56 credit hours that include a global experience and a modular curriculum, the Cox School's new program builds a strong portfolio of diverse international perspectives and course offerings for the Cox MBA student who is graduating in the twenty-first century. Also new is the e-Business Initiative at Cox (ebi@cox). In partnership with industry, the Cox School has established this program to better prepare its MBA students for the digital economy. ebi@cox offers a leading-edge curriculum to educate existing and future business leaders and provide real-time education through internships and on-site projects that enhance the experience of MBA students. Such courses include e-Commerce, Internet Marketing, Internet Entrepreneurship, and Venture Capital in the Internet Economy.

First-year students complete nine core courses, the Global Leadership Program (GLP), and a business elective course. Students commence their summer internships after they return from the GLP travel-abroad experience. Second-year students take courses from the new modular curriculum and one core course that builds upon the GLP experience. The new modular curriculum allows students to take up to 18 modules, which are 6.5-week short courses. Some of these courses are closely integrated, while others are short, stand-alone courses. This design provides students with greater curriculum flexibility, which allows students to build depth in an area of emphasis or create breadth for a broader perspective of business. MBAs can choose from such areas as e-business, finance, business policy, marketing, entrepreneurship, accounting, organizational behavior, business administration, information science and operations management, and real estate.

Cox's distinguished Business Leadership Center (BLC) complements the classroom curriculum throughout the two-year period. The BLC's innovative program is designed to help students develop effective management skills through seminars that center on interpersonal and communication skills, team building, and negotiation skills. Courses are organized by business leaders and taught by outside consultants from some of today's most progressive corporations.

In addition to the full-time two-year MBA program, Cox offers a part-time, three-year professional MBA program developed for working professionals and a 21-month executive MBA program for candidates with significant managerial experience.

Joint degree programs are offered in conjunction with the law school for a Juris Doctor/MBA (4.5 years) and with the Meadows School of Arts for a Master of Arts in administration/MBA (6 semesters).

Cox School of Business

Like the Business Leadership Center, Cox institutes provide a forum for students, faculty members, and the business community to participate in interactive programs and research. The Caruth Institute of Owner-Managed Business focuses on entrepreneurship, the Maguire Oil & Gas Institute promotes the study of oil and gas industry issues, and the SMU Finance Institute promotes interaction between financial practitioners and the SMU finance community.

Cox students benefit from a nationally recognized faculty that is approachable and accessible and is as dedicated to teaching as it is to research. Classes are taught using a variety of teaching methods that are best suited for the course material, including cases, lectures, class discussions, student presentations, team and field projects, and computer simulations. The Cox MBA curriculum is developed to equally emphasize quantitative and qualitative skills.

Today's business leaders must be global thinkers. At Cox, global thinking is incorporated into the MBA curriculum. The Global Leadership Program is a mandatory, three-week, travel-abroad course. All first-year students travel to one of three regions of the world—Asia, Europe, or Latin America—to meet with business and government leaders. The goal is to allow students to experience how business is conducted globally. In addition, the School's location at the gateway to NAFTA and Latin America is well positioned for enhancing international perspectives.

An international exchange program allows select students to experience their international business education firsthand by studying abroad. Cox has relationships with schools in Australia, Belgium, Brazil, Denmark, England, France, Hungary, Japan, Mexico, Singapore, Spain, and Venezuela.

CAMPUS LIFE

SMU, established in 1911, has six different schools and graduate programs in addition to its undergraduate program. The total undergraduate and graduate population is 10,361 students. The University's location in one of the world's major centers of commerce gives students an excellent advantage. The city of Dallas ranks third in the United States as a site of major corporate headquarters and sixth in the world for multinational corporate headquarters. Dallas offers a wide variety of cultural events and opportunities, from national league sports to the nationally renowned Myerson Symphony Center and the Dallas Museum of Art.

From state-of-the-art classrooms to the Business Information Center, the Cox School offers the latest in business technologies. As of fall 2000, the Cox School offers 802.11b Wireless Networking. This technology allows a student to use his or her own laptop computer on the network from a classroom. After class, students can walk from a classroom to a study room and continue to use the Internet from their computer on the network. Students utilize an in-house network (accessible from home) to communicate with other students and faculty members, connect with the Internet to conduct classroom assignments, and access numerous business databases and research tools.

The MBA Career Management Office (CMO) partners with students to help develop and implement successful career strategies. Students participate in the Career Management Training Program and receive individualized career counseling sessions year-round. In 2000, internship placement reached 100 percent, and graduates increased their salaries by 24 percent over 1999 graduates, which reflects the strength of the student body.

COSTS

The cost of tuition and fees for 2001–2002 is estimated at $25,946; books and supplies are approximately $1,200. Off-campus housing generally costs between $600 and $1,200 per month. Scholarships are available and are awarded strictly on merit.

ADMISSIONS

Admission to the MBA programs at the Edwin L. Cox School of Business is highly selective. The Admissions Committee seeks to admit students who represent various geographic, economic, religious, and ethnic groups and have a diverse set of work experiences.

Successful applicants are well-rounded individuals who have clearly demonstrated academic achievement in addition to a commitment and capacity for leadership in today's dynamic business world.

Students enter the full-time program in the fall semester only (orientation is held mid-August). Application deadlines for all applicants to the full-time MBA program are as follows: November 30, January 30, March 15, and May 1. To be considered for scholarships, students should apply by February 12. International students should apply by March 30. After May 1, admission decisions are made on a space-available basis.

Students enter the part-time program in the fall (orientation is held in August) and spring (orientation is held in January). The application deadline for fall admission is May 30; for spring admission, November 1. For more information, contact:

Director of MBA Admissions
Edwin L. Cox School of Business
Southern Methodist University
PO Box 750333
Dallas, TX 75275-0333
Telephone: 214-768-1214
800-472-3622 (toll free)
Fax: 214-768-3956
E-mail: M.B.A.info@mail.cox.smu.edu
World Wide Web: http://mba.cox.smu.edu

Admissions Contact: Arrion Rathsack, Associate Director, MBA Admissions
Address: PO Box 750333, Dallas, TX 75275
Admissions Phone: 214-768-1214 • Admissions Fax: 214-768-3956
Admissions E-mail: mbainfo@mail.cox.smu.edu • Web Address: mba.cox.smu.edu

SOUTHERN METHODIST UNIVERSITY
Cox School of Business

Admissions Contact: Arrion Rathsack, Associate Director, MBA Admissions
Address: PO Box 750333, Dallas, TX 75275
Admissions Phone: 214-768-1214 • *Admissions Fax:* 214-768-3956
Admissions E-mail: mbainfo@mail.cox.smu.edu • *Web Address:* mba.cox.smu.edu

"Open-door policy" doesn't even describe the amount of attention that the faculty at SMU's "state-of-the-art" Cox School of Business heap on the MBA students. "We can meet with our professors at any time," gloats one student. "We often have happy hours together." Cox students also laud the tremendously popular mentor program and the Business Leadership Center, and they tell us that "Dallas is an incredible resource for jobs and a great lifestyle."

INSTITUTIONAL INFORMATION
Public/Private: Private
Evening Classes Available? Yes
Total Faculty: 105
% Faculty Female: 29
% Faculty Minority: 10
% Faculty Part Time: 22
Student/Faculty Ratio: 4:1
Students in Parent Institution: 9,513
Academic Calendar: Semester

PROGRAMS
Degrees Offered: MBA (full time and part time, 2 to 3 years); Executive MBA (EMBA) (21 months); MSA (2 years)
Joint Degrees: JD/MBA (4 years + 1 semester); MA/MBA Arts Administration (24 months)
Academic Specialties: General Management, Accounting, Financial Consulting, Finance, Telecommunications and Electronic Commerce, Management Consulting and Strategy, Marketing, Strategy and Entrepreneurship
Special Opportunities: Executive Mentor Program, International Exchange Opportunities, Global Leadership Program, Career Management Training Program, FINA Foundation Business Leaders Spotlight Series, Management Briefing Series
Study Abroad Options: Australia, Belgium, Brazil, Mexico, Venezuela, Japan, Singapore, Denmark, England, France, Spain, China

STUDENT INFORMATION
Total Business Students: 843
% Full Time: 27
% Female: 28
% Minority: 10
% Out of State: 41
% International: 24
Average Age: 28

COMPUTER AND RESEARCH FACILITIES
Research Facilities: Caruth Institute of Owner Managed Business, Business Leadership Center, Finance Institute, Maguire Oil and Gas Institute, Business Information Center, Center for Research in Real Estate and Land Use Economics
Computer Facilities: Students have access to a variety of libraries, business-related CD-ROM products, and subscription Internet databases.
Campuswide Network? Yes
% of MBA Classrooms Wired: 100
Computer Model Recommended: Laptop
Internet Fee? No

EXPENSES/FINANCIAL AID
Annual Tuition: $26,090
Tuition Per Credit: $849
Room & Board (Off Campus): $8,398
Books and Supplies: $1,650
Average Grant: $12,500
% Receiving Financial Aid: 85
% Receiving Aid Their First Year: 85

ADMISSIONS INFORMATION
Application Fee: $50
Electronic Application? Yes
Early Decision Application Deadline: 11/30
Early Decision Notification: 1/30
Regular Application Deadline: 5/1
Regular Notification: 6/15
Length of Deferment: 1 year
Non-fall Admissions? No
Transfer Students Accepted? No
Need-Blind Admissions? Yes
Number of Applications Received: 597
% of Applicants Accepted: 32
% Accepted Who Enrolled: 64
Average GPA: 3.2
GPA Range: 2.8-3.5
Average GMAT: 651
GMAT Range: 580-720
Average Years Experience: 5
Other Admissions Factors Considered: Applicant's maturity, drive, initiative
Minority/Disadvantaged Student Recruitment Programs: NSHMBA and NBMBAA events
Other Schools to Which Students Applied: Duke, Emory, Georgetown, Rice, UT Austin, Vanderbilt, Washington U. in St. Louis

INTERNATIONAL STUDENTS
TOEFL Required of International Students? Yes
Minimum TOEFL: 600 (250 computer)

EMPLOYMENT INFORMATION

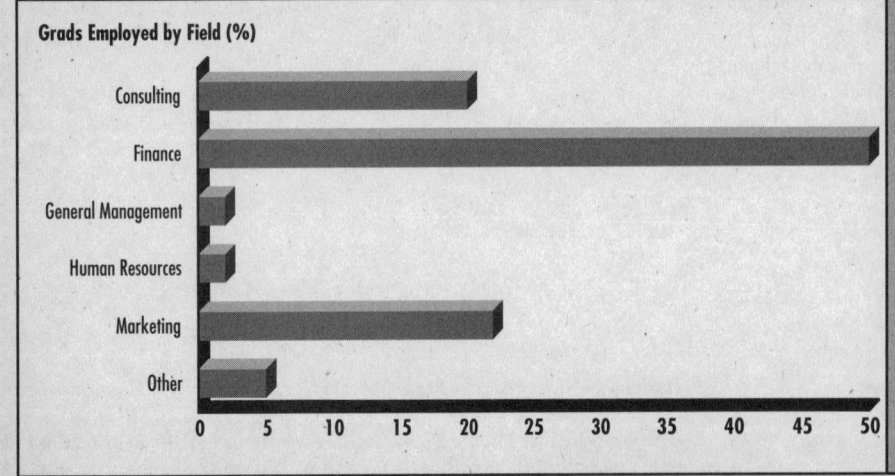

Grads Employed by Field (%)
- Consulting: 20
- Finance: 50
- General Management: 2
- Human Resources: 3
- Marketing: 22
- Other: 3

Placement Office Available? Yes
% Employed Within 3 Months: 91
Frequent Employers: American Airlines, SABRE, Deloitte Consulting, ExxonMobil, TXU, El Paso Corporation
Prominent Alumni: Thomas W. Horton, senior VP and CFO, American Airlines; David B. Miller, managing director, El Paso Energy; Ruth Ann Marshall, president, MasterCard; James MacNaughton, managing director, Rothschild, Inc.; C. Fred Ball, CEO, Bank of Texas

SOUTHWEST MISSOURI STATE UNIVERSITY
College of Business Administration

Admissions Contact: Derek Mallett, Graduate College Coordinator
Address: 901 S. National, Springfield, MO 65804
Admissions Phone: 417-836-5335 • Admissions Fax: 417-836-6888
Admissions E-mail: GraduateCollege@smsu.edu • Web Address: www.coba.smsu.edu

Breakfast of Champions is a lecture series at Southwest Missouri State's College of Business Administration, where local business executives speak and interact with the students, allowing connections to be made and opportunities to multiply. The long list of on-campus recruiters on SMSU's website further attests to the school's close ties to the business community. SMSU offers a general MBA and a Techno-MBA, designed for students seeking an MBA with a concentration in computer information systems. The quality and low cost of living in Springfield, located near the beautiful Ozark area, provides students with a comfortable arrangement and easy access to incredible recreational activities.

INSTITUTIONAL INFORMATION
Public/Private: Public
Evening Classes Available? Yes
Total Faculty: 70
Student/Faculty Ratio: 20:1
Students in Parent Institution: 17,733

PROGRAMS
Degrees Offered: Master in Business Administration (1 to 2 years); Master in Accountancy (1 to 2 years); Master in Health Administration (1 to 2 years)
Academic Specialties: Accounting, Computer Information Systems, Management, Marketing, Finance and General Business, Human Resource Management, International Management, Logistics

STUDENT INFORMATION
Total Business Students: 299
% Female: 41
% Minority: 33
% International: 33
Average Age: 29

COMPUTER AND RESEARCH FACILITIES
Computer Facilities: Computer labs in Glass Hall, Cheek Hall, and Public Affairs; computer facilities in dormitories
Campuswide Network? Yes
% of MBA Classrooms Wired: 100
Internet Fee? No

EXPENSES/FINANCIAL AID
Annual Tuition (Resident/Nonresident): $2,835/$5,670
Tuition Per Credit (Resident/Nonresident): $135/$270
Room & Board: $4,800
Books and Supplies: $800
Average Grant: $5,000
Average Loan: $10,000
% Receiving Financial Aid: 43

ADMISSIONS INFORMATION
Application Fee: $25
Electronic Application? Yes
Regular Application Deadline: Rolling
Regular Notification: Rolling
Deferment Available? Yes
Length of Deferment: 1 semester
Non-fall Admissions? Yes
Non-fall Application Deadline(s): 3 weeks before term begins
Transfer Students Accepted? Yes
Transfer Policy: With advisor permission
Need-Blind Admissions? No
Number of Applications Received: 361
% of Applicants Accepted: 88
% Accepted Who Enrolled: 18
Average GPA: 3.3
GPA Range: 2.2-4.0
Average GMAT: 520
GMAT Range: 430-630
Average Years Experience: 4
Other Schools to Which Students Applied: Arkansas State University, Central Missouri State University, Southeast Missouri State University, University of Arkansas-Little Rock, University of Missouri-Columbia, University of Missouri-Kansas City, University of Missouri-St. Louis

INTERNATIONAL STUDENTS
TOEFL Required of International Students? Yes
Minimum TOEFL: 550

EMPLOYMENT INFORMATION

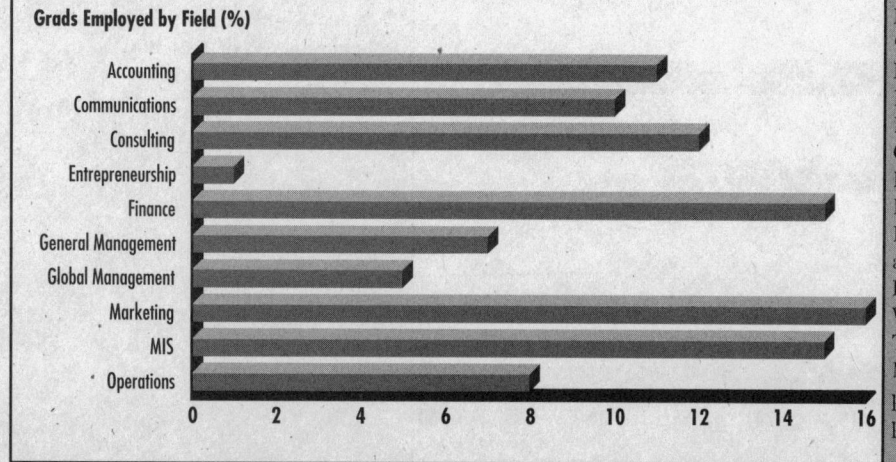

Placement Office Available? Yes
% Employed Within 3 Months: 79
Frequent Employers: Wal-Mart, Payless Shoes, Hallmark, Samson, Federal Express, Anheuser-Busch, DataTronics, Edward Jones, State Farm, Caterpillar, Occidental Petroleum, Renaissance Financial, John Hancock, Arthur Andersen, Boeing, State Street, Gateway Financial, Federal Reserve Bank, Cerner, Target, Toys R Us, Federated Insurance, Enterprise
Prominent Alumni: David Glass, former CEO, Wal-Mart, and CEO, Kansas City Royals; Todd Tiahrt, four-term U.S. Congressman; Richard McClure, president, Uni Group, Inc.; Jim Smith, president, ABA (2001-2002); Terry Thompson, president, Jack Henry

STANFORD UNIVERSITY
Stanford Graduate School of Business

Admissions Contact: Derrick Bolton, Director of MBA Admissions
Address: 518 Memorial Way, Stanford, CA 94305-5015
Admissions Phone: 650-723-2766 • Admissions Fax: 650-725-7831
Admissions E-mail: mba@gsb.stanford.edu • Web Address: www.gsb.stanford.edu

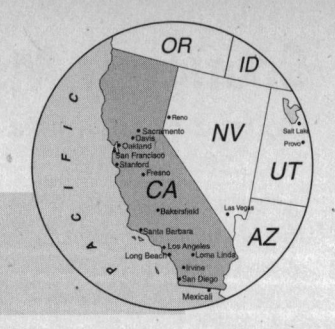

Feeling lucky? Got credentials out the wazoo? Check out Stanford's Graduate School of Business, home to an "entrepreneurial spirit," a "supportive and comfortable atmosphere," a great social life, and a Nobel Prize–winning faculty. Stanford MBAs are sane again after the demise of the heady days of the Silicon Valley rush, but this is still CEO training ground. Students graduate as stellar general managers (Stanford doesn't produce specialists) with a proclivity for networking and landing leadership posts.

INSTITUTIONAL INFORMATION
Public/Private: Private
Evening Classes Available? No
Total Faculty: 121
Student/Faculty Ratio: 6:1
Academic Calendar: Quarter

PROGRAMS
Degrees Offered: Sloan Program (leads to MS) (10 months); PhD (4 years)
Joint Degrees: It is possible to earn dual degrees with other departments. Common area is JD/MBA.
Academic Specialties: General Management includes all majors disciplines; Finance, Economics, Strategic Management, Marketing, Accounting, Human Resources/Organizational Behavior, Operations, Information and Technology, Political Science, Entrepreneurship
Special Opportunities: Global Management Program, Public Management Program

STUDENT INFORMATION
Total Business Students: 755
% Female: 38
% Minority: 24
% International: 26
Average Age: 27

COMPUTER AND RESEARCH FACILITIES
Research Facilities: Center for Entrepreneurial Studies at Stanford, Center for Electronic Business and Commerce, Center for Social Innovation, Alliance for Innovative Manufacturing, Global Organization of Business Enterprise, Global Supply Chain Management Forum, Stanford Project on Emerging Companies
Computer Facilities: The school has its own computer center state-of-the-art networking, online, and CD-ROM databases in the business school library. Schwab residence for first-year MBA students offers full network access.
Campuswide Network? Yes
% of MBA Classrooms Wired: 100
Computer Model Recommended: Laptop
Internet Fee? No

EXPENSES/FINANCIAL AID
Annual Tuition: $31,002
Room & Board (On Campus): $13,512
Average Grant: $11,355
% Receiving Financial Aid: 63

ADMISSIONS INFORMATION
Application Fee: $180
Electronic Application? Yes
Regular Application Deadline: Rolling
Regular Notification: Rolling
Deferment Available? Yes
Length of Deferment: Case-by-case basis
Non-fall Admissions? No
Transfer Students Accepted? No
Need-Blind Admissions? Yes
Number of Applications Received: 5,253
% of Applicants Accepted: 9
% Accepted Who Enrolled: 79
Average GPA: 3.5
GPA Range: 3.4-4.0
Average GMAT: 718
GMAT Range: 680-780
Average Years Experience: 5
Other Admissions Factors Considered: Strong academic aptitude, managerial potential, diversity among students
Minority/Disadvantaged Student Recruitment Programs: Partnership for Diversity Program offers financial support and professional experience to selected minority admits.
Other Schools to Which Students Applied: Harvard University

INTERNATIONAL STUDENTS
TOEFL Required of International Students? Yes

EMPLOYMENT INFORMATION

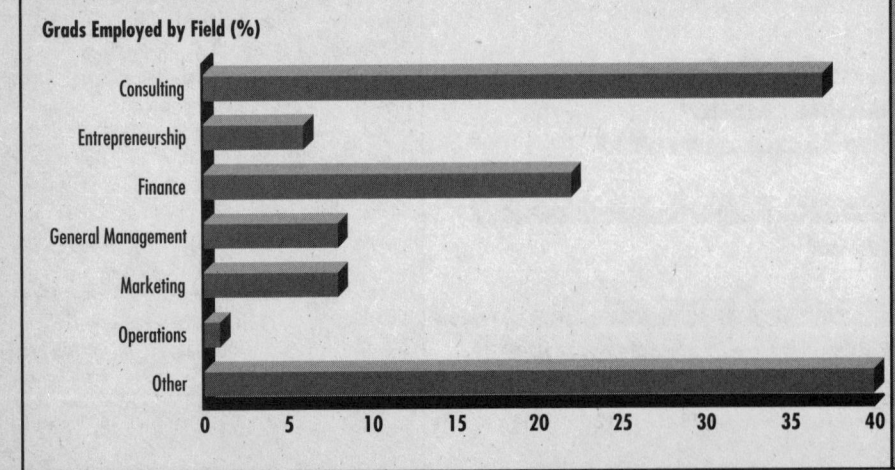

Grads Employed by Field (%)
- Consulting: ~38
- Entrepreneurship: ~5
- Finance: ~22
- General Management: ~8
- Marketing: ~7
- Operations: ~1
- Other: ~40

Placement Office Available? Yes
% Employed Within 3 Months: 94
Frequent Employers: McKinsey & Co., Boston Consulting Group, Goldman Sachs, Booz Allen Hamilton, Bain & Co., Siebel Systems Inc., Cisco Systems Inc., Deloitte Consulting, Monitor Company, Accenture, Merrill Lynch, The Bridgespan Group
Prominent Alumni: Phil Knight, chairman and CEO, Nike Inc.; Charles Schwab, chairman and CEO; Henry McKinnell, chairman and CEO, Pfizer Co.; Mads Ovlisen, president and CEO, Novo Nordisk A/S Denmark; Dominick Cadbury, chairman, Schwepps PLC

STATE UNIVERSITY OF WEST GEORGIA
Richards College of Business

Admissions Contact: John R. Wells, Director, MBA Program
Address: 1600 Maple Street, Carrollton, GA 30118-3000
Admissions Phone: 770-836-6467 • Admissions Fax: 770-836-6774
Admissions E-mail: jwells@westga.edu • Web Address: www.westga.edu

The Richards College of Business is proud to offer the Georgia Web MBA, an online degree opportunity available through a consortium of five University System of Georgia member institutions. The Web MBA is a 10-course distance learning program, designed for middle- and upper-management professionals who wish to attain an education without interrupting their careers. The general AACSB-accredited MBA is a nonthesis program with a broad-based curriculum designed to serve a whole range of students: those looking for a terminal degree to increase their competencies, those looking for in-service training, and those looking to prepare for doctoral studies in business.

INSTITUTIONAL INFORMATION
Public/Private: Public
Evening Classes Available? Yes
Total Faculty: 28
Student/Faculty Ratio: 19:1
Students in Parent Institution: 9,030
Academic Calendar: Semester

PROGRAMS
Degrees Offered: General MBA (12 months), Master of Professional Accountancy (12 months)
Academic Specialties: Case study, computer aided instruction, computer analysis, computer simulations, experiential learning, group discussion, lecture, research, seminars by members of the business community, simulations, student presentations, study groups, team projects

STUDENT INFORMATION
Total Business Students: 64
% Full Time: 52
% Female: 33
% Minority: 40
% Out of State: 48
% International: 52
Average Age: 30

COMPUTER AND RESEARCH FACILITIES
Research Facilities: Ingram Library
Computer Facilities: Computer labs with more than 100 seats, databases, and Microsoft applications
Campuswide Network? Yes
% of MBA Classrooms Wired: 100
Computer Model Recommended: No
Internet Fee? No

EXPENSES/FINANCIAL AID
Annual Tuition (Resident/Nonresident): $2,770/$9,526
Books and Supplies: $1,111

ADMISSIONS INFORMATION
Application Fee: $20
Electronic Application? Yes
Regular Application Deadline: 7/2
Regular Notification: 8/2
Deferment Available? Yes
Length of Deferment: 1 year
Non-fall Admissions? Yes
Non-fall Application Deadline(s): 12/10 spring, 5/28 summer
Transfer Students Accepted? Yes
Transfer Policy: Transfer students can transfer 2 courses from an accredited program.
Need-Blind Admissions? No
Average GPA: 3.0
GPA Range: 2.6-3.5
Other Admissions Factors Considered: Computer experience, résumé, GPA of last 2 years

INTERNATIONAL STUDENTS
TOEFL Required of International Students? Yes
Minimum TOEFL: 550 (213 computer)

EMPLOYMENT INFORMATION
Placement Office Available? Yes

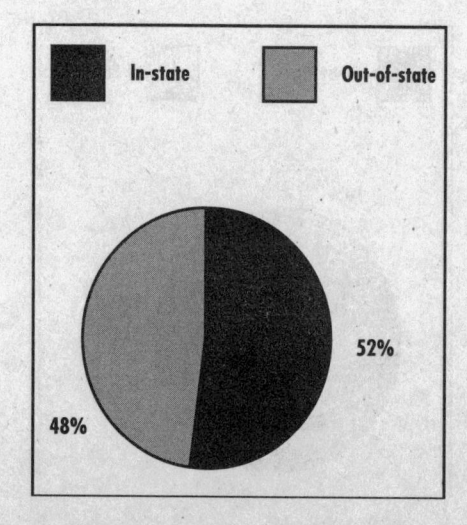

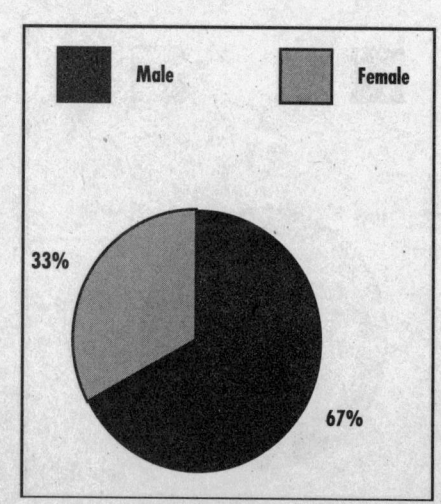

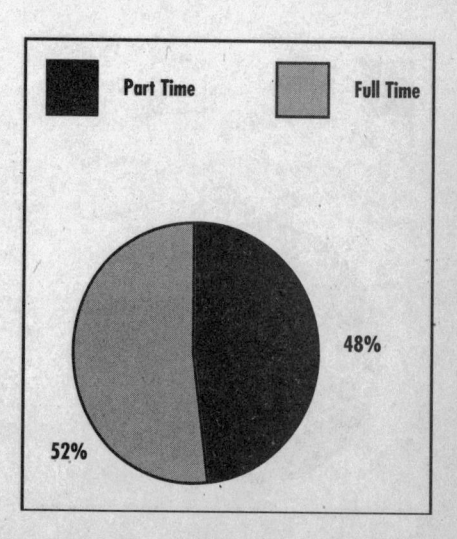

In-state: 48% / Out-of-state: 52%
Male: 67% / Female: 33%
Part Time: 52% / Full Time: 48%

STEPHEN F. AUSTIN STATE UNIVERSITY
College of Business

Admissions Contact: Violet Rogers, MBA Director
Address: PO Box 13004, Nacogdoches, TX 75962
Admissions Phone: 936-468-3101 • Admissions Fax: 936-468-1560
Web Address: www.cob.sfasu.edu

Make sure you can pronounce "Nacogdoches," the name of the city that Stephen F. Austin State University calls home, before you apply to the College of Business MBA program. The MBA program is designed primarily for part timers, as most classes are scheduled during evening hours, but full-time students may enroll as well. An SFASU MBA education provides advanced training in the theory and practice of management and exposes students to a wide assortment of fundamental business disciplines. At the host institution, business majors currently account for about 22 percent of the more than 11,000 students. Applicants to the College of Business also apply to Texas A&M and University of Texas at Tyler.

INSTITUTIONAL INFORMATION
Public/Private: Public
Evening Classes Available? Yes
Total Faculty: 25
% Faculty Female: 50
% Faculty Minority: 5
Student/Faculty Ratio: 16:1
Students in Parent Institution: 11,500

PROGRAMS
Degrees Offered: Master of Professional Accountancy (MPA) (36 hours); Master of Business Administration (MBA) (36 hours); Master of Science in Computer Science (MS) (36 hours)

STUDENT INFORMATION
Total Business Students: 65
% Full Time: 10
% Female: 40
% Minority: 11
% Out of State: 2
% International: 2
Average Age: 28

COMPUTER AND RESEARCH FACILITIES
Computer Facilities: Library research databases
Campuswide Network? Yes
Computer Model Recommended: Desktop
Internet Fee? No

EXPENSES/FINANCIAL AID
Annual Tuition (Resident/Nonresident): $432/$2,976
Tuition Per Credit (Resident/Nonresident): $120/$744
Room & Board (On/Off Campus): $4,500/$6,000
Books and Supplies: $1,000
Average Grant: $3,300
Average Loan: $3,300
% Receiving Financial Aid: 9
% Receiving Aid Their First Year: 9

ADMISSIONS INFORMATION
Electronic Application? Yes
Regular Application Deadline: 7/1
Regular Notification: 8/1
Deferment Available? Yes
Length of Deferment: 1 year
Non-fall Admissions? Yes
Non-fall Application Deadline(s): 12/1, 5/1
Transfer Students Accepted? Yes
Transfer Policy: May transfer 6 credits from an AACSB International-accredited school
Need-Blind Admissions? Yes
Number of Applications Received: 56
% of Applicants Accepted: 89
% Accepted Who Enrolled: 78
Average GPA: 3.0
GPA Range: 2.6-3.3
Average GMAT: 482
GMAT Range: 440-530
Average Years Experience: 5
Minority/Disadvantaged Student Recruitment Programs: Post minority scholarships on bulletin board

INTERNATIONAL STUDENTS
TOEFL Required of International Students? Yes
Minimum TOEFL: 550 (213 computer)

EMPLOYMENT INFORMATION
Placement Office Available? Yes
% Employed Within 3 Months: 100
Frequent Employers: Temple Inland, ExxonMobil, Andersen, Haliburton

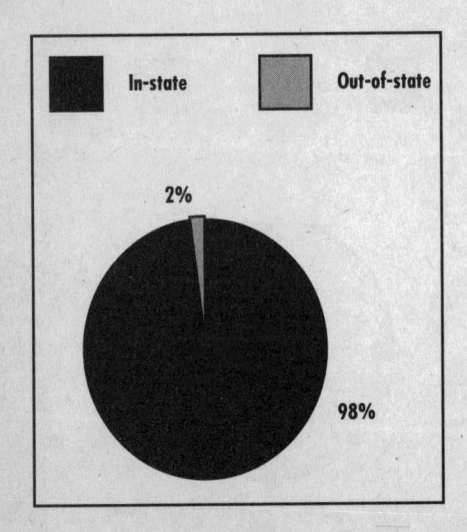

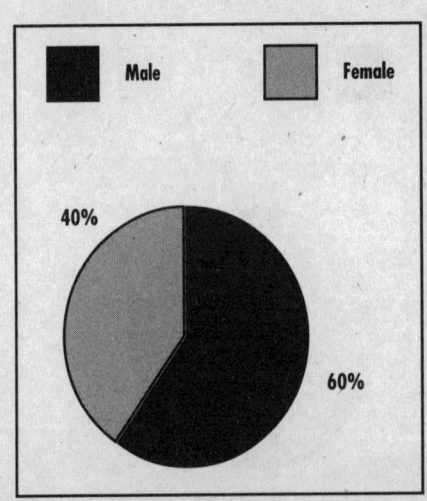

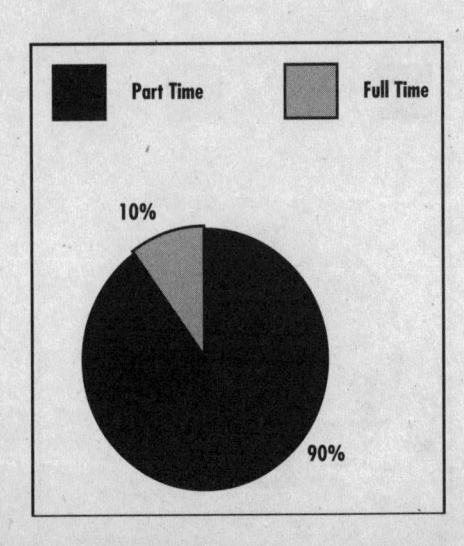

In-state: 98% / Out-of-state: 2%

Male: 60% / Female: 40%

Part Time: 90% / Full Time: 10%

SUFFOLK UNIVERSITY
Frank Sawyer School of Management

Admissions Contact: Judith L. Reynolds, Director of Graduate Admissions
Address: 8 Ashburton Place, Boston, MA 02108
Admissions Phone: 617-573-8302 • *Admissions Fax:* 617-523-0116
Admissions E-mail: grad.admission@admin.suffolk.edu • *Web Address:* www.sawyer.suffolk.edu

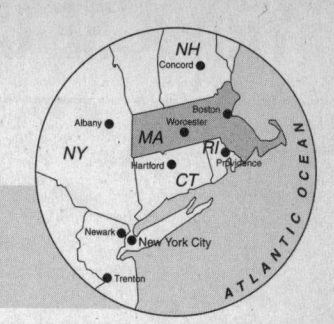

It would be nearly impossible for a prospective b-school student not to find a suitable MBA program at the Frank Sawyer School of Management. Students may enroll part time or full time, and classes are offered mostly at night but also during the day, on Saturdays, and during two summer sessions. Suffolk offers 13 MBA programs to choose from, including a general MBA and ranging from the MBA for pharmacists to the Accelerated MBA for music management majors at Berklee College of Music, as well as MBA programs at three other campuses and a summer session in Senegal. Frequent employers of Suffolk grads include Fidelity Investments, State Street Bank, and Fleet Financial.

INSTITUTIONAL INFORMATION
Public/Private: Private
Evening Classes Available? Yes
Total Faculty: 148
% Faculty Female: 26
% Faculty Minority: 5
% Faculty Part Time: 53
Student/Faculty Ratio: 12:1
Students in Parent Institution: 7,078
Academic Calendar: Semester

PROGRAMS
Degrees Offered: Accelerated MBA for attorneys (full time, 1 year); Executive MBA (15 to 21 months); MBA (full time, 10 to 16 months); MBA in Entrepreneurship (full time, 10 to 16 months)
Joint Degrees: JD/MPA (full time, 4 years); JD/MBA (part time, 5 years); MBA/MSA (full time, 2 years); MBA/MST (full time, 2 years); MBA/GDPA (1 to 2 years)
Academic Specialties: Entrepreneurship, International Business, Finance
Study Abroad Options: Italy, China, France, Argentina, Ireland, Spain, Prague (all 1- to 2-week seminars)

STUDENT INFORMATION
Total Business Students: 774
% Full Time: 21
% Female: 41
% Minority: 4
% Out of State: 4
% International: 61
Average Age: 33

COMPUTER AND RESEARCH FACILITIES
Computer Facilities: Lexis-Nexis, Info Track, ABI/Inform, Compustat, Dun & Bradstreet, PredicastsProut, General Business File ASAP, Wall Street Journal, Academic Universe, FIS Online, Reference USA
Campuswide Network? Yes
% of MBA Classrooms Wired: 8
Computer Model Recommended: Laptop
Internet Fee? No

EXPENSES/FINANCIAL AID
Annual Tuition: $20,440
Room & Board (Off Campus): $9,500
Books and Supplies: $700
Average Grant: $3,270
Average Loan: $14,259
% Receiving Financial Aid: 22

ADMISSIONS INFORMATION
Application Fee: $50
Electronic Application? No
Regular Application Deadline: 6/15
Regular Notification: Rolling
Deferment Available? Yes
Length of Deferment: 1 year
Non-fall Admissions? Yes
Non-fall Application Deadline(s): 11/15 spring, 4/15 summer
Transfer Students Accepted? Yes
Transfer Policy: Same as for regular applicants
Need-Blind Admissions? Yes
Number of Applications Received: 498
% of Applicants Accepted: 79
% Accepted Who Enrolled: 57
Average GPA: 3.2
GPA Range: 2.8-3.4
Average GMAT: 505
GMAT Range: 430-550
Average Years Experience: 3
Other Admissions Factors Considered: Length and quality of work experience
Minority/Disadvantaged Student Recruitment Programs: Attendance at underrepresented students' college fairs
Other Schools to Which Students Applied: Bentley College, Boston College, Boston University, Northeastern University, University of Massachusetts-Amherst

INTERNATIONAL STUDENTS
TOEFL Required of International Students? Yes
Minimum TOEFL: 550 (213 computer)

EMPLOYMENT INFORMATION

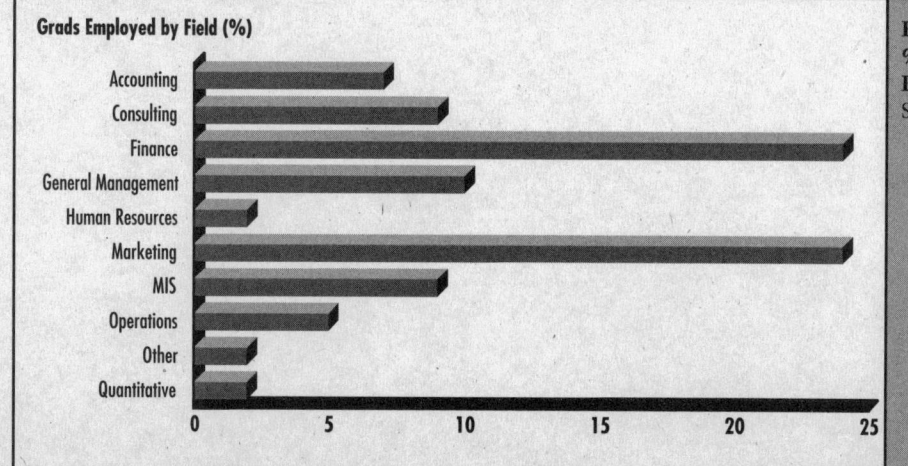

Placement Office Available? Yes
% Employed Within 3 Months: 95
Frequent Employers: Fidelity Investments, State Street Bank, Fleet Financial

Grads Employed by Field (%)

Field	%
Accounting	7
Consulting	7
Finance	24
General Management	9
Human Resources	2
Marketing	24
MIS	9
Operations	4
Other	2
Quantitative	1

SYRACUSE UNIVERSITY

THE SCHOOL AT A GLANCE

The School of Management (SOM) at Syracuse University offers one- and two-year full-time MBA programs; part-time evening MBA, Independent Study MBA (IS/MBA), and Executive MBA (EMBA) programs; three Master of Science (MS) programs; and dual degree programs. The SOM also offers a PhD program in management. All degree programs are accredited by AACSB—he International Association for Management Education.

Highlights of the program include the following:

Diverse degree offerings including Independent Study MBA
International business perspectives
Internship, study abroad, and fieldwork opportunities
Program accredited by AACSB

STUDENTS

International students comprise more than 30 percent of the student body at the SOM. International students on the SU campus come from over 100 countries, including Korea, China, Bulgaria, France, Canada, and Germany.

The Office of International Students (OIS) offers services ranging from immigration advice to personal counseling. OIS is housed in its own building and is a friendly place for all students to visit, relax, read a newspaper, and talk with staff. The office organizes many social and cultural events to promote on-campus diversity.

ACADEMICS

The SOM delivers MBA programs in various formats, including the traditional two-year MBA structure, a one-year Accelerated MBA, an EMBA program, an evening program, and an independent study program. The EMBA and evening and independent study programs can be completed without interruption to students' full-time careers. SOM's EMBA is designed for professionals with eight years of experience looking to move into senior-level management positions. The accelerated program is targeted to students who have an undergraduate degree in business from an accredited institution in the United States, and at least four years of full-time work experience. Applicants to this program must also achieve at least 650 points on the GMAT exam.

SOM's two-year MBA curriculum integrates the teaching of traditional management fundamentals and the innovations necessary for success in today's rapidly changing business world. At the beginning of the program, students are grouped into teams of five or six who work on a variety of group projects throughout the entire first year. First-year students follow a set of core courses, such as Accounting and Data Analysis. Classes are taught using forum-style lectures and often include other methods, such as case studies, computer simulations, and field studies.

The second year of the program offers students a high degree of flexibility. Students have the opportunity to select one or two areas of concentration. The SOM offers traditional concentrations such as accounting, finance, marketing management, and general management, as well as several progressive concentrations, including global entrepreneurship, innovation management, management of technology, and supply chain management. Students spend the summer between their first and second years in either an internship placement or in a study abroad program.

In their second year of studies, students begin the capstone challenge; two courses that require the integration of all the skills and tools gained throughout the program into one consulting project. Students work in their given teams, first on formulating strategy in the classroom and then on implementing these ideas in the business world.

International perspectives are incorporated throughout the program; more than half the professors at the SOM have experience in the global marketplace. With international students comprising 40 percent of the student population, each team is guaranteed to include an exciting mixture of nationalities and cultural perspectives.

Students can choose to spend the summer between their first and second year studying abroad in Shanghai. There are also international internship placements available in London or Singapore. The SOM is committed to providing students with a global outlook.

The SOM offers three master's programs, leading to an MS in accounting, finance, or media management. The School also works in cooperation with other graduate schools at SU to offer combined degrees in law, environmental science, media, public administration, and nursing.

School of Management

CAMPUS LIFE

Founded in 1870, Syracuse University is a private, nonsectarian research institution consisting of 13 colleges offering over 250 programs of study. One of the oldest schools in the state of New York, SU is also one of only 56 research universities in the U.S. to be elected to the prestigious Association of American Universities (AAU). SU offers a remarkable combination of academic excellence and a relaxed lifestyle amid the splendor of upstate New York.

The 220-acre campus rests on a hill overlooking the city of Syracuse, providing an ideal blend of urban and peaceful environments. SU consists of 170 buildings surrounding a historic central quadrangle. The University has more than 15,000 students; over 70 percent live in the 13 residence halls on campus. The student/faculty ratio is 12:1.

The Career Center at the SOM offers a wide variety of employment services for graduate business students. The center organizes workshops throughout the year on such topics as resume writing, career planning, interview skills, and job-search techniques. The School's extensive internship program is also run through the Center. The SOM actively promotes its graduates by participating in several MBA consortia and by organizing career fairs. Student resumes are also posted on the Internet. The Career Center library contains numerous online databases and other career resources such as newspapers and company profiles. High-profile executives are often on the SU campus to speak about current business trends, and students are encouraged to take advantage of the School's vast alumni network for career advice.

SU is a 20-minute walk from downtown Syracuse, a medium-sized city with many recreational and cultural options, including parks, museums, art galleries, and a symphony orchestra. Located in the geographical center of New York State, Syracuse enjoys four distinct seasons and is only a five-hour drive from the largest city in the U.S., New York City. We are also within easy driving distance of Boston, Toronto, Niagara Falls, and Providence.

ADMISSIONS

Admission to the SOM master's programs is highly selective; in a typical year, fewer than 25 percent of all applicants are selected for admission. The SOM seeks candidates who can contribute to SU and who aim to assume leadership roles in organizations around the world—individuals who have displayed the drive, the leadership potential, and the intellectual capacity to achieve their goals.

Individuals who have obtained the equivalent of a U.S. bachelor's degree from a fully accredited university are eligible for admission to the SOM. Previous study of business is not required; however, students are expected to be familiar with basic tools of quantitative analysis, including finite mathematics. Courses in introductory calculus and economics are also recommended. Students interested in the Accelerated MBA program must have a bachelor's degree in business and at least four years of full-time work experience, and must achieve a GMAT score of 650 or higher. For admission to the MS programs in accounting and finance, students should have appropriate backgrounds in accounting, finance, economics, and quantitative methods.

The admissions committee uses several criteria in their admissions decisions, including the applicant's academic achievement, communication skills, previous work history, and standardized test scores. A completed application form must be accompanied by two letters of recommendation from past supervisors or professors, a current resume, two copies of all academic transcripts, a GMAT score, essays, and a $50 application fee. The SOM strongly encourages students to participate in an evaluative interview, which can be done on campus or via the phone. Since the admissions decision involves several criteria, there are no set minimums for the GMAT or GPA average. The 2000 entering class had an average GPA of 3.2 on a 4.0 scale and an average GMAT score of 630.

In addition to the above, international students must also submit an official financial statement verifying access to at least $28,000 to cover the year's expenses. International students whose native language is not English are also required to submit a paper-based TOEFL score of 580 (237 on the computer-based test) in order to be considered for admission.

The SOM strongly encourages students to apply through the Internet at www.multi-app.com. The deadline for applications is May 1.

Admissions Contact: Carol J. Swanberg, Director of Admissions and Financial Aid
Address: 900 South Crouse Avenue, Suite 100, Syracuse, NY 13244-2130
Admissions Phone: 315-443-9214 • Admissions Fax: 315-443-9517
Admissions E-mail: MBAinfo@som.syr.edu • Web Address: www.som.syr.edu

SYRACUSE UNIVERSITY
School of Management

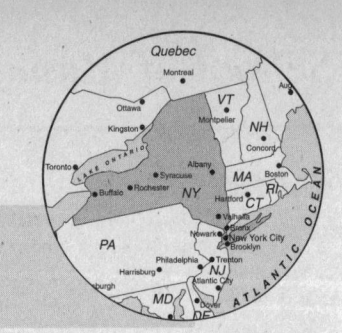

Admissions Contact: Carol J. Swanberg, Director of Admissions and Financial Aid
Address: 900 South Crouse Avenue, Suite 100, Syracuse, NY 13244-2130
Admissions Phone: 315-443-9214 • *Admissions Fax:* 315-443-9517
Admissions E-mail: MBAinfo@som.syr.edu • *Web Address:* www.som.syr.edu

Syracuse University's School of Management is, by its own account, "driven by the entrepreneurial spirit," and students say the "entrepreneurship professors are exceptional." The faculty in other areas are "spotty," though, and Syracuse winters can be brutal. Weather permitting, the generally "young" MBA students here enjoy a beautiful 200-acre campus replete with grassy lawns and historic buildings by day and a decent downtown bar and restaurant scene by night.

INSTITUTIONAL INFORMATION
Public/Private: Private
Evening Classes Available? Yes
Total Faculty: 58
% Faculty Female: 18
% Faculty Part Time: 10
Student/Faculty Ratio: 9:1
Students in Parent Institution: 18,186
Academic Calendar: Semester

PROGRAMS
Degrees Offered: MBA (2 years); MS Accounting (1 year); MS Media Management (1 year)
Joint Degrees: MBA/Juris Doctorate; MBA/MS Nursing Management
Academic Specialties: Accounting, Finance, Global Entrepreneurship, Marketing Management, Innovation Management, Management of Technology, Supply Chain Management, General Management
Special Opportunities: Full-Time MBA, Evening MBA, Independent Study MBA, Executive MBA
Study Abroad Options: International Campuses: London, England; Shanghai, China; Harare, South Africa; Madrid, Spain; Singapore. Exchange Programs: University of Shanghai for Science and Technology (Shanghai, China), National Chengchi University (Taipei, China), Kyung Hee University and Sejong University (Seoul, Korea), University of Limerick (Limerick, Ireland)

STUDENT INFORMATION
Total Business Students: 521
% Full Time: 36
% Female: 30
% Minority: 15
% International: 32
Average Age: 27

COMPUTER AND RESEARCH FACILITIES
Research Facilities: Ballentine Center (securities), Falcone Center (entrepreneurship), Kiebach Center (international business), Franklin Salzberg (logistics), Brethen Center (operations)
Computer Facilities: Library CD-ROM databases, electronic teaching stations, free dial-up Internet access, computers in group study areas, marketracks MX (stock market feed), high-performance Internet access, e-mail accounts
Campuswide Network? Yes
Computer Model Recommended: Laptop
Internet Fee? No

EXPENSES/FINANCIAL AID
Annual Tuition: $19,410
Tuition Per Credit: $647
Room & Board: $11,820
Books and Supplies: $1,270
Average Grant: $10,000
Average Loan: $17,000
% Receiving Financial Aid: 50
% Receiving Aid Their First Year: 50

ADMISSIONS INFORMATION
Application Fee: $50
Electronic Application? Yes
Regular Application Deadline: 5/1
Regular Notification: Rolling
Length of Deferment: 1 year
Non-fall Admissions? No
Transfer Students Accepted? No
Need-Blind Admissions? Yes
Number of Applications Received: 475
% of Applicants Accepted: 29
% Accepted Who Enrolled: 42
Average GPA: 3.2
Average GMAT: 636
GMAT Range: 570-700
Average Years Experience: 4
Other Admissions Factors Considered: Quality of full-time work experience, appropriateness for Syracuse's program, evidence of leadership potential, motivation, teamwork ability, perseverance
Minority/Disadvantaged Student Recruitment Programs: Feeder program with Florida A&M
Other Schools to Which Students Applied: Boston University, Cornell, NYU, Pennsylvania State—Harrisburg, U. of Illinois at Urbana-Champaign, U. of Rochester, U. of Wisconsin—Madison

INTERNATIONAL STUDENTS
TOEFL Required of International Students? Yes
Minimum TOEFL: 580 (237 computer)

EMPLOYMENT INFORMATION

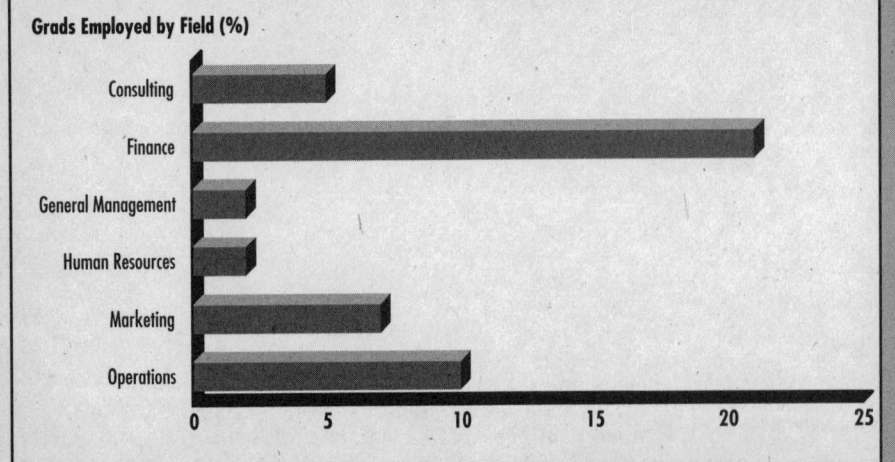

Grads Employed by Field (%)
- Consulting: ~5
- Finance: ~21
- General Management: ~7
- Human Resources: ~7
- Marketing: ~8
- Operations: ~10

Placement Office Available? Yes
% Employed Within 3 Months: 88
Frequent Employers: Eastman Kodak Company, Cisco Systems, United Technologies, IBM, American Airlines, Lockheed Martin, Intel, Goldman Sachs, Canon

TCU
M.J. Neeley School of Business

Admissions Contact: Peggy Conway, Director of MBA Admissions
Address: PO Box 298540, Fort Worth, TX 76129
Admissions Phone: 817-257-7531 • Admissions Fax: 817-257-6431
Admissions E-mail: mbainfo@tcu.edu • Web Address: www.mba.tcu.edu

Thanks to its prime location in the Dallas/Fort Worth Metroplex, students at TCU's very affordable Neeley School of Business have "great connections" all over the region. Neeley also offers a unique finance elective that allows students to manage the $1.3 million William C. Connor Educational Investment Fund. If you are looking for an affordable place to get your MBA, you will be hard-pressed to beat Neeley, especially if you want a career in Dallas.

INSTITUTIONAL INFORMATION
Evening Classes Available? Yes
Total Faculty: 61
% Faculty Female: 10
% Faculty Minority: 12
% Faculty Part Time: 21
Student/Faculty Ratio: 5:1
Students in Parent Institution: 8,054
Academic Calendar: Semester

PROGRAMS
Degrees Offered: MBA (full time, 21 months); Professional (evening, 28 to 33 months); Accelerated full-time (12 months) for applicants with a BBA, at least 3 years of postgraduate work experience, and minimum GMAT of 620; Executive MBA (21 months); MAcc (Master of Accounting) (1 year)
Joint Degrees: Educational Leadership MBA/EdD (3 years); Physics PhD/MBA (6 years including dissertation)
Academic Specialties: Finance, Corporate Finance, Investment Management, Marketing, Value-Chain Marketing, International Business, E-Business, Entrepreneurship, Management
Special Opportunities: Professional Development Program, Educational Investment Fund, MBA Enterprise Program, Center for Professional Communication, Global Experiences
Study Abroad Options: Germany, France, Hungary, Mexico

STUDENT INFORMATION
Total Business Students: 243
% Female: 28
% Minority: 8
% International: 40
Average Age: 28

COMPUTER AND RESEARCH FACILITIES
Research Facilities: Charles Tandy American Enterprise Center, Ryffel Entrepreneurship Center, Supply-Chain Management Institute
Computer Facilities: 2 on-site labs with more than 80 PCs, 8 other labs, wide variety of research databases available.
Campuswide Network? Yes
% of MBA Classrooms Wired: 100
Computer Model Recommended: No
Internet Fee? No

EXPENSES/FINANCIAL AID
Annual Tuition: $11,340
Tuition Per Credit: $420
Books and Supplies: $1,000
Average Grant: $9,647
Average Loan: $13,416
% Receiving Financial Aid: 80
% Receiving Aid Their First Year: 84

ADMISSIONS INFORMATION
Application Fee: $50
Electronic Application? Yes
Early Decision Application Deadline: Rolling; applications accepted as early as 9/1
Early Decision Notification: 12/1
Regular Application Deadline: 4/30
Regular Notification: Rolling
Length of Deferment: 1 year
Non-fall Admissions? No
Transfer Policy: 6 hours from AACSB-accredited institution
Need-Blind Admissions? Yes
Number of Applications Received: 229
% of Applicants Accepted: 53
% Accepted Who Enrolled: 48
Average GPA: 3.1
GPA Range: 2.7-3.5
Average GMAT: 601
GMAT Range: 540-630
Average Years Experience: 4
Other Admissions Factors Considered: Desire and ability to perform in a highly interactive, team-based environment
Minority/Disadvantaged Student Recruitment Programs: Henry B. Gonzalez and Martin Luther King, Jr. scholarships by the PepsiCo Foundation
Other Schools to Which Students Applied: Baylor, Southern Methodist, Texas A&M, Tulane, UT Arlington, UT Austin

INTERNATIONAL STUDENTS
TOEFL Required of International Students? Yes
Minimum TOEFL: 550 (213 computer)

EMPLOYMENT INFORMATION

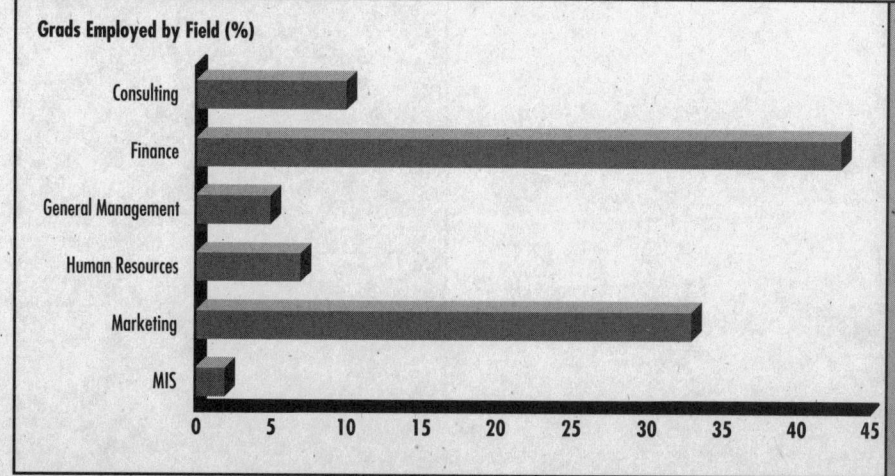

Grads Employed by Field (%)
- Consulting: ~10
- Finance: ~43
- General Management: ~5
- Human Resources: ~7
- Marketing: ~33
- MIS: ~2

Placement Office Available? Yes
% Employed Within 3 Months: 83
Frequent Employers: SABRE, Burlington Northern Santa Fe, Arthur Andersen, Accenture, Verizon, VHA/Novation, TXU, Alcon, AMR, Citigroup, Deloitte & Touche, Southwest Securities, Bank of America
Prominent Alumni: John Roach, Roach Investments/Field Electronics; Luther King, Luther King Capital Management; John Davis III, CEO and chairman, Pegasus Systems; Vivian Noble Dubose, president, Noble Properties

TEMPLE UNIVERSITY
Fox School of Business and Management

Admissions Contact: Natale A. Butto, Director, Graduate Admissions
Address: 1810 North 13th Street, Speakman Hall, Room 5, Philadelphia, PA 19122
Admissions Phone: 215-204-5890 • Admissions Fax: 215-204-1632
Admissions E-mail: masters@sbm.temple.edu • Web Address: www.sbm.temple.edu

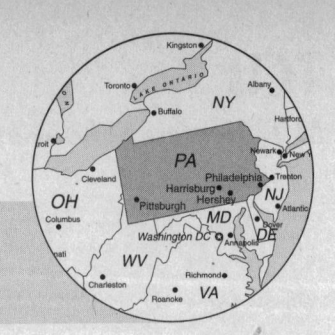

Temple University's Fox School of Business and Management, among the largest comprehensive business schools in the world, has 13 MBA programs available in the evening to part-time students. Fox promises a "results-oriented" and "student-centered" education to all students, although only 35 percent are registered as full timers. One of the Fox options is the unique International MBA, an 11-month tricontinent learning experience in the world's major economic regions—four months in Paris, six months in Philadelphia, and one month in Tokyo.

INSTITUTIONAL INFORMATION
Public/Private: Public
Evening Classes Available? Yes
Total Faculty: 153
% Faculty Female: 18
% Faculty Minority: 20
% Faculty Part Time: 17
Student/Faculty Ratio: 8:1
Students in Parent Institution: 29,872

PROGRAMS
Degrees Offered: MBA with 13 concentrations: Accounting, Business Administration, E-Business, Economics, Finance, General & Strategic Management, Healthcare Management, Human Resource Administration, International Business Administration, International Business (Tri-Continent), Management Information Systems, Management Science/Operations Management, and Risk Management & Insurance (1 year to 18 months); Executive MBA (Tokyo and Philadelphia) (2 years); MA in Economics; MS in Accounting, Actuarial Sciences, Finance, Healthcare Financial Management, Management Information Systems, Management Science/Operations Management, Marketing, or Statistics
Joint Degrees: JD/MBA; MD/MBA; DMD/MBA; MBA/MS in E-Business (2 years); MBA/MS in Healthcare Management/Healthcare Financial Management (2 years).
Study Abroad Options: Japan, France, Italy, India

STUDENT INFORMATION
Total Business Students: 868
% Full Time: 35
% Female: 35
% Minority: 13
% International: 47
% Out of State: 57
Average Age: 30

COMPUTER AND RESEARCH FACILITIES
Research Facilities: Irwin Gross eBusiness Institute; Innovation and Entrepreneurship Institute; Institute for Global Management Studies; Small Business Development Center.
Computer Facilities: 170 computers, 170 databases available through the Internet, IBM server lab
Campuswide Network? Yes
Computer Model Recommended: Laptop
Internet Fee? No

EXPENSES/FINANCIAL AID
Annual Tuition (Resident/Nonresident): $8,760/$14,040
Tuition Per Credit (Resident/Nonresident): $365/$585
Room & Board (On/Off Campus): $8,250/$11,000
Books and Supplies: $1,100

ADMISSIONS INFORMATION
Application Fee: $40
Electronic Application? Yes
Regular Application Deadline: 4/15
Regular Notification: Rolling
Length of Deferment: 1 year
Non-fall Application Deadline(s): 9/30, 3/15
Transfer Policy: Up to 6 upper-level credits
Need-Blind Admissions? Yes
Number of Applications Received: 574
% of Applicants Accepted: 63
% Accepted Who Enrolled: 50
Average GPA: 3.1
GPA Range: 2.9-3.5
Average GMAT: 565
GMAT Range: 530-600
Average Years Experience: 3
Other Admissions Factors Considered: Work experience and statement of goals that expresses the direction and how an MBA will serve that goal.
Minority/Disadvantaged Student Recruitment Programs: Participate in an annual state-wide conference for minority undergraduate students looking to further their education. Participate with KPMG in their diversity recruiting.
Other Schools to Which Students Applied: Drexel, Saint Joseph's, Villanova

INTERNATIONAL STUDENTS
TOEFL Required of International Students? Yes
Minimum TOEFL: 575 (230 computer)

EMPLOYMENT INFORMATION

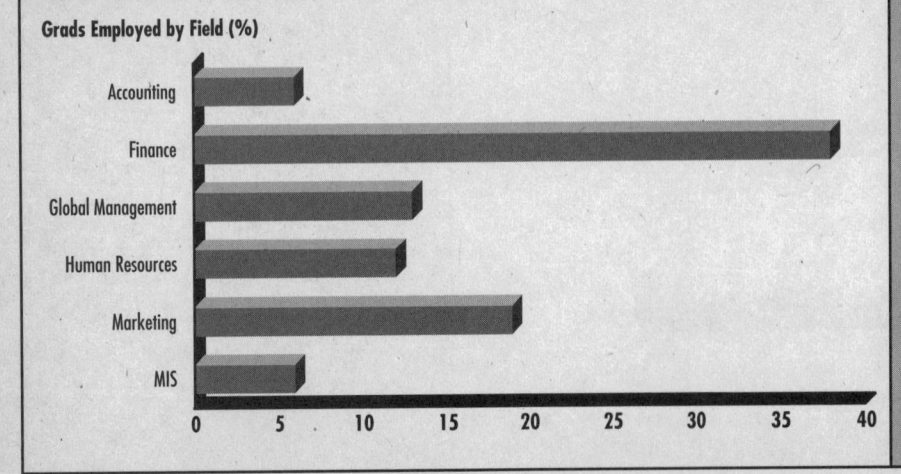

Grads Employed by Field (%)
- Accounting: ~5
- Finance: ~38
- Global Management: ~13
- Human Resources: ~13
- Marketing: ~19
- MIS: ~5

Placement Office Available? Yes
% Employed Within 3 Months: 100
Frequent Employers: Mass Mutual, Cigna, Vanguard, J.P. Morgan, William M. Mercer, Wyeth Ayerst, Merck, GlaxoSmithKline, IBM, Subaru of America, Independence Blue Cross, Eli Lilly, First Union, Lands End, Unisys, KPMG

TENNESSEE TECHNOLOGICAL UNIVERSITY
College of Business Administration

Admissions Contact: Dr. Virginia Moore, Director of MBA Studies
Address: Box 5023, Cookeville, TN 38505
Admissions Phone: 931-372-3600 • Admissions Fax: 931-372-6249
Admissions E-mail: mbastudies@tntech.edu • Web Address: www2.tntech.edu/mba

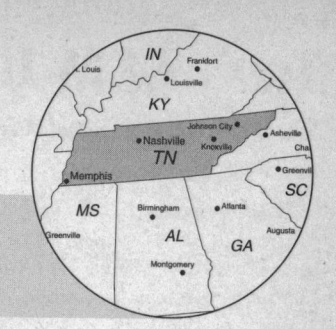

The Tennessee Technological University MBA program has a case method–based curriculum, and all applicants who haven't taken undergrad business prerequisites must take the Pre-MBA Foundation modules before getting started. TTU's one-year MBA program focuses on the advancement of written and oral communication skills and offers concentrations in accounting and management information. MBA students may start interviewing for jobs as soon as they matriculate, and should they happen to secure dream jobs while enrolled, they may simply complete the degree via Tennessee Tech's Distance MBA program.

INSTITUTIONAL INFORMATION
Public/Private: Public
Evening Classes Available? Yes
Total Faculty: 31
% Faculty Female: 23
Student/Faculty Ratio: 22:1
Students in Parent Institution: 8,500

PROGRAMS
Degrees Offered: MBA (36 credits, 12 months to 6 years)

STUDENT INFORMATION
Total Business Students: 122
% Full Time: 57
% Female: 24
% Minority: 10
% Out of State: 11
% International: 6
Average Age: 25

COMPUTER AND RESEARCH FACILITIES
Campuswide Network? Yes
% of MBA Classrooms Wired: 100
Computer Model Recommended: No
Internet Fee? No

EXPENSES/FINANCIAL AID
Annual Tuition (Resident): $6,472
Tuition Per Credit (Resident): $280
Room & Board (On Campus): $5,200
Books and Supplies: $800
Average Grant: $1,100
% Receiving Financial Aid: 38
% Receiving Aid Their First Year: 13

ADMISSIONS INFORMATION
Application Fee: $25
Electronic Application? Yes
Regular Application Deadline: Rolling
Regular Notification: Rolling
Deferment Available? Yes
Length of Deferment: 1 year
Non-fall Admissions? Yes
Non-fall Application Deadline(s): Rolling
Transfer Students Accepted? Yes
Transfer Policy: TTU will transfer 9 credits or less from an AACSB-accredited school.
Need-Blind Admissions? Yes
Number of Applications Received: 45
% of Applicants Accepted: 89
% Accepted Who Enrolled: 70
Average GPA: 3.3
GPA Range: 2.9-3.5

Average GMAT: 515
GMAT Range: 480-580
Average Years Experience: 3
Other Admissions Factors Considered: Interview, computer experience
Minority/Disadvantaged Student Recruitment Programs: Special minority fellowships and graduate assistantships

INTERNATIONAL STUDENTS
TOEFL Required of International Students? Yes
Minimum TOEFL: 550 (220 computer)

EMPLOYMENT INFORMATION
Placement Office Available? Yes
% Employed Within 3 Months: 95
Prominent Alumni: Harry Stonecipher, president and COO, Boeing; Lark Mason, VP, Sotheby's Inc. (world's largest auction house); Jimmy Bedford, master distiller, Jack Daniel's; Roger Crouch, astronaut; C. Stephen Lynn, former CEO, Shoney's Inc.

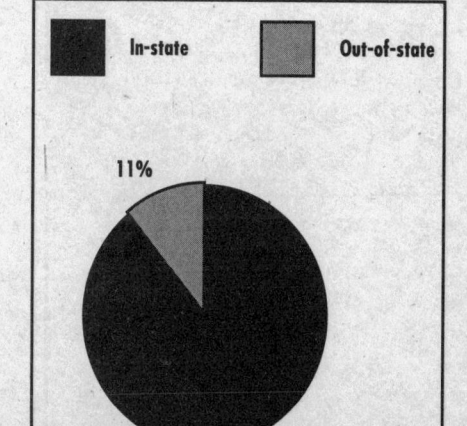

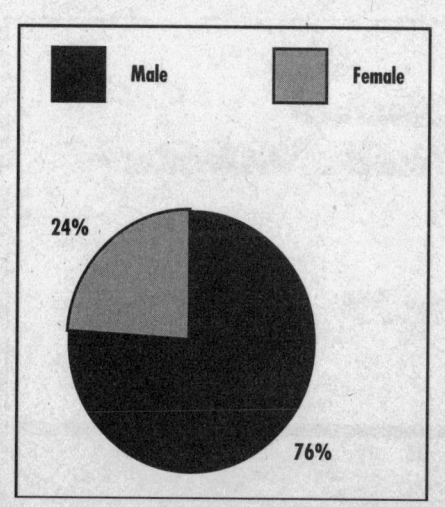

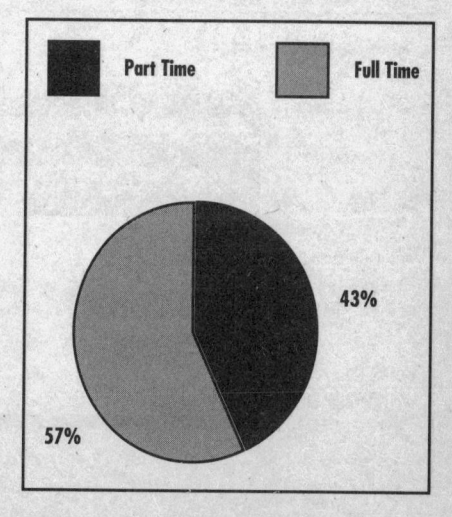

TEXAS A&M UNIVERSITY — COLLEGE STATION
Mays College and Graduate School of Business

Admissions Contact: Wendy Flynn, Assistant Director, Mays MBA
Address: TAMU 4117, College Station, TX 77845
Admissions Phone: 979-845-4714 • *Admissions Fax:* 979-862-2393
Admissions E-mail: maysmba@tamu.edu • *Web Address:* http://mba.tamu.edu

Texas A&M University's MBA program emphasizes extensive teamwork training and offers a great deal of program benefits, including business lectures with local business leaders and professional internship opportunities at home and abroad. Texas A&M is one of the few schools that offer students the chance to combine an MBA with a foreign business degree, available in conjunction with schools in Europe, Latin America, or the Pacific Rim. If you dazzle your professors, you may be chosen to participate in the Aggies on Wall Street program, which involves a three-week "immersion experience" or an enrichment experience in Washington, D.C.

INSTITUTIONAL INFORMATION
Public/Private: Public
Evening Classes Available? No
Total Faculty: 29
% Faculty Female: 35
% Faculty Minority: 10
Student/Faculty Ratio: 10:1
Students in Parent Institution: 43,000
Academic Calendar: Semester

PROGRAMS
Degrees Offered: MBA with concentrations in Accounting, Banking/Financial Markets, Consulting/Strategic Planning, E-Commerce, Finance, Human Resources, Management Information, Technology, International Business, Marketing Operations, Real Estate
Joint Degrees: Dual degree program (3 years)
Special Opportunities: 2-week intensive Wall Street program, 1-week program to explore business and government, Graduate Certificate in International Business
Study Abroad Options: Austria, China, England, France, Germany, Japan, Korea, Mexico, Netherlands, Switzerland

STUDENT INFORMATION
Total Business Students: 208
% Full Time: 100
% Female: 22
% Minority: 10
% Out of State: 30
% International: 27
Average Age: 29

COMPUTER AND RESEARCH FACILITIES
Research Facilities: Centers for Reliant Energy Securities and Commodities Trading, Real Estate, International Business, Retailing Management, Human Resources Development, and New Venture Capital
Computer Facilities: Fully furnished, Masters-student-only computer lab with 90+ Pentium computers available 24/7. MBA-only classrooms are equipped with the most current presentation technologies.
Campuswide Network? Yes
% of MBA Classrooms Wired: 100
Internet Fee? No

EXPENSES/FINANCIAL AID
Annual Tuition (Resident/Nonresident): $2,120/$7,818
Room & Board (Off Campus): $9,500
Books and Supplies: $700
Average Grant: $8,000
% Receiving Financial Aid: 90
% Receiving Aid Their First Year: 90

ADMISSIONS INFORMATION
Application Fee: $50
Electronic Application? Yes
Early Decision Application Deadline: Early application results in early decision
Early Decision Notification: 3/1
Regular Application Deadline: 5/1
Regular Notification: 6/1
Length of Deferment: 1 year
Non-fall Admissions? No
Transfer Students Accepted? No
Need-Blind Admissions? Yes
Number of Applications Received: 669
% of Applicants Accepted: 29
% Accepted Who Enrolled: 63
Average GPA: 3.3
GPA Range: 3.0-3.9
Average GMAT: 628
GMAT Range: 550-710
Average Years Experience: 5
Other Admissions Factors Considered: Work experience, 50th percentile on both sections of the GMAT
Minority/Disadvantaged Student Recruitment Programs: We aggressively seek to enhance diversity on all levels in our program and have recruitment programs in place.
Other Schools to Which Students Applied: Arizona State, Michigan State, Rice, University of Maryland—College Park, Notre Dame, Vanderbilt

INTERNATIONAL STUDENTS
TOEFL Required of International Students? Yes
Minimum TOEFL: 600 (250 computer)

EMPLOYMENT INFORMATION

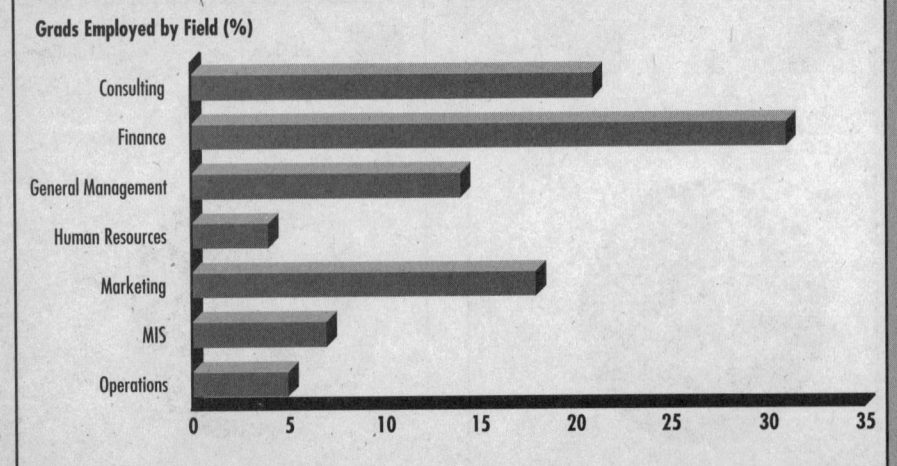

Placement Office Available? Yes
% Employed Within 3 Months: 98
Frequent Employers: Ford Motor Co., Duke Energy, Nortel Networks, Fed Ex, Dell, 3M, Accenture, PricewaterhouseCoopers, Compaq, Motorola, Exxon, Mobil, AT&T, Ernst & Young, Deloitte & Touche, Coral Energy, Reliant Energy, IBM, Halliburton, Texas Instruments, Hewlett Packard, Raytheon, Marathon Oil, Chevron, Ericsson, FMC Corp., Entergy

TEXAS A&M UNIVERSITY — COMMERCE
Graduate Programs in Business

Admissions Contact: Tammi Higginbotham, Admissions Advisor
Address: PO Box 3011, Commerce, TX 75429
Admissions Phone: 903-886-5167 • Admissions Fax: 903-886-5165
Admissions E-mail: graduate_school@tamu-commerce.edu • Web Address: www.tamu-commerce.edu/mba

Texas A&M—Commerce offers three MBA program options: the Fast-Track MBA for students with an undergraduate background in business; the Comprehensive MBA for students without substantial prior business course work; and the Weekend MBA for 9-to-5ers, with cohort-style Saturday classes. Students can also check out the MBA British summer study option at King's College in London for a change of pace and some invaluable international insight.

INSTITUTIONAL INFORMATION
Evening Classes Available? Yes
Total Faculty: 23
% Faculty Female: 33
% Faculty Minority: 25
% Faculty Part-Time: 4
Student/Faculty Ratio: 27:1
Students in Parent Institution: 7,661
Academic Calendar: Semester

PROGRAMS
Degrees Offered: MBA (30 to 48 credits, 12 months to 6 years); MS in Management (30 to 36 credits); MS in Marketing (30 to 36 credits); MS in Electronic Commerce (30 to 54 credits)
Joint Degrees: BPA/MBA with an emphasis on Accounting (4 years + 1 year)
Academic Specialties: Entrepreneurship, Strategy, Human Resources, Finance, Economics, International Business, Accounting. The curriculum has a General Management (Strategic Management) orientation.
Study Abroad Options: France, Germany, Italy, Jamaica, Mexico (ITESM), United Kingdom, China (CUG)

STUDENT INFORMATION
Total Business Students: 253
% Female: 43
% Minority: 23
% International: 32
Average Age: 31

COMPUTER AND RESEARCH FACILITIES
Computer Facilities: 60 Pentium-class Business PCs; 120 PCs in other parts of the campus; www.tamu-commerce.edu/geelibrary; various databases such as Lexis-Nexis and Internet resources; 25 Pentium-class computers (Mesquite, TX); graphics arts lab (downtown Dallas)
Campuswide Network? Yes
% of MBA Classrooms Wired: 60
Computer Model Recommended: No
Internet Fee? No

EXPENSES/FINANCIAL AID
Annual Tuition (Resident/Nonresident): $2,828/$7,942
Tuition Per Credit (Resident/Nonresident): $133/$344
Room & Board (On Campus): $4,100
Books and Supplies: $800
Average Grant: $4,798
% Receiving Financial Aid: 4

ADMISSIONS INFORMATION
Electronic Application? Yes
Regular Application Deadline: 6/1
Regular Notification: Rolling
Deferment Available? Yes
Length of Deferment: 2 semesters
Non-fall Admissions? Yes
Non-fall Application Deadline(s): 11/1, 3/15
Transfer Students Accepted? Yes
Transfer Policy: Students can transfer up to 12 semester hours in the 36- to 48-HR program and 9 semester hours for the 30- to 33-HR.
Need-Blind Admissions? No
Number of Applications Received: 175
% of Applicants Accepted: 86
% Accepted Who Enrolled: 83
Average GPA: 3.0
GPA Range: 2.5-3.6
Average GMAT: 460
GMAT Range: 380-620
Average Years Experience: 7
Other Admissions Factors Considered: Graduate work with an overall 3.0 GPA
Other Schools to Which Students Applied: University of Texas-Arlington, University of Dallas, Southern Methodist University, TCU.

INTERNATIONAL STUDENTS
TOEFL Required of International Students? Yes
Minimum TOEFL: 500 (173 computer)

EMPLOYMENT INFORMATION

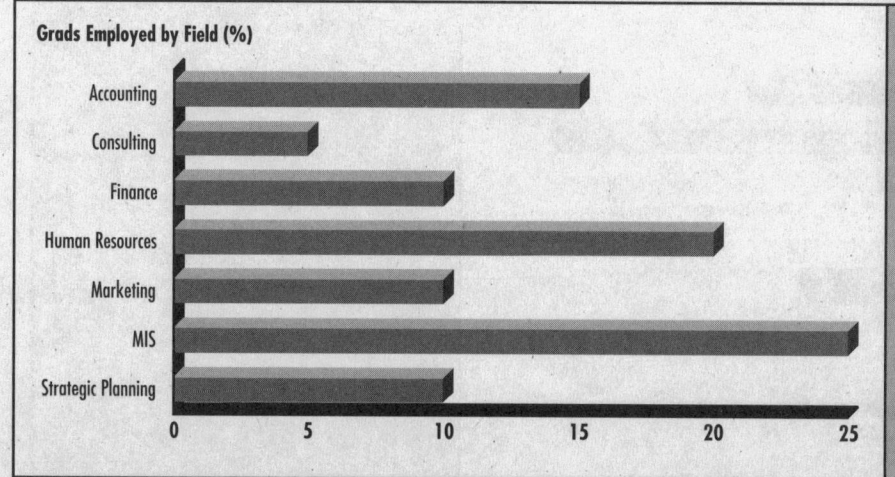

Grads Employed by Field (%)
- Accounting: 15
- Consulting: 5
- Finance: 15
- Human Resources: 20
- Marketing: 10
- MIS: 25
- Strategic Planning: 10

Placement Office Available? Yes
% Employed Within 3 Months: 95

TEXAS A&M UNIVERSITY — CORPUS CHRISTI
College of Business Administration

Admissions Contact: Betsy O'Lavin, Director of Master's Programs
Address: 6300 Ocean Drive, Corpus Christi, TX 78412-5503
Admissions Phone: 361-994-2655 • Admissions Fax: 361-994-2725
Admissions E-mail: eolavin@falcon.tamucc.edu • Web Address: www.enterprise.tamucc.edu

Deep in southern Texas lies Texas A&M—Corpus Christi, with a broad-based curriculum, churning out graduates who primarily go on to the fields of finance and consulting. Texas A&M offers a working model of a real business organization called Society for Advancement of Management, providing exceptional hands-on experience in multiple business disciplines and a personal introduction to practicing managers in the local community.

INSTITUTIONAL INFORMATION
Public/Private: Public
Evening Classes Available? No
Total Faculty: 37
% Faculty Part Time: 16
Students in Parent Institution: 6,161
Academic Calendar: Semester

PROGRAMS
Degrees Offered: MBA (36 to 60 credits, 12 months to 6 years), Master of Accountancy (36 to 60 credits, 12 months to 6 years)

STUDENT INFORMATION
Total Business Students: 144
% Full Time: 30
% Female: 47
% Minority: 38
% International: 1
Average Age: 32

COMPUTER AND RESEARCH FACILITIES
Number of Student Computers: 570
Campuswide Network? Yes
Computer Proficiency Required? No
Special Purchasing Agreements? No

EXPENSES/FINANCIAL AID
Room & Board (On/Off Campus): $5,106/$5,265

ADMISSIONS INFORMATION
Application Fee: $10
Electronic Application? No
Regular Application Deadline: 8/15
Regular Notification: Rolling
Deferment Available? Yes
Non-fall Admissions? Yes
Non-fall Application Deadline(s): 12/15, 5/15
Transfer Students Accepted? No
Need-Blind Admissions? No
Number of Applications Received: 65
% of Applicants Accepted: 96
% Accepted Who Enrolled: 90
Average GPA: 3.2
Average GMAT: 525

INTERNATIONAL STUDENTS
TOEFL Required of International Students? Yes
Minimum TOEFL: 550

EMPLOYMENT INFORMATION

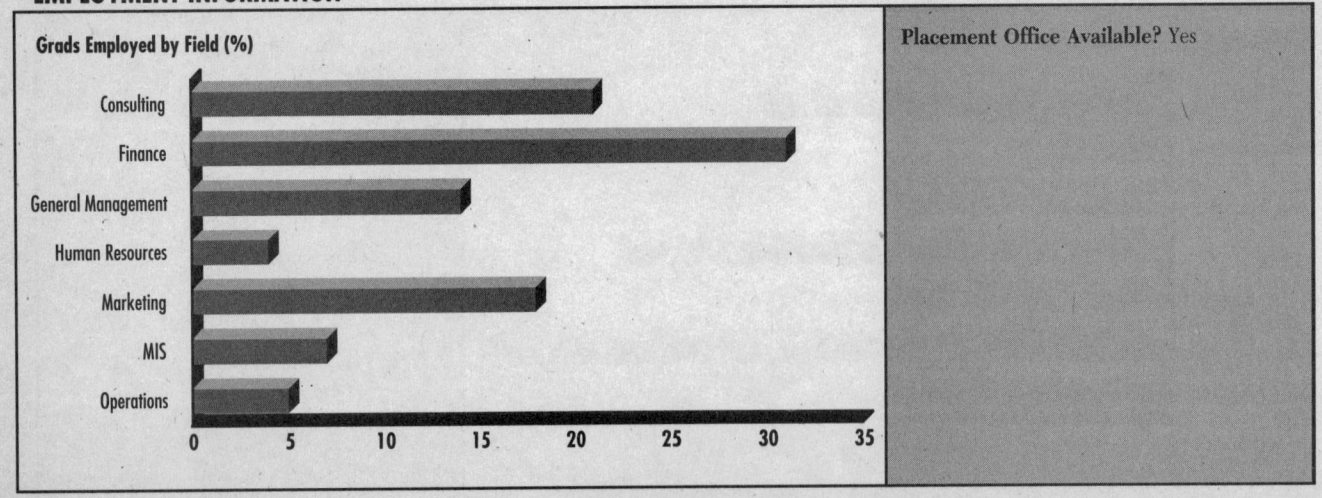

Grads Employed by Field (%)

Field	%
Consulting	21
Finance	31
General Management	14
Human Resources	2
Marketing	18
MIS	7
Operations	5

Placement Office Available? Yes

TEXAS TECH UNIVERSITY
Jerry S. Rawls College of Business Administration

Admissions Contact: Sheila Dixon, Academic Program Advisor
Address: Box 42101, Lubbock, TX 79409-2101
Admissions Phone: 806-742-3184 • Admissions Fax: 806-742-3958
Admissions E-mail: mba@ba.ttu.edu • Web Address: grad.ba.ttu.edu

Texas Tech University's MBA program is populated mostly by native Texans and offers a choice of academic concentrations to complement its general degree. A number of joint degrees are also offered, including MBAs coupled with MAs in French, German, and Spanish and the MBA/MD in health organization management, for physicians-to-be looking to gain advanced management know-how for use in the workplace. Student Naeem Malik comments that his team-building and critical thinking experiences at Texas Tech "reinforce the excellence and achievement that have always been in my vocabulary, and attending the Jerry S. Rawls College of Business adds them to my résumé."

INSTITUTIONAL INFORMATION
Public/Private: Public
Evening Classes Available? Yes
Total Faculty: 68
% Faculty Female: 7
% Faculty Minority: 2
% Faculty Part Time: 1
Student/Faculty Ratio: 4:1
Students in Parent Institution: 25,573
Academic Calendar: Rolling

PROGRAMS
Degrees Offered: MBA (1.5 years); MS Business Administration (2 years or less); PhD (4 years); MS Accounting (2 years or less)
Joint Degrees: MD/MBA (4 years); JD/MBA (3 years); BA Foreign Language/MBA (5 years); MA Foreign Language/MBA (2 years); MA Architecture/MBA (2.5 years); dual MBA
Academic Specialties: Taxation, Accounting, Controllership, Health Organization Management, High Performance Management, Marketing, Entrepreneurship, Agribusiness, E-Business, Finance, International Business, Management Information Systems
Study Abroad Options: Finland, Germany, UK, France, Mexico

STUDENT INFORMATION
Total Business Students: 213
% Full Time: 86
% Female: 27
% Minority: 13
% Out of State: 6
% International: 12
Average Age: 23

COMPUTER AND RESEARCH FACILITIES
Computer Facilities: Research databases, online computer-based training classes, eRaider account, interactive log-ons with open VMS cluster
Campuswide Network? Yes
% of MBA Classrooms Wired: 100
Computer Model Recommended: No
Internet Fee? No

EXPENSES/FINANCIAL AID
Annual Tuition (Resident/Nonresident): $1,920/$6,984
Tuition Per Credit (Resident/Nonresident): $80/$291
Room & Board (On/Off Campus): $4,500/$6,000
Books and Supplies: $1,500
Average Grant: $1,000
Average Loan: $9,210
% Receiving Financial Aid: 21
% Receiving Aid Their First Year: 31

ADMISSIONS INFORMATION
Application Fee: $25
Electronic Application? Yes
Regular Application Deadline: Rolling
Regular Notification: Rolling
Length of Deferment: 1 year
Non-fall Application Deadline(s): 9/1 spring, 3/1 fall
Transfer Policy: Up to 6 credits
Need-Blind Admissions? No
Number of Applications Received: 209
% of Applicants Accepted: 50
% Accepted Who Enrolled: 57
Average GPA: 3.4
Average GMAT: 580
Average Years Experience: 3
Other Admissions Factors Considered: Work experience, research, awards, leadership, unique perspective, civic and volunteer activities, motivation, past success, letters of recommendation
Minority/Disadvantaged Student Recruitment Programs: Advertise in minority magazines, recruit in minority colleges in New Mexico and Texas, attend and recruit at minority forums such as the National Black Graduate Student Conference
Other Schools to Which Students Applied: Texas A&M University

INTERNATIONAL STUDENTS
TOEFL Required of International Students? Yes
Minimum TOEFL: 550 (213 computer)

EMPLOYMENT INFORMATION

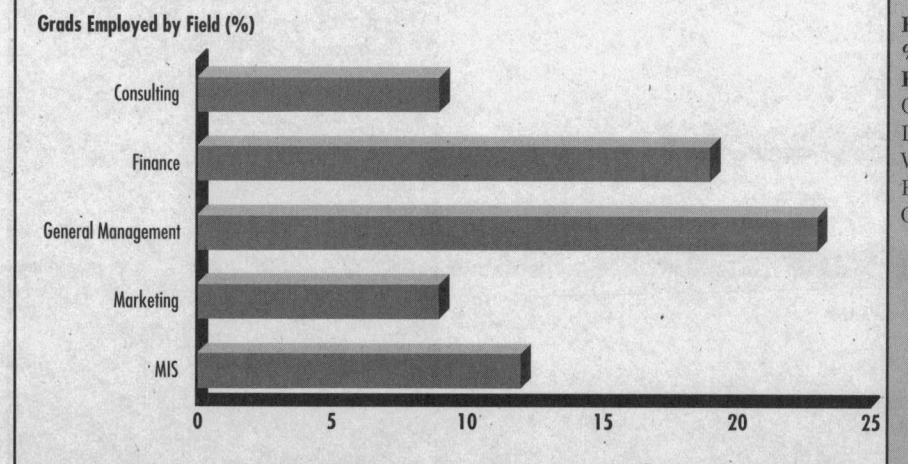

Grads Employed by Field (%)

Field	%
Consulting	~9
Finance	~19
General Management	~23
Marketing	~9
MIS	~12

Placement Office Available? Yes
% Employed Within 3 Months: 78
Frequent Employers: SBC, Pricewaterhouse-Coopers, Andersen, Deloitte & Touche, National Instruments, PNB Financial, Ryan and Company, Wells Fargo Financial, Accenture, Covenant Health Systems, Dell, Cap Gemini, KPMG, CINTAS, Comerica

THUNDERBIRD
American Graduate School of International Management

Admissions Contact: Judy Johnson, Dean of Admissions
Address: 15249 North 59th Avenue, Glendale, AZ 85306-6000
Admissions Phone: 602-978-7100 • Admissions Fax: 602-439-5432
Admissions E-mail: admissions@t-bird.edu • Web Address: www.thunderbird.edu

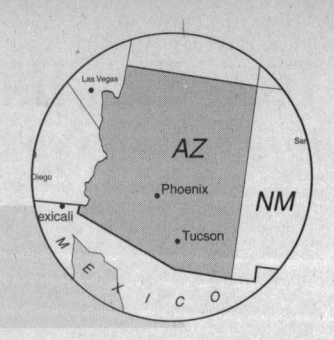

Like a great steak house that serves one dish exceedingly well, Thunderbird focuses on one thing: international business. Students here—who refer to themselves as T-Birds—study international economy and overseas markets, modern languages, and world business. That's pretty much it. Though the local area is "in need of a charm transfusion," T-Birds can easily head for nearby Phoenix or take "bonding trips to California and Vegas" to let off steam.

INSTITUTIONAL INFORMATION
Evening Classes Available? No
Total Faculty: 99
% Faculty Female: 26
% Faculty Minority: 35
% Faculty Part Time: 27
Student/Faculty Ratio: 11:1
Students in Parent Institution: 1,475
Academic Calendar: Trimester

PROGRAMS
Degrees Offered: MBA in International Management (full time, 48 to 60 credits, varies by track and specialization chosen, 12 months to 3 years), with concentrations in International Management, Global Marketing, Global Finance, and Global Development and Policy; Executive MBA in International Management (50 credits, up to 2 years), with concentration in International Management; program offered in Arizona, Sao Paolo, Brazil, and Taipei, Taiwan; Master of International Management Latin America (MIMLA) (full time. distance learning option, 50 credits, minimum 22 months); Post MBA Program, Master of International Management (MIM) (full time, 30 credits, 7 to 16 months)
Joint Degrees: MBA/Master of International Management in conjunction with 9 other schools
Academic Specialties: All aspects of International Management: Cross-Cultural Communication, Global Strategy, Emerging Market, and Regional Market Development; Corporate Marketing and Finance
Special Opportunities: Winterim, on campus; off campus: Kenya, South Africa, New York, San Francisco/Silicon Valley, Paris, India, Washington, D.C., Chile, Peru, Vietnam, London, Paris, Geneva, Cuba
Study Abroad Options: Japan, France/Geneva, Mexico, Republic of China, Czech Republic, Russia

STUDENT INFORMATION
Total Business Students: 1,100
% Full Time: 100
% Female: 32
% Minority: 4
% Out of State: 100
% International: 65
Average Age: 28

COMPUTER AND RESEARCH FACILITIES
Research Facilities: CIBER, IF&T, MyThunderbird, online services
Computer Facilities: IBIC: 42 databases, 1,200 periodicals; ITS: taping facilities
Campuswide Network? Yes
% of MBA Classrooms Wired: 15
Computer Model Recommended: Laptop
Internet Fee? Yes

EXPENSES/FINANCIAL AID
Annual Tuition: $25,500
Room & Board (On/Off Campus): $8,000/$9,500
Books and Supplies: $1,500
Average Grant: $2,500
Average Loan: $20,000
% Receiving Financial Aid: 67
% Receiving Aid Their First Year: 70

ADMISSIONS INFORMATION
Application Fee: $125
Electronic Application? Yes
Regular Application Deadline: 8/15
Regular Notification: Rolling
Length of Deferment: 1 year
Non-fall Application Deadline(s): 1/15 spring, 4/15 summer
Transfer Students Accepted? No
Need-Blind Admissions? Yes
Number of Applications Received: 1,126
% of Applicants Accepted: 78
% Accepted Who Enrolled: 49
Average GPA: 3.3
GPA Range: 3.1-3.9
Average GMAT: 600
GMAT Range: 545-725
Average Years Experience: 5
Other Admissions Factors Considered: Work experience, computer experience (Microsoft Office)
Other Schools to Which Students Applied: Arizona State, U. of Southern California, Vanderbilt, UT Austin, UCLA, Georgetown, U. of South Carolina

INTERNATIONAL STUDENTS
TOEFL Required of International Students? Yes
Minimum TOEFL: 600 (250 computer)

EMPLOYMENT INFORMATION

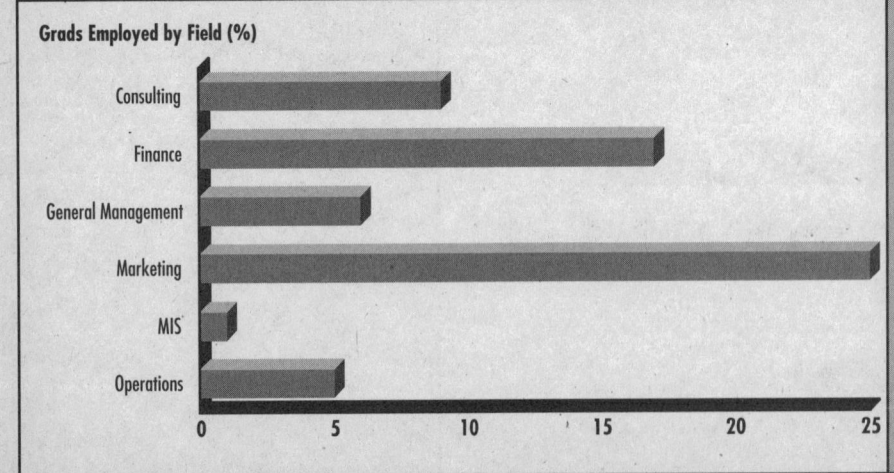

Grads Employed by Field (%)
- Consulting: ~9
- Finance: ~17
- General Management: ~6
- Marketing: ~25
- MIS: ~1
- Operations: ~5

Placement Office Available? Yes
% Employed Within 3 Months: 75
Frequent Employers: Citibank, General Motors, IBM, Intel, Merck, Enron, Johnson & Johnson
Prominent Alumni: John Lampe, CEO, Firestone Tire; Olga Reisler, regional VP, Infitiniti Division/Nissan; Sir Bruce Harris, executive director, Covenant House (Latin America); Sam Garvin, founder and CEO, Continental Promotion Group; Louis Moreno, Colombian ambassador to the U.S.

TULANE UNIVERSITY
A.B. Freeman School of Business

Admissions Contact: Bill D. Sandefer, Director for Admissions and Financial Aid
Address: 7 McAlister Drive, Suite 401, New Orleans, LA 70118
Admissions Phone: 504-865-5410 • Admissions Fax: 504-865-6770
Admissions E-mail: freeman.admissions@tulane.edu • Web Address: freeman.tulane.edu

Tulane University's "blissfully challenging" Freeman School of Business offers a wealth of excellent programs and a "superb," seven-story facility with computers galore and a laboratory for simulating manufacturing processes. The especially notable finance department is "filled with superstars" who share a "tremendous ability to articulate ideas." Beyond campus, of course, is the great city of New Orleans, America's preeminent party town.

INSTITUTIONAL INFORMATION
Public/Private: Private
Evening Classes Available? Yes
Total Faculty: 96
% Faculty Female: 15
% Faculty Minority: 15
% Faculty Part Time: 37
Student/Faculty Ratio: 20:1
Students in Parent Institution: 12,381
Academic Calendar: Semester

PROGRAMS
Degrees Offered: Master of Accounting (1 year with undergraduate business courses); PhD (5 years); MBA (2 years)
Joint Degrees: MBA/JD (4 years); MBA/MA Latin American Studies (2.5 years); MBA/Master of Public Health (3 years); Master of Accounting/JD (3 years); MAcc/MBA (2 years)
Academic Specialties: Career tracks, such as energy finance and information management
Special Opportunities: Faculty development doctoral program, joint-venture executive education programs
Study Abroad Options: Argentina, Australia, Austria, Brazil, Chile, Colombia, Czech Republic, Denmark, Ecuador, Finland, France, Germany, Hong Kong, Hungary, Mexico, Spain, Venezuela

STUDENT INFORMATION
Total Business Students: 150
% Full Time: 93
% Female: 28
% Minority: 12
% Out of State: 35
% International: 37
Average Age: 28

COMPUTER AND RESEARCH FACILITIES
Research Facilities: Institute for the Study of Ethics and Leadership in Management; Institute of International Business; Institute for Entrepreneurship; Center for Executive Education; Center for Research on Latin American Financial Markets; Fenner Fund
Computer Facilities: 116 Pentium-based workstations; Ethernet network drops; research databases including Bloomberg, Standard & Poor's, Compustat, CRSP, Lexis-Nexis, ABI/Inform, IBES, and others
Campuswide Network? Yes
% of MBA Classrooms Wired: 55
Computer Model Recommended: Laptop
Internet Fee? No

EXPENSES/FINANCIAL AID
Annual Tuition: $24,675
Tuition Per Credit: $823
Room & Board: $7,325
Books and Supplies: $1,600
Average Grant: $17,396
Average Loan: $15,000
% Receiving Financial Aid: 77
% Receiving Aid Their First Year: 77

ADMISSIONS INFORMATION
Application Fee: $40
Electronic Application? Yes
Regular Application Deadline: 3/15
Regular Notification: 4/15
Deferment Available? No
Non-fall Admissions? No
Transfer Students Accepted? No
Need-Blind Admissions? Yes
Number of Applications Received: 488
% of Applicants Accepted: 48
% Accepted Who Enrolled: 33
Average GPA: 3.3
Average GMAT: 653
Average Years Experience: 6
Other Admissions Factors Considered: Candidates should apply in earliest round possible.
Minority/Disadvantaged Student Recruitment Programs: Destination MBA, National Black MBA Association Career Fair, targeted GMASS searches, minority fellowships
Other Schools to Which Students Applied: Emory, Georgetown, NYU, U. of Maryland—College Park, UT Austin, Vanderbilt, Washington U.

INTERNATIONAL STUDENTS
TOEFL Required of International Students? Yes
Minimum TOEFL: 622 (263 computer)

EMPLOYMENT INFORMATION

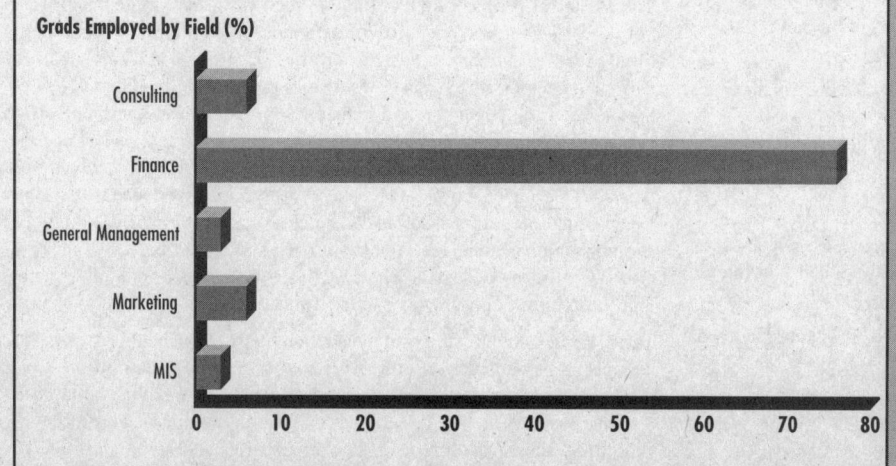

Grads Employed by Field (%)
- Consulting
- Finance
- General Management
- Marketing
- MIS

Placement Office Available? Yes
% Employed Within 3 Months: 90
Frequent Employers: Citibank, JPMorgan Chase, Federal Express, Entergy, TXU, D&T Management Solutions, Dynegy, Banc of America, Reliant Energy, Towers Perrin, Credit Suisse First Boston, First Union Securities, Jackson & Rhodes, PA Consulting, El Paso Energy, Mirant
Prominent Alumni: Berdon Lawrence, chairman, Kirby Corp. (nation's largest tank barge operator); Wayne A. Downing, national coordinator of counterterrorism, Homeland Security Council; Michael F. McKeever, managing director, Lehman Brothers Inc.

UNION COLLEGE

THE COLLEGE AT A GLANCE
Graduate management study at Union is a very special experience. Union's first-rate faculty delivers a relevant, accredited curriculum within a "small college" environment. Faculty at the MBA@Union program have distinguished careers in teaching, consulting, and research. It is Union's high-quality academic program, small size, and careful attention to the individual needs of each student that make graduate study at the College such a rewarding experience.

Small classes (average size 15) ensure that your Union education is not a "spectator sport." It is virtually impossible to become "lost" at GMI. Faculty are routinely accessible outside of class for individual student questions and conversation. Almost all classes meet in the evening, enabling Union to bring full- and part-time students together in exciting and educationally valuable ways.

STUDENTS
Union MBA students are a very diverse group. There is almost an even number of full- and part-time students, ranging from accelerated undergraduates to CEOs, doctors, lawyers, and entrepreneurs. Sixteen percent are international students. The program is designed for students ranging from those with no management background to those with years of experience. It is our philosophy that these diverse student populations experience a more rewarding and higher quality education when learning in a mixed environment. Thus, student populations are integrated in the same class and not taught separately.

ACADEMICS
MBA Curriculum
The MBA curriculum at Union consists of classes that incorporate a global business perspective. At a time when multinational corporations dominate the world's financial markets and e-commerce brings products and services to consumers across the globe, leaders in business and industry must possess both business acumen and an understanding of the peoples and customs of the world. At Union, we prepare students to succeed in the intensely competitive global environment.

Students must complete 20 courses (10 core courses and 10 electives) to fulfill MBA degree requirements. Course work is required in two areas: MBA core courses and electives. Typically, requirements are completed in two years of full-time study or four years of part-time study. Course waivers are dependent on prior course work and require approval of the program director. The MBA program may accept student requests for course waivers or course transfers up to a limit of eight courses.

MBA Core Courses (all students complete these required courses) are Managing Ethically in a Global Environment, Mathematics of Management (1/2), Introduction to Probability (1/2), Statistical Modeling in Management, Financial Accounting, Financial Analysis & Decision Making, Principles of Economics, Marketing Management and Strategy, Operations Management, Managing People & Teams in Organizations, and Legal Principles of Business.

Students are able to build a focus depending on their interests and career goals. Students take one course in each focus area listed below and three in the area(s) of their choice.

Finance Courses: Advanced Concepts of Financial Reporting I, Financial Management, Money & Banking, International Finance, Income Tax Accounting, Cost Accounting, Investments.

Economics Courses: Managerial Economics, International Economics, Monetary Economics, Efficient Management of Technology, Seminar in International Finance.

Marketing Courses: E-Commerce, Marketing Research Techniques, Industrial Marketing, International Marketing Management.

Operations/Management Science Courses: Quality Systems Management, Simulation, Lean Production Management, Statistical Methods.

Management Courses: Management for Information Systems, Organizational Theory, Organizational Development & Transformation, Human Resource Management, High Performance Leadership.

International Courses: International Economics, International Finance, Seminar in International Finance, International Marketing Management, International Business & Competitive Theory.

Capstone (all students take this course): Strategic Planning and Policy.

MBA Health Systems Curriculum
Faculty believe that in order to derive maximum benefit from the curriculum, theoretical insights generated during in-class discussion must be supplemented by practical, "hands-on" experience in the field. Consequently, a full-time internship is a program requirement. Normally, the internship is completed during the summer between the first and second years of study. This approach enables students to integrate practical work experience into the advanced portion of the academic program. Most students complete the internship within a health care institution.

Students must complete 20 courses (18 required and 2 elective) and an internship to fulfill MBA in Health Systems Administration degree requirements. Course work is required in three areas: MBA core courses, MBA Health Systems courses, and electives. Typically, requirements are completed in two academic years of full-time study or four years of part-time study. Course waivers are dependent on prior course work and require approval of the program director.

Required Core Courses (students must take each of these courses): Managing Ethically in a Global Environment, Introduction to Health Systems, Mathematics of Management (1/2), Introduction to Probability (1/2), Statistical Modeling in Management, Financial Accounting, Financial Analysis & Decision Making, Principles of Economics, Marketing Management & Strategy, and Operations Management.

Required Advanced Courses (students must take each of these courses): Health Care Finance, Health Economics, Health Systems Marketing and Planning, Structural Dynamics in Health Systems, Legal Aspects of Health Care, Health Policy and Information Systems, Strategic Issues for Health Care Organizations.

Elective Courses (students must take any three): Advanced Concepts in Financial Reporting, Money and Banking, International Finance, Industrial Marketing, E-Commerce, International Marketing Management, Quality Systems Management, Management Science, Organizational Development and Transformation, Management for Information Systems, High Performance Leadership, Human Resource Management, Group Practice Management, Issues in Long Term Care.

The Programs
The Master of Business Administration program prepares students for functional, managerial, and executive-level positions in a wide variety of manufacturing, service, and public policy enterprises. The design and delivery of the curriculum emphasize a broad exposure to core business disciplines, the building of analytical, computer, and human resource skills, and an emphasis on development of an ethical, systems-oriented, cross-functional view of management. Classes incorporate a global business perspective. Union graduates understand international business practices; many have experience working and living abroad, and all learn how to communicate cross-culturally. The Master of Business Administration is accredited by the AACSB International—The Association to Advance Collegiate Schools of Business. It is one of only 28 "graduate only" accredited MBA programs in the world.

The MBA in Health Systems Administration prepares graduates for careers as administrators and analysts in health care, governmental, and private-sector organizations with strong health care interests. Typical organizations hiring health systems graduates include hospitals, clinics, health maintenance organizations, consulting firms, planning and regulatory agencies, and research firms. The

Graduate Management Institute

MBA at UNION

curriculum is designed to help students understand the complexities of the health care system and to provide the skills necessary to allocate resources, execute programs, and manage health and health-related facilities more effectively.

The program is accredited by both the Accrediting Commission on Education for Health Services Administration (ACEHSA) and AACSB International. It is one of only 21 prestigious dually accredited health administration programs worldwide.

Union offers three joint degree programs. In cooperation with Albany Law School, students can obtain a JD and MBA, while in cooperation with Albany College of Pharmacy they offer a joint pharmacy degree. Union undergraduates may also pursue a joint degree program that leads to a bachelor's degree and MBA.

Internships are a crucial part of the Union MBA program. Through contacts in major businesses all over the world, we are able to help students find an internship in the industry and country of their choosing. Union students have interned at General Electric, Bank of America, Orion Consulting, PricewaterhouseCoopers, Morgan Stanley Dean Witter, Nestle, and other corporations. Often these experiences lead to full-time employment opportunities after graduation.

MBA faculty, in conjunction with Union's Career Development Center, offer a variety of opportunities for GMI students and alumni to explore career paths and learn the job search and career development skills needed to advance in their longer-term careers. Services and resources include one-on-one career counseling, self-assessment, workshops, videotaped mock interviews, resume development and critique, an online resume referral service, on-campus recruiting, "U-CAN" (the Union Career Advisory Network, a database of over 1,100 Union alumni representing 16 major career fields), an on-campus Career Festival, employer literature, and credential files.

Career advising and placement services are available to all matriculated full- and part-time graduate students. All MBA students are routinely apprised of upcoming events, workshops, and job opportunities.

A sampling of Organizations Employing Recent GMI Graduates includes Albany International Corp., Albany Medical Center Hospital, Albany Memorial Hospital, Andersen Consulting, Arthur Andersen & Co., Bank of New York, Blue Cross/Blue Shield, CHP/Kaiser Permanente, Deloitte & Touche, Ellis Hospital, Ernst & Young, General Electric, Health Association of New York State, KPMG, Moody's Investors Service, Morgan Stanley, New York State Department of Health, Nickelodeon, Novalis Corporation, Pharmacy Service Corporation of New York, PricewaterhouseCoopers, Saint Claire's Hospital, SONY Music, and Wells Fargo.

CAMPUS LIFE

Founded in 1795, Union College is located in Schenectady, New York, part of a metropolitan area of 850,000 centered in Albany, the state capital. The Capital District is a major education center with 55,000 students at a dozen colleges and universities, and the area's large array of businesses and government agencies offer extensive internship and career possibilities. Schenectady is three hours from both New York City and Boston, and four hours from Montreal, and the city is served by Albany International Airport and Amtrak. The 100-acre campus is the first united campus plan in America and combines classical architecture with modern academic facilities.

Numerous facilities, resources, and services are at the disposal of Union students. Schaffer Library holds over 50,000 volumes, approximately 2,000 current serials, government documents, a periodicals reading room, faculty studies, and more than 500 individual study spaces. A major renovation and expansion of the library was finished in 1998. The F.W. Olin Center, a $9 million high-technology classroom and laboratory building, is another major addition to the College. The Science and Engineering Center contains a number of specialized research tools available for student use. The Arts Center has been extensively renovated and the Morton and Helen Yulman Theater greatly enhances the art program.

Union's central computer facility consist of several multiuser servers on a campuswide fiber-optic-based network that includes UNIX, Windows T2000, and Apple Macintosh servers. The center hosts the College's main Web server and its library automation system. Connected to the network are more than 1,200 College-owned personal computers and workstations. More than 20 electronic classrooms are used to enhance the integration of technology and academic studies. Laboratories with Windows and Apple Macintosh computers and UNIX workstations are available for student use. Each residence hall room is wired (one Ethernet connection per resident), providing access to the College's computing resources and the World Wide Web.

The Murray and Ruth Reamer Campus Center provides space for social and community activities and services for the entire campus. Dining facilities, a pub, an auditorium, a radio station, and multiple student activities spaces are important parts of the building. The historic Nott Memorial has been renovated to become a display and discussion center. Highlights among the athletic facilities are the Alumni Gymnasium with an eight-lane swimming/diving pool and squash and racquetball courts, a 3,000-seat ice rink, an Astroturf field, and an all-weather track. A $10 million project to revitalize the neighborhood to the immediate west of campus was just completed. Key elements nclude apartment-style housing for 160 students, a security center, and a community center.

COSTS

Tuition for the MBA program for the academic year is $15,444. Program fees are $150. There is no on-campus housing for graduate students. Off-campus housing costs for room and board are approximately $9,600 per year.

Merit-based assistance is available to both U.S. and non-U.S. citizens. Competitive scholarships are awarded. Graduate student loans, co-op opportunities, part-time employment, and affordable graduate housing are available.

Graduate scholarships in the form of tuition waivers are available to full-time students. Students are selected for these competitive awards on the basis of prior academic performance, professional experience, and managerial potential. Student loans are available to both full- and part-time matriculated students.

ADMISSIONS

Applicants may seek admission to the MBA programs as matriculated graduate students throughout the year. Notification of an admissions decision is made within two weeks of receipt of a completed application. Students may begin their study in any term. Applications for admission are accepted on a rolling basis. International students whose native language is not English must take the TOFEL exam.

Criteria for admission to the MBA programs include a student's postsecondary academic record, career objectives, personal recommendations, and standardized test scores. Course waivers and transfer credit may be approved up to a maximum of eight courses. In general, a minimum GPA of 3.0 is expected in previous academic work. Applicants must submit a $50 application fee, essays, three letters of recommendation, official GMAT test scores, and official transcripts of all previous academic work.

UNION COLLEGE
Graduate Management Institute

Admissions Contact: Rhonda Sheehan, Coordinator of Recruiting and Admissions
Address: Lamont House, Schenectady, NY 12308
Admissions Phone: 518-388-6238 • Admissions Fax: 518-388-6754
Admissions E-mail: mba@union.edu • Web Address: www.mba.union.edu

Union College is a private institution in upstate New York with a small but diverse palette of MBA options. Classes with an average of 15 students "ensure that your education is not a 'spectator sport'" and the "global curriculum within a 'small college' environment" undoubtedly enhance the learning atmosphere. Union College also offers an MBA in health systems administrations, accelerated MBA courses, and a joint JD/MBA in conjunction with Albany Law School. Frequent employers of Union College MBA graduates are PricewaterhouseCoopers, IBM, and General Electric.

INSTITUTIONAL INFORMATION
Public/Private: Private
Evening Classes Available? Yes
Total Faculty: 11
% Faculty Female: 30
% Faculty Part Time: 20
Student/Faculty Ratio: 15:1
Students in Parent Institution: 2,427
Academic Calendar: Trimester

PROGRAMS
Degrees Offered: Master of Business Administration (2 years full time, 4 years part time); MBA in Health Systems Administration (2 years full time, 4 years part time)
Joint Degrees: JD/MBA (4 years), Accelerated MBA (BA-BS/MBA) (5 years), PharmD/MS (6 years)
Academic Specialties: Accounting, Economics, Finance, Health Care Management, Organizational Behavior, Operation Sciences, Statistics

STUDENT INFORMATION
Total Business Students: 118
% Full Time: 67
% Female: 42
% Minority: 5
% Out of State: 20
% International: 16
Average Age: 25

COMPUTER AND RESEARCH FACILITIES
Campuswide Network? Yes
% of MBA Classrooms Wired: 90
Computer Model Recommended: No
Internet Fee? No

EXPENSES/FINANCIAL AID
Annual Tuition: $14,640
Tuition Per Credit: $478
Room & Board (Off Campus): $6,000
Books and Supplies: $250
Average Grant: $16,000
Average Loan: $12,000
% Receiving Financial Aid: 75

ADMISSIONS INFORMATION
Application Fee: $50
Electronic Application? No
Regular Application Deadline: Rolling
Regular Notification: Rolling
Deferment Available? Yes
Non-fall Admissions? Yes
Non-fall Application Deadline(s): All terms are rolling admissions
Transfer Students Accepted? Yes
Transfer Policy: Will accept up to 8 courses (20 required)
Need-Blind Admissions? Yes
Number of Applications Received: 67
% of Applicants Accepted: 93
% Accepted Who Enrolled: 68
Average GPA: 3.2
GPA Range: 2.7-4.0
Average GMAT: 570
GMAT Range: 440-780
Average Years Experience: 2
Other Schools to Which Students Applied: University at Albany, Rensselaer Polytechnic Institute

INTERNATIONAL STUDENTS
TOEFL Required of International Students? Yes
Minimum TOEFL: 550 (213 computer)

EMPLOYMENT INFORMATION

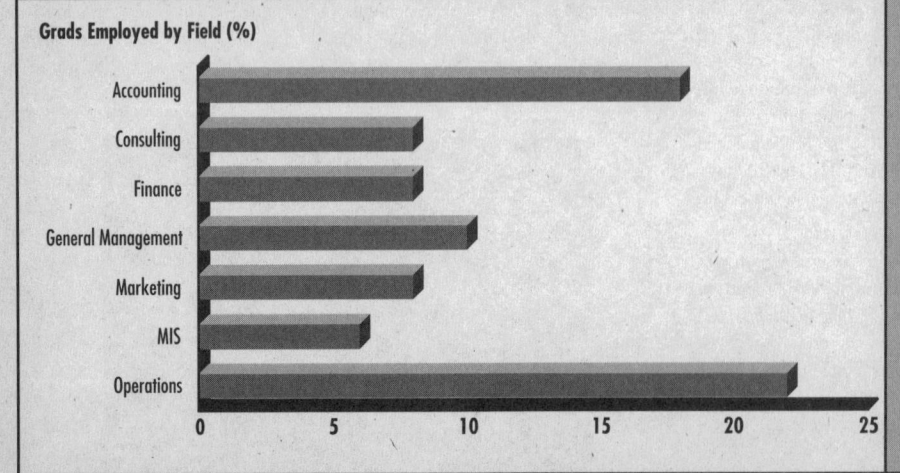

Grads Employed by Field (%)
- Accounting
- Consulting
- Finance
- General Management
- Marketing
- MIS
- Operations

Placement Office Available? Yes
% Employed Within 3 Months: 97
Frequent Employers: PricewaterhouseCoopers, Andersen Consulting, IBM, General Electric, KPMG Peat Marwick, Lehman Brothers

UNIVERSITY AT ALBANY (SUNY)
School of Business

Admissions Contact: Albina Y. Grignon, Assistant Dean
Address: UAB 121, 1400 Washington Ave., Albany, NY 12222
Admissions Phone: 518-442-4961 • *Admissions Fax:* 518-442-4975
Admissions E-mail: a.grignon@albany.edu • *Web Address:* www.albany.edu/business

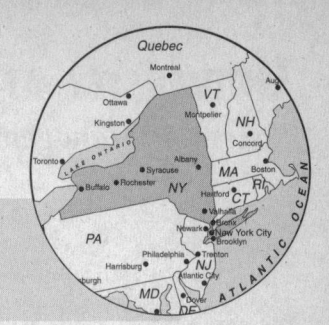

University at Albany is a branch of the State University of New York (SUNY) system, known for its academic excellence and experienced faculty. Full-time and part-time MBA schedules are available for completing the MBA program at SUNY Albany, where the tuition is affordable and the educational return on your investment is high. The curriculum is "focused on the information age," enabling graduates to enter the working world equipped with the skills of a confident manager who is comfortable with the various applications of technology in a business environment.

INSTITUTIONAL INFORMATION
Public/Private: Public
Evening Classes Available? Yes
Total Faculty: 45
% Faculty Female: 10
% Faculty Minority: 6
% Faculty Part Time: 20
Student/Faculty Ratio: 4:1
Students in Parent Institution: 17,000

PROGRAMS
Degrees Offered: MBA (2 years full time, up to 6 years part time), with concentrations in MIS, HR, IS; MS Accounting (1 year); MS Tax (1 year); MS Accounting (2 years)
Academic Specialties: Management Information Systems, Decision Support Systems, Knowledge Management, E-Commerce, Finance, Public Finance; HRIS—Compensation and Benefits Design, Entrepreneurship, Change Management. Albany's MIS program was ranked in the Top 10 in a ComputerWorld survey of corporate recruiters.
Study Abroad Options: Fudan University

STUDENT INFORMATION
Total Business Students: 148
% Full Time: 35
% Female: 40
% Minority: 8
% Out of State: 46
% International: 44
Average Age: 25

COMPUTER AND RESEARCH FACILITIES
Research Facilities: Center for Environmental Technology and Science, Small Business Development Center, Health Care Institute
Computer Facilities: A new library was built in 1999, completely wired for Internet access. Students have free access to Lexis-Nexis and Ebsco databases for research. There are 3 new computer labs available to MBA students in the business building, which were donated by prominent consulting firms that recruit from the program. There are more than 35 new systems with state-of-the-art application software.
Campuswide Network? Yes
% of MBA Classrooms Wired: 100
Computer Model Recommended: Laptop
Internet Fee? No

EXPENSES/FINANCIAL AID
Annual Tuition (Resident/Nonresident): $2,550/$4,208
Tuition Per Credit (Resident/Nonresident): $213/$351
Room & Board (On Campus): $3,255
Books and Supplies: $500
Average Grant: $10,500
Average Loan: $10,000
% Receiving Financial Aid: 90
% Receiving Aid Their First Year: 52

ADMISSIONS INFORMATION
Application Fee: $50
Electronic Application? Yes
Regular Application Deadline: 5/2
Regular Notification: 5/15
Deferment Available? Yes
Length of Deferment: 1 year
Non-fall Admissions? No
Transfer Students Accepted? No
Need-Blind Admissions? Yes
Number of Applications Received: 535
% of Applicants Accepted: 57
% Accepted Who Enrolled: 17
Average GPA: 3.3
GPA Range: 2.8-3.8
Average GMAT: 528
GMAT Range: 450-620
Average Years Experience: 3
Other Schools to Which Students Applied: University at Buffalo, State University of New York

INTERNATIONAL STUDENTS
TOEFL Required of International Students? Yes
Minimum TOEFL: 580 (237 computer)

EMPLOYMENT INFORMATION

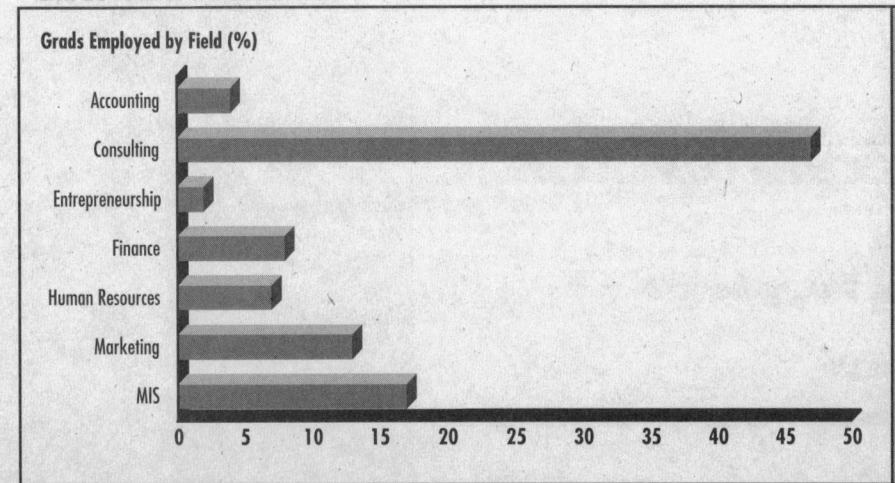

Grads Employed by Field (%)

Field	%
Accounting	~2
Consulting	~47
Entrepreneurship	~3
Finance	~7
Human Resources	~2
Marketing	~14
MIS	~18

Placement Office Available? Yes
% Employed Within 3 Months: 84
Frequent Employers: private law firms, government agencies, business and industry
Prominent Alumni: Herbert Lurie, managing director and cohead of investment banking, Merrill Lynch; Jeffrey Black, managing partner, assurance, Andersen LLP; Michael Weiss, CEO, Access Oncology, Inc.; Thomas Connolly, Sr., VP and controller, SUNY Music; David Light, managing director of fixed income securities, Salomon Smith Barney

UNIVERSITY AT BUFFALO (SUNY)
School of Management

Admissions Contact: Jaimie Taylor, MBA Admissions
Address: 206 Jacobs Management Center, Buffalo, NY 14260
Admissions Phone: 716-645-3204 • Admissions Fax: 716-645-2341
Admissions E-mail: som-mba@buffalo.edu • Web Address: www.mgt.buffalo.edu

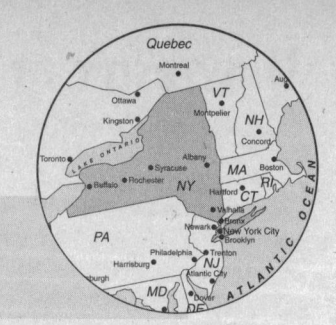

The University at Buffalo, a SUNY system school, has an "increasingly global business environment" and is dedicated to team-oriented learning. UAB offers an evening MBA, a three-year program structured for working professionals with at least one year of professional work experience under their belts. Any students itching to escape Buffalo for an academic stint elsewhere can travel to Singapore or Beijing on one of UB's international Executive MBA programs. UB's LEAP program provides an opportunity for graduate students to enroll in a practicum for formal real-world business exposure in a chosen area of concentration.

INSTITUTIONAL INFORMATION
Public/Private: Public
Evening Classes Available? Yes
Total Faculty: 61
% Faculty Female: 18
% Faculty Minority: 2
Student/Faculty Ratio: 8:1
Students in Parent Institution: 26,000
Academic Calendar: Semester

PROGRAMS
Degrees Offered: MBA (full time, 2 years); MS Accounting (1 year with undergraduate Accounting degree); MS Management Information Systems (1 year); MS Supply Chains and Operations Management (1 year)
Joint Degrees: JD/MBA; MD/MBA; Architecture/MBA; Pharmacy/MBA; Geography/MBA; BS/MBA Business or Engineering
Academic Specialties: Information Systems; Market Research; International; Competency Development
Study Abroad Options: Offered in 20 different countries

STUDENT INFORMATION
Total Business Students: 791
% Full Time: 75
% Female: 28
% Minority: 2
% Out of State: 2
% International: 60
Average Age: 25

COMPUTER AND RESEARCH FACILITIES
Computer Facilities: Wireless network on 2 floors of management building, large number of fully equipped computer labs, access to study rooms with computers, access to technically equipped classrooms across campus, Compustat PC Plus/Research Insight database, SPSS, Microsoft Software Suite (free to students)
Campuswide Network? Yes
% of MBA Classrooms Wired: 66
Computer Model Recommended: Laptop
Internet Fee? No

EXPENSES/FINANCIAL AID
Annual Tuition (Resident/Nonresident): $5,100/$8,416
Books and Supplies: $1,000
Average Grant: $5,100
Average Loan: $12,000
% Receiving Financial Aid: 32
% Receiving Aid Their First Year: 29

ADMISSIONS INFORMATION
Application Fee: $50
Electronic Application? Yes
Regular Application Deadline: 7/1
Regular Notification: Rolling
Deferment Available? No
Non-fall Admissions? No
Transfer Students Accepted? No
Need-Blind Admissions? Yes
Number of Applications Received: 1,187
% of Applicants Accepted: 47
% Accepted Who Enrolled: 80
Average GPA: 3.3
Average GMAT: 609
Average Years Experience: 3
Other Admissions Factors Considered: Work experience
Minority/Disadvantaged Student Recruitment Programs: The University at Buffalo offers competitive fellowships and assistantships to highly qualified minority applicants.
Other Schools to Which Students Applied: Baruch College (City University of New York), George Washington University, Syracuse University, University at Albany, University of Illinois at Urbana-Champaign, University of Rochester

INTERNATIONAL STUDENTS
TOEFL Required of International Students? Yes
Minimum TOEFL: 550 (213 computer)

EMPLOYMENT INFORMATION

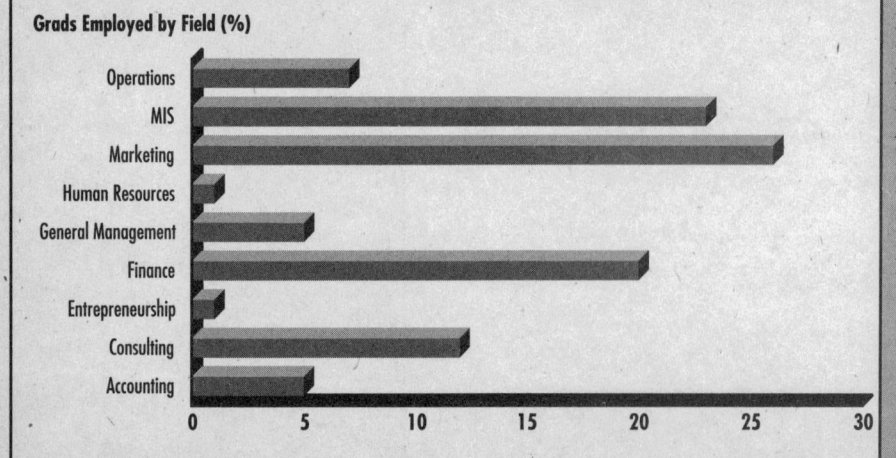

Grads Employed by Field (%):
- Operations
- MIS
- Marketing
- Human Resources
- General Management
- Finance
- Entrepreneurship
- Consulting
- Accounting

Placement Office Available? Yes
% Employed Within 3 Months: 86
Frequent Employers: Deloitte & Touche, M&T Bank Corp., PricewaterhouseCoopers, Andersen, IBM, Ernst & Young, HSBC Bank, D'Alba & Donovan, CPAs, Kaleida Health, GE, KeyCorp, Praxair Inc., AXA Advisors, Eastman Kodak Company, Electronic Data Systems, Eli Lilly, Goldman Sachs, KPMG, Lehman Brothers, National Fuel

UNIVERSITY OF AKRON
Graduate Programs in Business

Admissions Contact: Dr. James J. Divoky, Assistant Dean and Director
Address: The University of Akron, CBA 412, Arkon, OH 44325-4805
Admissions Phone: 330-972-7043 • Admissions Fax: 330-972-6588
Admissions E-mail: gradcba@uakron.edu • Web Address: www.uakron.edu/cba/grad

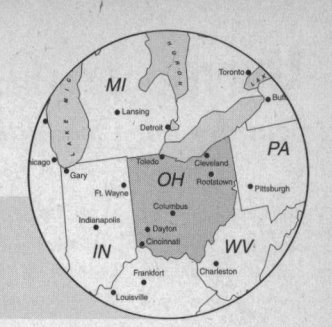

The University of Akron houses a student body that's half international and has an average age of 31, so expect a diverse, mature, and dedicated class of MBA business students. The College of Business Administration offers the unique IE-MBA program for midlevel executives involved in international finance, where students visit the headquarters of multinational corporations in the United States, in the UK, and throughout Europe, touring factories, interacting with executives, and attending presentations by internationally recognized business speakers. UA also offers the 1+1 MBA program, which involves one year of Web-based MBA classes followed by one year on campus.

INSTITUTIONAL INFORMATION
Public/Private: Public
Evening Classes Available? Yes
Total Faculty: 65
% Faculty Female: 11
% Faculty Minority: 25
Student/Faculty Ratio: 12:1
Students in Parent Institution: 23,400

PROGRAMS
Degrees Offered: MBA (34 to 58 credits), with concentrations in E-Business, Accounting, Finance, International Business, International Finance, Health Services Administration, Management of Technology and Innovation, Management, Marketing, Global Sales Management, and Supply Chain Management; MS Management (33 to 57 credits), with concentrations in Human Resources and Information Systems; Master of Taxation (30 to 48 credits); MSA (30 to 63 credits), with options in Professional Accounting and Accounting Information Systems
Joint Degrees: MBA/JD, MTax/JD, MSM-HR/JD
Study Abroad Options: France, Germany, Denmark, Mexico, Peru, Korea, UK, Thailand

STUDENT INFORMATION
Total Business Students: 306
% Full Time: 36
% Female: 45
% Minority: 5
% Out of State: 53
% International: 53
Average Age: 31

COMPUTER AND RESEARCH FACILITIES
Research Facilities: Member of Oracle DBMS Academic Initiative, Fisher Sales Laboratory, Fitzgerald Institute of Entrepreneurial Studies
Computer Facilities: Web-based MBA courses, Standard & Poor's Research Insight, CRSP Financial Database, and many others
Campuswide Network? Yes
% of MBA Classrooms Wired: 100
Computer Model Recommended: No
Internet Fee? No

EXPENSES/FINANCIAL AID
Annual Tuition (Resident/Nonresident): $7,786/$13,396
Tuition Per Credit (Resident/Nonresident): $229/$394
Room & Board: $8,050
Books and Supplies: $500
Average Grant: $10,567
% Receiving Financial Aid: 20
% Receiving Aid Their First Year: 12

ADMISSIONS INFORMATION
Application Fee: $25
Electronic Application? No
Regular Application Deadline: 8/1
Regular Notification: 8/15
Length of Deferment: 2 years
Non-fall Application Deadline(s): 12/1 spring, 5/1 summer
Transfer Policy: Up to 24 credits waived; 9 credits may transfer
Need-Blind Admissions? Yes
Number of Applications Received: 136
% of Applicants Accepted: 71
% Accepted Who Enrolled: 67
Average GPA: 3.3
Average GMAT: 561
Average Years Experience: 5
Other Admissions Factors Considered: Previous graduate and postbaccalaureate performance
Minority/Disadvantaged Student Recruitment Programs: The graduate school provides a minority recruitment program with Dr. Lathardus Goggins.
Other Schools to Which Students Applied: Case Western, John Carroll, Kent State, Ohio State, Youngstown State, Cleveland State, U. of Cincinnati

INTERNATIONAL STUDENTS
TOEFL Required of International Students? Yes
Minimum TOEFL: 550 (213 computer)

EMPLOYMENT INFORMATION

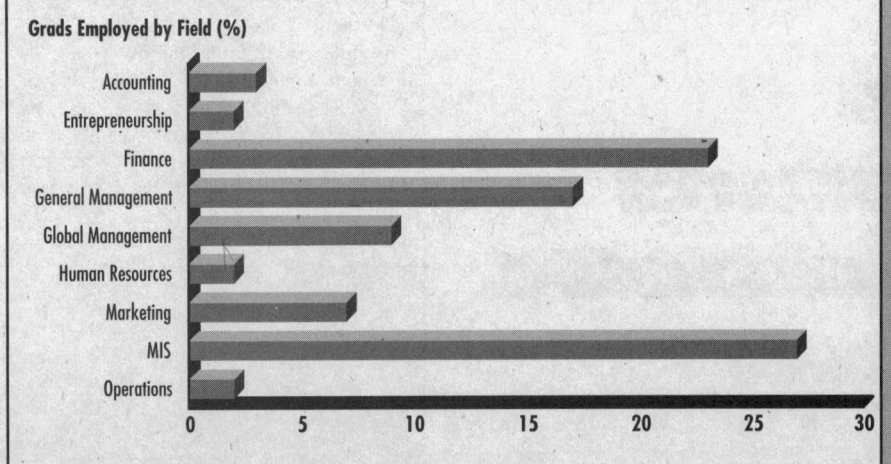

Grads Employed by Field (%): Accounting, Entrepreneurship, Finance, General Management, Global Management, Human Resources, Marketing, MIS, Operations

Placement Office Available? Yes
Frequent Employers: Buckingham, Doolittle & Burroughs; Brouse & McDowell; Roetzel & Andress; county prosecutor offices; Stark & Summit; County Courts of Common Pleas; 9th District Court of Appeals; Ernst & Young; Arthur Andersen; U.S. Army JAG Corps; CSFA; City of Akron Law Department; Jones, Day, Reavis & Pogue
Prominent Alumni: Peter Burg, chairman and CEO, First Energy; James McCready, chairman, Cypress Companies; John Piecuch, retired president and CEO, LaFarge Coppee; Joanne Rohrer, secretary/treasurer, Rohrer Corporation; Ernest Pouttu, VP of finance and CFO, Harwick Standard Distribution

UNIVERSITY OF ALABAMA — TUSCALOOSA
Manderson Graduate School of Business

Admissions Contact: Missy Strickland Brazil, Coordinator of Graduate Recruiting/Admissions MBA Program
Address: Box 870223, Tuscaloosa, AL 35487-0223 Canada
Admissions Phone: 205-348-6517 • Admissions Fax: 205-348-4504
Admissions E-mail: mba@cba.ua.edu • Web Address: www.cba.ua.edu/~mba

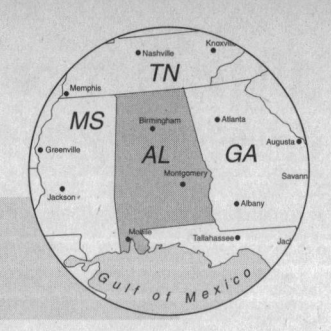

The Manderson Graduate School of Business has a unique student body, as it encourages students with varied, nonbusiness undergrad degrees as well as students with little or no work experience to apply to its MBA program. Manderson's MBA class has only about 65 students, so as you can imagine, students and faculty intermingle in a comfortable and personal learning environment. Aiming to provide a solid academic foundation, the Manderson MBA curriculum focuses on team-building skills; real-world experience, community involvement and networking, and achieving a "balance between personal and professional activities."

INSTITUTIONAL INFORMATION
Public/Private: Public
Evening Classes Available? No
Total Faculty: 86
% Faculty Female: 12
% Faculty Minority: 7
% Faculty Part Time: 3
Student/Faculty Ratio: 3:1
Students in Parent Institution: 19,000

PROGRAMS
Degrees Offered: Master of Arts (1 year), Master of Science (1 year), Master of Accountancy (1 year), Executive MBA (1.5 years), PhD (4 to 5 years), MA in Banking and Finance, MA in Economics, MA in Human Resources Management, MA in Management Science, MA in Marketing, MA in Statistics
Joint Degrees: MBA/Juris Doctor (4 years), 3/2 MBA + undergraduate (5 years)
Academic Specialties: Systems Consulting, Strategic Planning and Implementation, Strategic Business Management, Marketing, Statistics, Finance, Economics, Accounting
Study Abroad Options: Belgium, Italy

STUDENT INFORMATION
Total Business Students: 114
% Full Time: 100
% Female: 31
% Minority: 1
% Out of State: 25
% International: 12
Average Age: 24

COMPUTER AND RESEARCH FACILITIES
Research Facilities: Center for Business and Economic Research, Alabama Institute for Manufacturing Excellence, Alabama International Trade Center, Alabama Productivity Center, Alabama Real Estate Research and Education Center, Center for Economic Education, Enterprise Integration Lab, Small Business Development Center
Computer Facilities: Sloan Y. Bashinsky Computer Center, all campus libraries, computer labs, Enterprise Integration Lab
Campuswide Network? Yes
% of MBA Classrooms Wired: 100
Internet Fee? No

EXPENSES/FINANCIAL AID
Annual Tuition (Resident/Nonresident): $3,292/$8,912
Room & Board: $4,000
Books and Supplies: $700
Average Grant: $7,000
Average Loan: $8,000
% Receiving Financial Aid: 22
% Receiving Aid Their First Year: 15

ADMISSIONS INFORMATION
Application Fee: $25
Electronic Application? No
Regular Application Deadline: 4/15
Regular Notification: Rolling
Deferment Available? No
Non-fall Admissions? No
Transfer Students Accepted? Yes
Transfer Policy: The number of transferable credits is limited.
Need-Blind Admissions? Yes
Number of Applications Received: 213
% of Applicants Accepted: 50
% Accepted Who Enrolled: 64
Average GPA: 3.4
GPA Range: 2.8-3.8
Average GMAT: 607
GMAT Range: 560-680
Average Years Experience: 2
Other Schools to Which Students Applied: University of Georgia, Vanderbilt University

INTERNATIONAL STUDENTS
TOEFL Required of International Students? Yes
Minimum TOEFL: 575

EMPLOYMENT INFORMATION

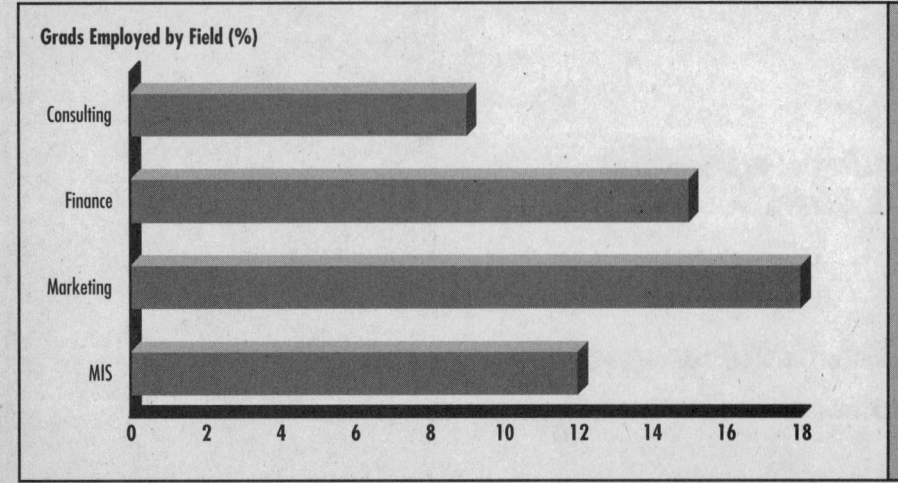

Grads Employed by Field (%)
- Consulting: ~9
- Finance: ~15
- Marketing: ~18
- MIS: ~12

Placement Office Available? Yes
% Employed Within 3 Months: 56
Frequent Employers: CSC Pinnacle, Andersen Consulting, AMS, Ernst & Young, MCI WorldCom, Procter & Gamble, International Paper, Federal Express
Prominent Alumni: Thomas Cross, managing partner, PricewaterhouseCoopers; Samuel D. DiPiazza, vice chairman, PricewaterhouseCoopers

UNIVERSITY OF ALBERTA
School of Business

Admissions Contact: Joan White, Executive Director, MBA Programs
Address: 2-30 Business Building, Edmonton, AB T6G 2R6 Canada
Admissions Phone: 780-492-3946 • Admissions Fax: 780-492-7825
Admissions E-mail: mba.programs@ualberta.ca • Web Address: www.bus.ualberta.ca/MBA

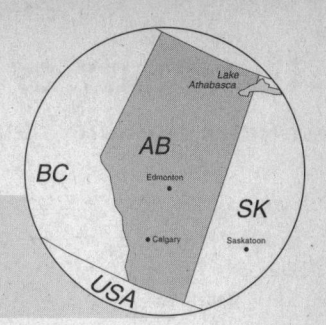

Edmonton, the capital of Alberta, is home to a dynamic and evolving business center. The class size at U of A's Faculty of Business is deliberately small, allowing for an intense amount of class interaction and access to faculty, and professors encourage participation in summer internships in Edmonton to exercise skills learned in the classroom. The Faculty of Business offers several unique joint degrees, including an MBA/Master of Agriculture, an MBA/Master of Forestry, and an MBA/Master of Engineering. UA also offers several interesting MBA concentrations, ranging from natural resources and energy to technology commercialization.

INSTITUTIONAL INFORMATION
Public/Private: Public
Evening Classes Available? Yes
Total Faculty: 105
% Faculty Female: 14
% Faculty Part Time: 17
Student/Faculty Ratio: 3:1
Students in Parent Institution: 29,859

PROGRAMS
Degrees Offered: MBA (20 months); Executive MBA (EMBA) (21 months); MBA with specialization in International Business (20 months), Leisure and Sport Management (20 months), Natural Resources and Energy (20 months), Technology Commercialization (20 months)
Joint Degrees: MBA/Bachelor of Law (4 years); MBA/Master of Engineering (2 years); MBA/Master of Agriculture (2 years); MBA/Master of Forestry (2 years)
Special Opportunities: Specializations offered in International Business, Leisure and Sport Management, Natural Resources and Energy, Technology Commercialization
Study Abroad Options: Australia, Austria, Finland, France, Germany, Japan, Mexico, United States, Switzerland, Scotland, Thailand, Chile, Denmark, United Kingdom, Hong Kong, Sweden

STUDENT INFORMATION
Total Business Students: 295
% Female: 42
% International: 40
Average Age: 27

COMPUTER AND RESEARCH FACILITIES
Research Facilities: Canadian Centre for Social Entrepreneurship; Centre for Applied Business Research in Energy and the Environment; Centre for Entrepreneurship and Family Enterprise; Centre for Executive and Management Development; Centre for Excellence in Operations; Centre for International Business Studies; Centre for Professional Service Firm Management; Chartered Accountants Centre; Canadian Institute of Retailing and Services; Cultural Industries Research Centre; Environmental Research Studies Centre; Institute for Financial Research; Western Centre for Economic Research
Computer Facilities: MBA computer lab equipped with 25 computers, a scanner, and a high-speed printer; database access for students
Campuswide Network? Yes
% of MBA Classrooms Wired: 70
Internet Fee? No

EXPENSES/FINANCIAL AID
Annual Tuition: $2,870
Tuition Per Credit (Resident): $100
Room & Board (On Campus): $4,700
Books and Supplies: $1,040

ADMISSIONS INFORMATION
Electronic Application? No
Regular Application Deadline: 4/30
Regular Notification: Rolling
Length of Deferment: 1 year
Non-fall Admissions? No
Transfer Students Accepted? No
Need-Blind Admissions? Yes
Number of Applications Received: 348
% of Applicants Accepted: 41
% Accepted Who Enrolled: 57
Average GPA: 3.2
Average GMAT: 627
GMAT Range: 570-710
Average Years Experience: 5

INTERNATIONAL STUDENTS
TOEFL Required of International Students? Yes
Minimum TOEFL: 600 (250 computer)

EMPLOYMENT INFORMATION
Placement Office Available? Yes
% Employed Within 3 Months: 88
Frequent Employers: PricewaterhouseCoopers, University of Alberta, University of Alberta Hospital, Canadian Imperial Bank of Commerce

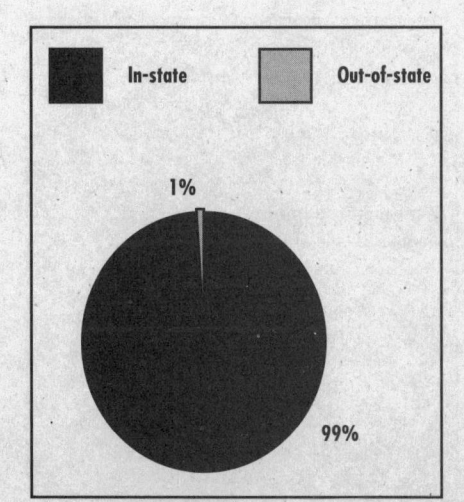

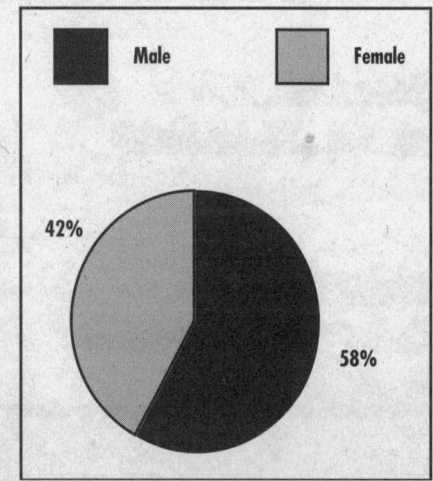

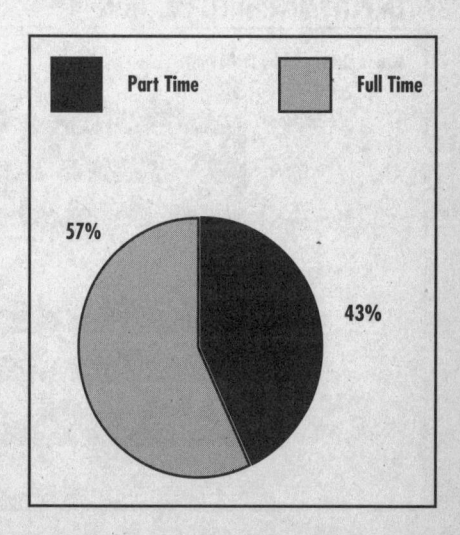

In-state / Out-of-state: 99% / 1%
Male / Female: 58% / 42%
Part Time / Full Time: 57% / 43%

UNIVERSITY OF ARIZONA
Eller Graduate School of Management

Admissions Contact: Cecilia Munoz-Escobedo, Admissions Counselor
Address: McClelland Hall 210, 1130 E. Helen, Tucson, AZ 85721-0108
Admissions Phone: 520-621-4008 • *Admissions Fax:* 520-621-2606
Admissions E-mail: mbaapp@bpa.arizona.edu • *Web Address:* www.eller.arizona.edu/mba

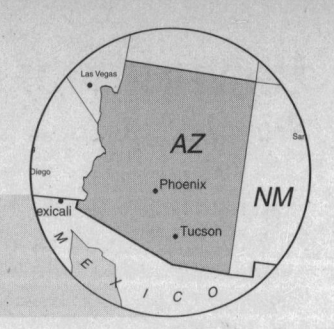

The tuition is dirt cheap at the University of Arizona's Eller School of Management, home to a nationally renowned information technology department, which draws substantial financial support from tech behemoths like IBM and Hewlett-Packard. U of A also boasts a "very well-respected entrepreneurial program," and MBA students here tell us that "Tucson is a great place to live" because "the cost of living is low and it has a laid-back environment."

INSTITUTIONAL INFORMATION
Public/Private: Public
Evening Classes Available? Yes
Total Faculty: 85
% Faculty Female: 20
Student/Faculty Ratio: 38:1
Students in Parent Institution: 35,000
Academic Calendar: Semester

PROGRAMS
Degrees Offered: MBA (21 months); MIS (10 to 21 months); MAC (10 months)
Joint Degrees: JD/MBA (4 years); MBA/MIM (2 to 4 years); MIS/MBA (3 years)
Academic Specialties: Entrepreneur; Management Information Systems; Research and Development; Finance

STUDENT INFORMATION
Total Business Students: 316
% Full Time: 100
% Female: 45
% Minority: 25
% Out of State: 85
% International: 25
Average Age: 28

COMPUTER AND RESEARCH FACILITIES
Computer Facilities: Graduate Computer Lab, Park Street Lab, Economics Lab (there are more on campus but these are specifically for business and MBA students)
Campuswide Network? Yes
% of MBA Classrooms Wired: 3
Internet Fee? No

EXPENSES/FINANCIAL AID
Annual Tuition (Nonresident): $15,804
Books and Supplies: $1,500
Average Grant: $10,000
Average Loan: $16,800

ADMISSIONS INFORMATION
Application Fee: $45
Electronic Application? Yes
Early Decision Application Deadline: 11/15
Early Decision Notification: 12/15
Regular Application Deadline: Rolling
Regular Notification: Rolling
Deferment Available? Yes
Length of Deferment: 1 year
Non-fall Admissions? No
Transfer Students Accepted? No
Need-Blind Admissions? Yes
Number of Applications Received: 1,124
% of Applicants Accepted: 23
% Accepted Who Enrolled: 62
Average GPA: 3.0
GPA Range: 2.0-3.0
Average GMAT: 656
GMAT Range: 580-790
Average Years Experience: 5
Other Admissions Factors Considered: Quality of work experience, performance on the quantitative section on the GMAT, performance on the analytical section of the GMAT, quality of application essays
Other Schools to Which Students Applied: Arizona State University, Cornell University, Purdue University, University of California-Berkeley, University of California-Los Angeles, University of Maryland-College Park, University of Texas-Austin

INTERNATIONAL STUDENTS
TOEFL Required of International Students? Yes
Minimum TOEFL: 600 (250 computer)

EMPLOYMENT INFORMATION

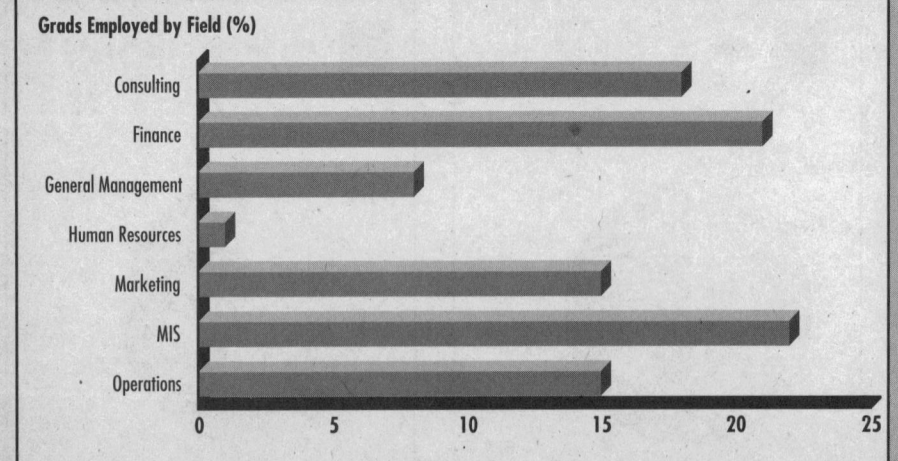

Grads Employed by Field (%)
- Consulting: ~18
- Finance: ~21
- General Management: ~8
- Human Resources: ~1
- Marketing: ~15
- MIS: ~22
- Operations: ~15

Placement Office Available? Yes
% Employed Within 3 Months: 95
Frequent Employers: Andersen Consulting, Intel, Hewlett-Packard, Agilent, E&J Gallo Winery, PCS Health Systems, Calence, Deloitte Consulting, IBM, American Management Systems
Prominent Alumni: Mark Hoffman, CEO, Commerce One; Robert Eckert, chairman, CEO, Mattel, Inc.; Jim Whims, managing partner, Tech Fund; Vicki Panhuise, VP of strategy, Honeywell/GE; Tom Hennings, president and CEO, OrderFusion

UNIVERSITY OF ARKANSAS—FAYETTEVILLE
Sam M. Walton College of Business

Admissions Contact: Michele Halsell, Managing Director, Graduate School of Business
Address: 475 Business Building, Fayetteville, AR 72701
Admissions Phone: 501-575-2851 • Admissions Fax: 501-575-8721
Admissions E-mail: gsb@walton.uark.edu • Web Address: waltoncollege.uark.edu/gsb/mba

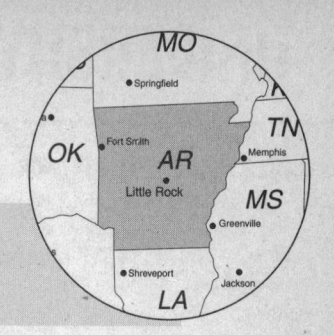

The Sam M. Walton College of Business Administration offers an accelerated one-year MBA program and a part-time managerial MBA program, and short preparatory courses are available to students who fail to meet the business admission requisites or score above 70 percent on the sample exams. A special feature of UA's business program takes place in mid-October of each year, when the MBA class travels to the Southwest MBA Fair, a regional career fair in Dallas that attracts big-name companies such as Intel, Nortel Networks, Deloitte & Touche, American Express, and Sprint. Applicants to UA Fayetteville also apply to East Tennessee State University, Arkansas State, Kansas State, Oklahoma State, and Vanderbilt, among others.

INSTITUTIONAL INFORMATION
Public/Private: Public
Evening Classes Available? Yes
Total Faculty: 85
% Faculty Female: 27
% Faculty Minority: 9
Student/Faculty Ratio: 20:1
Students in Parent Institution: 15,795

PROGRAMS
Degrees Offered: MBA (1 year); MAcc (1 year); MAECQN (18 months); MTLM (1 year); MIS (1 year)
Joint Degrees: MBA/JD (4 years)
Academic Specialties: 1-year program, 38 hours lockstep; consulting projects
Study Abroad Options: Italy, NAFTA, China, Japan, France

STUDENT INFORMATION
Total Business Students: 121
% Full Time: 39
% Female: 34
% Minority: 16
% Out of State: 32
% International: 28
Average Age: 28

COMPUTER AND RESEARCH FACILITIES
Research Facilities: Students Acquiring Knowledge Through Enterprise, a not-for-profit organization
Computer Facilities: More than 200 general-access lab computers, Graduate Student Lab with 20 computers. All computers have Internet access.
Campuswide Network? Yes
% of MBA Classrooms Wired: 100
Computer Model Recommended: No
Internet Fee? No

EXPENSES/FINANCIAL AID
Annual Tuition (Resident/Nonresident): $9,751/$20,007
Tuition Per Credit (Resident/Nonresident): $256/$526
Room & Board: $10,700
Books and Supplies: $1,000
Average Grant: $7,626
Average Loan: $11,064
% Receiving Financial Aid: 75
% Receiving Aid Their First Year: 75

ADMISSIONS INFORMATION
Application Fee: $40
Electronic Application? Yes
Regular Application Deadline: 2/15
Regular Notification: 3/15
Length of Deferment: 1 year
Non-fall Application Deadline(s): Summer only
Transfer Policy: Maximum 6 credits in electives from an AACSB-accredited school
Need-Blind Admissions? Yes
Number of Applications Received: 132
% of Applicants Accepted: 86
% Accepted Who Enrolled: 74
Average GPA: 3.4
GPA Range: 3.1-3.7
Average GMAT: 573
GMAT Range: 530-630
Average Years Experience: 2
Other Admissions Factors Considered: Those with significant business experience are given preference.
Minority/Disadvantaged Student Recruitment Programs: Special financial assistance is available to minority students.
Other Schools to Which Students Applied: Arkansas State, East Tennessee State, Kansas State, Oklahoma State, Pittsburg State, Vanderbilt, U. of Central Arkansas

INTERNATIONAL STUDENTS
TOEFL Required of International Students? Yes
Minimum TOEFL: 550 (213 computer)

EMPLOYMENT INFORMATION

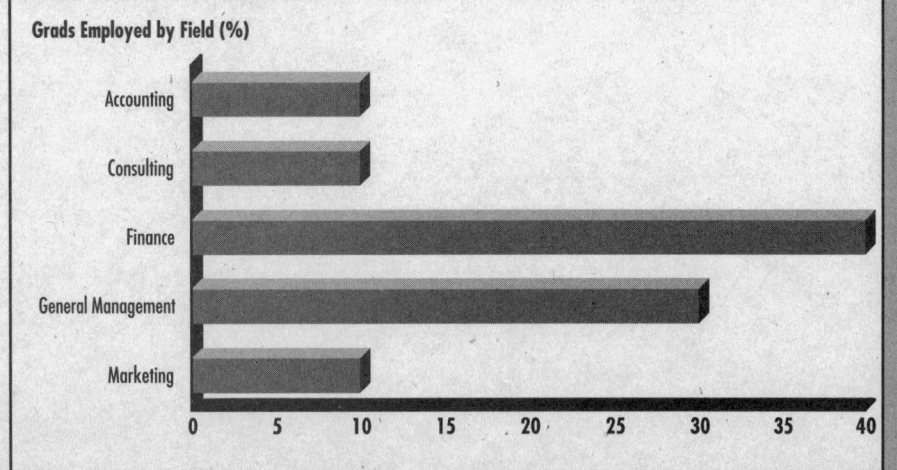

Grads Employed by Field (%)
- Accounting: ~10
- Consulting: ~10
- Finance: ~40
- General Management: ~30
- Marketing: ~10

Placement Office Available? Yes
% Employed Within 3 Months: 64
Frequent Employers: JB Hunt, Wal-Mart Stores Inc., Accenture, Tyson Foods, Whitehall Robin
Prominent Alumni: S. Robson Walton, chairman, Wal-Mart Stores Inc.; William Dillards, Sr., chairman, Dillard's Inc.; Frank Fletcher, entrepreneur; Jack Stephens, Stephens Inc.; Thomas F. McLarty, former U.S. presidential advisor

UNIVERSITY OF ARKANSAS—FAYETTEVILLE

THE UNIVERSITY AT A GLANCE
The University of Arkansas, Fayetteville, serves as the major center of liberal and professional education and as the primary land-grant campus for the state. The University offers graduate education leading to the master's degree in more than 82 fields and to the doctoral degree in more than 30 carefully selected areas.

The entire UA population is composed of approximately 15,000 students. The Sam M. Walton College of Business enrolls approximately 2,500 undergraduate students and approximately 200 graduate students.

STUDENTS
The UA MBA experience is different from the experience found in large MBA programs. Arkansas's small program size allows frequent and substantial contact among students and between students and faculty members. A very active graduate business student association plans and carries out community outreach work, professional development activities, and social functions.

Arkansas MBA students have widely varying backgrounds. More than 13 states and 20 countries are represented in the MBA student body. Students average 26 years of age and possess, on average, two years of professional work experience prior to joining the program. Approximately 42 percent of students are women, 16 percent are members of minority groups, and 26 percent are international students.

The MBA program is open to any undergraduate degree student. Nearly 20 percent of students possess undergraduate degrees and work experience in chemical, civil, electrical, industrial, or mechanical engineering. Other majors include business, biology, history, liberal arts, political science, psychology, and other social sciences.

ACADEMICS
The University of Arkansas Master of Business Administration program is designed to produce graduates with a broad view of the issues confronting managers in cutting-edge organizations. In a departure from the traditional collection of 3-hour courses, the Arkansas MBA program is organized around coordinated modules. UA MBA students are involved in classes and projects that ensure graduates possess the following five competencies: the skills, knowledge, and ability to lead change; the ability to approach problems from a managerial perspective; the ability to manage and work in teams; the ability to write and speak persuasively, based upon a comprehensive analysis of situations facing managers; and self-confidence grounded in one's abilities.

Both the full-time and the managerial (part-time) programs comprise five primary blocks: preparatory work, foundations, core modules, a partnering project, and a concentration in one of five areas: strategic retail alliances, finance, entrepreneurship and strategic innovation, global business, or a customized concentration. The customized concentration is designed by the student and can be completed with either business administration courses and/or courses outside of the College. A JD/MBA program is available.

The UA MBA program is a one-year program for all full-time students, regardless of their undergraduate degree. Through extensive self-study with preparatory materials, participation in prematriculation workshops, and completion of the foundations module, all students should have sufficient background to pursue the rigorous 38-hour, lock-step curriculum. The managerial program is a two-year (minimum) program. Initial matriculation is approximately July 1 for the full-time program and approximately August 25 for the managerial program.

UA MBA students have the opportunity to participate in numerous international programs and courses. Jointly taught summer classes are offered with the University of Quebec at Montreal and DUXX in Mexico. A dual master's degree program with ESC Toulouse in France allows French-speaking students to complete one year of study at the University of Arkansas and a second year of study in France, with degrees from both institutions being awarded at the completion of the second year. Many MBA students choose to participate in Sam M. Walton College of Business Administration classes in China, Italy, and Japan.

Future entrepreneurs can participate in the Students Acquiring Knowledge through Enterprise (SAKE) course. SAKE is a retail operation that offers high-quality, unique merchandise for college markets. Profits from the business are used to fund international travel; in the past, students have traveled to Hong Kong, China, and Costa Rica.

Arkansas MBA faculty members possess extensive experience in corporate problem solving for a variety of businesses and government agencies. Twenty-one percent of the graduate faculty are women and members of minority groups. Graduate faculty members have received doctoral degrees from major research institutions, including Carnegie Mellon, Duke, Georgia, Harvard, Indiana, Michigan State, MIT, North Carolina, Pennsylvania, Purdue, Tennessee, and Texas. Faculty members are active in research and professional publications.

Sam M. Walton College of Business

CAMPUS LIFE

The University is located in Fayetteville, a community of 60,000 residents. It is situated in the northwestern corner of the state in the heart of the Ozark Mountains at an elevation of 1,400 feet. Fayetteville is a two-hour drive from Tulsa, a four-hour drive from Kansas City, and a five-hour drive from Dallas and St. Louis. A regional airport offering daily flights to Atlanta, Chicago, Dallas, Memphis, New York, and St. Louis services the city.

All MBA classes are taught in state-of-the-art, dedicated rooms that allow technology to be fully integrated into classroom discussions. A separate graduate computer lab with the latest computer software is available for MBA students. A graduate lounge is available for student use for team meetings, study, and socializing.

For students' living needs, both on- and off-campus housing (within walking distance of the campus) is available. For on-campus housing, application should be made at least three months prior to the summer enrollment date. A mass transit system is available to all students for transportation in and around the surrounding areas. Transportation fees are nominal and are included as part of the total tuition fee expense.

The Sam M. Walton College of Business has a full-time placement director dedicated to supporting the career development needs of master's degree students. In addition, the University of Arkansas lends placement support through the Career Planning and Placement Office. Services that are provided include resume preparation, counseling, career workshops, employer information services, and employment search assistance. UA MBA graduates have been successful in finding jobs with partnering firms and with Fortune 500 companies. Eighty-two percent of Arkansas MBA graduates are in career positions or continue additional studies within three months of graduation.

The Dean's Executive Advisory Board utilizes its experience and expertise to assist the Sam M. Walton College of Business in defining and realizing its goals. The board consists of 34 corporate leaders, 27 of whom are chairmen, CEOs, presidents, or division presidents of large regional, national, or international corporations, including Wal-Mart Stores, Inc.; Tyson Foods, Inc.; J. B. Hunt Transport, Inc.; Entergy Corporation; ALLTEL Corporation; Beverly Enterprises; Southwestern Bell Telephone; Bank of America; American Freightways; Staffmark, Inc.; and Southwestern Energy Company. These corporate leaders provide valuable insight and contacts and play an integral part of the MBA experience, bridging academic learning with hands-on professional training.

The College also utilizes the services of the Business Alumni Advisory Council members. Council members serve as ambassadors to advance the presence of the College throughout the nation. The council comprises 38 members, all of whom are graduates of the University of Arkansas. Each member is a business leader in his or her field of expertise.

COSTS

Tuition and fees for one semester of the 2001–2002 academic year are $3,175 for Arkansas residents and $6,520 for nonresidents for 12 hours of graduate-level studies. In addition, students enrolled in six or more hours are assessed $200 for health, activity, technology, recreation, transportation, and facilities fees. International students must show proof of health insurance and are required to pay a nonimmigrant student service fee of $40 per semester.

Fayetteville consistently has been selected as one of the best cities in which to live in the United States. The area has a relatively low cost of living; students can expect to pay approximately $9,200 a year for living expenses, including room, board, books, supplies, and personal expenses.

Students may apply for graduate assistantships, which currently offer a tuition waiver and pay a stipend of $6,500 for 12 months. Students who are awarded graduate assistantships are required to work 12 hours per week to support the instructional or research needs of the faculty in the Sam M. Walton College of Business.

ADMISSIONS

Admission to the Master of Business Administration program is competitive and limited. Successful applicants are expected to rank in the 80th percentile on the GMAT and possess a cumulative undergraduate grade point average of 3.4. International applicants must score a minimum of 550 on the Test of English as a Foreign Language (TOEFL), and a TOEFL score of 600 is strongly recommended.

Although work experience is not required for the full-time program, applicants with a minimum of two years of professional work experience are given preference. Applicants to the managerial program must possess two years of full-time work experience prior to graduation. Letters of recommendation from those familiar with the applicant's aptitude for graduate-level work in business and essays from the applicant are weighted heavily in admission decisions.

International applicants, all applicants without an undergraduate business degree, and applicants who completed an undergraduate degree in business more than three years ago should submit their completed application materials by November 15. Admission decisions for early applicants are made by December 15, giving the successful applicant sufficient time to complete the preparatory work prior to matriculation in the summer. Preference in admission and financial aid is given to applicants who submit their application prior to February 15. All applications received after February 15 are processed on a space-available basis. In no case is an applicant admitted after May 15.

Admissions Contact: Michele Halsell, Managing Director, Graduate School of Business
Address: 475 Business Building, Fayetteville, AR 72701
Admissions Phone: 501-575-2851 • Admissions Fax: 501-575-8721
Admissions E-mail: gsb@walton.uark.edu • Web Address: waltoncollege.uark.edu/gsb/mba

UNIVERSITY OF BALTIMORE
Merrick School of Business

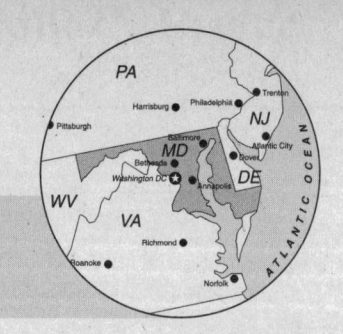

Admissions Contact: Jeffrey Zavronty, Assistant Director of Admissions
Address: 1420 North Charles Street, Baltimore, MD 21201
Admissions Phone: 877-277-5982 • Admissions Fax: 410-837-4793
Admissions E-mail: Admissions@ubmail.ubalt.edu • Web Address: www.ubalt.edu

"The career-minded university," University of Baltimore is 1 of 13 schools under the umbrella of the University System of Maryland. The Robert G. Merrick School of Business offers a multitude of MBA program options. The Advantage MBA is a one-year full-time track; the Saturday MBA is a two-year track designed for busy executives and managers; the Web MBA is designed for an online educational experience; and the Custom Track allows students to mix and match courses from the Advantage, Saturday, and Web MBA tracks to create a more personalized degree experience. To kick up the global perspective a notch, UB also offers the Executive MBA program in China and Chile.

INSTITUTIONAL INFORMATION
Public/Private: Public
Evening Classes Available? Yes
Total Faculty: 53
% Faculty Female: 25
% Faculty Minority: 34
Student/Faculty Ratio: 15:1
Students in Parent Institution: 4,639
Academic Calendar: Semester

PROGRAMS
Degrees Offered: Advantage MBA (30 to 48 credits, 12 months); Flex MBA (30 to 51 credits, 12 months to 7 years); MS in Finance (30 to 42 credits, 12 months to 7 years); MS in Information Systems (33 to 45 credits, 12 months to 7 years); MS in Taxation (30 credits, 12 months to 7 years); Professional MBA (48 credits, 23 months); MS in Accounting (30 to 51 credits, 12 months to 7 years); Chinese Executive MBA (48 credits, 12 months); Web MBA (48 credits, 2 years); MS in Marketing and Venturing (48 credits, 2 to 4 years)
Joint Degrees: MBA/MS in Nursing (66 credits, 2 to 7 years); MBA/PhD in Nursing (85 credits, 2 to 7 years); MBA/PharmD (155 credits, 2 to 7 years); MBA/JD (102 to 123 credits, 3 to 7 years)
Academic Specialties: International Business, Entrepreneurship, Finance, Information Systems, Accounting, Human Resource Management, Decision Technologies, Service and Manufacturing Operations, Marketing

STUDENT INFORMATION
Total Business Students: 506
% Full Time: 46
% Female: 43
% Minority: 18
% Out of State: 16
% International: 33
Average Age: 29

COMPUTER AND RESEARCH FACILITIES
Research Facilities: MBNA Information Systems Institute includes the Information Systems Research Center and the E-Learning Center.
Campuswide Network? Yes
% of MBA Classrooms Wired: 100
Computer Model Recommended: No
Internet Fee? No

EXPENSES/FINANCIAL AID
Annual Tuition (Resident/Nonresident): $5,941/$8,533
Tuition Per Credit (Resident/Nonresident): $294/$438
Books and Supplies: $900

ADMISSIONS INFORMATION
Application Fee: $30
Electronic Application? Yes
Regular Application Deadline: Rolling
Regular Notification: Rolling
Length of Deferment: 1 year
Non-fall Application Deadline(s): 12/1 spring, 4/1 summer
Transfer Policy: Maximum 6 credits; must be from an AACSB-accredited MBA program
Need-Blind Admissions? Yes
Number of Applications Received: 376
% of Applicants Accepted: 62
% Accepted Who Enrolled: 63
Average GPA: 3.0
Average GMAT: 500
Other Admissions Factors Considered: Work experience
Other Schools to Which Students Applied: Loyola College in Maryland, University of Maryland College Park

INTERNATIONAL STUDENTS
TOEFL Required of International Students? Yes
Minimum TOEFL: 550 (213 computer)

EMPLOYMENT INFORMATION
Placement Office Available? Yes
Frequent Employers: Government agencies, corporations
Prominent Alumni: William Donald Schaeffer, governor, state of Maryland; Peter Angelos, owner, Baltimore Orioles; Joseph Curran, attorney general, state of Maryland; Vernon Wright, vice chairman, MBNA America Bank

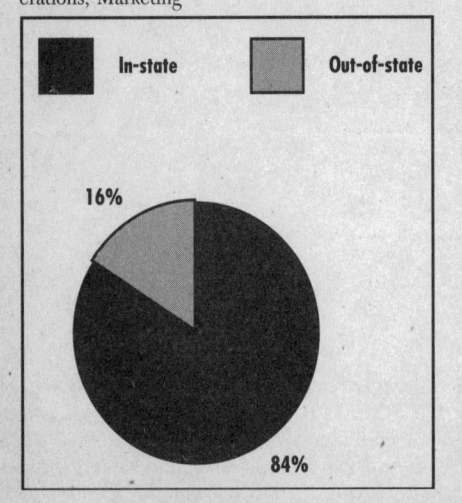

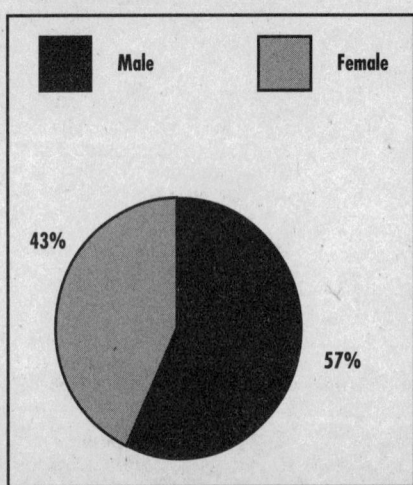

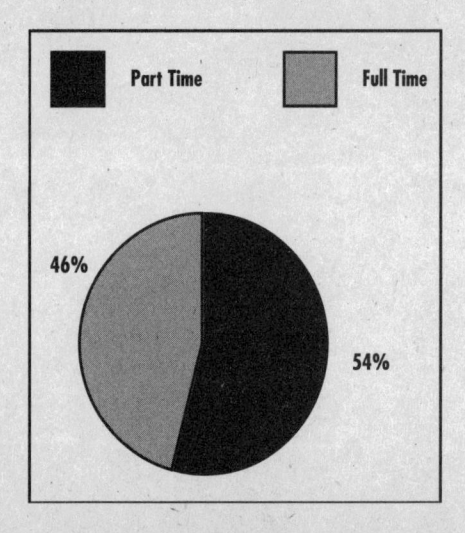

In-state: 84% / Out-of-state: 16%

Male: 57% / Female: 43%

Part Time: 54% / Full Time: 46%

UNIVERSITY OF BATH
School of Management

Admissions Contact: Ruth Cooper, MBA Admissions and Marketing Manager
Address: MBA Office, School of Management, Claverton Dewr., Bath, BA2 7AY, United Kingdom
Admissions Phone: 011 44 (0) 225 383432 • Admissions Fax: 011 44 (0) 225 386210
Admissions E-mail: mba-info@management.bath.ac.uk • Web Address: www.bath.ac.uk/management

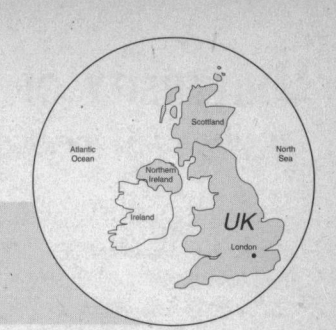

INSTITUTIONAL INFORMATION
Evening Classes Available? No
Total Faculty: 51
% Faculty Female: 22
% Faculty Part Time: 7
Student/Faculty Ratio: 8:1
Students in Parent Institution: 8,000

PROGRAMS
Degrees Offered: MBA (full time, 1 year); Executive MBA (Bath) (part time, 2 years); Executive MBA (Swindon) (part time, 3 years); Modular MBA (part time, 2 to 8 years, 3 or 4 average); MS in Management (full time, 1 year); MS in Responsibility and Business Practice (part time, 2 years)
Joint Degrees: BS in International Management and Modern Languages (IMML): French, German, Spanish (4 years)
Academic Specialties: Bath fosters an academically strong, friendly culture and avoids the "production line" approach of some MBA programs. The programs cover all the key quantitative techniques and subject areas, while the behavioral and values-based aspects of management are also key components. The School of Management has an excellent reputation for business education and research. Academic areas of expertise include Accounting and Finance, Business Economics and Strategy, Decision and Information Systems, Higher Education Management, Human Resource Management, International Business, Marketing, Operations Management and the Management of Supply, Organizational Behavior, and Risk Management.

Study Abroad Options: Czech Republic, Denmark, France, Germany, Netherlands, Canada, United States

STUDENT INFORMATION
Total Business Students: 293
% Female: 43
% International: 34
Average Age: 30

COMPUTER AND RESEARCH FACILITIES
Research Facilities: The strength of research in the School of Management lies in its multidisciplinary and issue-led focus. Academics from a range of disciplines work collaboratively in focused research centres. The centres currently based within the school are Centre for Action Research in Professional Practice, Centre for Technology and Innovation Management, Centre for Information Management, Centre for Research in Strategic Purchasing and Supply, Centre for the Study of Regulated Industries, Industrial Marketing and Purchasing Centre, International Centre for Higher Education Management, and Work and Employment Research Centre.
Computer Facilities: The Library and Learning Center is one of the few in the United Kingdom to offer 24-hour service during term time.
Campuswide Network? Yes
% of MBA Classrooms Wired: 50
Computer Model Recommended: No
Internet Fee? No

EXPENSES/FINANCIAL AID
Room & Board: $8,000

ADMISSIONS INFORMATION
Electronic Application? Yes
Regular Application Deadline: 1/6
Length of Deferment: 2 years
Non-fall Application Deadline(s): All terms
Transfer Policy: Normal application process
Need-Blind Admissions? No
Number of Applications Received: 400
% of Applicants Accepted: 23
% Accepted Who Enrolled: 87
Average GMAT: 580
GMAT Range: 450-710
Average Years Experience: 8
Other Admissions Factors Considered: Our selection process is designed to identify those students for whom the MBA represents more than just a "means to an end" and are able and willing to contribute their views and ideas to enrich the learning experience for all concerned. Although around 90 percent of participants hold a first degree, we believe experience, motivation, and commitment are just as important. Therefore, candidates without a degree or professional qualification but with valuable business experience are welcome to apply.
Other Schools to Which Students Applied: Manchester Business School, University of Warwick

INTERNATIONAL STUDENTS
TOEFL Required of International Students? Yes
Minimum TOEFL: 500 (250 computer)

EMPLOYMENT INFORMATION

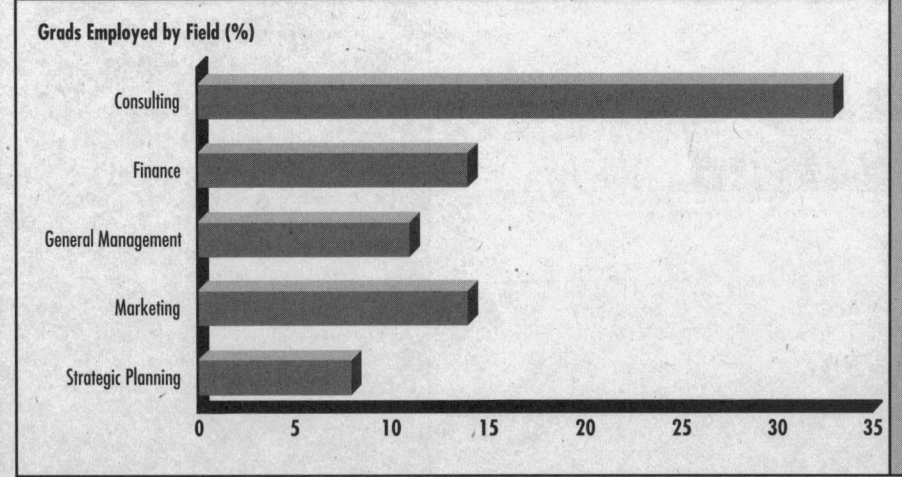

Grads Employed by Field (%)
- Consulting: ~33
- Finance: ~13
- General Management: ~13
- Marketing: ~13
- Strategic Planning: ~8

Placement Office Available? Yes
% Employed Within 3 Months: 80
Frequent Employers: BP Castrol, Lucent, Nortel Networks, Orange, Penna Change Consulting, Siemens

UNIVERSITY OF CALGARY
Faculty of Management

Admissions Contact: Penny O'Hearn, Admissions Officer
Address: 2500 University Drive, NW, Calgary, AB T2N 1N4 Canada
Admissions Phone: 403-220-3808 • Admissions Fax: 403-282-0095
Admissions E-mail: mbarequest@mgmt.ucalgary.ca • Web Address: www.ucalgary.ca/mg/mba

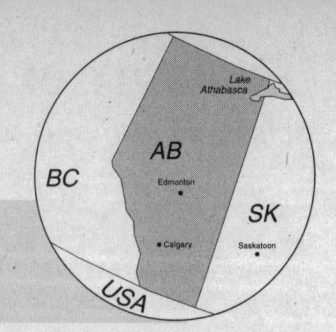

UC touches on Thornton May's rules about learning in the new economy by placing emphasis on conversation among workers, synergy, and meeting deadlines with efficiency and cooperation. Faculty members at U of Calgary also stress international finance, as well as the oh-so-necessary MBA requirements of a global perspective and a grasp on the ever-changing techno-economy. An especially unique feature of the MBA program is the presence of managers from a wide range of companies and industry sectors, who work in class alongside students as on-site mentors and consultants. An Executive MBA is also available, thanks to the combined forces of the University of Calgary and the University of Alberta.

INSTITUTIONAL INFORMATION
Evening Classes Available? Yes
Total Faculty: 85
% Faculty Female: 27
Students in Parent Institution: 25,500
Academic Calendar: Semester

PROGRAMS
Degrees Offered: MBA (2 years full time, up to 6 years part time, 4 to 4.5 years average); Thesis (2 to 5 years); PhD (4 to 6 years)
Joint Degrees: MBA/LLB (4 years), MBA/MSW
Academic Specialties: Finance, Entrepreneurship, E-Business
Study Abroad Options: European Summer School for Advanced Management, North American Summer School for Advanced Management, Asian Intensive School for Advanced Management, numerous exchange programs (see our Web page)

STUDENT INFORMATION
Total Business Students: 398
% Female: 43
% International: 35
Average Age: 30

COMPUTER AND RESEARCH FACILITIES
Research Facilities: Energy Centre, Centre for International Business, Canadian Association of Family Enterprise
Computer Facilities: Business Management databases include Bloomberg's Online Service; Canadian Business and Current Affairs; Canadian Labour Law Library; Canadian Newsdisc; Canadian Periodical Index; Canadian Research Index; Cancorp Financials; CCH Tax Works; CRSP; DRI PRO Global Economics; Dun & Bradstreet Industry Norms and Key Business Ratios; EconLit; Expanded Academic ASAPFP Analyser; Fund Profiler; Globe and Mail; Insite2; International Hospitality & Tourism Database; Investext; Lodging, Restaurant and Tourism Index; Moody's Company Data (FIS Online); PAIS International (Public Affairs Information Service); Political Risk Services; ProQuest Direct; Research Insight; STAT-USA; TableBase; Tax Partner; and Wall Street Journal on disc. Remote (off-campus) access is available for Internet subscription databases.
Campuswide Network? Yes
% of MBA Classrooms Wired: 25
Computer Model Recommended: Laptop
Internet Fee? No

EXPENSES/FINANCIAL AID
Annual Tuition (Resident/Nonresident): $6,000/$12,000
Tuition Per Credit (Resident/Nonresident): $528/$1,056
Books and Supplies: $1,500

ADMISSIONS INFORMATION
Application Fee: $60
Electronic Application? No
Regular Application Deadline: 5/1
Regular Notification: Rolling
Deferment Available? Yes
Length of Deferment: 1 year
Non-fall Admissions? No
Transfer Students Accepted? No
Need-Blind Admissions? No
Number of Applications Received: 299
% of Applicants Accepted: 81
% Accepted Who Enrolled: 65
Average GPA: 3.2
GPA Range: 3.0-4.0
Average GMAT: 598
GMAT Range: 550-740
Average Years Experience: 6

INTERNATIONAL STUDENTS
TOEFL Required of International Students? Yes
Minimum TOEFL: 600

EMPLOYMENT INFORMATION

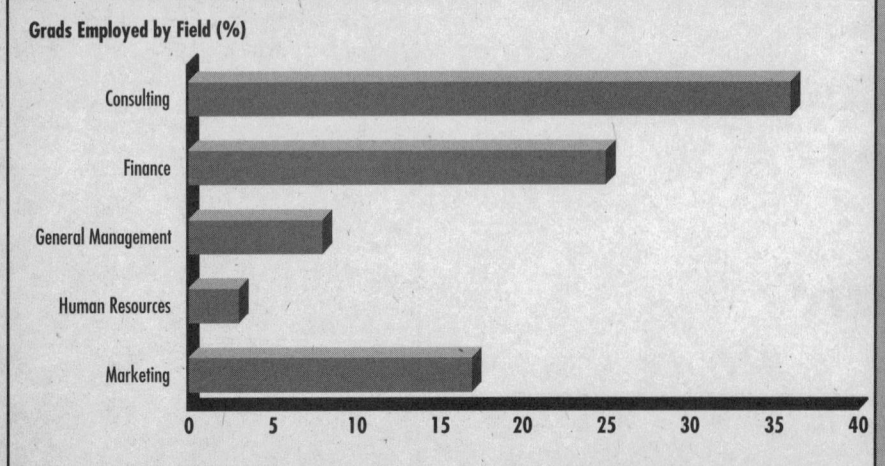

Grads Employed by Field (%)
- Consulting: ~37
- Finance: ~25
- General Management: ~8
- Human Resources: ~3
- Marketing: ~17

Placement Office Available? Yes
% Employed Within 3 Months: 95
Frequent Employers: SagaTech Electronic Inc., Calgary Catholic School Board, CIBC, PanCanadian Petroleum Limited, Cap Gemini Ernst & Young, Merak, Opportunity Capital Corporation, Deloitte & Touche Consulting, ENMAX, Rainbow Contractors, Canadian Natural Resources Limited, Encryption Systems Inc., TELUS Communications Inc., Dustsoft Technologies Inc., Gibson Petroleum, RLG International Ltd., SAP Canada, Coral Energy, Flare Consulting, Westlink Innovations Network, Pocket Connection Ltd., DCA Consulting Corp., WestCoast Energy, Burlington Resources

UNIVERSITY OF CALIFORNIA — BERKELEY
Haas School of Business

Admissions Contact: Peter Johnson, Director of International Admissions, Full-Time MBA Program
Address: 440 Student Services Building #1902, Berkeley, CA 94720-1902
Admissions Phone: 510-642-1405 • Admissions Fax: 510-643-6659
Admissions E-mail: mbaadms@haas.berkeley.edu • Web Address: haas.berkeley.edu

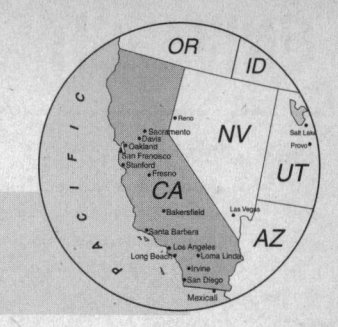

A strong international presence and "smart people" with "a wide variety of backgrounds" and "great stories to tell" are present in abundance at Berkeley's Haas School of Business. Students here laud their "top-notch" and "personable" professors, as well as the "challenging and demanding" course work and the "emphasis on learning, not grades." The San Francisco Bay Area location is also "superb"; students claim it "cannot be topped for climate and lifestyle."

INSTITUTIONAL INFORMATION
Public/Private: Public
Evening Classes Available? Yes
Total Faculty: 106
% Faculty Female: 18
% Faculty Minority: 16
% Faculty Part Time: 36
Student/Faculty Ratio: 8:1
Students in Parent Institution: 29,000
Academic Calendar: Semester

PROGRAMS
Degrees Offered: MBA (2 years full time, 3 years evening)
Joint Degrees: Concurrent degree programs lasting 3 years: JD/MBA in Law, MBA/MPH in Public Health, MBA/MA in Asian Studies, MBA/MIAS in International and Area Studies
Academic Specialties: E-Business, Entrepreneurship, International Business, Management of Technology, Finance, Marketing, Real Estate, Health Care Management, Organizational Behavior, Corporate Strategy
Special Opportunities: Certificate in Entrepreneurship and Innovation, Certificate in Global Management, Certificate in Management of Technology, Certificate in Health Services Management
Study Abroad Options: England, France, Spain, Netherlands, Italy, Hong Kong

STUDENT INFORMATION
Total Business Students: 840
% Full Time: 56
% Female: 30
% Minority: 7
% International: 33
Average Age: 28

COMPUTER AND RESEARCH FACILITIES
Research Facilities: Lester Center for Entrepreneurship and Innovation, Fisher Center for Strategic Use of Information Technology, Clausen Center for International Business and Policy, Fisher Center for Real Estate and Urban Economics
Computer Facilities: Access to a wide range of research databases
Campuswide Network? Yes
% of MBA Classrooms Wired: 9
Computer Model Recommended: Desktop
Internet Fee? No

EXPENSES/FINANCIAL AID
Room & Board: $11,258
Books and Supplies: $2,000
Average Grant: $15,320
Average Loan: $15,000
% Receiving Financial Aid: 60
% Receiving Aid Their First Year: 60

ADMISSIONS INFORMATION
Application Fee: $125
Electronic Application? Yes
Early Decision Application Deadline: November, December, February, March
Early Decision Notification: 2/21
Regular Application Deadline: 3/15
Regular Notification: 5/31
Deferment Available? No
Non-fall Admissions? No
Transfer Students Accepted? No
Need-Blind Admissions? Yes
Number of Applications Received: 3,265
% of Applicants Accepted: 15
% Accepted Who Enrolled: 50
Average GPA: 3.4
GPA Range: 3.1-3.7
Average GMAT: 690
Other Admissions Factors Considered: Quantitative ability, quality of work experience (including depth and breadth of responsibilities), leadership, letters of recommendation, extracurricular and community involvement, short answer and essays (including articulation of clear focus and goals)
Minority/Disadvantaged Student Recruitment Programs: We are members of the Consortium for Graduate Study in Management and the Toigo Fellowships Program, as well as the Diversity Alliance.
Other Schools to Which Students Applied: Columbia, Harvard, NYU, Northwestern, Stanford, UCLA, Penn

INTERNATIONAL STUDENTS
TOEFL Required of International Students? Yes
Minimum TOEFL: 570 (230 computer)

EMPLOYMENT INFORMATION

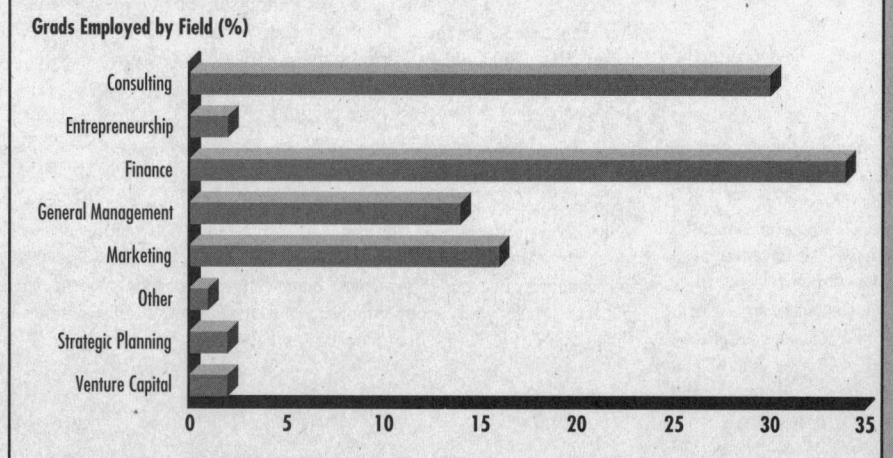

Grads Employed by Field (%)

Field	%
Consulting	~30
Entrepreneurship	~1
Finance	~34
General Management	~14
Marketing	~16
Other	~1
Strategic Planning	~2
Venture Capital	~2

Placement Office Available? Yes
% Employed Within 3 Months: 87
Frequent Employers: Clorox Company, Siebel Systems, Goldman Sachs, Hewlett-Packard, McKinsey & Co., Accenture, Dain Rauscher Wessels, AT Kearney, Credit Suisse First Boston, Deloitte Consulting
Prominent Alumni: Donald Fisher, chairman and founder, The Gap; Rodrigo Rato, deputy prime minister and minister of economy, Spain; Barbara Desoer, executive VP, Bank of America; Bengt Baron, president, Absolut Vodka; Jorge Montoya, president, Procter & Gamble Latin America

UNIVERSITY OF CALIFORNIA—DAVIS

THE SCHOOL AT A GLANCE

"At the Graduate School of Management at UC Davis, we believe that students learn best in a supportive, cooperative learning environment that encourages them to stretch intellectually. To create this environment, we've developed a rigorous program that features small classes, a faculty committed to excellence in teaching, and opportunities to work closely with that faculty and a select group of bright and energetic students. We then guide you to test your new knowledge and creative thinking in 'real world' business situations. I invite you to take advantage of an outstanding opportunity to fully develop your managerial potential and leadership skills."

—Robert H. Smiley, Dean

STUDENTS

UC Davis MBA students bring to the School a wide variety of academic and work experiences, and the School's personalized focus and "hands-on" teaching approach are augmented by this diversity. Because of the strong emphasis on technology management, the School is very attractive to students with backgrounds in engineering and the sciences as well as those with business and economics degrees. Over 35 percent of the fall 2002 entering class will come from undergraduate majors in the humanities and social sciences. The most recently admitted class represents over 44 undergraduate institutions.

The average full-time student is 28 years old and has five years of full-time work experience. Women make up 46 percent of the student population, and international students make up 20 percent.

The School encourages applications from international students. To be eligible for admission to the program, international students must take the TOEFL and earn a score of 250 or better on the computer-based test or 600 or better on the paper-based test. If admitted, international students must provide a Statement of Finances for visa purposes, showing at least $35,000 available to cover tuition and fees for their first year.

ACADEMICS

The UC Davis Graduate School of Management has accomplished what many in academic circles felt was impossible for such a small and young MBA program; it is being ranked among the top 50 in the nation. Conceived just 20 years ago, the program is recognized for the high quality of its graduates, its world-class faculty, and the excellence of its overall program.

The UC Davis MBA program cultivates each student's ability to deal successfully with the challenges of a continually changing, increasingly complex global business environment. The program's strengths come from:

- A managerial approach to the basic business disciplines
- A student/faculty ratio of 10:1
- A curriculum that integrates the technological, social, political, economic, and ethical aspects of business
- A variety of teaching methodologies, including case studies, lectures, class discussions, computer simulations, team projects, and "real world" applications.

The program is comprised of 24 classes (72 quarter units). Joint degrees are available in law (MBA/JD), engineering (MBA/MEng), medicine (MBA/MD), and agricultural management (MBA/MS). All students spend their first year in "core" classes mastering the curriculum, which provides a common foundation of fundamental management knowledge and skill. Elective concentrations available in the full-time day program or in the evening MBA Program for Working Professionals are accounting, corporate environmental management, e-commerce, environmental and natural resource management, finance, health services management, information technology, international management, marketing, not-for-profit management, technology management, and general management. Students can also design a customized concentration.

The first-year strategy course, Management Policy and Strategy, places students in teams and integrates their mastery of the core curriculum by giving them an opportunity to apply their decision-making and problem-solving skills developing a strategic plan in an experiential learning simulation.

UC Davis encourages students to take advantage of the many opportunities to participate in exchange programs with universities abroad. The invaluable experience at another university gives students a first-hand look at how companies are affected by fluctuations in the global marketplace. Students emerge from this experience with a comprehensive understanding of the "big picture."

As more students of diverse interests and backgrounds engage in MBA education, UC Davis is striving to expand the opportunities for students to study abroad. UC Davis has established student exchange programs with nine renowned international universities. Students can also take advantage of a "one-way" exchange with a number of other universities abroad. Established student exchange programs include Bocconi University in Milan, Italy; Hong Kong University of Science and Technology; Instituto Tenologico Antonomo de Mexico (ITAM); Erasmus University in Rotterdam, Holland; University of Lyon, France; Heinrich Heine Universitat Dusseldorf, Germany; Helsinki School of Economics and Business Administration in Helsinki, Finland; Groupe HEC, Institut Superieur des Affaires (ISA), France; and Manchester Business School, England.

To enhance preparation for the job market, the School requires students to participate in a videotaped mock interview with one of several executives drawn from both the public and private sector. This program gives students a unique chance to meet top executives face to face as well as to dramatically improve interviewing skills.

The annual Alumni Day gives current students the "inside track" on up-to-date industry information and career opportunities from alumni and also provides a valuable networking activity.

The School encourages prospective students to take advantage of the Visitation Program. While visiting the School, prospective students are able to talk one on one with current students and professors and can attend a class.

To enhance each student's learning and networking experience, the School has developed close ties with leaders throughout business and government. They are frequent visitors to campus, serving as guest lecturers in classes, as interviewers in the mock interview program, and as speakers at frequent School-sponsored events. Through these important contacts, students gain access to high-profile companies and establish relationships with potential employers.

The Executive-in-Residence program gives students and faculty members alike a unique opportunity to work closely with a top business leader during the executive's quarter-long visit to the School.

The Dean's Advisory Council, made up of many of California's top business leaders, provides the School with one of its strongest connections to the business community. The School's Business Partnership Program also provides an important avenue for top regional organizations to become involved with UC Davis MBAs. Students are invited to network with these corporate executives at breakfast meetings and special lectures.

The faculty of the UC Davis Graduate School of Management represent doctoral preparation from many of the most prestigious schools in the country and excel both as teachers and researchers. Their current consulting projects keep them in touch with managerial concerns of leading U.S. corporations as well as federal and state agencies. But one of the most distinctive features of this faculty is the close relationship they forge with students. The School recognizes the academic value students receive when given the opportunity to work closely and individually with faculty members, and offers many formal and informal chances to do so. The student/faculty ratio is 10:1.

Graduate School of Management

CAMPUS LIFE

With students comprising nearly half of the city's population, Davis is truly one of the few remaining "college towns" in this state or nation. As one of the country's great research universities and the most academically diverse of all the University of California campuses, UC Davis is home to scholars of worldwide reputation in more than 100 academic fields. They have found that UC Davis is an adventurous academic environment that is nurtured by dynamic interdisciplinary cooperation, entrepreneurial public-private partnerships, and a caring spirit. As progressive as the University's academic programs are, UC Davis has preserved the values of friendliness, openness, and cooperation.

The city of Davis is surrounded by some of the most economically vital, naturally magnificent communities in California. Close by, the state capital of Sacramento affords all the amenities expected in a metropolitan area and is home to the state legislature, an expanding high-technology manufacturing industry, and a community of data processing enterprises. A short distance to the southwest is the cosmopolitan San Francisco Bay Area and Silicon Valley. An hour's drive west is the beautiful Napa Valley wine country, and two hours east lies stunning Lake Tahoe.

Academic resources include a library of over 3.1 million volumes, ranked among the top research libraries in North America. A full-time Business Reference Librarian is available to assist students with the latest information-gathering strategies, including some of the most comprehensive online databases available today and access to over 1,000 scholarly and trade journals in business, management, finance, and economics. The School's newly remodeled classrooms feature state-of-the-art multimedia instructional support.

The School maintains a 24-hour computer lab with access to the University's high-speed network, the latest business software, networking to extensive library services, and the Internet and intranet. Access to the network within the Business School facility is wireless. Each student is issued a University computer account, which includes e-mail.

Prior to starting classes, the Career Services Center begins connecting with each student, offering support and personal guidance. Through workshops, on-campus recruiting, mock interviews, and an emphasis on internships, the Career Services Center provides students with the tools needed to build long-term relationships with the corporate community. In addition to an online application and job posting system, MBA students participate in on-campus interviewing for career and internship positions, career fairs, company information sessions, and on-site company tours. Approximately 39 percent of UC Davis's MBA students were placed in the high-tech industry, including positions in finance, marketing, consulting, and technology management. Over the past few years, an average of 92 percent of the School's students have been placed in internship positions after their first year in the program. The total compensation package for students graduating from the UC Davis GSM has averaged $86,500.

COSTS

The estimated fees for the 2002–2003 year for full-time study are $11,021 for California residents and $21,725 for nonresidents. These fees are subject to change. The 2002–2003 cost of the MBA Program for Working Professionals is $1,540 per class. Many reasonably priced apartments are within biking distance. Monthly rents range from $650 for a studio to $1,700 for a three-bedroom apartment. Student-family housing costs range from $486 per month for a one-bedroom apartment to $580 per month for a two-bedroom apartment. Books and supplies are approximately $1,000 for the academic year. Need-based grants, loans, and fee offsets are available, as is the merit-based GSM Scholar's Grant.

Financial aid eligibility at any school is based on the program's cost of attendance, a standard figure reflecting not only fees or tuition, but also basic expenses students incur during the academic year. Both the University of California and the Graduate School of Management have financial aid available for students, including grant funding. More than 90 percent of GSM students who apply for financial assistance receive some type of support. The UC Davis Graduate Financial Aid Office administers loans, grants, funds, and work-study employment that are available to all graduate and professional students. The Office also offers short-term and emergency loans designed to help students with unexpected expenses. The Graduate Financial Aid staff in that office can guide students in applying and qualifying for University grants, loans, work-study, and other financial support.

ADMISSIONS

Admission to the UC Davis Graduate School of Management is highly selective. Applicants are evaluated on the basis of demonstrated academic achievement, performance on the Graduate Management Admission Test (GMAT) and interest in professional management. Full-time business experience is considered an asset. No particular area of undergraduate preparation is required, but the University requires the completion of a bachelor's degree from an accredited college or university. The 2002 entering class has an average GMAT score of 674 and an average undergraduate GPA of 3.3.

Fall application deadlines for domestic applicants are December 1, February 1, and April 1. Deadlines for international applicants are December 1 and February 1. The deadline for the MBA Program for Working Professionals is April 1.

Admissions Contact: Donald A. Blodger, Assistant Dean of Admissions
Address: One Shields Ave., Davis, CA 95616
Admissions Phone: 530-752-7658 • Admissions Fax: 530-752-2924
Admissions E-mail: admissions@gsm.ucdavis.edu • Web Address: www.gsm.ucdavis.edu

UNIVERSITY OF CALIFORNIA — DAVIS
Graduate School of Management

Admissions Contact: Donald A. Blodger, Assistant Dean of Admissions
Address: One Shields Ave., Davis, CA 95616
Admissions Phone: 530-752-7658 • *Admissions Fax:* 530-752-2924
Admissions E-mail: admissions@gsm.ucdavis.edu • *Web Address:* www.gsm.ucdavis.edu

The Graduate School of Management provides a positive learning environment for the business-minded in northern California, as well as a cooperative and enthusiastic student spirit and an emphasis on management in high-tech environments. The MBA program options range from a Full-Time MBA to a Working MBA for busy daytime professionals to a Full-Time Interdisciplinary MBA, a dual degree program that requires serious dedication. The most notable dual degree programs available at UC Davis include an MBA/Juris Doctor, MBA/Doctor of Medicine, MBA/Master of Engineering, and an MBA/Master of Agricultural and Resource Economics.

INSTITUTIONAL INFORMATION
Public/Private: Public
Evening Classes Available? Yes
Total Faculty: 46
% Faculty Female: 13
% Faculty Minority: 11
% Faculty Part Time: 52
Student/Faculty Ratio: 10:1
Students in Parent Institution: 27,292
Academic Calendar: Quarter

PROGRAMS
Degrees Offered: MBA (2 years full time, 3 to 4 years Working Professional Program)
Joint Degrees: JD/MBA (4 years); MD/MBA (6 years); Engineering/MBA (2 years); Ag Econ/MBA (2 years)
Academic Specialties: Finance, Marketing, Technology Management
Study Abroad Options: Hong Kong, Mexico, Holland, Germany, Finland, France, England, Italy

STUDENT INFORMATION
Total Business Students: 131
% Full Time: 98
% Female: 42
% Minority: 4
% Out of State: 6
% International: 27
Average Age: 29

COMPUTER AND RESEARCH FACILITIES
Computer Facilities: Wireless local area network with high-speed Internet access, 2 student PC labs, access to CRSP and Compustat databases and several general databases, systemwide access to more than 1,000 scholarly and trade journals. Other data are available through the University's California Digital Library project.
Campuswide Network? Yes
% of MBA Classrooms Wired: 100
Computer Model Recommended: Laptop
Internet Fee? No

EXPENSES/FINANCIAL AID
Annual Tuition (Resident/Nonresident): $10,782/$21,027
Room & Board (On/Off Campus): $10,500/$10,300
Books and Supplies: $1,500
Average Grant: $7,200
Average Loan: $14,000
% Receiving Financial Aid: 73
% Receiving Aid Their First Year: 70

ADMISSIONS INFORMATION
Application Fee: $40
Electronic Application? Yes
Early Decision Application Deadline: 12/1
Early Decision Notification: 1/31
Regular Application Deadline: 4/1
Regular Notification: 5/31
Length of Deferment: 1 year
Non-fall Admissions? No
Transfer Students Accepted? No
Need-Blind Admissions? Yes
Number of Applications Received: 449
% of Applicants Accepted: 29
% Accepted Who Enrolled: 47
Average GPA: 3.3
GPA Range: 3.0-3.6
Average GMAT: 662
GMAT Range: 630-710
Average Years Experience: 6
Other Admissions Factors Considered: Motivation and leadership potential
Minority/Disadvantaged Student Recruitment Programs: The Michael Maher Scholarship, GSM Fellows Program
Other Schools to Which Students Applied: Stanford, U. of Arizona, UC Berkeley, UCLA, U. of Southern California, UT Austin, U. of Washington

INTERNATIONAL STUDENTS
TOEFL Required of International Students? Yes
Minimum TOEFL: 600 (250 computer)

EMPLOYMENT INFORMATION

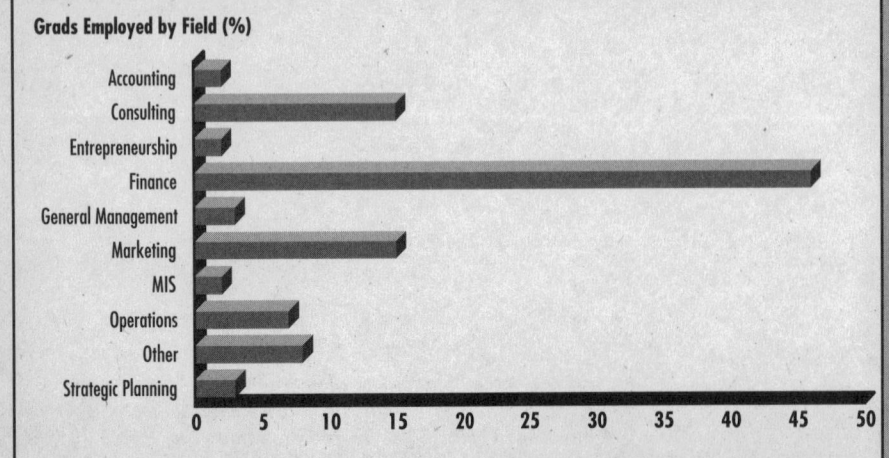

Grads Employed by Field (%)

Field	%
Accounting	~3
Consulting	~15
Entrepreneurship	~2
Finance	~47
General Management	~5
Marketing	~15
MIS	~2
Operations	~7
Other	~5
Strategic Planning	~2

Placement Office Available? Yes
% Employed Within 3 Months: 82
Frequent Employers: Intel, Hewlett-Packard, Agilent, Wells Fargo, GATX Capital, Lam Research, Barclay's Global Investors, Deloitte & Touche, Sun Microsystems, Cisco, Gartner Group, National Parks Conservation Association, CalPERS, California State Auditors, E&J Gallo Winery, Morgan Stanley, KPMG, Mervyn's-Dayton Hudson
Prominent Alumni: David H. Russ, UC treasurer and VP of investments; Christine Smith, Global Catalyst Partners; Gordon C. Hunt, Jr., M.D., senior VP, and chief, Clinical Integration

UNIVERSITY OF CALIFORNIA — IRVINE
Graduate School of Management

Admissions Contact: Francine Matijak, Associate Director, Marketing
Address: 202 GSM, Irvine, CA 92697-3125
Admissions Phone: 949-824-4622 • Admissions Fax: 949-824-2944
Admissions E-mail: gsm-mba@uci.edu • Web Address: www.gsm.uci.edu

UC Irvine is part of the 10-campus California university system. "It works and sprawls like Silicon Valley, but looks and lives like Mediterranean Europe," bubbles the website. How can you blame them, when you can kick back California-style and still have access to nearby big-city business opportunities? UC Irvine MBA programs are offered for full-time and part-time students, and Information Technology for Management is a theme that's integrated into every core class and many electives, including an extensive series of e-commerce courses.

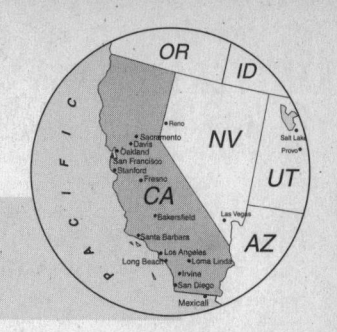

INSTITUTIONAL INFORMATION
Public/Private: Public
Evening Classes Available? Yes
Total Faculty: 77
% Faculty Female: 30
% Faculty Minority: 1
% Faculty Part Time: 43
Student/Faculty Ratio: 8:1
Students in Parent Institution: 21,550

PROGRAMS
Degrees Offered: MBA (2 years), Executive MBA (2 years), Health Care Executive MBA (2 years), Fully Employed MBA (3 years), PhD (4 years)
Joint Degrees: MD/MBA (5 years)
Academic Specialties: Distinguished faculty has an international impact on management knowledge, deepening our understanding of how technological innovations are transforming the way business is done. Our full-time program is widely recognized for integrating the principles of information and technology into the MBA curriculum.
Special Opportunities: Elective course work is offered in Accounting, Business and Government, Economics, Finance, Health Care Management, Information Systems, Marketing, Operations and Decisions Technologies, Organization and Strategy, Real Estate Management, and Management of Innovation and Growth.

Study Abroad Options: France, Belgium, China, Hungary, Austria, Hong Kong, Singapore

STUDENT INFORMATION
Total Business Students: 638
% Full Time: 38
% Female: 25
% Minority: 3
% Out of State: 29
% International: 26
Average Age: 29

COMPUTER AND RESEARCH FACILITIES
Research Facilities: Center for Research on Information Technology and Organizations, National Science Foundation, Irvine Innovation Initiative
Computer Facilities: Standard & Poor's, Compustat, CRSP, and many other databases
Campuswide Network? Yes
% of MBA Classrooms Wired: 100
Computer Model Recommended: Laptop
Internet Fee? No

EXPENSES/FINANCIAL AID
Annual Tuition (Resident): $10,244
Room & Board (On/Off Campus): $6,686/$10,510
Books and Supplies: $5,200
Average Grant: $6,000
Average Loan: $12,500
% Receiving Financial Aid: 85
% Receiving Aid Their First Year: 70

ADMISSIONS INFORMATION
Application Fee: $75
Electronic Application? Yes
Regular Application Deadline: 5/1
Regular Notification: 6/30
Deferment Available? Yes
Length of Deferment: 1 year
Non-fall Admissions? No
Transfer Students Accepted? No
Need-Blind Admissions? Yes
Number of Applications Received: 815
% of Applicants Accepted: 29
% Accepted Who Enrolled: 41
Average GPA: 3.3
GPA Range: 3.1-3.5
Average GMAT: 654
GMAT Range: 623-680
Average Years Experience: 5
Other Admissions Factors Considered: Career progression, well-articulated educational and professional goals, clear understanding of MBA programs, presentation skills, leadership potential
Minority/Disadvantaged Student Recruitment Programs: The Educational Opportunity Program
Other Schools to Which Students Applied: UC Berkeley, UCLA, U. of Southern California, UT Austin, U. of Washington

INTERNATIONAL STUDENTS
TOEFL Required of International Students? Yes
Minimum TOEFL: 600 (250 computer)

EMPLOYMENT INFORMATION

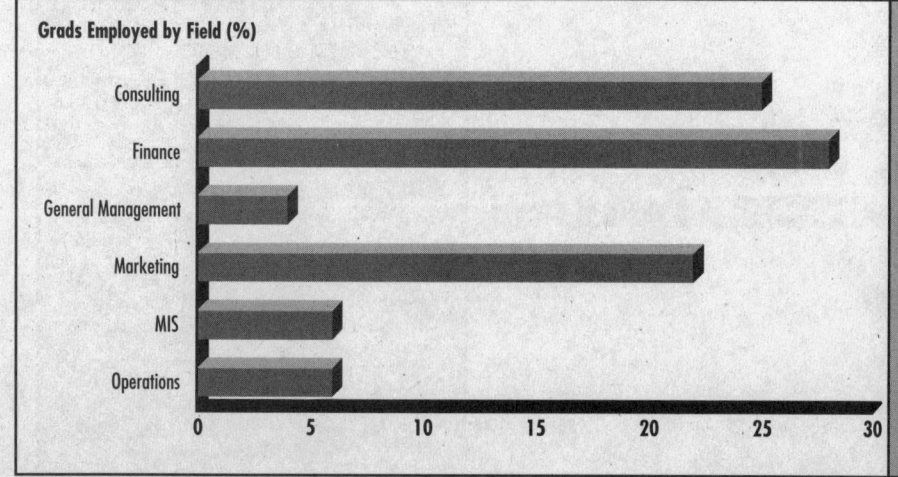

Grads Employed by Field (%)

Field	%
Consulting	25
Finance	28
General Management	5
Marketing	22
MIS	6
Operations	6

Placement Office Available? Yes
% Employed Within 3 Months: 82
Frequent Employers: Deloitte & Touche, PacifiCare, Intel, Conexant, Disney, Nissan, Gateway, Accenture, Wells Fargo, Bristol-Myers Squibb
Prominent Alumni: Afshin Mohebbi, president and COO, Qwest; Darcy B. Kopcho, executive VP, Capital Group Companies; George W. Kessinger, president and CEO, Goodwill Industries International; Norman Witt, VP of community development, The Irvine Co.; Lisa Locklear, VP of operations and resort support finance

UNIVERSITY OF CALIFORNIA — LOS ANGELES
The Anderson School at UCLA

Admissions Contact: Linda Baldwin, Director of Admissions
Address: 110 Westwood Plaza, Los Angeles, CA 90095-1481
Admissions Phone: 310-825-6944 • Admissions Fax: 310-825-8582
Admissions E-mail: mba.admissions@anderson.ucla.edu • Web Address: www.anderson.ucla.edu

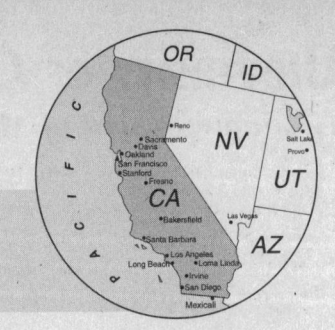

You just can't beat living on the beach with an ocean view, contend the "very active and entrepreneurial" MBA students at UCLA's Anderson School, where "life is good" thanks to an "unbeatable location" and, of course, "February beach parties." The Career Center is fabulous as well, but students sing their highest praises for Anderson's entrepreneurship program, which gives MBAs a chance to study under professors like "Wild Bill" Cockrum—arguably "the top entrepreneurial professor in the nation"—and "Big Al" Osborne.

INSTITUTIONAL INFORMATION
Public/Private: Public
Evening Classes Available? No
Total Faculty: 134
% Faculty Female: 15
% Faculty Minority: 16
% Faculty Part Time: 40
Student/Faculty Ratio: 9:1
Students in Parent Institution: 36,890
Academic Calendar: Quarter

PROGRAMS
Degrees Offered: MBA (2 years); Executive MBA (2 years); Fully Employed MBA (3 years); PhD (4 years)
Joint Degrees: MBA/JD; MBA/MD; MBA/MA Latin American Studies; MBA/MA Urban Planning; MBA/MLIS; MBA/MN; MBA/MPH; MBA/MS Computer Science
Academic Specialties: Finance, Marketing, Management in the Information Economy, Entrepreneurship, Entertainment Management
Study Abroad Options: Philippines, Australia, Argentina, Hong Kong, Denmark, France, Netherlands, Peru, Spain, Venezuela, Mexico, Japan, Germany, England, Norway, Chile, Italy, Switzerland, Belgium, South Africa, Austria, Sweden, New Zealand, China, Brazil, India

STUDENT INFORMATION
Total Business Students: 1,388
% Full Time: 47
% Female: 30
% Minority: 21
% Out of State: 54
% International: 28
Average Age: 28

COMPUTER AND RESEARCH FACILITIES
Research Facilities: Harold Price Center for Entrepreneurial Studies, UCLA Anderson Forecast Center, Center for International Business Education and Research, Center for Management in the Information Economy, Center for Communication Policy and Entertainment Management, Richard S. Ziman Center for Real Estate
Campuswide Network? Yes
% of MBA Classrooms Wired: 100
Computer Model Recommended: Laptop
Internet Fee? No

EXPENSES/FINANCIAL AID
Annual Tuition (Resident/Nonresident): $11,744/$22,448
Room & Board (On Campus): $9,351
Books and Supplies: $5,293
Average Grant: $6,000
Average Loan: $24,500
% Receiving Financial Aid: 70
% Receiving Aid Their First Year: 65

ADMISSIONS INFORMATION
Application Fee: $125
Electronic Application? Yes
Early Decision Application Deadline: 11/15
Early Decision Notification: 1/16
Regular Application Deadline: 4/5
Regular Notification: 6/17
Deferment Available? No
Non-fall Admissions? No
Transfer Students Accepted? No
Need-Blind Admissions? Yes
Number of Applications Received: 3,907
% of Applicants Accepted: 17
% Accepted Who Enrolled: 49
Average GPA: 3.5
Average GMAT: 700
Average Years Experience: 4
Other Admissions Factors Considered: Managerial potential, leadership qualities, interpersonal skills, personal values, special character
Minority/Disadvantaged Student Recruitment Programs: The Anderson School actively seeks highly qualified minority applicants for the MBA Program through graduate advisors, MBA Information Day, LEAD Program, and Riordan Programs.
Other Schools to Which Students Applied: Harvard, Northwestern, Stanford, Penn

INTERNATIONAL STUDENTS
TOEFL Required of International Students? Yes
Minimum TOEFL: 600 (260 computer)

EMPLOYMENT INFORMATION

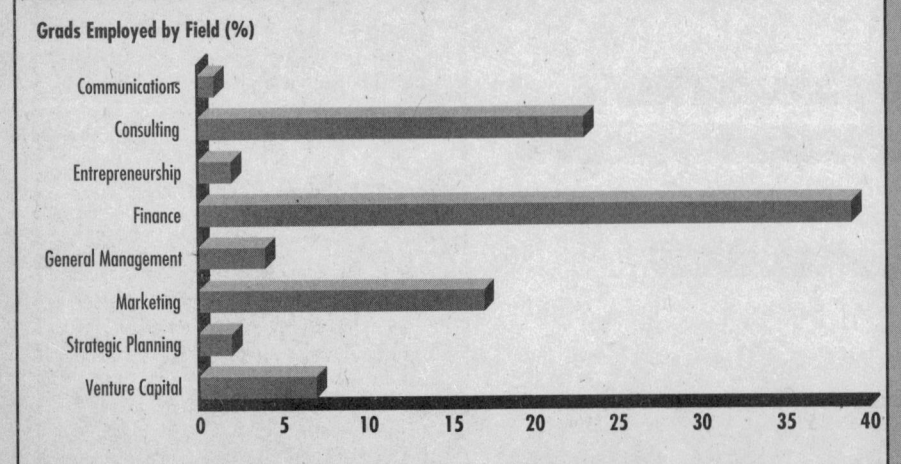

Grads Employed by Field (%)
- Communications
- Consulting
- Entrepreneurship
- Finance
- General Management
- Marketing
- Strategic Planning
- Venture Capital

Placement Office Available? Yes
% Employed Within 3 Months: 98
Frequent Employers: Intel Corporation, Goldman Sachs, Lehman Brothers, Morgan Stanley Dean Witter, Robertson Stephens, McKinsey & Co., Salomon Smith Barney, Diamond Technology Partners
Prominent Alumni: Jeff Henley, CFO, Oracle; Mark Zoradi, president, Buena Vista International; Chris Zyda, international CFO, Amazon; Lisa Brummel, VP of home products, Microsoft; William Gross, investment management,

UNIVERSITY OF CENTRAL FLORIDA
College of Business Administration

Admissions Contact: Judy Ryder, Director of Graduate Studies
Address: PO Box 161400, Orlando, FL 32816
Admissions Phone: 407-823-2184 • Admissions Fax: 407-823-6206
Admissions E-mail: cbagrad@bus.ucf.edu • Web Address: www.bus.ucf.edu

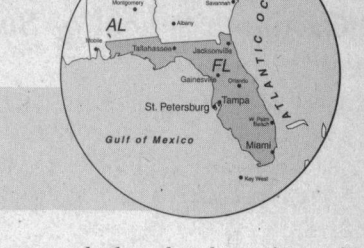

The University of Central Florida is located just 13 miles east of downtown Orlando, a huge center of international commerce and culture that's home of some of the world's best and most popular theme parks. The UCF curriculum is designed to develop a student's analytical, problem-solving, and decision-making capabilities instead of just focusing on the theoretical concepts of finance. Prospective MBA students may choose from a selective one-year daytime MBA program for honors students, an evening MBA program for part-time and full-time students, and an Executive MBA program, composed of 13 Friday or Saturday courses and two off-campus residencies.

INSTITUTIONAL INFORMATION
Public/Private: Public
Evening Classes Available? Yes
Student/Faculty Ratio: 30:1
Students in Parent Institution: 36,000
Academic Calendar: Semester

PROGRAMS
Degrees Offered: Master of Business Administration (MBA) (39 credits, up to 3 years); Master of Arts in Applied Economics (MAAE) (30 credits, up to 1.5 years); Master of Science in Accounting (MSA) (30 credits, up to 1.5 years); Master of Science in Taxation (MST) (30 credits, up to 1.5 years); Executive MBA (EMBA) (39 credits, up to 21 months); Master of Science in Management/Human Resources and Change Management (30 credits, up to 2 years); Master of Science/Management Information Systems (30 credits, up to 1.5 years)

STUDENT INFORMATION
Total Business Students: 725
% Full Time: 21
% Female: 50
% Minority: 50
% Out of State: 13
% International: 25
Average Age: 29

COMPUTER AND RESEARCH FACILITIES
Research Facilities: Small Business Development Center, UCF Incubator, Executive Development Center
Computer Facilities: Access to more than 100 data sources, such as Lexis-Nexis and Academic Universe, is available online to all students.
Campuswide Network? Yes
% of MBA Classrooms Wired: 100
Computer Model Recommended: No
Internet Fee? No

EXPENSES/FINANCIAL AID
Annual Tuition (Resident/Nonresident): $4,000/$14,000
Tuition Per Credit (Resident/Nonresident): $162/$569
Books and Supplies: $1,200

ADMISSIONS INFORMATION
Application Fee: $20
Electronic Application? Yes
Regular Application Deadline: 6/15
Regular Notification: Rolling
Deferment Available? Yes
Length of Deferment: 1 semester
Non-fall Admissions? Yes
Non-fall Application Deadline(s): 11/1 spring, 3/15 summer
Transfer Students Accepted? Yes
Transfer Policy: Transfer applicants must be from an AACSB-accredited university.
Need-Blind Admissions? Yes
Number of Applications Received: 289
% of Applicants Accepted: 84
% Accepted Who Enrolled: 78
Average GPA: 3.3
GPA Range: 3.0-3.5
Average GMAT: 556
GMAT Range: 500-600
Average Years Experience: 7

INTERNATIONAL STUDENTS
TOEFL Required of International Students? Yes

EMPLOYMENT INFORMATION
Placement Office Available? Yes
% Employed Within 3 Months: 98

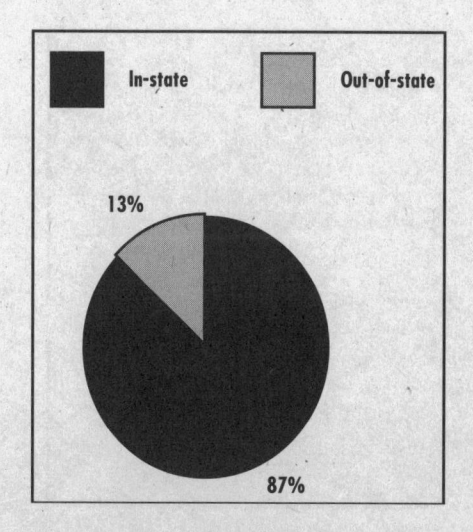

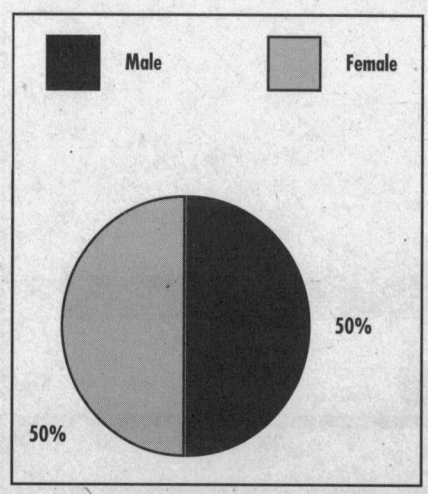

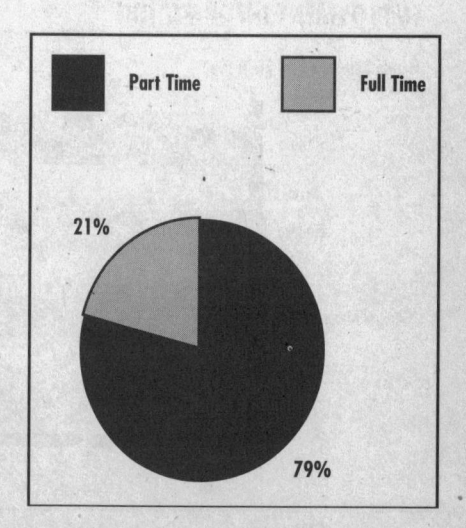

In-state 87% / Out-of-state 13%

Male 50% / Female 50%

Part Time 79% / Full Time 21%

UNIVERSITY OF CHICAGO
Graduate School of Business

Admissions Contact: Don Martin, Associate Dean for Enrollment Management
Address: 1101 East 58th Street, Chicago, IL 60637
Admissions Phone: 773-702-7369 • *Admissions Fax:* 773-702-9085
Admissions E-mail: admissions@gsb.uchicago.edu • *Web Address:* gsb.uchicago.edu

"I would pit my instructors against any other faculty in the nation, bar none," boasts one confident student at the University of Chicago's Graduate School of Business Administration where Nobel laureates abound and social life takes a back seat to "business, business, business!" Though Chicago is best known for finance and economics and is considered "numbers-heavy," it offers much more, including an International MBA, which "builds truly global management skills."

INSTITUTIONAL INFORMATION
Public/Private: Private
Evening Classes Available? Yes
Total Faculty: 174
% Faculty Female: 14
Students in Parent Institution: 12,989
Academic Calendar: Quarter

PROGRAMS
Degrees Offered: PhD (5.5 years)
Joint Degrees: MBA/AM Area Studies and Business; MBA/AM International Relations and Business; JD/MBA Law and Business; MD/MBA Medicine and Business; MBA/MPP Public Policy Studies and Business; MBA/AM Social Service Administration and Business
Academic Specialties: Finance, Marketing, General Management, International Business, Accounting, Organizational Behavior and Strategy, Entrepreneurship
Special Opportunities: IMBA (International MBA Program)
Study Abroad Options: Australia, Hong Kong, France, Spain, Netherlands, Brazil, Mexico, Israel, United Kingdom, Chile, Sweden, Austria, Belgium, Japan, China, Italy, South Korea, Switzerland, Germany, Singapore, South Africa

STUDENT INFORMATION
Total Business Students: 3,060
% Female: 24
% Minority: 6
% International: 36
Average Age: 29

COMPUTER AND RESEARCH FACILITIES
Research Facilities: Center for Research in Security Prices, Center for Decision Research, Center for the Study of the Economy and State, Center for Population Economics
Computer Facilities: Students have access to both mainframe and personal computers through the school's computing services department. Databases include Center for Research in Security Prices, Compustat, and DRI. Online services include Bloomberg, Datastream, Investext, and One Source as well as most electronic services provided through the U of C library.
Campuswide Network? Yes
Internet Fee? Yes

EXPENSES/FINANCIAL AID
Annual Tuition: $30,500
Room & Board (On Campus): $13,500
Books and Supplies: $1,500
Average Grant: $10,000
Average Loan: $42,657

ADMISSIONS INFORMATION
Application Fee: $175
Electronic Application? Yes
Regular Application Deadline: 11/30
Regular Notification: 1/28
Deferment Available? Yes
Length of Deferment: 1 year
Non-fall Admissions? Yes
Non-fall Application Deadline(s): Winter, spring
Transfer Students Accepted? No
Need-Blind Admissions? Yes
Number of Applications Received: 2,779
% of Applicants Accepted: 28
% Accepted Who Enrolled: 62
Average GPA: 3.4
GPA Range: 2.8-3.8
Average GMAT: 695
GMAT Range: 640-750
Average Years Experience: 5
Minority/Disadvantaged Student Recruitment Programs: Minority scholarship program

INTERNATIONAL STUDENTS
TOEFL Required of International Students? Yes
Minimum TOEFL: 600 (250 computer)

EMPLOYMENT INFORMATION

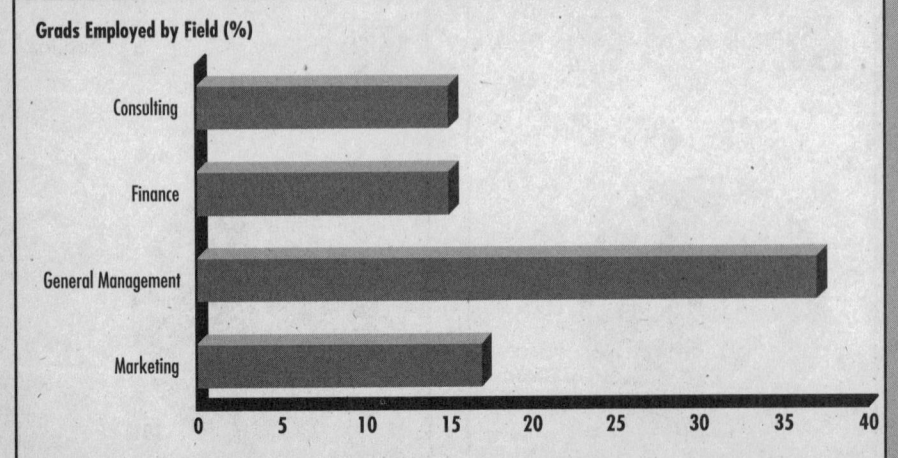

Grads Employed by Field (%)

Field	%
Consulting	~15
Finance	~15
General Management	~37
Marketing	~17

Placement Office Available? Yes
% Employed Within 3 Months: 95
Frequent Employers: McKinsey & Co., Lehman Brothers, Merrill Lynch, Goldman Sachs, Boston Consulting Group, JPMorgan Chase, Morgan Stanley, Credit Suisse First Boston, Deloitte Consulting, Salomon Smith Barney, Bear Stearns, Booz Allen Hamilton, Bain & Co.
Prominent Alumni: Basil L. Anderson, vice chairman, Staples, Inc.; Judith G. Boynton, CFO, Royal Dutch/Shell Group; Arthur Velasquez, chairman, president, and CEO, Azteca Foods Inc.; James Kilts, chairman and CEO, Gillette Company; R. Philip Purcell, chairman and CEO, Morgan Stanley

UNIVERSITY OF CINCINNATI
College of Business Administration

Admissions Contact: Valerie Robinson, Assistant Director, Graduate Programs
Address: Carl H. Linder Hall, Suite 103, Cincinnati, OH 45221
Admissions Phone: 513-556-7020 • Admissions Fax: 513-558-7006
Admissions E-mail: graduate@uc.edu • Web Address: www.cba.uc.edu/mba

"An MBA is a business investment," declares the University of Cincinnati's website, and it means business. The MBA curriculum at Cincinnati's Graduate School of Business Administration is as solid as the walls of Carl H. Linder Hall, where its classes are held. UC offers an excellent opportunity for working professionals to earn an MBA in the evenings and on Saturdays, as well as a full-time program and an MBA that combines on-campus course work with online instruction. The UC MBA student will benefit from the Graduate School's close ties to Cincinnati's business leaders through field studies, job placement services, and many other hands-on opportunities within the community.

INSTITUTIONAL INFORMATION
Public/Private: Public
Evening Classes Available? Yes
Total Faculty: 45
% Faculty Female: 13
% Faculty Part Time: 2
Student/Faculty Ratio: 7:1
Students in Parent Institution: 37,000
Academic Calendar: Quarter

PROGRAMS
Degrees Offered: MBA (12 months full time, 24 to 33 months part time); MS in Quantitative Analysis (12 months); MSBA in Accounting (12 to 15 months); MS in Taxation (12 months)
Joint Degrees: MBA/JD (4 years); MBA/MA in Arts Administration (3 years); MBA/MS in Industrial Engineering (2 to 3 years); MBA/MD (5 years); MBA/Nursing (3 years)
Academic Specialties: Marketing, Supply Chain, General Management, International
Special Opportunities: International Seminars (7 to 10 abroad), weekend courses
Study Abroad Options: Austria, Czech Republic, Germany, France, Spain, Thailand, Chile

STUDENT INFORMATION
Total Business Students: 307
% Full Time: 27
% Female: 34
% Minority: 18
% Out of State: 46
% International: 18
Average Age: 27

COMPUTER AND RESEARCH FACILITIES
Research Facilities: Centers for Management & Executive Development, Family & Private Businesses, Entrepreneurship Education and Research, Total Quality Management, and Global Competitiveness
Computer Facilities: Numerous computer labs across campus
Campuswide Network? Yes
% of MBA Classrooms Wired: 80
Computer Model Recommended: No
Internet Fee? No

EXPENSES/FINANCIAL AID
Annual Tuition (Resident/Nonresident): $12,916/$16,348
Tuition Per Credit: $328
Room & Board (On/Off Campus): $6,500/$5,400
Books and Supplies: $3,136
Average Grant: $7,664
Average Loan: $12,000
% Receiving Financial Aid: 100
% Receiving Aid Their First Year: 100

EMPLOYMENT INFORMATION

Grads Employed by Field (%)
- Consulting: ~20
- Entrepreneurship: ~3
- Finance: ~28
- General Management: ~12
- Human Resources: ~2
- Marketing: ~8
- MIS: ~5

ADMISSIONS INFORMATION
Application Fee: $30
Electronic Application? Yes
Early Decision Application Deadline: 2/1
Early Decision Notification: 2/15
Regular Application Deadline: 5/30
Regular Notification: Rolling
Length of Deferment: 1 year
Non-fall Application Deadline(s): 3/30 summer
Transfer Policy: No more than 9 quarter hours from an AACSB-accredited institution
Need-Blind Admissions? Yes
Number of Applications Received: 159
% of Applicants Accepted: 70
% Accepted Who Enrolled: 76
Average GPA: 3.2
Average GMAT: 579
Average Years Experience: 4
Other Admissions Factors Considered: Interview, leadership, extracurricular activities
Minority/Disadvantaged Student Recruitment Programs: Albert C. Yates Scholarships and Fellowship
Other Schools to Which Students Applied: Xavier University, Northern Kentucky University, Ohio State University, Miami University

INTERNATIONAL STUDENTS
TOEFL Required of International Students? Yes
Minimum TOEFL: 600 (250 computer)

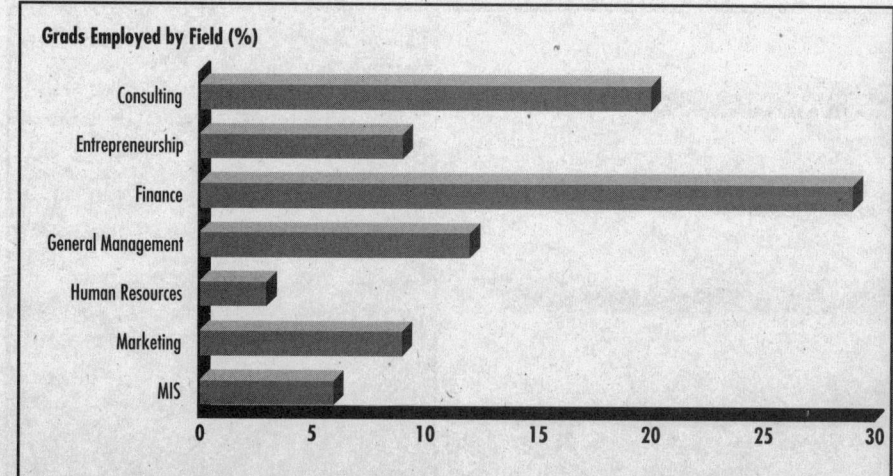

Placement Office Available? Yes
% Employed Within 3 Months: 71
Frequent Employers: Accenture; Alliance Data Systems; Cincinnati Bell; Cintas; Ethicon Endo Surgery; Executive Benefits; Fidelity Investments; Fifth Third Bank; Johnson Investments; Northlich, Stolle & LaWarre; Procter & Gamble
Prominent Alumni: Robert Taft, governor, state of Ohio; John F. Barrett, president and CEO, Western-Southern Life; Myron E. Ullman III, group managing director, LVMH Moet Hennessy; Dr. Candace Kendle Bryan, chairman and CEO, Kendle International; Richard E. Thornburgh, vice chairman, Credit Suisse First Boston

UNIVERSITY OF COLORADO — BOULDER
Leeds School of Business

Admissions Contact: Colette Stiglich, MBA Program Assistant
Address: Business 204, UCB 419, Boulder, CO 80309
Admissions Phone: 303-492-8397 • *Admissions Fax:* 303-492-1727
Admissions E-mail: LeedsMBA@colorado.edu • *Web Address:* leeds.colorado.edu

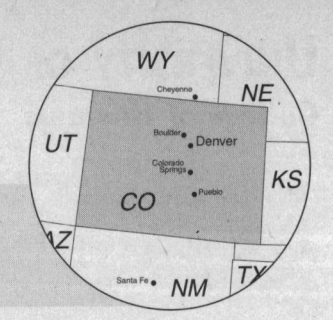

Students at the "well-run" Leeds School of Business can boast one of "the best" entrepreneurship programs in the nation, as well as enjoy the benefits that accompany a sizable school endowment. Said endowment is primarily the result of the sixth largest donation ever ($35 million) to an American b-school, made by Michael Leeds (hence the school's re-christening), former president and CEO of CMP Media. And "if you enjoy balancing social life with a solid academic life" and skiing, "Boulder offers the perfect mix."

INSTITUTIONAL INFORMATION
Public/Private: Public
Evening Classes Available? Yes
Total Faculty: 74
% Faculty Female: 19
% Faculty Minority: 23
% Faculty Part Time: 41
Student/Faculty Ratio: 25:1
Students in Parent Institution: 25,000
Academic Calendar: Semester

PROGRAMS
Degrees Offered: MBA (2 years full time), Professional Evening MBA (33 months)
Joint Degrees: JD/MBA (4 years full time); MBA/MS in Telecommunications (3 to 3.5 years full time); MBA/MA in Fine Arts (3 years full time)
Academic Specialties: Small class sizes, close ties to the Colorado business community, "free electives" in other graduate programs on the University of Colorado—Boulder campus, nationally ranked entrepreneurship program
Special Opportunities: Summer course held in London studies international finance and economics

STUDENT INFORMATION
Total Business Students: 181
% Full Time: 61
% Female: 30
% Minority: 11

% Out of State: 23
% International: 20
Average Age: 28

COMPUTER AND RESEARCH FACILITIES
Research Facilities: Business Research Division, Real Estate Center, Center for Entrepreneurship, Burridge Center for Securities Analysis & Valuation
Computer Facilities: Lexis-Nexis, ABI/Inform, Compact Disclosure, Infotrac PC, Compustat, Dun & Bradstreet, Corp Tech, Disclosure Select. MBA Business Center is a dedicated facility for MBA students that provides computer workstations plus fax, phone, and conference facilities.
Campuswide Network? No
% of MBA Classrooms Wired: 100
Computer Model Recommended: Laptop
Internet Fee? No

EXPENSES/FINANCIAL AID
Annual Tuition (Resident/Nonresident): $4,418/$17,750
Tuition Per Credit: $706
Room & Board: $16,000
Books and Supplies: $1,500
Average Grant: $2,242
Average Loan: $5,750
% Receiving Financial Aid: 35
% Receiving Aid Their First Year: 30

ADMISSIONS INFORMATION
Application Fee: $52
Electronic Application? Yes
Early Decision Application Deadline: 12/1
Early Decision Notification: 2/15
Regular Application Deadline: 2/1
Regular Notification: 4/15
Deferment Available? No
Non-fall Admissions? No
Transfer Students Accepted? No
Need-Blind Admissions? Yes
Number of Applications Received: 303
% of Applicants Accepted: 38
% Accepted Who Enrolled: 45
Average GPA: 3.2
Average GMAT: 648
Average Years Experience: 5
Other Admissions Factors Considered: Ability to add diversity to student body, to work well with a team/group focus, and to make unique contributions to the program
Other Schools to Which Students Applied: Arizona State, UCLA, UC—Berkeley, U. of Colorado—Denver, U. of Denver, U. of Southern California, U. of Washington

INTERNATIONAL STUDENTS
TOEFL Required of International Students? Yes
Minimum TOEFL: 600 (250 computer)

EMPLOYMENT INFORMATION

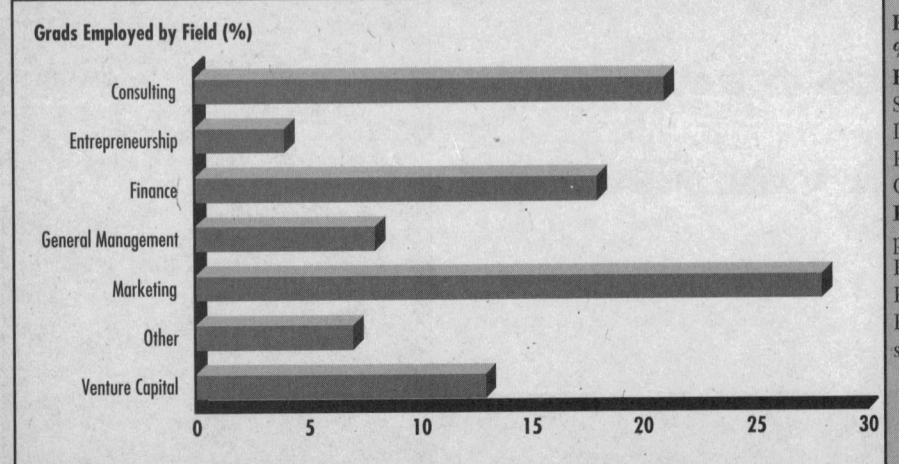

Grads Employed by Field (%)
- Consulting: ~22
- Entrepreneurship: ~4
- Finance: ~17
- General Management: ~8
- Marketing: ~28
- Other: ~7
- Venture Capital: ~13

Placement Office Available? Yes
% Employed Within 3 Months: 90
Frequent Employers: IBM Global Services, Sun Microsystems, Millennium Venture Group, IBM Printing Systems, Softsource, Hewlett-Packard, Agilent Technologies, Cap Gemini, Gartner Solista, Intel, Qwest
Prominent Alumni: Kevin Burns, managing principal, Lazard Technology Partners; John Puerner, president and CEO, Los Angeles Times; Patrick Tierney, president and CEO, Thompson Financial; Dick Fuld, CEO, banking; Jeanne Jackson, CEO, Walmart.com

UNIVERSITY OF COLORADO — DENVER
Graduate School of Business Administration

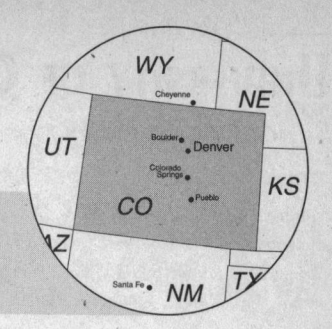

Admissions Contact: Graduate Admissions Coordinator
Address: Campus Box 165, PO Box 173364, Denver, CO 80217-3364
Admissions Phone: 303-556-5900 • Admissions Fax: 303-556-5904
Admissions E-mail: none • Web Address: www.business.cudenver.edu

Located in the heart of Denver's business community, UC Denver offers several MBA programs. The 11-Month MBA program meets during the day in the historic Masonic Temple Building on the 16th Street Mall in Denver, and the Individualized MBA allows students to advance at their own pace. Students can also choose from the Cohort MBA or the On-Site MBA. The curriculum of each MBA program includes case studies, computer simulations, and interaction with Colorado businesses, and the MBA programs are self-contained, requiring no preliminary course work. UC Denver encourages its students to participate in Mentor Programs, where students learn from those who've already been there, done that.

INSTITUTIONAL INFORMATION
Public/Private: Public
Evening Classes Available? Yes
Total Faculty: 95
Student/Faculty Ratio: 35:1
Students in Parent Institution: 11,050
Academic Calendar: Semester

PROGRAMS
Degrees Offered: MBA (16 months to 5 years), Executive MBA (22 months), MBA/Master of Science (2 to 3 years), MBA/Master of International Management (2 to 3 years), Master of Science (9 months to 5 years), 11-Month MBA (11 months)
Academic Specialties: Technology-Global, Entrepreneurship
Special Opportunities: An intership is available.
Study Abroad Options: Belgium, France, Spain

STUDENT INFORMATION
Total Business Students: 1,249
% Full Time: 29
% Female: 11
% Minority: 10
% Out of State: 1
% International: 14
Average Age: 25

COMPUTER AND RESEARCH FACILITIES
Research Facilities: Bard Center for Entrepreneurship, Center for Information Technology Innovation
Computer Facilities: J.D. Edward
Campuswide Network? Yes
Computer Model Recommended: No
Internet Fee? No

EXPENSES/FINANCIAL AID
Annual Tuition (Resident/Nonresident): $3,956/$13,818
Average Grant: $1,000
% Receiving Financial Aid: 29

ADMISSIONS INFORMATION
Application Fee: $50
Electronic Application? No
Regular Application Deadline: 6/15
Regular Notification: Rolling
Deferment Available? Yes
Length of Deferment: 1 year
Non-fall Admissions? Yes
Non-fall Application Deadline(s): 11/1 spring, 4/1 summer
Transfer Students Accepted? Yes
Transfer Policy: Varies by student and program
Need-Blind Admissions? Yes
Number of Applications Received: 547
% of Applicants Accepted: 74
% Accepted Who Enrolled: 64
Average Years Experience: 5
Other Admissions Factors Considered: GRE score accepted, resume, work experience, computer experience

INTERNATIONAL STUDENTS
TOEFL Required of International Students? Yes
Minimum TOEFL: 525 (197 computer)

EMPLOYMENT INFORMATION
Placement Office Available? Yes
% Employed Within 3 Months: 90

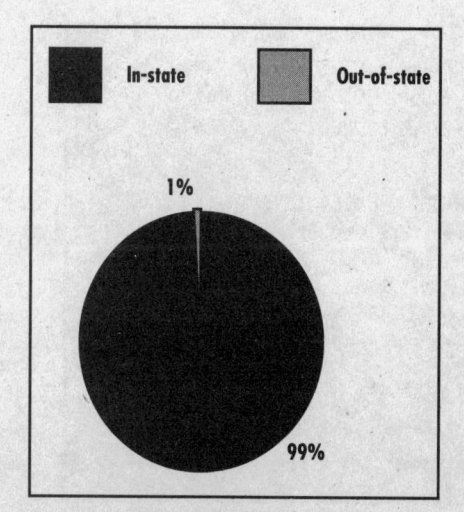

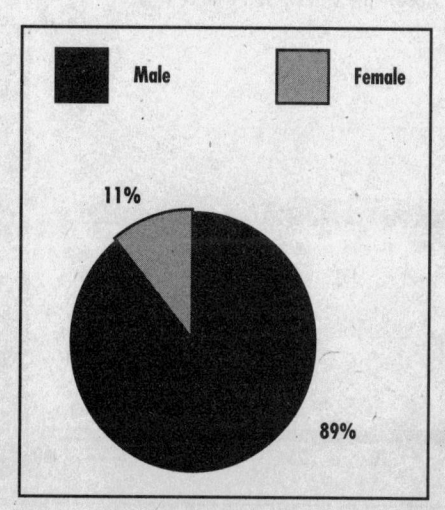

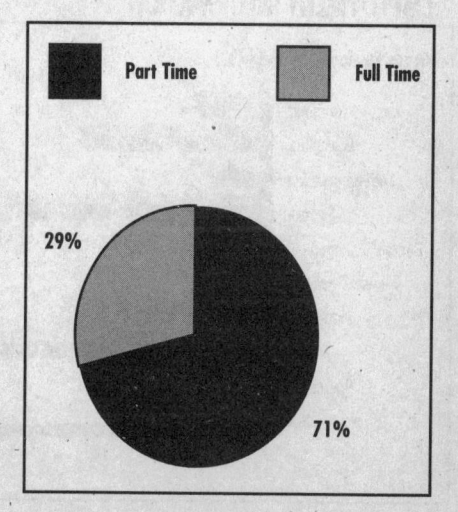

UNIVERSITY OF CONNECTICUT
School of Business

Admissions Contact: Richard N. Dino, Associate Dean
Address: 2100 Hillside Road, Unit 1041, Storrs, CT 06269-1041
Admissions Phone: 860-486-2872 • Admissions Fax: 860-486-5222
Admissions E-mail: uconnmba@business.uconn.edu • Web Address: www.business.uconn.edu

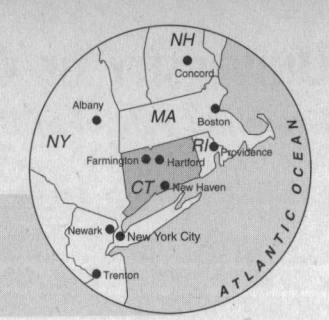

Reasonable tuition and a variety of programs attract MBAs to the University of Connecticut's School of Business Administration. The top brass here is "constantly seeking ways to improve" the school, and professors—though they "pile the work up"—are "well respected," especially in management, operations, and finance. UConn also boasts a "tremendous number of international students" and an "excellent," "rural and quaint" location "between New York and Boston."

INSTITUTIONAL INFORMATION
Public/Private: Public
Evening Classes Available? Yes
Total Faculty: 97
% Faculty Female: 15
% Faculty Minority: 14
% Faculty Part Time: 19
Student/Faculty Ratio: 13:1
Students in Parent Institution: 24,051
Academic Calendar: Semester

PROGRAMS
Degrees Offered: MBA (2 years); EMBA (21 months); PhD (4 years); MS Accounting (1 year); Professional MBA (part time, 3 to 6 years)
Joint Degrees: JD/MBA; MD/MBA; MSW/MBA; MBA/MA International Studies; MBA/Master of International Management; MBA/MS Nursing (2.5 years)
Academic Specialties: Information Technology, Finance, Management Consulting, Interactive Marketing, Accounting, and Health Systems. Curriculum emphasizes information technology and globalization. Laptop computer required and integrated into the curriculum.
Special Opportunities: Student Managed Fund, Wolff Program in Entrepreneurship, Advanced Business Certificates, MBA Business Plan Competition, Mentor Program
Study Abroad Options: EM Lyon, France

STUDENT INFORMATION
Total Business Students: 783
% Full Time: 13
% Female: 40
% Minority: 6
% Out of State: 10
% International: 56
Average Age: 29

COMPUTER AND RESEARCH FACILITIES
Research Facilities: Edgelab; Center for International Business, Education and Research; GE Global Learning Center; Real Estate Center; Health Systems Center
Computer Facilities: 10 labs and 8 databases; Academic Universe; UCONN Online catalog; Survey of Current Business; ABI Global; National Trade Data Bank; CCH Internet Tax Research; D&B Millennium Dollar Database; Primark Global Access; Dow Jones Interactive; Infotrac; EconLit
Campuswide Network? Yes
% of MBA Classrooms Wired: 100
Computer Model Recommended: Laptop
Internet Fee? No

EXPENSES/FINANCIAL AID
Annual Tuition (Resident/Nonresident): $5,478/$14,230
Tuition Per Credit: $465
Room & Board (On/Off Campus): $7,634/$8,500
Books and Supplies: $2,000
% Receiving Financial Aid: 60
% Receiving Aid Their First Year: 76

ADMISSIONS INFORMATION
Application Fee: $52
Electronic Application? Yes
Regular Application Deadline: 4/1
Regular Notification: Rolling
Length of Deferment: 11 months
Non-fall Admissions? No
Transfer Policy: Meet with director of the MBA Program; maximum of 15 credits accepted
Need-Blind Admissions? Yes
Number of Applications Received: 177
% of Applicants Accepted: 42
% Accepted Who Enrolled: 45
Average GPA: 3.4
GPA Range: 3.0-3.9
Average GMAT: 640
GMAT Range: 600-670
Average Years Experience: 7
Other Admissions Factors Considered: Quality of undergraduate degree, granting institution, quality and length of professional work experience
Minority/Disadvantaged Student Recruitment Programs: Specialized recruiting by the MBA Program and the Office of Diversity Initiatives
Other Schools to Which Students Applied: Babson, Boston College, George Washington University, Ohio State, Pennsylvania State

INTERNATIONAL STUDENTS
TOEFL Required of International Students? Yes
Minimum TOEFL: 575 (233 computer)

EMPLOYMENT INFORMATION

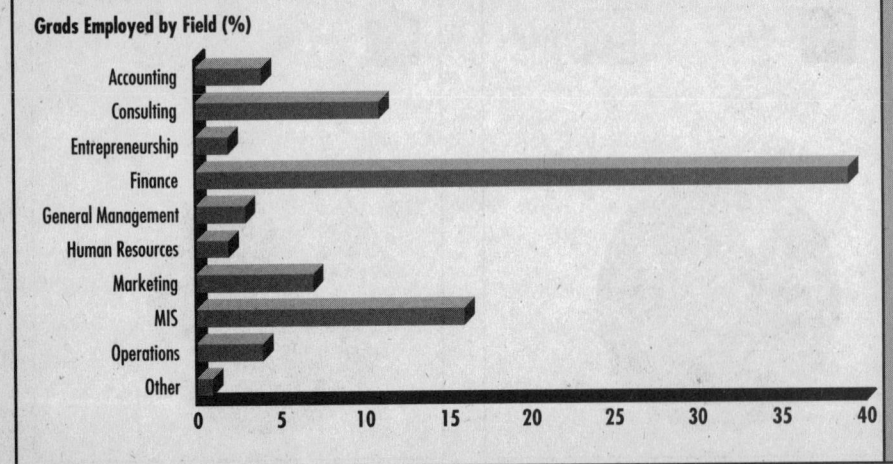

Grads Employed by Field (%)
- Accounting
- Consulting
- Entrepreneurship
- Finance
- General Management
- Human Resources
- Marketing
- MIS
- Operations
- Other

Placement Office Available? Yes
% Employed Within 3 Months: 83
Frequent Employers: United Technologies, CIGNA, IBM, Arthur Andersen, GE/GE Capital, The Hartford, Travelers/Citigroup, ESPN, Aetna, General Dynamics
Prominent Alumni: Denis J. Nayden, chairman, president, and CEO, GE Capital Corp.; Janice Brandt, vice chairwoman and chief marketing officer, AOL, Inc.; John Y. Kim, president, CIGNA Retirement and Investment Service; Christopher P.A. Komisarjevsky, president and CEO, Burston-Marsteller Worldwide; Penelope A. Dobkin, portfolio manager, Fidelity Investments

UNIVERSITY OF DAYTON
School of Business Administration

Admissions Contact: Janis Glynn, Director
Address: 300 College Park Avenue, Dayton, OH 45469
Admissions Phone: 937-229-3733 • Admissions Fax: 937-229-3882
Admissions E-mail: mba@udayton.edu • Web Address: www.sba.udayton.edu/mba

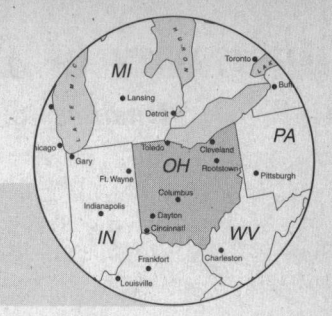

UD's School of Business Administration's catchphrase is "Integrating Technology Across the School of Business Administration." The Catholic University of Dayton boasts university centers and state-of-the-art computer and research facilities that grant students the opportunity to meet local business leaders and potential future employers, as well as participate in experiential learning through the use and application of cutting-edge technology. Full timers and part timers alike will find a place in UD's MBA program, where internships, capstone consulting projects, fellowships, assistantships, and study abroad opportunities abound.

INSTITUTIONAL INFORMATION
Public/Private: Private
Evening Classes Available? Yes
Total Faculty: 38
% Faculty Female: 11
Students in Parent Institution: 10,180
Academic Calendar: Semester

PROGRAMS
Degrees Offered: Master of Business Administration (MBA) (1 to 2 years full time, 2 to 3 years part time)
Joint Degrees: Juris of Doctor of Law/Master of Business Administration (JD/MBA) (3 to 5 years)
Academic Specialties: Accounting, Finance, International Business, Management Information Systems, Operations Management, Marketing, Technology-Enhanced Business; special strength in integrative team-teaching
Special Opportunities: We offer a Post-Master's Certificate Program for students holding an MBA or similar graduate degree.
Study Abroad Options: Germany—University of Augsburg; France—University of Toulouse; China; Finland; Czech Republic

STUDENT INFORMATION
Total Business Students: 431
% Female: 46
Average Age: 29

COMPUTER AND RESEARCH FACILITIES
Research Facilities: Center for Portfolio Management and Security Analysis, Center for Business and Economic Research, Center for Leadership and Executive Development
Computer Facilities: Lexis-Nexis, Ryan C. Harris Learning-Teaching Center
Campuswide Network? Yes
Computer Model Recommended: Laptop
Internet Fee? No

EXPENSES/FINANCIAL AID
Annual Tuition: $8,658
Tuition Per Credit: $481
Books and Supplies: $600

ADMISSIONS INFORMATION
Electronic Application? Yes
Regular Application Deadline: Rolling
Regular Notification: Rolling
Deferment Available? Yes
Length of Deferment: 1 year
Non-fall Admissions? Yes
Non-fall Application Deadline(s): Rolling
Transfer Students Accepted? Yes
Transfer Policy: Students may request up to 12 semester hours of approved graduate transfer credit for course work of B or better quality.
Need-Blind Admissions? Yes
Number of Applications Received: 368
% of Applicants Accepted: 80
% Accepted Who Enrolled: 80
Average GPA: 3.2
Average GMAT: 543
Average Years Experience: 7
Other Admissions Factors Considered: Trend in grade point average, grade point average within major, possible work experience
Other Schools to Which Students Applied: Xavier University, University of Cincinnati, Wright State University, Miami University

INTERNATIONAL STUDENTS
TOEFL Required of International Students? Yes
Minimum TOEFL: 550 (213 computer)

EMPLOYMENT INFORMATION
Placement Office Available? Yes
% Employed Within 3 Months: 95
Prominent Alumni: Allen Hill, president and CEO, Dayton Power and Light; Philip Parker, president and CEO, Dayton Area Chamber of Commerce; Mike Turner, former mayor, city of Dayton

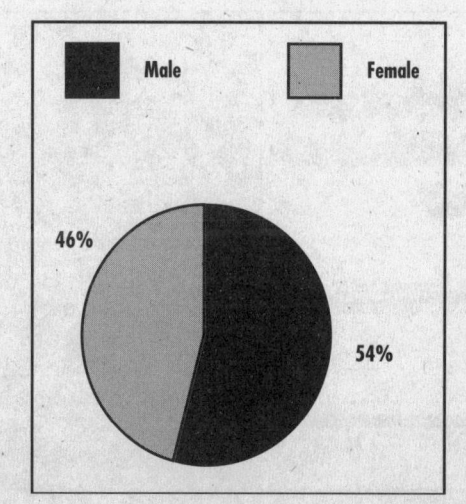

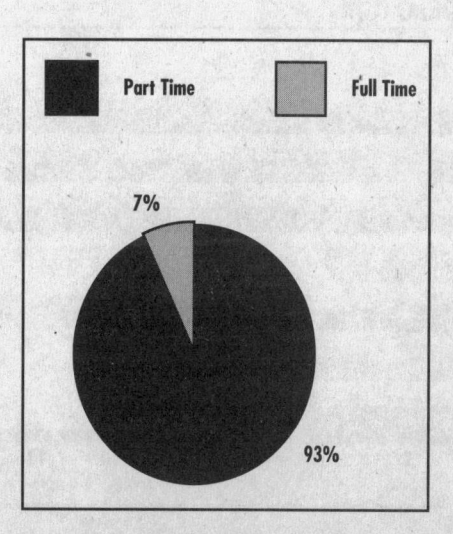

UNIVERSITY OF DELAWARE
College of Business and Economics

Admissions Contact: Ronald I. Sibert, Director of MBA Programs
Address: 103 MBNA America Hall, Newark, DE 19716
Admissions Phone: 302-831-2221 • Admissions Fax: 302-831-3329
Admissions E-mail: mbaprogram@udel.edu • Web Address: www.mba.udel.edu

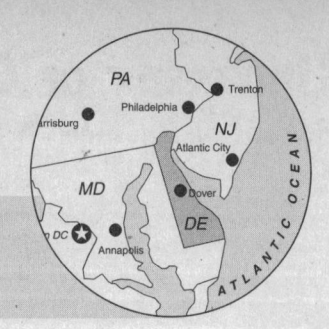

University of Delaware students are enraptured with their campus, "absolutely the most gorgeous campus anywhere." The College of Business and Economics offers full- and part-time MBA programs, with a self-contained curriculum requiring no specific prerequisites as well as the unique MBA concentration in museum leadership and management. Most MBA students go into finance upon graduation, and many are employed by companies like Citibank, JPMorgan Chase, and IBM.

INSTITUTIONAL INFORMATION
Public/Private: Public
Evening Classes Available? Yes
Total Faculty: 64
% Faculty Female: 14
% Faculty Minority: 3
% Faculty Part Time: 5
Student/Faculty Ratio: 30:1
Students in Parent Institution: 20,949
Academic Calendar: Semester

PROGRAMS
Degrees Offered: MBA (48 credits, 16 months to 5 years); Executive MBA (48 credits, 19 months); MS Accounting (48 credits, 16 months to 5 years)
Joint Degrees: MA Economics/MBA (57 credits), MIB/MBA (57 credits)
Academic Specialties: Corporate Governance, DE Audit Institute
Study Abroad Options: France

STUDENT INFORMATION
Total Business Students: 302
% Full Time: 24
% Female: 51
% Minority: 5
% Out of State: 27
% International: 50
Average Age: 27

COMPUTER AND RESEARCH FACILITIES
Research Facilities: Center for Corporate Governance, Small Business Development Center
Computer Facilities: 800 databases (major resources related to business and economics), top national award for Excellence in Campus Networking (CAUSE), number 2 Most Wired College (2000) by Yahoo!, state-of-the-art technology in case rooms, newly outfitted computer labs, ERP software and site server, Web server for classrooms applications, wireless networking
Campuswide Network? Yes
% of MBA Classrooms Wired: 100
Computer Model Recommended: No
Internet Fee? No

EXPENSES/FINANCIAL AID
Annual Tuition (Resident/Nonresident): $6,020/$13,860
Tuition Per Credit (Resident/Nonresident): $334/$770
Room & Board (On/Off Campus): $6,200/$7,200
Books and Supplies: $1,400
Average Grant: $3,940
% Receiving Financial Aid: 60
% Receiving Aid Their First Year: 26

ADMISSIONS INFORMATION
Application Fee: $50
Electronic Application? Yes
Regular Application Deadline: 5/1
Regular Notification: Rolling
Length of Deferment: 1 year
Non-fall Application Deadline(s): 11/1 spring (part time only)
Transfer Policy: Up to 9 semester hours (12 by special request)—must submit a written request
Need-Blind Admissions? Yes
Number of Applications Received: 259
% of Applicants Accepted: 75
% Accepted Who Enrolled: 65
Average GPA: 3.0
GPA Range: 2.1-3.9
Average GMAT: 555
GMAT Range: 330-750
Average Years Experience: 5
Other Admissions Factors Considered: Work experience, undergraduate and graduate work, GMAT/TOEFL scores, letters of recommendation, statement of objectives
Other Schools to Which Students Applied: Temple, Penn, Villanova

INTERNATIONAL STUDENTS
TOEFL Required of International Students? Yes
Minimum TOEFL: 587 (240 computer)

EMPLOYMENT INFORMATION

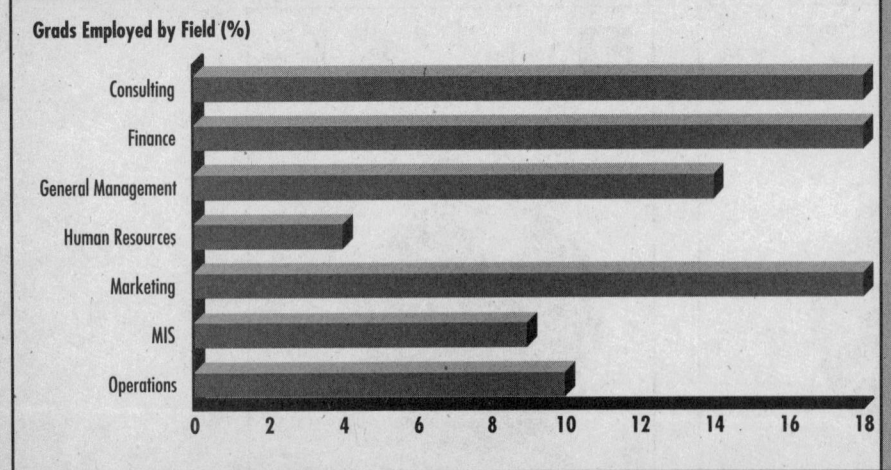

Grads Employed by Field (%)

Field	%
Consulting	18
Finance	18
General Management	14
Human Resources	4
Marketing	18
MIS	9
Operations	10

Placement Office Available? Yes
% Employed Within 3 Months: 2
Frequent Employers: Agilent Technologies, JPMorgan Chase, Cigna, Citicorp, Deloitte Consulting, Dade Behring, FMC, FNX, IBM, Johnson & Johnson, MIDI, Siegfried Group, TransUnion LLC, Wilmington Trust, W.L. Gore and Associates
Prominent Alumni: Hon. Thomas R. Carper, governor, state of Delaware, and candidate for U.S. Senate; Leonard Quill, CEO and chairman of the board, Wilmington Trust Corp.; Howard Cosgrove, chairman and CEO, Conectiv; Dennis Sheehy, partner, Deloitte & Touche

UNIVERSITY OF DENVER
Daniels College of Business

Admissions Contact: Admissions Staff
Address: 2101 South University Blvd. #255, Denver, CO 80208
Admissions Phone: 303-871-3416 • Admissions Fax: 303-871-4466
Admissions E-mail: daniels@du.edu • Web Address: www.daniels.du.edu

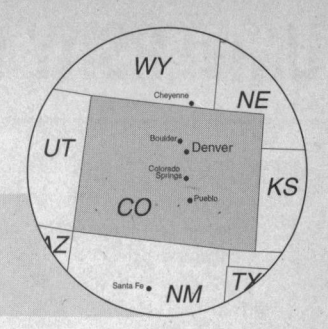

A "great city, great mountains," and "great outdoor life" are a few of the perks available at the University of Denver's Daniels College of Business, "one of the nation's most technologically advanced business schools" and home to a sizable international student contingent. Scheduling is "flexible" and the range of courses is broad, though the academic pressure can be "intense" thanks largely to a "hectic" quarter system.

INSTITUTIONAL INFORMATION
Public/Private: Private
Evening Classes Available? Yes
Total Faculty: 78
% Faculty Female: 12
% Faculty Minority: 5
% Faculty Part Time: 5
Student/Faculty Ratio: 15:1
Students in Parent Institution: 9,100
Academic Calendar: Quarter

PROGRAMS
Degrees Offered: Executive MBA (60 credits), Accelerated MBA (60 credits), Full-Time and Evening MBA (minimum 72 credits), Full-Time and Evening International MBA (78 credits), Master of Accountancy (minimum 48 credits), MS Finance (64 credits), MS Real Estate and Construction Management (64 credits), MS Management (54 to 68 credits), MS Information Technology
Joint Degrees: JD/MBA, JD/IMBA, JD/MSRECM (approximately 4 years), Flexible Dual Degree with any other University of Denver degree; Combined Degree with other Daniels degrees
Academic Specialties: MBA and IMBA specializations include Accounting, Finance, Marketing, Real Estate and Construction Management, Entrepreneurship, Information Technology and Electronic Commerce, Hospitality Property Development and Asset Management, Hospitality Information Technology, and E-Business. MSM concentrations include Training and Development, Cable Telecommunication, Applied Communication, and Sport Management.

STUDENT INFORMATION
Total Business Students: 180
% Full Time: 71
% Female: 32
% Minority: 7
% Out of State: 40
% International: 22
Average Age: 27

COMPUTER AND RESEARCH FACILITIES
Computer Facilities: Access server for class notes, discussion, and updates; access to new technologies through the Technology Center; Lexis-Nexis statistical software and numerous other databases; real estate/construction management software
Campuswide Network? Yes
% of MBA Classrooms Wired: 100
Computer Model Recommended: Laptop
Internet Fee? No

EXPENSES/FINANCIAL AID
Annual Tuition: $21,456
Tuition Per Credit: $596
Room & Board: $8,000
Books and Supplies: $1,000
Average Grant: $3,500
Average Loan: $19,500
% Receiving Financial Aid: 60
% Receiving Aid Their First Year: 60

ADMISSIONS INFORMATION
Application Fee: $50
Electronic Application? Yes
Early Decision Application Deadline: 1/15
Early Decision Notification: 3/1
Regular Application Deadline: 5/15
Regular Notification: 7/1
Length of Deferment: 1 year
Non-fall Application Deadline(s): 12/15
Transfer Policy: 12 quarter hours (9 semester hours) toward electives
Need-Blind Admissions? Yes
Number of Applications Received: 438
% of Applicants Accepted: 70
% Accepted Who Enrolled: 50
Average GPA: 3.0
GPA Range: 2.6-3.6
Average GMAT: 560
GMAT Range: 470-630
Average Years Experience: 5
Other Admissions Factors Considered: Community service
Minority/Disadvantaged Student Recruitment Programs: Limited amount of need-based scholarships
Other Schools to Which Students Applied: Arizona State, Colorado State, Thunderbird, U. of Arizona, Southern Methodist, U. of Colorado,

INTERNATIONAL STUDENTS
TOEFL Required of International Students? Yes
Minimum TOEFL: 550 (213 computer)

EMPLOYMENT INFORMATION

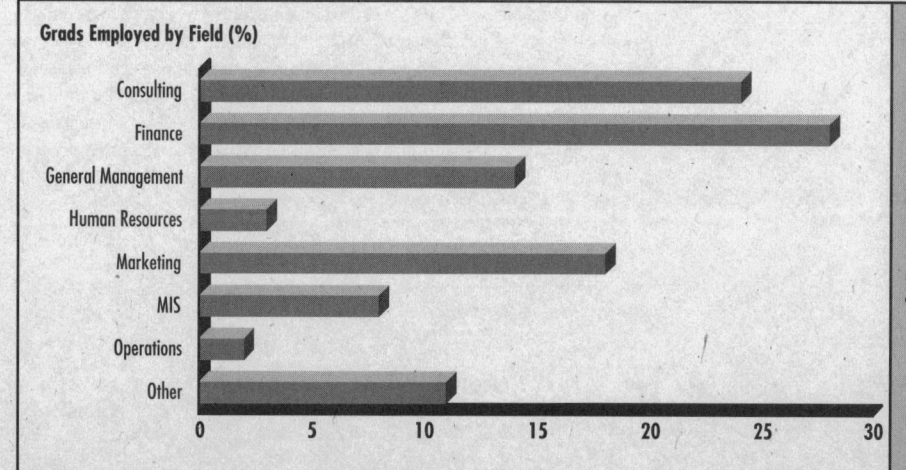

Grads Employed by Field (%)
- Consulting: ~24
- Finance: ~28
- General Management: ~8
- Human Resources: ~3
- Marketing: ~18
- MIS: ~7
- Operations: ~2
- Other: ~11

Placement Office Available? Yes
% Employed Within 3 Months: 81
Frequent Employers: Accenture, AIMCO, Andersen, Citigroup, Coors Brewing Company, IBM, J.D. Edwards, Keane Consulting Group, Lockheed Martin, PricewaterhouseCoopers
Prominent Alumni: Peter Coors, CEO, Coors Brewing Company; Andrew Daly, president, Vail Resorts; Michael Enzi, U.S. Senator, Wyoming; Gale Norton, U.S. Secretary of the Interior; Carol Tome, executive VP and CFO, Home Depot

UNIVERSITY OF DENVER

THE COLLEGE AT A GLANCE
"At the Daniels College of Business, we are committed to your success—as a highly competent professional, a team builder and leader, and a valued member of your community. Founded in 1908, the Daniels College of Business is the nation's eighth-oldest accredited collegiate business school and a leader in management education. With one of the nation's premier MBA programs, we put you at the cutting edge of knowledge, present an educational experience that prepares you for a lifetime of leadership, and provide our commitment to your career placement and development. We do all this in a classic campus setting located in Denver, a wonderful city that symbolizes the dynamic business environment of the Rocky Mountain West."

—James R. Griesemer, Dean

STUDENTS
Daniels College of Business students have a wide range of academic and professional backgrounds and represent more than 30 countries around the world. Insights and skills from an average of more than six years of professional experience and undergraduate majors, including business, engineering, international studies, history, and economics provide diverse perspectives that add to dynamic classroom environments and group projects. Of the approximately 560 MBA students in the Evening, Accelerated, and Executive MBA programs, 51 percent are working professionals, 34 percent are women, and 15 percent are international students.

Prominent alumni include James Unruh, chairman and CEO, Unisys; Peter Coors, CEO, Coors Brewing Company; June Travis, executive vice president, National Cable Television Association; Andy Daly, president, Vail Associates; Thomas Marsico, CEO, Marsico Capital Management; and David Bailey, CEO, Wells Fargo Bank West (retired).

ACADEMICS
The Daniels College of Business MBA program presents a forward-thinking curriculum that challenges students through an active learning environment. The new core curriculum incorporates experiential elements in leadership, career management, technology, and group work in addition to traditional methods of learning. Through this exciting experience, students learn technical business knowledge, refine skills that are key to managerial excellence, and gain an appreciation for values-based leadership.

Mirroring the cross-functional involvement of management decision making, the courses combine the business technical fundamentals and management skills into a more applications-oriented format from which students develop a comprehensive view of business the way it actually operates. Included in the experience are an outdoor leadership and team-building program, opportunities for volunteer participation, and a team field-study project in which students work with Denver-based organizations.

Students move through the core into elective or specialization courses that provide focus to their degree. Specializations in accounting, construction management, electronic commerce, entrepreneurship, finance, information technology, marketing, real estate, and resort and tourism management are available, or students may create their own specializations from courses offered at the University.

A part-time MBA program is available. Other options include an MBA/JD joint-degree program and a flexible dual-degree program that allows students to combine their MBA degree with programs from other schools and departments within the University of Denver.

The Executive MBA program is an 18-month program designed to strengthen the management skills and leadership abilities of middle- and upper-level managers and managing professionals. Intensive course work, creative problem solving, and an international cultural travel seminar provide firsthand knowledge of management, international, and emerging business opportunities.

The Accelerated MBA is a cutting-edge graduate study program designed for high-potential men and women with at least two years of management experience who want to strengthen technical business skills and enhance leadership abilities.

The integrated curriculum helps develop creative critical thinking and decision making through courses that focus on applying business tools in an interrelated format. Exciting core courses have replaced traditional individual function courses to combine tools and skills as students use them.

A three-day outdoor leadership experience provides an arena for students to learn key elements of communication skills, team building, and consensus problem solving. Added to the managerial excellence focus are negotiation skills and Myers-Briggs testing.

The Daniels College of Business's 83 full-time faculty members have a balance of industry experience and academic dedication, providing a classroom environment that is diverse and exciting. They have developed the curriculum with outside business leaders and continue to refine the program as well as maintain their excellence in teaching, research, and consulting. They are recognized worldwide for their industry knowledge and work with educational organizations such as the Fulbright Foundation.

The Daniels College of Business's MBA program emphasizes international business and a global understanding of cultures and perspectives. Core courses focus on global perspectives, and elective courses include international marketing, comparative management, and multinational finance. In addition, courses in international politics, economics, and policy analysis are available from the University's Graduate School of International Studies.

The Daniels College of Business works with corporate advisors in a multitude of program areas. The curriculum continues to be shaped by faculty members and corporate advisors. The Career Placement Center works with executives in operations and panel discussions, and the team field study course, Integrative Challenge, is a partnership with Denver-area corporations and businesses that utilize Daniels students to address management problems. In addition, the Career Placement Center alumni mentor program provides contacts with alumni in a wide range of industries and positions for placement counseling and assistance.

Daniels College of Business

CAMPUS LIFE

The University of Denver is the largest independent, private university in the Rocky Mountain region, with more than 8,800 students from more than 80 countries. Founded in 1864 by John Evans, the Colorado Territory Governor for Abraham Lincoln, the 125-acre University of Denver campus is located in a quiet neighborhood in Denver, Colorado, providing students an academic atmosphere with access to the cosmopolitan population, activities, and lifestyle of Denver, with the Rocky Mountains nearby.

In September 1999, the $25 million Daniels College of Business building opened. One of the nation's most technologically advanced business school facilities, the building has more than 3,000 data ports for instant access to the Internet. It houses the Advanced Technology Center, a state-of-the-art laboratory with more than $1 million worth of the latest software and hardware.

Computer facilities include labs with 125 networked PCs that support word processing, spreadsheet and visual presentation software, UNIX mainframes that provide statistical packages, and Internet and information research database access.

The Daniels Career Placement Center helps students assess career choices and develop effective career strategies using a wide range of resources. Workshops and personal counseling are available to help students enhance job search skills, techniques, and knowledge. Career forums, job fairs, alumni networking events, regional consortium events, computerized job and internship listing databases, a research library, and an alumni mentor program provide access to employers from around the nation.

COSTS

For the academic year 2001–2002, tuition for full-time students attending three quarters was $21,456. Books, supplies, fees, housing, and meal expenses vary, depending on the number of courses taken per quarter and extracurricular activities. Even though Denver is the largest city in the Rocky Mountain region, the cost of living is well below other major U.S. cities.

ADMISSIONS

The Daniels College of Business enrolls students in September and March. Applications are reviewed on a rolling basis through a comprehensive process that evaluates previous academic performance and completion of an undergraduate degree from an accredited college or university, results of the GMAT, professional work experience, responses to essay questions, two letters of recommendation, and a completed application form. International students whose primary language is not English or who graduated from an institution where English is not the primary language of instruction are required to submit TOEFL results. Interviews are not always required.

Applications are evaluated on a rolling basis as they are received and completed, with a decision response within five weeks of completion. The deadline for September enrollment is May 1, and the deadline for March enrollment is January 1. Applications received after these dates are reviewed on a space-available basis. For inquiries, students should contact:

Rifkin Center for Student Services
Daniels College of Business
University of Denver
2101 South University Boulevard
Denver, CO 80208
Telephone: 303-871-3416
800-622-4723 (toll-free)
Fax: 303-871-4466
E-mail: daniels@du.edu
World Wide Web: www.daniels.du.edu

Admissions Contact: Admissions Staff
Address: 2101 South University Blvd. #255, Denver, CO 80208
Admissions Phone: 303-871-3416 • Admissions Fax: 303-871-4466
Admissions E-mail: daniels@du.edu • Web Address: www.daniels.du.edu

UNIVERSITY OF DETROIT MERCY
College of Business Administration

Admissions Contact: Dr. Bahman Mirshab, Director of Graduate Business Programs
Address: College of Business Administration, Detroit, MI 48219-0900
Admissions Phone: 313-993-1202 • Admissions Fax: 313-993-1673
Admissions E-mail: admissions@udmercy.edu • Web Address: www.business.udmercy.edu

The University of Detroit—Mercy, Michigan's largest and most comprehensive Catholic university, boasts small class sizes and a strong dedication to the education of the whole person. Some proud themes of the MBA program include "teaching students self-reflection, teamwork with diverse peoples, and responsible stewardship for the common good." The student body is composed of nearly all part-time MBA students. Intensive courses with an emphasis on global business are offered during the summer in England, Ireland, China, Brazil, and Mexico.

INSTITUTIONAL INFORMATION
Public/Private: Private
Evening Classes Available? Yes
Total Faculty: 53
% Faculty Part Time: 38
Student/Faculty Ratio: 30:1
Students in Parent Institution: 5,843
Academic Calendar: Semester

PROGRAMS
Degrees Offered: MBA (37 to 55 credits, 12 months to 5 years); MS in Computer and Information Systems (33 to 36 credits, 12 months to 5 years); MS in Product Development (45 credits, 2 years)
Joint Degrees: JD/MBA
Study Abroad Options: Brazil, People's Republic of China, United Kingdom, France, Mexico

STUDENT INFORMATION
Total Business Students: 235
% Full Time: 9
% Female: 35
% Minority: 26
% Out of State: 1
% International: 8
Average Age: 29

COMPUTER AND RESEARCH FACILITIES
Campuswide Network? Yes
% of MBA Classrooms Wired: 12
Computer Model Recommended: Laptop
Internet Fee? No

EXPENSES/FINANCIAL AID
Tuition Per Credit: $640

ADMISSIONS INFORMATION
Application Fee: $30
Electronic Application? Yes
Regular Application Deadline: 7/15
Regular Notification: 8/1
Deferment Available? Yes
Length of Deferment: 2 years
Non-fall Admissions? Yes
Non-fall Application Deadline(s): 10/15, 3/15, 4/15
Transfer Students Accepted? Yes
Transfer Policy: Up to 12 credits from AACSB programs
Need-Blind Admissions? No
Number of Applications Received: 65
% of Applicants Accepted: 94
% Accepted Who Enrolled: 59
Average GPA: 3.1
Average GMAT: 513
Average Years Experience: 6
Other Schools to Which Students Applied: University of Pittsburgh, University of Scranton.

EMPLOYMENT INFORMATION
Placement Office Available? Yes
% Employed Within 3 Months: 95

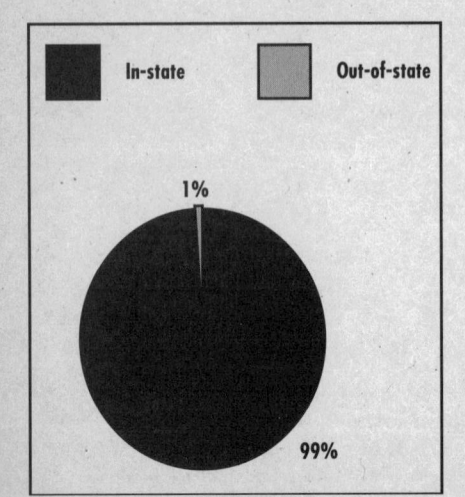

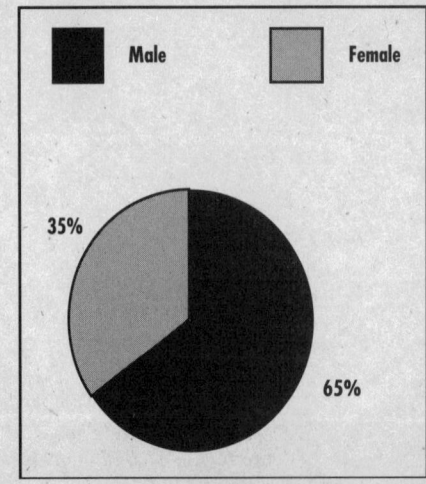

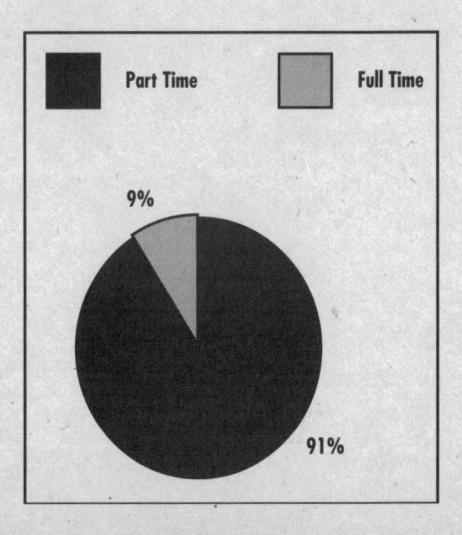

UNIVERSITY OF FINDLAY
College of Business

Admissions Contact: MBA Program Director
Address: 1000 N. Main Street, Findlay, OH 45840
Admissions Phone: 419-434-4676 • Admissions Fax: 419-434-6781
Admissions E-mail: obenour@findlay.edu • Web Address: www.findlay.edu/academic_programs/business/index.html

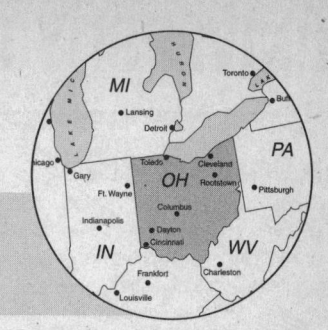

INSTITUTIONAL INFORMATION
Public/Private: Private
Evening Classes Available? Yes
Total Faculty: 18
% Faculty Female: 17
% Faculty Minority: 39
% Faculty Part Time: 25
Student/Faculty Ratio: 25:1
Students in Parent Institution: 4,405
Academic Calendar: Semester

PROGRAMS
Degrees Offered: MBA (33 credits, 18 months to 5 years)
Academic Specialties: Program blends theory, research, problem solving, and decision making; PhD in Marketing Management, Finance, Accounting, Operations, Strategy, and International Business

STUDENT INFORMATION
Total Business Students: 450
% Full Time: 12
% Female: 19
% Minority: 80
% Out of State: 95
% International: 90
Average Age: 32

COMPUTER AND RESEARCH FACILITIES
Research Facilities: Center for Management Development
Computer Facilities: Website and numerous computer labs on campus
Campuswide Network? Yes
% of MBA Classrooms Wired: 70
Computer Model Recommended: No
Internet Fee? Yes

EXPENSES/FINANCIAL AID
Annual Tuition: $13,572
Tuition Per Credit: $377
Books and Supplies: $2,000
Average Grant: $5,000
Average Loan: $10,000

ADMISSIONS INFORMATION
Application Fee: $25
Electronic Application? Yes
Regular Application Deadline: Rolling
Regular Notification: Rolling
Deferment Available? Yes
Length of Deferment: Varies upon reason
Non-fall Admissions? Yes
Non-fall Application Deadline(s): Winter, spring, summer
Transfer Students Accepted? Yes
Transfer Policy: May transfer up to 9 credits of similar courses of the program
Need-Blind Admissions? No
Number of Applications Received: 282
% of Applicants Accepted: 83
% Accepted Who Enrolled: 165
Average GPA: 3.3
Average GMAT: 550
Average Years Experience: 6
Other Schools to Which Students Applied: Bowling Green State University, University of Toledo

INTERNATIONAL STUDENTS
TOEFL Required of International Students? Yes
Minimum TOEFL: 525

EMPLOYMENT INFORMATION
Placement Office Available? Yes
% Employed Within 3 Months: 95

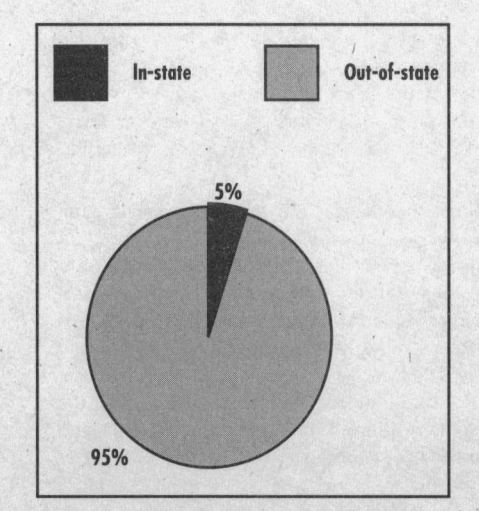

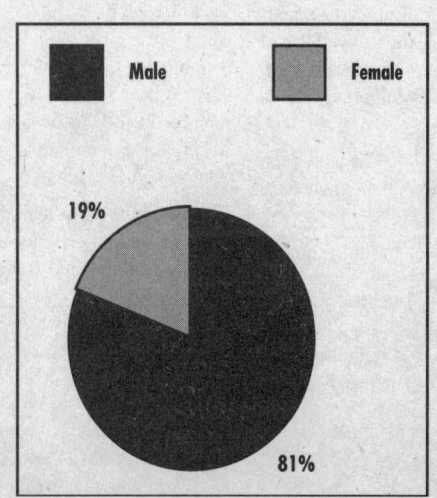

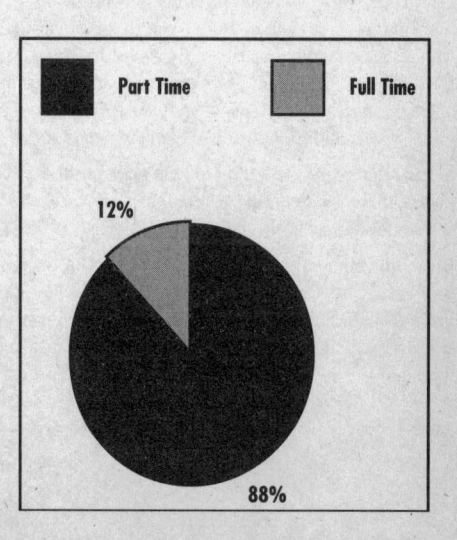

In-state 5% / Out-of-state 95%

Male 81% / Female 19%

Part Time 88% / Full Time 12%

UNIVERSITY OF FLORIDA

THE UNIVERSITY AT A GLANCE

"For more than 50 years, the University of Florida (UF) has developed successful leaders and managers to meet the challenges of a rapidly changing business environment. We are committed to promoting academic excellence, creating innovative programs, and fostering a collegial environment. Innovative new programs and curricular enhancements provide improved accessibility and greater flexibility for all students. Small class sizes, a low student/faculty ratio, and an expanded program staff ensure that individual needs are met throughout the program. Tremendous value results from the combination of our nationally recognized MBA program, the comparatively low cost of attendance, and Gainesville's high quality of life. We look toward a bright future with renewed focus, ambition, and spirit. We invite you to join the dynamic Florida MBA community.

—*John Kraft, Dean*

STUDENTS

Florida's programs integrate distinguished faculty, talented students, a dedicated staff, and successful alumni to form a cooperative and supportive community.

Florida MBA students come from diverse backgrounds and average approximately five years of work experience. They come from a variety of academic backgrounds, ranging from philosophy to engineering. Traditional MBA students benefit from involvement in various extracurricular activities, including student organizations such as the MBA Association, MBA Ambassadors, the Investment Club, Graduate Women in Business, and the International Business Association.

ACADEMICS

The University of Florida is nationally recognized for the academic excellence of its MBA programs and for the exceptional value that it provides. The MBA experience at Florida is unique in that it empowers students to tailor their education according to their individual needs. The University offers 9 distinct MBA program options, 15 academic concentrations, 6 certificate programs, 7 joint-degree programs, and a dual-degree program.

Florida's full-time traditional program options include the two-year program as well as a one-year program for students with an undergraduate degree in business. Both are delivered in a modular format composed of eight-week quarters.

Students can focus their studies in one or more of the following areas: finance, competitive strategy, marketing, entrepreneurship, security analysis, decision and information sciences, arts administration, general business, global management, international studies, human resources management, Latin American business, management, real estate, and sports administration.

Florida also provides an opportunity for its students to dedicate themselves to a more intensive course of study. The program awards certificates to students who allocate a large majority of their elective hours toward the study of one of the following functional areas: financial services, supply chain management, entrepreneurship and technology management, decision and information sciences, electronic commerce, and global management.

Seven joint degree programs enable students to combine the MBA with a UF degree in law, engineering, exercise and sport sciences, biotechnology, medical sciences, pharmacy, or medicine.

Busy professionals who want to earn the MBA degree without interrupting a successful career may elect to enroll in one of Florida's programs for working professionals. Students in the Executive MBA Program and MBA for Professionals Programs (two-year and one-year options) meet on campus just one weekend per month. Our newest professional program, the MBA for Engineers and Scientists, was tailor-made for people with technical backgrounds and follows the same weekend format.

Florida also offers its Internet MBA in two-year and one-year options. The Internet MBA utilizes leading-edge interactive technology to deliver a high-caliber graduate degree via flexible distance learning. The program requires only occasional visits to the campus: for orientation and one weekend at the end of each term.

MBA students have the opportunity to study abroad via one of 16 international exchange programs. In addition, they have the option to pursue a dual degree—the MBA/Master of International Management (MIM), offered in conjunction with Thunderbird, The American Graduate School of International Management. For those interested in an international experience, our newest full-time option, the International MBA, is an exciting degree track that allows students to earn a MBA in about one year.

Corporate Partnerships

Corporate leaders are an integral part of Florida's business school community. The program is supported largely by the contributions of its executive advisory board, corporate recruiters, and alumni.

Prominent business leaders routinely visit the University to speak to students via the Distinguished Speaker Series or by invitation from various professors. Recent speakers include Craig R. Barrett (CEO of Intel Corporation), Warren Buffet (chairman, Berkshire Hathaway), Richard Teerlink (former chairman of the board for Harley Davidson), and Mary Alice Taylor (chairperson and CEO of HomeGrocer.com).

Prominent Alimni

Prominent Alumni include John Dasburg (CEO of Burger King), Hal Steinbrenner (general partner, New York Yankees), Allen Lastinger (former president/COO, Barnett Banks), Jonathan Root (general partner, US Venture Partners), Bill Gurley (general partner, Benchmark Capital), Manny Fernandez (UF Board of Trustees), Judith Rosenblum (chief learning officer, Coca-Cola), Chris Verlander (president and COO, American Heritage Life), and Randall P. Bast (co-founder of Innovex Group).

Florida's MBA faculty members possess exceptional credentials and are recognized by industry leaders and their peers for contributions to various areas of expertise. With small average class sizes for electives, students have maximum access to these top-notch instructors. The Departments of Accounting, Marketing, Finance, and Management are consistently ranked among the top 25 in the country. Individual faculty members have been honored with national awards for their excellence in research. Members of the faculty serve as editors for major journals of marketing, finance, accounting, management, and business law. They also direct 13 research centers, which explore emerging trends in a wide array of business disciplines. These faculty members are not just preeminent researchers, they are outstanding teachers as well.

CAMPUS LIFE

The University of Florida is a comprehensive, public research university that was founded in 1853. With more than 44,000, students it is the 6th largest university in the nation. It is the only public university in the southeast that is a member of the prestigious Association of American Universities. The University of Florida has established a place for itself among the country's elite institutions of higher learning.

Florida's business school is located in the northeast corner of campus, in an area known as the "Business Triangle." It is adjacent to the University's administration building and the main library facilities. Bryan Hall contains a computer lab and a study lounge (exclusively for MBA students), along with a student information center and offices for the MBA program staff members. Classrooms, faculty offices, and academic research centers are housed in Stuzin and Matherly Halls, the other two buildings that comprise the Business Triangle. Florida's 2,000-acre campus features athletic facilities that are among the Nation's finest—including two state-of-the-art fitness centers and a championship golf course. The campus also has a performing arts center, a wildlife sanctuary, and several museums for students to enjoy.

Warrington College of Business

The classrooms and study areas utilized by the MBA program are all linked to the business school's computer network. MBA students are required to have a notebook computer in order to be able to participate in this interactive learning environment.

Florida features a staff of dedicated career services professionals who assist MBA students with their career development. The staff uses a series of skill assessments and other activities to help students develop comprehensive career plans. These tools include workshops for creating effective resumes and improving interview skills. The staff also develops and maintains working relationships with corporate recruiters, coordinates recruiting events, and maintains an extensive list of job postings for positions in major cities. MBA students also may utilize the University's Career Resource Center, widely regarded as one of the Nation's best.

COSTS

The Florida MBA is consistently rated as one of the best buys in business education. Nationally ranked academic programs, low cost of attendance, and Gainesville's high quality of life combine to provide students with tremendous value. A limited number of merit-based MBA fellowships and graduate assistantships are available to help traditional students reduce their educational expenses.

ADMISSIONS

Candidates are evaluated based on their academic achievement and aptitude, professional experience, community involvement, and personal character. All applicants must have a bachelor's degree from an accredited U.S. institution or its international equivalent. Additional requirements include at least two years of significant post-baccalaureate work experience, official GMAT scores, official transcripts, two letters of recommendation, four essays, and completed application forms. All one-year program options require an acceptable undergraduate business degree. Official TOEFL scores are required for applicants whose native language is not English. Other requirements vary by program. Students should refer to the application packet for details.

The Traditional MBA Program (two-year option), the MBA for Professionals (one-year option), and the Executive MBA Program begin each August; the MBA for Professionals Program (two-year option), the Internet MBA Programs (one and two-year options), and the MBA for Engineers and Scientists Programs begin each January; and the Traditional MBA Program (one-year option) commences in June. The start date for the International MBA Program varies depending on the partner school chosen. For additional information on the International MBA Program please contact admissions. Prospective students should refer to the application packet or the Florida MBA Programs' website for specific application deadlines, program calendars, and budgets. An online inquiry and application system is available through the website as well.

Admissions Contact: Amanda Moore, Admissions Coordinator
Address: 134 Bryan Hall, PO Box 117152, Gainesville, FL 32611-7152
Admissions Phone: 352-392-7992 • Admissions Fax: 352-392-8791
Admissions E-mail: floridamba@notes.cba.ufl.edu • Web Address: www.floridamba.ufl.edu

UNIVERSITY OF FLORIDA
Warrington College of Business

Admissions Contact: Amanda Moore, Admissions Coordinator
Address: 134 Bryan Hall, PO Box 117152, Gainesville, FL 32611-7152
Admissions Phone: 352-392-7992 • Admissions Fax: 352-392-8791
Admissions E-mail: floridamba@notes.cba.ufl.edu • Web Address: www.floridamba.ufl.edu

Strong programs in entrepreneurship and finance, diverse course offerings, and a paradise-like atmosphere draw future MBAs to the "practical" University of Florida Graduate School of Business. It's also "a bargain financially"—particularly for in-staters—and the sweltering, hopping, activity-laden college town of Gainesville "is probably unparalleled socially."

INSTITUTIONAL INFORMATION
Public/Private: Public
Evening Classes Available? No
Total Faculty: 91
% Faculty Female: 13
% Faculty Minority: 14
Student/Faculty Ratio: 6:1
Academic Calendar: Semester

PROGRAMS
Degrees Offered: MBA (14 to 33 months); MS in Management (1 year); MA in International Business (1 year); MA in Real Estate (1 year); MS in Decision and Information Sciences (1 year); MAcc (1 year); MS in Finance (1 year); PhD in Marketing, Finance, Management, DIS, or Economics (3 to 6 years)
Joint Degrees: MBA/JD (4 years); MBA/Master of Exercise and Sport Science (3 years); MBA/MS in Biotechnology; MBA/Doctor of Pharmacy; MBA/PhD in Medical Sciences; MBA/MD
Academic Specialties: Electronic Commerce, Supply Chain Management, Entrepreneurship, Management of Technology, Financial Services
Special Opportunities: Traditional MBA; Executive MBA; MBA for Professionals (1- and 2-year options); Internet MBA (1- and 2-year options); International MBA; MBA for Engineers and Scientists
Study Abroad Options: Belgium, Chile, China (Hong Kong), Denmark, Finland, France, Germany, Great Britain, Italy, Netherlands, Norway, Spain, Turkey, Venezuela, Japan

STUDENT INFORMATION
Total Business Students: 457
% Full Time: 76
% Female: 24
% Minority: 10
% Out of State: 52
% International: 21
Average Age: 27

COMPUTER AND RESEARCH FACILITIES
Research Facilities: Bureau of Economic & Business Research; Business Ethics Education & Research Center; Center for Accounting Research & Professional Education; Center for International Economic & Business Studies; Center for Public Policy Research; Consumer Research, Decision & Information Sciences Forum; Entrepreneurship & Innovation Center; Florida Insurance Research Center; Human Resource Research Center; Public Utilities Research Center; Real Estate Research Center; Retailing Education & Research Center
Computer Facilities: Technology Assistance Ctr.
Campuswide Network? Yes
% of MBA Classrooms Wired: 100
Computer Model Recommended: Laptop
Internet Fee? No

EXPENSES/FINANCIAL AID
Annual Tuition (Resident/Nonresident): $4,620/$16,018
Room & Board (Off Campus): $6,800
Books and Supplies: $2,935

Average Grant: $4,750
Average Loan: $10,000

ADMISSIONS INFORMATION
Application Fee: $20
Electronic Application? Yes
Early Decision Application Deadline: 12/15 fall
Early Decision Notification: 2/15
Regular Application Deadline: 4/15
Regular Notification: 6/15
Deferment Available? No
Non-fall Application Deadline(s): 10/15 (spring programs for working professionals), 6/1 (fall programs for working professionals)
Transfer Students Accepted? No
Need-Blind Admissions? Yes
Number of Applications Received: 491
% of Applicants Accepted: 22
% Accepted Who Enrolled: 46
Average GPA: 3.3
Average GMAT: 655
Average Years Experience: 4
Other Admissions Factors Considered: Leadership potential
Minority/Disadvantaged Student Recruitment Programs: Graduate Minority Campus Visitation
Other Schools to Which Students Applied: UT Austin, U. of Georgia, U. of Miami, Arizona State, Emory, Georgetown, Texas A&M

INTERNATIONAL STUDENTS
TOEFL Required of International Students? Yes
Minimum TOEFL: 600 (250 computer)

EMPLOYMENT INFORMATION

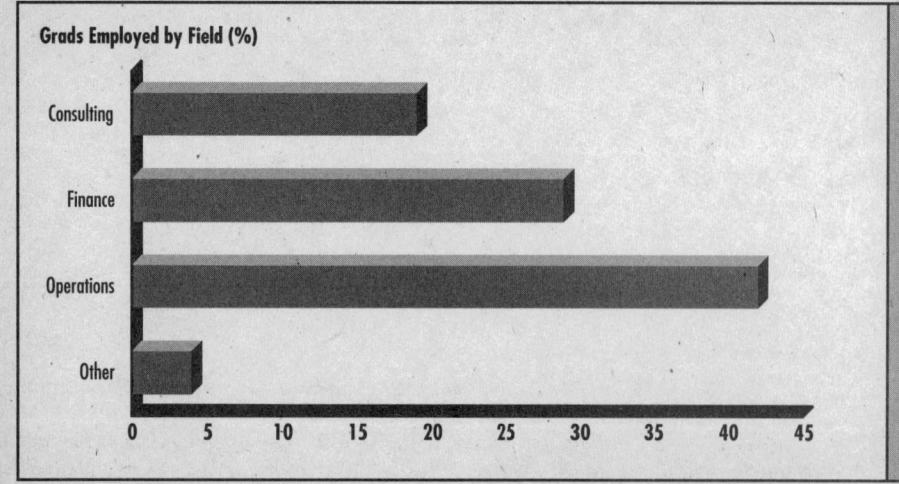

Grads Employed by Field (%)
- Consulting: ~20
- Finance: ~28
- Operations: ~43
- Other: ~3

Placement Office Available? Yes
% Employed Within 3 Months: 93
Frequent Employers: Deloitte & Touche, ExxonMobil, General Electric, Arthur Andersen, Ford Motor Co., PricewaterhouseCoopers, Samsung, SunTrust Bank
Prominent Alumni: John Dasburg (MBA '70), president and CEO, Burger King; Don McKinney (MBA '72), venture capitalist and partner, Watershed Capital; William R. Hough (MBA '48), president, William R. Hough & Co. and WRH Mortgage

UNIVERSITY OF GEORGIA
Terry College of Business,
Graduate School of Business Administration

Admissions Contact: Anne C. Cooper, Director, MBA Admissions
Address: 346 Brooks Hall, Athens, GA 30602-6264
Admissions Phone: 706-542-5671 • Admissions Fax: 706-542-5351
Admissions E-mail: terrymba@terry.uga.edu • Web Address: www.terry.uga.edu/mba

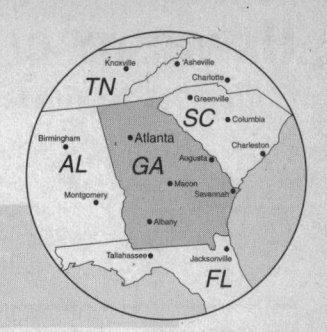

What with "state-of-the-art" facilities and flexible degree programs, the University of Georgia's Terry College of Business is "an excellent value" and one of the nation's best public business schools. You certainly can't beat its location; students say the "comfortable" environs of Athens provide "a broad spectrum of individuals and culture" and "epitomize what a college town should be." As an added bonus, Atlanta—the "Capital of the New South"—is a mere 70 miles away.

INSTITUTIONAL INFORMATION
Public/Private: Public
Evening Classes Available? Yes
Total Faculty: 132
Student/Faculty Ratio: 25:1
Students in Parent Institution: 32,500
Academic Calendar: Semester

PROGRAMS
Degrees Offered: MBA (41 to 66 credits, 11 to 22 months), with concentrations in Accounting, Economics, Entrepreneurship, Finance, Insurance, International Business, Real Estate, Risk Management, Organizational Consulting, and Productivity/Quality Management; MAcc (30 credits, 9 months to 2 years) with concentrations in Economics, Financial Economics, and International Economics; MA Economics (30 to 36 credits, 9 months to 2 years); Master of Marketing Research (40 credits, 18 months)
Joint Degrees: JD/MBA (4 years)
Academic Specialties: MIS, Corporate Finance, Investments, Marketing
Special Opportunities: Progressive Partners Program (minority initiative)
Study Abroad Options: Netherlands

STUDENT INFORMATION
Total Business Students: 368
% Full Time: 68
% Female: 31
% Minority: 13
% Out of State: 54
% International: 21
Average Age: 28

COMPUTER AND RESEARCH FACILITIES
Research Facilities: Institute for Leadership Advancement, Center for Enterprise Risk Management, Center for Information Systems Leadership, Ramsey Center for Private Enterprise, Coca-Cola Center for International Business, Coca-Cola Center for Marketing Studies, Bonbright Utilities Center, Selig Center for Economic Growth
Computer Facilities: GALIN online library search service; sizable library of software provided by professors from their classes; more than 900 seats in new classroom, Sanford Hall, with laptop connectivity to the campus network
Campuswide Network? Yes
% of MBA Classrooms Wired: 100
Computer Model Recommended: Laptop
Internet Fee? No

EXPENSES/FINANCIAL AID
Annual Tuition (Resident/Nonresident): $3,549/$13,017
Room & Board (On/Off Campus): $4,870/$6,825
Books and Supplies: $900
Average Grant: $2,705
% Receiving Financial Aid: 65
% Receiving Aid Their First Year: 75

ADMISSIONS INFORMATION
Application Fee: $30
Electronic Application? Yes
Regular Application Deadline: 5/1
Regular Notification: Rolling
Length of Deferment: 1 year
Non-fall Application Deadline(s): 2/1 summer
Transfer Students Accepted? No
Need-Blind Admissions? Yes
Number of Applications Received: 734
% of Applicants Accepted: 28
% Accepted Who Enrolled: 50
Average GPA: 3.3
Average GMAT: 659
Average Years Experience: 5
Minority/Disadvantaged Student Recruitment Programs: Progressive Partners Program
Other Schools to Which Students Applied: Emory University, Vanderbilt University

INTERNATIONAL STUDENTS
TOEFL Required of International Students? Yes
Minimum TOEFL: 577 (233 computer)

EMPLOYMENT INFORMATION
Placement Office Available? Yes
% Employed Within 3 Months: 93
Frequent Employers: Federal Express, Andersen Consulting, Wachovia, International Paper, SunTrust Bank, BellSouth, Delta Airlines, Shopping Center Properties, Fannie Mae, Cintas, Coca-Cola

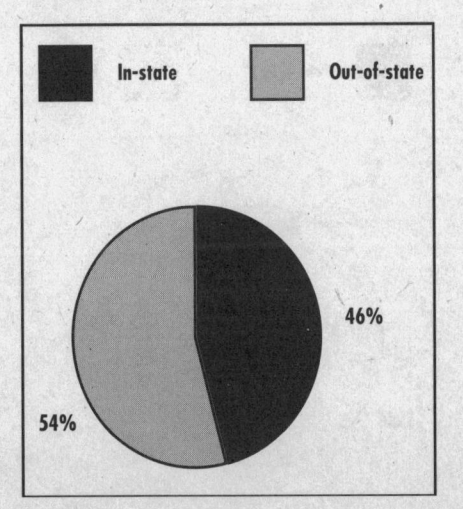

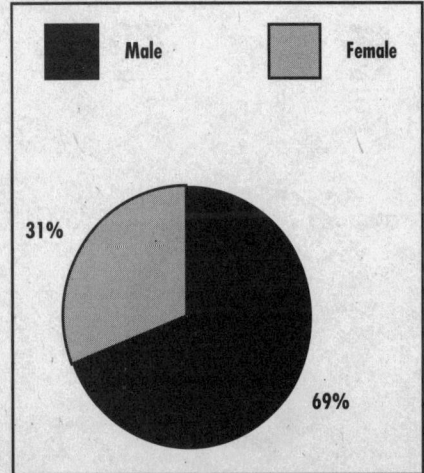

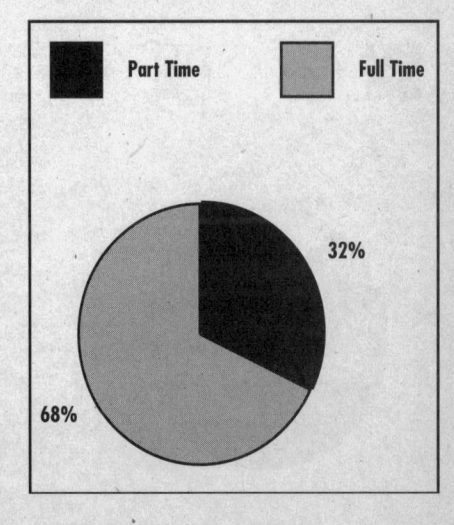

UNIVERSITY OF HAWAII — MANOA
College of Business Administration

Admissions Contact: Marsha Anderson, Assistant Dean
Address: 2404 Maile Way B201, Honolulu, HI 96822
Admissions Phone: 808-956-8266 • Admissions Fax: 808-956-9890
Admissions E-mail: osasgrad@busadm.cba.hawaii.edu • Web Address: www.cba.hawaii.edu

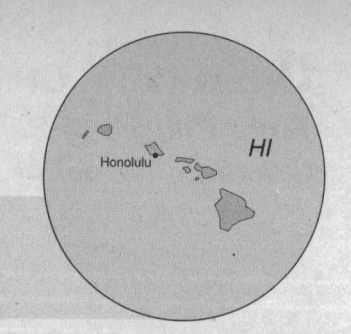

INSTITUTIONAL INFORMATION
Public/Private: Public
Evening Classes Available? Yes
Total Faculty: 65
% Faculty Female: 5
% Faculty Minority: 10
% Faculty Part Time: 22
Student/Faculty Ratio: 25:1
Students in Parent Institution: 17,532
Academic Calendar: Semester

PROGRAMS
Degrees Offered: MBA (42 to 48 credits, 2 to 7 years); Executive MBA (EMBA) (48 credits, 22 months); Master of Accounting (MAcc) (30 credits, 12 months to 7 years); Japan-Focused Executive MBA (MBA) (48 credits, 15 months); China-Focused Executive MBA (MBA) (48 credits, 15 months); PhD in International Management (3 to 7 years)
Joint Degrees: MBA/JD (122 to 128 credits, 5 to 7 years)
Academic Specialties: International Business, Entrepreneurship, Information Technology Management
Special Opportunities: Internship program
Study Abroad Options: Denmark, Germany, Hong Kong, Japan, Korea, Saipan, Thailand, France, Finland

STUDENT INFORMATION
Total Business Students: 319
% Full Time: 52
% Female: 39
% Minority: 18
% Out of State: 8
% International: 21

COMPUTER AND RESEARCH FACILITIES
Research Facilities: Instructional Resource Center, Behavior Research Laboratory, The Sunset Reference Center, The Asia-Pacific Center for Executive Development, Academy of International Business, The Asia Pacific Economic Corporation Study Center, The Center for Japanese Global Investment and Finance, The Pacific Asian Management Institute, The Center for International Business Education and Research, The Hawaii Real Estate Research and Education Center, The Pacific Business Center, and The Pacific Research Institute for Information Systems and Management.
Computer Facilities: 2 computer labs at the College of Business Administration. 10 computers in the graduate reading room area. Access to online bibliographic retrieval systems and online databases, including ABI Inform, Disclosure, Dissertation Abstracts, Lexis/Nexis, Periodicals Abstracts Research, and Public Affairs Info Service.
Campuswide Network? Yes
Computer Model Recommended: Laptop
Internet Fee? No

EXPENSES/FINANCIAL AID
Annual Tuition (Resident/Nonresident): $4,920/$10,954
Tuition Per Credit (Resident/Nonresident): $205/$456
Room & Board (On/Off Campus): $12,000/$14,000
Books and Supplies: $950
Average Grant: $25,000
Average Loan: $10,900
% Receiving Financial Aid: 25

ADMISSIONS INFORMATION
Application Fee: $25
Electronic Application? Yes
Regular Application Deadline: 5/1
Regular Notification: Rolling
Length of Deferment: one semester
Non-fall Application Deadline(s): 11/1 spring
Transfer Policy: Credits may be transferred into the MBA program from other AACSB-accredited business schools, from other University of Hawaii graduate programs, or by petition. Transfer credit is appropriate for both Core (upon approval) and electives.
Need-Blind Admissions? No
Number of Applications Received: 313
% of Applicants Accepted: 67
% Accepted Who Enrolled: 46
Other Admissions Factors Considered: Computer experience required (ICS 101 or equivalent)

INTERNATIONAL STUDENTS
TOEFL Required of International Students? Yes
Minimum TOEFL: 550 (220 computer)

EMPLOYMENT INFORMATION
Placement Office Available? Yes
% Employed Within 3 Months: 80
Frequent Employers: First Hawaiian Bank, Bank of Hawaii, City Bank, KPMG LLP, Star Supermarket, State of Hawaii, City and County of Honolulu, Andersen Consulting, Hewlett Packard, Microsoft
Prominent Alumni: Robin Campaniano, president and CEO, Insurance; Brenda Lei Foster, executive assistant, Governor State of Hawaii; Sharon Weiner, VP, DFS Hawaii; C. Dudley Pratt, Jr., former trustee, Campbell Estate; David McCoy, CEO, Campbell Estate

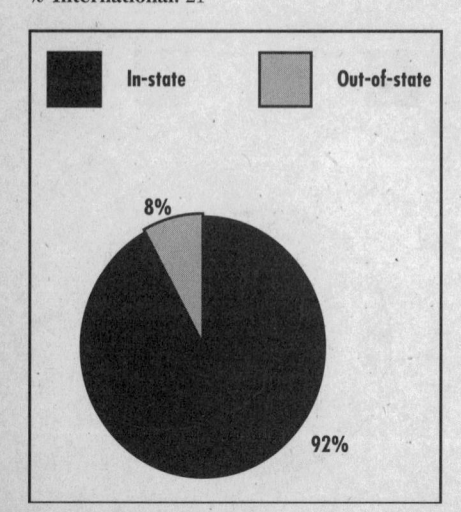

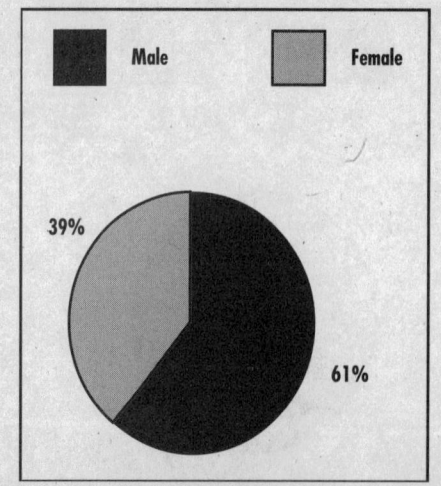

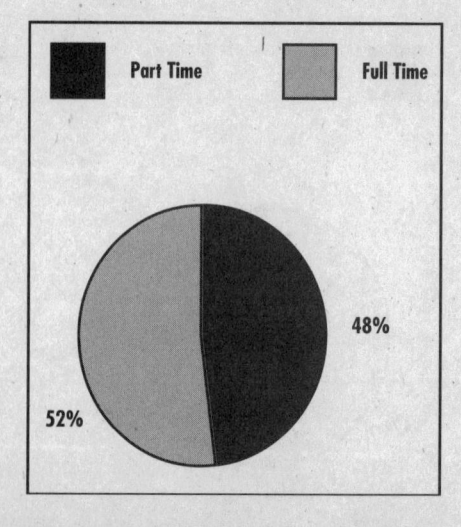

In-state: 92% / Out-of-state: 8%

Male: 61% / Female: 39%

Part Time: 52% / Full Time: 48%

UNIVERSITY OF ILLINOIS — CHICAGO
UIC MBA Program

Admissions Contact: Rita Rackauskas, Recruitment and Admissions Counselor
Address: 815 West Van Buren, Suite 220, Chicago, IL 60607
Admissions Phone: 312-996-4573 • Admissions Fax: 312-413-0338
Admissions E-mail: mba@uic.edu • Web Address: www.uic.edu/cba/mba

University of Illinois at Chicago caters to the demands of students' varying schedules and offers both full-time and part-time MBA programs. In addition, UI sends 8 to 12 students per semester off to foreign countries, including Germany, Mexico, France, and Malaysia, for unforgettable experiences working with companies such as Kellogg's, American Express, Deutsche Bank, and Nestle. Such foreign business opportunities may or may not be in conjunction with study abroad and typically last from six to nine months. Dual degrees, including an MBA/Master in Public Health and MBA/Doctor of Medicine, are also available.

INSTITUTIONAL INFORMATION
Public/Private: Public
Evening Classes Available? Yes
Student/Faculty Ratio: 30:1
Students in Parent Institution: 24,865
Academic Calendar: Semester

PROGRAMS
Degrees Offered: Master of Business Administration (MBA) (full time or part time, 54 credits, 2 to 6 years)
Joint Degrees: Master of Business Administration/Master of Science in Accounting (MBA/MS) (full time or part time, 68 credits, 2.5 to 6 years); Master of Business Administration/Master of Public Health (MBA/MPH) (full time or part time, 70 credits, 2.5 to 6 years); Master of Business Administration/Master of Science in Nursing (MBA/MS) (full time or part time, 67 credits, 2 to 6 years); Master of Business Administration/Master of Arts in Economics (MBA/MA) (full time or part time, 72 credits, 2.5 to 6 years); Master of Business Administration/Master of Science in Management Information Systems (70 credits, 2.5 to 6 years); Master of Business Administration/Doctor of Medicine (medical curriculum and 48 MBA credits, 5 years)
Academic Specialties: Same professors teaching full- and part-time programs; flexible pace for students; students can switch between full time and part time to accommodate individual schedules; day, evening, and online courses available

STUDENT INFORMATION
Total Business Students: 499
% Female: 39
% Minority: 19
% International: 30
Average Age: 28

COMPUTER AND RESEARCH FACILITIES
Research Facilities: Center for Urban Business, Family Business Council, Institute for Entrepreneurial Studies, Thursday Business Forum
Computer Facilities: Multiple on-campus computer labs. UIC website offers access to much individual class information from remote locations. On-campus labs offer SPSS, OmniPro, and all current Office software.
Campuswide Network? Yes
Computer Model Recommended: No
Internet Fee? No

EXPENSES/FINANCIAL AID
Annual Tuition (Resident/Nonresident): $11,078/$18,334
Tuition Per Credit (Resident/Nonresident): $462/$764
Room & Board (Off Campus): $9,900
Books and Supplies: $1,290

ADMISSIONS INFORMATION
Application Fee: $40
Electronic Application? Yes
Regular Application Deadline: 6/1
Regular Notification: Rolling
Length of Deferment: 1 year
Non-fall Application Deadline(s): 10/15 spring, 4/1 summer; international applicants: 4/1 fall, 9/15 spring, 3/1 summer
Transfer Policy: Need to apply and be accepted to the UIC MBA Program; can submit transcripts from previous course work with a grade of B or better and a course description; must be from an AACSB-accredited institution; maximum of 24 semester hours
Need-Blind Admissions? Yes
Number of Applications Received: 568
% of Applicants Accepted: 59
% Accepted Who Enrolled: 53
Average GPA: 3.1
Average GMAT: 580
Average Years Experience: 5
Other Schools to Which Students Applied: DePaul University, Northwestern University, University of Chicago

INTERNATIONAL STUDENTS
TOEFL Required of International Students? Yes
Minimum TOEFL: 570 (230 computer)

EMPLOYMENT INFORMATION

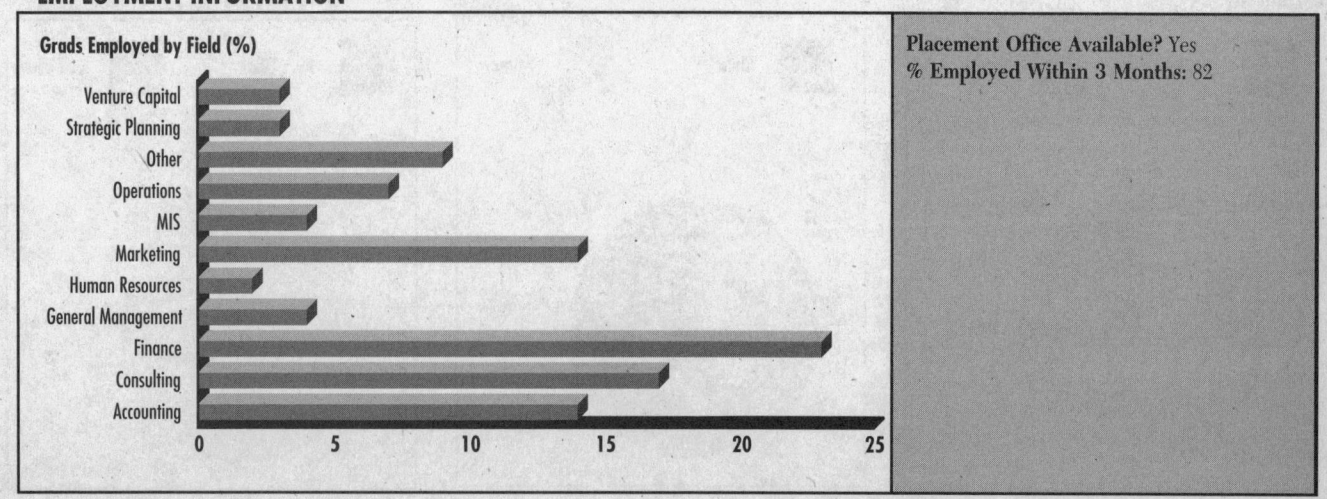

Grads Employed by Field (%)

Field	%
Venture Capital	~2
Strategic Planning	~3
Other	~9
Operations	~7
MIS	~3
Marketing	~14
Human Resources	~2
General Management	~4
Finance	~23
Consulting	~17
Accounting	~14

Placement Office Available? Yes
% Employed Within 3 Months: 82

UNIVERSITY OF ILLINOIS — URBANA-CHAMPAIGN
College of Commerce and Business Administration

Admissions Contact: Camille Gilmore, Director of Admission and Recruiting
Address: 410 David Kinley Hall, 1407 West Gregory Drive, Urbana, IL 61801
Admissions Phone: 800-622-8482 • Admissions Fax: 217-333-1156
Admissions E-mail: mba@uiuc.edu • Web Address: www.mba.uiuc.edu

Because the University of Illinois's MBA program boasts a "huge international population," one benefit of coming here is that you can almost "study abroad without going abroad." At the least, students tell us you'll come away with "very cool global business experience." Illinois's "integrated" first-year curriculum allows for seriously "hands-on" learning, and the Office for the Study of Business Issues allows MBAs to work with engineers and entrepreneurs to evaluate the commercial potential of their innovations.

INSTITUTIONAL INFORMATION
Public/Private: Public
Evening Classes Available? Yes
Total Faculty: 191
% Faculty Female: 16
% Faculty Minority: 11
% Faculty Part Time: 31
Students in Parent Institution: 36,000
Academic Calendar: Semester

PROGRAMS
Degrees Offered: MBA (2 years), Master of Science of Business Administration (1 year), Master of Science in Accounting (1 year), MS in International Finance (1 year), Master of Accounting Science (MAS) (1 year), Executive MBA (21 months)
Joint Degrees: Architecture (3 years), Computer Science (3 years), Civil and Environmental Engineering (3 years), Electrical Engineering (3 years), Mechanical Engineering (3 years), Medicine (5 years), Journalism (3 years), Law (4 years), Education (3 years), Human Resource Development (3 years), custom-designed joint degree
Academic Specialties: Finance, Accounting, Marketing, MIS
Special Opportunities: Custom Executive Development Program
Study Abroad Options: Formalized programs in United Kingdom, Germany, France, Spain, Norway, Denmark, Canada, Netherlands, Brazil, and the Phillippines. Students can study in virtually any country through university-to-university agreements.

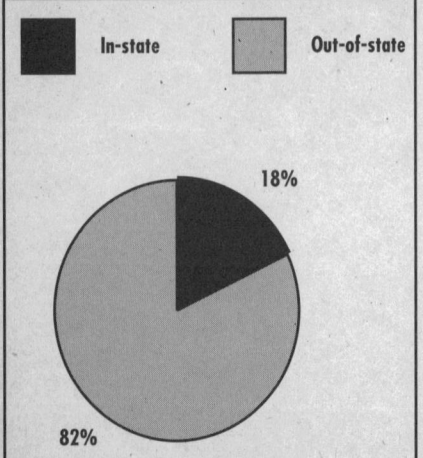

STUDENT INFORMATION
Total Business Students: 148
% Full Time: 100
% Female: 43
% Minority: 41
% Out of State: 82
% International: 71
Average Age: 28

COMPUTER AND RESEARCH FACILITIES
Research Facilities: National Center for Supercomputing Applications, Office for Strategic Business Initiatives
Computer Facilities: National Center for Supercomputing Applications and many more online databases
Number of Student Computers: Thousands
Campuswide Network? Yes
% Who Own Computers: 100
Computer Proficiency Required? Yes
Computer Model Recommended: Laptop
Special Purchasing Agreements? Yes
Companies with Agreements: IBM
Internet Fee? No

EXPENSES/FINANCIAL AID
Annual Tuition (Resident/Nonresident): $11,050/$18,776
Room & Board (On/Off Campus): $7,510/$7,510
Books and Supplies: $1,154
Average Grant: $6,360

ADMISSIONS INFORMATION
Application Fee: $40
Electronic Application? Yes
Early Decision Application Deadline: 12/15
Regular Application Deadline: 4/1
Regular Notification: Rolling
Length of Deferment: 1 year
Non-fall Admissions? No
Transfer Students Accepted? Yes
Need-Blind Admissions? Yes
Number of Applications Received: 948
% of Applicants Accepted: 36
% Accepted Who Enrolled: 43
Average GPA: 3.4
Average GMAT: 620
Average Years Experience: 4
Other Admissions Factors Considered: Work experience, essays, letter of recommendation, extracurricular activities, intership, military experience
Minority/Disadvantaged Student Recruitment Programs: Diversity Preview Weekends
Other Schools to Which Students Applied: Carnegie Mellon, Indiana Univ., Purdue, Univ. of Maryland, UNC—Chapel Hill

INTERNATIONAL STUDENTS
TOEFL Required of International Students? Yes
Minimum TOEFL: 600

EMPLOYMENT INFORMATION
Placement Office Available? Yes

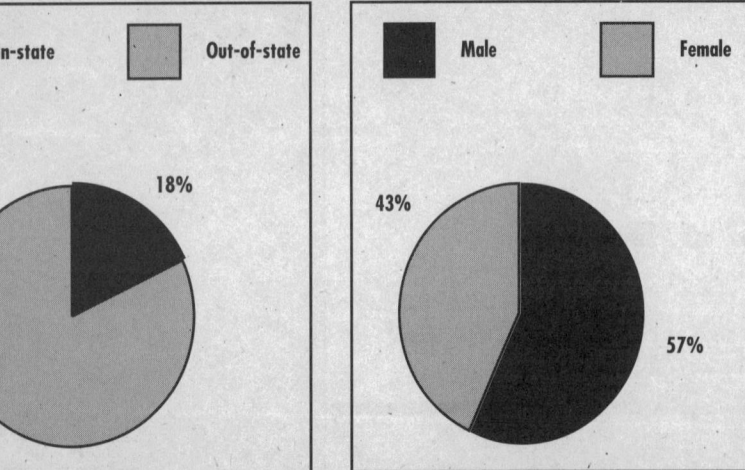

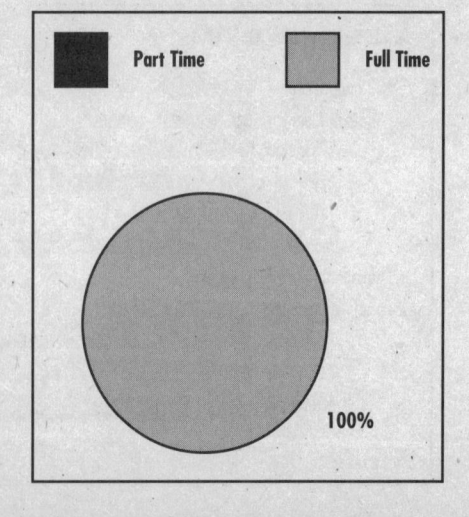

UNIVERSITY OF IOWA
Henry B. Tippie School of Management

Admissions Contact: Admissions Office, Director of MBA Admissions and Financial Aid
Address: 108 Pappajohn Business Administration Building, Iowa City, IA 52242-1000
Admissions Phone: 319-335-1039 • Admissions Fax: 319-335-3604
Admissions E-mail: iowamba@uiowa.edu • Web Address: www.biz.uiowa.edu/mba

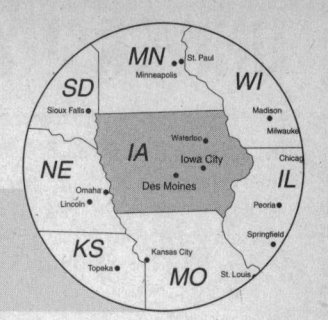

The "immensely talented and cooperative" students at the University of Iowa say theirs is "an MBA program on the rise." Iowa boasts an "incredibly advanced" facility complete "with the latest multimedia," a "fantastic" administration, and an "ever-improving atmosphere." Finance is probably the strongest discipline here, thanks to innovative programs like "the Applied Securities Management program, which allows students to apply classroom ideas to manage real portfolios."

INSTITUTIONAL INFORMATION
Public/Private: Public
Evening Classes Available? Yes
Total Faculty: 142
% Faculty Female: 21
% Faculty Minority: 15
% Faculty Part Time: 30
Student/Faculty Ratio: 5:1
Students in Parent Institution: 29,000
Academic Calendar: Semester

PROGRAMS
Degrees Offered: MBA (21 months); MAcc in Accounting (9 to 21 months depending on undergraduate degree); PhD in Business Administration; PhD in Economics (4 years)
Joint Degrees: MBA and Law (4 years), Hospital and Health Administration (2.5 years), Library Science (3 years), Nursing (3 years)
Academic Specialties: Finance/Investments, Marketing, Entrepreneurship, Accounting and Management Information Systems
Special Opportunities: Summer internships program, consulting projects (in U.S. and abroad)
Study Abroad Options: Greece, Austria, Germany, Hungary, Netherlands, Australia

STUDENT INFORMATION
Total Business Students: 910
% Full Time: 25
% Female: 29
% Minority: 5
% Out of State: 24
% International: 43
Average Age: 29

COMPUTER AND RESEARCH FACILITIES
Research Facilities: Pappajohn Entrepreneurial Center, Iowa Electronic Markets, Behavioral Research Laboratory, Small Business Development Center, Iowa Institute for International Business, Pomerantz Business Library, Economic Research Institute, Hawkinson Institute of Business Finance, Stead Advanced Learning Technologies Center
Computer Facilities: Computer laboratory set aside for MBA students; software and hardware provided including Bloomberg, Lexis-Nexis, and Dow Jones News Retrieval Service.
Campuswide Network? Yes
% of MBA Classrooms Wired: 100
Computer Model Recommended: No
Internet Fee? No

EXPENSES/FINANCIAL AID
Annual Tuition (Resident/Nonresident): $7,440/$15,752
Tuition Per Credit: $359
Room & Board (On/Off Campus): $9,088/$13,120
Books and Supplies: $1,400
Average Grant: $2,188
% Receiving Financial Aid: 52
% Receiving Aid Their First Year: 54

ADMISSIONS INFORMATION
Application Fee: $30
Electronic Application? Yes
Regular Application Deadline: 7/15
Regular Notification: Rolling
Length of Deferment: 1 year
Non-fall Application Deadline(s): 11/1 Evening, spring; 12/15 early application deadline
Transfer Policy: Maximum number of transferable credits is 9 (from an AACSB-accredited program).
Need-Blind Admissions? Yes
Number of Applications Received: 395
% of Applicants Accepted: 38
% Accepted Who Enrolled: 49
Average GPA: 3.3
Average GMAT: 631
Average Years Experience: 5
Other Admissions Factors Considered: Management and business experience, demonstrated leadership abilities
Minority/Disadvantaged Student Recruitment Programs: Minority MBA Association; financial aid available due to a FIPSE grant to the Iowa Electronic Markets' initiative to promote knowledge of markets among minority students
Other Schools to Which Students Applied: Indiana U., Purdue, U. of Illinois at Urbana-Champaign, U. of Minnesota, U. of Wisconsin—Madison

INTERNATIONAL STUDENTS
TOEFL Required of International Students? Yes
Minimum TOEFL: 600 (250 computer)

EMPLOYMENT INFORMATION

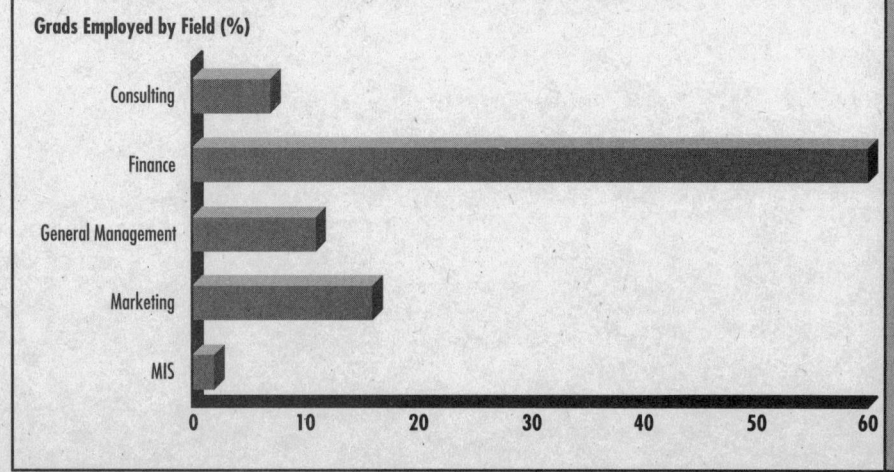

Grads Employed by Field (%)

Field	%
Consulting	~7
Finance	~60
General Management	~12
Marketing	~17
MIS	~2

Placement Office Available? Yes
% Employed Within 3 Months: 98
Frequent Employers: HON Industries, Deere & Co., Northwest Airlines, Kraft Foods, Allsteel Inc., GE, Rockwell Collins Inc., U.S. Bancorp, Pillsbury Company, Procter & Gamble
Prominent Alumni: Steven L. Caves, president, Firstar Bank Iowa; Kathleen A. Dore, president, Bravo Networks; Kerry Killinger, chairman, president, and CEO, Washington Mutual Savings Bank; Mark McCormack, president, Skymast; Sheryl K. Sunderman, partner, Accenture

UNIVERSITY OF IOWA

THE SCHOOL AT A GLANCE

Founded in 1847, The University of Iowa is the oldest and largest public university in the state. The University, with a population of nearly 30,000 students, offers renowned professional graduate programs in medicine, law, writing, and business. The Henry B. Tippie School of Management houses the MBA program at the University.

ACADEMICS

Students in the MBA program at the Tippie School of Management soon discover that the guiding principles of the program reflect those of its namesake, Henry B. Tippie. The program emphasizes:

- A solid foundation of knowledge
- Application of the latest technology to solve problems
- Leadership based on integrity and hard work

Throughout the program, MBAs work together on group projects and in study groups, learning how to practice team-based management as well as individual leadership.

The MBA program starts with an interdisciplinary core of courses that includes key functional areas of finance, marketing, statistics, and organizational behavior. Next, students choose a 12-credit concentration within the disciplines of:

Accounting
Entrepreneurship
Finance
Human Resources/Organizational Consulting
Management Information Systems (MIS)
Marketing
Operations Management

Within the MIS concentration, students can further focus in areas such as E-Commerce or Software Engineering Management. Students may also develop an area of MBA concentration tailored to their personal goals.

To enhance leadership abilities, the Tippie School encourages students to get involved in one of several peer organizations that sponsor community service, social events, workshops, seminars, and corporate trips. During winter break, the School sponsors an intensive semester course in finance or marketing in Europe. Students can also work with an international business on a specific project and travel to the relevant destination during spring break.

Iowa MBA faculty members hold doctoral degrees from some of the world's top educational institutions, and all bring practical experience into the classroom. They combine theoretical frameworks, case studies, and real projects to impart not just knowledge, but understanding, of business problems. The MBA faculty take personal interest in their students and take the time to get to know them and meet them outside the classroom.

CAMPUS LIFE

The Iowa City community of 60,000 residents combines with the University to offer a small-town atmosphere with the cultural and recreational benefits of a Big Ten university. Iowa City is within easy reach of the major metropolitan areas of Chicago, St. Louis, Kansas City, and Minneapolis.

The John Pappajohn Business Building integrates multimedia capabilities and instructional technology within a structure of striking neo-classic design. The 187,000-square-foot building includes an Instructional Technology Center with a 100-station computer laboratory (the largest on campus), an operations/behavioral laboratory, and two 32-seat computer classrooms. The Advanced Real-Time Information Center provides students with live access to 135 financial markets.

The Marvin A. Pomerantz Business Library features a collection of more than 30,000 volumes. Its computerized catalog service connects to all the University libraries and other Big Ten libraries. The library computers also carry numerous news and research services, including Bridge Telerate, Lexis-Nexis, Bloomberg, and National Trade Data Bank.

MBA Career Services partners with students to achieve their career goals, helping them refine their interviewing and career-planning skills. The Career Services staff develops corporate relationships and focuses on the *best fit* between individual and employer. Students interact with employers through on-campus recruiting and off-campus consortiums. Career Services also maintains direct referral relationships with top MBA employers and continually cultivates new relationships.

Henry B. Tippie School of Management

Henry B. Tippie School of Management
THE UNIVERSITY OF IOWA

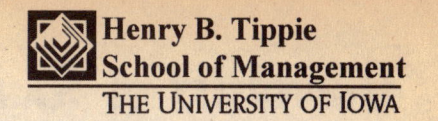

COSTS

Tuition and Fees 2000-2001:
Annual Tuition (Resident/Nonresident): $5,568/$13,322
Computer Fee: $110
Health and Health Facility Fee: $112
Student Activity and Student Service Fee: $76
Total Tuition and Fees (Resident/Nonresident): $5,866/$13,620

Living Costs:
Off-Campus Housing Per Month: $435–$760
University Apartments Per Month: $250–$419
Textbooks and Supplies: $1,400
Personal Expenses: $4,060
Total Estimated Cost Per Year (12 Months):
Resident: $14,226–$20,346
Nonresident: $21,980–$28,100

The Tippie School offers merit-based financial aid awards to highly qualified applicants. Scholarships are direct grants to recipients, varying in amount from $1,000 to $4,000 per year. Graduate assistantships provide a quarter-time position with salary ($7,076 per year for 2000–2001) and qualify the recipient for resident tuition rates. The application form for merit-based aid is included in the application packet, and the deadline for applying for financial aid is April 15.

ADMISSIONS

Application forms and instructions are available via www.biz.uiowa.edu/mba, or Multi-app.com. Contact the Tippie School at the address below to request an application packet by mail.

In addition to the application materials, MBA candidates are evaluated on their work experience, GMAT scores, prior academic experience, references, and personal interview. The deadline for international applicants is April 15; priority deadline for U.S. applicants is the same date. U.S. citizens and permanent residents may be accepted until July 15 on a space-available basis.

Admissions Contact: Admissions Office, Director of MBA Admissions and Financial Aid
Address: 108 Pappajohn Business Administration Building, Iowa City, IA 52242-1000
Admissions Phone: 319-335-1039 • Admissions Fax: 319-335-3604
Admissions E-mail: iowamba@uiowa.edu • Web Address: www.biz.uiowa.edu/mba

UNIVERSITY OF KANSAS
School of Business

Admissions Contact: Dee Steinle, Associate Director of Master's Programs
Address: 206 Summerfield Hall, Lawrence, KS 66045
Admissions Phone: 785-864-3844 • Admissions Fax: 785-864-5328
Admissions E-mail: bschoolgrad@ku.edu • Web Address: www.business.ku.edu

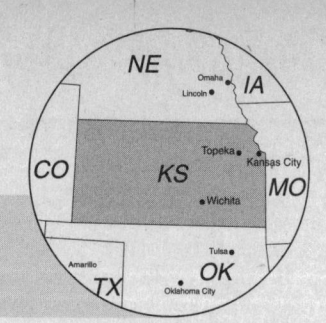

The management program is king at the University of Kansas School of Business, and the "highly competitive" and "ambitious" students here tell us that "the KU MBA program provides a great education for the money." The campus is "beautiful" as well, and Lawrence is by all accounts an "ideal college town." When life gets dull, students can head to the more bustling metropolis of Kansas City, "which is only 30 minutes away and has a lot to offer."

INSTITUTIONAL INFORMATION
Public/Private: Public
Evening Classes Available? Yes
Total Faculty: 55
% Faculty Female: 16
% Faculty Minority: 12
% Faculty Part Time: 3
Student/Faculty Ratio: 8:1
Students in Parent Institution: 26,894
Academic Calendar: Semester

PROGRAMS
Degrees Offered: MBA (2 years full time, 3 years part time); MS Human Resources Management; MS Organizational Behavior (1 year); MS Information Systems (2 years or 1 year + BS in Business); MAIS (2 years or 1 year + bachelor's in Accounting)
Joint Degrees: JD/MBA (4 years)
Academic Specialties: Strengths of faculty include strong research and consulting records and a genuine commitment to teaching.
Study Abroad Options: France, Italy, England, Japan, Brazil

STUDENT INFORMATION
Total Business Students: 477
% Full Time: 21
% Female: 31
% Minority: 1
% Out of State: 33
% International: 25
Average Age: 28

COMPUTER AND RESEARCH FACILITIES
Research Facilities: Watson Library plus 12 additional on-campus libraries; total holdings of 3,292,923 volumes, 2,797,658 microforms, 33,051 current periodical subscriptions; CD player(s) available for graduate student use; access to online bibliographic retrieval services and online databases
Campuswide Network? Yes
Internet Fee? No

EXPENSES/FINANCIAL AID
Annual Tuition (Resident/Nonresident): $3,434/$11,212
Books and Supplies: $800
Average Grant: $1,200

ADMISSIONS INFORMATION
Application Fee: $60
Electronic Application? Yes
Regular Application Deadline: 4/1
Regular Notification: Rolling
Deferment Available? Yes
Length of Deferment: 1 year
Non-fall Admissions? Yes
Non-fall Application Deadline(s): 10/1 spring
Transfer Students Accepted? Yes
Transfer Policy: Maximum number of transferable credit hours is 6.
Need-Blind Admissions? Yes
Number of Applications Received: 124
% of Applicants Accepted: 73
% Accepted Who Enrolled: 64
Average GPA: 3.3
GPA Range: 3.1-3.5
Average GMAT: 606
GMAT Range: 540-690
Average Years Experience: 1
Minority/Disadvantaged Student Recruitment Programs: Some scholarship money is available to minority students. Recruiting is conducted at MBA Forums, local employer fairs, and paid ads in certain minority magazines, such as Minority MBA Magazine.
Other Schools to Which Students Applied: University of Iowa, University of Missouri-Columbia, Iowa State University, University of Oklahoma, University of Nebraska-Lincoln

INTERNATIONAL STUDENTS
TOEFL Required of International Students? Yes
Minimum TOEFL: 600 (250 computer)

EMPLOYMENT INFORMATION

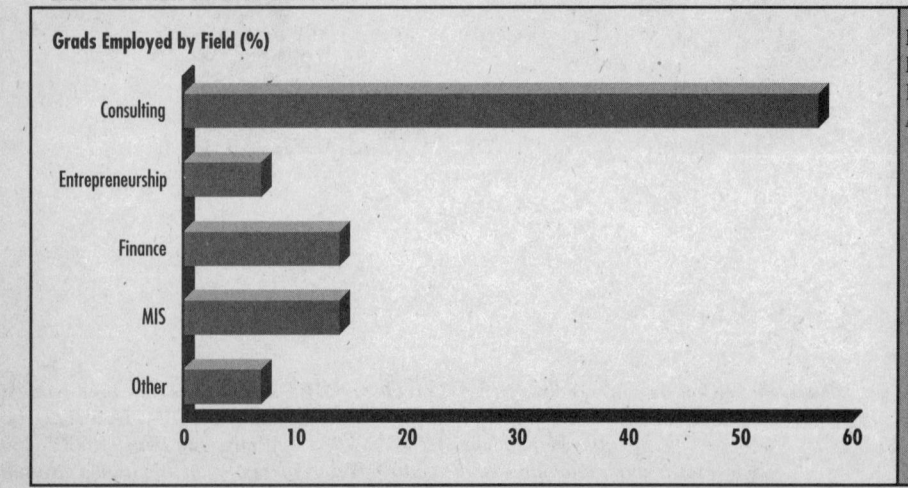

Grads Employed by Field (%)
- Consulting: ~57
- Entrepreneurship: ~13
- Finance: ~14
- MIS: ~14
- Other: ~7

Placement Office Available? Yes
Frequent Employers: Andersen Consulting, Deloitte Consulting, Payless Shoes, Sprint, Aquila, Cap Gemini, Accenture, Cerner

UNIVERSITY OF KENTUCKY
Gatton College of Business and Economics

Admissions Contact: Dr. Fred Morgan, MBA Director
Address: 145 Carol Martin Gatton College of Business and Economics, Lexington, KY 40506-0034
Admissions Phone: 859-257-5889 • Admissions Fax: 859-323-9971
Admissions E-mail: fwmorg1@uky.edu • Web Address: gatton.uky.edu

The MBA program at the University of Kentucky offers two distinct tracks: a business track for students with undergraduate business degrees and a nonbusiness track for everybody else. Each can be completed in three semesters, but the business track is a lot more flexible. Students here say one of the main advantages of UK is its location: a "safe" college town in a region of strong economic growth. When monotony sets in, more metropolitan Louisville is a short drive away.

INSTITUTIONAL INFORMATION
Public/Private: Public
Evening Classes Available? Yes
Total Faculty: 73
% Faculty Female: 25
Student/Faculty Ratio: 5:1
Students in Parent Institution: 32,549
Academic Calendar: Semester

PROGRAMS
Degrees Offered: PhD in Business Administration (4 years); PhD in Economics (4 years); MS in Economics (2 years); MS in Accountancy (1 year)
Joint Degrees: MBA/JD (4 years); BS Engineering/MBA (5 years); MD/MBA (5 years); DPharm/MBA (4 years)
Academic Specialties: DSIS, Finance, Management/Organizational Behavior, Marketing, Management Information Systems, Marketing Distribution, Finance, Banking, Corporate Finance
Special Opportunities: Internships, Summer Study Abroad
Study Abroad Options: Austria, England, France, Italy, Germany, Australia, ISEP schools worldwide (200 through study-abroad office)

STUDENT INFORMATION
Total Business Students: 233
% Full Time: 64
% Female: 31
% Minority: 14
% Out of State: 24
% International: 10
Average Age: 26

COMPUTER AND RESEARCH FACILITIES
Research Facilities: Center for Business & Economics Research, Center for Business Development, Small Business Development Center, Center for Labor Education & Research, Real Estate Studies, International Business & Management Center, Center for Entrepreneurial Studies
Computer Facilities: High-level systems supporting research and networking plus state-of-the-art business database access and terminals
Campuswide Network? Yes
% of MBA Classrooms Wired: 100
Internet Fee? No

EXPENSES/FINANCIAL AID
Annual Tuition (Resident/Nonresident): $3,610/$10,830
Tuition Per Credit (Resident/Nonresident): $201/$602
Room & Board (On/Off Campus): $6,500/$7,100
Books and Supplies: $800
Average Grant: $3,615
% Receiving Financial Aid: 35
% Receiving Aid Their First Year: 33

ADMISSIONS INFORMATION
Application Fee: $30
Electronic Application? Yes
Early Decision Notification: 4/1
Regular Application Deadline: 7/15
Regular Notification: Rolling
Length of Deferment: 3 years
Non-fall Admissions? No
Transfer Policy: Maximum credits is 9.
Need-Blind Admissions? Yes
Number of Applications Received: 296
% of Applicants Accepted: 45
% Accepted Who Enrolled: 80
Average GPA: 3.3
Average GMAT: 613
Average Years Experience: 3
Other Admissions Factors Considered: Communication skills; international experience; work experience; TWE for foreign applicants
Minority/Disadvantaged Student Recruitment Programs: Kentucky Scholars Program; Lyman T. Johnson Fellowships; Commonwealth Minority Scholarship Program; Academic Excellence
Other Schools to Which Students Applied: U. of Tennessee, Ohio State, Indiana U., Vanderbilt, U. of Georgia, U. of Alabama-Birmingham, UT Austin

INTERNATIONAL STUDENTS
TOEFL Required of International Students? Yes
Minimum TOEFL: 550 (213 computer)

EMPLOYMENT INFORMATION

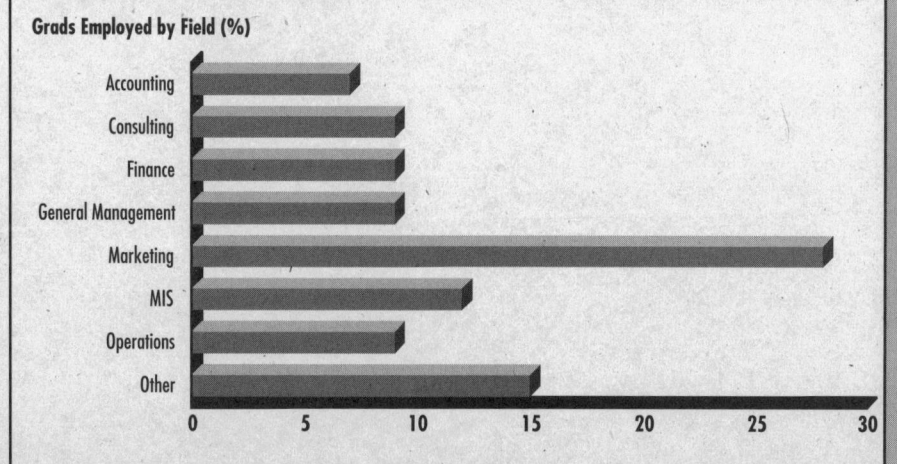

Grads Employed by Field (%)
- Accounting
- Consulting
- Finance
- General Management
- Marketing
- MIS
- Operations
- Other

Placement Office Available? Yes
% Employed Within 3 Months: 94
Frequent Employers: Accenture; Bank One; Central Bank & Trust Co.; Dillard's; Ernst & Young; General Motors; KPMG; Lehman Brothers; New York Life Insurance; Procter & Gamble; Schlumberger; Toyota Tusho; Valvoline; Verizon; Wal-Mart; Wells Fargo; Western Southern Life; Yellow Freight; Yorkshire Restaraunts
Prominent Alumni: Paul Chellgren, chairman and CEO, Ashland, Inc.; Kim Hatch Burse, president and CEO, Louisville Devil-Bancorp

UNIVERSITY OF KENTUCKY

THE COLLEGE AT A GLANCE
The MBA program at the University of Kentucky offers two distinct tracks: a business track for students with undergraduate business degrees and a nonbusiness track for everybody else. Both can be completed in three semesters, but the business track is a lot more flexible. Students here say one of the main advantages of UK is its location: a "safe" college town in a region of strong economic growth. When monotony sets in, more metropolitan Louisville is a short drive away.

STUDENTS
In 2001–2002, the College enrolled 233 graduate students. Of the 2001 MBA class, women represented 31 percent, international students 6 percent, and members of minority groups 11 percent of the student body. Thirty-six percent of the students were part-time. The average age of students was 26, the average work experience was 2.95 years, and the average GMAT score was 608. The program offers a judicious mix of teamwork and individual projects, case study, and lectures, designed to improve analytic, technical, and communications skills. Students are selected on the basis of proven academic excellence and a commitment to succeed. A significant percentage of full-time MBA students have internships.

There are more than 1,300 MBA alumni in all 50 states and in 22 other countries. Prominent alumni of the College include the presidents and CEOs of numerous corporations including public companies listed on the NYSE. Inductees into the College's Hall of Fame include former State Governor Edward T. Breathitt; Carl F. Pollard, former chairman and CEO of Columbia Healthcare, Inc.; James E. Rogers, chairman, president, and CEO, PSI Holdings, Inc.; Warren W. Rosenthal; Chris Sullivan, CEO, Outback Steakhouse; Paul Chellgren, CEO, Ashland Oil, Inc.; and Carol Martin Gatton.

ACADEMICS
The Gatton College of Business and Economics was named for Carol Martin Gatton, a distinguished alumnus, after he contributed the single largest gift in the history of the University of Kentucky (UK). Graduate programs include the PhD in business administration and economics and the master's degree in business administration, accounting, and economics. Joint degrees are offered between the Master of Business Administration program and the Juris Doctorate, Bachelor's of Engineering, and Pharmaceutical Doctorate.

The MBA program enrolls approximately 100 new students each year; the entering class size is deliberately limited to ensure personal contact with graduate faculty members and individualized attention. The program is designed to provide students with the education needed to prepare them for upper-level managerial responsibilities. Two 36-hour programs are offered: one is for those with an undergraduate degree in business who desire more specialized skills, the other is for students without an undergraduate degree in business but who are interested in acquiring a broad-based management training. A basic common core of seven courses provide an understanding of business enterprise, an understanding of quantitative methods and the applications of analysis to business decision making, development of leadership skills, the ability to solve complicated and realistic business problems, and an understanding of managing a business enterprise in a global environment. For the business undergraduate, the remaining courses are electives that permit the development of skills in a particular area. Concentrations are offered in accounting and corporate finance; finance, real estate, and banking; international business; management information systems; and marketing and distribution. For the nonbusiness undergraduate, the remaining required courses provide an understanding of problems encountered in business enterprise as related to organizational behavior, production, marketing, and finance.

The College, headed by Dean Richard W. Furst and Associate Dean Michael G. Tearney, consists of three divisions; the School of Accountancy, with 18 faculty members; the School of Management, incorporating the areas of decision sciences and information systems, finance, management, and marketing, with a total of 43 faculty members under the direction of Dr. Donald Mullineaux; and the Department of Economics, with 19 faculty members under the chairmanship of Dr. Glenn Blomquist. Faculty members have achieved both national and international recognition for excellence in teaching and research as well as for service to the commonwealth of Kentucky and the business community. Many of the faculty members are presently actively engaged in joint research projects with faculty members at institutions around the world including Austria, England, China, Indonesia, Kazakhstan, Sweden, and Croatia.

Students seeking an understanding of the global business environment find that the curriculum and the program supplies them with this opportunity. A core course on global business management provides the essential foundation, which can be supplemented by appropriate electives. The concentration in international business is available for those wishing to specialize. Study abroad is made possible by exchange agreements with premier institutions in Europe and Asia. There are a number of opportunities to interact with the many visiting faculty members and business experts from abroad who come to the college to share their expertise and culture with their U.S. counterparts. Facility in foreign language can be acquired or improved through the many courses offered at the University.

Gatton College of Business and Economics

CAMPUS LIFE

The UK campus and the Gatton College of Business and Economics are close to the heart of downtown Lexington, a city with a population of 243,000, where many of the cultural and recreational amenities of a large city are combined with the charm and traditions of a small town. Famed for its horse farms, Lexington lies within a 500-mile radius of nearly three fourths of the manufacturing, employment, retail sales, and population of the United States. Established in 1865, the University of Kentucky has more than 23,000 students, of whom approximately 6,200 are graduate students. Founded in 1925 as the College of Commerce, the Gatton College of Business and Economics occupies a modern building with all the facilities needed to fulfill the mission of excellence in teaching, research, and service. The College is accredited by AACSB International—The Association to Advance Collegiate Schools of Business.

As befits a Carnegie Foundation Research University of the first class, the University of Kentucky has excellent facilities. The $58 million William T. Young Library, which opened in spring 1998, contains more than 2.5 million volumes and receives more than 27,000 periodical and serial titles. The M. I. King Library houses several special and rare books collections. The Computing Center has several high-level systems supporting research and networking needs. Within the College are the electronic Business Information Center for state-of-the-art business database access and seven centers of research that serve as resources to the state, local, and international business community. At sites throughout the campus, computer workstations cater to the computing needs of all students.

Major corporations, such as Procter & Gamble, National City, Cinergy, Brown & Williamson, Aegon, Humana, Accenture, and Eli Lilly are among several that recruit graduates of the University of Kentucky's Master of Business Administration program. Seventy percent of the graduates of the MBA program choose to stay in the Kentucky/Ohio region due to career opportunities and the low cost of living. The average compensation for the 2001–2002 graduates was $65,000, which would be equivalent to $203,000 in New York, $131,000 in Chicago, $99,000 in Los Angeles, and $90,000 in Atlanta. Janie Thomas, MBA Director of Recruitment and Placement, provides many employment opportunities for students through the MBA Center, Business Career Fair, Career Center, and professional organizations. She also provides assistance in resume writing, interviewing, and all aspects of job search through both seminars and one-on-one consultations. Prospective students may contact her for more information by telephone or e-mail, listed below.

The College's University of Kentucky Business Partnership Foundation consists of prominent individuals in the business and academic communities. The Board of Directors of the Foundation fulfills an important role in assessing the present and future needs of the business world and in advising the College on how to provide the education necessary to meet those needs in a manner consistent with the College's missions of excellence in teaching, research, and service. Local businesses provide scholarships and internships for MBA students. Guest speakers from the business community visit the college on a regular basis throughout the year.

COSTS

The College and Graduate School offer merit-based scholarships and fellowships. Approximately 21 percent of the fall 2001 entering class received some form of College-based aid, including scholarships for members of minority groups and disadvantaged students. Students of outstanding merit are nominated for Graduate School Fellowships. Eligible students may also obtain on-campus employment through the UK STEPS service and the UK work-study program.

The University of Kentucky operates on the semester system. For 20001–2002, in-state graduate tuition for a full-time student was $2,037 per semester. Part-time in-state students paid $213 per credit hour. Nonresident full-time graduate tuition was $5,647 per semester. Part-time nonresident tuition was $614 per credit hour. The registration fee for full-time students was $232 per semester. Part-time students paid $12 per credit hour. A full-time nonresident student can expect to pay approximately $19,000 per academic year for tuition, fees, books, supplies, room, meals, and health insurance. On-campus housing rents range from $403 to $635 per

ADMISSIONS

Admission to the full- and part-time programs are for the fall semester only. An undergraduate degree with a minimum GPA of 2.75 is required, together with the following course work: two principles of accounting courses (financial, managerial), two principles of economics courses (micro, macro), a course in statistics and probability, and an elementary calculus course. All prerequisite courses should be equivalent to at least three semester hours. Applicants must also submit a GMAT score, and international applicants must also present a minimum TOEFL score of 550 (paper-based) or 213 (computer-based) overall and a minimum Test of Written English (TWE) score of 4.5. Academic background, GMAT score, personal recommendations, and the applicant's statement of purpose are all considered in the evaluation for admission. Demonstrated academic ability and potential for subsequent success in the business world are qualities that are looked for in applicants.

Admission to the College's graduate business programs is achieved by applying to both the Graduate School and the MBA program. The MBA program accepts applicants for the fall semester only. Deadlines for applying are as follows: for international students, February 1; priority deadline for domestic students and financial aid consideration for full-time students, April 1; final deadline for completed applications to be submitted for consideration, July 19.

Successful applicants are usually notified two to four weeks after the receipt of all required documentation. For information, applicants should contact:

Ms. Janie Thomas
MBA Center
Gatton College of Business and Economics
University of Kentucky
Lexington, KY 40506
Telephone: 859-257-4605
Fax: 859-323-9971
E-mail: jmthom5@uky.edu

For application materials, students should contact:

Admissions
MBA Center
Gatton College of Business and Economics
University of Kentucky
Lexington, KY 40506
Telephone: 859-257-1306
Fax: 859-323-9971
E-mail: kemper@uky.edu
World Wide Web: http://gatton.uky.edu/

UNIVERSITY OF LOUISIANA — MONROE
College of Business Administration

Admissions Contact: Jacqueline O'Neal, Director, MBA Program
Address: 700 University Avenue, Monroe, LA 71209-0100
Admissions Phone: 318-342-1100 • Admissions Fax: 318-342-1101
Admissions E-mail: econeal@ulm.edu • Web Address: ele.ulm.edu/MBA

Small class sizes, less than 100 students enrolled in the MBA program, and a diverse student makeup that's nearly one-third international: This is the UL Monroe experience. MBA applicants can enroll during any semester, take day or night classes, and study full time or part time, while full-time students will enjoy the benefit of completing their MBA program in only one year. UL Monroe offers standard academic concentrations in e-commerce, health care administration, and entrepreneurship and also makes the unique offer to study business with a concentration in gerontology. Located between Dallas, Texas, and Jackson, Mississippi, the university is accessible to all neighboring states and their businesses.

INSTITUTIONAL INFORMATION
Evening Classes Available? Yes
Total Faculty: 34
Student/Faculty Ratio: 2:1
Students in Parent Institution: 10,942
Academic Calendar: Semester

PROGRAMS
Degrees Offered: Master of Business Administration (1 year full time, 2 years part time), with concentrations in Entrepreneurship, Health Care Administration, E-Commerce, and Gerontology
Academic Specialties: Case studies, computer aided instruction, computer analysis, computer simulations, faculty seminars, group discussion, research, student presentations, study groups, team projects

STUDENT INFORMATION
Total Business Students: 78
% Full Time: 81
% Female: 40
% Minority: 5
% Out of State: 14
% International: 32
Average Age: 27

COMPUTER AND RESEARCH FACILITIES
Campuswide Network? Yes
Internet Fee? No

EXPENSES/FINANCIAL AID
Annual Tuition (Resident/Nonresident): $1,900/$7,858
Room & Board (On Campus): $2,560
Books and Supplies: $600
Average Grant: $5,000
Average Loan: $5,000

ADMISSIONS INFORMATION
Application Fee: $20
Electronic Application? No
Regular Application Deadline: 7/1
Regular Notification: 7/15
Deferment Available? Yes
Length of Deferment: 1 year
Non-fall Admissions? Yes
Non-fall Application Deadline(s): 11/1 spring, 4/1 summer I, 5/1 summer II
Transfer Students Accepted? Yes
Transfer Policy: Varies according to individual
Need-Blind Admissions? No
Number of Applications Received: 57
% of Applicants Accepted: 79
% Accepted Who Enrolled: 78
Average GPA: 3.0
GPA Range: 2.2-4.0
Average GMAT: 500
GMAT Range: 390-710
Other Admissions Factors Considered: Work experience

INTERNATIONAL STUDENTS
TOEFL Required of International Students? Yes
Minimum TOEFL: 480 (157 computer)

EMPLOYMENT INFORMATION
Placement Office Available? Yes

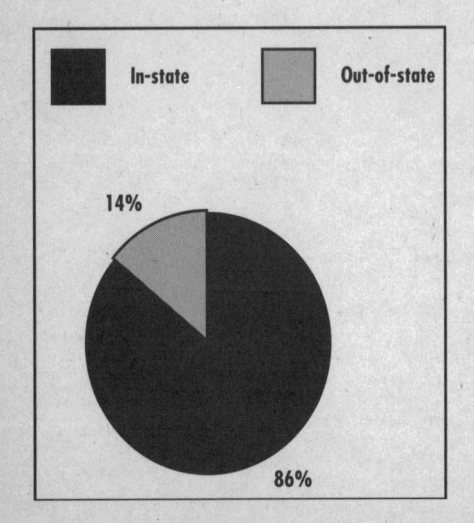

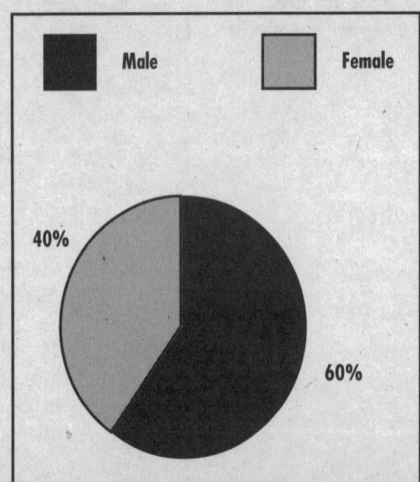

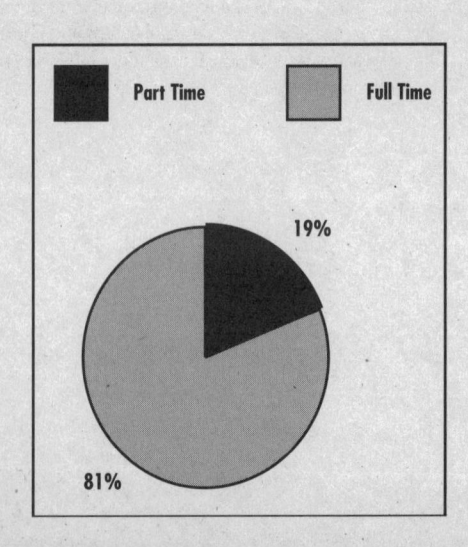

In-state 86% / Out-of-state 14%

Male 60% / Female 40%

Part Time 19% / Full Time 81%

UNIVERSITY OF MAINE
Maine Business School

Admissions Contact: Mary Cady, Assistant to the Director of Graduate Programs
Address: 5723 DP Corbett Business Building, Orono, ME 04469-5723
Admissions Phone: 207-581-1973 • Admissions Fax: 207-581-1930
Admissions E-mail: mba@maine.edu • Web Address: www.umaine.edu/business

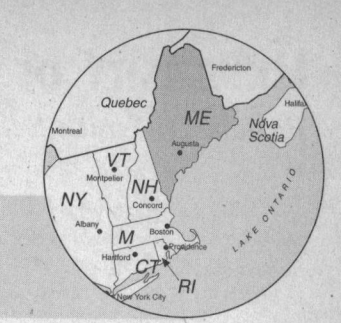

The University of Maine's MBA class size is less than 100 students, enabling the university's focus on student-centered learning to hold true. MBA applicants to the Maine Business School, who come from a great variety of backgrounds, can matriculate in the fall, spring, or summer, allowing for flexibility with the student's schedule. The MBA program provides students with a business education that's both broad and deep and is designed to "equip the candidate with concepts, analytical tools, and supervisory skills" necessary to hold responsible management positions.

INSTITUTIONAL INFORMATION
Public/Private: Public
Evening Classes Available? Yes
Total Faculty: 20
% Faculty Female: 50
Student/Faculty Ratio: 12:1
Students in Parent Institution: 10,282
Academic Calendar: Semester

PROGRAMS
Degrees Offered: MBA (12 to 24 months full time, up to 6 years part time); MS in Accounting (12 to 24 months full time, up to 6 years part time)
Academic Specialties: Electives continually change with current business trends; small classes with group work and presentations; small faculty-student ratio; latest classroom technology

STUDENT INFORMATION
Total Business Students: 95
% Full Time: 42
% Female: 52
% Minority: 18
% Out of State: 40
% International: 30
Average Age: 30

COMPUTER AND RESEARCH FACILITIES
Computer Facilities: Computer lab only for business students located in Business Building, where all classes meet; convenient hours for graduate students; other computer facilities in library and student union
Campuswide Network? Yes
% of MBA Classrooms Wired: 50
Internet Fee? No

EXPENSES/FINANCIAL AID
Annual Tuition (Resident/Nonresident): $3,780/$10,728
Tuition Per Credit (Resident/Nonresident): $210/$596
Room & Board: $5,728
Books and Supplies: $600
Average Grant: $2,500

ADMISSIONS INFORMATION
Application Fee: $50
Electronic Application? No
Regular Application Deadline: 2/1
Regular Notification: 3/1
Deferment Available? Yes
Length of Deferment: 1 year
Non-fall Admissions? Yes
Non-fall Application Deadline(s): 12/1 spring
Transfer Students Accepted? Yes
Transfer Policy: Maximum of 6 hours accepted from accredited schools with approval
Need-Blind Admissions? Yes
Number of Applications Received: 23
% of Applicants Accepted: 100
% Accepted Who Enrolled: 96
Average GPA: 3.2
Average GMAT: 530
Average Years Experience: 6

INTERNATIONAL STUDENTS
TOEFL Required of International Students? Yes
Minimum TOEFL: 550 (213 computer)

EMPLOYMENT INFORMATION
Placement Office Available? No

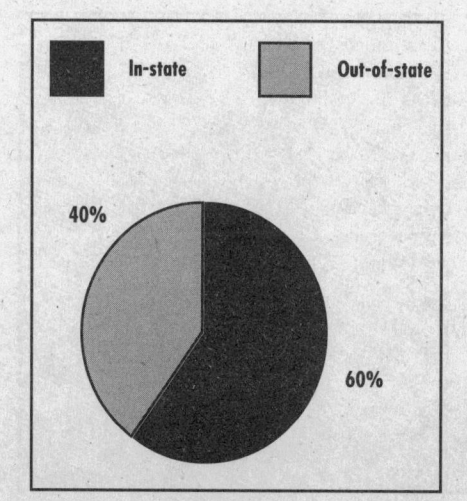

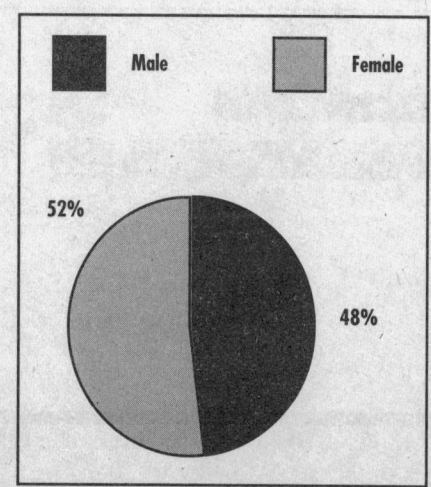

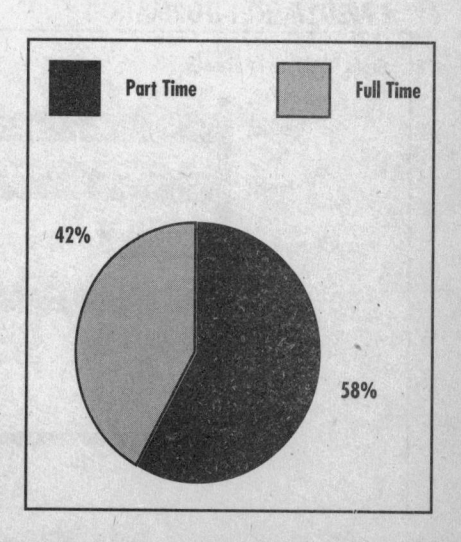

In-state 60% / Out-of-state 40%

Male 48% / Female 52%

Part Time 58% / Full Time 42%

UNIVERSITY OF MARYLAND—COLLEGE PARK
Robert H. Smith School of Business

Admissions Contact: Sabrina White, Director, MBA and MS Admissions
Address: 2308 Van Munching Hall, University of Maryland, College Park, MD 20742-1871
Admissions Phone: 301-405-2278 • Admissions Fax: 301-314-9862
Admissions E-mail: mba_info@rhsmith.umd.edu • Web Address: www.rhsmith.umd.edu

Registration, billing, and everything else is online at the University of Maryland's state-of-the-art School of Business, where there is a "strong technology emphasis." The "intelligent, fun, and personable" students here "are of exceptional character," and "the business school is like a campus in itself: tight-knit, easy to get to know others," and boasting many of the assets of a smaller school. Nearby Washington, D.C., "Mecca for high tech" and government, "provides plenty of cultural, political, and nightlife activities."

INSTITUTIONAL INFORMATION
Public/Private: Public
Evening Classes Available? Yes
Total Faculty: 177
% Faculty Female: 19
% Faculty Minority: 19
% Faculty Part Time: 31
Student/Faculty Ratio: 11:1
Students in Parent Institution: 33,000
Academic Calendar: Semester

PROGRAMS
Degrees Offered: MBA (54 credits, 18 months to 5 years); MS (30 credits, 12 months to 5 years)
Joint Degrees: MBA/MS (66 credits, 21 months to 5 years); MBA/JD (108 credits, 3 to 5 years); MBA/Master of Public Management (66 credits, 2.3 to 5 years); MBA/Master of Social Work (88 credits, 2.3 to 5 years)
Academic Specialties: Accounting, Entrepreneurship, Finance, Logistics and Supply Chain Management, Decision and Information Technologies, Management and Organization, Marketing, E-Commerce, Telecommunications, Financial Engineering, Technology Management, Global Business, and Entrepreneurship
Special Opportunities: 7- to 10-day programs abroad, member of the MBA Enterprise Corps, Global Executive Breakfast Seminars

Study Abroad Options: Australia, Denmark, France, Germany, Hong Kong, Italy, Mexico, United Kingdom

STUDENT INFORMATION
Total Business Students: 1,111
% Female: 32
% Minority: 13
% International: 40
Average Age: 28

COMPUTER AND RESEARCH FACILITIES
Research Facilities: Center for Career Management; Center for e-Service; Center for Electronic Markets and Enterprises; Center for Executive Education; Center for Global Business; Center for Human Capital, Innovation, and Technology; Dingman Center for Entrepreneurship; Netcentric Financial Markets Laboratory; Netcentricity Laboratory; Supply Chain Management Center
Computer Facilities: Dual-display advanced teaching theatre, IT wireless access, collection of electronic and print business resources
Campuswide Network? Yes
% of MBA Classrooms Wired: 100
Computer Model Recommended: No
Internet Fee? No

EXPENSES/FINANCIAL AID
Annual Tuition (Resident/Nonresident): $11,466/$16,992

Tuition Per Credit (Resident/Nonresident): $637/$944
Room & Board (Off Campus): $13,650

ADMISSIONS INFORMATION
Application Fee: $50
Electronic Application? Yes
Regular Application Deadline: 2/1
Regular Notification: 4/1
Length of Deferment: 1 year
Non-fall Admissions? No
Transfer Students Accepted? No
Need-Blind Admissions? No
Number of Applications Received: 1,554
% of Applicants Accepted: 24
% Accepted Who Enrolled: 59
Average GPA: 3.4
Average GMAT: 658
Average Years Experience: 5
Other Admissions Factors Considered: GRE, work experience, letters of recommendation, essay response
Other Schools to Which Students Applied: Carnegie Mellon, Georgetown, Purdue, UNC Chapel Hill, UT Austin, U. of Virginia, Vanderbilt

INTERNATIONAL STUDENTS
TOEFL Required of International Students? Yes
Minimum TOEFL: 600

EMPLOYMENT INFORMATION

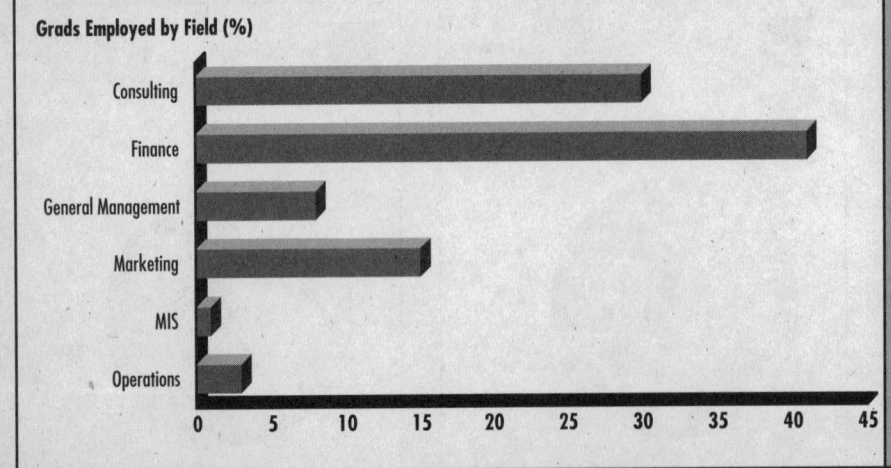

Grads Employed by Field (%)
- Consulting: ~30
- Finance: ~42
- General Management: ~5
- Marketing: ~15
- MIS: ~1
- Operations: ~3

Placement Office Available? Yes
% Employed Within 3 Months: 81
Frequent Employers: Andersen, Booz Allen Hamilton, Citigroup, Deloitte Consulting, Legg Mason Wood Walker, Marriott International, Accenture, Intel, Deutsche Financial Services, Campbell Soup Co., AT&T Corp., IBM, Johnson & Johnson
Prominent Alumni: Carly Fiorina, chairman and CEO, Hewlett-Packard

UNIVERSITY OF MASSACHUSETTS — AMHERST
Isenberg School of Management

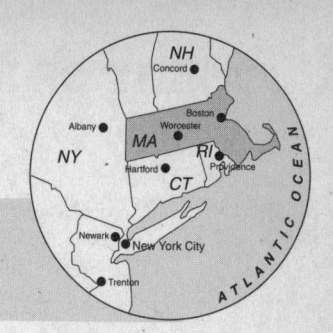

Admissions Contact: Jessica Zalewski, Admissions Coordinator
Address: 209 Isenberg School of Management, UMASS, Amherst, MA 01003
Admissions Phone: 413-545-5608 • Admissions Fax: 413-545-3858
Admissions E-mail: gradprog@som.umass.edu • Web Address: www.umass.edu/mba

Professors are excellent and administrators are very supportive at the intimate Isenberg School of Management at the University of Massachusetts. "There's a good team spirit within the classes" here, and students who choose to specialize in finance and operations management have access to the Center for International Security and Derivatives Markets, a real-time trading room.

INSTITUTIONAL INFORMATION
Public/Private: Public
Evening Classes Available? Yes
Total Faculty: 55
% Faculty Female: 22
% Faculty Minority: 11
Student/Faculty Ratio: 8:1
Students in Parent Institution: 24,726
Academic Calendar: Semester

PROGRAMS
Degrees Offered: MBA (2 years); PhD (4 years); Professional MBA (2 to 3 years)
Joint Degrees: MBA/MS in Sport Management (2 years)
Academic Specialties: Research orientation of the faculty; the small, intimate nature of the program; the quality of educational material; presentation of a very committed faculty
Study Abroad Options: France, Sweden, Germany

STUDENT INFORMATION
Total Business Students: 260
% Full Time: 26
% Female: 51
% Minority: 10
% Out of State: 43
% International: 28
Average Age: 27

COMPUTER AND RESEARCH FACILITIES
Research Facilities: Massachusetts Small Business Development Center, Family Business Center, Center for International Security and Derivations Markets, Massachusetts Institute for Social and Economic Research, Strategic Information Technology Center, Electronic Enterprise Center, Graduate Business Association
Computer Facilities: 75-PC lab facility, local area network, access to Internet and World Wide Web, e-mail accounts, Infotrac, Compustat, SAS, Lexis-Nexis, Windows NT, Microsoft Professional Office for Windows 2000, Investext, Worldscope, Hoover's Company Profile Database, American Business Information Company Directory, Standard & Poor's Corporation Description
Campuswide Network? Yes
% of MBA Classrooms Wired: 100
Computer Model Recommended: No
Internet Fee? No

EXPENSES/FINANCIAL AID
Annual Tuition (Resident/Nonresident): $2,640/$9,937
Tuition Per Credit: $490
Room & Board (On/Off Campus): $5,115/$8,100
Books and Supplies: $2,000
Average Grant: $10,000
Average Loan: $9,207
% Receiving Financial Aid: 96
% Receiving Aid Their First Year: 91

ADMISSIONS INFORMATION
Application Fee: $40
Electronic Application? Yes
Regular Application Deadline: 2/1
Regular Notification: 3/15
Length of Deferment: 1 year
Non-fall Admissions? No
Transfer Students Accepted? No
Need-Blind Admissions? Yes
Number of Applications Received: 207
% of Applicants Accepted: 30
% Accepted Who Enrolled: 53
Average GPA: 3.3
GPA Range: 3.0-3.7
Average GMAT: 640
GMAT Range: 590-710
Average Years Experience: 4
Other Admissions Factors Considered: We like to see at least 3 to 5 years of professional work experience, with 2 professional (rather than academic) letters of recommendation.
Minority/Disadvantaged Student Recruitment Programs: Diversity Recruitment Committee, including current Isenberg School students and administrators, meets regularly to design and implement effective strategies to continue development of diversity in the program.

INTERNATIONAL STUDENTS
TOEFL Required of International Students? Yes
Minimum TOEFL: 600 (250 computer)

EMPLOYMENT INFORMATION

Grads Employed by Field (%)
- Consulting
- Finance
- General Management
- Human Resources
- Marketing
- MIS
- Operations
- Other

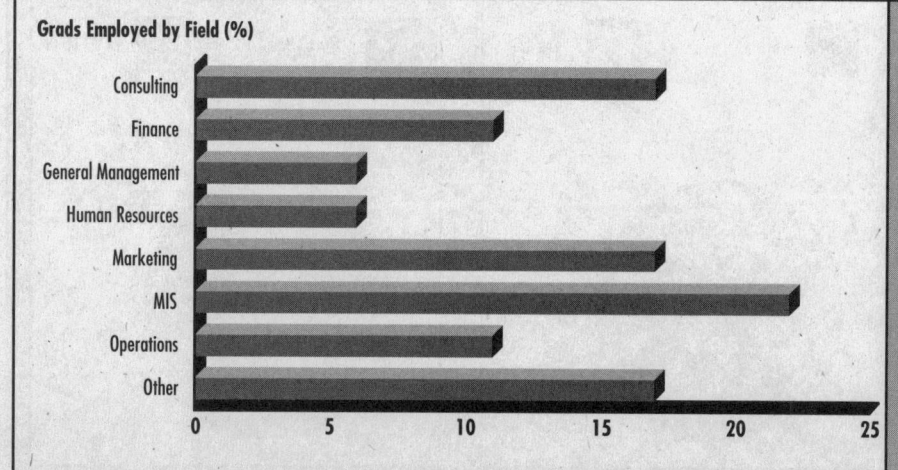

Placement Office Available? Yes
% Employed Within 3 Months: 88
Frequent Employers: United Technologies Corporation; PricewaterhouseCoopers; Teradyne; IBM; MassMutual; Accenture; Morgan Stanley Dean Witter; Avery Dennison; Siemens, Inc.; Tillion, Inc.; Frito-Lay; Baystate Health System
Prominent Alumni: John P. Flavin, chairman of the board, Flavin, Blake & Co. Inc.; Eugene M. Isenberg, chairman and CEO, Nabors Industries, Inc.; Jayne A. McMellen, VP of fund administration, State Street Bank & Trust Co. Inc.; John F. Smith, Jr., chairman of the board, General Motors Corporation; Michael Philipp, chairman and CEO, Deutsche Asset Management

UNIVERSITY OF MIAMI
School of Business Administration

Admissions Contact: Dierdre Lacativa, Director, Graduate Recruiting and Admissions
Address: 5250 University Drive, Jenkins 221, Coral Gables, FL 33124
Admissions Phone: 305-284-4607 • Admissions Fax: 305-284-1878
Admissions E-mail: mba@miami.edu • Web Address: www.bus.miami.edu/grad

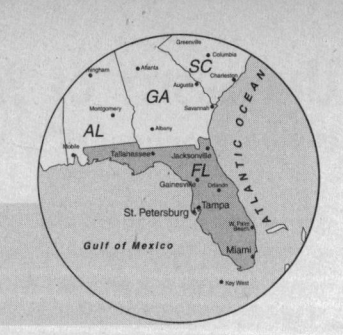

"Diversity" is the catchword at the University of Miami Business School. Enjoying a location "in the midst of one of the most dynamic areas of international business growth in the western hemisphere," relishing the fact that one-third of its student body is international, and offering 27 specializations from which MBA candidates can choose, the Business School has a pretty apt catchword. The Global Master of Science for Business Executives and Professionals is a unique 13-month track designed to develop the skills necessary to analyze "issues and policies affecting the relations of states and world regions" while allowing candidates to hold on to their regular jobs.

INSTITUTIONAL INFORMATION
Public/Private: Private
Evening Classes Available? Yes
Total Faculty: 90
% Faculty Female: 5
% Faculty Minority: 6
Student/Faculty Ratio: 13:1
Students in Parent Institution: 13,715
Academic Calendar: August-May

PROGRAMS
Degrees Offered: MBA (1 to 2 years full time), MS (1 to 2 years full time), PhD (4 years)
Joint Degrees: Juris Doctor/MBA, MBA/MS, Computer Information Systems
Academic Specialties: The University of Miami School of Business takes pride in being a solid traditional school, offering full-time MBA programs as well as extensive executive MBA programs throughout Florida. Specializations offered in E-Commerce, Enterprise and Resource Planning, International Business, and more.

STUDENT INFORMATION
Total Business Students: 529
% Full Time: 75
% Female: 35
% Minority: 15
% Out of State: 34

% International: 42
Average Age: 26

COMPUTER AND RESEARCH FACILITIES
Campuswide Network? Yes
Computer Proficiency Required? Yes
Special Purchasing Agreements? Yes
Internet Fee? No

EXPENSES/FINANCIAL AID
Annual Tuition: $21,576
Room & Board (On Campus): $5,946
Books and Supplies: $700
Average Grant: $12,730
Average Loan: $18,520
% Receiving Financial Aid: 50
% Receiving Aid Their First Year: 61

ADMISSIONS INFORMATION
Application Fee: $50
Electronic Application? Yes
Regular Application Deadline: Rolling
Regular Notification: Rolling
Length of Deferment: 1 year
Non-fall Application Deadline(s): Rolling
Transfer Policy: 6 credits
Need-Blind Admissions? Yes
Number of Applications Received: 730

% of Applicants Accepted: 47
% Accepted Who Enrolled: 42
Average GPA: 3.1
GPA Range: 2.5-3.6
Average GMAT: 620
GMAT Range: 550-690
Average Years Experience: 3
Minority/Disadvantaged Student Recruitment Programs: Florida A&M University Program
Other Schools to Which Students Applied: Florida International, Florida State, Georgetown, NYU, University of Florida

INTERNATIONAL STUDENTS
TOEFL Required of International Students? Yes
Minimum TOEFL: 550

EMPLOYMENT INFORMATION
Placement Office Available? Yes
% Employed within 6 months: 92
Frequent Employers: IBM, Nortel, Deloitte & Touche, Arthur Andersen, Walt Disney, American Express, Fedex, Ernst & Young, Procter and Gamble, Citicorp, Siemens, Motorola, KPMG, Johnson & Johnson, Hershey International
Prominent Alumni: Jose S. Suquet (MBA '91), senior executive vice president, AXA Financial, Inc.; Dr. Martin E. Zweig (MBA '67), president, Zweig Consulting

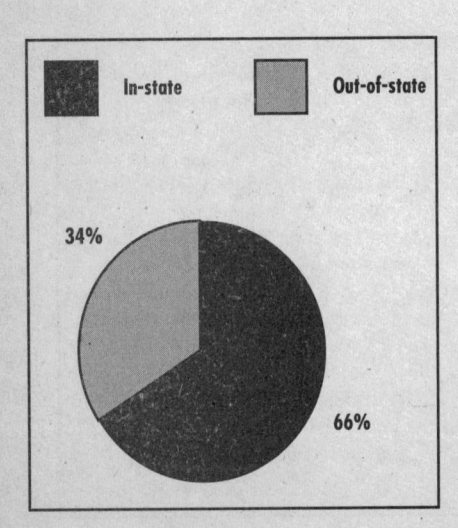

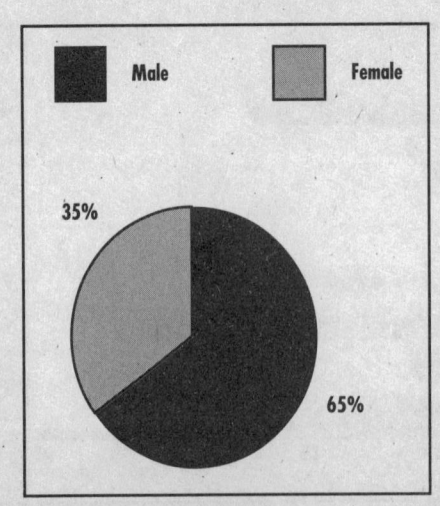

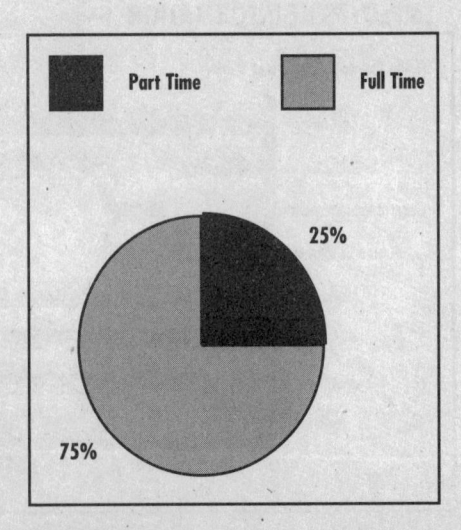

UNIVERSITY OF MICHIGAN—ANN ARBOR
Business School

Admissions Contact: Cynthia Shaw, Office of Communications
Address: 701 Tappan Street, Ann Arbor, MI 48109
Admissions Phone: 734-763-5796 • *Admissions Fax:* 734-763-7804
Admissions E-mail: umbsmba@umich.edu • *Web Address:* www.bus.umich.edu

The University of Michigan Business School—possibly "the world's most innovative business school"—"has strength across all business disciplines." Consequently, according to the "down-to-earth, humble, smart risk-takers" here, "you cannot say Michigan is just a 'fill in the blank: finance, marketing, etc.' school." When they begin their job searches, Michigan Business School alums can cash in on an alumni network that numbers some 30,000.

INSTITUTIONAL INFORMATION
Public/Private: Public
Evening Classes Available? Yes
Total Faculty: 174
% Faculty Female: 25
% Faculty Minority: 19
% Faculty Part Time: 20
Student/Faculty Ratio: 17:1
Students in Parent Institution: 38,100
Academic Calendar: Semester

PROGRAMS
Degrees Offered: MAcc
Joint Degrees: 21 joint degrees available
Academic Specialties: Particularly strong general management program but also depth of expertise in specializations
Special Opportunities: Executive Skills Seminars; Leadership Development Program; international in-company learning (Europe, Asia, Africa, South America); required in-company immersion/development experience; international network of corporate partnerships
Study Abroad Options: Australia, Austria, Costa Rica, Denmark, Finland, France, Hong Kong, Italy, Netherlands, Singapore, Spain, Sweden, Switzerland, United Kingdom

STUDENT INFORMATION
Total Business Students: 1,813
% Female: 28
% Minority: 12
% International: 29
Average Age: 28

COMPUTER AND RESEARCH FACILITIES
Research Facilities: Special institutes for environmental management, manufacturing, and entrepreneurship; electronic library; financial trading floor; eCommerce Research Lab; Global Learning Center; Career Resource Center; M-Track
Computer Facilities: High-performance research computing, including large-volume statistical, mathematical, and geographic information system data analysis. Resources to help students complete multimedia class projects with current software, scanners, MIDI stations, and personal studios for digitizing and editing audio and video.
Campuswide Network? Yes
% of MBA Classrooms Wired: 38
Computer Model Recommended: Laptop
Internet Fee? No

EXPENSES/FINANCIAL AID
Annual Tuition (Resident/Nonresident): $25,500/$30,500
Tuition Per Credit: $835
Room & Board (Off Campus): $13,864
Books and Supplies: $1,000
Average Grant: $16,026
Average Loan: $37,500

ADMISSIONS INFORMATION
Application Fee: $125
Electronic Application? Yes
Early Decision Application Deadline: 11/1
Early Decision Notification: 1/15
Regular Application Deadline: 1/15
Regular Notification: 3/15
Deferment Available? No
Non-fall Admissions? No
Transfer Policy: Welcome to apply, but no credits will transfer
Need-Blind Admissions? Yes
Number of Applications Received: 3,764
% of Applicants Accepted: 20
% Accepted Who Enrolled: 58
Average GPA: 3.3
Average GMAT: 676
Average Years Experience: 5
Other Admissions Factors Considered: Track record of success, clarity of goals, management and leadership potential
Minority/Disadvantaged Student Recruitment Programs: Member of Consortium for Graduate Study in Management; UpClose Program, a weekend for prospective minority students; Robert F. Toigo Fellowships in Finance; Management Leadership for Tomorrow; mentorship opportunities; National Society of Hispanic MBA Conference; National Black MBA Conference; faculty and alumni outreach; student Phonathon
Other Schools to Which Students Applied: Duke, Northwestern, U. of Chicago, Penn

INTERNATIONAL STUDENTS
TOEFL Required of International Students? Yes
Minimum TOEFL: 600 (250 computer)

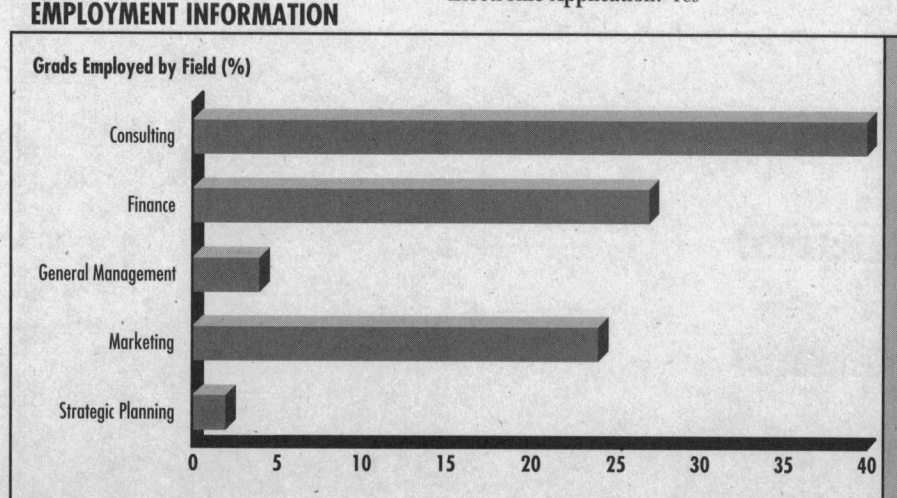

EMPLOYMENT INFORMATION

Grads Employed by Field (%)

Field	%
Consulting	40
Finance	27
General Management	4
Marketing	24
Strategic Planning	2

Placement Office Available? Yes
% Employed Within 3 Months: 94
Frequent Employers: AT Kearney, McKinsey & Co., Deloitte Consulting, Booz Allen Hamilton, Accenture, Bear Stearns, Kraft Foods Inc., Boston Consulting Group, Diamond, Cluster International, Ford Motor Co., General Motors Corporation, Goldman Sachs, Bristol-Myers Squibb, PricewaterhouseCoopers, Lehman Brothers Inc., Mercer Management Consulting, Salomon Smith Barney, Banc of America Securities, Citigroup/Citibank, IBM Corp., Pittiglio Rabin Todd & McGrath, SC Johnson & Son, Inc.,

UNIVERSITY OF MICHIGAN—DEARBORN
School of Management

Admissions Contact: Janet McIntire, Graduate Programs Advisor
Address: School of Management, 4901 Evergreen Road, Dearborn, MI 48128-1491
Admissions Phone: 313-593-5460 • Admissions Fax: 313-593-4071
Admissions E-mail: gradbusiness@umd.umich.edu • Web Address: www.som.umd.umich.edu

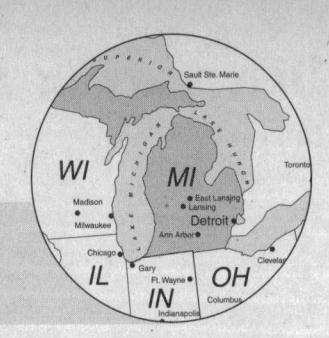

The University of Michigan—Dearborn School of Management is a solid choice for business school students looking to build a career in Michigan. UM—Dearborn offers a unique dual Master of Business Administration/Master of Science in Industrial and Systems Engineering. Developed to produce management- and technology-savvy MBAs for "the corporate/manufacturing/industrial center that is southeast Michigan," the program is popular and pretty selective. Dearborn also offers a WebMBA (entirely online course work), which takes most candidates two to four years to complete.

INSTITUTIONAL INFORMATION
Public/Private: Public
Evening Classes Available? Yes
Total Faculty: 30
% Faculty Female: 20
% Faculty Minority: 30
Student/Faculty Ratio: 22:1
Students in Parent Institution: 8,386
Academic Calendar: Semester

PROGRAMS
Degrees Offered: MBA (part time, 2 to 4 years), with concentrations in Accounting, Finance, International Business, Marketing, Workforce Management, and Management Information Systems. Web MBA (entirely online, part time, 2 to 4 years); Master of Science in Accounting (1 year full time, 2 years part time); Master of Science in Finance (1 year full time, 2 years part time)
Joint Degrees: MBA/MS Industrial Engineering (part time, 4 to 5 years)
Academic Specialties: Accounting, Finance, Marketing, Strategy, Management Information Systems, Organizational Behavior and Human Resources, Operations Management
Study Abroad Options: Master of Science in Finance offered in Hong Kong; Germany; Spain; University of Oviedo

STUDENT INFORMATION
Total Business Students: 396
% Female: 26
% Minority: 20
Average Age: 29

COMPUTER AND RESEARCH FACILITIES
Research Facilities: Mardigian Library with total holdings of 299,792 volumes, 432,298 microforms, 1,169 periodical subscriptions; CD players available for graduate students; access to online bibliographic retrieval services and online databases; alumni network; career counseling/planning; career fairs; career library; career placement; job interviews arranged; résumé referral to employers; résumé preparation
Campuswide Network? Yes
Internet Fee? No

EXPENSES/FINANCIAL AID
Annual Tuition (Resident/Nonresident): $10,700/$19,955
Tuition Per Credit (Resident/Nonresident): $370/$826
Books and Supplies: $1,200
Average Grant: $1,500
Average Loan: $5,000

ADMISSIONS INFORMATION
Application Fee: $55
Electronic Application? No
Regular Application Deadline: 8/1
Regular Notification: 8/20
Deferment Available? Yes
Length of Deferment: 1 year
Non-fall Admissions? Yes
Non-fall Application Deadline(s): Fall, winter, summer
Transfer Students Accepted? Yes
Transfer Policy: For equivalent courses to our MBA core courses, waivers will be given. Up to si6x credits of transfer may be given for other MBA courses.
Need-Blind Admissions? Yes
Number of Applications Received: 143
% of Applicants Accepted: 69
% Accepted Who Enrolled: 76
Average GPA: 3.2
Average GMAT: 565
Average Years Experience: 5
Other Admissions Factors Considered: 2 years full-time professional work experience required
Other Schools to Which Students Applied: University of Michigan, Wayne State University, Oakland University, University of Detroit-Mercy, Eastern Michigan University, Michigan State University

INTERNATIONAL STUDENTS
TOEFL Required of International Students? Yes
Minimum TOEFL: 560 (222 computer)

EMPLOYMENT INFORMATION

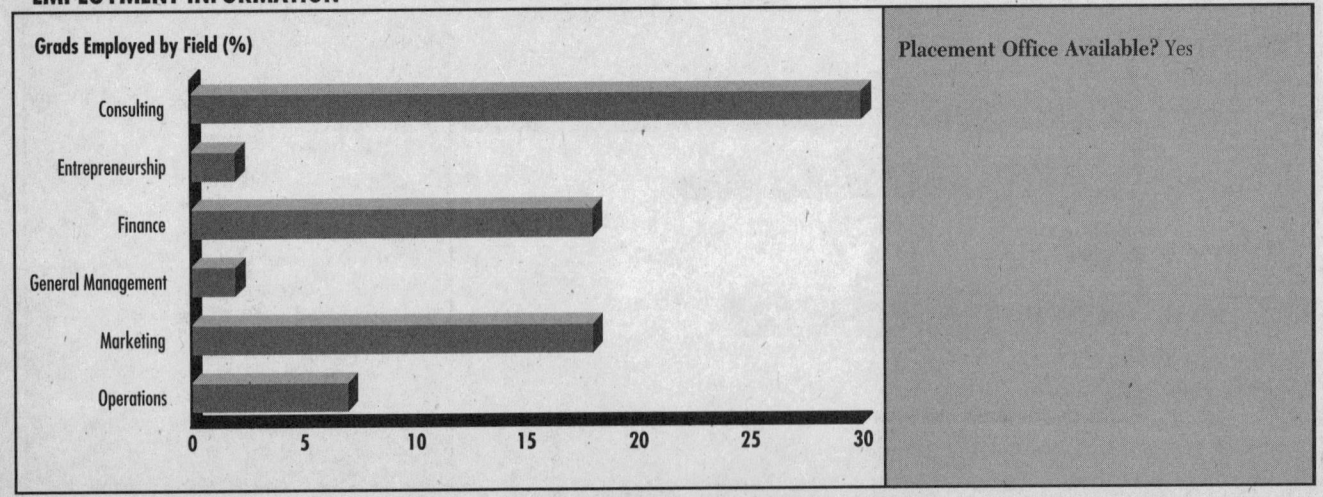

Grads Employed by Field (%)

Field	%
Consulting	30
Entrepreneurship	2
Finance	18
General Management	2
Marketing	18
Operations	7

Placement Office Available? Yes

UNIVERSITY OF MICHIGAN — FLINT
School of Management

Admissions Contact: Cheryl Tabachki, MBA, NetPlus! MBA Coordinator
Address: UM-F, MBA Office, 364 French Hall, 303 E. Kearsley, Flint, MI 48502-1950
Admissions Phone: 810-761-3163 • Admissions Fax: 810-762-0736
Admissions E-mail: ctabachk@umflint.edu • Web Address: www.flint.umich.edu/departments/som/MBA

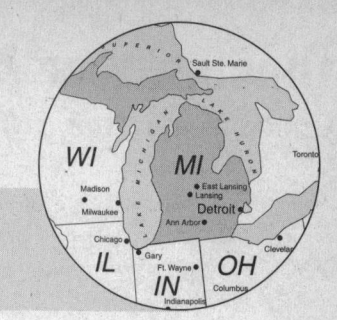

Whether you're a resident or not, the tuition song remains the same, and it's a pretty good deal either way you slice it. Most UM—Flint students are from the upper central states, and that's where most Flint MBAs expect to work when they graduate. If cold winters don't entice you, how does a 100 percent chance of snagging a job within three months of graduation sound?

INSTITUTIONAL INFORMATION
Public/Private: Public
Evening Classes Available? Yes
Total Faculty: 23
% Faculty Female: 26
% Faculty Minority: 39
% Faculty Part Time: 35
Student/Faculty Ratio: 35:1
Academic Calendar: Semester

PROGRAMS
Degrees Offered: Master of Business Administration, Traditional MBA (3 years or 33 months), Master of Business Administration, NetPlus! MBA (mixed mode delivery, 2 years)

STUDENT INFORMATION
Total Business Students: 225

COMPUTER AND RESEARCH FACILITIES
Computer Facilities: Labs and classrooms contain 140 computers. LANs provide additional storage. UNIX machines provide e-mail services. Campus users connect to the Internet thorough the MichNet Computer System.
Campuswide Network? Yes
% of MBA Classrooms Wired: 6
Computer Model Recommended: No
Internet Fee? Yes

EXPENSES/FINANCIAL AID
Annual Tuition: $8,420
Tuition Per Credit: $370
Books and Supplies: $1,200
Average Grant: $1,000
Average Loan: $5,700

ADMISSIONS INFORMATION
Application Fee: $50
Electronic Application? No
Regular Application Deadline: 7/1
Regular Notification: 8/1
Deferment Available? Yes
Length of Deferment: 3 years
Non-fall Admissions? Yes
Non-fall Application Deadline(s): 11/1 winter
Transfer Students Accepted? Yes
Transfer Policy: AACSB-accredited, B or better, graduate level, 6 credits only, not part of any other degree
Need-Blind Admissions? Yes
Number of Applications Received: 71
% of Applicants Accepted: 96
% Accepted Who Enrolled: 76
Average GPA: 3.1
Average GMAT: 530

INTERNATIONAL STUDENTS
TOEFL Required of International Students? Yes
Minimum TOEFL: 550 (213 computer)

EMPLOYMENT INFORMATION

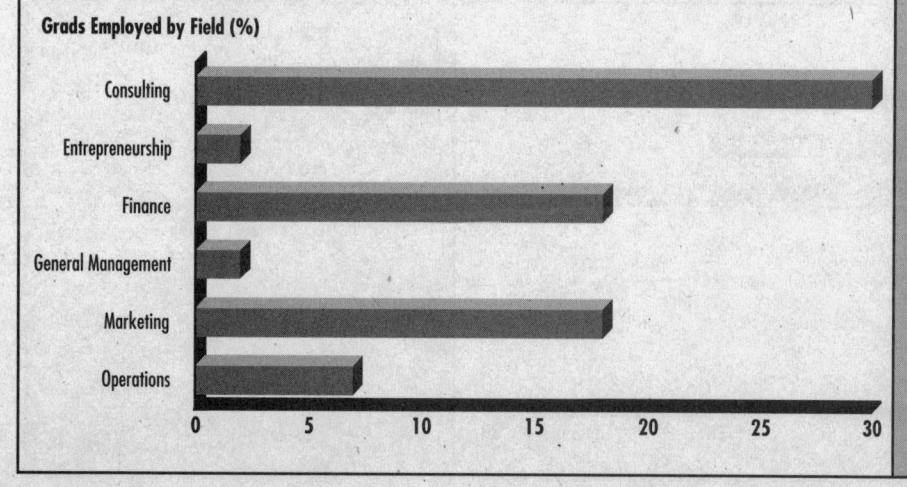

Grads Employed by Field (%)

Field	%
Consulting	~30
Entrepreneurship	~2
Finance	~18
General Management	~3
Marketing	~18
Operations	~7

Placement Office Available? No
% Employed Within 3 Months: 100

UNIVERSITY OF MINNESOTA — MINNEAPOLIS
Curtis L. Carlson School of Management

Admissions Contact: Sandra Kelzenberg, Interim Director, Full-Time MBA Program
Address: 321 19th Avenue South, Minneapolis, MN 55455
Admissions Phone: 612-625-5555 • Admissions Fax: 612-626-7785
Admissions E-mail: mbaoffice@csom.umn.edu • Web Address: www.CarlsonSchool.umn.edu

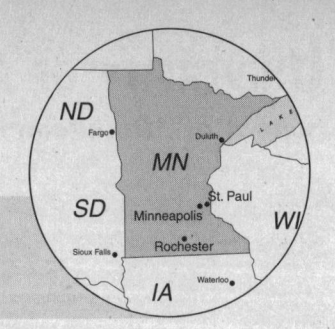

Winters are "too long and too cold" at the University of Minnesota's Carlson School of Management. Other than that, though, the "mature, helpful, friendly" midwesterners here have practically no complaints. They say the "small and comfortable" Carlson School has "accessible professors" and "a very cooperative learning environment." Also, student life here is particularly "active." There are "regular happy hours" and "many clubs and organizations," and "classmates enjoy being in activities with each other."

INSTITUTIONAL INFORMATION
Evening Classes Available? Yes
Total Faculty: 124
% Faculty Female: 16
Student/Faculty Ratio: 3:1
Academic Calendar: Semester

PROGRAMS
Degrees Offered: Bachelor of Science in Business (BSB) (4 years); MBA (2 years); Carlson Executive MBA (2 years); Master of Arts in Human Resources in Industrial Relations (2 years); Master of Healthcare Administration (2 years); Master of Business Taxation (1 year); Master of Science in Management of Technology (2 years); PhD Business (4 years); PhD Human Resources and Industrial Relations (4 years); PhD Health Services Administration (4 years)
Joint Degrees: JD/MBA (4 years), MHA/MBA (3 years), MD/MBA (6 years)
Academic Specialties: Accounting, Finance, Information Systems, Marketing, Entrepreneurship, Operations, E-Business, International Business, Supply Chain Management, Strategic Management, Healthcare Management.
Special Opportunities: MBA Enterprise Corps
Study Abroad Options: Australia, New Zealand, Japan, Austria, Belgium, Brazil, Costa Rica, England, France, Italy, Norway, Spain, Sweden, Switzerland

STUDENT INFORMATION
Total Business Students: 1,243
% Full Time: 19
% Female: 31
% Minority: 8
% Out of State: 31
% International: 26
Average Age: 28

COMPUTER AND RESEARCH FACILITIES
Research Facilities: Financial Markets Lab & Golden Gopher Growth Fund (investments), Juran Center (quality management), Center for Corporate Responsibility (ethics), Center for Industrial Relations, Strategic Management Research Center, Center for Entrepreneurial Studies, MIS Research Center
Computer Facilities: 5 computer labs, MIS lab, Financial Markets Lab, wide variety of research databases
Campuswide Network? Yes
% of MBA Classrooms Wired: 100
Computer Model Recommended: No
Internet Fee? No

EXPENSES/FINANCIAL AID
Annual Tuition (Resident/Nonresident): $14,683/$19,200
Tuition Per Credit (Resident/Nonresident): $562/$822
Room & Board (On/Off Campus): $5,000/$7,500
Books and Supplies: $2,000
Average Grant: $10,000
Average Loan: $15,000

ADMISSIONS INFORMATION
Application Fee: $60
Electronic Application? Yes
Early Decision Application Deadline: 1/1
Early Decision Notification: 2/15
Regular Application Deadline: 4/1
Regular Notification: 5/15
Length of Deferment: 1 year
Non-fall Admissions? No
Transfer Students Accepted? No
Need-Blind Admissions? Yes
Number of Applications Received: 759
% of Applicants Accepted: 34
% Accepted Who Enrolled: 41
Average GPA: 3.3
Average GMAT: 645
Average Years Experience: 5
Other Admissions Factors Considered: Interview recommended
Minority/Disadvantaged Student Recruitment Programs: Minnesota Boulevard Program; minority scholarships; close ties with National Black MBA Association and NSHMBA

INTERNATIONAL STUDENTS
TOEFL Required of International Students? Yes
Minimum TOEFL: 580 (240 computer)

EMPLOYMENT INFORMATION

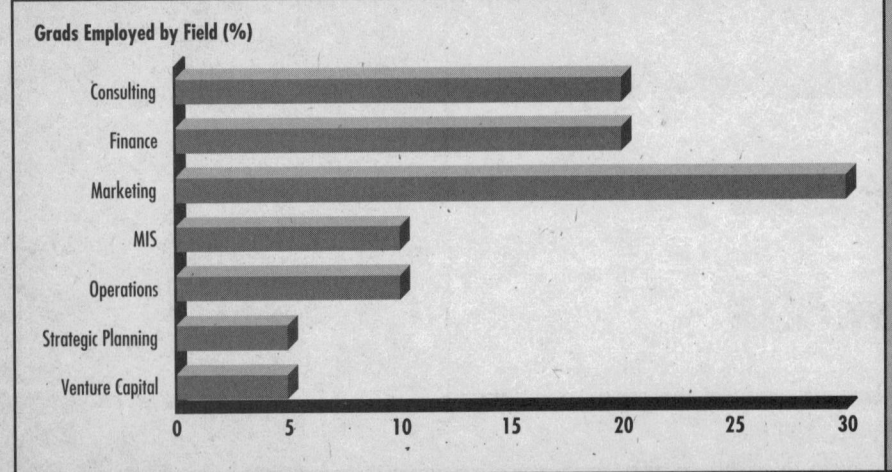

Grads Employed by Field (%)
- Consulting: ~20
- Finance: ~10
- Marketing: ~30
- MIS: ~10
- Operations: ~10
- Strategic Planning: ~5
- Venture Capital: ~5

Placement Office Available? Yes
% Employed Within 3 Months: 95
Frequent Employers: Accenture, US Bancorp, Pillsbury, General Mills, Northwest Airlines, Medtronic, 3M, HB Fuller, Cargill, Deloitte & Touche, Ecolab, ADC Telecommunications, Intel, Guidant

UNIVERSITY OF MINNESOTA — DULUTH
School of Business and Economics

Admissions Contact: M.J. Leone
Address: 431 Darland Administration Building, Duluth, MN 55812-2496
Admissions Phone: 218-726-7523 • Admissions Fax: 218-726-6970
Admissions E-mail: grad@d.umn.edu • Web Address: sbe.d.umn.edu/sem_description

U of M—Duluth offers one track: a part-time evening program that takes most students between two and seven years to complete. For those anti–standardized test activists, U of M—Duluth can waive the GMAT requirement for admission if you're a CPA or have obtained some other graduate degree from a regionally accredited institution.

INSTITUTIONAL INFORMATION
Public/Private: Public
Evening Classes Available? Yes
Students in Parent Institution: 10,000
Academic Calendar: Semester

PROGRAMS
Degrees Offered: Evening MBA (2 to 7 years)
Academic Specialties: Case study, computer-aided instruction, computer simulations, field projects, group discussion, lecture, simulations, student presentations, team projects

STUDENT INFORMATION
Average Age: 30

COMPUTER AND RESEARCH FACILITIES
Number of Student Computers: 250
Campuswide Network? Yes
Computer Proficiency Required? No
Special Purchasing Agreements? No
Internet Fee? No

EXPENSES/FINANCIAL AID
Annual Tuition: $6,000
Room & Board (On/Off Campus): $6,000/$6,500
% Receiving Financial Aid: 35

ADMISSIONS INFORMATION
Application Fee: $50
Electronic Application? No
Regular Application Deadline: 7/15
Deferment Available? Yes
Non-fall Admissions? Yes
Non-fall Application Deadline(s): 11/1, 5/1
Transfer Students Accepted? No
Need-Blind Admissions? No
Number of Applications Received: 20
% of Applicants Accepted: 75
% Accepted Who Enrolled: 80
Average GPA: 3.3
Average GMAT: 550
Other Admissions Factors Considered: GRE scores, work experience, word processing experience, spreadsheet experience

INTERNATIONAL STUDENTS
TOEFL Required of International Students? Yes
Minimum TOEFL: 550

EMPLOYMENT INFORMATION

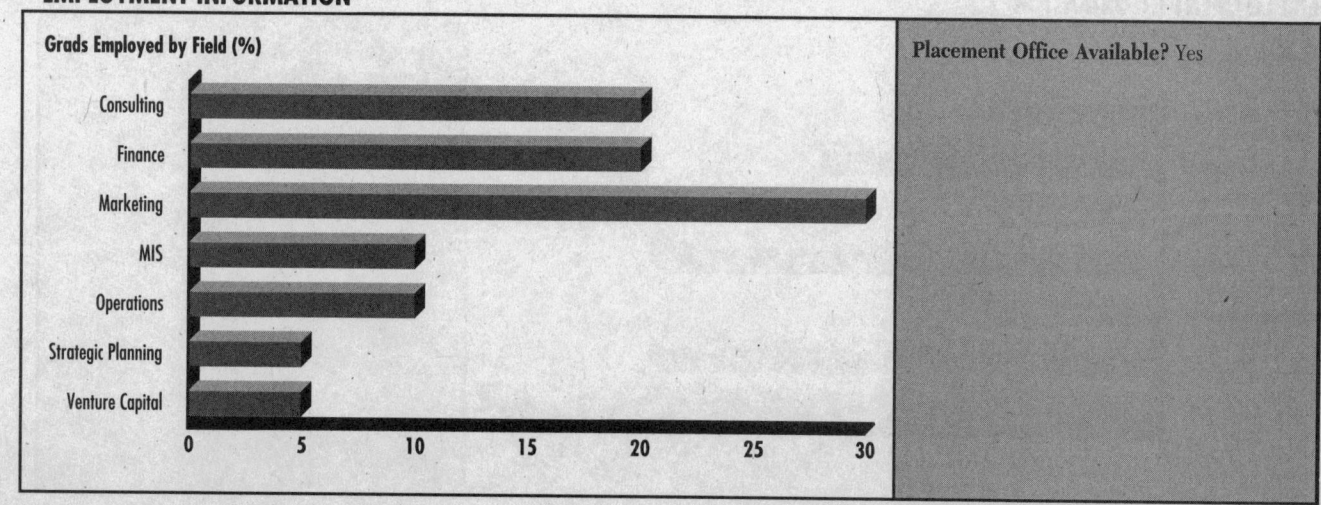

Grads Employed by Field (%)

Field	%
Consulting	20
Finance	20
Marketing	30
MIS	10
Operations	10
Strategic Planning	5
Venture Capital	5

Placement Office Available? Yes

UNIVERSITY OF MISSISSIPPI
School of Business Adminstration

Admissions Contact: Dr. John Holleman, Director of MBA Adminstration
Address: 319 Conner Hall, University, MS 38677
Admissions Phone: 662-915-5483 • Admissions Fax: 662-915-7968
Admissions E-mail: jholleman@bus.olemiss.edu • Web Address: www.bus.olemiss.edu/mba

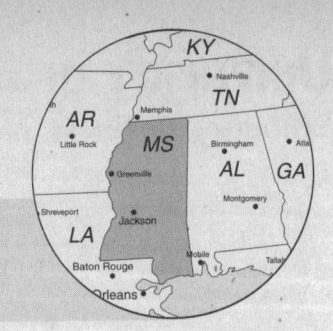

When your business school is in the hometown of Faulkner, you're expected to master people skills. Indeed, the School of Business Administration, one of the oldest in the United States, encourages students to build relationships with the faculty, the surrounding community, and one another. Even though "no academic regimen has [a] better grasp of today's new technology," Ole Miss knows that some things never change, including the fact "that leaders achieve success by gaining the cooperation of those who work with them." Fittingly, many an MBA candidate cites "the importance of balancing work and play." So if you've got the technical skills but don't know how to schmooze—or vice versa—you'll leave Ole Miss as the total package: a dealmaker and a code breaker.

INSTITUTIONAL INFORMATION
Public/Private: Public
Evening Classes Available? Yes
Total Faculty: 57
% Faculty Female: 18
% Faculty Minority: 2
Student/Faculty Ratio: 30:1
Students in Parent Institution: 11,500
Academic Calendar: Semester

PROGRAMS
Degrees Offered: MBA with concentration in Management, Accounting, Banking, Economics, Finance, International Business, Management information Systems, Marketing, Operations Management, Organizational Behavior/Development, Quantitative Analysis, Real Estate, Financial Management/Planning, Human Resources, Information Management, Insurance, Managerial Economics System Management (18 months to 2.2 years)
Academic Specialties: Case study, computer analysis, computer simulations, experiential learning, field projects, group discussion, lecture, seminars by members of the business community, student presentations, study groups, team projects

STUDENT INFORMATION
Total Business Students: 90
% Full Time: 100
% Female: 40
% Minority: 8
% Out of State: 48
% International: 8
Average Age: 28

COMPUTER AND RESEARCH FACILITIES
Campuswide Network? Yes
% of MBA Classrooms Wired: 100
Computer Model Recommended: Laptop
Internet Fee? No

EXPENSES/FINANCIAL AID
Room & Board (On/Off Campus): $8,800/ $10,000
Average Grant: $1,377
Average Loan: $10,000

ADMISSIONS INFORMATION
Electronic Application? Yes
Regular Application Deadline: 4/1
Regular Notification: Rolling
Deferment Available? No
Non-fall Admissions? Yes
Non-fall Application Deadline(s): 4/1 summer
Transfer Students Accepted? No
Need-Blind Admissions? Yes
Number of Applications Received: 573
% of Applicants Accepted: 21
% Accepted Who Enrolled: 84
Average GPA: 3.3
GPA Range: 3.0-3.7
Average GMAT: 560
GMAT Range: 500-610

INTERNATIONAL STUDENTS
TOEFL Required of International Students? Yes
Minimum TOEFL: 600

EMPLOYMENT INFORMATION

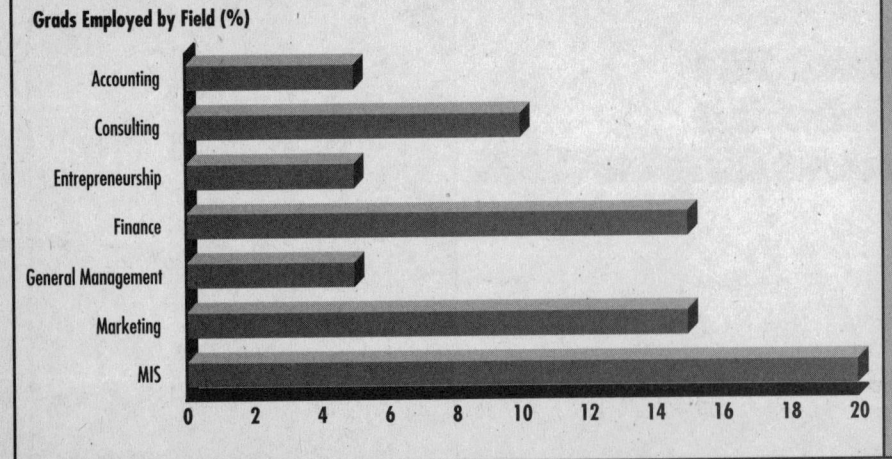

Grads Employed by Field (%)

Field	%
Accounting	5
Consulting	10
Entrepreneurship	5
Finance	15
General Management	5
Marketing	15
MIS	20

Placement Office Available? Yes
% Employed Within 3 Months: 100
Frequent Employers: Top regional employers from across the South and Southeast

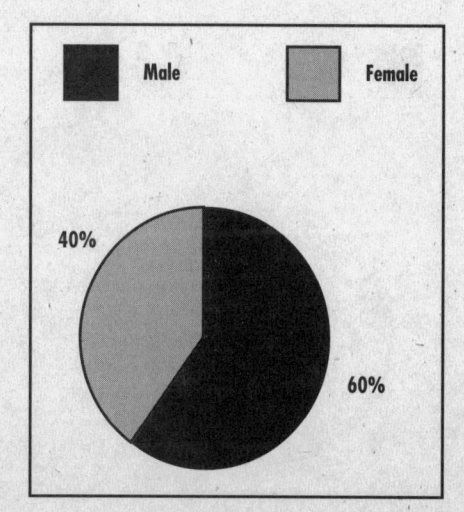

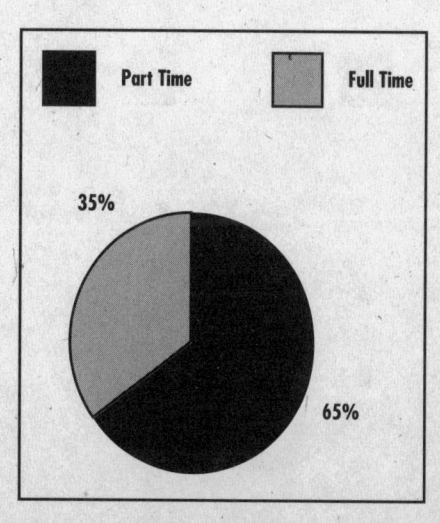

UNIVERSITY OF MISSOURI—KANSAS CITY
Henry W. Bloch School of Business & Public Administration

Admissions Contact: Director of Admissions
Address: 5100 Rockhill Road, Kansas City, MO 64110
Admissions Phone: 816-235-1111 • Admissions Fax: 816-235-5544
Admissions E-mail: admit@umkc.edu • Web Address: www.umkc.edu/bloch

To budding entrepreneurs from the state of Missouri, hark! You will find an environment ripe with opportunity to hone the skills you'll need to make your own business thrive at the Bloch School of Business and Public Administration. Students with an emphasis in entrepreneurship (one of six options) can give themselves a baptism of fire with the Entrepreneurial Growth Resource Center, which basically outsources undergraduate and graduate business students to small businesses to help them with their needs, whether it be "business plan[s], a website, [or] assistance in getting government contracts."

INSTITUTIONAL INFORMATION
Public/Private: Public
Evening Classes Available? Yes
Total Faculty: 44
% Faculty Female: 23
% Faculty Minority: 7
% Faculty Part Time: 4
Student/Faculty Ratio: 25:1
Students in Parent Institution: 10,016
Academic Calendar: Semester

PROGRAMS
Degrees Offered: Master of Business Administration (12 months to 7 years), with concentrations in Entrepreneurship, Finance, Human Resources, Management, Management Information Systems, Marketing, Operations Management, and Organizational Behavior; Master of Science in Accounting (12 months to 7 years); Master of Public Administration (12 months to 7 years), with concentrations in Nonprofit Management, Organizational Behavior, Human Resources, City/Urban Administration, and Health Care; Executive MBA (21 months)
Joint Degrees: JD/MBA (4 years)
Academic Specialties: Case study, computer aided instruction, computer analysis, computer simulations, experimental learning, faculty seminars, field projects, group discussion, lecture, research, seminars by members of the business community, simulations, student presentations, study groups, team projects
Study Abroad Options: International exchange programs in Germany, Malaysia, Singapore, United Kingdom, France

STUDENT INFORMATION
Total Business Students: 403
% Female: 40
% Minority: 9
% International: 29
Average Age: 31

COMPUTER AND RESEARCH FACILITIES
Campuswide Network? Yes
Internet Fee? No

EXPENSES/FINANCIAL AID
Annual Tuition (Resident/Nonresident): $3,582/$9,842

ADMISSIONS INFORMATION
Application Fee: $25
Electronic Application? No
Regular Application Deadline: 5/1
Regular Notification: Rolling
Deferment Available? Yes
Length of Deferment: 1 year
Non-fall Admissions? Yes
Non-fall Application Deadline(s): 10/1 winter, 3/1 summer
Transfer Students Accepted? Yes
Transfer Policy: We will accept up to 6 hours of graduate credit from an AACSB-accredited institution.
Need-Blind Admissions? Yes
Number of Applications Received: 349
% of Applicants Accepted: 54
% Accepted Who Enrolled: 74
Average GPA: 3.3
Average GMAT: 559
Average Years Experience: 5

INTERNATIONAL STUDENTS
TOEFL Required of International Students? Yes
Minimum TOEFL: 550

EMPLOYMENT INFORMATION
Placement Office Available? Yes
% Employed Within 3 Months: 90
Frequent Employers: prosecutor's office, Jackson County, Missouri; Shook Hardy & Bacon; Blackwell Sanders Peper Martin LLP; Bryan Cave LLP; United Missouri Bank; Shughart Thomson & Kilroy, PC; Lathrop & Gage LC; Stinson, Mag & Fizzell, PC; Morrison & Hecker LLP; Husch & Eppenberger, LLC

Male 60% / Female 40%

Part Time 65% / Full Time 35%

UNIVERSITY OF MONTANA — MISSOULA
School of Business Administration

Admissions Contact: Kathleen Spritzer, Administrative Officer
Address: School of Business Administration, University of Montana, Missoula, MT 59812
Admissions Phone: 406-243-4983 • *Admissions Fax:* 406-243-2086
Admissions E-mail: kathleen.spritzer@business.umt.edu • *Web Address:* www.mba-macct.umt.edu

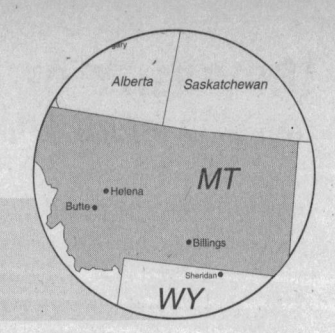

You can work toward a UM—Missoula MBA from just about any big city in Big Sky country, including Billings, Bozeman, Butte, Helena, Great Falls, Kalispell, and Missoula, with the Off-Campus MBA. A low cost of living and low tuition make UM—Missoula a terrific choice for in-state and out-of-state students alike. No matter which city you choose to do your course work in, bring a serious jacket. And gloves. And lip balm.

INSTITUTIONAL INFORMATION
Public/Private: Public
Evening Classes Available? Yes
Total Faculty: 30
% Faculty Female: 24
% Faculty Minority: 1
% Faculty Part Time: 12
Student/Faculty Ratio: 21:1
Students in Parent Institution: 12,413
Academic Calendar: Semester

PROGRAMS
Degrees Offered: MBA (1 calendar year), MAcc (1 calendar year)
Combined Degrees: JD/MBA (3 years)
Academic Specialties: The general MBA, with ten semester credits of electives available, allows students to specialize in an area of their interest. Specialities include Accounting Theory, Banking, Business Law, Corporate Finance, Entrepreneurship, Financial Accounting, Human Resource Management, Income Taxation, Information Systems, International Management, Investments, Management, Communications, Marketing, Operations Management, Research Methods, and Strategic Marketing.

STUDENT INFORMATION
Total Business Students: 132
% Full Time: 60
% Female: 48
% Minority: 19
% International: 20
Average Age: 29

COMPUTER AND RESEARCH FACILITIES
Research Facilities: Bureau of Business and Economic Resources, Montana World Trade Center, American Indian Business Leaders, Montana Business Connections
Computer Facilities: The Gallagher Business Building has two open computer labs of 50 stations each, a 50-station computer classroom, 3 interactive distance-learning classrooms, as well as 8 additional classrooms equipped with computers, VCRs, projectors, and audio systems for classroom presentations. Microsoft and Hewlett-Packard have partnered to provide the building with the latest software and hardware on an ongoing basis.
Campuswide Network? Yes
% of MBA Classrooms Wired: 50
Internet Fee? No

EXPENSES/FINANCIAL AID
Annual Tuition (Resident/Nonresident): $3,500/$9,820
Tuition Per Credit (Resident/Nonresident): $195/$415
Room and Board (On Campus): $7,500
Average Grant: $8,490
Average Loan: $10,970
% Receiving Aid: 66

ADMISSIONS INFORMATION
Application Fee: $45
Electronic Application? No
Regular Application Deadline: 5/1
Regular Notification: 5/15
Length of Deferment: 1 year
Non-fall Application Deadline(s): 11/1 spring, 5/1 summer
Transfer Policy: Up to 9 semester credits
Need-Blind Admissions? Yes
Number of Applications Received: 119
% of Applicants Accepted: 80
% Accepted Who Enrolled: 83
Average GPA: 3.3
Average GMAT: 570
Average Years Experience: 2.5
Other Admissions Factors Considered: Resume
Minority/Disadvantaged Student Recruitment Programs: One graduate assistantship for member of a Native American tribe
Other Schools to Which Students Applied: Montana State, U. of Colorado, U. of Oregon, U. of Washington, Washington State

INTERNATIONAL STUDENTS
TOEFL Required of International Students? Yes
Minimum TOEFL: 580 (237 computer)

EMPLOYMENT INFORMATION
Placement Office Available? Yes
Frequent Employers: Andersen Consulting, Arthur Andersen, Cargill, Deloitte Consulting, Ernst & Young, GTE, Hewlett-Packard, KPMG, Microsoft, PricewaterhouseCoopers, Safeco, U.S. Bank, Wells Fargo Bank, U.S. Marines

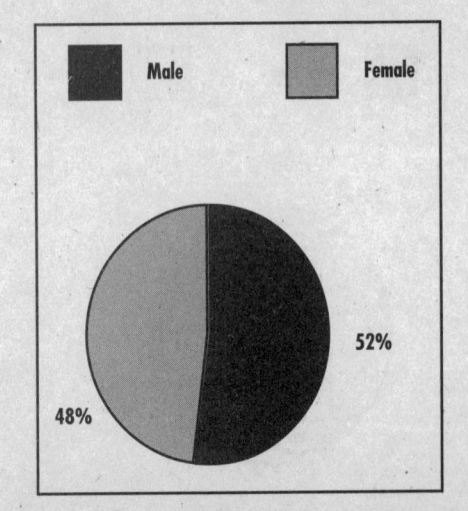

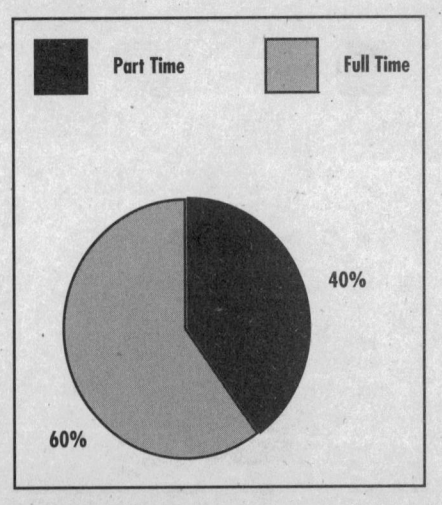

UNIVERSITY OF NAVARRA
IESE International Graduate School of Management

Admissions Contact: Alberto Arribas, Director of MBA Admissions
Address: Av. Pearson 21, Barcelona, Spain 08034
Admissions Phone: 011-34-93-253-4227 • *Admissions Fax:* 011-34-93-253-4343
Admissions E-mail: mbainfo@iese.edu • *Web Address:* www.iese.edu

INSTITUTIONAL INFORMATION
Public/Private: Private
Evening Classes Available? No
Total Faculty: 111
% Faculty Part Time: 34
Student/Faculty Ratio: 5:1
Students in Parent Institution: 16,000
Academic Calendar: Trimester

PROGRAMS
Degrees Offered: MBA (2 years), PhD in Management (3 years)
Academic Specialties: General Management, Entrepreneurship, IT Management, Organizational Behavior, Business Ethics
Study Abroad Options: University of California—Berkeley, USA; China Europe International Business School, China; University of Chicago, USA; Columbia Business School, USA; Cornell University, USA; Chinese University of Hong Kong, Hong Kong; University of Virginia, USA; Duke University, USA; Georgetown University, USA; Instituto Centroamericano de Administración de Empresas, Costa Rica; Instituto Panamericano de Alta Dirección de Empresa, Mexico; Keio University, Japan; Northwestern University, USA; University of London, U.K.; University of Michigan, USA; Massachusetts Institute of Technology, USA; Erasmus University, The Netherlands; Dartmouth College, USA; Univeristy of California—Los Angeles, USA; University of Western Ontario, Canada; University of Pennsylvania, USA

STUDENT INFORMATION
Total Business Students: 220
% Full Time: 100
% Female: 22
% International: 59
Average Age: 27

COMPUTER AND RESEARCH FACILITIES
Research Facilities: The International Center for Financial Investigation, The Center for Operations Excellence, The Center for Entrepreneurship and Family-Owned Business, The International Research Center on Organizations, The Center for Enterprise in Latin America, The International Research Center on Logistics
Computer Facilities: Databases include Proquest Direct, BOENET, DOGC, Lexis-Nexis Academic Universe, Hoover's Online, International Financial Statistics, SABE, Snapshots, WorldScope among others.
Number of Computer Labs: 10
Number of Student Computers: 90
Campuswide Network? Yes
% Who Own Computers: 95
Computer Proficiency Required? No
Special Purchasing Agreements? No
Internet Fee? No

EXPENSES/FINANCIAL AID
Annual Tuition: $17,000
Books and Supplies: $500
Average Grant: $9,100
Average Loan: $32,000

ADMISSIONS INFORMATION
Application Fee: $60
Electronic Application? Yes
Regular Application Deadline: 4/3
Regular Notification: Rolling
Deferment Available? Yes
Length of Deferment: 1 year
Non-fall Admissions? No
Transfer Students Accepted? No
Need-Blind Admissions? No
Number of Applications Received: 1,289
% of Applicants Accepted: 21
% Accepted Who Enrolled: 75
Average GMAT: 640
Average Years Experience: 4

INTERNATIONAL STUDENTS
TOEFL Required of International Students? Yes
Minimum TOEFL: 600

EMPLOYMENT INFORMATION

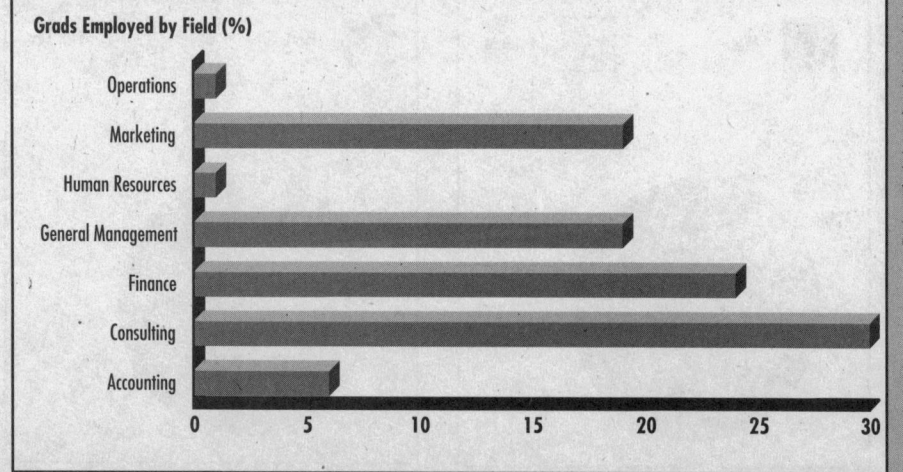

Grads Employed by Field (%)
- Operations: ~1
- Marketing: ~19
- Human Resources: ~2
- General Management: ~19
- Finance: ~24
- Consulting: ~29
- Accounting: ~6

Placement Office Available? Yes
% Employed Within 6 Months: 100
Frequent Employers: Cluster Consulting, Arthur D. Little, Andersen Consulting, McKinsey & Company
Prominent Alumni: Jan Oosterveld, Philips; vice president for corporate strategy; Harry Anderson; vice president, The Boston Consulting Group; David Stead, partner, Andersen Consulting

UNIVERSITY OF NEBRASKA — LINCOLN
College of Business Administration

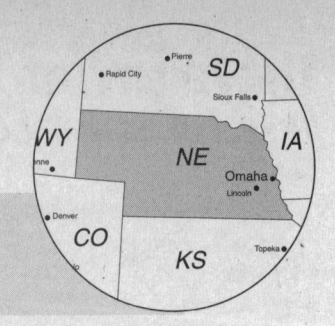

Admissions Contact: Judy Shutts, Graduate Advisor
Address: CBA 126, Lincoln, NE 68588-0405
Admissions Phone: 402-472-2338 • *Admissions Fax:* 402-472-5180
Admissions E-mail: cgraduate@unlnotes.unl.edu • *Web Address:* www.cba.unl.edu

Present at the creation? UN—Lincoln was a charter member (along with Harvard, Northwestern, and the University of Texas) of the AACSB. Entrepreneurial then and entrepreneurial now, UN—Lincoln's Center for Entrepreneurship was recently named tops in the nation by the U.S. Association for Small Business and Entrepreneurship. UN—Lincoln isn't sitting on its laurels, though. Plans for the inauguration of a PhD specialization in leadership, to be offered in partnership with the Gallup Organization, are currently in the works.

INSTITUTIONAL INFORMATION
Public/Private: Public
Evening Classes Available? No
Total Faculty: 56
% Faculty Female: 18
% Faculty Minority: 11
% Faculty Part Time: 1
Student/Faculty Ratio: 6:1
Students in Parent Institution: 22,268
Academic Calendar: Semester

PROGRAMS
Degrees Offered: MA (2 years); MBA (2 years); Master of Professional Accountancy (2 years)
Joint Degrees: MBA/JD (4 years); MBA/Arch (3 years)
Special Opportunities: CIMBA (Italy), Consortium of International MBA; Oxford Summer Program; Senshu University (Senshu, Japan)
Study Abroad Options: Italy, Mexico, Japan, England, Germany, France

STUDENT INFORMATION
Total Business Students: 159
% Full Time: 51
% Female: 30
% Out of State: 30
% International: 20
Average Age: 28

COMPUTER AND RESEARCH FACILITIES
Research Facilities: Bureau of Business Research, Public Policy Center
Computer Facilities: CRSP, Research Insight, ExecuComp
Campuswide Network? Yes
% of MBA Classrooms Wired: 100
Internet Fee? No

EXPENSES/FINANCIAL AID
Annual Tuition (Resident/Nonresident): $3,216/$8,298
Tuition Per Credit (Resident/Nonresident): $134/$346
Room & Board (On/Off Campus): $5,110/$6,100
Books and Supplies: $740
Average Grant: $1,000
% Receiving Financial Aid: 44
% Receiving Aid Their First Year: 57

ADMISSIONS INFORMATION
Application Fee: $35
Electronic Application? Yes
Regular Application Deadline: 6/15
Regular Notification: Rolling
Deferment Available? No
Non-fall Admissions? Yes
Non-fall Application Deadline(s): 11/15 spring, 4/15 summer
Transfer Students Accepted? Yes
Transfer Policy: 12 credit hours may be accepted from an AACSB-accredited institution if approved by the Graduate Committee.
Need-Blind Admissions? Yes
Number of Applications Received: 78
% of Applicants Accepted: 60
% Accepted Who Enrolled: 64
Average GPA: 3.4
GPA Range: 3.1-3.6
Average GMAT: 596
GMAT Range: 560-660
Average Years Experience: 3
Minority/Disadvantaged Student Recruitment Programs: Fellowships for minority students

INTERNATIONAL STUDENTS
TOEFL Required of International Students? Yes
Minimum TOEFL: 550 (213 computer)

EMPLOYMENT INFORMATION
Placement Office Available? Yes
% Employed Within 3 Months: 9
Frequent Employers: Novartis, Merck, Sprint, IBM, Qwest, Gallup Inc.
Prominent Alumni: Marsha Lommel, president and CEO, Madonna Rehabilitation Hospital; Vinod Gupta, founder and chairman, InfoUSA; David Maurstad, lieutenant governor, state of Nebraska; Bernard Reznicek, national director, Central States Indemnity Co.; William Ruud, policy director, state of Idaho

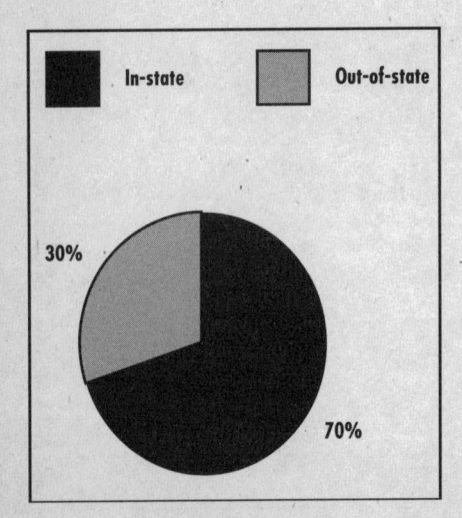

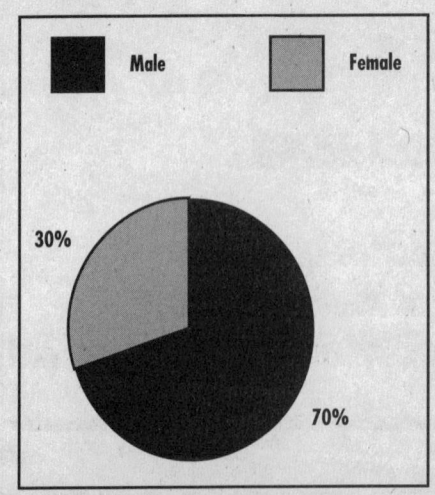

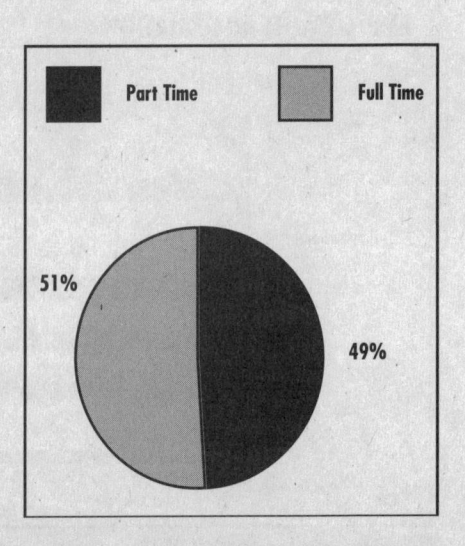

UNIVERSITY OF NEVADA—LAS VEGAS
College of Business

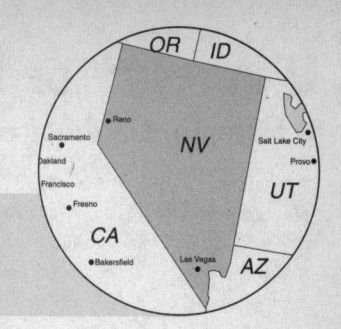

Admissions Contact: *Nasser Daneshvary, MBA Director/Associate Dean, College of Business*
Address: *4505 Maryland Parkway, Box 456031, Las Vegas, NV 89154-6031*
Admissions Phone: 702-895-3655 • Admissions Fax: 702-895-4090
Admissions E-mail: *cobmba@ccmail.nevada.edu* • Web Address: *www.unlv.edu*

For MBAs who want an edge in the hospitality industry, take a look at the recently initiated combined MBA/Master of Hotel Administration program at UNLV. And it can't hurt that the school happens to be in one of the most popular vacation cities in the world. (Vegas, baby. Vegas!) While the school wants to graduate "visionary...executive leaders," accountants who want to audit evil companies in dark, quiet rooms and economists who want to pontificate from ivory towers will find master's degree programs to prepare them to achieve their dreams.

INSTITUTIONAL INFORMATION
Public/Private: Public
Evening Classes Available? Yes
Total Faculty: 75
% Faculty Female: 10
% Faculty Minority: 5
Student/Faculty Ratio: 25:1
Students in Parent Institution: 24,000
Academic Calendar: Semester

PROGRAMS
Degrees Offered: MBA (2 years full time evening, 3 to 4 years part time evening); EMBA (18 months block attendance)
Joint Degrees: MS Hotel Administration/MBA (2.5 years)
Academic Specialties: Teamwork emphasis, case study approach

STUDENT INFORMATION
Total Business Students: 191
% Full Time: 45
% Female: 17
% Minority: 6
% Out of State: 10
% International: 12
Average Age: 28

COMPUTER AND RESEARCH FACILITIES
Research Facilities: Center for Business and Economic Research
Computer Facilities: ABI/Inform, Compustat, CRSP, Dissertation abstracts, Ebsco, FirstSearch, Infotrac, Lexis-Nexis, Moody's, PAIS, Simmons Study Media/Markets, STAT-USA
Campuswide Network? Yes
Computer Model Recommended: No
Internet Fee? No

EXPENSES/FINANCIAL AID
Annual Tuition (Resident): $7,215
Tuition Per Credit (Resident/Nonresident): $104/$209
Room & Board (On/Off Campus): $5,000/$7,000
Books and Supplies: $600
Average Grant: $2,500
Average Loan: $2,500
% Receiving Financial Aid: 20
% Receiving Aid Their First Year: 10

ADMISSIONS INFORMATION
Application Fee: $40
Electronic Application? No
Regular Application Deadline: 6/1
Regular Notification: 7/1
Deferment Available? Yes
Length of Deferment: 1 semester
Non-fall Admissions? Yes
Non-fall Application Deadline(s): 6/1 fall, 11/15 spring
Transfer Students Accepted? Yes
Transfer Policy: Total of 6 credits from an AACSB-accredited school
Need-Blind Admissions? Yes
Number of Applications Received: 146
% of Applicants Accepted: 53
% Accepted Who Enrolled: 71
Average GPA: 3.3
GPA Range: 3.0-3.6
Average GMAT: 588
GMAT Range: 540-620
Average Years Experience: 5

INTERNATIONAL STUDENTS
TOEFL Required of International Students? Yes
Minimum TOEFL: 550 (213 computer)

EMPLOYMENT INFORMATION
Placement Office Available? No

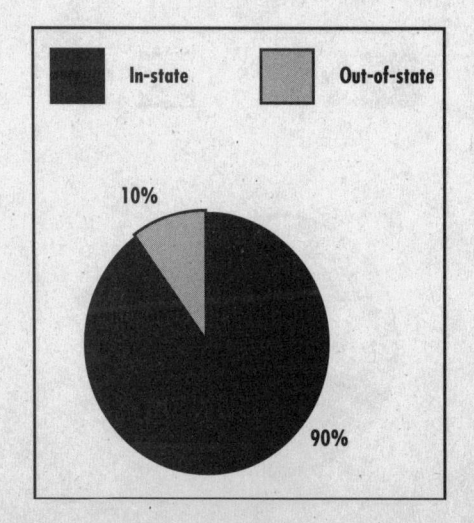

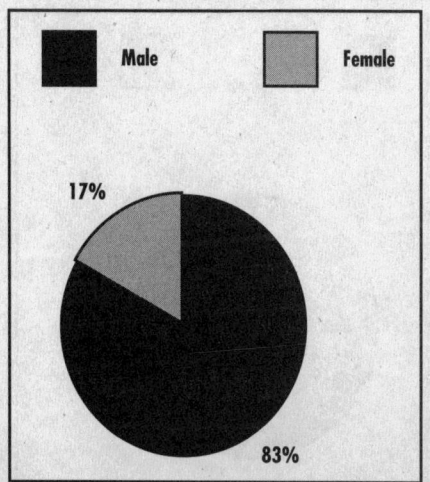

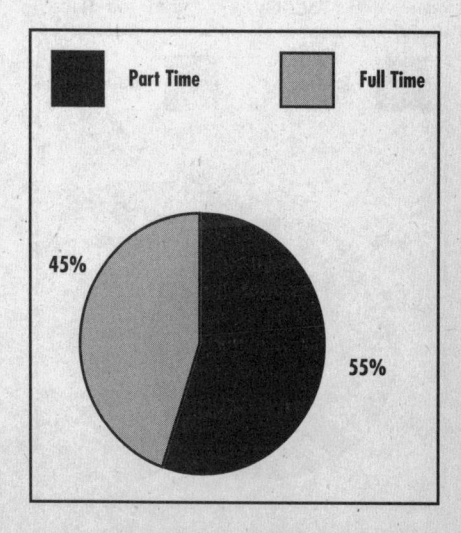

In-state 90% / Out-of-state 10%

Male 83% / Female 17%

Part Time 45% / Full Time 55%

UNIVERSITY OF NEW HAMPSHIRE
Whittemore School of Business and Economics

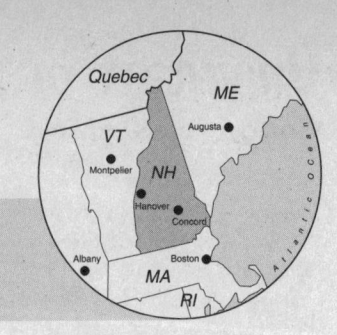

Admissions Contact: George Abraham, Director, Graduate and Executive Programs
Address: 116 McConnell Hall, 15 College Road, Durham, NH 03824
Admissions Phone: 603-862-1367 • Admissions Fax: 603-862-4468
Admissions E-mail: wsbe.grad@unh.edu • Web Address: www.mba.unh.edu

UNH offers your basic garden variety of graduate business degrees. A new master's in the management of technology brings candidates who pursue it through a teamwork-focused curriculum. Three-quarters of graduates end up working in New England making not too shabby a salary, so if you're looking to make a life in the region, Whittemore is a solid choice.

INSTITUTIONAL INFORMATION
Public/Private: Public
Evening Classes Available? Yes
Total Faculty: 63
% Faculty Female: 27
% Faculty Minority: 11
% Faculty Part Time: 33
Student/Faculty Ratio: 3:1
Students in Parent Institution: 12,000
Academic Calendar: Trimester

PROGRAMS
Degrees Offered: MBA (19 months full time, 2.5 to 3 years part time); Executive MBA (19 months); MS Accounting (1 year full time, 2.5 years part time); MA Economics (1.5 years); PhD Economics (4 to 5 years)
Joint Degrees: BA/MA Economics (5 years)
Academic Specialties: The full-time MBA program begins with a month-long residency in September and the remainder of the first year is devoted to completion of core courses. The second year requires a corporate field-based project with electives/specializations. Currently, specializations in Entrepreneurship, Managing Technology and Innovation, Accounting, Finance, and General Management are available. The part-time MBA program typically takes 2.5 to 3 years to complete and is offered in both Durham and Manchester, New Hampshire. The curriculum is currently under revision. Specializations have been proposed in Entrepreneurship, Technology and Operations Management, Accounting, Finance, and Health Management. The Executive MBA is designed to provide a flexible full-time program for professionals or managers with a minimum of 7 years of work experience. The 19-month program meets on alternating Fridays and Saturdays so that students can continue to work while enrolled.

STUDENT INFORMATION
Total Business Students: 210
% Full Time: 32
% Female: 31
% Minority: 1
% Out of State: 39
% International: 16
Average Age: 30

COMPUTER AND RESEARCH FACILITIES
Computer Facilities: All graduate students are able to utilize computers and printers in the Graduate Conference Room. In addition, there are several computer clusters open to all university students throughout the campus.
Campuswide Network? Yes
Computer Model Recommended: Laptop
Internet Fee? No

EXPENSES/FINANCIAL AID
Annual Tuition (Resident/Nonresident): $6,300/$15,720
Tuition Per Credit (Resident/Nonresident): $427/$497
Room & Board (On Campus): $5,804
Books and Supplies: $1,250
Average Grant: $3,000

ADMISSIONS INFORMATION
Application Fee: $50
Electronic Application? Yes
Early Decision Application Deadline: 4/1
Early Decision Notification: 5/15
Regular Application Deadline: 7/1
Regular Notification: Rolling
Length of Deferment: 1 year
Non-fall Application Deadline(s): The part-time program, on a space-available basis, admits for the winter term by 11/15.
Transfer Policy: A maximum of 3 courses from an AACSB institution.
Need-Blind Admissions? Yes
Number of Applications Received: 123
% of Applicants Accepted: 89
% Accepted Who Enrolled: 66
Average GPA: 3.0
Average GMAT: 560
Average Years Experience: 8
Other Schools to Which Students Applied: Babson, Bentley, UMass Amherst

INTERNATIONAL STUDENTS
TOEFL Required of International Students? Yes
Minimum TOEFL: 550 (213 computer)

EMPLOYMENT INFORMATION
Placement Office Available? Yes
% Employed Within 3 Months: 60
Prominent Alumni: Dan Burnham, president, Raytheon Defense; Beth Baldwin, vice president, Lycos

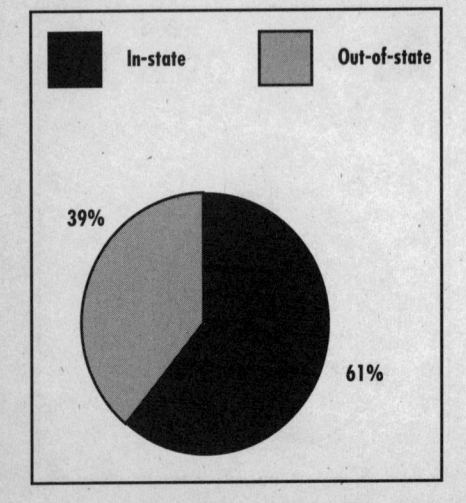

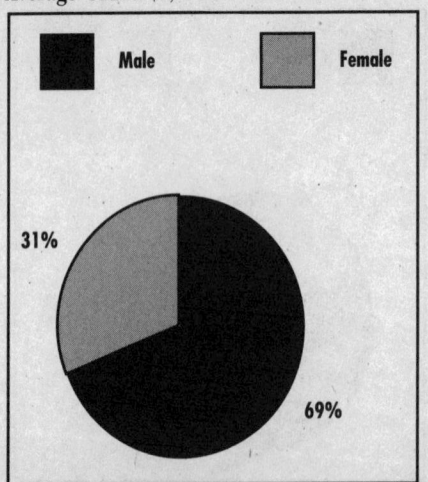

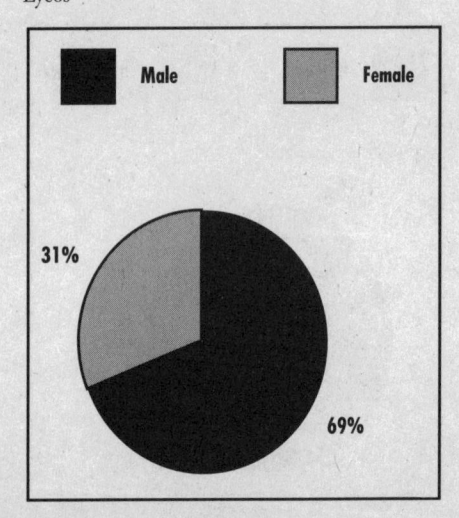

UNIVERSITY OF NEW MEXICO
Robert O. Anderson Graduate School of Management

Admissions Contact: Loyola Chastain, MBA Program Manager
Address: University of New Mexico, Albuquerque, NM 87131
Admissions Phone: 505-277-3147 • Admissions Fax: 505-277-9356
Admissions E-mail: chastain@mgt.unm.edu • Web Address: asm.unm.edu

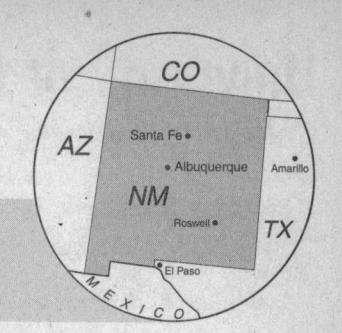

Hispanic Magazine ranked Anderson's MBA program as one of the top 10 nationally for Hispanic students. With a starting salary well above the region's average, more than a quarter of its students of minority status, and more than 40 percent of its students women, Anderson is sitting pretty. Its MBA candidates are sure to have a dynamic academic experience and one that pays off nicely after graduation.

INSTITUTIONAL INFORMATION
Public/Private: Public
Evening Classes Available? Yes
Total Faculty: 86
% Faculty Female: 33
% Faculty Part Time: 46
Student/Faculty Ratio: 30:1
Students in Parent Institution: 23,956
Academic Calendar: Semester

PROGRAMS
Degrees Offered: MBA (48 credits, 18 months to 3 years); MS in Accounting (33 credits, 2 to 5 years); Executive MBA (50 credits, 2 years)
Joint Degrees: MBA/MA in Latin American Studies (72 credits, 4.4 to 6 years); MBA/JD (129 credits, 5 to 8 years)
Study Abroad Options: France, Mexico, United Kingdom, western Europe, Hong Kong

STUDENT INFORMATION
Total Business Students: 431
% Full Time: 57
% Female: 43
% Minority: 26
% Out of State: 4
% International: 9
Average Age: 31

COMPUTER AND RESEARCH FACILITIES
Research Facilities: Bureau of Business and Economic Research
Computer Facilities: ASM has 2 computer pods available for students.
Campuswide Network? Yes
% of MBA Classrooms Wired: 100
Internet Fee? No

EXPENSES/FINANCIAL AID
Annual Tuition (Resident/Nonresident): $3,301/$11,737
Tuition Per Credit (Resident/Nonresident): $139/$491
Room & Board: $10,200
Books and Supplies: $1,200
Average Grant: $4,500
Average Loan: $18,000
% Receiving Financial Aid: 75

ADMISSIONS INFORMATION
Application Fee: $40
Electronic Application? No
Regular Application Deadline: 6/1
Regular Notification: Rolling
Deferment Available? Yes
Length of Deferment: 1 year
Non-fall Admissions? Yes
Non-fall Application Deadline(s): 11/1, 4/1, 6/1
Transfer Students Accepted? Yes
Transfer Policy: Up to 6 credits may transfer.
Need-Blind Admissions? No
Number of Applications Received: 129
% of Applicants Accepted: 57
% Accepted Who Enrolled: 100
Average GPA: 3.2
GPA Range: 2.7-3.8
Average GMAT: 562
GMAT Range: 420-740

INTERNATIONAL STUDENTS
TOEFL Required of International Students? Yes
Minimum TOEFL: 550 (213 computer)

EMPLOYMENT INFORMATION

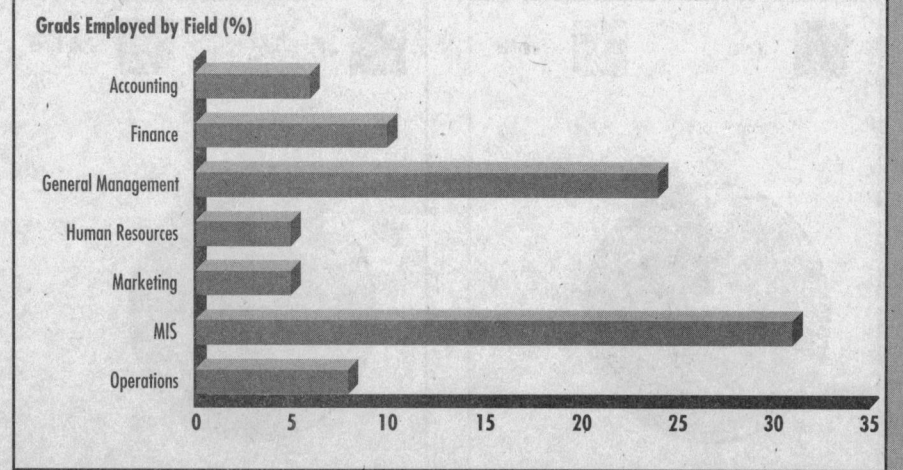

Grads Employed by Field (%)
- Accounting
- Finance
- General Management
- Human Resources
- Marketing
- MIS
- Operations

Placement Office Available? Yes
% Employed Within 3 Months: 86
Frequent Employers: Intel, Sandia National Laboratories, Ford Motor Company, IBM, KPMG

UNIVERSITY OF NEW ORLEANS
College of Business Administration

Admissions Contact: Rosyln Sheley, Director of Admissions
Address: Administration Building, Room 103, New Orleans, LA 70148
Admissions Phone: 504-280-6595 • Admissions Fax: 504-280-5522
Admissions E-mail: admissions@uno.edu • Web Address: www.uno.edu

The student body of UNO's College of Business Administration reflects the changing face of the MBA: women and minorities each comprise more than half of the overall population. The recently introduced EMBA-Kinston (Jamaica) is drawing applications by the score. It's no wonder. What MBA candidate wouldn't want to enjoy the Mai Tai life most other already made MBAs are working long hours to achieve? The tuition is low, the temperature is high, and there's no city that makes it easier to network than the Big Easy.

INSTITUTIONAL INFORMATION
Public/Private: Public
Evening Classes Available? Yes
Total Faculty: 58
% Faculty Female: 28
% Faculty Minority: 80
% Faculty Part Time: 5
Student/Faculty Ratio: 17:1
Students in Parent Institution: 17,014
Academic Calendar: Semester

PROGRAMS
Degrees Offered: Master of Business Administration (16 months to 8 years), with concentrations in Finance, International Business, Marketing, Real Estate, Human Resources, Travel Industry/Tourism Management, Management Information Systems, Technology Management, and Health Care; Executive Master of Business Administration (18 months); Master of Science in Accounting (16 months to 8 years); Master of Science in Taxation (16 months to 8 years); Master of Philosophy in Financial Education (3 to 10 years); Master in Health Care Management (18 months to 8 years); Master of Science in Health Care Management (13 months)
Academic Specialties: Case study, computer analysis, computer simulations, faculty seminars, field projects, group discussion, lecture, research, seminars by members of the business community, student presentations, study groups, team projects

Study Abroad Options: International exchange program in Austria

STUDENT INFORMATION
Total Business Students: 792
% Full Time: 44
% Female: 54
% Minority: 59
% Out of State: 39
% International: 33
Average Age: 31

COMPUTER AND RESEARCH FACILITIES
Computer Facilities: University Computing & Communications Lab, Library Lab, Business Lab
Campuswide Network? Yes
Internet Fee? No

EXPENSES/FINANCIAL AID
Annual Tuition (Resident/Nonresident): $2,748/$9,792
Tuition Per Credit (Resident/Nonresident): $435/$1,773
Room & Board: $3,900
Books and Supplies: $1,150
Average Grant: $4,200
Average Loan: $5,000

ADMISSIONS INFORMATION
Application Fee: $20
Electronic Application? No
Regular Application Deadline: 8/21
Regular Notification: 9/1
Deferment Available? Yes
Length of Deferment: 1 semester
Non-fall Admissions? Yes
Non-fall Application Deadline(s): 11/15, 5/1
Transfer Students Accepted? Yes
Transfer Policy: Maximum number of credits transferable is 12.
Need-Blind Admissions? No
Number of Applications Received: 623
% of Applicants Accepted: 70
% Accepted Who Enrolled: 68
Average GPA: 3.5
Average GMAT: 461
GMAT Range: 400-520
Other Admissions Factors Considered: Computer experience

INTERNATIONAL STUDENTS
TOEFL Required of International Students? Yes
Minimum TOEFL: 550

EMPLOYMENT INFORMATION
Placement Office Available? No
Prominent Alumni: Dr. James Clark, chairman of the board, Netscape Communications; Michael Fitzpatrick, CEO, Rohm & Haas; Erving Johnson, starting center, Milwaukee Bucks; Mike Kettenring, president and general manager, Gillett Broadcasting; Dr. Reuben Arminana, president, Sonoma State University

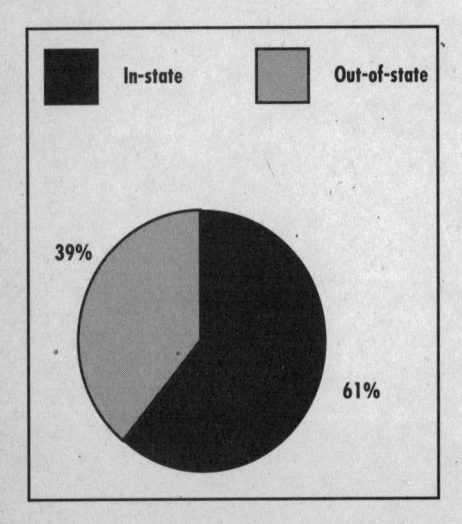

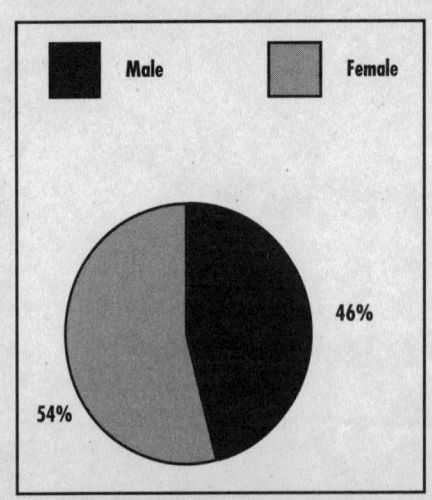

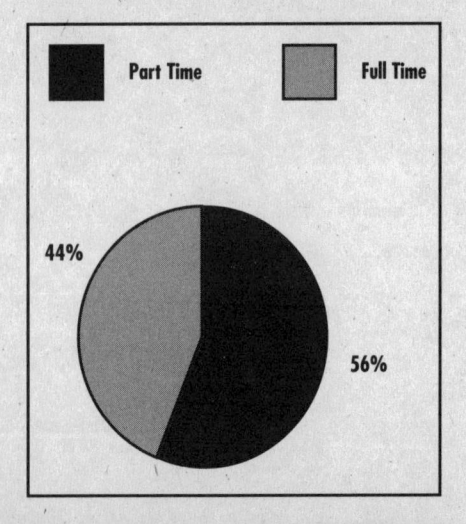

In-state 61% / Out-of-state 39%

Male 54% / Female 46%

Part Time 56% / Full Time 44%

UNIVERSITY OF NORTH CAROLINA — CHAPEL HILL
Kenan-Flagler Business School

Admissions Contact: Sherry Wallace, Director, MBA Admissions
Address: CB #3490, McColl Building, Chapel Hill, NC 27599-3490
Admissions Phone: 919-962-3236 • Admissions Fax: 919-962-0898
Admissions E-mail: mba_info@unc.edu • Web Address: www.kenan-flagler.unc.edu

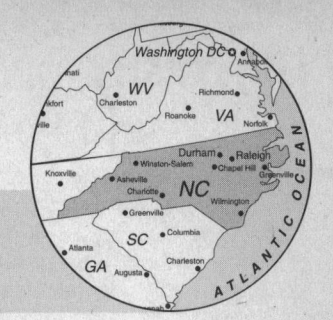

The "pace is very fast and sometimes stressful," but "the faculty are outstanding, jobs are plentiful, students are intelligent, and everyone loves one another" at the Kenan-Flagler Business School at the University of North Carolina at Chapel Hill. Seriously. Students also appreciate the "global focus throughout the curriculum," and the surrounding area provides a "relaxed atmosphere" and a good social scene.

INSTITUTIONAL INFORMATION
Public/Private: Public
Evening Classes Available? Yes
Total Faculty: 93
% Faculty Female: 19
% Faculty Minority: 3
Student/Faculty Ratio: 4:1
Students in Parent Institution: 23,000
Academic Calendar: Semester

PROGRAMS
Degrees Offered: MBA; Executive MBA (24 months evening, 20 months weekend); Global OneMBA (EMBA) (21 months); PhD (4 years); Master of Accounting (12 months)
Joint Degrees: MBA/JD (4 years); MBA/Master of Regional Planning (3 years); MBA/Master of Health Care Administration (3 years); MBA/MS in Information Sciences
Academic Specialties: MBA second-year concentrations in Corporate Finance, Customer and Product Management, Investment Management, Management Consulting, Real Estate, Global Supply Chain Management, Entrepreneurship and Venture Development, Electronic Business and Digital Commerce, Sustainable Enterprise and International Business
Special Opportunities: International internships, global immersion electives, Washington campus, and Launcher (a business incubator)

Study Abroad Options: Dozens of opportunities around the world

STUDENT INFORMATION
Total Business Students: 554
% Female: 30
% Minority: 15
% International: 33
Average Age: 27

COMPUTER AND RESEARCH FACILITIES
Research Facilities: Centers for Entrepreneurship and Technology Venturing, Sustainable Enterprise, Real Estate Development, Community Capitalism, Logistics and Digital Strategy, Economic Development, Emerging Markets, International Business Education and Research, Innovation in Learning, Technology and Advanced Commerce
Computer Facilities: Wireless access, state-of-the-art Trading Room, 40-workstation multimedia classroom, Lexis-Nexis, UMI ProQuest, Hoover's, STAT-USA, additional stand-alone CD-ROM and electronic databases, company-specific information for approximately 2,000 organizations
Campuswide Network? Yes
% of MBA Classrooms Wired: 100
Computer Model Recommended: Laptop
Internet Fee? No

EXPENSES/FINANCIAL AID
Annual Tuition (Resident/Nonresident): $12,082/$25,524
Room & Board (Off Campus): $8,736

Books and Supplies: $4,700
Average Grant: $19,399

ADMISSIONS INFORMATION
Application Fee: $100
Electronic Application? Yes
Regular Application Deadline: 3/8
Regular Notification: 5/3
Length of Deferment: 1 year (emergency only)
Non-fall Admissions? No
Transfer Students Accepted? No
Need-Blind Admissions? Yes
Number of Applications Received: 2,644
% of Applicants Accepted: 24
% Accepted Who Enrolled: 44
Average GPA: 3.3
Average GMAT: 674
Average Years Experience: 5
Other Admissions Factors Considered: Achieving well-balanced class
Minority/Disadvantaged Student Recruitment Programs: Inside Kenan-Flagler Weekend Workshop presented by current minority students; member of the Consortium for Graduate Study in Management; exhibitor at National Black MBA Association annual conference; exhibitor at National Society of Hispanic MBAs annual conference

INTERNATIONAL STUDENTS
TOEFL Required of International Students? Yes
Minimum TOEFL: 600 (250 computer)

EMPLOYMENT INFORMATION

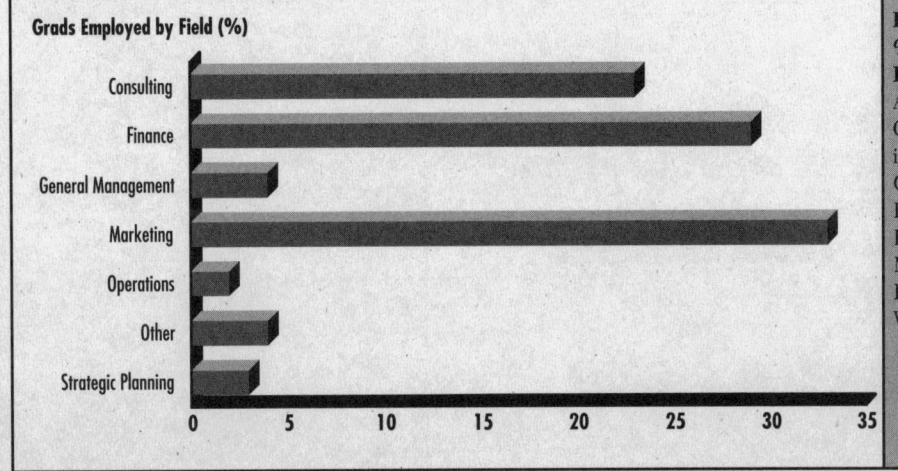

Grads Employed by Field (%)
- Consulting: ~23
- Finance: ~29
- General Management: ~4
- Marketing: ~33
- Operations: ~2
- Other: ~3
- Strategic Planning: ~3

Placement Office Available? Yes
% Employed Within 3 Months: 95
Frequent Employers: Accenture, Bank of America, Bear Stearns, Bristol-Myers Squibb, Chase Bank, Dell Computer, Deloitte Consulting, Dupont, Eli Lilly, Ericsson, First Union, GlaxoSmithKline, Goldman Sachs, Hewlett-Packard, IBM, JP Morgan, Johnson & Johnson, Kraft Foods, Lehman Brothers, McKinsey & Co., Merrill Lynch, Nabisco, Nortel Networks, Procter & Gamble, Salomon Smith Barney, UPS, Walt Disney

UNIVERSITY OF NORTH CAROLINA — CHARLOTTE
Belk College of Business Administration

Admissions Contact: Johnna Watson, Assistant Dean for Enrollment Services
Address: 9201 University City Boulevard, Charlotte, NC 28223-0001
Admissions Phone: 704-687-3366 • Admissions Fax: 704-687-3279
Admissions E-mail: gradadm@email.uncc.edu • Web Address: www.belkcollege.uncc.edu

If you're a North Carolina resident looking to stay in the region and make some good money for low opportunity costs, you'd better take a look at UNC—Charlotte. The Bank of America, a perennially high-placing company on the Fortune 500, is one of the major employers of UNC—Charlotte MBAs, which is fitting, since its world headquarters happen to be in Charlotte.

INSTITUTIONAL INFORMATION
Public/Private: Public
Evening Classes Available? Yes
Total Faculty: 56
% Faculty Female: 23
% Faculty Minority: 9
% Faculty Part Time: 1
Student/Faculty Ratio: 8:1
Students in Parent Institution: 18,308
Academic Calendar: Semester

PROGRAMS
Degrees Offered: Master of Business Administration (2 to 3 years); Master of Accountancy (1 to 2 years); MS in Economics (2 years)
Academic Specialties: UNC Charlotte's MBA program is designed to suit the schedule of working professionals so that students can earn their degree by attending evening classes without interrupting their careers. The program provides a balance of lectures, case analysis, and projects, and a balance between individual and team assignments. Students have the option of pursuing areas of concentration such as Business Finance, Information and Technology Management, E-Business, Management, Marketing, Economics, and Financial Institutions/Commercial Banking. Students may also self-structure their own area of concentration in consultation with the MBA director in areas such as International Business, Health Care, and other areas of interest. A new concentration in Real Estate Development should be available in 2002-2003.
Study Abroad Options: Pending; possible locations may include Mexico, Germany, or France.

STUDENT INFORMATION
Total Business Students: 372
% Full Time: 23
% Female: 32
% Minority: 10
% Out of State: 5
% International: 51
Average Age: 29

COMPUTER AND RESEARCH FACILITIES
Computer Facilities: Compact Disclosure, Dow Jones News Retrieval, National Trade Bank, FirstSearch, Academic Universe, CCH Tax Research Network, Choices II, MasterFile Full Test 1500, ProQuest Direct, Research Bank Web, STAT-USA
Campuswide Network? Yes
% of MBA Classrooms Wired: 50
Computer Model Recommended: No
Internet Fee? No

EXPENSES/FINANCIAL AID
Annual Tuition (Resident/Nonresident): $2,526/$10,456
Tuition Per Credit (Resident/Nonresident): $139/$661
Room & Board (On/Off Campus): $5,100/$5,600
Books and Supplies: $750
Average Grant: $500
Average Loan: $8,500

ADMISSIONS INFORMATION
Application Fee: $35
Electronic Application? No
Regular Application Deadline: 7/1
Regular Notification: Rolling
Length of Deferment: 1 year
Non-fall Application Deadline(s): 11/1 spring
Transfer Policy: Up to 12 credits of graduate-level work from an AACSB-accredited university. This will be considered when the application materials are officially reviewed.
Need-Blind Admissions? Yes
Number of Applications Received: 234
% of Applicants Accepted: 76
% Accepted Who Enrolled: 69
Average GPA: 3.2
GPA Range: 2.9-3.4
Average GMAT: 552
GMAT Range: 500-600
Average Years Experience: 5
Other Admissions Factors Considered: Work experience, extracurricular activities, professional designations

INTERNATIONAL STUDENTS
TOEFL Required of International Students? Yes
Minimum TOEFL: 550 (220 computer)

EMPLOYMENT INFORMATION

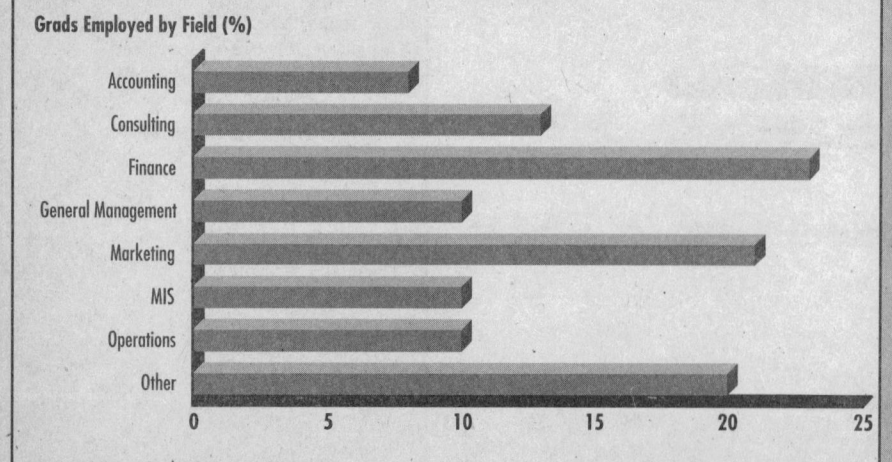

Grads Employed by Field (%)

Field	%
Accounting	8
Consulting	13
Finance	23
General Management	10
Marketing	21
MIS	5
Operations	10
Other	20

Placement Office Available? Yes
% Employed Within 3 Months: 93
Frequent Employers: Bank of America, Wachovia, Duke Energy, Vanguard Group, IBM, BB&T, Accenture, Royal and SunAlliance, KPMG Peat Marwick, Potter and Company
Prominent Alumni: David Hauser, executive VP and treasurer, Duke Energy; Robert Rucho, Senator, North Carolina General Assembly; Manuel Zapata, president, Zapata Engineering

UNIVERSITY OF NORTH CAROLINA—GREENSBORO
Joseph M. Bryan School of Business & Economics

Admissions Contact: Dr. Catherine Holderness, Associate Director for MBA Student Services
Address: PO Box 26165, Greensboro, NC 27402-6165
Admissions Phone: 336-334-5390 • Admissions Fax: 336-334-4209
Admissions E-mail: mba@uncg.edu • Web Address: www.uncg.edu/bae/mba

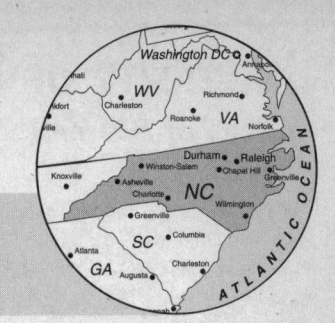

The study abroad opportunities are fat and the tuition is thin at the Bryan School. And even if you don't go international, that's okay. Bryan has brought international to you with a student body that's 50 percent non-American. You can take only evening MBA classes here, so if you're a late riser, welcome home. But if you're a nighttime social bug, you'd better clear your schedule.

INSTITUTIONAL INFORMATION
Public/Private: Public
Evening Classes Available? Yes
Total Faculty: 45
% Faculty Female: 17
% Faculty Minority: 9
% Faculty Part Time: 12
Student/Faculty Ratio: 9:1
Students in Parent Institution: 13,200
Academic Calendar: Semester

PROGRAMS
Degrees Offered: Full-Time MBA (evening, 36 to 48 credits, 2 years); Part-Time MBA (evening, 36 to 48 credits, 2 to 4 years); MSITM (full time, 36 credits, 2 years); MSA (full time, 30 credits, 1.5 years)
Joint Degrees: MSN/MBA (42 to 54 credits, 2 to 5 years)
Academic Specialties: Elective courses in Advanced Accounting, Management Information Systems, and Economics, as well as the usually offered MBA electives in Finance, Marketing, and International Business. The school has internationally recognized faculty in the areas of International Business, Operations Management, and Economics. Students may also take graduate electives in related programs such as the Master of Textile Design and Marketing Program.
Study Abroad Options: Australia, Austria, Canada, Estonia, Finland, France, Germany, Israel, Japan, Mexico, Poland, Spain, Sweden, United Kingdom

STUDENT INFORMATION
Total Business Students: 214
% Female: 40
% Minority: 12
% International: 50
Average Age: 30

COMPUTER AND RESEARCH FACILITIES
Research Facilities: SAP Alliance, Center for Global Business Research and Education, Center for Applied Research
Computer Facilities: There are 3 computer labs in the business school and several other labs across campus, including a computing superlab in the library. An extensive assortment of databases, as well as software, is available to students. We are an SAP Alliance School, and SAP software is loaded in our labs and utilized in classroom instruction. Each classroom is equipped with a computer and projection system.
Campuswide Network? Yes
% of MBA Classrooms Wired: 20
Computer Model Recommended: No
Internet Fee? No

EXPENSES/FINANCIAL AID
Annual Tuition (Resident/Nonresident): $2,675/$12,057
Tuition Per Credit (Resident/Nonresident): $179/$1,173
Books and Supplies: $1,000
Average Grant: $14,000

ADMISSIONS INFORMATION
Application Fee: $35
Electronic Application? Yes
Regular Application Deadline: 7/1
Regular Notification: Rolling
Length of Deferment: 1 year
Non-fall Application Deadline(s): 11/1
Transfer Policy: Good standing at AACSB-accredited institution; may transfer uo to 12 credits.
Need-Blind Admissions? Yes
Number of Applications Received: 175
% of Applicants Accepted: 61
% Accepted Who Enrolled: 67
Average GPA: 3.3
Average GMAT: 573
Average Years Experience: 6
Other Admissions Factors Considered: Maturity achieved through work or other experience, demonstrated ability to succeed academically
Other Schools to Which Students Applied: UNC—Chapel Hill, Wake Forest

INTERNATIONAL STUDENTS
TOEFL Required of International Students? Yes
Minimum TOEFL: 550 (213 computer)

EMPLOYMENT INFORMATION

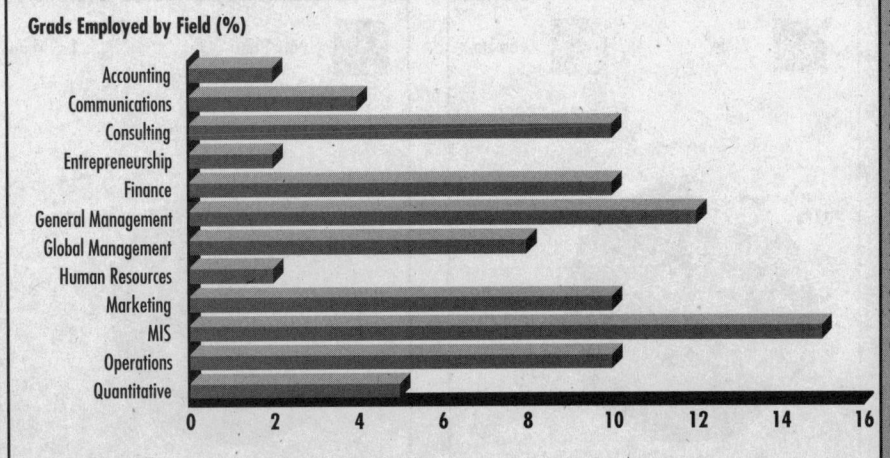

Grads Employed by Field (%)

Field	%
Accounting	4
Communications	2
Consulting	10
Entrepreneurship	2
Finance	10
General Management	12
Global Management	8
Human Resources	2
Marketing	10
MIS	15
Operations	10
Quantitative	5

Placement Office Available? Yes
% Employed Within 3 Months: 95
Frequent Employers: Wachovia, VF Corporation, Sara Lee, Volvo Finance, American Express, Gilbarco Inc., Syngenta, Konica, Moses Cone Health Care System, Center for Creative Leadership, Eveready Battery Co., Kayser-Roth, Stockhausen Inc., Dow Corning, Labcorps, Banner Pharmacaps, North Carolina Baptist Hospital
Prominent Alumni: Nido R. Qubein, founder, chairman, and CEO, Creative Services, Inc.; Sue W. Cole, president, U.S. Trust Company of North Carolina; Joe K. Pickett, chairman and CEO, HomeSide International, Inc.; Lee McGehee Porter III, managing director, Weiss, Peck & Greer, LLC

UNIVERSITY OF NORTH TEXAS
College of Business Administration

Admissions Contact: Denise Galubenski or Konni Stubblefield, Graduate Degree Program Advisors
Address: PO Box 311160, Denton, TX 76203
Admissions Phone: 940-369-8977 • Admissions Fax: 940-369-8978
Admissions E-mail: MBA@cobaf.unt.edu • Web Address: www.coba.unt.edu

Offering more graduate business degrees and degree combos than your average b-school, UNT maintains a people-oriented approach to the MBA. Specializations within the MBA program are operations management science, human resource management, and administrative management, all designed "to present a realistic, relevant, and thorough view of people working in organizations." Denton lies about 25 miles northwest of the so-called Dallas/Fort Worth Metroplex near the shores of one of the many lakes in the area.

INSTITUTIONAL INFORMATION
Public/Private: Public
Evening Classes Available? Yes
Total Faculty: 99
Student/Faculty Ratio: 30:1
Students in Parent Institution: 27,000
Academic Calendar: Semester

PROGRAMS
Degrees Offered: Master of Business Administration (MBA) (up to 6 years); Master of Science in Accounting (MS) (up to 6 years); Master of Science (MS) (up to 6 years); Executive Master of Business Administration (EMBA) (up to 20 months)
Joint Degrees: MBA Operations Management Science/MS Engineering Technology (48 credits); MBA (any professional field)/MS Merchandising (54 credits); MBA (any professional field)/MS Hospitality Management (54 credits)
Study Abroad Options: Mexico, United Kingdom

STUDENT INFORMATION
Total Business Students: 412
% Full Time: 45
% Female: 37
% Minority: 8
% Out of State: 1
% International: 15

COMPUTER AND RESEARCH FACILITIES
Computer Facilities: More computers per student than other comparable Texas institutions, 14 general-access computer labs with more than 550 microcomputers (including 1 lab available 24 hours and 1 adaptive lab for students with special needs)
Campuswide Network? Yes
Internet Fee? No

EXPENSES/FINANCIAL AID
Tuition Per Credit (Resident/Nonresident): $146/$272

ADMISSIONS INFORMATION
Application Fee: $25
Electronic Application? Yes
Regular Application Deadline: Rolling
Regular Notification: Rolling
Deferment Available? Yes
Length of Deferment: 3 semesters
Non-fall Admissions? Yes
Non-fall Application Deadline(s): Spring, May mini-mester, summer I, summer II
Transfer Students Accepted? Yes
Transfer Policy: Transfer applicants must meet the same university application deadline. Only 9 to 9 credits may transfer into our program. These credits will be determined by the departmental advisor.
Need-Blind Admissions? No
Number of Applications Received: 324
% of Applicants Accepted: 43
% Accepted Who Enrolled: 60
Average GPA: 2.9
Average GMAT: 560
Other Admissions Factors Considered: GRE scores accepted

INTERNATIONAL STUDENTS
TOEFL Required of International Students? Yes
Minimum TOEFL: 550 (213 computer)

EMPLOYMENT INFORMATION
Placement Office Available? Yes

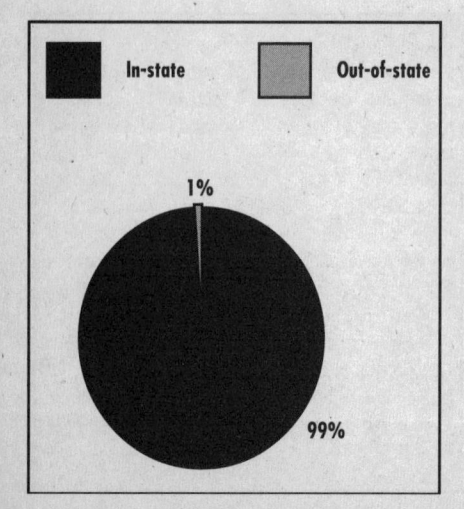

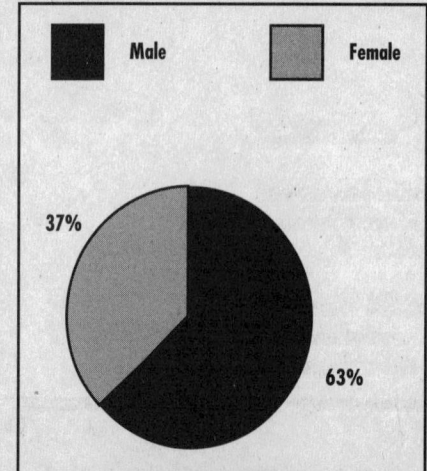

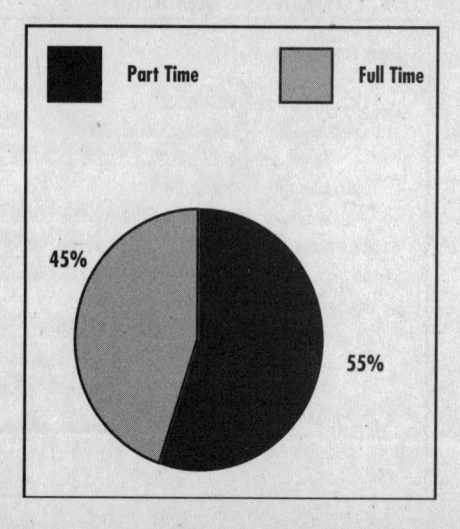

In-state 99% / Out-of-state 1%

Male 63% / Female 37%

Part Time 55% / Full Time 45%

UNIVERSITY OF NOTRE DAME
Mendoza College of Business

Admissions Contact: Hayden Estrada IV, Director of Admissions
Address: 276 Mendoza College of Business, Notre Dame, IN 46556-4656
Admissions Phone: 219-631-8488 • Admissions Fax: 219-631-8800
Admissions E-mail: mba1@nd.edu • Web Address: www.nd.edu/~mba

Would it surprise you to learn that Notre Dame's "small" and "well-rounded" College of Business Administration takes a traditional approach to the MBA? We hope not. Among the academic departments here, finance gets the highest marks among students, and management scores high as well. Students tell us "the people are, without question, the greatest strength of this school. People care about one another and all learning takes place in that context."

INSTITUTIONAL INFORMATION
Public/Private: Private
Evening Classes Available? No
Total Faculty: 92
% Faculty Female: 16
Student/Faculty Ratio: 4:1
Students in Parent Institution: 10,800
Academic Calendar: Semester

PROGRAMS
Degrees Offered: Executive MBA (2 years), MS in Administration (3 years), MS in Accountancy (1 year)
Joint Degrees: Juris Doctor/MBA (4 years), Master of Engineering/MBA (2 years), MS/MBA (2 years)
Study Abroad Options: Instituto Latino Americano de Doctrina y Estudios Sociales (ILADES), Santiago, Chile; Notre Dame London Centre, London, England

STUDENT INFORMATION
Total Business Students: 332
% Full Time: 100
% Female: 30
% Minority: 5
% International: 30
Average Age: 27

COMPUTER AND RESEARCH FACILITIES
Research Facilities: Irich Angles, Fanning Communication Center, Gigot Center
Computer Facilities: Dial-up to NT network
Campuswide Network? Yes
% of MBA Classrooms Wired: 100
Internet Fee? No

EXPENSES/FINANCIAL AID
Annual Tuition: $24,969
Room & Board (On Campus): $4,800
Books and Supplies: $1,300
Average Grant: $14,000
Average Loan: $28,000

ADMISSIONS INFORMATION
Application Fee: $100
Electronic Application? Yes
Early Decision Application Deadline: 11/15
Regular Application Deadline: 1/15
Regular Notification: 5/30
Deferment Available? Yes
Length of Deferment: 1 year
Non-fall Admissions? No
Transfer Students Accepted? No
Need-Blind Admissions? Yes
Number of Applications Received: 813
% of Applicants Accepted: 29
% Accepted Who Enrolled: 82
Average GPA: 3.2
GPA Range: 3.1-3.8
Average GMAT: 659
GMAT Range: 610-710
Average Years Experience: 5
Other Admissions Factors Considered: Desire to attend Notre Dame, a track record of community service and leadership
Minority/Disadvantaged Student Recruitment Programs: Ford Review Weekend
Other Schools to Which Students Applied: Northwestern University, University of Michigan, University of Texas—Austin, Vanderbilt University

INTERNATIONAL STUDENTS
TOEFL Required of International Students? Yes
Minimum TOEFL: 600

EMPLOYMENT INFORMATION

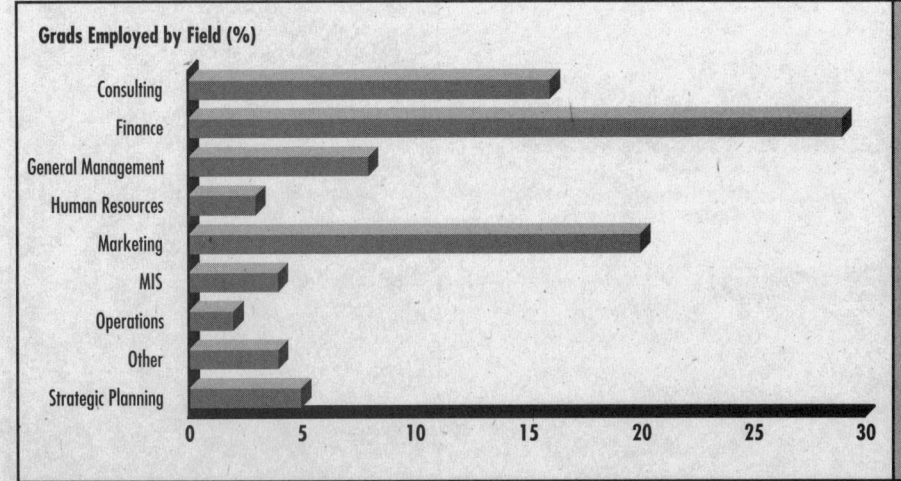

Grads Employed by Field (%)
- Consulting: ~16
- Finance: ~29
- General Management: ~8
- Human Resources: ~2
- Marketing: ~20
- MIS: ~3
- Operations: ~2
- Other: ~4
- Strategic Planning: ~5

Placement Office Available? Yes
% Employed Within 3 Months: 97
Frequent Employers: Ford, IBM, Dell, Sprint, Intel, Corning, Andersen Consulting, Procter & Gamble, PricewaterhouseCoopers LLP, Deloitte & Touche LLP, Hewlett Packard, CAP Gemini Ernst & Young LLC
Prominent Alumni: Marc Fields, Raytheon; Justin Johnson, Major League Baseball

UNIVERSITY OF OREGON
Charles H. Lundquist College of Business

Admissions Contact: Ms. Laura Balaty, Admissions Clerk
Address: 300 Gilbert Hall, 1208 University of Oregon, Eugene, OR 97403-1208
Admissions Phone: 541-346-1462 • Admissions Fax: 541-346-0073
Admissions E-mail: mbainfo@biz.uoregon.edu • Web Address: http://biz.uoregon.edu

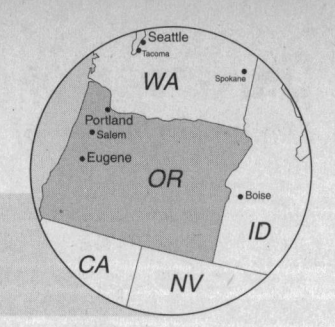

The rain is almost relentless in Eugene, but so is the praise that Lundquist receives from industry watchdogs like Forbes and Success magazines. The faculty are well honored and the student body is active in intercollegiate business competitions. You won't find too many consultant types coming out of Lundquist, but if sports marketing is what you want to do, you've hit the mother lode. The Warsaw Sports Marketing Center is instrumental in getting Lundquist MBAs hired by the likes of the NFL, the NBA, VISA, the U.S. Olympic Committee, SFX, EA Sports, and Yahoo!

INSTITUTIONAL INFORMATION
Public/Private: Public
Evening Classes Available? No
Total Faculty: 43
% Faculty Female: 16
% Faculty Minority: 22
% Faculty Part Time: 16
Student/Faculty Ratio: 4:1
Students in Parent Institution: 17,843
Academic Calendar: Quarter

PROGRAMS
Degrees Offered: MBA (2 years); Master of Accounting (1 year); PhD in Accounting, Decision Sciences, Finance, Management, Marketing (average of 5 years)
Joint Degrees: Juris Doctor/MBA (4 years), MA/MBA in International Studies or Asian Studies (3 years)
Academic Specialties: Corporate Finance, Financial Institutions, Sports, Business Services, Marketing and Management, International Strategic Management and Marketing, Entrepreneurship, Environmental Management
Study Abroad Options: China, Denmark, Finland, France, Germany, Japan, Russia, South Korea

STUDENT INFORMATION
Total Business Students: 139
% Full Time: 100
% Female: 26
% Minority: 6
% Out of State: 30
% International: 29
Average Age: 27

COMPUTER AND RESEARCH FACILITIES
Research Facilities: Lundquist Center for Entrepreneurship, Lundquist Center Student Business Incubator, James Warsaw Sports Marketing Center, LCB Business Technology Center
Computer Facilities: LCB Business Technology Center, University Computing Center, University Library and Information Technology System, including the central Knight Library
Campuswide Network? Yes
% of MBA Classrooms Wired: 100
Computer Model Recommended: Laptop
Internet Fee? No

EXPENSES/FINANCIAL AID
Annual Tuition (Resident/Nonresident): $7,056/$11,958
Room & Board (On/Off Campus): $5,750/$9,800
Books and Supplies: $831
Average Grant: $5,000
Average Loan: $17,209
% Receiving Financial Aid: 65
% Receiving Aid Their First Year: 61

ADMISSIONS INFORMATION
Application Fee: $50
Electronic Application? Yes
Early Decision Application Deadline: 12/15
Early Decision Notification: 1/31
Regular Application Deadline: 4/15
Regular Notification: 5/15
Deferment Available? Yes
Length of Deferment: 1 year
Non-fall Admissions? No
Transfer Students Accepted? No
Need-Blind Admissions? Yes
Number of Applications Received: 233
% of Applicants Accepted: 46
% Accepted Who Enrolled: 52
Average GPA: 3.2
GPA Range: 2.9-3.4
Average GMAT: 601
GMAT Range: 570-640
Average Years Experience: 3
Minority/Disadvantaged Student Recruitment Programs: Minority scholarships
Other Schools to Which Students Applied: Arizona State University, Ohio State University, University of California—Davis, University of California—Irvine, University of Colorado—Boulder, University of Illinois, University of Washington

INTERNATIONAL STUDENTS
TOEFL Required of International Students? Yes
Minimum TOEFL: 600 (250 computer)

EMPLOYMENT INFORMATION

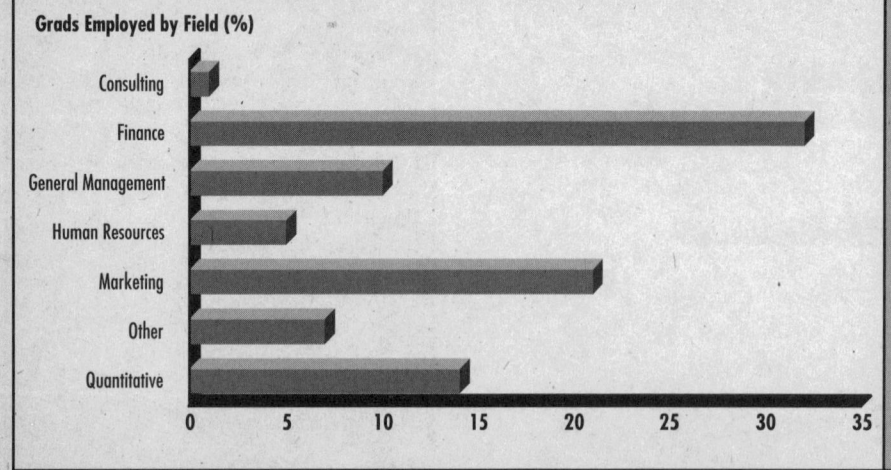

Grads Employed by Field (%)

Field	%
Consulting	1
Finance	32
General Management	10
Human Resources	7
Marketing	21
Other	7
Quantitative	14

Placement Office Available? Yes
% Employed Within 3 Months: 96
Frequent Employers: Hewlett-Packard Co., Intel Corp., Wells Fargo Bank, Enron Energy, Tektronix, Xerox, Lattice Semiconductor, Bear Creek Corp.
Prominent Alumni: Bard Buneas, CEO and president, Sirius America Insurance Co.; David Petrone, former vice chair, Wells Fargo Bank; Richard Wills, president and CEO, Tektronix Inc.

UNIVERSITY OF OXFORD
Saïd Business School

Admissions Contact: Alison Owen, Planning and Admissions Manager
Address: Saïd Business School, Park End Street, Oxford, OX1 1HP United Kingdom
Admissions Phone: 011-44-186-528-8830 • Admissions Fax: 011-44-186-528-8831
Admissions E-mail: enquiries@sbs.ox.ac.uk • Web Address: www.sbs.ox.ac.uk

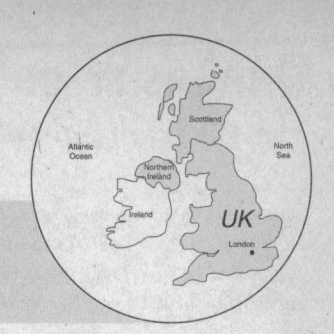

INSTITUTIONAL INFORMATION
Evening Classes Available? No
Total Faculty: 29
% Faculty Female: 10
Student/Faculty Ratio: 4:1

PROGRAMS
Degrees Offered: MBA (1 year); MS in Management Research (1 year); MS in Industrial Relation and Human Resource Management (1 year); DPhil in Management Studies (Doctoral Program) (3 to 4 years)
Academic Specialties: Entrepreneurship, Finance

STUDENT INFORMATION
Total Business Students: 120
% Female: 16
% International: 85
Average Age: 29

COMPUTER AND RESEARCH FACILITIES
Computer Facilities: In-house Virtual Library; gateway to business information resources including Fame, Amadeus, Mintel, Profound, EIU Country Data, Reuters Business Briefing, Reuters Business Insight, Business Source Premier, ProQuest Direct, Datastream Advance, Bloomberg; access to Oxford University database resources using Oxlip
Campuswide Network? Yes
% of MBA Classrooms Wired: 100
Computer Model Recommended: Laptop
Internet Fee? No

EXPENSES/FINANCIAL AID
Annual Tuition: $27,440
Room & Board (On Campus): $11,200
Books and Supplies: $700

ADMISSIONS INFORMATION
Application Fee: $140
Electronic Application? Yes
Regular Application Deadline: 6/5
Regular Notification: 1/7
Deferment Available? Yes
Length of Deferment: 1 year
Non-fall Admissions? Yes
Non-fall Application Deadline(s): Winter/spring
Transfer Students Accepted? No
Need-Blind Admissions? Yes
Number of Applications Received: 400
% of Applicants Accepted: 30
% Accepted Who Enrolled: 100
Average GPA: 3.5
Average GMAT: 671
Average Years Experience: 5

INTERNATIONAL STUDENTS
TOEFL Required of International Students? Yes
Minimum TOEFL: 600 (250 computer)

EMPLOYMENT INFORMATION

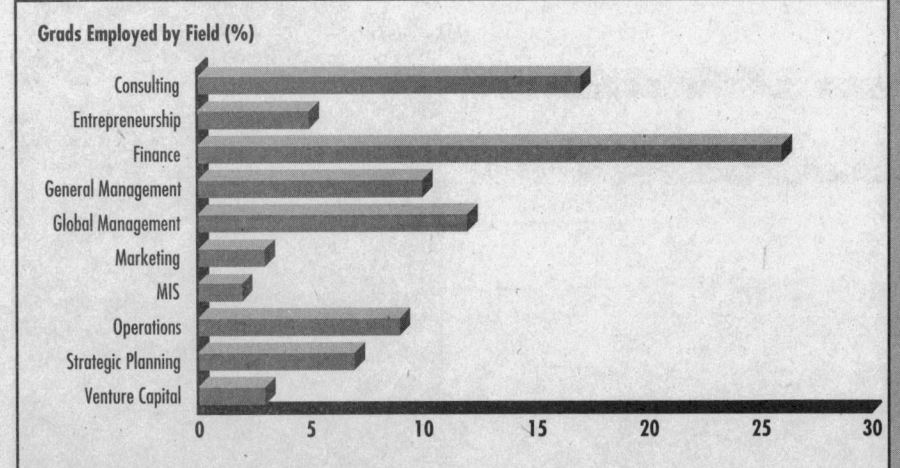

Grads Employed by Field (%)

- Consulting: ~17
- Entrepreneurship: ~3
- Finance: ~26
- General Management: ~11
- Global Management: ~12
- Marketing: ~4
- MIS: ~1
- Operations: ~9
- Strategic Planning: ~7
- Venture Capital: ~3

Placement Office Available? Yes
% Employed Within 3 Months: 75
Frequent Employers: Finance and banking: Barclays Capital, Bear Stearns, Citibank, Credit Suisse First Boston, Deutsche Bank, Goldman Sachs, HSBC, Lehman Brothers, Merrill Lynch, Morgan Stanley Dean Witter, Pricewaterhouse-Coopers, Royal Bank of Scotland; management consulting: AT Kearney, Bain & Co., Boston Consulting Group, IBM Consulting, McKinsey & Co., Oxford Analytical, PRTM, Roland Berger; diversified industries: Electrocomponents, Eli Lilly, Lucent Technologies, Nortel Networks, P&O, Reuters Group, Shell International, Virgin

UNIVERSITY OF PENNSYLVANIA
The Wharton School, Graduate Division

Admissions Contact: Rosemaria Martinelli, Director of Admissions and Financial Aid
Address: 102 Vance Hall, 3733 Spruce Street, Philadelphia, PA 19104-6361
Admissions Phone: 215-898-6183 • Admissions Fax: 215-898-0120
Admissions E-mail: mba.admissions@wharton.upenn.edu • Web Address: www.wharton.upenn.edu/mba

The Wharton School's MBA program is the Rolls Royce of business programs: It's big, it's expensive, its name impresses people, and it offers many luxurious options. Wharton built its reputation as a premier finance program, and finance continues to hold a prominent place here, but the other concentrations are outstanding as well (the entrepreneurial program is reportedly "a real standout"). Students need not look far for jobs because "all the best companies come here," which makes the opportunities "unbelievable."

INSTITUTIONAL INFORMATION
Public/Private: Private
Evening Classes Available? No
Total Faculty: 190
Student/Faculty Ratio: 8:1
Students in Parent Institution: 20,000
Academic Calendar: Semester

PROGRAMS
Degrees Offered: MBA (2 years full time)
Joint Degrees: MBA/JD; MBA/MD; MBA/DMD-Dental; MBA/MSE Engineering; Communication; MBA/MA; MBA/MSW; MBA/PhD; MBA/Animal Health Economics Training Program; MBA/VMD (Veterinary); MBA/MSN (Nursing)
Academic Specialties: From its founding in 1881 as the world's first school of management, Wharton has always been the leader in extending the frontiers of management education. The program builds upon Wharton's substantial strengths—our expertise across the widest range of areas, our extensive global initiatives, and our long-standing commitment to innovation and entrepreneurship.
Special Opportunities: Wharton's Sol C. Snider Entrepreneurial Center; Lauder Institute's Program in International Studies (paid consulting available); summer pre-enrollment "pre-term"
Study Abroad Options: Australia, Brazil, England, France, Italy, Japan, Netherlands, Philippines, Spain, Sweden, Thailand

STUDENT INFORMATION
Total Business Students: 1,573
% Female: 31
% Minority: 21
% International: 36
Average Age: 28

COMPUTER AND RESEARCH FACILITIES
Research Facilities: Leonard Davis Institute of Health Economics, Sol C. Snider Entrepreneurial Research Center, SEI Center for Advanced Studies in Management, Samuel Zell and Robert Lurie Real Estate Center, Weiss Center for International Financial Research, Small Business Development Center
Computer Facilities: The school provides students with access to a wide range of specialized instructional software and data. These resources are available through Wharton's computer labs and group workstations at dedicated financial information terminals and from home over Wharton's Intranet.
Campuswide Network? Yes
% of MBA Classrooms Wired: 50
Computer Model Recommended: Laptop
Internet Fee? No

EXPENSES/FINANCIAL AID
Annual Tuition: $28,970
Books and Supplies: $1,682
Average Grant: $5,000
% Receiving Financial Aid: 87
% Receiving Aid Their First Year: 60

ADMISSIONS INFORMATION
Application Fee: $175
Electronic Application? Yes
Regular Application Deadline: 4/10
Regular Notification: 4/30
Length of Deferment: Case-by-case basis
Non-fall Admissions? No
Transfer Students Accepted? No
Need-Blind Admissions? Yes
Number of Applications Received: 7,274
% of Applicants Accepted: 26
% Accepted Who Enrolled: 42
Average GPA: 3.5
Average GMAT: 703
Average Years Experience: 5
Other Admissions Factors Considered: Timing and overall presentation of candidacy
Minority/Disadvantaged Student Recruitment Programs: Outreach through targeted repetitions and programs.

INTERNATIONAL STUDENTS
TOEFL Required of International Students? Yes

EMPLOYMENT INFORMATION

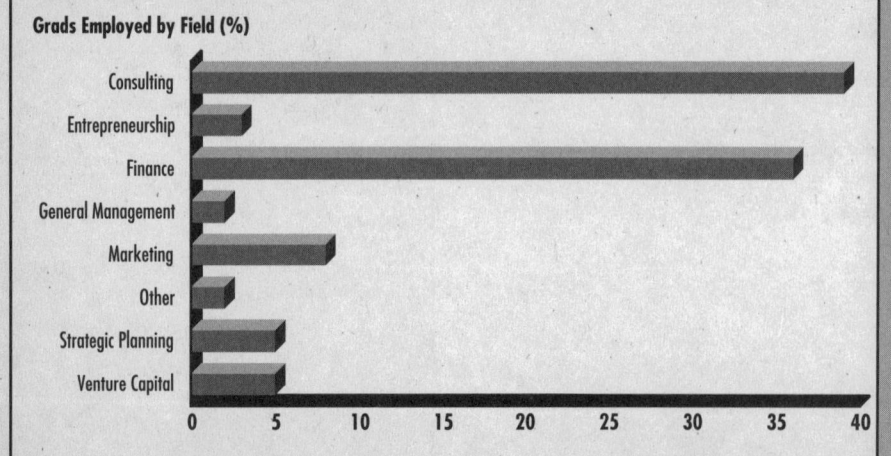

Grads Employed by Field (%)

Field	%
Consulting	~40
Entrepreneurship	~3
Finance	~37
General Management	~2
Marketing	~8
Other	~3
Strategic Planning	~3
Venture Capital	~4

Placement Office Available? Yes
% Employed Within 3 Months: 91
Frequent Employers: McKinsey & Co., Bain & Co., Goldman Sachs, Boston Consulting Group, JPMorgan Chase, Credit Suisse First Boston, Morgan Stanley, Deloitte Consulting, Merrill Lynch, Accenture, Lehman Brothers, Booz Allen Hamilton, AT Kearney, Deutsche Bank Alex. Brown, Siebel Systems Inc., Salomon Smith Barney, Monitor Group, Microsoft Corporation
Prominent Alumni: J.D. Power III, founder and chairman, JD Power & Associates; Klaus Zumwinkel, chairman and CEO, Deutsche Post AG; Lewis Platt, former chairman, Hewlett-Packard; Arthur D. Wollins, president and CEO, Medtronic, Inc.

UNIVERSITY OF PITTSBURGH
Katz Graduate School of Business

Admissions Contact: Kelly R. Wilson, Director, Office of Enrollment Management
Address: 272 Mervis Hall, Roberto Clemente Drive, Pittsburgh, PA 15260
Admissions Phone: 412-648-1700 • Admissions Fax: 412-648-1659
Admissions E-mail: mba@katz.pitt.edu • Web Address: www.katz.pitt.edu

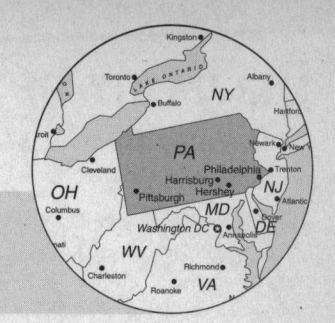

The University of Pittsburgh's Katz Graduate School of Business offers an "aggressive" one-year program that students describe as "an academic boot camp" complete with an "intense workload" and midterms or finals "every three to four weeks." It's a tremendous opportunity to jump-start a business career, though. You can also stay here for two years and pretty easily graduate with a dual degree.

INSTITUTIONAL INFORMATION
Public/Private: Public
Evening Classes Available? Yes
Total Faculty: 92
% Faculty Part Time: 27
Student/Faculty Ratio: 40:1
Students in Parent Institution: 36,000
Academic Calendar: Module

PROGRAMS
Degrees Offered: PhD
Joint Degrees: MBA/MA in areas of specialization such as East Asia, Latin America, and eastern Europe; MBA/MS Information Systems; JD/MBA (Business and Law); MBA/Master of Public and International Affairs (MPIA)
Academic Specialties: Finance, Marketing, Information Systems, Strategy
Special Opportunities: Study abroad modules in eastern and western Europe and Latin America; international research (14-week course) in various countries (recently Austria and Czech and Slovak Republics); summer internships abroad
Study Abroad Options: Czech Republic, Slovak Republic, Brazil

STUDENT INFORMATION
Total Business Students: 633
% Full Time: 22
% Female: 32
% Minority: 8
% Out of State: 80
% International: 44
Average Age: 27

COMPUTER AND RESEARCH FACILITIES
Research Facilities: Katz Center for Research on Contracts and the Structure of Enterprise, Institute for Industrial Competitiveness, International Business Centers, Center for International Enterprise Development
Computer Facilities: Databases include ABI/Inform Global, Academic Universe, Barron's, Business Source Elite, CCH Business Research Network, CCH Human Resources Research Network, and CCH Tax Research Network. Two labs in business school: 56 ported stations for laptops and 40 Pentium desktops. Eight general-access labs on campus: 377 Windows NT, 265 Macintosh, and 58 Sun Spark Ultra UNIX workstations.
Campuswide Network? Yes
Computer Model Recommended: Laptop
Internet Fee? No

EXPENSES/FINANCIAL AID
Annual Tuition (Resident/Nonresident): $19,707/$33,570
Tuition Per Credit (Resident/Nonresident): $542/$1,016
Room & Board (Off Campus): $12,500
Books and Supplies: $1,400
Average Grant: $10,000

ADMISSIONS INFORMATION
Application Fee: $50
Electronic Application? Yes
Regular Application Deadline: 1/15
Regular Notification: 3/15
Deferment Available? No
Non-fall Admissions? No
Transfer Students Accepted? Yes
Transfer Policy: Matching course work, up to 17 credits from an AACSB MBA program, provided that credits were not used to complete a previous MBA degree
Need-Blind Admissions? Yes
Number of Applications Received: 562
% of Applicants Accepted: 48
% Accepted Who Enrolled: 50
Average GPA: 3.2
Average GMAT: 621
Average Years Experience: 4
Other Admissions Factors Considered: Any graduate education completed
Minority/Disadvantaged Student Recruitment Programs: Presidential Fellowship Program, a scholarship opportunity for graduates of historically black colleges and universities; participation in destination MBA; alumni referral; Roberto Clemente Association

INTERNATIONAL STUDENTS
TOEFL Required of International Students? Yes
Minimum TOEFL: 600 (250 computer)

EMPLOYMENT INFORMATION

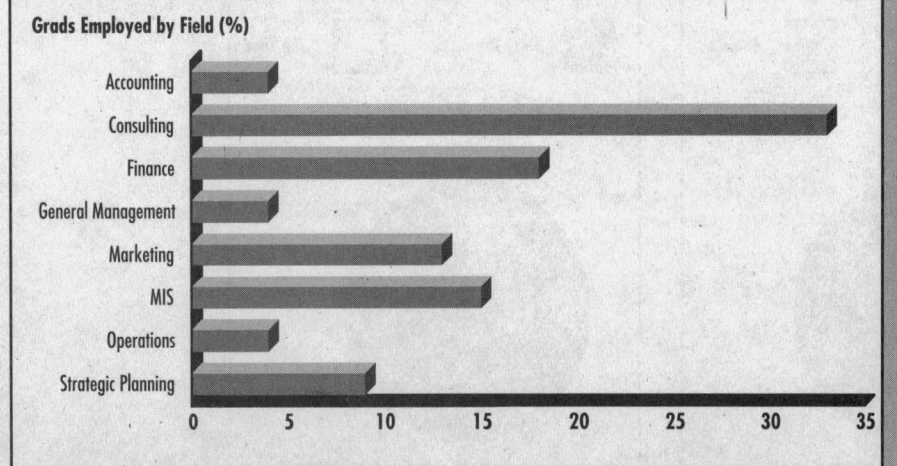

Grads Employed by Field (%)

Field	%
Accounting	3
Consulting	33
Finance	18
General Management	4
Marketing	13
MIS	15
Operations	4
Strategic Planning	9

Placement Office Available? Yes
% Employed Within 3 Months: 83
Frequent Employers: Buchanan Ingersoll; Kirkpatrick & Lockhart; Reed, Smith, Shaw & McClay; Morgan, Lewis & Bockius; Jones, Day, Reavis & Pogue; Pepper Hamilton; Milbank Tweed

UNIVERSITY OF RHODE ISLAND
College of Business Administration

Admissions Contact: Lisa Lancellotta, Coordinator, MBA Programs
Address: 210 Flagg Road, Kingston, RI 02881
Admissions Phone: 401-874-5000 • Admissions Fax: 401-874-7047
Admissions E-mail: mba@etal.uri.edu • Web Address: www.cba.uri.edu/graduate/mba.htm

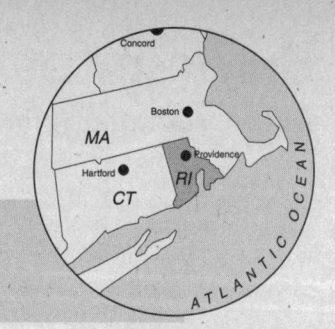

The quintessential New England campus is what you'll find at the University of Rhode Island: somewhere between rural and urban, just the right size, and not far from another major hub (in this case, both New York and Boston are accessible). The College of Business Administration aims to "instill excellence, confidence, and strong leadership skills" in its grads, emphasizing critical thinking and personal responsibility. MBA students at URI can choose between a one-year full-time program in Kingston, a part-time program in Providence, or the Executive MBA with integrated weekend sessions held at the W. Alton Jones campus.

INSTITUTIONAL INFORMATION
Public/Private: Public
Evening Classes Available? Yes
Total Faculty: 55
% Faculty Female: 20
Student/Faculty Ratio: 4:1
Academic Calendar: Semester

PROGRAMS
Degrees Offered: MBA (1 year, August-July); Providence Evening MBA (4 years average); Executive MBA (18 months, August-February); MS Accounting (2 years average); PhD (4 years average)
Joint Degrees: MBA/PharmD (6 years); MBA/Marine Affairs (5 years); MBA/Engineering (5 years)
Academic Specialties: Our 1-year full-time MBA program takes the traditional curriculum and integrates the materials into modules. Modules include Basic Conceptual and Functional Module, Developing/Growing a Business Module, and Strategic Thinking.
Study Abroad Options: Germany—Braunschweig University; France—Marseille University

STUDENT INFORMATION
Total Business Students: 220
% Female: 45
% Minority: 9
% International: 33

COMPUTER AND RESEARCH FACILITIES
Research Facilities: Institute for International Business, Research Institute for Telecommunications and Information Marketing, Research Center in Business and Economics, Pacific-Basin Capital Markets Research Center
Computer Facilities: Computer facilities are available at all URI campuses. Students get a student ID, which lets them access any computer lab. Laptops are given to students in the Executive MBA program.
Campuswide Network? Yes
Computer Model Recommended: Laptop
Internet Fee? No

EXPENSES/FINANCIAL AID
Annual Tuition (Resident/Nonresident): $7,800/$22,155
Tuition Per Credit (Resident/Nonresident): $209/$599
Books and Supplies: $2,000

ADMISSIONS INFORMATION
Application Fee: $30
Electronic Application? No
Regular Application Deadline: 6/1
Regular Notification: Rolling
Deferment Available? Yes
Length of Deferment: 1 year
Non-fall Admissions? Yes
Non-fall Application Deadline(s): 11/15 spring (part time only)
Transfer Students Accepted? Yes
Transfer Policy: Can transfer up to 20 percent of total credits from another AACSB-accredited college/university
Need-Blind Admissions? Yes
Number of Applications Received: 126
% of Applicants Accepted: 78
% Accepted Who Enrolled: 82
Average GPA: 3.0
Average GMAT: 620
Other Schools to Which Students Applied: Babson College, Boston College, Boston University, Bryant College, Northeastern University, Suffolk University, University of Connecticut

INTERNATIONAL STUDENTS
TOEFL Required of International Students? Yes
Minimum TOEFL: 575 (233 computer)

EMPLOYMENT INFORMATION
Placement Office Available? Yes
% Employed Within 3 Months: 100

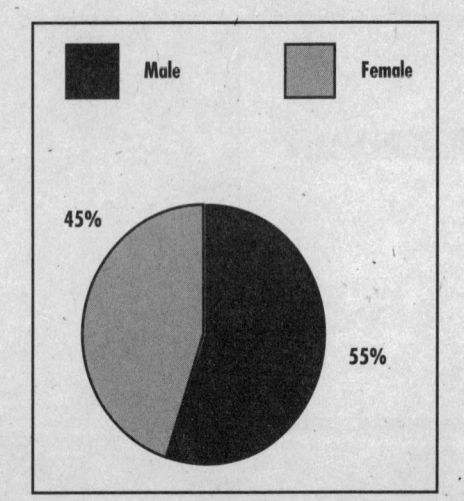

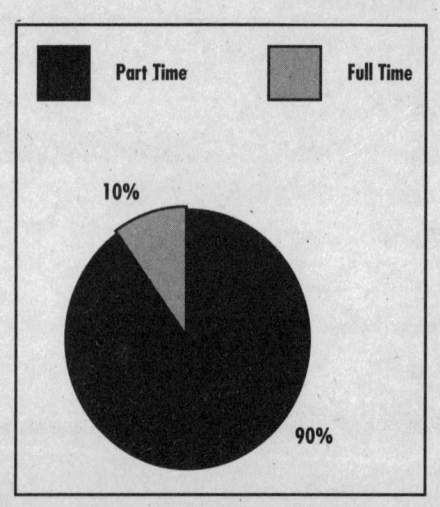

UNIVERSITY OF ROCHESTER
William E. Simon Graduate School of Business Administration

Admissions Contact: Pamela A. Black-Colton, Assistant Dean for MBA Admissions and Administration
Address: 305 Schlegel Hall, Rochester, NY 14627
Admissions Phone: 585-275-3533 • Admissions Fax: 585-271-3907
Admissions E-mail: mbaadm@simon.rochester.edu • Web Address: www.simon.rochester.edu

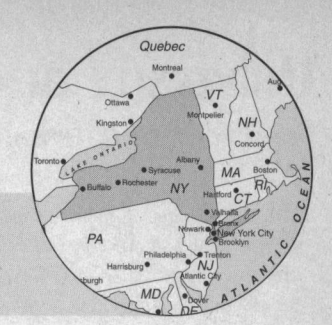

Finance is the magic word at the University of Rochester's Simon Graduate School of Business Administration in "beautiful" upstate New York, where the "world-class, research-oriented faculty" happen to be "excellent teachers." The vaunted finance faculty here feature Gregg A. Jarrell, onetime chief economist of the U.S. Securities and Exchange Commission, and Clifford W. Smith Jr., author of numerous books and winner of even more teaching awards. Accounting is the other standout department at Simon.

INSTITUTIONAL INFORMATION
Public/Private: Private
Evening Classes Available? Yes
Total Faculty: 64
% Faculty Female: 14
% Faculty Minority: 1
% Faculty Part Time: 12
Student/Faculty Ratio: 14:1
Students in Parent Institution: 8,351
Academic Calendar: Quarter

PROGRAMS
Degrees Offered: MBA (2 years); PhD (5 years); MS in Business Administration (9 months)
Joint Degrees: MBA/Master of Public Health (3 years), MD/MBA (5 years)
Academic Specialties: 14 concentrations, ranging from the more broad-based, such as Finance, to the more specialized, such as E-Commerce and Health Care Management.
Special Opportunities: VISION, Coach-Mentor Program, Broaden Your Horizons Intercultural Seminar Series, Fredrick Kalmbach Executive Seminar Series, International Exchange Programs
Study Abroad Options: Argentina, Australia, Belgium, Finland, China, Israel, Japan, Norway

STUDENT INFORMATION
Total Business Students: 703
% Full Time: 68
% Female: 25
% Minority: 10
% Out of State: 68
% International: 54
Average Age: 28

COMPUTER AND RESEARCH FACILITIES
Research Facilities: The Bradley Policy Research Center
Computer Facilities: More than 72 microcomputers with high-speed Internet access as well as laser printing and other output devices. The Simon School Intranet serves as a portal to a wide array of databases and information services.
Campuswide Network? Yes
% of MBA Classrooms Wired: 50
Computer Model Recommended: Laptop
Internet Fee? No

EXPENSES/FINANCIAL AID
Annual Tuition: $28,320
Tuition Per Credit: $944
Room & Board: $8,185
Books and Supplies: $1,425
Average Grant: $11,134
Average Loan: $25,350

ADMISSIONS INFORMATION
Application Fee: $90
Electronic Application? Yes
Regular Application Deadline: 6/1
Regular Notification: 7/1
Deferment Available? No
Non-fall Application Deadline(s): 11/1 winter
Transfer Students Accepted? Yes
Transfer Policy: No more than 9 credits
Need-Blind Admissions? Yes
Number of Applications Received: 1,428
% of Applicants Accepted: 31
% Accepted Who Enrolled: 42
Average GPA: 3.3
GPA Range: 3.1-3.8
Average GMAT: 640
GMAT Range: 560-740
Average Years Experience: 5
Minority/Disadvantaged Student Recruitment Programs: Member of the Consortium for Graduate Study in Management
Other Schools to Which Students Applied: Carnegie Mellon, Columbia, Cornell, NYU, Penn

INTERNATIONAL STUDENTS
TOEFL Required of International Students? Yes
Minimum TOEFL: 600 (250 computer)

EMPLOYMENT INFORMATION

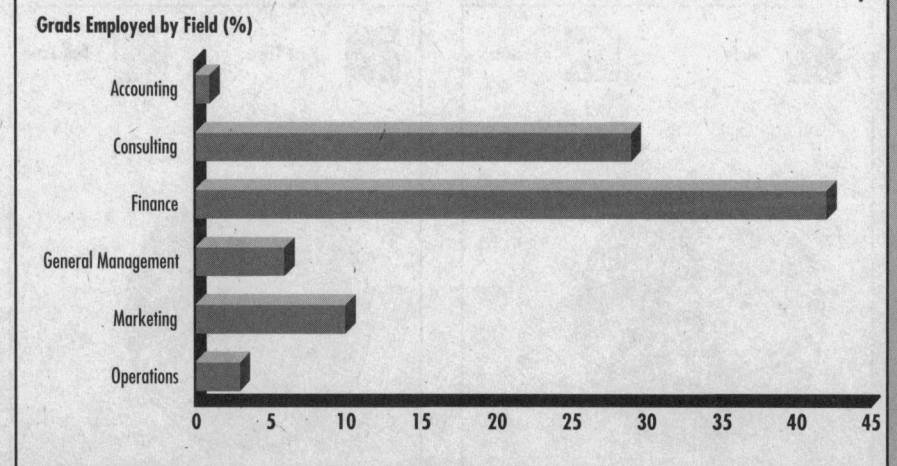

Grads Employed by Field (%)

Field	%
Accounting	~2
Consulting	~30
Finance	~43
General Management	~6
Marketing	~10
Operations	~3

Placement Office Available? Yes
% Employed Within 3 Months: 97
Frequent Employers: AT Kearney; Accenture; Dresdner Kleinwort Benson; Eastman Kodak Company; ExxonMobil; Intel; JP Morgan Chase; Kraft Foods; Oasis Venture Capital; Pershing; Pratt & Whitney; SCM LLC; Standard and Poor's; State Street Bank & Trust; Stern Stewart & Co.; SunTrust Bank; TD Securities; United Technologies; UTC
Prominent Alumni: Richard Couch, CEO, Diablo Management Group; Jack Davies, senior advisor, America Online; Janina Pawlowski, president, E-Loan

UNIVERSITY OF SAN FRANCISCO
School of Business and Management

Admissions Contact: Graduate Admissions
Address: 2130 Fulton Street, San Francisco, CA 94117-1045
Admissions Phone: 415-422-4723 • Admissions Fax: 415-422-2217
Admissions E-mail: graduate@usfca.edu • Web Address: www.usfca.edu/sobam

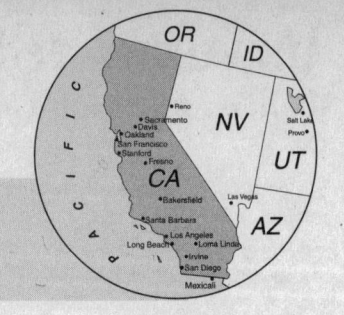

San Francisco's first university, University of San Francisco, is a Jesuit institution with a hearty plateful of MBA options and beautiful views from campus of the Pacific Ocean, the San Francisco Bay, and the downtown skyline. USF has an "outstanding faculty" who come to teach after pursuing successful careers in their areas of expertise and an advisory board that benefits from almost 150 CEOs and executives of prominent stature. USF's position among a network of Jesuit colleges and universities allows its students not only access to loads of study abroad options, but also the option to easily transfer graduate credits to another Jesuit university in the event of relocation.

INSTITUTIONAL INFORMATION
Public/Private: Private
Evening Classes Available? Yes
Total Faculty: 78
% Faculty Female: 20
% Faculty Minority: 25
% Faculty Part Time: 23
Student/Faculty Ratio: 10:1
Students in Parent Institution: 8,130

PROGRAMS
Degrees Offered: Master of Business Administration (MBA); Executive MBA (EMBA); Professional MBA (PMBA)
Joint Degrees: JD/MBA; MS/MBA (Nursing); MAPS/MBA (Asian Pacific Studies)
Study Abroad Options: University of Beijing

STUDENT INFORMATION
Total Business Students: 460
% Full Time: 63
% Female: 42
% Minority: 37
% Out of State: 48
% International: 40
Average Age: 26

COMPUTER AND RESEARCH FACILITIES
Campuswide Network? Yes
% of MBA Classrooms Wired: 68
Computer Model Recommended: No
Internet Fee? No

EXPENSES/FINANCIAL AID
Annual Tuition: $19,200
Tuition Per Credit: $800
Room & Board (On Campus): $8,324
Books and Supplies: $1,250

ADMISSIONS INFORMATION
Application Fee: $55
Electronic Application? Yes
Regular Application Deadline: 6/1
Regular Notification: Rolling
Deferment Available? Yes
Length of Deferment: 1 year
Non-fall Admissions? Yes
Non-fall Application Deadline(s): 11/10 spring, 4/1 summer
Transfer Students Accepted? Yes
Transfer Policy: May transfer up to 6 credits from another AACSB-accredited program
Need-Blind Admissions? No
Number of Applications Received: 501

% of Applicants Accepted: 73
% Accepted Who Enrolled: 42
Average GPA: 3.0
GPA Range: 2.0-3.5
Average GMAT: 541
GMAT Range: 450-650
Average Years Experience: 5
Other Admissions Factors Considered: GPA, letters of recommendation, essays, work experience
Other Schools to Which Students Applied: San Francisco State University

INTERNATIONAL STUDENTS
TOEFL Required of International Students? Yes
Minimum TOEFL: 600 (250 computer)

EMPLOYMENT INFORMATION
Placement Office Available? Yes
% Employed Within 3 Months: 77
Frequent Employers: Hewlett-Packard, Sun Microsystems, Gatx Capital, Clorox, New Channel Inc., Key3media, Chevron, AC Nielson, Kenson Ventures
Prominent Alumni: Gordon Smith, CEO, PG&E; Mary Cannon, treasurer (retired), county and city of San Francisco

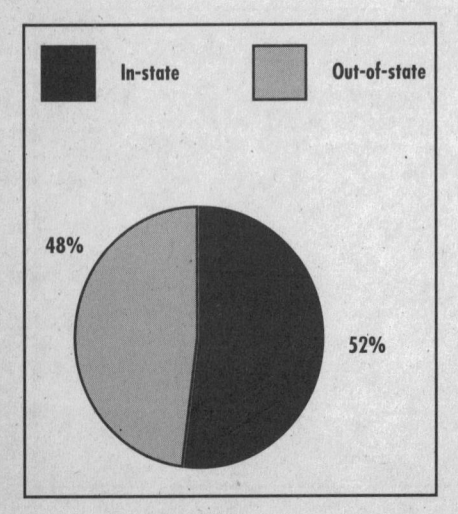

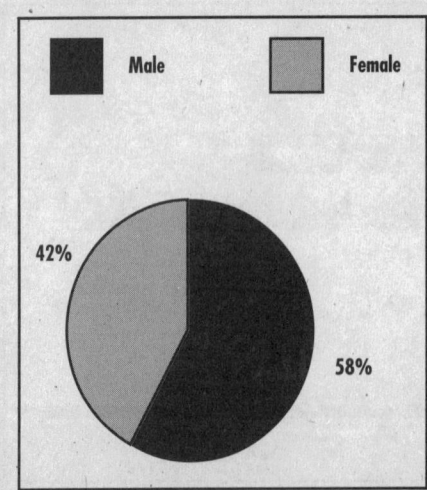

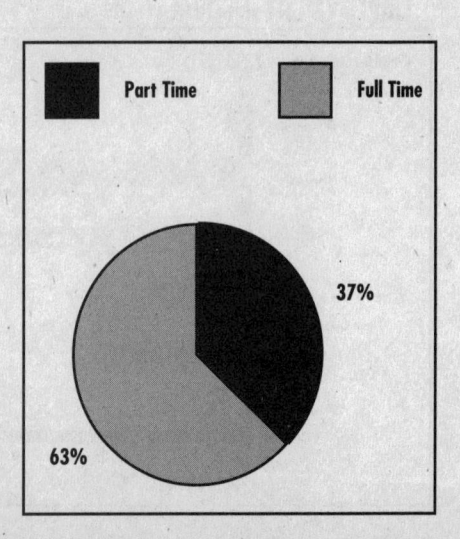

UNIVERSITY OF SOUTH CAROLINA
Darla Moore School of Business

Admissions Contact: Reena Lichtenfeld, Managing Director, Graduate Admissions
Address: Darla Moore School of Business, Columbia, SC 29208
Admissions Phone: 803-777-4346 • Admissions Fax: 803-777-0414
Admissions E-mail: gradadmit@darla.badm.sc.edu • Web Address: darlamoore.badm.sc.edu

The International MBA at Darla offers several program options: the Language Track, providing intense study and immersion in the language and culture of a specific chosen region (available to non-U.S. residents); the Global Track, for students who may already know another language but wish to acquire a global approach to the global economy; and the Vienna program, an accelerated program offered in partnership with the Vienna University of Business and Economics in Vienna, Austria. Talk about options. Large and in charge, Darla Moore students should expect decently sized classes, great computer and research facilities, many international students, and happy graduates who are courted by companies like Intel, General Motors, Deloitte & Touche, and Federal Express.

INSTITUTIONAL INFORMATION
Evening Classes Available? Yes
Total Faculty: 124
% Faculty Female: 17
% Faculty Minority: 2
% Faculty Part Time: 15
Student/Faculty Ratio: 30:1
Academic Calendar: Semester

PROGRAMS
Degrees Offered: MBA (2 years); MIBS (2 to 3 years); IMBA (15 months); MACE (1 year); MTax (1 year); MHA (1.5 years); MSBA (2 years); MAECON (2 years); PMBA (31 months)
Joint Degrees: JD/MBA (3 years); JD/MAcc (3 years); JD/MIBS (3 to 4 years); JD/MHR (3 years); JD/MSBA (3 years); JD/MA Economics (3 years)
Academic Specialties: International Business, Finance, Marketing, Information Systems, Operations, Accounting, Entrepreneurship, Human Resources, Strategic Management, Economics
Special Opportunities: MBA Enterprise Corps; MBA Accord (nonprofit consulting); Field Study Program
Study Abroad Options: Denmark, Holland, Germany, France, Finland, UK, Australia, Norway, Belgium

STUDENT INFORMATION
Total Business Students: 653
% Full Time: 62
% Female: 35
% Minority: 7
% Out of State: 72
% International: 28
Average Age: 28

COMPUTER AND RESEARCH FACILITIES
Research Facilities: Small Business Development Center; Division of Research; Center for International Business Education and Research; Center for Entrepreneurship; Center for Process Research in Information Systems, Services, and Manufacturing
Computer Facilities: More than 150 PCs and numerous databases
Campuswide Network? Yes
% of MBA Classrooms Wired: 30
Computer Model Recommended: No
Internet Fee? No

EXPENSES/FINANCIAL AID
Room & Board: $8,000
Books and Supplies: $2,000
Average Grant: $3,000
Average Loan: $10,000
% Receiving Financial Aid: 41
% Receiving Aid Their First Year: 34

ADMISSIONS INFORMATION
Application Fee: $35
Electronic Application? Yes
Early Decision App. Deadline: 12/1 IMBA
Early Decision Notification: 1/1
Regular Application Deadline: 2/1
Regular Notification: 3/15
Length of Deferment: 1 year
Non-fall Application Deadline(s): 12/1 summer IMBA and MIBS
Transfer Policy: Up to 12 credit hours
Need-Blind Admissions? Yes
Number of Applications Received: 748
% of Applicants Accepted: 57
% Accepted Who Enrolled: 50
Average GPA: 3.2
Average GMAT: 610
Average Years Experience: 4
Minority/Disadvantaged Student Recruitment Programs: Minority fellowships/assistantships; assistance for GMAT test preparation; recruit at National Black MBA Association meeting; recruit at historically black colleges and universities
Other Schools to Which Students Applied: Thunderbird, U. of Florida, U. of Georgia, UNC—Chapel Hill, Penn, UT Austin, U. of Virginia

INTERNATIONAL STUDENTS
TOEFL Required of International Students? Yes
Minimum TOEFL: 600 (250 computer)

EMPLOYMENT INFORMATION

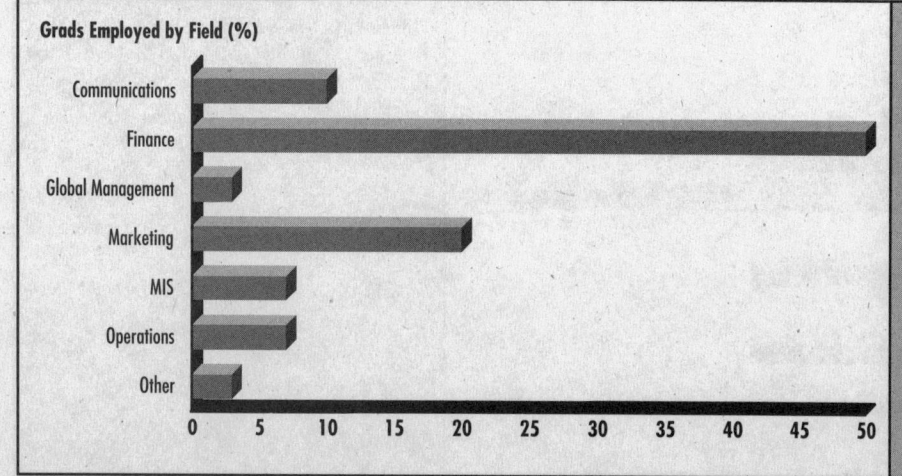

Grads Employed by Field (%)
- Communications: ~10
- Finance: ~50
- Global Management: ~5
- Marketing: ~20
- MIS: ~7
- Operations: ~7
- Other: ~4

Placement Office Available? Yes
% Employed Within 3 Months: 91
Frequent Employers: Nelson Mullins Riley & Scarborough; Kennedy, Covington, Labdell, & Hickman; Alston and Bird

UNIVERSITY OF SOUTH FLORIDA
College of Business Administration

Admissions Contact: Wendy Baker, Assistant Director of Graduate Studies
Address: 4202 E. Fowler Ave., BSN 3403, Tampa, FL 33620
Admissions Phone: 813-974-8800 • *Admissions Fax:* 813-974-7343
Admissions E-mail: mba2@grad.usf.edu • *Web Address:* www.coba.usf.edu

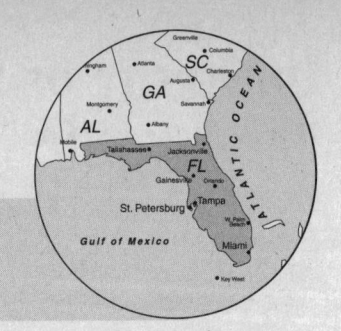

Tuition is manageable at USF, and students can look forward to an abundance of study abroad opportunities in countries like Spain, Costa Rica, Denmark, Wales, Japan, and France. USF's Evening MBA candidates meet for classes in the state-of-the-art USF Downtown Center in the Tampa Port Authority building. Most graduates go into general management, though finance and marketing draw significant portions of freshly minted USF MBAs.

INSTITUTIONAL INFORMATION
Public/Private: Public
Evening Classes Available? Yes
Total Faculty: 124
Student/Faculty Ratio: 4:1
Students in Parent Institution: 95

PROGRAMS
Degrees Offered: Master of Business Administration (MBA) (1 to 5 years); Master of Accountancy (MAcc) (12 months); Master of Arts in Economics (MA) (12 months); Executive MBA (20 months); MBA for Physicians (21 months); Saturday MBA for Professionals (30 months); Master of Science in Management Information Systems (MSM) (12 months); Master of Science in Management in Leadership and Organizational Effectiveness (MSM) (12 months)
Joint Degrees: -Master of Business Administration/Master of Science in Management Information Systems (MBA/MSM) (2 to 5 years)
Study Abroad Options: France—Universite Paris-Dauphine, Paris, and ESC Normandie, Normandy Business School, Le Havre-Caen, and ESC Rennes; Spain—Instituto de Empresa, Madrid; Great Britain—University of Glamorgan, Pontypridd, Wales, and University of Brighton; Denmark—Aarhus School of Business; Japan—Kagawa University, Takamatsu; Costa Rica—University of Costa Rica, San Jose; Brazil—Fundacao Getulio Vargas, Sao Paulo

STUDENT INFORMATION
Total Business Students: 503
% Full Time: 34
% Female: 40
% Minority: 15
% Out of State: 40
% International: 29
Average Age: 28

COMPUTER AND RESEARCH FACILITIES
Campuswide Network? Yes
% of MBA Classrooms Wired: 14
Computer Model Recommended: No
Internet Fee? No

EXPENSES/FINANCIAL AID
Annual Tuition (Resident/Nonresident): $2,789/$9,606
Tuition Per Credit (Resident/Nonresident): $166/$573
Books and Supplies: $700

ADMISSIONS INFORMATION
Application Fee: $20
Electronic Application? Yes
Regular Application Deadline: 5/15
Regular Notification: 5/15
Deferment Available? Yes
Length of Deferment: 1 year
Non-fall Admissions? Yes
Non-fall Application Deadline(s): 10/15 spring
Transfer Students Accepted? Yes
Transfer Policy: 9 credits from an AACSB university
Need-Blind Admissions? Yes
Number of Applications Received: 624
% of Applicants Accepted: 73
% Accepted Who Enrolled: 61
Average GPA: 3.3
Average GMAT: 560
GMAT Range: 490-630
Average Years Experience: 5
Other Schools to Which Students Applied: Florida State University, University of Central Florida, University of Florida

INTERNATIONAL STUDENTS
TOEFL Required of International Students? Yes
Minimum TOEFL: 550 (213 computer)

EMPLOYMENT INFORMATION

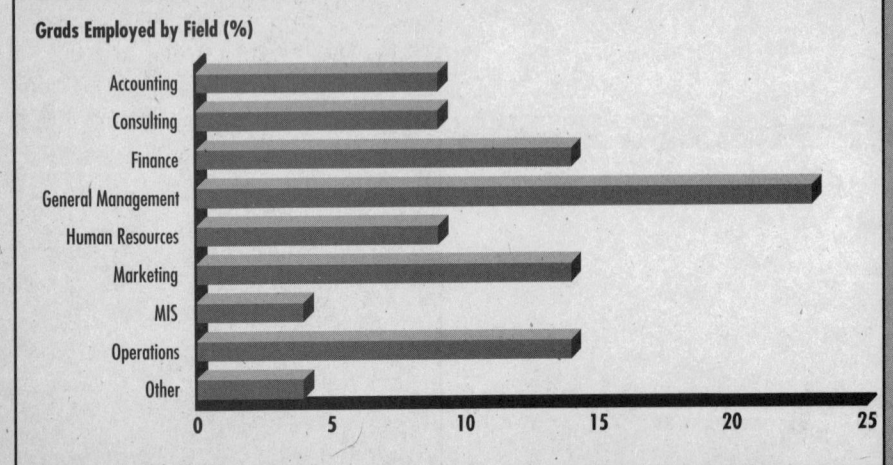

Grads Employed by Field (%)

Field	%
Accounting	9
Consulting	9
Finance	14
General Management	23
Human Resources	9
Marketing	14
MIS	2
Operations	14
Other	4

Placement Office Available? Yes
Frequent Employers: Andersen Consulting, Eckerd Corp., First Investors Corp., John Hancock Financial Services

UNIVERSITY OF SOUTHERN CALIFORNIA
Marshall School of Business

Admissions Contact: A. Keith Vaughn, Director of MBA Admissions
Address: Popovich Hall Room 308, Los Angeles, CA 90089-2633
Admissions Phone: 213-740-7846 • *Admissions Fax:* 213-749-8520
Admissions E-mail: marshallmba@marshall.usc.edu • *Web Address:* www.marshall.usc.edu

USC's Marshall School of Business boasts "strong academic programs" in an impressive array of areas including finance, marketing, information systems, and entrepreneurship. Students also praise the Pacific Rim Education program here, which consists of a short course covering business practices and management styles on the Pacific Rim and concludes with a field trip to China, Japan, or Mexico. However, students save their highest praise for Marshall's legendary "active and eager" alumni network.

INSTITUTIONAL INFORMATION
Public/Private: Private
Evening Classes Available? Yes
Total Faculty: 180
Student/Faculty Ratio: 8:1
Students in Parent Institution: 28,000
Academic Calendar: Semester

PROGRAMS
Degrees Offered: MBA, MS of Business Administration, Executive MBA, Master of Accounting, Master of Business Taxation, International Business Education and Research MBA, Master of Medical Management
Joint Degrees: MBA/Doctor of Dental Surgery, MBA/MA in East Asian Studies, MS in Gerontology/MBA, MBA/MS in Industrial and Systems Engineering, MBA/MA in Jewish Communal Service, JD/MBA, MD/MBA, MBA/MS in Nursing, MBA/Master of Planning, Doctor of Pharmacy/MBA, MBA/Master of Real Estate Development
Special Opportunities: MBA Enterprise Corps, Entrepreneurship Program, Program in Real Estate, travel abroad
Study Abroad Options: Argentina, Australia, Austria, Brazil, Chile, China, Costa Rica, Denmark, France, Germany, Hong Kong, Indonesia, Japan, Korea, Mexico, Phillipines, Singapore, Spain, Switzerland, Taiwan, Thailand, United Kingdom

STUDENT INFORMATION
Total Business Students: 1,477
% Female: 33
% Minority: 10
% Out of State: 70
% International: 23
Average Age: 28

COMPUTER AND RESEARCH FACILITIES
Research Facilities: Center for Effective Organizations, Center for Telecommunications Management, Center for International Business Education and Research, Family and Closely-Held Business Program, Experiential Learning Center, Instructional Services Center, Electronic Economy Research Lab (Ebizlab)
Campuswide Network? Yes
% of MBA Classrooms Wired: 100
Computer Model Recommended: No
Internet Fee? No

EXPENSES/FINANCIAL AID
Annual Tuition: $28,677
Books and Supplies: $2,200
Average Grant: $20,000
Average Loan: $25,000
% Receiving Financial Aid: 95
% Receiving Aid Their First Year: 95

ADMISSIONS INFORMATION
Application Fee: $90
Electronic Application? Yes
Regular Application Deadline: 4/1
Regular Notification: Rolling
Deferment Available? No
Non-fall Admissions? No
Transfer Students Accepted? No
Need-Blind Admissions? Yes
Number of Applications Received: 2,583
% of Applicants Accepted: 25
% Accepted Who Enrolled: 46
Average GPA: 3.3
GPA Range: 3.1-3.5
Average GMAT: 670
GMAT Range: 640-700
Average Years Experience: 4
Other Admissions Factors Considered: Leadership, interview (if requested), "fit" with the program
Minority/Disadvantaged Student Recruitment Programs: Member of the Consortium for Graduate Study in Management (provides merit-based full-tuition scholarships), annual Diversity Weekend
Other Schools to Which Students Applied: Duke, NYU, UC Berkeley, UCLA, U. of Chicago

INTERNATIONAL STUDENTS
TOEFL Required of International Students? Yes
Minimum TOEFL: 250

EMPLOYMENT INFORMATION

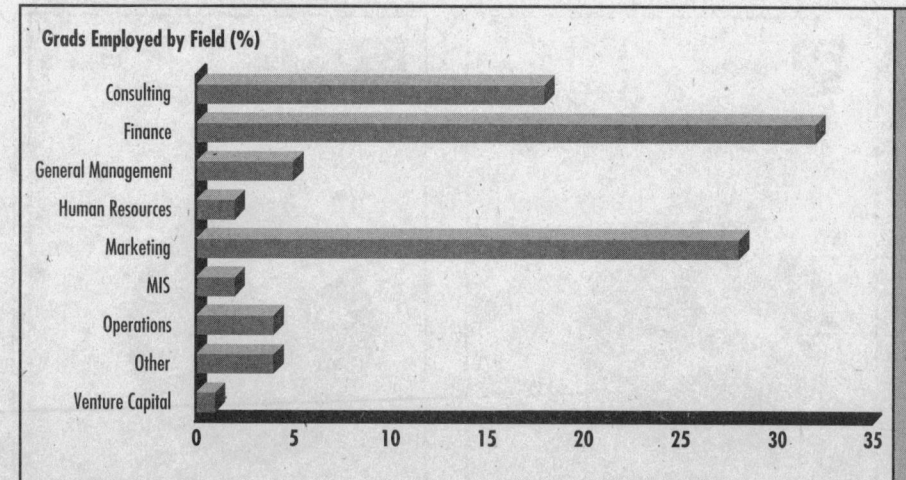

Grads Employed by Field (%)

Field	%
Consulting	~18
Finance	~32
General Management	~5
Human Resources	~2
Marketing	~28
MIS	~1
Operations	~4
Other	~4
Venture Capital	~1

Placement Office Available? Yes
% Employed Within 3 Months: 98
Frequent Employers: Private firms, corporations, federal judges, government, public-interest nonprofits. Private corporations include: Hewlett Packard, Bank of America Securities, Deloitte & Touche, PricewaterhouseCoopers, Wells Fargo, ClickTex.com, Intel, Mattel, American Express, Artisan Entertainment, Dell, Ernst & Young, Walt Disney Co., Viant, Amgen, Arthur Andersen, ConAgra Grocery Products, Honeywell, Kraft Foods, Nestle USA, Teradyne, Toyota.

UNIVERSITY OF SOUTHERN MAINE
School of Business

Admissions Contact: Alice B. Cash, MBA Program Manager
Address: PO Box 9300, Portland, ME 04104
Admissions Phone: 207-780-4184 • Admissions Fax: 207-780-4662
Admissions E-mail: mba@usm.maine.edu • Web Address: www.usm.maine.edu/sb

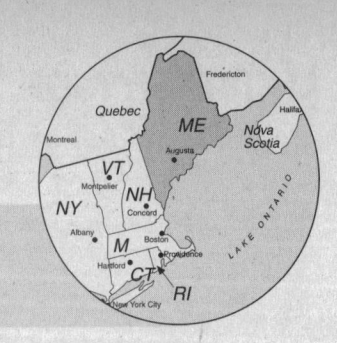

If you're not a Mainah (and not knowing what a Mainah is would mean you aren't), then you might feel like a fish out of water at the University of Southern Maine. A whopping 96 percent of USM students are Maine residents. There's a good reason, too: if you're a resident, you pay about a third of what nonresidents pay. Another stat: Nearly everyone in the MBA program is part time. USM's School of Business greatly boasts its Internship Program, in which many local businesses employ students, eventually hiring them full time after graduation. And it's close to Canada. Go NAFTA.

INSTITUTIONAL INFORMATION
Public/Private: Public
Evening Classes Available? Yes
Total Faculty: 17
% Faculty Female: 35
% Faculty Minority: 6
Student/Faculty Ratio: 15:1
Students in Parent Institution: 10,966
Academic Calendar: Semester

PROGRAMS
Special Opportunities: Master of Business Administration, Master of Science in Accounting

STUDENT INFORMATION
Total Business Students: 121
% Full Time: 17
% Female: 38
% Out of State: 4
% International: 3
Average Age: 32

COMPUTER AND RESEARCH FACILITIES
Campuswide Network? Yes
% of MBA Classrooms Wired: 1
Internet Fee? No

EXPENSES/FINANCIAL AID
Annual Tuition (Resident/Nonresident): $4,620/$12,912
Tuition Per Credit (Resident/Nonresident): $193/$538
Room & Board (On Campus): $6,116
Books and Supplies: $825
Average Grant: $1,000

ADMISSIONS INFORMATION
Application Fee: $50
Electronic Application? No
Regular Application Deadline: 8/1
Regular Notification: Rolling
Deferment Available? Yes
Length of Deferment: 1 year
Non-fall Admissions? Yes
Non-fall Application Deadline(s): 12/1 spring
Transfer Students Accepted? Yes
Transfer Policy: Please see catalog.
Need-Blind Admissions? Yes
Number of Applications Received: 38
% of Applicants Accepted: 79
% Accepted Who Enrolled: 87
Average GPA: 3.2
GPA Range: 2.8-3.5
Average GMAT: 566
GMAT Range: 505-589
Average Years Experience: 5
Other Admissions Factors Considered: Performance in outside activities, evidence of creativity and leadership, record of accomplishment in business

INTERNATIONAL STUDENTS
TOEFL Required of International Students? Yes
Minimum TOEFL: 550 (213 computer)

EMPLOYMENT INFORMATION
Placement Office Available? No

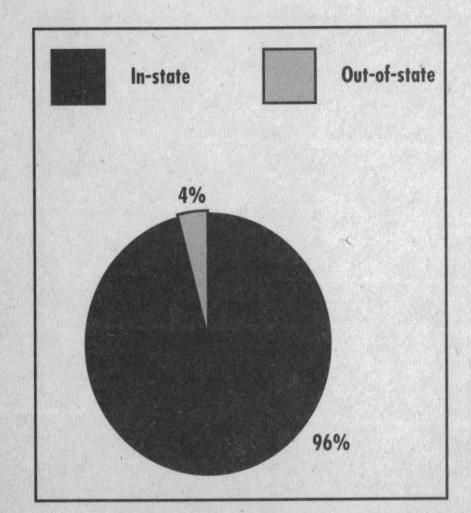

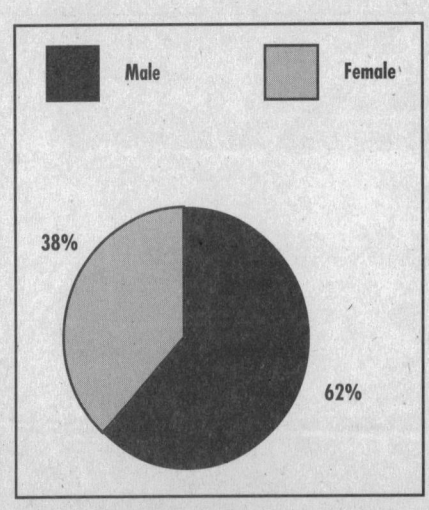

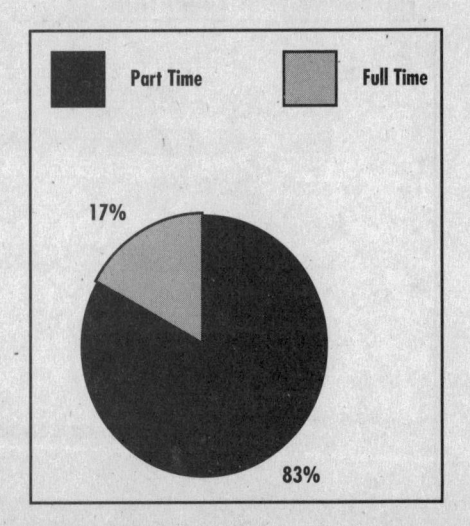

UNIVERSITY OF TAMPA
John H. Sykes College of Business

Admissions Contact: Fernando Nolasco, Associate Director, Graduate Studies in Business
Address: 401 W. Kennedy Blvd., Tampa, FL 33606-1490
Admissions Phone: 813-258-7409 • Admissions Fax: 813-259-5403
Admissions E-mail: mba@ut.edu • Web Address: mba.ut.edu

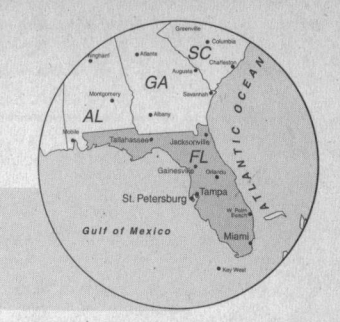

Located in west central Florida's center of commerce and culture, the University of Tampa has a low student/faculty ratio and claims to house not just professors, but mentors who offer continual personal attention and care to the students. Business events on campus include the Backstage Tour, Executive Luncheon Series, and Executive Tune-Up; students can reap the benefits of these great career-building programs and also attend the meeting where local alumni plan the events for each academic year, providing multiple opportunities to meet future employers and mentors.

INSTITUTIONAL INFORMATION
Public/Private: Private
Evening Classes Available? Yes
Total Faculty: 42
% Faculty Female: 31
Student/Faculty Ratio: 12:1
Students in Parent Institution: 3,957
Academic Calendar: Semester

PROGRAMS
Degrees Offered: Master of Business Administration (accelerated full time and flexible part time), Master of Science in Technology and Innovation Management, Master of Science in Nursing
Joint Degrees: MSN/MBA
Academic Specialties: Strong Accounting, Economics, Finance, and Information Systems Management curriculum
Study Abroad Options: Monterrey Tech, Mexico

STUDENT INFORMATION
Total Business Students: 387
% Full Time: 37
% Female: 41
% Minority: 6
% Out of State: 4
% International: 66
Average Age: 28

COMPUTER AND RESEARCH FACILITIES
Research Facilities: Center for Ethics, Center for Innovation and Knowledge Management, TECO Energy Center for Leadership, Human Resource Institute, Institute for World Commerce Education, Naimoli Institute for Business Strategy, Huizenga Family Foundation Trading Center
Computer Facilities: ABI/Inform, Disclosure, Lexis-Nexis, National Trade Data Bank, 1,300 data ports
Campuswide Network? Yes
% of MBA Classrooms Wired: 100
Computer Model Recommended: Laptop
Internet Fee? No

EXPENSES/FINANCIAL AID
Annual Tuition: $8,400
Tuition Per Credit: $352
Room & Board (On Campus): $5,890
Books and Supplies: $1,000
Average Grant: $9,048
Average Loan: $9,608
% Receiving Financial Aid: 37
% Receiving Aid Their First Year: 32

ADMISSIONS INFORMATION
Application Fee: $35
Electronic Application? Yes
Regular Application Deadline: Rolling
Regular Notification: Rolling
Deferment Available? Yes
Length of Deferment: 1 year
Non-fall Admissions? Yes
Non-fall Application Deadline(s): Rolling
Transfer Students Accepted? Yes
Transfer Policy: Up to 9 credits from an AACSB-accredited school
Need-Blind Admissions? Yes
Number of Applications Received: 349
% of Applicants Accepted: 43
% Accepted Who Enrolled: 67
Average GPA: 3.4
GPA Range: 2.9-3.9
Average GMAT: 529
GMAT Range: 460-600
Average Years Experience: 4
Other Schools to Which Students Applied: University of Florida, University of South Florida

INTERNATIONAL STUDENTS
TOEFL Required of International Students? Yes
Minimum TOEFL: 577 (230 computer)

EMPLOYMENT INFORMATION

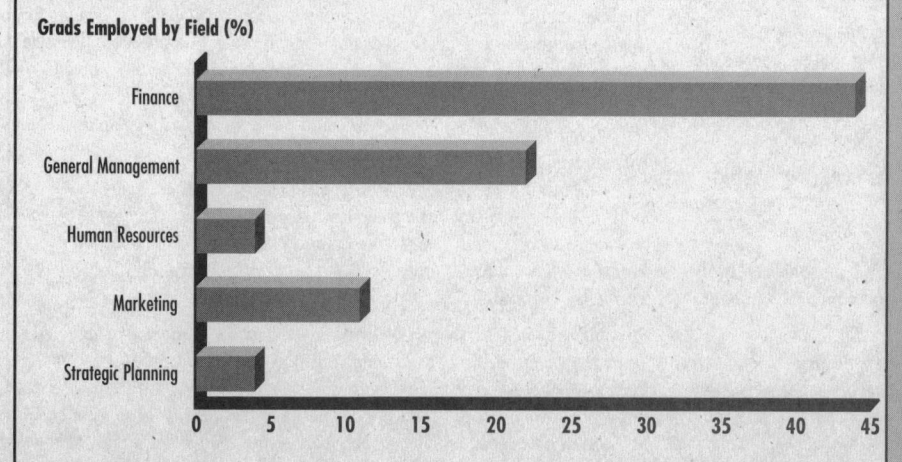

Grads Employed by Field (%)

Field	%
Finance	~44
General Management	~22
Human Resources	~10
Marketing	~11
Strategic Planning	~4

Placement Office Available? Yes
% Employed Within 3 Months: 100
Frequent Employers: Tampa Electric, Franklin Templeton, GATX Capital, Am South, SunTrust Bank
Prominent Alumni: Dennis Zank, COO, Raymond James; Lyndon Martin, member, legislative assembly, Cayman Islands; Jorgen Adolfsson, Swedish technology entrepreneur

THE UNIVERSITY OF TAMPA

THE COLLEGE AT A GLANCE

Congratulations! By exploring your MBA Program you've recognized that a leading twenty-first-century enterprise requires rethinking of yourself and your career. Technological, environmental, demographic, and political changes are transforming the world, creating new demands for performance. Our goal is to provide you with perspective, skills, mentoring, and lots of opportunities for fully expressing your potential and meeting those demands.

We can help you prepare you for leadership responsibilities in a technically sophisticated, diverse global environment where change rules. We're part of one of the nation's most vibrant regional economies. Whether it's the Internet, computer technology, financial services, telecommunications, international trade and tourism, or one of a dozen other industries, we have experience and contacts. More than 700 community and business leaders serve on the University's boards, as classroom advisors, as executive coaches, and as members of academic support groups. Together we are preparing students and business leaders to create and grow twenty-first-century enterprises.

The University was founded in 1931 by visionary community leaders who wanted to provide the best possible educational opportunity for their community. UT has excelled in its mission of preparing a growing and culturally diverse student body for rewarding careers and responsible citizenship. Through a highly qualified faculty, challenging classes, learning experiences, and state-of-the facilities, we deliver an exceptional and exciting educational experience that pays off over your entire life.

The John H. Sykes College of Business is accredited by AACSB International—The Association to Advance Collegiate Schools of Business. The University is also accredited by the Commission on Colleges of the Southern Association of Colleges and Schools to award associate, baccalaureate, and master's degrees.

STUDENTS

Interaction with local community leaders and organizations is part of your MBA education. The University of Tampa is woven into the Tampa Bay community through internships, experiential learning opportunities, community forums, advisory boards, and business outreach programs.

The University sponsors numerous business and community events that give you the opportunity to learn from local business leaders, complementing your academic learning. Among the discussion and speaker groups that meet regularly on campus are the Fellows Forum, Business Network, and several centers and institutes.

Career Services offers MBA students individualized attention from the professional staff. Services include resume critique, design, and referral; personal career advising; interview skills refreshers; on-campus interview opportunities; and informational interviews with professional MBAs from the greater Tampa Bay area.

Whether the MBA student is looking for employment while enrolled, at graduation, or as alumni, our innovative HIRE-UT Job Listing System and Resume Database is available 24 hours a day, 7 days a week. Since its inception in September 1999, over 400 employers have registered with the HIRE-UT program. With its combination of a resume database, online employer access, and job listings, the HIRE-UT system is the epitome of online career services, perfectly suited for today's busy professionals.

ACADEMICS

Because of your hectic schedule, business obligations, and personal and professional deadlines, we offer you unequalled flexibility as you pursue your degree. In short, you may complete the MBA program at your own pace.

Full-time students can complete the entire program in as little as 16 months in the accelerated Full-Time Day Program. Students who work full time can complete the course work in less than three years in the Flex Part-Time Evening Program. It's important to note, however, that you have up to seven years from your time of entry to complete the entire program.

The program requirements will vary from 39 to 51 hours depending on the student's undergraduate major and background.

Our program theme, Creating Value Through Strategic Leadership, helps you develop the sophisticated strategic perspectives and mindset demonstrated by successful executives. Any enterprise, if it is to grow and prosper, must deliver a clear and compelling value proposition. Leaders must continuously apply sophisticated concepts and practices across the business' entire value chain or network if it is to deliver that value to all it's stakeholders—owners, investors, employees, suppliers, customers, and communities. Such a perspective asks students to appreciate how key enterprise functions such as marketing and sales, operations, finance, human resources, and information systems add value and interact to optimize value delivery.

You want a solid foundation of core business concepts and techniques to prepare you for the Integrated Core and the specialized electives that follow. The goal is to help you move confidently and capably into your program. We deliver these through the required preliminary program elements:

- Fast Start Workshop
- High-Performance Leadership Workshop
- Developing Software Competencies
- Analytic Skills

The Fast Start Workshop is a two-and-a-half-day weekend program that introduces you to your new colleagues—students, faculty, and staff—and gives you the understanding and skills to start the program. You participate in a team-based business simulation that demonstrates essential business concepts and perspectives, how to work in and lead a team, and how to make effective oral and written presentations. An elective executive coaching program supports the student's achievement of the Personal Commitment Plan throughout the remainder of their MBA program.

The High Performance Leadership Workshop is part of a total MBA program experience specifically designed to assess and build your leadership skills. You will develop a Personal Commitment Plan that will guide actions to improve your personal health and fitness as well as your leadership skills. You will have access to an entire team composed of management, psychology, exercise, fitness, and nutrition faculty and staff.

Developing Software Competencies is a course required of all students in their first semester to help freshen basic computer skills, specifically using Microsoft 2000 Word, Excel, PowerPoint, and Access programs. Faculty lectures and tutorial support are provided. You may elect to test out of a specific course section or take a brief quiz on that section. You can confidently enter your later courses knowing that your basic software skills are there.

Each student's required curriculum is determined by their academic background. Students with a strong formal business education participate in Analytic Skills to help freshen basic concepts of accounting, finance, operations, and statistics. Students with less business education participate in the Foundation Course Sequence consisting of half- or full-semester courses covering accounting, economics, finance, marketing, statistics, and professional writing topics.

Integrated Core

The Integrated Core engages you in a series of 12 intellectually challenging half-semester course modules designed to help you develop the practical hands-on business knowledge and tools required to lead the value creation process. Modules include such topics as Building Customer Value, Creating Value Through Financial Strategies, and Leading Strategic Change.

Specialization with Depth & Impact—Program Concentrations

You have the opportunity to deepen your business knowledge of specific topics by taking 12 credits in one of seven different MBA Concentrations: Accounting, Entrepreneurship, Finance, International Business, Information Systems Management, Management, and Marketing. Students electing not to declare

John H. Sykes College of Business

an MBA Concentration may take their 12 credits from two or more of these Concentration areas.

The Capstone Experience—Real World, Hands-on Strategy

You will work as part of a student team in performing a strategic business assessment and then creating an oral and written presentation for the top leadership of an actual company. Our student teams have helped take companies into new international markets, redirect marketing and financial strategies, and restructure entire organizations—well beyond textbook case studies and solutions.

To make sure projects of such importance are executed well, students will also take a course on Effective Project Management. You will see the results of your course work in action, confident that you have the skills to deliver the high quality expected of a University of Tampa MBA graduate.

We place the highest priority on the teaching and mentoring role of our faculty. It shows! We maintain a low student-faculty ratio to fulfill our commitment to working with you individually and ensuring that you get the best education possible.

All of our MBA faculty members have PhDs. More than half of our graduate faculty have won awards for teaching and professional excellence. Many of our faculty have owned their own businesses, have helped lead and build major companies, or are engaged in consulting at the highest leadership levels. Faculty members serve on boards and councils throughout the community. They've been routinely quoted in Fortune, Barron's, The Wall Street Journal, and in dozens of local, national, and international media.

Faculty are experienced in working with students who must integrate academic, career, and family responsibilities. They understand your world.

CAMPUS LIFE

The 80-acre University of Tampa campus offers a full-service educational setting that includes a comprehensive library, a broad range of technology and support, an active Career Services and Placement Center, and many student programs.

There is much more to Tampa's location than beautiful beaches and pleasant year-round temperatures. Tampa Bay is among the top 10 fastest-growing areas in the U.S. and a great place to be for career building. Tampa is Florida's West Coast center for the arts, banking, real estate, law, transportation, international business, education, communications, health care, and scientific research.

When it comes to technology, the John H. Sykes College of Business is keeping pace! The new 80,000-square-foot facility boasts more than 1,300 data ports for high-speed networking and access to the Internet. You can log onto the information highway in all 30 classrooms, student break-out rooms, three computer labs, and even in the hallways and vending area. Use these to communicate with your professors, classmates, and students here and around the world.

The Huizenga Family Foundation Trading Center is one of the technological centerpieces of the building, providing a significant hands-on dimension to finance education. The Trading Center offers Bloomberg Professional real-time trading information on large plasma screens and workstations.

COSTS

Tuition for 2002–2003 is $352 per credit hour. Tuition is payable at registration each semester. In addition, a $35 student services fee is required each term and a one-time $100 fee is required for the Fast Start Workshop. The cost of books, supplies, health insurance, and personal expenses is additional.

Graduate Assistantships are available each academic year. Assistantships provide tuition waiver for up to six classes per year plus a $3,000 stipend. Recipients must be full-time students and work 20 hours per week. Federal Stafford Student Loans are also available. The graduate and financial aid offices assist students with preparation of necessary application forms. Graduate students who are not currently employed may apply for a noncredit internship with a local business.

ADMISSIONS

Admission to UT's MBA Program is competitive and is based on a number of factors. Applications are processed on a rolling basis and students are admitted for the fall, spring, or summer sessions. Individual interviews are encouraged but not required. All students admitted to the MBA program must have earned four-year undergraduate degrees. A specific undergraduate degree is not required.

Students entering the MBA program are expected to be competent in mathematics, have strong communications skills (both written and oral), and be competent with use of computers.

To be considered for graduate admissions, applicants must submit the following information:

- Completed application
- $35 application fee
- Official transcripts of all previous college work received directly from each institution
- Graduate Management Admissions Test (GMAT) score report—WRI 520 can be waived if a writing score of 4.0 or greater is obtained on teh Analytical Writing Assessment of the GMAT.
- Two letters of recommendation from professionals (e.g., employers or professors) familiar with the applicant's academic potential
- International applicants must submit a Test of English as a Foreign Language (TOEFL) score report

Applicants for the Masters of Business Administration (MBA) Graduate Program should submit materials to:

Graduate Studies in Business
The University of Tampa
Box O
401 West Kennedy Blvd.
Tampa, FL 33606-1490
Telephone: 813-258-7409
Fax: 813-259-5403
E-mail: mba@ut.edu
Website: mba.ut.edu

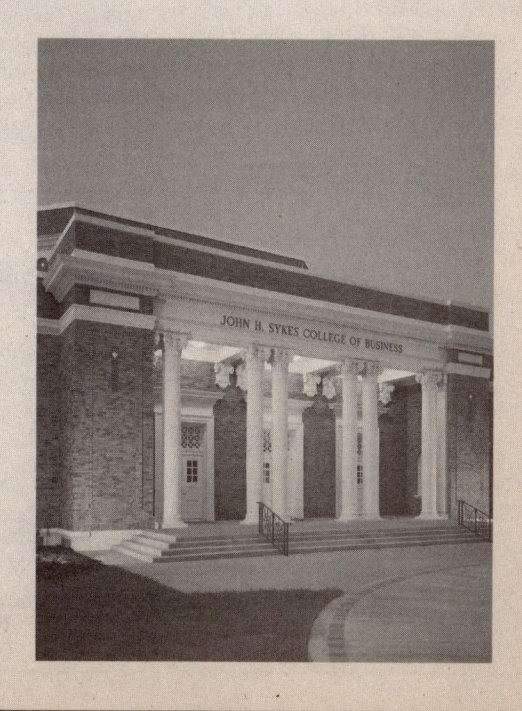

UNIVERSITY OF TENNESSEE—KNOXVILLE
College of Business Administration

Admissions Contact: Donna Potts, Director of Admissions, MBA Program
Address: 527 Stokely Management Center, Knoxville, TN 37996-0552
Admissions Phone: 865-974-5033 • Admissions Fax: 865-974-3826
Admissions E-mail: mba@utk.edu • Web Address: mba.bus.utk.edu

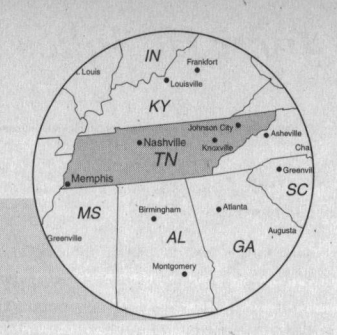

The small and intimate University of Tennessee College of Business Administration offers a "very strong academic program" that students call a "great value for the money." The core curriculum centers on a yearlong case experience in which teams of students run their own businesses, "taking a company from its birth through the entire business cycle." As for Knoxville, "it's a great little city" with "excellent restaurants," and the Smoky Mountains are only a short drive away.

INSTITUTIONAL INFORMATION
Public/Private: Public
Evening Classes Available? No
Total Faculty: 43
% Faculty Female: 18
% Faculty Minority: 6
Student/Faculty Ratio: 15:1
Students in Parent Institution: 26,979
Academic Calendar: Semester

PROGRAMS
Degrees Offered: MBA (2 years with internship between the 1st and 2nd years)
Joint Degrees: Juris Doctor/MBA (4 to 4.4 years), BA/MBA (5 years), MBA/Masters in Industrial Engineering (2 years and half summer session)
Academic Specialties: Technology, Entrepreneurship, Logistics/Transportation, Marketing, Supply Chain, Management Information Systems
Special Opportunities: The MBA Symposia, Tennessee Organization of MBAs, summer internships, corporate connections, community connections, E-Biz Club (E-Commerce), New Venture Now Club, MBA Marketing Association, Clayton Torch Fund and Haslam Torch Fund, 6 national and international case competition teams
Study Abroad Options: The Consortium International Master of Business Administration (CIMBA) in Italy, Slovenia, and Austria; IEFSI, France; University of Santiago, Chile; University of Greenwich, London; Reims School of Management in France and China

STUDENT INFORMATION
Total Business Students: 195
% Full Time: 100
% Female: 26
% Minority: 5
% Out of State: 62
% International: 18
Average Age: 26

COMPUTER AND RESEARCH FACILITIES
Computer Facilities: Multiple DII labs plus 2 College of Business Labs
Number of Computer Labs: 48
Number of Student Computers: 26
Campuswide Network? Yes
% Who Own Computers: 100
Computer Proficiency Required? Yes
Computer Model Recommended: Laptop
Special Purchasing Agreements? Yes
Companies with Agreements: Dell, Gateway, IBM
Internet Fee? Yes

EXPENSES/FINANCIAL AID
Annual Tuition (Resident/Nonresident): $3,306/$9,374
Room & Board (On/Off Campus): $3,500/$6,000
Books and Supplies: $1,622
Average Grant: $3,000
Average Loan: $11,353
Average Total Debt: $6,000
% Receiving Financial Aid: 90
% Receiving Aid Their First Year: 80

ADMISSIONS INFORMATION
Application Fee: $35
Electronic Application? Yes
Early Decision Application Deadline: 3/1
Regular Application Deadline: 3/1
Regular Notification: Rolling
Deferment Available? No
Non-fall Admissions? No
Transfer Students Accepted? No
Need-Blind Admissions? No
Number of Applications Received: 737
% of Applicants Accepted: 31
% Accepted Who Enrolled: 42
Average GPA: 3.3
GPA Range: 2.9-3.8
Average GMAT: 625
GMAT Range: 490-740
Average Years Experience: 5
Minority/Disadvantaged Student Recruitment Programs: THEC Black Graduate Fellowship
Other Schools to Which Students Applied: Arizona State University, University of Texas—Austin, Michigan State University, Pennsylvania State University, University of Arizona, University of Georgia

INTERNATIONAL STUDENTS
TOEFL Required of International Students? Yes
Minimum TOEFL: 600

EMPLOYMENT INFORMATION

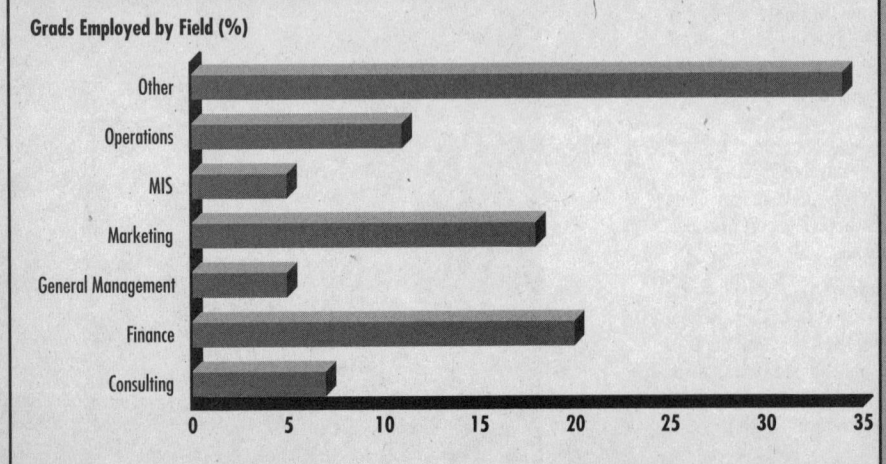

Grads Employed by Field (%)
- Other: ~34
- Operations: ~11
- MIS: ~5
- Marketing: ~18
- General Management: ~5
- Finance: ~20
- Consulting: ~7

Placement Office Available? Yes
% Employed Within 6 Months: 100
Frequent Employers: Dell Computer Corporation, IBM, Procter & Gamble, Lexmark, Federal Express, PricewaterhouseCoopers, Ernst & Young, Andersen Consulting, General Motors, Ford, SunTrust Bank, Wal-Mart, Deere & Company, Caterpillar, Inc., Fleetguard/Cummins
Prominent Alumni: William E. Dickenson, president and chief executive, Hagler Bailly, Inc.; Tom Morgan, CEO, enfoTrust Networks

UNIVERSITY OF TEXAS — ARLINGTON
College of Business Administration

Admissions Contact: Davis Hall, Assistant Vice President
Address: Box 19167, Arlington, TX 76019
Admissions Phone: 817-272-2688 • Admissions Fax: 817-272-2627
Admissions E-mail: graduate.school@uta.edu • Web Address: www2.uta.edu/gradbiz

Chief among the assets of the University of Texas at Arlington's MBA program is its location in the Dallas/Fort Worth Metroplex region, a hub of the active, high-stakes Texas business world. UTA offers flexibility to MBA students, "with most classes held in the evening," and the surrounding area provides a fertile lab for the exploration and pursuit of hundreds of career alternatives. Many of UTA's "hardworking, hard-earning, future-focused" MBA students are part-time and "commuter students."

INSTITUTIONAL INFORMATION
Evening Classes Available? Yes
Total Faculty: 149
% Faculty Female: 25
% Faculty Minority: 13
% Faculty Part Time: 2
Student/Faculty Ratio: 7:1
Academic Calendar: Semester

PROGRAMS
Degrees Offered: MBA, online MBA, Accelerated MBA, MA Economics, MS Accounting, MS Taxation, MS Human Resource Management, MS Marketing Research, MS Information Systems, MS Real Estate, Master of Professional Accounting, PhD Business Administration, MS Health Care Admin.
Joint Degrees: A variety of joint programs are available, usually MBA and specialized program
Academic Specialties: Finance, Accounting, Information Systems, International Business, Marketing Research, Real Estate, Human Resource Management, Electronic Commerce, Enterprise Resource Planning
Study Abroad Options: Norway, England, France, Australia, Mexico, Germany, Korea

STUDENT INFORMATION
Total Business Students: 536
% Female: 13
% Minority: 5
% International: 14
Average Age: 32

COMPUTER AND RESEARCH FACILITIES
Research Facilities: Center for Information Technologies Management, Center for Research on Organizational and Managerial Excellence, Center for Urban Land Utilization
Computer Facilities: Variety and software databases available
Campuswide Network? Yes
% of MBA Classrooms Wired: 7
Internet Fee? No

EXPENSES/FINANCIAL AID
Annual Tuition (Resident/Nonresident): $2,400/$9,180
Tuition Per Credit (Resident/Nonresident): $80/$306
Books and Supplies: $1,000
Average Grant: $1,070
Average Loan: $8,576
% Receiving Financial Aid: 14
% Receiving Aid Their First Year: 13

ADMISSIONS INFORMATION
Application Fee: $25
Electronic Application? Yes
Early Decision Application Deadline: Rolling
Early Decision Notification: 1/1
Regular Application Deadline: 6/15
Regular Notification: Rolling
Length of Deferment: 1 year
Non-fall Application Deadline(s): Mid-October, spring; mid-March, summer
Transfer Policy: Up to 9 credits with B or better from AACSB-accredited university.
Need-Blind Admissions? Yes
Number of Applications Received: 591
% of Applicants Accepted: 46
% Accepted Who Enrolled: 61
Average GPA: 3.2
Average GMAT: 542
Average Years Experience: 5
Other Admissions Factors Considered: Degree held, college/university attended, professional certifications held, professional experience after earning bachelor's degree
Minority/Disadvantaged Student Recruitment Programs: Activities sponsored by the McNair Scholar Program and the National Black MBA Association

INTERNATIONAL STUDENTS
TOEFL Required of International Students? Yes
Minimum TOEFL: 550 (213 computer)

EMPLOYMENT INFORMATION
Placement Office Available? Yes
Frequent Employers: Alcon Laboratories, SABRE, Nokia, American Airlines, Bank of America
Prominent Alumni: Lee Thurburn, founder, FlashNet; John McMichael, executive VP of business operations, Southwest Sports Group

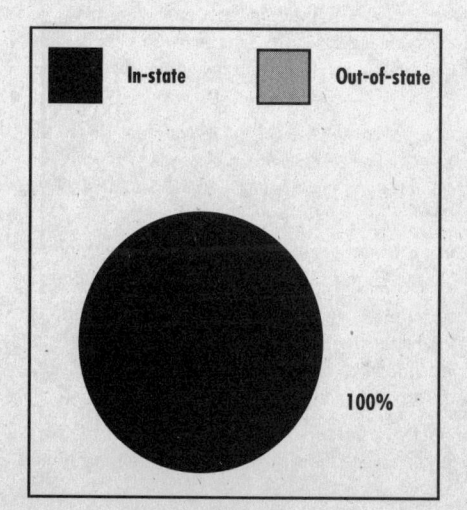

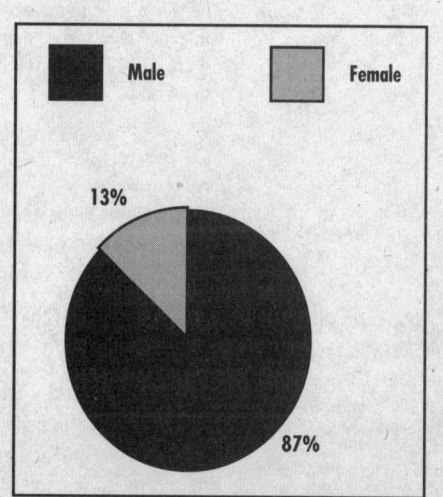

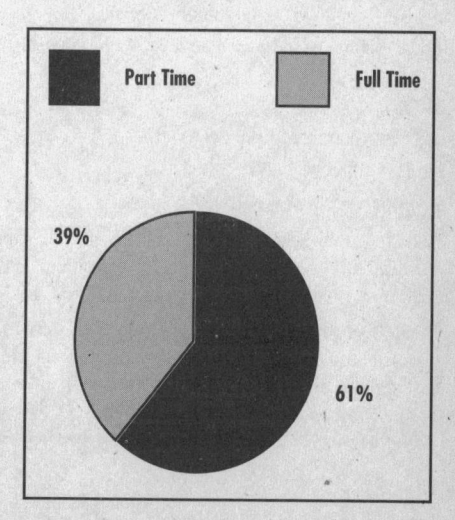

In-state / Out-of-state: 100% In-state

Male / Female: 87% Male, 13% Female

Part Time / Full Time: 61% Part Time, 39% Full Time

UNIVERSITY OF TEXAS—AUSTIN

THE SCHOOL AT A GLANCE

MBAs at the McCombs School of Business enjoy the depth and accessibility of the faculty, close ties to the Austin business community, the emphasis on collaboration over competition, and the infusion of technology, entrepreneurship, and globalization throughout the curriculum. McCombs is strong in all major disciplines, and is consistently ranked as a top 20 business school in the major national rankings. The program's hometown of Austin also routinely rates as one of the best places in the country to live and work.

In the fall of 2001, the school received endowment revenues from a $50 million gift from entrepreneur Red McCombs, implementing a strategic plan to rise to the next level of excellence in business education.

Technology and entrepreneurship are already especially strong, anchored by a distinguished information management program that includes the country's preeminent e-business research center and a model entrepreneurship curriculum anchored by the MOOT CORP business plan competition awarding over $130,000 in prizes annually.

McCombs supports a diverse student body, which provides the opportunity for expansion professionally, academically, and personally. McCombs MBA students represent more than 30 different countries, allowing for intense cultural exchange, and with students from every race and religion and a vast range of professional experiences, the community is rich and lively. The school aspires to continue to grow the awareness of diversity issues in both the business school, and, ultimately, in the workplace. As we expand our community, we will continue to increase the interaction between our current students and prospective students—broadening the scale and scope of our outreach.

Partnerships with three of the top Latin American business schools enable us to maintain a strong presence and continue to build mutually beneficial relationships for the university and our corporate partners. McCombs has been recognized as the number one business school for Hispanic students for two years running.

With more than 20 alumni chapters worldwide, the McCombs MBA network grows stronger each year—providing students and alumni the opportunity to maintain close ties to the school and reap the benefits of the resources created for them.

STUDENTS

There are 800 MBA students in the full-time program on average, and typically about 25 percent are female. The average age is 28. These students enter with an average of five years work experience, an average GMAT score of 680, and an average undergraduate GPA of 3.4. About 30 percent of the class has an undergraduate degree in business, 23 percent in the liberal arts, 33 percent in a technical field, and 11 percent in economics. The McCombs School counts diversity among its strong points, and over 25 percent of the class is international, hailing from more than 30 different countries worldwide.

Class of 2001 Statistics
Average Salary: $87,874
Average Guaranteed Bonus: $18,824
Average Signing Bonus: $21,335

ACADEMICS

The McCombs School of Business offers the following degree programs: BBA, MBA, PPA (Professional Program in Accounting), MPA (Master of Professional Accounting), and PhD.

In addition to the traditional, full-time MBA program, the McCombs School offers an Executive MBA program in Austin that meets on Fridays and Saturdays on alternate weekends called Option II, an Executive MBA program in Mexico City, an Executive MBA program in Dallas, and an Evening MBA program that meets on Monday and Tuesday evenings called TEMBA.

The hallmarks of the McCombs MBA include a common educational experience that prepares all students for success, a collaborative rather than competitive learning environment, market-driven concentrations, and program flexibility. In addition, our three core program strengths—technology, entrepreneurship, and globalization—are infused throughout the curriculum from day one.

Our goal is to give all MBAs the same grounding in the fundamentals of business and to endow them with general management competence. Through the core, the faculty seeks to instill these essential business skills and values:

- A contemporary, real-world managerial perspective
- Business ethics
- Teamwork and leadership skills
- Cross-functional problem solving
- Effective written and oral communications
- The ability to manage change, risk, and crises
- The ability to manage human resources and diversity
- Personal presentation skills

The core consists of seven required classes (21 hours) taken over the first year: financial accounting, statistics, information technology management, managerial economics, operations management, marketing management, and financial management.

A student may choose to earn a general MBA degree, or may concentrate in an academic discipline, such as marketing, by taking at least 15 hours of coursework within that discipline. Students may also choose a specialization, which is a specifically designed set of courses. Our market-driven specializations are designed to give graduates outstanding employment prospects. McCombs also offers a wide array of electives that provide for a flexible curriculum that allows students to tailor their education.

For specializations in each of our five major disciplines, please visit our website: http://texasmba.bus.utexas.edu/admissions/cur/.

When McCombs MBAs describe their favorite aspects of the school, they often cite the quality and accessibility of the faculty. These gifted men and women—more than 150 of them—understand their roles as teachers, but also as mentors whose advice, contacts, and guidance can transform your career. Among our many star faculty, we have Andrew Whinston, internationally renowned for his e-commerce insight; preeminent finance researchers Laura Starks and Sheridan Titman; Vijay Mahajan, digital marketing guru; and Robert Green, a key globalizer of business education.

MBA Investment Fund was established in 1994. The MBA Investment Fund, LLC is the first legally constituted, private investment company to be managed by students.

EDS Financial Trading and Technology Center serves the student managers of the MBA Investment Fund, as well as other students of finance. The center houses a state-of-the-art trading facility replicating those on Wall Street. Live financial data feeds, videoconferencing capability, and access to satellite links dramatically reduce the distance between Austin and financial capitals around the world.

Electronic Digital Economy is part of the Center for Research in Electronic Commerce, where internationally known researchers Andrew Whinston and Anitesh Barua run a living laboratory of e-commerce and MBA students form and operate online companies.

MOOT CORP® International Business Plan Competition places McCombs at the top as founder and host of the "Super Bowl of business plan competitions."

Quality Management Consortia is an entrepreneurial venture run jointly by business and engineering graduate students and serves as a consulting company for local-area companies. Students solve real business problems while earning part-time salaries and University benefits.

Venture Capital Fellows evaluate business plans received from their VC partners and help groom entrepreneurs and their companies for presenting to potential investors.

McCombs School of Business

Community Consulting Program is a student initiative. This program partners McCombs MBA students with Austin-area nonprofit organizations to tackle real management issues.

This fall marks the introduction of TEXAS+ to the standard curriculum—an exciting curriculum change that incorporates comprehensive development into the McCombs MBA.

In the spring of 2001, the McCombs School's commitment to hands-on learning and market-driven education led to an exciting change in the MBA program—the approval of TEXAS+. This curriculum enhancement is aimed at the comprehensive development of MBA students. Under the new arrangement, to be rolled out for incoming students in the fall of 2002, each academic semester will break into two seven-week modules with a two-week period in between (the "Plus") dedicated to short programs that enrich the standard curriculum. Ranging from international business tours to professional development seminars, the two-week programs will help develop the broad perspective and total character that are the hallmark of a well-rounded corporate leader.

CAMPUS LIFE

The University of Texas at Austin's 357-acre main campus sits in the heart of Austin, Texas—the state's capital, and home to hundreds of major employers like Dell, Motorola, IBM, Applied Materials, 3M, Samsung, AMD, and National Instruments. It also boasts a nurturing climate for start-ups, as home to the Austin Technology Incubator, Austin Ventures, and a slew of investment banks and traditional firms. UT Austin has the fifth largest academic library system in the U.S., which includes 20 libraries, and is listed among the greatest libraries of the world.

A city of lakes, hills, live music, and cosmopolitan culture, Austin used to be the big surprise awaiting prospective students. Today, the secret is pretty much out, but the quality of life that made Austin great remains. The moderate climate makes outdoor recreation a year-round pleasure. In addition to its scenic beauty, laid-back atmosphere, and great sense of history, Austin has a lively arts and music scene.

The McCombs School of Business is a four-building complex of 350,000 square feet that houses classrooms, offices, research centers, and computer laboratories. It features a three-story atrium and cafeteria, a state-of-the-art multimedia service center, and the Ford Career Center—one of the country's best corporate interviewing facilities. The business school is home to cutting-edge facilities with nearly 900 workstations in seven different computer labs and an NT lab equipped with 142 state-of-the-art workstations. The school runs a common, wireless operating environment modeled on the highest corporate standards. All graduate classrooms have Ethernet ports and power at each seat. In fact, just about anywhere you are within the McCombs School—private study rooms, our huge tech workroom, the dining and lounge areas—you can sit down and connect to a virtual learning community that runs 24 hours a day.

Every year, recruiters from more than 400 public and private companies come to the McCombs School of Business to recruit. They find our students to be more than prepared to meet the challenges they will face in today's rapidly changing workplace.

The Ford Career Center at McCombs is a remarkable 10,290-square-foot interviewing suite comprised of 43 professional interviewing rooms and a recruiter lounge, fronted by a single-point-of-service foyer. Beautifully designed and supremely practical, as much thought went into the facility's psychological impact as into its functionality. The Center's recruiter lounge contains private restrooms and phone booths, a kitchen area with vending machines and free coffee, fax and copy machines, and laptop ports. Each interview room is wired for laptop use, and one of the larger rooms has videoconferencing and remote interviewing capabilities. Outside the facility, a bank of changing rooms and suit lockers make preparation for interviews hassle-free for students. The Ford Career Center posts opportunities on AccessUT (https://accessut.utexas.edu), a free service that employers use to advertise immediate vacancies to business school students and alumni. We receive an average of 90 full-time, part-time, and internship postings each week.

COSTS

The McCombs School is simply one of the best values among top business schools due mainly to the comparatively lower cost of living in the South and a Texas state mandate that education be widely accessible. Estimated expenses for one year of the two-year, full-time MBA program at the McCombs School are as follows:

Tuition & Fees: $11,540 in state, $24,200 out of state, $24,350 international

Estimated Books: $1,400

Housing: $11,812

Laptop (required): $2,000

One-year costs: $26,952 in state, $39,612 out of state, $39,762 international

Financial aid usually comes in the form of student loans for first-year students. Applicants can apply for most loans and scholarships through the University's Office of Student Financials Services (OSFS). To apply for federal, state, and institutional assistance, students will need OSFS's Application Guide: Steps to Financing Your Education and the Free Application for Federal Student Aid (FAFSA). Interested applicants should see www.utexas.edu/student/finaid.

The recommended deadline for most financial aid applications is March 31. Additional information is available through the School's in-house financial aid officer at 512-471-7698.

The McCombs MBA offers several different means of direct assistance.

Longhorn Business and Admissions Scholarships: Longhorn Business and Admissions Scholarships provide assistance with tuition and fees for a limited number of outstanding applicants. Consideration for the scholarship is automatic at the time of admission. Scholarships are offered to students who demonstrate a superior record of academic and professional accomplishment through their application materials. Additionally, the McCombs School of Business offers scholarships in smaller amounts ranging from $2,000 to $5,000 throughout the application season.

Continuing Student Scholarships and Awards: During their first year's enrollment, continuing students may apply for a number of scholarships and awards sponsored by the McCombs School of Business and its corporate supporters.

Loans: There are many organizations both inside and outside of the United States that offer school loan programs.

For Minority Students: Texas is a member of The Consortium for Graduate Study in Management, a 14-university alliance that seeks to increase the number of minorities in MBA programs and in managerial positions in business.

For International Students: We have Tuition Assistance for Mexican Students. For more information please visit www.utexas.edu/international/cs/finaid.html.

We also offer Good Neighbor Scholarships for students holding residency status of countries in the Caribbean and North, Central, or South America (except the U.S. and Cuba). For more information please visit www.utexas.edu/international/cs/finaid.html.

ADMISSIONS

Admission to the McCombs School is highly competitive. Last year we received 2,552 applications and admitted 765 students. In reviewing applications, the admissions committee seeks to assess an individual's potential for academic success and future professional growth.

All applicants are urged to meet the December 15 early application date. April 15 is the application deadline for domestic applicants; February 1 for international applicants. Application reviews begin as early as mid-December and are reviewed on a rolling admissions basis in order of their receipt.

The McCombs School of Business accepts the McCombs MBA online application (http://texasmba.bus.utexas.edu/admissions/) or a pdf version of the application (downloadable from PrincetonReview.com and other sites).

UNIVERSITY OF TEXAS — AUSTIN
McCombs School of Business

Admissions Contact: Dr. Matt Turner, Director of Admission, MBA Programs
Address: MBA Program Office, CBA 2.316, Austin, TX 78712
Admissions Phone: 512-471-7612 • Admissions Fax: 512-471-4243
Admissions E-mail: texasmba@bus.utexas.edu • Web Address: texasmba.bus.utexas.edu

You can't beat the bang for the buck you get at the University of Texas at Austin's Graduate School of Business. Perks at this "strong quantitative school" include the EDS Financial Trading and Technology Center, a state-of-the-art research facility, and the Austin Technology Incubator, which assists start-up technology entrepreneurs and provides more than 150 students with hands-on entrepreneurial experience. The "beautiful" city of Austin has "a wonderful culture of live music," a vibrant bar scene, and a climate that allows "outdoor sports all year."

INSTITUTIONAL INFORMATION
Public/Private: Public
Evening Classes Available? Yes
Total Faculty: 154
% Faculty Female: 20
% Faculty Minority: 2
Student/Faculty Ratio: 5:1
Students in Parent Institution: 50,000
Academic Calendar: Semester

PROGRAMS
Degrees Offered: McCombs MBA (2 years); Option II Executive MBA (2 years); Texas Evening MBA (TEMBA) (3 years); PhD (5 years); Master of Public Accounting (MPA) (2 years); Professional Program in Accounting (PPA) (1 year)
Joint Degrees: MBA/MA Asian Studies, Latin American Studies, Middle Eastern Studies, Public Affairs, Post-Soviet Studies, Communications; MBA/MS Manufacturing Systems Engineering or Nursing; MBA/JD.
Academic Specialties: Finance, Management Science and Information Systems, Marketing, Entrepreneurship, Operations, Information Technology
Special Opportunities: Spanish Language Track, MBA Investment Fund, Quality Management Consortium, MOOT Corp
Study Abroad Options: Australia, Europe, Latin America, Asia, Canada

STUDENT INFORMATION
Total Business Students: 783
% Full Time: 100
% Female: 33
% Minority: 4
% Out of State: 31
% International: 26
Average Age: 28

COMPUTER AND RESEARCH FACILITIES
Research Facilities: Centers for Business Research, Electronic Commerce, International Business Education, Management Operations & Logistics, Financial Trading & Technology, Computational/Finance, Energy Finance
Campuswide Network? Yes
Computer Model Recommended: Laptop
Internet Fee? No

EXPENSES/FINANCIAL AID
Annual Tuition (Resident/Nonresident): $3,600/$14,850
Room & Board (Off Campus): $11,386
Books and Supplies: $1,400
Average Grant: $4,054
Average Loan: $16,000
% Receiving Financial Aid: 70
% Receiving Aid Their First Year: 80

ADMISSIONS INFORMATION
Application Fee: $125
Electronic Application? Yes
Regular Application Deadline: 4/15
Regular Notification: 5/1
Length of Deferment: 1 year
Non-fall Admissions? No
Transfer Students Accepted? No
Need-Blind Admissions? Yes
Number of Applications Received: 2,552
% of Applicants Accepted: 30
% Accepted Who Enrolled: 52
Average GPA: 3.3
Average GMAT: 680
Average Years Experience: 5
Other Admissions Factors Considered: Communication skills displayed in essays, diversity of professional skills experiences, optional interview
Minority/Disadvantaged Student Recruitment Programs: Consortium for Graduate Study in Management, GMAC Forums, Texas Tour, Top Ten Schools Forum, Toigo Fellowship, National Society for Hispanic MBAs, National Black MBA Association, National Organization to Increase Women in Business Leadership

INTERNATIONAL STUDENTS
TOEFL Required of International Students? Yes
Minimum TOEFL: 620 (260 computer)

EMPLOYMENT INFORMATION

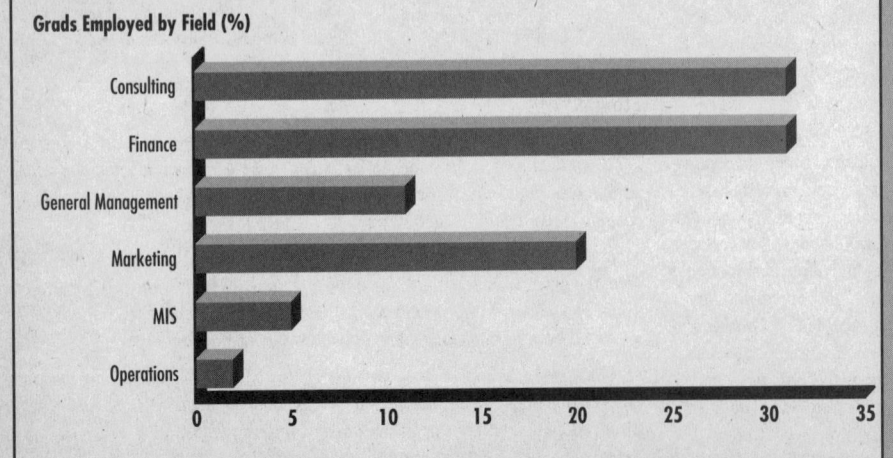

Grads Employed by Field (%)
- Consulting: ~31
- Finance: ~31
- General Management: ~11
- Marketing: ~20
- MIS: ~3
- Operations: ~2

Placement Office Available? Yes
% Employed Within 3 Months: 78
Frequent Employers: IBM, Accenture, Dell, Deloitte Consulting, Frito-Lay, American Airlines, AT Kearney, Diamond Technology Partners, Microsoft Corp., PwC, Deloitte & Touche, Goldman Sachs, JPMorgan Chase, Booz Allen Hamilton, Conoco, Credit Suisse First Boston, Hines, Intel, McKinsey & Co., Motorola
Prominent Alumni: William Johnson, CEO, HJ Heinz; Bill Gurley, general partner, Benchmark Capital; Don Evans, U.S. Secretary of Commerce; Sara Martinez Tucker, CEO, Hispanic Scholarship Fund; Pat Frost, president, Frost National Bank

UNIVERSITY OF TEXAS — SAN ANTONIO
College of Business

Admissions Contact: Suzette Vallejo, Supervisor Graduate Admissions
Address: 6900 N. Loop 1604 West, San Antonio, TX 78249-0603
Admissions Phone: 210-458-4330 • Admissions Fax: 210-458-4332
Admissions E-mail: graduatestudies@utsa.edu • Web Address: business.utsa.edu

The University of Texas at San Antonio offers its students a solid, broad-based education with comprehensive business goals. UTSA provides students with a handful of MBA programs to choose from and opportunities to interact with top local business leaders with programs like the Frost Bank Distinguished Lecture Series and the Business Ethics Symposium. The Executive MBA is a five-semester plan designed for executives and entrepreneurs with significant managerial experience, while the International MBA is designed for students with proficiency in one of the six modern languages, enabling them to study business administration in the context of a global business outlook. The Weekend MBA and Online MBA are also available.

INSTITUTIONAL INFORMATION
Public/Private: Public
Evening Classes Available? Yes
Total Faculty: 71
% Faculty Female: 24
Students in Parent Institution: 19,843
Academic Calendar: Semester

PROGRAMS
Degrees Offered: MBA (33 to 57 credits, 12 months to 6 years); MBA in International Business (MBA) (33 to 63 credits, 12 months to 6 years); Master of Science in Accounting (MS) (30 to 60 credits, 12 months to 6 years); Master of Taxation (MTax) (30 to 60 credits, 12 months to 6 years); Master of Science in Management of Technology (MSMOT) (30 credits, 12 months to 6 years); Executive MBA (MBA) (42 credits, 21 months); Master of Arts in Economics (MA) (33 to 48 credits, 12 months to 6 years); Master of Science in Finance (MS) (33 to 48 credits, 12 months to 6 years); Master of Science in Information Technology (MS) (33 to 51 credits, 12 months to 6 years)
Special Opportunities: Internship program; UNAM program; NAFTA class
Study Abroad Options: Canada, Mexico

STUDENT INFORMATION
Total Business Students: 311
% Female: 38
% Minority: 21
% International: 38
Average Age: 29

COMPUTER AND RESEARCH FACILITIES
Computer Facilities: Access to online bibliographic retrieval services and online databases
Campuswide Network? Yes
Internet Fee? No

EXPENSES/FINANCIAL AID
Annual Tuition (Resident/Nonresident): $2,268/$6,066
Tuition Per Credit (Resident/Nonresident): $126/$337

ADMISSIONS INFORMATION
Application Fee: $25
Electronic Application? Yes
Regular Application Deadline: 7/1
Regular Notification: Rolling
Deferment Available? Yes
Length of Deferment: 3 terms
Non-fall Admissions? Yes
Non-fall Application Deadline(s): 11/1 spring, 5/1 summer
Transfer Students Accepted? Yes
Transfer Policy: Please refer to current graduate catalog.
Need-Blind Admissions? Yes
Number of Applications Received: 169
% of Applicants Accepted: 68
% Accepted Who Enrolled: 67
Average GPA: 3.2
Average GMAT: 564
GMAT Range: 530-590
Other Admissions Factors Considered: Letters of reference, a current résumé, and a personal statement are strongly recommended.

INTERNATIONAL STUDENTS
TOEFL Required of International Students? Yes
Minimum TOEFL: 500

EMPLOYMENT INFORMATION
Placement Office Available? Yes

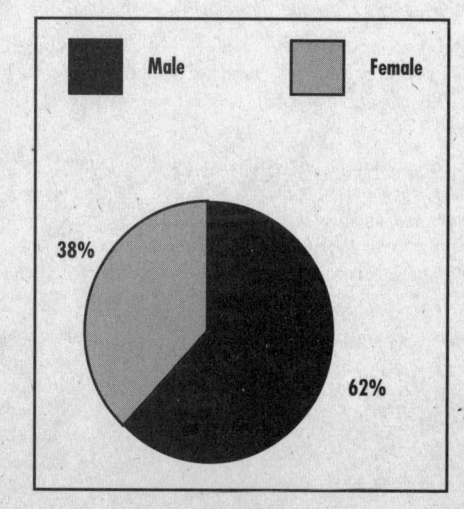

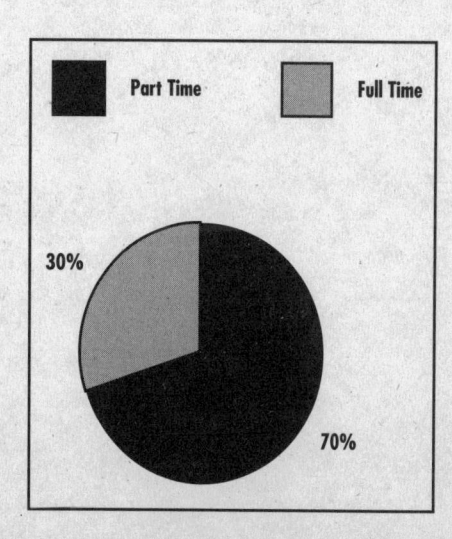

Male 62% / Female 38%

Part Time 70% / Full Time 30%

UNIVERSITY OF THE PACIFIC

THE UNIVERSITY AT A GLANCE

The University of the Pacific was recently ranked as a top 10 national "hidden treasure" in the Kaplan/Newsweek College Guide. This ranking is due in large part to the student-centered focus and emphasis on learning that have been a hallmark of a Pacific education since its founding in 1851.

The Pacific MBA is designed to place young managers on the fast track to a successful and rewarding career. The earlier one is recognized as having rapid promotion potential, the quicker one's career advances. This is the key to becoming a senior executive. The Pacific curriculum focuses on the skills and knowledge recent college graduates and young professionals need to be future business leaders. Pacific's mission is to provide an MBA education that expands an individual's competitive edge.

The Eberhardt School of Business strives to meet the challenges of a dynamic, technology-driven, global business environment. In the classroom and in the outside business world, students are exposed to the latest in technology development and and new management concepts. For example, all students have the opportunity to participate in a global competitiveness business course, and all students take at least one course in the management of technology and innovation.

The Eberhardt School of Business (ESB) is AACSB-accredited and takes the accrediting body's standards delivering a quality education and commiting to continuous improvement seriously. The School also understands that the classroom is not always the most effective place to learn the skills of successful management and makes extensive use of successful business leaders and their organizations to provide both role models and practice settings.

STUDENTS

The Pacific MBA Program usually enrolls approximately 70 students--of this enrollment 40 percent are female and 15 percent are international. The average student is 23.5 years old with two years of work experience, a 570 GMAT score, and an average undergraduate GPA of 3.40.

About 55 percent of the class possesses undergraduate degrees in business, 21 percent in science or technical majors, 17 percent in liberal arts areas, and 7 percent in social sciences.

A large percentage of ESB's students are from California, although there are students from many leading universities.

ACADEMICS

The hallmark of a Pacific MBA is a student-centered learning environment that prepares students with various academic backgrounds and experiences for success in a collaborative, team-based effort between students, faculty, and administrators. In addition, our three core program strengths—leadership, innovation, and globalization—are infused throughout the curriculum.

The School's mission is to prepare students for successful careers as leaders of business, government, and nonprofit organizations by integrating a broad-based educational foundation with business principles in a personalized learning environment that emphasizes small classes and opportunities for extensive interaction between students, faculty, and practitioners.

For its students, ESB strives to:

- Develop skills in leadership and innovation
- Develop technical and analytical competence
- Develop an understanding of the global business environment
- Instill concern for issues of ethics and social responsibility
- Encourage community service

The MBA Program consists of two phases:

Phase I: Foundation Courses: This phase includes 10 courses covering basic business skills. Students who have successfully completed similar courses at the undergraduate or graduate level with a B or better letter grade can waive each of these foundation courses. Students able to waive all 10 of the Phase I courses are eligible to enter into the Pacific MBA One-Year Accelerated Program. The phase I courses are Data and Decisions, The Firm and Competition, Financial Accounting, Managerial Accounting, Management Information Systems, Legal Environments of Business, Operations Management, Financial Management, Marketing Management, and Organizational Behavior.

Phase II: Integrative Courses: Phase II contains the advanced conceptual and skill courses of the Pacific MBA. Students may choose either a General Management, Entrepreneurship, Finance, or Marketing specialization. All specializations emphasize leadership and innovation, and take an integrative approach to studying business administration. Each specialization focuses on providing a career pathway for each student:

- The Entrepreneurship specialization is designed to provide young professionals with the skill sets to start or manage a rapidly growing company.
- The General Management specialization is designed for those seeking careers in human resource managemnt, strategic planning, strategy consulting, and international business.
- The Finance specialization is designed for young professionals seeking careers in investments, portfolio management, and corporate finance.
- The Marketing specialization is designed for students who have career goals in the areas of product management, marketing research, relationship management, and value chain management.

In addition, to the MBA, ESB has jointly developed the following programs: JD/MBA (Juris Doctorate in law and MBA), Master's Internationalist (MBA with a Peace Corps service), and PharmD/MBA (Doctor of Pharmacy and MBA).

Graduating Pacific MBAs rank the quality and accessibility of the faculty as one of the top reasons for their satisfaction in attending Pacific. The Eberhardt School of Business is committed to teaching excellence. ESB believes teaching is the primary responsibility of the faculty. Faculty research is viewed as a complement to the teaching mission and allows faculty to offer instruction that is relevant and current. In addition, close ties to industry allow faculty to provide real-world applications to students, which assist in the development of marketable job skills.

Currently, the MBA student/faculty ratio is 7:1. Because of this low ratio, MBA faculty members are able to devote considerable time and effort to the personal and professional development of students. This mentoring opportunity is one of the key ingredients in the development focus that characterizes the UOP MBA.

Other special opportunities available at Eberhardt include the following:

CFA Preparation: The Finance specialization offers the opportunity to review and prepare for the Chartered Financial Analysts (CFA) examination, Level I. This is offered through comprehensive training with assigned Eberhardt School of Business faculty members.

The Center for Entrepreneurship: The Center houses programs and services that foster the spirit of entrepreneurship. The mission of the Center is to bring together academic, community, and business resources to foster a greater understanding of entrepreneurship, to support family businesses, and to engender interest in entrepreneurship as a viable life-long career option. Center programs include:

- Invention Evaluation Service (IES): Every year several students are selected to staff the IES. These students gain intense hands-on practical training completing feasibility studies for inventors considering launch of their inventions.

Eberhardt School of Business

- **Institute for Family Business (IFB):** Students participating in or simply interested in the dynamics of family business can participate in activities run through IFB. These include seminars, conferences, and workshops with nationally renowned experts in the areas of family business.
- **Entrepreneur in Residence:** ESB students have access to successful entrepreneurs who work with the School to conduct seminars and work shops and provide consulting services to those students majoring in or with strong interest in entrepreneurial ventures.

CAMPUS LIFE

The University of the Pacific's 150-acre Stockton campus is located in the center of the city affectionately known as "California's Sunrise Seaport." The University and the School of Business have taken advantage of their Central Valley location to develop a close working relationship with many regional employers in the Central Valley, Sacramento, and the Bay Area. These employers also provide the MBA students with a variety of fieldwork opportunities, including internships, mentorships, and class-based consulting assignments.

Stockton is a city of just over 250,000 people blessed with a rich cultural history and many recreational opportunities, including over 1,000 miles of winding Delta waterways. In addition, a short road trip of 1.5 to 2.5 hours will land you in San Francisco, Monterey, and the Central California Coast to the West or Lake Tahoe, the Sierra ski resorts, and Yosemite National Park to the East. The University is also home each July to the San Francisco 49ers professional football team's training camp.

The Eberhardt School of Business houses one of eight main computing labs on campus. The ESB computer lab presently maintains state-of-the-art hardware and software and provides easy access to all of the campus computing resources and the Internet. The UOP Information Commons, located in the main library, provides 55 computer workstations as well as carrels equipped for laptops. These workstations have access to library databases, Web-based resources, and word processing and spreadsheet software. MBA students are provided disk space for maintaining their materials and are allowed to create their own websites on ESB's server.

The library website (http://library.uop.edu) is also a portal to the library's catalog, which allows access to electronic databases, e-mail reference service, interlibrary loan services, Internet resource guides and other library services. Most of the databases are available from any off-campus location through the off-campus link. Wireless internet access is available across campus providing connections for laptop users in many areas of the campus.

Our students often choose to take advantage of the network of relationships that ESB has developed with the corporate community. ESB strives to use this network to integrate the classroom with the business world. Business world experiences include the Pacific Business Forum, which brings nationally and internationally recognized corporate or governmental leaders to campus to speak about current issues in the world today and how they affect businesses. ESB also runs the Westgate Center for Management Development, which provides management training for the regional business community. The School's Business Advisory Board includes 30 executives from local, regional, and national businesses who work with the School to integrate the School's curriculum and programs with the needs of the business world. Finally, the Mentorship and Internship program allows students to be matched with business leaders and help make decisions regarding classes, careers, and the job search process; or to gain business exposure on an individual basis or as part of a consulting team.

The ESB Office of Career Services works in close proximity with the University's Career and Internship Center to offer many services to help develop MBA student capabilities and provide access to employers. This begins with a full-time Director of Employment and Internships who is constantly seeking new and unusual opportunities for our students. In addition, the Office provides workshops, individual counseling, and mentoring opportunities to develop students' career skills. Also, career fairs and campus recruiting sessions provide students with the chance to meet individually with employers and present themselves and their capabilities.

COSTS

The University of the Pacific was recently named by Kaplan/Newsweek as one of the top 10 regional universities with respect to Return on Student Investment.

Annual full-time costs for the 2002–2003 MBA Program for all students, including international and out-of state students, are as follows:

Tuition and fees: $20,820
Housing and living expenses (estimated): $10,500
Books and personal expenses (estimated): $ 2,100
Total annual costs: $33,420

From day one assistance is available including scholarships, graduate assistantships, and loans. We make it a point to make sure our high-achieving MBA students get the assistance they deserve upon entry into the Pacific MBA Program.

To be considered for any federal or state assistance, you must file a Free Application for Federal Student Aid (FAFSA). This form is available through the Office of Financial Assistance at the University, (209-946-2629) or on the Internet at www.fafsa.ed.gov. The recommended due date for the FAFSA is February 15 each year for the upcoming academic year.

In addition to federal, state, and corporate assistance, the Eberhardt School of Business offers several sources of direct aid for its students:

Eberhardt School of Business Scholarships: The ESB scholarships provides direct tuition and fee assistance to a number of academically outstanding students each year. To be considered, a student must complete a scholarship application with their application for admission.

ESB Graduate Assistantships: A limited number of Graduate Assistantships are awarded to students who wish to earn tuition remission by being assigned to an MBA faculty member to support his/her teaching and research efforts. Generally students may earn up to one-third of a semester's tuition through a Graduate Assistantship.

Additionally, those students who have a minimum 3.25 undergraduate GPA and a 600 GMAT score may apply for an Eberhardt MBA Scholars Assistantship. Students awarded these assistantships may earn up to half of a semester's tuition for their Graduate Assistantship assignment.

ADMISSIONS

The MBA Admissions Committee completes a personalized review of each application evaluating each individual's potential for a successful professional career. In addition to GPA, GMAT scores and recommendations, factors such as professional, managerial and leadership background from internships and work experience are used as indicators of potential for career success.

The Pacific MBA offers three enrollment options with the following application dates preferred:

Fall Semester: March 1

Spring Semester: November 1

Summer Session: March 15

Applications are reviewed on a rolling basis year round in the order of receipt and completion. International students and students applying to joint programs (i.e. MBA/JD, PharmD/MBA, or MBA/Peace Corps) are encouraged to apply at least 6 to 9 months in advance of planned enrollment.

Admissions Contact: Christopher Lozano, ESB Director, Student Recruitment
Address: MBA Program, 3601 Pacific Avenue, Stockton, CA 95211
Admissions Phone: 800-952-3179 • Admissions Fax: 209-946-2586
Admissions E-mail: mba@uop.edu • Web Address: www.uop.edu/esb

UNIVERSITY OF THE PACIFIC
Eberhardt School of Business

Admissions Contact: Christopher Lozano, ESB Director, Student Recruitment
Address: MBA Program, 3601 Pacific Avenue, Stockton, CA 95211
Admissions Phone: 800-952-3179 • Admissions Fax: 209-946-2586
Admissions E-mail: mba@uop.edu • Web Address: www.uop.edu/esb

The Eberhardt School of Business provides its MBA students with a wagonload of academic options. They begin with numerous study abroad opportunities, including locales like South Korea, Singapore (can you say "Asian Tigers"?) Chile, Malaysia, Spain, Ireland, France, and England. Full-time students with limited prior work experience should participate in an internship between the first and second years. Pacific's tuition is that of a private school, and the student body is small. Most MBA grads go into general management and consulting.

INSTITUTIONAL INFORMATION
Public/Private: Private
Evening Classes Available? Yes
Total Faculty: 12
% Faculty Female: 12
% Faculty Minority: 6
Student/Faculty Ratio: 8:1
Students in Parent Institution: 5,800
Academic Calendar: Semester

PROGRAMS
Degrees Offered: MBA (full time, 1 to 2 years)
Joint Degrees: MBA/JD (4 years), Peace Corps MBA (4.5 years)
Academic Specialties: MIS/E-Commerce, Strategy, Commercial Law, Real Estate Law, Residential and Commercial Real Estate, Marketing Research Methods, Consumer Behavior, Small Business Strategy, Entrepreneurship, Production/Operations Management
Study Abroad Options: All Peace Corps sites; global study-abroad trip offered at various locations

STUDENT INFORMATION
Total Business Students: 61
% Full Time: 52
% Female: 30
% Minority: 15
% Out of State: 10
% International: 10
Average Age: 27

COMPUTER AND RESEARCH FACILITIES
Research Facilities: Wireless Internet
Computer Facilities: Dow Jones Retrieval; Business Index ASAP; all databases (about 50-75) available through Pacificat
Campuswide Network? Yes
% of MBA Classrooms Wired: 6
Computer Model Recommended: Laptop
Internet Fee? No

EXPENSES/FINANCIAL AID
Annual Tuition: $19,830
Tuition Per Credit: $661
Room & Board (On/Off Campus): $7,350/$8,000
Books and Supplies: $2,000
Average Grant: $3,000
Average Loan: $18,000
% Receiving Financial Aid: 95
% Receiving Aid Their First Year: 95

ADMISSIONS INFORMATION
Application Fee: $50
Electronic Application? Yes
Regular Application Deadline: 5/1
Regular Notification: Rolling
Length of Deferment: 1 year
Non-fall Application Deadline(s): 11/1 spring, 3/15 summer
Transfer Policy: Students may waive all first-year courses if they have completed them with a B or better from another AACSB-accredited college. Students may transfer up to 2 Phase II courses from another AACSB-accredited MBA program.
Need-Blind Admissions? Yes
Number of Applications Received: 60
% of Applicants Accepted: 73
% Accepted Who Enrolled: 68
Average GPA: 3.4
GPA Range: 3.0-3.5
Average GMAT: 553
GMAT Range: 500-590
Average Years Experience: 4
Other Admissions Factors Considered: Grade trends, formula score (GPA x 200 + GMAT must be 1100 or higher)
Other Schools to Which Students Applied: California Polytechnic State University, San Luis Obispo, California State University-Sacramento, Saint Mary's College of California, Santa Clara University, University of California-Berkeley, University of California-Davis, University of San Francisco

INTERNATIONAL STUDENTS
TOEFL Required of International Students? Yes
Minimum TOEFL: 550 (213 computer)

EMPLOYMENT INFORMATION

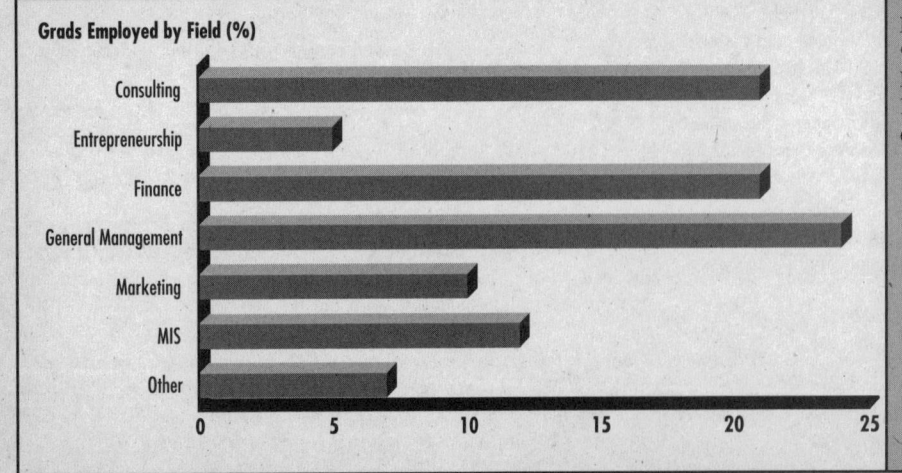

Grads Employed by Field (%)
- Consulting: 21
- Entrepreneurship: 5
- Finance: 21
- General Management: 24
- Marketing: 10
- MIS: 12
- Other: 7

Placement Office Available? Yes
% Employed Within 3 Months: 90
Frequent Employers: Andersen Consulting, Pac West Telecommunications, E&J Gallo Winery, Lawrence Livermore National Lab

UNIVERSITY OF TOLEDO
College of Business Administration

Admissions Contact: John Reynolds, Jr., Director, MBA and EMBA Programs
Address: College of Business Administration, University of Toledo, Toledo, OH 43606-3390
Admissions Phone: 419-530-2775 • Admissions Fax: 419-530-7260
Admissions E-mail: mba@utoledo.edu • Web Address: www.business.utoledo.edu/degrees/mba

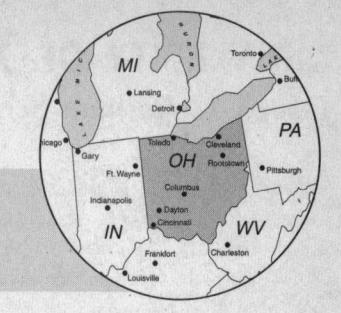

DaimlerChrysler, General Motors, Ford, and Owens Corning: These are some of the big names that hire UT MBA graduates. The MBA program houses less than 100 students who are mostly male part timers. A multitude of study abroad opportunities are available around the globe, including Australia, the Czech Republic, England, Ireland, Japan, Mexico, and Thailand. The MBA program offers an Executive MBA for mid-career working professionals and the option of a Juris Doctor/MBA dual degree in four years.

INSTITUTIONAL INFORMATION
Public/Private: Public
Evening Classes Available? Yes
Total Faculty: 58
% Faculty Female: 20
% Faculty Part Time: 2
Student/Faculty Ratio: 10:1
Students in Parent Institution: 20,313
Academic Calendar: Semester

PROGRAMS
Degrees Offered: MBA (30 to 60 credits, 12 to 24 months); Executive MBA (42 credits, 15 months); MS in Accounting (30 credits, 12 to 24 months); MS in Manufacturing Management (33 credits, 12 to 24 months)
Joint Degrees: JD/MBA (3 years)
Study Abroad Options: Italy, Chile, Spain, Israel, China, France, Ireland, England, Scotland, Germany, Thailand, Australia, Denmark, Costa Rica, New Zealand, Czech Republic, Japan, Mexico

STUDENT INFORMATION
% Female: 39
% Minority: 6
% International: 48
Average Age: 27

COMPUTER AND RESEARCH FACILITIES
Campuswide Network? Yes
% of MBA Classrooms Wired: 80
Computer Model Recommended: Desktop
Internet Fee? No

EXPENSES/FINANCIAL AID
Annual Tuition (Resident/Nonresident): $6,335/$13,694
Tuition Per Credit (Resident/Nonresident): $264/$571
Room & Board (Off Campus): $5,500
Books and Supplies: $1,000
Average Grant: $12,564
Average Loan: $18,500

ADMISSIONS INFORMATION
Application Fee: $30
Electronic Application? Yes
Regular Application Deadline: Rolling
Regular Notification: Rolling
Deferment Available? Yes
Length of Deferment: 1 year
Non-fall Admissions? Yes
Non-fall Application Deadline(s): 8/1, 4/15, 11/15; international: 5/1, 10/1, 3/1
Transfer Students Accepted? Yes
Transfer Policy: Maximum 10 credits with at least a B from an AACSB-accredited school
Need-Blind Admissions? No
Number of Applications Received: 213
% of Applicants Accepted: 87
% Accepted Who Enrolled: 52
Average GPA: 3.3
Average GMAT: 517
Other Admissions Factors Considered: Work/research/computer experience, type of undergraduate or professional degree
Other Schools to Which Students Applied: Bowling Green State University, University of Findlay, Wayne State University

INTERNATIONAL STUDENTS
TOEFL Required of International Students? Yes
Minimum TOEFL: 550 (213 computer)

EMPLOYMENT INFORMATION
Placement Office Available? Yes
Frequent Employers: Dana Corporation, Owens Corning, Owens Illinois, DaimlerChrysler, Dana Commercial Credit, Libbey, Ford Motor Co., General Motors Corp., Sun Oil Co., Eaton Aeroquip
Prominent Alumni: Edward Kinsey, cofounder, Ariba, Inc.; Ora Alleman, VP, National City Bank; Michael Durik, executive VP, The Limited Stores, Inc.; Marvin Herb, CEO, Coca-Cola Bottling Company; Julie Higgins, executive VP, Trust Company of Toledo

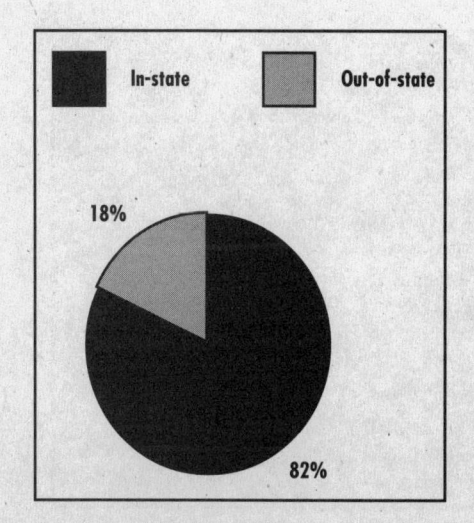

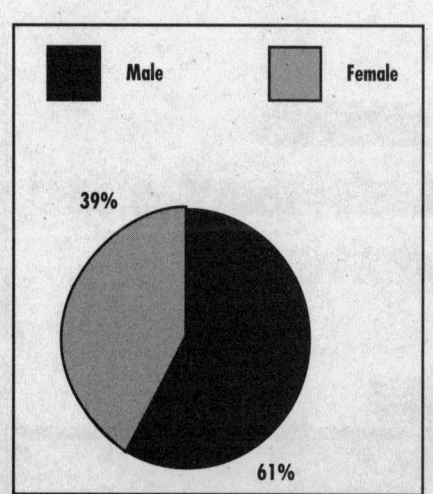

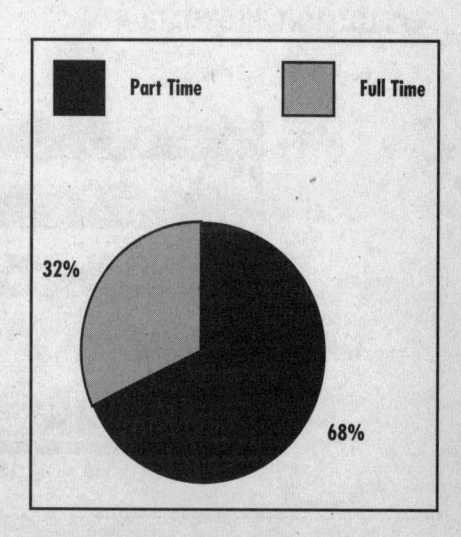

In-state: 82% / Out-of-state: 18%
Male: 61% / Female: 39%
Part Time: 68% / Full Time: 32%

UNIVERSITY OF TORONTO
Joseph L. Rotman School of Management

Admissions Contact: Cheryl Millington, Director, MBA Recruitment and Admissions
Address: 105 St. George Street, Toronto, ON M5S 3E6 Canada
Admissions Phone: 416-978-3499 • Admissions Fax: 416-978-5812
Admissions E-mail: mba@rotman.utoronto.ca • Web Address: www.rotman.utoronto.ca

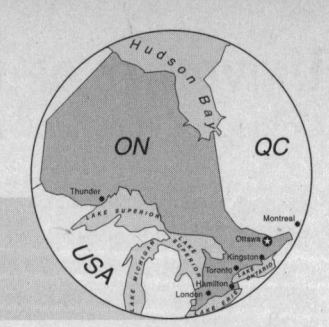

The average starting salary of an MBA graduate for the 2001 class of U Toronto's Rotman School of Management was $102,000. Not bad, eh? MBA program options include the Part-Time MBA, the Full-Time MBA, and the Executive MBA, completed in one year. The Joseph L. Rotman School of Management also offers two strong dual degree programs, the Juris Doctor/MBA and the Master of Nursing/MBA, and both are well regarded in their respective fields. The Rotman MBA also offers opportunities to study in France, the Czech Republic, Israel, Hong Kong, and Singapore, but you'll have to work hard to earn that global advantage, as admission to the study abroad program is pretty selective.

INSTITUTIONAL INFORMATION
Public/Private: Public
Evening Classes Available? Yes
Total Faculty: 81
% Faculty Female: 23
% Faculty Part Time: 17
Student/Faculty Ratio: 3:1
Students in Parent Institution: 52,797

PROGRAMS
Degrees Offered: MBA (2 years full time, 3 years part time); Executive MBA (20 months); Master of Management and Professional Accounting (27 months)
Joint Degrees: JD/MBA (4 years); BASC/MBA (5.6); Master of Nursing/MBA (4 years); MA Russian and Eastern European Studies/MBA (4 years)
Academic Specialties: Finance, Marketing, Strategic Management
Special Opportunities: MBA Exchange Program for second-year students
Study Abroad Options: Austria, China, Singapore, Israel, Mexico, France, Germany, Czech Republic

STUDENT INFORMATION
Total Business Students: 264
% Full Time: 100
% Female: 26
% International: 30
Average Age: 27

COMPUTER AND RESEARCH FACILITIES
Research Facilities: Business Information Centre (student library), Institute for International Business, Clarkson Centre for Business Ethics, Capital Markets Institute
Computer Facilities: EMBAnet: online community for all Rotman students; Rotman Online: access to course materials, study groups, etc.
Campuswide Network? Yes
% of MBA Classrooms Wired: 100
Computer Model Recommended: Laptop
Internet Fee? No

EXPENSES/FINANCIAL AID
Annual Tuition (Resident/Nonresident): $41,000/$47,150
Room & Board (Off Campus): $10,000
Books and Supplies: $800
Average Grant: $1,000
Average Loan: $30,000

ADMISSIONS INFORMATION
Application Fee: $125
Electronic Application? Yes
Early Decision Application Deadline: Domestic students only
Early Decision Notification: 1/15
Regular Application Deadline: 4/30
Regular Notification: 7/1
Length of Deferment: 1 year
Non-fall Admissions? No
Transfer Students Accepted? No
Need-Blind Admissions? Yes
Number of Applications Received: 905
% of Applicants Accepted: 24
% Accepted Who Enrolled: 62
Average GPA: 3.7
GPA Range: 3.6-3.8
Average GMAT: 674
Average Years Experience: 4
Other Admissions Factors Considered: Interview if requested by Admissions Committee
Other Schools to Which Students Applied: Queen's University, University of Western Ontario

INTERNATIONAL STUDENTS
TOEFL Required of International Students? Yes
Minimum TOEFL: 600 (250 computer)

EMPLOYMENT INFORMATION

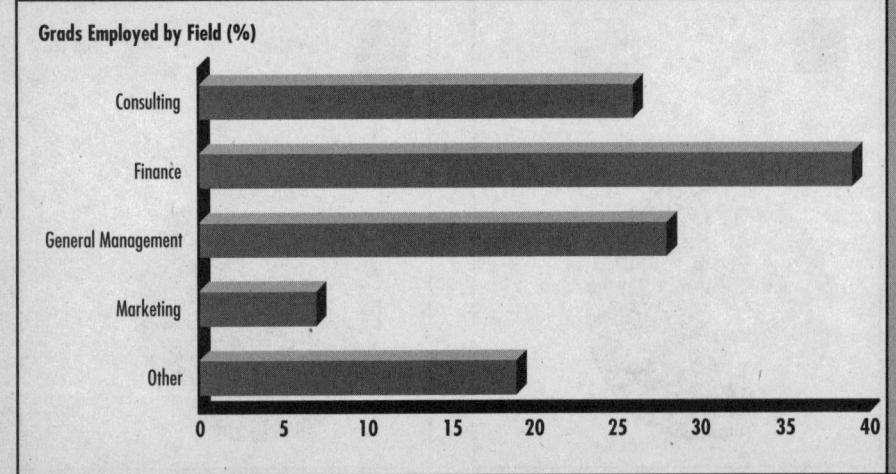

Grads Employed by Field (%)
- Consulting: ~26
- Finance: ~39
- General Management: ~28
- Marketing: ~7
- Other: ~19

Placement Office Available? Yes
% Employed Within 3 Months: 100
Frequent Employers: Manulife Financial, Canadian Imperial Bank of Commerce, Ernst & Young Corporate Finance, Mercer, RBC Dominion Securities, Cap Gemini, PricewaterhouseCoopers, AT&T, Boston Consulting Group, Bank of Montreal
Prominent Alumni: Joseph L. Rotman, founder and chairman, Clairvest Group Inc.; Ian Locke, former VP, Netscape Communications Corp.; Jim Balsillie, chairman and co-CEO, Research in Motion

UNIVERSITY OF TULSA
College of Business Administration

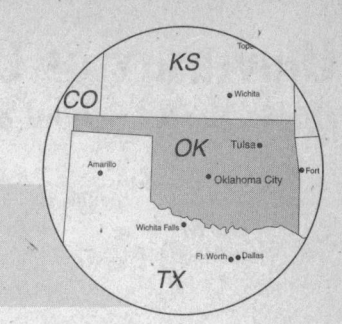

Admissions Contact: Rebecca Holland, Director of Graduate Business Programs
Address: BAH 215, 600 S. College Avenue, Tulsa, OK 74104-3189
Admissions Phone: 918-631-2242 • Admissions Fax: 918-631-2142
Admissions E-mail: graduate.business@tulsa.edu • Web Address: www.utulsa.edu

The UT College of Business Administration offers a private education with a global focus. The low student/faculty ratio allows students to feel immediately "at home" with their professors and in the classroom. UT has multimedia classrooms, several internship opportunities in the Tulsa region, and numerous community service business projects that connect MBA students with the business community. Don't come to Tulsa expecting to globetrot your way through the program, though, as study abroad options are limited to undergraduate students. Frequent employers include PricewaterhouseCoopers, Microsoft, and Boeing.

INSTITUTIONAL INFORMATION
Public/Private: Private
Evening Classes Available? Yes
Total Faculty: 56
% Faculty Female: 24
% Faculty Minority: 8
Student/Faculty Ratio: 7:1
Students in Parent Institution: 4,100
Academic Calendar: Semester

PROGRAMS
Degrees Offered: Master of Taxation (30 credits); MS in Finance (30 credits); MBA (30 credits); Internet-mediated MBA (iMBA) (36 credits including foundation work)
Joint Degrees: JD/MBA (78 law credits and 24 hours of business courses); JD/MTax (78 law credits and 24 hours of business courses); Master of Engineering/Technology Management (36 credits; 18 engineering and 18 business)
Academic Specialties: Taxation; Management Information Systems. Finance program offers 4 options including Risk Management, Corporate Finance, Investments and Portfolio Management, and International Finance. Special lab offering experiential learning has been built for the Finance graduate program.
Study Abroad Options: One international course involving travel abroad for 2 to 6 weeks is offered at least once per year.

STUDENT INFORMATION
Total Business Students: 203
% Full Time: 22
% Female: 30
% Minority: 6
% Out of State: 11
% International: 4
Average Age: 26

COMPUTER AND RESEARCH FACILITIES
Computer Facilities: Computer labs available; databases include Lexis-Nexis, Innopac, and a variety of academic resources.
Campuswide Network? Yes
% of MBA Classrooms Wired: 100
Computer Model Recommended: No
Internet Fee? No

EXPENSES/FINANCIAL AID
Tuition Per Credit: $560

ADMISSIONS INFORMATION
Application Fee: $30
Electronic Application? Yes
Regular Application Deadline: Rolling
Regular Notification: Rolling
Length of Deferment: 1 year
Non-fall Application Deadline(s): 1/5 fall, 5/15 spring, 8/15 summer

Transfer Policy: Up to 6 credits
Need-Blind Admissions? Yes
Number of Applications Received: 90
% of Applicants Accepted: 69
% Accepted Who Enrolled: 56
Average GPA: 3.2
GPA Range: 2.5-4.0
Average GMAT: 520
GMAT Range: 400-660
Average Years Experience: 3
Other Admissions Factors Considered: Work experience
Minority/Disadvantaged Student Recruitment Programs: GM minority scholarship
Other Schools to Which Students Applied: Oklahoma State University, University of Oklahoma

INTERNATIONAL STUDENTS
TOEFL Required of International Students? Yes
Minimum TOEFL: 575 (232 computer)

EMPLOYMENT INFORMATION
Placement Office Available? Yes
% Employed Within 3 Months: 95
Frequent Employers: Williams, Boeing, CITGO, Dollar-Thrifty, Hilti, Arthur Andersen, SABRE, Prime America, American Electric Power, KPMG, Deloitte & Touche, WorldCom, Pennwell Publishing

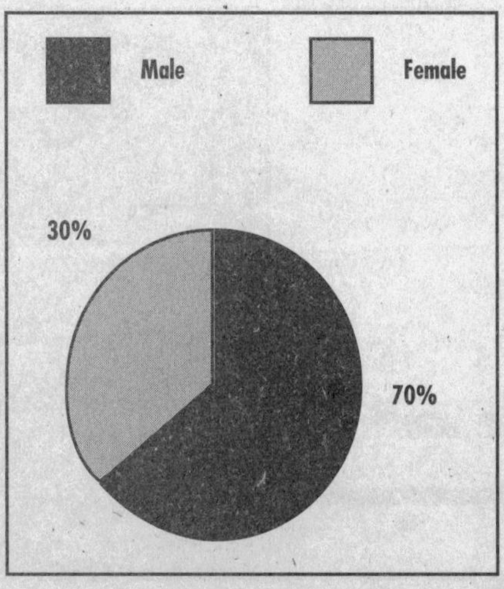

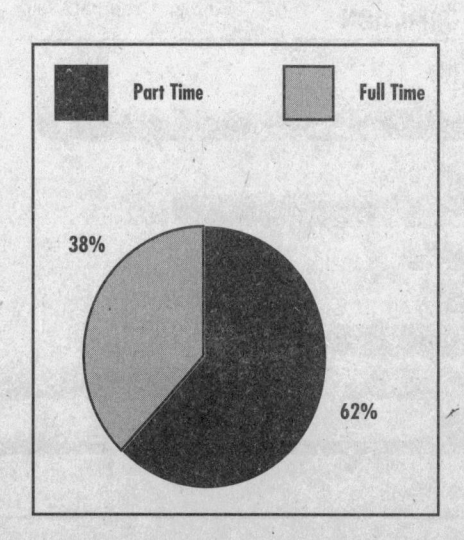

UNIVERSITY OF UTAH
David Eccles School of Business

Admissions Contact: Carrie Radmall, Admissions and Scholarship Coordinator
Address: 1645 East Campus Center Drive, Room 101, Salt Lake City, UT 84112-9301
Admissions Phone: 801-581-7785 • Admissions Fax: 801-581-3666
Admissions E-mail: masters@business.utah.edu • Web Address: www.business.utah.edu/masters

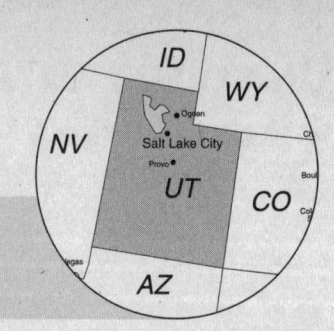

Utilizing its solid computer and research facilities, the MBA curriculum at the David Eccles School of Business emphasizes the importance of information technology and a deep understanding of the global economy. The MBA program promotes "e-business savvy, a global perspective, an entrepreneurial spirit, and professional integrity," and two powerful joint degrees offered by UT are the MBA/Juris Doctor and the unique MBA/Master of Architecture. Frequent employers of Utah MBA grads are Accenture, American Express, Intel, IBM, and PricewaterhouseCoopers.

INSTITUTIONAL INFORMATION
Public/Private: Public
Evening Classes Available? Yes
Total Faculty: 60
% Faculty Female: 28
% Faculty Minority: 16
% Faculty Part Time: 25
Student/Faculty Ratio: 5:1
Students in Parent Institution: 25,500
Academic Calendar: Semester

PROGRAMS
Degrees Offered: Accelerated MBA Program (1 year); Executive MBA (21 months); Professional MBA Program (21 to 32 months); 2-year MBA Program (21 months); Master of Professional Accountancy (9 months); Master of Statistics (minimum 9 months); Master of Science in Finance (minimum 9 months)
Joint Degrees: MBA/JD (3 to 4 years depending on undergraduate degree), MBA/Master of Architecture (3 to 4 years depending on undergraduate degree)
Academic Specialties: Information Systems, Corporate Finance, Entrepreneurship and Emerging Business, International Business (we are 1 of only 25 business schools designated as a Center for International Business Education and Research in the country)

Special Opportunities: MBA exchange programs
Study Abroad Options: Germany, Denmark, Holland

STUDENT INFORMATION
Total Business Students: 370
% Full Time: 49
% Female: 31
% Minority: 7
% Out of State: 34
% International: 22
Average Age: 29

COMPUTER AND RESEARCH FACILITIES
Computer Facilities: Software includes statistical analysis, database management, spreadsheets, financial modeling, graphics, and word processing. Databases or networks in the field of business include ABI/Inform, Lexis-Nexis, Infotrac, CCH Internet Tax Network, and UMI ProQuest Direct.
Campuswide Network? Yes
% of MBA Classrooms Wired: 100
Computer Model Recommended: Laptop
Internet Fee? No

EXPENSES/FINANCIAL AID
Annual Tuition (Resident/Nonresident): $4,300/$11,900
Room & Board (On/Off Campus): $6,000/$11,000
Books and Supplies: $1,500
Average Grant: $12,200

ADMISSIONS INFORMATION
Application Fee: $40
Electronic Application? Yes
Regular Application Deadline: 3/15
Regular Notification: 5/10
Deferment Available? No
Non-fall Application Deadline(s): 1/15 summer
Transfer Students Accepted? No
Need-Blind Admissions? Yes
Number of Applications Received: 230
% of Applicants Accepted: 69
% Accepted Who Enrolled: 69
Average GPA: 3.4
Average GMAT: 600
Average Years Experience: 4
Other Admissions Factors Considered: TSE score (minimum 50) required from international applicants
Minority/Disadvantaged Student Recruitment Programs: Several privately donated scholarships reserved for underrepresented groups and to help us build the gender, ethnic, and geographic diversity of our student body.

INTERNATIONAL STUDENTS
TOEFL Required of International Students? Yes
Minimum TOEFL: 600 (250 computer)

EMPLOYMENT INFORMATION

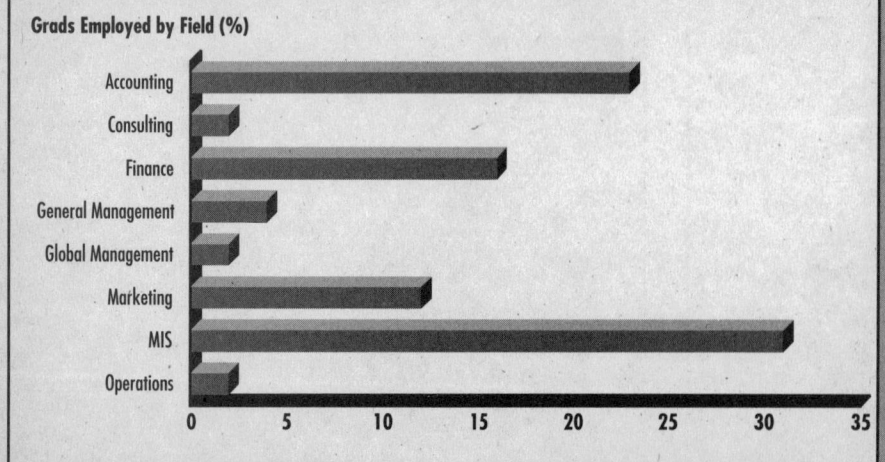

Grads Employed by Field (%)

Field	%
Accounting	23
Consulting	2
Finance	16
General Management	3
Global Management	2
Marketing	12
MIS	31
Operations	2

Placement Office Available? Yes
% Employed Within 3 Months: 91
Frequent Employers: Accenture, American Express, Arthur Andersen, Swloirrw Xonaulrinf, Intermountain Health Care, DMR Consulting, Eaton Corp., IBM, Iomega, Intel, KPMG, PricewaterhouseCoopers
Prominent Alumni: Stephen Covey, cofounder and VP, Franklin Covey; Spencer Eccles, chairman and CEO, First Security Corp.; E. Jake Garn, former U.S. Senator; J. Willard Marriott, chairman, president, and CEO, Marriott Corp.; Geoffrey Wooley, founding partner, Dominion Ventures

UNIVERSITY OF VIRGINIA
Darden Graduate School of Business Administration

Admissions Contact: A. Jon Megibow, Director of Admissions
Address: PO Box 6550, Charlottesville, VA 22906-6550
Admissions Phone: 800-882-6221 • Admissions Fax: 804-243-5033
Admissions E-mail: darden@virginia.edu • Web Address: www.darden.virginia.edu

The academics are "certainly rigorous" and the "quality of life is outstanding" at the University of Virginia's "intense but enjoyable and rewarding" Darden School. The administration here does a good job promoting the "Darden community," and students tell us that low tuition, a state-of-the-art facility, and an "incredibly loyal and tight alumni base" round out "an experience beyond expectations."

INSTITUTIONAL INFORMATION
Public/Private: Public
Evening Classes Available? No
Total Faculty: 87
% Faculty Female: 28
% Faculty Minority: 2
% Faculty Part Time: 42
Student/Faculty Ratio: 8:1
Students in Parent Institution: 18,500
Academic Calendar: Semester

PROGRAMS
Degrees Offered: PhD (3 years)
Joint Degrees: MBA/Juris Doctor (4 years); MBA/MA in Asian Studies (3 years); MBA/MA in Government, Foreign Affairs, or Public Administration (3 years); MBA/Master of Engineering (3 years); MBA/Master of Science in Nursing (3 years); MBA/PhD (4 years)
Academic Specialties: Excellent teachers—most have business experience, over half have taught overseas, 14 percent international. Curriculum strengths: general management; case method; integrated, holistic curriculum; required ethics course; teamwork; student-centered learning.
Study Abroad Options: Hong Kong University of Science and Technology, China; Solvay Business School, Belgium; China Europe International Business School, China; Universite Libre de Bruxelles, Belgium; International Univeristy of Japan; Sweden; Finland; Mexico; Australia; Canada

STUDENT INFORMATION
Total Business Students: 491
% Full Time: 100
% Female: 30
% Minority: 15
% Out of State: 52
% International: 20
Average Age: 27

COMPUTER AND RESEARCH FACILITIES
Research Facilities: Olsson Center for Applied Ethics, Balten Center for Entreprenuerial Leadership, Tayloe Murphy Center for International Business Studies
Computer Facilities: Internet, University of Virginia Commonwealth Network, Dow Jones News/Retrieval, Nexis, Compustat, remote dialing, classroom hookups and much more
Campuswide Network? No
Computer Proficiency Required? No
Special Purchasing Agreements? No

EXPENSES/FINANCIAL AID
Annual Tuition (Resident/Nonresident): $16,060/$21,480
Room & Board (Off Campus): $11,900
Books and Supplies: $2,000
Average Grant: $9,050
Average Loan: $17,850
% Receiving Financial Aid: 75
% Receiving Aid Their First Year: 60

ADMISSIONS INFORMATION
Application Fee: $100
Electronic Application? Yes
Regular Application Deadline: 3/15
Regular Notification: 5/1
Deferment Available? No
Non-fall Admissions? Yes
Non-fall Application Deadline(s): 11/2, 12/2, 1/15, 2/15, 3/15
Transfer Students Accepted? No
Need-Blind Admissions? Yes
Number of Applications Received: 3,277
% of Applicants Accepted: 14
% Accepted Who Enrolled: 48
Average GPA: 3.3
Average GMAT: 660
Minority/Disadvantaged Student Recruitment Programs: Consortium for Graduate Study in Management

INTERNATIONAL STUDENTS
TOEFL Required of International Students? Yes

EMPLOYMENT INFORMATION

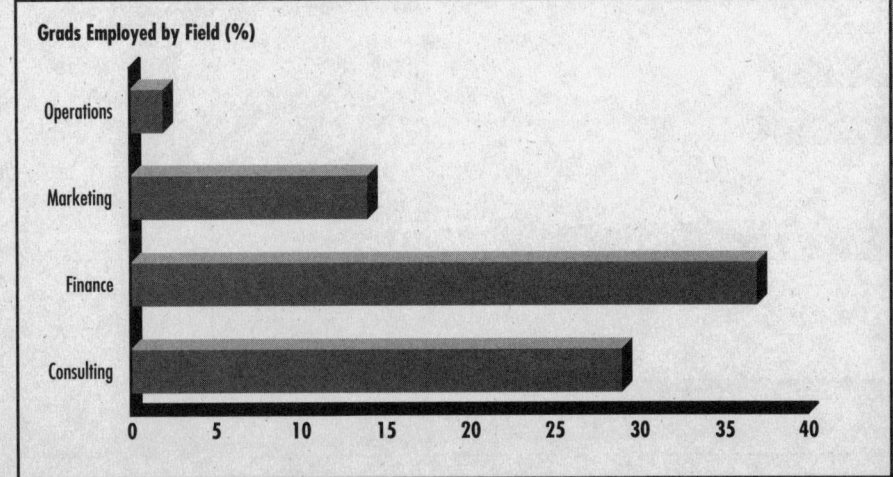

Grads Employed by Field (%)
- Operations: ~2
- Marketing: ~15
- Finance: ~37
- Consulting: ~29

Placement Office Available? Yes
% Employed Within 6 Months: 100
Frequent Employers: Deloitte & Touche; PricewaterhouseCoopers; Booz-Allen & Hamilton; McKinsey & Company
Prominent Alumni: George David, chairman, CEO, United Technologies; Steven S. Reinemund, chairman and CEO, Frito-Lay; Henri A.M. Termeer, president CEO, and chairman, Genzyme Corporation

UNIVERSITY OF WASHINGTON
Business School

Admissions Contact: Janna Trefren, Assistant Director, MBA Admissions
Address: 110 Mackenzie Hall, Box 353200, Seattle, WA 98195-3200
Admissions Phone: 206-543-4661 • Admissions Fax: 206-616-7351
Admissions E-mail: mba@u.washington.edu • Web Address: www.mba.washington.edu

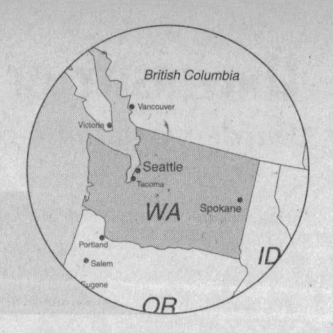

The University of Washington's affordable MBA program "has a great reputation," and it boasts "proximity to a high-tech and rapidly growing economy" in "safe," "fun-filled" but expensive Seattle, the capital of the Pacific Northwest. UW draws heavily from the Pacific Rim, a situation agreeable to students from both sides of the Pacific, as "international students add a much needed layer of depth and insight to our education."

INSTITUTIONAL INFORMATION
Public/Private: Public
Evening Classes Available? Yes
Total Faculty: 102
% Faculty Female: 11
% Faculty Minority: 7
Student/Faculty Ratio: 8:1
Students in Parent Institution: 34,400
Academic Calendar: Quarter

PROGRAMS
Degrees Offered: MBA (day, 2 years; evening, 3 years); MP Accounting (1 year); PhD (4 to 5 years); Program in Engineering and Manufacturing Management (PEMM) (3 years)
Joint Degrees: JD/MBA (4 years); MBA/MAIS (3 years); MBA/Master of Health Administration (3 years)
Academic Specialties: Marketing, Finance, Entrepreneurship, International Business, E-Business, Accounting, Management, Production Management, Quantitative Methods
Special Opportunities: Business and Economic Development Program, EDGE Program in International Business, PEI Consulting Network
Study Abroad Options: Chile, Mexico, China, Denmark, England, Finland, France, Germany, India, Japan, Spain, Switzerland, Singapore

STUDENT INFORMATION
Total Business Students: 417
% Full Time: 64
% Female: 34
% Minority: 3
% Out of State: 28
% International: 31
Average Age: 29

COMPUTER AND RESEARCH FACILITIES
Research Facilities: Center for Technology Entrepreneurship, Center for International Business Education and Research
Computer Facilities: Computer labs, special E-Business Lab, online and database resources such as Lexis-Nexis, Dow Jones, and other systems; wireless access
Campuswide Network? Yes
% of MBA Classrooms Wired: 20
Computer Model Recommended: Laptop
Internet Fee? No

EXPENSES/FINANCIAL AID
Annual Tuition (Resident/Nonresident): $5,859/$15,988
Room & Board (On/Off Campus): $8,319/$9,564
Books and Supplies: $1,500
Average Grant: $4,250
Average Loan: $14,300
% Receiving Financial Aid: 70
% Receiving Aid Their First Year: 65

ADMISSIONS INFORMATION
Application Fee: $50
Electronic Application? Yes
Early Decision Application Deadline: 12/1
Early Decision Notification: 1/19
Regular Application Deadline: Rolling
Regular Notification: 4/20
Deferment Available? No
Non-fall Admissions? No
Transfer Students Accepted? No
Need-Blind Admissions? Yes
Number of Applications Received: 801
% of Applicants Accepted: 38
% Accepted Who Enrolled: 43
Average GPA: 3.3
Average GMAT: 657
Average Years Experience: 5
Other Admissions Factors Considered: Diverse class in terms of academic background, work experience, and personal experience—nonbusiness backgrounds encouraged to apply.
Minority/Disadvantaged Student Recruitment Programs: All-day campus-visit programs and receptions for students from underrepresented groups
Other Schools to Which Students Applied: Seattle U., Stanford, UC Berkeley, UC Davis, UCLA, U. of Southern California, UT Austin

INTERNATIONAL STUDENTS
TOEFL Required of International Students? Yes
Minimum TOEFL: 600 (250 computer)

EMPLOYMENT INFORMATION

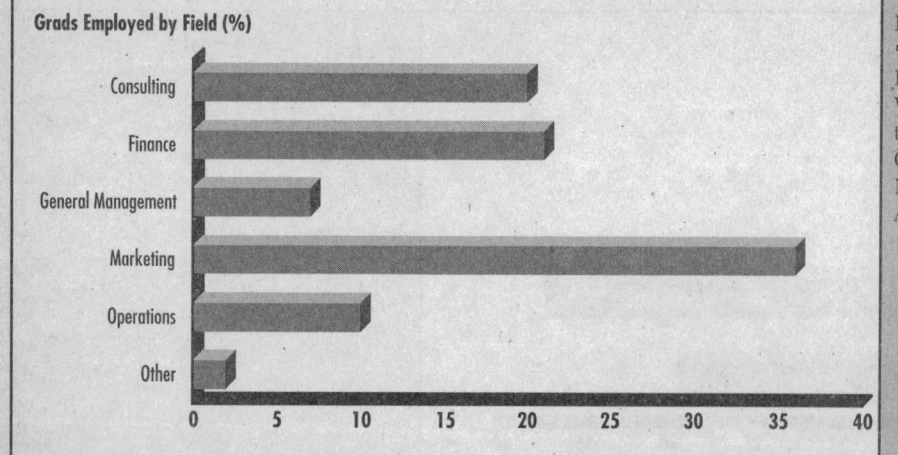

Grads Employed by Field (%)

Field	%
Consulting	20
Finance	21
General Management	7
Marketing	37
Operations	10
Other	2

Placement Office Available? Yes
% Employed Within 3 Months: 85
Frequent Employers: Arthur Andersen, AT&T Wireless, Deloitte & Touche Management Solutions, Deloitte Consulting, ECG Management Consultants, Hewlett-Packard, Intel, Microsoft, Nordstrom, Oracle, Paccar, Starbucks, Amazon.com

UNIVERSITY OF WESTERN ONTARIO
Richard Ivey School of Business

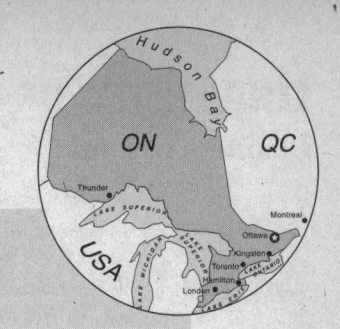

Admissions Contact: Larysa Gamula, Director, MBA Program Office
Address: 1151 Richmond Street North, London, ON N6A 3K7 Canada
Admissions Phone: 519-661-3212 • Admissions Fax: 519-661-3431
Admissions E-mail: mba@ivey.uwo.ca • Web Address: www.ivey.uwo.ca/mba

The workload is heavy and fast-paced and there is a "strong focus on general management" at the University of Western Ontario's Ivey School of Business, which reportedly boasts "the best MBA program in Canada." The average incoming student here is 29 and has five years of work experience, and students describe their "helpful, interesting, and sophisticated" classmates as "diverse in perspectives, experiences, age, and career goals."

INSTITUTIONAL INFORMATION
Evening Classes Available? No
Total Faculty: 70
% Faculty Female: 15
Student/Faculty Ratio: 7:1
Students in Parent Institution: 26,000
Academic Calendar: Semester

PROGRAMS
Degrees Offered: MBA (2 years), Executive MBA (2 years)
Joint Degrees: MBA/Bachelor of Laws (4 years)
Academic Specialties: Global Orientation, General Management, Extensive Exchange Program, Integrated Program, Consulting, E-Business, Globalization
Study Abroad Options: Australia, Austria, Brazil, Chile, China, Denmark, England, France, Germany, Hong Kong, India, Israel, Japan, Korea, Mexico, Netherlands, Philippines, Singapore, South Korea, Spain, Sweden, Switzerland, Thailand

STUDENT INFORMATION
Total Business Students: 600
% Full Time: 100
% Female: 25
% Out of State: 60
% International: 35
Average Age: 29

COMPUTER AND RESEARCH FACILITIES
Research Facilities: Asian Management Institute; Centre for International Business Studies; Institute for Entrepreneurship, Innovation, and Growth; National Centre for Management Research and Development
Computer Facilities: All campus facilities are available to MBA students. The Business Library also has an extensive resource of databases.
Campuswide Network? Yes
% of MBA Classrooms Wired: 100
Computer Model Recommended: Laptop
Internet Fee? No

EXPENSES/FINANCIAL AID
Annual Tuition: $22,000
Room & Board: $6,000
Books and Supplies: $2,000
Average Grant: $2,000

ADMISSIONS INFORMATION
Application Fee: $125
Electronic Application? Yes
Early Decision Application Deadline: Rolling
Regular Application Deadline: 4/1
Regular Notification: Rolling
Deferment Available? Yes
Length of Deferment: 1 year
Non-fall Admissions? No
Transfer Students Accepted? No
Need-Blind Admissions? Yes
Number of Applications Received: 1,100
Average GPA: 3.3
GPA Range: 2.7-3.7
Average GMAT: 660
GMAT Range: 600-710
Minority/Disadvantaged Student Recruitment Programs: Information sessions

INTERNATIONAL STUDENTS
TOEFL Required of International Students? Yes
Minimum TOEFL: 600 (250 computer)

EMPLOYMENT INFORMATION

Grads Employed by Field (%)

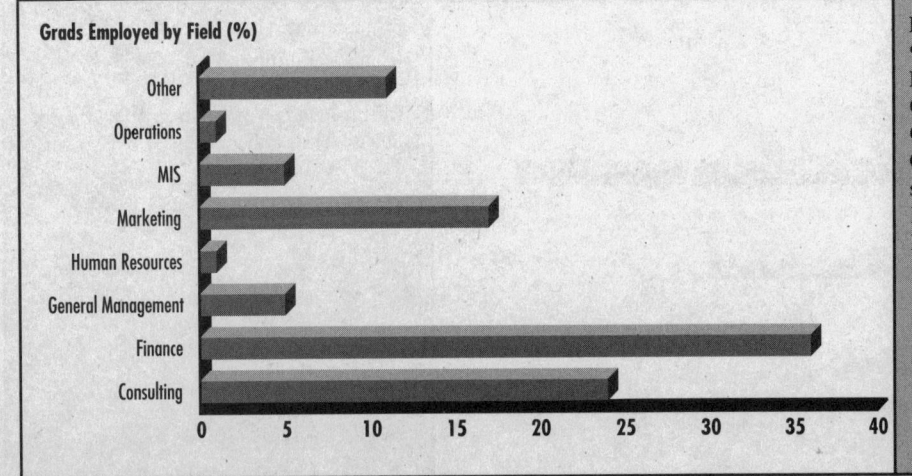

Field	%
Other	~11
Operations	~3
MIS	~1
Marketing	~17
Human Resources	~1
General Management	~5
Finance	~36
Consulting	~24

Placement Office Available? Yes
% Employed Within 3 Months: 96
Frequent Employers: Deloitte & Touche, CAP Gemini Ernst & Young, Salomon Smith Barney, General Motors, Boston Consulting Group, CIBC, Bain and Co., Mercer Management Consulting, Scotiabank, IBM, Credit Suisse First Boston, Manulife Financial, McKinsey and Co., Dell Computer Corp.

UNIVERSITY OF WISCONSIN—MADISON
Business School

Admissions Contact: Director of Marketing and Recruiting
Address: 2266 Grainger Hall, 975 University Avenue, Madison, WI 53706
Admissions Phone: 608-262-4000 • Admissions Fax: 608-265-4192
Admissions E-mail: uwmadmba@bus.wisc.edu • Web Address: www.wisc.edu/bschool

The placement office bends over backward for students, and there are many "high-quality specialty/niche programs" at the University of Wisconsin—Madison's School of Business. Among the best of these is the one and only AC Neilsen Center for Market Research, "which provides top-notch training" and "great connections to the industry." After class, "Madison is a wonderful place to be a student—what with its "plethora of restaurants, bars, and arts activities"—and "the city is great for outdoor enthusiasts."

INSTITUTIONAL INFORMATION
Public/Private: Public
Evening Classes Available? Yes
Total Faculty: 85
% Faculty Female: 15
% Faculty Minority: 5
Student/Faculty Ratio: 6:1
Students in Parent Institution: 40,196
Academic Calendar: Semester

PROGRAMS
Degrees Offered: MBA (3 to 4 semesters), MA (3 to 4 semesters), MS (2 to 4 semesters), MAcc (2 to 4 semesters)
Joint Degrees: JD/MBA (4 years), Agribusiness MBA (2 years)
Academic Specialties: New MBA curriculum enables students to build on their strengths. Seven-week modules combined with semester courses allows for the best mix of core courses and electives. Schedule allows greater opportunity for students to take electives in their majors, both inside and outside the Business School.
Special Opportunities: Marketing Research, Arts Administration, Applied Security Analysis, Real Estate, Enterprise, Distribution Management, Manufacturing and Technology Management, and Agribusiness.
Study Abroad Options: Germany, France, Chile, Mexico, Denmark, Austria, Thailand, China, England

STUDENT INFORMATION
Total Business Students: 489
% Full Time: 93
% Female: 32
% Minority: 13
% Out of State: 50
% International: 31
Average Age: 28

COMPUTER AND RESEARCH FACILITIES
Research Facilities: Bolz Center for Arts Administration, Center for Applied Security Analysis, Enterprise Center, Neilsen Center for Marketing Research, Grainger Center for Distribution Management, Erdman Center for Manufacturing and Technology Management
Computer Facilities: Graduate students have their own computer lab. Library has databases such as Lexis-Nexis, Dow Jones, and ABI/Inform.
Campuswide Network? Yes
Computer Model Recommended: Laptop
Internet Fee? No

EXPENSES/FINANCIAL AID
Annual Tuition (Resident/Nonresident): $5,950/$16,230
Books and Supplies: $665
Average Grant: $500
Average Loan: $11,089
% Receiving Financial Aid: 46
% Receiving Aid Their First Year: 43

ADMISSIONS INFORMATION
Application Fee: $45
Electronic Application? Yes
Regular Application Deadline: 5/1
Regular Notification: Rolling
Deferment Available? No
Non-fall Application Deadline(s): 10/1 spring
Transfer Policy: Waiver of up to 13 credits
Need-Blind Admissions? Yes
Number of Applications Received: 799
% of Applicants Accepted: 48
% Accepted Who Enrolled: 39
Average GPA: 3.3
GPA Range: 3.1-3.6
Average GMAT: 612
GMAT Range: 550-640
Minority/Disadvantaged Student Recruitment Programs: Consortium for Graduate Study in Management, Minority Fellowship Program, advanced opportunity fellowships, Wisconsin Investment Scholars Program

INTERNATIONAL STUDENTS
TOEFL Required of International Students? Yes
Minimum TOEFL: 600

EMPLOYMENT INFORMATION

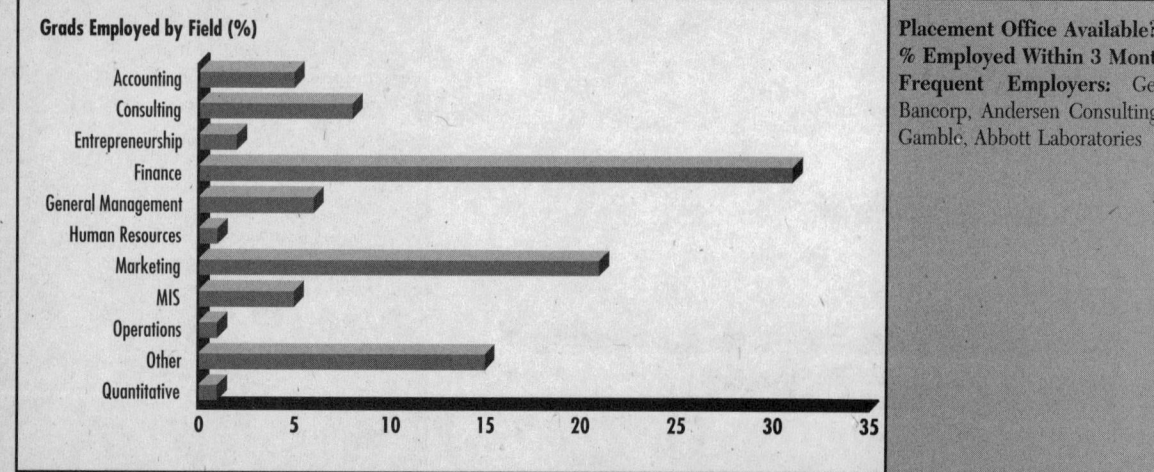

Grads Employed by Field (%)

Field	%
Accounting	4
Consulting	8
Entrepreneurship	1
Finance	31
General Management	6
Human Resources	1
Marketing	21
MIS	4
Operations	2
Other	15
Quantitative	1

Placement Office Available? Yes
% Employed Within 3 Months: 97
Frequent Employers: General Mills, US Bancorp, Andersen Consulting, IBM, Procter & Gamble, Abbott Laboratories

UNIVERSITY OF WISCONSIN—MILWAUKEE
School of Business Administration

Admissions Contact: Sarah M. Sandin, MBA/MS Program Manager
Address: PO Box 742, Milwaukee, WI 53201-0742
Admissions Phone: 414-229-5403 • Admissions Fax: 414-229-2372
Admissions E-mail: uwmbusmasters@uwm.edu • Web Address: www.uwm.edu/Dept/Business/SBA

Available for the business-minded at UW—Milwaukee, near the shores of beautiful Lake Michigan, are the standard MBA, a dynamic and flexible program with more than 10 elective tracks, and the MS/MBA Coordinated Degree program, which prepares its grads for managerial positions in information technology and related fields.

INSTITUTIONAL INFORMATION
Public/Private: Public
Evening Classes Available? Yes
Total Faculty: 62
% Faculty Female: 22
% Faculty Minority: 27
% Faculty Part Time: 20
Student/Faculty Ratio: 10:1
Students in Parent Institution: 23,828
Academic Calendar: Semester

PROGRAMS
Degrees Offered: Master of Business Administration (MBA) (2 to 7 years); Executive MBA (EMBA) (22 months); Master of Science in Management (MS) (2 to 7 years); Master of Human Resources and Labor Relations (2 to 7 years); Engineering Management Master Program (17 months); Master of Public Administration, Non-Profit Management (2 to 7 years)
Academic Specialties: Management Information Systems, E-Business, Taxation, Management
Study Abroad Options: France, England, Ireland

STUDENT INFORMATION
Total Business Students: 274
% Female: 51
% Minority: 2
% International: 40
Average Age: 30

COMPUTER AND RESEARCH FACILITIES
Research Facilities: Bostrom Center for Business Competitiveness, Innovation and Entrepreneurship; School of Business Administration Center for Technology Innovation; Deloitte & Touche Center for Multistate Taxation; Helen Bader Institute for Nonprofit Management; International Business Center; Low Income Taxpayer Clinic; Minority Entrepreneurship Program; Institute for Global Studies
Computer Facilities: Disclosure (Thomson Financial), CRSP, and Compustat through Wharton Research Data Services
Campuswide Network? Yes
Internet Fee? No

EXPENSES/FINANCIAL AID
Annual Tuition (Resident/Nonresident): $7,471/$20,839
Tuition Per Credit (Resident/Nonresident): $616/$1,451
Room & Board (On/Off Campus): $6,000/$4,850
Books and Supplies: $700

ADMISSIONS INFORMATION
Application Fee: $45
Electronic Application? Yes
Regular Application Deadline: Rolling
Regular Notification: Rolling
Deferment Available? Yes
Length of Deferment: 1 year
Non-fall Admissions? Yes
Non-fall Application Deadline(s): Rolling
Transfer Students Accepted? Yes
Transfer Policy: The application process is the same for all applicants.
Need-Blind Admissions? Yes
Number of Applications Received: 173
% of Applicants Accepted: 60
% Accepted Who Enrolled: 49
Average GPA: 3.1
GPA Range: 2.0-4.0
Average GMAT: 535
Average Years Experience: 6
Other Admissions Factors Considered: GMAT and GRE scores accepted for MS program
Minority/Disadvantaged Student Recruitment Programs: The UWM Graduate School offers an Advanced Opportunity Program fellowship.
Other Schools to Which Students Applied: Marquette University, University of Wisconsin-Madison, University of Wisconsin-Whitewater

INTERNATIONAL STUDENTS
TOEFL Required of International Students? Yes
Minimum TOEFL: 550 (213 computer)

EMPLOYMENT INFORMATION

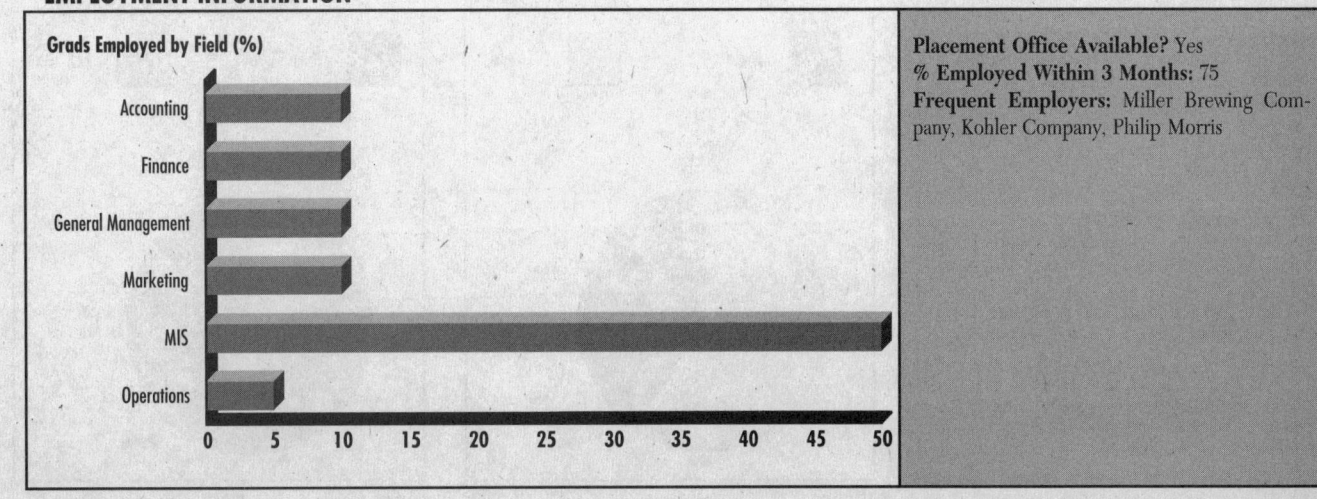

Grads Employed by Field (%)
- Accounting
- Finance
- General Management
- Marketing
- MIS
- Operations

Placement Office Available? Yes
% Employed Within 3 Months: 75
Frequent Employers: Miller Brewing Company, Kohler Company, Philip Morris

UNIVERSITY OF WISCONSIN—WHITEWATER
College of Business and Economics

Admissions Contact: Donald K. Zahn, Associate Dean
Address: 800 West Main Street, Whitewater, WI 53190
Admissions Phone: 262-472-1945 • Admissions Fax: 262-472-4863
Admissions E-mail: zandh@uww.edu • Web Address: www.uww.edu

UW—Whitewater is known mostly for its degree programs in accounting, but its management programs are starting to gain recognition. Daytime or evening and part-time or full-time students can take advantage of UW—Whitewater's MBA programs, and students anywhere in the world can obtain an MBA in marketing, finance, management, or international business via the Internet with the AACSB-accredited Online MBA.

INSTITUTIONAL INFORMATION
Public/Private: Public
Evening Classes Available? Yes
Total Faculty: 62
% Faculty Female: 20
% Faculty Minority: 5
Student/Faculty Ratio: 28:1
Students in Parent Institution: 10,521
Academic Calendar: Semester

PROGRAMS
Degrees Offered: Master of Business Administration (MBA) (full time or part time, 36 to 51 credits, minimum of 18, months), with concentrations in Accounting, Decision Support Systems, Finance, Human Resource Management, International Business, Management, Marketing, Technology and Training, Health Care, Operations, and Supply Chain Management; Master of Science in Management Computer Systems (MS) (part time, 36 credits, 3 years); Master of Professional Accountancy (MPA) (full time or part time, 30 to 60 credits, 12 months to 2 years)
Study Abroad Options: France, Czech Republic, Mexico, Netherlands, Russia, Sweden

STUDENT INFORMATION
Total Business Students: 405
% Full Time: 21
% Female: 60
% Minority: 1
% Out of State: 5
% International: 75
Average Age: 30

COMPUTER AND RESEARCH FACILITIES
Campuswide Network? Yes
Internet Fee? No

EXPENSES/FINANCIAL AID
Annual Tuition (Resident/Nonresident): $5,023/$14,871
Tuition Per Credit (Resident/Nonresident): $279/$826
Room & Board (On Campus): $3,412
Books and Supplies: $2,400
Average Grant: $500

ADMISSIONS INFORMATION
Application Fee: $45
Electronic Application? Yes
Regular Application Deadline: Rolling
Regular Notification: Rolling
Deferment Available? Yes
Length of Deferment: 1 year
Non-fall Admissions? Yes
Non-fall Application Deadline(s): Rolling; international students: 6/1 fall, 10/1 spring
Transfer Students Accepted? Yes
Transfer Policy: Transfer students must meet the same requirements as nontransfer students; 9 credits may be transferred into the program.
Need-Blind Admissions? No
Number of Applications Received: 111
% of Applicants Accepted: 93
% Accepted Who Enrolled: 100
Average GPA: 3.1
GPA Range: 2.1-3.9
Average GMAT: 523
GMAT Range: 320-720
Average Years Experience: 5
Other Admissions Factors Considered: A résumé, work experience, and computer experience are all recommended for application.
Other Schools to Which Students Applied: Marquette University, University of Wisconsin—Madison, University of Wisconsin—Milwaukee, University of Wisconsin—Oshkosh, University of Wisconsin—Parkside

INTERNATIONAL STUDENTS
TOEFL Required of International Students? Yes
Minimum TOEFL: 550 (213 computer)

EMPLOYMENT INFORMATION
Placement Office Available? No
% Employed Within 3 Months: 82

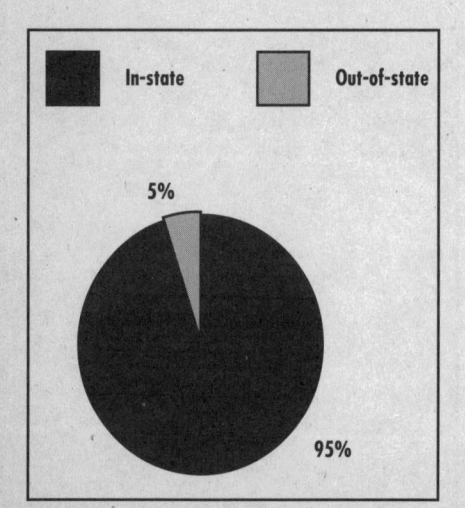

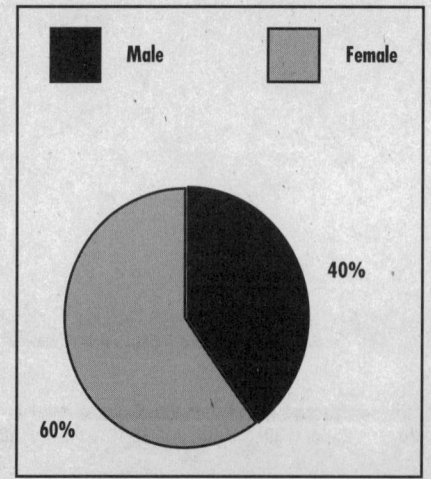

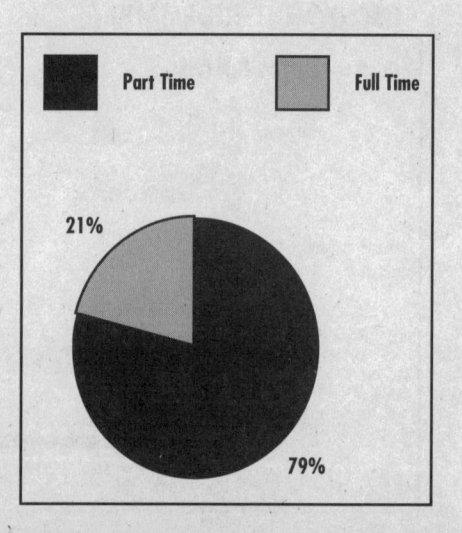

UNIVERSITY OF WYOMING
College of Business

Admissions Contact: Martin M. Greller, Director of MBA Program
Address: PO Box 3275, Laramie, WY 82071
Admissions Phone: 307-766-2449 • *Admissions Fax:* 307-766-4028
Admissions E-mail: MBA@uwyo.edu • *Web Address:* www.business.uwyo.edu/grad/mba

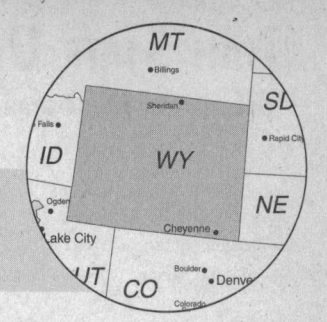

Anyone possessing an undergraduate degree, including a student with no previous formal business experience, is invited to apply to the University of Wyoming's MBA program. Students should expect to receive a formidable education, stressing effective communication and writing, presentations, and teamwork.

INSTITUTIONAL INFORMATION
Public/Private: Public
Evening Classes Available? Yes
Total Faculty: 30
% Faculty Female: 20
% Faculty Minority: 2
Student/Faculty Ratio: 3:1
Students in Parent Institution: 10,774
Academic Calendar: Semester

PROGRAMS
Degrees Offered: MBA (11 months without foundation year, 23 months if foundation year is necessary)
Academic Specialties: Strengths of faculty and curriculum in solving business problems, decision-making, interpersonal skills, balancing human and quantitative management tools
Study Abroad Options: Ecole Superieure de commerce (ESC), Tours, France

STUDENT INFORMATION
Total Business Students: 90
% Full Time: 48
% Female: 23
% International: 12

COMPUTER AND RESEARCH FACILITIES
Number of Computer Labs: 12
Number of Student Computers: 100
Campuswide Network? Yes
% Who Own Computers: 95
Computer Proficiency Required? No
Special Purchasing Agreements? No
Internet Fee? Yes

EXPENSES/FINANCIAL AID
Annual Tuition (Resident/Nonresident): $2,816/$7,906
Room & Board (On/Off Campus): $2,772/$550
Books and Supplies: $300
Average Grant: $1,000
Average Loan: $8,000
Average Total Debt: $10,000

ADMISSIONS INFORMATION
Application Fee: $40
Electronic Application? Yes
Regular Application Deadline: 3/3
Regular Notification: Rolling
Deferment Available? Yes
Length of Deferment: 1 year
Non-fall Admissions? No
Transfer Students Accepted? Yes
Transfer Policy: Maximum number of transferable credits is 9 with a minimum grade of B from an AACSB-accredited school
Need-Blind Admissions? Yes
Number of Applications Received: 50
% of Applicants Accepted: 72
Average GPA: 3.4
GPA Range: 2.2-3.9
Average GMAT: 555
GMAT Range: 420-690
Other Admissions Factors Considered: Work experience and time since acquiring baccalaureate degree

INTERNATIONAL STUDENTS
TOEFL Required of International Students? Yes
Minimum TOEFL: 540

EMPLOYMENT INFORMATION
Placement Office Available? Yes
Prominent Alumni: Solomon Trujillo, CEO, US West

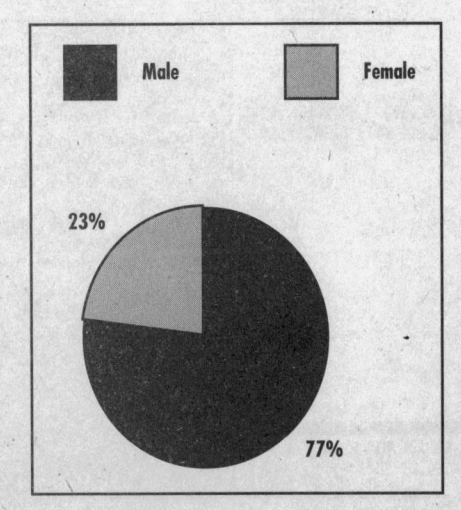

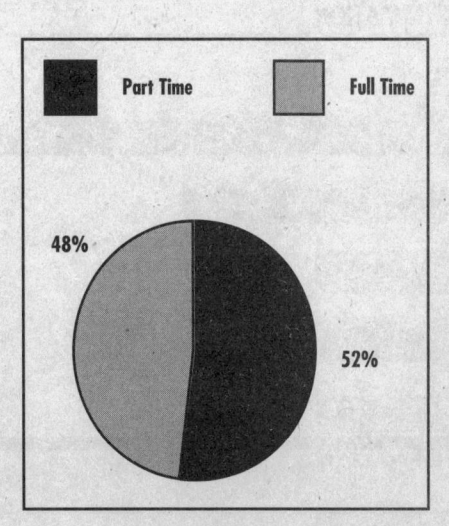

Utah State University
College of Business

Admissions Contact: Graduate School, Admissions Assistant
Address: 900 Old Main Hill, Logan, UT 84322-0900
Admissions Phone: 435-797-1189 • *Admissions Fax:* 435-797-1192
Admissions E-mail: mjh@grad.usu.edu • *Web Address:* www.usu.edu/mba/pages/main.html

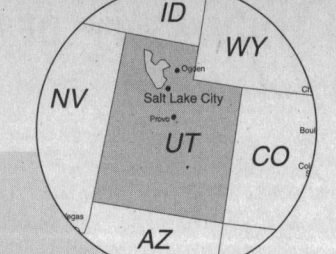

Utah recently evaluated its offerings in comparison to other fully accredited schools, establishing an accelerated team-oriented business core and a choice of nine specializations. It introduced "intrasessions," nonacademic courses intended to "develop personal skills related to employment and the 'corporate culture.'" Utah State's Partners in Business program draws local, national, and international leaders to campus for seven featured programs each year, as well as the Shingo Prize competition, giving MBAs access to a multitude of business personalities and the chance to evaluate real corporate proposals.

INSTITUTIONAL INFORMATION
Public/Private: Public
Evening Classes Available? Yes
Total Faculty: 81
% Faculty Part Time: 8
Student/Faculty Ratio: 30:1
Students in Parent Institution: 20,808
Academic Calendar: Semester

PROGRAMS
Degrees Offered: Master of Accountancy (MAcc), Master of Science in Business Information Systems and Education (MS), Master of Science in Economics (MBA), Master of Social Science in Human Resource Management (MSS) (all 2 years)
Study Abroad Options: Oslo, Italy Consortium, Netherlands

STUDENT INFORMATION
Total Business Students: 370
% Female: 27
% Minority: 4
% International: 20
Average Age: 30

COMPUTER AND RESEARCH FACILITIES
Computer Facilities: Learning Resource Center provides access to online databases and bibliographies.
Campuswide Network? Yes
% of MBA Classrooms Wired: 30
Computer Model Recommended: No
Internet Fee? No

EXPENSES/FINANCIAL AID
Annual Tuition (Resident/Nonresident): $2,426/$7,438
Average Grant: $2,800
Average Loan: $3,000
% Receiving Financial Aid: 5
% Receiving Aid Their First Year: 5

ADMISSIONS INFORMATION
Application Fee: $40
Electronic Application? Yes
Regular Application Deadline: Rolling
Regular Notification: Rolling
Deferment Available? Yes
Length of Deferment: 1 year
Non-fall Admissions? Yes
Non-fall Application Deadline(s): 10/1 spring, 3/1 summer
Transfer Students Accepted? No
Need-Blind Admissions? No
Number of Applications Received: 105
% of Applicants Accepted: 81
% Accepted Who Enrolled: 94
Average GPA: 3.5
GPA Range: 3.0-4.0
Average GMAT: 590
GMAT Range: 500-720
Average Years Experience: 10
Other Schools to Which Students Applied: Brigham Young University, University of Utah, Weber State University

INTERNATIONAL STUDENTS
TOEFL Required of International Students? Yes
Minimum TOEFL: 550

EMPLOYMENT INFORMATION

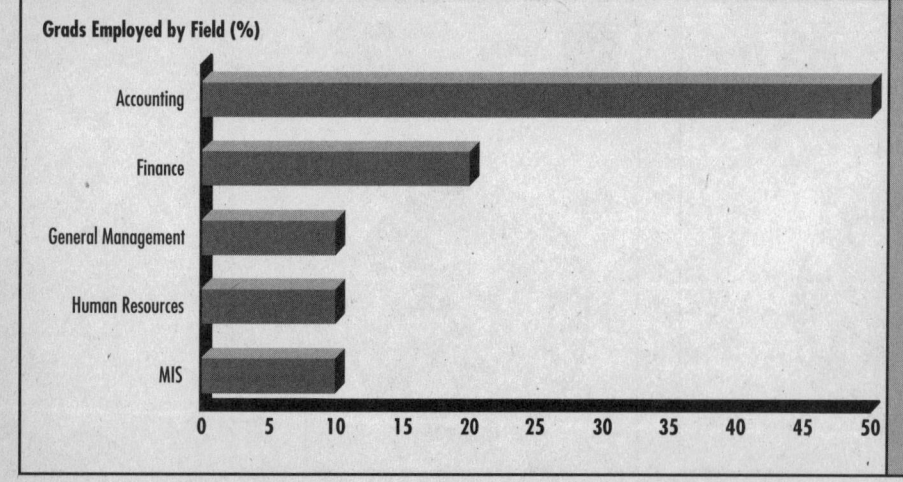

Grads Employed by Field (%)
- Accounting: 50
- Finance: 20
- General Management: 10
- Human Resources: 10
- MIS: 10

Placement Office Available? Yes
% Employed Within 3 Months: 80
Frequent Employers: Allegiance Health Care, Micron, Hewlett-Packard, Ernst & Young

VANDERBILT UNIVERSITY
Owen Graduate School of Management

Admissions Contact: Todd Reale, Director, MBA Admissions and Marketing
Address: 401 21st Avenue South, Nashville, TN 37203
Admissions Phone: 615-322-6469 • Admissions Fax: 615-343-1175
Admissions E-mail: admissions@owen.vanderbilt.edu • Web Address: mba.vanderbilt.edu

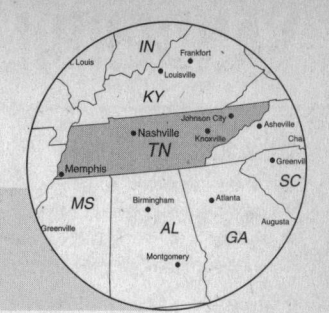

An intimate setting, innovative programs, and a top-flight faculty are the distinguishing characteristics of the Owen Graduate School of Management at Vanderbilt University. There is also a "unique" electronic commerce program here, and students say they really benefit from Vanderbilt's genial, laid-back southern setting. Additional amenities of the Vanderbilt experience include a "great gym," low cost of living, and nightlife that is reportedly "a blast."

INSTITUTIONAL INFORMATION
Public/Private: Private
Evening Classes Available? No
Total Faculty: 63
% Faculty Female: 14
% Faculty Minority: 10
% Faculty Part Time: 41
Student/Faculty Ratio: 9:1
Students in Parent Institution: 10,291
Academic Calendar: Semester

PROGRAMS
Degrees Offered: Full-Time MBA (2 years), Executive MBA (2 years), PhD Program (4+ years)
Joint Degrees: MBA/JD (4 years), MBA/MD (5 years), MBA/MSN (5 semesters), MBA/ME (5 semesters), MBA/MLAS (3 years), MBA/BA or MBA/BS (5 years)
Academic Specialties: Accounting, Brand Management, Electronic Commerce, Entrepreneurship, Environmental Management, Finance, General Management, Health Care, Human and Organizational Performance, Information Technology, International Business, Law and Business, Marketing, Operations Management, Strategy
Special Opportunities: Exchange experiences, internship opportunities
Study Abroad Options: Mexico, Venezuela, Costa Rica, Chile, Brazil, Germany, France, Austria, Spain, Norway, Germany, UK, Japan, Hong Kong, South Africa

STUDENT INFORMATION
Total Business Students: 438
% Full Time: 100
% Female: 26
% Minority: 12
% Out of State: 82
% International: 26
Average Age: 28

COMPUTER AND RESEARCH FACILITIES
Research Facilities: Financial Markets Research Center, eLab, Owen Entrepreneurship Center, Vanderbilt Center for Environmental Studies
Computer Facilities: Wireless computer network, Internet connections from remote locations, extensive Intranet resources, dozens of online databases
% of MBA Classrooms Wired: 100
Computer Model Recommended: Laptop
Internet Fee? No

EXPENSES/FINANCIAL AID
Annual Tuition: $27,560
Room & Board (Off Campus): $8,780
Books and Supplies: $1,256
Average Grant: $17,000
Average Loan: $27,000
% Receiving Financial Aid: 37

ADMISSIONS INFORMATION
Application Fee: $100
Electronic Application? Yes
Regular Application Deadline: 4/15
Regular Notification: 5/31
Deferment Available? No
Non-fall Admissions? No
Transfer Students Accepted? No
Need-Blind Admissions? Yes
Number of Applications Received: 1,237
% of Applicants Accepted: 38
% Accepted Who Enrolled: 44
Average GPA: 3.3
Average GMAT: 638
Average Years Experience: 5
Other Admissions Factors Considered: Undergraduate institution; difficulty of major; prior work experience; professional responsibilities and accomplishments; career progression/advancement; well-defined career goals; extracurricular/professional/community involvement; leadership potential; interpersonal skills; communication skills; team orientation; diversity (gender, ethnic, cultural, geographic, academic, professional, etc.); cross-cultural awareness/understanding/experience/appreciation
Minority/Disadvantaged Student Recruitment Programs: Diversity Weekend is specially targeted to prospective female, U.S. minority, and international students.
Other Schools to Which Students Applied: Carnegie Mellon, Duke, Emory, Indiana U., UNC—Chapel Hill, U. of Virginia, Washington U.

INTERNATIONAL STUDENTS
TOEFL Required of International Students? Yes
Minimum TOEFL: 600 (250 computer)

EMPLOYMENT INFORMATION

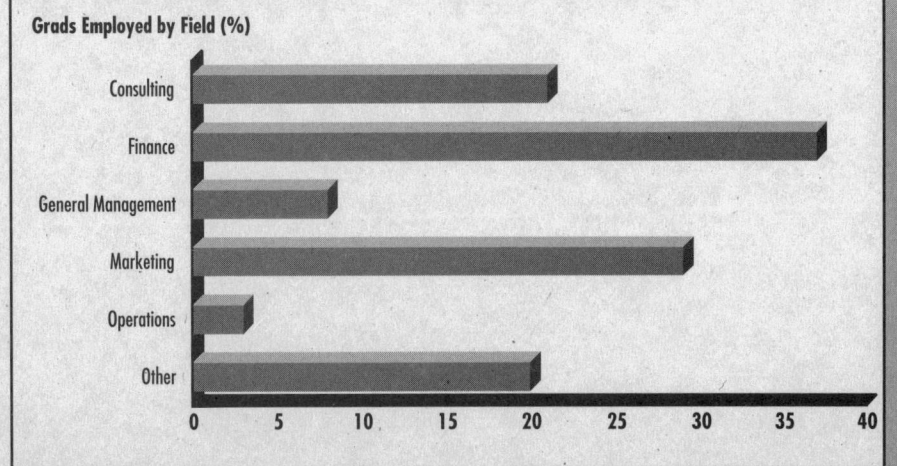

Grads Employed by Field (%)

Field	%
Consulting	21
Finance	38
General Management	8
Marketing	29
Operations	3
Other	20

Placement Office Available? Yes
% Employed Within 3 Months: 90
Frequent Employers: Accenture; AT Kearney; Capital One; Compaq; Cummins, Inc.; Darwin Networks; Dell Computer; Deloitte Consulting; Deutsche Bank Alex. Brown; Federal Express; First Union Securities; Ford Motor Co.; General Motors; Goldman Sachs; Intel; International Paper; Investment Scorecard; Kraft Foods; Lehman Brothers; Lucent Technologies; Mattel Toys; Morgan Stanley Dean Witter; PricewaterhouseCoopers; Procter & Gamble; Proxicom, Inc.; Reliant Energy; Southern Company; SunTrust Bank; Unilever; Wachovia Bank

VANDERBILT UNIVERSITY

THE SCHOOL AT A GLANCE
Innovative ideas help set Owen@Vanderbilt apart from other business schools. We take seriously our role of getting students on the "fast track" in all areas of study. Our faculty brings their research, consulting, and previous professional experience into the classroom.

STUDENTS
Owen@Vanderbilt offers a sense of community and teamwork that students will not find at larger schools. We are one of the most personalized graduate business schools around.

Owen@Vanderbilt is a hub for global study. The school's focus on international and global business activities has attracted the attention of students and the business world alike. Students from outside the United States make up 30 percent of the total enrollment in Owen's full-time program; many of our domestic students also have international experience. We welcome the diversity international students bring to the classroom and encourage academic and social interaction at all levels.

ACADEMICS
The Owen@Vanderbilt MBA program requires completing 60 credit hours in eight 7-week modules: 22 hours of core curriculum courses, one area of concentration, and 38 hours of elective courses. Students customize 60 percent of their course work by choosing from 150 elective courses.

Owen@Vanderbilt offers concentrations in the following functional areas: accounting, finance, human and organizational performance, marketing, operations management, electronic commerce, information technology, and strategic management. Owen@Vanderbilt was the first school to offer electronic commerce to it's students.

Owen's groundbreaking curriculum focuses on business and financial markets.

The mission of the Career Management Center is to assist students in developing their abilities and experience toward their future success.

What distinguishes Owen@Vanderbilt from other business schools is its highly personal approach to career management. By partnering with students, the CMC supports the professional development of all students by providing a weekly newsletter, one-on-one counseling sessions, career skills workshops, industry-related seminars, company information sessions, on-campus interviews, recruiter feedback, networking trips, off-campus career consortia, and more.

Owen Graduate School of Management

CAMPUS LIFE

With 1.2 million residents in the metropolitan area, Nashville is one of the Southeast's booming and most vibrant, sophisticated, and livable cities. In addition to its world-renowned music industry, Nashville combines big-city amenities and small-town values to create a community that is enthusiastically touted by Owen@Vanderbilt students as an ideal place to go to.

ADMISSIONS

We rely on the applicant's academic records and test scores to assess his or her ability to succeed in the Owen@Vanderbilt MBA program. The ideal candidate has earned at least a four-year U.S. bachelor's degree, or its equivalent, from a top quality college or university.

To apply to Owen@Vanderbilt a candidate must submit the results of the Graduate Management Admissions Test (GMAT). International applicants from non-English-speaking countries must also submit scores from the Test of English as a Second Language (TOEFL).

Full-time post-baccalaureate work experience is strongly recommended, but not required. No minimum amount is specified, as we believe there are exceptional candidates who are able to assume leadership roles, inside the classroom and out, despite little or no work experience. However, most incoming students find that substantial prior work experience enables them to understand new concepts more fully and apply them more quickly; to make relevant and meaningful contributions to the learning community; and to realize a greater return on their MBA investment with access to more and better career options. In recent years, 90 percent of Vanderbilt MBA students have worked three or more years prior to enrollment.

Admissions Contact: Todd Reale, Director, MBA Admissions and Marketing
Address: 401 21st Avenue South, Nashville, TN 37203
Admissions Phone: 615-322-6469 • Admissions Fax: 615-343-1175
Admissions E-mail: admissions@owen.vanderbilt.edu • Web Address: mba.vanderbilt.edu

VILLANOVA UNIVERSITY
College of Commerce and Finance

Admissions Contact: Christopher Ore, Assistant Director, Graduate Studies in Business
Address: 800 Lancaster Avenue, Bartley Hall, Villanova, PA 19085
Admissions Phone: 610-519-4336 • Admissions Fax: 610-519-6273
Admissions E-mail: mba@villanova.edu • Web Address: www.mba.villanova.edu

Villanova features a unique pass/fail three-day "orientation" called the Leadership Skills Lab, where students get a taste of what is expected of them while they focus on communication and negotiation in a "cohesive team atmosphere." Villanova's broad-based MBA curriculum was recently revamped to increase emphasis on technology integration, cross-functional solutions, teamwork, and strategic decision-making. Villanova makes the claim that "we align our program with work and life realities," so expect the program to practice flexibility regarding obligations that exist outside the classroom.

INSTITUTIONAL INFORMATION
Public/Private: Private
Evening Classes Available? Yes
Total Faculty: 95
Student/Faculty Ratio: 12:1
Students in Parent Institution: 10,330
Academic Calendar: Semester

PROGRAMS
Degrees Offered: MBA, Executive MBA, Master of Taxation, Master of Accounting and Professional Consultancy
Joint Degrees: JD/MBA
Study Abroad Options: China—East China Normal University; Russia—Nizhny Novgorod State University; Germany—European Business School; Costa Rica—Universidad Catolica De Valparaio; Poland—University of Warsaw

STUDENT INFORMATION
Total Business Students: 585
% Full Time: 7
% Female: 35
% Minority: 2
% Out of State: 3
% International: 5
Average Age: 27

COMPUTER AND RESEARCH FACILITIES
Campuswide Network? Yes
% of MBA Classrooms Wired: 100
Computer Model Recommended: Laptop
Internet Fee? No

EXPENSES/FINANCIAL AID
Annual Tuition: $15,000
Tuition Per Credit: $555
Books and Supplies: $700
Average Grant: $27,000

ADMISSIONS INFORMATION
Application Fee: $40
Electronic Application? Yes
Regular Application Deadline: 6/30
Regular Notification: Rolling
Deferment Available? Yes
Length of Deferment: 1 year
Non-fall Admissions? Yes
Non-fall Application Deadline(s): 11/15 spring, 3/31 summer
Transfer Students Accepted? Yes
Transfer Policy: Up to 9 credits from an AACSB-accredited MBA program
Need-Blind Admissions? Yes
Number of Applications Received: 453
% of Applicants Accepted: 69
% Accepted Who Enrolled: 68
Average GPA: 3.2
GPA Range: 2.6-3.4
Average GMAT: 582
GMAT Range: 540-620
Average Years Experience: 5
Other Schools to Which Students Applied: Temple University, Drexel University

INTERNATIONAL STUDENTS
TOEFL Required of International Students? Yes
Minimum TOEFL: 600 (250 computer)

EMPLOYMENT INFORMATION
Placement Office Available? Yes
% Employed Within 3 Months: 98

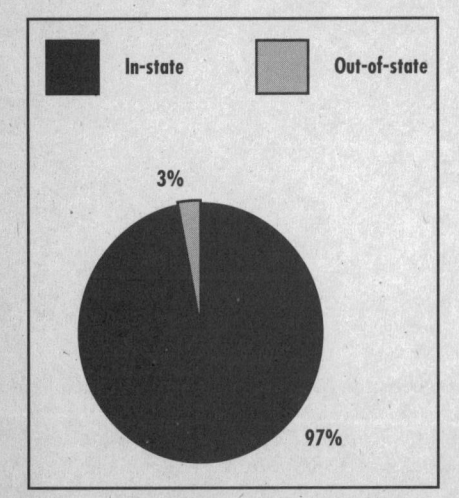

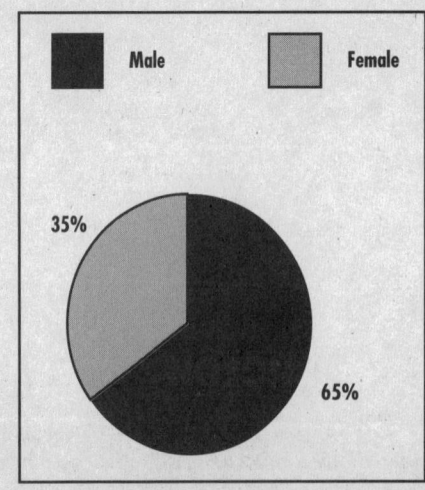

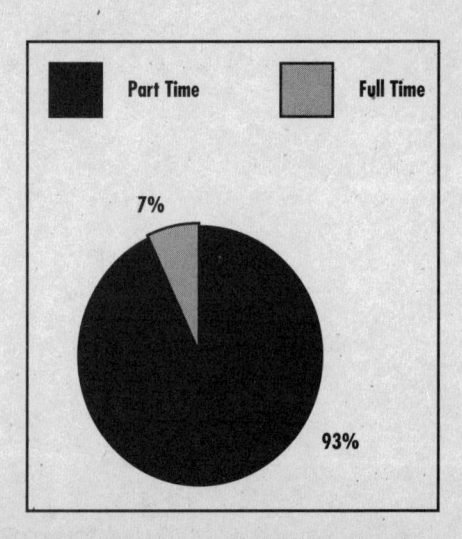

In-state 97% / Out-of-state 3%

Male 65% / Female 35%

Part Time 93% / Full Time 7%

VIRGINIA COMMONWEALTH UNIVERSITY
School of Business

Admissions Contact: Tracy S. Green, Director of Graduate Programs
Address: Box 844000, University Hill, Richmond, VA 23284-4000
Admissions Phone: 804-828-1741 • *Admissions Fax:* 804-828-7174
Admissions E-mail: tsgreen@vcu.edu • *Web Address:* www.vcu.edu/busweb/gsib

The Virginia Commonwealth University owns a suite of great historical buildings; one is the Ritter-Hickok House, in which spies were imprisoned during the Civil War. There's more to this school than a full-flavored southern history, though: VCU recently turned its Classic MBA into a Technology-Focused MBA with the help of its information systems faculty. The Fast-Track MBA is also available for the instruction of professionals with six or seven years of experience.

INSTITUTIONAL INFORMATION
Public/Private: Public
Evening Classes Available? Yes
Total Faculty: 93
Student/Faculty Ratio: 19:1
Students in Parent Institution: 22,000
Academic Calendar: Semester

PROGRAMS
Degrees Offered: MBA (2 years); Master of Science in Business (2 years), with multiple concentration choices; Master of Accountancy (2 years); Master of Taxation (2 years); Master of Arts in Economics (2 years); Doctor of Philosophy (5 years)
Joint Degrees: Master of Accountancy (5 years), for entering undergraduate students; BS Engineering/MBA
Special Opportunities: Focused MS degrees in Decision Sciences, Finance, Global Marketing Management, Human Resource Management and Industrial Relations, Information Systems, and Real Estate Valuation
Study Abroad Options: Italy; France; exchange with Ecole Superieure de Commerce Marseille, Provence

STUDENT INFORMATION
Total Business Students: 289
% Full Time: 20
% Female: 13
% Minority: 12
% Out of State: 35
% International: 6
Average Age: 30

COMPUTER AND RESEARCH FACILITIES
Research Facilities: Alfred L. Blake Chair of Real Estate, Center for Corporate Education, Employment Support Institute, Family Business Forum, Information Systems Research Institute, Insurance Studies Center, Philip Morris Chair in International Business, VCU Center for Economic Education, Virginia Council for Economic Education, Virginia Real Estate Research Center, Virginia Labor Studies Center
Computer Facilities: University Library Services maintains all database access.
Campuswide Network? Yes
Computer Model Recommended: Desktop
Internet Fee? No

EXPENSES/FINANCIAL AID
Books and Supplies: $600
Average Grant: $8,375
Average Loan: $12,000

ADMISSIONS INFORMATION
Application Fee: $30
Electronic Application? No
Regular Application Deadline: 6/1
Regular Notification: 6/30
Deferment Available? Yes
Length of Deferment: 1 year
Non-fall Admissions? Yes
Non-fall Application Deadline(s): 11/1, 3/1
Transfer Students Accepted? Yes
Transfer Policy: Students who were admitted to and completed course work at other AACSB-accredited institutions may apply to VCU and seek transfer of up to 6 semester hours of work toward the VCU graduate degree. Students must have earned no less than a B in each class to be transferred. The decision to transfer courses is left to the discretion of the Director of Graduate Programs.
Need-Blind Admissions? Yes
Number of Applications Received: 4,127
% of Applicants Accepted: 8
% Accepted Who Enrolled: 53
Average Years Experience: 5
Other Schools to Which Students Applied: University of Virginia, College of William and Mary, University of Richmond, George Mason University, Southern Methodist University

INTERNATIONAL STUDENTS
TOEFL Required of International Students? Yes
Minimum TOEFL: 600

EMPLOYMENT INFORMATION
Placement Office Available? No

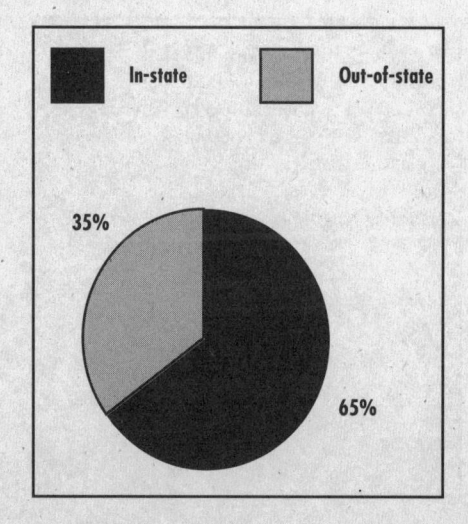

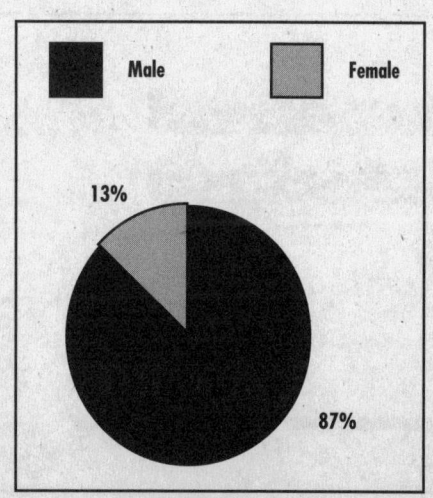

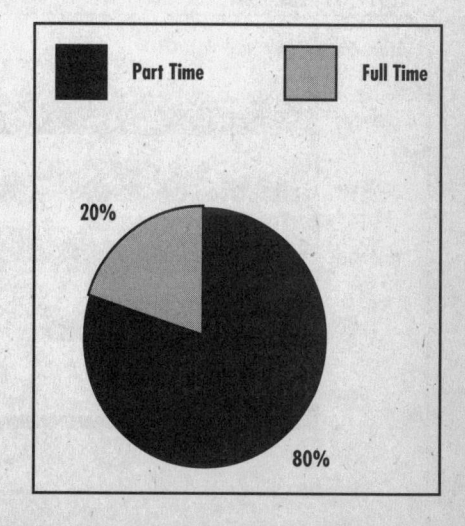

VIRGINIA POLYTECHNIC INSTITUTE AND STATE UNIVERSITY
Pamplin College of Business

Admissions Contact: Susan Vest, Enrollment Coordinator
Address: 1044 Pamplin Hall, Virginia Tech, Blacksburg, VA 24061
Admissions Phone: 540-231-6152 • Admissions Fax: 540-231-4487
Admissions E-mail: mba_info@vt.edu • Web Address: www.mba.vt.edu

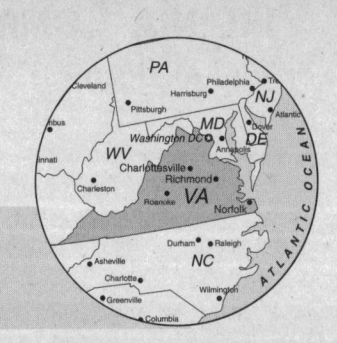

Students are enthusiastic about Pamplin's growing reputation. Active student participation is a distinguishing factor of Pamplin's MBA education, which focuses on "the interrelationships among the various functions within a firm" and is available on a full-time or part-time basis. Upon graduation, students will "bask in the reputation" of the program, as recent grads have been hired by a long list of companies that includes Lucent Technologies, Pfizer pharmaceuticals, and Ford Motor Company.

INSTITUTIONAL INFORMATION
Public/Private: Public
Evening Classes Available? Yes
Total Faculty: 116
Students in Parent Institution: 27,800

PROGRAMS
Degrees Offered: Accounting and Information Systems: Master of Accountancy (30 credits), PhD Program; Finance, Insurance, and Business Law: PhD Program; Management: PhD Program; Business Information Technology: PhD Program; Marketing: PhD Program; MBA Program (48 credits); concentrations: Information Systems Technology, Systems Engineering Management, Electronic Commerce, Executive Leadership, Human Resources, Investment and Financial Services Management, Corporate Financial Management, Financial Risk Management, Global Business, Marketing in High Technology Industries
Joint Degrees: MBA/Master of International Management (33 semester hours in the Pamplin MBA Program and 30 trimester hours at Thunderbird); l'Institute National des Telecommunications (INT) in France
Study Abroad Options: Short Programs: INTOP III (Austria), International Business Consulting (Slovenia); Semester Abroad: CIU Spring Semester in Europe (Italy), Fall Semester in Europe (Switzerland); Summer Abroad: European Integration/Business and Accounting Issues (western and central Europe), Global Workplace (eastern Europe), Marketing in the EU (France), International Electronic Commerce (Austria), Business in the EU (Germany), London Internships (England); Managerial and Ethical Challenges in the Global Marketplace (Asia); China/HK/Vietnam Program in Finance (China, Hong Kong, Vietnam); China/HK/Vietnam Program in Marketing (China, Hong Kong, and Vietnam)

STUDENT INFORMATION
Total Business Students: 393
% Female: 31
% Minority: 8
Average Age: 23

COMPUTER AND RESEARCH FACILITIES
Campuswide Network? Yes
% of MBA Classrooms Wired: 100
Computer Model Recommended: Laptop
Internet Fee? No

EXPENSES/FINANCIAL AID
Annual Tuition: $2,174
Tuition Per Credit (Resident/Nonresident): $242/$407
Room & Board (Off Campus): $800
Books and Supplies: $8,200
Average Grant: $2,000
% Receiving Aid Their First Year: 14

ADMISSIONS INFORMATION
Application Fee: $45
Electronic Application? Yes
Regular Application Deadline: 2/1
Regular Notification: Rolling
Deferment Available? Yes
Length of Deferment: 1 year
Non-fall Admissions? No
Transfer Students Accepted? No
Need-Blind Admissions? Yes
Number of Applications Received: 239
% of Applicants Accepted: 38
% Accepted Who Enrolled: 56
Average GPA: 3.3
GPA Range: 3.0-3.6
Average GMAT: 630
GMAT Range: 590-690
Average Years Experience: 4

INTERNATIONAL STUDENTS
TOEFL Required of International Students? Yes
Minimum TOEFL: 550

EMPLOYMENT INFORMATION

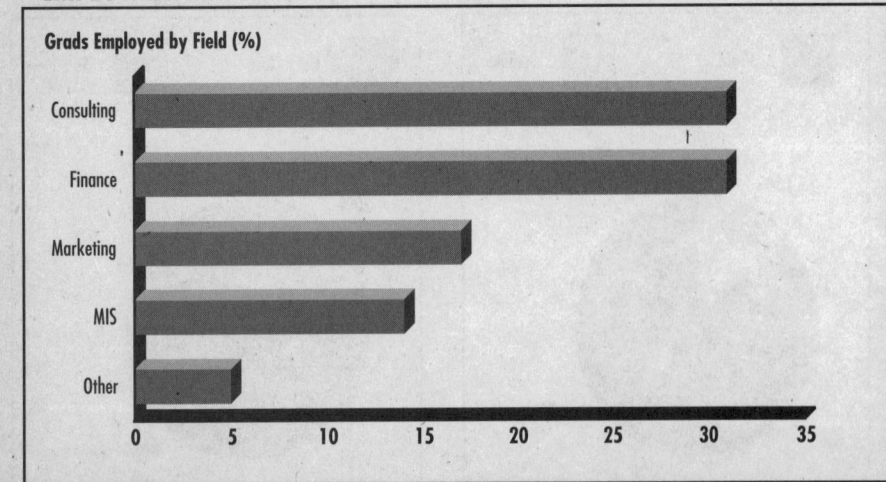

Grads Employed by Field (%)
- Consulting: ~31
- Finance: ~31
- Marketing: ~17
- MIS: ~14
- Other: ~5

Placement Office Available? No
% Employed Within 3 Months: 85
Frequent Employers: Corning Cable Systems, Deloitte & Touche, PricewaterhouseCoopers, Lockheed Martin, GMAC, First USA, Federal Express, National Basketball Association, Accenture, Lucent Technologies, Eastman Chemical, Cap Gemini Ernst & Young, Free Markets, Norfolk Southern

WAKE FOREST UNIVERSITY
Babcock Graduate School of Management

Admissions Contact: Mary Goss, Assistant Dean
Address: PO Box 7659, Winston-Salem, NC 27109
Admissions Phone: 336-758-5422 • Admissions Fax: 336-758-5830
Admissions E-mail: admissions@mba.wfu.edu • Web Address: www.mba.wfu.edu

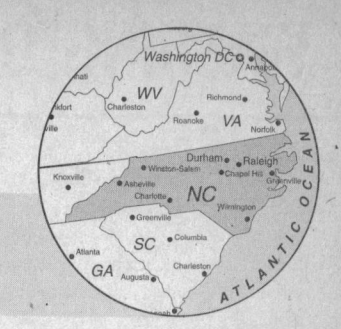

The campus is gorgeous, the "brilliant" professors are "real people" who are "fun to go to lunch with," and there are some of "the smallest section sizes of any major MBA program" in the country at Wake Forest University's Babcock School of Management. "Students get to know each other pretty well," which creates "an environment of free interaction" and "a genuine sense of community here that extends to faculty, staff, students, and their families."

INSTITUTIONAL INFORMATION
Public/Private: Private
Evening Classes Available? Yes
Total Faculty: 57
% Faculty Female: 19
% Faculty Minority: 10
% Faculty Part Time: 15
Student/Faculty Ratio: 7:1
Students in Parent Institution: 6,258
Academic Calendar: Semester

PROGRAMS
Degrees Offered: Full-time and evening MBA (2 years); Fast-track executive MBA (17 months)
Joint Degrees: JD/MBA (4 years); MD/MBA (5 years); PhD/MBA (5 years)
Academic Specialties: Operations, Finance, Marketing, Management Consulting, Entrepreneurship, Family Business, Information Technology, E-Business
Special Opportunities: Babcock Leadership Series; Mentor Program; Management Practicum Program; Family Business Center; Capital Market Training Center; Marketing Case Competition; Elevator Case Competition; New Business Incubator; Case Writing Competition
Study Abroad Options: France, Germany, Austria, Russia, England, Japan, China

STUDENT INFORMATION
Total Business Students: 660
% Full Time: 35
% Female: 24
% Minority: 9
% Out of State: 62
% International: 30
Average Age: 27

COMPUTER AND RESEARCH FACILITIES
Research Facilities: Centers and institutes for Economic Studies, International Studies, Executive Education, Entrepreneurship and Family Business, Venture Capital Incubator, and Capital Market Training
Computer Facilities: IBM laptop computer is part of tuition; computer lab has desktop computers with 20 software packages; multiple databases online; Internet access; Interactive Whiteboards
Campuswide Network? Yes
% of MBA Classrooms Wired: 100
Computer Model Recommended: Laptop
Internet Fee? No

EXPENSES/FINANCIAL AID
Annual Tuition: $23,000
Tuition Per Credit: $958
Room & Board (Off Campus): $5,600
Books and Supplies: $1,500
Average Grant: $12,570
Average Loan: $26,718
% Receiving Financial Aid: 72
% Receiving Aid Their First Year: 82

ADMISSIONS INFORMATION
Application Fee: $50
Electronic Application? Yes
Early Decision Application Deadline: 12/1
Early Decision Notification: 12/25
Regular Application Deadline: 4/1
Regular Notification: Rolling
Length of Deferment: 1 year
Non-fall Admissions? No
Transfer Students Accepted? No
Need-Blind Admissions? Yes
Number of Applications Received: 468
% of Applicants Accepted: 49
% Accepted Who Enrolled: 47
Average GPA: 3.2
Average GMAT: 643
Average Years Experience: 4
Other Admissions Factors Considered: Academic achievement, professional experience, and community involvement
Minority/Disadvantaged Student Recruitment Programs: Diversity Day and participation in the National Black MBA Association and the National Hispanic Society of MBAs Career Forums.
Other Schools to Which Students Applied: U. of Virginia, Washington U. in St. Louis, Duke, Emory, UNC—Chapel Hill, Vanderbilt, Indiana U.

INTERNATIONAL STUDENTS
TOEFL Required of International Students? Yes
Minimum TOEFL: 600 (250 computer)

EMPLOYMENT INFORMATION

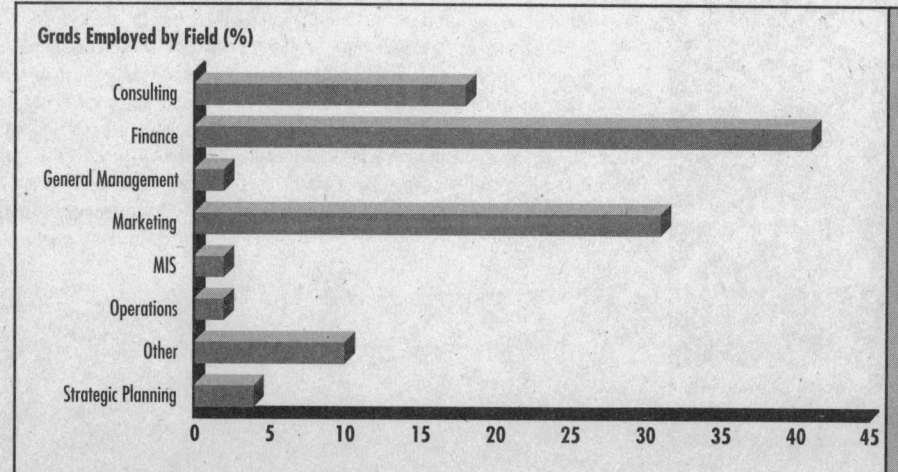

Grads Employed by Field (%)
- Consulting: ~18
- Finance: ~42
- General Management: ~3
- Marketing: ~31
- MIS: ~2
- Operations: ~3
- Other: ~10
- Strategic Planning: ~4

Placement Office Available? Yes
% Employed Within 3 Months: 92
Frequent Employers: Wachovia, Dell Computer, Bank of America, Nabisco, Coca-Cola, Sara Lee, Corning, Lego Systems, RJ Reynolds
Prominent Alumni: Charles Ergen, CEO, EchoStar; Ken Thompson, president and CEO, First Union Corp.; William Taylor, president, The Springs Co.; Charles Nesbit, Jr., president and CEO, Sara Lee Intimate Apparel; John Thompson, president, Southwest Medical Services

WASHINGTON UNIVERSITY

THE SCHOOL AT A GLANCE
MBA students at Washington University's Olin School of Business tell us that its intimate size, flexible curriculum, and faculty composed of "heavy hitters" make it a worthwhile choice. Experiential learning is another major focal point of the Olin approach. Practicum allows students to consult for area companies on matters ranging from marketing to strategy. Thus far, a slew of firms, including Enterprise Rent-A-Car, Ford Motor Company, PriceWaterhouseCoopers, Ralston Purina, and Monsanto, have asked Olin students for their advice.

STUDENTS
The full-time MBA program enrolls approximately 150 new students each year. They have diverse undergraduate backgrounds ranging from business and the humanities to engineering and the sciences. On average, an entering class includes students from more than 30 states and as many as 26 foreign countries. Students also have the opportunity to participate in one or more of Olin's 15 student organizations. These organizations allow students to further expand their professional network and hone leadership skills. A student-administered honor code designed to govern full-time MBA students represents Olin MBAs' commitment to excellence in the classroom, and sends a direct message to future employers: students are graduating from a community that actively practices an exemplary standard of integrity.

ACADEMICS
At Olin, you'll find a supportive community where each person's interests and ideas make a difference. With approximately 160 MBA students in a class, you're assured of receiving individual attention from our faculty and staff. And it's likely that you'll get to know our dean, Stuart Greenbaum.

Olin's curriculum is based on the understanding that no two students are identical--therefore, no single, prescribed curriculum is expected to meet everyone's needs. That's what makes the Olin curriculum different: it's flexible, it's based on a relatively small set of required classes and a large number of electives, and it acknowledges students' individual strengths and career aspirations.

Simon Hall, the hub of MBA student activity, contains spacious student lounges, classrooms, seminar rooms, faculty offices, a library, a computer lab, rooms for small-group study, offices for student organizations and clubs, and a deli.

Experiential learning is an important element in your learning strategy. We offer a broad and innovative menu of hands-on learning opportunities that enable you to apply your classroom knowledge to real-life business situations. These programs help you develop confidence in your leadership ability, gain consulting experience, and hone your communication and teamwork skills.

For more information on the Olin experience at Washington University in St. Louis, visit our website at www.olin.wustl.edu.

The following degrees are offered:

BSBA
MSBA
MBA (full-time)
MBA (part-time)
Executive degree programs
PhD

Approximately 24 tenured professors, 30 additional tenure-track professors, 8 visiting professors, and 16 part-time professors who are world-class scholars serve on Olin's faculty. They hold positions on editorial boards, publish articles in top journals, and earn distinction as exemplary teachers and strong community builders who further the vision of the Olin School. They are instrumental in developing the curriculum to reflect state-of-the-art business practices. Twenty adjunct faculty members who are leaders in the business community bring to the classroom a passion for merging business theory with cutting-edge business practices.

Washington University and the Olin School are located in a lovely suburban setting within walking distance of the largest park in St. Louis. You're minutes away from recreation facilities, including art and history museums, a science center, a skating rink, and a world-class zoo.

John M. Olin School of Business

CAMPUS LIFE

Founded in 1853, Washington University is recognized among the Top 20 universities in the United States, according to *U.S. News & World Report*. The University is located in a picturesque suburban setting and is within walking distance of Forest Park. The Hilltop Campus, where Olin is situated, is seven miles west of the Mississippi Riverfront and the St. Louis Arch. Learning takes place in the supportive, comfortable atmosphere of a small college with the resources and amenities of a larger university. St. Louis is a thriving metropolitan center with notable art galleries, museums, theatre, sporting events, and bustling ethnic neighborhoods. It is home to a dynamic corporate community that fosters projects, internships, and mentoring programs for Olin MBAs.

John E. Simon Hall: Opened in 1986, the Olin School occupies John E. Simon Hall. The 80,000-square-foot building houses modern classrooms and study areas, an extensive library with online computer linkups to all major data systems, modern faculty and administrative offices, and a 70-unit computer lab for student use.

Charles F. Knight Executive Education Center: The Knight Center, Olin's new executive residential living and learning facility, reflects Washington University's tradition of world-class scholarship and research, as well as the Olin School's philosophy of education for a lifetime of achievement. The 135,000-square-foot building includes classrooms, breakout rooms, lounges, a dining area, 66 bedrooms, administrative offices, a fitness center, and a pub.

ADMISSIONS

Admission to Olin is selective. The Olin Admissions Committee reviews applications based on a series of four deadlines with the earliest falling in mid-November. Qualified full-time MBA students are admitted to start in the fall semester only. The committee reviews all information in the application to determine a candidate's ability to perform in an intensely rigorous academic environment. The committee also seeks to identify students who will add significantly to the academic, cultural, and social character of the School. Prospective students must submit an Olin application in hard copy, online, or through MBA Multi-App interactive software. The committee also requires a current GMAT score, results of the TOEFL exam (if applicable), official transcripts from each university previously attended, a work history form, essays, a resume, and two letters of recommendation. Interviews are strongly encouraged.

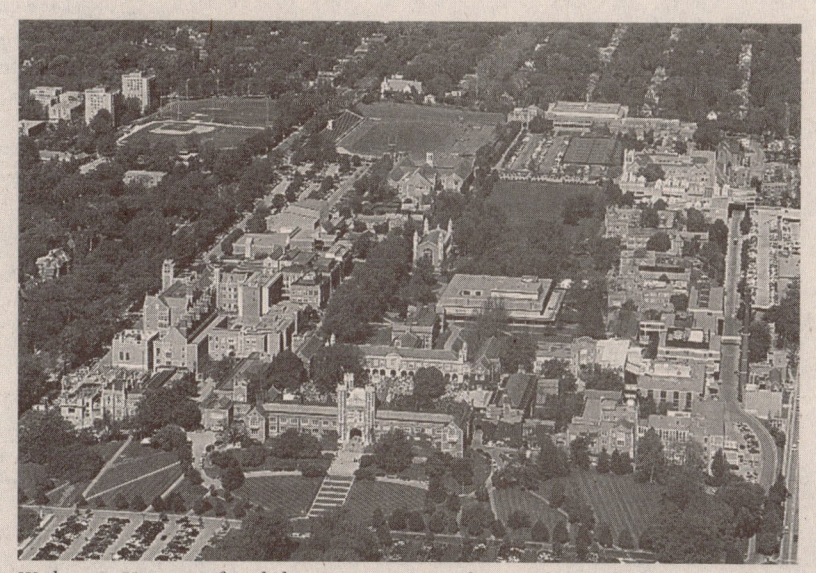

Washington University, founded in 1853, is recognized among the Top 20 national universities in the U.S., according to *U.S. News & World Report*. It draws more than 11,500 student annually from all 50 states and more than 80 countries.

Admissions Contact: Brad Pearson, Director of MBA Admissions
Address: Campus Box 1133, One Brookings Drive, St. Louis, MO 63130
Admissions Phone: 314-935-7301 • Admissions Fax: 314-935-6309
Admissions E-mail: mba@olin.wustl.edu • Web Address: www.olin.wustl.edu

WASHINGTON UNIVERSITY
John M. Olin School of Business

Admissions Contact: Brad Pearson, Director of MBA Admissions
Address: Campus Box 1133, One Brookings Drive, St. Louis, MO 63130
Admissions Phone: 314-935-7301 • Admissions Fax: 314-935-6309
Admissions E-mail: mba@olin.wustl.edu • Web Address: www.olin.wustl.edu

MBA students at Washington University's Olin School of Business tell us that its intimate size, flexible curriculum, and faculty composed of "heavy hitters" make it a worthwhile choice. Experiential learning is another major focal point of the Olin approach. Practicum allows students to consult for area companies on matters ranging from marketing to strategy. Thus far, a slew of firms, including Enterprise Rent-A-Car, Ford Motor Company, PricewaterhouseCoopers, Ralston Purina, and Monsanto, have asked Olin students for their advice.

INSTITUTIONAL INFORMATION
Public/Private: Private
Evening Classes Available? Yes
Total Faculty: 81
% Faculty Female: 18
% Faculty Minority: 3
% Faculty Part Time: 29
Student/Faculty Ratio: 14:1
Students in Parent Institution: 11,606
Academic Calendar: Semester

PROGRAMS
Degrees Offered: Full-Time MBA (20 months); Executive MBA (20 months), with academic paths in General Management, Health Services Management, and Manufacturing and Operations; Professional MBA (part time, 3 years); PhD (5 years)
Joint Degrees: MBA/Master of Health Administration (3 years); MBA/Master of Architecture (3 years); MBA/MA East Asian Studies (3 years); MBA/Master of Social Work (3 years); MBA/MA International Affairs (3 years); MBA/JD (4 years)
Academic Specialties: Curriculum is designed to focus on the individual student; mini-semester gives students more choice in electives; Professional Development Planning.
Special Opportunities: Experiential learning through management consulting, business plan development for entrepreneurs, investment management and global fund activities, global management studies, use of total quality management techniques, MBA Enterprise Corps.
Study Abroad Options: France, Germany, England, Venezuela

STUDENT INFORMATION
Total Business Students: 664
% Full Time: 45
% Female: 25
% Minority: 9
% Out of State: 90
% International: 32
Average Age: 28

COMPUTER AND RESEARCH FACILITIES
Research Facilities: Business, Law and Economics Center; Boeing Center for Technology, Information, and Manufacturing
Computer Facilities: 60-unit computer lab, "Express Lab" for checking e-mail and printing papers between classes; full range of research databases
Campuswide Network? Yes
Computer Model Recommended: Laptop
Internet Fee? No

EXPENSES/FINANCIAL AID
Annual Tuition: $28,300
Tuition Per Credit: $760
Room & Board (Off Campus): $10,000
Books and Supplies: $2,000
Average Grant: $11,524
Average Loan: $26,086
% Receiving Financial Aid: 70
% Receiving Aid Their First Year: 71

ADMISSIONS INFORMATION
Application Fee: $100
Electronic Application? Yes
Regular Application Deadline: 4/29
Regular Notification: 6/14
Deferment Available? No
Non-fall Admissions? No
Transfer Policy: Up to 9 credits from an AACSB-accredited graduate program
Need-Blind Admissions? Yes
Number of Applications Received: 4,376
% of Applicants Accepted: 7
% Accepted Who Enrolled: 38
Average GPA: 3.2
Average GMAT: 660
Average Years Experience: 5
Minority/Disadvantaged Student Recruitment Programs: Consortium for Graduate Study in Management (funds fellowships for talented minorities)
Other Schools to Which Students Applied: Emory, Northwestern, U. of Chicago, U. of Michigan, UNC—Chapel Hill, Vanderbilt

INTERNATIONAL STUDENTS
TOEFL Required of International Students? Yes
Minimum TOEFL: 590

EMPLOYMENT INFORMATION

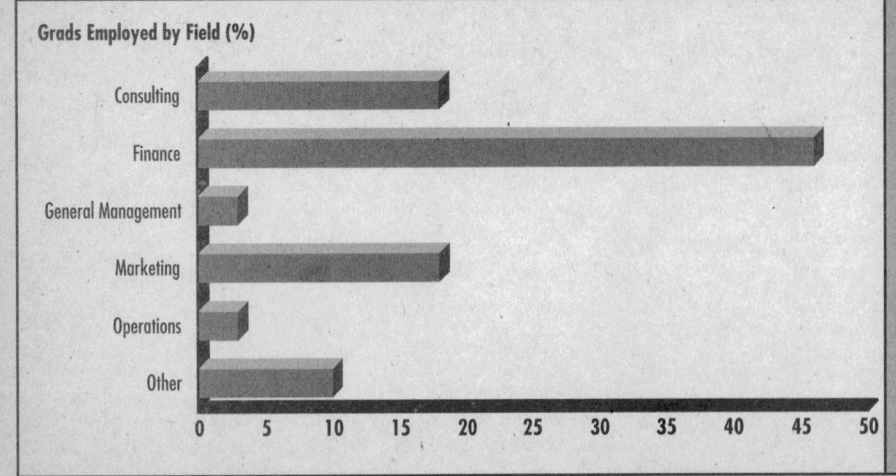

Grads Employed by Field (%)
- Consulting: ~19
- Finance: ~47
- General Management: ~3
- Marketing: ~18
- Operations: ~3
- Other: ~10

Placement Office Available? Yes
% Employed Within 3 Months: 97
Frequent Employers: Northwest Airlines, SBC Communications, Bank of America, A.G. Edwards, Anheuser-Busch, Charter Communications, Ernst & Young, Goldman Sachs, Ralston Purina Company, Procter & Gamble
Prominent Alumni: Priscilla L. Hill-Ardoin (MBA '88), senior VP, FCC, SBC Communications; Jerald L. Kent (BS, BA '78, MBA '79), president and CEO, Charter Communications; W. Patrick McGinnis (MBA '72), president and CEO, Ralston Purina Company; William J. Shaw, president and COO, Marriott International

WEBER STATE UNIVERSITY
John B. Goddard School of Business and Economics

Admissions Contact: Dr. Mark A. Stevenson, MBA Enrollment Director
Address: 3806 University Circle, Ogden, UT 84408-3806
Admissions Phone: 801-626-7545 • Admissions Fax: 801-626-7423
Admissions E-mail: mba@weber.edu • Web Address: goddard.weber.edu/dp/mba

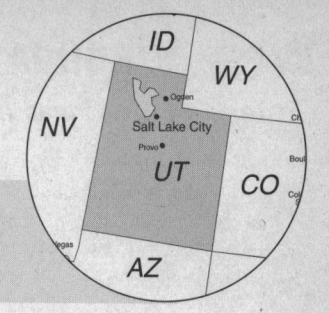

Weber State's MBA programs are only a couple of years old, but they are already reputedly "personalized, flexible, and thought-provoking." Classes (called "hybrid courses" because they combine traditional face-to-face instruction with online course work) are taught at night at the WSU—Davis campus in Layton. The program accepts applicants with undergraduate degrees in any discipline, whereas only business undergraduates need apply to the Fast-Track MBA, completed in as little as 56 weeks. Goddard's MBA students have, on average, four years of work experience, and are split about 50-50 between the two available programs.

INSTITUTIONAL INFORMATION
Public/Private: Public
Evening Classes Available? Yes
Total Faculty: 18
% Faculty Female: 38
Student/Faculty Ratio: 5:1
Students in Parent Institution: 16,800

PROGRAMS
Degrees Offered: MBA, MPAcc (Master of Professional Accountancy)
Academic Specialties: The John B. Goddard School of Business and Economics Master of Business Administration degree is fully accredited by AACSB International, the Association to Advance Collegiate Schools of Business. The Goddard School MBA is designed to meet the needs of working professionals who wish to advance in their careers. MBA courses are taught in the evenings at the WSU Davis campus in Layton. Our general management graduate curriculum consists of "hybrid courses," which blend the best of traditional classroom instruction with online educational tools and the power of the Internet.
Special Opportunities: The Goddard School MBA Program offers two different tracks. The Fast-Track MBA program is open only to students who have completed an undergraduate business degree from an AACSB-accredited school within the past 10 years. Students eligible for this option complete 36 credit hours of MBA course work. Full-time students who pursue this option can complete the Fast-Track program in as little as 56 weeks. The Non-Business Major Track is for nonbusiness undergraduates. We welcome applications from those who have undergraduate degrees in fields other than business. Half of our current students fall into this category. Our 55-credit MBA program can be completed in 2 years of full-time study. We have designed a set of foundations courses to prepare these students to move into the advanced MBA curriculum.

STUDENT INFORMATION
Total Business Students: 75
% Female: 32
% Minority: 4
% International: 9
Average Age: 31

COMPUTER AND RESEARCH FACILITIES
Campuswide Network? Yes
Computer Model Recommended: No
Internet Fee? No

EXPENSES/FINANCIAL AID
Annual Tuition (Resident/Nonresident): $6,000/$13,000
Books and Supplies: $2,000
Average Grant: $3,145
Average Loan: $6,000

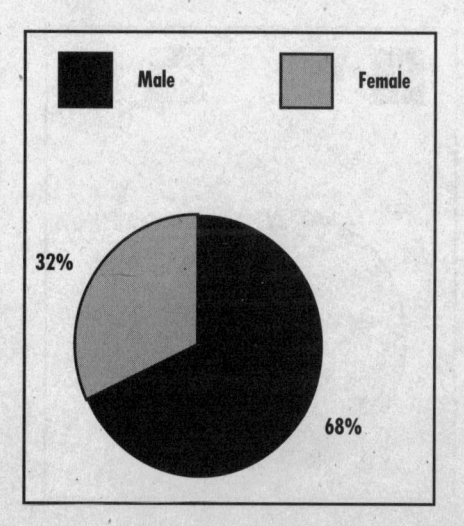

ADMISSIONS INFORMATION
Application Fee: $30
Electronic Application? Yes
Regular Application Deadline: 6/1
Regular Notification: Rolling
Deferment Available? Yes
Length of Deferment: 1 year
Non-fall Admissions? Yes
Non-fall Application Deadline(s): 11/1 spring
Transfer Students Accepted? Yes
Transfer Policy: Transfer credits from AACSB-accredited programs are accepted.
Need-Blind Admissions? Yes
Number of Applications Received: 63
% of Applicants Accepted: 75
% Accepted Who Enrolled: 94
Average GPA: 3.4
GPA Range: 3.1-3.7
Average GMAT: 571
GMAT Range: 530-620
Average Years Experience: 5
Other Admissions Factors Considered: Candidates from non-English-speaking countries are required to take the Test of English as a Foreign Language (TOEFL), unless they received their bachelor's degree from a university in which the language of instruction was English. Transcript evaluations are also required for international applicants.
Other Schools to Which Students Applied: Utah State University, University of Utah

INTERNATIONAL STUDENTS
TOEFL Required of International Students? Yes
Minimum TOEFL: 550 (213 computer)

EMPLOYMENT INFORMATION
Placement Office Available? Yes

West Virginia University
College of Business and Economics

Admissions Contact: Jennifer Butler, Associate Director
Address: PO Box 6025, Morgantown, WV 26506-6025
Admissions Phone: 304-293-5408 • Admissions Fax: 304-293-2385
Admissions E-mail: mba@wvu.edu • Web Address: www.be.wvu.edu

Touted as a great educational buy, West Virginia University offers a business education that covers all bases. Whether you're an executive looking for additional theoretical grounding or a beginner with an undergrad degree and a curiosity about the backbone of business, WVU has a program catered to your needs and schedule.

INSTITUTIONAL INFORMATION
Public/Private: Public
Evening Classes Available? Yes
Total Faculty: 65
% Faculty Female: 18
% Faculty Minority: 2
% Faculty Part Time: 6
Student/Faculty Ratio: 18:1
Students in Parent Institution: 22,000
Academic Calendar: Semester

PROGRAMS
Degrees Offered: MBA (1 year); Executive MBA (2 years); International MBA (1 year accelerated); Master of Science in Industrial Relations (MSIR) (1 year); Master of Professional Accountancy (MPA) (2 years); PhD in Economics
Joint Degrees: MBA/JD
Academic Specialties: AACSB-accredited; Carnegie research-extensive institution
Study Abroad Options: Germany, Italy, selected destinations in MBA International Business Trip

STUDENT INFORMATION
Total Business Students: 187
% Full Time: 18
% Female: 42
% Minority: 6
% Out of State: 73
% International: 36
Average Age: 30

COMPUTER AND RESEARCH FACILITIES
Campuswide Network? Yes
% of MBA Classrooms Wired: 100
Computer Model Recommended: Laptop
Internet Fee? No

EXPENSES/FINANCIAL AID
Annual Tuition (Resident/Nonresident): $11,300/$30,800
Tuition Per Credit (Resident/Nonresident): $383/$804
Books and Supplies: $1,500

ADMISSIONS INFORMATION
Application Fee: $50
Electronic Application? Yes
Regular Application Deadline: 3/1
Regular Notification: 3/31
Deferment Available? Yes
Length of Deferment: 1 year
Non-fall Admissions? Yes
Non-fall Application Deadline(s): July
Transfer Students Accepted? No
Need-Blind Admissions? Yes

Number of Applications Received: 156
% of Applicants Accepted: 24
% Accepted Who Enrolled: 89
Average GPA: 3.3
GPA Range: 3.0-3.7
Average GMAT: 560
GMAT Range: 520-630
Average Years Experience: 7
Other Schools to Which Students Applied: Marshall University, Pennsylvania State University, Syracuse University, Temple University, University of Kentucky, University of Pittsburgh, Virginia Polytechnic Institute and State University

INTERNATIONAL STUDENTS
TOEFL Required of International Students? Yes
Minimum TOEFL: 580

EMPLOYMENT INFORMATION
Placement Office Available? Yes
% Employed Within 3 Months: 98
Prominent Alumni: John Chambers, CEO, Cisco Systems; Glen Hiner, CEO, Owens Corning; Homer Hickam, author; Ray Lane, former president and COO, Oracle; Jerry West, general manager, Los Angeles Lakers

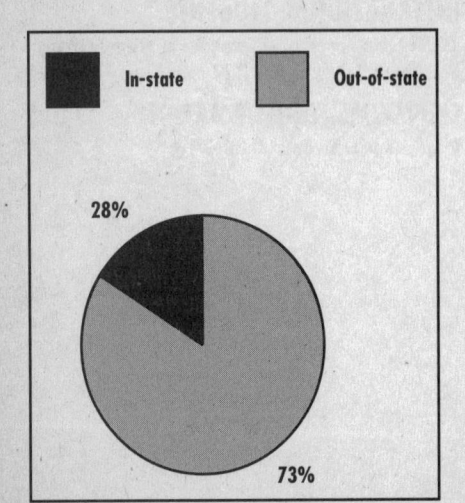

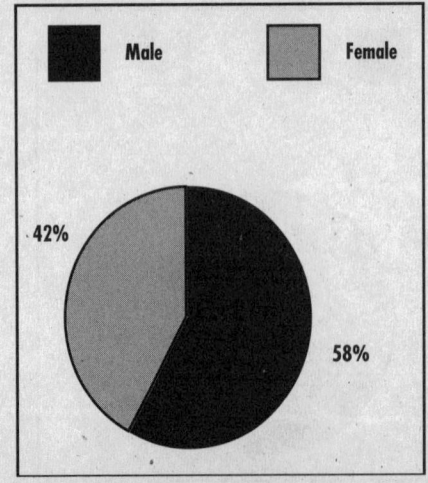

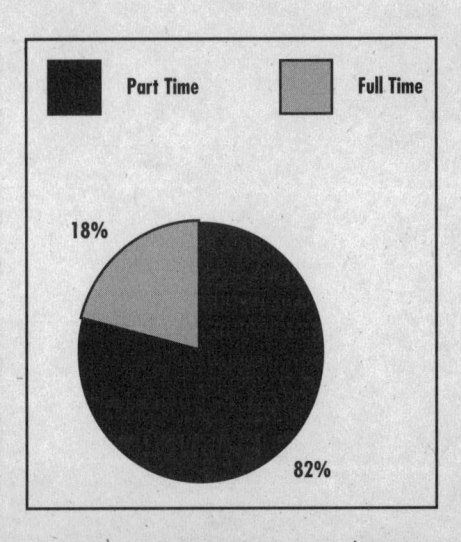

WESTERN CAROLINA UNIVERSITY
College of Business

Admissions Contact: Phillip Little, Director of MBA Program
Address: 112 Forsyth Building, Cullowhee, NC 28723
Admissions Phone: 828-227-7402 • Admissions Fax: 828-227-7414
Admissions E-mail: fdeitz@email.wcu.edu • Web Address: www.wcu.edu/cob/gradprograms.html

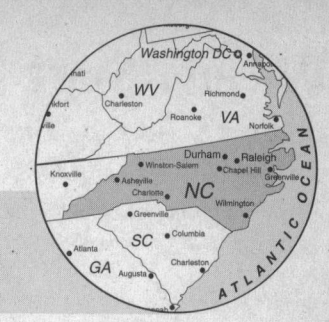

Located "in a rural valley between the Blue Ridge and Great Smoky Mountains," Western Carolina University's main campus in Cullowhee is a beautiful wooded area with all of the modern amenities a prospective b-school student could want: great academic, residential, and recreational facilities and a spot on Yahoo! Internet Life magazine's "100 Most Wired Campuses" list. Class sizes are small, and professors use a mixture of teaching methods to best "balance theory with practical application" and prepare students to "handle the business complexities of the global marketplace."

INSTITUTIONAL INFORMATION
Public/Private: Public
Evening Classes Available? Yes
Total Faculty: 47
% Faculty Female: 30
% Faculty Minority: 9
Student/Faculty Ratio: 3:1
Students in Parent Institution: 6,863
Academic Calendar: Semester

PROGRAMS
Degrees Offered: Master of Business Administration (MBA) (full time, 1.5 years); Master of Accountancy (full time, 1.5 years); Master of Project Management (online, 2 years)
Academic Specialties: The graduate faculty have PhD degrees in all areas of business; combined with real-world experience, they provide students with a broad knowledge of the business world.

STUDENT INFORMATION
Total Business Students: 126
% Full Time: 38
% Female: 35
% Minority: 6
% Out of State: 20
% International: 38
Average Age: 26

COMPUTER AND RESEARCH FACILITIES
Computer Facilities: All resources in library, career, and placement centers are available.
Campuswide Network? Yes
% of MBA Classrooms Wired: 12
Internet Fee? No

EXPENSES/FINANCIAL AID
Annual Tuition (Resident/Nonresident): $1,072/$8,704
Books and Supplies: $1,000
Average Grant: $9,154
Average Loan: $8,285
% Receiving Financial Aid: 58
% Receiving Aid Their First Year: 53

ADMISSIONS INFORMATION
Application Fee: $35
Electronic Application? No
Regular Application Deadline: Rolling
Regular Notification: Rolling
Deferment Available? Yes
Length of Deferment: 1 year
Non-fall Admissions? Yes
Non-fall Application Deadline(s): Rolling, spring, summer
Transfer Students Accepted? Yes
Transfer Policy: Up to 6 hours of graduate credit may be transferred.
Need-Blind Admissions? Yes
Number of Applications Received: 79
% of Applicants Accepted: 91
% Accepted Who Enrolled: 44
Average GPA: 3.4
GPA Range: 3.0-3.7
Average GMAT: 509
GMAT Range: 440-570
Average Years Experience: 6
Other Admissions Factors Considered: Computer experience

INTERNATIONAL STUDENTS
TOEFL Required of International Students? Yes
Minimum TOEFL: 550 (213 computer)

EMPLOYMENT INFORMATION
Placement Office Available? Yes

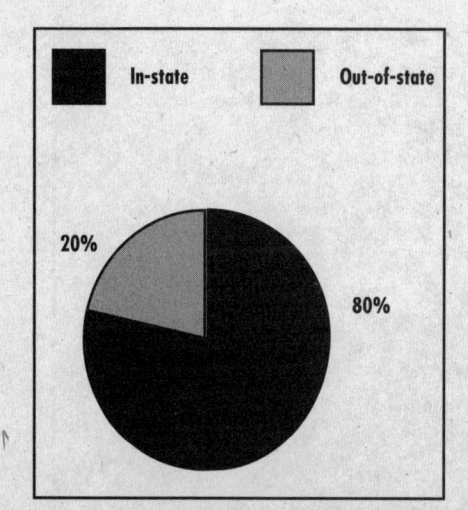

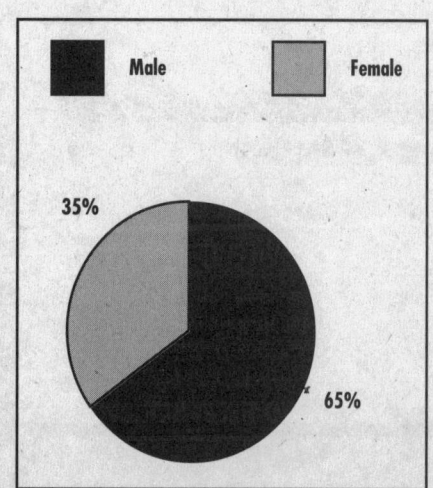

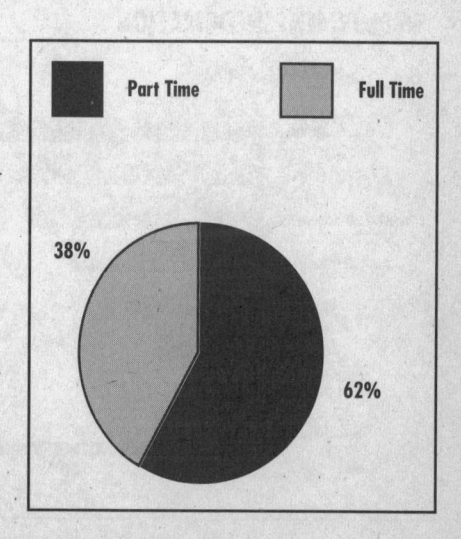

In-state: 80% / Out-of-state: 20%

Male: 65% / Female: 35%

Part Time: 62% / Full Time: 38%

WICHITA STATE UNIVERSITY
Barton School of Business

Admissions Contact: Dorothy Harpool, Associate Director of Graduate Studies in Business
Address: 1845 N. Fairmount, Wichita, KS 67260-0048
Admissions Phone: 316-978-3230 • Admissions Fax: 316-978-3767
Admissions E-mail: grad.business@wichita.edu • Web Address: business.twsu.edu

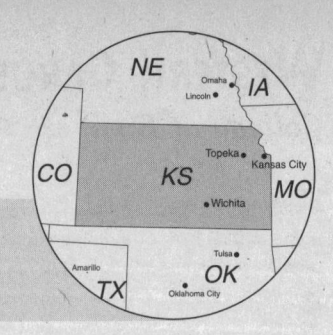

Entrepreneurship is a major focus at the Barton School of Business, and Wichita is the birthplace of some top-flight companies, including Cessna, Beech, Coleman, Learjet aircraft companies, and Koch Industries. You can find the original Pizza Hut building on the Wichita State campus, since two of Barton's alumni, Dan and Frank Carney, started the business in Wichita in 1958 with $600 and some used equipment. Barton's "traditional, managed-based" MBA focuses on perceiving an organization as an integrated system and offers "a unique blend of cutting-edge classroom instruction and practical business application" to its students.

INSTITUTIONAL INFORMATION
Public/Private: Public
Evening Classes Available? Yes
Total Faculty: 60
% Faculty Female: 12
% Faculty Minority: 15
Student/Faculty Ratio: 3:1
Academic Calendar: Semester

PROGRAMS
Degrees Offered: MBA (2 years); EMBA (22 months); MBA/MS Nursing (4 years)
Joint Degrees: MBA/MS in Nursing (66 credits: 30 MBA, 36 Nursing)

STUDENT INFORMATION
Total Business Students: 222
% Female: 38
% Minority: 9
% International: 43
Average Age: 25

COMPUTER AND RESEARCH FACILITIES
Research Facilities: Ablah Library; total holdings of 938,817 volumes, 907,837 microforms, 6,319 current periodical subscriptions; CD player(s) available
Campuswide Network? Yes
% of MBA Classrooms Wired: 75
Computer Model Recommended: No
Internet Fee? No

EXPENSES/FINANCIAL AID
Annual Tuition (Resident/Nonresident): $3,095/$8,856
Tuition Per Credit (Resident/Nonresident): $129/$369
Books and Supplies: $800
Average Grant: $6,000
Average Loan: $2,000

ADMISSIONS INFORMATION
Application Fee: $25
Electronic Application? Yes
Regular Application Deadline: 7/1
Regular Notification: 7/15
Deferment Available? Yes
Length of Deferment: 1 year
Non-fall Admissions? Yes
Non-fall Application Deadline(s): 12/1 spring
Transfer Students Accepted? Yes
Transfer Policy: Only AACSB-accredited classes may be transferred.
Need-Blind Admissions? Yes
Number of Applications Received: 173
% of Applicants Accepted: 58
% Accepted Who Enrolled: 82
Average GPA: 3.3
Average GMAT: 520
Average Years Experience: 3

INTERNATIONAL STUDENTS
TOEFL Required of International Students? Yes
Minimum TOEFL: 550 (213 computer)

EMPLOYMENT INFORMATION

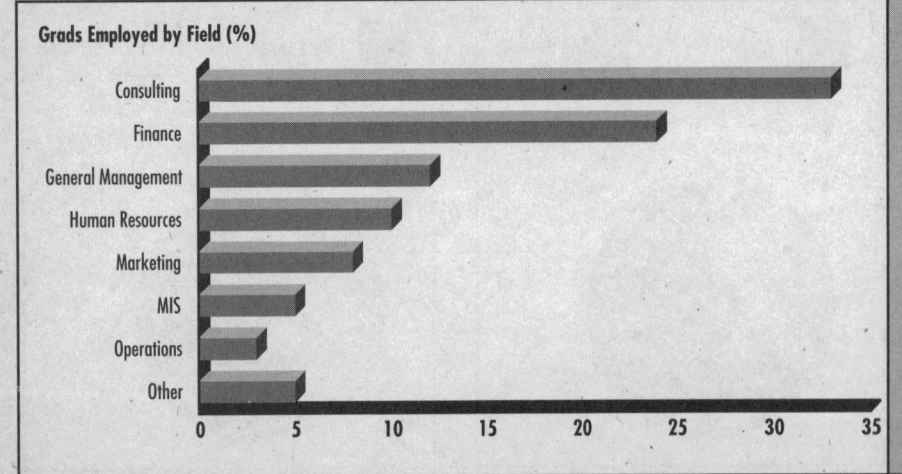

Grads Employed by Field (%)
- Consulting: ~34
- Finance: ~24
- General Management: ~12
- Human Resources: ~10
- Marketing: ~8
- MIS: ~3
- Operations: ~3
- Other: ~5

Placement Office Available? Yes
% Employed Within 3 Months: 90
Frequent Employers: Koch Industries, Raytheon, Boeing

WIDENER UNIVERSITY
School of Business Administration

Admissions Contact: Lisa Bussom, Assistant Dean
Address: 1 University Place, Chester, PA 19013
Admissions Phone: 610-499-4305 • Admissions Fax: 610-499-4615
Admissions E-mail: gradbus.advise@widener.edu • Web Address: www.sba.widener.edu

"We take your education personally" is the credo of Widener University, where the student/faculty relationship is based on personal attention. Widener has recently revamped its MBA program to offer students a modern ethical, global, and technological approach to business education.

INSTITUTIONAL INFORMATION
Public/Private: Private
Evening Classes Available? No
Total Faculty: 46
% Faculty Female: 33
% Faculty Part Time: 26
Student/Faculty Ratio: 6:1
Students in Parent Institution: 5,680
Academic Calendar: Semester

PROGRAMS
Degrees Offered: MBA (36 to 54 credits, 1.5 to 7 years, average of 4 years part time); MBA with concentration in Health and Medical Services (40 to 59 credits, 1.5 years to 7 years, average of 4 years part time); MS in Accounting Information Systems (33 credits); MS in Taxation (33 credits); MS in Human Resources Management (33 credits); MS in Information Systems (33 credits); MS in Management and Technology (36 credits); Master of Health Administration (33 credits)
Joint Degrees: MBA/Juris Doctor (3 years full time, 4 years part time); MBA/Master of Engineering (2 years full time, 5 years part time); MBA/Doctor of Clinical Psychology (5 years full time); MBA in Health and Medical Services Administration/Doctor of Clinical Psychology (5 years full time)
Academic Specialties: Financial Planning, Technology Management, Information Systems, Health Administration
Special Opportunities: Internship program available

STUDENT INFORMATION
Total Business Students: 318
% Female: 50
% Minority: 11
Average Age: 31

COMPUTER AND RESEARCH FACILITIES
Research Facilities: MBA students have access to all computer facilities on the main campus in Chester and the Delaware campus. Students can search databases from home through the library website. Specialized computer lab for MIS/IS courses includes SAP software.
Computer Facilities: MBA students have full access to the Law Library.
Campuswide Network? Yes
Internet Fee? No

EXPENSES/FINANCIAL AID
Annual Tuition: $12,800
Books and Supplies: $900
Average Grant: $12,725
Average Loan: $8,525
% Receiving Financial Aid: 14
% Receiving Aid Their First Year: 14

ADMISSIONS INFORMATION
Application Fee: $25
Electronic Application? No
Regular Application Deadline: 8/1
Regular Notification: Rolling
Deferment Available? Yes
Non-fall Admissions? Yes
Non-fall Application Deadline(s): 12/1 spring, 4/1 summer
Transfer Students Accepted? No
Need-Blind Admissions? No
Number of Applications Received: 126
% of Applicants Accepted: 73
% Accepted Who Enrolled: 62
Average GPA: 3.1
Average GMAT: 500
Other Schools to Which Students Applied: Drexel University, La Salle University, Pennsylvania State University Great Valley Campus, Temple University, University of Delaware, Villanova University

INTERNATIONAL STUDENTS
TOEFL Required of International Students? Yes
Minimum TOEFL: 550

EMPLOYMENT INFORMATION
Placement Office Available? Yes
Frequent Employers: The MBA program is part time, with more than 85 percent of our students working full time while earning their degree. Employers of our students include Boeing Co., PFPC, MBNA, DuPont, and First Union.
Prominent Alumni: Leslie C. Quick, founder, Quick & Reilly; H. Edward Hanway, CEO, Cigna Corp.; Paul Biederman, chairman, Mellon Mid-Atlantic; Mary McKenney, CEO, ManageMyProperty.com

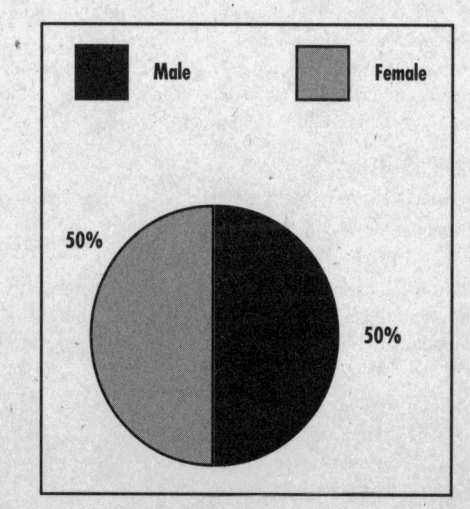

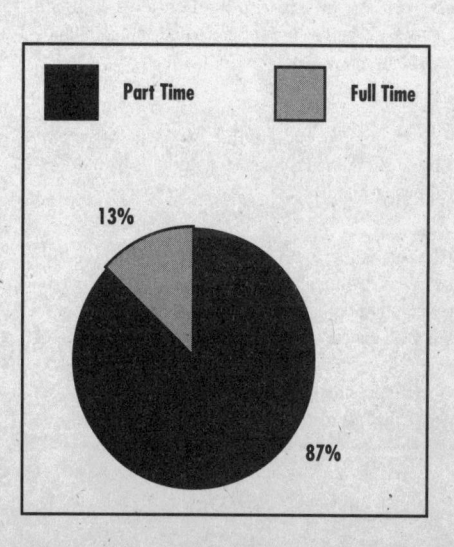

WILLAMETTE UNIVERSITY

THE SCHOOL AT A GLANCE
Willamette University's Atkinson Graduate School of Management offers the only MBA program in the nation accredited by the two most prestigious organizations governing management education: AACSB International (business) and NASPAA (public administration). The distinctive dual accreditation provides professional recognition and respect in all sectors, and prepares students for careers in entrepreneurial, business, consulting, government, and not-for-profit organizations. The School has also been recognized as one of the country's best business schools by *Business Week* and *U.S. News & World Report*.

The learning environment emphasizes excellent teaching, teamwork, and the practical application of management theory to managerial decision-making. From the first day of class, Atkinson students apply what they learn to real organizations. The Atkinson School PaCE Project (where teams of students create and run a real enterprise), case studies, internships, simulations, and consulting projects provide multiple opportunities to "learn by doing" and build their professional work experience while completing their MBA.

Curricular areas of interest include accounting, finance, general management, human resources, information technology, international management, marketing, organizational analysis, public management, and quantitative analysis/management science. A joint degree in management and law (MBA/JD) and a certificate in dispute resolution are also available.

The Atkinson School is part of Willamette University. Willamette University is widely recognized for the excellence of its academic programs, the quality of its students, the dedication of its faculty, and the success of its alumni. The University offers 34 undergraduate majors and three graduate professional degrees: the MBA (Master of Business Administration for Business, Government, and Not-for-Profit Management), the MAT (Master of Arts in Teaching) and the JD (Doctor of Jurisprudence).

Willamette University's campus is spacious and beautiful, and located in Salem, Oregon. Our Salem location offers the advantages of one of the nation's most livable small cities (population 122,000), and easy access to the professional and recreational resources of the Pacific Northwest.

STUDENTS
The Atkinson student profile is characterized by the same diversity of age and experience that is common to the work environment of most organizations. Students come to the Atkinson School with a variety of academic backgrounds and work experience. Some have years of management experience and are pursuing career advancement or change. Others have recently completed their bachelor's degree and are preparing for entry-level management positions.

Students also come to the Atkinson School with differing aspirations and career goals. Future business leaders work side-by-side with future leaders of public and not-for-profit organizations—each gaining insight and a better understanding of the role of a manager in the organizational environment.

ACADEMICS
The Atkinson School MBA has two program options; the "two-year" MBA program and the "accelerated" option. Both are designed for students with different academic and professional backgrounds.

The Two-Year MBA Program
The traditional "two-year" Atkinson School MBA program is designed for full-time students who have a bachelor's degree in the liberal arts (humanities, social sciences, science, math, etc.), engineering, or other areas of study. It is also designed for full-time students who have a major in business from a college of liberal arts or a business program that is not accredited for business administration by AACSB International (note: less than 50 percent of business programs in the U.S. are accredited by AACSB International) or students with a business degree who are not eligible for the accelerated program.

During the first year of study, students complete the required core curriculum; a set of 10 courses where students learn the financial, marketing, accounting, human resource, international, organizational, statistical, economic, quantitative, and information technology tools that support managerial decision-making. Students immediately apply what they learn through the unique Private, Public, and Community Enterprise Project (PaCE)—an extensive "hands-on" management project where teams of students create a business, make a profit, close the business, and donate their profits to a local not-for-profit organization.

During the second year of study, students use the elective curriculum to design a program that meets their individual career goals. Students may choose to pursue a broad background in general management or develop greater depth of knowledge in one or more career areas of interest. Elective courses include classes that involve projects and consulting for organizations, internships, independent study, industry analysis, case studies, research, study abroad programs, and traditional management classes.

The Accelerated Option
The "accelerated" option of the Atkinson School MBA for Business, Government, and Not-for-Profit Management is designed for people who have a strong background in the academic study of business as well as professional work experience. Through this program, admitted students may be eligible to waive up to 30 credits of the required core curriculum, and complete the Atkinson School MBA in approximately one academic year of full-time study (or longer as a part-time student).

Placement
The Atkinson School works with students and employers to provide a complete program of services connecting students and alumni with employment opportunities. Career service programs help students develop strategic career management skills, improve job search skills, and obtain internships and employment. Services include workshops, internship programs, on-campus interviews, employment opportunity postings, national employment databases, individual counseling, mentoring programs, and career/networking fairs.

Willamette University's Atkinson Graduate School of Management offers the MBA for Business, Government, and Not-for-Profit Management. The Atkinson School degree is the first and only MBA program accredited for both business (AACSB International) and public administration (NASPAA). It is a multi-sector, multi-opportunity degree that prepares students for the business of management—whether it is managing the business of business, the business of government, or the business of not-for-profit organizations.

Students may also pursue a joint degree in management and law (MBA/JD) through a cooperative agreement between Willamette University's College of Law and Atkinson Graduate School of Management. Candidates for the MBA/JD joint degree program must apply and be admitted to both the College of Law and the Atkinson School. During the first two years of the program, students complete one academic year in each school. During the third and fourth years, two-thirds of the student's courses are taken at the College of Law and one-third at the Atkinson School.

CAMPUS LIFE
Willamette University is located in Salem, Oregon. The University's campus is spacious and one of the most beautiful college campuses in the United States. The Willamette campus is comprised of 43 buildings on 61 acres of land.

Atkinson School classrooms are spacious, modern, and facilitate interaction among students and between students and faculty. Two classrooms are fully electronic and feature network computer-assisted instruction. The main lecture hall also features a visualizer and video-television projection unit.

Atkinson students have 24-hour-a-day access to the Internet, e-mail and local network services. Students are required to have a laptop computer with wireless LAN capability and a standard suite of software for word processing, spreadsheets, and presentations.

Atkinson Graduate School of Management

The University's Mark O. Hatfield Library and the J.W. Long Law Library support the research needs of Atkinson students. Services include a Management/Economics Librarian who assists students and faculty, electronic databases, books, periodicals, journals, newspapers, specialized materials, and programs that provide access to more than four million books, journals, and library resources.

Seventy percent of Atkinson alumni choose to live and work in the Pacific Northwest after graduation. The Salem-Portland I-5 corridor is home to a multitude of businesses (including Northwest legends Nike, Intel, and Tektronix) and hosts a large variety of government and not-for-profit organizations.

Barbecues, receptions, the international dinner, community service projects, food drives, holiday celebrations, alumni activities, pizza nights, traditional Thursday nights out, and the time-honored Brownwater Regatta (a celebration of spring) balance the academic demands of the program. University programs popular with Atkinson students include films, art shows, nationally recognized speakers, athletics, intramural sports, concerts of the Oregon Symphony Orchestra, the Willamette University Hallie Ford Museum of Art, and numerous music and theater productions.

Beyond campus life, students can ski the Cascade Mountains, enjoy the beaches of the Pacific Ocean, hike and mountain bike the Willamette National Forest, windsurf and hike the Columbia River Gorge—or explore the urban and cultural offerings of the Portland metropolitan area. Graduate students don't live by classes alone—there is perhaps no environment better than Salem and Oregon to prove that point.

COSTS

Willamette University's Atkinson School provides a nationally recognized MBA education at a reasonable and manageable cost. Atkinson School tuition for full-time students enrolled in 12 to 18 semester credits of course work is $9,025 per semester or $18,050 for the 2002-2003 academic year. Tuition for part-time students is $602 per semester credit.

The budget for full-time Atkinson School students includes the estimated costs of tuition, books, fees, and living expenses (living expenses include room, board, and personal expenses). Tuition, books, and fees are common costs among students. Living expenses vary with the needs and choices of individuals. Students are also required to have a laptop computer with 802.11b wireless LAN capability and a standard suite of software. If you need to purchase a laptop, the cost to purchase the required laptop can be included in your financial aid budget. For planning purposes, students should assume an annual tuition increase of 4 to 5 percent for the following academic year.

Estimated Expenses for 2002–2003
Tuition: $18,050
Student Body Fee: $50
Books: $1,200
Living Expenses: $7,550 to $11,350

Full-time students may be eligible for Atkinson School scholarships. Scholarships are awarded on the basis of merit as measured by GMAT/GRE scores, undergraduate grade point average, and experience. Scholarships range in value from one-third to two-thirds of tuition.

U.S. citizens and permanent residents may be eligible to borrow up to $18,500 per year through the Federal Stafford Loan Programs. Eligibility for the Stafford Loan Programs is determined by submission and analysis of the FAFSA (Free Application for Federal Student Aid). U.S. citizens and permanent residents may also be eligible for private credit-based educational loans and campus work programs.

International students may be eligible for Atkinson School merit-based scholarships, and may be eligible for private credit-based educational loans if they have a co-signer who is a U.S. citizen or permanent resident. However, international applicants and/or their sponsor should be prepared to fund the entire cost of educational and living expenses for the two-year program.

ADMISSIONS

Admission to the Atkinson School is based on academic ability and managerial potential. Academic ability is evaluated by the applicant's past academic performance, recommendations, and performance on the GMAT or GRE. Managerial potential is evaluated by the applicant's general experience, work experience, motivation, leadership, involvement in organizational or community activities, communication skills, and commitment to attain a graduate management education. These characteristics are evaluated through information provided on the Application for Admission, letters of recommendation, personal statement of experience/goals, and often, an interview with the applicant. Candidates are also evaluated on their potential to contribute to and benefit from the learning environment of the Atkinson School.

Each applicant is evaluated individually. Applicants must have a baccalaureate degree from an accredited college or university in the United States or an equivalent degree from another country. There are no specific course prerequisites for admission, but students should have an understanding of mathematical principles and well-developed writing skills. Experience with word processing and spreadsheet applications is also helpful.

Applicants requesting admission to the Atkinson School must submit the following materials to the Atkinson School Admission Office: application for admission (paper or online), personal statement of experiences and professional goals, two letters of evaluation, official transcripts of all undergraduate and graduate course work, official GMAT or GRE scores, and a $50 nonrefundable application fee.

In addition to the documents listed above, international applicants must submit the following: English translation of academic records and transcripts, and Statement of Financial Responsibility and official bank verification showing sufficient resources to cover educational and personal expenses. International students for whom English is not the first language must also submit a TOEFL score of 213 or higher on the computer-based test.

The Atkinson School has a rolling admission process and reviews applications throughout the year. Applications completed by March 31 receive priority in admission and scholarship decisions. Applications submitted after March 31 may also receive consideration for admission and scholarship assistance.

Applicants will be notified of the admission decision within three weeks of completion of the application process.

Applicants are always welcome to contact the Atkinson School Admission Office at agsm-admission@willamette.edu or 503-370-6167 to check on the status of the application and communicate with members of the admission staff.

Applicants for the Willamette University MBA/JD joint degree program must also complete the application process of the Willamette University College of Law.

Admissions Contact: Judy O'Neill, Assistant Dean and Director of Admission
Address: 900 State Street, Salem, OR 97301
Admissions Phone: 503-370-6167 • Admissions Fax: 503-370-3011
Admissions E-mail: agsm-admission@willamette.edu
Web Address: www.willamette.edu/agsm

WILLAMETTE UNIVERSITY
Atkinson Graduate School of Management

Admissions Contact: Judy O'Neill, Assistant Dean/Director of Admission
Address: 900 State Street, Salem, OR 97301
Admissions Phone: 503-370-6167 • Admissions Fax: 503-370-3011
Admissions E-mail: agsm-admission@williamette.edu • Web Address: www.willamette.edu/agsm

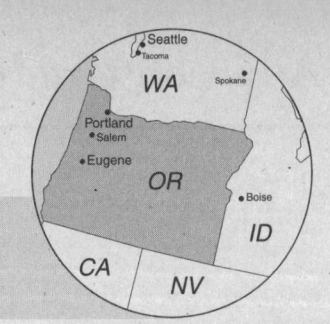

The Atkinson School has the only graduate management program in the nation accredited for both business administration and public administration. Accordingly, its MBA for business, government, and not-for-profit management is the only degree that grants its recipients the benefits of an MBA and an MPA. Atkinson has a progressive outlook, claiming that the school "goes far beyond existing ideas of management education," providing programs "that redefine real-world experience" and enabling students to "receive an unprecedented multi-sector, multi-opportunity education."

INSTITUTIONAL INFORMATION
Public/Private: Private
Evening Classes Available? No
Total Faculty: 14
% Faculty Female: 14
Student/Faculty Ratio: 12:1
Students in Parent Institution: 2,353
Academic Calendar: Semester

PROGRAMS
Degrees Offered: MBA for Business, Government, and Not-for-Profit Management (2 years full time, 4 to 6 years part time); Accelerated MBA (1 year full time
Joint Degrees: MBA/JD (4 years)
Academic Specialties: General Business, Government, and Not-for-Profit Management; Accounting; Finance; Human Resources; Marketing; Organizational Analysis; Public Management; Management Science; Negotiation/Dispute Resolution. Real-world experiences include the Atkinson School PaCE Project, in which students create and run a real enterprise, internships, class consulting projects, case studies, simulations, etc. Curriculum stresses the practical application of management theory to real-world organizations.
Study Abroad Options: Denmark, Sweden

STUDENT INFORMATION
Total Business Students: 168
% Full Time: 90
% Female: 37
% Minority: 8
% Out of State: 58
% International: 32
Average Age: 26

COMPUTER AND RESEARCH FACILITIES
Research Facilities: Centers for Public Policy Research and Dispute Resolution
Computer Facilities: Library databases include Academic Search Elite, Business Dateline, Congressional Universe, Standard & Poor's NetAdvantage, Statistical Universe, STAT-USA, Wilson Business Abstracts
Campuswide Network? Yes
% of MBA Classrooms Wired: 20
Computer Model Recommended: Laptop
Internet Fee? No

EXPENSES/FINANCIAL AID
Annual Tuition: $17,150
Tuition Per Credit: $572
Books and Supplies: $1,900
Average Grant: $7,300
Average Loan: $12,000
% Receiving Financial Aid: 70
% Receiving Aid Their First Year: 70

ADMISSIONS INFORMATION
Application Fee: $50
Electronic Application? Yes
Regular Application Deadline: Rolling
Regular Notification: Rolling
Length of Deferment: 1 year
Non-fall Admissions? No
Transfer Policy: Up to 6 credits with approval of the dean
Need-Blind Admissions? Yes
Number of Applications Received: 175
% of Applicants Accepted: 75
% Accepted Who Enrolled: 63
Average GPA: 3.2
GPA Range: 2.9-3.7
Average GMAT: 564
GMAT Range: 520-600
Average Years Experience: 3
Minority/Disadvantaged Student Recruitment Programs: University-endowed scholarships
Other Schools to Which Students Applied: U. of Oregon, U. of Washington, Thunderbird, Brigham Young, Portland State, Arizona State, Pepperdine

INTERNATIONAL STUDENTS
TOEFL Required of International Students? Yes
Minimum TOEFL: 550 (213 computer)

EMPLOYMENT INFORMATION

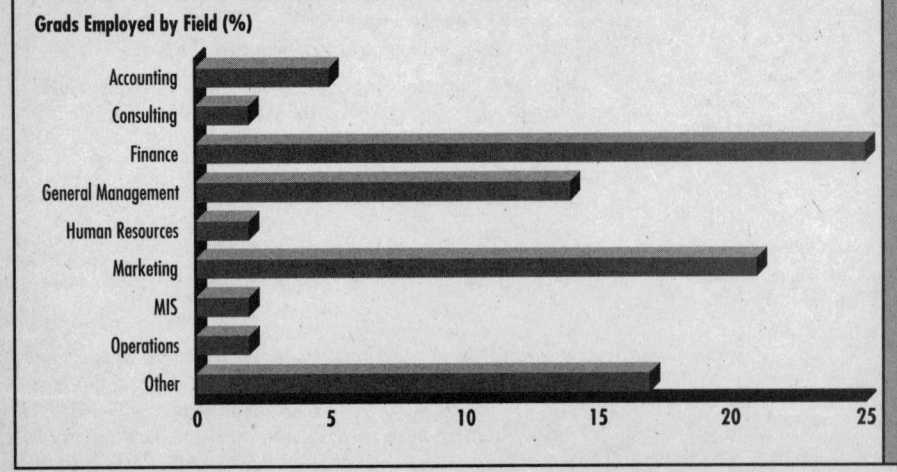

Grads Employed by Field (%)

Field	%
Accounting	5
Consulting	2
Finance	25
General Management	14
Human Resources	2
Marketing	21
MIS	2
Operations	2
Other	17

Placement Office Available? Yes
% Employed Within 3 Months: 87
Frequent Employers: Intel Corporation, Andersen, Deloitte & Touche, state of Oregon, Hewlett-Packard, Tektronix Inc., Nike Inc., U.S. government, Planar Systems, Xerox, Bonneville Power Administration
Prominent Alumni: Marcus Robins, investments; Grace Crunican, U.S. government; Tom Hoover, marketing research; Ann Jackson, not-for-profit management; Tom Neilsen, general management

WRIGHT STATE UNIVERSITY
College of Business and Administration

Address: 3640 Colonel Glenn Highway, Dayton, OH 45435
Admissions Phone: 937-775-2437
Admissions Fax: 937-775-3545

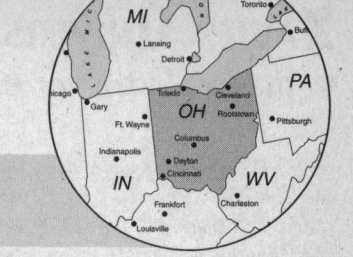

Thankfully, voters decided to name the school Wright State University in '65 to honor Dayton's Wright Brothers instead of other title suggestions, such as Whatsamatta U. The MBA program offered at the Raj Soin School of Business has an incredibly flexible curriculum, so if you're totally unsure about what you'll be doing over the next year or more between your job, kids, and school, Wright State may very well be a fit for you. Students can choose from nine concentrations in order to gain specialized knowledge as their business talents mature in the program, and they can earn the degree in as little as 11 months or stretch it out for five years.

INSTITUTIONAL INFORMATION
Public/Private: Public
Evening Classes Available? Yes
Total Faculty: 50
% Faculty Female: 24
Student/Faculty Ratio: 8:1
Academic Calendar: Quarter

PROGRAMS
Degrees Offered: MBA (1 to 5 years), MS Social and Applied Economics (1 to 5 years), Master of Accountancy (1 to 5 years)
Joint Degrees: MBA/MS Nursing (2 to 5 years), MBA/MS Economics (2 to 5 years)

STUDENT INFORMATION
Total Business Students: 435
% Full Time: 33
% Female: 35
Average Age: 29

COMPUTER AND RESEARCH FACILITIES
Campuswide Network? Yes
Computer Proficiency Required? Yes
Special Purchasing Agreements? No
Internet Fee? No

EXPENSES/FINANCIAL AID
Annual Tuition (Resident/Nonresident): $5,847/$10,182
Room & Board (On Campus): $6,000
Books and Supplies: $90/course

ADMISSIONS INFORMATION
Application Fee: $25
Electronic Application? Yes
Deferment Available? Yes
Length of Deferment: 4 quarters
Non-fall Admissions? Yes
Transfer Students Accepted? Yes
Transfer Policy: Must meet WSU admissions requirements; can transfer up to 4 classes, with faculty approval
Need-Blind Admissions? Yes
Number of Applications Received: 314
% of Applicants Who Accepted: 83
% Accepted Who Enrolled: 53
Average GPA: 3.15
Average GMAT: 535
Average Years Experience: 5

INTERNATIONAL STUDENTS
TOEFL Required of International Students? Yes
Minimum TOEFL: 550

EMPLOYMENT INFORMATION
Placement Office Available? No

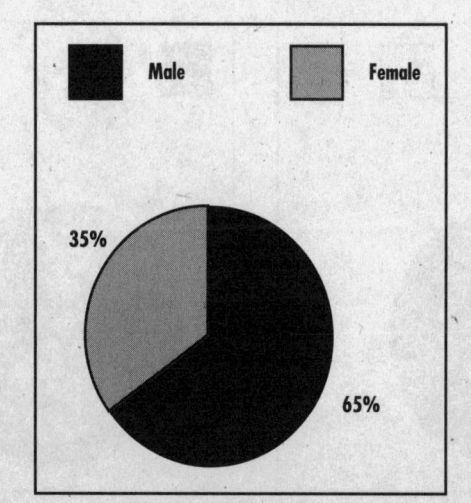

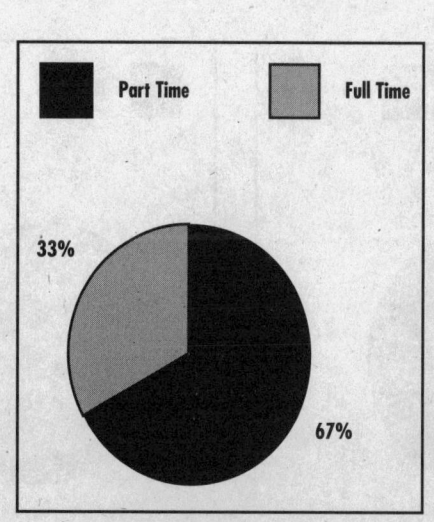

XAVIER UNIVERSITY
Williams College of Business

Admissions Contact: Jennifer Bush, Director, MBA Enrollment Services
Address: 3800 Victory Parkway, Cincinnati, OH 45207
Admissions Phone: 513-745-3525 • Admissions Fax: 513-745-2929
Admissions E-mail: XUMBA@xu.edu • Web Address: www.xavier.edu/mba

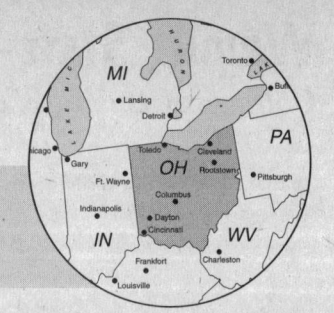

The Xavier MBA has a team-based curriculum that "emphasizes the dynamic nature of business and teaches the skills to grow and change with it." Students may cater the broad-based On-Site MBA program to their specific goals and interests by choosing from nine concentrations. Experienced professionals who can make it to class once a week will be able to earn an Executive MBA in just 19 months. Xavier is a Jesuit university, so the curriculum has roots in Jesuit philosophy, stressing ethical and moral issues while encouraging the development of the whole person.

INSTITUTIONAL INFORMATION
Public/Private: Private
Evening Classes Available? Yes
Total Faculty: 75
% Faculty Female: 35
% Faculty Part Time: 25
Student/Faculty Ratio: 18:1
Students in Parent Institution: 6,660
Academic Calendar: Semester

PROGRAMS
Degrees Offered: Weekend (Saturday) MBA; Executive MBA; on-site MBA; add-on concentration for post-MBA graduates in 9 areas, approximate length 2 semesters
Joint Degrees: Master of Health Services Administration/MBA (3 years), MS in Nursing/MBA (3 years)
Academic Specialties: Accounting, E-Business, Entrepreneurship, Finance, General Business, Human Resources, Information Systems, International Business, Marketing
Study Abroad Options: France—ESC, Bordeaux; China—Beijing International MBA at Peking University; Annual Summer Study trips to South America, Asia, and Europe. Through Jesuit Business School Network agreement, students have access to study-abroad trips with 23 Jesuit AACSB MBA schools.

STUDENT INFORMATION
Total Business Students: 997
% Full Time: 19
% Female: 29
% Minority: 10
% Out of State: 17
% International: 20
Average Age: 28

COMPUTER AND RESEARCH FACILITIES
Research Facilities: Xavier University Entrepreneurial Center
Computer Facilities: ABI/Inform, CCH Tax Research Network, Business and Industry, Business and Management Practices, Business Dataline, Compustat, Computer Select, Congressional University, Disclosure Global Access, E-Marketer Reports, EconLit, FirstSearch, Infotrac, General Business File, Lexis-Nexis Academic Universe, STAT-USA
Campuswide Network? Yes
% of MBA Classrooms Wired: 50
Internet Fee? No

EXPENSES/FINANCIAL AID
Annual Tuition: $7,830
Tuition Per Credit: $435
Books and Supplies: $600
Average Grant: $743

ADMISSIONS INFORMATION
Application Fee: $35
Electronic Application? Yes
Regular Application Deadline: Rolling
Regular Notification: Rolling
Deferment Available? Yes
Length of Deferment: 1 year
Non-fall Admissions? Yes
Non-fall Application Deadline(s): Rolling
Transfer Students Accepted? Yes
Transfer Policy: 6 hours of core curriculum from AACSB-accredited programs only; up to 18 hours of core curriculum from AACSB-accredited Jesuit MBA Network Schools
Need-Blind Admissions? Yes
Number of Applications Received: 357
% of Applicants Accepted: 60
% Accepted Who Enrolled: 97
Average GPA: 3.2
GPA Range: 2.9-3.5
Average GMAT: 550
GMAT Range: 500-590
Average Years Experience: 5
Other Schools to Which Students Applied: Northern Kentucky University, University of Cincinnati

INTERNATIONAL STUDENTS
TOEFL Required of International Students? Yes
Minimum TOEFL: 550 (213 computer)

EMPLOYMENT INFORMATION
Placement Office Available? Yes

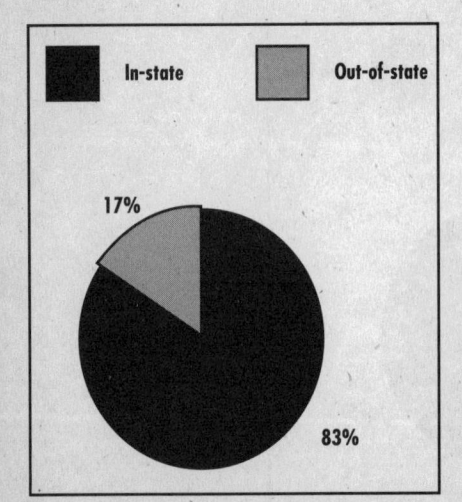

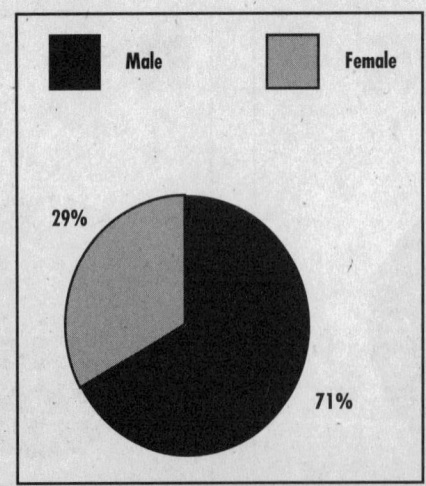

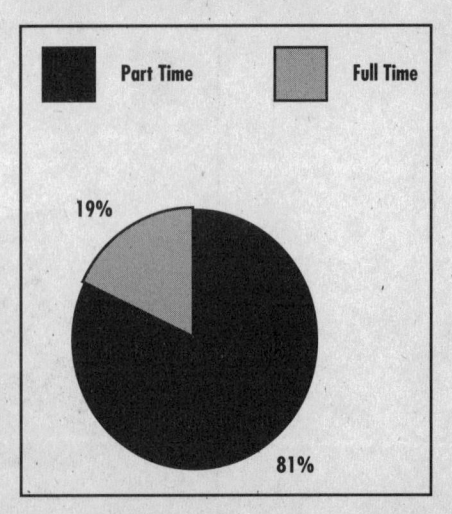

In-state 83% / Out-of-state 17%

Male 71% / Female 29%

Part Time 81% / Full Time 19%

YALE UNIVERSITY
Yale School of Management

Admissions Contact: James R. Stevens, Director of Admissions
Address: 135 Prospect Street, PO Box 208200, New Haven, CT 06520-8200
Admissions Phone: 203-432-5932 • Admissions Fax: 203-432-7004
Admissions E-mail: mba.admissions@yale.edu • Web Address: www.mba.yale.edu

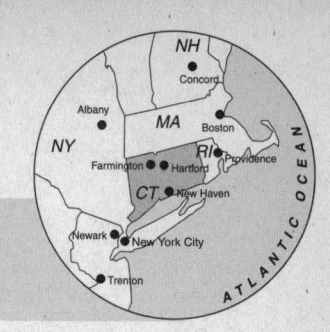

Where do "the best, brightest, and most diverse management students" go for their MBAs? Yale, of course, where "brilliant, accomplished," and "innovative" professors are "well published" and "100 percent accessible." Yale's nontraditional (i.e., "noncompetitive") grading system "encourages students to take risks with difficult course work," and while students report a fair amount of academic pressure, they say it "varies because it's self-imposed."

INSTITUTIONAL INFORMATION
Public/Private: Private
Evening Classes Available? No
Total Faculty: 84
% Faculty Female: 14
% Faculty Part Time: 38
Student/Faculty Ratio: 8:1
Students in Parent Institution: 11,039
Academic Calendar: Semester

PROGRAMS
Degrees Offered: MBA (full time, 2 years), PhD
Joint Degrees: MBA/JD (4 years); MBD/MD (5 years); MBA/MArch (4 years); MBA/MFA Drama (4 years); MBA/MSN (3 years); MBA/MDiv (3 years); MBA/MES or MF Environment (3 years); MBA/MA International Relations (3 years); MBA/MPH (3 years); MBA/MA (East Asian Studies or International and Development Economics or International Relations or Russia and East European Studies) (3 years)
Academic Specialties: Finance, Accounting, Strategy, International and General Management
Special Opportunities: International Institute for Corporate Governance, Yale SOM-Goldman Sachs Foundation Partnership on Nonprofit Ventures, Leaders Forum, Sachem Ventures (MBA-managed venture capital fund), Enterprise Center, Connecticut Venture Group, Office of Cooperative, Yale SOM Outreach (pro bono consulting)

Study Abroad Options: Summer internships throughout the world.

STUDENT INFORMATION
Total Business Students: 440
% Female: 28
% Minority: 5
% International: 39
Average Age: 28

COMPUTER AND RESEARCH FACILITIES
Research Facilities: International Center for Finance housed at the Yale School of Management: viking.som.yale.edu/finance.center
Computer Facilities: See our website at www.mba.yale.edu.
Campuswide Network? Yes
Computer Model Recommended: Laptop
Internet Fee? No

EXPENSES/FINANCIAL AID
Annual Tuition: $31,500
Room & Board (On Campus): $10,125
Books and Supplies: $4,070
Average Grant: $6,870
Average Loan: $29,484
% Receiving Financial Aid: 65
% Receiving Aid Their First Year: 55

ADMISSIONS INFORMATION
Application Fee: $175
Electronic Application? Yes
Regular Application Deadline: 3/15

Regular Notification: 5/31
Deferment Available? Yes
Length of Deferment: 1 year
Non-fall Admissions? No
Transfer Students Accepted? No
Need-Blind Admissions? No
Number of Applications Received: 2,101
% of Applicants Accepted: 20
% Accepted Who Enrolled: 57
Average GPA: 3.5
GPA Range: 3.3-3.7
Average GMAT: 686
GMAT Range: 660-710
Average Years Experience: 4
Other Admissions Factors Considered: Career goals, demonstrated leadership
Minority/Disadvantaged Student Recruitment Programs: Minority MBA student workshops held in major cities nationwide, Pre-MBA Prep programs, scholarships, annual Minority Student Receptions, Minority Student Weekend, participation in Destination MBA, the National Black MBA Association, the National Society of Hispanic MBAs Conference, Management Leadership for Tomorrow's mentoring program
Other Schools to Which Students Applied: Columbia, Cornell, Harvard, NYU, Northwestern, Stanford, Penn

INTERNATIONAL STUDENTS
TOEFL Required of International Students? Yes
Minimum TOEFL: 600 (250 computer)

EMPLOYMENT INFORMATION

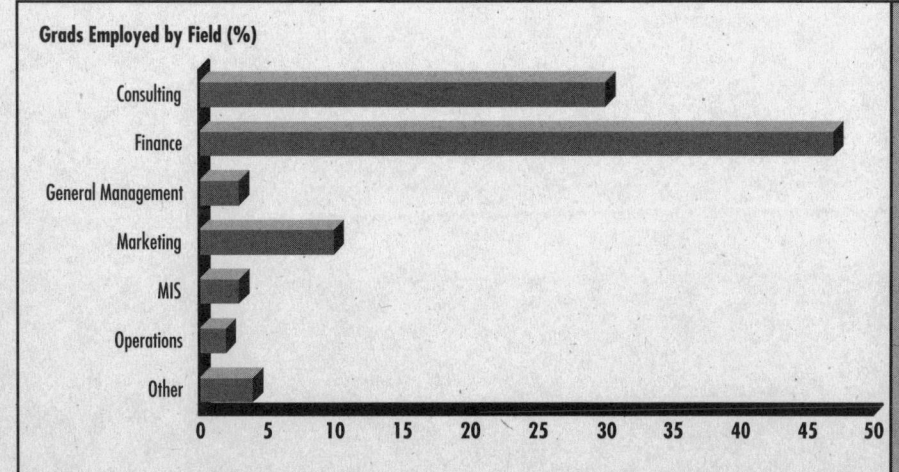

Grads Employed by Field (%)
- Consulting: ~30
- Finance: ~48
- General Management: ~3
- Marketing: ~10
- MIS: ~1
- Operations: ~2
- Other: ~5

Placement Office Available? Yes
% Employed Within 3 Months: 97
Frequent Employers: McKinsey & Co., Deutsche Bank, IBM, American Express, Goldman Sachs, Lehman Brothers, Booz Allen Hamilton, Standard & Poor's, Citigroup/Citibank, Salomon Smith Barney, Credit Suisse First Boston
Prominent Alumni: John Thornton, president and co-COO, Goldman Sachs; Nancy Peretsman, executive VP and managing director, Allen & Company; Indra Nooyi, president and CFO, PepsiCo Inc.; Fred Terrell, managing partner and CEO, Provender Capital Group; Thomas Krens, director, Solomon R. Guggenheim Foundation

ADDITIONAL B-SCHOOLS

In this section, you'll find detailed profiles of a few business schools that are not yet accredited by the AACSB, with information about their programs, faculty, facilities, and admissions. The Princeton Review charges each school a small fee to be listed, and the editorial responsibility is solely that of the college.

AUDREY COHEN COLLEGE

THE SCHOOL AT A GLANCE

Audrey Cohen College's Graduate School of Business was established to accommodate the growing need for continuing professional education in today's rapidly changing business world. The Graduate School of Business offers the following day, evening, and weekend programs: the Bachelor of Business Administration; the Master of Business Administration in Media Management; the Master of Business Administration in General Management; the Master of Business Administration in Multimedia Industry and E-Commerce; and the Master of Business Administration in Sports, Recreation, and Leisure Service Management.

In addition to the MBA degrees, The Graduate School also offers a dual MS/MBA Media Management degree based on the current MBA in Media Management. Students earn the MS/MBA by completing 1) the current Media Management MBA, plus 2) a specialization semester in Multimedia and E-commerce or Sports, Recreation, and Leisure Service Management, plus 3) a thesis.

The College has adapted its Purpose-Centered System of Education to the elementary/secondary experience, and this system is being used by schools around the country.

STUDENTS

Students in the Graduate School of Business work full-time for the most part. This limits the number of hours for activities not related to the classroom. Still, student government functions, a yearly school dance, yearbook, and journalistic activities are sources for student involvement. Mentoring and tutoring opportunities are encouraged. A comfortable student lounge provides a quiet space for socializing and networking.

ACADEMICS

The Constructive Action

The Constructive Action is the core of the College model. Each selected Constructive Action creates an opportunity for the customized integration of class work and practice for a given Purpose. The developmentally designed Constructive Actions undertaken in each program form a capstone experience for the business management student.

Students select a significant and beneficial professional purpose to work on—for example, solving an industry problem or establishing a new venture using knowledge gleaned from their classes and applying that knowledge to their immediate career or circumstances. In order to earn the Master of Business Administration degree, each student must design, implement, and document three interrelated Constructive Actions at a given work site or through their own entrepreneurial effort. The Constructive Actions will be planned, carried out, and assessed under the guidance of a Purpose Instructor and program faculty members who are experienced high-level industry specialists.

International Study Abroad Component

All our MBA programs have an exciting, built-in, international study component. Each student is required to design and implement a practical project that will be both pertinent and beneficial to his or her stateside career, organization, or job-related responsibilities. The study abroad component prepares students to become business professionals capable of negotiating cultural diversity and understanding first-hand the purposes, systems, and skills that comprise the conduct of international business and world markets. Current study abroad programs are held in England and France.

Our One-Year Executive MBAs

- Media Management
- Sports, Recreation, and Leisure Service Management

The Core Curriculm & Specialization Series

Our innovative, achievement-oriented one year Executive MBA Programs consist of 2 required Core Semesters which provide students from ANY field with the fundamental skills necessary for managerial success. Students then select their 3rd Semester area of specialization from of the following specialization options:

- General Management
- Multimedia Industry and E-Commerce

While the College offers three full semesters of study each calendar year, there is no requirement that students attend without interruption. However, the majority of students do, permitting them to complete their degree in one year.

Audrey Cohen College Graduate School of Business offers both MBA and MS degrees. The programs are as follows:

- Master of Business Administration in General Management
- Master of Business Administration in Media Management
- Master of Business Administration in Multimedia Industry and E-Commerce
- Master of Business Administration in Sports, Recreation, and Leisure Service Management
- MS/MBA: MS in Sports, Recreation, and Leisure Service Management/MBA in Media Management
- MS/MBA: MS in Multimedia Industry and E-Commerce/MBA in Media Management

The Graduate School for Business has 2 full-time faculty and over 20 adjunct members. Faculty are affiliated with leading media organizations and major international corporations such as NBC, Disney, A&E, and New York's leading radio stations, to name a few. The faculty also have significant experience in accounting; arts administration; banking; e-commerce management; entertainment, labor, and business law; entrepreneurship; film; human resource management; Internet marketing; management theory and practice; managerial economics; managerial finance; media economics and finance; MIS; MIS and e-commerce; multimedia industry; music; operations management; organizational behavior; organizational behavior design and development; portfolio asset management; publishing; sports, recreation, and leisure service management; statistics; strategic management; technology and the arts; television; and theater. Full-time faculty serve as mentors and advisors to students, monitor student performance in the internship, and work closely with students in the planning and execution of all phases of their program.

In addition to the MBA programs, students enrolled in the MBA in Media Management Program have the option of a dual degree. The degree consists of the current Media Management MBA plus a specialization semester and thesis, resulting in an MS/MBA (6 semesters and 72 credits).

Two tracks are available:

- MS/MBA - MS in Sports, Recreation & Leisure Service Management/MBA Media Management
- MS/MBA - MS in Multimedia Industry and E-Commerce/MBA Media Management

Graduate School of Business

CAMPUS LIFE

The College's main location is in lower Manhattan at 75 Varick Street, adjacent to New York's Greenwich Village, the financial district, and SoHo and TriBeCa's flourishing media and artistic communities. It is convenient to all public transportation and easily accessible to major thoroughfares.

The College offers a variety of support services and maintains a state-of-the-art library of business literature. This technologically sophisticated library provides storage, retrieval, and dissemination of both in-house library materials and outside online information sources, including the Internet. The collection is cataloged using the Library of Congress system. The Learning Center provides the College with expanded applications that support undergraduate and graduate education. These applications include Windows 98 and Microsoft Office Professional. Additionally, an innovative "video network" provides instructors with a sophisticated means of distributing problems and complete flexibility in involving students in the solution process. The Student Services Office provides an array of curricular and co-curricular support services to assist students with their academic programs.

Career Services Offered

In partnership with the Career Center, monstertrak.com provides full-time, part-time, temporary, and internship opportunities targeted by employers to "Your School" students and alumni.

- Workshops in Resume Writing, Interviewing Skills, Business Etiquette.
- Utilizing the Computer and Electronic Job-Hunting
- Resume Critiques and Revisions
- Job and Internship Fairs
- Assistance in Drafting the Cover Letter and Follow-Up/Thank You Letter
- Interviewing Tips, Questions, Format, and Content
- Negotiating Salary
- Strategies for Beginning and Retaining Employment
- Professional and Networking Etiquette
- Employment and Internship Search Assistance
- Current Job Postings
- Long-Distance Job Search Assistance
- General Organizational Skills

The Career Services Staff is always available to assist students in optimizing their internship and employment experiences and to answer their questions. Career Services offers a range of services to our students and functions as the liaison between prospective employers and our students. Audrey Cohen students get hands-on experience in real work settings as part of their studies, and the Career Services Office assists students with getting the internships or jobs that will lead them to truly rewarding careers. Students can make appointments to see a career counselor at their convenience to discuss job searches, internship sites, or career development issues. Students can also discuss the different career possibilities open to them after graduation and attend workshops that build their job search skills and prepare them for fall or spring career fairs. Also, supervisors can download information about the curriculum.

COSTS

Audrey Cohen College participates in the federally administered Pell Grant, Federal Stafford Student Loan, and Federal PLUS Loan programs, and in the Tuition Assistance Program (TAP) sponsored and administered by New York State for its state residents. The College also has limited resources under two other federal financial aid programs: the Federal Supplemental Educational Opportunity Grant Program and the Federal Work-Study Program. In addition, the College has its own scholarship program. Applicants may file through the College Scholarship Service or apply for federal funds directly at the College following their admission. State TAP applications are sent directly to the student once the federal applications have been processed.

ADMISSIONS

All applicants to the MBA degree programs at Audrey Cohen College must complete and return the application with a $45 application fee, appear at the College for a personal interview with an admissions counselor, submit two letters of reference, provide official transcripts for secondary and any postsecondary schools attended, and submit the results of GRE or GMAT. In addition, an topic statement regarding your proposed Constuctive Action is required. Also, the student must submit proof of immunizations for measles, mumps, and rubella. Applicants are informed of admissions decisions on a rolling basis.

For additional information, please contact:

Admissions Office
Audrey Cohen College
75 Varick Street
New York, NY 10013
Telephone: 212-343-1234, ext. 5001
Fax: 212 343-8470
E-mail: mbarecruiter@audreycohen.edu
World Wide Web: www.audreycohen.edu

HAWAI'I PACIFIC UNIVERSITY

THE UNIVERSITY AT A GLANCE
Hawai'i Pacific University is a dynamic and innovative institution of higher learning strategically located in the heart of the Pacific Rim. Students are provided a rigorous and contemporary education with undergraduate degrees available in nearly 50 different areas. HPU's Center for Graduate Studies offers nine graduate degree programs, including the largest MBA program in the State of Hawai'i.

The university is a private, not-for-profit, coeducational, career-oriented postsecondary institution founded in 1965. The experienced faculty challenges students with an exciting integration of theory and practical application. Hawai'i Pacific University's goal is to provide students the knowledge and resources they need to become distinguished and productive leaders in their field of study, in the local community and throughout the world.

Hawai'i Pacific University is accredited by the Accrediting Commission for Senior Colleges and Universities of the Western Association of Schools and Colleges (WASC) and the National League for Nursing Accrediting Commission (NLNAC). The University is a member of the International Association for Management Education (AACSB), recognized by the Hawai'i Commission of Postsecondary Education, and approved by the Hawai'i Board of Nursing.

STUDENTS
HPU is a dynamic community of 7,626 undergraduate and 1,283 graduate students. The student body is comprised of individuals from all 50 U.S. states and more than 100 countries, making HPU one of the most culturally diverse universities in the world. This global influence results in a microcosm of the world's cultures: students learn from each other, build lifelong friendships and important future business contacts.

All registered students are members of the Associated Students of Hawai'i Pacific University (ASHPU), which is headed by elected officers and class representatives. ASHPU supervises many clubs, organizations, and activities, including a literary magazine, a student newspaper, a pep band, professional, cultural and social organizations, service societies, dances, luaus, and cheerleading. Graduate students may also participate in the Graduate Student Organization (GSO), a professional student organization that provides graduate students opportunities to meet and network with fellow students, faculty, staff, and leaders from the local business community.

ACADEMICS
MBA
Hawai'i Pacific University's Master of Business Administration (MBA) offers the ideal balance of modern computer technology, leading business and management theory, and opportunities for practical application. Through core courses, concentration options, electives, two capstone courses, and an optional internship, graduate students gain a solid foundation in modern business and management principles. Within the 45-credit-hour curriculum, 27 credit hours are spent in the core to ensure an in-depth understanding of the latest developments in computer technology, business simulations, marketing and communication theory, and strategic planning.

Because each MBA participant possesses varying career interests and goals, HPU students decide which elective courses they wish to pursue from ten different areas of concentration.

- Accounting/CPA
- E-Business
- Economics
- Finance
- Human Resource Management
- Information Systems
- International Business
- Management
- Marketing
- Travel Industry Management

12-Month MBA
The 12-Month MBA is designed for full-time students who have completed an undergraduate business degree or have satisfied the necessary business prerequisites at an accredited college or university. The program consists of 45 semester hours of full-time study with a fall entry only. The student's graduate education is divided into 4 terms (fall, winter, spring, and summer) and offers a distinctive combination of theory and practice. Students are provided with multiple opportunities for study across a variety of fundamental areas. Concentrations are not available in this 12-Month MBA Program, instead 12 semester hours of electives are required and will enable students to tailor the curriculum to address specific long-term career goals.

Weekend MBA for Business Professionals
HPU's 18-month Weekend MBA program is structured to accommodate the demanding lifestyle of working professionals. Recognized as a model for group-oriented learning that engages students in projects that hone leadership, communication, and collaborative skills, the program is intensely team-based and diverse with a cross-section of participants from Hawai'i's leading businesses, including physicians, lawyers, and entrepreneurs. The Weekend MBA program includes a cluster of professional courses that focus on marketing, economics, accounting, quantitative methods, human resource management, and information systems. These courses are combined with a series of "contemporary" courses that examine twenty-first-century management challenges at both the micro and macro levels. Topics dealing with the global environment, change and innovation, team building, technology, and strategic planning are examined in detail and provide a unifying theme throughout the course of study.

FlexMBA
Hawai'i Pacific University offers another option for aspiring nontraditional MBA students who have busy personal and professional lives. HPU's FlexMBA provides a tailor-made format for students who need flexibility in pursuing an MBA degree. The FlexMBA allows students to switch between full- and part-time study; attend evening, day, or weekend classes; meet with a personal advisor to plan their schedule; and arrange a convenient payment plan. Students also have a choice of seven start dates throughout the year.

Degrees Offered
Master of Business Administration
Master of Arts in Communication
Master of Arts in Global Leadership
Master of Arts in Organizational Change
Master of Arts in Human Resource Management
Master of Science in Information Systems
Master of Arts in Diplomacy and Military Studies
Master of Arts in Teaching English as a Second Language
Master of Science in Nursing

Faculty
Hawai'i Pacific University's faculty are noted scholars who conduct and publish research and come from some of the top academic institutions around the world. Eighty percent of the faculty hold doctorate degrees or the equivalent in their field of specialty.

The MBA faculty has distinguished academic backgrounds and relationships to the corporate world, bringing years of experience to the classroom. They make valuable contributions to business through leadership positions in professional organizations, executive development programs, consulting, and service on advisory boards. This hands-on involvement keeps HPU's MBA faculty in tune with today's business practices and emerging trends. With a student/faculty ratio of 18:1, professors can maintain their commitment to teaching excellence.

MBA Program

Hawai'i Pacific University
CENTER FOR GRADUATE STUDIES

CAMPUS LIFE

With two campuses on the island of Oahu, Hawai'i Pacific University combines the excitement of an urban downtown campus with the serenity of a residential campus set in the green foothills of the Ko'olau mountains. The main campus is ideally located in downtown Honolulu, the business and financial center of the Pacific. Eight miles away, situated on 135 acres in Kaneohe, the windward Hawai'i Loa campus is the site of the nursing program, the marine biology, oceanography, and environmental sciences programs, and several liberal arts programs. Students can travel between the two campuses via the convenient HPU shuttle service.

There are also seven military campuses on the island of O'ahu located at Pearl Harbor Naval Base, Hickam Air Force Base, Schofield Army Barracks, Fort Shafter, Tripler Army Medical Center, Marine Corps Base Hawai'i—Kaneohe, and Marine Corps Base Hawai'i—Camp H.M. Smith to provide U.S. service members with educational opportunities.

To support graduate studies, HPU's libraries, with a collection exceeding 159,000 volumes, add an average of 2,500 volumes annually, 15 percent of which are on business topics. A significant number of business reference books, including national and international business directories, investment and financial services, accounting and tax information sources, and a collection of annual reports are available.

The University's accessible on-campus computer center houses more than 100 IBM-compatible microcomputers with stand-alone and networked configurations.

Career development and preparation is an integral part of Hawai'i Pacific University's MBA education. The University's key location in downtown Honolulu, in the heart of the business and financial community of the Asia-Pacific region, serves as an immense asset to MBA students seeking interaction with potential employers and mentors. Hawai'i Pacific University's Career Services Center offers students professional support and consultations on services that range from career counseling to job preparation, job search assistance, employment listing, cooperative education and internships, and career opportunity referrals.

COSTS

Full-time status per semester for a graduate student is nine credits; however, tuition is calculated on a per-credit basis. Graduate tuition for 2002–2003 is $410 per credit hour.

The cost of books, supplies, health insurance and personal expenses is additional.

Life as a graduate student demands that much time be spent on campus attending classes, conducting research, participating in group meetings, and attending cultural events. Living near campus makes the obligations of graduate student life easier.

Hawai'i Pacific University's on-campus housing options are open to graduate students, but most graduate students prefer independent off-campus rentals because of the convenient locations close to the downtown Honolulu campus. The University works closely with an apartment referral service to assist students in placement.

Hawai'i Pacific University offers several types of institutional graduate scholarships and assistantships to new, full-time, degree-seeking students. HPU's graduate scholarships range from 20 percent to 50 percent tuition waivers for one or two semesters. Graduate assistantships provide a 50 percent tuition waiver for one semester and require the student to commit to a 10-hour-per-week work assignment.

Federal Stafford Student Loans are also available. Hawai'i Pacific University's Graduate Admissions Office will work with the Financial Aid office to assist students with preparation of necessary application forms.

ADMISSIONS

Admission to the MBA at Hawai'i Pacific University is based on academic ability and potential for success at the graduate level. Academic ability is evaluated by the applicant's past academic performance, recommendations, and performance on the GMAT. Although not required for admission, professional work experience as well as involvement in organizational or community activities may be used in the evaluation. A comprehensive approach is used when considering an application, and no one factor will exclude an applicant from consideration. The University is seeking students who have demonstrated the ability and motivation to do graduate level work.

Applicants must have a baccalaureate degree from an accredited college or university in the United States or an equivalent degree from another country. All applicants must submit certified copies of their post-secondary work showing completion of the undergraduate degree, plus two letters of recommendation. These letters should be from professors, counselors, employers, and others who can attest to your achievements and potential for success at the graduate level.

Applicants who have not satisfied pre-requisite requirements may still apply to the graduate program. However, prior to beginning certain graduate-level courses, students may be required to complete the required pre-requisite courses.

The University has a rolling admission process and reviews applications throughout the year. In order to ensure adequate time for evaluation and correspondence, it is strongly recommended that applications be submitted early.

When reviewing an application for graduate admission, the Admission Committee considers several factors including:

- Completion of a baccalaureate degree (or its equivalent) from an accredited college or university
- Undergraduate grade point average
- Letters of recommendation
- GMAT results
- Work experience (if applicable)
- Personal statement/essay questions

All applicants to the Master of Business Administration (MBA) graduate program at Hawai'i Pacific University must submit the following documents:

- A signed and completed application form
- U.S. $50 nonrefundable application fee
- An official/certified transcript from every college or university attended, showing course work, grades, and conferral of bachelor's degree. Official transcripts must be sent directly from the college or university to Hawai'i Pacific University. Applicants may also submit official transcripts in an unopened envelope sealed by the college or university.
- Personal statement/essay describing applicant's academic and career goals
- Resume (optional)
- GMAT scores (sent directly to the Graduate Admissions Office)

Application materials should be sent to:

Hawai'i Pacific University
Graduate Admissions
1164 Bishop Street, Suite 911
Honolulu, HI 96813
Telephone: 808-544-0279
Toll free: 866-GRAD-HPU
Fax: 808-544-0280
E-mail: graduate@hpu.edu

Students may also apply for Hawai'i Pacific University's MBA program online by visiting www.hpu.edu/grad.

YORK UNIVERSITY

THE SCHOOL AT A GLANCE

Located in the country's financial center, the Schulich School of Business is Canada's Global Business School. At Schulich students are provided with choice, relevance, and opportunity as they design their programs. The MBA program offers students 18 different specializations to choose from. Canada's only IMBA program provides students with the opportunity to pursue global interests and opportunities. Critical skills are developed and honed as students move through the core of the program. One CEO, who worked with students on the Strategy Field Study, said "the students knocked [the company management team's] socks off! [The study] was state-of-the-art in strategic planning. To this day it continues to inform our strategic thinking." Graduates from Schulich are employed around the world. Many of our students benefit from the Alumni Mentorship Program as they prepare for job search and reentry into the work force.

STUDENTS

Average age: 29
Average years work experience: 5
Average GMAT: 645
Average GPA: 3.3/4.0 (B+)
Male: 58%
Female: 42%
International Students: 47%

ACADEMICS

Study Abroad Opportunities
- Argentina
- Australia
- Austria
- Brazil
- Canada
- Chile
- China
- Denmark
- England
- France
- Germany
- Hong Kong
- Hungary
- India
- Italy
- Israel
- Japan
- Korea
- Mexico
- The Netherlands
- Philippines
- Singapore
- Spain
- Sweden
- South Korea
- Switzerland
- Taiwan
- Thailand
- Uruguay
- Venezuela

Degrees offered:
- MBA Full Time: 4-semester program can be completed in 16 months
- MBA Part Time: Completed in 3.5 years or 18 semesters
- IMBA Full Time: 4 academic semesters and one semester for internships
- EMBA (Kellogg/Schulich): 2 years
- Post MBA Diploma in Advanced Management: 15 credit hours of study can be done full time or part time

Joint combined degrees offered:
- MBA/LLB: 4 years
- MBA/MFA/MA: 3 years
- MBA (Schulich/SASIN joint degree)
- MBA (Schulich/Laval University joint degree)

Schulich School of Business

CAMPUS LIFE

The new Schulich School of Business and Executive Learning Center, scheduled to open in September 2003, was designed following intensive study of the best features of the world's top business schools. Attributes such as technology-enhanced classrooms, state-of-the-art library and computer facilities, wireless Internet cafes, courtyards, and a 300-seat auditorium will greatly enhance future teaching, learning, and research at Schulich.

In addition, the Career Center annually attracts close to 2,000 Canadian, U.S. and offshore companies to recruit for over 4,000 full-time and summer postings. Our students have access to Monster.ca, which provides them with a greater number and variety of opportunities. Workshops, counseling, resume directories, and Company Information Sessions are all examples of the Career Center services offered to Schulich students.

Employed in 3 months: 92%
Average Starting Salary: $89,600 Canadian

COSTS

Domestic Tuition: $18,790 U.S. International: $25,054 U.S.
Receiving Aid: 70% Scholarships and Bursaries Awarded: 1,388

ADMISSIONS

Admissions Statistics

Average Undergraduate GPA (4.0 scale): 3.3
Average GMAT: 645

Admission Deadlines

September start deadline (international): March 1
September start deadline (national): April 1
January start deadline (international): August 15
January start deadline (national): October 1

For more information, contact:

York University
Schulich School of Business
4700 Keele Street
Toronto, Ontario M3J 1P3
Canada
Phone: 416-736-5060
Fax: 416-650-8174
Domestic admissions e-mail: admissions@schulich.yorku.ca
International admissions e-mail: intladmissions@schulich.yorku.ca
World Wide Web: www.schulich.yorku.ca

INDEXES

Alphabetical List of Schools

A

American University	202
Appalachian State University	203
Arizona State University	204-206
Arizona State University West	207
Auburn University	208
Audrey Cohen College	510-511
Augusta State University	209

B

Babson College	210
Ball State University	211
Baruch College (City University of New York)	212-214
Baylor University	215
Bentley College	216
Binghamton University (SUNY)	217
Boise State University	218
Boston College	219
Boston University	220
Bowling Green State University	221-223
Brigham Young University	224

C

California Polytechnic State University—San Luis Obispo	225
California State University—Chico	226
California State University—Fullerton	227
California State University—Hayward	228
California State University—Sacramento	229
California State University—San Bernardino	230
Canisius College	231
Carnegie Mellon University	232
Case Western Reserve University	233
Central Missouri State University	234
Chapman University	235
Claremont Graduate University	236-238
Clarkson University	239
Clemson University	240-242
Cleveland State University	243
College of William and Mary	244-246
Columbia University	247
Concordia University	248
Cornell University	249
Creighton University	250

D

Dartmouth College	251
DePaul University	252
Duke University	253

E

Eastern Michigan University	254
Eastern Washington University	255
Emory University	256
Erasmus Graduate School of Business	257-259
ESADE	260

F

Fairfield University	261
FIU College of Business Administration	262
Florida Atlantic University	263
Florida State University	264
Fordham University	265

G

George Mason University	266
The George Washington University	267
Georgetown University	268
Georgia College & State University	269
Georgia Institute of Technology	270
Georgia Southern University	271
Georgia State University	272
Golden Gate University	273-275
Grand Valley State University	276

H

Harvard University	277
Hawai'i Pacific University	512-513
Hofstra University	278-280
Hong Kong University of Science and Technology	281
Howard University	282

I

Illinois Institute of Technology	283
Indiana University	284
INSEAD	285
International Institute for Management Development	286
Iowa State University	287

J

Jacksonville State University	288
John Carroll University	289

K

Kansas State University	290
Kent State University	291

L

Lehigh University	292
Louisiana State University	293
Loyola College in Maryland	294
Loyola Marymount University	295
Loyola University Chicago	296-298
Loyola University New Orleans	299

M

Marshall University	300
Massachusetts Institute of Technology	301
Michigan State University	302
Mississippi State University	303
Monmouth University	304-306

N

New Jersey Institute of Technology	307
New York University	308
Nicholls State University	309

Northeastern University	310	Saint Louis University	346	University of Dayton	409
Northern Arizona University	311	San Diego State University	347	University of Delaware	410
Northern Illinois University	312	San Francisco State University	348	University of Denver	411-413
Northwestern University	313	San Jose State University	349-351	University of Detroit Mercy	414
		Santa Clara University	352	University of Findlay	415
		Seattle University	353	University of Florida	416-418
		Seton Hall University	354	University of Georgia	419
		Simmons College	355-357	University of Hawaii—Manoa	420
		Southeast Missouri State University	358	University of Illinois—Chicago	421

O

		Southeastern Louisiana University	359	University of Illinois—	
		Southern Illinois University—		Urbana-Champaign	422
Oakland University	314	Carbondale	360	University of Iowa	423-425
Ohio State University	315	Southern Illinois University—		University of Kansas	426
Ohio University	316	Edwardsville	361	University of Kentucky	427-429
Oklahoma State University	317	Southern Methodist University	362-364	University of Louisiana—Monroe	430
Old Dominion University	318	Southwest Missouri State University	365	University of Maine	431
Oregon State University	319	Stanford University	366	University of Maryland—College Park	432
		State University of West Georgia	367	University of Massachusetts—Amherst	433
		Stephen F. Austin State University	368	University of Miami	434
		Suffolk University	369	University of Michigan—Ann Arbor	435
		Syracuse University	370-372	University of Michigan—Dearborn	436
				University of Michigan—Flint	437
				University of Minnesota—Duluth	438

P

				University of Minnesota—Minneapolis	439
Pace University	320-322			University of Mississippi	440
Pennsylvania State University—				University of Missouri—Kansas City	441
Erie, Behrend College	323			University of Montana—Missoula	442
Pennsylvania State University—				University of Navarra	443
Harrisburg	324	TCU	373	University of Nebraska—Lincoln	444
Pennsylvania State University—		Temple University	374	University of Nevada—Las Vegas	445
University Park	325	Tennessee Technological University	375	University of New Hampshire	446
Pepperdine University	326	Texas A&M University—College Station	376	University of New Mexico	447
Pittsburg State University	327	Texas A&M University—Commerce	377	University of New Orleans	448
Portland State University	328	Texas A&M University—Corpus Christi	378	University of North Carolina—	
Purdue University—Calumet	329	Texas Tech University	379	Chapel Hill	449
Purdue University—West Lafayette	330	Thunderbird	380	University of North Carolina—Charlotte	450
		Tulane University	381	University of North Carolina—	
				Greensboro	451

Q

				University of North Texas	452
				University of Notre Dame	453
				University of Oregon	454

U

				University of Oxford	455
				University of Pennsylvania	456
Queen's University	331			University of Pittsburgh	457
		Union College	382-384	University of Rhode Island	458
		University at Albany (SUNY)	385	University of Rochester	459
		University at Buffalo (SUNY)	386	University of San Francisco	460

R

		University of Akron	387	University of South Carolina	461
		University of Alabama—Tuscaloosa	388	University of South Florida	462
		University of Alberta	389	University of Southern California	463
Rensselaer Polytechnic Institute	332-334	University of Arizona	390	University of Southern Maine	464
Rice University	335-337	University of Arkansas—		University of Tampa	465-467
Rider University	338	Fayetteville	391-393	University of Tennessee—Knoxville	468
Rochester Institute of Technology	339	University of Baltimore	394	University of Texas—Arlington	469
Rollins College	340	University of Bath	395	University of Texas—Austin	470-472
Rutgers University—Camden	341	University of Calgary	396	University of Texas—San Antonio	473
Rutgers University—Newark	342	University of California—Berkeley	397	University of the Pacific	474-476
		University of California—Davis	398-400	University of Toledo	477
		University of California—Irvine	401	University of Toronto	478
		University of California—Los Angeles	402	University of Tulsa	479

S

		University of Central Florida	403	University of Utah	480
		University of Chicago	404	University of Virginia	481
		University of Cincinnati	405	University of Washington	482
		University of Colorado—Boulder	406	University of Western Ontario	483
St. Cloud State University	343	University of Colorado—Denver	407	University of Wisconsin—Madison	484
St. John's University	344	University of Connecticut	408	University of Wisconsin—Milwaukee	485
Saint Joseph's University	345				

University of Wisconsin—Whitewater 486
University of Wyoming 487
Utah State University 488

V

Vanderbilt University 489-491
Villanova University 492
Virginia Commonwealth University 493
Virginia Polytechnic Institute
   and State University 494

W

Wake Forest University 495
Washington University 496-498
Weber State University 499
West Virginia University 500
Western Carolina University 501
Wichita State University 502
Widener University 503
Willamette University 504-506
Wright State University 507

X

Xavier University 508

Y

Yale University 509
York University 514-515

Business Program Name

A. B. Freeman School of Business	381	
Albers School of Business and Economics	353	
Alvah H. Chapman, Jr., Graduate Schoolf of Business	262	
American Graduate School of International Management	380	
Anderson School at UCLA	402	
Atkinson Graduate School of Management	504-506	
Babcock Graduate School of Management	495	
Barton School of Business	502	
Belk College of Business Administration	450	
Carroll School of Management	219	
Charles F. Dolan School of Business	261	
Charles H. Lundquist College of Business	454	
Cox School of Business	362-364	
Crummer Graduate School of Business	340	
Curtis L. Carlson School of Management	439	
Daniels College of Business	411-413	
Darden Graduate School of Business Administration	481	
Darla Moore School of Business	461	
David Eccles School of Business	480	
Donald L. Harrison College of Business	358	
DuPree School of Management	270	
E.J. Ourso College of Business Administration	293	
Eberhardt School of Business	474-476	
Edward S. Ageno School of Business	273-275	
Eli Broad Graduate School of Management	302	
Eller Graduate School of Management	390	
Erivan K. Haub School of Business	345	
European Institute of Business Administration	285	
F. W. Olin Graduate School of Business	210	
Fisher College of Business	315	
Fox School of Business and Management	374	
Frank G. Zarb School of Business	278-280	
Frank Sawyer School of Management	369	
Fuqua School of Business	253	
Gatton College of Business and Economics	427-429	
George L. Argyros School of Business and Economics	235	
Gladys A. Kelce College of Business	327	
Goizueta Business School	256	
Graziadio School of Business and Management	326	
Haas School of Business	397	
Hankamer School of Business	215	
Harmon College of Business Administration	234	
Henry B. Tippie School of Management	423-425	
Henry W. Bloch School of Business & Public Administration	441	
Herberger College of Business	343	
IESE International Graduate School of Management	443	
Isenberg School of Management	433	
J. L. Kellogg Graduate School of Management	313	
J. Mack Robinson College of Business	272	
James J. Nance College of Business Administration	243	
Jerry S. Rawls College of Business Administration	379	
Jesse H. Jones Graduate School of Management	335-337	
John B. Goddard School of Buisness and Economics	499	
John Cook School of Business	346	
John H. Sykes College of Business	465-467	
John M. and Mary Jo Boler School of Business	289	
John M. Olin School of Business	496-498	
John Molson School of Business	248	
Johnson Graduate School of Management	249	
Joseph A. Butt, S.J. College of Business Administration	299	
Joseph L. Rotman School of Management	478	
Joseph M. Bryan School of Business & Economics	451	
Katz Graduate School of Business	457	
Kelley School of Business	284	
Kellstadt Graduate School of Business	252	
Kenan-Flagler Business School	449	
Kogod College of Business Administration	202	
Krannert Graduate School of Management	330	
Lally School of Management and Technology	332-334	
Leavey School of Business	352	
Leeds School of Business	406	
Leonard N. Stern School of Business	308	
Lubin School of Business	320-322	
M.J. Neeley School of Business	373	
Manderson Graduate School of Business	388	
Marriott School of Management	224	
Marshall School of Business	463	
Mays College and Graduate School of Business	376	
McCallum Graduate School of Business	216	
McCombs School of Business	470-472	
Mendoza College of Business	453	
Merrick School of Business	394	
Owen Graduate School of Management	489-491	
Pamplin College of Business	494	
Peter F. Drucker Graduate School of Management	236-238	
Peter J. Tobin College of Business	344	
Richard Ivey School of Business	483	
Richard Wehle School of Business	231	
Richards College of Business	367	
Robert H. Smith School of Business	432	
Robert O. Anderson Graduate School of Management	447	
Rotterdam School of Management	257-259	
Said Business School	455	
Sam M. Walton College of Business Administration	391-393	
Seidman School of Business	276	
Sellinger School of Business and Management	294	
Sloan School of Management	301	
Smeal College of Business Administration	325	
Stillman School of Business	354	
Stuart Graduate School of Business	283	
Terry College of Business, Graduate School of Business Administration	419	
The J. Whitney Bunting School of Business	269	
Tuck School of Business	251	
Walker College of Business	203	
Warrington College of Business	416-418	
Weatherhead School of Management	233	
Wharton School, Graduate Division	456	
William E. Simon Graduate School of Business Administration	459	
Williams College of Business	508	
Wittemore School of Buisness and Economics	446	
Zicklin School of Business	212-214	

Location

USA

Alabama

Auburn University	208
Jacksonville State University	288
University of Alabama—Tuscaloosa	388

Arizona

Arizona State University	204-206
Arizona State University West	207
Northern Arizona University	311
Thunderbird	380
University of Arizona	390

Arkansas

University of Arkansas—Fayetteville	391-393

California

California Polytechnic State University—San Luis Obispo	225
California State University—Chico	226
California State University—Fullerton	227
California State University—Hayward	228
California State University—Sacramento	229
California State University—San Bernardino	230
Chapman University	235
Claremont Graduate University	236-238
Golden Gate University	273-275
Loyola Marymount University	295
Pepperdine University	326
San Diego State University	347
San Francisco State University	348
San Jose State University	349-351
Santa Clara University	352
Stanford University	366
University of California—Berkeley	397
University of California—Davis	398-400
University of California—Irvine	401
University of California—Los Angeles	402
University of San Francisco	460
University of Southern California	463
University of the Pacific	474-476

Colorado

University of Colorado—Boulder	406
University of Colorado—Denver	407
University of Denver	411-413

Connecticut

Fairfield University	261
University of Connecticut	408
Yale University	509

Delaware

University of Delaware	410

District of Columbia

American University	202
The George Washington University	267
Georgetown University	268
Howard University	282

Florida

FIU College of Business Administration	262
Florida Atlantic University	263
Florida State University	264
Rollins College	340
University of Central Florida	403
University of Florida	416-418
University of Miami	434
University of South Florida	462
University of Tampa	465-467

Georgia

Augusta State University	209
Emory University	256
Georgia College & State University	269
Georgia Institute of Technology	270
Georgia Southern University	271
Georgia State University	272
State University of West Georgia	367
University of Georgia	419

Hawaii

University of Hawaii—Manoa	420

Idaho

Boise State University	218

Illinois

DePaul University	252
Illinois Institute of Technology	283
Loyola University Chicago	296-298
Northern Illinois University	312
Northwestern University	313
Southern Illinois University—Carbondale	360
Southern Illinois University—Edwardsville	361
University of Chicago	404
University of Illinois—Chicago	421
University of Illinois—Urbana-Champaign	422

Indiana

Ball State University	211
Indiana University	284
Purdue University—Calumet	329
Purdue University—West Lafayette	330
University of Notre Dame	453

Iowa

Iowa State University	287
University of Iowa	423-425

Kansas

Kansas State University	290
Pittsburg State University	327
University of Kansas	426
Wichita State University	502

Kentucky

University of Kentucky	427-429

Louisiana

Louisiana State University	293
Loyola University New Orleans	299
Nicholls State University	309
Southeastern Louisiana University	359
Tulane University	381
University of Louisiana—Monroe	430
University of New Orleans	448

Maine

University of Maine	431
University of Southern Maine	464

Maryland

Loyola College in Maryland	294
University of Baltimore	394
University of Maryland—College Park	432

Massachusetts

Babson College	210
Bentley College	216
Boston College	219
Boston University	220
Harvard University	277
Massachusetts Institute of Technology	301
Northeastern University	310
Simmons College	355-357
Suffolk University	369
University of Massachusetts—Amherst	433

Michigan

Eastern Michigan University	254
Grand Valley State University	276
Michigan State University	302
Oakland University	314
University of Detroit Mercy	414
University of Michigan—Ann Arbor	435
University of Michigan—Dearborn	436
University of Michigan—Flint	437

Minnesota

St. Cloud State University	343
University of Minnesota—Duluth	438
University of Minnesota—Minneapolis	439

Mississippi

Mississippi State University	303
University of Mississippi	440

Missouri

Central Missouri State University	234
Saint Louis University	346
Southeast Missouri State University	358
Southwest Missouri State University	365
University of Missouri—Kansas City	441
Washington University	496-498

Montana

University of Montana—Missoula	442

Nebraska

Creighton University	250
University of Nebraska—Lincoln	444

Nevada

University of Nevada—Las Vegas	445

New Hampshire

Dartmouth College	251
University of New Hampshire	446

New Jersey

Monmouth University	304-306
New Jersey Institute of Technology	307
Rider University	338
Rutgers University—Camden	341
Rutgers University—Newark	342
Seton Hall University	354

New Mexico

University of New Mexico	447

New York

Baruch College (City University of New York)	212-214
Binghamton University (SUNY)	217
Canisius College	231
Clarkson University	239
Columbia University	247
Cornell University	249
Fordham University	265
Hofstra University	278-280
New York University	308
Pace University	320-322
Rensselaer Polytechnic Institute	332-334
Rochester Institute of Technology	339
St. John's University	344
Syracuse University	370-372
Union College	382-384
University at Albany (SUNY)	385
University at Buffalo (SUNY)	386
University of Rochester	459

North Carolina

Appalachian State University	203
Duke University	253
University of North Carolina—Chapel Hill	449
University of North Carolina—Charlotte	450
University of North Carolina—Greensboro	451
Wake Forest University	495
Western Carolina University	501

Ohio

Bowling Green State University	221-223
Case Western Reserve University	233
Cleveland State University	243
John Carroll University	289
Kent State University	291
Ohio State University	315
Ohio University	316
University of Akron	387
University of Cincinnati	405
University of Dayton	409
University of Findlay	415
University of Toledo	477
Wright State University	507
Xavier University	508

Oklahoma

Oklahoma State University	317
University of Tulsa	479

Oregon

Oregon State University	319
Portland State University	328
University of Oregon	454
Willamette University	504-506

Pennsylvania

Carnegie Mellon University	232
Lehigh University	292
Pennsylvania State University—Erie, Behrend College	323
Pennsylvania State University—Harrisburg	324
Pennsylvania State University—University Park	325
Saint Joseph's University	345
Temple University	374
University of Pennsylvania	456
University of Pittsburgh	457
Villanova University	492
Widener University	503

Rhode Island

University of Rhode Island	458

South Carolina

Clemson University	240-242
University of South Carolina	461

Tennessee

Tennessee Technological University	375
University of Tennessee—Knoxville	468
Vanderbilt University	489-491

Texas

Baylor University	215
Rice University	335-337
Southern Methodist University	362-364
Stephen F. Austin State University	368
TCU	373
Texas A&M University—College Station	376
Texas A&M University—Commerce	377
Texas A&M University—Corpus Christi	378
Texas Tech University	379
University of North Texas	452
University of Texas—Arlington	469
University of Texas—Austin	470-472
University of Texas—San Antonio	473

Utah

Brigham Young University	224
University of Utah	480
Utah State University	488
Weber State University	499

Virginia

College of William and Mary	244-246
George Mason University	266
Old Dominion University	318
University of Virginia	481
Virginia Commonwealth University	493
Virginia Polytechnic Institute and State University	494

Washington

Eastern Washington University	255
Seattle University	353
University of Washington	482

West Virginia

Marshall University	300
West Virginia University	500

Wisconsin

University of Wisconsin—Madison	484
University of Wisconsin—Milwaukee	485
University of Wisconsin—Whitewater	486

Wyoming

University of Wyoming	487

International

Canada

Concordia University	248
Queen's University	331
University of Alberta	389
University of Calgary	396
University of Toronto	478
University of Western Ontario	483

France

INSEAD	285

Hong Kong

Hong Kong University of Science and Technology	281

The Netherlands

Erasmus Graduate School of Business	257-259

Spain

ESADE	260
University of Navarra	443

Switzerland

International Institute for Management Development	286

United Kingdom

University of Bath	395
University of Oxford	455

COST

(IN-STATE TUITION)

Less than $3,500

Appalachian State University	203
Auburn University	208
Augusta State University	209
California Polytechnic State University— San Luis Obispo	225
California State University—Chico	226
California State University—Fullerton	227
California State University—Hayward	228
California State University—Sacramento	229
California State University— San Bernardino	230
Concordia University	248
Georgia Southern University	271
Jacksonville State University	288
Kansas State University	290
Louisiana State University	293
Marshall University	300
New Jersey Institute of Technology	307
Nicholls State University	309
Northern Illinois University	312
Oklahoma State University	317
Pace University	320-322
Pittsburg State University	327
Purdue University—Calumet	329
St. Cloud State University	343
San Diego State University	347
San Francisco State University	348
San Jose State University	349-351
Southeast Missouri State University	358
Southeastern Louisiana University	359
Southern Illinois University— Edwardsville	361
Southwest Missouri State University	365
State University of West Georgia	367
Stephen F. Austin State University	368
Tennessee Technological University	375
Texas A&M University—College Station	376
Texas A&M University—Commerce	377
Texas Tech University	379
University at Albany (SUNY)	385
University of Alabama—Tuscaloosa	388
University of Alberta	389
University of California—Irvine	401
University of Kansas	426
University of Louisiana—Monroe	430
University of Massachusetts—Amherst	433
University of Nebraska—Lincoln	444
University of Nevada—Las Vegas	445
University of New Mexico	447
University of New Orleans	448
University of North Carolina—Charlotte	450
University of North Carolina— Greensboro	451
University of North Texas	452
University of South Florida	462
University of Texas—Arlington	469
University of Texas—San Antonio	473
University of Tulsa	479
Utah State University	488
Virginia Polytechnic Institute and State University	494
Western Carolina University	501
Wichita State University	502

$3,500 to $14,000

Arizona State University	204-206
Ball State University	211
Baruch College (City University of New York)	212-214
Binghamton University (SUNY)	217
Bowling Green State University	221-223
Brigham Young University	224
Central Missouri State University	234
Clemson University	240-242
Cleveland State University	243
College of William and Mary	244-246
Creighton University	250
Eastern Michigan University	254
Eastern Washington University	255
Florida Atlantic University	263
George Mason University	266
Georgia College & State University	269
Georgia Institute of Technology	270
Grand Valley State University	276
Howard University	282
Indiana University	284
Iowa State University	287
John Carroll University	289
Kent State University	291
Loyola College in Maryland	294
Loyola Marymount University	295
Loyola University New Orleans	299
Michigan State University	302
Mississippi State University	303
Monmouth University	304-306
Northern Arizona University	311
Oakland University	314
Ohio University	316
Old Dominion University	318
Oregon State University	319
Pennsylvania State University— Harrisburg	324
Pennsylvania State University— University Park	325
Portland State University	328
Purdue University—West Lafayette	330
Rider University	338
Rutgers University—Newark	342
Saint Joseph's University	345
Seattle University	353
Southern Illinois University— Carbondale	360
TCU	373
Temple University	374
University at Buffalo (SUNY)	386
University of Akron	387
University of Arizona	390
University of Arkansas— Fayetteville	391-393
University of Baltimore	394
University of Calgary	396
University of California—Davis	398-400
University of California—Los Angeles	402
University of Central Florida	403
University of Cincinnati	405
University of Colorado—Boulder	406
University of Colorado—Denver	407
University of Connecticut	408
University of Dayton	409
University of Delaware	410
University of Findlay	415
University of Florida	416-418
University of Georgia	419
University of Illinois—Chicago	421
University of Illinois— Urbana-Champaign	422
University of Iowa	423-425
University of Kentucky	427-429
University of Maine	431
University of Maryland—College Park	432
University of Michigan—Dearborn	436
University of Michigan—Flint	437
University of Missouri—Kansas City	441
University of Montana—Missoula	442
University of New Hampshire	446
University of North Carolina— Chapel Hill	449
University of Oregon	454
University of Rhode Island	458
University of Southern Maine	464
University of Tampa	465-467
University of Texas—Austin	470-472
University of Toledo	477
University of Utah	480
University of Washington	482
University of Wisconsin—Madison	484
University of Wisconsin—Milwaukee	485
University of Wisconsin—Whitewater	486
Weber State University	499
West Virginia University	500
Widener University	503
Wright State University	507
Xavier University	508

More than $14,000

American University	202
Babson College	210
Baylor University	215
Bentley College	216
Boston College	219
Boston University	220
Canisius College	231
Carnegie Mellon University	232
Case Western Reserve University	233
Chapman University	235
Claremont Graduate University	236-238
Clarkson University	239
Columbia University	247
Cornell University	249
Dartmouth College	251
DePaul University	252
Duke University	253
Emory University	256
Erasmus Graduate School of Business	257-259
ESADE	260
Fairfield University	261
FIU College of Business Administration	262
Fordham University	265
The George Washington University	267
Georgetown University	268
Harvard University	277
Hofstra University	278-280
Illinois Institute of Technology	283
INSEAD	285
International Institute for Management Development	286
Lehigh University	292
Loyola University Chicago	296-298
Massachusetts Institute of Technology	301
New York University	308
Northeastern University	310
Northwestern University	313
Pepperdine University	326
Queen's University	331
Rensselaer Polytechnic Institute	332-334
Rice University	335-337
Rochester Institute of Technology	339
Rollins College	340
St. John's University	344
Saint Louis University	346
Santa Clara University	352
Seton Hall University	354
Simmons College	355-357
Southern Methodist University	362-364
Stanford University	366
Suffolk University	369
Syracuse University	370-372
Thunderbird	380
Tulane University	381
Union College	382-384
University of Chicago	404
University of Denver	411-413
University of Miami	434
University of Michigan—Ann Arbor	435
University of Minnesota—Minneapolis	439
University of Navarra	443
University of Notre Dame	453
University of Oxford	455
University of Pennsylvania	456
University of Pittsburgh	457
University of Rochester	459
University of San Francisco	460
University of Southern California	463
University of the Pacific	474-476
University of Toronto	478
University of Western Ontario	483
Vanderbilt University	489-491
Villanova University	492
Wake Forest University	495
Washington University	496-498
Willamette University	504-506
Yale University	509

Enrollment of Business School

Less than 200 Students

American University	202
Appalachian State University	203
Augusta State University	209
Ball State University	211
Baylor University	215
Binghamton University (SUNY)	217
Bowling Green State University	221-223
California Polytechnic State University—San Luis Obispo	225
California State University—Chico	226
Central Missouri State University	234
Chapman University	235
Clarkson University	239
Creighton University	250
Eastern Washington University	255
Fairfield University	261
Florida State University	264
George Mason University	266
Georgia College & State University	269
Hong Kong University of Science and Technology	281
Howard University	282
International Institute for Management Development	286
Jacksonville State University	288
Kansas State University	290
Louisiana State University	293
Loyola University New Orleans	299
Marshall University	300
Mississippi State University	303
Nicholls State University	309
Northern Arizona University	311
Northwestern University	313
Ohio University	316
Oregon State University	319
Pennsylvania State University—Erie, Behrend College	323
Pennsylvania State University—University Park	325
Pittsburg State University	327
Queen's University	331
St. Cloud State University	343
Southeast Missouri State University	358
Southern Illinois University—Carbondale	360
State University of West Georgia	367
Stephen F. Austin State University	368
Tennessee Technological University	375
Texas A&M University—Corpus Christi	378
Tulane University	381
Union College	382-384
University at Albany (SUNY)	385
University of Alabama—Tuscaloosa	388
University of Arkansas—Fayetteville	391-393
University of California—Davis	398-400
University of Colorado—Boulder	406
University of Denver	411-413
University of Louisiana—Monroe	430
University of Maine	431
University of Mississippi	440
University of Montana—Missoula	442
University of Nebraska—Lincoln	444
University of Nevada—Las Vegas	445
University of Oregon	454
University of Oxford	455
University of Southern Maine	464
University of Tennessee—Knoxville	468
University of the Pacific	474-476
University of Wyoming	487
Weber State University	499
West Virginia University	500
Western Carolina University	501
Willamette University	504-506

200 to 450 Students

Arizona State University West	207
Boise State University	218
Brigham Young University	224
California State University—Sacramento	229
California State University—San Bernardino	230
Canisius College	231
Claremont Graduate University	236-238
Clemson University	240-242
College of William and Mary	244-246
Concordia University	248
Dartmouth College	251
ESADE	260
Georgia Institute of Technology	270
Georgia Southern University	271
Grand Valley State University	276
Illinois Institute of Technology	283
Iowa State University	287
John Carroll University	289
Kent State University	291
Lehigh University	292
Loyola Marymount University	295
Michigan State University	302
Monmouth University	304-306
New Jersey Institute of Technology	307
Oklahoma State University	317
Pennsylvania State University—Harrisburg	324
Portland State University	328
Purdue University—West Lafayette	330
Rensselaer Polytechnic Institute	332-334
Rice University	335-337
Rider University	338
Rochester Institute of Technology	339
Rollins College	340
Rutgers University—Camden	341
Saint Louis University	346
Simmons College	355-357
Southeastern Louisiana University	359
Southern Illinois University—Edwardsville	361
Southwest Missouri State University	365
TCU	373
Texas A&M University—College Station	376
Texas A&M University—Commerce	377
Texas Tech University	379
University of Akron	387
University of Alberta	389
University of Arizona	390
University of Bath	395
University of Calgary	396
University of Cincinnati	405
University of Dayton	409
University of Delaware	410
University of Detroit Mercy	414
University of Georgia	419
University of Hawaii—Manoa	420
University of Illinois—Urbana-Champaign	422
University of Kentucky	427-429
University of Massachusetts—Amherst	433
University of Michigan—Dearborn	436
University of Michigan—Flint	437
University of Missouri—Kansas City	441
University of Navarra	443
University of New Hampshire	446
University of New Mexico	447
University of North Carolina—Charlotte	450
University of North Carolina—Greensboro	451
University of North Texas	452
University of Notre Dame	453
University of Rhode Island	458
University of Tampa	465-467
University of Texas—San Antonio	473
University of Toledo	477
University of Toronto	478
University of Tulsa	479
University of Utah	480
University of Washington	482
University of Wisconsin—Milwaukee	485
University of Wisconsin—Whitewater	486
Utah State University	488
Vanderbilt University	489-491
Virginia Commonwealth University	493
Virginia Polytechnic Institute and State University	494
Wichita State University	502
Widener University	503
Wright State University	507
Yale University	509

More than 450 Students

Arizona State University	204-206
Auburn University	208
Babson College	210
Baruch College (City University of New York)	212-214
Bentley College	216
Boston College	219
Boston University	220
California State University—Fullerton	227
California State University—Hayward	228
Carnegie Mellon University	232
Case Western Reserve University	233
Cleveland State University	243
Columbia University	247
Cornell University	249
DePaul University	252
Duke University	253
Eastern Michigan University	254
Emory University	256
Erasmus Graduate School of Business	257-259
FIU College of Business Administration	262
Florida Atlantic University	263
Fordham University	265
The George Washington University	267
Georgetown University	268
Georgia State University	272
Harvard University	277
Hofstra University	278-280
Indiana University	284
INSEAD	285
Loyola College in Maryland	294
Loyola University Chicago	296-298
Massachusetts Institute of Technology	301
New York University	308
Northeastern University	310
Northern Illinois University	312
Oakland University	314
Ohio State University	315
Old Dominion University	318
Pace University	320-322
Pepperdine University	326
Purdue University—Calumet	329
Rutgers University—Newark	342
St. John's University	344
Saint Joseph's University	345
San Diego State University	347
San Francisco State University	348
San Jose State University	349-351
Santa Clara University	352
Seattle University	353
Seton Hall University	354
Southern Methodist University	362-364
Stanford University	366
Suffolk University	369
Syracuse University	370-372
Temple University	374
Thunderbird	380
University at Buffalo (SUNY)	386
University of Baltimore	394
University of California—Berkeley	397
University of California—Irvine	401
University of California—Los Angeles	402
University of Central Florida	403
University of Chicago	404
University of Colorado—Denver	407
University of Connecticut	408
University of Findlay	415
University of Florida	416-418
University of Illinois—Chicago	421
University of Iowa	423-425
University of Kansas	426
University of Maryland—College Park	432
University of Miami	434
University of Michigan—Ann Arbor	435
University of Minnesota—Duluth	438
University of Minnesota—Minneapolis	439
University of New Orleans	448
University of North Carolina—Chapel Hill	449
University of Pennsylvania	456
University of Pittsburgh	457
University of Rochester	459

Average GMAT

Less than 550

Appalachian State University	203
Augusta State University	209
Ball State University	211
Bentley College	216
Bowling Green State University	221-223
California State University—Hayward	228
California State University—San Bernardino	230
Canisius College	231
Chapman University	235
Cleveland State University	243
Eastern Michigan University	254
Eastern Washington University	255
Fairfield University	261
FIU College of Business Administration	262
Florida Atlantic University	263
Georgia College & State University	269
Georgia Southern University	271
Howard University	282
Jacksonville State University	288
John Carroll University	289
Kansas State University	290
Kent State University	291
Loyola College in Maryland	294
Loyola University Chicago	296-298
Marshall University	300
Mississippi State University	303
Monmouth University	304-306
Nicholls State University	309
Northern Arizona University	311
Northern Illinois University	312
Oakland University	314
Old Dominion University	318
Pennsylvania State University—Erie, Behrend College	323
Pennsylvania State University—Harrisburg	324
Pittsburg State University	327
Rider University	338
St. Cloud State University	343
St. John's University	344
Saint Joseph's University	345
San Francisco State University	348
Seton Hall University	354
Southeast Missouri State University	358
Southern Illinois University—Carbondale	360
Southern Illinois University—Edwardsville	361
Southwest Missouri State University	365
Stephen F. Austin State University	368
Suffolk University	369
Tennessee Technological University	375
Texas A&M University—Commerce	377
University at Albany (SUNY)	385
University of Baltimore	394
University of Dayton	409
University of Detroit Mercy	414
University of Louisiana—Monroe	430
University of Maine	431
University of Michigan—Flint	437
University of New Orleans	448
University of San Francisco	460
University of Tampa	465-467
University of Texas—Arlington	469
University of Toledo	477
University of Tulsa	479
University of Wisconsin—Milwaukee	485
University of Wisconsin—Whitewater	486
Western Carolina University	501
Wichita State University	502
Widener University	503

550 to 625

American University	202
Arizona State University West	207
Auburn University	208
Baylor University	215
Binghamton University (SUNY)	217
California Polytechnic State University—San Luis Obispo	225
California State University—Chico	226
California State University—Fullerton	227
California State University—Sacramento	229
Case Western Reserve University	233
Claremont Graduate University	236-238
Clarkson University	239
Clemson University	240-242
College of William and Mary	244-246
Creighton University	250
DePaul University	252
Erasmus Graduate School of Business	257-259
Florida State University	264
George Mason University	266
The George Washington University	267
Georgia State University	272
Grand Valley State University	276
Hofstra University	278-280
Illinois Institute of Technology	283
Iowa State University	287
Lehigh University	292
Louisiana State University	293
Loyola Marymount University	295
Northeastern University	310
Ohio University	316
Oklahoma State University	317
Oregon State University	319
Pennsylvania State University—University Park	325
Portland State University	328
Rochester Institute of Technology	339
Rollins College	340
Rutgers University—Newark	342
Saint Louis University	346
San Diego State University	347
San Jose State University	349-351
Santa Clara University	352
Seattle University	353
Simmons College	355-357
TCU	373
Texas Tech University	379
Thunderbird	380
Union College	382-384
University at Buffalo (SUNY)	386
University of Akron	387
University of Alabama—Tuscaloosa	388
University of Arkansas—Fayetteville	391-393
University of Bath	395
University of Calgary	396
University of Central Florida	403
University of Cincinnati	405
University of Delaware	410
University of Denver	411-413
University of Findlay	415
University of Illinois—Chicago	421
University of Illinois—Urbana-Champaign	422
University of Kansas	426
University of Kentucky	427-429
University of Michigan—Dearborn	436
University of Mississippi	440
University of Missouri—Kansas City	441
University of Montana—Missoula	442
University of Nebraska—Lincoln	444
University of Nevada—Las Vegas	445
University of New Hampshire	446
University of New Mexico	447
University of North Carolina—Charlotte	450
University of North Carolina—Greensboro	451
University of North Texas	452
University of Oregon	454
University of Pittsburgh	457
University of Rhode Island	458
University of South Carolina	461
University of South Florida	462
University of Southern Maine	464
University of Texas—San Antonio	473
University of the Pacific	474-476
University of Utah	480
University of Wisconsin—Madison	484
University of Wyoming	487
Utah State University	488
Villanova University	492
Weber State University	499
West Virginia University	500
Willamette University	504-506
Xavier University	508

More than 625

Arizona State University	204-206
Babson College	210
Baruch College (City University of New York)	212-214
Boston College	219
Boston University	220
Brigham Young University	224
Carnegie Mellon University	232
Columbia University	247
Concordia University	248
Cornell University	249
Dartmouth College	251
Duke University	253
Emory University	256
ESADE	260
Georgetown University	268
Georgia Institute of Technology	270
Indiana University	284
International Institute for Management Development	286
Massachusetts Institute of Technology	301
Michigan State University	302
New York University	308
Northwestern University	313
Ohio State University	315
Pepperdine University	326
Purdue University—West Lafayette	330
Queen's University	331
Rensselaer Polytechnic Institute	332-334
Rice University	335-337
Southern Methodist University	362-364
Stanford University	366
Syracuse University	370-372
Texas A&M University—College Station	376
Tulane University	381
University of Alberta	389
University of Arizona	390
University of California—Berkeley	397
University of California—Davis	398-400
University of California—Irvine	401
University of California—Los Angeles	402
University of Chicago	404
University of Colorado—Boulder	406
University of Connecticut	408
University of Florida	416-418
University of Georgia	419
University of Iowa	423-425
University of Maryland—College Park	432
University of Massachusetts—Amherst	433
University of Michigan—Ann Arbor	435
University of Minnesota—Minneapolis	439
University of North Carolina—Chapel Hill	449
University of Notre Dame	453
University of Oxford	455
University of Pennsylvania	456
University of Rochester	459
University of Southern California	463
University of Tennessee—Knoxville	468
University of Texas—Austin	470-472
University of Toronto	478
University of Virginia	481
University of Washington	482
University of Western Ontario	483
Vanderbilt University	489-491
Virginia Polytechnic Institute and State University	494
Wake Forest University	495
Washington University	496-498
Yale University	509

Average Undergrad GPA

Less than 3.2

Appalachian State University	203
Augusta State University	209
Baylor University	215
Boston University	220
Bowling Green State University	221-223
California State University—Hayward	228
Canisius College	231
Chapman University	235
Clarkson University	239
Cleveland State University	243
DePaul University	252
Eastern Michigan University	254
George Mason University	266
The George Washington University	267
Georgia Southern University	271
Georgia State University	272
Howard University	282
Illinois Institute of Technology	283
Jacksonville State University	288
Kent State University	291
Loyola University Chicago	296-298
Monmouth University	304-306
Nicholls State University	309
Oakland University	314
Old Dominion University	318
Pennsylvania State University—Harrisburg	324
Pepperdine University	326
Rollins College	340
St. John's University	344
Simmons College	355-357
State University of West Georgia	367
Stephen F. Austin State University	368
TCU	373
Texas A&M University—Commerce	377
University of Arizona	390
University of Baltimore	394
University of Delaware	410
University of Denver	411-413
University of Detroit Mercy	414
University of Illinois—Chicago	421
University of Illinois—Urbana-Champaign	422
University of Louisiana—Monroe	430
University of Michigan—Flint	437
University of New Hampshire	446
University of North Texas	452
University of Rhode Island	458
University of San Francisco	460
University of Wisconsin—Milwaukee	485
University of Wisconsin—Whitewater	486
Widener University	503

3.2 to 3.3

American University	202
Auburn University	208
Babson College	210
Ball State University	211
Boston College	219
California State University—Fullerton	227
California State University—Sacramento	229
California State University—San Bernardino	230
Carnegie Mellon University	232
Case Western Reserve University	233
Claremont Graduate University	236-238
College of William and Mary	244-246
Creighton University	250
Eastern Washington University	255
Fairfield University	261
Florida State University	264
Hofstra University	278-280
John Carroll University	289
Lehigh University	292
Loyola Marymount University	295
Northeastern University	310
Northern Illinois University	312
Pennsylvania State University—University Park	325
Portland State University	328
Purdue University—West Lafayette	330
Queen's University	331
Rensselaer Polytechnic Institute	332-334
Rochester Institute of Technology	339
Rutgers University—Newark	342
St. Cloud State University	343
Saint Joseph's University	345
Saint Louis University	346
San Diego State University	347
San Francisco State University	348
Santa Clara University	352
Seattle University	353
Southeast Missouri State University	358
Southern Illinois University—Edwardsville	361
Southern Methodist University	362-364
Suffolk University	369
Syracuse University	370-372
Union College	382-384
University of Alberta	389
University of Calgary	396
University of Cincinnati	405
University of Colorado—Boulder	406
University of Dayton	409
University of Maine	431
University of Michigan—Dearborn	436
University of New Mexico	447
University of North Carolina—Charlotte	450
University of Notre Dame	453
University of Oregon	454
University of Pittsburgh	457
University of South Carolina	461
University of Southern Maine	464
University of Texas—Arlington	469
University of Texas—San Antonio	473
University of Tulsa	479
Villanova University	492
Wake Forest University	495
Washington University	496-498
Willamette University	504-506
Xavier University	508

More than 3.3

Arizona State University West	207
Arizona State University	204-206
Baruch College (City University of New York)	212-214
Binghamton University (SUNY)	217
Brigham Young University	224
California Polytechnic State University—San Luis Obispo	225
California State University—Chico	226
Clemson University	240-242
Columbia University	247
Concordia University	248
Cornell University	249
Dartmouth College	251
Duke University	253
Emory University	256
FIU College of Business Administration	262
Florida Atlantic University	263
Georgetown University	268
Georgia College & State University	269
Georgia Institute of Technology	270
Grand Valley State University	276
Harvard University	277
Indiana University	284
Iowa State University	287
Kansas State University	290
Louisiana State University	293
Marshall University	300
Massachusetts Institute of Technology	301
Michigan State University	302
Mississippi State University	303
New York University	308
Northern Arizona University	311
Northwestern University	313
Ohio State University	315
Ohio University	316
Oklahoma State University	317
Oregon State University	319
Pennsylvania State University—Erie, Behrend College	323
Pittsburg State University	327
Rice University	335-337
Rider University	338

San Jose State University	349-351
Seton Hall University	354
Southern Illinois University—Carbondale	360
Southwest Missouri State University	365
Stanford University	366
Tennessee Technological University	375
Texas A&M University—College Station	376
Texas Tech University	379
Thunderbird	380
Tulane University	381
University at Albany (SUNY)	385
University at Buffalo (SUNY)	386
University of Akron	387
University of Alabama—Tuscaloosa	388
University of Arkansas—Fayetteville	391-393
University of California—Berkeley	397
University of California—Davis	398-400
University of California—Irvine	401
University of California—Los Angeles	402
University of Central Florida	403
University of Chicago	404
University of Connecticut	408
University of Findlay	415
University of Florida	416-418
University of Georgia	419
University of Iowa	423-425
University of Kansas	426
University of Kentucky	427-429
University of Maryland—College Park	432
University of Massachusetts—Amherst	433
University of Michigan—Ann Arbor	435
University of Minnesota—Minneapolis	439
University of Mississippi	440
University of Missouri—Kansas City	441
University of Montana—Missoula	442
University of Nebraska—Lincoln	444
University of Nevada—Las Vegas	445
University of New Orleans	448
University of North Carolina—Chapel Hill	449
University of North Carolina—Greensboro	451
University of Oxford	455
University of Pennsylvania	456
University of Rochester	459
University of South Florida	462
University of Southern California	463
University of Tampa	465-467
University of Tennessee—Knoxville	468
University of Texas—Austin	470-472
University of the Pacific	474-476
University of Toledo	477
University of Toronto	478
University of Utah	480
University of Virginia	481
University of Washington	482
University of Western Ontario	483
University of Wisconsin—Madison	484
University of Wyoming	487
Utah State University	488
Vanderbilt University	489-491
Virginia Polytechnic Institute and State University	494
Weber State University	499
West Virginia University	500
Western Carolina University	501
Wichita State University	502
Yale University	509

Average Starting Salary

Less than $52,000

California State University—Sacramento	229
Canisius College	231
Clarkson University	239
Eastern Michigan University	254
Florida Atlantic University	263
Florida State University	264
Georgia State University	272
Hong Kong University of Science and Technology	281
Kansas State University	290
Kent State University	291
Loyola University New Orleans	299
Marshall University	300
Old Dominion University	318
Oregon State University	319
Pennsylvania State University—Harrisburg	324
Pittsburg State University	327
Purdue University—Calumet	329
Rollins College	340
St. Cloud State University	343
Southeast Missouri State University	358
Southwest Missouri State University	365
State University of West Georgia	367
Stephen F. Austin State University	368
Tennessee Technological University	375
Texas Tech University	379
University at Buffalo (SUNY)	386
University of Akron	387
University of Arkansas—Fayetteville	391-393
University of Bath	395
University of Texas—San Antonio	473
University of Tulsa	479
University of Hawaii—Manoa	420
University of Mississippi	440
University of Missouri—Kansas City	441
University of Nebraska—Lincoln	444
University of South Carolina	461
University of South Florida	462
University of Tennessee—Knoxville	468
University of Utah	480
University of Wisconsin—Whitewater	486
University of Wyoming	487
Utah State University	488
Wichita State University	502
Willamette University	504-506

$52,000 to $70,000

Auburn University	208
Baruch College (City University of New York)	212-214
Baylor University	215
Bentley College	216
Binghamton University (SUNY)	217
Brigham Young University	224
California Polytechnic State University—San Luis Obispo	225
California State University—Chico	226
California State University—Fullerton	227
Clemson University	240-242
Cleveland State University	243
Concordia University	248
DePaul University	252
ESADE	260
FIU College of Business Administration	262
The George Washington University	267
Hofstra University	278-280
Illinois Institute of Technology	283
Iowa State University	287
Louisiana State University	293
Loyola University Chicago	296-298
Northeastern University	310
Northern Arizona University	311
Oklahoma State University	317
Pace University	320-322
Pepperdine University	326
Portland State University	328
Queen's University	331
Rensselaer Polytechnic Institute	332-334
Rochester Institute of Technology	339
Saint Louis University	346
Seton Hall University	354
Suffolk University	369
TCU	373
Texas A&M University—Commerce	377
Union College	382-384
University at Albany (SUNY)	385
University of Alabama—Tuscaloosa	388
University of Alberta	389
University of Cincinnati	405
University of Colorado—Denver	407
University of Connecticut	408
University of Delaware	410
University of Denver	411-413
University of Detroit Mercy	414
University of Findlay	415
University of Florida	416-418
University of Georgia	419
University of Kansas	426
University of Kentucky	427-429
University of Massachusetts—Amherst	433
University of Miami	434
University of New Hampshire	446
University of New Mexico	447
University of North Carolina—Charlotte	450
University of North Carolina—Greensboro	451
University of Oregon	454
University of Rhode Island	458
University of Tampa	465-467
University of the Pacific	474-476
University of Wisconsin—Madison	484
University of Wisconsin—Milwaukee	485
Virginia Polytechnic Institute and State University	494

More than $70,000

Arizona State University	204-206
Babson College	210
Boston College	219
Boston University	220
Carnegie Mellon University	232
Case Western Reserve University	233
Claremont Graduate University	236-238
College of William and Mary	244-246
Columbia University	247
Cornell University	249
Dartmouth College	251
Duke University	253
Emory University	256
Erasmus Graduate School of Business	257-259
Fordham University	265
George Mason University	266
Georgetown University	268
Georgia Institute of Technology	270
Harvard University	277
Howard University	282
Indiana University	284
INSEAD	285
International Institute for Management Development	286
Lehigh University	292
Massachusetts Institute of Technology	301
Michigan State University	302
New York University	308
Northwestern University	313
Ohio State University	315
Pennsylvania State University—University Park	325
Purdue University—West Lafayette	330
Rice University	335-337
Rutgers University—Camden	341
Rutgers University—Newark	342
St. John's University	344
Santa Clara University	352
Southern Methodist University	362-364
Stanford University	366
Syracuse University	370-372
Temple University	374
Texas A&M University—College Station	376
Thunderbird	380
Tulane University	381
University of Arizona	390
University of Calgary	396
University of California—Berkeley	397
University of California—Davis	398-400
University of California—Irvine	401

University of California—Los Angeles 402
University of Chicago 404
University of Colorado—Boulder 406
University of Illinois—
　Urbana-Champaign 422
University of Iowa 423-425
University of Maryland—College Park 432
University of Michigan—Ann Arbor 435
University of Minnesota—Minneapolis 439
University of Navarra 443
University of Notre Dame 453
University of Oxford 455
University of Pennsylvania 456
University of Pittsburgh 457
University of Rochester 459
University of San Francisco 460
University of Southern California 463
University of Texas—Austin 470-472
University of Toronto 478
University of Virginia 481
University of Washington 482
University of Western Ontario 483
Vanderbilt University 489-491
Wake Forest University 495
Washington University 496-498
Yale University 509

ABOUT THE AUTHOR

Nedda Gilbert is a graduate of the University of Pennsylvania and holds a master's degree from Columbia University. She has worked for The Princeton Review since 1985. In 1987, she created The Princeton Review corporate test preparation service, which provides Wall Street firms and premier companies tailored educational programs for their employees. She currently resides in New Jersey.

NOTES

NOTES

NOTES

NOTES

NOTES

NOTES

NOTES

NOTES

NOTES

Understanding the Test

About the GRE.
The best way to prepare for the GRE is to know as much about the exam as possible. Here is some information to help you prepare.

What is the GRE and how is it structured?
The Graduate Record Examinations (GRE) General Test is a three-part admission test for applicants to graduate schools.

- One 30-minute, 30-question "Verbal Ability" (vocabulary and reading) section
- One 45-minute, 28-question "Quantitative Ability" (math) section
- An Analytical Writing Assessment, consisting of two essay tasks
  - One 45-minute "Analysis of an Issue" task
  - One 30-minute "Analysis of an Argument" task

How does the GRE work?
The GRE is a computer-adaptive test, which means that the test software uses your performance on previous questions to determine which question you will be asked next. The software calculates your score based on the number of questions you answer correctly, the difficulty of the questions you answer, and the number of questions you complete. Questions that appear early in the test impact your score to a greater degree than do those that come toward the end of the test.

How important are my GRE scores?
The weights placed on the different factors in the admissions process vary tremendously, so contact schools about their specific requirements. Be aware that your GRE scores are a major factor in determining the elements of your financial aid package, such as assistantships or fellowships.

Can I cancel my scores?
Yes. However, you must make the decision at the testing center before you see your scores. Score cancellations will be noted on your official GRE score report.

Where can I get more information about the GRE?
The Princeton Review
800-2Review
www.PrincetonReview.com

Educational Testing Service (ETS)
609-771-7670
www.gre.org

How can I register to take the test?
Call 1-800-GRE-CALL or register online at www.gre.org.

Sample GRE Problems
Verbal Ability

Analogies
Directions: In each of the following questions, a related pair of words or phrases is followed by five pairs of words or phrases. Select the pair that best expresses a relationship similar to that expressed in the original pair.

ANESTHETIC : NUMBNESS ::
- meditation : happiness
- antibiotic : illness
- food : hunger
- fear : alertness
- intoxicant : drunkenness

DECIBEL : LOUDNESS ::
- circumference : circle
- spectrum : color
- light-year : distance
- meter : mile
- clock : duration

Sentence Completions
Directions: Each sentence below has one or two blanks, each blank indicating that something has been omitted. Beneath the sentence are five words or sets of words. Choose the word or set of words for each blank that best fits the meaning of the sentence as a whole.

Under the new ruler's leadership, _____ between the parties diminished, and _____ was quickly restored.
- cooperation. .order
- enmity. .harmony
- dogma. .rectitude
- unity. .innovation
- apathy. ,economy

Antonyms
Directions: Each question below consists of a word printed in capital letters, followed by five words or phrases. Choose the word or phrase that is most nearly opposite in meaning to the word in capital letters.

PROVIDENCE :
- conjecture
- wrath
- equanimity
- alacrity
- contentment

Correct Answers
Analogies: 1-e, 2-c
Sentence Completions: b
Antonyms: b

Sample GRE Problems
Quantitative Ability

Problem Solving

Solve the problem and indicate the best of the answer choices given.

Eleven years ago, Lauren was half as old as Mike will be in 4 years. If Mike is m years old now, how old is Lauren now in terms of m?

- 4m − 11
- $\frac{1}{2}$ (m + 4) + 11
- $\frac{1}{2}$ (m - 11)
- 4m + $\frac{11}{2}$
- 2m − 7

What is the sum of the distinct prime numbers between 50 and 60?

- 104
- 108
- 110
- 112
- 116

Quantitative Comparison

The following consists of two quantities, one in Column A and one in Column B. You are to compare the two quantities.

x>0

Column A	Column B
2x	$4x^2$

- the quantity in Column A is greater
- the quantity in Column B is greater
- the two quantities are equal
- the relationship cannot be determined from the information given

Column A	Column B
$(0.4)^6$	$(1-0.6)^4$

- the quantity in Column A is greater
- the quantity in Column B is greater
- the two quantities are equal
- the relationship cannot be determined from the information given

Correct Answers
Problem Solving: 1-b, 2-d
Quantitative Comparison: 1-b, 2-d

800-2Review | www.PrincetonReview.com

Getting Ready for the GRE

Registering for the GRE
You should schedule you test as soon as you know when you want to take it. Certain time slots, particularly weekends, are filled quickly, and the further ahead you call, the more likely you are to get one of your first-choice appointments. You can register online at www.gre.org, or by calling 1-800-GRE-CALL. The fee to take the GRE is $105 within the United States, some U.S. Territories, and Puerto Rico, and $130 in all other locations. You can pay by credit card, check, or money order.

The Day Before the Test
Investigate the logistics – figure out how to get to the test center and where to go once you're there. This will prevent a lot of stress on test day. Put away your study materials – you're not really going to learn anything from last-minute cramming. Instead, do something low-key to help you relax. Make sure you get a good night's sleep so you'll be at your best for the test.

The Day of the Test
Have a good breakfast and do a few GRE questions you've already seen in order to get your mind working. Walk through the steps and remind yourself what you're supposed to do with each type of question. Dress comfortably and in layers – you don't want to be too hot or too cold in the test center. Give yourself plenty of time to get to the test site, and bring snacks for your breaks. You'll need energy to keep your mind working.

At the Testing Center
You'll be asked for two forms of identification, one of which must be a photo ID with your signature. You'll have to sign some forms and put your personal items in a locker – you can only bring your pens and pencils in with you. There may be additional security procedures, such as fingerprinting or digital photographs.

You'll be taking your test in a room with several computers, some or all of which will probably be occupied by other people taking standardized tests, but not necessarily the same test as you. The testing center hosts everything from architectural licensing to nursing.

12 Tips to Improve your Score

1. Work on vocab
Half of the verbal portion of the GRE is vocabulary-based. Learning new words takes time, so start now. Carry flashcards with you to write down new words. Try to use your new vocabulary in conversation.

2. Brush up on math formulas
Remember _ bh? What about pr²? Refresh yourself on common math formulas to save frustration on test day.

3. Don't walk into traps
Reread each question before you answer it. ETS loves to try to trap you. They'll tell you 4n=100 and ask you for the value of 2n. If you answer 25, you're sunk.

4. Use your scratch paper
You won't need to do any work in your head. In fact, you shouldn't. You're more likely to make mistakes. On the GRE CAT, you have unlimited scratch paper.

5. Ballpark
Many math questions ask for approximate values. Round to the nearest hundred or thousand and estimate. Remember, you can't use a calculator on the GRE. If you need one, you're probably doing too much work.

6. Know the directions ahead of time
Nothing is a bigger waste of time than trying to figure out what to do with a Quantitative Comparison problem while the clock is ticking. Read and understand the directions ahead of time.

7. Slow down
Rushing can cause careless mistakes. Answering all of the questions and having time to spare does you no good if you've made errors in your haste.

8. Take your breaks
Use your break time to rest your eyes and clear your head. Don't think about the section you've just finished—try to concentrate on doing your best on the remaining sections.

9. Familiarize yourself with the test
Preview the types of questions you'll see before you sit down on test day. Some questions are harder than they look, and working on them ahead of time can help you know what you're getting into.

10. All questions are not created equal
On the GRE CAT, questions that appear earlier in the test tend to have a greater impact on your score than do later questions.

11. Get used to typing
As silly as it may sound, if you're handy with a keyboard you'll be able to write more quickly on the Analytic Writing section. That means a more thorough treatment of the topic, more time to plan and edit, and a higher score.

12. Hone your critical skills
Whether it's by reading opinion columns in your local paper or by participating in the lively debate of an online discussion group, practice analyzing others' arguments and making effective points.

800-2Review | www.PrincetonReview.com

ClassSize-8 *Classroom Course*

Top of the Class
Our premium classroom instruction and powerful online lessons and drills will help you get your best score. Reap the benefits of integrated test prep–only at The Princeton Review.

Small Classes
We know students learn better in smaller classes. With no more than eight students in a Princeton Review GRE class, your instructor knows who you are, and works closely with you to identify your strengths and weaknesses. You will be as prepared as possible. When it comes to your future, you shouldn't be lost in a crowd of students.

Guaranteed Satisfaction
A GMAT prep course is a big investment – in terms of both time and money. At The Princeton Review, your investment will pay off. Our GRE students boast an average score improvement of 212 points.* We guarantee that you will be satisfied with your results. If you're not, we'll work with you again for free.**

Expert Instructors
What's worse than sitting in a classroom for hours on end? Having to listen to a boring instructor. Princeton Review instructors are energetic and smart – they've all scored in the 95th percentile or higher on standardized tests. Our instructors will make your experience engaging and effective.

Free Extra Help
We want you to get your best possible score on the GMAT. If you need extra help on a particular topic, your instructor is happy to meet with you outside of class to make sure you are comfortable with the material – at no extra charge!

Online Lessons, Tests, and Drills
Princeton Review *ClassSize-8* GRE Courses are the only classroom courses that have online lessons designed to support each class session. You can practice concepts you learn in class, spend some extra time on topics that you find challenging, or prepare for an upcoming class. You'll also gain comfort with the computer-based testing environment by taking online tests. And you'll have access as soon as you enroll, so you can get a head start on your GRE preparation.

The Most Comprehensive, Up-to-Date Materials
Look on the bright side – once you take the test, you won't have to study it anymore. But our research and development team studies the test year-round to stay on top of GMAT trends and to make sure you learn what you need to get your best score. You course includes The Princeton Review's Manual for the GRE Exam, and *Practicing to take the GRE General Test, 9th Edition*, the official ETS publication – more than enough material to help you excel.

*Independently verified by International Communications Research (ICR).
**Some restrictions apply.

Online *and* LiveOnline *Courses*

The Best of Both Worlds
We've combined our high-quality, comprehensive test preparation with a convenient, multimedia format that works around your schedule and your needs.

Online *and* LiveOnline *Courses*
Lively, Engaging Lessons
If you think taking an online course means staring at a screen and struggling to pay attention, think again. Our lessons are engaging and interactive – you'll never just read blocks of text or passively watch video clips. Princeton Review online courses feature animation, audio, interactive lessons, and self-directed navigation.

Customized, Focused Practice
The course software will discover your personal strengths and weaknesses. It will help you to prioritize and focus on the areas that are most important to your success. Of course, you'll have access to dozens of hours' worth of lessons and drills covering all areas of the test, so you can practice as much or as little as you choose.

Help at your Fingertips
Even though you'll be working on your own, you won't be left to fend for yourself. We're ready to help at any time of the day or night: you can chat online with a live Coach, check our Frequently Asked Questions database, or talk to other students in our discussion groups.

LiveOnline *Course*
Extra Features
In addition to self-directed online lessons, practice tests, drills, and more, you'll participate in five live class sessions and three extra help sessions given in real time over the Internet. You'll get the live interaction of a classroom course from the comfort of your own home.

ExpressOnline *Course*
The Best in Quick Prep
If your test is less than a month away, or you just want an introduction to our legendary strategies, this mini-course may be the right choice for you. Our multimedia lessons will walk you through basic test-taking strategies to give you the edge you need on test day.

800-2Review | www.PrincetonReview.com

1-2-1 *Private Tutoring*

The Ultimate in Personalized Attention
If you're too busy for a classroom course, prefer learning at your kitchen table, or simply want your instructor's undivided attention, 1-2-1 Private Tutoring may be for you.

Focused on You
In larger classrooms, there is always one student who monopolizes the instructor's attention. With *1-2-1* Private Tutoring, that student is you. Your instructor will tailor the course to your needs – greater focus on the subjects that cause you trouble, and less focus on the subjects that you're comfortable with. You can get all the instruction you need in less time than you would spend in a class.

Expert Tutors
Our outstanding tutoring staff is comprised of specially selected, rigorously trained GMAT instructors who have performed exceptionally in the classroom. They have scored in the top percentiles on standardized tests and received the highest student evaluations.

Schedules to Meet Your Needs
We know you are busy, and preparing for the GMAT is perhaps the last thing you want to do in your "spare" time. The Princeton Review *1-2-1* Private Tutoring Program will work around your schedule.

Additional Online Lessons and Resources
The learning continues outside of your tutoring sessions. Within the Online Student Center, you will have access to math, verbal, AWA, and general strategy lessons to supplement your private instruction. Best of all, they are accessible to you 24 hours a day, 7 days a week.

The Princeton Review
www.PrincetonReview.com

The Princeton Review Admissions Services

At The Princeton Review, we genuinely care about your academic success, which involves much more than just the SATs and other standardized tests. Admissions Services' PrincetonReview.com is the best online resource available for finding, researching, applying to, and learning how to pay for the right school for you.

No matter what type of program you're applying to—undergrad, graduate, law, business, or medical—you'll find an entire center dedicated to it on PrincetonReview.com, with a main page that acts as a portal sending you directly to all the free information and services you need. When you register, you gain access to even more specific free services tailored to your profile.

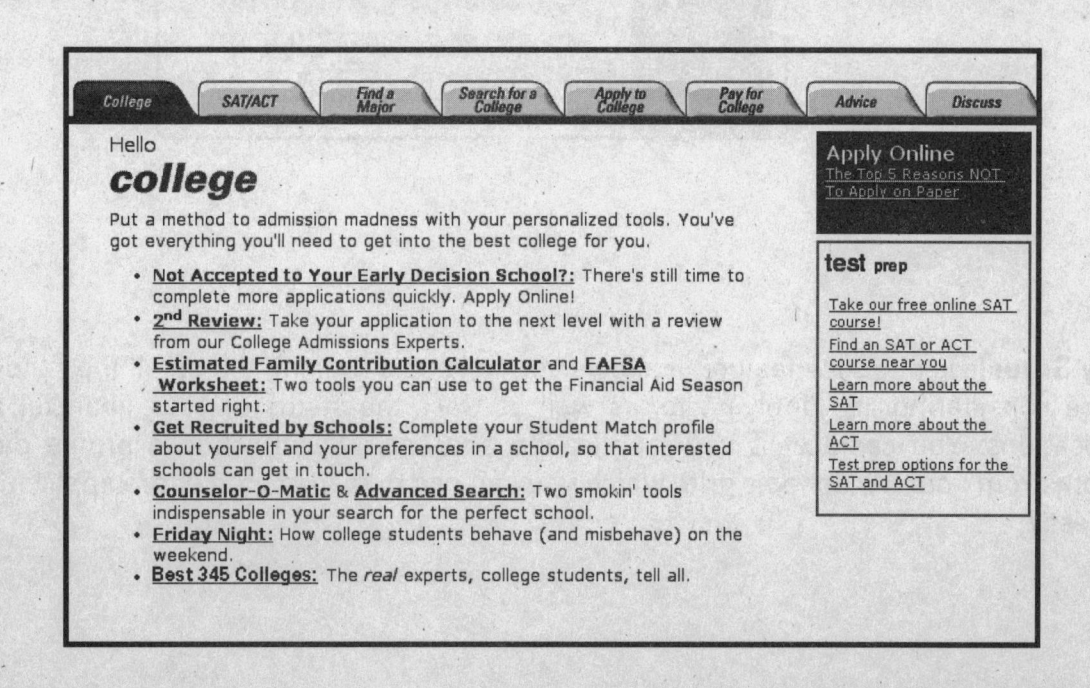

| College | SAT/ACT | Find a Major | Search for a College | Apply to College | Pay for College | Advice | Discuss |

Hello
college
Put a method to admission madness with your personalized tools. You've got everything you'll need to get into the best college for you.

- **Not Accepted to Your Early Decision School?:** There's still time to complete more applications quickly. Apply Online!
- **2nd Review:** Take your application to the next level with a review from our College Admissions Experts.
- **Estimated Family Contribution Calculator** and **FAFSA Worksheet:** Two tools you can use to get the Financial Aid Season started right.
- **Get Recruited by Schools:** Complete your Student Match profile about yourself and your preferences in a school, so that interested schools can get in touch.
- **Counselor-O-Matic** & **Advanced Search:** Two smokin' tools indispensable in your search for the perfect school.
- **Friday Night:** How college students behave (and misbehave) on the weekend.
- **Best 345 Colleges:** The *real* experts, college students, tell all.

Apply Online
The Top 5 Reasons NOT To Apply on Paper

test prep
Take our free online SAT course!
Find an SAT or ACT course near you
Learn more about the SAT
Learn more about the ACT
Test prep options for the SAT and ACT

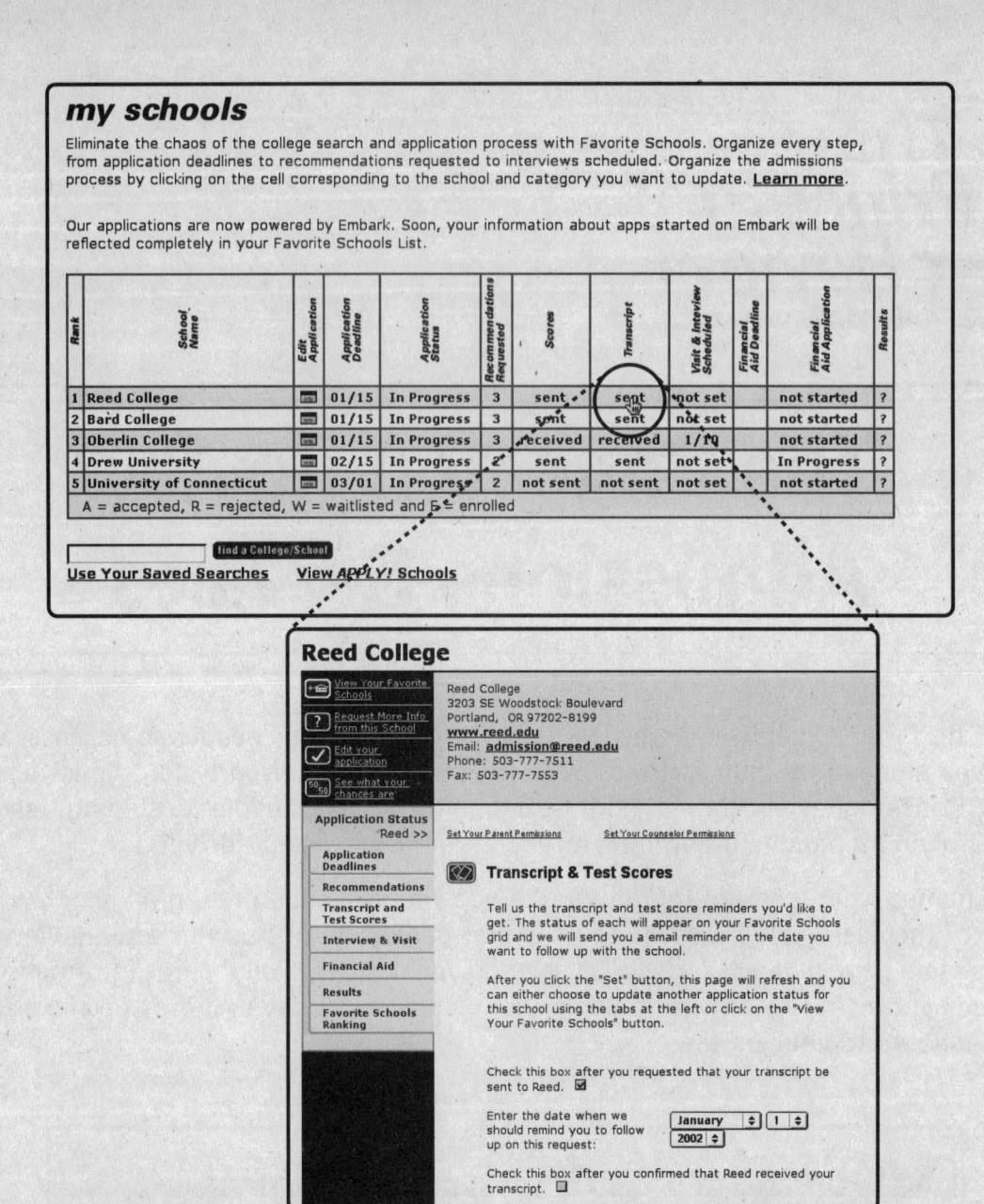

my schools

Eliminate the chaos of the college search and application process with Favorite Schools. Organize every step, from application deadlines to recommendations requested to interviews scheduled. Organize the admissions process by clicking on the cell corresponding to the school and category you want to update. **Learn more**.

Our applications are now powered by Embark. Soon, your information about apps started on Embark will be reflected completely in your Favorite Schools List.

Rank	School Name	Edit Application	Application Deadline	Application Status	Recommendations Requested	Scores	Transcript	Visit & Interview Scheduled	Financial Aid Deadline	Financial Aid Application	Results
1	Reed College		01/15	In Progress	3	sent	sent	not set		not started	?
2	Bard College		01/15	In Progress	3	sent	sent	not set		not started	?
3	Oberlin College		01/15	In Progress	3	received	received	1/10		not started	?
4	Drew University		02/15	In Progress	2	sent	sent	not set		In Progress	?
5	University of Connecticut		03/01	In Progress	2	not sent	not sent	not set		not started	?

A = accepted, R = rejected, W = waitlisted and E = enrolled

[find a College/School]

Use Your Saved Searches   View **APPLY! Schools**

Reed College

- View Your Favorite Schools
- Request More Info from this School
- Edit your application
- See what your chances are

Reed College
3203 SE Woodstock Boulevard
Portland, OR 97202-8199
www.reed.edu
Email: **admission@reed.edu**
Phone: 503-777-7511
Fax: 503-777-7553

Application Status
Reed >>

- Application Deadlines
- Recommendations
- Transcript and Test Scores
- Interview & Visit
- Financial Aid
- Results
- Favorite Schools Ranking

Set Your Parent Permissions   Set Your Counselor Permissions

Transcript & Test Scores

Tell us the transcript and test score reminders you'd like to get. The status of each will appear on your Favorite Schools grid and we will send you a email reminder on the date you want to follow up with the school.

After you click the "Set" button, this page will refresh and you can either choose to update another application status for this school using the tabs at the left or click on the "View Your Favorite Schools" button.

Check this box after you requested that your transcript be sent to Reed. ☑

Enter the date when we should remind you to follow up on this request: January ▾ 1 ▾   2002 ▾

Check this box after you confirmed that Reed received your transcript. ☐

   My Schools is one such feature. It allows you to keep a running tab on all the schools you're considering and applying to, as well as track the status of your financial aid applications. You can access your application and each saved school's profile page directly from your My Schools grid, which you can use to manage the entire application process.

ONLINE APPLICATIONS

Applying to college online is faster and easier! Just ask any of the 450,000 students entering college in the fall of 2002 who applied online using our Embark technology. Worried about how the schools you're applying to will feel about electronic applications? The apps that we have on our site are the genuine school applications—and we have more than 700 of them. Every line that you scrawl by hand on a paper application has to be hand-entered by someone at the school's admissions office anyway. Why not save yourself and the school some time and trouble by using the more efficient e-application? Just a few of the perks include not having to fill out basic information more than once for a whole set of applications, being able to stop and save your application at any time and come back to it later, and of course, no need for a postage stamp. **Did we mention that there's no fee to apply online with The Princeton Review? Yes, it's free.**

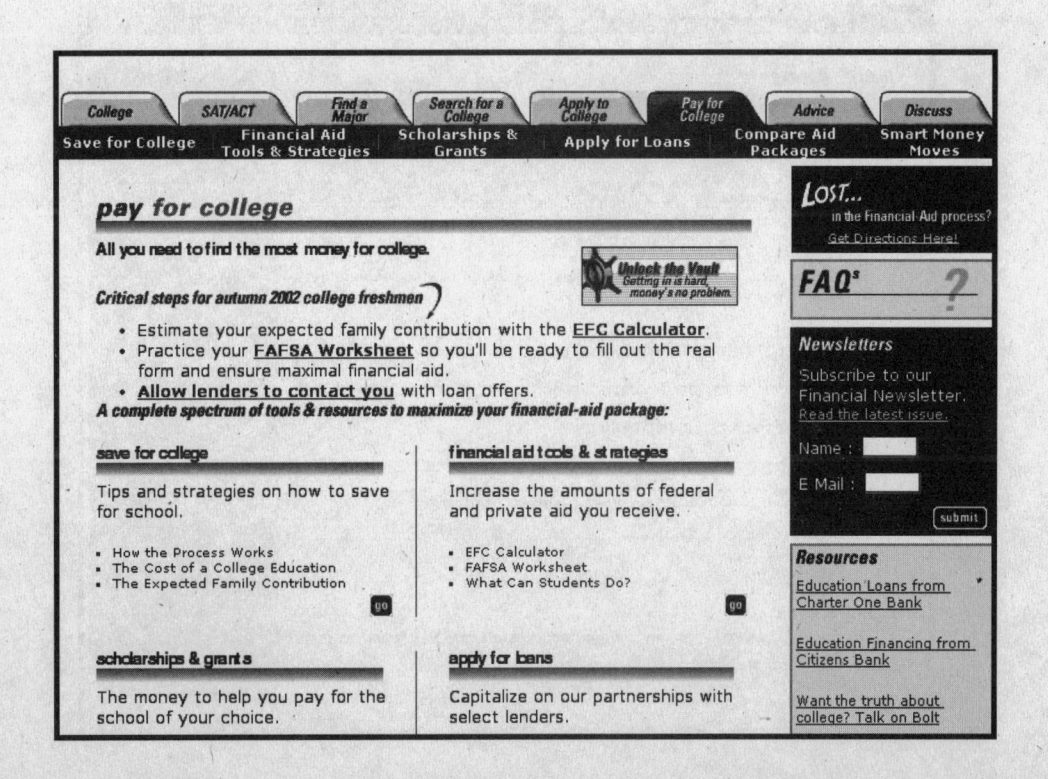

FINANCIAL CENTER

Our revamped Financial Center is a unique resource for parents and students alike. You'll find everything from helpful tips on saving money, tax forms, aid, loans, and scholarships to tools that allow you to compare aid packages and calculate your expected financial contribution. We'll also tell you things you didn't know and were afraid to ask about, such as credit cards, debt, and insurance. For those of you who are completely lost, we can show you the way: we have a straightforward financial timeline telling you exactly what to do and when to do it so you can get the maximum amount of aid.

Two outstanding financial tools you'll find on PrincetonReview.com are the EFC Calculator and the FAFSA Worksheet. **The Need Analysis/Expected Family Contribution Calculator** allows you to calculate your approximate Expected Family Contribution (EFC), which both colleges and the federal government use to determine what they think you and your family should be able to pay for a year's worth of higher education. This is an essential starting point for financial aid, as it helps you understand the federal methodology and gives you a ballpark figure with which you can start the financial aid process.

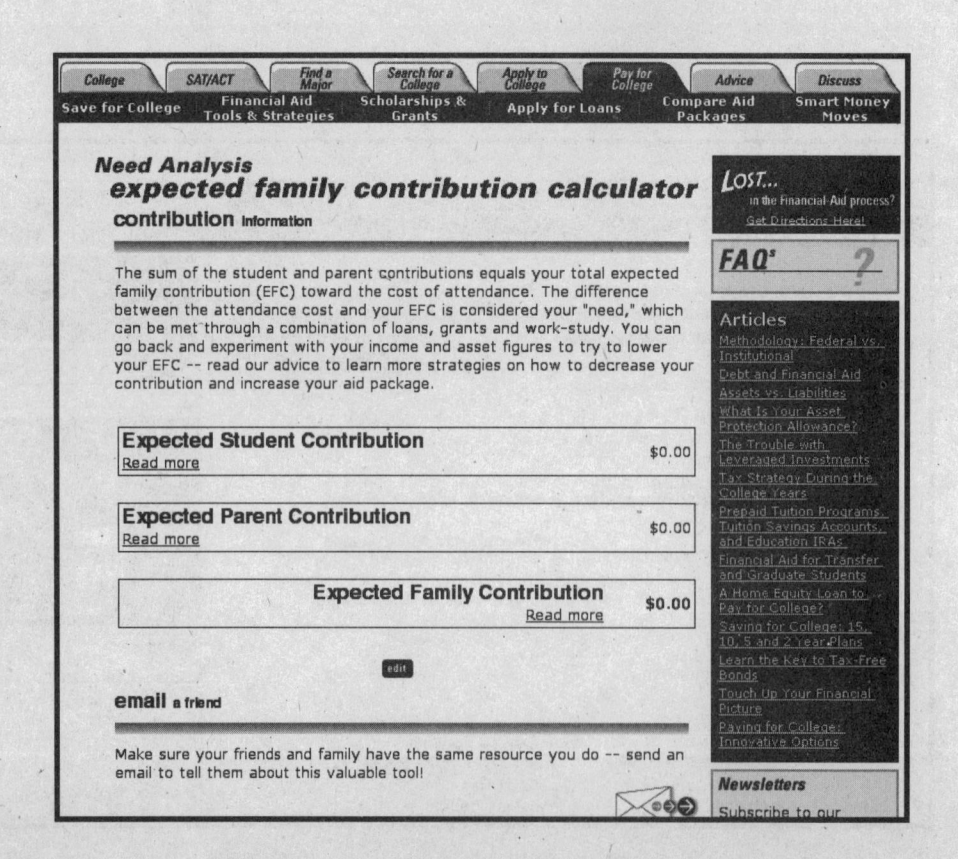

The FAFSA Worksheet is a virtual dress rehearsal for the official FAFSA form. You will *have* to complete the FAFSA if you want any federal financial aid at all. Each question on the worksheet has its own pop-up window with a detailed explanation and tips for entering the response that will benefit you the most.

Note: This worksheet has been known to radically reduce the likelihood that parents and students will suffer from the panic attacks and financial nightmares often attributed to filling out the FAFSA.

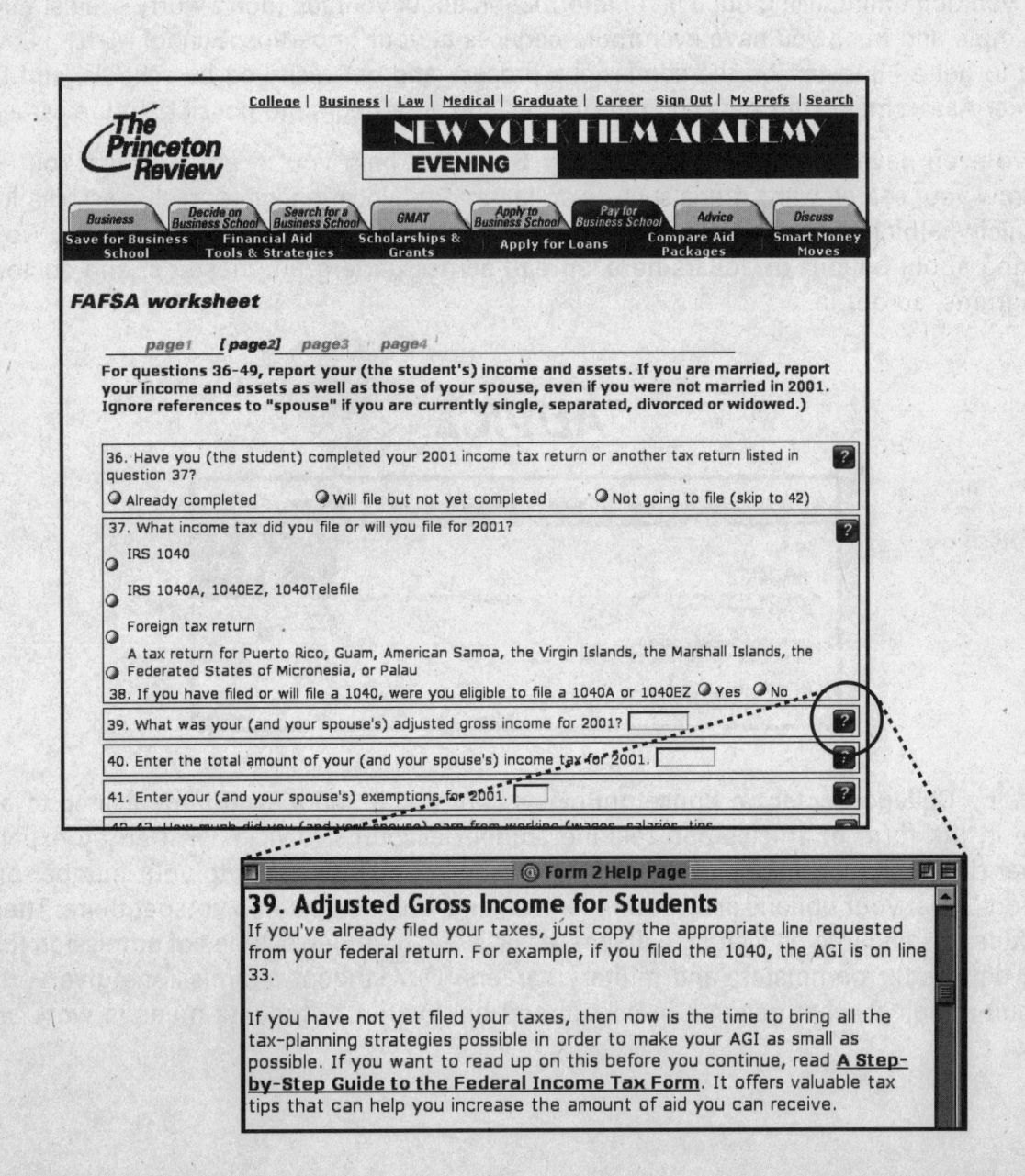

39. Adjusted Gross Income for Students

If you've already filed your taxes, just copy the appropriate line requested from your federal return. For example, if you filed the 1040, the AGI is on line 33.

If you have not yet filed your taxes, then now is the time to bring all the tax-planning strategies possible in order to make your AGI as small as possible. If you want to read up on this before you continue, read **A Step-by-Step Guide to the Federal Income Tax Form**. It offers valuable tax tips that can help you increase the amount of aid you can receive.

SEARCHABLE DATABASES

Visitors to PrincetonReview.com can take advantage of our wealth of data by searching for schools, majors, and careers. Each **Major's** profile provides information on curriculum, salaries, careers, and the appropriate high school preparation, as well as colleges that offer it. You can use the feature to search for hundreds of majors, browse an alphabetical list, or search by category. The same thing goes for searching for schools. Our undergrad database alone consists of nearly 2,000 schools, with hundreds more available in the two-year college and career and technical databases. You'll find a detailed profile on almost any school you can think of. **Advanced School Search** helps you find four-year schools based on cost, curriculum, student body, or other categories that might be of primary interest to you.

If you don't mind filling out a bit of information about yourself (don't worry—registration is simple and free), you have even more services at your fingertips: **School Match** allows you to get a jumpstart on the admissions process and get recruited by schools, and the **Career Assessment Quiz** gets you thinking beyond your degree to possible future careers.

We even have an excellent **Scholarship Search** to help you locate funding. You can narrow your search with criteria such as dollar amount, location, gender, club association, ethnicity, athletics, and talent and prospective prizes will appear before your eyes. We're talking about billions of dollars here, spread across undergrad, master's, and doctoral programs, so opt in.

ADVICE

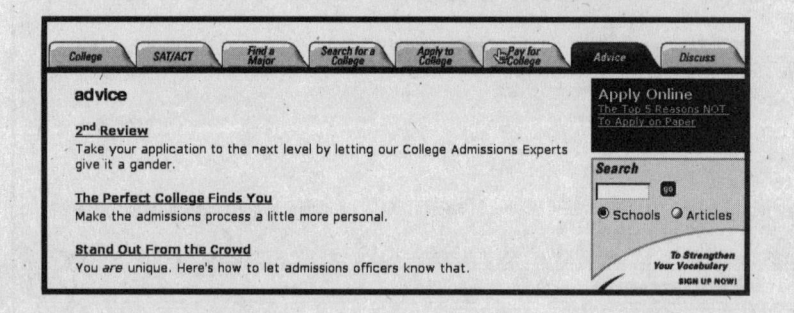

In the **College Center** on PrincetonReview.com you'll find a section dedicated to advice in the form of articles and real-life student accounts. Articles written by experts cover different aspects of each stage of the process: how to get in to your number-one school, what your options are, what to expect, and what to do when you get there. These include tips and info on visiting colleges, essays and interviews, types of admission (EA, ED, deferred), roommates, and military careers. Our student submissions give you a genuine look at what goes on in school and how various students manage work *and* play.

TUFTS UNIVERSITY

BENDETSON HALL, MEDFORD, MA 02155 • ADMISSIONS: 617-627-3170 • FAX: 617-627-3860

CAMPUS LIFE

Quality of Life Rating	87
Type of school	private
Affiliation	none
Environment	suburban

STUDENTS

Total undergrad enrollment	4,869
% male/female	47/53
% from out of state	77
% from public high school	60
% live on campus	80
% in (# of) fraternities	15 (10)
% in (# of) sororities	3 (3)
% African American	7
% Asian	14
% Caucasian	80
% Hispanic	7
% international	7

SURVEY SAYS...
Campus feels safe
Great library
Beautiful campus
Campus easy to get around
Great off-campus food
Student publications are ignored
(Almost) no one listens to college radio
Students are cliquish
(Almost) no one smokes

ACADEMICS

Academic Rating	89
Calendar	semester
Student/faculty ratio	9:1
Profs interesting rating	85
Profs accessible rating	96
% profs teaching UG courses	100
% classes taught by TAs	1
Avg lab size	10-19 students
Avg reg class size	10-19 students

MOST POPULAR MAJORS
international relations
biology
English

STUDENTS SPEAK OUT

Academics

Known for stealing the Ivy wait-list population, Tufts University offers rigorous academics that keep the school's hard-working, career-driven students on their toes. With its small class size, ample funding, and noteworthy professors, Tufts offers a wide variety of solid departments. Of particular renown is the international relations major, which draws in students from all over. Notes one student, "The best part of academics at Tufts are the small classes, the accessible faculty and staff, and the fact that NO classes are taught by TAs." Another opines, "Academically Tufts is impressive. The teachers are always available and ready to help, and if you look well, there are some really interesting classes: History of Reggae, Negotiation and Conflict Resolution, and Yoga." Requirements for first-year students are stiff, and some freshmen are hung up on "pointless requirements," but says one older and wiser student, "As an incoming freshman, it was good to have some idea of what to take. The advising program is excellent." Professors are highly regarded: reports one student, "My professors are incredible! From an astronomy professor who was late to class because he was rushing back from a NASA meeting in Houston to a political science professor who accidentally caught Justice Sandra Day O'Connor with food in her teeth, I have had fantastic and knowledgeable professors throughout my Tufts career. They're all open, honest, and enthusiastic educators with whom it is a pleasure to learn." Administrators "are great.... The president takes a very personal interest in the lives of the students. He is one of three professors leading a community dialogue/class on Leadership for Active Citizenship." On the downside, "Classrooms are ugly at best.... On the outside the buildings are pretty, but our lack of a large endowment has allowed many of them to become somewhat dilapidated on the inside."

Life

Tufts students describe an active campus life, one cram-packed with both class-related activities and extracurriculars. Writes one, "Even though most people are very focused on academics, most find plenty of time to be active in several of our 150-plus diverse activities. We have fantastic volunteer organizations, for example." Agrees another, "School spirit lies primarily in the 150 student activities groups. Within these groups, the most incredible bonds are formed. From the moment I arrived on campus, I joined everything! The daily newspaper, film series, debate team, tutoring, musical theater, etc. There's so much to do, my parents often question when I do my work." Students report that "everyone at this school is either dating someone here or someone at another school. This is far from a 'frat party and hook up' school." As for the Greeks, students explain that "although the fraternities and sororities make up only a fraction of the student body, they are pretty much the center of freshman life on campus. Once you become an upperclassman, though, you realize there is life beyond the Greek system." That life usually takes students into Boston, fortuitously "nearby to offer an outlet for students to live life. A lot of people go to Boston for fun, movies, dinner, and dance clubs." Then it's back to the beautiful campus, secluded in the suburban hills just a short commuter train ride away.

Student Body

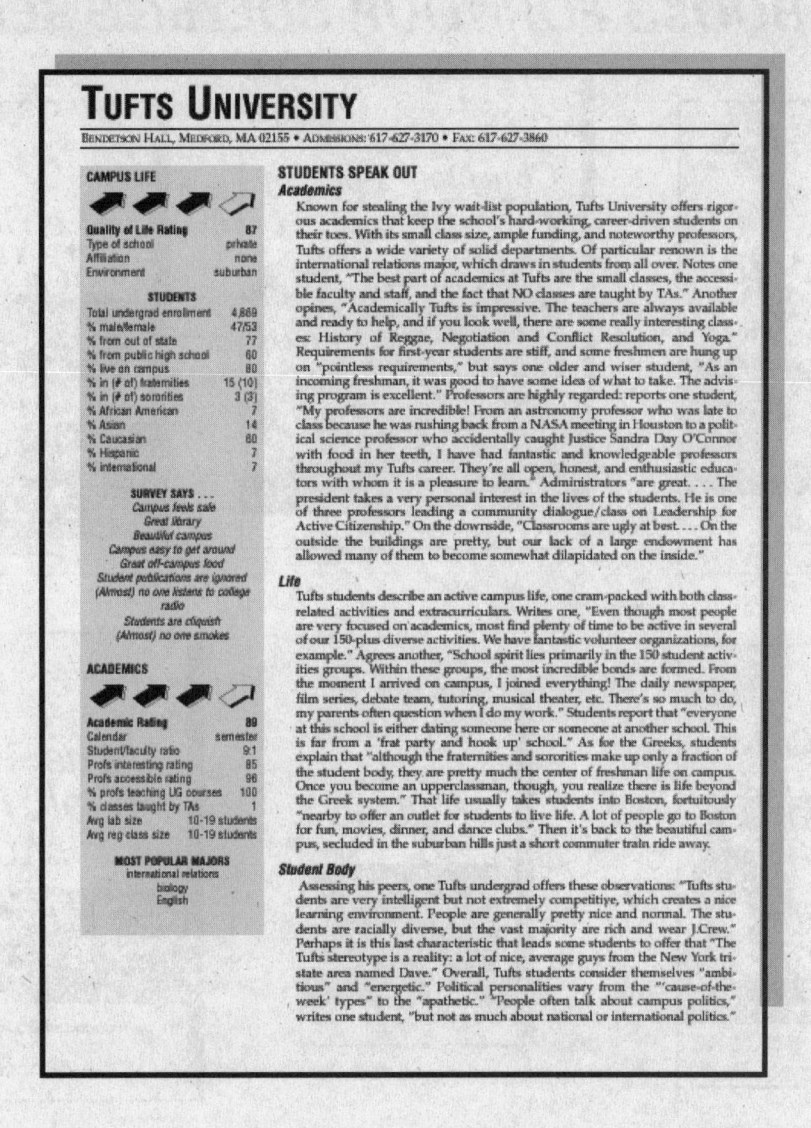

Assessing his peers, one Tufts undergrad offers these observations: "Tufts students are very intelligent but not extremely competitive, which creates a nice learning environment. People are generally pretty nice and normal. The students are racially diverse, but the vast majority are rich and wear J.Crew." Perhaps it is this last characteristic that leads some students to offer that "The Tufts stereotype is a reality: a lot of nice, average guys from the New York tri-state area named Dave." Overall, Tufts students consider themselves "ambitious" and "energetic." Political personalities vary from the "'cause-of-the-week' types" to the "apathetic." "People often talk about campus politics," writes one student, "but not as much about national or international politics."

BOOKS

Admissions Services publishes great data and advice books on undergrad, graduate, and professional schools, as well as careers. As the number-one student advocate in the business, we have the most updated student opinion data on colleges available. Just a few of the college titles we offer are *The Best 345 Colleges*, *The Complete Book of Colleges*, *The K&W Guide to Colleges for Students with Learning Disabilities or Attention Deficit Disorder*, *Visiting College Campuses*, *America's Elite Colleges*, *Paying for College Without Going Broke*, *The Scholarship Advisor*, *The Internship Bible*, and our brand new *Guide to College Majors*. For a complete listing of our available titles, check out our books page at PrincetonReview.com/college and click on Bookstore..

MORE BOOKS FOR YOUR COLLEGE SEARCH

Members SAVE More

Join the Student Advantage Membership® Program to save hundreds of dollars a year on food, clothing, travel and more! Members enjoy exclusive, on-going savings at more than 15,000 locations nationwide. Here are just a few:

The Princeton Review
$50 off any GMAT, LSAT, GRE or MCAT course

U·S AIRWAYS
Member-only discounts and bonus Dividend Miles®

BARNES & NOBLE.com
www.bn.com
Save an additional 5% on new and used textbooks

Liberty Mutual
Save up to $300 or more a year on auto insurance

Plus, receive the **Student Advantage Bonus Savings Book** with over $200 in additional savings from Art.com, Student Advantage Tech Store, Timberland® and more!

HOW TO JOIN...

Go to studentadvantage.com or call 1.877.2JOINSA and use promotion code TPR88P9001. Get a 1-Year Membership for only $20*!

*Plus $2.50 shipping and handling. Student Advantage® is a registered trademark and product of Student Advantage, Inc.

MORE EXPERT ADVICE FROM THE PRINCETON REVIEW

If you want to give yourself the best chances for getting into the business school of your choice, we can help you get higher test scores, make the most informed choices, and make the most of your experience once you get there. We can also help you make the career move that will let you use your skills and education to their best advantage.

CRACKING THE GMAT
2003 EDITION
0-375-76249-3 $20.00

CRACKING THE GMAT WITH SAMPLE TESTS ON CD-ROM
2003 EDITION
0-375-76250-7 $35.95
MAC AND WINDOWS COMPATIBLE

MATH WORKOUT FOR THE GMAT
0-679-78373-3 $16.00

VERBAL WORKOUT FOR THE GMAT
0-375-75417-2 $16.00

THE BEST 106 INTERNSHIPS
8TH EDITION
0-375-75637-X $21.00

BUSINESS SCHOOL COMPANION
0-679-76463-1 $15.00

COMPLETE BOOK OF BUSINESS SCHOOLS
2003 EDITION
0-375-76270-1 $23.00

THE INTERNSHIP BIBLE
2002 EDITION
0-375-76239-6 $25.00

MATH SMART FOR BUSINESS
0-679-77356-8 $12.00

WORD SMART FOR BUSINESS
0-679-78391-1 $12.95

The Princeton Review

Available at Bookstores Everywhere.
www.review.com